Less managing. More teaching. Greater learning.

 INSTRUCTORS...

Would you like your **students** to show up for class **more prepared**?
(Let's face it, class is much more fun if everyone is engaged and prepared...)

Want an **easy way to assign** homework online and track student **progress**?
(Less time grading means more time teaching...)

Want an **instant view** of student or class performance relative to learning objectives? *(No more wondering if students understand...)*

Need to **collect data and generate reports** required for administration or accreditation? *(Say goodbye to manually tracking student learning outcomes...)*

Want to **record and post your lectures** for students to view online?

 With McGraw-Hill's *Connect® Plus Business Statistics*,

INSTRUCTORS GET:

- Simple **assignment management**, allowing you to spend more time teaching.

- **Auto-graded** assignments, quizzes, and tests.

- **Detailed Visual Reporting** where student and section results can be viewed and analyzed.

- Sophisticated **online testing** capability.

- A **filtering and reporting** function that allows you to easily select Excel-based homework problems as well as assign and report on materials that are correlated to accreditation standards, learning outcomes, and Bloom's taxonomy.

- An easy-to-use **lecture capture** tool.

- The option to **upload course documents** for student access.

Want an online, **searchable version** of your textbook?

Wish your textbook could be **available online** while you're doing your assignments?

 ### *Connect® Plus Business Statistics* eBook

If you choose to use *Connect® Plus Business Statistics*, you have an affordable and searchable online version of your book integrated with your other online tools.

Connect® Plus Business Statistics eBook offers features like:

- Topic search
- Direct links from assignments
- Adjustable text size
- Jump to page number
- Print by section
- highlight
- take notes
- access instructor highlights/notes

 Want to get more **value** from your textbook purchase?

Think learning business statistics should be a bit more **interesting**?

 ### Check out the STUDENT RESOURCES section under the *Connect®* Library tab.

Here you'll find a wealth of resources designed to help you achieve your goals in the course. You'll find things like **quizzes, guided examples, PowerPoints, and Internet activities** to help you study. Every student has different needs, so explore the STUDENT RESOURCES to find the materials best suited to you.

Applied Statistics

in Business and Economics

Fourth Edition

David P. Doane
Oakland University

Lori E. Seward
University of Colorado

McGraw-Hill Irwin

APPLIED STATISTICS IN BUSINESS AND ECONOMICS

Published by McGraw-Hill/Irwin, a business unit of The McGraw-Hill Companies, Inc., 1221.
Avenue of the Americas, New York, NY, 10020. Copyright © 2013, 2011, 2009, 2007 by
The McGraw-Hill Companies, Inc. All rights reserved. Printed in the United States of America.
No part of this publication may be reproduced or distributed in any form or by any means,
or stored in a database or retrieval system, without the prior written consent of The McGraw-Hill
Companies, Inc., including, but not limited to, in any network or other electronic storage or
transmission, or broadcast for distance learning.

Some ancillaries, including electronic and print components, may not be available to customers outside the
United States.

This book is printed on acid-free paper.

3 4 5 6 7 8 9 0 DOW/DOW 1 0 9 8 7 6 5 4 3

ISBN   978-0-07-352148-0
MHID 0-07-352148-5

Vice president and editor-in-chief: *Brent Gordon*
Publisher: *Tim Vertovec*
Executive editor: *Steve Schuetz*
Executive director of development: *Ann Torbert*
Senior development editor: *Wanda J. Zeman*
Vice president and director of marketing: *Robin J. Zwettler*
Marketing director: *Brad Parkins*
Marketing manager: *Dean Karampelas*
Vice president of editing, design, and production: *Sesha Bolisetty*
Senior project manager: *Dana M. Pauley*
Senior buyer: *Michael R. McCormick*
Senior designer: *Matt Diamond*
Senior photo research coordinator: *Keri Johnson*
Photo researcher: *Allison Grimes*
Media project manager: *Rachel Townsend*
Media project manager: *Ron Nehms*
Typeface: *10/12 Times New Roman MT Std*
Compositor: *MPS Limited, a Macmillan Company*
Printer: *R. R. Donnelley*

Library of Congress Cataloging-in-Publication Data

Doane, David P.
   Applied statistics in business and economics / David P. Doane, Lori E. Seward. — 4th ed.
      p. cm.
   1. Commercial statistics. 2. Management—Statistical methods. 3. Economics—Statistical methods.
   4. Statistics. I. Seward, Lori Welte, 1962- II. Title.
HF1017.D55 2013
519.5—dc23
                                                                          2011042028

David P. Doane

David P. Doane is a Certified Professional Statistician (PStat™) by the American Statistical Association. He is a professor of quantitative methods in Oakland University's Department of Decision and Information Sciences. He earned his Bachelor of Arts degree in mathematics and economics at the University of Kansas and his PhD from Purdue University's Krannert Graduate School. His research and teaching interests include applied statistics, forecasting, and statistical education. He is corecipient of three National Science Foundation grants to develop software to teach statistics and to create a computer classroom. He is a longtime member of the American Statistical Association, serving in 2002 as president of the Detroit ASA chapter, where he remains on the board. He has consulted with government, health care organizations, and local firms. He has published articles in many academic journals and is the author of *LearningStats* (McGraw-Hill, 2003, 2007) and co-author of *Visual Statistics* (McGraw-Hill, 1997, 2001).

Lori E. Seward

Lori E. Seward is a senior instructor of Operations Management in The Leeds School of Business at the University of Colorado in Boulder. She earned her Bachelor of Science and Master of Science degrees in Industrial Engineering at Virginia Tech. After several years working as a reliability and quality engineer in the paper and automotive industries, she earned her PhD from Virginia Tech and joined the faculty at The Leeds School in 1998. She has been the coordinator of the undergraduate core business statistics course and currently teaches the core MBA statistics course. She is also responsible for coordinating the undergraduate program in Operations Management. She served as the chair of the INFORMS Teachers' Workshop for the annual 2004 meeting. Her teaching interests focus on developing pedagogy that uses technology to create a collaborative learning environment in large undergraduate and MBA statistics courses. Her most recent article, co-authored with David Doane, was published in the *Journal of Statistics Education* (2011).

DEDICATION

To Robert Hamilton Doane-Solomon

David

To all my students who challenged me to make statistics relevant to their lives.

Lori

"How often have you heard people/students say about a particular subject, 'I'll never use this in the real world?' I thought statistics was a bit on the 'math-geeky' side at first. Imagine my horror when I saw α, R^2, and correlations on several financial reports at my current job (an intern position at a financial services company). I realized then that I had better try to understand some of this stuff."

—*Jill Odette (an introductory statistics student)*

As recently as a decade ago our students used to ask us, "**How** do I use statistics?" Today we more often hear, "**Why** should I use statistics?" *Applied Statistics in Business and Economics* has attempted to provide real meaning to the use of statistics in our world by using real business situations and real data and appealing to your need to know *why* rather than just *how*.

With over 50 years of teaching statistics between the two of us, we feel we have something to offer. Seeing how students have changed as the new century unfolds has required us to adapt and seek out better ways of instruction. So we wrote *Applied Statistics in Business and Economics* to meet four distinct objectives.

Objective 1: Communicate the Meaning of Variation in a Business Context   Variation exists everywhere in the world around us. Successful businesses know how to measure variation. They also know how to tell when variation should be responded to and when it should be left alone. We'll show how businesses do this.

Objective 2: Use Real Data and Real Business Applications   Examples, case studies, and problems are taken from published research or real applications whenever possible. Hypothetical data are used when it seems the best way to illustrate a concept. You can usually tell the difference by examining the footnotes citing the source.

Objective 3: Incorporate Current Statistical Practices and Offer Practical Advice With the increased reliance on computers, statistics practitioners have changed the way they use statistical tools. We'll show the current practices and explain why they are used the way they are. We will also tell you when each technique should *not* be used.

Objective 4: Provide More In-Depth Explanation of the Why and Let the Software Take Care of the How   It is critical to understand the importance of communicating with data. Today's computer capabilities make it much easier to summarize and display data than ever before. We demonstrate easily mastered software techniques using the common software available. We also spend a great deal of time on the idea that there are risks in decision making and those risks should be quantified and directly considered in every business decision.

Our experience tells us that students want to be given credit for the experience they bring to the college classroom. We have tried to honor this by choosing examples and exercises set in situations that will draw on students' already vast knowledge of the world and knowledge gained from other classes. Emphasis is on thinking about data, choosing appropriate analytic tools, using computers effectively, and recognizing limitations of statistics.

What's New in This Fourth Edition?

In this fourth edition we have listened to you and have made many changes that you asked for. We sought advice from students and faculty who are currently using the textbook, objective reviewers at a variety of colleges and universities, and participants in focus groups on teaching statistics with technology. At the end of this preface is a detailed list of chapter-by-chapter improvements, but here are just a few of them:

* Step-by-step instructions and many new screen shots on using Excel 2010 for descriptive statistics, histograms, scatter plots, line charts, fitting trends, and probability calculations.

* Appendix J—a new reference tool for Excel 2010 functions using standard textbook notation.

* Substantially updated exercises with emphasis on compatibility with Connect.

* Well-indexed exercises, quizzes, and test bank questions matched with topics and learning objectives.

* Addition of topics requested by reviewers, including stem-and-leaf displays, weighted mean, finite populations, and logistic regression.

* Lots of updated exercises and skill-focused "business context" exercises.

* Rewritten instructor's manual with step-by-step solutions.

* New and updated Mini Cases for economics and business.

AUTHORS

- Improved explanations of data types, random sampling, probability, and distributions.

- Improved discussion and visuals for quartiles, percentiles, outliers, and boxplots.

- Reorganized and expanded discussion of sampling error and estimating from finite populations.

- Streamlined sections on Types I and II error, hypothesis formulation, and decision rules.

- More focus on one-factor ANOVA and interpreting ANOVA results.

- Better articulated learning objectives for regression with new visuals, improved notation, and intuitive explanations of error assumptions, residual tests, and categorical variables.

- Excel's CHISQ.TEST function and new exercises on the multinomial and Poisson GOF tests.

- New treatment of Wilcoxon rank sum test (Mann–Whitney test) with illustration of two versions.

- Condensed material on quality management with more focus on tools and service quality.

- Updated treatment of simulation based on new Excel functions and new @Risk software.

- End of each chapter guides to downloads from the **Online Learning Center** (simulations, demonstrations, tips, and video tutorials for Excel, *MegaStat,* and MINITAB).

Software

Excel is used throughout this book because it is available everywhere. Some calculations are illustrated using *MegaStat*, an Excel add-in whose Excel-based menus and spreadsheet format offer more capability than Excel's Data Analysis Tools. MINITAB menus and examples are also included to point out similarities and differences of these tools. To assist students who need extra help or "catch up" work, the text website contains tutorials or demonstrations on using Excel, MINITAB, or *MegaStat* for the tasks of each chapter. At the end of each chapter is a list of *LearningStats* demonstrations that illustrate the concepts from the chapter. These demonstrations can be downloaded from the text website (**www.mhhe.com/doane4e**).

Math Level

The assumed level of mathematics is pre-calculus, though there are rare references to calculus where it might help the better-trained reader. All but the simplest proofs and derivations are omitted, though key assumptions are stated clearly. The learner is advised what to do when these assumptions are not fulfilled. Worked examples are included for basic calculations, but the textbook does assume that computers will do the calculations after the statistics class is over, so, *interpretation* is paramount. End-of-chapter references and suggested websites are given so that interested readers can deepen their understanding.

Exercises

Simple practice exercises are placed within each section. End-of-chapter exercises tend to be more integrative or to be embedded in more realistic contexts. Attention has been given to revising exercises so that they have clear-cut answers that are matched to specific learning objectives. A few exercises invite short answers rather than just quoting a formula. Answers to most odd-numbered exercises are in the back of the book (all of the answers are in the instructor's manual).

LearningStats

LearningStats is a downloadable collection of Excel spreadsheets, Word documents, and PowerPoints for each chapter. It is intended to let students explore data and concepts at their own pace, ignoring material they already know and focusing on things that interest them. *LearningStats* includes explanations on topics that are not covered in other software packages, such as how to write effective reports, how to perform calculations, or how to make effective charts. It also includes topics that did not appear prominently in the textbook (e.g., partial F-test, Durbin–Watson test, sign test, bootstrap simulation, and logistic regression). Instructors can use *LearningStats* PowerPoint presentations in the classroom, but students can also use them for self-instruction. No instructor can "cover everything," but students can be encouraged to explore *LearningStats* data sets and/or demonstrations perhaps with an instructor's guidance.

David P. Doane
Lori E. Seward

HOW ARE CHAPTERS ORGANIZED

Chapter Contents

Each chapter begins with a short list of section topics that are covered in the chapter.

Chapter Learning Objectives

Each chapter includes a list of learning objectives students should be able to attain upon reading and studying the chapter material. Learning objectives give students an overview of what is expected and identify the goals for learning. Learning objectives also appear next to chapter topics in the margins.

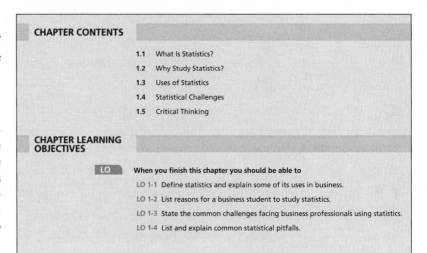

CHAPTER CONTENTS

1.1 What Is Statistics?

1.2 Why Study Statistics?

1.3 Uses of Statistics

1.4 Statistical Challenges

1.5 Critical Thinking

CHAPTER LEARNING OBJECTIVES

LO When you finish this chapter you should be able to

LO 1-1 Define statistics and explain some of its uses in business.

LO 1-2 List reasons for a business student to study statistics.

LO 1-3 State the common challenges facing business professionals using statistics.

LO 1-4 List and explain common statistical pitfalls.

Section Exercises

Multiple section exercises are found throughout the chapter so that students can focus on material just learned.

SECTION EXERCISES

connect

4.34 Scores on an accounting exam ranged from 42 to 96, with quartiles $Q_1 = 61$, $Q_2 = 77$, and $Q_3 = 85$. (a) Sketch a simple boxplot (5-number summary without fences) using a nicely scaled X-axis. (b) Describe its shape (skewed left, symmetric, skewed right).

4.35 In 2007, total compensation (in thousands of dollars) for 40 randomly chosen CEOs ranged from 790 to 192,920, with quartiles $Q_1 = 3,825$, $Q_2 = 8,890$, and $Q_3 = 17,948$. (a) Sketch a simple boxplot (5-number summary without fences) using a nicely scaled X-axis. (b) Describe its shape (skewed left, symmetric, skewed right).

4.36 The Comer-Correr Taco Wagon is only open from 11:00 a.m. to 2:00 p.m. on Saturday. The owner kept track of the number of customers served on Saturday for 60 weeks. (a) Visually estimate the quartiles Q_1, Q_2, Q_3. (b) Approximately how many customers were served on the busiest day? The slowest day? (c) Is the distribution symmetric? **Customers**

Customers per Day

Mini Cases

Every chapter includes two or three mini cases, which are solved applications. They show and illlustrate the analytical application of specific statistical concepts at a deeper level than the examples.

Mini Case 4.7

Vail Resorts Customer Satisfaction

Figure 4.35 is a matrix showing correlations between several satisfaction variables from a sample of respondents to a Vail Resorts' satisfaction survey. The correlations are all positive, suggesting that greater satisfaction with any one of these criteria tends to be associated with greater satisfaction with the others (positive covariance). The highest correlation ($r = 0.488$) is between *SkiSafe* (attention to skier safety) and *SkiPatV* (Ski Patrol visibility). This makes intuitive sense. When a skier sees a ski patroller, you would expect increased perception that the organization is concerned with skier safety. While many of the correlations seem small, they are all *statistically significant* (as you will learn in Chapter 12).

FIGURE 4.35 Correlation Matrix of Skier Satisfaction Variables ($n = 502$)
VailGuestSat

	LiftOps	LiftWait	TrailVar	SnoAmt	GroomT	SkiSafe	SkiPatV
LiftOps	1.000						
LiftWait	0.180	1.000					
TrailVar	0.206	0.128	1.000				
SnoAmt	0.242	0.227	0.373	1.000			
GroomT	0.271	0.251	0.221	0.299	1.000		
SkiSafe	0.306	0.196	0.172	0.200	0.274	1.000	
SkiPatV	0.190	0.207	0.172	0.184	0.149	0.488	1.000

Figures and Tables

Throughout the text, there are hundreds of charts, graphs, tables, and spreadsheets to illustrate statistical concepts being applied. These visuals help stimulate student interest and clarify the text explanations.

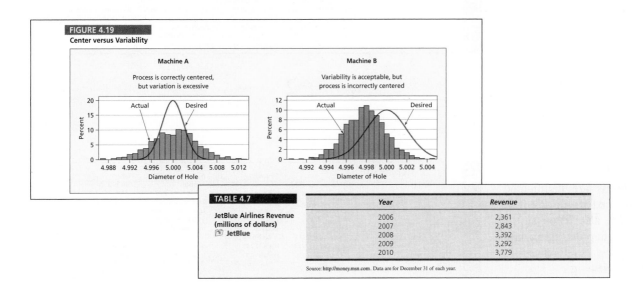

Examples

Examples of interest to students are taken from published research or real applications to illustrate the statistics concept. For the most part, examples are focused on business, but there are also some that are more general and don't require any prerequisite knowledge. And there are some that are based on student projects.

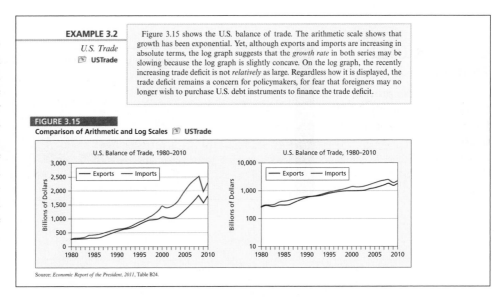

Data Set Icon

A data set icon is used throughout the text to identify data sets used in the figures, examples, and exercises that are included on the Online Learning Center (OLC) for the text.

 USTrade

Chapter Summary

Chapter summaries provide an overview of the material covered in the chapter.

CHAPTER SUMMARY For a set of observations on a single numerical variable, a **stem-and-leaf plot** or a **dot plot** displays the individual data values, while a **frequency distribution** classifies the data into classes called **bins** for a **histogram** of **frequencies** for each bin. The number of bins and their limits are matters left to your judgment, though **Sturges' Rule** offers advice on the number of bins. The **line chart** shows values of one or more **time series** variables plotted against time. A **log scale** is sometimes used in time series charts when data vary by orders of magnitude. The **bar chart** or **column chart** shows a **numerical** data value for each category of an **attribute.** However, a bar chart can also be used for a time series. A **scatter plot** can reveal the association (or lack of association) between two variables X and Y. The **pie chart** (showing a **numerical** data value for each category of an **attribute** if the data values are parts of a whole) is common but should be used with caution. Sometimes a **simple table** is the best visual display. Creating effective visual displays is an acquired skill. Excel offers a wide range of charts from which to choose. Deceptive graphs are found frequently in both media and business presentations, and the consumer should be aware of common errors.

Key Terms

Key terms are highlighted and defined within the text. They are also listed at the ends of chapters, along with chapter page references, to aid in reviewing.

KEY TERMS

Center	Variability	Shape	Other
geometric mean, 123	Chebyshev's	bimodal	box plot, 143
mean, 113	Theorem, 134	distribution, 118	covariance, 148
median, 115	coefficient of	kurtosis, 155	five-number
midhinge, 145	variation, 130	leptokurtic, 155	summary, 143
midrange, 124	Empirical Rule, 134	mesokurtic, 155	interquartile
mode, 116	mean absolute	multimodal	range, 140
trimmed mean, 124	deviation, 131	distribution, 118	method of
weighted mean, 152	outliers, 135	negatively	medians, 141
	population	skewed, 118	quartiles, 140
	variance, 128	platykurtic, 155	sample correlation
	range, 127	positively skewed, 118	coefficient, 147

Commonly Used Formulas

Some chapters provide a listing of commonly used formulas for the topic under discussion.

Commonly Used Formulas in Descriptive Statistics

Sample mean: $\bar{x} = \frac{1}{n}\sum_{i=1}^{n} x_i$

Geometric mean: $G = \sqrt[n]{x_1 x_2 \ldots x_n}$

Growth rate: $GR = \sqrt[n-1]{\frac{x_n}{x_1}} - 1$

Range: $\text{Range} = x_{max} - x_{min}$

Midrange: $\text{Midrange} = \frac{x_{max} + x_{min}}{2}$

Sample standard deviation: $s = \sqrt{\frac{\sum_{i=1}^{n}(x_i - \bar{x})^2}{n - 1}}$

Chapter Review

Each chapter has a list of questions for student self-review or for discussion.

CHAPTER REVIEW

1. Define (a) random process; (b) random variable; (c) discrete random variable; and (d) probability distribution.
2. Without using formulas, explain the meaning of (a) expected value of a random variable; (b) actuarial fairness; and (c) variance of a random variable.
3. What is the difference between a PDF and a CDF? Sketch a picture of each.
4. (a) What are the two parameters of a uniform distribution? (b) Why is the uniform distribution the first one considered in this chapter?
5. (a) Describe a Bernoulli experiment and give two examples. (b) What is the connection between a Bernoulli experiment and a binomial distribution?

Chapter Exercises

Exercises give students an opportunity to test their understanding of the chapter material. Exercises are included at the ends of sections and at the ends of chapters. Some exercises contain data sets, identified by data set icons. Data sets can be accessed on the Online Learning Center and used to solve problems in the text.

Online Learning Resources

LearningStats, included on the Online Learning Center (OLC: **www.mhhe.com/doane4e**), provides a means for students to explore data and concepts at their own pace. Applications that relate to the material in the chapter are identified by topic at the ends of chapters under Online Learning Resources.

Exam Review Questions

At the end of a group of chapters, students can review the material they covered in those chapters. This provides them with an opportunity to test themselves on their grasp of the material.

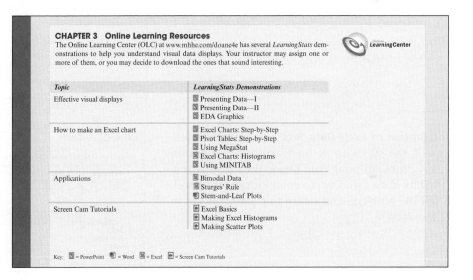

4.85 (a) Sort the data and find X_{min} and X_{max}. (b) Choose a data set and prepare a brief, descriptive report. You may use any computer software you wish (e.g., Excel, MegaStat, MINITAB). Include relevant worksheets or graphs in your report. If some questions do not apply to your data set, explain why not. Make a histogram. Describe its shape. (c) Calculate the mean and median. Are the data skewed? (d) Calculate the standard deviation. (e) Standardize the data and check for outliers. (f) Calculate the quartiles and make a box plot. Describe its appearance.

DATA SET A	Advertising Dollars as Percent of Sales in Selected Industries ($n = 30$) Ads	
	Industry	*Percent*
	Accident and health insurance	0.9
	Apparel and other finished products	5.5
	Beverages	7.4
	⋮	⋮
	Steel works and blast furnaces	1.9
	Tires and inner tubes	1.8
	Wine, brandy, and spirits	11.3

Source: George E. Belch and Michael A. Belch, *Advertising and Promotion*, pp. 219–220. Copyright © 2004 Richard D. Irwin. Used with permission of McGraw-Hill Companies, Inc.

CHAPTER 3 Online Learning Resources

The Online Learning Center (OLC) at www.mhhe.com/doane4e has several *LearningStats* demonstrations to help you understand visual data displays. Your instructor may assign one or more of them, or you may decide to download the ones that sound interesting.

Topic	*LearningStats Demonstrations*
Effective visual displays	Presenting Data—I
	Presenting Data—II
	EDA Graphics
How to make an Excel chart	Excel Charts: Step-by-Step
	Pivot Tables: Step-by-Step
	Using MegaStat
	Excel Charts: Histograms
	Using MINITAB
Applications	Bimodal Data
	Sturges' Rule
	Stem-and-Leaf Plots
Screen Cam Tutorials	Excel Basics
	Making Excel Histograms
	Making Scatter Plots

Key: = PowerPoint = Word = Excel = Screen Cam Tutorials

EXAM REVIEW QUESTIONS FOR CHAPTERS 5–7

1. Which type of probability (empirical, classical, subjective) is each of the following?
   a. On a given Friday, the probability that Flight 277 to Chicago is on time is 23.7%.
   b. Your chance of going to Disney World next year is 10%.
   c. The chance of rolling a 3 on two dice is 1/8.

2. For the following contingency table, find (a) $P(H \cap T)$; (b) $P(S \mid G)$; (c) $P(S)$

	R	S	T	Row Total
G	10	50	30	90
H	20	50	40	110
Col Total	30	100	70	200

3. If $P(A) = .30$, $P(B) = .70$, and $P(A \cap B) = .25$, are A and B independent events? Explain.

4. Which statement is *false*? Explain.
   a. If $P(A) = .05$, then the odds against event *A*'s occurrence are 19 to 1.
   b. If *A* and *B* are mutually exclusive events, then $P(A \cup B) = 0$.
   c. The number of permutations of 5 things taken 2 at a time is 20.

McGraw-Hill Connect®
Business Statistcs

McGraw-Hill *Connect® Business Statistics* is an online assignment and assessment solution that connects students with the tools and resources they'll need to achieve success through faster learning, higher retention, and more efficient studying. It provides instructors with tools to quickly pick content and assignments according to the topics they want to emphasize.

Online Assignments. *Connect Business Statistics* helps students learn more efficiently by providing practice material and feedback when they are needed. Connect grades homework automatically and provides feedback on any questions that students may have missed.

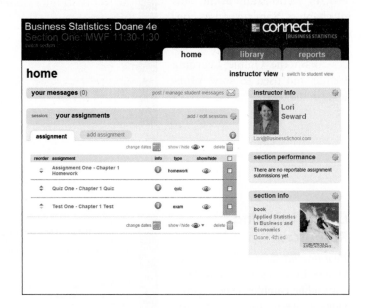

Integration of Excel Data Sets. A convenient feature is the inclusion of an Excel data file link in many problems using data files in their calculation. The link allows students to easily launch into Excel, work the problem, and return to *Connect* to key in the answer.

Chapter Exercise 5-74

High levels of cockpit noise in an aircraft can damage the hearing of pilots who are exposed to this hazard for many hours. Cockpit noise in a jet aircraft is mostly due to airflow at hundreds of miles per hour. This 3×3 contingency table shows 61 observations of data collected by an airline pilot using a handheld sound meter in a Boeing 727 cockpit. Noise level is defined as "low" (under 88 decibels), "medium" (88 to 91 decibels), or "high" (92 decibels or more). There are three flight phases (climb, cruise, descent).

Cockpit Noise

Noise Level	Flight Phase			
	Climb(B)	Cruise(C)	Descent(D)	Row Total
Low(L)	6	2	6	14
Medium(M)	18	3	8	29
High(H)	1	3	14	18
Column Total	25	8	28	61

Click here for the Excel Data File

(a) Calculate the following probabilities: (Round your answers to 4 decimal places.)

P(B)	
P(L)	
P(H)	

Student Resource Library. The *Connect Business Statistics* Student Library is the place for students to access additional resources. The Student Library provides quick access to recorded lectures, practice materials, eBooks, data files, PowerPoint files, and more.

Guided Examples. These narrated video walkthroughs provide students with step-by-step guidelines for solving selected exercises similar to those contained in the text. The student is given personalized instruction on how to solve a problem by applying the concepts presented in the chapter. The narrated voiceover shows the steps to take to work through an exercise. Students can go through each example multiple times if needed.

Simple Assignment Management and Smart Grading. When it comes to studying, time is precious. *Connect Business Statistics* helps students learn more efficiently by providing feedback and practice material when they need it, where they need it. When it comes to teaching, your time also is precious. The grading function enables you to:

- Have assignments scored automatically, giving students immediate feedback on their work and side-by-side comparisons with correct answers.
- Access and review each response; manually change grades or leave comments for students to review.

Student Reporting. *Connect Business Statistics* keeps instructors informed about how each student, section, and class is performing, allowing for more productive use of lecture and office hours. The progress-tracking function enables you to:

- View scored work immediately and track individual or group performance with assignment and grade reports.
- Access an instant view of student or class performance relative to learning objectives.
- Collect data and generate reports required by many accreditation organizations, such as AACSB.

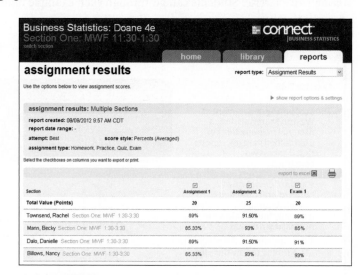

Instructor Library. The *Connect Business Statistics* Instructor Library is your repository for additional resources to improve student engagement in and out of class. You can select and use any asset that enhances your lecture. The *Connect Business Statistics* Instructor Library includes:

- eBook
- PowerPoint presentations
- Test Bank
- Instructor's Solutions Manual
- Digital Image Library

McGraw-Hill Connect® Plus Business Statistcs

Connect® Plus Business Statistics includes a seamless integration of an eBook and *Connect Business Statistics, Connect* with rich functionality integrated into the product.

Integrated Media-Rich eBook. An integrated media-rich eBook allows students to access media in context with each chapter. Students can highlight, take notes, and access shared instructor highlights/notes to learn the course material.

Dynamic Links. Dynamic links provide a connection between the problems or questions you assign to your students and the location in the eBook where that problem or question is covered.

Powerful Search Function. A powerful search function pinpoints and connects key concepts in a snap. This state-of-the-art, thoroughly tested system supports you in preparing students for the world that awaits. For more information about *Connect*, go to **www.mcgrawhillconnect.com** or contact your local McGraw-Hill sales representative.

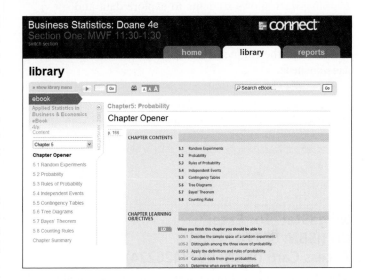

Tegrity Campus: Lectures 24/7

Tegrity Campus is a service that makes class time available 24/7. With Tegrity, you can automatically capture every lecture in a searchable format for students to review when they study and complete assignments. With a simple one-click start-and-stop process, you capture all computer screens and corresponding audio. Students can replay any part of any class with easy-to-use browser-based viewing on a PC or Mac.

Educators know that the more students can see, hear, and experience class resources, the better they learn. In fact, studies prove it. With *Tegrity Campus*, students quickly recall key moments by using *Tegrity Campus*'s unique search feature. This search helps students efficiently find what they need, when they need it, across an entire semester of class recordings. Help turn all your students' study time into learning moments immediately supported by your lecture. To learn more about *Tegrity*, watch a two-minute Flash demo at **http://tegritycampus.mhhe.com**.

The following software tools are available to assist students in understanding concepts and solving problems.

LearningStats

LearningStats allows students to explore data and concepts at their own pace. It includes demonstrations, simulations, and tutorials that can be downloaded from the Online Learning Center **www.mhhe.com/doane4e**.

MegaStat® for Excel®
CD (ISBN: 0077496442)
Access Card (ISBN: 0077426274)

MegaStat is a full-featured Excel add-in that is available with this text. It performs statistical analyses within an Excel workbook. It does basic functions such as descriptive statistics, frequency distributions, and probability calculations as well as hypothesis testing, ANOVA, and regression.

MegaStat output is carefully formatted, and ease-of-use features include Auto Expand for quick data selection and Auto Label detect. Since *MegaStat* is easy to use, students can focus on learning statistics without being distracted by the software. MegaStat is always available from Excel's main menu. Selecting a menu item pops up a dialog box. Descriptive statistics screen's are shown here. MegaStat works with all recent versions of Excel including Excel 2010 for Windows and Excel 2011 for Macintosh.

Minitab® SV14 (ISBN: 007305237X)
SPSS® SV18 (ISBN: 0077327144)
JMP® SE8 (ISBN: 007739030X)

MINITAB® Student Version 14, SPSS® Student Version 18, and JMP Student Edition version 8 are software tools that are available to help students solve the business statistics exercises in the text. Each is available in the student version and can be packaged with any McGraw-Hill business statistics text.

Online Learning Center: www.mhhe.com/doane4e

The Online Learning Center (OLC) provides the instructor with a complete Instructor's Manual in Word format, the complete Test Bank in both Word files and computerized EZ Test format, Instructor Power-Point slides, text art files, an introduction to ALEKS®, an introduction to McGraw-Hill Connect™ Business Statistics, access to the eBook, and more.

 Online

All test bank questions are available in an EZ Test electronic format. Included are a number of multiple-choice, true–false, and short-answer questions and problems. The answers to all questions are given, along with a rating of the level of difficulty, topic, chapter learning objective, Bloom's taxonomy question type, and AACSB knowledge category.

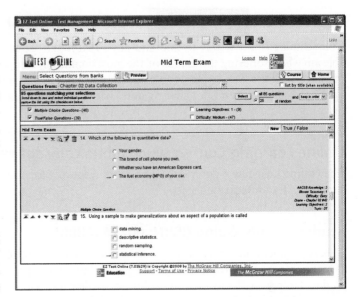

Online Course Management

No matter what online course management system you use (WebCT, Blackboard, or eCollege), we have a course content ePack available for your course. Our new ePacks are specifically designed to make it easy for students to navigate and access content online. For help, our online Digital Learning Consultants are ready to assist you with your online course needs. They provide training and will answer any questions you have throughout the life of your adoption.

The **Best** of **Both Worlds**

McGraw-Hill Higher Education and Blackboard have teamed up. What does this mean for you?

1. **Single sign-on.** Now you and your students can access McGraw-Hill's Connect™ and Create™ right from within your Blackboard course—all with one single sign-on.
2. **Integration of content and tools.** You get a single sign-on with Connect™ and Create™, and you also get integration of McGraw-Hill content and content engines right into Blackboard. Whether you're choosing a book for your course or building Connect™ assignments, all the tools you need are right where you want them—inside of Blackboard.
3. **One grade book.** Keeping several grade books and manually synchronizing grades into Blackboard is no longer necessary. When a student completes an integrated Connect™ assignment, the grade for that assignment automatically (and instantly) feeds your Blackboard grade center.
4. **A solution for everyone.** Whether your institution is already using Blackboard or you just want to try Blackboard on your own, we have a solution for you. McGraw-Hill and Blackboard can now offer you easy access to industry-leading technology and content, whether your campus hosts it, or we do. Be sure to ask your local McGraw-Hill representative for details.

McGraw-Hill Customer Experience Information

For Customer Support, call **800-331-5094** or visit **www.mhhe.com/support.** One of our customer experience team members will be able to assist you in a timely fashion.

CourseSmart CourseSmart (ISBN: 0077416848)

CourseSmart is a new way to find and buy eTextbooks. CourseSmart has the largest selection of eTextbooks available anywhere, offering thousands of the most commonly adopted textbooks from a wide variety of higher education publishers. CourseSmart eTextbooks are available in one standard online reader with full text search, notes and highlighting, and e-mail tools for sharing notes between classmates. Visit **www.CourseSmart.com** for more information on ordering.

Online Learning Center: www.mhhe.com/doane4e

The Online Learning Center (OLC) provides resources for students including quizzes, powerpoint, data sets, screencam tutorials, and learning stats.

Student Study Guide (ISBN: 0077416880)

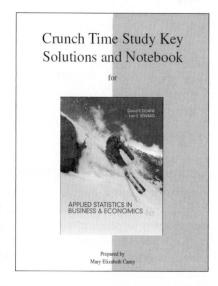

This supplement has been created to help students master the course content. It highlights the important ideas in the text and provides opportunities for students to review the worked-out solutions, review terms and concepts, and practice. The Study Guide is available through Primis Online at **www.mhhe.com/primis.** Instructors can order the Study Guide in either print or eBook format for their students.

ALEKS®

ALEKS is an assessment and learning system that provides individualized instruction in business statistics. Available from McGraw-Hill/Irwin over the World Wide Web, ALEKS delivers precise assessments of students' knowledge, guides them in the selection of appropriate new study material, and records their progress toward mastery of goals.

ALEKS interacts with students much as a skilled human tutor would, moving between explanation and practice as needed, correcting and analyzing errors, defining terms, and changing topics on request. By accurately assessing their knowledge, ALEKS focuses precisely on what to learn next, helping them master the course content more quickly and easily.

ACKNOWLEDGMENTS

The authors would like to acknowledge some of the many people who have helped with this book. Thomas W. Lauer and Floyd G. Willoughby permitted quotation of a case study. Morgan Elliott, Karl Majeske, Robin McCutcheon, Kevin Murphy, John Sase, T. J. Wharton, and Kenneth M. York permitted questionnaires to be administered in their classes. Mark Isken, Ron Tracy, and Robert Kushler gave generously of their time as expert statistical consultants. Jonathan G. Koomey of E.O. Lawrence Berkeley National Laboratory offered valuable suggestions on visual data presentation.

Mark Isken has reliably provided Excel expertise and has suggested health care applications for examples and case studies. John Seeley and Jeff Whitbey provided regression databases. John Savio and the Michigan State Employees Credit Union provided ATM data. The Siena Research Institute has made its poll results available. J.D. Power and Associates generously provided permission to use vehicle quality data. The Public Interest Research Group of Michigan (PIRGIM) has generously shared data from its field survey of prescription drug prices.

We owe special thanks to Aaron Kennedy and Dave Boennighausen of Noodles & Company, to Mark Gasta, Anja Wallace, and Clifton Pacaro of Vail Resorts, to Jim Curtin and Gordon Backman of Ball Corporation, and to Santosh Lakhan from The Verdeo Group for providing suggestions and access to data for mini cases and examples. For reviewing the material on quality, we wish to thank Kay Beauregard, administrative director at William Beaumont Hospital, and Ellen Barnes and Karry Roberts of Ford Motor Company.

A special debt of gratitude is due to Steve Schuetz for his direction and support and Wanda Zeman for coordinating the project. Thanks to Lloyd Jasingh, Morehead State University, for updating the PowerPoint slides and Mary Beth Camp, Indiana University, for writing an excellent Study Guide. Special thanks to the accuracy checkers: Kevin Schaub, University of Colorado; Paul Kuzdrall, Akron University; and David Meyer, Akron University. Thanks to the many reviewers who provided such valuable feedback including criticism that made the book better, some of whom reviewed several drafts of the manuscript. Any remaining errors or omissions are the authors' responsibility. Thanks too, to the participants in our focus groups and symposia on teaching business statistics, who have provided so many teaching ideas and insights into their particular students and courses. We hope you will be able to see in the book and the teaching package consideration of those ideas and insights.

Sung Ahn, *Washington State University*
Mostafa Aminzadeh, *Towson University*
Scott Bailey, *Troy University*
Hope Baker, *Kennesaw State University*
Saad Taha Bakir, *Alabama State University*
Katherine Broneck, *Pima Community College—Downtown*
Mary Beth Camp, *Indiana University—Bloomington*
Alan Cannon, *University of Texas—Arlington*
Deborah Carter, *Coahoma Community College*
Michael Cervetti, *University of Memphis*
Alan Chesen, *Wright State University*
Chia-Shin Chung, *Cleveland State University*
Joseph Coleman, *Wright State University—Dayton*
Robert Cutshall, *Texas A&M University—Corpus Christi*
Terry Dalton, *University of Denver*
Douglas Dotterweich, *East Tennessee State University*
Michael Easley, *University of New Orleans*
Mark Farber, *University of Miami*
Soheila Kahkashan Fardanesh, *Towson University*
Mark Ferris, *St. Louis University*
Stergios Fotopoulos, *Washington State University*
Vickie Fry, *Westmoreland County Community College*
Joseph Fuhr, *Widener University*
Bob Gillette, *University of Kentucky*
Don Gren, *Salt Lake City Community College*

Clifford Hawley, *West Virginia University*
Natalie Hegwood, *Sam Houston State University*
Alam M. Imam, *University of Northern Iowa*
Marc Isaacson, *Augsburg College*
Kishen Iyengar, *University of Colorado—Boulder*
Christopher Johnson, *University of North Florida*
Jerzy Kamburowski, *University of Toledo*
Bob Kitahara, *Troy University*
Drew Koch, *James Madison University*
Bob Lynch, *University of Northern Colorado*
Bradley McDonald, *Northern Illinois University*
Richard McGowan, *Boston College*
Larry McRae, *Appalachian State University*
Kelly McKillop, *University of Massachusetts*
Robert Mee, *University of Tennessee—Knoxville*
John Miller, *Sam Houston State University*
James E. Moran, Jr., *Oregon State University*
Geraldine Moultine, *Northwood University*
Joshua Naranjo, *Western Michigan University*
Anthony Narsing, *Macon State College*
Pin Ng, *Northern Arizona University*
Thomas Obremski, *University of Denver*
Mohammad Reza Oskoorouchi, *California State University—San Marcos*
Mahour Mellat Parast, *University of North Carolina—Pembroke*
Eddy Patuwo, *Kent State University*

John Pickett, *University of Arkansas—Little Rock*
James Pokorski, *Virginia Polytechnic Institute & State University*
Stephan Pollard, *California State University—Los Angeles*
Tammy Prater, *Alabama State University*
Michael Racer, *University of Memphis*
Azar Raiszadeh, *Chattanooga State Community College*
Sue Schou, *Idaho State University*
Sankara N. Sethuraman, *Augusta State University*
Thomas R. Sexton, *Stony Brook University*
Murali Shanker, *Kent State University*
Gary W. Smith, *Florida State University*
Courtenay Stone, *Ball State University*
Paul Swanson, *Illinois Central College*
Deborah Tesch, *Xavier University*
Dharma S. Thiruvaiyaru, *Augusta State University*
Jesus M. Valencia, *Slippery Rock University*
Rachel Webb, *Portland State University*
Simone A. Wegge, *City University of New York*
Alan Wheeler, *University of Missouri—St. Louis*
Blake Whitten, *University of Iowa*
Charles Wilf, *Duquesne University*
Janet Wolcutt, *Wichita State University*
Ye Zhang, *Indiana University—Purdue University Indianapolis*
Mustafa R. Yilmaz, *Northeastern University*

Many changes were motivated by advice from dozens of reviewers and users of the textbook. We wanted to make chapter material easier for students to understand and to sharpen our focus on essential concepts. Besides thousands of small edits, six changes were common to all chapters:

- Reorganized and streamlined presentations of key topics with simple visuals and intuitive explanations.
- Thorough coverage of new Excel functions with updated screen shots and examples in each chapter.
- Updated data sets, new practice exercises, and exercises matched to chapter learning objectives.

- New Appendix J with detailed comparison of old and new Excel statistical functions—an outstanding reference tool.
- Closer compatibility of exercises with *Connect Plus* online homework assignments.
- Updated *Related Readings* and *Web Sources* for students who want to "dive deeper."

Chapter 1—Overview of Statistics

Revised material on motivation, business ethics, critical thinking, and communication.

Revised Vail Resorts and NASA Mini Cases.

Three new critical thinking exercises, one deleted exercise.

Five revised exercises to match learning objective and Connect.

Updated references (delete three, add two).

Chapter 2—Data Collection

Clarified definitions of categorical and numerical data.

Eleven new exercises, seven updated exercises, and 10 deleted exercises.

Consolidated discussion on time series data, simplified discussion on random sampling, and deletion of redundant figures and tables resulting in a more concise chapter.

Emphasized difference between random and nonrandom sampling.

New Mini Case "Pricing Accuracy."

Chapter 3—Describing Data Visually

New common terminology (center, variability).

Added stem-and-leaf plots, with illustrations and practice exercises, as requested by several reviewers.

Reorganized material on dotplots, pie charts, and deceptive graphs.

Updated examples (price/earnings, school spending, medical school applicants by gender, U.S. trade balance).

Updated Mini Case on U.S. business cycles with discussion of the latest recession.

Twenty new Excel screen shots (histograms, line and bar charts, scatter plots, pivot tables).

Updated MegaStat and Minitab screen shots to reflect latest versions.

Updated exercises (e.g., J.D. Power vehicle defects, LCD shipments, Rose Bowl scores, U.S. gas prices, petroleum and energy use).

Delete four exercises and three figures to reduce clutter and condense the material.

Four new exercises (home sales, civil service exams, power outages, package weights).

Chapter 4—Descriptive Statistics

New common terminology (center, variability).

Updated data sets (e.g., vehicle defects, SuperBowl scores, microprocessor speed, weighted means, tax preparation time).

Two deleted figures, 13 revised figures.

Rewritten quartiles and percentiles with new Excel functions and simplified exercises.

More on variance and covariance with new and old Excel functions compared.

New visuals for quartiles, IQR, and fences.

Six updated exercises, seven deleted exercises, and 13 revised exercises.

Exercise content more closely matched with learning objectives and Connect.

Ten new exercises (e.g., days on market, civil service exams, fuel economy, unusual observations, quartiles, boxplots, Chebychev).

Updated chapter references.

Chapter 5—Probability

Clarified notation on calculating relative frequencies.

Two new figures illustrating coin flips and conditional probabilities.

Six new exercises on recognizing probability types, odds, and independent events.

Expanded discussion of Law of Addition and Law of Multiplication and one new example.

New "boxed" format for most formulas.

Clarified and reorganized discussion on independent events.

Consolidated discussion of disjoint events and deleted five figures and tables to reduce clutter.

Ten revised exercises and five deleted exercises.

Chapter 6—Discrete Probability Distributions

Improved notation for variance of a random variable.

Updated three examples and one Mini Case with current data.

Updated four figures with Excel 2010 screenshots.

Updated all Excel functions for Excel 2010.

Three deleted exercises and 15 revised or updated exercises.

Delete three figures to reduce clutter.

Ten new exercises.

Clarified discussion and examples for compound events.

Clarified description of covariance.

Chapter 7—Continuous Probability Distributions

Enhanced definitions throughout chapter.

New tables showing important normal areas.

Clarified step-by-step solutions for examples.

Modifications in one figure and two examples for the exponential distribution.

Added a new application for triangular distribution.

Added a new *LearningStats* module for Rule of 10 for normal-binomial equivalency.

Twelve new exercises on standard normal, finding areas, inverse normal, and normal approximations to discrete probabilities.

Five revised exercises and two deleted exercises.

New figures, tables, and Excel 2010 screen shots on normal probabilities.

New Excel 2010 functions.

Chapter 8—Sampling Distributions and Estimation

Reorganized and expanded discussion of sampling error.

New section on estimating from finite populations.

Rewritten discussion on how to deal with outliers and messy data.

Clarified interpretation of confidence intervals for proportions.

Three revised examples and two new examples.

Two new exercises on the standard error and sampling distributions.

Two new exercises on calculating a confidence interval for μ with σ known.

Two new Student's t "practice" exercises on confidence intervals for μ.

Four new exercises using the FPCF.

Three new end-of-chapter exercises for confidence intervals.

One new student MiniProject on sampling NYSE stock prices for IPOs.

Deleted two figures and revised one figure.

Deleted six exercises and revised seven exercises.

Updated all Excel functions for Excel 2010.

Chapter 9—One-Sample Hypothesis Tests

Reorganized and streamlined sections on Types I and II error, hypothesis formulation.

Consistent use of five steps in hypothesis testing in examples.

Improved visuals for decision rules.

Coverage of new Excel functions with updated screen shots and examples.

Nine new exercises (Types I and II error, formulating H_0 and H_1, critical z and t values, p-values) and six revised exercises.

New Mini Case showing how Ball Corporation uses statistics to compare metal suppliers.

Chapter 10—Two-Sample Hypothesis Tests

Reorganized hypothesis testing presentation for tests of means in two independent samples.

Consistent use of five-step hypothesis testing method with updates for new Excel functions.

New Mini Case on greenhouse gas emissions from pneumatic controllers.

Deleted two figures and one Mini Case (JASA).

Improved visuals for paired t-tests and four new exercises, as requested by reviewers.

Added two new exercises on independent means and deleted four exercises.

Chapter 11—Analysis of Variance

Simplified chapter introduction with visuals that focus on one-factor ANOVA.

Four new exercises on interpreting ANOVA results rather than working from raw data.

Two new practice exercises that focus on setting up Tukey and Hartley tests.

Consistent use of five-step method of hypothesis testing.

Chapter 12—Simple Regression

Better articulated learning objectives.

Expanded introduction with a new figure and a new example.

More intuitive description of correlation.

Clarified interpretation of linear model.

Rewritten discussion of population model.

Improved notation for regression statistics.

Expanded discussion of most formulas.

New illustration for regression parameters and error assumptions.

Rewritten section on residual tests to enhance diagnostic steps.

One new example and two revised examples.

Two new exercises on interpreting the regression line, four new exercises on unusual residuals, and two new exercises on residual assumptions.

Three new end-of-chapter data sets, five revised exercises, and four deleted exercises.

Updated figures and functions for Excel 2010.

Chapter 13—Multiple Regression

Rewritten introduction to provide more intuitive motivation for topic.

Better definitions of technical terms and motivation for using F test.

Added formula for standard error of regression coefficients.

Improved notation for regression statistics.

Clarified discussion of categorical predictors.

Replaced Mini Cases 13.3 and 13.5 with current data.

New figure illustrating nonlinear relationship.

Modified section 13.8 to reduce redundancy with section 12.8.

Added discussion on logistic regression.

Two new exercises on nonlinear and interaction terms.

One new exercise on leverage, one on error assumptions, and added two new data sets to end of chapter.

Chapter 14—Time-Series Analysis

New examples for labor market participation, dollar exchange rates, Amazon sales, hospital costs, and space launches.

New data for exercises on work stoppages, new car dealerships, Swiss watch exports, TV viewing, voter participation, consumer credit, beverage consumption, PepsiCo, JetBlue,

Olympic 100m times, U.S. federal budget, Boston Marathon, student pilots, Coca Cola.

Updated Mini Case on the U.S. trade deficit.

Deleted four exercises and added one exercise.

New Excel 2010 screen shots, updated chapter references, and updated examples.

Chapter 15—Chi-Square Tests

Added discussion on how to use Excel's CHISQ.TEST function.

Updated Excel or MegaStat screen shots and new content for one figure.

Updated example on Supreme Court appointees.

Deleted two figures and one table.

Reorganized section 15.6.

Added three new exercises on the multinomial GOF test.

Added one new exercise on the Poisson GOF test and revised two exercises.

Chapter 16—Nonparametric Tests

New treatment of Wilcoxon rank sum test (Mann-Whitney test) with restaurant quality illustration of two versions of the test.

Two new exercises (Mann-Whitney test for salaries in two industries, rank correlation in movie review ratings).

New data for EU fertility rates.

Updated chapter references.

Chapter 17—Quality Management

Deleted two sections and merged content with existing sections.

Rewritten discussions on productivity, types of variation, and statisticians' roles in quality improvement.

Condensed discussion of quality experts.

Added discussion on service quality tools.

New figure illustrating process capability.

Added four exercises on definitions and six exercises on quality programs and tools.

Chapter 18—Simulation

Updated treatment of random data generation based on new Excel functions.

Updated @Risk discussion corresponding to newer software version.

Ten new @Risk and Excel screen shots based on newer software versions.

Updated chapter references and Web links for simulation and queuing software (e.g., Visio, Arena, YASAI, XLMiner).

BRIEF CONTENTS

CONTENTS

Applied
Statistics

in Business and Economics

Fourth Edition

Overview of Statistics

CHAPTER LEARNING OBJECTIVES

LO

When you finish this chapter you should be able to

LO 1-1   Define statistics and explain some of its uses in business.

LO 1-2   List reasons for a business student to study statistics.

LO 1-3   State the common challenges facing business professionals using statistics.

LO 1-4   List and explain common statistical pitfalls.

Prelude

When managers are well informed about a company's internal operations (e.g., sales, production, inventory levels, time to market, warranty claims) and competitive position (e.g., market share, customer satisfaction, repeat sales) they can take appropriate actions to improve their business. Managers need reliable, timely information so they can analyze market trends and adjust to changing market conditions. Better data can also help a company decide which types of strategic information they should share with trusted business partners to improve their supply chain. *Statistics* and *statistical analysis* permit *data-based decision making* and reduce managers' need to rely on guesswork.

Statistics is a key component of the field of *business intelligence,* which encompasses all the technologies for collecting, storing, accessing, and analyzing data on the company's operations in order to make better business decisions. Statistics helps convert unstructured "raw" data (e.g., point-of-sale data, customer spending patterns) into *useful information* through online analytical processing (OLAP) and data mining, terms that you may have encountered in your other business classes. Statistical analysis focuses attention on key problems and guides discussion toward issues, not personalities or territorial struggles. While powerful database software and query systems are the key to managing a firm's data warehouse, relatively small Excel spreadsheets are often the focus of discussion among managers when it comes to "bottom line" decisions. That is why Excel is featured prominently in this textbook.

In short, companies increasingly are using *business analytics* to support decision making, to recognize anomalies that require tactical action, or to gain strategic insight to align business processes with business objectives. Answers to questions such as "How likely is this event?" or "What if this trend continues?" will lead to appropriate actions. Businesses that combine managerial judgment with statistical analysis are more successful.

1.1 WHAT IS STATISTICS?

Statistics is the science of collecting, organizing, analyzing, interpreting, and presenting data. Some experts prefer to call statistics *data science,* a trilogy of tasks involving data modeling, analysis, and decision making. Here are some alternative definitions.

Statistics

"I like to think of statistics as the science of learning from data . . ."
Jon Kettenring, American Statistical Association President, 1997

"The mathematics of the collection, organization, and interpretation of numerical data, especially the analysis of population characteristics by inference from sampling."
American Heritage Dictionary®*

"Statistical analysis involves collecting information, evaluating it, drawing conclusions, and providing guidance in what information is reliable and which predictions can be trusted."
American Statistical Association

In contrast, a **statistic** is a single measure, reported as a number, used to summarize a sample data set. Many different measures can be used to summarize data sets. You will learn throughout this textbook that there can be different measures for different sets of data and different measures for different types of questions about the same data set. Consider, for example, a sample data set that consists of heights of students in a university. There could be many different uses for this data set. Perhaps the manufacturer of graduation gowns wants to know how long to make the gowns; the best *statistic* for this would be the *average* height of the students. But an architect designing a classroom building would want to know how high the doorways should be, and would base measurements on the *maximum* height of the students. Both the average and the maximum are examples of a *statistic*.

You may not have a trained statistician in your organization, but any college graduate is expected to know something about statistics, and anyone who creates graphs or interprets data is "doing statistics" without an official title.

VAILRESORTS

Mini Case	1.1

Vail Resorts

What do the following experiences have in common with *statistics:* an epic ski down a snowy mountain, a superb day of golf, a restful night's sleep, and plentiful clean water for wildlife? Vail Resorts, Inc., has been successfully providing these experiences through the use of rigorous data analysis.

How does Vail Resorts achieve growth? One way is to increase ski lift ticket revenue. Prior to the 2008/2009 ski season, Vail Resorts management asked their marketing group to figure out how to increase the number of annual visits from their destination guests. Customer surveys indicated that having more flexibility around vacation planning would increase the chance that they visited more than once per year. A new season pass of some sort that allowed multiple ski days throughout the ski season was one possible solution. Vail Resorts currently offers The Colorado Pass, which is attractive to in-state guests. But this pass product was not available to out-of-state guests. Vail Resorts needed answers to questions such as: Which resorts should be included on the pass? How many ski days should the pass offer? Should there be blackout dates or not? What price would make the pass attractive?

Four market surveys were sent out to random samples of current and potential guests, including out-of-state guests, in-state guests, and Vail Valley residents. The responses were then used in a statistical analysis to determine relative importance of the various pass features so that the optimal pass product could be offered. What the Vail Resorts marketing team found was that guests were most concerned about the pass price but still wanted to be able to ski at all five ski areas owned by Vail Resorts: Vail, Beaver Creek, Breckenridge, Keystone, and Heavenly. Guests also wanted unlimited days of skiing at Vail and Beaver Creek, and did not want any dates blacked out.

The Epic Pass was first offered for sale on March 18, 2008, for a price of $579. Customers kept their word. By December 9, 2008, over 59,000 Epic Passes had been purchased for total sales revenue of $32.5 million. The number of total passes sold had increased by 18 percent and total pass revenue had increased by 29 percent over the previous pass sales season.

American Heritage Dictionary of the English Language, 4th ed. Copyright © 2000 by Houghton Mifflin Company. Used with permission.

www.vailresorts.com

In the following chapters, look for the Vail Resorts logo VAIL RESORTS next to examples and exercises to learn more about how Vail Resorts uses data analysis and statistics to:

- Decrease waiting times to purchase lift tickets.
- Maintain a healthy ratio of out-of-state to in-state guests.
- Help guests feel safe on the mountain.
- Keep hotel rooms booked.
- Increase the percentage of employees who return each season.
- Ensure a healthy environment for wildlife at Grand Teton National Park.

1.2 WHY STUDY STATISTICS?

A 2006 *BusinessWeek* article called statistics and probability "core skills for businesspeople" in order to know when others are dissembling, to build financial models, or to develop a marketing plan. This same report also said that "B-school grads with strong calculus will find far more opportunities." Each year, *The Wall Street Journal* asks corporate recruiters to rate U.S. business schools on various attributes. In a 2006 *WSJ* survey, recruiters said that the top five attributes were (1) communication and interpersonal skills; (2) ability to work well within a team; (3) personal ethics and integrity; (4) analytical and problem-solving skills; and (5) work ethic. (See "Why Math Will Rock Your World," *BusinessWeek*, January 23, 2006, p. 60; and *The Wall Street Journal*, Sept. 20, 2006.)

LO 1-2

List reasons for a business student to study statistics.

Data Skills Count

"We look to recruit and groom leaders in our organization who possess strong quantitative skills in addition to a passion for what we do—delivering exceptional experiences at our extraordinary resorts every day. Knowing how to use and interpret data when making important business decisions is one of the keys to our Company's success."

Rob Katz, chairman and chief executive officer of Vail Resorts

Knowing statistics will make you a better consumer of other people's data analyses. You should know enough to handle everyday data problems, to feel confident that others cannot deceive you with spurious arguments, and to know when you've reached the limits of your expertise. Statistical knowledge gives your company a competitive advantage versus those that cannot understand their internal or external market data. Mastery of basic statistics gives you, the individual manager, a competitive advantage as you work your way through the promotion process, or when you move to a new employer. Here are some more reasons to study statistics.

Communication   The language of statistics is widely used in science, social science, education, health care, engineering, and even the humanities. In all areas of business (accounting, finance, human resources, marketing, information systems, operations management), workers use statistical jargon to facilitate communication. In fact, statistical terminology has reached the highest corporate strategic levels (e.g., "Six Sigma" at GE and Motorola). And in the multinational environment, the specialized vocabulary of statistics permeates language barriers to improve problem solving across national boundaries.

Computer Skills   Whatever your computer skill level, it can be improved. Every time you create a spreadsheet for data analysis, write a report, or make an oral presentation, you bring together skills you already have, and learn new ones. Specialists with advanced training design the databases and decision support systems, but you must handle daily data problems *without* experts. Besides, you can't always find an "expert," and, if you do, the "expert" may not understand your application very well. You need to be able to analyze data, use software with confidence, prepare your own charts, write your own reports, and make electronic presentations on technical topics.

Information Management   Statistics can help you handle either too little or too much information. When insufficient data are available, statistical surveys and samples can be used to obtain the necessary market information. But most large organizations are closer to drowning in data than starving for it. Statistics can help summarize large amounts of data and reveal underlying relationships. You've heard of data mining? Statistics is the pick and shovel that you take to the data mine.

Technical Literacy   Many of the best career opportunities are in growth industries propelled by advanced technology. Marketing staff may work with engineers, scientists, and manufacturing experts as new products and services are developed. Sales representatives must understand and explain technical products like pharmaceuticals, medical equipment, and industrial tools to potential customers. Purchasing managers must evaluate suppliers' claims about the quality of raw materials, components, software, or parts.

Process Improvement   Large manufacturing firms like Boeing or Toyota have formal systems for continuous quality improvement. The same is true of insurance companies and financial service firms like Vanguard or Fidelity, and the federal government. Statistics helps firms oversee their suppliers, monitor their internal operations, and identify problems. Quality improvement goes far beyond statistics, but every college graduate is expected to know enough statistics to understand its role in quality improvement.

Mini Case   1.2

Can Statistics Predict Airfares?

When you book an airline ticket online, does it annoy you when the next day you find a cheaper fare on exactly the same flight? Or do you congratulate yourself when you get a "good" fare followed by a price rise? This ticket price volatility led to the creation of a new company called Farecast that examines over 150 billion "airfare observations" and tries to use the data to predict whether or not the fare for a given ticket is likely to rise. The company's prediction accuracy so far is estimated at 61 percent (in independent tests) and 75 percent (the company's tests). In this case, the benchmark is a coin toss (50 percent). The company offers price rise insurance for a small fee. If you travel a lot and like to play the odds, such predictions could save money. With online air bookings at $44 billion, a few dollars saved here and there can add up. (See *Budget Travel,* February 2007, p. 37; and *The New York Times,* "An Insurance Policy for Low Airfares," January 22, 2007, p. C10.)

1.3 USES OF STATISTICS

There are two primary kinds of statistics:

- **Descriptive statistics** refers to the collection, organization, presentation, and summary of data (either using charts and graphs or using a numerical summary).
- **Inferential statistics** refers to generalizing from a sample to a population, estimating unknown population parameters, drawing conclusions, and making decisions.

Figure 1.1 identifies the tasks and the text chapters for each.

FIGURE 1.1

Overview of Statistics

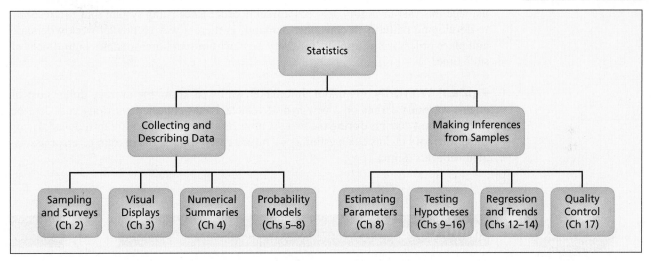

Now let's look at some of the ways statistics is used in business.

Auditing   A large firm pays over 12,000 invoices to suppliers every month. The firm has learned that some invoices are being paid incorrectly, but they don't know how widespread the problem is. The auditors lack the resources to check all the invoices, so they decide to take a sample to estimate the proportion of incorrectly paid invoices. How large should the sample be for the auditors to be confident that the estimate is close enough to the true proportion?

Marketing   A marketing consultant is asked to identify likely repeat customers for Amazon.com, and to suggest co-marketing opportunities based on a database containing records of 5 million Internet purchases of books, CDs, and DVDs. How can this large database be mined to reveal useful patterns that might guide the marketing strategy?

Health Care   Health care is a major business (1/6 of the U.S. GDP). Hospitals, clinics, and their suppliers can save money by finding better ways to manage patient appointments, schedule procedures, or rotate their staff. For example, an outpatient cognitive retraining clinic for victims of closed-head injuries or stroke evaluates 56 incoming patients using a 42-item physical and mental assessment questionnaire. Each patient is evaluated independently by two experienced therapists. Are there statistically significant differences between the two therapists' evaluations of incoming patients' functional status? Are some assessment questions redundant? Do the initial assessment scores accurately predict the patients' lengths of stay in the program?

Quality Improvement   A manufacturer of rolled copper tubing for radiators wishes to improve its product quality. It initiates a triple inspection program, sets penalties for workers who produce poor-quality output, and posts a slogan calling for "zero defects." The approach fails. Why?

Purchasing   A retailer's shipment of 200 DVD players reveals 4 with defects. The supplier's historical defect rate is .005. Has the defect rate really risen, or is this simply a "bad" batch?

Medicine   An experimental drug to treat asthma is given to 75 patients, of whom 24 get better. A placebo is given to a control group of 75 volunteers, of whom 12 get better. Is the new drug better than the placebo, or is the difference within the realm of chance?

Operations Management   The Home Depot carries 50,000 different products. To manage this vast inventory, it needs a weekly order forecasting system that can respond to developing patterns in consumer demand. Is there a way to predict weekly demand and place orders from suppliers for every item, without an unreasonable commitment of staff time?

Product Warranty   A major automaker wants to know the average dollar cost of engine warranty claims on a new hybrid vehicle. It has collected warranty cost data on 4,300 warranty claims during the first six months after the engines are introduced. Using these warranty claims as an estimate of future costs, what is the margin of error associated with this estimate?

Mini Case	1.3

How Do You Sell Noodles with Statistics?

"The best answer starts with a thorough and thoughtful analysis of the data," says Aaron Kennedy, founder and chairman of Noodles & Company.

(Visit www.noodles.com to find a Noodles & Company restaurant near you.)

Noodles & Company introduced the *quick casual* restaurant concept, redefining the standard for modern casual dining in the United States in the 21st century. Noodles & Company first opened in Colorado in 1995 and has not stopped growing since. As of June 2009, they had over 210 restaurants all across the United States from Portland and Encinitas to Alexandria and Silver Spring with stops in cities such as Omaha and Naperville.

Noodles & Company has achieved this success with a customer-driven business model and fact-based decision making. Their widespread popularity and high growth rate have been supported by careful consideration of data and thorough statistical analysis that provide answers to questions such as:

- Should we offer continuity/loyalty cards for our customers?
- How can we increase the use of our extra capacity during the dinner hours?
- Which new city should we open in?
- Which location should we choose for the new restaurant?
- How do we determine the effectiveness of a marketing campaign?
- Which meal maximizes the chance that a new customer will return?
- Are Rice Krispies related to higher sales?
- Does reducing service time increase sales?

Aaron Kennedy, founder of Noodles & Company, says that "using data is the strongest way to inform good decisions. By assessing our internal and external environments on a continuous basis, our Noodles management team has been able to plan and execute our vision."

"I had no idea as a business student that I'd be using statistical analysis as extensively as I do now," says Dave Boennighausen, vice president of finance at Noodles & Company. In the coming chapters, as you learn about the statistical tools businesses use today, look for the Noodles logo ⬭ next to examples and exercises that show how Noodles uses data and statistical methods in its business functions.

SECTION EXERCISES

1.1 Give an example of how statistics might be useful to the person in the scenario.

   a. An auditor is looking for inflated broker commissions in stock transactions.

   b. An industrial marketer is representing her firm's compact, new low-power OLED screens to the military.

   c. A plant manager is studying absenteeism at vehicle assembly plants in three states.

   d. An automotive purchasing agent is comparing defect rates in steel shipments from three vendors of steel.

1.2 Give an example of how statistics might be useful to the person in the scenario.

   a. A personnel executive is examining job turnover by gender in different restaurants in a fast-food chain.

   b. An intranet manager is studying e-mail usage rates by employees in different job classifications.

   c. A retirement planner is studying mutual fund performance for six different types of asset portfolios.

   d. A hospital administrator is studying surgery scheduling to improve facility utilization rates at different times of day.

1.3 (a) Should the average business school graduate expect to use computers to manipulate data, or is this a job better left to specialists? (b) What problems arise when an employee is weak in quantitative skills? Based on your experience, is that common?

1.4 "Many college graduates will not use very much statistics during their 40-year careers, so why study it?" (a) List several arguments for and against this statement. Which position do you find more convincing? (b) Replace the word "statistics" with "accounting" or "foreign language" and repeat this exercise.

1.5 (a) How much statistics does a student need in *your* chosen field of study? Why not more? Why not less? (b) How can you tell when the point has been reached where you should call for an expert statistician? List some costs and some benefits that would govern this decision.

1.4 STATISTICAL CHALLENGES

LO 1-3

State the common challenges facing business professionals using statistics.

Business professionals who use statistics are not mere number crunchers who are "good at math." As Jon Kettenring succinctly said, "Industry needs holistic statisticians who are nimble problem solvers" (www.amstat.org). Consider the criteria listed below:

The ideal data analyst

- Is technically current (e.g., software-wise).
- Communicates well.
- Is proactive.
- Has a broad outlook.
- Is flexible.
- Focuses on the main problem.
- Meets deadlines.
- Knows his/her limitations and is willing to ask for help.
- Can deal with imperfect information.
- Has professional integrity.

Clearly, many of these characteristics would apply to any *business* professional.

Role of Communication Skills

"Leaders differentiate themselves by *how* they get jobs done. The how is largely about communication. By communication, I mean both written and oral skills, and both listening and presentation skills. Leaders are able to present their ideas and knowledge in complete thoughts that leave no room for guessing. They are able to achieve funding for projects by using data to articulate a strong written business case and return on investment. They effectively engage and listen to others, ultimately gaining buy-in and a comprehensive solution. These tasks are dependent upon excellent communication skills—a core competency for leaders at all levels."

Comments on leadership skills by Mark Gasta, senior vice president and chief human resources officer, Vail Resorts Management Company

Imperfect Data and Practical Constraints

In mathematics, exact answers are expected. But statistics lies at the messy interface between theory and reality. For instance, suppose a new air bag design is being tested. Is the new air bag design safer for children? Test data indicate the design may be safer in some crash situations, but the old design appears safer in others. The crash tests are expensive and time-consuming, so the sample size is limited. A few observations are missing due to sensor failures in the crash dummies. There may be random measurement errors. If you are the data analyst, what can you do? Well, you can know and use generally accepted statistical methods, clearly state any assumptions you are forced to make, and honestly point out the limitations of your analysis. You can use statistical tests to detect unusual data points or to deal with missing data. You can give a range of answers under varying assumptions. But occasionally, you need the courage to say, "No useful answer can emerge from these data."

You will face constraints on the type and quantity of data you can collect. Automobile crash tests can't use human subjects (*too risky*). Telephone surveys can't ask a female respondent whether or not she has had an abortion (*sensitive question*). We can't test everyone for HIV (*the world is not a laboratory*). Survey respondents may not tell the truth or may not answer all the questions (*human behavior is unpredictable*). Every analyst faces constraints of time and money (*research is not free*).

Business Ethics

In your business ethics class, you learned (or will learn) the broad ethical responsibilities of business, such as treating customers in a fair and honest manner, complying with laws that prohibit discrimination, ensuring that products and services meet safety regulations, standing behind warranties, and advertising in a factual and informative manner. You learned that organizations should encourage employees to ask questions and voice concerns about the company's business practices, and give employees access to alternative channels of communication if they fear reprisal. But as an individual employee, *you* are responsible for accurately reporting information to management, including potential sources of error, material inaccuracies, and degrees of uncertainty. A data analyst faces a more specific set of ethical requirements.

Surveys of corporate recruiters show that ethics and personal integrity rank high on their list of hiring criteria. The respected analyst is an honest broker of data. He or she uses statistics to find out the truth, not to represent a popular point of view. Scrutinize your own motives carefully. If you manipulate numbers or downplay inconvenient data, you may succeed in fooling your competitors (or yourself) for a while. But what is the point? Sooner or later the facts will reveal themselves, and you (or your company) will be the loser. Quantitative analyses in business can quantify the risks of alternative courses of action and events. For example, statistics can help managers set realistic expectations on sales volume, revenues, and costs. An inflated sales forecast or an understated cost estimate may propel a colleague's favorite product program from the planning board to an actual capital investment. But a poor analysis may cost both of you your jobs.

Headline scandals such as Bernard L. Madoff's financial pyramid that cost investors as much as $65 billion (*The New York Times,* April 11, 2009, p. B1) or tests of pain relievers financed by drug companies whose results turned out to be based on falsified data (*NewScientist,* March 21, 2009, p. 4) are easily recognizable as willful lying or criminal acts. You might say, "I would never do things like that." Yet in day-to-day handling of data, you may not *know* whether the data are accurate or not. You may not *know* the uses to which the data will be put. You may not *know* of potential conflicts of interest. You and other employees (including top management) will need training to recognize the boundaries of what is or is not ethical within the context of your organization and the decision at hand.

Find out whether your organization has a code of ethics. If not, initiate efforts to create such a code. Fortunately, ideas and help are available (e.g., www.ethicsweb.ca/codes/). Since every organization is different, the issues will depend on your company's business environment. Creating or improving a code of ethics will generally require employee involvement to identify likely conflicts of interest, to look for sources of data inaccuracy, and to update company policies on disclosure and confidentiality. Everyone must understand the code and know the rules for follow-up when ethics violations are suspected.

Upholding Ethical Standards

Let's look at how ethical requirements might apply to anyone who analyzes data and writes reports for management. You need to know the specific rules to protect your professional integrity and to minimize the chance of inadvertent ethical breaches. Ask questions, think about hidden agendas, and dig deeper into how data were collected. Here are some basic rules for the data analyst:

- Know and follow accepted procedures.
- Maintain data integrity.
- Carry out accurate calculations.
- Report procedures faithfully.
- Protect confidential information.
- Cite sources.
- Acknowledge sources of financial support.

Because legal and ethical issues are intertwined, there are specific ethical guidelines for statisticians concerning treatment of human and animal subjects, privacy protection, obtaining informed consent, and guarding against inappropriate uses of data. For further information about ethics, see the American Statistical Association's ethical guidelines (www.amstat.org), which have been extensively reviewed by the statistics profession.

Ethical dilemmas for a nonstatistician are likely to involve conflicts of interest or competing interpretations of the validity of a study and/or its implications. For example, suppose a market research firm is hired to investigate a new corporate logo. The CEO lets you know that she strongly favors a new logo, and it's a big project that could earn you a promotion. Yet, the market data have a high error margin and could support either conclusion. As a manager, you will face such situations. Statistical practices and statistical data can clarify your choices.

A *perceived* ethical problem may be just that—*perceived*. For example, it may appear that a company promotes more men than women into management roles while, in reality, the promotion rates for men and women are the same. The perceived inequity could be a result of fewer female employees to begin with. In this situation, organizations might work hard to hire more women, thus increasing the pool of women who are promotable. Statistics plays a role in sorting out ethical business dilemmas by using data to uncover *real* versus *perceived* differences, identify root causes of problems, and gauge public attitudes toward organizational behavior.

Using Consultants

Students often comment on the first day of their statistics class that they don't need to learn statistics because businesses rely on consultants to do the data analyses. This is a misconception. Today's successful companies expect their employees to be able to perform all types of statistical analyses, from the simple descriptive analyses to the more complex inferential analyses. They also expect their employees to be able to interpret the results of a statistical analysis, even if it was completed by an outside consultant. Organizations have been asking business schools across the nation to increase the level of quantitative instruction that students receive and, when hiring, are increasingly giving priority to candidates with strong quantitative skills.

This is not to say that statistical consultants are a dying breed. When an organization is faced with a decision that has serious public policy implications or high cost consequences, hiring a consultant can be a smart move. An hour with an expert at the *beginning* of a project could be the smartest move a manager can make. When should a consultant be hired? When your team lacks certain critical skills, or when an unbiased or informed view cannot be found inside your organization. Expert consultants can handle domineering or indecisive team members, personality clashes, fears about adverse findings, and local politics. Large and medium-sized companies may have in-house statisticians, but smaller firms only hire them as needed. Obtain agreement at the outset on the consultant's rates and duties. Fees should be by the hour or job (never contingent on the findings). If you hire a statistical expert, you can make better use of the consultant's time by learning how consultants work. Read books about statistical consulting. If your company employs a statistician, take him or her to lunch!

Keep It Simple

"When we communicate statistics, there are two things I want to make sure don't happen. One is showing off and using too much statistical jargon to our clients. The second thing is adding too many details . . . I prefer a two-sentence explanation or overview in language that would be clear to our clients."

From an interview with Mary Batcher, executive director of Ernst and Young's Quantitative Economics and Statistics Group. Reprinted with permission from Amstat News, *July 2010, p. 29. Copyright 2010 by the American Statistical Association. All rights reserved.*

Communicating with Numbers

Numbers have meaning only when communicated in the context of a certain situation. Busy managers rarely have time to read and digest detailed explanations of numbers. **Appendix I** contains advice on technical report writing and oral presentations. But you probably already know that attractive graphs will enhance a technical report, and help other managers quickly understand the information they need to make a good decision. Chapter 3 will give detailed directions for effective tables and graphs using Excel.

But how do we present a table or graph in a written report? Tables should be embedded in the narrative (*not* on a separate page) near the paragraph in which they are cited. Each table should have a number and title. Graphs should be embedded in the narrative (*not* on a separate page) near the paragraph in which they are discussed. Each table or graph should have a title and number. A graph may make things clearer. For example, compare Table 1.1 and Figure 1.2. Which is more helpful in understanding U.S. trademark activity in recent years?

TABLE 1.1	U.S. Trademarks, 1999–2005 (thousands)						
	1999	*2000*	*2001*	*2002*	*2003*	*2004*	*2005*
Applications Filed	328.6	361.8	277.3	264.1	271.7	304.5	334.7
Trademarks Issued	191.9	115.2	142.9	176.0	166.6	146.0	154.8

Source: U.S. Census Bureau, *Statistical Abstract of the United States, 2007*, p. 507. A trademark (identified with ®) is a name or symbol identifying a product, registered with the U.S. Patent and Trademark Office and restricted by law to use by its owner.

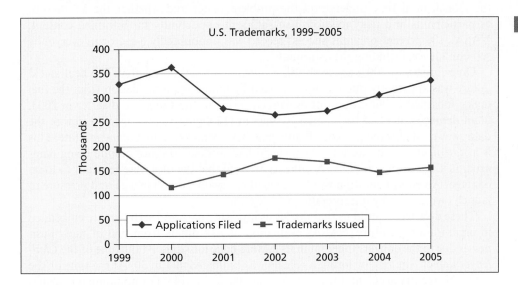

FIGURE 1.2

U.S. Trademarks, 1999–2005

SECTION EXERCISES

1.6   The U.S. Public Interest Research Group Education Fund, USPIRG, recently published a report titled *The Campus Credit Card Trap: A Survey of College Students about Credit Card Marketing*. You can find this report and more information about campus credit card marketing at www.truthaboutcredit.org. Read this report and then answer the following questions about how statistics plays a role in resolving ethical dilemmas.

    a. What is the perceived ethical issue highlighted in this report?

    b. How did USPIRG conduct their study to collect information and data?

    c. What broad categories did their survey address?

    d. Did the survey data verify that the issue was a real, instead of a perceived, ethical problem?

    e. Do you agree with the study's assessment of the issue? Why or why not?

    f. Based on the results of the survey, is the issue widespread? Explain.

    g. Describe the report's suggested solutions to confront unethical business practices.

1.7   Using your favorite Web browser, enter the search string "business code of ethics." List five examples of features that a business ethics code should have.

Mini Case   1.4

Lessons from NASA

The late President Lyndon Baines Johnson observed, "A President's hardest task is not to *do* what is right, but to *know* what is right." What's missing is wisdom, not courage. Given incomplete or contradictory data, people have trouble making decisions (remember *Hamlet*?). Sometimes the correct choice is obvious in retrospect, as in NASA's space shuttle disasters. On January 28, 1986, *Challenger* exploded shortly after takeoff, due to erosion of O-rings that had become brittle in freezing overnight temperatures at Cape Canaveral. The crux of the matter was a statistical relationship between brittleness and temperature. Data on O-ring erosion were available for 22 prior shuttle flights. The backup O-rings (there were two layers of O-rings) had suffered no erosion in 9 prior flights at launch temperatures in the range 72°F–81°F, but they had suffered significant erosion in 4 of 13 prior flights at temperatures in the range 53°F–70°F. However, the role of temperature was by no means clear. NASA and Morton-Thiokol engineers had debated the erratic data inconclusively, including the night before the launch.

After the *Challenger* accident, it was clear that the risk was underestimated. Two *statistical* issues were the degree to which backup layer O-rings provided redundant protection and the correct way to predict O-ring erosion at the *Challenger* launch temperature of 36°F when the lowest previous launch temperature had been 53°F. Two possible *ethical* questions were whether NASA officials should have postponed the launch until they understood the problem better and whether the astronauts, as participants in a risky mission, had sufficient opportunity for informed consent. NASA's 100 percent previous success record was undoubtedly a factor in everyone's self-confidence, including the astronauts'.

On February 1, 2003, space shuttle *Columbia* burned on reentry. The heat shield failure was apparently due to tiles damaged by falling foam insulation from the fuel tanks, loosened by vibration during launch. Prior to the *Columbia* disaster in 2003, foam-damaged tiles had been noted 70 times in 112 flights. In retrospect, review of the data showed that some previous flights may have come close to *Columbia*'s fate. This is a *statistical* issue because the heat shield had worked 70 times despite being damaged. Is it surprising that NASA officials believed that the tiles were resistant to foam damage? An *ethical* question would be whether organizational inertia and pressure to launch favored a risky interpretation of the data.

These disasters remind us that decisions involving data and statistics are embedded in organizational culture. NASA's evaluation of risk differs from that of most businesses due to the dangers inherent in its cutting-edge missions. At the time of the *Challenger* launch, the risk of losing a vehicle was estimated at 1 in 30. At the time of the *Columbia* reentry accident, the risk was estimated at 1 in 145. For nonhuman launches the risk is about 1 in 50 (2 percent) compared with 2 space shuttle losses in 113 flights (1.8 percent). By comparison, the risk of losing a commercial airline flight is about 1 in 2,000,000.

Sources: yahoo.com; www.nasa.gov; *The New York Times*, February 2, 2003.

1.5 CRITICAL THINKING

Statistics is an essential part of **critical thinking** because it allows us to test an idea against empirical evidence. Random occurrences and chance variation inevitably lead to occasional outcomes that could support one viewpoint or another. But the science of statistics tells us whether the sample evidence is convincing. In this book, you will learn how to use statistics correctly in accordance with professional standards to make the best decision.

"Critical thinking means being able to evaluate evidence, to tell fact from opinion, to see holes in an argument, to tell whether cause and effect has been established, and to spot illogic."
The Wall Street Journal, October 20, 2006.

We use statistical tools to compare our prior ideas with **empirical data** (data collected through observations and experiments). If the data do not support our theory, we can reject or revise our theory. In *The Wall Street Journal,* in *Money* magazine, and on CNN you see stock market experts with theories to "explain" the current market (bull, bear, or pause). But each year brings new experts and new theories, and the old ones vanish. Logical pitfalls abound in both the data collection process and the reasoning process. Let's look at some.

Pitfall 1: Conclusions from Small Samples

"My Aunt Harriet smoked all her life and lived to 90. Smoking doesn't hurt you." Good for her. But does one case prove anything? Five customers are asked if the new product design is an improvement. If three say yes, should the company implement the new design? If 10 patients try a new asthma medication and one gets a rash, can we conclude that the medication caused the rash? How large a sample is needed to make reliable conclusions? Statisticians have developed clear rules about sample sizes. Until you learn them in Chapter 8, it's OK to raise your pennant hopes when your favorite baseball team wins five games in a row.

> **LO 1-4**
> List and explain common statistical pitfalls.

Pitfall 2: Conclusions from Nonrandom Samples

"Rock stars die young. Look at Buddy Holly, Jimi Hendrix, Janis Joplin, Jim Morrison, John Lennon, and Kurt Cobain." But we are looking only at those who *did* die young. What about the thousands who are alive and well or who lived long lives? Similarly, we should be careful about generalizing from retrospective studies of people who have heart attacks, unless we also study those who do not have heart attacks. (From Arnold Barnett, "How Numbers Can Trick You," *Technology Review,* October 1994, p. 40.) In Chapter 2, you will learn proper sampling methods to make reliable inferences.

Pitfall 3: Conclusions from Rare Events

Unlikely events happen if we take a large enough sample. In Chapter 5, you will learn about the law of large numbers, which explains unlikely events such as these:

- "Mary in my office won the lottery. Her system must have worked." Millions of people play the lottery. Someone will eventually win.
- "Bill's a sports genius. He predicted every Notre Dame football win last season." Millions of sports fans make predictions. A few of them will call every game correctly.
- "Tom's SUV rolled over. SUVs are dangerous." Millions of people drive SUVs. Some will roll over.

Pitfall 4: Poor Survey Methods

Did your instructor ever ask a question like "How many of you remember the simplex method from your math class?" One or two timid hands (or maybe none) are raised, even though the topic was covered. Did the math department not teach the simplex method? Or did students not "get it"? Actually, the instructor has used a poor sampling method and a vaguely worded question. It's difficult for students to respond to such a question in public, for they assume (often correctly) that if they raise a hand, the instructor is going to ask them to explain it, or that their peers will think they are showing off. An anonymous survey or a quiz on the simplex method would provide better insight. In Chapter 2, you will learn rules for survey design and response scaling.

Pitfall 5: Assuming a Causal Link

In your economics class, you may have learned about the **post hoc fallacy** (the mistaken conclusion that if *A* precedes *B* then *A* is the *cause* of *B*). For example, the divorce rate in

Mississippi fell in 2005 after Hurricane Katrina. Did the hurricane cause couples to stay together? A little research reveals that the divorce rate had been falling for the previous two years, so Hurricane Katrina could hardly be credited.

The *post hoc fallacy* is a special case of the general fallacy of *assuming causation* anytime there is a *statistical association* between events. For example, there is the "curse of the ballfield," which says that teams who play in named ballparks (e.g., Citi Field for the New York Mets) tend to lose more games than they win (see *The New York Times*, November 15, 2006, p. C16). Perhaps in a statistical sense this may be true. But it is actually the players and managers who determine whether a team wins. Association does not prove causation. You've probably heard that. But many people draw unwarranted conclusions when no cause-and-effect link exists. Consider anecdotes like these:

- "Murder rates were higher during the full moon in Miami last year. I guess the moon makes people crazy." But what about cities that saw a *decrease* in murders during the same full moon?

- "Most shark attacks occur between 12 p.m. and 2 p.m. Sharks must be hungrier then." But more people go swimming near midday. If a causal link exists, it would have to be shown in a carefully controlled experiment.

On the other hand, association may warrant further study when common sense suggests a potential causal link. For example, is there any link between cell phones and cancer (see *Scientific American,* Vol. 305, No. 2, August 2011, p. 96)? In Chapter 12, you will learn tests to decide whether a correlation is within the realm of chance.

Pitfall 6: Generalization to Individuals

"Men are taller than women." Yes, but only in a statistical sense. Men are taller *on average,* but many women are taller than many men. "Japanese cars have high quality." Yes, but not all of them. We should avoid reading too much into **statistical generalizations**. Instead, ask how much *overlap* is in the populations that are being considered. Often, the similarities transcend the differences. In Chapter 10, you will learn precise tests to compare two groups.

Pitfall 7: Unconscious Bias

Without obvious fraud (tampering with data), researchers can unconsciously or subtly allow bias to color their handling of data. For example, for many years it was assumed that heart attacks were more likely to occur in men than women. But symptoms of heart disease are usually more obvious in men than women and so doctors tend to catch heart disease earlier in men. Studies show that heart disease is the number one cause of death for American women (www.americanheart.org). In Chapter 2, you will learn about sources of bias and error in surveys.

Pitfall 8: Significance versus Importance

Statistically significant effects may lack practical importance. A study of over 500,000 Austrian military recruits showed that those born in the spring averaged 0.6 cm taller than those born in the fall (J. Utts, *The American Statistician* 57, no. 2 (May 2003), pp. 74–79). But who would notice? Would prospective parents change their timing in hopes of having a child 0.6 cm taller? Cost-conscious businesses know that some product improvements cannot support a valid business case. Consumers cannot perceive small improvements in durability, speed, taste, and comfort if the products already are "good enough." For example, Seagate's Cheetah 147GB disk drive already has a mean time between failure (MTBF) rating of 1.4 million hours (about 160 years in continuous use). Would a 10 percent improvement in MTBF matter to anyone?

1.8 In 2007, the same five winning numbers [4, 21, 23, 34, 39] came up both on Monday and on Wednesday in the North Carolina Lottery. "That's so unlikely that it must be rigged," said Mary. Which fallacy, if any, do you see in Mary's reasoning? (See Leonard A. Stefanski, "The North Carolina Lottery Coincidence," *The American Statistician* 62, no. 2, p. 130.)

1.9 A National Health Interview Survey conducted by the U.S. Centers for Disease Control reported that using a cell phone instead of a landline appeared to double a person's chances of binge drinking. "I guess I'd better give up my cell phone," said Bob. Which fallacy, if any, do you see in Bob's reasoning?

1.10 A study found that radar detector users have lower accident rates, wear their seat belts more, and even vote more than nonusers. (a) Assuming that the study is accurate, do you think there is cause-and-effect? (b) If everyone used radar detectors, would voting rates and seat-belt usage rise?

1.11 A lottery winner told how he picked his six-digit winning number (5-6-8-10-22-39): number of people in his family, birth date of his wife, school grade of his 13-year-old daughter, sum of his birth date and his wife's, number of years of marriage, and year of his birth. He said, "I try to pick numbers that mean something to me." The State Lottery Commissioner called this method "the screwiest I ever heard of . . . but apparently it works." (a) From a statistical viewpoint, do you agree that this method "works"? (b) Based on your understanding of how a lottery works, would someone who picks 1-2-3-4-5-6 because "it is easy to remember" have a lower chance of winning?

1.12 "Smokers are much more likely to speed, run red lights, and get involved in car accidents than nonsmokers." (a) Can you think of reasons why this statement might be misleading? *Hint:* Make a list of six factors that you think would cause car accidents. Is smoking on your list? (b) Can you suggest a causal link between smoking and car accidents?

1.13 An ad for a cell phone service claims that its percent of "dropped calls" was significantly lower than that of its main competitor. In the fine print, the percents were given as 1.2 percent versus 1.4 percent. Is this reduction likely to be *important* to customers (as opposed to being *significant*)?

1.14 What logical or ethical problems do you see in these hypothetical scenarios?

   a. Dolon Privacy Consultants concludes that its employees are not loyal because a few samples of employee e-mails contained comments critical of the company's management.
   b. Calchas Financial Advisors issues a glowing report of its new stock market forecasting system, based on testimonials of five happy customers.
   c. Five sanitation crew members at Malcheon Hospital are asked to try a new cleaning solvent to see if it has any allergic or other harmful side effects.
   d. A consumer group rates a new personal watercraft from Thetis Aquatic Conveyances as "Unacceptable" because two Ohio teens lost control and crashed into a dock.

1.15 In 2007, a study of 231,164 New Jersey heart attack patients showed that those admitted on a weekday had a 12.0 percent death rate in the next three years, compared with 12.9 percent for those admitted on a weekend. This difference was statistically significant. (a) "That's too small to have any practical importance," said Sarah. Do you agree with Sarah's conclusion? Explain. (See *The New York Times,* March 15, 2007, p. A19.)

1.16 In 2003, Pennsylvania repealed a law that required motorcycle riders to wear helmets. A 2008 news headline reported, "Deaths Soar After Repeal of Helmet Law." After reading the story, Bill said, "But it's just a correlation, not causation." Do you agree with Bill's conclusion? Explain. (See *The New York Times,* June 24, 2008, p. D6.)

CHAPTER SUMMARY

Statistics is the science of collecting, organizing, analyzing, interpreting, and presenting data. A **statistician** is an expert with a degree in mathematics or statistics, while a **data analyst** is anyone who works with data. **Descriptive statistics** is the collection, organization, presentation, and summary of data with charts or numerical summaries. **Inferential statistics** refers to generalizing from a sample to a population, estimating unknown parameters, drawing conclusions, and making decisions. Statistics is used in all branches of business. **Statistical challenges** include imperfect data, practical constraints, and ethical dilemmas. Statistical tools are used to test theories against empirical data. Pitfalls include nonrandom samples, incorrect sample size, and lack of causal links. The field of statistics is relatively new and continues to grow as mathematical frontiers expand.

KEY TERMS

critical thinking, *14*

descriptive statistics, *7*

empirical data, *15*

inferential statistics, *7*

post hoc fallacy, *15*

statistic, *4*

statistics, *3*

statistical generalization, *16*

CHAPTER REVIEW

1. Define (a) statistic; (b) statistics.

2. List three reasons to study statistics.

3. List three applications of statistics.

4. List four skills needed by statisticians. Why are these skills important?

5. List three *practical* challenges faced by statisticians.

6. List three *ethical* challenges faced by statisticians.

7. List five pitfalls or logical errors that may ensnare the unwary statistician.

CHAPTER EXERCISES

connect

1.17 A survey of beginning students showed that a majority strongly agreed with the statement, "I am afraid of statistics." (a) Why might this attitude exist among students who have not yet taken a statistics class? (b) Would a similar attitude exist toward an ethics class? Explain your reasoning.

1.18 Under a recent U.S. Food and Drug Administration (FDA) standard for food contaminants, 3.5 ounces of tomato sauce can have up to 30 fly eggs, and 11 ounces of wheat flour can contain 450 insect fragments. How could statistical sampling be used to see that these standards of food hygiene are being met by producers? (Source: www.fda.gov)

1.19 A statistical consultant was retained by a linen supplier to analyze a survey of hospital purchasing managers. After looking at the data, she realized that the survey had missed several key geographic areas and included some that were outside the target region. Some survey questions were ambiguous. Some respondents failed to answer all the questions or gave silly replies (one manager said he worked 40 hours a day). Of the 1,000 surveys mailed, only 80 were returned. (a) What alternatives are available to the statistician? (b) Might an imperfect analysis be better than none?

1.20 Ergonomics is the science of making sure that human surroundings are adapted to human needs. How could statistics play a role in the following:

a. Choosing the height of an office chair so that 95 percent of the employees (male and female) will feel it is the "right height" for their legs to reach the floor comfortably.

b. Designing a drill press so its controls can be reached and its forces operated by an "average employee."

c. Defining a doorway width so that a "typical" wheelchair can pass through without coming closer than 6 inches from either side.

d. Setting the width of a parking space to accommodate 95 percent of all vehicles at your local Walmart.

e. Choosing a font size so that a highway sign can be read in daylight at 100 meters by 95 percent of all drivers.

1.21 Analysis of 1,064 deaths of famous popular musicians (rock, punk, rap, R&B, electronic, and new age) showed that 31 percent were related to alcohol or drug abuse. "But that is just a sample. It proves nothing," said Hannah. Do you agree with Hannah's conclusion? Explain. (See *Scientific American,* November 2007, p. 34.)

1.22 A recent study showed that women who lived near a freeway had an unusually high rate of rheumatoid arthritis. Sarah said, "They should move away from freeways." Is there a fallacy in Sarah's reasoning? Explain.

1.23 "Lacrosse helmets are not needed," said Tom. "None of the guys on my team have ever had head injuries." Is there a fallacy in Tom's reasoning? Explain.

1.24 In 2009, a European study of thousands of men found that the PSA screening for prostate cancer reduced the risk of a man's dying from prostate cancer from 3.0 percent to 2.4 percent. "But it's already a small risk. I don't think a difference of less than 1 percent would be of practical importance," said Ed. Do you agree with Ed's conclusion? Explain. (See *The New York Times,* March 24, 2009, p. D5.)

1.25 A research study showed that 7 percent of "A" students smoke, while nearly 50 percent of "D" students do. (a) List in rank order six factors that you think affect grades. Is smoking on your list? (b) If smoking is not a likely cause of poor grades, can you suggest reasons why these results were observed? (c) Assuming these statistics are correct, would "D" students who give up smoking improve their grades? Why or why not?

1.26 A research study by the Agency for Healthcare Research Quality showed that adolescents who watched more than 4 hours of TV per day were more than five times as likely to start smoking as those who watched less than 2 hours a day. The researchers speculate that TV actors' portrayals of smoking as personally and socially rewarding were an effective indirect method of tobacco promotion (*Note:* Paid television tobacco ads are illegal). List in rank order six factors that you think cause adolescents to start smoking. Did TV portrayals of attractive smokers appear on your list? (See *AHRQ Newsletter,* no. 269, January 2003, p. 12.)

1.27 The Graduate Management Admission Test (GMAT) is used by many graduate schools of business as one of their admission criteria. GMAT scores for selected undergraduate majors are shown below. Using your own reasoning and concepts in this chapter, criticize each of the following statements.

    a. "Philosophy majors must not be interested in business since so few take the GMAT."
    b. "More students major in engineering than in English."
    c. "If marketing students majored in physics, they would score better on the GMAT."
    d. "Physics majors would make the best managers."

GMAT Scores and Undergraduate Major, 1984–1989   GMAT

Major	*Average GMAT Score*	*Number Taking Test*
Accounting	483	25,233
Computer Science	508	7,573
Economics	513	16,432
Engineering	544	29,688
English	507	3,589
Finance	489	20,001
Marketing	455	15,925
Philosophy	546	588
Physics	575	1,223

Source: Graduate Management Admission Council, *Admission Office Profile of Candidates,* October 1989, pp. 27–30.

1.28 (a) Which of these two displays (table or graph) is more helpful in visualizing the relationship between restaurant size and interior seating for 74 Noodles restaurants? Explain your reasoning. (b) Do you see anything unusual in the data? (*Source:* Noodles & Company)   **NoodlesSqFt**

Number of Restaurants in Each Category (*n* = 74 restaurants)

Interior Seats	*Square Feet Inside Restaurant*				*Row Total*
	1000 < 1750	*1750 < 2500*	*2500 < 3250*	*3250 < 4000*	
105 < 130	0	0	0	3	3
80 < 105	0	4	17	0	21
55 < 80	0	21	24	0	45
30 < 55	1	4	0	0	5
Col Total	1	29	41	3	74

1.29 (a) Which of these two displays (table or graph) is more helpful in describing the salad sales by Noodles & Company? Why? (b) Write a one-sentence summary of the data. (*Source:* Noodles & Company) **NoodlesSalad**

2005 Average Daily Salads Sold by Month, Noodles & Company			
Month	*Salads*	*Month*	*Salads*
Jan	2847	Jul	2554
Feb	2735	Aug	2370
Mar	2914	Sep	2131
Apr	3092	Oct	1990
May	3195	Nov	1979
Jun	3123	Dec	1914

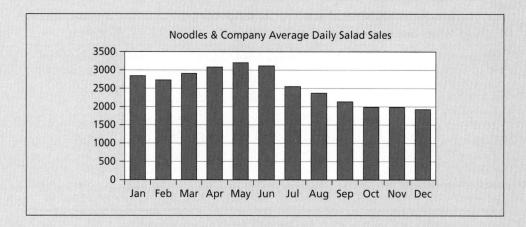

1.30 Choose *three* of the following statisticians and use the web to find out a few basic facts about them (e.g., list some of their contributions to statistics, when they did their work, whether they are still living, etc.).

Florence Nightingale	John Wilder Tukey	Genichi Taguchi
Gertrude Cox	William Cochran	Helen Walker
Sir Francis Galton	Siméon Poisson	George Box
W. Edwards Deming	S. S. Stevens	Sam Wilks
The Bernoulli family	R. A. Fisher	Carl F. Gauss
Frederick Mosteller	George Snedecor	William S. Gosset
William H. Kruskal	Karl Pearson	Thomas Bayes
Jerzy Neyman	C. R. Rao	Bradley Efron
Egon Pearson	Abraham De Moivre	
Harold Hotelling	Edward Tufte	

RELATED READING   *Practical Guides*

Baker, Stephen. *The Numerati.* Houghton-Mifflin, 2008.

Best, Joel. *Stat-Spotting: A Field Guide to Dubious Data.* University of California Press, 2008.

Davenport, Thomas H.; and Jeanne G. Harris. *Competing on Analytics: The New Science of Winning.* Harvard Business School Press, 2007.

Dodge, Yadolah. *The Concise Encyclopedia of Statistics.* Springer, 2008.

Everitt, B. S. *The Cambridge Dictionary of Statistics.* 2nd ed. Cambridge University Press, 2002.

Fung, Kaiser. *Numbers Rule Your World: The Hidden Influence of Probabilities and Statistics on Everything You Do.* McGraw-Hill, 2010.

John, J. A.; and D. Whitaker. *Statistical Thinking in Business.* 2nd ed. Chapman and Hall, 2005.

Newton, Rae R. *Your Statistical Consultant*. Sage Publications, 1999.

Sahei, Hardeo; and Anwer Khurshid. *Pocket Dictionary of Statistics*. McGraw-Hill, 2002.

Seife, Charles. *Proofiness: The Dark Arts of Mathematical Deception*. Viking, 2010.

Utts, Jessica. "What Educated Citizens Should Know About Statistics and Probability." *The American Statistician* 57, no. 2 (May 2003), pp. 74–79.

Ethics

Badaracco, Joseph L., Jr. *Defining Moments: When Managers Must Choose between Right and Right*. Harvard Business School Press, 1997.

Gardner, Howard; Mihaly Csikszentmihalyi; and William Damon. *Good Work: When Excellence and Ethics Meet*. Basic Books, 2001.

Hartman, Laura P. *Perspectives in Business Ethics*. McGraw-Hill, 2002.

Nash, Laura L. *Good Intentions Aside: A Manager's Guide to Resolving Ethical Problems*. Harvard Business School Press, 1990.

Seglin, Jeffrey L. *The Right Thing: Conscience, Profit and Personal Responsibility in Today's Business*. Spiro Press, 2003.

Vardeman, Stephen B.; and Max D. Morris. "Statistics and Ethics: Some Advice for Young Statisticians." *The American Statistician* 57 (February 2003), pp. 21–26.

CHAPTER 1   Online Learning Resources

The Online Learning Center (OLC) at www.mhhe.com/doane4e has several *LearningStats* demonstrations to give you an overview of statistics. Your instructor may assign one or more of them, or you may decide to download the ones that seem interesting.

Topic	LearningStats Demonstrations
Microsoft® Office	Excel Tips Word Tips PowerPoint Tips
Excel	Excel Functions
Math Review	Math Review Significant Digits
Web Stuff	Web Resources Statistics Software

Key: = PowerPoint   = Word   = Excel

CHAPTER

2

Data Collection

CHAPTER CONTENTS

CHAPTER LEARNING OBJECTIVES

LO   **When you finish this chapter you should be able to**

LO 2-1   Use basic terminology for describing data and samples.

LO 2-2   Explain the distinction between numerical and categorical data.

LO 2-3   Explain the difference between time series and cross-sectional data.

LO 2-4   Recognize levels of measurement in data and ways of coding data.

LO 2-5   Recognize a Likert scale and know how to use it.

LO 2-6   Use the correct terminology for samples and populations.

LO 2-7   Explain the common sampling methods and how to implement them.

LO 2-8   Find everyday print or electronic data sources.

LO 2-9   Describe basic elements of survey design, survey types, and sources of error.

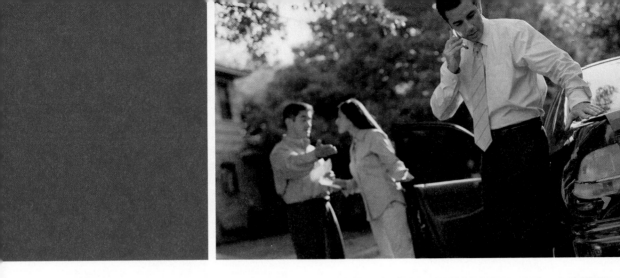

2.1 DEFINITIONS

LO 2-1

Use basic terminology for describing data and samples.

In scientific research, data arise from experiments whose results are recorded systematically. In business, data usually arise from accounting transactions or management processes (e.g., inventory, sales, payroll). Much of the data that statisticians analyze were recorded without explicit consideration of their statistical uses, yet important decisions may depend on the data. How many pints of type A blood will be required at Mt. Sinai Hospital next Thursday? How many dollars must State Farm keep in its cash account to cover automotive accident claims next November? How many yellow three-quarter-sleeve women's sweaters will Lands' End sell this month? To answer such questions, we usually look at historical data.

Data: Singular or Plural?

Data is the plural of the Latin *datum* (a "given" fact). This traditional usage is preferred in Britain, and especially in scientific journals, where over 90 percent of the references use data as a plural ("These data show a correlation . . ."). But in the popular press (newspapers, magazines) you will often see "data" used synonymously with "information" and hence as a singular ("The compressed data is stored on a CD . . ."). The singular usage is especially common in the United States and is becoming more common in the United Kingdom, rather to the chagrin of the educated populace.

Observations, Variables, and Data Sets

An **observation** is a single member of a collection of items that we want to study, such as a person, firm, or region. An example of an observation is an employee or an invoice mailed last month. A **variable** is a characteristic of the subject or individual, such as an employee's income or an invoice amount. The **data set** consists of all the values of all of the variables for all of the observations we have chosen to observe. In this book, we will use **data** as a plural, and data set to refer to a collection of observations taken as a whole. Data usually are entered into a spreadsheet or database as an $n \times m$ matrix. Specifically, each column is a variable (m columns) and each row is an observation (n rows). Table 2.1 shows a small data set with eight observations (8 rows) and five variables (5 columns).

A data set may consist of many variables. The questions that can be explored and the analytical techniques that can be used will depend upon the data type and the number of variables. This textbook starts with **univariate data sets** (one variable), then moves to **bivariate data sets** (two variables) and **multivariate data sets** (more than two variables), as illustrated in Table 2.2.

TABLE 2.1

A Small Multivariate
Data Set (5 variables,
8 observations)
📁 SmallData

Obs	Name	Age	Income	Position	Gender
1	Frieda	45	$67,100	Personnel director	F
2	Stefan	32	56,500	Operations analyst	M
3	Barbara	55	88,200	Marketing VP	F
4	Donna	27	59,000	Statistician	F
5	Larry	46	36,000	Security guard	M
6	Alicia	52	68,500	Comptroller	F
7	Alec	65	95,200	Chief executive	M
8	Jaime	50	71,200	Public relations	M

TABLE 2.2

Number of Variables
and Typical Tasks

Data Set	Variables	Example	Typical Tasks
Univariate	One	Income	Histograms, basic statistics
Bivariate	Two	Income, Age	Scatter plots, correlation
Multivariate	More than two	Income, Age, Gender	Regression modeling

Data Types

LO 2-2

Explain the distinction
between numerical
and categorical data.

A data set may contain a mixture of *data types*. Two broad categories are **categorical data** and **numerical data**, as shown in Figure 2.1.

Categorical Data   *Categorical* data (also called *qualitative* data) have values that are described by words rather than numbers. For example, structural lumber can be classified by the lumber type (e.g., fir, hemlock, pine), automobile styles can be classified by size (e.g., full, midsize, compact, subcompact), and movies can be categorized using common movie classifications (e.g., action and adventure, children and family, classics, comedy, documentary).

Because categorical variables have nonnumerical values, it might seem that categorical data would be of limited statistical use. In fact, there are many statistical methods that can handle categorical data, which we will introduce in later chapters. On occasion

FIGURE 2.1

Data Types and Examples

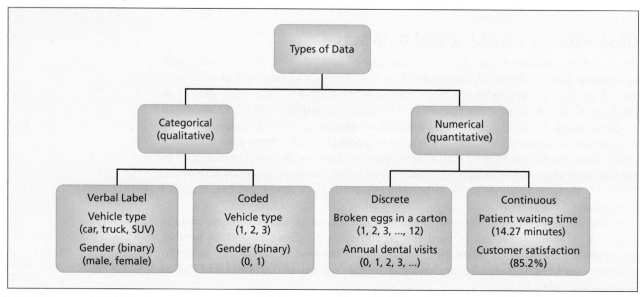

the values of the categorical variable might be represented using numbers. This is called **coding**. For example, a database might code payment methods using numbers:

1 = cash 2 = check 3 = credit/debit card 4 = gift card

Coding a category as a number does *not* make the data numerical and the numbers do not typically imply a rank. But on occasion a ranking does exist. For example, a database might code education degrees using numbers:

1 = Bachelor's 2 = Master's 3 = Doctorate

Some categorical variables have only two values. We call these **binary variables**. Examples include employment status (e.g., employed or unemployed), mutual fund type (e.g., load or no-load), and marital status (e.g., currently married or not currently married). Binary variables are often coded using a 1 or 0. For a binary variable, the 0-1 coding is arbitrary, so the choice is equivalent. For example, a variable such as gender could be coded as:

1 = female 0 = male

or as

1 = male 0 = female

Numerical Data   *Numerical* or *quantitative* data arise from counting, measuring something, or some kind of mathematical operation. For example, we could count the number of auto insurance claims filed in March (e.g., 114 claims) or sales for last quarter (e.g., $4,920), or we could measure the amount of snowfall over the last 24 hours (e.g., 3.4 inches). Most accounting data, economic indicators, and financial ratios are quantitative, as are physical measurements.

Numerical data can be broken down into two types. A variable with a countable number of distinct values is **discrete**. Often, such data are integers. You can recognize integer data because their description begins with "number of." For example, the number of Medicaid patients in a hospital waiting room (e.g., 2) or the number of takeoffs at Chicago O'Hare International Airport in an hour (e.g., 37). Such data are integer variables because we cannot observe a fractional number of patients or takeoffs.

A numerical variable that can have any value within an interval is **continuous**. This would include things like physical measurements (e.g., distance, weight, time, speed) or financial variables (e.g., sales, assets, price/earnings ratios, inventory turns); for example, runner Usain Bolt's time in the 100 meter dash (e.g., 9.58 seconds) or the weight of a package of Sun-Maid raisins (e.g., 427.31 grams). These are continuous variables because any interval such as [425, 429] grams can contain infinitely many possible values. Sometimes we round a continuous measurement to an integer (e.g., 427 grams), but that does not make the data discrete.

Apparent ambiguity between *discrete* and *continuous* is introduced when we round continuous data to whole numbers (e.g., your weight this morning). However, the underlying measurement scale is continuous. That is, a package of Sun-Maid raisins is labeled 425 grams, but on an accurate scale its weight would be a noninteger (e.g., 427.31). Precision depends on the instrument we use to measure the continuous variable. We generally treat financial data (dollars, euros, pesos) as continuous even though retail prices go in discrete steps of .01 (i.e., we go from $1.25 to $1.26). The FM radio spectrum is continuous, but only certain discrete values are observed (e.g., 104.3) because of Federal Communications Commission rules. Conversely, we sometimes treat discrete data as continuous when the range is very large (e.g., SAT scores) and when small differences (e.g., 604 or 605) aren't of much importance. This topic will be discussed in later chapters. If in doubt, just think about how X was measured and whether or not its values are countable.

Time Series Data

LO 2-3

If each observation in the sample represents a different equally spaced point in time (years, months, days), we have **time series data**. The *periodicity* is the time between observations. It may be annual, quarterly, monthly, weekly, daily, hourly, etc. Examples of *macroeconomic* time series data would include national income (GDP, consumption,

Explain the difference between time series and cross-sectional data.

FIGURE 2.2

Examples of Time Series versus Cross-Sectional Data

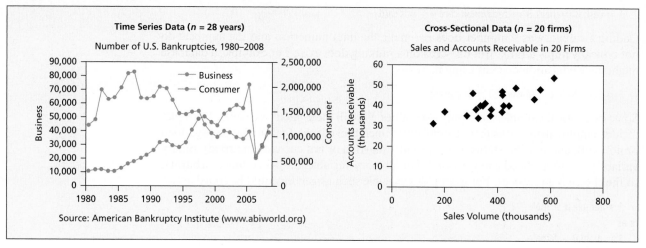

Source: American Bankruptcy Institute (www.abiworld.org)

investment), economic indicators (Consumer Price Index, unemployment rate, Standard & Poor's 500 Index), and monetary data (M1, M2, M3, prime rate, T-bill rate, consumer borrowing, federal debt). Examples of *microeconomic* time series data would include a firm's sales, market share, debt/equity ratio, employee absenteeism, inventory turnover, and product quality ratings. For time series, we are interested in *trends and patterns over time* (e.g., personal bankruptcies from 1980 to 2008 as shown in Figure 2.2).

Cross-Sectional Data

If each observation represents a different individual unit (e.g., a person, firm, geographic area) at the same point in time, we have **cross-sectional data**. Thus, traffic fatalities in the 50 U.S. states for a given year, debt/equity ratios for the Fortune 500 firms in the last quarter of a certain year, last month's Visa balances for a bank's new mortgage applicants, or GPAs of students in a statistics class would be cross-sectional data. For cross-sectional data, we are interested in *variation among observations* (e.g., accounts receivable in 20 Subway franchises) or in *relationships* (e.g., whether accounts receivable are related to sales volume in 20 Subway franchises as shown in Figure 2.2).

Some variables (such as unemployment rates) could be either time series (monthly data over each of 60 months) or cross-sectional (January's unemployment rate in 50 different cities). We can combine the two (e.g., monthly unemployment rates for the 13 Canadian provinces or territories for the last 60 months) to obtain *pooled cross-sectional and time series data.*

SECTION EXERCISES

connect

2.1   What type of data (categorical, discrete numerical, or continuous numerical) is each of the following variables? If there is any ambiguity about the data type, explain why the answer is unclear.

    a. The manufacturer of your car.

    b. Your college major.

    c. The number of college credits you are taking.

2.2   What type of data (categorical, discrete numerical, or continuous numerical) is each of the following variables? If there is any ambiguity, explain why the answer is unclear.

    a. Length of a TV commercial.

    b. Number of peanuts in a can of Planter's Mixed Nuts.

    c. Occupation of a mortgage applicant.

    d. Flight time from London Heathrow to Chicago O'Hare.

2.3 What type of data (categorical, discrete numerical, or continuous numerical) is each of the following variables? If there is any ambiguity about the data type, explain why the answer is unclear.

    a. The miles on your car's odometer.
    b. The fat grams you ate for lunch yesterday.
    c. The name of the airline with the cheapest fare from New York to London.
    d. The brand of cell phone you own.

2.4 (a) Give three original examples of discrete data. (b) Give three original examples of continuous data. In each case, explain and identify any ambiguities that might exist. *Hint:* Do not restrict yourself to published data. Consider data describing your own life (e.g., your sports performance, financial data, or academic data). You need *not* list all the data, merely describe them and show a few typical data values.

2.5 Which type of data (cross-sectional or time series) is each variable?

    a. Scores of 50 students on a midterm accounting exam last semester.
    b. Bob's scores on 10 weekly accounting quizzes last semester.
    c. Average score by all takers of the state's CPA exam for each of the last 10 years.
    d. Number of years of accounting work experience for each of the 15 partners in a CPA firm.

2.6 Which type of data (cross-sectional or time series) is each variable?

    a. Value of Standard & Poor's 500 stock price index at the close of each trading day last year.
    b. Closing price of each of the 500 stocks in the S&P 500 index on the last trading day this week.
    c. Dividends per share paid by General Electric common stock for the last 20 quarters.
    d. Latest price/earnings ratios of 10 stocks in Bob's retirement portfolio.

2.7 Which type of data (cross-sectional or time series) is each variable?

    a. Mexico's GDP for each of the last 10 quarters.
    b. Unemployment rates in each of the 31 states in Mexico at the end of last year.
    c. Unemployment rate in Mexico at the end of each of the last 10 years.
    d. Average home value in each of the 10 largest Mexican cities today.

2.8 Give an original example of a time series variable and a cross-sectional variable. Use your own experience (e.g., your sports activities, finances, education).

2.2 LEVEL OF MEASUREMENT

Statisticians sometimes refer to four levels of measurement for data: *nominal, ordinal, interval,* and *ratio.* This typology was proposed over 60 years ago by psychologist S. S. Stevens. The allowable statistical tests depend on the measurement level. The criteria are summarized in Figure 2.3.

LO 2-4

Recognize levels of measurement in data and ways of coding data.

Nominal Measurement

Nominal measurement is the weakest level of measurement and the easiest to recognize. **Nominal data** (from Latin *nomen,* meaning "name") merely identify a *category.* "Nominal" data are the same as "qualitative," "categorical," or "classification" data. To be sure that the categories are collectively exhaustive, it is common to use **Other** as the last item on the list. For example, the following survey questions yield nominal data:

Did you file an insurance claim last month?

1. Yes   2. No

Which cell phone service provider do you use?

1. AT&T   2. Sprint-Nextel   3. T-Mobile   4. Verizon   5. Other

We usually code nominal data numerically. However, the codes are arbitrary placeholders with no numerical meaning, so it is improper to perform mathematical analysis on them. For example, we would not calculate an average using the cell phone service data

FIGURE 2.3

Determining the Measurement Level

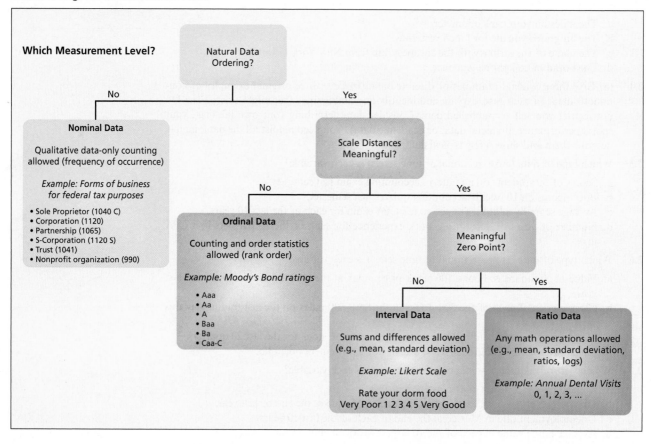

(1 through 5). This may seem obvious, yet people have been known to do it. Once the data are in the computer, it's easy to forget that the "numbers" are only categories. With nominal data, the only permissible mathematical operations are counting (e.g., frequencies) and a few simple statistics such as the mode.

Ordinal Measurement

Ordinal data codes connote a *ranking* of data values. For example:

What size automobile do you usually drive?

1. Full-size   2. Compact   3. Subcompact

How often do you use Microsoft Access?

1. Frequently   2. Sometimes   3. Rarely   4. Never

Thus, a 2 (Compact) implies a larger car than a 3 (Subcompact). Like nominal data, these ordinal numerical codes lack the properties that are required to compute many statistics, such as the average. Specifically, there is no clear meaning to the *distance* between 1 and 2, or between 2 and 3, or between 3 and 4 (what would be the distance between "Rarely" and "Never"?). Other examples of ordinal scales can be found in a recruiter's rating of job candidates (outstanding, good, adequate, weak, unsatisfactory), S&P credit ratings (AAA, AA+, AA, AA−, A+, A, A−, B+, B, B−, etc.) or job titles (president, group vice president, plant manager, department head, clerk). Ordinal data can be treated as nominal, but not vice versa. Ordinal data are especially common in social sciences, marketing, and human resources research. There are many useful statistical tests for ordinal data.

Interval Measurement

The next step up the measurement scale is **interval data**, which not only is a rank but also has meaningful intervals between scale points. Examples are the Celsius or Fahrenheit scales of temperature. The interval between 60°F and 70°F is the same as the interval between 20°F and 30°F. Since intervals between numbers represent *distances,* we can do mathematical operations such as taking an average. But because the zero point of these scales is arbitrary, we can't say that 60°F is twice as warm as 30°F, or that 30°F is 50 percent warmer than 20°F. That is, ratios are not meaningful for interval data. The absence of a meaningful zero is a key characteristic of interval data.

Likert Scales   The **Likert scale** is a special case that is frequently used in survey research. You have undoubtedly seen such scales. Typically, a statement is made and the respondent is asked to indicate his or her agreement/disagreement on a five-point or seven-point scale using verbal anchors. The *coarseness* of a Likert scale refers to the number of scale points (typically 5 or 7). For example:

"College-bound high school students should be required to study a foreign language." (check one)

❏	❏	❏	❏	❏
Strongly Agree	Somewhat Agree	Neither Agree Nor Disagree	Somewhat Disagree	Strongly Disagree

LO 2-5

Recognize a Likert scale and know how to use it.

A neutral midpoint ("Neither Agree Nor Disagree") is allowed if we use an *odd* number of scale points (usually 5 or 7). Occasionally, surveys may omit the neutral midpoint to force the respondent to "lean" one way or the other. Likert data are coded numerically (e.g., 1 to 5), but any equally spaced values will work, as shown in Table 2.3.

TABLE 2.3

Examples of Likert-Scale Coding: "How will deflation affect the investment climate?"

Likert Coding: 1 to 5 scale	Likert Coding: −2 to +2 scale
5 = Will help a lot	+2 = Will help a lot
4 = Will help a little	+1 = Will help a little
3 = No effect on investment climate	0 = No effect on investment climate
2 = Will hurt a little	−1 = Will hurt a little
1 = Will hurt a lot	−2 = Will hurt a lot

But do Likert data qualify as interval measurements? By choosing the verbal anchors carefully, many researchers believe that the *intervals* are the same (e.g., the distance from 1 to 2 is "the same" as the *interval,* say, from 3 to 4). However, ratios are not meaningful (i.e., here 4 is not twice 2). The assumption that Likert scales produce interval data justifies a wide range of statistical calculations, including averages, correlations, and so on. Researchers use many Likert-scale variants.

"How would you rate your Internet service provider?" (check one)

❏ Terrible   ❏ Poor   ❏ Adequate   ❏ Good   ❏ Excellent

Instead of labeling every response category, many marketing surveys put verbal anchors only on the endpoints. This avoids intermediate scale labels and permits any number of scale points. For example, Vail Resorts includes the following question on their guest satisfaction survey that they administer at their ski resorts. This survey question has a *Likert-type* scale with 11 response points, verbal anchors at each endpoint, and a neutral anchor at the midpoint.

"On a scale of 0 to 10, how likely would you be to recommend this resort to your friends and family?"

0	1	2	3	4	5	6	7	8	9	10
❏	❏	❏	❏	❏	❏	❏	❏	❏	❏	❏
Not likely at all to recommend					Neither likely nor unlikely to recommend					Highly likely to recommend

Likert data usually are discrete, but some web surveys now use a continuous response scale that allows the respondent to position a "slider" anywhere along the scale to produce continuous data (actually the number of positions is finite but very large). For example:

Likert (using scale points)

Very Poor 1 2 3 4 5 6 7 Very Good

Likert (using a slider)

Very Poor ▼ Very Good

Ratio Measurement

Ratio measurement is the strongest level of measurement. **Ratio data** have all the properties of the other three data types, but in addition possess a *meaningful zero* that represents the absence of the quantity being measured. Because of the zero point, ratios of data values are meaningful (e.g., $20 million in profit is twice as much as $10 million). Balance sheet data, income statement data, financial ratios, physical counts, scientific measurements, and most engineering measurements are ratio data because zero has meaning (e.g., a company with zero sales sold nothing). Having a zero point does *not* restrict us to positive data. For example, profit is a ratio variable (e.g., $4 million is twice $2 million), yet firms can have negative profit (i.e., a loss).

Zero does *not* have to be observable in the data. Newborn babies, for example, cannot have zero weight, yet baby weight clearly is ratio data (i.e., an 8-pound baby is 33 percent heavier than a 6-pound baby). What matters is that the zero is an absolute reference point. The Kelvin temperature scale is a ratio measurement because its absolute zero represents the absence of molecular vibration, while zero on the Celsius scale is merely a convenience (note that 30°C is not "twice as much temperature" as 15°C).

Lack of a true zero is often the quickest test to defrock variables masquerading as ratio data. For example, a Likert scale ($+2, +1, 0, -1, -2$) is *not* ratio data despite the presence of zero because the zero (neutral) point does not connote the absence of anything. As an acid test, ask yourself whether 2 (strongly agree) is twice as much "agreement" as 1 (slightly agree). Some classifications are debatable. For example, college GPA has a zero, but does it represent the absence of learning? Does 4.00 represent "twice as much" learning as 2.00? Is there an underlying reality ranging from 0 to 4 that we are measuring? Most people seem to think so, although the conservative procedure would be to limit ourselves to statistical tests that assume only ordinal data.

Although beginning statistics textbooks usually emphasize interval or ratio data, there are textbooks that emphasize other kinds of data, notably in behavioral research (e.g., psychology, sociology, marketing, human resources).

Changing Data by Recoding

We can recode ratio measurements *downward* into ordinal or nominal measurements (but not conversely). For example, doctors may classify systolic blood pressure as "normal" (under 130), "elevated" (130 to 140), or "high" (140 or over). The recoded data are ordinal, since the ranking is preserved. Intervals may be unequal. For example, U.S. air traffic controllers classify planes as "small" (under 41,000 pounds), "large" (41,001 to 254,999 pounds), and "heavy" (255,000 pounds or more). Such recoding is done to simplify the data when the exact data magnitude is of little interest; however, it discards information by mapping stronger measurements into weaker ones.

SECTION EXERCISES

connect

2.9 Which measurement level (nominal, ordinal, interval, ratio) is each of the following variables? Explain.

a. Number of hits in Game 1 of the next World Series.
b. Baltimore's standing in the American League East (among five teams).
c. Field position of a baseball player (catcher, pitcher, etc.).
d. Temperature on opening day (Celsius).
e. Salary of a randomly chosen American League pitcher.
f. Freeway traffic on opening day (light, medium, heavy).

2.10 Which measurement level (nominal, ordinal, interval, ratio) is each of the following variables? Explain.
- a. Number of employees in the Walmart store in Hutchinson, Kansas.
- b. Number of merchandise returns on a randomly chosen Monday at a Walmart store.
- c. Temperature (in Fahrenheit) in the ice-cream freezer at a Walmart store.
- d. Name of the cashier at register 3 in a Walmart store.
- e. Manager's rating of the cashier at register 3 in a Walmart store.
- f. Social Security number of the cashier at register 3 in a Walmart store.

2.11 Give an original example of each type of data (nominal, ordinal, interval, ratio) from your own life (e.g., your finances, sporting activities, education).

2.12 Which measurement level (nominal, ordinal, interval, ratio) is the response to each question? If you think that the level of measurement is ambiguous, explain why.
- a. How would you describe your level of skill in using Excel? (check one)
  - ❏ Low   ❏ Medium   ❏ High
- b. How often do you use Excel? (check one)
  - ❏ Rarely   ❏ Often   ❏ Very Often
- c. Which version of Excel do you use? (check one)
  - ❏ 2003   ❏ 2007   ❏ 2010   ❏ Other
- d. I spend _____ hours a day using Excel.

2.13 Vail Resorts uses various types of scales and questions on their surveys. Here is a question from their guest satisfaction survey that uses a five-point scale. (a) Would the measurement level for the data collected from this question be nominal, ordinal, interval, or ratio? (b) Would it be appropriate to calculate an average rating for the various items? Explain. (c) Would a 10-point scale be better? Explain. (Source: Vail Resorts, Inc. Used with permission.)   **VAIL**RESORTS

"Rate your satisfaction level on numerous aspects of *today's* experience, where 1=Extremely Dissatisfied & 5=Extremely Satisfied."

1. Value for Price Paid:	1	2	3	4	5
2. Ticket Office Line Wait (if went to ticket window):	1	2	3	4	5
3. Friendliness/Helpfulness of Lift Operators:	1	2	3	4	5
4. Lift Line Waits:	1	2	3	4	5
5. Variety of Trails:	1	2	3	4	5
6. Amount of Snow Coverage:	1	2	3	4	5
7. Level of Crowding on Trails:	1	2	3	4	5
8. Clearly Marked Trail Signs:	1	2	3	4	5
9. Attention to Skier Safety:	1	2	3	4	5
10. Ski Patrol Visibility:	1	2	3	4	5

2.14 (a) Would the measurement level for the data collected from this Microsoft® survey question be nominal, ordinal, interval, or ratio? (b) Would a "6" response be considered twice as good as a "3" response? Why or why not? (c) Would a 1–5 scale be adequate? Explain.

Microsoft **Quality of Support Survey**

Please rate the overall quality of support you received from Microsoft on this particular issue, using a 9-point scale where 9 is Excellent and 1 is Very Poor.

Excellent								Very Poor	Don't Know
9	8	7	6	5	4	3	2	1	
○	○	○	◉	○	○	○	○	○	○

2.3 SAMPLING CONCEPTS

There are almost 2 million retail businesses in the United States. It is unrealistic for market researchers to study them all or in a timely way. But since 2001, a new firm called ShopperTrak RCT (www.shoppertrak.com) has been measuring purchases at a sample of 45,000 mall-based stores, and using this information to advise clients quickly of changes in shopping trends. This application of sampling is part of the relatively new field of *retail intelligence*. In this section, you will learn the differences between a **sample** and a **population**, and why sometimes a sample is necessary or desirable.

LO 2-6

Use the correct terminology for samples and populations.

Population or Sample?

Population	All of the items that we are interested in. May be either finite (e.g., all of the passengers on a particular plane) or effectively infinite (e.g., all of the Cokes produced in an ongoing bottling process).
Sample	A subset of the population that we will actually analyze.

Sample or Census?

A *sample* involves looking only at some items selected from the population, while a **census** is an examination of all items in a defined population. The accuracy of a census can be illusory. For example, the U.S. decennial census cannot locate every individual in the United States (the 1990 census is thought to have missed 8 million people while the 2000 census is believed to have overcounted 1.3 million people). Reasons include the extreme mobility of the U.S. population and the fact that some people do not want to be found (e.g., illegal immigrants) or do not reply to the mailed census form. Further, budget constraints make it difficult to train enough census field workers, install data safeguards, and track down incomplete responses or nonresponses. For these reasons, U.S. censuses have long used sampling in certain situations. Many statistical experts advised using sampling more extensively in the 2000 decennial census, but the U.S. Congress concluded that an actual headcount must be attempted.

When the quantity being measured is volatile, there cannot be a census. For example, The Arbitron Company tracks American radio listening habits using over 2.6 million "Radio Diary Packages." For each "listening occasion," participants note start and stop times for each station. Panelists also report their age, sex, and other demographic information. Table 2.4 outlines some situations where a sample rather than a census would be preferred, and vice versa.

TABLE 2.4   Sample or Census?

Situations Where a Sample May Be Preferred	Situations Where a Census May Be Preferred
Infinite Population No census is possible if the population is of indefinite size (an assembly line can keep producing bolts, a doctor can keep seeing more patients).	**Small Population** If the population is small, there is little reason to sample, for the effort of data collection may be only a small part of the total cost.
Destructive Testing The act of measurement may destroy or devalue the item (battery life, vehicle crash tests).	**Large Sample Size** If the required sample size approaches the population size, we might as well go ahead and take a census.
Timely Results Sampling may yield more timely results (checking wheat samples for moisture content, checking peanut butter for salmonella contamination).	**Database Exists** If the data are on disk, we can examine 100% of the cases. But auditing or validating data against physical records may raise the cost.
Accuracy Instead of spreading resources thinly to attempt a census, budget might be better spent to improve training of field interviewers and improve data safeguards.	**Legal Requirements** Banks must count *all* the cash in bank teller drawers at the end of each business day. The U.S. Congress forbade sampling in the 2000 decennial population census.
Cost Even if a census is feasible, the cost, in either time or money, may exceed our budget.	
Sensitive Information A trained interviewer might learn more about sexual harassment in an organization through confidential interviews of a small sample of employees.	

Parameters and Statistics

From a sample of n items, chosen from a population, we compute **statistics** that can be used as estimates of **parameters** found in the population. To avoid confusion, we use different symbols for each parameter and its corresponding statistic. Thus, the population mean is denoted μ (the lowercase Greek letter mu) while the sample mean is $\bar{x}$. The population proportion is denoted π (the lowercase Greek letter pi) while the sample proportion is p. Figure 2.4 illustrates this idea.

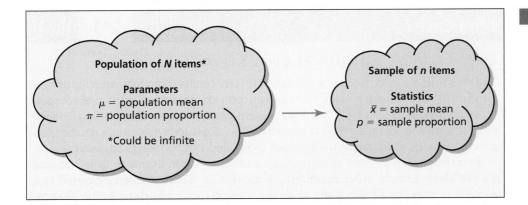

FIGURE 2.4

Population versus Sample

Parameter or Statistic?

Parameter	A measurement or characteristic of the population (e.g., a mean or proportion). Usually unknown since we can rarely observe the entire population. Usually (but not always) represented by a Greek letter (e.g., μ or π).
Statistic	A numerical value calculated from a sample (e.g., a mean or proportion). Usually (but not always) represented by a Roman letter (e.g., $\bar{x}$ or p).

For example, suppose we want to know the mean (average) repair cost for auto air-conditioning warranty claims, or the proportion (percent) of 25-year-old concertgoers who have permanent hearing loss. Since a census is impossible, these parameters would be estimated using a sample. For the sample statistics to provide good estimates of the population parameters, the population must be carefully specified and the sample must be drawn scientifically so the sample items are representative of the population.

Target Population

A population may be defined either by a list (e.g., the names of the passengers on Flight 234) or by a rule (e.g., the customers who eat at Noodles & Company). The **target population** contains all the individuals in which we are interested. Suppose we wish to estimate the proportion of potential consumers who would purchase a $20 Harley-Davidson desk calendar. Is the target population all drivers? Only male drivers over age 16? Only drivers with incomes over $25,000? Only motorcycle owners? By answering questions such as these, we not only identify the target population but also are forced to define our business goals more clearly. The **sampling frame** is the group from which we take the sample. If the frame differs from the target population, then our estimates might not be accurate. Examples of frames are phone directories, voter registration lists, alumni association mailing lists, or marketing databases. Other examples might be:

- Names and addresses of all registered voters in Colorado Springs, Colorado.
- Names and addresses of all vehicle owners in Ventura County, California.
- E-mail addresses of all L. L. Bean customers who have placed online orders.

EXAMPLE 2.1

Gasoline Price Survey

The sample for the U.S. Energy Information Administration's survey of gasoline prices is drawn from a frame of approximately 115,000 retail gasoline outlets, constructed from purchased private commercial sources and EIA sources, combined with zip codes from private lists. Individual frames are mapped to the county level by using zip codes, and outlets are assigned to standard metropolitan statistical areas from Census Bureau definitions. (For details, see www.eia.doe.gov.)

Mini Case   2.1

College Students—You Have a Voice in TV Ratings!

Nielsen Media Research (see www.nielsenmedia.com) conducts random sampling using a panel of 10,000 television households in order to provide viewing information to advertisers and broadcast companies. Advertising agencies use the viewing ratings to decide which programs are best for airing their commercials. Broadcast companies make decisions on advertising rates, which nights to run which shows, and which shows to keep on the air.

In 2006, Nielsen decided to add college students living in dorms to their National People Meter Sample. After monitoring their viewing habits, Nielsen estimated that 636,000 women age 18–24, living in dorms, viewed *Grey's Anatomy* during November 2006. This implied a 50 percent jump in the program ranking and elevated *Grey's Anatomy* to a top spot in the TV rankings. But to calculate their estimates, Nielsen is extrapolating from the viewing habits of *just 130 students* around the country who have agreed to have electronic monitors installed in their dorm rooms. That means that a handful of students can lead to a huge swing in ratings. For example, an estimated 163,000 jump in viewers for *Drawn Together* was based on only 12 people in the survey group who tuned in to the show. Later in this textbook, you will learn how to estimate the *margin of error* in a sample like this. But advertisers clearly believe that the information is reliable enough to use in making their decisions (for a discussion of Nielson's margin of error, see *The New York Times,* April 8, 2007, p. 10).

Does Nielsen accept volunteers in their National People Meter Sample? No. According to the Nielsen website, the firm draws its samples in a way that offers every American household with a television an equal chance of being selected. They go on to say that "[t]o include volunteers would violate basic laws of random sampling practice and skew our results. A truly representative sample of the population can only be generated using statistical methods of selection."

SECTION EXERCISES

connect

2.15 Would you use a sample or a census to measure each of the following? Why?
  a. The model years of the cars driven by each of your five closest friends.
  b. The model years of the cars driven by each student in your statistics class.
  c. The model years of the cars driven by each student in your university.
  d. The model years of the cars driven by each professor whose classes you are taking.

2.16 Would you use a sample or a census to measure each of the following? Why? If you are uncertain, explain the issues.

  a. The mean time battery life of your laptop computer in continuous use.
  b. The number of students in your statistics class who brought laptop computers to class today.
  c. The average price paid for a laptop computer by students at your university.
  d. The percentage of disk space available on laptop computers owned by your five closest friends.

2.17 The target population is all stocks in the S&P 500 index. Is each of the following a parameter or a statistic?

  a. The average price/earnings ratio for all 500 stocks in the S&P index.
  b. The proportion of all stocks in the S&P 500 index that had negative earnings last year.
  c. The proportion of energy-related stocks in a random sample of 50 stocks.
  d. The average rate of return for 20 stocks recommended by a broker.

2.4 SAMPLING METHODS

There are two main categories of sampling methods. In **random sampling** items are chosen by randomization or a chance procedure. The idea of random sampling is to produce a sample that is representative of the population. **Non-random sampling** is less scientific but is sometimes used for expediency. We will first discuss the four random sampling techniques shown in Table 2.5 and then describe three commonly used non-random sampling techniques, summarized in Table 2.8.

TABLE 2.5

Random Sampling Methods

Simple Random Sample	Use random numbers to select items from a list (e.g., Visa cardholders).
Systematic Sample	Select every kth item from a list or sequence (e.g., restaurant customers).
Stratified Sample	Select randomly within defined strata (e.g., by age, occupation, gender).
Cluster Sample	Select random geographical regions (e.g., zip codes) that represent the population.

Simple Random Sample

We denote the population size by N and the sample size by n. In a **simple random sample**, every item in the population of N items has the same chance of being chosen in the sample of n items. A physical experiment to accomplish this would be to write each of the N data values on a poker chip, and then to draw n chips from a bowl after stirring it thoroughly. But we can accomplish the same thing if the N population items appear on a numbered list, by choosing n integers between 1 and N that we match up against the numbered list of the population items.

LO 2-7

Explain the common sampling methods and how to implement them.

For example, suppose we want to select one student at random from a list of 15 students (see Figure 2.5). If you were asked to "use your judgment," you would probably pick a name in the middle, thereby biasing the draw against those individuals at either end of the list. Instead we rely on a **random number** to "pick" the name. How do we determine the random number? Before computers, statisticians relied on published tables of random numbers. The process is simpler today. Even most pocket calculators have a key to produce a random decimal in the interval [0, 1] which can be converted to a random integer. In this example, we used Excel's function =RANDBETWEEN(1,15) to pick a random integer between 1 and 15. The number was 12, so Stephanie was selected. There is no bias since all values from 1 to 15 are *equiprobable* (i.e., equally likely to occur).

Sampling without replacement means that once an item has been selected to be included in the sample, it cannot be considered for the sample again. The Excel function =RANDBETWEEN(a,b) uses **sampling with replacement**. This means that the same random number could show up more than once. Using the bowl analogy, if we throw each chip back in the bowl and stir the contents before the next draw, an item can be chosen again. Instinctively most people believe that sampling without replacement is preferred over sampling with replacement because allowing duplicates in our sample seems odd. In reality, sampling without replacement can be a problem when our sample size n is close to our population size N. At some point in the sampling process, the remaining items in the population will no longer have the same probability of being selected as the items

FIGURE 2.5

Picking on Stephanie

Random person **12**

1	Adam	6	Haitham	11	Moira
2	Addie	7	Jackie	12	**Stephanie**
3	Don	8	Judy	13	Stephen
4	Floyd	9	Lindsay	14	Tara
5	Gadis	10	Majda	15	Xander

we chose at the beginning of the sampling process. This could lead to a bias (a tendency to overestimate or underestimate the parameter we are trying to measure) in our sample results. Sampling with replacement does not lead to bias.

When should we worry about sampling without replacement? Only when the population is finite and the sample size is close to the population size. Consider the Russell 3000® Index, which has 3000 stocks. If you sample 100 stocks, without replacement, you have "used" only about 3 percent of the population. The sample size $n = 100$ is considered small relative to the population size $N = 3000$. A common criterion is that a finite population is *effectively infinite* if the sample is less than 5 percent of the population (i.e., if $n/N \leq .05$). In Chapter 8, you will learn how to adjust for the effect of population size when you make a sample estimate. For now, you only need to recognize that such adjustments are of little consequence when the population is large.

Rule of Thumb

When the sample is less than 5 percent of the population (i.e., when $n/N \leq .05$), then the population is effectively infinite. An equivalent statement is that a population is effectively infinite when it is at least 20 times as large as the sample (i.e., when $N/n \geq 20$).

Because computers are easier, we rarely use random number tables. Table 2.6 shows a few alternative ways to choose 10 integers between 1 and 875. All are based on a software algorithm that creates uniform decimal numbers between 0 and 1. Excel's function =RAND( ) does this, and many pocket calculators have a similar function. We call these *pseudorandom* generators because even the best algorithms eventually repeat themselves (after a cycle of millions of numbers). Thus, a software-based random data encryption scheme could conceivably be broken. To enhance data security, Intel and other firms are examining hardware-based methods (e.g., based on thermal noise or radioactive decay) to prevent patterns or repetition. Fortunately, most applications don't require that degree of randomness. For example, the iPod Shuffle's song choices are not strictly random because its random numbers are generated by an algorithm from a "seed number" that eventually repeats. However, the repeat period is so great that an iPod user would never notice. Excel's and MINITAB's random numbers are good enough for most purposes.

TABLE 2.6		
Some Ways to Get 10 Random Integers between 1 and 875	Excel—Option A	Enter the Excel function =RANDBETWEEN(1,875) into 10 spreadsheet cells. Press **F9** to get a new sample.
	Excel—Option B	Enter the function =INT(1+875*RAND()) into 10 spreadsheet cells. Press **F9** to get a new sample.
	Internet	The website www.random.org will give you many kinds of excellent random numbers (integers, decimals, etc).
	MINITAB	Use MINITAB's Random Data menu with the Integer option.
	Pocket Calculator	Press the **RAND** key to get a random number in the interval [0,1], multiply by 875, then round up to the next integer.

Randomizing a List

To randomize a list (assuming it is in a spreadsheet) we can insert the Excel function =RAND( ) beside each row. This creates a column of random decimal numbers between 0 and 1. Copy the random numbers and paste them in the same column using Paste Special > Values to "fix" them (otherwise they will keep changing). Then sort all the columns by the random number column, and *voilà*—the list is now random! The first n items on the randomized list can now be used as a random sample. This method is especially useful when the list is very long (perhaps millions of lines). The first n items are a random sample of the entire list, for they are as likely as any others.

Systematic Sample

Another method of random sampling is to choose every kth item from a sequence or list, starting from a randomly chosen entry among the first k items on the list. This is called **systematic sampling**. Figure 2.6 shows how to sample every fourth item, starting from item 2, resulting in a sample of $n = 20$ items.

FIGURE 2.6

Systematic Sampling

An attraction of systematic sampling is that it can be used with unlistable or infinite populations, such as production processes (e.g., testing every 5,000th light bulb) or political polling (e.g., surveying every tenth voter who emerges from the polling place). Systematic sampling is also well-suited to linearly organized physical populations (e.g., pulling every tenth patient folder from alphabetized filing drawers in a veterinary clinic).

A systematic sample of n items from a population of N items requires that periodicity k be approximately N/n. For example, to choose 25 companies from a list of 500 companies in Example 2.2 (Table 2.7), we chose every twentieth stock ($k = 500/25 = 20$).

To sample the compensation of the CEOs of the 500 largest companies in the United States listed in *Forbes'* annual survey, take every twentieth company in the alphabetized list, starting (randomly) with the thirteenth company. The starting point (the thirteenth company) is chosen at random. This yields the sample of 25 CEOs, shown in Table 2.7. While it would be very time-consuming to examine all 500 executives, this sample should provide a representative cross-section.

EXAMPLE 2.2

CEO Compensation

TABLE 2.7

CEO Compensation in 25 Large U.S. Firms
📁 **CEOComp**

Observation	Firm	CEO	One-Year Total ($mil)
1	AK Steel Holding	James L Wainscott	11.82
2	Anadarko Petroleum	James T Hackett	19.65
3	Avnet	Roy Vallee	10.16
4	Bristol-Myers Squibb	James M Cornelius	5.06
5	Charter Communications	Neil Smith	5.63
6	Commercial Metals	Murray R McClean	3.84
7	CVS Caremark	Thomas M Ryan	19.55
8	Dynegy	Bruce A Williamson	8.70
9	Estee Lauder Cos	William P Lauder	5.32
10	FPL Group	Lewis Hay III	14.25
11	Google	Eric E Schmidt	0.48
12	Huntington Bancshares	Thomas E Hoaglin	0.98
13	Johnson Controls	Stephen A Roell	15.69
14	Leucadia National	Ian M Cumming	1.21
15	MBIA	Joseph W Brown	22.20
16	Morgan Stanley	John J Mack	17.65
17	Northeast Utilities	Charles W Shivery	5.91
18	People's United	Philip R Sherringham	2.22
19	Progress Energy	William D Johnson	4.11
20	Rockwell Collins	Clayton M Jones	11.31
21	Sovereign Bancorp	Joseph P Campanelli	2.48
22	TD Ameritrade Holding	Joseph H Moglia	3.76
23	Union Pacific	James R Young	7.19
24	Wal-Mart Stores	H Lee Scott Jr	8.65
25	Wynn Resorts	Stephen A Wynn	11.25

Source: *Forbes.com*, April 30, 2008. Compensation is for 2007.

Systematic sampling should yield acceptable results unless patterns in the population happen to recur at periodicity k. For example, weekly pay cycles ($k = 7$) would make it illogical to sample bank check cashing volume every Friday. A less obvious example would be a machine that stamps a defective part every twelfth cycle due to a bad tooth in a 12-tooth gear, which would make it misleading to rely on a sample of every twelfth part ($k = 12$). But periodicity coincident with k is not typical or expected in most situations.

Stratified Sample

Sometimes we can improve our sample efficiency by utilizing prior information about the population. This method is applicable when the population can be divided into relatively homogeneous subgroups of known size (called *strata*). Within each *stratum,* a simple random sample of the desired size could be taken. Alternatively, a random sample of the whole population could be taken, and then individual strata estimates could be combined using appropriate weights. This procedure, called **stratified sampling**, can reduce cost per observation and narrow the error bounds. For a population with L strata, the population size N is the sum of the stratum sizes: $N = N_1 + N_2 + \cdots + N_L$. The weight assigned to stratum j is $w_j = N_j/N$ (i.e., each stratum is weighted by its known proportion of the population).

To illustrate, suppose we want to estimate MMR (measles-mumps-rubella) vaccination rates among employees in state government, and we know that our target population (those individuals we are trying to study) is 55 percent male and 45 percent female. Suppose our budget only allows a sample of size 200. To ensure the correct gender balance, we could sample 110 males and 90 females. Alternatively, we could just take a random sample of 200 employees. Although our random sample probably will not contain *exactly* 110 males and 90 females, we can get an overall estimate of vaccination rates by *weighting* the male and female sample vaccination rates using $w_M = 0.55$ and $w_F = 0.45$ to reflect the known strata sizes.

Mini Case   2.2

Sampling for Safety

To help automakers and other researchers study the causes of injuries and fatalities in vehicle accidents, the U.S. Department of Transportation developed the National Accident Sampling System (NASS) Crashworthiness Data System (CDS). Because it is impractical to investigate every accident (there were 6,159,000 police-reported accidents in 2005), detailed data are collected in a common format from 24 primary sampling units, chosen to represent all serious police-reported motor vehicle accidents in the United States during the year. Selection of sample accidents is done in three stages: (1) The country is divided into 1,195 geographic areas called Primary Sampling Units (PSUs) grouped into 12 strata based on geographic region. Two PSUs are selected from each stratum using weights roughly proportional to the number of accidents in each stratum. (2) In each sampled PSU, a second stage of sampling is performed using a sample of Police Jurisdictions (PJs) based on the number, severity, and type of accidents in the PJ. (3) The final stage of sampling is the selection of accidents within the sampled PJs. Each reported accident is classified into a stratum based on type of vehicle, most severe injury, disposition of the injured, tow status of the vehicles, and model year of the vehicles. Each team is assigned a fixed number of accidents to investigate each week, governed by the number of researchers on a team. Weights for the strata are assigned to favor a larger percentage of higher severity accidents while ensuring that accidents in the same stratum have the same probability of being selected, regardless of the PSU. The NASS CDS database is administered by the National Center for Statistics and Analysis (NCSA) of the National Highway Traffic Safety Administration (NHTSA). These data are currently helping to improve the government's "5 Star" crashworthiness rating system for vehicles.

(Source: www-nrd.nhtsa.dot.gov/Pubs/NASS94.PDF)

Cluster Sample

Cluster samples are taken from strata consisting of geographical regions. We divide a region (say, a city) into subregions (say, blocks, subdivisions, or school districts). In one-stage cluster sampling, our sample consists of all elements in each of k randomly chosen subregions (or clusters). In two-stage cluster sampling, we first randomly select k subregions (clusters) and then choose a random sample of elements within each cluster. Figure 2.7 illustrates how four elements could be sampled from each of three randomly chosen clusters using two-stage cluster sampling.

FIGURE 2.7

Two-Stage Cluster Sampling: Randomly choose three clusters, then randomly choose four items in each cluster

Because elements within a cluster are proximate, travel time and interviewer expenses are kept low. Cluster sampling is useful when:

- Population frame and stratum characteristics are not readily available.
- It is too expensive to obtain a simple or stratified sample.
- The cost of obtaining data increases sharply with distance.
- Some loss of reliability is acceptable.

Although cluster sampling is cheap and quick, it is often reasonably accurate because people in the same neighborhood tend to be similar in income, ethnicity, educational background, and so on. Cluster sampling is useful in political polling, surveys of gasoline pump prices, studies of crime victimization, vaccination surveys, or lead contamination in soil. A hospital may contain clusters (floors) of similar patients. A warehouse may have clusters (pallets) of inventory parts. Forest sections may be viewed as clusters to be sampled for disease or timber growth rates.

Cluster sampling is also widely used in marketing and economic surveys. The Bureau of Labor Statistics relies on multistage cluster sampling for estimating economic indicators such as the Consumer Price Index (CPI) and employment rates. The CPI measures the average change in price for a "market basket" of goods and services typically used by urban consumers. The CPI is estimated from a two-stage cluster sampling process. The sampling process begins with 87 urban areas in the United States. Within these urban areas, prices on over 200 categories are gathered from approximately 50,000 housing units and 23,000 retail establishments.

Table 2.8 describes three commonly used non-random sampling techniques. Businesses often rely on these techniques to quickly gather data that might be used to guide informal decisions or as preliminary data to help design formal studies that use random samples.

TABLE 2.8

Non-Random Samples

Judgment Sample	Use expert knowledge to choose "typical" items (e.g., which employees to interview).
Convenience Sample	Use a sample that happens to be available (e.g., ask co-workers' opinions at lunch).
Focus Groups	In-depth dialog with a representative panel of individuals (e.g., iPod users).

Judgment Sample

Judgment sampling is a non-random sampling method that relies on the expertise of the sampler to choose items that are representative of the population. For example, to estimate the corporate spending on research and development (R&D) in the medical equipment industry, we might ask an industry expert to select several "typical" firms. Unfortunately, subconscious biases can affect experts, too. In this context, "bias" does not mean prejudice, but rather *non-randomness* in the choice. Judgment samples may be the best alternative in some cases, but we can't be sure whether the sample was random. *Quota sampling* is a special kind of judgment sampling in which the interviewer chooses a certain number of people in each category (e.g., men/women).

Convenience Sample

The sole virtue of **convenience sampling** is that it is quick. The idea is to grab whatever sample is handy. An accounting professor who wants to know how many MBA students would take a summer elective in international accounting can just survey the class she is currently teaching. The students polled may not be representative of all MBA students, but an answer (although imperfect) will be available immediately. A newspaper reporter doing a story on perceived airport security might interview co-workers who travel frequently. An executive might ask department heads if they think nonbusiness web surfing is widespread.

You might think that convenience sampling is rarely used or, when it is, that the results are used with caution. However, this does not appear to be the case. Since convenience samples often sound the first alarm on a timely issue, their results have a way of attracting attention and have probably influenced quite a few business decisions. The mathematical properties of convenience samples are unknowable, but they do serve a purpose and their influence cannot be ignored.

Focus Groups

A **focus group** is a panel of individuals chosen to be representative of a wider population, formed for open-ended discussion and idea gathering about an issue (e.g., a proposed new product or marketing strategy). Typically 5–10 people are selected, and the interactive discussion lasts 1–2 hours. Participants are usually individuals who do not know each other, but who are prescreened to be broadly compatible yet diverse. A trained moderator guides the focus group's discussion and keeps it on track. Although not a random sampling method, focus groups are widely used, both in business and in social science research, for the insights they can yield beyond "just numbers."

Mini Case   2.3

Pricing Accuracy

Bar code price scanning using the Universal Product Code (UPC) became the standard in most retail businesses following the rapid improvement in scanning technology during the 1970s. Since that time, federal and state agencies have monitored businesses to regulate pricing accuracy at their checkouts. Because a census is impossible for checking price accuracy, sampling is an essential tool in enforcing consumer protection laws. The National Institute for Standards and Technology (NIST) has developed a handbook for inspection agencies that provides guidance on how to conduct a pricing sampling inspection.

Arizona's Department of Weights and Measures (DWM) has set up a UPC scanner pricing sampling inspection process for the retail establishments in their state. A UPC inspection will be based on either a stratified sample (i.e., a cosmetics department) or a simple random sample from throughout the store. The inspector will select between 25 and 50 items based on the sample size recommendation from NIST. The items will be taken to the register for scanning and the inspector will count the number of items that show a difference between the display and scanned price. Arizona requires that the retail store have 98 percent accuracy.

Between 2001 and 2006, in the state of Arizona, Walmart failed 526 price accuracy inspections. The Arizona attorney general filed a lawsuit against Walmart in 2006. The lawsuit was settled when Walmart agreed to a financial settlement of $1 million and modifications of their pricing practices.

Source: http://www.azag.gov/press_releases/may/2009/WM%20Settlement%20Release.pdf, accessed February 10, 2011.

Sample Size

The necessary sample size depends on the inherent variability of the quantity being measured and the desired precision of the estimate. For example, the caffeine content of Mountain Dew is fairly consistent because each can or bottle is filled at the factory, so a small sample size would suffice to estimate the mean. In contrast, the amount of caffeine in an individually brewed cup of Bigelow Raspberry Royale tea varies widely because people let it steep for varying lengths of time, so a larger sample would be needed to estimate the mean. The purposes of the investigation, the costs of sampling, the budget, and time constraints are also taken into account in deciding on sample size. Setting the sample size is worth a detailed discussion, found in later chapters.

Sources of Error

No matter how careful you are when conducting a survey, you will encounter potential sources of error. Let's briefly review a few, summarized in Table 2.9.

In sampling, the word *bias* does not refer to prejudice. Rather, it refers to a systematic tendency to over- or underestimate a population parameter of interest. The word "error" generally refers to problems in sample methodology that lead to inaccurate estimates of a population parameter.

TABLE 2.9

Potential Sources of Survey Error

Source of Error	Characteristics
Nonresponse bias	Respondents differ from nonrespondents
Selection bias	Self-selected respondents are atypical
Response error	Respondents give false information
Coverage error	Incorrect specification of frame or population
Measurement error	Unclear survey instrument wording
Interviewer error	Responses influenced by interviewer
Sampling error	Random and unavoidable

Nonresponse bias occurs when those who respond have characteristics different from those who don't respond. For example, people with caller ID, answering machines, blocked or unlisted numbers, or cell phones are likely to be missed in telephone surveys. Since these are generally more affluent individuals, their socioeconomic class may be underrepresented in the poll. A special case is **selection bias**, a self-selected sample. For example, a talk show host who invites viewers to take a web survey about their sex lives will attract plenty of respondents. But those who are willing to reveal details of their personal lives (and who have time to complete the survey) are likely to differ substantially from those who dislike nosy surveys or are too busy (and probably weren't watching the show anyway).

Further, it is easy to imagine that hoax replies will be common to such a survey (e.g., a bunch of college dorm students giving silly answers on a web survey). **Response error** occurs when respondents deliberately give false information to mimic socially acceptable answers, to avoid embarrassment, or to protect personal information.

Coverage error occurs when some important segment of the target population is systematically missed. For example, a survey of Notre Dame University alumni will fail to represent noncollege graduates or those who attended public universities. **Measurement error** results when the survey questions do not accurately reveal the construct being assessed. When the interviewer's facial expressions, tone of voice, or appearance influences the responses, data are subject to **interviewer error**.

Finally, **sampling error** is uncontrollable random error that is inherent in any random sample. Even when using a random sampling method, it is possible that the sample will contain unusual responses. This cannot be prevented and is generally undetectable. It is *not* an error on your part.

Mini Case   2.4

Making Commercials Work Better

A new company has sprung up to offer advertisers help in improving their targeting of commercial messages on various broadcast media, using digital technology. Integrated Media Measurement (IMMI, Inc.) tracks the behavior of 3,000 panel members (including teenagers) by having them carry a special cell phone (the panelists get free cell phone usage for two years). The phones capture samples of audio 24/7 from the surrounding environment. Samples are then analyzed digitally and matched against known ad content to see what the participant is listening to, and where the participant heard the ad (TV, radio, internet, DVD, etc.). This technology has the potential to inform marketers of ways to reach those who watch TV online, a group who tend to be missed through traditional television ads. Another new potential ad content stream being explored is movie theatre ads. Traditional Nielson ratings (see Mini Case 2.1) only cover television viewers, so there is considerable investor interest in this emerging high-tech sampling method. A carefully designed *stratified* sample of panelists is needed to permit estimation of ad exposure of listener populations by age, ethnicity, education, income, and other relevant demographics.

Source: *The New York Times*, September 7, 2007, p. B4; immi.com; www.tradevibes.com.

SECTION EXERCISES

connect

2.18   The target population is all students in your university. You wish to estimate the average current Visa balance for each student. How large would the university student population have to be in order to be regarded as effectively infinite in each of the following samples?

   a. A sample of 10 students.
   b. A sample of 50 students.
   c. A sample of 100 students.

2.19   Suppose you want to know the ages of moviegoers who attend the latest *Harry Potter* movie. What kind of sample is it if you (a) survey the first 20 persons to emerge from the theater, (b) survey every tenth person to emerge from the theater, and (c) survey everyone who looks under age 12?

2.20 Referring to the previous question, would a simple random sample be possible?

2.21 Below is a 6 × 8 array containing the ages of moviegoers (see file 📄 **HarryPotter**). Treat this as a population. Select a random sample of 10 moviegoers' ages by using (a) simple random sampling with a random number table, (b) simple random sampling with Excel's =RANDBETWEEN( ) function, (c) systematic sampling, (d) judgment sampling, and (e) convenience sampling. Explain your methods.

32	34	33	12	57	13	58	16
23	23	62	65	35	15	17	20
14	11	51	33	31	13	11	58
23	10	63	34	12	15	62	13
40	11	18	62	64	30	42	20
21	56	11	51	38	49	15	21

2.22 (a) In the previous population, what was the proportion of all 48 moviegoers who were under age 30? (b) For each of the samples of size $n = 10$ that you took, what was the proportion of moviegoers under age 30? (c) Was each sample proportion close to the population proportion?

2.23 In Excel, type a list containing names for 10 of your friends into cells B1:B10. Choose three names at random by randomizing this list. To do this, enter =RAND( ) into cells A1:A10, copy the random column and paste it using Paste Special > Values to fix the random numbers, and then sort the list by the random column. The first three names are the random sample.

2.5 DATA SOURCES

LO 2-8

Find everyday print or electronic data sources.

One goal of a statistics course is to help you learn where to find data that might be needed. Fortunately, many excellent sources are widely available, either in libraries or through private purchase. Table 2.10 summarizes a few of them.

The *Statistical Abstract of the United States* is the largest, most general, and widely available annual compendium of facts and figures from public sources. You can purchase it at government bookstores in major cities, order it by mail, or use it for free on the web. It covers a wide range of cross-sectional data (e.g., states, cities) as well as time series data. Subjects include population, vital statistics, immigration, health, nutrition, education, law enforcement, geography, environment, parks, recreation, elections, government, national defense, social insurance, human services, labor force, income, prices, banking, finance, insurance, communications, energy, science, transportation, agriculture, forests, fisheries, mining, construction, housing, manufactures, and international statistics. No business statistician should be without this reference.

For annual and monthly time series economic data, try the *Economic Report of the President* (*ERP*), which is published every February. The tables in the *ERP* can be downloaded for free in Excel format. Data on cities, counties, and states can be found in the *State and Metropolitan Area Data Book,* published every few years by the Bureau of the Census and available on CD-ROM in many libraries.

Annual almanacs from several major publishers are sold at most bookstores. These include data reprinted from the above sources, but also information on recent events, sports, stock market, elections, Congress, world nations, states, and higher education. One of these almanacs should be on every informed citizen's shelf.

TABLE 2.10

Useful Data Sources

Type of Data	Examples
U.S. general data	*Statistical Abstract of the United States*
U.S. economic data	*Economic Report of the President*
Almanacs	*World Almanac, Time Almanac*
Periodicals	*Economist, Bloomberg Businessweek, Fortune, Forbes*
Indexes	*The New York Times, The Wall Street Journal*
Databases	Compustat, Citibase, U.S. Census
World data	*CIA World Factbook*
Web	Google, Yahoo!, MSN

Annual surveys of major companies, markets, and topics of business or personal finance are found in magazines such as *Bloomberg Businessweek, Consumer Reports, Forbes, Fortune,* and *Money.* Indexes such as the *Business Periodical Index, The New York Times Index,* and *The Wall Street Journal Index* are useful for locating topics. Libraries have web search engines that can access many of these periodicals in abstract or full-text form.

Specialized computer databases (e.g., CRSP, Compustat, Citibase, U.S. Census) are available (at a price) for research on stocks, companies, financial statistics, and census data. An excellent summary of sources is F. Patrick Butler's *Business Research Sources: A Reference Navigator.* The web allows us to use search engines (e.g., Google, Yahoo!, MSN) to find information. Sometimes you may get lucky, but web information is often undocumented, unreliable, or unverifiable. Better information is available through private companies or trade associations, though often at a steep price. Related Reading and Web Data Sources are listed at the end of this chapter.

Often overlooked sources of help are your university librarians. University librarians understand how to find databases and how to navigate databases quickly and accurately. Librarians can help you distinguish between valid and invalid Internet sources and then help you put the source citation in the proper format when writing reports.

Copying Data to a Spreadsheet

If your data set contains commas (e.g., 42,586), dollar signs (e.g., $14.88), or percents (e.g., 7.5%), your statistics package (e.g., MINITAB or SPSS) may treat the data as text. A numerical variable may only contain the digits 0–9, a decimal point, and a minus sign. Format the data column as plain numbers with the desired number of decimal places *before* you copy the data to whatever package you are using. Excel can display a value such as 32.8756 as 32.9 if you set only one decimal digit, but it is the *displayed* number that is copied, so your Excel statistics may not agree with the package you are using.

Web Data Sources

Source	*Website*
Bureau of Economic Analysis	www.bea.gov
Bureau of Justice Statistics	www.ojp.usdoj.gov/bjs
Bureau of Labor Statistics	www.bls.gov
Central Intelligence Agency	www.cia.gov
Economic Report of the President	www.gpoaccess.gov/eop
Environmental Protection Agency	www.epa.gov
Federal Reserve System	www.federalreserve.gov
Food and Drug Administration	www.fda.gov
National Agricultural Statistics Service	www.nass.usda.gov
National Center for Education Statistics	www.nces.ed.gov
National Center for Health Statistics	www.cdc.gov/nchs
State and Metropolitan Area Data Book	www.census.gov/statab/www/smadb.html
Statistical Abstract of the United States	www.census.gov/compendia/statab/
Statistics Canada	www.statcan.gc.ca
U.N. Dept of Economic and Social Affairs	www.un.org/depts/unsd
U.S. Census Bureau	www.census.gov
U.S. Federal Statistics	www.fedstats.gov
World Bank	www.worldbank.org
World Demographics	www.demographia.com
World Health Organization	www.who.int/en

2.6 SURVEYS

Most survey research follows the same basic steps. These steps may overlap in time:

- Step 1: State the goals of the research.
- Step 2: Develop the budget (time, money, staff).
- Step 3: Create a research design (target population, frame, sample size).
- Step 4: Choose a survey type and method of administration.
- Step 5: Design a data collection instrument (questionnaire).
- Step 6: Pretest the survey instrument and revise as needed.
- Step 7: Administer the survey (follow up if needed).
- Step 8: Code the data and analyze it.

LO 2-9

Describe basic elements of survey design, survey types, and sources of error.

Survey Types

Surveys fall into five general categories: mail, telephone, interview, web, and direct observation. They differ in cost, response rate, data quality, time required, and survey staff training requirements. Table 2.11 lists some common types of surveys and a few of their salient strengths/weaknesses.

Response Rates

Consider the *cost per valid response*. A telephone survey might be cheapest to conduct, but bear in mind that over half the households in some metropolitan areas have unlisted phones, and many have answering machines or call screening. The sample

TABLE 2.11

Common Types of Surveys

Survey Type	Characteristics
Mail	Mail requires a well-targeted and current mailing list (people move a lot). Expect low response rates and nonresponse bias (nonrespondents differ from those who respond). Zip code lists (often costly) are an attractive option to define strata of similar income, education, and attitudes. To encourage participation, a cover letter should explain the uses of the survey data. Plan for follow-up mailings.
Telephone	Random dialing yields low response and is poorly targeted. Purchased phone lists help reach the target population, though a low response rate still is typical (disconnected phones, caller screening, answering machines, work hours, no-call lists). Other sources of nonresponse bias include the growing number of cell phones, non-English speakers, and distrust caused by scams.
Interviews	Interviewing is expensive and time-consuming, yet a trade-off between sample size for high-quality results may be worth it. Interviewers must be well-trained—an added cost. Interviewers can obtain information on complex or sensitive topics (e.g., gender discrimination in companies, birth control practices, diet and exercise).
Web	Web surveys are growing in popularity but are subject to nonresponse bias because they miss those who feel too busy, don't own computers, or distrust your motives (scams and spam). This type of survey works best when targeted to a well-defined interest group on a question of self-interest (e.g., views of CPAs on Sarbanes-Oxley accounting rules, frequent flyer views on airline security).
Direct Observation	Observation can be done in a controlled setting (e.g., psychology lab) but requires informed consent, which can change behavior. Unobtrusive observation is possible in some nonlab settings (e.g., what percentage of airline passengers carry on more than two bags, what percentage of SUVs carry no passengers, what percentage of drivers wear seat belts).

you get may not be very useful in terms of reaching the target population. Telephone surveys (even with random dialing) do lend themselves nicely to cluster sampling (e.g., using each three-digit area code as a cluster and each three-digit exchange as a cluster) to sample somewhat homogeneous populations. Similarly, mail surveys can be clustered by zip code, which is a significant attraction. Web surveys are cheap, but rather uncontrolled. Nonresponse bias is a problem with all of these. Interviews or observational experiments are expensive and labor-intensive, but they may provide higher quality data. Large-scale national research projects (e.g., mental health status of U.S. household members) offer financial incentives to encourage participants who otherwise would not provide information. Research suggests that adjustments can be made for whatever biases may result from such incentives. Table 2.12 offers some tips to conduct successful surveys.

TABLE 2.12 **Survey Guidelines**	Planning	What is the survey's purpose? What do you really need to know? What staff expertise is available? What skills are best hired externally? What degree of precision is required? What is your budget?
	Design	To ensure a good response and useful data, you must invest time and money in designing the survey. Take advantage of many useful books and references so that you do not make unnecessary errors.
	Quality	Care in preparation is needed. Glossy printing and advertising have raised people's expectations about quality. A scruffy questionnaire will be ignored. Some surveys (e.g., web-based) may require special software.
	Pilot Test	Questions that are clear to you may be unclear to others. You can pretest the questionnaire on friends or co-workers, but using a small test panel of naive respondents who don't owe you anything is best.
	Buy-In	Response rates may be improved by stating the purpose of the survey, by offering a token of appreciation (e.g., discount coupon, free gift), or with endorsements (e.g., from a trusted professional group).
	Expertise	Consider hiring a consultant at the early stages, even if you plan to do your own data collection and tabulation. Early consultation is more effective than waiting until you get in trouble.

Questionnaire Design

You should consider hiring a consultant, at least in the early stages, to help you get your survey off the ground successfully. Alternatively, resources are available on the web to help you plan a survey. The American Statistical Association (www.amstat.org) offers brochures *What Is a Survey* and *How to Plan a Survey*. Additional materials are available from the Research Industry Coalition, Inc. (www.researchindustry.org) and the Council of American Survey Research Organizations (www.casro.org). Entire books have been written to help you design and administer your own survey (see Related Reading).

The layout must not be crowded (use lots of white space). Begin with very short, clear instructions, stating the purpose, assuring anonymity, and explaining how to submit the completed survey. Questions should be numbered. Divide the survey into sections if the topics fall naturally into distinct areas. Let respondents bypass sections that aren't relevant to them (e.g., "If you answered no to Question 7, skip directly to Question 15"). Include an "escape option" where it seems appropriate (e.g., "Don't know or Does not apply"). Use wording and response scales that match the reading ability and knowledge level of the intended respondents. Pretest and revise. Keep the questionnaire as short as possible. Table 2.13 lists a few common question formats and response scales.

TABLE 2.13

Question Format and Response Scale

Type of Question	Example
Open-ended	Briefly describe your job goals.
Fill-in-the-blank	How many times did you attend formal religious services during the last year? _____ times
Check boxes	Which of these statistics packages have you used? ❏ SAS ❏ Visual Statistics ❏ SPSS ❏ MegaStat ❏ Systat ❏ MINITAB

Ranked choices

Please evaluate your dining experience:

	Excellent	Good	Fair	Poor
Food	❏	❏	❏	❏
Service	❏	❏	❏	❏
Ambiance	❏	❏	❏	❏
Cleanliness	❏	❏	❏	❏
Overall	❏	❏	❏	❏

Pictograms

What do you think of the president's economic policies? (circle one)

☺ ☺ ☺ ☹ ☹

Likert scale

Statistics is a difficult subject.

Strongly Agree	Slightly Agree	Neither Agree nor Disagree	Slightly Disagree	Strongly Disagree
❏	❏	❏	❏	❏

Question Wording

The way a question is asked has a profound influence on the response. For example, in a *Wall Street Journal* editorial, Fred Barnes tells of a *Reader's Digest* poll that asked two similar questions:

Version 1: I would be disappointed if Congress cut its funding for public television.

Version 2: Cuts in funding for public television are justified to reduce federal spending.

The same 1,031 people were polled in both cases. Version 1 showed 40 percent in favor of cuts, while version 2 showed 52 percent in favor of cuts. The margin of error was ± 3.5 percent (in "How to Rig a Poll," June 14, 1995, p. A18). To "rig" the poll, emotional overlays or "loaded" mental images can be attached to the question. In fact, it is often difficult to ask a neutral question without any context. For example:

Version 1: Shall state taxes be cut?

Version 2: Shall state taxes be cut, if it means reducing highway maintenance?

Version 3: Shall state taxes be cut, if it means firing teachers and police?

An unconstrained choice (version 1) makes tax cuts appear to be a "free lunch," while versions 2 and 3 require the respondent to envision the consequences of a tax cut. An alternative is to use version 1 but then ask the respondent to list the state services that should be cut to balance the budget after the tax cut.

Another problem in wording is to make sure you have covered all the possibilities. For example, how could a widowed independent voter answer questions like these?

Are you married? What is your party preference?

❏ Yes ❏ Democrat

❏ No ❏ Republican

Avoid overlapping classes or unclear categories. What if the respondent's father is deceased or is 45 years old?

How old is your father?

❏ 35–45   ❏ 45–55   ❏ 55–65   ❏ 65 or older

Coding and Data Screening

Survey responses usually are coded numerically (e.g., 1 = male, 2 = female), although some software packages can also tabulate text variables (nominal data) and use them in certain kinds of statistical tests. Most packages require you to denote missing values by a special character (e.g., blank, period, or asterisk). If too many entries on a given respondent's questionnaire are flawed or missing, you may decide to discard the entire response.

Other data screening issues include multiple responses (i.e., the respondent chose two responses where one was expected), outrageous replies on fill-in-the-blank questions (e.g., a respondent who claims to work 640 hours a week), "range" answers (e.g., 10–20 cigarettes smoked per day), or inconsistent replies (e.g., a 55-year-old respondent who claims to receive Medicare benefits). Sometimes a follow-up is possible, but in anonymous surveys you must make the best decisions you can about how to handle anomalous data. Be sure to document your data-coding decisions—not only for the benefit of others but also in case you are asked to explain how you did it (it is easy to forget after a month or two, when you have moved on to other projects).

SECTION EXERCISES

connect

2.24   What sources of error might you encounter if you want to know (a) about the dating habits of college men, so you go to a dorm meeting and ask students how many dates they have had in the last year; (b) how often people attend religious services, so you stand outside a particular church on Sunday and ask entering individuals how often they attend; (c) how often people eat at McDonald's, so you stand outside a particular McDonald's and ask entering customers how often they eat at McDonald's?

2.25   What kind of survey (mail, telephone, interview, web, direct observation) would you recommend for each of the following purposes, and why? What problems might be encountered?

a.   To estimate the proportion of students at your university who would prefer a web-based statistics class to a regular lecture.

b.   To estimate the proportion of students at your university who carry backpacks to class.

c.   To estimate the proportion of students at your university who would be interested in taking a two-month summer class in international business with tours of European factories.

d.   To estimate the proportion of U.S. business graduates who have taken a class in international business.

2.26   What kind of survey (mail, telephone, interview, web, direct observation) would you recommend that a small laundry and dry cleaning business use for each of the following purposes, and why?

a.   To estimate the proportion of customers preferring opening hours at 7 a.m. instead of 8 a.m.

b.   To estimate the proportion of customers who have only laundry and no dry cleaning.

c.   To estimate the proportion of residents in the same zip code who spend more than $20 a month on dry cleaning.

d.   To estimate the proportion of its seven employees who think it is too hot inside the building.

2.27   What would be the difference in student responses to the two questions shown?

Version 1:   I would prefer that tuition be reduced.

Version 2:   Cuts in tuition are a good idea even if some classes are canceled.

2.28   What problems are evident in the wording of these two questions?

What is your race?   What is your religious preference?

❏ White   ❏ Christian

❏ Black   ❏ Jewish

Mini Case   2.5

Roles of Colleges

A survey of public opinion on the role of colleges was conducted by *The Chronicle of Higher Education*. Results of the survey showed that 77 percent of respondents agreed it was highly important that colleges prepare its undergraduate students for a career. The percentage of respondents who agreed it was highly important for colleges to prepare students to be responsible citizens was slightly lower, at 67 percent. The survey utilized 1,000 telephone interviews of 20 minutes each, using a random selection of men and women aged 25 through 65. It was conducted February 25, 2004. The survey was administered by TMR Inc. of Broomall, Pennsylvania. Data were collected and analyzed by GDA Integrated Services, a market research firm in Old Saybrook, Connecticut.

The Likert-type scale labels are weighted toward the positive, which is common when the survey items (roles for colleges in this case) are assumed to be potentially important and there is little likelihood of a strong negative response. Respondents were also asked for demographic information. Fifty-eight percent were women and 42 percent were men, coming from all states except Alaska and Hawaii. Eleven percent were African American (similar to the national average), but only 6 percent were Hispanic (about 8 percent below the national average). The underrepresentation of Hispanics was due to language barriers, illustrating one difficulty faced by surveys. However, the respondents' incomes, religious affiliations, and political views were similar to the general U.S. population. The random selection method was not specified. Note that firms that specialize in survey sampling generally have access to commercial lists and use their own proprietary methods.

CHAPTER SUMMARY

A **data set** consists of all the values of all the variables we have chosen to observe. It often is an array with n rows and m columns. Data sets may be **univariate** (one variable), **bivariate** (two variables), or **multivariate** (three or more variables). There are two basic data types: **categorical data** (categories that are described by labels) or **numerical** (meaningful numbers). Numerical data are **discrete** if the values are integers or can be counted or **continuous** if any interval can contain more data values. **Nominal** measurements are names, **ordinal** measurements are ranks, **interval** measurements have meaningful distances between data values, and **ratio** measurements have meaningful ratios and a zero reference point. **Time series** data are observations measured at n different points in time or over sequential time intervals, while **cross-sectional** data are observations among n entities such as individuals, firms, or geographic regions. Among **random samples, simple random** samples pick items from a list using random numbers, **systematic** samples take every kth item, **cluster** samples select geographic regions, and **stratified** samples take into account known population proportions. **Nonrandom** samples include convenience or judgment samples, gaining time but sacrificing randomness. **Focus groups** give in-depth information. **Survey design** requires attention to question **wording** and **scale definitions**. **Survey techniques** (mail, telephone, interview, web, direct observation) depend on time, budget, and the nature of the questions and are subject to various sources of error.

KEY TERMS

binary variable, *25*
bivariate data sets, *23*
categorical data, *24*
census, *32*
cluster sample, *39*
coding, *25*
continuous data, *25*
convenience sampling, *40*
coverage error, *42*
cross-sectional data, *26*
data, *23*
data set, *23*

discrete data, *25*
focus group, *40*
interval data, *29*
interviewer error, *42*
judgment sampling, *40*
Likert scale, *29*
measurement error, *42*
multivariate data sets, *23*
nominal data, *27*
non-random sampling, *35*
nonresponse bias, *42*
numerical data, *24*

observation, *23*
ordinal data, *28*
parameter, *33*
population, *31*
random numbers, *35*
random sampling, *35*
ratio data, *30*
response error, *42*
sample, *31*
sampling error, *42*
sampling frame, *33*
sampling with replacement, *35*

CHAPTER REVIEW

1. Define (a) data, (b) data set, (c) observation, and (d) variable.

2. How do business data differ from scientific experimental data?

3. Distinguish (a) univariate, bivariate, and multivariate data; (b) discrete and continuous data; (c) numerical and categorical data.

4. Define the four measurement levels and give an example of each.

5. Explain the difference between cross-sectional data and time series data.

6. (a) List three reasons why a census might be preferred to a sample. (b) List three reasons why a sample might be preferred to a census.

7. (a) What is the difference between a parameter and a statistic? (b) What is a target population?

8. (a) List four methods of random sampling. (b) List two methods of non-random sampling. (c) Why would we ever use non-random sampling? (d) Why is sampling usually done without replacement?

9. List five (a) steps in a survey, (b) issues in survey design, (c) survey types, (d) question scale types, and (e) sources of error in surveys.

10. List advantages and disadvantages of different types of surveys.

CHAPTER EXERCISES

connect

DATA TYPES

2.29 Which type of data (categorical, discrete numerical, continuous numerical) is each of the following variables?

a. Age of a randomly chosen tennis player in the Wimbledon tennis tournament.
b. Nationality of a randomly chosen tennis player in the Wimbledon tennis tournament.
c. Number of double faults in a randomly chosen tennis game at Wimbledon.

2.30 Which type of data (categorical, discrete numerical, continuous numerical) is each of the following variables?

a. Number of spectators at a randomly chosen Wimbledon tennis match.
b. Water consumption (liters) by a randomly chosen Wimbledon player during a match.
c. Gender of a randomly chosen tennis player in the Wimbledon tennis tournament.

2.31 Which measurement level (nominal, ordinal, interval, ratio) is each of the following variables?

a. A customer's ranking of five new hybrid vehicles.
b. Noise level 100 meters from the Dan Ryan Expressway at a randomly chosen moment.
c. Number of occupants in a randomly chosen commuter vehicle on the San Diego Freeway.

2.32 Which measurement level (nominal, ordinal, interval, ratio) is each of the following variables?

a. Number of annual office visits by a particular Medicare subscriber.
b. Daily caffeine consumption by a six-year-old child.
c. Type of vehicle driven by a college student.

2.33 Below are 15 questions from a survey that was administered to a sample of MBA students (see *LearningStats,* Cross-Sectional Data, Surveys). Answers were recorded on paper in the blank at the left of each question. For each question, state the data type (categorical, discrete numerical, or continuous numerical) and measurement level (nominal, ordinal, interval, ratio). Explain your reasoning. If there is doubt, discuss the alternatives.

_____ Q1   What is your gender? (Male = 0, Female = 1)
_____ Q2   What is your approximate undergraduate college GPA? (1.0 to 4.0)
_____ Q3   About how many hours per week do you expect to work at an outside job this semester?
_____ Q4   What do you think is the ideal number of children for a married couple?
_____ Q5   On a 1 to 5 scale, which best describes your parents?
            1 = Mother clearly dominant ↔ 5 = Father clearly dominant
_____ Q6   On a 1 to 5 scale, assess the current job market for your undergraduate major.
            1 = Very bad ↔ 5 = Very good

_____ Q7   During the last month, how many times has your schedule been disrupted by car trouble?

_____ Q8   About how many years of college does the more-educated one of your parents have? (years)

_____ Q9   During the last year, how many traffic tickets (excluding parking) have you received?

_____ Q10   Which political orientation most nearly fits you? (1 = Liberal, 2 = Middle-of-Road, 3 = Conservative)

_____ Q11   What is the age of the car you usually drive? (years)

_____ Q12   About how many times in the past year did you attend formal religious services?

_____ Q13   How often do you read a daily newspaper? (0 = Never, 1 = Occasionally, 2 = Regularly)

_____ Q14   Can you conduct simple transactions in a language other than English? (0 = No, 1 = Yes)

_____ Q15   How often do you exercise (aerobics, running, etc)? (0 = Not at All, 1 = Sometimes, 2 = Regularly)

2.34 Identify the following data as either time series or cross-sectional.

a. The 2007 CEO compensation of the 500 largest U.S. companies.
b. The annual compensation for the CEO of Coca-Cola Enterprises from 1990 to 2009.
c. The weekly revenue for a Noodles & Company restaurant for the 52 weeks in 2009.
d. The number of skiers on the mountain on Christmas Day 2009 at each of the ski mountains owned by Vail Resorts.

2.35 Identify the following data as either time series or cross-sectional.

a. The number of rooms booked each night for the month of January 2010 at a Vail Resorts hotel.
b. The amount spent on books at the start of this semester by each student in your statistics class.
c. The number of Caesar salads sold for the week of April 19, 2010, at each Noodles & Company restaurant.
d. The stock price of Coca-Cola Enterprises on May 1st for each of the last 10 years.

SAMPLING METHODS

2.36 Would you use a sample or a census to measure each of the following? Why? If you are uncertain, explain the issues.

a. The number of cans of Campbell's soup on your local supermarket's shelf today at 6:00 p.m.
b. The proportion of soup sales last week in Boston that was sold under the Campbell's brand.
c. The proportion of Campbell's brand soup cans in your family's pantry.

2.37 Would you use a sample or census to measure each of the following?

a. The number of workers currently employed by Campbell Soup Company.
b. The average price of a can of Campbell's Cream of Mushroom soup.
c. The total earnings of workers employed by Campbell Soup Company last year.

2.38 Is each of the following a parameter or a statistic? If you are uncertain, explain the issues.

a. The number of cans of Campbell's soup sold last week at your local supermarket.
b. The proportion of all soup in the United States that was sold under the Campbell's brand last year.
c. The proportion of Campbell's brand soup cans in the family pantries of 10 students.

2.39 Is each of the following a parameter or statistic?

a. The number of visits to a pediatrician's office last week.
b. The number of copies of John Grisham's most recent novel sold to date.
c. The total revenue realized from sales of John Grisham's most recent novel.

2.40 In 2008, researchers estimated that 76.8 percent of global e-mail traffic was spam. Could a census be used to update this estimate? Why or why not?

2.41 A certain health maintenance organization (HMO) is studying its daily office routine. They collect information on three variables: the number of patients who visit during a day, the patient's complaint, and the waiting time until each patient sees a doctor. (a) Which variable is categorical? (b) Identify the two quantitative variables and state whether they are discrete or continuous.

2.42 There are 327 official ports of entry in the United States. The Department of Homeland Security selects 15 ports of entry at random to be audited for compliance with screening procedures of incoming travelers through the primary and secondary vehicle and pedestrian lanes. What kind of sample is this (simple random, systematic, stratified, cluster)?

2.43 The IRS estimates that the average taxpayer spent 3.7 hours preparing Form 1040 to file a tax return. Could a census be used to update this estimate for the most recent tax year? Why or why not?

2.44 The General Accounting Office conducted random testing of retail gasoline pumps in Michigan, Missouri, Oregon, and Tennessee. The study concluded that 49 percent of gasoline pumps nationwide are mislabeled by more than one-half of an octane point. What kind of sampling technique was most likely to have been used in this study?

2.45 Arsenic (a naturally occurring, poisonous metal) in home water wells is a common threat. (a) What sampling method would you use to estimate the arsenic levels in wells in a rural county to see whether the samples violate the EPA limit of 10 parts per billion (ppb)? (b) Is a census possible?

2.46 The average American male wears a size 10 shoe and spends 4 hours a year tying a tie. The average American female college student owns 3.5 pairs of jeans. The average American laughs 15 times daily, swallows 215 aspirin tablets a year, and has a dog weighing 32 pounds. (a) Choose one of these estimates. How do you suppose it was derived? (b) What sampling method would *you* use to update each of these statistics? What problems would you anticipate? (c) Could a census be used? (Data are from Mike Feinsilber and William B. Mead, *American Averages: Amazing Facts of Everyday Life* [Doubleday-Dolphin, 1980].)

2.47 Would you expect Noodles & Company to use a sample or census to measure each of the following? Explain.

a. The annual average weekly revenue of each Noodles restaurant.
b. The average number of weekly lunch visits by customers.
c. The customer satisfaction rating of a new dessert.
d. The number of weeks in a year that a restaurant sells more bottled beverages than fountain drinks.

2.48 A financial magazine publishes an annual list of major stock funds. Last year, the list contained 1,699 funds. What method would you recommend to obtain a sample of 20 stock funds to estimate the 10-year percent return?

2.49 Examine each of the following statistics. Which sampling method was most likely to have been used (simple random, systematic, stratified, cluster)?

a. A survey showed that 30 percent of U.S. businesses have fired an employee for inappropriate web surfing, such as gambling, watching porn, or shopping.
b. Surveyed doctors report that 59 percent of patients do not follow their prescribed treatment.
c. The Internal Revenue Service reports that, based on a sample of individual taxpayers, 80 percent of those who failed to pay what they owed did so through honest errors or misinterpretation of the tax code.
d. In Spain, per capita consumption of cigarettes is 2,274 compared with 1,230 in the United States.

2.50 The National Claims History (NCH) contains records for 999,645 Medicare patients who were discharged from acute care hospitals in October 2008. The Department of Health and Human Services performed a detailed audit of adverse medical events on a random sample of 780 drawn at random without replacement by assigning a random number to each patient on the list and then choosing random integers between 1 and 999,645. (a) What kind of sample is this (random, systematic, stratified, cluster)? (b) Is this population effectively infinite?

2.51 Prior to starting a recycling program, a city decides to measure the quantity of garbage produced by single-family homes in various neighborhoods. This experiment will require weighing garbage on the day it is set out. (a) What sampling method would you recommend, and why? (b) What would be a potential source of sampling error?

2.52 As a statistics project, a student examined every cigarette butt along the sidewalk and curb along one block near his home. Of 47 identifiable butts, 22 were Marlboro. (a) What sampling method is this (if any)? (b) Is it correct to infer that 47 percent of all smokers prefer Marlboro? (c) What potential sources of error are likely in this sample?

2.53 To protect baby scallops and ensure the survival of the species, the U.S. Fisheries and Wildlife Service requires that an average scallop must weigh at least 1/36 pound. The harbormaster at a Massachusetts port randomly selected 18 bags of scallops from 11,000 bags on an arriving vessel. From each bag, agents took a large scoop of scallops, separated and weighed the meat, and divided by the number of scallops in the scoop, finding a mean weight of 1/39 pound. (a) Would the population of 11,000 bags be considered effectively infinite in this case? (b) Which value represents a sample statistic: 1/36 or 1/39? (Data are from *Interfaces* 25, no. 2 [March–April 1995], p. 18.)

2.54 A marketing research group wanted to collect information from existing and potential customers on the appeal of a new product. They sent out surveys to a random sample of 1,200 people from their database of over 25,000 current and potential customers. Would you consider this population to be effectively infinite?

2.55 A survey of 500 potential customers for new vehicles across the United States indicated that 37 percent expected their next vehicle to be a hybrid. What kind of sampling method do you suppose was used to arrive at this estimate?

2.56 Blood lead levels exceeding 10 micrograms per deciliter have been shown to be harmful to mental and physical development in children. The U.S. Centers for Disease Control and Prevention in Atlanta estimated that about 500,000 children in the United States have blood concentrations of lead higher than this level. Which sampling method do you suppose was used to measure blood levels of lead in U.S. children to reach this conclusion?

2.57 Households can sign up for a telemarketing "no-call list." How might households who sign up differ from those who don't? What biases might this create for telemarketers promoting (a) financial planning services, (b) carpet cleaning services, and (c) vacation travel packages?

SURVEYS AND SCALES

2.58 Suggest response check boxes for these questions. In each case, what difficulties do you encounter as you try to think of appropriate check boxes?

a. Where are you employed?
b. What is the biggest issue facing the next U.S. president?
c. Are you happy?

2.59 Suggest both a Likert scale question and a response scale to measure the following:

a. A student's rating of a particular statistics professor.
b. A voter's satisfaction with the president's economic policy.
c. An HMO patient's perception of waiting time to see a doctor.

2.60 What level of measurement (nominal, ordinal, interval, ratio) is appropriate for the movie rating system that you see in *TV Guide* (☆, ☆☆, ☆☆☆, ☆☆☆☆)? Explain your reasoning.

2.61 Insurance companies are rated by several rating agencies. The Fitch 20-point scale is AAA, AA+, AA, AA−, A+, A, A−, BBB+, BBB, BBB−, BB+, BB, BB−, B+, B, B−, CCC+, CCC, CCC−, DD. (a) What level of measurement does this scale use? (b) To assume that the scale uses interval measurements, what assumption is required? (Scales are from *Weiss Ratings Guide to HMOs and Health Insurers,* Summer 2003, p. 15.)

2.62 A tabletop survey by a restaurant asked the question shown below. (a) What kind of response scale is this? (b) Suggest an alternative response scale that would be more sensitive to differences in opinion. (c) Suggest possible sources of bias in this type of survey.

Were the food and beverage presentations appealing?

    ❑ Yes   ❑ No

MINI-PROJECTS

2.63 Give *two* original examples of (a) discrete data and (b) continuous data. In each example, explain and identify any ambiguities that might exist. *Hint:* Consider data describing your own life (e.g., your sports performance or financial or academic data). You need *not* list all the data, merely describe them and show a few typical data values.

2.64 Give *two* original examples of (a) time series data and (b) cross-sectional data. *Hint:* Do not restrict yourself to published data. You need *not* list all the data, merely describe them and show a few typical data values.

2.65 Devise a practical sampling method to collect data to estimate each of the following parameters.

a. Percentage of an HMO's patients who make more than five office visits per year.
b. Noise level (measured in decibels) in neighborhoods 100 meters from a certain freeway.
c. Percentage of bank mortgages issued to first-time borrowers last year.

2.66 Devise a practical sampling method to collect data to estimate each of the following parameters.

  a. Percentage of peanuts in a can of Planter's Mixed Nuts.
  b. Average price of gasoline in your area.
  c. Average flight departure delay for Southwest Airlines in Salt Lake City.

2.67 Below are 64 names of employees at NilCo. Colors denote different departments (finance, marketing, purchasing, engineering). Sample eight names from the display shown by using (a) simple random sampling, (b) systematic sampling, and (c) cluster sampling. Try to ensure that every name has an equal chance of being picked. Which sampling method seems most appropriate? **PickEight**

Floyd	Sid	LaDonna	Tom	Mabel	Nicholas	Bonnie	Deepak
Nathan	Ginnie	Mario	Claudia	Dmitri	Kevin	Blythe	Dave
Lou	Tim	Peter	Jean	Mike	Jeremy	Chad	Doug
Loretta	Erik	Jackie	Juanita	Molly	Carl	Buck	Janet
Anne	Joel	Moira	Marnie	Ted	Greg	Duane	Amanda
Don	Gadis	Balaji	Al	Takisha	Dan	Ryan	Sam
Graham	Scott	Lorin	Vince	Jody	Brian	Tania	Ralph
Bernie	Karen	Ed	Liz	Erika	Marge	Gene	Pam

2.68 From the display below pick five cards (without replacement) by using random numbers. Explain your method. Why would the other sampling methods not work well in this case?

A ♠	A ♥	A ♣	A ♦
K ♠	K ♥	K ♣	K ♦
Q ♠	Q ♥	Q ♣	Q ♦
J ♠	J ♥	J ♣	J ♦
10 ♠	10 ♥	10 ♣	10 ♦
9 ♠	9 ♥	9 ♣	9 ♦
8 ♠	8 ♥	8 ♣	8 ♦
7 ♠	7 ♥	7 ♣	7 ♦
6 ♠	6 ♥	6 ♣	6 ♦
5 ♠	5 ♥	5 ♣	5 ♦
4 ♠	4 ♥	4 ♣	4 ♦
3 ♠	3 ♥	3 ♣	3 ♦
2 ♠	2 ♥	2 ♣	2 ♦

2.69 Treating this textbook as a population, select a sample of 10 pages at random by using (a) simple random sampling, (b) systematic sampling, (c) cluster sampling, and (d) judgment sampling. Explain your methodology carefully in each case. (e) Which method would you recommend to estimate the mean number of formulas per page? Why not the others?

2.70 Photocopy the exhibit below (omit these instructions) and show it to a friend or classmate. Ask him/her to choose a number at random and write it on a piece of paper. Collect the paper. Repeat for *at least* 20 friends/classmates. Tabulate the results. Were all the numbers chosen equally often? If not, which were favored or avoided? Why? *Hint:* Review section 2.6. **PickOne**

0	11	17	22
8	36	14	18
19	28	6	41
12	3	5	0

2.71 Ask each of 20 friends or classmates to choose a whole number between 1 and 5. Tabulate the results. Do the results seem random? If not, can you think of any reasons?

2.72 You can test Excel's algorithm for selecting random integers with a simple experiment. Enter =RANDBETWEEN(1,2) into cell A1 and then copy it to cells A1:E20. This creates a data block of 100 cells containing either a one or a two. In cell G1 type =COUNTIF(A1:E20,"=1") and in cell G2 type

=COUNTIF(A1:E20,"=2"). Highlight cells G1 and G2 and use Excel's Chart Wizard to create a bar chart. Click on the vertical axis scale and set the lower limit to 0 and upper limit to 100. You will see something like the example shown below. Then hold down the F9 key and observe the chart. Are you convinced that, on average, you are getting about 50 ones and 50 twos? *Ambitious Students:* Generalize this experiment to integers 1 through 5. **RandBetween**

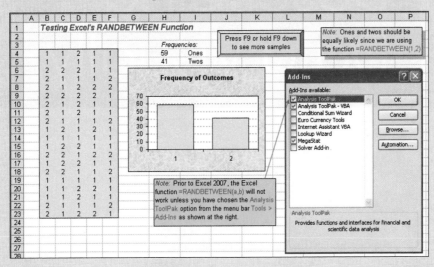

Guides to Data Sources

Butler, F. Patrick. *Business Research Sources: A Reference Navigator.* http://www.businessresearchsources.com/business-school/.

Clayton, Gary E.; and Martin Giesbrecht. *A Guide to Everyday Economic Statistics.* 6th ed. Irwin/McGraw-Hill, 2003.

Sampling and Surveys

Cooper, Donald R.; and Pamela S. Schindler. *Business Research Methods.* 11th ed. Irwin/McGraw-Hill, 2011.

Fowler, Floyd J. *Survey Research Methods.* 3rd ed. Sage, 2001.

Groves, Robert M., et al. *Survey Methodology.* Wiley, 2004.

Groves, Robert M.; Paul P. Biemer; and Lars E. Lyberg. *Telephone Survey Methodology.* Wiley, 2001.

Levy, Paul S.; and Stanley Lemeshow. *Sampling of Populations.* 3rd ed. Wiley, 2003.

Lyberg, Lars; and Paul Blemer. *Introduction to Survey Quality.* Wiley Europe, 2003.

Mathieson, Kieran; and David P. Doane. "Using Fine-Grained Likert Scales in Web Surveys." *Alliance Journal of Business Research* 1, no. 1 (2006), pp. 27–34.

Scheaffer, Richard L.; William Mendenhall; and R. Lyman Ott. *Elementary Survey Sampling.* 6th ed. Duxbury, 2006.

Thompson, Steven K. *Sampling.* 2nd ed. Wiley, 2002.

RELATED READING

CHAPTER 2   Online Learning Resources

The Online Learning Center (OLC) at www.mhhe.com/doane4e has several *LearningStats* demonstrations to help you understand random sampling. Your instructor may assign one or more of them, or you may decide to download the ones that sound interesting.

Online
LearningCenter

Topic	LearningStats Demonstrations
Sampling	Sampling Methods Who Gets Picked? Randomizing a File Pick a Card Excel's RANDBETWEEN Function
Data sources	Web Data Sources

Key: = Word   = Excel

Describing Data Visually

CHAPTER LEARNING OBJECTIVES

LO

When you finish this chapter you should be able to

LO 3-1 Make a stem-and-leaf or dot plot by hand or by computer.

LO 3-2 Create a frequency distribution for a data set.

LO 3-3 Make a histogram with appropriate bins.

LO 3-4 Identify skewness, modal classes, and outliers in a histogram.

LO 3-5 Make an effective line chart using Excel.

LO 3-6 Know the rules for effective bar charts and pie charts.

LO 3-7 Make and interpret a scatter plot using Excel.

LO 3-8 Make simple tables and pivot tables.

LO 3-9 Recognize deceptive graphing techniques.

3.1 STEM-AND-LEAF DISPLAYS AND DOT PLOTS

Managers need information that can help them identify trends and adjust to changing conditions. But it is hard to assimilate piles of raw data. How can a business analyst convert raw data into useful information? Statistics offers many methods that can help organize, explore, and summarize data in a succinct way. The methods may be *visual* (charts and graphs) or *numerical* (statistics or tables). In this chapter, you will see how visual displays can provide insight into the characteristics of a data set *without* using mathematics. We begin with a set of n observations $x_1, x_2, \ldots, x_n$ on one variable (univariate data). Such data can be discussed in terms of three characteristics: center, variability, and shape. Table 3.1 summarizes these characteristics as *questions* that we will be asking about the data.

TABLE 3.1

Characteristics of Univariate Data

Characteristic	Interpretation
Measurement	What are the units of measurement? Are the data integer or continuous? Any missing observations? Any concerns with accuracy or sampling methods?
Center	Where are the data values concentrated? What seem to be typical or middle data values?
Variability	How much dispersion is there in the data? How spread out are the data values? Are there unusual values?
Shape	Are the data values distributed symmetrically? Skewed? Sharply peaked? Flat? Bimodal?

EXAMPLE 3.1

Price/Earnings Ratios

Price/earnings (P/E) ratios—current stock price divided by earnings per share in the last 12 months—show how much an investor is willing to pay for a stock based on the stock's earnings. P/E ratios are also used to determine how optimistic the market is for a stock's growth potential. Investors may be willing to pay more for a lower-earning stock than a higher-earning stock if they see potential for growth. Table 3.2 shows P/E ratios for a random sample of companies ($n = 44$) from Standard & Poor's 500 index. We are interested in learning how the P/E ratios of the companies in the S&P 500 compare to each other and what the distribution of P/E ratios looks like. Visual displays can help us describe and summarize the main characteristics of this sample.

TABLE 3.2	P/E Ratios for 44 Companies	PERatios			
Company	**P/E Ratio**	**Company**	**P/E Ratio**	**Company**	**P/E Ratio**
Amer Tower Corp A	59	FMC Corporation	20	NetApp	37
Analog Devices Inc	16	Gap (The)	12	Occidental Petroleum	19
Applied Materials Inc	20	Hartford Finan Svc Gp	11	O'Reilly Automotive	22
Best Buy Co Inc	10	Hess Corporation	7	PepsiCo Inc	16
Big Lots Inc	11	Hospira Inc	24	PG&E Corp	16
Carefusion Corp	38	Intel Corp	11	PPL Corp	14
Coventry Health Care Inc	10	Invesco Ltd	27	Reynolds Amer Inc	19
Cummins Inc	23	Johnson Controls	17	Roper Industries	26
Dell Inc	13	King Pharmaceuticals	42	Starbucks Corp	26
Dentsply International	18	Kroger Co	13	Sunoco Inc	28
Donnelley (RR) & Sons	31	Macy's Inc	17	Titanium Metals Corp	50
Eastman Chemical	16	Mattel Inc	14	United Health Grp Inc	9
Entergy Corp	10	Medco Health Sols Inc	21	Ventas Inc	37
Exelon Corp	10	MetroPCS Comm Inc	21	Walmart Stores	13
Fiserv Inc	18	Murphy Oil	15		

Source: www.finance.yahoo.com, accessed December 30, 2010. Each of the 500 companies on an alphabetical list was assigned a random number using Excel's =RAND( ) function. Companies were then sorted on the =RAND( ) column, and the first 44 companies on the sorted list were chosen as a random sample.

Preliminary Assessment

Before calculating any statistics or drawing any graphs, it is a good idea to *look at the data* and try to visualize how it was collected. Because the companies in the S&P 500 index are publicly traded, they are required to publish verified financial information, so the accuracy of the data is not an issue. Since the intent of the analysis is to study the S&P 500 companies at a *point in time,* these are *cross-sectional* data. (Financial analysts also study time series data on P/E ratios, which vary daily as stock prices change.) Although rounded to integers, the measurements are continuous. For example, a stock price of $43.22 divided by earnings per share of $2.17 gives a P/E ratio $(43.22)/(2.17) = 19.92$, which would be rounded to 20 for convenience. Since there is a true zero, we can speak meaningfully of ratios and can perform any standard mathematical operations. Because the analysis is based on a sample (not a census), we must allow for *sampling error,* that is, the possibility that our sample is not representative of the population of all 500 S&P 500 firms, due to the nature of random sampling.

Sorting

As a first step, it is helpful to sort the data. This is a visual display, although a very simple one. From the sorted data, we can see the range, the frequency of occurrence for each data value, and the data values that lie near the middle and ends.

				44 Sorted Price/Earnings Ratios						
7	9	10	10	10	10	11	11	11	12	13
13	13	14	14	15	16	16	16	16	17	17
18	18	19	19	20	20	21	21	22	23	24
26	26	27	28	31	37	37	38	42	50	59

When the number of observations is large, a sorted list of data values is difficult to analyze. Further, a simple list of numbers may not reveal very much about center, variability, and shape. To see broader patterns in the data, analysts often prefer a *visual display* of the data. The type of graph you use to display your data is dependent on the type of data you have. Some charts are better suited for quantitative data, while others are better for displaying categorical data. This chapter explains several basic types of charts, offers guidelines on when to use them, advises you how to make them effective, and warns of ways that charts can be deceptive.

Stem-and-Leaf Display

One simple way to visualize small data sets is a **stem-and-leaf plot**. The stem-and-leaf plot is a tool of *exploratory data analysis* (EDA) that seeks to reveal essential data features in an intuitive way. A stem-and-leaf plot is basically a frequency tally, except that we use digits instead of tally marks. For two-digit or three-digit integer data, the *stem* is the tens digit of the data, and the *leaf* is the ones digit. For the 44 P/E ratios, the stem-and-leaf plot would be:

Frequency	Stem	Leaf
2	0	7 9
24	1	0 0 0 0 1 1 1 2 3 3 3 4 4 5 6 6 6 6 7 7 8 8 9 9
11	2	0 0 1 1 2 3 4 6 6 7 8
4	3	1 7 7 8
1	4	2
2	5	0 9
44		

For example, the data values in the fourth stem are 31, 37, 37, 38. We always use equally spaced stems (even if some stems are empty). The stem-and-leaf can reveal *central tendency* (24 of the 44 P/E ratios were in the 10–19 stem) as well as *dispersion* (the range is from 7 to 59). In this illustration, the leaf digits have been sorted, although this is not necessary. The stem-and-leaf has the advantage that we can retrieve the raw data by concatenating a *stem digit* with each of its *leaf digits*. For example, the last stem has data values 50 and 59.

A stem-and-leaf plot works well for small samples of integer data with a limited range but becomes awkward when you have decimal data (e.g., $60.39) or multidigit data (e.g., $3,857). In such cases, it is necessary to round the data to make the display "work." Although the stem-and-leaf plot is rarely seen in presentations of business data, it is a useful tool for a quick tabulation of small data sets.

Dot Plots

A **dot plot** is another simple graphical display of *n* individual values of numerical data. The basic steps in making a dot plot are to (1) make a scale that covers the data range, (2) mark axis demarcations and label them, and (3) plot each data value as a dot above the scale at its approximate location. If more than one data value lies at approximately the same *X*-axis location, the dots are piled up vertically. Figure 3.1 shows a dot plot for 44 P/E ratios.

Dot plots are an attractive tool for data exploration because they are easy to understand. A dot plot shows *variability* by displaying the range of the data. It shows the *center* by revealing where the data values tend to cluster and where the midpoint lies. A dot plot can also reveal some things about the *shape* of the distribution if the sample is large enough. For the P/E ratios, the dot plot in Figure 3.1 shows that:

- The range is from 7 to 59.
- All but a few data values lie between 10 and 25.
- A typical "middle" data value would be around 17 or 18.
- The data are not symmetric due to a few large P/E ratios.

> **LO 3-1**
>
> Make a stem-and-leaf or dot plot by hand or by computer.

FIGURE 3.1

Dot Plot of 44 P/E Ratios   PERatios

You can make a dot plot yourself (if the sample is small) using a straightedge and a pencil. Excel doesn't offer dot plots, but you can get them from MegaStat or MINITAB. Figure 3.2 shows menus from MegaStat and MINITAB with marked options to choose a dot plot or stem-and-leaf plot.

FIGURE 3.2

MegaStat and MINITAB Menus for Dot Plot and Stem-and-Leaf Plot

Comparing Groups

A **stacked dot plot** can be used to compare two or more groups. For example, Figure 3.3 shows a stacked dot plot for median home prices for 150 U.S. cities in four different regions. A common *X*-axis scale is used for all four dot plots. This stacked dot plot shows the range of data values and gives an idea of typical home values within each region. (MegaStat doesn't offer stacked dot plots, but MINITAB does.) Could a table show this amount of information as clearly?

FIGURE 3.3

Stacked Dot Plot For Home Prices (*n* = 150 cities)   HomePrices

Source: www.realtor.org

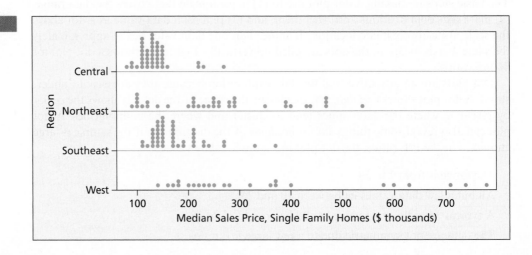

While they are easy to understand, dot plots have limitations. They don't reveal very much information about the data set's shape when the sample is small, and they become awkward when the sample is large (what if you have 100 dots at the same point?) or when you have decimal data. The next section of this textbook explains some widely used methods for creating visual displays that work for any sample size.

Software

There are different types of software tools for statistical analysis, ranging from Excel's basic functions to stand-alone packages such as MINITAB, SAS, and SPSS. Excel is emphasized throughout this book because it is widely available and is used extensively in business. We will also illustrate graphs and calculations using MegaStat, an Excel add-in that is available with your textbook. MegaStat augments Excel's functions with drop-down menus and spreadsheet formats that offer more capability than Excel's Data Analysis. You will also see examples from MINITAB, a comprehensive software system for statistical analysis that is *not* part of Excel. However, you can copy data from Excel to a MINITAB worksheet (and vice versa) to obtain attractive graphs and statistics from MINITAB. Although MINITAB is not included with this textbook, it is available at most colleges and universities.

Online Learning Center Resources

The Online Learning Center (OLC) website www.mhhe.com/doane4e has 5-minute video tutorials and demonstrations on Excel, MegaStat, and MINITAB, tailored to the material in this textbook. Also on this website are downloadable data files for examples and textbook exercises. Downloadable data files are indicated by the 📁 symbol followed by a file name (e.g., 📁 Housing). At the end of each chapter, there are additional learning resources that expand on topics in the textbook (e.g., Excel demonstrations).

SECTION EXERCISES

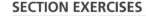

3.1   (a) Make a stem-and-leaf plot for these 24 observations on the number of customers who used a downtown CitiBank ATM during the noon hour on 24 consecutive workdays. (b) Make a dot plot of the ATM data. (c) Describe these two displays. (*Hint:* Refer to center, variability, and shape.) 📁 **CitiBank**

39	32	21	26	19	27	32	25
18	26	34	18	31	35	21	33
33	9	16	32	35	42	15	24

3.2   (a) Make a stem-and-leaf plot for the number of defects per 100 vehicles for these 32 brands. (b) Make a dot plot of the defects data. (c) Describe these two displays. (*Hint*: Refer to center, variability, and shape.) 📁 **JDPower**

Defects per 100 Vehicles (alphabetical by brand)					
Brand	**Defects**	**Brand**	**Defects**	**Brand**	**Defects**
Acura	86	Hyundai	102	Mini	133
Audi	111	Infiniti	107	Mitsubishi	146
BMW	113	Jaguar	130	Nissan	111
Buick	114	Jeep	129	Porsche	83
Cadillac	111	Kia	126	Ram	110
Chevrolet	111	Land Rover	170	Scion	114
Chrysler	122	Lexus	88	Subaru	121
Dodge	130	Lincoln	106	Toyota	117
Ford	93	Mazda	114	Volkswagen	135
GMC	126	Mercedes-Benz	87	Volvo	109
Honda	95	Mercury	113		

Source: J. D. Power and Associates 2010 Initial Quality Study™. Used with permission.

3.3   Sarah and Bob share a 1,000-minute cell phone calling plan. (a) Make a *stacked dot plot* to compare the lengths of cell phone calls by Sarah and Bob during the last week. (b) Describe what the dot plots tell you.   📁 **PhoneCalls**

Sarah's calls: 1, 1, 1, 1, 2, 3, 3, 3, 5, 5, 6, 6, 7, 8, 8, 12, 14, 14, 22, 23, 29, 33, 38, 45, 66

Bob's calls: 5, 8, 9, 14, 17, 21, 23, 23, 24, 26, 27, 27, 28, 29, 31, 33, 35, 39, 41

Mini Case   3.1

U.S. Business Cycles

Although many businesses anticipated the recession that followed the housing price bubble of the early 2000s, they needed to anticipate its probable length to form strategies for debt management and future product releases. Fortunately, good historical data are available from the National Bureau of Economic Research, which keeps track of business cycles. The length of a contraction is measured from the peak of the previous expansion to the beginning of the next expansion based on the real gross domestic product (GDP). Table 3.3 shows the durations, in months, of 33 U.S. recessions.

TABLE 3.3   **U.S. Business Contractions, 1857–2010 (*n* = 33)** 📁 Recessions

Peak	Trough	Months	Peak	Trough	Months
Jun 1857	Dec 1858	18	May 1923	Jul 1924	14
Oct 1860	Jun 1861	8	Oct 1926	Nov 1927	13
Apr 1865	Dec 1867	32	Aug 1929	Mar 1933	43
Jun 1869	Dec 1870	18	May 1937	Jun 1938	13
Oct 1873	Mar 1879	65	Feb 1945	Oct 1945	8
Mar 1882	May 1885	38	Nov 1948	Oct 1949	11
Mar 1887	Apr 1888	13	Jul 1953	May 1954	10
Jul 1890	May 1891	10	Aug 1957	Apr 1958	8
Jan 1893	Jun 1894	17	Apr 1960	Feb 1961	10
Dec 1895	Jun 1897	18	Dec 1969	Nov 1970	11
Jun 1899	Dec 1900	18	Nov 1973	Mar 1975	16
Sep 1902	Aug 1904	23	Jan 1980	Jul 1980	6
May 1907	Jun 1908	13	Jul 1981	Nov 1982	16
Jan 1910	Jan 1912	24	Jul 1990	Mar 1991	8
Jan 1913	Dec 1914	23	Mar 2001	Nov 2001	8
Aug 1918	Mar 1919	7	Dec 2007	Jun 2009	18
Jan 1920	Jul 1921	18			

Source: U.S. Business Contractions found at www.nber.org. Copyright © 2012 National Bureau of Economic Research, Inc. Used with permission.

From the dot plot in Figure 3.4, we see that the 65-month contraction (1873–1879) was quite unusual, although four recessions did exceed 30 months. Most recessions have lasted less than 20 months. Only 7 of 33 lasted less than 10 months. The 8-month 2001 recession was among the shortest. Although the recession that began in December 2007 had unique features (major financial crisis, steep rise in unemployment, sluggish recovery), its duration (18 months) was not extreme.

FIGURE 3.4	Dot Plot of Business Cycle Duration ($n = 33$)

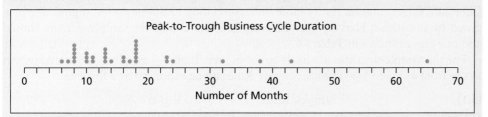

The table supplies information that the dot plot cannot. For example, during the 1930s there were actually *two* major contractions (43 months from 1929 to 1933, 13 months from 1937 to 1938) which is one reason why that period seemed so terrible to those who lived through it. The Great Depression of the 1930s was so named because it lasted a long time and the economic decline was deeper than in most recessions.

3.2 FREQUENCY DISTRIBUTIONS AND HISTOGRAMS

Bins and Bin Limits

A **frequency distribution** is a table formed by classifying n data values into k classes called *bins* (we adopt this terminology from Excel). The *bin limits* define the values to be included in each bin. Usually, all the bin widths are the same. The table shows the *frequency* of data values within each bin. Frequencies can also be expressed as *relative frequencies* or *percentages* of the total number of observations.

Frequency Distribution

A tabulation of n data values into k classes called *bins,* based on values of the data. The *bin limits* are cutoff points that define each bin. Bins generally have equal interval widths and their limits cannot overlap.

The basic steps for constructing a frequency distribution are to (1) sort the data in ascending order, (2) choose the number of bins, (3) set the bin limits, (4) put the data values in the appropriate bin, and (5) create the table. Let's walk through these steps.

Constructing a Frequency Distribution

Step 1: Find Smallest and Largest Data Values

				Sorted Price/Earnings Ratios						
7	9	10	10	10	10	11	11	11	12	13
13	13	14	14	15	16	16	16	16	17	17
18	18	19	19	20	20	21	21	22	23	24
26	26	27	28	31	37	37	38	42	50	59

For the P/E data, we get $x_{min} = 7$ and $x_{max} = 59$ (highlighted). You might be able to find x_{min} and x_{max} without sorting the entire data set, but it is easier to experiment with bin choices if you have already sorted the data.

Step 2: Choose Number of Bins   Since a frequency distribution seeks to condense many data points into a small table, we expect the number of bins k to be much smaller

than the sample size n. When you use *too many* bins, some bins are likely to be sparsely populated, or even empty. With *too few* bins, dissimilar data values are lumped together. Left to their own devices, people tend to choose similar bin limits for a given data set. Generally, larger samples justify more bins. According to **Sturges' Rule**, a guideline proposed by statistician Herbert Sturges, every time we double the sample size, we should add one bin, as shown in Table 3.4.

For the sample sizes you are likely to encounter, Table 3.4 says that you would expect to use from $k = 5$ to $k = 11$ bins. Sturges' Rule can be expressed as a formula:

(3.1)   Sturges' Rule: $k = 1 + 3.3 \log(n)$

For the P/E data ($n = 44$), Sturges' Rule says:

$$k = 1 + 3.3 \log(n) = 1 + 3.3 \log(44) = 1 + 3.3(1.6435) = 6.42 \text{ bins}$$

Using either Table 3.4 or Sturges' formula, we would consider using 6 or 7 bins for the P/E data. To get "nice" bin limits, you may choose more or fewer bins. Picking attractive bin limits is often an overriding consideration (not Sturges' Rule). When the data are skewed by unusually large or small data values, we may need more classes than Sturges' Rule suggests. This will be illustrated in a moment.

TABLE 3.4		
Sturges' Rule	**Sample Size (n)**	**Suggested Number of Bins (k)**
	16	5
	32	6
	64	7
	128	8
	256	9
	512	10
	1,024	11

Step 3: Set Bin Limits   Just as choosing the number of bins requires judgment, setting the bin limits also requires judgment. For guidance, find the approximate width of each bin by dividing the data range by the number of bins:

(3.2) $$\text{Bin width} \approx \frac{x_{max} - x_{min}}{k}$$

Round the bin width *up* to an appropriate value, then set the lower limit for the first bin as a multiple of the bin width. What does "appropriate" mean? If the data are discrete, then it makes sense to have a width that is an integer value. If the data are continuous, then setting a bin width equal to a fractional value may be appropriate. Experiment until you get bins that cover the data range.

For example, for this data set, the smallest P/E ratio was 7 and the largest P/E ratio was 59, so if we want to use $k = 6$ bins, we calculate the approximate bin width as:

$$\text{Bin width} \approx \frac{59 - 7}{6} = \frac{52}{6} = 8.67$$

To obtain "nice" limits, we could round the bin width up to 10 and choose bin limits of 0, 10, 20, 30, 40, 50, 60. Usually "nice" bin limits are 2, 5, or 10 multiplied by an appropriate integer power of 10. As a starting point for the lowest bin, we choose the largest multiple of the bin width smaller than the lowest data value. Here, the bin width is 10 and the smallest data value is 7, so the first bin would start at 0.

Step 4: Count the Data Values in Each Bin   In general, the lower limit is *included* in the bin, while the upper limit is *excluded*. MegaStat and MINITAB follow this convention. However, Excel's histogram option *includes* the upper limit and *excludes* the lower limit. There are advantages to either method. Our objective is to make sure that none of the bins overlap and that data values are counted in only one bin.

Step 5: Prepare a Table You can choose to show only the absolute frequencies, or counts, for each bin, but we often also include the relative frequencies and the cumulative frequencies. Relative frequencies are calculated as the absolute frequency for a bin divided by the total number of data values. Cumulative relative frequencies accumulate relative frequency values as the bin limits increase. Table 3.5 shows the frequency distribution we've created for the P/E ratio data. Sometimes the relative frequencies do not sum to 1 due to rounding.

Bin Limits		Frequency	Relative		Cumulative	
Lower	Upper	(f)	Frequency (f/n)	Percent	Frequency	Percent
0 <	10	2	2/44 = .0455	4.55	2	4.55
10 <	20	24	24/44 = .5455	54.55	26	59.09
20 <	30	11	11/44 = .2500	25.00	37	84.09
30 <	40	4	4/44 = .0909	9.09	41	93.18
40 <	50	1	1/44 = .0227	2.27	42	95.45
50 <	60	2	2/44 = .0455	4.55	44	100.00
		44		100.00		

TABLE 3.5

Frequency Distribution of P/E Ratios Using Six Bins
PERatios

Histograms

A **histogram** is a graphical representation of a frequency distribution. A histogram is a bar chart whose *Y*-axis shows the number of data values (or a percentage) within each bin of a frequency distribution and whose *X*-axis ticks show the end points of each bin. There should be no gaps between bars (except when there are no data in a particular bin) as shown in Figure 3.5. The appearance of a histogram is identical, regardless of whether the vertical axis displays *frequency, relative frequency,* or *percent.* It is only a matter of scaling the *Y*-axis because a percent is $100f/n$ (the bin frequency divided by the sample size and multiplied by 100).

FIGURE 3.5

Three Histograms for P/E Ratios PERatios

Choosing the number of bins and bin limits requires judgment on our part. Creating a histogram is often a trial-and-error process. Our first choice of bins and limits may not be our final choice for presentation. Figure 3.5 shows histograms for the P/E ratio sample using three different bin definitions.

LO 3-3

Make a histogram with appropriate bins.

k	$(x_{max} - x_{min})/k$	Nice Bin Width
6	8.7	10
8	6.5	8
9	5.8	6

Bin Limits

0	10	20	30	40	50	60			
0	8	16	24	32	40	48	56	64	
6	12	18	24	30	36	42	48	54	60

Our perception of the shape of the distribution depends on how the bins are chosen. The skewed shape of the distribution becomes more obvious when we use more than six bins. In this example, we might wish to depart from Sturges' Rule to show additional detail. You can use your own judgment to determine which histogram you would ultimately include in a report.

Making an Excel Histogram

Excel will produce histograms. Click on the menu bar Data ribbon. If you don't see Data Analysis on the Data ribbon, click **File** (upper left corner), click the Excel Options button at the bottom of the screen, click Add-Ins, select Analysis Tool Pak, and click OK. Once the Data Analysis icon appears on the Data ribbon, follow these steps to create your histogram:

Step 1: Open an existing data file or key in your own data. Key in the upper bin limits that will cover the data range (smallest through largest data values). Each bin upper limit will be *included* in the bin. Only the *upper* bin limit is used by Excel (both are shown here for clarity). You may wish to experiment with different bin limits, as illustrated in the example shown here. Click on the Data ribbon, select the Data Analysis icon, choose the Histogram option, and click OK.

Step 2: Enter the cell range for your data values. Enter the cell range for the upper bin limits. Specify a cell for the upper left corner of the histogram output range (or choose a new worksheet ply). Check Chart Output and click OK.

Step 3: Excel's default histogram is quite basic, so you will most likely want to customize it. To do this, click on the chart so the Chart Tools ribbon appears at the top of the screen. Click on the Design ribbon to try different Chart Layout graph templates, or click on the Layout ribbon and select an icon to edit a specific chart feature (e.g., *Chart Title, Axis Labels, Gridlines*). You can also right-click on any feature of the chart (e.g., bars, axis label, chart area, plot area) and choose the edit options you want. For example, to improve Excel's skinny histogram bars, right-click on the histogram bars, choose Format Data Series, and reduce the gap width. Alternatively, you can make a new column chart (highlight the frequency range, click on the Insert ribbon, choose Column, and then customize the resulting chart).

Making a MegaStat Histogram

MegaStat will automatically make a nice histogram, although you can specify your own bins if you wish. It also provides a table of frequencies (including percent and cumulative) for each interval. On the histogram's *Y*-axis, MegaStat shows *percents* (not frequencies), which will give exactly the same view of the data (as you saw in Figure 3.5).

Step 1:   Open an existing file or key in the data. Click on Add-Ins and select MegaStat. Select Frequency Distribution. Choose the Input Range for the data. MegaStat will automatically detect the column heading and use it to label the histogram, regardless of whether or not you include it in the input range. You may enter an interval width and lower boundary for the first bin. If you leave them blank, MegaStat will create a nice histogram using its own judgment. As an option, you can create a frequency polygon, ogive, or custom histogram with unequal bins (the default is equal bins).

Step 2:   MegaStat provides a table with bin limits, frequencies, percent frequencies, and cumulative frequencies. Its nicely labeled histogram shows *percent* (not frequencies) on the vertical axis, though, as you have seen, the appearance of the histogram is the same either way. The histogram can be edited (e.g., title, colors, axis labels), but if you want different bins, you must revisit the MegaStat menu.

MINITAB Histograms

Figure 3.6 shows how MINITAB creates a histogram for the same data. Copy the data from the spreadsheet and paste it into MINITAB's worksheet, then choose Graphs > Histogram from the top menu bar. Let MINITAB use its default options. Once the histogram has been created, you can right-click the *X*-axis to adjust the bins, axis tick marks, and so on.

FIGURE 3.6

MINITAB Histogram
PERatios

Shape

A histogram suggests the *shape* of the population we are sampling, but, unless the sample is large, we must be cautious about making inferences. Our perception is also influenced by the number of bins and the way the bin limits are chosen. The following terminology is helpful in discussing shape.

A **modal class** is a histogram bar that is higher than those on either side. A histogram with a single modal class is *unimodal*, one with two modal classes is *bimodal*, and one with more than two modes is *multimodal*. However, modal classes may be artifacts of the way the bin limits are chosen. It is wise to experiment with various ways of binning and to make cautious inferences about modality unless the modes are strong and invariant to binning. Figure 3.6 shows a single modal class for P/E ratios between 10 and 20.

A histogram's *skewness* is indicated by the direction of its longer tail. If neither tail is longer, the histogram is **symmetric**. A **right-skewed** (or positively skewed) histogram has a longer right tail, with most data values clustered on the left side. A **left-skewed** (or negatively skewed) histogram has a longer left tail, with most data values clustered on the right side. Few histograms are exactly symmetric. Business data tend to be right-skewed because they are often bounded by zero on the left but are unbounded on the right (e.g., number of employees). You may find it helpful to refer to the templates shown in Figure 3.7.

An **outlier** is an extreme value that is far enough from the majority of the data that it probably arose from a different cause or is due to measurement error. We will define outliers more precisely in the next chapter. For now, think of outliers as unusual points located in the histogram tails. None of the histograms shown so far has any obvious outliers.

Tips for Effective Frequency Distributions

LO 3-4

Identify skewness, modal classes, and outliers in a histogram.

Here are some general tips to keep in mind when making frequency distributions and histograms.

1. Check Sturges' Rule first, but only as a suggestion for the number of bins.
2. Choose an appropriate bin width.

FIGURE 3.7

Prototype Distribution Shapes

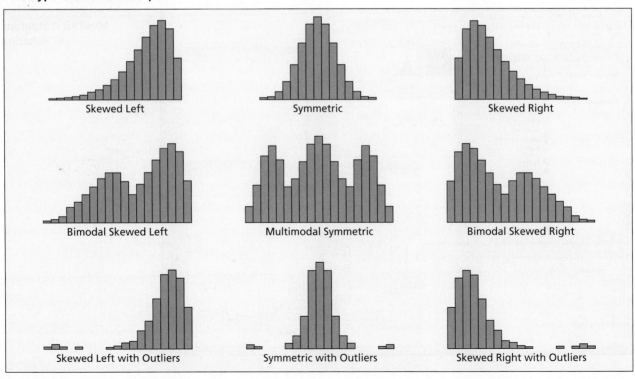

Skewed Left	Symmetric	Skewed Right
Bimodal Skewed Left	Multimodal Symmetric	Bimodal Skewed Right
Skewed Left with Outliers	Symmetric with Outliers	Skewed Right with Outliers

3. Choose bin limits that are multiples of the bin width.
4. Make sure that the range is covered, and add bins if necessary.
5. Skewed data may require more bins to reveal sufficient detail.

Frequency Polygon and Ogive

Figure 3.8 shows two more graphs offered by MegaStat. A **frequency polygon** is a line graph that connects the midpoints of the histogram intervals, plus extra intervals at the beginning and end so that the line will touch the X-axis. It serves the same purpose as a histogram, but is attractive when you need to compare two data sets (since more than one frequency polygon can be plotted on the same scale). An *ogive* (pronounced "oh-jive") is a line graph of the cumulative frequencies. It is useful for finding percentiles or in comparing the shape of the sample with a known benchmark such as the normal distribution (that you will be seeing in the next chapter).

FIGURE 3.8

MegaStat's Frequency Polygon and Ogive (embellished) 📁 PERatios

Mini Case   3.2

Duration of U.S. Recessions

Table 3.6 shows two "nice" ways to bin the data on the duration of 33 U.S. recessions (for details, see **Mini Case 3.1**). Sturges would recommend using six bins, i.e., $k = 1 + 3.3 \log(n) = 1 + 3.3 \log(33) = 5.97$. Using six bins works out well, using a bin size of 12 months (one year). However, we also can create a nice histogram using seven bins of width 10 months. You can surely think of other valid possibilities.

TABLE 3.6   Some Ways to Tabulate 33 Business Contractions 📁 Recessions

Using k = 6 bins			Using k = 7 bins		
From	*To (not inclusive)*	*f*	*From*	*To (not inclusive)*	*f*
0	12	12	0	10	7
12	24	16	10	20	19
24	36	2	20	30	3
36	48	2	30	40	2
48	60	0	40	50	1
60	72	1	50	60	0
			60	70	1
	Total	33		Total	33

Both histograms in Figure 3.9 suggest right-skewness (long right tail, most values cluster to the left). Each histogram has a single modal class (e.g., the $k = 7$ bin histogram says that a recession most often lasts between 10 and 20 months). The long recession of 1873–79 (65 months) can be seen as a possible outlier in the right tail of both histograms.

FIGURE 3.9   **Histograms for 6 and 7 Bins**

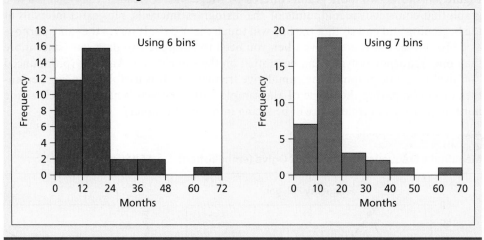

SECTION EXERCISES

connect™

3.4   (a) The table shows the number of days on the market for the 36 recent home sales in the city of Sonando Hills. Construct a frequency distribution and histogram, using nice (round) bin limits. (b) Describe the distribution and note any unusual features. 📄 **Homes**

18	70	52	17	86	121	86	3	66
96	41	50	176	26	28	6	55	21
43	20	56	71	57	16	20	30	31
44	44	92	179	80	98	44	66	15

3.5   (a) The table shows raw scores on a state civil service exam taken by 24 applicants for positions in law enforcement. Construct a frequency distribution and histogram, using nice (round) bin limits. (b) Describe the distribution and note any unusual features. 📄 **Civil**

83	93	74	98	85	82	79	78
82	68	67	82	78	83	70	99
18	96	93	62	64	93	27	58

3.6   (a) Make a frequency distribution and histogram (using appropriate bins) for these 28 observations on the amount spent for dinner for four in downtown Chicago on Friday night. (b) Repeat the exercise, using a different number of bins. Which is preferred? Why? 📄 **Dinner**

95	103	109	170	114	113	107
124	105	80	104	84	176	115
69	95	134	108	61	160	128
68	95	61	150	52	87	136

3.7   (a) Make a frequency distribution and histogram for the monthly off-campus rent paid by 30 students. (b) Repeat the exercise, using a different number of bins. Which is preferred? Why? 📄 **Rents**

730	730	730	930	700	570
690	1030	740	620	720	670
560	740	650	660	850	930
600	620	760	690	710	500
730	800	820	840	720	700

3.8 (a) Make a frequency distribution and histogram for the 2007 annual compensation of 40 randomly chosen CEOs (millions of dollars). (b) Describe the shape of the histogram. (c) Identify any unusual values. (Source: www.forbes.com.) 📄 **CEOComp40**

5.33	18.3	24.55	9.08	12.22	5.52	2.01	3.81
192.92	17.83	23.77	8.7	11.15	4.87	1.72	3.72
66.08	15.41	22.59	6.75	9.97	4.83	1.29	3.72
28.09	12.32	19.55	5.55	9.19	3.83	0.79	2.79
34.91	13.95	20.77	6.47	9.63	4.47	1.01	3.07

3.9 For each frequency distribution, suggest "nice" bins. Did your choice agree with Sturges' Rule? If not, explain.

    a. Last week's MPG for 35 student vehicles ($x_{min} = 9.4$, $x_{max} = 38.7$).
    b. Ages of 50 airplane passengers ($x_{min} = 12$, $x_{max} = 85$).
    c. GPAs of 250 first-semester college students ($x_{min} = 2.25$, $x_{max} = 3.71$).
    d. Annual rates of return on 150 mutual funds ($x_{min} = .023$, $x_{max} = .097$).

3.10 Below are sorted data showing average spending per customer (in dollars) at 74 Noodles & Company restaurants. (a) Construct a frequency distribution. Explain how you chose the number of bins and the bin limits. (b) Make a histogram and describe its appearance. (c) Repeat, using a larger number of bins and different bin limits. (d) Did your visual impression of the data change when you increased the number of bins? Explain. *Note:* You may use MegaStat or MINITAB if your instructor agrees. 📄 **NoodlesSpending**

6.54	6.58	6.58	6.62	6.66	6.70	6.71	6.73	6.75	6.75	6.76	6.76
6.76	6.77	6.77	6.79	6.81	6.81	6.82	6.84	6.85	6.89	6.90	6.91
6.91	6.92	6.93	6.93	6.94	6.95	6.95	6.95	6.96	6.96	6.98	6.99
7.00	7.00	7.00	7.02	7.03	7.03	7.03	7.04	7.05	7.05	7.07	7.07
7.08	7.11	7.11	7.13	7.13	7.16	7.17	7.18	7.21	7.25	7.28	7.28
7.30	7.33	7.33	7.35	7.37	7.38	7.45	7.56	7.57	7.58	7.64	7.65
7.87	7.97										

3.3 EXCEL CHARTS

Excel has strong graphics capabilities. Once you become proficient at making effective visuals in Excel, you will possess a skill that will make you a valuable team member and employee. Making your own charts in Excel is something you will have to learn by experience. Professionals who use Excel say that they learn new things every day. Excel offers a vast array of charts. While only a few of them are likely to be used in business, it is fun to review the whole list.

Excel charts are represented by icons (see Figure 3.10). The icons are designed to be visually self-explanatory. We will discuss those (circled in red) that are most useful in business and economics, paying special attention to line charts (used by analysts to reveal trends) and scatter plots (used by analysts to reveal relationships between two variables).

Excel's default charts tend to be very plain. But business charts need not be dull. You can customize any graph to your taste. For example, you can

- Improve the titles (main, *x*-axis, *y*-axis).
- Change the axis scales (minimum, maximum, ticks).
- Display the data values (not always a good idea).
- Add a data table underneath the graph (if there is room).
- Change color or patterns in the plot area or chart area.
- Format decimals to make axis scales more readable.
- Edit the gridlines and borders (dotted or solid, colors).
- Alter the appearance of bars (color, pattern, gap width).
- Change markers and lines on a scatter plot (size, color).

FIGURE 3.10

Excel Chart Types

Once you have inserted a chart into your worksheet, click on the chart to select it, and the Chart Tools ribbon will appear at the top of the screen. There are three ribbons (Design, Layout, Format) that you can use to customize the chart you have created, as illustrated in Figure 3.11 for a line chart. Although certain features are unique to each chart type, these three menus are similar for all chart types.

FIGURE 3.11

Chart Tool Ribbons

The Design ribbon's Chart Layouts menu lets you apply different style templates to your chart (e.g., adding gridlines, axis labels, or legends). The design layout templates will depend on the chart type. Click on any layout template; if you don't like the result, just click the ⤴ Undo icon (or Ctrl-Z).

Use the Layout ribbon to select an icon to customize specific features of your graph. Each Layout icon is clearly labeled (e.g., *Chart Title, Axis Titles, Gridlines*). Figure 3.12 shows the drop-down menus for several of the most-used Layout icons. You can generally accomplish the same thing by right-clicking a particular graph feature (e.g., the *x*-axis) and using the menu of options that come up.

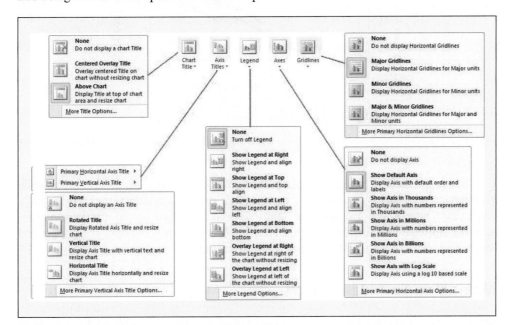

FIGURE 3.12

Drop-Down Menus for Layout Icons

3.4 LINE CHARTS

Simple Line Charts

A **line chart** like the one shown in Figure 3.13 is used to display a time series, to spot trends, or to compare time periods. Line charts can be used to display several variables at once. If two variables are displayed, the right and left scales can differ, using the right scale for one variable and the left scale for the other. Excel's *two-scale line chart,* illustrated in Figure 3.14, lets you compare variables that *differ in magnitude* or are measured in *different units*. But keep in mind that someone who only glances at the chart may mistakenly conclude that both variables are of the same magnitude.

LO 3-5

Make an effective line chart using Excel.

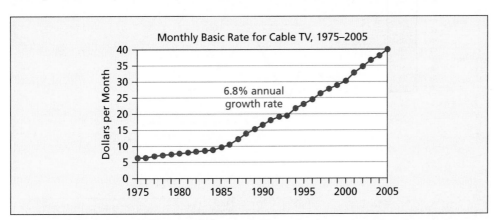

FIGURE 3.13

Line Chart CableTV

Source: *Statistical Abstract of the U.S., 2007*, p. 717.

How many variables can be displayed at once on a line graph? Too much clutter ruins any visual display. If you try to display half a dozen time series variables at once, no matter how cleverly you choose symbols and graphing techniques, the result is likely to be unsatisfactory. You will have to use your judgment.

FIGURE 3.14

Two Scales
CellPhones

Source: *Statistical Abstract of the U.S., 2007*, p. 720.

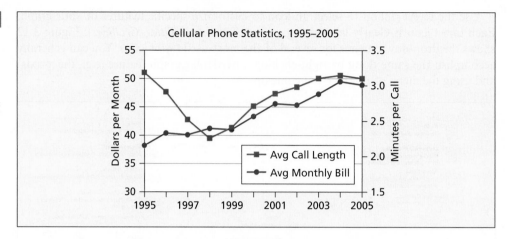

A line graph usually has no vertical gridlines. What about horizontal gridlines? While gridlines do add background clutter, they make it easier to establish the *Y* value for a given year. One compromise is to use lightly colored dashed or dotted gridlines to minimize the clutter, and to increase gridline spacing. If the intent is to convey only a general sense of the data magnitudes, gridlines may be omitted.

Making an Excel Line Chart

Step 1:   Highlight the data that you want to display in the line chart, click on the Insert ribbon, click on the Line icon, and choose a line chart style. *Hint:* Do *not* highlight the *X*-axis labels (if any). You can add *X*-axis labels later. The default line plot is quite basic, so you may wish to customize it.

Step 2:   If you wish to add a fitted trend, right-click on the data series on the line chart and choose Add Trendline. By default, the fitted trend will be linear. There is an option to display the trend equation and its R^2 statistic (a measure of "fit" of the line).

Step 3:   To customize your graph, click on it. Its border will change to show that it has been selected, and the Chart Tools ribbon will become active (at the top of the screen). Click on the Design ribbon and try different Chart Layout graph templates, or click on the Layout ribbon and select an edit icon (e.g., *Chart Title, Axis Titles, Gridlines*). Instead, you could simply right-click on any feature of your graph (e.g., chart area, plot area, *X*-axis, *Y*-axis, gridlines) and explore the options until you are satisfied with the graph's appearance. To add *X*-axis labels, right-click on the chart, choose Select Data, click on the Edit button for *Horizontal (Category) Axis Labels,* and then enter the cell range for the *X*-axis labels (A2:B13 in this example).

Log Scales

On the customary **arithmetic scale**, distances on the Y-axis are proportional to the magnitude of the variable being displayed. But on a **logarithmic scale**, equal distances represent equal *ratios* (for this reason, a log scale is sometimes called a *ratio scale*). When data vary over a wide range, say, by more than an order of magnitude (e.g., from 6 to 60), we might prefer a *log scale* for the vertical axis, to reveal more detail for small data values. A log graph reveals whether the quantity is growing at an *increasing percent* (convex function), *constant percent* (straight line), or *declining percent* (concave function). On a log scale, *equal distances* represent *equal ratios*. That is, the distance from 100 to 1,000 is the same as the distance from 1,000 to 10,000 (because both have the same 10:1 ratio). Since logarithms are undefined for negative or zero values (try it on your calculator), a log scale is only suited for positive data values.

A log scale is useful for time series data that might be expected to grow at a compound annual percentage rate (e.g., GDP, the national debt, or your future income). Log scales are common in financial charts that cover long periods of time or for data that grow rapidly (e.g., revenues for a start-up company). Some experts feel that corporate annual reports and stock prospectuses should avoid ratio scales, on the grounds that they may be misleading to uninformed individuals. But then how can we fairly portray data that vary by orders of magnitude? Should investors become better informed? The bottom line is that business students must understand log scales because they are sure to run into them.

EXAMPLE 3.2

U.S. Trade

📂 USTrade

Figure 3.15 shows the U.S. balance of trade. The arithmetic scale shows that growth has been exponential. Yet, although exports and imports are increasing in absolute terms, the log graph suggests that the *growth rate* in both series may be slowing because the log graph is slightly concave. On the log graph, the recently increasing trade deficit is not *relatively* as large. Regardless how it is displayed, the trade deficit remains a concern for policymakers, for fear that foreigners may no longer wish to purchase U.S. debt instruments to finance the trade deficit.

FIGURE 3.15

Comparison of Arithmetic and Log Scales 📂 USTrade

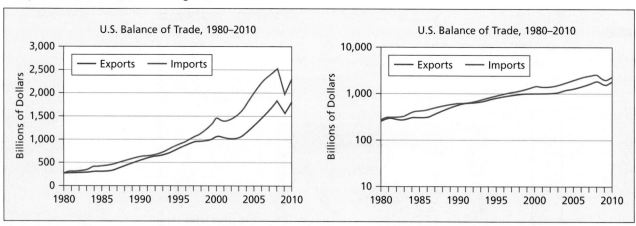

Source: *Economic Report of the President, 2011*, Table B24.

Tips for Effective Line Charts

Here are some general tips to keep in mind when creating line charts:

1. Line charts are used for *time series data* (never for cross-sectional data).
2. The numerical variable is shown on the Y-axis, while the time units go on the X-axis with time increasing from left to right. Business audiences expect this rule to be followed.

3. Except for log scales, use a zero origin on the *Y*-axis (this is the default in Excel) unless more detail is needed. The zero-origin rule is mandatory for a corporate annual report or investor stock prospectus.

4. To avoid graph clutter, numerical labels usually are *omitted* on a line chart, especially when the data cover many time periods. Use gridlines to help the reader read data values.

5. Data markers (squares, triangles, circles) are helpful. But when the series has many data values or when many variables are being displayed, they clutter the graph.

6. If the lines on the graph are too thick, the reader can't ascertain graph values.

SECTION EXERCISES

connect

3.11 (a) Use Excel to prepare a line chart to display the data on housing starts. Modify the default colors, fonts, etc., to make the display effective. (b) Describe the pattern, if any. 📄 **Housing**

U.S. Housing Starts (thousands), 1990–2007

Year	Housing Starts	Year	Housing Starts	Year	Housing Starts
1990	895	1996	1,161	2002	1,359
1991	840	1997	1,134	2003	1,499
1992	1,030	1998	1,271	2004	1,611
1993	1,126	1999	1,302	2005	1,716
1994	1,198	2000	1,231	2006	1,465
1995	1,076	2001	1,273	2007	1,046

Source: *Statistical Abstract of the U.S., 2009*, Table 930.

3.12 (a) Use Excel to prepare a line chart to display the skier/snowboarder data. Modify the default colors, fonts, etc., to make the display effective. (b) Describe the pattern, if any. 📄 **Snowboards**

U.S. Skier/Snowboarder Visits (Millions), 1984–2007

Season	Visits	Season	Visits	Season	Visits
1984–1985	51.354	1992–1993	54.032	2000–2001	57.337
1985–1986	51.921	1993–1994	54.637	2001–2002	54.411
1986–1987	53.749	1994–1995	52.677	2002–2003	57.594
1987–1988	53.908	1995–1996	53.983	2003–2004	57.067
1988–1989	53.335	1996–1997	52.520	2004–2005	56.882
1989–1990	50.020	1997–1998	54.122	2005–2006	58.897
1990–1991	46.722	1998–1999	52.089	2006–2007	55.068
1991–1992	50.835	1999–2000	52.198		

Source: www.nsaa.org/nsaa/press/.

3.13 (a) Use Excel to prepare a line chart to display the lightning death data. Modify the default colors, fonts, etc., as you judge appropriate to make the display effective. (b) Describe the pattern, if any.

U.S. Deaths by Lightning, 1940–2005 📄 **Lightning**

Year	Deaths	Year	Deaths
1940	340	1975	91
1945	268	1980	74
1950	219	1985	74
1955	181	1990	74
1960	129	1995	85
1965	149	2000	51
1970	122	2005	38

Sources: *Statistical Abstract of the United States, 2007*, p. 228; and www.nws.noaa.gov.

3.14 (a) Use Excel to prepare a line chart to display the following transplant data. Modify the default colors, fonts, etc., to make the display effective. (b) Describe the pattern, if any.

California Living Organ Transplants, 1988–2004 📄 Transplants					
Year	Transplants	Year	Transplants	Year	Transplants
1988	12,786	1994	18,170	2000	23,004
1989	13,471	1995	19,264	2001	23,942
1990	15,462	1996	19,566	2002	24,552
1991	15,687	1997	20,093	2003	25,083
1992	16,043	1998	21,313	2004	26,539
1993	17,533	1999	21,824		

Source: www.gsds.org.

3.5 BAR CHARTS

LO 3-6

Know the rules for effective bar charts and pie charts.

Simple Bar Charts 📄 Tires

The **bar chart** is probably the most common type of data display in business. Attribute data are typically displayed using a bar chart. Each bar represents a category or attribute. The length of each bar reflects a frequency or a value for that category. Each bar has a label showing the category name or time period. Figure 3.16 shows simple column and bar charts comparing market shares among tire manufacturers. Each bar is separated from its neighbors by a slight gap to improve legibility (you can control gap width in Excel). *Vertical* bar charts (called **column charts**) are the most common, but *horizontal* bar charts can be useful when the axis labels are long or when there are many categories.

FIGURE 3.16
Same Data Displayed Two Ways

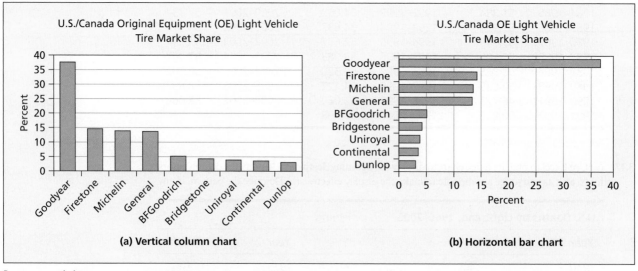

(a) Vertical column chart

(b) Horizontal bar chart

Source: www.mtdealer.com

Pareto Charts

A special type of column chart used in business is the **Pareto chart**. A Pareto chart displays categorical data, with categories displayed in descending order of frequency, so that the most common categories appear first. Typically, only a few categories account for the majority of observations. This phenomenon is called the *80/20 Rule*. This rule holds true for many aspects of business. For example, in a sample of U.S. guests responding to a Vail Resorts' guest satisfaction survey, 80 percent of the respondents were visiting from just 20 percent of the states in the United States.

Pareto charts are commonly used in quality management to display the *frequency* of defects or errors of different types. The majority of quality problems can usually be traced to only a few sources or causes. Sorting the categories in descending order helps managers focus on the *vital few* causes of problems rather than the *trivial many*.

Figure 3.17 shows a Pareto chart for complaints collected from a sample of $n = 398$ customers at a concession stand. Notice that the top three categories make up 76 percent of all complaints. The owners of the concession stand can concentrate on ensuring that their food is not cold, on decreasing the time their customers spend in line, and on providing vegetarian choices.

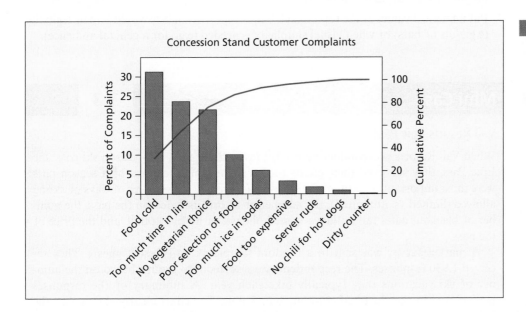

FIGURE 3.17

Pareto Chart

Concessions

Note: The cumulative percentage was added as a second data series on a secondary axis.

Stacked Column Chart

In a **stacked column chart** like Figure 3.18, the bar height is the sum of several subtotals. Areas may be compared by color to show patterns in the subgroups, as well as showing the total. Stacked column charts can be effective for any number of groups but work best when you have only a few. Use numerical labels if exact data values are of importance.

FIGURE 3.18

Stacked Column Chart

MedSchool

Source: www.aamc.org.

Tips for Effective Bar and Column Charts

The following guidelines will help you to create the most effective bar charts:

1. The numerical variable of interest usually is shown with vertical bars on the Y-axis, while the category labels go on the X-axis.

2. If the quantity displayed is a time series, the category labels (e.g., years) are displayed on the horizontal X-axis with time increasing from left to right.

3. The height or length of each bar should be proportional to the quantity displayed. This is easy, since most software packages default to a zero origin on a bar graph. The zero-origin rule is essential for a corporate annual report or investor stock prospectus (e.g., to avoid overstating earnings). However, nonzero origins may be justified to reveal sufficient detail.

4. Put numerical values at the top of each bar, except when labels would impair legibility (e.g., lots of bars) or when visual simplicity is needed (e.g., for a general audience).

VAILRESORTS·

Mini Case	3.3

Vail Resorts Epic Pass

When Vail Resorts was conducting market research for their new season ski pass, the Epic Pass, they surveyed their guests to determine which features of a season pass were most important. Features of a season pass include the number of days of skiing allowed (limited vs. unlimited), the number of resorts included on the pass, the number of blackout dates (all holidays, some holidays, or no blackouts), and the price of the pass.

A market survey was sent to a random sample of Vail Resort guests. They received 1,930 responses. The respondents were sorted into groups based on the number of ski vacations they typically take each year. A summary of the responses is displayed in the clustered column chart below. The chart clearly shows that the feature considered most important to all three groups was the price of the pass. Determining the right price of the pass was critical in order to create a valuable product that a skier would purchase. Subsequent surveys provided more data that was used to price the Epic Pass at $579. Charts can be effective communication tools by allowing the analyst to compare and summarize information from many different groups and across different variables. Decision makers can then see in a snapshot the areas on which to focus.

3.15 (a) Use Excel to prepare a line chart to display the following gasoline price data. Modify the default colors, fonts, etc., to make the display effective. (b) Change it to a *2-D column chart*. Modify the display if necessary to make the display attractive. (c) Do you prefer the line chart or bar chart? Why? *Hint:* Do *not* include the years when you make the chart. After the chart is completed, you can right-click the chart, choose Select Data, select Horizontal Axis Labels, and then click Edit to insert the range for the years as *X*-axis labels.

Average U.S. Retail Price of Gasoline (dollars per gallon) GasPrice			
Year	*Price*	*Year*	*Price*
1960	0.31	1990	1.16
1965	0.31	1995	1.15
1970	0.36	2000	1.51
1975	0.57	2005	2.30
1980	1.25	2010	3.02
1985	1.20		

Sources: www.fueleconomy.gov and eia.doe.gov. Pre-1980 prices are for unleaded gas.

3.16 (a) Use Excel to prepare a *2-D stacked column chart* for television sales by year. Modify the colors, fonts, etc., to make the display effective. (b) Change your graph to a *3-D stacked column chart*. Modify the chart if necessary to make it attractive. (c) Is 3-D better than 2-D? Why? (d) Right-click the data series, choose Add Data Labels, and add labels to the data. Do the labels help?

U.S. Television Sales, 2002–2005 ($ thousands) TVSales			
Year	*Projection TV*	*LCD TV*	*Plasma TV*
2002	3,574	246	515
2003	4,351	664	1,590
2004	6,271	1,579	2,347
2005	5,320	3,295	4,012

Source: *Statistical Abstract of the United States, 2007*, p. 643.

3.17 (a) Use Excel to prepare a Pareto chart of the following data. (b) Which three complaint categories account for approximately 80 percent of all complaints? (c) Which category should the telephone company focus on first? **Complaints**

Telephone Company Service Complaints, *n* = 791		
Customer Complaints	*Frequency*	*Percent*
Wait too long	350	44.2%
Service person rude	187	23.6%
Difficult to reach a real person	90	11.4%
Service person not helpful	85	10.7%
Automated instructions confusing	45	5.7%
Customer service phone number hard to find	21	2.7%
Automated voice annoying	13	1.6%

3.6 PIE CHARTS

LO 3-6

Know the rules for effective bar charts and pie charts.

An Oft-Abused Chart 🖙 PieCharts

Many statisticians feel that a table or bar chart is a better choice than a **pie chart** for several reasons. But, because of their visual appeal, pie charts appear daily in company annual reports and the popular press (e.g., *USA Today, The Wall Street Journal, Scientific American*), so you must understand their uses and misuses. A pie chart can only convey a *general idea of the data* because it is hard to assess areas precisely. It should have only a few slices (typically two to five) and the slices should be labeled with data values or percents. The only correct use of a pie chart is to *portray data that sum to a total* (e.g., percent market shares). A pie chart is never used to display time series data.

Pie Chart Options 🖙 PieCharts

A simple *2-D pie chart* is best, as in Figure 3.19. The *3-D pie chart* (Figure 3.20) adds visual interest, but the sizes of pie slices are harder to assess. Nonetheless, you will see 3-D charts in business publications because of their strong visual impact. A simple bar chart (Figure 3.21) can be used to display the same data, and would be preferred by many statisticians. Black-and-white charts may be used internally in business, but color is typically preferred for customers, stockholders, or investors. Practices may change as color copiers become more cost-effective. *Caution*: If you use Excel to make pie charts with data labels on the slices, the chart itself can shrink so much that it is difficult to read.

FIGURE 3.19

2-D Pie with Labels
🖙 **Textbook**

Source: Web survey of 269 students at two large public universities in 2007.

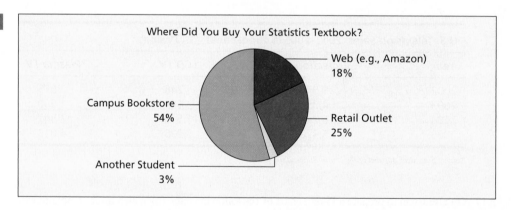

FIGURE 3.20

3-D Exploded Pie Chart

Source: Based on data from www.tiaa-cref.org.

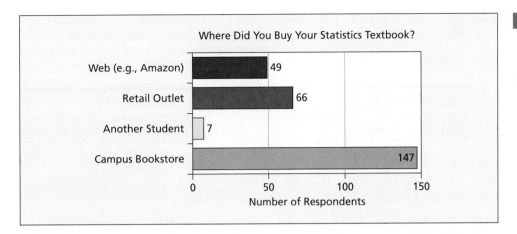

FIGURE 3.21

Bar Chart Alternative
🗇 **Textbook**

Source: Web survey of 269 students at
two large public universities in 2007.

Common Errors in Pie Chart Usage

- Pie charts can only convey a general idea of the data values.
- Pie charts are ineffective when they have too many slices.
- Pie chart data must represent *parts of a whole* (e.g., percent market share).

SECTION EXERCISES

connect

3.18 (a) Use Excel to prepare a *2-D pie chart* for these web-surfing data. Modify the default colors, fonts, etc., as you judge appropriate to make the display effective. (b) Right-click the chart area, select Chart Type, and change to an *exploded 2-D pie chart*. (c) Right-click the chart area, select Chart Type, and change to a *bar chart*. Which do you prefer? Why? *Hint:* Include data labels with the percent *values.*

Are You Concerned About Being Tracked While Web Surfing? 🗇 WebSurf	
Level of Concern	*Percent*
Very concerned	68
Somewhat concerned	23
Not very concerned	9
Total	100

3.19 (a) Use Excel to prepare a *2-D pie chart* for the following data. Modify the default colors, fonts, etc., as you judge appropriate to make the display effective. (b) Right-click the chart area, select Chart Type, and change to a *3-D pie chart*. (c) Right-click the chart area, select Chart Type, and change to a *bar chart*. Which do you prefer? Why? *Hint:* Include data labels with the percent *values.*

Dolon Corporation Medical Claims in 2011 🗇 Dolon	
Spent On	*Percent of Total*
Hospital services	47.5
Physicians	27.0
Pharmaceuticals	19.5
Mental health	5.0
Other	1.0
Total	100.0

3.20 (a) Use Excel to prepare a *2-D pie chart* for these LCD (liquid crystal display) shipments data. Modify the default colors, fonts, etc., as you judge appropriate to make the display effective. (b) Do you feel that the chart has become too cluttered (i.e., are you displaying too many slices)? Would a bar chart be better? Explain. *Hint:* Include data labels with the percent *values.*

World Market Share of LCD Shipments in 2010 LCDMarket	
Company	**Percent**
Samsung	18.0
Vizio	16.7
Sony	11.3
Sanyo	8.0
LG Electronics	7.8
Others	38.1
Total	100.0

Source: http://news.cnet.com/. Data are for first quarter of 2010. Percents may not add to 100 due to rounding.

3.7 SCATTER PLOTS

LO 3-7

Make and interpret a scatter plot using Excel.

A **scatter plot** shows *n* pairs of observations $(x_1, y_1), (x_2, y_2), \ldots, (x_n, y_n)$ as dots (or some other symbol) on an *X-Y* graph. This type of display is so important in statistics that it deserves careful attention. A scatter plot is a starting point for bivariate data analysis. We create scatter plots to investigate the relationship between two variables. Typically, we would like to know if there is an *association* between two variables and, if so, what kind of association exists. As we did with univariate data analysis, let's look at a scatter plot to see what we can observe.

EXAMPLE 3.3

Birth Rates and Life Expectancy

Source: *The CIA World Facebook 2003, www.cia.gov.*

Figure 3.22 shows a scatter plot with life expectancy on the *X*-axis and birth rates on the *Y*-axis. In this illustration, there seems to be an association between *X* and *Y*. That is, nations with higher birth rates tend to have lower life expectancy (and vice versa). No cause-and-effect relationship is implied, since in this example both variables could be influenced by a third variable that is not mentioned (e.g., GDP per capita).

FIGURE 3.22   Scatter Plot of Birth Rates and Life Expectancy (*n* = 153 nations)   BirthLife

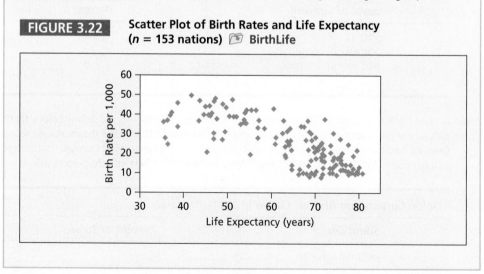

Figure 3.23 shows some scatter plot patterns similar to those that that you might observe when you have a sample of (*X, Y*) data pairs. A scatter plot can convey patterns in data pairs that would not be apparent from a table. Compare the scatter plots in Figure 3.24 with the prototypes and use your own words to describe the patterns that you see.

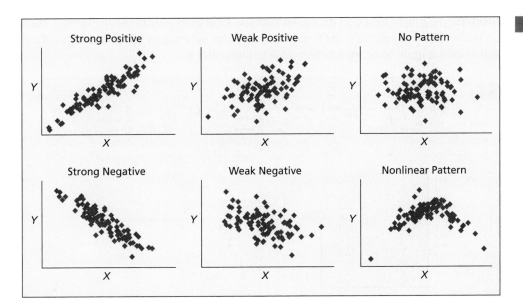

FIGURE 3.23

Prototype Scatter Plot Patterns

FIGURE 3.24

Four Scatter Plots

Very Strong Positive Association

Source: *National Center for Education Statistics.*

Strong Positive Association

Moderate Positive Association

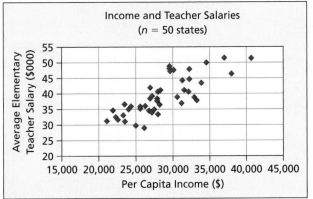

Source: *Statistical Abstract of the United States, 2001,* p. 151.

Little or No Association

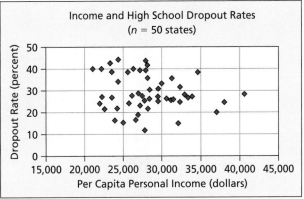

Source: *Statistical Abstract of the United States, 2001,* p. 141.

Making an Excel Scatter Plot

Making a scatter plot is easy using Excel. However, you will probably want to improve the graph after making it, as explained in the following steps. Note that Excel assumes that the first column is *X* and the second column is *Y*.

LO 3-7

Make and interpret a scatter plot using Excel.

Step 1: Highlight the (x, y) data pairs that you want to display in the scatter plot, click on the Insert ribbon, click on the Scatter icon, and choose a scatter plot style. The default scatter plot is quite basic, so you may wish to customize it.

Step 2: If you wish to add a fitted trend, right-click on the data series on the scatter plot and choose Add Trendline. By default, the fitted trend will be linear. There is an option to display the trend equation and its R^2 statistic (a measure of "fit" of the line).

Step 3: To customize your graph, click on it. Its border will change to show that it has been selected, and the Chart Tools ribbon will become active. Click on the Design ribbon and try different Chart Layout scatter plot templates, or click on the Layout ribbon and select a

specific edit icon (e.g., *Chart Title, Axis Titles, Gridlines*). Alternatively, you can just right-click on any feature of your graph (e.g., chart area, plot area, *X*-axis, *Y*-axis, gridlines) and explore the options until you are satisfied with the graph's appearance. Here is an example of a customized scatter plot.

Interpreting a Linear Trend

Figure 3.25 shows Excel's fitted linear trend for X = total gross leasable area and Y = total retail sales for a sample of 28 states. The slope of the line (0.2594) suggests that a unit change in X (each "unit" is one million square feet) is associated with an extra $0.2594 billion in retail sales, on average. The intercept is near zero, suggesting that a shopping center with no leasable area would have no sales. Later (in Chapter 12) you will learn how Excel fits a **trend line**, how to interpret it, and when such a line is meaningful. But since almost every student discovers this option the first time he or she makes a scatter plot, we must mention Excel's fitted trend line here purely as a *descriptive tool* that may help you find patterns in (X, Y) data.

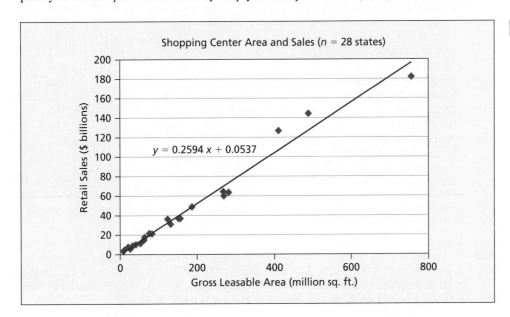

FIGURE 3.25

Excel Scatter Plot with Fitted Trend Line (n = 28 states)
RetailSales

Source: *Statistical Abstract of the United States, 2007*, p. 660.

SECTION EXERCISES

connect™

3.21 (a) Use Excel to make a scatter plot of the data for bottled water sales for 10 weeks, placing Price on the X-axis and Units Sold on the Y-axis. Add titles and modify the default colors, fonts, etc., as you judge appropriate to make the scatter plot effective. (b) Describe the relationship (if any) between X and Y. Weak? Strong? Negative? Positive? Linear? Nonlinear? ☞ **WaterSold**

Unit Price	Units Sold
1.15	186
0.94	216
1.04	173
1.05	182
1.08	183
1.33	150
0.99	190
1.25	165
1.16	190
1.11	201

3.22 (a) Use Excel to make a scatter plot of these vehicle data, placing Weight on the X-axis and City MPG on the Y-axis. Add titles and modify the default colors, fonts, etc., as you judge appropriate to make the scatter plot effective. (b) Describe the relationship (if any) between X and Y. Weak? Strong? Negative? Positive? Linear? Nonlinear?

Weight and MPG for 20 Randomly Selected Vehicles ☞ **CityMPG**

Vehicle	City MPG	Weight (lbs.)
Acura TSX	23	3,320
BMW 3-Series	19	3,390
Chevrolet Corvette	19	3,255
Chevrolet Silverado 1500	14	4,935
Chrysler Pacifica	17	4,660
Dodge Caravan	18	4,210
Ford Focus	26	2,760
Infiniti FX	16	4,295
Jaguar XJ8	18	3,805
Lexus IS300	18	3,390
Lincoln Aviator	13	5,000
Mazda 6	19	3,355
Land Rover Freelander	17	3,640
Mercedes-Benz S-Class	17	4,195
Nissan 350Z	20	3,345
Nissan Xterra	16	4,315
Pontiac Vibe	28	2,805
Pontiac Grand Am	25	3,095
Toyota Sienna	19	4,120
Volvo C70	20	3,690

Source: © 2003 by Consumers Union of U.S., Inc. Yonkers, NY, a nonprofit organization. From *Consumer Reports New Car Buying Guide, 2003–2004.* Used with permission.

3.23 (a) Use Excel to make a scatter plot of the following exam score data, placing Midterm on the X-axis and Final on the Y-axis. Add titles and modify the default colors, fonts, etc., as you judge appropriate to make the scatter plot effective. (b) Describe the relationship (if any) between X and Y. Weak? Strong? Negative? Positive? Linear? Nonlinear?

Exam Scores for 18 Statistics Students 🔄 **ExamScores**

Name	Midterm Score	Final Score	Name	Midterm Score	Final Score
Aaron	50	30	Joe	68	83
Angela	95	83	Lisa	75	58
Brandon	75	90	Liz	70	83
Buck	60	83	Michele	60	73
Carole	60	75	Nancy	88	78
Cecilia	63	45	Ryan	93	100
Charles	90	100	Tania	73	83
Dmitri	88	90	Ursula	33	53
Ellie	75	68	Xiaodong	60	70

3.24 (a) Use Excel to make a scatter plot of the data, placing Floor Space on the X-axis and Weekly Sales on the Y-axis. Add titles and modify the default colors, fonts, etc., as you judge appropriate to make the scatter plot effective. (b) Describe the relationship (if any) between X and Y. Weak? Strong? Negative? Positive? Linear? Nonlinear? 🔄 **FloorSpace**

Floor Space (sq. ft.)	Weekly Sales (dollars)
6,060	16,380
5,230	14,400
4,280	13,820
5,580	18,230
5,670	14,200
5,020	12,800
5,410	15,840
4,990	16,610
4,220	13,610
4,160	10,050
4,870	15,320
5,470	13,270

3.8 TABLES

Tables are the simplest form of data display, yet creating effective tables is an acquired skill. By arranging numbers in rows and columns, their meaning can be enhanced so it can be understood at a glance.

EXAMPLE 3.4

School Expenditures

Table 3.7 is a *compound table* that contains time series data (going down the columns) on seven variables (going across the rows). The data can be viewed in several ways. We can focus on the time pattern (going down the columns) or on comparing public and private spending (between columns) for a given school level (elementary/secondary or college/university). Or we can compare spending by school level (elementary/secondary or college/university) for a given type of control (public or private). Figures are rounded to three or four significant digits to make it easier for the reader. Units of measurement are stated in the footnote to keep the column headings simple. Columns are grouped using merged heading cells (blank columns could be inserted to add vertical separation). Presentation tables can be linked dynamically to spreadsheets so that slides can be updated quickly, but take care that data changes do not adversely affect the table layout.

TABLE 3.7	School Expenditures by Control and Level, 1980–2005 Schools						
		Elementary and Secondary			**Colleges and Universities**		
Year	*All Schools*	*Public*	*Private*	*Total*	*Public*	*Private*	*Total*
1980	442.6	265.3	19.9	285.2	104.4	52.9	157.4
1985	485.8	278.0	25.2	303.2	118.4	64.2	182.6
1990	618.4	359.7	31.1	390.8	145.0	82.6	227.6
1995	692.4	398.2	33.1	431.3	164.8	96.3	261.1
2000	823.3	484.2	38.9	523.1	193.1	107.1	300.2
2005	980.9	559.4	46.4	605.8	241.6	133.5	375.2

Source: U.S. Census Bureau, *Statistical Abstract of the United States, 2011,* p. 143. All figures are in constant 2008–2009 dollars.

Tips for Effective Tables

LO 3-8

Make simple tables and pivot tables.

Here are some tips for creating effective tables:

1. Keep the table simple, consistent with its purpose. Put summary tables in the *main body* of the written report and detailed tables in an *appendix*. In a slide presentation, the main point of the table should be clear to the reader within *10 seconds*. If not, break the table into parts or aggregate the data.

2. Display the data to be compared in columns rather than rows. Research shows that people find it easier to compare across rather than down.

3. For presentation purposes, round off to three or four significant digits (e.g., 142 rather than 142.213). People mentally round numbers anyway. Exceptions: when accounting requirements supersede the desire for rounding or when the numbers are used in subsequent calculations.

4. Physical table layout should guide the eye toward the comparison you wish to emphasize. Spaces or shading may be used to separate rows or columns. Use lines sparingly.

5. Row and column headings should be simple yet descriptive.

6. Within a column, use a consistent number of decimal digits. Right-justify or decimal-align the data unless all field widths are the same within the column.

Pivot Tables PivotTable

One of Excel's most popular and powerful features is the **pivot table**, which provides interactive analysis of a data matrix. The simplest kind of pivot table has rows and columns. Each of its cells shows a statistic for a row and column combination. The row and column variables must be either *categorical* or *discrete numerical* and the variable for the table cells must be *numerical* (review Chapter 2 if you do not remember these terms). After the table is created, you can change the table by dragging variable names from the list specified in your data matrix. You can change the displayed statistic in the cells (sum, count, average, maximum, minimum, product) by right-clicking the display and selecting from the *field settings* menu. We show here the steps needed to create a pivot table for a small data matrix (25 homes, 3 variables). The first table shows the *sum* of square feet for all the homes in each category. The second table was created by copying the first table and then changing the cells to display the *average* square feet of homes in that cell.

Step 1:   Select the Insert tab and specify the data range.

Step 2:   Drag and drop desired fields for rows, columns, and the table body.

Step 3:   Now you can format the table or right-click to choose desired field setting.

The Online Learning Center (OLC) website has a more detailed step-by-step guide to creating a pivot table (see the end of this chapter list of *LearningStats* demonstrations). A pivot table is especially useful when you have a large data matrix with several variables. For example, Figure 3.26 shows two pivot tables based on tax return data for $n = 4{,}801$ U.S. taxpayers. The first pivot table shows the number of taxpayers by filing type (single, married joint, married separate, head of household) cross-tabulated against the number of child exemptions (0, 1, 2, . . . , 10). The second pivot table shows average tax rate (percent) for each cell in the cross-tabulation. Note that some of the averages are based on small cell counts.

FIGURE 3.26

Two Pivot Tables for U.S. Income Tax Returns (n = 4,801) 📂 **Taxes**

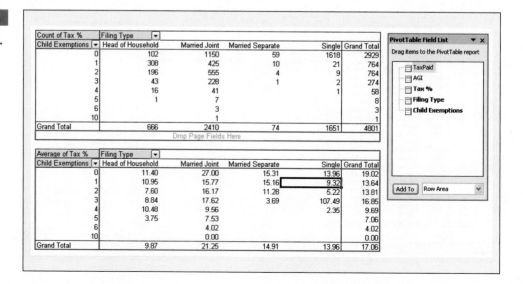

3.9 DECEPTIVE GRAPHS

We have explained how to create *good* graphs. Now, let's turn things around. As an impartial consumer of information, you need a checklist of errors to beware. Those who want to slant the facts may do these things deliberately, although most errors occur through ignorance. Use this list to protect yourself against ignorant or unscrupulous practitioners of the graphical arts.

LO 3-9

Recognize deceptive graphing techniques.

Error 1: Nonzero Origin A nonzero origin will exaggerate the trend. Measured distances do not match the stated values or axis demarcations. The accounting profession is particularly aggressive in enforcing this rule. Although zero origins are preferred, sometimes a nonzero origin is needed to show sufficient detail. Here are two charts of the same data. The first chart (nonzero origin) exaggerates the trend.

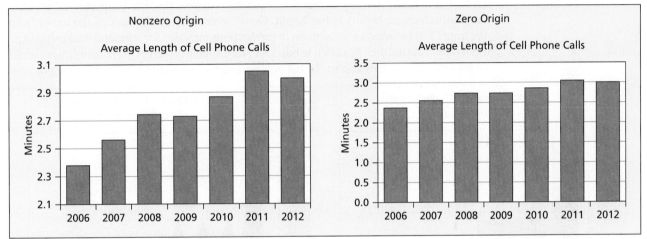

Error 2: Elastic Graph Proportions By shortening the *X*-axis in relation to the *Y*-axis, vertical change is exaggerated. For a time series (*X*-axis representing time), this can make a sluggish sales or profit curve appear steep. Conversely, a wide *X*-axis and short *Y*-axis can downplay alarming changes (recalls, industrial accidents). Keep the *aspect ratio* (width/height) below 2.00. Excel graphs use a default aspect ratio of about 1.68. The Golden Ratio you learned in art history suggests that 1.62 is ideal. Older TV screens use a 1.33 ratio, as do older PCs (640 × 480 pixels). Movies use a wide-screen format (up to 2.55) but VHS tapes and DVDs may crop it to fit on a television screen. HDTV and multimedia computers use a 16:9 aspect ratio (about 1.78). Newer ultrawide monitors offer ratios of 21:9 (about 2.33). Charts whose height exceeds their width don't fit well on pages or computer screens. These two charts show the same data. Which seems to be growing faster?

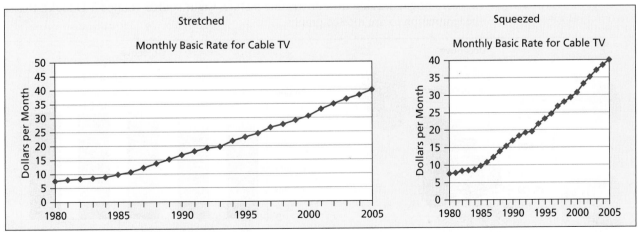

Source: *Statistical Abstract of the United States, 2007,* p. 717.

Error 3: Dramatic Titles and Distracting Pictures

The title often is designed more to grab the reader's attention than to convey the chart's content (Criminals on a Spree, Deficit Swamps Economy). Sometimes the title attempts to draw your conclusion for you (Inflation Wipes Out Savings, Imports Dwarf Exports). A title should be short but adequate for the purpose.

To add visual pizzazz, artists may superimpose the chart on a photograph (e.g., a gasoline price chart atop a photo of an oil-drilling platform) or add colorful cartoon figures, banners, or drawings. This is mostly harmless but can distract the reader or impart an emotional slant. Advertisements sometimes feature mature, attractive, conservatively attired actors portraying scientists, doctors, or business leaders examining scientific-looking charts. Because the public respects science's reputation, such displays impart credibility to self-serving commercial claims. The medical school applications graph illustrates these deceptive elements.

Error 4: 3-D and Novelty Graphs

Depth may enhance the visual impact of a bar chart, but it introduces ambiguity in bar height. Do we measure from the back of the bar or from the front? *3-D bar charts* are common in publications intended for a general readership (e.g., *USAToday*) but are seen less often in business. Novelty charts such as the *pyramid chart* should be avoided because they distort the bar volume and make it hard to measure bar height.

(a) 3-D column Chart

(b) Pyramid Chart (avoid it)

Source: www.mtdealer.com.

Error 5: Rotated Graphs

By making a graph 3-dimensional and rotating it through space, the author can make trends appear to dwindle into the distance or loom alarmingly toward you. This example (medical school applications) combines several errors (nonzero origin, leading title, distracting picture, vague source, rotated 3-D look). Resist the temptation to use rotated graphs.

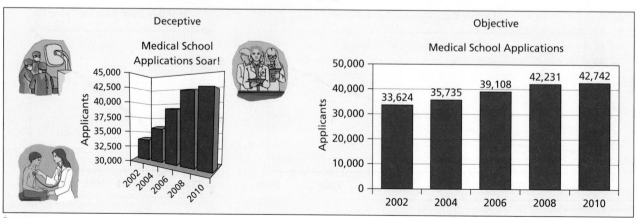

Source: www.aamc.org.

Error 6: Unclear Definitions or Scales Missing or unclear units of measurement (dollars? percent?) can render a chart useless. Even if the vertical scale is in dollars, we must know whether the variable being plotted is sales, profits, assets, or whatever. If percent, indicate clearly *percentage of what*. Without "tick" marks on the axis, the reader cannot identify individual data values. Gridlines help the viewer compare magnitudes but are often omitted to avoid graph clutter. For maximum clarity in a bar graph, label each bar with its numerical value, unless the scale is clearly demarcated and labeled.

Error 7: Vague Sources Large federal agencies or corporations employ thousands of people and issue hundreds of reports per year. Vague sources like "Department of Commerce" may indicate that the author lost the citation, didn't know the data source, or mixed data from several sources. Scientific publications insist on complete source citations. Rules are less rigorous for publications aimed at a general audience.

Error 8: Complex Graphs Complicated visual displays make the reader work harder. Keep your main objective in mind. Omit "bonus" detail or put it in the appendix. Apply the *10-second rule* to graphs. If the message really is complex, can it be broken into smaller parts? This example (surgery volume) combines several errors (silly subtitle, distracting pictures, no data labels, no definitions, vague source, too much information).

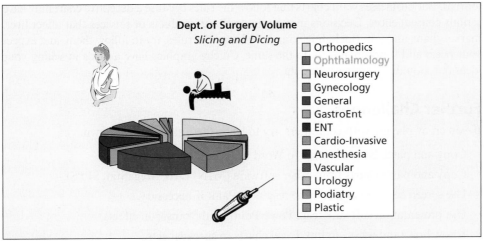

Source: Hospital reports.

Error 9: Gratuitous Effects Slide shows often use color and special effects (sound, interesting slide transitions, spinning text, etc.) to attract attention. But once the novelty wears off, audiences may find special effects annoying.

Error 10: Estimated Data In a spirit of zeal to include the "latest" figures, the last few data points in a time series are often estimated. Or perhaps a couple of years were missing or incompatible, so the author had to "fill in the blanks." At a minimum, estimated points should be noted.

Error 11: Area Trick One of the most pernicious visual tricks is simultaneously enlarging the width of the bars as their height increases, so the bar area misstates the true proportion (e.g., by replacing graph bars with figures like human beings, coins, or gas pumps). As figure height increases, so does width, distorting the area. This example (physician salaries) illustrates this distortion.

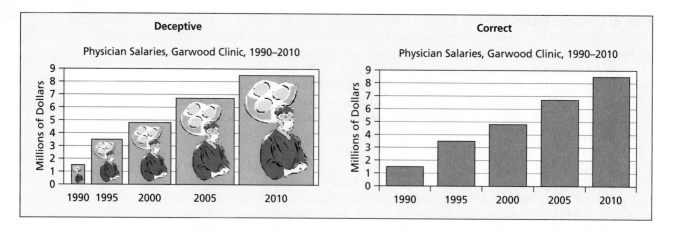

Final Advice

Can you trust any visual display (unless you created it yourself)? Be a skeptic, and be pleasantly surprised if the graph lives up to the best standards. Print media compete with TV and the web, so newspapers and magazines must use colorful charts to attract reader interest. People enjoy visual displays, so we accept some artistic liberties. Mass-readership publications like *U.S. News & World Report, Time, Newsweek, USA Today,* or even specialized business-oriented publications like *Forbes, Fortune, Bloomberg Businessweek,* and *The Wall Street Journal* should not be judged by the same standards you would apply to an academic journal. But businesses want charts that follow the rules because a deceptive chart may have serious consequences. Decisions may be made about products or services that affect lives, market share, and jobs (including yours). So know the rules, try to follow them, and expect your peers and subordinates to do the same. Catchy graphics have a place in selling your ideas but shouldn't dominate the data.

Further Challenges

If you enjoy playing with computers, try to learn these skills on your own:

- Copy and paste Excel charts into Word or PowerPoint.
- Copy and paste charts from other software (MINITAB, MegaStat, SPSS).
- Use screen captures and edit the results in Paint if necessary.
- Use presentation software (e.g., PowerPoint) with transition effects.
- Know how (and when) to link Excel charts to spreadsheets.
- Use clip art and create your own graphics.

CHAPTER SUMMARY

For a set of observations on a single numerical variable, a **stem-and-leaf plot** or a **dot plot** displays the individual data values, while a **frequency distribution** classifies the data into classes called **bins** for a **histogram** of **frequencies** for each bin. The number of bins and their limits are matters left to your judgment, though **Sturges' Rule** offers advice on the number of bins. The **line chart** shows values of one or more **time series** variables plotted against time. A **log scale** is sometimes used in time series charts when data vary by orders of magnitude. The **bar chart** or **column chart** shows a **numerical** data value for each category of an **attribute.** However, a bar chart can also be used for a time series. A **scatter plot** can reveal the association (or lack of association) between two variables X and Y. The **pie chart** (showing a **numerical** data value for each category of an **attribute** if the data values are parts of a whole) is common but should be used with caution. Sometimes a **simple table** is the best visual display. Creating effective visual displays is an acquired skill. Excel offers a wide range of charts from which to choose. Deceptive graphs are found frequently in both media and business presentations, and the consumer should be aware of common errors.

CHAPTER REVIEW

1. Name two attractive features and two limitations of the (a) stem-and-leaf plot and (b) dot plot.

2. (a) What is a frequency distribution? (b) What are the steps in creating one?

3. (a) What is a histogram? (b) What does it show?

4. (a) What is a bimodal histogram? (b) Explain the difference between left-skewed, symmetric, and right-skewed histograms. (c) What is an outlier?

5. (a) What is a scatter plot? (b) What do scatter plots reveal? (c) Sketch a scatter plot with a moderate positive correlation. (d) Sketch a scatter plot with a strong negative correlation.

6. For what kind of data would we use a bar chart? List three tips for creating effective bar charts.

7. For what kind of data would we use a line chart? List three tips for creating effective line charts.

8. (a) List the three most common types of charts in business, and sketch each type (no real data, just a sketch). (b) List three specialized charts that can be created in Excel, and sketch each type (no real data, just a sketch).

9. (a) For what kind of data would we use a pie chart? (b) Name two common pie chart errors. (c) Why are pie charts regarded with skepticism by some statisticians?

10. Which types of charts can be used for time series data?

11. (a) When might we need a log scale? (b) What do equal distances on a log scale represent? (c) State one drawback of a log scale graph.

12. When might we use a stacked column chart? An area chart? A Pareto chart?

13. List five deceptive graphical techniques.

14. What is a pivot table? Why is it useful?

CHAPTER EXERCISES

Note: In these exercises, you may use a software package if your instructor agrees. For example, use MegaStat's Descriptive Statistics for dot plots or Frequency Distributions for histograms. Use MINITAB's Graphs or a similar software package to create the dot plot or histogram. Data files may be downloaded from the Online Learning Center website www.mhhe.com/doane4e.

3.25 The durations (minutes) of 26 electric power outages in the community of Sonando Heights over the past five years are shown below. (a) Make a stem-and-leaf diagram. (b) Make a histogram. (c) Describe the shape of the distribution. **Duration**

32	44	25	66	27	12	62	9	51	4	17	50	35
99	30	21	12	53	25	2	18	24	84	30	17	17

3.26 The U.S. Postal Service will ship a Priority Mail® Large Flat Rate Box (12" × 12" × 5½") anywhere in the United States for a fixed price, regardless of weight. The weights (ounces) of 20 randomly chosen boxes are shown below. (a) Make a stem-and-leaf diagram. (b) Make a histogram. (c) Describe the shape of the distribution. **Weights**

72	86	28	67	64	65	45	86	31	32
39	92	90	91	84	62	80	74	63	86

3.27 A study of 40 U.S. cardiac care centers showed the following ratios of nurses to beds. (a) Prepare a dot plot. (b) Prepare a frequency distribution and histogram (you may either specify the bins yourself or use automatic bins). (c) Describe the distribution, based on these displays. 📄 **Nurses**

1.48	1.16	1.24	1.52	1.30	1.28	1.68	1.40	1.12	0.98	0.93	2.76
1.34	1.58	1.72	1.38	1.44	1.41	1.34	1.96	1.29	1.21	2.00	1.50
1.68	1.39	1.62	1.17	1.07	2.11	2.40	1.35	1.48	1.59	1.81	1.15
1.35	1.42	1.33	1.41								

3.28 The first Rose Bowl (football) was played in 1902. The next was not played until 1916, but a Rose Bowl has been played every year since then. The margin of victory in each of the 95 Rose Bowls from 1902 through 2011 is shown below (0 indicates a tie). (a) Prepare a stem-and-leaf plot. (b) Prepare a frequency distribution and histogram (you may either specify the bins yourself or use automatic bins). (c) Describe the distribution, based on these displays. (Data are from http://en.wikipedia.org) 📄 **RoseBowl**

0	7	7	7	7	7	7	7	8	9	10	10	13	13
14	14	14	14	14	14	14	14	14	14	17	17	17	17
17	17	17	17	18	20	20	20	20	20	20	20	21	21
21	21	21	21	21	22	22	23	23	24	24	25	26	27
27	27	27	28	28	28	28	29	29	32	34	34	34	34
34	35	35	37	38	38	38	38	38	38	40	41	41	42
42	42	44	45	45	45	46	47	49	49	49			

3.29 An executive's telephone log showed the following data for the length of 65 calls initiated during the last week of July. (a) Prepare a dot plot. (b) Prepare a frequency distribution and histogram (you may either specify the bins yourself or use automatic bins). (c) Describe the distribution, based on these displays. 📄 **CallLength**

1	2	10	5	3	3	2	20	1	1
6	3	13	2	2	1	26	3	1	3
1	2	1	7	1	2	3	1	2	12
1	4	2	2	29	1	1	1	8	5
1	4	2	1	1	1	1	6	1	2
3	3	6	1	3	1	1	5	1	18
2	13	13	1	6					

3.30 Below are batting averages of the New York Yankees players who were at bat five times or more in 2006. (a) Construct a frequency distribution. Explain how you chose the number of bins and the bin limits. (b) Make a histogram and describe its appearance. (c) Repeat, using a different number of bins and different bin limits. (d) Did your visual impression of the data change when you changed the number of bins? Explain. 📄 **Yankees**

Batting Averages for the 2006 New York Yankees

Player	Avg	Player	Avg	Player	Avg
Derek Jeter	0.343	Miguel Cairo	0.239	Sal Fasano	0.143
Johnny Damon	0.285	Bobby Abreu	0.330	Terrence Long	0.167
Alex Rodriguez	0.290	Hideki Matsui	0.302	Kevin Thompson	0.300
Robinson Cano	0.342	Gary Sheffield	0.298	Kevin Reese	0.417
Jorge Posada	0.277	Craig Wilson	0.212	Andy Cannizaro	0.250
Melky Cabrera	0.280	Bubba Crosby	0.207	Randy Johnson	0.167
Jason Giambi	0.253	Aaron Guiel	0.256	Wil Nieves	0.000
Bernie Williams	0.281	Kelly Stinnett	0.228		
Andy Phillips	0.240	Nick Green	0.240		

Source: www.thebaseballcube.com.

3.31 Download the full data set of measurements of cockpit noise level for a commercial jet airliner from the OLC (only six data values are shown). (a) Use Excel to make a scatter plot, placing

Airspeed on the X-axis and Noise Level on the Y-axis. Add titles and modify the default colors, fonts, etc., as you judge appropriate to make the scatter plot effective. (b) Describe the relationship (if any) between X and Y. Weak? Strong? Negative? Positive? Linear? Nonlinear? *Hint:* You may need to rescale the X and Y axes to see more detail.

Airspeed and Cockpit Noise ($n = 61$ measurements) 📄 CockpitNoise

Obs	Airspeed (knots)	Noise Level (dB)
1	250	83
2	340	89
3	320	88
.	.	.
.	.	.
.	.	.
59	370	91
60	405	93
61	250	82

Note: The decibel (dB) is a logarithmic unit that indicates the ratio of measured sound pressure to a benchmark. Some familiar examples for comparison: Vuvuzela horn at 1 m (120 dB), jack hammer at 1 m (100 dB), handheld electric mixer (65 dB).

3.32 Download the full data set from the OLC (only six data values are shown). (a) Use Excel to make a scatter plot, placing Revenue on the X-axis and Net Income on the Y-axis. Add titles and modify the default colors, fonts, etc., as you judge appropriate to make the scatter plot effective. (b) Describe the relationship (if any) between X and Y. Weak? Strong? Negative? Positive? Linear? Nonlinear?

Revenue and Net Income (millions) for 27 Randomly Chosen Fortune 1000 Companies 📄 RevenueIncome

Company	Revenue	Net Income
1	1,494.9	30.8
2	1,523.2	328.9
3	1,565.8	90.5
.	.	.
.	.	.
.	.	.
25	11,066.8	168.2
26	11,164.2	253.6
27	19,468.0	496.5

Source: money.cnn.com/magazines/fortune/fortune500/2006/full_list/301_400.html. Data are from the April 17, 2006, issue.

3.33 Download the full data set from the OLC (only six data values are shown). (a) Use Excel to make a scatter plot, placing GDP per Capita on the X-axis and Birth Rate on the Y-axis. Add titles and modify the default colors, fonts, etc., as you judge appropriate to make the scatter plot effective. (b) Describe the relationship (if any) between X and Y. Weak? Strong? Negative? Positive? Linear? Nonlinear?

GDP per Capita and Birth Rate ($n = 153$ nations) 📄 GDPBirthRate

Nation	GDP per Capita	Birth Rate
Afghanistan	800	41.03
Albania	3800	18.59
Algeria	5600	22.34
.	.	.
.	.	.
.	.	.
Yemen	820	43.30
Zambia	870	41.01
Zimbabwe	2450	24.59

Source: Central Intelligence Agency, *The World Factbook*, 2003.

3.34   (a) What kind of display is this? (b) Identify its strengths and weaknesses, using the tips and checklists shown in this chapter. (c) Can you suggest any improvements? Would a different type of display be better? **WomenPilots**

Source: www.faa.gov.

3.35   (a) What kind of display is this? (b) Identify its strengths and weaknesses, using the tips and checklists shown in this chapter. (c) Can you suggest any improvements? Would a different type of display be better? **MedError**

3.36   (a) What kind of display is this? (b) Identify its strengths and weaknesses, using the tips and checklists shown in this chapter. (c) Can you suggest any improvements? Would a different type of display be better? **Oxnard**

3.37   (a) What kind of display is this? (b) Identify its strengths and weaknesses, using the tips and checklists shown in this chapter. (c) Can you suggest any improvements? Would a different type of display be better?

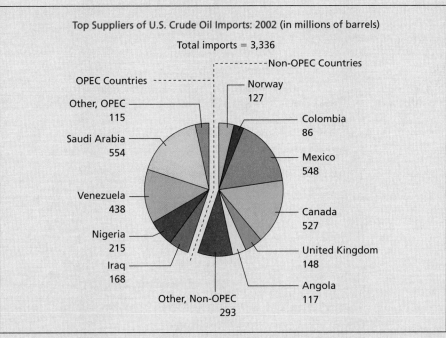

Source: *Statistical Abstract of the United States, 2003.*

3.38 (a) What kind of display is this? (b) Identify its strengths and weaknesses, using the tips and checklists shown in this chapter. (c) Can you suggest any improvements? Would a different type of display be better? 🖻 **BirthRate**

3.39 (a) What kind of display is this? (b) Identify its strengths and weaknesses, using the tips and checklists shown in this chapter. (c) Can you suggest any improvements? Would a different type of display be better? 🖻 **Advertising**

Source: *Statistical Abstract of the United States, 2002,* p. 772.

3.40   (a) What kind of display is this? (b) Identify its strengths and weaknesses, using the tips and checklists shown in this chapter. (c) Can you suggest any improvements? Would a different type of display be better?

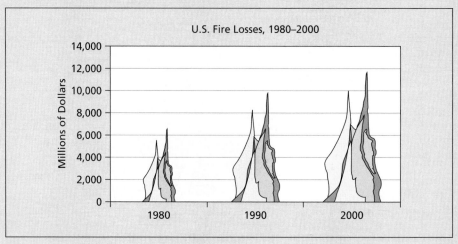

Source: *Statistical Abstract of the United States, 2001*, p. 340.

3.41   (a) What kind of display is this? (b) Identify its strengths and weaknesses, using the tips and checklists shown in this chapter. (c) Can you suggest any improvements? Would a different type of display be better?   **Bankruptcies**

Source: *American Bankruptcy Institute*, www.abiworld.org.

3.42   (a) What kind of display is this? (b) Identify its strengths and weaknesses, using the tips and checklists shown in this chapter. (c) Can you suggest any improvements? Would a different type of display be better?

3.43 (a) Use Excel to prepare an appropriate type of chart (bar, line, pie, scatter) to display the following data. Modify the default colors, fonts, etc., as you judge appropriate to make the display effective. (b) Would more than one kind of display be acceptable? Why or why not?

Where Did You Purchase Your Statistics Textbook? ⬚ **Textbook**

Response	Count
Campus Bookstore	147
Retail Outlet	66
Web (e.g., Amazon)	49
Another Student	7
Total	269

Source: Survey of statistics students in 2007 at two large public universities.

3.44 (a) Use Excel to prepare an appropriate type of chart (bar, line, pie, scatter) to display the following data. Modify the default colors, fonts, etc., as you judge appropriate to make the display effective. (b) Would more than one kind of display be acceptable? Why or why not?

New Car Color Preferences for U.S. Buyers ⬚ **CarColor**

Color	Percent
Blue	12
Green	7
Natural	12
Red	13
Silver/Grey	24
White	16
Black	13
Other	3
Total	100

Source: *Detroit Auto Scene* 24, no. 1 (2006), p. 1.

3.45 (a) Use Excel to prepare an appropriate type of chart (bar, line, pie, scatter) to display the following data. Modify the default colors, fonts, etc., as you judge appropriate to make the display effective. (b) Would more than one kind of display be acceptable? Why or why not?

Domestic Market Share, Ten Largest U.S. Airlines ⬚ **AirlineMkt**

Airline	Percent
AirTran	3.3
Alaska	2.9
American	14.3
Continental	7.6
Delta	10.8
JetBlue	4.3
Northwest	6.4
Southwest	13.0
United	11.0
US Airways	8.3
Other	18.1
Total	100.0

Source: www.transtats.bts.gov. Data are for February 2008 to January 2009. Based on revenue passenger miles.

3.46 (a) Use Excel to prepare an appropriate type of chart (bar, line, pie, scatter) to display the following data. Modify the default colors, fonts, etc., as you judge appropriate to make the display effective. (b) Would more than one kind of display be acceptable? Why or why not?

U.S. and World Petroleum Usage (millions of barrels per day) Petroleum

Used by	1996	1998	2000	2002	2004	2006	2007	2008	2009	2010
U.S.	18.3	18.9	19.7	19.8	20.7	20.7	20.7	19.5	18.8	19.3
Non-U.S.	53.2	55.1	57.0	58.4	61.9	64.6	65.6	66.3	65.6	67.7

Source: www.eia.doe.gov.

3.47 (a) Use Excel to prepare an appropriate type of chart (bar, line, pie, scatter) to display the following data. Modify the default colors, fonts, etc., as you judge appropriate to make the display effective. (b) Would more than one kind of display be acceptable? Why or why not?

Operating Expenses per Seat Mile for U.S. Airlines (cents) SeatMile

Carrier	Cost	Carrier	Cost
AirTran	10.9	JetBlue	9.5
Alaska	13.1	Northwest	16.0
Allegiant	9.6	Southwest	9.7
American	14.4	Spirit	9.8
Continental	14.9	United	14.9
Delta	16.5	US Airways	17.0
Frontier	12.0		

Source: Bureau of Transportation Statistics, Form 41, Schedule P1.2. Data are for 1Q 2008.

3.48 (a) Use Excel to prepare an appropriate type of chart (bar, line, pie, scatter) to display the following data. Modify the default colors, fonts, etc., as you judge appropriate to make the display effective. (b) Would more than one kind of display be acceptable? Why or why not?

Licensed Drivers and Fatal Accidents in the United States Fatal

Age Group	Percent of Drivers	Percent of Fatal Crashes
15–19	4.7	11.0
20–24	8.5	14.3
25–34	18.2	18.1
35–44	20.5	16.5
45–54	19.7	15.6
55–64	13.8	9.8
65–74	8.2	6.3
75 and over	6.4	8.4
Total	100.0	100.0

Source: *Statistical Abstract of the United States, 2007*, p. 696.

3.49 (a) Use Excel to prepare an appropriate type of chart (bar, line, pie, scatter) to display the following data. Modify the default colors, fonts, etc., as you judge appropriate to make the display effective. (b) Would more than one kind of display be acceptable? Why or why not?

U.S. Market Share for Search Engines WebSearch

Search Engine	Percent
Google	45.4
Yahoo	28.2
Microsoft	11.7
Ask	5.8
AOL/Time Warner	5.4
All Others	3.5
Total	100.0

Source: *The New York Times*, December 4, 2006, p. C1.

3.50 (a) Use Excel to prepare an appropriate type of chart (bar, line, pie, scatter) to display the following data. Modify the default colors, fonts, etc., as you judge appropriate to make the display effective. (b) Would more than one kind of display be acceptable? Why or why not?

U.S. Energy Consumption in 2010 by Source 📂 **Energy**

Source	Quad BTU	Percent
Petroleum	37.06	38.4%
Natural Gas	23.15	24.0%
Coal	20.49	21.2%
Nuclear	8.52	8.8%
Renewables	7.17	7.4%
Other	0.21	0.2%
Total	96.60	100.0%

Source: *Statistical Abstract of the United States, 2011*, p. 583.

3.51 (a) Use Excel to prepare a Pareto chart of the following data. (b) Which three service providers account for approximately 80 percent of all responses? (Source: 2007 web survey of 158 statistics students).

Cell Phone Service Provider (2007) *n* = 158 📂 **CellPhone**

Service Provider	Percent	Cumulative Percent
Verizon	37.3	37.3
Cingular	29.7	67.1
T-Mobile	13.3	80.4
Sprint	8.9	89.2
Other	4.4	93.7
Nextel	3.2	96.8
Alltel	2.5	99.4
Virgin	0.6	100.0

DO-IT-YOURSELF

3.52 (a) Clip an example of a deceptive visual data presentation from a recent magazine or newspaper (if it is from a library, make a photocopy instead). Try to choose an outrageous example that violates many principles of ideal graphs. (b) Cite the exact source where you found the display. (c) What do you think is its presumed purpose? (d) Write a short, critical evaluation of its strengths and weaknesses. Be sure to attach the original clipping (or a good photocopy) to your analysis.

RELATED READING

Visual Displays

Cleveland, William S. *The Elements of Graphing Data.* Hobart Press, 1994.

Cleveland, William S. *Visualizing Data.* Hobart Press, 1993.

Huff, Darrell; and Irving Geiss. *How to Lie with Statistics.* W. W. Norton, 1954.

Jones, Gerald E. *How to Lie with Charts.* Sybex, 1995.

Monmonier, Mark. *How to Lie with Maps.* University of Chicago Press, 1996.

Tufte, Edward R. *The Visual Display of Quantitative Information.* 2nd ed. Graphics Press, 2004.

Wilkinson, Leland. *The Grammar of Graphics.* Springer, 2005.

Wong, Dona M. *The Wall Street Journal Guide to Information Graphics: The Dos and Don'ts of Presenting Data, Facts, and Figures.* W. W. Norton, 2010.

Zelazny, Gene. *Say It with Charts: The Executive's Guide to Visual Communication.* Irwin Professional Publishers, 1995.

CHAPTER 3   Online Learning Resources

The Online Learning Center (OLC) at www.mhhe.com/doane4e has several *LearningStats* demonstrations to help you understand visual data displays. Your instructor may assign one or more of them, or you may decide to download the ones that sound interesting.

Topic	LearningStats Demonstrations
Effective visual displays	Presenting Data—I Presenting Data—II EDA Graphics
How to make an Excel chart	Excel Charts: Step-by-Step Pivot Tables: Step-by-Step Using MegaStat Excel Charts: Histograms Using MINITAB
Applications	Bimodal Data Sturges' Rule Stem-and-Leaf Plots
Screen Cam Tutorials	Excel Basics Making Excel Histograms Making Scatter Plots

Key: = PowerPoint   = Word   = Excel   = Screen Cam Tutorials

MegaStat for Excel by J. B. Orris of Butler University is an Excel add-in that can be downloaded from the Online Learning Center (OLC) to be installed on your own computer. The setup will guide you through the installation process. MegaStat goes beyond Excel's built-in statistical functions to offer a full range of statistical tools to help you analyze data, create graphs, and perform calculations. MegaStat examples are shown throughout this textbook.

After installing MegaStat, you should see MegaStat appear on the left when you click the Add-Ins tab on the top menu bar (right side in the illustration above). If not, click File in the upper left. Click Options > Add Ins > Manage Excel Add-Ins > Go and check the box that says MegaStat. If you do not see a check box for MegaStat, go to the Online Learning Center at www.mhhe.com/doane4e for further instructions.

CHAPTER CONTENTS

CHAPTER LEARNING OBJECTIVES

LO

When you finish this chapter you should be able to

LO 4-1   Explain the concepts of center, variability, and shape.

LO 4-2   Use Excel to obtain descriptive statistics and visual displays.

LO 4-3   Calculate and interpret common measures of center.

LO 4-4   Calculate and interpret common measures of variability.

LO 4-5   Transform a data set into standardized values.

LO 4-6   Apply the Empirical Rule and recognize outliers.

LO 4-7   Calculate quartiles and other percentiles.

LO 4-8   Make and interpret box plots.

LO 4-9   Calculate and interpret a correlation coefficient and covariance.

LO 4-10 Calculate the mean and standard deviation from grouped data.

LO 4-11 Assess skewness and kurtosis in a sample.

4.1 NUMERICAL DESCRIPTION

The last chapter explained *visual* descriptions of data (e.g., histograms, dot plots, scatter plots). This chapter explains *numerical* descriptions of data. Descriptive measures derived from a sample (n items) are *statistics,* while for a population (N items or infinite) they are *parameters*. For a sample of numerical data, we are interested in three key characteristics: center, variability, and shape. Table 4.1 summarizes the questions that we will be asking about the data.

Characteristic	Interpretation
Center	Where are the data values concentrated? What seem to be typical or middle data values? Is there central tendency?
Variability	How much dispersion is there in the data? How spread out are the data values? Are there unusual values?
Shape	Are the data values distributed symmetrically? Skewed? Sharply peaked? Flat? Bimodal?

EXAMPLE 4.1

Vehicle Quality

Every year, J.D. Power and Associates issues its initial vehicle quality ratings. These ratings are of interest to consumers, dealers, and manufacturers. Table 4.2 shows defect rates for 33 vehicle brands. We will demonstrate how numerical statistics can be used to summarize a data set like this. The reported defect rates are based on a random sample of vehicles within each brand.

TABLE 4.2 Defects per 100 Vehicles 📁 JDPower

Brand	Defects	Brand	Defects	Brand	Defects
Acura	86	Hyundai	102	MINI	133
Audi	111	Infiniti	107	Mitsubishi	146
BMW	113	Jaguar	130	Nissan	111
Buick	114	Jeep	129	Porsche	83
Cadillac	111	Kia	126	Ram	110
Chevrolet	111	Land Rover	170	Scion	114
Chrysler	122	Lexus	88	Suburu	121
Dodge	130	Lincoln	106	Suzuki	122
Ford	93	Mazda	114	Toyota	117
GMC	126	Mercedes-Benz	87	Volkswagen	135
Honda	95	Mercury	113	Volvo	109

Source: J.D. Power and Associates 2010 Initial Quality Study™. Used with permission. Ratings are intended for educational purposes only, and should not be used as a guide to consumer decisions.

Preliminary Analysis

Before calculating any statistics, we consider how the data were collected. A web search reveals that J.D. Power and Associates is a well-established independent company whose methods are widely considered to be objective. Data on defects are obtained by inspecting randomly chosen vehicles for each brand, counting the defects, and dividing the number of defects by the number of vehicles inspected. J.D. Power multiplies the result by 100 to obtain defects per 100 vehicles, rounded to the nearest integer. The underlying measurement scale is continuous (e.g., if 4 defects were found in 3 vehicles, the defect rate would be 1.333333, or 133 defects per 100 vehicles). Defect rates would vary from year to year, and perhaps even within a given model year, so the timing of the study could affect the results. Since the analysis is based on sampling of vehicles within each brand, we must allow for the possibility of sampling error. With these cautions in mind, we look at the data. A good first step is to sort the data, as shown in Table 4.3.

TABLE 4.3

Defects per 100 Vehicles Ranked Lowest to Highest 📋 **JDPower**

Brand	Defects	Brand	Defects	Brand	Defects
Porsche	83	Audi	111	Chrysler	122
Acura	86	Cadillac	111	Suzuki	122
Mercedes-Benz	87	Chevrolet	111	GMC	126
Lexus	88	Nissan	111	Kia	126
Ford	93	BMW	113	Jeep	129
Honda	95	Mercury	113	Dodge	130
Hyundai	102	Buick	114	Jaguar	130
Lincoln	106	Mazda	114	MINI	133
Infiniti	107	Scion	114	Volkswagen	135
Volvo	109	Toyota	117	Mitsubishi	146
Ram	110	Suburu	121	Land Rover	170

The sorted data in Table 4.3 provide insight into both *center* and *variability*. The values range from 83 (Porsche) to 170 (Land Rover), while the middle values seem mostly to lie between 110 and 120. The dot plot in Figure 4.1 reveals additional detail, including one unusual value.

FIGURE 4.1

Dot Plot of J.D. Power Data (*n* = 33) 📋 **JDPower**

Except for tiny samples, sorting would be done in Excel. As illustrated in Figure 4.2, highlight the data array (including the headings), right-click, choose Sort > Custom Sort, select the column to sort on, and click OK.

The next visual step is a histogram, shown in Figure 4.3. The modal class (largest frequency) between 100 and 120 reveals the *center*. The *shape* of the histogram is right-skewed.

FIGURE 4.2

Sorting Data in Excel
📁 JDPower

LO 4-2

Use Excel to obtain descriptive statistics and visual displays.

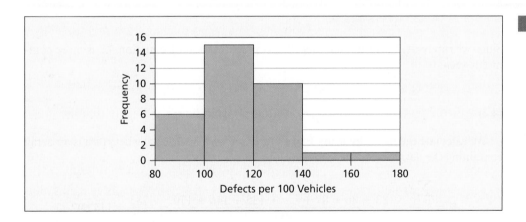

FIGURE 4.3

Histogram of J.D. Power Data (*n* = 33)
📁 JDPower

4.2 MEASURES OF CENTER

When we speak of *center*, we are trying to describe the middle or typical values of a distribution. You can assess central tendency in a general way from a dot plot or histogram, but numerical statistics allow more precise statements. Table 4.4 lists six common measures of center. Each has strengths and weaknesses. We need to look at several of them to obtain a clear picture of central tendency.

LO 4-3

Calculate and interpret common measures of center.

Mean

The most familiar statistical measure of center is the **mean**. It is the sum of the data values divided by the number of data items. For a population we denote it μ, while for a sample we call it $\bar{x}$. We use equation 4.1 to calculate the mean of a population:

$$\mu = \frac{\sum_{i=1}^{N} x_i}{N} \qquad \text{(population definition)} \qquad \textbf{(4.1)}$$

TABLE 4.4		Six Measures of Center		
Statistic	**Formula**	**Excel Formula**	**Pro**	**Con**
Mean	$\dfrac{1}{n}\displaystyle\sum_{i=1}^{n} x_i$	=AVERAGE(Data)	Familiar and uses all the sample information.	Influenced by extreme values.
Median	Middle value in sorted array	=MEDIAN(Data)	Robust when extreme data values exist.	Ignores extremes and can be affected by gaps in data values.
Mode*	Most frequently occurring data value	=MODE.SNGL(Data)	Useful for attribute data or discrete data with a small range.	May not be unique, and is not helpful for continuous data.
Midrange	$\dfrac{x_{min} + x_{max}}{2}$	=0.5*(MIN(Data) +MAX(Data))	Easy to understand and calculate.	Influenced by extreme values and ignores most data values.
Geometric mean (G)	$\sqrt[n]{x_1 x_2 \cdots x_n}$	=GEOMEAN(Data)	Useful for growth rates and mitigates high extremes.	Less familiar and requires positive data.
Trimmed mean	Same as the mean except omit highest and lowest k% of data values (e.g., 5%)	=TRIMMEAN(Data, Percent)	Mitigates effects of extreme values.	Excludes some data values that could be relevant.

*Equivalent to =MODE(Data) in earlier versions of Excel (see Appendix J for further discussion).

Since we rarely deal with populations, the sample notation of equation 4.2 is more commonly seen:

$$\bar{x} = \frac{\displaystyle\sum_{i=1}^{n} x_i}{n} \qquad \text{(sample definition)}$$

(4.2)

We calculate the mean by using Excel's function =AVERAGE(Data) where Data is an array containing the data. So for the sample of $n = 33$ car brands:

$$\bar{x} = \frac{\displaystyle\sum_{i=1}^{n} x_i}{n} = \frac{83 + 86 + 87 + \cdots + 135 + 146 + 170}{33} = \frac{3785}{33} = 114.697$$

Characteristics of the Mean

The arithmetic mean is the "average" with which most of us are familiar. The mean is affected by every sample item. It is the balancing point or fulcrum in a distribution if we view the X-axis as a lever arm and represent each data item as a physical weight, as illustrated in Figure 4.4 for the J.D. Power data.

FIGURE 4.4

Mean as Fulcrum (n = 33 vehicles)
📁 JDPower

The mean is the balancing point because it has the property that distances from the mean to the data points *always* sum to zero:

(4.3)
$$\sum_{i=1}^{n} (x_i - \bar{x}) = 0$$

This statement is true for *any* sample or population, regardless of its shape (skewed, symmetric, bimodal, etc.). Even when there are extreme values, the distances below the mean are *exactly* counterbalanced by the distances above the mean.

For example, Bob's scores on five quizzes were 42, 60, 70, 75, 78. His mean is pulled down to 65, mainly because of his poor showing on one quiz, as illustrated in Figure 4.5. Although the data are asymmetric, the three scores above the mean exactly counterbalance the two scores below the mean:

$$\sum_{i=1}^{n}(x_i - \overline{x}) = (42 - 65) + (60 - 65) + (70 - 65) + (75 - 65) + (78 - 65)$$
$$= (-23) + (-5) + (5) + (10) + (13) = -28 + 28 = 0$$

FIGURE 4.5

Bob's Quiz Scores (n = 5 quizzes)

Median

The **median** (denoted M) is the 50th percentile or midpoint of the *sorted* sample data set $x_1, x_2, \ldots, x_n$. It separates the upper and lower halves of the sorted observations:

The median is the middle observation in the sorted array if n is odd, but the average of the middle two observations if n is even, as illustrated in Figure 4.6.

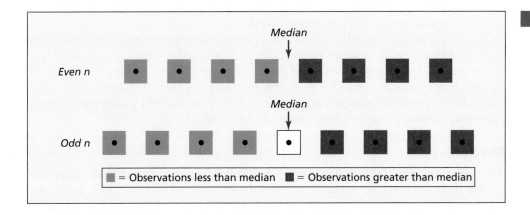

FIGURE 4.6

Illustration of the Median

For example, if we have an even n, say $n = 6$, then the median is halfway *between* the third and fourth observation in the sorted array: $M = (x_3 + x_4)/2 = (15 + 17)/2 = 16$.

Median

11   12   15   17   21   32

But for an odd n, say $n = 7$, the median is the fourth observation in the sorted array: $M = x_4 = 25$.

It is tempting to imagine that half the observations are less than the median, but this is not necessarily the case. For example, here are 11 exam scores in ascending order:

Their median is 78. But only three data values are *below* 78, while five data values are *above* 78. This median did not provide a clean "50-50 split" in the data because there were several identical exam scores clustered at the middle of the distribution. This situation is not so unusual. In fact, we might expect it when there is strong central tendency in a data set.

Excel's function for the median is =MEDIAN(Data) where Data is the data array. For the 33 vehicle quality ratings (odd n) the median is the 17th observation (16 below, 16 above), which is $x_{17} = 113$. However, you can verify that 113 occurs twice, so this does not provide a clean "50-50 split" in the data.

The median is especially useful when there are extreme values. For example, government statistics use the median income because a few very high incomes will render the mean atypical. The median's insensitivity to extremes may seem advantageous or not, depending on your point of view. Consider three students' scores on five quizzes:

Tom's scores: 20, 40, 70, 75, 80   Mean = 57, Median = 70

Jake's scores: 60, 65, 70, 90, 95   Mean = 76, Median = 70

Mary's scores: 50, 65, 70, 75, 90   Mean = 70, Median = 70

Each student has the same median quiz score (70). Tom, whose mean is pulled down by a few low scores, would rather have his grade based on the median. Jake, whose mean is pulled up by a few high scores, would prefer the mean. Mary is indifferent, since her measures of center agree (she has symmetric scores).

The median lacks some of the mean's useful mathematical properties. For example, if we multiply the mean by the sample size, we get the sum of the data values. But this is not true for the median. For instance, Tom's total points on all five quizzes (285) are the product of the sample size times his mean ($5 \times 57 = 285$). But this is not true for his median ($5 \times 70 = 350$). That is one reason why instructors tend to base their semester grades on the mean. Otherwise, the lowest and highest scores would not "count."

Mode

The **mode** is the most frequently occurring data value. It may be similar to the mean and median if data values near the center of the sorted array tend to occur often. But it may also be quite different from the mean and median. A data set may have multiple modes or no mode at all. For example, consider these four students' scores on five quizzes:

Lee's scores: 60, 70, 70, 70, 80   Mean = 70, Median = 70, Mode = 70

Pat's scores: 45, 45, 70, 90, 100   Mean = 70, Median = 70, Mode = 45

Sam's scores: 50, 60, 70, 80, 90   Mean = 70, Median = 70, Mode = none

Xiao's scores: 50, 50, 70, 90, 90   Mean = 70, Median = 70, Modes = 50, 90

Each student has the same mean (70) and median (70). Lee's mode (70) is the same as his mean and median, but Pat's mode (45) is nowhere near the "middle." Sam has no mode, while Xiao has two modes (50, 90). These examples illustrate some quirks of the mode.

The mode is easy to define, but *not* easy to calculate (except in very small samples), because it requires tabulating the frequency of occurrence of every distinct data value. For example, the sample of $n = 33$ brands has a unique mode at 111 (occurs four times), although several other data values have multiple occurrences.

83	86	87	88	93	95	102	106	107	109	110
111	111	111	111	113	113	114	114	114	117	121
122	122	126	126	129	130	130	133	135	146	170

Excel's function =MODE.SNGL(Data) will return #N/A if there is no mode. If there are multiple modes, =MODE.SNGL(Data) will return the first one it finds. Sometimes the mode is far from the "middle" of the distribution and may not be at all "typical." For *continuous* data, the mode generally isn't useful because continuous data values rarely repeat. To assess central tendency in continuous data, we would rely on the mean or median. But the mode is good for describing central tendency in *categorical data* such as gender (male, female) or college major (accounting, finance, etc.). Indeed, the mode is the *only* useful measure of central tendency for categorical data. The mode is also useful to describe a *discrete* variable with a *small range* (e.g., responses to a five-point Likert scale).

> *Tip* The mode is most useful for discrete or categorical data with only a few distinct data values. For continuous data or data with a wide range, the mode is rarely useful.

Two Illustrations of the Mode Figure 4.7 shows a dot plot of P/E ratios (current stock price divided by the last 12 months' earnings) for a random sample of 44 Standard & Poor's 500 stocks (see Chapter 3, Table 3.2). Although P/E ratios are continuous, the data are rounded to the nearest integer.

FIGURE 4.7

Dot Plot for P/E Ratios
(*n* = 44 stocks)
PERatios

For these 44 observations, there are modes at 10 and 16 (each occurs four times), suggesting that these are somewhat "typical" P/E ratios. However, 11 and 13 occur three times, suggesting that the mode is not a robust measure of center for this data set. That is, we suspect that these modes would be unlikely to recur if we were to take a different sample of 44 stocks.

There may be a logical reason for the existence of modes. For example, points scored by winning college football teams on a given Saturday will tend to have modes at multiples of 7 (e.g., 7, 14, 21, etc.) because each touchdown yields 7 points (counting the extra point). Other mini-modes in football scores reflect commonly occurring combinations of scoring events. Figure 4.8 shows a dot plot of the points scored by the winning team in the first 95 Rose Bowl games (one game was a scoreless tie). The mode is 14 (occurs 10 times), but there are several other local modes. If you are a football fan, you can figure out, for example, why 20 points occur so often.

FIGURE 4.8

Dot Plot of Rose Bowl
Winners' Points
(*n* = 95 games)
RoseBowl

A **bimodal distribution** or a **multimodal distribution** occurs when dissimilar populations are combined into one sample. For example, if heights of 500 adult men and 500 adult women are combined into a single sample of 1,000 adults, we would get something like the second polygon in Figure 4.9.

Frequency Polygons of Heights of 1,000 Men and Women 📁 **Heights**

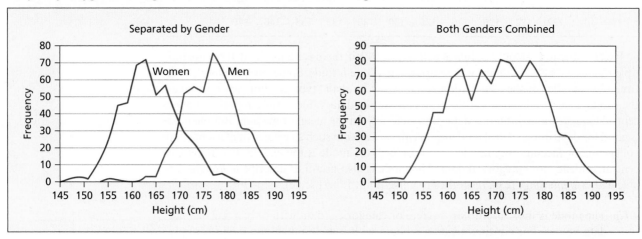

In such a case, the mean of all 1,000 adults would not represent central tendency for either gender. When heterogeneity is known to exist, it would be better to create separate histograms or frequency polygons and carry out the analysis on each group separately. Unfortunately, we don't always know when heterogeneous populations have been combined into one sample.

Shape

LO 4-1

Explain the concepts of center, variability, and shape.

The shape of a distribution may be judged by looking at the histogram or by comparing the mean and median. In **symmetric data**, the mean and median are about the same. When the data are **skewed right** (or **positively skewed**), the mean exceeds the median. When the data are **skewed left** (or **negatively skewed**), the mean is below the median. Figure 4.10 shows prototype population shapes showing varying degrees of **skewness**.

FIGURE 4.10

Skewness Prototype Populations

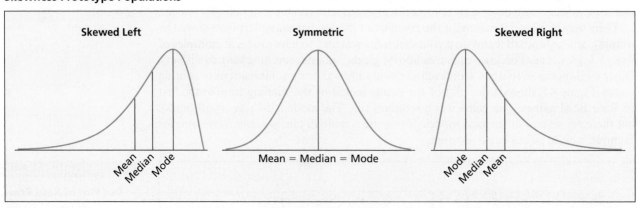

Table 4.5 summarizes the symptoms of skewness in a sample. Since few data sets are exactly symmetric, skewness is a matter of degree. Due to the nature of random sampling, the mean and median may differ, even when a symmetric population is being sampled. Small differences between the mean and median do not indicate significant skewness and may lack practical importance.

TABLE 4.5

Symptoms of Skewness

Distribution's Shape	Histogram Appearance	Statistics
Skewed left (negative skewness)	Long tail of histogram points left (a few low values but most data on right)	Mean < Median
Symmetric	Tails of histogram are balanced (low/high values offset)	Mean ≈ Median
Skewed right (positive skewness)	Long tail of histogram points right (most data on left but a few high values)	Mean > Median

For example, in Figure 4.11 the average spending per customer at 74 Noodles & Company restaurants appears somewhat right-skewed, so we would expect the mean to exceed the median. Actually, the difference is slight (using the spreadsheet raw data, the mean is $7.04 and the median is $7.00). The student GPA histogram in Figure 4.11 appears left-skewed, so we would expect the mean to be lower than the median. But again, the difference is slight (using the spreadsheet raw data, the mean is 3.17 and the median is 3.20). Since a histogram's appearance is affected by the way its bins are set up, its shape offers only a rough guide to skewness.

FIGURE 4.11

Histograms to Illustrate Skewness

For the sample of J.D. Power quality ratings, the mean (114.17) exceeds the median (113), which suggests right-skewness. However, this small difference between the mean and median may lack practical importance. The histograms in Figure 4.3 suggest that the skewness is minimal. In Section 4.8, we will introduce more precise tests for skewness.

Business data tend to be right-skewed because financial variables often are unlimited at the top but are bounded from below by zero (e.g., salaries, employees, inventory). This is also true for engineering data (e.g., time to failure, defect rates) and sports (e.g., scores in soccer). Even in a Likert scale (1, 2, 3, 4, 5) a few responses in the opposite tail can skew the mean if most replies are clustered toward the top or bottom of the scale.

Descriptive Statistics in Excel

As shown in Figure 4.12, select the Data tab and click the Data Analysis icon (on the far right side of the top menu). When the Data Analysis menu appears, select Descriptive Statistics. On the Descriptive Statistics menu form, click anywhere inside the Input Range field, then highlight the data block (in this case C4:C37). Specify a destination cell for the upper left corner of the output range (cell K1 in this example). Notice that we checked the Labels in first row box, since cell C4 is actually a column heading that will be used to label the output in cell K1. Check the Summary Statistics box and then click OK. The resulting statistics are shown in Figure 4.12. You probably recognize some of them (e.g., mean, median, mode) and the others will be covered later in this chapter.

LO 4-2

Use Excel to obtain descriptive statistics and visual displays.

FIGURE 4.12

Excel's Data Analysis and Descriptive Statistics JDPower

Note: If Data Analysis does not appear on the upper right of the Data tab, click File in the extreme upper left corner, select Add-Ins, and then check the box for Analysis ToolPak.

Descriptive Statistics Using MegaStat

You can get similar statistics (and more) from MegaStat as illustrated in Figure 4.13. Click the Add-Ins tab on the top menu, and then click on the MegaStat icon (left side of the top menu in this example). On the list of MegaStat procedures, click Descriptive Statistics. On the new menu, enter the data range (in this case C4:C37) in the Input range field (or highlight the data block on the worksheet. You can see that MegaStat offers you many statistics, plus some visual displays such as a dot plot, stem-and-leaf, and other graphs. We have only chosen a few of them for this illustration. MegaStat output normally appears on a separate worksheet, but the results have been copied to the data worksheet so that everything can be seen

FIGURE 4.13

MegaStat's Descriptive Statistics JDPower

Note: MegaStat is available as a download from the OLC. Instructions for installing MegaStat as an Add-In are found on the last page of Chapter 3.

in one picture. Try using both Excel and MegaStat to see the similarities and differences in their interfaces and results. At the end of this chapter, look for a list of Online Learning Center (OLC) PowerPoint demonstrations and ScreenCam tutorials with more detailed explanations of how to use Excel and MegaStat for statistical data description.

Descriptive Statistics Using MINITAB

MINITAB is a comprehensive software system for statistical analysis. It has nothing to do with Excel, although you can copy data from Excel to MINITAB's worksheet (and vice versa). You can get a wide range of statistics and attractive graphs from MINITAB. Although MINITAB is not on the textbook CD, it is widely available at colleges and universities. This textbook emphasizes Excel and MegaStat, but it is wise to learn about other software that may give you just the result you want (or in a more attractive form), so we will show MINITAB results when they are appropriate. The OLC resources at www.mhhe.com/doane4e/ include a PowerPoint demonstration with more detailed explanations of how to use MINITAB. Figure 4.14 shows MINITAB's menus and a graphical summary of descriptive statistics for the J.D. Power data.

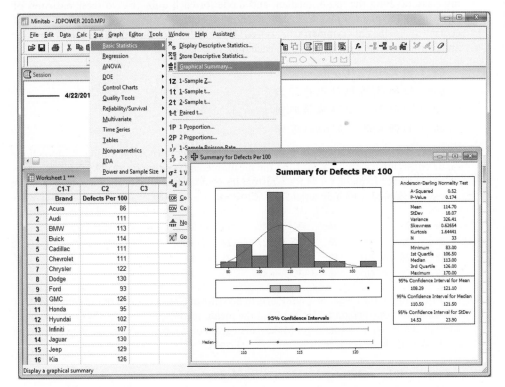

FIGURE 4.14

MINITAB's Basic Statistics > Graphical Summary

4.1   (a) For each data set, find the mean, median, and mode. (b) Discuss anything about the data that affects the usefulness of each statistic as a measure of center.

    a. Class absences (12 students):   0, 0, 0, 0, 0, 1, 2, 3, 3, 5, 5, 15
    b. Exam scores (9 students):   40, 40, 65, 71, 72, 75, 76, 78, 98
    c. GPAs (8 students):   2.25, 2.55, 2.95, 3.02, 3.04, 3.37, 3.51, 3.66

4.2   For each data set, is the mode a good measure of center? Explain.

    a. Genders of 12 CEOs: M, M, F, M, F, M, M, M, F, M, M, M
    b. Ages of 10 college freshmen: 17, 17, 18, 18, 18, 18, 18, 18, 19, 20
    c. Ages of 8 MBA students: 24, 26, 27, 28, 30, 31, 33, 37

4.3   For each data set, which best indicates a "typical" data value (mean, median, either)?

    a. MPG for 7 Honda Civics: 21.8, 24.1, 24.6, 26.2, 28.4, 35.2, 36.3
    b. Number of riders in 8 cars: 1, 1, 1, 1, 1, 1, 4, 6
    c. Diners at 10 restaurant tables: 1, 2, 2, 2, 3, 3, 4, 4, 4, 5

SECTION EXERCISES

connect

4.4   Days on the market are shown for the 36 most recent home sales in the city of Sonando Hills. (a) Calculate the mean, median, and mode. (b) Is the distribution skewed? Explain. (c) Is the mode a useful measure of center for this data set? 🖾 **Homes**

18	70	52	17	86	121	86	3	66
96	41	50	176	26	28	6	55	21
43	20	56	71	57	16	20	30	31
44	44	92	179	80	98	44	66	15

4.5   Scores are shown for the most recent state civil service exam taken by 24 applicants for positions in law enforcement. (a) Calculate the mean, median, and mode. (b) Is the distribution skewed? Explain. (c) Is the mode a useful measure of center for this data set? 🖾 **Civil**

83	93	74	98	85	82	79	78
82	68	67	82	78	83	70	99
18	96	93	62	64	93	27	58

4.6   Prof. Hardtack gave four Friday quizzes last semester in his 10-student senior tax accounting class. (a) Find the mean, median, and mode for each quiz. (b) Do these measures of center agree? Explain. (c) For each data set, note strengths or weaknesses of each statistic of center. (d) Are the data symmetric or skewed? If skewed, which direction? (e) Briefly describe and compare student performance on each quiz. 🖾 **Quizzes**

Quiz 1: 60, 60, 60, 60, 71, 73, 74, 75, 88, 99

Quiz 2: 65, 65, 65, 65, 70, 74, 79, 79, 79, 79

Quiz 3: 66, 67, 70, 71, 72, 72, 74, 74, 95, 99

Quiz 4: 10, 49, 70, 80, 85, 88, 90, 93, 97, 98

4.7   CitiBank recorded the number of customers to use a downtown ATM during the noon hour on 32 consecutive workdays. (a) Find the mean, median, and mode. (b) Do these measures of center agree? Explain. (c) Make a histogram or dot plot. (d) Are the data symmetric or skewed? If skewed, which direction? 🖾 **CitiBank**

25	37	23	26	30	40	25	26
39	32	21	26	19	27	32	25
18	26	34	18	31	35	21	33
33	9	16	32	35	42	15	24

4.8   On Friday night, the owner of Chez Pierre in downtown Chicago noted the amount spent for dinner for 28 four-person tables. (a) Find the mean, median, and mode. (b) Do these measures of center agree? Explain. (c) Make a histogram or dot plot. (d) Are the data symmetric or skewed? If skewed, which direction? 🖾 **Dinner**

95	103	109	170	114	113	107
124	105	80	104	84	176	115
69	95	134	108	61	160	128
68	95	61	150	52	87	136

4.9   An executive's telephone log showed the lengths of 65 calls initiated during the last week of July. (a) Sort the data. (b) Find the mean, median, and mode. (c) Do the measures of center agree? Explain. (d) Are the data symmetric or skewed? If skewed, which direction? 🖾 **CallLength**

1	2	10	5	3	3	2	20	1	1
6	3	13	2	2	1	26	3	1	3
1	2	1	7	1	2	3	1	2	12
1	4	2	2	29	1	1	1	8	5
1	4	2	1	1	1	1	6	1	2
3	3	6	1	3	1	1	5	1	18
2	13	13	1	6					

Mini Case   4.1

ATM Deposits

Table 4.6 shows a sorted random sample of 100 deposits at an ATM located in the student union on a college campus. The sample was selected at random from 1,459 deposits in one 30-day month. Deposits range from $3 to $1,341. The dot plot shown in Figure 4.15 indicates a right-skewed distribution with a few large values in the right tail and a strong clustering on the left (i.e., most ATM deposits are small). Excel's Descriptive Statistics indicate a very skewed distribution, since the mean (233.89) greatly exceeds the median (135). The mode (100) is somewhat "typical," occurring five times. However, 40 and 50 each occurs four times (mini-modes).

TABLE 4.6		100 ATM Deposits (dollars)		ATMDeposits							
3	10	15	15	20	20	20	22	23	25	26	26
30	30	35	35	36	39	40	40	40	40	47	50
50	50	50	53	55	60	60	60	67	75	78	86
90	96	100	100	100	100	100	103	105	118	125	125
130	131	139	140	145	150	150	153	153	156	160	163
170	176	185	198	200	200	200	220	232	237	252	259
260	268	270	279	295	309	345	350	366	375	431	433
450	450	474	484	495	553	600	720	777	855	960	987
1,020	1,050	1,200	1,341								

Source: Michigan State University Federal Credit Union.

FIGURE 4.15   **Dot Plot for ATM Deposits (*n* = 100)**

Geometric Mean

The **geometric mean** (denoted *G*) is a multiplicative average, obtained by multiplying the data values and then taking the *n*th root of the product. This is a measure of central tendency used when all the data values are positive (greater than zero).

LO 4-3

Calculate and interpret common measures of center.

$$G = \sqrt[n]{x_1 x_2 \cdots x_n} \quad \text{for the geometric mean} \tag{4.4}$$

For example, the geometric mean for *X* = 2, 3, 7, 9, 10, 12 is:

$$G = \sqrt[6]{(2)(3)(7)(9)(10)(12)} = \sqrt[6]{45,360} = 5.972$$

The product of *n* numbers can be quite large. For the J.D. Power quality data:

$$G = \sqrt[33]{(83)(86)(87) \cdots (135)(146)(170)} = \sqrt[33]{6.25105 \times 10^{67}} = 113.35$$

The calculation is easy using Excel's function =GEOMEAN(Data). Scientific calculators have a y^x key whose inverse permits taking the *n*th root needed to calculate *G*. However, if the data values are large, the product can exceed the calculator's capacity. The geometric mean tends to mitigate the effects of high outliers.

Growth Rates

We can use a variation on the geometric mean to find the *average growth rate* for a time series (e.g., sales in a growing company):

(4.5) $$GR = \sqrt[n-1]{\frac{x_n}{x_1}} - 1 \qquad \text{(average growth rate of a time series)}$$

For example, from 2006 to 2010, JetBlue Airlines' revenues grew as shown in Table 4.7.

	Year	Revenue
TABLE 4.7		
	2006	2,361
JetBlue Airlines Revenue	2007	2,843
(millions of dollars)	2008	3,392
JetBlue	2009	3,292
	2010	3,779

Source: http://money.msn.com. Data are for December 31 of each year.

The *average growth rate* is given by taking the geometric mean of the ratios of each year's revenue to the preceding year. However, due to cancellations, only the first and last years are relevant:

$$GR = \sqrt[4]{\left(\frac{2843}{2361}\right)\left(\frac{3392}{2843}\right)\left(\frac{3292}{3392}\right)\left(\frac{3779}{3292}\right)} - 1 = \sqrt[4]{\frac{3779}{2361}} = 1.125 - 1 = 0.125$$

or 12.5 percent per year. In Excel, we could use the formula =(3779/2361)^(1/4)−1 to get the same result.

Midrange

The **midrange** is the point halfway between the lowest and highest values of X. It is easy to calculate but is not a robust measure of central tendency because it is sensitive to extreme data values. It is useful when you only have x_{min} and x_{max}.

(4.6) $$\text{Midrange} = \frac{x_{min} + x_{max}}{2}$$

For the J.D. Power data:

$$\text{Midrange} = \frac{x_1 + x_{33}}{2} = \frac{83 + 170}{2} = 126.5$$

For the J.D. Power data, the midrange is higher than the mean (114.70) or median (113), and is a dubious measure of center because it is "pulled up" by one high data value $x_{max} = 170$.

Trimmed Mean

The **trimmed mean** is calculated like any other mean, except that the highest and lowest k percent of the observations in the sorted data array are removed. The trimmed mean mitigates the effects of extreme high values on either end. For a 5 percent trimmed mean, the Excel function is =TRIMMEAN(Data, 0.10) because .05 + .05 = .10. For the J.D. Power data ($n = 33$), we would remove only one observation from each end because .05 × 33 = 1.65 = 1 (truncated to the next *lower* integer) and then take the average of the middle 31 observations.

Excel's measures of center for the J.D. Power data:

Mean:	=AVERAGE(Data)	= 114.70
Median:	=MEDIAN(Data)	= 113
Mode:	=MODE.SNGL(Data)	= 111
Geo Mean:	=GEOMEAN(Data)	= 113.35
Midrange:	=(MIN(Data)+MAX(Data))/2	= 126.5
5% Trim Mean:	=TRIMMEAN(Data,0.1)	= 113.94

FIGURE 4.16

16 Percent Trimmed-Mean for CPI

Source: Federal Reserve Bank of Cleveland, www.clevelandfed.org

The Federal Reserve uses a 16 percent trimmed mean to mitigate the effect of extremes in its analysis of trends in the Consumer Price Index, as illustrated in Figure 4.16.

Mini Case   4.2

Prices of Lipitor®

Prescription drug prices vary across the United States and even among pharmacies in the same city. A consumer research group examined prices for a 30-day supply of Lipitor® (a cholesterol-lowering prescription drug) in three U.S. cities at various pharmacies. Attention has recently been focused on prices of such drugs because recent medical research has suggested more aggressive treatment of high cholesterol levels in patients at risk for heart disease. This poses an economic issue for government because Medicare is expected to pay some of the cost of prescription drugs. It is also an issue for Pfizer, the maker of Lipitor®, who expects a fair return on its investments in research and patents. Finally, it is an issue for consumers who seek to shop wisely.

From the dot plots in Figure 4.17, we gain an impression of the *variability* of the data (the *range* of prices for each drug) as well as the *center* of the data (the middle or typical data values). Lipitor® prices vary from about $60 to about $91 and typically are in the $70s. The dot plots suggest that Providence tends to have higher prices, and New Orleans lower prices, though there is considerable variation among pharmacies.

FIGURE 4.17 **Dot Plots for Lipitor® Prices**

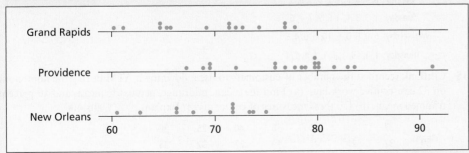

In Table 4.8, the measures of center unanimously say that Providence has higher prices. New Orleans and Grand Rapids are similar, although Grand Rapids has slightly higher prices. The means and medians for each city are similar, suggesting no significant skewness. Because these are decimal data values, the mode is not appropriate, and is therefore omitted.

TABLE 4.8	Measures of Center for Lipitor® Prices 🖅 Lipitor		
Statistic	**New Orleans**	**Providence**	**Grand Rapids**
Sample size	12	20	15
Mean	69.27	77.54	69.73
Median	70.70	78.75	71.56
Geometric mean	69.14	77.33	69.51
Midrange	67.77	79.18	69.19
5% Trim mean	69.57	77.36	69.81

Source: Survey by the Public Interest Research Group (www.pirg.org) in March/April 2003. Prices were studied for 10 drugs in 555 pharmacies in 48 cities in 19 states. Public Interest Research Groups are an alliance of state-based, citizen-funded advocacy organizations that seek to protect the environment, encourage a fair marketplace for consumers, and foster responsive, democratic government. Data used with permission. Mode is omitted (decimal data).

SECTION EXERCISES

connect

4.10 (a) For each data set, find the median, midrange, and geometric mean. (b) Are they reasonable measures of central tendency? Explain.

    a. Exam scores (9 students)   42, 55, 65, 67, 68, 75, 76, 78, 94
    b. GPAs (8 students)   2.25, 2.55, 2.95, 3.02, 3.04, 3.37, 3.51, 3.66
    c. Class absences (12 students)   0, 0, 0, 0, 0, 1, 2, 3, 3, 5, 5, 15

4.11 (a) Write the Excel function for the 10 percent trimmed mean of a data set in cells A1:A50. (b) How many observations would be trimmed in each tail? (c) How many would be trimmed overall?

4.12 In the Excel function =TRIMMEAN(Data,.10), how many observations would be trimmed from each end of the sorted data array named Data if (a) $n = 41$, (b) $n = 66$, and (c) $n = 83$?

4.13 The city of Sonando Hills has 8 police officers. In January, the work-related medical expenses for each officer were 0, 0, 0, 0, 0, 0, 150, 650. (a) Calculate the mean, median, mode, midrange, and geometric mean. (b) Which measure of center would you use to budget the expected medical expenses for the whole year by all officers?

4.14 Spirit Airlines kept track of the number of empty seats on flight 308 (DEN–DTW) for 10 consecutive trips on each weekday except Friday. (a) Sort the data for each day. (b) Find the mean, median, mode, midrange, geometric mean, and 10 percent trimmed mean (i.e., dropping the first and last sorted observations) for each day. (c) Do the measures of center agree? Explain. (d) Note strengths or weaknesses of each statistic of center for the data. 🖅 **EmptySeats**

      Monday: 6, 1, 5, 9, 1, 1, 6, 5, 5, 1
      Tuesday: 1, 3, 3, 1, 4, 6, 9, 7, 7, 6
   Wednesday: 6, 0, 6, 0, 6, 10, 0, 0, 4, 6
     Thursday: 1, 1, 10, 1, 1, 1, 1, 1, 1, 1

4.15 CitiBank recorded the number of customers to use a downtown ATM during the noon hour on 32 consecutive workdays. (a) Find the mean, midrange, geometric mean, and 10 percent trimmed mean. (b) Do these measures of center agree? Explain. 🖅 **CitiBank**

25	37	23	26	30	40	25	26
39	32	21	26	19	27	32	25
18	26	34	18	31	35	21	33
33	9	16	32	35	42	15	24

4.16   On Friday night, the owner of Chez Pierre in downtown Chicago noted the amount spent for dinner at 28 four-person tables. (a) Find the mean, midrange, geometric mean, and 10 percent trimmed mean. (b) Do these measures of center agree? Explain.   📁 **Dinner**

95	103	109	170	114	113	107
124	105	80	104	84	176	115
69	95	134	108	61	160	128
68	95	61	150	52	87	136

4.17   An executive's telephone log showed the lengths of 65 calls initiated during the last week of July. (a) Find the mean, median, mode, midrange, geometric mean, and 10 percent trimmed mean. (b) Are the data symmetric or skewed? If skewed, which direction?   📁 **CallLength**

1	2	10	5	3	3	2	20	1	1
6	3	13	2	2	1	26	3	1	3
1	2	1	7	1	2	3	1	2	12
1	4	2	2	29	1	1	1	8	5
1	4	2	1	1	1	1	6	1	2
3	3	6	1	3	1	1	5	1	18
2	13	13	1	6					

4.18   The number of Internet users in Latin America grew from 78.5 million in 2000 to 156.6 million in 2010. Use the geometric mean to find the annual growth rate. *Source:* www.internetworldstats.com (accessed April 5, 2011).

4.3 MEASURES OF VARIABILITY

We can use a statistic such as the mean to describe the *center* of a distribution. But it is just as important to look at how individual data values vary around the mean. For example, if two *NYSE* stocks *A* and *B* have the same mean return over the last 100 trading days, but *A* has more day-to-day variation, then the portfolio manager who wants a stable investment would prefer *B*. Or consider possible sample distributions of study time spent by several college students taking an economics class:

LO 4-4

Calculate and interpret common measures of variability.

Each diagram has the same mean, but they differ in dispersion around the mean. The problem is: how do we *describe* variability in a sample? Because different variables have different means and different units of measurement (dollars, pounds, yen), we are looking for measures of variability that can be applied to many situations.

Histograms and dot plots tell us something about variation in a data set (the "spread" of data points about the center), but formal measures of dispersion are needed. Table 4.9 lists several common measures of variability. All formulas shown are for sample data sets.

Range

The **range** is the difference between the largest and smallest observations:

$$\text{Range} = x_{\max} - x_{\min} \qquad \textbf{(4.7)}$$

For the J.D. Power data the range is:

$$\text{Range} = 170 - 83 = 87$$

TABLE 4.9		Five Measures of Variability for a Sample			
Statistic	Formula	Excel*	Pro	Con	
Range (R)	$x_{max} - x_{min}$	=MAX(Data)-MIN(Data)	Easy to calculate and easy to interpret.	Sensitive to extreme data values.	
Sample variance (s^2)	$\dfrac{\sum\limits_{i=1}^{n}(x_i - \bar{x})^2}{n - 1}$	=VAR.S(Data)	Plays a key role in mathematical statistics.	Less intuitive meaning.	
Sample standard deviation (s)	$\sqrt{\dfrac{\sum\limits_{i=1}^{n}(x_i - \bar{x})^2}{n - 1}}$	=STDEV.S(Data)	Most common measure. Same units as the raw data ($, £, ¥, grams, etc.).	Less intuitive meaning.	
Coefficient of variation (CV)	$100 \times \dfrac{s}{\bar{x}}$	None	Expresses relative variation in *percent* so can compare data sets with different units of measurement.	Requires nonnegative data.	
Mean absolute deviation (MAD)	$\dfrac{\sum\limits_{i=1}^{n}|x_i - \bar{x}|}{n}$	=AVEDEV(Data)	Easy to understand.	Lacks "nice" theoretical properties.	

*Excel 2010's sample functions =VAR.S(Data) and =STDEV.S(Data) give the same results as the older functions =VAR(Data) and =STDEV(Data). These Excel 2010 functions will not work in previous versions of Excel, but the old functions work in all versions of Excel as of the publication date of this textbook.

Although it is easy to calculate, a drawback of the range is that it only considers the two extreme data values. It seems desirable to seek a broad-based measure of variability that is based on *all* the data values $x_1, x_2, \ldots, x_n$.

Variance and Standard Deviation

If we calculate the differences between each data value x_i and the mean, we would have both positive and negative differences. The mean is the balancing point of the distribution, so if we just sum these differences and take the average, we will always get zero, which obviously doesn't give us a useful measure of variability. One way to avoid this is to *square* the differences before we find the average. Following this logic, the **population variance** (denoted σ^2, where σ is the lowercase Greek letter "sigma") is defined as the sum of squared deviations from the mean divided by the population size:

$$\text{(4.8)} \qquad \sigma^2 = \frac{\sum\limits_{i=1}^{N}(x_i - \mu)^2}{N}$$

If we have a sample (i.e., most of the time), we replace μ with $\bar{x}$ to get the **sample variance** (denoted s^2):

$$\text{(4.9)} \qquad s^2 = \frac{\sum\limits_{i=1}^{n}(x_i - \bar{x})^2}{n - 1}$$

A variance is basically a mean squared deviation. But why then do we divide by $n - 1$ instead of n when using sample data? This question perplexes many students. A sample contains n pieces of information, each of which can have any value, independently from the others. But once you have calculated the sample mean (as you must in order to find the variance), there are only $n - 1$ pieces of independent information left (since the sample values must add to a fixed total that gives the mean). We divide the sum of squared deviations by $n - 1$ instead of n because we have "lost" one piece of information. Otherwise, s^2 would tend to underestimate the unknown population variance σ^2.

In describing variability, we most often use the **standard deviation** (the square root of the variance). The standard deviation is a single number that helps us understand how individual values in a data set vary from the mean. Because the square root has been taken, its units of measurement are the same as X (e.g., dollars, kilograms, miles). To find the standard deviation of a population we use:

$$\sigma = \sqrt{\frac{\sum_{i=1}^{N}(x_i - \mu)^2}{N}} \qquad (4.10)$$

and for the standard deviation of a sample:

$$s = \sqrt{\frac{\sum_{i=1}^{n}(x_i - \bar{x})^2}{n - 1}} \qquad (4.11)$$

Many inexpensive calculators have built-in formulas for the standard deviation. To distinguish between the population and sample formulas, some calculators have one function key labeled σ_x and another labeled s_x. Others have one key labeled σ_n and another labeled σ_{n-1}. The only question is whether to divide the numerator by the number of data items or the number of data items minus one. Computers and calculators don't know whether your data are a sample or a population. They will use whichever formula you request. It is up to you to know which is appropriate for your data. Excel has built-in functions for these calculations:

	Excel 2010		Pre-2010 Excel	
	Sample	*Population*	*Sample*	*Population*
Variance	=VAR.S(Data)	=VAR.P(Data)	=VAR(Data)	=VARP(Data)
Std deviation	=STDEV.S(Data)	=STDEV.P(Data)	=STDEV(Data)	=STDEVP(Data)

Calculating a Standard Deviation

Table 4.10 illustrates the calculation of a standard deviation using Stephanie's scores on five quizzes (40, 55, 75, 95, 95). Her mean is 72.

i	x_i	$x_i - \bar{x}$	$(x_i - \bar{x})^2$	x_i^2
1	40	$40 - 72 = -32$	$(-32)^2 = 1{,}024$	$40^2 = 1{,}600$
2	55	$55 - 72 = -17$	$(-17)^2 = 289$	$55^2 = 3{,}025$
3	75	$75 - 72 = +3$	$(3)^2 = 9$	$75^2 = 5{,}625$
4	95	$95 - 72 = +23$	$(23)^2 = 529$	$95^2 = 9{,}025$
5	95	$95 - 72 = +23$	$(23)^2 = 529$	$95^2 = 9{,}025$
Sum	360	0	2,380	28,300
Mean	72			

TABLE 4.10

Worksheet for Standard Deviation Stephanie

Notice that the deviations around the mean (column three) sum to zero, an important property of the mean. Because the mean is rarely a "nice" number, such calculations typically require a spreadsheet or a calculator. Stephanie's sample standard deviation is:

$$s = \sqrt{\frac{\sum_{i=1}^{n}(x_i - \bar{x})^2}{n - 1}} = \sqrt{\frac{2{,}380}{5 - 1}} = \sqrt{595} = 24.39$$

Alternatively, the **two-sum formula** can also be used to calculate the standard deviation:

$$s = \sqrt{\frac{\sum_{i=1}^{n}x_i^2 - \frac{\left(\sum_{i=1}^{n}x_i\right)^2}{n}}{n - 1}} \qquad (4.12)$$

This formula avoids calculating the mean and subtracting it from each observation. Scientific calculators use this formula and also give the sums $\sum_{i=1}^{n} x_i$ and $\sum_{i=1}^{n} x_i^2$. For Stephanie's five quiz scores, using the sums shown in Table 4.10, we get the same result as from the definitional formula:

$$s = \sqrt{\frac{\sum_{i=1}^{n} x_i^2 - \frac{\left(\sum_{i=1}^{n} x_i\right)^2}{n}}{n - 1}} = \sqrt{\frac{28,300 - \frac{(360)^2}{5}}{5 - 1}} = \sqrt{\frac{28,300 - 25,920}{5 - 1}} = \sqrt{595} = 24.39$$

Because it is less intuitive (and because we usually rely on spreadsheets, calculators, or statistical software), some textbooks omit the two-sum formula. For business data, either formula should be OK.

Characteristics of the Standard Deviation

The standard deviation is nonnegative because the deviations around the mean are squared. When every observation is exactly equal to the mean, then the standard deviation is zero (i.e., there is no variation). For example, if every student received the same score on an exam, the numerators of formulas 4.8 through 4.12 would be zero because every student would be at the mean. At the other extreme, the greatest dispersion would be if the data were concentrated at x_{min} and x_{max} (e.g., if half the class scored 0 and the other half scored 100).

But the standard deviation can have any nonnegative value, depending on the unit of measurement. For example, yields on n randomly chosen investment bond funds (e.g., Westcore Plus at 7.2 percent in 2010) would have a small standard deviation compared to annual revenues of n randomly chosen Fortune 500 corporations (e.g., Walmart at $429 billion in 2010).

Standard deviations can be compared *only* for data sets measured in the same units. For example, prices of hotel rooms in Tokyo (yen) cannot be compared with prices of hotel rooms in Paris (euros). Also, standard deviations should not be compared if the means differ substantially, even when the units of measurement are the same. For instance, weights of apples (ounces) have a smaller mean than weights of watermelons (ounces).

Standard Deviation Used to Compare Risks

"Generally speaking, standard deviation is how much an investment's returns have varied historically from its average. The statistical measure is usually computed using monthly returns for the most recent three-year period . . . Standard deviation can be useful when comparing the investment risk of various mutual funds. If two funds have similar average returns but different standard deviations, the fund with the higher standard deviation is the more volatile of the two."

From *T. Rowe Price Investor,* September 2009, p. 8. Used with permission.

Coefficient of Variation

To compare dispersion in data sets with dissimilar units of measurement (e.g., kilograms and ounces) or dissimilar means (e.g., home prices in two different cities), we define the **coefficient of variation** (CV), which is a unit-free measure of dispersion:

(4.13) $CV = 100 \times \frac{s}{\bar{x}}$

The *CV* is the standard deviation expressed as a percent of the mean. In some data sets, the standard deviation can actually exceed the mean, so the *CV* can exceed 100 percent. The *CV* is useful for comparing variables measured in different units. For example:

Defect rates: $s = 24.94$, $\bar{x} = 134.51$ $CV = 100 \times (24.94)/(134.51) = 19\%$

ATM deposits: $s = 280.80$, $\bar{x} = 233.89$ $CV = 100 \times (280.80)/(233.89) = 120\%$

P/E ratios: $s = 14.08$, $\bar{x} = 22.72$ $CV = 100 \times (14.08)/(22.72) = 62\%$

Despite the different units of measurement, we can say that ATM deposits have much greater relative dispersion (120 percent) than either defect rates (18 percent) or P/E ratios (62 percent). The chief weakness of the *CV* is that it is undefined if the mean is zero or negative, so it is appropriate only for positive data.

Mean Absolute Deviation

An additional measure of dispersion is the **mean absolute deviation** (*MAD*). This statistic reveals the average distance from the center. Absolute values must be used since otherwise the deviations around the mean would sum to zero.

$$MAD = \frac{\sum_{i=1}^{n}|x_i - \bar{x}|}{n}$$

(4.14)

The *MAD* is appealing because of its simple, concrete interpretation. Using the lever analogy, the *MAD* tells us what the average distance is from an individual data point to the fulcrum. Excel's function =AVEDEV(Data) will calculate the *MAD*.

Mini Case   4.3

Bear Markets

Investors know that stock prices have extended cycles of downturns ("bear markets") or upturns ("bull markets"). But how long must an investor be prepared to wait for the cycle to end? Table 4.11 shows the duration of 15 bear markets since 1929 and the decline in the S&P 500 stock index.

TABLE 4.11   Duration of 15 Bear Markets   BearMarkets

Peak	Trough	Duration (months)	S&P Loss (%)
Sep 1929	Jun 1932	34	83.4
Jun 1946	Apr 1947	11	21.0
Aug 1956	Feb 1957	7	10.2
Aug 1957	Dec 1957	5	15.0
Jan 1962	Jun 1962	6	22.3
Feb 1966	Sep 1966	8	15.6
Dec 1968	Jun 1970	19	29.3
Jan 1973	Sep 1974	21	42.6
Jan 1977	Feb 1978	14	14.1
Dec 1980	Jul 1982	20	16.9
Sep 1987	Nov 1987	3	29.5
Jun 1990	Oct 1990	5	14.7
Jul 1998	Aug 1998	2	15.4
Sep 2000	Mar 2003	31	42.0
Oct 2007	Mar 2009	17	50.6

Source: TIAA/CREF, *Balance*, Summer 2004, p. 15. Downturns are defined as a loss in value of 10 percent or more. Standard & Poor's 500 stock index and S&P 500 are registered trademarks. Calculations for the bear market that began in 2007 are based on a 30-day trailing moving average of the S&P 500 index.

Figure 4.18 shows that bear markets typically are short-lived (under 1 year) but may last nearly 3 years. S&P losses generally are in the 10–40 percent range, with one notable exception (the 1929 crash).

FIGURE 4.18   **Dot Plots of Bear Market Measurements**

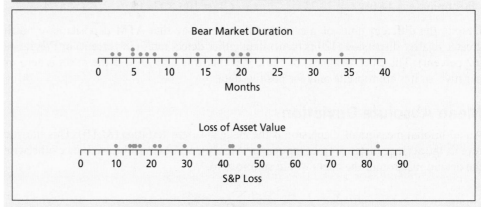

Table 4.12 shows that both duration (months) and S&P loss (percent) are right-skewed (mean substantially exceeding median) and have similar coefficients of variation. The other measures of center and variability cannot be compared because the units of measurement differ.

TABLE 4.12   **Statistical Summary of 15 Bear Markets**

Statistic	Duration (months)	S&P Loss (%)
Count	15	15
Mean	13.53	28.173
Median	11.00	21.000
Sample variance	99.27	383.266
Sample standard deviation	9.96	19.577
Minimum	2	10.2
Maximum	34	83.4
Range	32	73.2
Coefficient of variation	73.6%	69.5%
Mean absolute deviation (MAD)	8.17	14.45

SECTION EXERCISES

connect

4.19 (a) Find the mean and standard deviation for each sample. (b) What does this exercise show about the standard deviation?

Sample A: 6, 7, 8

Sample B: 61, 62, 63

Sample C: 1000, 1001, 1002

4.20 For each data set: (a) Find the mean. (b) Find the standard deviation, treating the data as a sample. (c) Find the standard deviation, treating the data as a population. (d) What does this exercise show about the two formulas?

Data Set A: 6, 7, 8

Data Set B: 4, 5, 6, 7, 8, 9, 10

Data Set C: 1, 2, 3, 4, 5, 6, 7, 8, 9, 10, 11, 12, 13

4.21   In fuel economy tests in city driving conditions, a hybrid vehicle's mean was 43.2 mpg with a standard deviation of 2.2 mpg. A comparably sized gasoline vehicle's mean was 27.2 mpg with a standard deviation of 1.9 mpg. Which vehicle's mpg was more consistent in relative terms?

4.22   Find the mean absolute deviation (MAD) of these five numbers: 12, 18, 21, 22, 27.

4.23   (a) Find the coefficient of variation for prices of these three stocks. (b) Which stock has the greatest relative variation? (c) To measure variability, why not just compare the standard deviations?

> Stock A: $\bar{x}$ = $24.50, s = 5.25
>
> Stock B: $\bar{x}$ = $147.25, s = 12.25
>
> Stock C: $\bar{x}$ = $5.75, s = 2.08

4.24   Prof. Hardtack gave four Friday quizzes last semester in his 10-student senior tax accounting class. (a) Find the sample mean, standard deviation, and coefficient of variation for each quiz. (b) How do these data sets differ in terms of center and variability? (c) Briefly describe and compare student performance on each quiz. 📄 **Quizzes**

> Quiz 1: 60, 60, 60, 60, 71, 73, 74, 75, 88, 99
>
> Quiz 2: 65, 65, 65, 65, 70, 74, 79, 79, 79, 79
>
> Quiz 3: 66, 67, 70, 71, 72, 72, 74, 74, 95, 99
>
> Quiz 4: 10, 49, 70, 80, 85, 88, 90, 93, 97, 98

4.25   Noodles and Company tested consumer reaction to two spaghetti sauces. Each of 70 raters assessed both sauces on a scale of 1 (worst) to 10 (best) using several taste criteria. To correct for possible bias in tasting order, half the raters tasted *Sauce A* first, while the other half tasted *Sauce B* first. Actual results are shown below for "overall liking." (a) Calculate the mean and standard deviation for each sample. (b) Calculate the coefficient of variation for each sample. (c) What is your conclusion about consumer preferences for the two sauces? (Source: Noodles and Company) 📄 **Spaghetti**

Sauce A:

6, 7, 7, 8, 8, 6, 8, 6, 8, 7, 8, 8, 6, 8, 7, 7, 7, 8, 8, 8, 7, 7, 6, 7, 7,
8, 3, 8, 8, 7, 8, 6, 7, 8, 7, 7, 3, 6, 8, 7, 1, 8, 8, 7, 6, 7, 7, 4, 8, 8,
3, 8, 7, 7, 7, 5, 7, 7, 7, 9, 5, 7, 6, 8, 8, 8, 4, 5, 9, 8

Sauce B:

7, 7, 7, 8, 8, 7, 8, 6, 8, 7, 7, 6, 7, 7, 8, 7, 8, 7, 8, 8, 7, 8, 5, 7, 7,
9, 4, 8, 8, 7, 8, 8, 8, 8, 7, 7, 3, 7, 9, 8, 9, 7, 8, 8, 6, 7, 7, 7, 8, 8,
7, 7, 8, 6, 6, 7, 7, 9, 7, 9, 8, 8, 6, 7, 7, 9, 4, 4, 9, 8

Mini Case   4.4

What Is the DJIA? 📄 DJIA

The Dow Jones Industrial Average (commonly called the DJIA) is the oldest U.S. stock market price index, based on the prices of 30 large, widely held, and actively traded "blue chip" public companies in the United States (e.g., Coca-Cola, Microsoft, Walmart, Walt Disney). Actually, only a few of its 30 component companies are "industrial." The DJIA is measured in "points" rather than dollars. Originally, a simple mean of stock prices, the DJIA now is the sum of the 30 stock prices divided by a "divisor" to compensate for stock splits and other changes over time. The divisor is revised as often as necessary (see www.djindexes.com/mdsidx or www.cbot.com for the latest value). Since high-priced stocks comprise a larger proportion of the sum, the DJIA is more strongly affected by changes in high-priced stocks. That is, a 10 percent price increase in a $10 stock would have less effect than a 10 percent price increase in a $50 stock, even if both companies have the same total market capitalization (the total number of shares times the price per share; often referred to as "market cap"). Broad-based market price indexes (e.g., NSDQ, AMEX, NYSE, S&P 500, Russ 2K) are widely used by fund managers, but the venerable "Dow" is still the one you see first on CNN or MSNBC.

Center versus Variability

LO 4-1

Explain the concepts of center, variability, and shape.

Figure 4.19 shows histograms of hole diameters drilled in a steel plate during a manufacturing process. The desired distribution is shown in red. The samples from Machine *A* have the desired *mean* diameter (5 mm) but too much *variation* around the mean. It might be an older machine whose moving parts have become loose through normal wear, so there is greater variation in the holes drilled. Samples from Machine *B* have acceptable *variation* in hole diameter, but the *mean* is incorrectly adjusted (less than the desired 5 mm). To monitor quality, we would take frequent samples from the output of each machine, so that the process can be stopped and adjusted if the sample statistics indicate a problem.

FIGURE 4.19
Center versus Variability

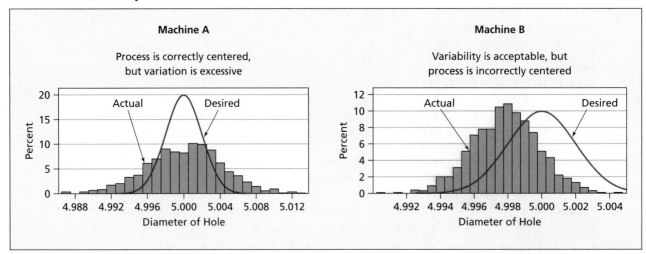

4.4 STANDARDIZED DATA

The standard deviation is an important measure of variability because of its many roles in statistics. One of its main uses is to gauge the position of items within a data array.

Chebyshev's Theorem

LO 4-5

Transform a data set into standardized values.

The French mathematician Jules Bienaymé (1796–1878) and the Russian mathematician Pafnuty Chebyshev (1821–1894) proved that, for any data set, no matter how it is distributed, the percentage of observations that lie within k standard deviations of the mean (i.e., within $\mu \pm k\sigma$) must be at least $100\,[1 - 1/k^2]$. Commonly called **Chebyshev's Theorem**, it says that for *any population* with mean μ and standard deviation σ:

$k = 2$ at least 75.0% will lie within $\mu \pm 2\sigma$.

$k = 3$ at least 88.9% will lie within $\mu \pm 3\sigma$.

$k = 4$ at least 93.8% will lie within $\mu \pm 4\sigma$.

For example, for an exam with $\mu = 72$ and $\sigma = 8$, at least 75 percent of the scores will be within the interval $72 \pm 2(8)$ or $[56, 88]$ regardless how the scores are distributed. Although applicable to any data set, these limits tend to be rather wide.

The Empirical Rule

More precise statements can be made about data from a normal or Gaussian distribution, named for its discoverer Karl Gauss (1777–1855). The Gaussian distribution is the well-known bell-shaped curve. Commonly called the **Empirical Rule**, it says that for data from a *normal distribution* we expect the interval $\mu \pm k\sigma$ to contain a known percentage of the data:

$k = 1$ 68.26% will lie within $\mu \pm 1\sigma$.
$k = 2$ 95.44% will lie within $\mu \pm 2\sigma$.
$k = 3$ 99.73% will lie within $\mu \pm 3\sigma$.

The Empirical Rule is illustrated in Figure 4.20. The Empirical Rule does *not* give an upper bound, but merely describes what is *expected*. Rounding off a bit, we say that in samples from a normal distribution we expect 68 percent of the data within 1 standard deviation, 95 percent within 2 standard deviations, and virtually all of the data within 3 standard deviations. Data values outside $\mu \pm 3\sigma$ are rare (less than 1%) in a normal distribution and are called **outliers**.

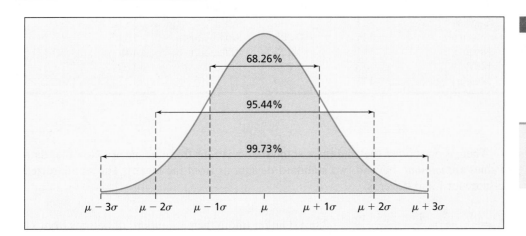

FIGURE 4.20

The Empirical Rule for a Normal Population

LO 4-6

Apply the Empirical Rule and recognize outliers.

EXAMPLE 4.2

Exam Scores

Suppose 80 students take an exam. How many students will score within 2 standard deviations of the mean? Assuming that exam scores follow a normal or bell-shaped curve, we might be willing to rely on the Empirical Rule, which predicts that 95.44% × 80 or approximately 76 students will score within 2 standard deviations from the mean. Since a normal distribution is symmetric about the mean, we expect that about 2 students will score more than 2 standard deviations above the mean, and 2 below the mean. Using the Empirical Rule, we can further say that it is unlikely that any student will score more than 3 standard deviations from the mean (99.73% × 80 = 79.78 ≈ 80).

Standardized Data

A general approach to identifying unusual observations is to redefine each observation in terms of its distance from the mean in standard deviations to obtain **standardized data**. We get the standardized value (called a **z-score**) by transforming each value of the observed data:

$$z_i = \frac{x_i - \mu}{\sigma} \quad \textit{for a population} \tag{4.15}$$

$$z_i = \frac{x_i - \bar{x}}{s} \quad \textit{for a sample} \tag{4.16}$$

By looking at the standardized z-score (z_i), we can tell at a glance how far away from the mean an observation lies. Excel's function =STANDARDIZE(XValue, Mean, StDev) makes it easy to calculate standardized values from a column of data. For the J.D. Power data, we set Mean = 114.697 and StDev = 18.067 and then use Excel to produce Table 4.13.

TABLE 4.13

Standardized *z*-Scores for Vehicle Brands (*n* = 33)
JDPower

Brand	Defects per 100	z-Score	Brand	Defects per 100	z-Score
Porsche	83	−1.754	Buick	114	−0.039
Acura	86	−1.588	Mazda	114	−0.039
Mercedes-Benz	87	−1.533	Scion	114	−0.039
Lexus	88	−1.478	Toyota	117	0.127
Ford	93	−1.201	Suburu	121	0.349
Honda	95	−1.090	Chrysler	122	0.404
Hyundai	102	−0.703	Suzuki	122	0.404
Lincoln	106	−0.481	GMC	126	0.626
Infiniti	107	−0.426	Kia	126	0.626
Volvo	109	−0.315	Jeep	129	0.792
Ram	110	−0.260	Dodge	130	0.847
Audi	111	−0.205	Jaguar	130	0.847
Cadillac	111	−0.205	MINI	133	1.013
Chevrolet	111	−0.205	Volkswagen	135	1.124
Nissan	111	−0.205	Mitsubishi	146	1.733
BMW	113	−0.094	Land Rover	170	3.061
Mercury	113	−0.094			

There is one *outlier* (beyond three standard deviations from the mean). No other data values are *unusual* (beyond two standard deviations from the mean). The standardized *z*-score for Land Rover is:

$$z_i = \frac{x_i - \bar{x}}{s} = \frac{170 - 114.697}{18.067} = 3.061 \quad \text{Outlier (more than 3 standard deviations from } \bar{x})$$

By tabulating the standardized *z*-scores, we can compare our sample with the Empirical Rule. For the J.D. Power data, you can verify from Table 4.13 that 23 of 33 observations (69.70 percent) lie within the range $\bar{x} \pm 1s$ (i.e., standardized *z*-score within the range −1 to +1). This compares favorably with the Empirical Rule (68.26 percent if the distribution is normal). Further, 32 of 33 observations (96.97 percent) lie within the range $\bar{x} \pm 2s$ (i.e., standardized *z*-score within the range −2 to +2). This compares favorably with the Empirical Rule (95.44 percent if the distribution is normal). However, the existence of an outlier casts doubt on the idea of a normal distribution.

In its Descriptive Statistics menu, MegaStat has an option to tabulate sample frequencies within each interval ($\bar{x} \pm 1s$, $\bar{x} \pm 2s$, $\bar{x} \pm 3s$) based on *z*-scores. Figure 4.21 shows the Empirical Rule for the J.D. Power data.

FIGURE 4.21

Empirical Rule Using MegaStat (*n* = 33)
JDPower

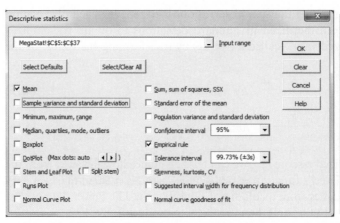

For a large sample (e.g., $n = 1,000$), it would *not* be surprising to see a few data values outside the three standard deviation range (e.g., 99.73 percent of 1,000 is 997, so we would expect three outliers). For a small sample (say, fewer than 30 observations), comparing the sample frequencies with a normal distribution may be risky because we really don't have much information about *shape*.

What to Do about Outliers?

Extreme values of a variable are vexing, but what do we do about them? It is tempting to discard unusual data points. Discarding an outlier would be reasonable only if we had reason to suppose it is erroneous data. For example, a blood pressure reading of 1200/80 seems impossible (probably was supposed to be 120/80). Perhaps the lab technician was distracted by a conversation while marking down the reading. An outrageous observation may be invalid. But how do we guard against self-deception? More than one scientist has been convinced to disregard data that didn't fit the pattern, when in fact the weird observation was trying to say something important. For example, in the 1980s, instruments monitoring the ozone layer over Antarctica automatically disregarded readings two standard deviations from the long-term mean as likely due to measurement error (*New Scientist,* December 6, 2008, p. 32). Fortunately, the raw data were retrievable, and scientists were able to spot an increase in the number of discarded readings as the "ozone hole" grew. Strict new regulations on the release of chlorofluorocarbons have been successful in restoring the ozone in the atmosphere. At this stage of your statistical training, it suffices to *recognize* unusual data points and outliers and their potential impact, and to know that there are entire books that cover the topic of outliers (see Related Reading).

Unusual Observations

Based on its standardized z-score, a data value is classified as:

Unusual   if $|z_i| > 2$ (beyond $\mu \pm 2\sigma$)

Outlier   if $|z_i| > 3$ (beyond $\mu \pm 3\sigma$)

Estimating Sigma

For a normal distribution, essentially all the observations lie within $\mu \pm 3\sigma$, so the range is approximately 6σ (from $\mu - 3\sigma$ to $\mu + 3\sigma$). Therefore, if you know the range $x_{max} - x_{min}$, you can estimate the standard deviation as $\sigma = (x_{max} - x_{min})/6$. This rule can come in handy for approximating the standard deviation when all you know is the range. For example, the caffeine content of a cup of tea depends on the type of tea and length of time the tea steeps, with a range of 20 to 90 mg. Knowing the range, we could estimate the standard deviation as $s = (90 - 20)/6$, or about 12 mg. This estimate assumes that the caffeine content of a cup of tea is normally distributed.

Mini Case   4.5

Presidential Ages

At 47, President Barack Obama was perceived to be unusually young when he became president. But how unusual was he? Table 4.14 shows the sorted ages at inauguration of the first 44 U.S. Presidents. President Obama is tied as the fourth youngest president. For these 44 presidents, the mean is 54.68 years with a standard deviation of 6.227 years. In terms of his standardized z-score, President Obama ($x = 47$, $z = -1.23$) is not unusual. Only our youngest president, Theodore Roosevelt ($x = 42$, $z = -2.04$) was unusual, as were our two oldest presidents, William Henry Harrison ($x = 68$, $z = 2.14$) and Ronald Reagan ($x = 69$, $z = 2.30$).

TABLE 4.14		Ages at Inauguration of 44 U.S. Presidents (sorted)		Presidents	
President	**Age**	**President**	**Age**	**President**	**Age**
T. Roosevelt	42	Lincoln	52	Washington	57
Kennedy	43	Carter	52	Jefferson	57
Grant	46	Van Buren	*54*	Madison	57
Cleveland	47	Hayes	*54*	J. Q. Adams	57
Clinton	47	McKinley	*54*	Monroe	58
Obama	47	Hoover	*54*	Truman	60
Pierce	48	G. W. Bush	*54*	J. Adams	61
Polk	49	B. Harrison	55	Jackson	61
Garfield	49	Cleveland	55	Ford	61
Fillmore	50	Harding	55	Eisenhower	62
Tyler	*51*	L. Johnson	55	Taylor	64
Arthur	*51*	A. Johnson	56	G. H. W. Bush	64
Taft	*51*	Wilson	56	Buchanan	65
Coolidge	*51*	Nixon	56	W. H. Harrison	68
F. Roosevelt	*51*			Reagan	69

Source: Ken Parks, *The World Almanac and Book of Facts 2002*, p. 545. Copyright © 2005 The World Almanac Education Group, Inc.

The dot plot in Figure 4.22 shows modes at 51 and 54 (five times each).

FIGURE 4.22   **Dot Plot of Presidents' Ages at Inauguration**

Using six classes, based on Sturges' Rule, Figure 4.23 shows that the modal class is 50 to 55 (13 presidents are in that class). However, since the next higher class has almost as many observations, it might be more helpful to say that presidents tend to be between 50 and 59 years of age upon inauguration (25 presidents are within this range). By that criterion, President Obama was relatively young.

FIGURE 4.23   **Histogram of Presidents' Ages at Inauguration**

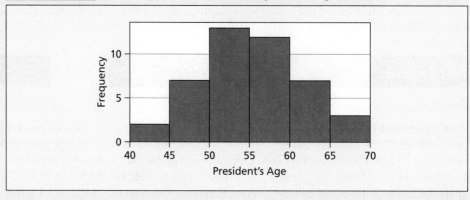

SECTION EXERCISES

connect

4.26 (a) By Chebychev's Theorem, at least how many students in a class of 200 would score within the range $\mu \pm 2\sigma$? (b) By the Empirical Rule, how many students in a class of 200 would score within the range $\mu \pm 2\sigma$? (c) What assumption is required in order to apply the Empirical Rule?

4.27 An exam has a mean of 70 with a standard deviation of 10. Use Chebyshev's Theorem to find a lower bound for the number of students in a class of 400 who scored between 50 and 90.

4.28 The mean monthly rent of students at Oxnard University is $875 with a standard deviation of $219. (a) John's rent is $1,325. What is his standardized z-score? (b) Is John's rent an outlier? (c) How high would the rent have to be to qualify as an outlier?

4.29 Convert each individual X data value to a standardized Z value and interpret it.

   a. Class exam: John's score is 91, $\mu = 79$, $\sigma = 5$
   b. Student GPA: Mary's GPA is 3.18, $\mu = 2.87$, $\sigma = 0.31$
   c. Weekly study hours: Jaime studies 18 hours, $\mu = 15.0$, $\sigma = 5.0$

4.30 In a regional high school swim meet, women's times (in seconds) in the 200-yard freestyle ranged from 109.7 to 126.2. Estimate the standard deviation, using the Empirical Rule.

4.31 Find the original data value corresponding to each standardized z-score.

   a. Student GPAs: Bob's z-score $z = +1.71$, $\mu = 2.98$, $\sigma = 0.36$
   b. Weekly work hours: Sarah's z-score $z = +1.18$, $\mu = 21.6$, $\sigma = 7.1$
   c. Bowling scores: Dave's z-score $z = -1.35$, $\mu = 150$, $\sigma = 40$

4.32 CitiBank recorded the number of customers to use a downtown ATM during the noon hour on 32 consecutive workdays. (a) Use Excel or MegaStat to sort and standardize the data. (b) Based on the Empirical Rule, are there outliers? Unusual data values? (c) Compare the percent of observations that lie within 1 and 2 standard deviations of the mean with a normal distribution. What is your conclusion? 📁 **CitiBank**

25	37	23	26	30	40	25	26
39	32	21	26	19	27	32	25
18	26	34	18	31	35	21	33
33	9	16	32	35	42	15	24

4.33 An executive's telephone log showed the lengths of 65 calls initiated during the last week of July. (a) Use Excel or MegaStat to sort and standardize the data. (b) Based on the standardized z-scores, are there outliers? Unusual data values? (c) Compare the percent of observations that lie within 1 and 2 standard deviations of the mean with a normal distribution. What is your conclusion? 📁 **CallLength**

1	2	10	5	3	3	2	20	1	1
6	3	13	2	2	1	26	3	1	3
1	2	1	7	1	2	3	1	2	12
1	4	2	2	29	1	1	1	8	5
1	4	2	1	1	1	1	6	1	2
3	3	6	1	3	1	1	5	1	18
2	13	13	1	6					

4.5 PERCENTILES, QUARTILES, AND BOX PLOTS

Percentiles

You are familiar with percentile scores of national educational tests such as ACT, SAT, and GMAT, which tell you where you stand in comparison with others. For example, if you are in the 83rd percentile, then 83 percent of the test-takers scored below you, and you are in the top 17 percent of all test-takers. However, only when the sample is large can we meaningfully divide the data into 100 groups (*percentiles*). Alternatively, we can divide the data into 10 groups (*deciles*), 5 groups (*quintiles*), or 4 groups (*quartiles*).

LO 4-7

Calculate quartiles and other percentiles.

Percentiles in Excel

The Pth percentile of a sorted data array $x_1, x_2, \ldots, x_n$ is the value of x that defines the lowest P percent of the data values. Excel's formula for the Pth percentile is =PERCENTILE .EXC(Data, Proportion), where Proportion is the *proportion* below the Pth percentile. For example, =PERCENTILE.EXC(Data, .95) returns the 95th percentile. In older versions of Excel, the function =PERCENTILE(Data, Proportion) will give somewhat different results (see Appendix J).

Percentiles generally have to be interpolated *between* two data values. For example, suppose you want the 95th percentile for a sample of $n = 73$ items. Since $.95 \times 73 = 69.35$, you would have to interpolate between the 69th and 70th observations (i.e., between x_{69} and x_{70}) to obtain the 95th percentile. The Excel formula =PERCENTILE.EXC(Data, .95) handles this interpolation automatically.

In health care, manufacturing, and banking, selected percentiles (e.g., 5, 25, 50, 75, and 95 percent) are calculated to establish *benchmarks* so that any firm can compare itself with similar firms (i.e., other firms in the same industry) in terms of profit margin, debt ratio, defect rate, or any other relevant performance measure. In finance, quartiles (25, 50, and 75 percent) are commonly used to assess financial performance of companies and stock portfolio performances. In human resources, percentiles are used in employee salary benchmarking. Occupational Employment Statistics (OES) published by the U.S. Bureau of Labor Statistics (www.bls.gov) show the 25th, 50th, and 75th percentiles for over 800 occupations in different metropolitan areas. An individual could use these benchmarks to assess his/her potential earnings in different locations, or an employer could use them to estimate the cost of hiring its employees. The number of groups depends on the task at hand and the sample size, but quartiles deserve special attention because they are meaningful even for fairly small samples.

Quartiles

The **quartiles** (denoted Q_1, Q_2, Q_3) are scale points that divide the sorted data into four groups of approximately equal size, that is, the 25th, 50th, and 75th percentiles, respectively.

The second quartile Q_2 is the *median*. Since equal numbers of data values lie below and above the median, it is an important indicator of *center*.

The first and third quartiles Q_1 and Q_3 indicate *center* because they define the boundaries for the middle 50 percent of the data. But Q_1 and Q_3 also indicate *variability* because the **interquartile range** $Q_3 - Q_1$ (denoted IQR) measures the degree of spread in the data (the middle 50 percent).

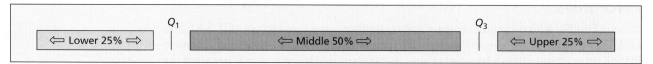

Conceptually, the first quartile Q_1 is the median of the data values below Q_2, and the third quartile Q_3 is the median of the data values above Q_2. Depending on n, the quartiles

FIGURE 4.24
Possible Quartile Positions

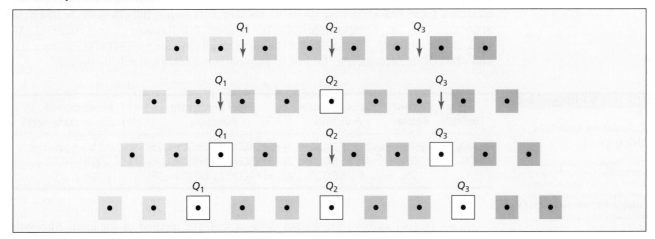

Q_1, Q_2, Q_3 may be members of the data set or may lie *between* two of the sorted data values. Figure 4.24 shows four possible situations.

Method of Medians

For small data sets, you can find the quartiles using the **method of medians**, as illustrated in Figure 4.25.

- Step 1:   Sort the observations.
- Step 2:   Find the median Q_2.
- Step 3:   Find the median of the data values that lie below Q_2.
- Step 4:   Find the median of the data values that lie above Q_2.

When interpolation is necessary, we simply go halfway between the two data values. This method is attractive because it is quick and logical (see Freund 1987 in Related Reading). However, Excel uses a different method.

EXAMPLE 4.3

Method of Medians

A financial analyst has a portfolio of 12 energy equipment stocks. She has data on their recent price/earnings (P/E) ratios. To find the quartiles, she sorts the data, finds Q_2 (the median) halfway between the middle two data values, and then finds Q_1 and Q_3 (medians of the lower and upper halves, respectively) as illustrated in Figure 4.25.

FIGURE 4.25   **Method of Medians**

Company	Sorted P/E
Maverick Tube	7
BJ Services	22
FMC Technologies	25
Nabors Industries	29
Baker Hughes	31
Varco International	35
National-Oilwell	36
Smith International	36
Cooper Cameron	39
Schlumberger	42
Halliburton	46
Transocean	49

Q_1 is between x_3 and x_4 so
$Q_1 = (x_3 + x_4)/2 = (25 + 29)/2 = 27.0$

Q_2 is between x_6 and x_7 so
$Q_2 = (x_6 + x_7)/2 = (35 + 36)/2 = 35.5$

Q_3 is between x_9 and x_{10} so
$Q_3 = (x_9 + x_{10})/2 = (39 + 42)/2 = 40.5$

Source: Data are from *BusinessWeek,* November 22, 2004, pp. 95–98.

Excel Quartiles

Excel does not use the method of medians, but instead uses a formula[1] to interpolate its quartiles. Excel has a function =QUARTILE.EXC(Data, k) to return the kth quartile in a data array $x_1, x_2, \ldots, x_n$. For example =QUARTILE.EXC(Data, 1) will return Q_1 and =QUARTILE.EXC (Data, 3) will return Q_3. You could get the same results by using =PERCENTILE.EXC(Data, .25) and =PERCENTILE.EXC(Data, .75). Table 4.15 summarizes Excel's quartile methods.

TABLE 4.15

Calculating Quartiles Using Excel

Note: The older Excel functions =QUARTILE and =PERCENTILE will give different results from the functions shown in this table. The functions ending in .EXC will match MINITAB and other statistical packages.

Quartile	Percent Below	Excel Quartile Function	Excel Percentile Function	Interpolated Position in Data Array
Q_1	25%	=QUARTILE.EXC(Data,1)	=PERCENTILE.EXC(Data,.25)	$.25n + .25$
Q_2	50%	=QUARTILE.EXC(Data,2)	=PERCENTILE.EXC(Data,.50)	$.50n + .50$
Q_3	75%	=QUARTILE.EXC(Data,3)	=PERCENTILE.EXC(Data,.75)	$.75n + .75$

Excel's Q_2 (the median) will be the same as with the method of medians. Although Excel's Q_1 and Q_3 may differ from the method of medians, the differences are usually unimportant. Figure 4.26 illustrates calculations for Excel's interpolation methods for a small sample of 12 P/E ratios.

EXAMPLE 4.4

Excel Formula Method

Figure 4.26 illustrates Excel's quartile calculations using =QUARTILE.EXC for the same sample of P/E ratios. The resulting quartiles are similar to those using the method of medians.

FIGURE 4.26   **Excel's Quartile Interpolation Method**

Source: Data are from *BusinessWeek,* November 22, 2004, pp. 95–98.

Tip

Whether you use the method of medians or Excel, your quartiles will be about the same. Small differences in calculation techniques typically do not lead to different conclusions in business applications.

[1]There are several acceptable ways to define the quartile position within a data array. Excel's QUARTILE.EXC and PERCENTILE.EXC functions define the Pth percentile position as $pn + p$ where $p = P/100$. See Eric Langford, "Quartiles in Elementary Statistics," *Journal of Statistics Education* 14, no. 3, November 2006. Different interpolation formulas generally give similar results.

Quartiles are robust statistics that generally resist outliers. However, quartiles do not always provide clean cutpoints in the sorted data, particularly in small samples or when there are repeating data values. For example:

These two data sets have identical quartiles, but are not really similar. Because of the small sample size and "gaps" in the data, the quartiles do not represent either data set well.

Box Plots

A useful tool of *exploratory data analysis* (EDA) is the **box plot** (also called a *box-and-whisker plot*) based on the **five-number summary**:

$$x_{min}, Q_1, Q_2, Q_3, x_{max}$$

The box plot is displayed visually, like this.

LO 4-8

Make and interpret box plots.

A box plot shows *center* (position of the median Q_2). A box plot shows *variability* (width of the "box" defined by Q_1 and Q_3 and the range between x_{min} and x_{max}). A box plot shows *shape* (skewness if the whiskers are of unequal length and/or if the median is not in the center of the box). Figure 4.27 shows simple boxplots and histograms for samples drawn from different types of populations. Despite sampling variation, the shape of each boxplot reveals the shape of its parent population. A boxplot gives a simple visual complement to the histogram and/or numerical statistics that we use to

FIGURE 4.27
Sample Boxplots from Four Populations (*n* = 1000)

describe data. For example, the five-number summary for the J.D. Power data ($n =$ 33 vehicle brands) is:

$$x_{\min} = 83, \ Q_1 = 107, \ Q_2 = 113, \ Q_3 = 126, \ x_{\max} = 170$$

Figure 4.28 shows a box plot of the J.D. Power data. Below the box plot there is a well-labeled scale showing the values of X. The vertical lines that define the ends of the box are located at Q_1 and Q_3 on the X-axis. The vertical line within the box is the median (Q_2). The "whiskers" are the horizontal lines that connect each side of the box to $x_{\min}$ and $x_{\max}$ and their length suggests the length of each tail of the distribution. The long right whisker suggests right-skewness, a conclusion also suggested by the fact that the median is to the left of the center of the box.

FIGURE 4.28

Simple Box Plot of J.D. Power Data ($n = 33$ brands) JDPower

Fences and Unusual Data Values

We can use the quartiles to identify unusual data points. The idea is to detect data values that are far below Q_1 or far above Q_3. The *fences* are based on the *interquartile range* $Q_3 - Q_1$:

		Inner fences	*Outer fences*
(4.17)	Lower fence:	$Q_1 - 1.5(Q_3 - Q_1)$	$Q_1 - 3.0(Q_3 - Q_1)$
(4.18)	Upper fence:	$Q_3 + 1.5(Q_3 - Q_1)$	$Q_3 + 3.0(Q_3 - Q_1)$

On a boxplot, MegaStat and other software packages define observations outside the inner fences as *outliers* while those outside the outer fences are *extreme outliers*. For the J.D. Power data ($Q_1 = 107$ and $Q_3 = 126$), the fences are:

	Inner fences	*Outer fences*
Lower fence:	$107 - 1.5(126 - 107) = 78.5$	$107 - 3.0(126 - 107) = 50$
Upper fence:	$126 + 1.5(126 - 107) = 154.5$	$126 + 3.0(126 - 107) = 183$

In this example, there is one outlier (170) that lies above the *inner* fence. There are no extreme outliers that exceed the *outer* fence. Outliers are shown on a box plot by truncating the whisker at the fences and displaying the unusual data points as dots or asterisks, as in Figure 4.29. MegaStat shows fences *only if there are outliers*. Note that this "fences" criterion for "outliers" is not the same as the Empirical Rule.

FIGURE 4.29

Box Plot with Fences JDPower

A diagram helps to visualize the fence calculations. To get the fences, we merely add or subtract a multiple of the *IQR* from Q_1 and Q_3.

Midhinge

Quartiles can be used to define an additional measure of center that has the advantage of not being influenced by outliers. The **midhinge** is the average of the first and third quartiles:

$$\text{Midhinge} = \frac{Q_1 + Q_3}{2}$$ **(4.19)**

The name "midhinge" derives from the idea that, if the "box" were folded at its halfway point, it would resemble a hinge:

Since the midhinge is always exactly *halfway* between Q_1 and Q_3 while the median Q_2 can be *anywhere* within the "box," we have a new way to describe skewness:

$$\begin{array}{ll} \text{Median} < \text{Midhinge} & \Rightarrow \text{Skewed right (longer right tail)} \\ \text{Median} \cong \text{Midhinge} & \Rightarrow \text{Symmetric (tails roughly equal)} \\ \text{Median} > \text{Midhinge} & \Rightarrow \text{Skewed left (longer left tail)} \end{array}$$

The 24 boxplots in Figure 4.30 show occupied beds in a hospital emergency room hour by hour. Each boxplot is based on $n = 52$ Saturdays in one year. There are 24 hourly readings, so the total sample is $24 \times 52 = 1,248$ data points. Boxplots are shown vertically to facilitate comparisons over time. The median (50th percentile) and quartiles (25th and 75th percentiles) change slowly and predictably over the course of the day. In several boxplots there are unusual values (very high occupancy) marked with an asterisk. Since the upper whiskers are longer than the lower whiskers, the occupancy rates are positively skewed. On several occasions (e.g., between midnight and 8 a.m.) there were Saturdays with zero bed occupancy. Similar charts can be prepared for each day of the week, aiding the hospital in planning its emergency room staffing and bed capacity.

EXAMPLE 4.5

Hospital Bed Occupancy

FIGURE 4.30   **Boxplots of Hospital Emergency Room Bed Occupancy**

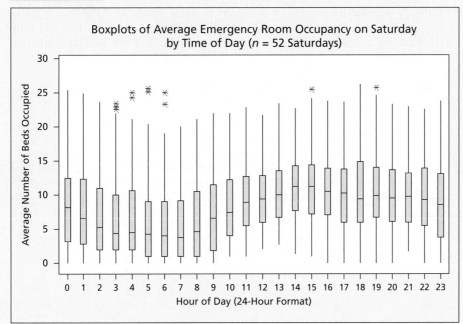

SECTION EXERCISES

connect

4.34 Scores on an accounting exam ranged from 42 to 96, with quartiles $Q_1 = 61$, $Q_2 = 77$, and $Q_3 = 85$. (a) Sketch a simple boxplot (5-number summary without fences) using a nicely scaled X-axis. (b) Describe its shape (skewed left, symmetric, skewed right).

4.35 In 2007, total compensation (in thousands of dollars) for 40 randomly chosen CEOs ranged from 790 to 192,920, with quartiles $Q_1 = 3,825$, $Q_2 = 8,890$, and $Q_3 = 17,948$. (a) Sketch a simple boxplot (5-number summary without fences) using a nicely scaled X-axis. (b) Describe its shape (skewed left, symmetric, skewed right).

4.36 The Comer-Correr Taco Wagon is only open from 11:00 a.m. to 2:00 p.m. on Saturday. The owner kept track of the number of customers served on Saturday for 60 weeks. (a) Visually estimate the quartiles Q_1, Q_2, Q_3. (b) Approximately how many customers were served on the busiest day? The slowest day? (c) Is the distribution symmetric? **Customers**

4.37 On San Martin Boulevard, embedded sensors kept track of the vehicle traffic count each hour for five weekdays, Monday through Friday between 6 a.m. and 8 p.m. (5 weeks $\times$ 14 hours = 70 observations). (a) Visually estimate the quartiles Q_1, Q_2, Q_3. (b) Estimate x_{min} and x_{max}. (c) Is the distribution symmetric? **Traffic**

4.38 CitiBank recorded the number of customers to use a downtown ATM during the noon hour on 32 consecutive workdays. (a) Use Excel to find the quartiles. What do they tell you? (b) Find the midhinge. What does it tell you? (c) Make a box plot and interpret it. **CitiBank**

25	37	23	26	30	40	25	26
39	32	21	26	19	27	32	25
18	26	34	18	31	35	21	33
33	9	16	32	35	42	15	24

4.39 An executive's telephone log showed the lengths of 65 calls initiated during the last week of July. (a) Use Excel to find the quartiles. What do they tell you? (b) Find the midhinge. What does it tell you? (c) Make a box plot and interpret it. **CallLength**

1	2	10	5	3	3	2	20	1	1
6	3	13	2	2	1	26	3	1	3
1	2	1	7	1	2	3	1	2	12
1	4	2	2	29	1	1	1	8	5
1	4	2	1	1	1	1	6	1	2
3	3	6	1	3	1	1	5	1	18
2	13	13	1	6					

Mini Case   4.6

Airline Delays   UnitedAir

In 2005, United Airlines announced that it would award 500 frequent flier miles to every traveler on flights that arrived more than 30 minutes late on all flights departing from Chicago O'Hare to seven other hub airports (see *The Wall Street Journal,* June 14, 2005). What is the likelihood of such a delay? On a randomly chosen day (Tuesday, April 26, 2005), the Bureau of Transportation Statistics website (www.bts.gov) showed 278 United Airlines departures from O'Hare. The mean arrival delay was -7.45 minutes (i.e., flights arrived early, on average). The quartiles were $Q_1 = -19$ minutes, $Q_2 = -10$ minutes, and $Q_3 = -3$ minutes. While these statistics show that most of the flights arrive early, we must look further to estimate the probability of a frequent flier bonus.

In the box plot with fences (Figure 4.31), the "box" is entirely below zero. In the right tail, one flight was slightly above the inner fence (unusual) and eight flights were above the outer fence (outliers). An empirical estimate of the probability of a frequent flier award is 8/278 or about a 3 percent chance. A longer period of study might alter this estimate (e.g., if there were days of bad winter weather or traffic congestion).

FIGURE 4.31   **Box Plot of Flight Arrival Delays**

The dot plot (Figure 4.32) shows that the distribution of arrival delays is rather bell-shaped, except for the unusual values in the right tail. This is consistent with the view that "normal" flight operations are predictable, with only random variation around the mean. While it is difficult for flights to arrive earlier than planned, unusual factors could delay them by a lot.

FIGURE 4.32   **Dot Plot of Flight Arrival Delays**

4.6 CORRELATION AND COVARIANCE

LO 4-9

Calculate and interpret a correlation coefficient and covariance.

You often hear the term "significant correlation" in casual use, often imprecisely or incorrectly. Actually, the **sample correlation coefficient** is a well-known statistic that describes the degree of linearity between *paired* observations on two quantitative variables X and Y. The data set consists of n pairs (x_i, y_i) that are usually displayed on a *scatter* *plot* (review Chapter 3 if you need to refresh your memory about making scatter plots). The formula for the sample correlation coefficient is:

(4.20)
$$r = \frac{\sum_{i=1}^{n}(x_i - \bar{x})(y_i - \bar{y})}{\sqrt{\sum_{i=1}^{n}(x_i - \bar{x})^2}\sqrt{\sum_{i=1}^{n}(y_i - \bar{y})^2}}$$

Its range is $-1 \le r \le +1$. When r is near 0 there is little or no linear relationship between X and Y. An r value near $+1$ indicates a strong positive relationship, while an r value near -1 indicates a strong negative relationship. In Chapter 12, you will learn how to determine when a correlation is "significant" in a statistical sense (i.e., significantly different than zero), but for now it is enough to recognize the correlation coefficient as a *descriptive statistic*.

Excel's formula =CORREL(XData,YData) will return the sample correlation coefficient for two columns (or rows) of paired data. In fact, many scientific pocket calculators will calculate r. The diagrams in Figure 4.33 will give you some idea of what various correlations look like. The correlation coefficient is a measure of the *linear relationship*—so take special note of the last scatter plot, which shows a relationship but not a *linear* one.

FIGURE 4.33

Illustration of Correlation Coefficients

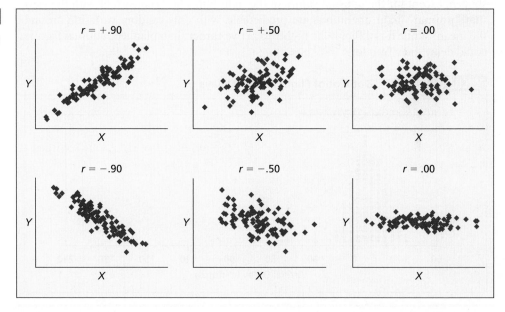

Covariance

The **covariance** of two random variables X and Y is denoted Cov(X,Y) or simply σ_{XY}. The covariance measures the degree to which the values of X and Y change together. This concept is particularly important in financial portfolio analysis. For example, if the prices of two stocks X and Y tend to move in the same direction, their covariance is positive ($\sigma_{XY} > 0$), and conversely if their prices tend to move in opposite directions ($\sigma_{XY} < 0$). If the prices of X and Y are unrelated, their covariance is zero ($\sigma_{XY} = 0$). A portfolio manager can apply this concept to reduce volatility in the overall portfolio, by combining stocks in a way that reduces variation. To estimate the covariance, we would generally use the sample formula.

For a population:
$$\sigma_{XY} = \frac{\sum_{i=1}^{N}(x_i - \mu_X)(y_i - \mu_Y)}{N}$$
(4.21)

For a sample:
$$s_{XY} = \frac{\sum_{i=1}^{n}(x_i - \bar{x})(y_i - \bar{y})}{n - 1}$$
(4.22)

The units of measurement for the covariance are unpredictable because the means and/or units of measurement of X and Y may differ. For this reason, analysts generally work with the correlation coefficient, which is a standardized value of the covariance. As you have already learned, the correlation coefficient always lies between -1 and $+1$. Conceptually, a correlation coefficient is the covariance divided by the product of the standard deviations of X and Y. For a population, the correlation coefficient is indicated by the lowercase Greek letter ρ (rho), while for a sample we use the lowercase Roman letter r (as you saw in formula 4.20 in the previous section).

Population correlation coefficient:
$$\rho = \frac{\sigma_{XY}}{\sigma_X \sigma_Y}$$
(4.23)

where

σ_X = population standard deviation of X

σ_Y = population standard deviation of Y

Sample correlation coefficient:
$$r = \frac{s_{XY}}{s_X s_Y}$$
(4.24)

where

s_X = sample standard deviation of X

s_Y = sample standard deviation of Y

Application: Stock Prices 📄 TwoStocks   The prices of two stocks are recorded at the close of trading each Friday for 12 weeks, as displayed in Figure 4.34.

Closing Price for Week ($n = 8$ weeks)								
Company	*1*	*2*	*3*	*4*	*5*	*6*	*7*	*8*
X (AardCo)	41.87	47.87	43.26	37.76	45.86	45.22	46.83	46.49
Y (Zymurgy)	9.11	8.07	11.02	13.24	9.14	12.04	6.96	9.27

We can see that these two stock prices tend to move in opposite directions, so we anticipate a negative covariance (and a negative correlation). We can do the calculations using Excel functions with named data ranges. Because Excel's =COVAR function uses the population formula, we must make an adjustment to get a *sample* covariance (since here we have only a sample of stock prices). To avoid this extra step, Excel 2010 introduced =COVARIANCE.S for a sample or =COVARIANCE.P for a population (but these two functions are not available in earlier versions of Excel).

Scatter Plot of Two Stock Prices (*n* = 8)
📂 **TwoStocks**

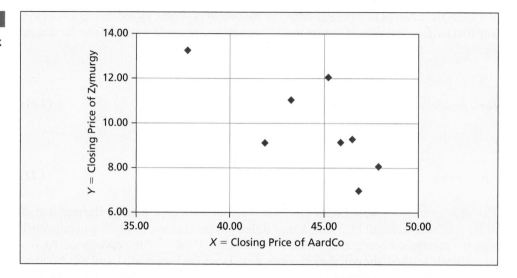

Statistic	Result	Excel 2010 Formula	Excel 2007 Formula
Sample covariance:	$s_{XY} = -5.0890$	=COVARIANCE.S (XData, YData)	=COVAR(XData, YData)*(n/(n-1)
Std. dev. of X:	$s_X = 3.3146$	=STDEV.S(Xdata)	=STDEV(XData)
Std. dev. of Y:	$s_Y = 2.0896$	=STDEV.S(Ydata)	=STDEV(YData)
Sample correlation:	$r = -0.7347$	=CORREL(Xdata,YData)	=CORREL(Xdata,YData)
Sample size:	$n = 8$ weeks	=COUNT(XData)	=COUNT(XData)

Applying the formula for a sample correlation coefficient:

$$r = \frac{s_{XY}}{s_X s_Y} = \frac{-5.0890}{(3.3146)(2.0896)} = -0.7347$$

This is the same value for the correlation coefficient that we would get from formula 4.20. Using this type of information, a financial analyst can construct a portfolio whose total value is more stable, knowing that these stock prices tend to move in opposite directions.

Correlations Help Portfolio Design

"A good way to decrease the standard deviation of your portfolio is through diversification. By investing in different types of funds, you can minimize the impact that any one sub-asset class may have on your total holding."

From T. Rowe Price Investor, *September 2009, p. 8. Used with permission.*

VAILRESORTS   **Mini Case**   **4.7**

Vail Resorts Customer Satisfaction

Figure 4.35 is a matrix showing correlations between several satisfaction variables from a sample of respondents to a Vail Resorts' satisfaction survey. The correlations are all positive, suggesting that greater satisfaction with any one of these criteria tends to be associated with greater satisfaction with the others (positive covariance). The highest correlation ($r = 0.488$) is between *SkiSafe* (attention to skier safety) and *SkiPatV* (Ski Patrol visibility). This makes intuitive sense. When a skier sees a ski patroller, you would expect increased perception that the organization is concerned with skier safety. While many of the correlations seem small, they are all *statistically significant* (as you will learn in Chapter 12).

FIGURE 4.35 **Correlation Matrix of Skier Satisfaction Variables ($n = 502$)**
VailGuestSat

	LiftOps	LiftWait	TrailVar	SnoAmt	GroomT	SkiSafe	SkiPatV
LiftOps	1.000						
LiftWait	0.180	1.000					
TrailVar	0.206	0.128	1.000				
SnoAmt	0.242	0.227	0.373	1.000			
GroomT	0.271	0.251	0.221	0.299	1.000		
SkiSafe	0.306	0.196	0.172	0.200	0.274	1.000	
SkiPatV	0.190	0.207	0.172	0.184	0.149	0.488	1.000

where

LiftOps = helpfulness/friendliness of lift operators

LiftWait = lift line wait

TrailVar = trail variety

SnoAmt = amount of snow

GroomTr = amount of groomed trails

SkiSafe = attention to skier safety

SkiPatV = Ski Patrol visibility

SECTION EXERCISES

connect

4.40 For each *X-Y* data set ($n = 12$): (a) Make a scatter plot. (b) Find the sample correlation coefficient. (c) Is there a linear relationship between *X* and *Y*? If so, describe it. *Note:* Use Excel or MegaStat or MINITAB if your instructor permits. XYDataSets

Data Set (a)

X	64.7	25.9	65.6	49.6	50.3	26.7	39.5	56.0	90.8	35.9	39.9	64.1
Y	5.8	18.1	10.6	11.9	11.4	14.6	15.7	4.4	2.2	15.4	14.7	9.9

Data Set (b)

X	55.1	59.8	72.3	86.4	31.1	41.8	40.7	36.8	42.7	28.9	24.8	16.2
Y	15.7	17.5	15.2	20.6	7.3	8.2	9.8	8.2	13.7	11.2	7.5	4.5

Data Set (c)

X	53.3	18.1	49.8	43.8	68.3	30.4	18.6	45.8	34.0	56.7	60.3	29.3
Y	10.2	6.9	14.8	13.4	16.8	9.5	16.3	16.4	1.5	11.4	10.9	19.7

4.41 Your laptop gets warm (even hot) when you place it on your lap because it is dissipating heat from its microprocessor and related components. (a) Use the information in the following table to make a scatter plot. (b) Describe the relationship between *Microprocessor Speed* and *Power Dissipation*. (c) Calculate the correlation coefficient. MicroSpeed

Chip	Microprocessor Speed (MHz)	Power Dissipation (watts)
1989 Intel 80486	20	3
1993 pentium	100	10
1997 Pentium II	233	35
1998 Intel Celeron	300	20
1999 Pentium III	600	42
1999 AMD Athlon	600	50
2000 Pentium 4	1300	51
2004 Celeron D	2100	73
2004 Pentium 4	3800	115
2005 Pentium D	3200	130
2007 AMD Phenom	2300	95
2008 Intel Core 2	3200	136
2009 Intel Core i7	2900	95
2009 AMD Phenom II	3200	125

Source: *New Scientist,* 208, no. 2780 (October 2, 2010), p. 41.

4.42 For a sample of (X, Y) data values, the covariance is 48.724, the standard deviation of X is 11.724, and the standard deviation of Y is 8.244. (a) Find the sample correlation coefficient. (b) What does the sample correlation coefficient suggest about the relationship between X and Y? (c) Why is the sample correlation easier to interpret than the sample covariance?

4.43 (a) Make a scatter plot of the following data on $X =$ home size and $Y =$ selling price (thousands of dollars) for new homes ($n = 20$) in a suburb of an eastern city. (b) Find the sample correlation coefficient. (c) Is there a linear relationship between X and Y? If so, describe it. *Note:* Use Excel or MegaStat or MINITAB if your instructor permits. **HomePrice**

Square Feet	Selling Price (thousands)	Square Feet	Selling Price (thousands)
3,570	861	3,460	737
3,410	740	3,340	806
2,690	563	3,240	809
3,260	698	2,660	639
3,130	624	3,160	778
3,460	737	3,310	760
3,340	806	2,930	729
3,240	809	3,020	720
2,660	639	2,320	575
3,160	778	3,130	785

4.7 GROUPED DATA

Weighted Mean

LO 4-10

Calculate the mean and standard deviation from grouped data.

The **weighted mean** is a sum that assigns each data value a weight w_j that represents a fraction of the total (i.e., the k weights must sum to 1).

(4.25)
$$\bar{x} = \sum_{j=1}^{k} w_j x_j \quad \text{where} \quad \sum_{j=1}^{k} w_j = 1.00$$

For example, your instructor might give a weight of 30 percent to homework, 20 percent to the midterm exam, 40 percent to the final exam, and 10 percent to a term project (so that .30 + .20 + .40 + .10 = 1.00). Suppose your scores on these were 85, 68, 78, and 90. Your weighted average for the course would be

$$\bar{x} = \sum_{j=1}^{k} w_j x_j = .30 \times 85 + .20 \times 68 + .40 \times 78 + .10 \times 90 = 79.3$$

Despite a low score on the midterm exam, you are right at the borderline for an 80 (if your instructor rounds up). The weighted mean is widely used in cost accounting (weights for cost categories), finance (asset weights in investment portfolios), and other business applications.

Grouped Data

We can apply the idea of a weighted mean when we must work with observations that have been grouped. When a data set is tabulated into bins, we lose information about the location of the x values within bins but gain clarity of presentation because grouped data can be displayed more compactly than raw data. As long as the bin limits are given, we can estimate the mean and standard deviation using weights based on the bin frequencies. The accuracy of the grouped estimates will depend on the number of bins, distribution of data within bins, and bin frequencies.

Grouped Mean and Standard Deviation

Table 4.16 shows a frequency distribution for prices of Lipitor®, a cholesterol-lowering prescription drug, for three cities (see **Mini Case 4.2**). The observations are classified into bins of equal width 5. When calculating a mean or standard deviation from grouped data, we treat all observations within a bin *as if they were located at the midpoint*. For example, in the third class (70 but less than 75), we pretend that all 11 prices were equal to $72.50 (the interval midpoint). In reality, observations may be scattered within each interval, but we assume that *on average* they are located at the class midpoint.

TABLE 4.16			Worksheet for Grouped Lipitor® Data (*n* = 47) LipitorGrp				
From	*To*	f_j	m_j	$f_j m_j$	$m_j - \bar{x}$	$(m_j - \bar{x})^2$	$f(m - \bar{x})^2$
60	65	6	62.5	375.0	−10.42553	108.69172	652.15029
65	70	11	67.5	742.5	−5.42553	29.43640	323.80036
70	75	11	72.5	797.5	−0.42553	0.18108	1.99185
75	80	13	77.5	1,007.5	4.57447	20.92576	272.03486
80	85	5	82.5	412.5	9.57447	91.67044	458.35220
85	90	0	87.5	0.0	14.57447	212.41512	0.00000
90	95	1	92.5	92.5	19.57447	383.15980	383.15980
	Sum	47	Sum	3,427.5		Sum	2,091.48936
			Mean ($\bar{x}$)	72.925532		Std Dev (*s*)	6.74293408

Each interval j has a midpoint m_j and a frequency f_j. We calculate the estimated mean by multiplying the midpoint of each class by its class frequency, taking the sum over all k classes, and dividing by sample size n.

$$\bar{x} = \frac{\sum_{j=1}^{k} f_j m_j}{n} = \frac{3,427.5}{47} = 72.9255 \qquad \textbf{(4.26)}$$

We then estimate the standard deviation by subtracting the estimated mean from each class midpoint, squaring the difference, multiplying by the class frequency, taking the sum over all classes to obtain the sum of squared deviations about the mean, dividing by $n - 1$, and taking the square root. *Avoid the common mistake of "rounding off" the mean before subtracting it from each midpoint.*

(4.27)
$$s = \sqrt{\sum_{j=1}^{k} \frac{f_j(m_j - \bar{x})^2}{n - 1}} = \sqrt{\frac{2,091.48936}{47 - 1}} = 6.74293$$

Once we have the mean and standard deviation, we can estimate the coefficient of variation in the usual way:

$$CV = 100(s/\bar{x}) = 100\,(6.74293/72.925532) = 9.2\%$$

Accuracy Issues

How accurate are grouped estimates of $\bar{x}$ and s? To the extent that observations are *not* evenly spaced within the bins, accuracy would be lost. But, unless there is systematic skewness (say, clustering at the low end of each class), the effects of uneven distributions within bins will tend to average out.

Accuracy tends to improve as the number of bins increases. If the first or last class is open-ended, there will be no class midpoint, and therefore no way to estimate the mean. For nonnegative data (e.g., GPA), we can assume a lower limit of zero when the first class is open-ended, although this assumption may make the first class too wide. Such an assumption may occasionally be possible for an open-ended top class (e.g., the upper limit of people's ages could be assumed to be 100), but many variables have no obvious upper limit (e.g., income). It is usually possible to estimate the median and quartiles from grouped data even with open-ended classes (the end of chapter *LearningStats* demonstrations give the formulas and illustrate grouped quartile calculations).

4.8 SKEWNESS AND KURTOSIS

Skewness

In a general way, *skewness* (as shown in Figure 4.36) may be judged by looking at the sample histogram, or by comparing the mean and median. However, this comparison is imprecise and does not take account of sample size. When more precision is needed, we look at the sample's **skewness coefficient** provided by Excel and MINITAB:

(4.28)
$$\text{Skewness} = \frac{n}{(n - 1)(n - 2)} \sum_{i=1}^{n} \left(\frac{x_i - \bar{x}}{s}\right)^3$$

FIGURE 4.36

Skewness Prototype Populations

| Skewed Left | Normal | Skewed Right |
| Skewness < 0 | Skewness = 0 | Skewness > 0 |

This unit-free statistic can be used to compare two samples measured in different units (say, dollars and yen) or to compare one sample with a known reference distribution such as the symmetric normal (bell-shaped) distribution. The skewness coefficient is obtained from Excel's Tools > Data Analysis > Descriptive Statistics or by the function =SKEW(Data).

Table 4.17 shows the expected range within which the sample skewness coefficient would be expected to fall 90 percent of the time if the population being sampled were normal. A sample skewness statistic within the 90 percent range may be attributed to random variation, while coefficients outside the range would suggest that the sample came from a nonnormal population. As *n* increases, the range of chance variation narrows.

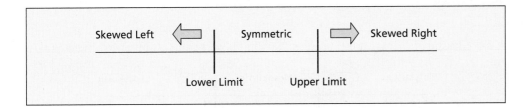

n	Lower 5%	Upper 5%	n	Lower 5%	Upper 5%	
20	−0.84	+0.84	90	−0.41	+0.41	**TABLE 4.17**
30	−0.69	+0.69	100	−0.40	+0.40	
40	−0.61	+0.61	150	−0.33	+0.33	**90 Percent Range for Excel's Sample Skewness Coefficient**
50	−0.55	+0.55	200	−0.28	+0.28	
60	−0.51	+0.51	300	−0.23	+0.23	Source: Simulation of 100,000 samples using R with CRAN e1071 library.
70	−0.47	+0.47	400	−0.20	+0.20	
80	−0.44	+0.44	500	−0.18	+0.18	

Kurtosis

Kurtosis refers to the relative length of the tails and the degree of concentration in the center. A normal bell-shaped population is called **mesokurtic** and serves as a benchmark (see Figure 4.37). A population that is flatter than a normal (i.e., has heavier tails) is called **platykurtic** while one that is more sharply peaked than a normal (i.e., has thinner tails) is **leptokurtic**. Kurtosis is *not* the same thing as variability, although the two are easily confused.

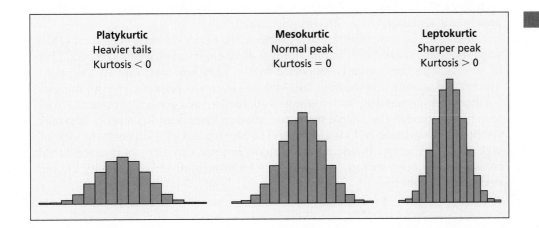

FIGURE 4.37

Kurtosis Prototype Shapes

A histogram is an unreliable guide to kurtosis because its scale and axis proportions may vary, so a numerical statistic is needed. Excel and MINITAB use this statistic:

$$(4.29) \quad \text{Kurtosis} = \frac{n(n+1)}{(n-1)(n-2)(n-3)} \sum_{i=1}^{n} \left(\frac{x_i - \bar{x}}{s}\right)^4 - \frac{3(n-1)^2}{(n-2)(n-3)}$$

The sample kurtosis coefficient is obtained from Excel's function =KURT(Data). Table 4.18 shows the expected range within which sample kurtosis coefficients would be expected to fall 90 percent of the time if the population is normal. A sample coefficient within the ranges shown may be attributed to chance variation, while a coefficient outside this range would suggest that the sample differs from a normal population. As sample size increases, the chance range narrows. Unless you have at least 50 observations, inferences about kurtosis are risky.

TABLE 4.18						
90 Percent Range for Excel's Sample Kurtosis Coefficient	*n*	*Lower 5%*	*Upper 5%*	*n*	*Lower 5%*	*Upper 5%*
	40	−0.89	1.35	100	−0.62	0.88
	50	−0.82	1.23	150	−0.53	0.71
	60	−0.76	1.13	200	−0.47	0.62
Source: Simulation of 100,000 samples using R with CRAN e1071 library.	70	−0.72	1.04	300	−0.40	0.50
Note that lower and upper table limits	80	−0.68	0.98	400	−0.35	0.44
are *not* symmetric.	90	−0.65	0.92	500	−0.32	0.39

Mini Case   4.8

Stock Prices 📁 **StockPrices**

An investor is tracking four stocks, two in the computer data services sector (IBM and EDS) and two in the consumer appliance sector (Maytag and Whirlpool). The analyst chose a two-month period of observation and recorded the closing price of each stock (42 trading days). Figure 4.38 shows MINITAB box plots for the stock prices (note that each has a different price scale).

Looking at the numerical statistics (Table 4.19), EDS's skewness coefficient (1.04) suggests a right-skewed distribution (for $n = 40$, the normal skewness range is −.594 to +.594). This conclusion is supported by the EDS box plot, with its long right whisker and an outlier in the right tail. Maytag's kurtosis coefficient (−1.40) suggests a flatter-than-normal distribution (for $n = 50$, the kurtosis coefficient range is −0.81 to +1.23), although the sample size is too small to assess kurtosis reliably. Maytag's coefficient of variation (CV) is also high. The Maytag box plot supports the view of high relative variation. In addition to patterns in price variation, an investor would consider many other factors (e.g., prospects for growth, dividends, stability, etc.) in evaluating a portfolio.

FIGURE 4.38   **Box Plots for Prices of Four Stocks**

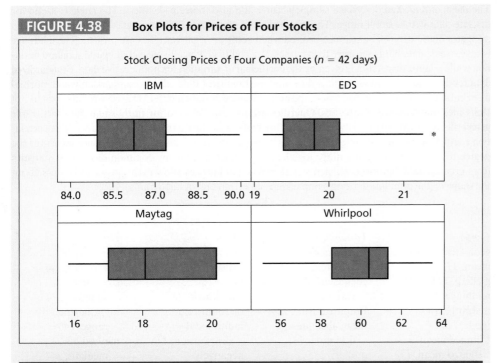

Stock Closing Prices of Four Companies (*n* = 42 days)

TABLE 4.19   **Four Companies' Stock Prices**

Statistic	IBM	EDS	Maytag	Whirlpool
Mean	86.40	19.86	18.39	59.80
Standard deviation	1.70	0.59	1.59	1.94
Skewness	0.51	1.04	0.23	−0.48
Kurtosis	−0.62	0.72	−1.40	−0.16
CV (%)	2.0%	3.0%	8.6%	3.2%
Quartile 1	84.97	19.40	17.07	58.53
Quartile 2	86.25	19.80	18.10	60.20
Quartile 3	87.37	20.13	20.11	61.28

Source: Data are from the Center for Research in Security Prices (CRSP®), a financial research center at the University of Chicago Graduate School of Business. Example is for statistical education only, and not as a guide to investment decisions. Maytag was acquired by Whirlpool in 2006.

Excel Hints

Hint 1: Formats When You Copy Data from Excel

Excel's dollar format (e.g., $214.07) or comma format (e.g., 12,417) will cause many statistical packages (e.g., MINITAB) to interpret the pasted data as text (because "$" and "," are not numbers). For example, in MINITAB a column heading C1-T indicates that the data column is text. Text cannot be analyzed numerically, so you can't get means, medians, etc. Check the format before you copy and paste.

Hint 2: Decimals When You Copy Data from Excel

Suppose you have adjusted Excel's decimal cell format to display 2.4 instead of 2.35477. When you copy this cell and paste it into MINITAB, the pasted cell contains 2.4 (not 2.35477). Thus, Excel's statistical calculations (based on 2.35477) will not agree with MINITAB. If you copy several columns of data (e.g., for a regression model), the differences can be serious.

CHAPTER SUMMARY

The **mean** and **median** describe a sample's **center** and also indicate **skewness.** The **mode** is useful for discrete data with a small range. The **trimmed mean** eliminates extreme values. The **geometric mean** mitigates high extremes but cannot be used when zeros or negative values are present. The **midrange** is easy to calculate but is sensitive to extremes. Variability is typically measured by the **standard deviation** while relative dispersion is given by the **coefficient of variation** for nonnegative data. **Standardized data** reveal **outliers** or unusual data values, and the **Empirical Rule** offers a comparison with a normal distribution. In measuring dispersion, the **mean absolute deviation** or **MAD** is easy to understand but lacks nice mathematical properties. **Quartiles** are meaningful even for fairly small data sets, while **percentiles** are used only for large data sets. **Box plots** show the quartiles and data range. The **correlation coefficient** measures the degree of linearity between two variables. The **covariance** measures the degree to which two variables move together. We can estimate many common descriptive statistics from **grouped data.** Sample coefficients of **skewness** and **kurtosis** allow more precise inferences about the **shape** of the population being sampled instead of relying on histograms.

KEY TERMS

Center	*Variability*	*Shape*	*Other*
geometric mean, *123*	Chebyshev's	bimodal	box plot, *143*
mean, *113*	Theorem, *134*	distribution, *118*	covariance, *148*
median, *115*	coefficient of	kurtosis, *155*	five-number
midhinge, *145*	variation, *130*	leptokurtic, *155*	summary, *143*
midrange, *124*	Empirical Rule, *134*	mesokurtic, *155*	interquartile
mode, *116*	mean absolute	multimodal	range, *140*
trimmed mean, *124*	deviation, *131*	distribution, *118*	method of
weighted mean, *152*	outliers, *135*	negatively	medians, *141*
	population	skewed, *118*	quartiles, *140*
	variance, *128*	platykurtic, *155*	sample correlation
	range, *127*	positively skewed, *118*	coefficient, *147*
	sample variance, *128*	skewed left, *118*	
	standard	skewed right, *118*	
	deviation, *128*	skewness, *118*	
	standardized	skewness	
	data, *135*	coefficient, *154*	
	two-sum formula, *129*	symmetric data, *118*	
	z-score, *135*		

Commonly Used Formulas in Descriptive Statistics

Sample mean: $\bar{x} = \dfrac{1}{n}\sum_{i=1}^{n} x_i$

Geometric mean: $G = \sqrt[n]{x_1 x_2 \ldots x_n}$

Growth rate: $GR = \sqrt[n-1]{\dfrac{x_n}{x_1}} - 1$

Range: $\text{Range} = x_{\max} - x_{\min}$

Midrange: $\text{Midrange} = \dfrac{x_{\max} + x_{\min}}{2}$

Sample standard deviation: $s = \sqrt{\dfrac{\sum_{i=1}^{n}(x_i - \bar{x})^2}{n - 1}}$

Coefficient of variation:

Population   Sample

$CV = 100 \times \dfrac{\sigma}{\mu}$ $CV = 100 \times \dfrac{s}{\bar{x}}$

Standardized variable:

Population   Sample

$z_i = \dfrac{x_i - \mu}{\sigma}$ $z_i = \dfrac{x_i - \bar{x}}{s}$

Midhinge: $\text{Midhinge} = \dfrac{Q_1 + Q_3}{2}$

Sample correlation coefficient: $r = \dfrac{\displaystyle\sum_{i=1}^{n}(x_i - \bar{x})(y_i - \bar{y})}{\sqrt{\displaystyle\sum_{i=1}^{n}(x_i - \bar{x})^2}\sqrt{\displaystyle\sum_{i=1}^{n}(y_i - \bar{y})^2}}$ or $r = \dfrac{s_{XY}}{s_X s_Y}$

Weighted mean: $\bar{x} = \displaystyle\sum_{j=1}^{k} w_j x_j$ where $\displaystyle\sum_{j=1}^{k} w_j = 1.00$

Grouped mean: $\bar{x} = \displaystyle\sum_{j=1}^{k} \dfrac{f_j m_j}{n}$

CHAPTER REVIEW

1. What are descriptive statistics? How do they differ from visual displays of data?

2. Explain each concept: (a) center, (b) variability, and (c) shape.

3. (a) Why is sorting usually the first step in data analysis? (b) Why is it useful to begin a data analysis by thinking about how the data were collected?

4. List strengths and weaknesses of each measure of center and write its Excel function: (a) mean, (b) median, and (c) mode.

5. (a) Why must the deviations around the mean sum to zero? (b) What is the position of the median in the data array when n is even? When n is odd? (c) Why is the mode of little use in continuous data? (d) For what type of data is the mode most useful?

6. (a) What is a bimodal distribution? (b) Explain two ways to detect skewness.

7. List strengths and weaknesses of each measure of center and give its Excel function (if any): (a) midrange, (b) geometric mean, and (c) 10 percent trimmed mean.

8. (a) What is variability? (b) Name five measures of variability. List the main characteristics (strengths, weaknesses) of each measure.

9. (a) Which standard deviation formula (population, sample) is used most often? Why? (b) When is the coefficient of variation useful?

10. (a) To what kind of data does Chebyshev's Theorem apply? (b) To what kind of data does the Empirical Rule apply? (c) What is an outlier? An unusual data value?

11. (a) In a normal distribution, approximately what percent of observations are within 1, 2, and 3 standard deviations of the mean? (b) In a sample of 10,000 observations, about how many observations would you expect beyond 3 standard deviations of the mean?

12. (a) Write the mathematical formula for a standardized variable. (b) Write the Excel formula for standardizing a data value in cell F17 from an array with mean Mu and standard deviation Sigma.

13. (a) Why is it dangerous to delete an outlier? (b) When might it be acceptable to delete an outlier?

14. (a) Explain how quartiles can measure both center and variability. (b) Why don't we calculate percentiles for small samples?

15. (a) Explain the method of medians for calculating quartiles. (b) Write the Excel formula for the first quartile of an array named XData.

16. (a) What is a box plot? What does it tell us? (b) What is the role of fences in a box plot? (c) Define the midhinge and interquartile range.

17. What does a correlation coefficient measure? What is its range? Why is a correlation coefficient easier to interpret than a covariance?

18. (a) Why is some accuracy lost when we estimate the mean or standard deviation from grouped data? (b) Why do open-ended classes in a frequency distribution make it impossible to estimate the mean and standard deviation? (c) When would grouped data be presented instead of the entire sample of raw data?

19. (a) What is the skewness coefficient of a normal distribution? A uniform distribution? (b) Why do we need a table for sample skewness coefficients that is based on sample size?

20. (a) What is kurtosis? (b) Sketch a platykurtic population, a leptokurtic population, and a mesokurtic population. (c) Why can't we rely on a histogram to assess kurtosis?

CHAPTER EXERCISES

connect

4.44 For each data set: (a) Find the mean, median, and mode. (b) Which, if any, of these three measures is the weakest indicator of a "typical" data value? Why?

a. 100 m dash times ($n = 6$ top runners):   9.87, 9.98, 10.02, 10.15, 10.36, 10.36

b. Number of children ($n = 13$ families):   0, 1, 1, 2, 2, 2, 2, 2, 2, 2, 2, 2, 6

c. Number of cars in driveway ($n = 8$ homes):   0, 0, 1, 1, 2, 2, 3, 5

4.45 During a rock concert, the noise level (in decibels) in front row seats has a mean of 95 dB with a standard deviation of 8 dB. Without assuming a normal distribution, find the minimum percentage of noise level readings within 3 standard deviations of the mean.

4.46 Bags of jelly beans have a mean weight of 396 gm with a standard deviation of 5 gm. Use Chebyshev's Theorem to find a lower bound for the number of bags in a sample of 200 that weigh between 386 and 406 gm.

4.47 Based on experience, the Ball Corporation's aluminum can manufacturing facility in Ft. Atkinson, Wisconsin, knows that the metal thickness of incoming shipments has a mean of 0.2731 mm with a standard deviation of 0.000959 mm. (a) A certain shipment has a diameter of 0.2761. Find the standardized z-score for this shipment. (b) Is this an outlier?

4.48 SAT scores for the entering class of 2010 at Oxnard University were normally distributed with a mean of 1340 and a standard deviation of 90. Bob's SAT score was 1430. (a) Find Bob's standardized z-score. (b) By the Empirical Rule, is Bob's SAT score unusual?

4.49 Find the data value that corresponds to each of the following z-scores.

a. Final exam scores: Allison's z-score $= 2.30$, $\mu = 74$, $\sigma = 7$

b. Weekly grocery bill: James' z-score $= -1.45$, $\mu = \$53$, $\sigma = \$12$

c. Daily video game play time: Eric's z-score $= -0.79$, $\mu = 4.00$ hours, $\sigma = 1.15$ hours

4.50 The average time a Boulder High varsity lacrosse player plays in a game is 30 minutes with a standard deviation of 7 minutes. Nolan's playing time in last week's game against Fairview was 48 minutes. (a) Calculate the z-score for Nolan's playing time against Fairview. (b) By the Empirical Rule, was Nolan's playing time *unusual* when compared to the typical playing time?

4.51 The number of blueberries in a blueberry muffin baked by EarthHarvest Bakeries can range from 18 to 30 blueberries. (a) Use the Empirical Rule to estimate the standard deviation of the number of blueberries in a muffin. (b) What assumption did you make about the distribution of the number of blueberries?

Note: Unless otherwise instructed, you may use any desired statistical software for calculations and graphs in the following problems.

DESCRIBING DATA

4.52 Below are monthly rents paid by 30 students who live off campus. (a) Find the mean, median, and mode. (b) Do the measures of central tendency agree? Explain. (c) Calculate the standard deviation. (d) Sort and standardize the data. (e) Are there outliers or unusual data values? (f) Using the Empirical Rule, do you think the data could be from a normal population? Rents

730	730	730	930	700	570
690	1,030	740	620	720	670
560	740	650	660	850	930
600	620	760	690	710	500
730	800	820	840	720	700

4.53 How many days in advance do travelers purchase their airline tickets? Below are data showing the advance days for a sample of 28 passengers on United Airlines Flight 815 from Chicago to Los Angeles. (a) Calculate the mean, median, mode, and midrange. (b) Calculate the quartiles and midhinge. (c) Why can't you use the geometric mean for this data set? Days

11	7	11	4	15	14	71	29	8	7	16	28	17	249
0	20	77	18	14	3	15	52	20	0	9	9	21	3

4.54   The durations (minutes) of 26 electric power outages in the community of Sonando Heights over the past five years are shown below. (a) Find the mean, median, and mode. (b) Are the mean and median about the same? (c) Is the mode a good measure of center for this data set? Explain. (d) Is the distribution skewed? Explain. ⌦ **Duration**

32	44	25	66	27	12	62	9	51	4	17	50	35
99	30	21	12	53	25	2	18	24	84	30	17	17

4.55   The U.S. Postal Service will ship a Priority Mail® Large Flat Rate Box (12″ × 12″ × 5½″) anywhere in the United States for a fixed price, regardless of weight. The weights (ounces) of 20 randomly chosen boxes are shown below. (a) Find the mean, median, and mode. (b) Are the mean and median about the same? If not, why not? (c) Is the mode a "typical" data value? Explain. (d) Is the distribution skewed? Explain. ⌦ **Weights**

72	86	28	67	64	65	45	86	31	32
39	92	90	91	84	62	80	74	63	86

4.56   A sample of size $n = 70$ showed a skewness coefficient of 0.773 and a kurtosis coefficient of 1.277. What is the distribution's shape?

4.57   The "expense ratio" is a measure of the cost of managing the portfolio. Investors prefer a low expense ratio, all else equal. Below are expense ratios for 23 randomly chosen stock funds and 21 randomly chosen bond funds. (a) Calculate the mean and median for each sample. (b) Calculate the standard deviation and coefficient of variation for each sample. (c) Which type of fund has more variability? Explain. ⌦ **Funds**

23 Stock Funds

1.12	1.44	1.27	1.75	0.99	1.45	1.19	1.22	0.99	3.18	1.21	1.89
0.60	2.10	0.73	0.90	1.79	1.35	1.08	1.28	1.20	1.68	0.15	

21 Bond Funds

1.96	0.51	1.12	0.64	0.69	0.20	1.44	0.68	0.40	0.94	0.75	1.77
0.93	1.25	0.85	0.99	0.95	0.35	0.64	0.41	0.90			

4.58   Statistics students were asked to fill a one-cup measure with raisin bran, tap the cup lightly on the counter three times to settle the contents, if necessary add more raisin bran to bring the contents to the one-cup line, spread the contents on a large plate, and count the raisins. The 13 students who chose Kellogg's Raisin Bran obtained the results shown below. (a) Use Excel to calculate the mean, median, mode, and midrange. (b) Which is the best measure of center, and why? (c) Calculate the standard deviation. (d) Is the highest data value an outlier? ⌦ **Raisins**

23	33	44	36	29	42	31	33	61	36	34	23	24

4.59   The table below shows estimates of the total cost of repairs in four bumper tests (full frontal, front corner, full rear, rear corner) on 17 cars. (a) Calculate the mean and median. (b) Would you say the data are skewed? (c) Why is the mode not useful for these data? (Data are from Insurance Institute for Highway Safety, *Detroit Free Press*, March 1, 2007, p. 2E). ⌦ **CrashDamage**

Car Tested	Damage	Car Tested	Damage	Car Tested	Damage
Chevrolet Malibu	6,646	Mazda 6	4,961	Suburu Legacy	7,448
Chrysler Sebring	7,454	Mitsubishi Galant	4,277	Toyota Camry	4,911
Ford Fusion	5,030	Nissan Altima	6,459	Volkswagen Jetta	9,020
Honda Accord	8,010	Nissan Maxima	9,051	Volkswagen Passat	8,259
Hyundai Sonata	7,565	Pontiac G6	8,919	Volvo S40	5,600
Kia Optima	5,735	Saturn Aura	6,374		

4.60   Grace took a random sample of the number of steps per minute from the electronic readout of her aerobic climbing machine during a 1-hour workout. (a) Calculate the mean, median, and mode. (b) Which is the best measure of center? The worst? Why? (Data are from a project by Grace Obringer, MBA student.) 📄 **Steps**

| 90 | 110 | 97 | 144 | 54 | 60 | 156 | 86 | 82 | 64 | 100 | 47 | 80 | 164 | 93 |

4.61   How much revenue does it take to maintain a cricket club? The following table shows annual income for 18 first-class clubs that engage in league play. (a) Calculate the mean and median. (b) Describe a "typical" cricket club's income. (Data are from *The Economist* 367, no. 8329 [June 21, 2003], p. 47.)

Annual Income of First-Class Cricket Clubs in England 📄 **Cricket**

Club	Income (£000)	Club	Income (£000)
Lancashire	5,366	Durham	3,009
Surrey	6,386	Worcestershire	2,446
Derbyshire	2,088	Gloucestershire	2,688
Middlesex	2,280	Northamptonshire	2,416
Somerset	2,544	Glamorgan	2,133
Nottinghamshire	3,669	Essex	2,417
Kent	2,894	Warwickshire	4,272
Leicestershire	2,000	Yorkshire	2,582
Sussex	2,477	Hampshire	2,557

4.62   A plumbing supplier's mean monthly demand for vinyl washers is 24,212 with a standard deviation of 6,053. The mean monthly demand for steam boilers is 6.8 with a standard deviation of 1.7. Compare the variability of these distributions. Which demand pattern has more relative variation? Explain.

4.63   The table below shows average daily sales of Rice Krispies in the month of June in 74 Noodles & Company restaurants. (a) Make a histogram for the data. (b) Would you say the distribution is skewed? (c) Calculate the mean and standard deviation. (d) Are there any outliers? 📄 **RiceKrispies**

32	8	14	20	28	19	37	31	16	16
16	29	11	34	31	18	22	17	27	16
24	49	25	18	25	21	15	16	20	11
21	29	14	25	10	15	8	12	12	19
21	28	27	26	12	24	18	19	24	16
17	20	23	13	17	17	19	36	16	34
25	15	16	13	20	13	13	23	17	22
11	17	17	9						

4.64   Analysis of portfolio returns over a 20-year period showed the statistics below. (a) Calculate and compare the coefficients of variation. (b) Why would we use a coefficient of variation? Why not just compare the standard deviations? (c) What do the data tell you about risk and return? 📄 **Returns**

Comparative Returns on Four Types of Investments

Investment	Mean Return	Standard Deviation	Coefficient of Variation
Venture funds	19.2	14.0	
Common stocks	15.6	14.0	
Real estate	11.5	16.8	
Federal short-term paper	6.7	1.9	

4.65   Analysis of annualized returns over a 10-year period showed that prepaid tuition plans had a mean return of 6.3 percent with a standard deviation of 2.7 percent, while the Standard & Poor's 500 stock index had a mean return of 12.9 percent with a standard deviation of

15.8 percent. (a) Calculate and compare the coefficients of variation. (b) Why would we use a coefficient of variation? Why not just compare the standard deviations?

4.66   Caffeine content in a 5-ounce cup of brewed coffee ranges from 60 to 180 mg, depending on brew time, coffee bean type, and grind. (a) Use the midrange as a measure of center. (b) Use the Empirical Rule to estimate the standard deviation. (c) Why is the assumption of a normal, bell-shaped distribution important in making these estimates? (d) Why might caffeine content of coffee *not* be normal?

4.67   Chlorine is added to city water to kill bacteria. In a certain year, chlorine content in water from the Lake Huron Water Treatment plant ranged from 0.79 ppm (parts per million) to 0.92 ppm. (a) Use the midrange as a measure of center. (b) Use the Empirical Rule to estimate the standard deviation.

THINKING ABOUT DISTRIBUTIONS

4.68   At the Midlothian Independent Bank, a study shows that the mean ATM transaction takes 74 seconds, the median 63 seconds, and the mode 51 seconds. (a) Sketch the distribution, based on these statistics. (b) What factors might cause the distribution to be like this?

4.69   At the Eureka library, the mean time a book is checked out is 13 days, the median is 10 days, and the mode is 7 days. (a) Sketch the distribution, based on these statistics. (b) What factors might cause the distribution to be like this?

4.70   On Professor Hardtack's last cost accounting exam, the mean score was 71, the median was 77, and the mode was 81. (a) Sketch the distribution, based on these statistics. (b) What factors might cause the distribution to be like this?

4.71   The median life span of a mouse is 118 weeks. (a) Would you expect the mean to be higher or lower than 118? (b) Would you expect the life spans of mice to be normally distributed? Explain.

4.72   The median waiting time for a liver transplant in the United States is 321 days. Would you expect the mean to be higher or lower than 321 days? Explain. (See http://www.livermd.org/.)

4.73   A small suburban community agreed to purchase police services from the county sheriff's department. The newspaper said, "In the past, the charge for police protection from the Sheriff's Department has been based on the median cost of the salary, fringe benefits, etc. That is, the cost per deputy was set halfway between the most expensive deputy and the least expensive." (a) Is this the median? If not, what is it? (b) Which would probably cost the city more, the midrange or the median? Why?

4.74   A company's contractual "trigger" point for a union absenteeism penalty is a certain distance above the *mean* days missed by all workers. Now the company wants to switch the trigger to a certain number of days above the *median* days missed for all workers. (a) Visualize the distribution of missed days for all workers (symmetric, skewed left, skewed right). (b) Discuss the probable effect on the trigger point of switching from the mean to the median. (c) What position would the union be likely to take on the company's proposed switch?

EXCEL PROJECTS

4.75   (a) Use Excel functions to calculate the mean and standard deviation for weekend occupancy rates (percent) in nine resort hotels during the off-season. (b) What conclusion would a casual observer draw about center and variability, based on your statistics? (c) Now calculate the median for each sample. (d) Make a dot plot for each sample. (e) What did you learn from the medians and dot plots that was not apparent from the means and standard deviations? 🖫 **Occupancy**

Observation	Week 1	Week 2	Week 3	Week 4
1	32	33	38	37
2	41	35	39	42
3	44	45	39	45
4	47	50	40	46
5	50	52	56	47
6	53	54	57	48
7	56	58	58	50
8	59	59	61	67
9	68	64	62	68

4.76 (a) Enter the Excel function =ROUND(NORMINV(RAND(),70,10),0) in cells B1:B100. This will create 100 random data points from a normal distribution using parameters $\mu = 70$ and $\sigma = 10$. Think of these numbers as exam scores for 100 students. (b) Use the Excel functions =AVERAGE(B1:B100) and =STDEV.S(B1:B100) to calculate the sample mean and standard deviation for your data array. (c) Write down the sample mean and standard deviation. (d) Compare the sample statistics with the desired parameters $\mu = 70$ and $\sigma = 10$. Do Excel's random samples have approximately the desired characteristics?

GROUPED DATA

Note: In each of the following tables, the upper bin limit is excluded from that bin but is included as the lower limit of the next bin.

4.77 A random sample of individuals who filed their own income taxes were asked how much time (hours) they spent preparing last year's federal income tax forms. (a) Estimate the mean. (b) Estimate the standard deviation. (c) Do you think the observations would be distributed uniformly within each interval? Why would that matter? (d) Why do you imagine that unequal bin sizes (interval widths) were used?

From	To (not incl)	f
0	2	7
2	4	42
4	8	33
8	16	21
16	32	11
32	64	6

4.78 This table shows the distribution of winning times in the Kentucky Derby (a horse race) over 80 years. Times are recorded to the nearest $\frac{1}{5}$ second (e.g., 121.4). (a) From the grouped data, calculate the mean. Show your calculations clearly in a worksheet. (b) What additional information would you have gained by having the raw data? (c) Do you think it likely that the distribution of times within each interval might not be uniform? Why would that matter?

Kentucky Derby Winning Times, 1930–2009 (seconds) 📄 Derby

From	To	f
119	120	2
120	121	4
121	122	18
122	123	25
123	124	12
124	125	9
125	126	5
126	127	3
127	128	2
	Total	80

Source: *Sports Illustrated 2004 Sports Almanac, Detroit Free Press, The New York Times,* and www.horse-races.net.

4.79 The self-reported number of hours worked per week by 204 top executives is given below. (a) Estimate the mean, standard deviation, and coefficient of variation, using an Excel worksheet to organize your calculations. (b) Do the unequal class sizes hamper your calculations? Why do you suppose that was done?

Weekly Hours of Work by Top Executives 📄 Work

From	To	f
40	50	12
50	60	116
60	80	74
80	100	2
	Total	204

4.80 How long does it take to fly from Denver to Atlanta on Delta Airlines? The table below shows 56 observations on flight times (in minutes) for the first week of March 2005. (a) Use the grouped data formula to estimate the mean and standard deviation. (b) Using the ungrouped data (not shown), the *ungrouped* sample mean is 161.63 minutes and the ungrouped standard deviation is 8.07 minutes. How close did your *grouped* estimates come? (c) Why might flight times *not* be uniformly distributed within the second and third class intervals? (*Source:* www.bts.gov.)

Flight Times DEN to ATL (minutes) 📄 DeltaAir

From		To	frequency
140	<	150	1
150	<	160	25
160	<	170	24
170	<	180	4
180	<	190	2
		Total	56

DO-IT-YOURSELF SAMPLING PROJECTS

4.81 (a) Record the points scored by the winning team in 30 college football games played last weekend (if it is not football season, do the same for basketball or another sport of your choice). If you can't find 30 scores, do the best you can. (b) Make a frequency distribution and histogram. Describe the histogram. (c) Calculate the mean, median, and mode. Which is the best measure of center? Why? (d) Calculate the standard deviation and coefficient of variation. (e) Standardize the data. Are there any outliers? (f) Make a box plot. What does it tell you?

4.82 (a) Record the length (in minutes) of 30 movies chosen at random from your cable TV guide (or a similar source). Include the name of each movie. (b) Make a frequency distribution and histogram. Describe the histogram. (c) Calculate the mean, median, and mode. Which is the best measure of center? Why? (d) Standardize the data. Are there any outliers?

SCATTER PLOTS AND CORRELATION

Note: Obtain these data sets from the OLC website www.mhhe.com/doane4e/.

4.83 (a) Make an Excel scatter plot of X = 1990 assault rate per 100,000 population and Y = 2004 assault rate per 100,000 population for the 50 U.S. states. (b) Use Excel's =CORREL function to find the correlation coefficient. (c) What do the graph and correlation coefficient say about assault rates by state for these two years? (d) Use MegaStat or Excel to find the mean, median, and standard deviation of assault rates in these two years. What does this comparison tell you? 📄 Assault

4.84 (a) Make an Excel scatter plot of X = airspeed (nautical miles per hour) and Y = cockpit noise level (decibels) for 61 aircraft flights. (b) Use Excel's =CORREL function to find the correlation coefficient. (c) What do the graph and correlation coefficient say about the relationship between airspeed and cockpit noise? Why might such a relationship exist? *Optional:* Fit an Excel trend line to the scatter plot and interpret it. 📄 CockpitNoise

MINI-PROJECTS

Note that in the following data sets, only the first three and last three observations are shown. Download the full data sets from the OLC website www.mhhe.com/doane4e/

4.85   (a) Sort the data and find X_{min} and X_{max}. (b) Choose a data set and prepare a brief, descriptive report. You may use any computer software you wish (e.g., Excel, MegaStat, MINITAB). Include relevant worksheets or graphs in your report. If some questions do not apply to your data set, explain why not. Make a histogram. Describe its shape. (c) Calculate the mean and median. Are the data skewed? (d) Calculate the standard deviation. (e) Standardize the data and check for outliers. (f) Calculate the quartiles and make a box plot. Describe its appearance.

DATA SET A   **Advertising Dollars as Percent of Sales in Selected Industries (*n* = 30)** 📂 **Ads**

Industry	Percent
Accident and health insurance	0.9
Apparel and other finished products	5.5
Beverages	7.4
⋮	⋮
Steel works and blast furnaces	1.9
Tires and inner tubes	1.8
Wine, brandy, and spirits	11.3

Source: George E. Belch and Michael A. Belch, *Advertising and Promotion,* pp. 219–220. Copyright © 2004 Richard D. Irwin. Used with permission of McGraw-Hill Companies, Inc.

DATA SET B   **Maximum Rate of Climb for Selected Piston Aircraft (*n* = 54)** 📂 **ClimbRate**

Manufacturer/Model	Year	Climb (ft./min.)
AMD CH 2000	2000	820
Beech Baron 58	1984	1,750
Beech Baron 58P	1984	1,475
⋮	⋮	⋮
Sky Arrow 650 TC	1998	750
Socata TB20 Trinidad	1999	1,200
Tiger AG-5B	2002	850

Source: *Flying Magazine* (various issues from 1997 to 2002).

DATA SET C   **December Heating Degree-Days for Selected U.S. Cities (*n* = 35)** 📂 **Heating**

City	Degree-Days
Albuquerque	911
Baltimore	884
Bismarck	1,538
⋮	⋮
St. Louis	955
Washington, D.C.	809
Wichita	949

Source: U.S. Bureau of the Census, *Statistical Abstract of the United States.*

Note: A degree-day is the sum over all days in the month of the difference between 65 degrees Fahrenheit and the daily mean temperature of each city.

DATA SET D   **Commercial Bank Profit as Percent of Revenue, 2003** 📁 **Banks**

Bank	Percent
AmSouth Bancorp	21
Bank of America Corp.	22
Bank of New York Co.	18
⋮	⋮
Wachovia Corp.	19
Wells Fargo	20
Zions Bancorp	18

Source: *Fortune* 149, no. 7 (April 5, 2004). Copyright © 2004 Time Inc. All rights reserved.
Note: These banks are in the Fortune 1000 companies.

DATA SET E   **Caffeine Content of Randomly Selected Beverages (*n* = 32)** 📁 **Caffeine**

Company/Brand	mg/oz.
Barq's Root Beer	1.83
Coca-Cola Classic	2.83
Cool from Nestea	1.33
⋮	⋮
Snapple Sweet Tea	1.00
Sunkist Orange Soda	3.42
Vanilla Coke	2.83

Source: National Soft Drink Association (www.nsda.org).

DATA SET F   **Super Bowl Scores 1967–2011 (*n* = 45 games)** 📁 **SuperBowl**

Year	Teams and Scores
1967	Green Bay 35, Kansas City 10
1968	Green Bay 33, Oakland 14
1969	NY Jets 16, Baltimore 7
⋮	⋮
2009	Pittsburgh 27, Arizona 23
2010	New Orleans 31, Indianapolis 17
2011	Green Bay 31, Pittsburgh 25

Source: *Sports Illustrated 2004 Sports Almanac, Detroit Free Press,* www.cbs.sportsline.com, www.nfl.com, and en.wikipedia.org.

DATA SET G   **Property Crimes per 100,000 Residents (*n* = 68 cities)** 📁 **Crime**

City and State	Crime
Albuquerque, NM	8,515
Anaheim, CA	2,827
Anchorage, AK	4,370
⋮	⋮
Virginia Beach, VA	3,438
Washington, DC	6,434
Wichita, KS	5,733

Source: *Statistical Abstract of the United States, 2002.*

DATA SET H   **Size of Whole Foods Stores (*n* = 171)** 🖾 **WholeFoods**

Location (Store Name)	Sq. Ft.
Albuquerque, NM (Academy)	33,000
Alexandria, VA (Annandale)	29,811
Ann Arbor, MI (Washtenaw)	51,300
⋮	⋮
Winter Park, FL	20,909
Woodland Hills, CA	28,180
Wynnewood, PA	14,000

Source: www.wholefoodsmarket.com/stores/.

RELATED READING

Freund, John E.; and Benjamin M. Perles. "A New Look at Quartiles of Ungrouped Data." *The American Statistician* 41, no. 3 (August 1987), pp. 200–203.

Pukelsheim, Friedrich. "The Three Sigma Rule." *The American Statistician* 48, no. 2 (May 1994), pp. 88–91.

Little, Roderick J. A., and Donald B. Rubin. *Statistical Analysis with Missing Data.* 2nd ed. John Wiley and Sons, 2002.

CHAPTER 4   Online Learning Resources

The Online Learning Center (OLC) at www.mhhe.com/doane4e has several *LearningStats* demonstrations to help you understand descriptive statistics. Your instructor may assign one or more of them, or you may decide to download the ones that sound interesting.

Topic	*LearningStats Demonstrations*
Overview	🅖 Describing Data 🅖 Using MegaStat 🅖 Using MINITAB
Descriptive statistics	🅧 Basic Statistic 🅧 Quartiles 🅧 Box Plots 🅧 Grouped Data 🆆 Significant Digits
ScreenCam Tutorials	🅡 Using MegaStat 🅡 Excel Descriptive Statistics 🅡 Excel Scatter Plots

Key: 🅖 = PowerPoint   🆆 = Word   🅧 = Excel   🅡 = ScreenCam Tutorials

EXAM REVIEW QUESTIONS FOR CHAPTERS 1–4

1. Which type of statistic (descriptive, inferential) is each of the following?

   a. Estimating the default rate on all U.S. mortgages from a random sample of 500 loans.
   b. Reporting the percent of students in your statistics class who use Verizon.
   c. Using a sample of 50 iPhones to predict the average battery life in typical usage.

2. Which is *not* an ethical obligation of a statistician? Explain.

   a. To know and follow accepted procedures.
   b. To ensure data integrity and accurate calculations.
   c. To support client wishes in drawing conclusions from the data.

3. "Driving without a seat belt is not risky. I've done it for 25 years without an accident." This *best* illustrates which fallacy?

   a. Unconscious bias.
   b. Conclusion from a small sample.
   c. *Post hoc* reasoning.

4. Which data type (categorical, numerical) is each of the following?

   a. Your current credit card balance.
   b. Your college major.
   c. Your car's odometer mileage reading today.

5. Give the type of measurement (nominal, ordinal, interval, ratio) for each variable.

   a. Length of time required for a randomly chosen vehicle to cross a toll bridge.
   b. Student's ranking of five cell phone service providers.
   c. The type of charge card used by a customer (Visa, MasterCard, AmEx, Other).

6. Tell if each variable is continuous or discrete.

   a. Tonnage carried by an oil tanker at sea.
   b. Wind velocity at 7 o'clock this morning.
   c. Number of text messages you received yesterday.

7. To choose a sample of 12 students from a statistics class of 36 students, which type of sample (simple random, systematic, cluster, convenience) is each of these?

   a. Picking every student who was wearing blue that day.
   b. Using Excel's =RANDBETWEEN(1,36) to choose students from the class list.
   c. Selecting every 3rd student starting from a randomly chosen position.

8. Which of the following is *not* a reason for sampling? Explain.

   a. The destructive nature of some tests.
   b. High cost of studying the entire population.
   c. The expense of obtaining random numbers.

9. Which statement is *correct*? Why not the others?

   a. Likert scales are interval if scale distances are meaningful.
   b. Cross-sectional data are measured over time.
   c. A census is always preferable to a sample.

10. Which statement is *false*? Explain.

    a. Sampling error can be reduced by using appropriate data coding.
    b. Selection bias means that respondents are not typical of the target population.
    c. Simple random sampling requires a list of the population.

11. The management of a theme park obtained a random sample of the ages of 36 riders of its Space Adventure Simulator. (a) Make a nice histogram. (b) Did your histogram follow Sturges' Rule? If not, why not? (c) Describe the distribution of sample data. (d) Make a dot plot of the data. (e) What can be learned from each display (dot plot and histogram)?

39	46	15	38	39	47	50	61	17
40	54	36	16	18	34	42	10	16
16	13	38	14	16	56	17	18	53
24	17	12	21	8	18	13	13	10

12. Which one of the following is *true*? Why not the others?

    a. Histograms are useful for visualizing correlations.
    b. Pyramid charts are generally preferred to bar charts.
    c. A correlation coefficient can be negative.

13. Which data would be most suitable for a pie chart? Why not the others?

    a. Presidential vote in the last election by party (Democratic, Republican, Other).
    b. Retail prices of six major brands of color laser printers.
    c. Labor cost per vehicle for 10 major world automakers.

14. Find the mean, standard deviation, and coefficient of variation for $X = 5, 10, 20, 10, 15$.

15. Here are the ages of a random sample of 20 CEOs (chief executive officers) of Fortune 500 U.S. corporations. (a) Find the mean, median, and mode. (b) Discuss advantages and disadvantages of each of these measures of center for this data set. (c) Find the quartiles and interpret them. (d) Sketch a box plot and describe it.

57	56	58	46	70	62	55	60	59	64
62	67	61	55	53	58	63	51	52	77

16. A consulting firm used a random sample of 12 CIOs (chief information officers) of large businesses to examine the relationship (if any) between salary (in thousands) and years of service in the firm. (a) Make a scatter plot and describe it. (b) Calculate a correlation coefficient and interpret it.

Years (X)	4	15	15	8	11	5	5	8	10	1	6	17
Salary (Y)	133	129	143	132	144	61	128	79	140	116	88	170

17. Which statement is *true*? Why not the others?

   a. We expect the median to exceed the mean in positively skewed data.
   b. The geometric mean is not possible when there are negative data values.
   c. The midrange is resistant to outliers.

18. Which statement is *false*? Explain.

   a. If $\mu = 52$ and $\sigma = 15$, then $X = 81$ would be an outlier.
   b. If the data are from a normal population, about 68 percent of the values will be within $\mu \pm \sigma$.
   c. If $\mu = 640$ and $\sigma = 128$ then the coefficient of variation is 20 percent.

19. Which is *not* a characteristic of using a log scale to display time series data? Explain.

   a. A log scale helps if we are comparing changes in two time series of dissimilar magnitude.
   b. General business audiences find it easier to interpret a log scale.
   c. If you display data on a log scale, equal distances represent equal ratios.

Probability

CHAPTER CONTENTS

CHAPTER LEARNING OBJECTIVES

LO　**When you finish this chapter you should be able to**

LO 5-1　Describe the sample space of a random experiment.

LO 5-2　Distinguish among the three views of probability.

LO 5-3　Apply the definitions and rules of probability.

LO 5-4　Calculate odds from given probabilities.

LO 5-5　Determine when events are independent.

LO 5-6　Apply the concepts of probability to contingency tables.

LO 5-7　Interpret a tree diagram.

LO 5-8　Use Bayes' Theorem to calculate revised probabilities.

LO 5-9　Apply counting rules to calculate possible event arrangements.

You've learned that a statistic is a measurement that describes a sample data set of observations. Descriptive statistics allow us to describe a business process that we have already observed. But how will that process behave in the future? Nothing makes a business person more nervous than not being able to anticipate customer demand, supplier delivery dates, or their employees' output. Businesses want to be able to quantify the *uncertainty* of future events. What are the chances that revenue next month will exceed last year's average? How likely is it that our new production system will help us decrease our product defect rate? Businesses also want to understand how they can increase the chance of positive future events (increasing market share) and decrease the chance of negative future events (failing to meet forecasted sales.) The field of study called *probability* allows us to understand and quantify the uncertainty about the future. We use the rules of probability to bridge the gap between what we know now and what is unknown about the future.

5.1 RANDOM EXPERIMENTS

Sample Space

A **random experiment** is an observational process whose results cannot be known in advance. For example, when a customer enters a Lexus dealership, will the customer buy a car or not? How much will the customer spend? The set of all possible *outcomes* (denoted S) is the **sample space** for the experiment. Some sample spaces can be enumerated easily, while others may be immense or impossible to enumerate. For example, when CitiBank makes a consumer loan, we might define a sample space with only two outcomes:

LO 5-1

Describe the sample space of a random experiment.

$$S = \{\text{default, no default}\}$$

The sample space describing a Walmart customer's payment method might have four outcomes:

$$S = \{\text{cash, debit card, credit card, check}\}$$

The sample space to describe rolling a die has six outcomes:

$$S = \{\boxdot, \boxdot, \boxdot, \boxdot, \boxdot, \boxdot\}$$

When two dice are rolled, the sample space consists of 36 outcomes, each of which is a pair:

A sample space could be so large that it is impractical to enumerate the possibilities (e.g., the 12-digit UPC bar code on a product in your local Walmart could have 1 trillion values). If the outcome of the experiment is a *continuous* measurement, the sample space cannot be listed, but it can be described by a rule. For example, the sample space for the length of a randomly chosen cell phone call would be

$$S = \{\text{all } X \text{ such that } X \geq 0\}$$

and the sample space to describe a randomly chosen student's GPA would be

$$S = \{\text{all } X \text{ such that } 0.00 \leq X \leq 4.00\}$$

Similarly, some *discrete* measurements are best described by a rule. For example, the sample space for the number of hits on a YouTube website on a given day is:

$$S = \{\text{all } X \text{ such that } X = 0, 1, 2, \ldots\}$$

Event

An **event** is any subset of outcomes in the sample space. A **simple event**, or *elementary event,* is a single outcome. A discrete sample space S consists of all the simple events, denoted $E_1, E_2, \ldots, E_n$.

(5.1) $$S = \{E_1, E_2, \ldots, E_n\}$$

Consider the random experiment of tossing a balanced coin. The sample space for this experiment would be $S = \{\text{heads, tails}\}$. The chance of observing a head is the same as the chance of observing a tail. We say that these two elementary events are *equally likely*. When you buy a lottery ticket, the sample space $S = \{\text{win, lose}\}$ also has two elementary events; however, these events are not equally likely.

Simple events are the building blocks from which we can define a **compound event** consisting of two or more simple events. For example, Amazon's website for "Books & Music" has seven categories that a shopper might choose: $S = \{\text{Books, DVD, VHS, Magazines, Newspapers, Music, Textbooks}\}$. Within this sample space, we could define compound events "electronic media" as $A = \{\text{Music, DVD, VHS}\}$ and "print periodicals" as $B = \{\text{Newspapers, Magazines}\}$.

5.1   A credit card customer at Barnes and Noble can use Visa (*V*), MasterCard (*M*), or American Express (*A*). The merchandise may be books (*B*), electronic media (*E*), or other (*O*). (a) Enumerate the elementary events in the sample space describing a customer's purchase. (b) Would each elementary event be equally likely? Explain.

5.2   A survey asked tax accounting firms their business form (*S* = sole proprietorship, *P* = partnership, *C* = corporation) and type of risk insurance they carry (*L* = liability only, *T* = property loss only, *B* = both liability and property). (a) Enumerate the elementary events in the sample space. (b) Would each elementary event be equally likely? Explain.

5.3   A baseball player bats either left-handed (*L*) or right-handed (*R*). The player either gets on base (*B*) or does not get on base (*B'*). (a) Enumerate the elementary events in the sample space. (b) Would these elementary events be equally likely? Explain.

5.4   A die is thrown (1, 2, 3, 4, 5, 6) and a coin is tossed (*H*, *T*). (a) Enumerate the elementary events in the sample space for the die/coin combination. (b) Are the elementary events equally likely? Explain.

5.2 PROBABILITY

The concept of probability is so familiar to most people that it can easily be misused. Therefore, we begin with some precise definitions and a few rules.

Definitions

The **probability** of an event is a number that measures the relative likelihood that the event will occur. The probability of an event *A*, denoted $P(A)$, must lie within the interval from 0 to 1:

$$0 \leq P(A) \leq 1 \tag{5.2}$$

$P(A) = 0$ means the event cannot occur (e.g., a naturalized citizen becoming president of the United States) while $P(A) = 1$ means the event is certain to occur (e.g., rain occurring in Hilo, Hawaii, sometime this year). In a discrete sample space, the probabilities of all simple events must sum to 1, since it is certain that one of them will occur:

$$P(S) = P(E_1) + P(E_2) + \cdots + P(E_n) = 1 \tag{5.3}$$

For example, if 32 percent of purchases are made by credit card, 15 percent by debit card, 35 percent by cash, and 18 percent by check, then:

$P(\text{credit card}) + P(\text{debit card}) + P(\text{cash}) + P(\text{check}) = .32 + .15 + .35 + .18 = 1$

LO 5-2

Distinguish among the three views of probability.

What Is "Probability"?

There are three distinct ways of assigning probability, listed in Table 5.1. Many people mix them up or use them interchangeably; however, each approach must be considered separately.

TABLE 5.1

Three Views of Probability

Approach	*How Assigned?*	*Example*
Empirical	Estimated from observed outcome frequency	There is a 2 percent chance of twins in a randomly chosen birth.
Classical	Known *a priori* by the nature of the experiment	There is a 50 percent chance of heads on a coin flip.
Subjective	Based on informed opinion or judgment	There is a 75 percent chance that England will adopt the euro currency by 2012.

Empirical Approach

Sometimes we can collect empirical data through observations or experiments. We can use the **empirical** or **relative frequency approach** to assign probabilities by counting the frequency of observed outcomes (f) defined in our experimental sample space and dividing by the number of observations (n). The estimated probability is f/n. For example, we could estimate the reliability of a bar code scanner:

$$P(\text{a missed scan}) = \frac{\text{number of missed scans}}{\text{number of items scanned}}$$

or the default rate on student loans:

$$P(\text{a student defaults}) = \frac{\text{number of defaults}}{\text{number of loans}}$$

As we increase the number of observations (n) or the number of times we perform the experiment, our estimate will become more and more accurate. We use the ratio f/n to represent the probability. Here are some examples of empirical probabilities:

- An industrial components manufacturer interviewed 280 production workers before hiring 70 of them.

  H = event that a randomly chosen interviewee is hired

  $$P(H) = f/n = \frac{70}{280} = .25$$

- Over 20 years, a medical malpractice insurer saw only one claim for "wrong-site" surgery (e.g., amputating the wrong limb) in 112,994 malpractice claims.

  M = event that malpractice claim is for wrong-site surgery

  $$P(M) = f/n = \frac{1}{112,994} = .00000885$$

- On average, 2,118 out of 100,000 Americans live to age 100 or older.

  C = event that a randomly chosen American lives to 100 or older

  $$P(C) = f/n = \frac{2,118}{100,000} = .02118$$

Law of Large Numbers An important probability theorem is the **law of large numbers**, which says that as the number of trials increases, any empirical probability approaches its theoretical limit. Imagine flipping a coin 50 times. You know that the proportion of heads should be near .50. But in any finite sample it will be probably not be .50, but something like 7 out of 13 (.5385) or 28 out of 60 (.4667). Coin flip experiments show that a large n may be needed before the proportion gets really close to .50, as illustrated in Figure 5.1.

A common variation on the law of large numbers says that, as the sample size increases, there is an increased probability that any event (even an unlikely one) will occur. For example, the same five winning numbers [4, 21, 23, 34, 39] came up twice in a three-day period in the North Carolina Cash-5 game.[1] Was something wrong with the lottery? The odds on this event are indeed small (191,919 to 1), but in a large number of drawings, an event like this becomes less surprising. Similarly, the odds that one ticket will win the lottery are low; yet the probability is high that *someone* will win the lottery because so many people buy lottery tickets. Gamblers tend to misconstrue this principle as implying that a streak of bad luck is "bound to change" if they just keep betting. Unfortunately, the necessary number of tries is likely to exhaust the gambler's bankroll.

Practical Issues for Actuaries You may know that **actuarial science** is a high-paying career that involves estimating empirical probabilities. Actuaries help companies

---

[1]See Leonard A. Stefanski, "The North Carolina Lottery Coincidence," *The American Statistician* 62, no. 2 (May 2008), pp. 130–134.

FIGURE 5.1

Results of 10, 20, 50, and 200 Coin Flips **CoinFlips**

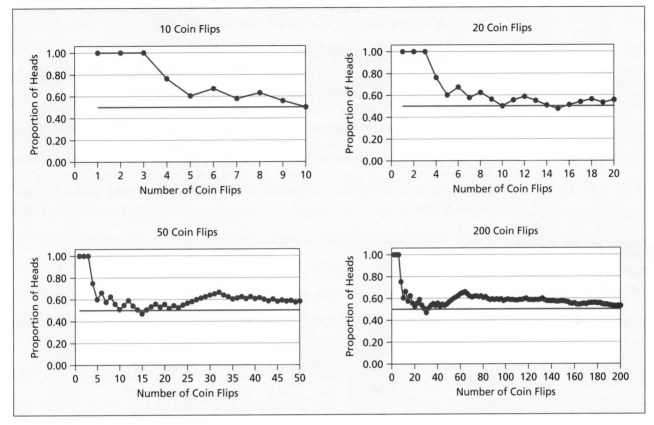

calculate payout rates on life insurance, pension plans, and health care plans. Actuaries created the tables that guide IRA withdrawal rates for individuals from age 70 to 99. Here are a few challenges that actuaries face:

- Is n "large enough" to say that f/n has become a good approximation to the probability of the event of interest? Data collection costs money, and decisions must be made. The sample should be large enough but not larger than necessary for a given level of precision.

- Was the experiment repeated identically? Subtle variations may exist in the experimental conditions and data collection procedures.

- Is the underlying process stable over time? For example, default rates on 2007 student loans may not apply in 2017, due to changes in attitudes and interest rates.

- Do nonstatistical factors override data collection? Drug companies want clinical trials of a promising AIDS treatment to last long enough to ascertain its adverse side effects, yet ethical considerations forbid withholding a drug that could be beneficial.

- What if repeated trials are impossible? A good example occurred when Lloyd's of London was asked to insure a traveling exhibition of Monet paintings that was sent on a tour of the United States. Such an event only occurs once, so we have no f/n to help us.

Classical Approach

Statisticians use the term *a priori* to refer to the process of assigning probabilities before we actually observe the event or try an experiment. When flipping a coin or rolling a pair of dice, we do not actually have to perform an experiment because the nature of the process allows us to envision the entire sample space. Instead, we can use deduction to determine $P(A)$. This is the **classical approach** to probability. For example, in the sample space for the two-dice experiment shown in Figure 5.2, there are 36 possible outcomes, so the probability of rolling a seven is known to be:

$$P(\text{rolling a seven}) = \frac{\text{number of possible outcomes with 7 dots}}{\text{number of outcomes in sample space}} = \frac{6}{36} = .1667$$

The probability is obtained *a priori* without actually doing an experiment. We can apply pure reason to cards, lottery numbers, and roulette. Also, in some physical situations we can assume that the probability of an event such as a defect (leak, blemish) occurring in a particular unit of area, volume, or length is proportional to the ratio of that unit's size to the total area, volume, or length. Examples would be pits on rolled steel, stress fractures in concrete, or leaks in pipelines. These are *a priori* or *classical* probabilities if they are based on logic or theory, not on experience. Such calculations are rarely possible in business situations.

FIGURE 5.2

Sample Space for Rolling Two Dice 🖬 DiceRolls

(1,1)	(1,2)	(1,3)	(1,4)	(1,5)	**(1,6)**
(2,1)	(2,2)	(2,3)	(2,4)	**(2,5)**	(2,6)
(3,1)	(3,2)	(3,3)	**(3,4)**	(3,5)	(3,6)
(4,1)	(4,2)	**(4,3)**	(4,4)	(4,5)	(4,6)
(5,1)	**(5,2)**	(5,3)	(5,4)	(5,5)	(5,6)
(6,1)	(6,2)	(6,3)	(6,4)	(6,5)	(6,6)

Subjective Approach

A *subjective* probability reflects someone's informed judgment about the likelihood of an event. The **subjective approach** to probability is needed when there is no repeatable random experiment. For example:

- What is the probability that Ford's new supplier of plastic fasteners will be able to meet the September 23 shipment deadline?
- What is the probability that a new truck product program will show a return on investment of at least 10 percent?
- What is the probability that the price of Ford's stock will rise within the next 30 days?

In such cases, we rely on personal judgment or expert opinion. However, such a judgment is not random because it is typically based on experience with similar events and knowledge of the underlying causal processes. Assessing the New York Knicks's chances of an NBA title next year would be an example. Thus, subjective probabilities have something in common with empirical probabilities, although their empirical basis is informal and not quantified.

SECTION EXERCISES

connect

Instructions for Exercises 5.5–5.12: Which kind of probability is it (empirical, classical, subjective)?

5.5 "There is a 20% chance that a new stock offered in an initial public offering (IPO) will reach or exceed its target price on the first day."

5.6 "There is a 25% chance that AT&T Wireless and Verizon will merge."

5.7 "Commercial rocket launches have a 95% success rate."

5.8 "The probability of rolling three sevens in a row with dice is .0046."

5.9   The probability that a randomly selected student in your class is celebrating a birthday today is 1/365.

5.10   More than 30 percent of the results from major search engines for the keyword phrase "ring tone" are fake pages created by spammers.

5.11   Based on the reported experience of climbers from a given year, a climber who attempts Everest has a 31 percent chance of success.

5.12   An entrepreneur who plans to open a Cuban restaurant in Nashville has a 20 percent chance of success.

5.3 RULES OF PROBABILITY

The field of probability has a distinct vocabulary that is important to understand. This section reviews the definitions of probability terms and illustrates how to use them.

Complement of an Event

The **complement** of an event A is denoted A' and consists of everything in the sample space S except event A, as illustrated in the **Venn diagram** in Figure 5.3.

Since A and A' together comprise the sample space, their probabilities sum to 1:

$$P(A) + P(A') = 1 \qquad \textbf{(5.4)}$$

The probability of the complement of A is found by subtracting the probability of A from 1:

$$P(A') = 1 - P(A) \qquad \textbf{(5.5)}$$

For example, it has been reported that about 33 percent of all new small businesses fail within the first 2 years. From this we can determine that the probability that a new small business will survive at least 2 years is:

$$P(\text{survival}) = 1 - P(\text{failure}) = 1 - .33 = .67, \text{ or } 67\%$$

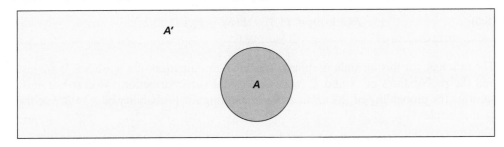

FIGURE 5.3

Complement of Event A

Union of Two Events

The **union** of two events consists of all outcomes in the sample space S that are contained either in event A or in event B or in both. The union of A and B is sometimes denoted $A \cup B$ or "A or B" as illustrated in the Venn diagram in Figure 5.4. The symbol $\cup$ may be read "or" since it means that either or both events occur. For example, when we choose a card at random from a deck of playing cards, if Q is the event that we draw a queen and R is the event that we draw a red card, $Q \cup R$ consists of getting *either* a

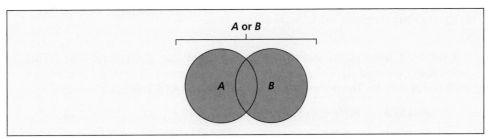

FIGURE 5.4

Union of Two Events

queen (4 possibilities in 52) *or* a red card (26 possibilities in 52) or *both* a queen and a red card (2 possibilities in 52).

Intersection of Two Events

The **intersection** of two events A and B is the event consisting of all outcomes in the sample space S that are contained in both event A and event B. The intersection of A and B is denoted $A \cap B$ or "A and B" as illustrated in the Venn diagram in Figure 5.5. The probability of $A \cap B$ is called the **joint probability** and is denoted $P(A \cap B)$.

FIGURE 5.5

Intersection of Two Events

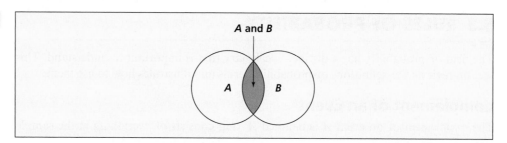

The symbol $\cap$ may be read "and" since the intersection means that both events occur. For example, if Q is the event that we draw a queen and R is the event that we draw a red card, then, $Q \cap R$ is the event that we get a card that is both a queen and red. That is, the intersection of sets Q and R consists of two cards ($Q\heartsuit$ and $Q\diamondsuit$).

General Law of Addition

The **general law of addition** says that the probability of the union of two events A and B is the sum of their probabilities less the probability of their intersection.

General Law of Addition

(5.6)
$$P(A \cup B) = P(A) + P(B) - P(A \cap B)$$

The rationale for this formula is apparent from an examination of Figure 5.5. If we just add the probabilities of A and B, we would count the intersection twice, so we must subtract the probability of $A \cap B$ to avoid overstating the probability of $A \cup B$. For the card example:

Queen: $P(Q) = 4/52$	(there are 4 queens in a deck)
Red: $P(R) = 26/52$	(there are 26 red cards in a deck)
Queen and Red: $P(Q \cap R) = 2/52$	(there are 2 red queens in a deck)

Therefore,

$$\text{Queen or Red:} \quad P(Q \cup R) = P(Q) + P(R) - P(Q \cap R)$$
$$= 4/52 + 26/52 - 2/52$$
$$= 28/52 = .5385, \text{ or a } 53.85\% \text{ chance}$$

This result, while simple to calculate, is not obvious.

EXAMPLE 5.1

Cell Phones and Credit Cards WebSurvey

A survey of introductory statistics students showed that 29.7 percent have AT&T wireless service (event A), 73.4 percent have a Visa card (event B), and 20.3 percent have both (event $A \cap B$). The probability that a student uses AT&T *or* has a Visa card is:

$$P(A \cup B) = P(A) + P(B) - P(A \cap B) = .297 + .734 - .203 = .828$$

Mutually Exclusive Events

Events A and B are **mutually exclusive** (or **disjoint**) if their intersection is the **empty set** (a set that contains no elements). In other words, one event precludes the other from occurring. The null set is denoted ϕ.

$$\text{If } A \cap B = \phi, \text{ then } P(A \cap B) = 0 \qquad (5.7)$$

As illustrated in Figure 5.6, the probability of $A \cap B$ is zero when the events do not overlap. For example, if A is the event that an Applebee's customer finishes her lunch in less than 30 minutes and B is the event that she takes 30 minutes or more, then $P(A \cap B) = P(\phi) = 0$. Here are examples of events that are mutually exclusive (cannot be in both categories):

- *Customer age:* A = under 21, B = over 65
- *Purebred dog breed:* A = border collie, B = golden retriever
- *Business form:* A = corporation, B = sole proprietorship

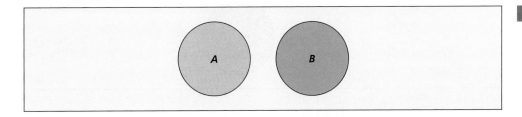

FIGURE 5.6

Mutually Exclusive Events

These events may not cover all of the possibilities (e.g., a business could also be a partnership or S-corporation). The only issue is whether the categories overlap. Here are examples of events that are *not* mutually exclusive (can be in both categories):

- *Student's major:* A = marketing major, B = economics major
- *Bank account:* A = Bank of America, B = J.P. Morgan Chase Bank
- *Credit card held:* A = Visa, B = MasterCard, C = American Express

Special Law of Addition

If A and B are mutually exclusive events, then $P(A \cap B) = 0$ and the general addition law can be simplified to the sum of the individual probabilities for A and B, the **special law of addition**.

Special Law of Addition

$$P(A \cup B) = P(A) + P(B) \qquad \text{(addition law for mutually exclusive events)} \qquad (5.8)$$

For example, if we look at a person's age, then $P(\text{under 21}) = .28$ and $P(\text{over 65}) = .12$, so $P(\text{under 21 } or \text{ over 65}) = .28 + .12 = .40$ since these events do not overlap.

Collectively Exhaustive Events

Events are **collectively exhaustive** if their union is the entire sample space S (i.e., all the events that can possibly occur). Two mutually exclusive, collectively exhaustive events are **binary** (or *dichotomous*) **events**. For example, a car repair is either covered by the warranty (A) or is not covered by the warranty (A'). There can be more than two mutually exclusive, collectively exhaustive events. For example, a Walmart customer can pay by credit card (A), debit card (B), cash (C), or check (D).

Conditional Probability

The probability of event *A* *given* that event *B* has occurred is a **conditional probability**, denoted $P(A \mid B)$ which is read "the probability of *A* given *B*." The vertical line is read as "given." The conditional probability is the joint probability of *A* and *B* divided by the probability of *B*.

(5.9)
$$P(A \mid B) = \frac{P(A \cap B)}{P(B)} \quad \text{for } P(B) > 0$$

The logic of formula 5.9 is apparent by looking at the Venn diagram in Figure 5.7. The sample space is restricted to *B*, an event that we know has occurred (the green shaded circle). The intersection, $(A \cap B)$, is the part of *B* that is also in *A* (the blue shaded area). The ratio of the relative size of set $(A \cap B)$ to set *B* is the conditional probability $P(A \mid B)$.

FIGURE 5.7

Conditional Probability

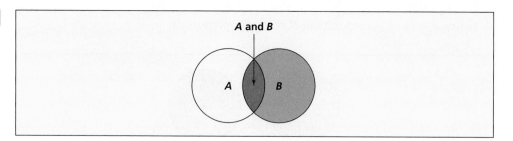

EXAMPLE 5.2

High School Dropouts

Of the population aged 16–21 and not in college, 13.50 percent are unemployed, 29.05 percent are high school dropouts, and 5.32 percent are unemployed high school dropouts. What is the conditional probability that a member of this population is unemployed, given that the person is a high school dropout? To answer this question, define:

U = the event that the person is unemployed

D = the event that the person is a high school dropout

This "story problem" contains three facts:

$$P(U) = .1350 \qquad P(D) = .2905 \qquad P(U \cap D) = .0532$$

So by formula 5.9 the conditional probability of an unemployed youth given that the person dropped out of high school is:

$$P(U \mid D) = \frac{P(U \cap D)}{P(D)} = \frac{.0532}{.2905} = .1831, \text{ or } 18.31\%$$

The *conditional* probability of being unemployed is $P(U \mid D) = .1831$ (18.31 percent), which is greater than the *unconditional probability* of being unemployed $P(U) = .1350$ (13.50 percent). In other words, knowing that someone is a high school dropout alters the probability that the person is unemployed.

Using algebra we can rewrite formula 5.9, resulting in a **general law of multiplication** for the joint probability of two events.

General Law of Multiplication

(5.10)
$$P(A \cap B) = P(A \mid B)P(B)$$

EXAMPLE 5.3

Video Game Purchases

Suppose 30 percent of video games are purchased as digital content. Of those games purchased as digital content, 47 percent are acquired from a gaming website. What is the joint probability that a video game was purchased as digital content through a gaming website? To answer this question, define:

D = the event that a video game was purchased as digital content

G = the event that a video game was purchased through a gaming website

This "story problem" contains two facts:

$$P(D) = .30 \qquad P(G \mid D) = .47$$

So by formula 5.10 the joint probability that a video game was purchased as digital and through a gaming website is:

$$P(D \cap G) = .30 \times .47 = .141.$$

Therefore, 14.1 percent of video games are purchased as digital content through a gaming website.

Odds of an Event

LO 5-4

Calculate odds from given probabilities.

Statisticians usually speak of probabilities rather than odds, but in sports and games of chance, we often hear **odds** quoted. We define the *odds in favor* of an event A as the ratio of the probability that event A will occur to the probability that event A will not occur. Its reciprocal is the *odds against* event A.

Odds *in favor* of A:

$$\frac{P(A)}{P(A')} = \frac{P(A)}{1 - P(A)}$$

Odds *against* A:

$$\frac{P(A')}{P(A)} = \frac{1 - P(A)}{P(A)}$$

If a probability is expressed as a percentage, you can easily convert it to odds. For example, suppose the IRS tax audit rate is 1.41 percent among taxpayers earning between \$100,000 and \$199,999. Let A = the event that the taxpayer is audited and set $P(A) = .0141$. The odds against an audit are:

$$\frac{P(\text{no audit})}{P(\text{audit})} = \frac{1 - P(A)}{P(A)} = \frac{1 - .0141}{.0141} = 70 \text{ to } 1 \text{ } against \text{ being audited}$$

In horse racing and other sports, odds usually are quoted *against* winning. If the odds against event A are quoted as b to a, then the implied probability of event A is:

$$P(A) = \frac{a}{a + b}$$

For example, if a race horse has 4 to 1 odds *against* winning, this is equivalent to saying that the odds-makers assign the horse a 20 percent chance of winning:

$$P(\text{win}) = \frac{a}{a + b} = \frac{1}{1 + 4} = \frac{1}{5} = .20, \text{ or } 20\%$$

SECTION EXERCISES

connect

5.13 Are these characteristics of a student at your university mutually exclusive or not? Explain.

a. A = works 20 hours or more, B = majoring in accounting
b. A = born in the United States, B = born in Canada
c. A = owns a Toyota, B = owns a Honda

5.14 Are these events collectively exhaustive or not? Explain.

    a. A = college grad, B = some college, C = no college
    b. A = born in the United States, B = born in Canada, C = born in Mexico
    c. A = full-time student, B = part-time student, C = not enrolled as a student

5.15 Given $P(A)$ = .40, $P(B)$ = .50, and $P(A \cap B)$ = .05, find (a) $P(A \cup B)$, (b) $P(A \mid B)$, and (c) $P(B \mid A)$. (d) Sketch a Venn diagram.

5.16 Given $P(A)$ = .70, $P(B)$ = .30, and $P(A \cap B)$ = .00, find (a) $P(A \cup B)$ and (b) $P(A \mid B)$. (c) Sketch a Venn diagram.

5.17 Suppose Samsung ships 21.7 percent of the liquid crystal displays (LCDs) in the world. Let S be the event that a randomly selected LCD was made by Samsung. Find (a) $P(S)$, (b) $P(S')$, (c) the odds *in favor* of event S, and (d) the odds *against* event S.

5.18 Suppose the probability of an IRS audit is 1.7 percent for U.S. taxpayers who file form 1040 and who earned $100,000 or more. (a) What are the odds that such a taxpayer will be audited? (b) What are the odds *against* such a taxpayer being audited?

5.19 List *two* mutually exclusive events that describe the possible outcomes of each situation.

    a. A pharmaceutical firm seeks FDA approval for a new drug.
    b. A baseball batter goes to bat.
    c. A woman has a mammogram test.

5.20 List *more than two* events (i.e., categorical events) that might describe the outcome of each situation.

    a. A student applies for admission to Oxnard University.
    b. A football quarterback throws a pass.
    c. A bank customer makes an ATM transaction.

5.21 Let S be the event that a randomly chosen female aged 18–24 is a smoker. Let C be the event that a randomly chosen female aged 18–24 is a Caucasian. Given $P(S)$ = .246, $P(C)$ = .830, and $P(S \cap C)$ = .232, find each probability and express the event in words.

    a. $P(S')$.
    b. $P(S \cup C)$.
    c. $P(S \mid C)$.
    d. $P(S \mid C')$.

5.4 INDEPENDENT EVENTS

LO 5-5

Determine when events are independent.

When $P(A)$ differs from $P(A \mid B)$, the events are **dependent**. You can easily think of examples of dependence. For example, cell phone text messaging is more common among young people, while arteriosclerosis is more common among older people. Therefore, knowing a person's age would affect the *probability* that the individual uses text messaging or has arteriosclerosis. Dependent events may be causally related, but statistical dependence does *not* prove cause and effect. It only means that knowing that event B has occurred will affect the *probability* that event A will occur.

When knowing that event B has occurred does *not* affect the probability that event A will occur, then events A and B are **independent**. In other words, event A is independent of event B if the conditional probability $P(A \mid B)$ is the same as the unconditional probability $P(A)$; that is, if the probability of event A is the same whether event B occurs or not. For example, if text messaging among high school students is *independent* of gender, this means that knowing whether a student is a male or female does not *change* the probability that the student uses text messaging.

Independent Events

(5.11)   Event A is independent of event B if and only if $P(A \mid B) = P(A)$.

If A and B are independent events, we can simplify the general law of multiplication (formula 5.10) to show that the joint probability of events A and B is the product of their individual probabilities. Recall the general law of multiplication:

$$P(A \cap B) = P(A \mid B)P(B)$$

If A and B are independent, then we can substitute $P(A)$ for $P(A \mid B)$. The result is shown in formula 5.12, the **special law of multiplication**.

Special Law of Multiplication

If events A and B are independent, then

$$P(A \cap B) = P(A)P(B) \tag{5.12}$$

Based on past data, the probability that a customer at a certain Noodles & Company restaurant will order a dessert (event D) with the meal is .08. The probability that a customer will order a bottled beverage (event B) is .14. The joint probability that a customer will order both a dessert *and* a bottled beverage is .0112. Is ordering a dessert independent of ordering a bottled beverage?

$$P(D) = .08 \qquad P(B) = .14 \qquad P(D \cap B) = .0112$$
$$P(D) \times P(B) = .08 \times .14 = .0112 = P(D \cap B)$$

We see that $P(D \cap B) = P(D) \times P(B)$, so D and B are independent of each other. If we know that a customer has ordered a bottled beverage, does this information change the probability that he or she will also order a dessert? No, because the events are independent.

EXAMPLE 5.4

Restaurant Orders

The target audience is 2,000,000 viewers. Ad A reaches 500,000 viewers, ad B reaches 300,000 viewers, and both ads reach 100,000 viewers. That is:

$$P(A) = \frac{500,000}{2,000,000} = .25 \quad P(B) = \frac{300,000}{2,000,000} = .15 \quad P(A \cap B) = \frac{100,000}{2,000,000} = .05$$

Applying the definition of conditional probability from formula 5.9, the conditional probability that ad A reaches a viewer *given* that ad B reaches the viewer is:

$$P(A \mid B) = \frac{P(A \cap B)}{P(B)} = \frac{.05}{.15} = .3333 \text{ or } 33.3\%$$

We see that A and B are not independent because $P(A) = .25$ is not equal to $P(A \mid B) = .3333$. That is, knowing that ad B reached the viewer raises the probability that ad A reached the viewer from $P(A) = .25$ to $P(A \mid B) = .3333$. Alternatively, since $P(A) P(B) = (.25)(.15) = .0375$ is not equal to $P(A \cap B) = .05$, we know that events A and B are not independent.

EXAMPLE 5.5

Television Ads

Applications of the Multiplication Law

The probability of more than two independent events occurring simultaneously is the product of their separate probabilities, as shown in formula 5.13 for n independent events $A_1, A_2, \ldots, A_n$.

$$P(A_1 \cap A_2 \cap \cdots \cap A_n) = P(A_1) P(A_2) \cdots P(A_n) \quad \text{if the events are independent} \tag{5.13}$$

The special multiplication law for independent events can be applied to system reliability. To illustrate, suppose a website has two independent file servers (i.e., no shared power or other components). Each server has 99 percent reliability (i.e., is "up" 99 percent of the time). What is the total system reliability? Let F_1 be the event that server 1 fails, and F_2 be the event that server 2 fails. Then

$$P(F_1) = 1 - 0.99 = .01$$
$$P(F_2) = 1 - 0.99 = .01$$

Applying the rule of independence:

$$P(F_1 \cap F_2) = P(F_1)\, P(F_2) = (.01)(.01) = .0001$$

The probability that at least one server is up is 1 minus the probability that both servers are down, or $1 - .0001 = .9999$. Dual file servers dramatically improve reliability to 99.99 percent.

When individual components have a low reliability, high reliability can still be achieved with massive redundancy. For example, a Teramac supercomputer has over 7 million components. About 3 percent are defective (nanodevices are extremely difficult to manufacture). Yet programs can run reliably because there is significant redundancy in the interconnect circuitry, so that a valid path can almost always be found (see *Scientific American* 293, no. 5 [November 2005], p. 75).

EXAMPLE 5.6

Space Shuttle

Redundancy can increase system reliability even when individual component reliability is low. For example, the NASA space shuttle has three flight computers. Suppose that they function independently but that each has an unacceptable .03 chance of failure (3 failures in 100 missions). Let F_j = event that computer j fails. Then

$$
\begin{aligned}
P(\text{all 3 fail}) &= P(F_1 \cap F_2 \cap F_3) \\
&= P(F_1)\, P(F_2)\, P(F_3) \quad \text{(presuming that failures are independent)} \\
&= (.03)\,(.03)\,(.03) \\
&= .000027, \text{ or 27 in } 1,000,000 \text{ missions.}
\end{aligned}
$$

Triple redundancy can reduce the probability of computer failure to .000027 (27 failures in 1,000,000 missions). Of course, in practice, it is very difficult to have truly independent computers, since they may share electrical buses or cables. On one shuttle mission, two of the three computers actually did fail, which proved the value of redundancy. Another example of space shuttle redundancy is the four independent fuel gauges that prevent the shuttle's main engines from shutting down too soon. Initial launch rules allowed the shuttle to fly as long as two of them were functional, but after the *Challenger* launch explosion, the rules were modified to require that 3 of 4 be functional, and were modified again after the *Columbia* accident to require that all 4 be functional (see http://aolsvc.news.aol.com).

The Five Nines Rule

How high must reliability be? Prime business customers expect public carrier-class telecommunications data links to be available 99.999 percent of the time. This so-called five nines rule implies only 5 minutes of downtime per year. Such high reliability is needed not only in telecommunications but also for mission-critical systems such as airline reservation systems or banking funds transfers. Table 5.2 shows some expected system reliabilities in contemporary applications.

Suppose a certain network web server is up only 94 percent of the time (i.e., its probability of being down is .06). How many independent servers are needed to ensure that the system is up at least 99.99 percent of the time? This is equivalent to requiring that

Type of System	Typical Reliability (%)
Commercial fiber-optic cable systems	99.999
Cellular-radio base stations with mobile switches connected to public-switched telephone networks	99.99
Private-enterprise networking (e.g., connecting two company offices)	99.9
Airline luggage systems	99

TABLE 5.2

Typical System Reliabilities in Various Applications

the probability of all the servers being down is .0001 (i.e., $1 - .9999$). Four servers will accomplish the goal*:

2 servers: $P(F_1 \cap F_2) = (.06)(.06) = .0036$

3 servers: $P(F_1 \cap F_2 \cap F_3) = (.06)(.06)(.06) = .000216$

4 servers: $P(F_1 \cap F_2 \cap F_3 \cap F_4) = (.06)(.06)(.06)(.06) = .00001296$

Applications of Redundancy

The principle of redundancy is found in many places. Basketball teams have more than five players, even though only five can play at once. You set two alarm clocks in case the first doesn't wake you up. The Embraer Legacy 13-passenger jet ($21.2 million) has two identical generators on each of its two engines to allow the plane to be used as a commercial regional jet (requiring 99.5 percent dispatch reliability) as well as for private corporate travel. With four generators, plus an auxiliary power unit that can be started and run in flight, the Legacy can fly even after the failure of a generator or two (*Flying* 131, no. 9 [September 2004], p. 50).

Older airliners (e.g., Boeing 747) had four engines, not only because older engine designs were less powerful but also because they were less reliable. Particularly for transoceanic flights, four-engine planes could fly even if one engine failed (or maybe even two). Modern airliners (e.g., Boeing 777) have only two engines because newer engines are more powerful and more reliable.

It is not just a matter of individual component reliability but also of cost and consequence. Cars have only one battery because the consequence of battery failure (walking home or calling AAA) does not justify the expense of having a backup battery. But spare tires are cheap enough that most cars carry one (maybe two, if you are driving in Alaska).

Redundancy is not required when components are highly reliable, cost per component is high, and consequences of system failure are tolerable (e.g., cell phone, alarm clock). Unfortunately, true component independence is difficult to achieve. The same catastrophe (fire, flood, etc.) that damages one component may well damage the backup system. On August 24, 2001, a twin-engine Air Transat Airbus A330 transiting the Atlantic Ocean did have a double engine shutdown with 293 passengers aboard. Fortunately, the pilot was able to glide 85 miles to a landing in the Azores, resulting in only minor injuries (*Aviation Week and Space Technology*, September 3, 2001, p. 34).

Dependent Events in Business

Banks and credit unions know that the probability that a customer will default on a car loan is dependent on his/her past record of unpaid credit obligations. That is why lenders consult credit bureaus (e.g., Equifax, Experian, and TransUnion) before they make a loan. Your credit score is based on factors such as the ratio of your credit card balance to your credit limit, length of your credit history, number of accounts with balances, and

---

*In general, if p is the probability of failure, we can set $p^k = .0001$, plug in $p = .06$, take the log of both sides, and solve for k. In this case, $k = 3.27$, so we can then round up to the next higher integer.

frequency of requests for credit. Your score can be compared with actuarial data and national averages to see what percentile you are in. The lender can then decide whether your loan is worth the risk.

Automobile insurance companies (e.g., AAA, Allstate, State Farm) know that the probability that a driver will be involved in an accident depends on the driver's age, past traffic convictions, and similar factors. This actuarial information is used in deciding whether to accept you as a new customer and in setting your insurance premium. The situation is similar for life insurance. Can you think of factors that might affect a person's life insurance premium?

In each of these loan and insurance examples, knowing B will affect our estimate of the likelihood of A. Obviously, bankers and insurance companies need to quantify these conditional probabilities precisely. An *actuary* studies conditional probabilities empirically, using accident statistics, mortality tables, and insurance claims records. Although few people undergo the extensive training to become actuaries, many businesses rely on actuarial services, so a business student needs to understand the concepts of conditional probability and statistical independence.

SECTION EXERCISES

connect

5.22 Given $P(A) = .40$, $P(B) = .50$. If A and B are independent, find $P(A \cap B)$.

5.23 Given $P(A) = .40$, $P(B) = .50$, and $P(A \cap B) = .05$. (a) Find $P(A \mid B)$. (b) In this problem, are A and B independent? Explain.

5.24 Which pairs of events are independent?

a. $P(A) = .60$, $P(B) = .40$, $P(A \cap B) = .24$.
b. $P(A) = .90$, $P(B) = .20$, $P(A \cap B) = .18$.
c. $P(A) = .50$, $P(B) = .70$, $P(A \cap B) = .25$.

5.25 The probability that a student has a Visa card (event V) is .73. The probability that a student has a MasterCard (event M) is .18. The probability that a student has both cards is .03. (a) Find the probability that a student has either a Visa card or a MasterCard. (b) In this problem, are V and M independent? Explain.

5.26 Bob sets two alarm clocks (battery-powered) to be sure he arises for his Monday 8:00 a.m. accounting exam. There is a 75 percent chance that either clock will wake Bob. (a) What is the probability that Bob will oversleep? (b) If Bob had three clocks, would he have a 99 percent chance of waking up?

5.27 A hospital's backup power system has three independent emergency electrical generators, each with uptime averaging 95 percent (some downtime is necessary for maintenance). Any of the generators can handle the hospital's power needs. Does the overall reliability of the backup power system meet the five nines test?

5.28 Over 1,000 people try to climb Mt. Everest every year. Of those who try to climb Everest, 31 percent succeed. The probability that a climber is at least 60 years old is .04. The probability that a climber is at least 60 years old and succeeds in climbing Everest is .005. (a) Find the probability of success, given that a climber is at least 60 years old. (b) Is success in climbing Everest independent of age?

5.29 Suppose 50 percent of the customers at Pizza Palooza order a square pizza, 80 percent order a soft drink, and 40 percent order both a square pizza and a soft drink. Is ordering a soft drink independent of ordering a square pizza? Explain.

5.5 CONTINGENCY TABLES

LO 5-6

Apply the concepts of probability to contingency tables.

In Chapter 3, you saw how Excel's pivot tables can be used to display the frequency of co-occurrence of data values (e.g., how many taxpayers in a sample are filing as "single" and also have at least one child?). Since a probability usually is estimated as a *relative frequency*, we can use tables of relative frequencies to learn about relationships (e.g., dependent events or conditional probabilities) that are extremely useful in business planning. Data for the table may be from a survey or from actuarial records.

What Is a Contingency Table?

To better understand dependent events and conditional probability, let's look at some real data. A **contingency table** is a cross-tabulation of frequencies into rows and columns. The intersection of each row and column is a *cell* that shows a frequency. A contingency table is like a frequency distribution for a single variable, except it has *two* variables (rows and columns). A contingency table with r rows and c columns has rc cells and is called an $r \times c$ table. Contingency tables often are used to report the results of a survey.

Table 5.3 shows a cross-tabulation of tuition cost versus five-year net salary gains for MBA degree recipients at 67 top-tier graduate schools of business. Here, salary gain is compensation after graduation, minus the sum of tuition and forgone compensation. Are large salary gains more likely for graduates of high-tuition MBA programs?

| Tuition | Salary Gain | | | |
	Small (S_1) Under $50K	Medium (S_2) $50K–$100K	Large (S_3) $100K+	Row Total
Low (T_1) Under $40K	5	10	1	16
Medium (T_2) $40K–$50K	7	11	1	19
High (T_3) $50K+	5	12	15	32
Column Total	17	33	17	67

TABLE 5.3

Contingency Table of Frequencies (n = 67 MBA programs)
📁 **MBASalary**

Source: Data are from *Forbes* 172, no. 8 (October 13, 2003), p. 78. Copyright © 2005 Forbes, Inc.

Inspection of this table reveals that MBA graduates of the high-tuition schools do tend to have large salary gains (15 of the 67 schools) and that about half of the top-tier schools charge high tuition (32 of 67 schools). We can make more precise interpretations of these data by applying the concepts of probability.

Marginal Probabilities

The **marginal probability** of an event is a relative frequency that is found by dividing a row or column total by the total sample size. For example, using the column totals, 33 out of 67 schools had medium salary gains, so the marginal probability of a medium salary gain is $P(S_2) = 33/67 = .4925$. In other words, salary gains at about 49 percent of the top-tier schools were between $50,000 and $100,000. This calculation is shown in Table 5.4.

| Tuition | Salary Gain | | | |
	Small (S_1)	Medium (S_2)	Large (S_3)	Row Total
Low (T_1)	5	10	1	16
Medium (T_2)	7	11	1	19
High (T_3)	5	12	15	32
Column Total	17	33	17	67

TABLE 5.4

Marginal Probability of Event S_2

Using the row totals, for example, we see that 16 of the 67 schools had low tuition so the marginal probability of low tuition is $P(T_1) = 16/67 = .2388$. In other words, there is a 24 percent chance that a top-tier school's MBA tuition is under $40,000. This calculation is illustrated in Table 5.5.

TABLE 5.5

Marginal Probability of Event T_1

Tuition	Salary Gain			Row Total
	Small (S_1)	Medium (S_2)	Large (S_3)	
Low (T_1)	5	10	1	16
Medium (T_2)	7	11	1	19
High (T_3)	5	12	15	32
Column Total	17	33	17	67

Joint Probabilities

Each of the nine main cells is used to calculate a *joint probability* representing the intersection of *two* events. For example, the upper right-hand cell is the joint event that the school has low tuition (T_1) *and* has large salary gains (S_3). We can write this probability either as $P(T_1$ and $S_3)$ or as $P(T_1 \cap S_3)$. Since only 1 out of 67 schools is in this category, the joint probability is $P(T_1$ and $S_3) = 1/67 = .0149$. In other words, there is less than a 2 percent chance that a top-tier school has *both* low tuition *and* high salary gains. This calculation is illustrated in Table 5.6.

TABLE 5.6

Joint Probability of Event $T_1 \cap S_3$

Tuition	Salary Gain			Row Total
	Small (S_1)	Medium (S_2)	Large (S_3)	
Low (T_1)	5	10	1	16
Medium (T_2)	7	11	1	19
High (T_3)	5	12	15	32
Column Total	17	33	17	67

Conditional Probabilities

Conditional probabilities may be found by *restricting* ourselves to a single row or column (the *condition*). For example, suppose we know that a school's MBA tuition is high (T_3). When we restrict ourselves to the 32 schools in the third row (those with high tuition) the conditional probabilities of any event may be calculated. For example, Table 5.7 illustrates the calculation of the conditional probability that salary gains are small (S_1) *given* that the MBA tuition is large (T_3). This conditional probability may be written $P(S_1 \mid T_3)$. We see that $P(S_1 \mid T_3) = 5/32 = .1563$, so there is about a 16 percent chance that a top-tier school's salary gains will be small despite its high tuition because there were 5 small-gain schools out of the 32 high-tuition schools.

TABLE 5.7

Conditional Probability $P(S_1 \mid T_3)$

Tuition	Salary Gain			Row Total
	Small (S_1)	Medium (S_2)	Large (S_3)	
Low (T_1)	5	10	1	16
Medium (T_2)	7	11	1	19
High (T_3)	5	12	15	32
Column Total	17	33	17	67

Here are some other conditional probabilities and their interpretations:

Low Tuition MBA Program

$P(S_1 \mid T_1) = 5/16 = .3125$ There is a 31 percent probability that schools whose tuition is low will have small MBA salary gains.

$P(S_2 \mid T_1) = 10/16 = .6250$ There is a 63 percent probability that schools whose tuition is low will have medium MBA salary gains.

$P(S_3 \mid T_1) = 1/16 = .0625$ There is a 6 percent probability that schools whose tuition is low will have large MBA salary gains.

High Tuition MBA Program

$P(S_1 \mid T_3) = 5/32 = .1563$ There is a 16 percent probability that schools whose tuition is high will have small MBA salary gains.

$P(S_2 \mid T_3) = 12/32 = .3750$ There is a 38 percent probability that schools whose tuition is high will have medium MBA salary gains.

$P(S_3 \mid T_3) = 15/32 = .4688$ There is a 47 percent probability that schools whose tuition is high will have large MBA salary gains.

Caveat   Conditional probabilities show, as we would expect, that higher tuition is associated with higher MBA salary gains (and conversely). But these results pertain only to a set of elite universities at a particular point in time, and few MBA students actually have access to such schools. Data from different universities or at a different point in time might show a different pattern.

Independence

To check whether events in a contingency table are independent, we can look at *conditional probabilities*. For example, if large salary gains (S_3) were independent of low tuition (T_1), then the conditional probability $P(S_3 \mid T_1)$ would be the same as the marginal probability $P(S_3)$. But this is not the case:

Conditional   *Marginal*

$P(S_3 \mid T_1) = 1/16 = .0625$ $P(S_3) = 17/67 = .2537$

Thus, large salary gains (S_3) are *not* independent of low tuition (T_1). Alternatively, we could ask whether $P(S_3 \text{ and } T_1) = P(S_3)P(T_1)$ is a necessary condition for independence. But

$$P(S_3)P(T_1) = (17/67)(16/67) = .0606$$

which is *not* equal to the observed joint probability

$$P(S_3 \text{ and } T_1) = 1/67 = .0149$$

Therefore, large salary gains (S_3) are *not* independent of low tuition (T_1).

Relative Frequencies

To facilitate probability calculations, we can divide each cell frequency f_{ij} by the total sample size ($n = 67$) to get the *relative frequencies* f_{ij}/n shown in Table 5.8. For example, the upper left-hand cell becomes $5/67 = .0746$.

TABLE 5.8

**Relative Frequency Table
Each Cell Is f_{ij}/n**

Tuition	Salary Gains			Row Total
	Small (S_1)	Medium (S_2)	Large (S_3)	
Low (T_1)	.0746	.1493	.0149	.2388
Medium (T_2)	.1045	.1642	.0149	.2836
High (T_3)	.0746	.1791	.2239	.4776
Column Total	.2537	.4926	.2537	1.0000

The nine joint probabilities sum to 1.0000 since these are all the possible intersections. Except for rounding, summing the joint probabilities across a row or down a column gives marginal (or *unconditional*) probabilities for the respective row or column. The marginal row and column probabilities sum to 1.0000 (except for rounding):

$$\text{Columns (Salary): } P(S_1) + P(S_2) + P(S_3) = .2537 + .4926 + .2537 = 1.0000$$
$$\text{Rows (Tuition): } P(T_1) + P(T_2) + P(T_3) = .2388 + .2836 + .4776 = 1.0000$$

Table 5.8 may be written in symbolic form as shown in Table 5.9.

TABLE 5.9

Symbolic Notation for Relative Frequencies

Tuition	Salary Gains			Row Total
	Small (S_1)	Medium (S_2)	Large (S_3)	
Low (T_1)	$P(T_1 \text{ and } S_1)$	$P(T_1 \text{ and } S_2)$	$P(T_1 \text{ and } S_3)$	$P(T_1)$
Medium (T_2)	$P(T_2 \text{ and } S_1)$	$P(T_2 \text{ and } S_2)$	$P(T_2 \text{ and } S_3)$	$P(T_2)$
High (T_3)	$P(T_3 \text{ and } S_1)$	$P(T_3 \text{ and } S_2)$	$P(T_3 \text{ and } S_3)$	$P(T_3)$
Column Total	$P(S_1)$	$P(S_2)$	$P(S_3)$	1.0000

EXAMPLE 5.7

Payment Method and Purchase Quantity

📁 **Payment**

A small grocery store would like to know if the number of items purchased by a customer is independent of the type of payment method the customer chooses to use. Having this information can help the store manager determine how to set up his/her various checkout lanes. The manager collected a random sample of 368 customer transactions. The results are shown in Table 5.10.

TABLE 5.10   Contingency Table for Payment Method by Number of Items Purchased

Number of Items Purchased	Payment Method			Row Total
	Cash	Check	Credit/ Debit Card	
5 or fewer	30	15	43	88
6 to 9	46	23	66	135
10 to 19	31	15	43	89
20 or more	19	10	27	56
Column Total	126	63	179	368

Looking at the frequency data presented in the table we can calculate the marginal probability that a customer will use cash to make the payment. Let C be the event that the customer chose cash as the payment method.

$$P(C) = \frac{126}{368} = .3424$$

Is $P(C)$ the same if we condition on number of items purchased?

$$P(C \mid 5 \text{ or fewer}) = \frac{30}{88} = .3409 \qquad P(C \mid 6 \text{ to } 9) = \frac{46}{135} = .3407$$

$$P(C \mid 10 \text{ to } 19) = \frac{31}{89} = .3483 \qquad P(C \mid 20 \text{ or more}) = \frac{19}{56} = .3393$$

Notice that there is little difference in these probabilities. If we perform the same type of analysis for the next two payment methods, we find that *payment method* and *number of items purchased* are essentially independent. Based on this study, the manager might decide to offer a cash-only checkout lane that is *not* restricted to the number of items purchased.

How Do We Get a Contingency Table?

Contingency tables do not just "happen" but require careful data organization and fore-thought. They are constructed from raw data. In this example, numerical values were mapped into discrete codes, as shown in Table 5.11. If the data were already categorical (e.g., a survey with discrete responses), this step would have been unnecessary. Once the data are coded, we tabulate the frequency in each cell of the contingency table. The tabulation would be done using Excel's pivot table or another software package (e.g., MINITAB's Stat > Tables > Cross Tabulation).

| School | Original Data ($000) | | Coded Data | |
	Tuition	Gain	Tuition	Gain
Alabama (Manderson)	67	21	T_3	S_1
Arizona (Eller)	69	42	T_3	S_1
Arizona State (Carey)	70	41	T_3	S_1
Auburn	46	18	T_2	S_1
Babson (Olin)	22	53	T_1	S_2
⋮	⋮	⋮	⋮	⋮
Wake Forest (Babcock)	91	50	T_3	S_2
Washington U.—St. Louis (Olin)	120	61	T_3	S_2
William & Mary	94	45	T_3	S_1
Wisconsin—Madison	81	48	T_3	S_1
Yale	137	65	T_3	S_2

TABLE 5.11

Data Coding for MBA Data 📄 **MBASalary**

Note: S_1 is salary gain under $50K, S_2 = salary gain $50K–$100K, and S_3 is salary gain $100K+. T_1 is tuition under $40K, T_2 is tuition from $40K–$50K, and T_3 is tuition of $50K+. Data are provided for educational purposes and not as a guide to financial gains.

Source: *Forbes* 172, no. 8 (October 13, 2003), p. 78. Copyright © 2005 Forbes, Inc. Data used with permission of *Forbes* magazine.

Mini Case   5.1

Smoking and Gender

Table 5.12 shows that the proportion of women over age 65 who have never smoked is much higher than for men, that a higher proportion of men than women used to smoke but have quit, and that the number of current smokers over 65 is about the same for men and women, although the *proportion* is lower for women.

TABLE 5.12   **Smoking and Gender for Persons Age 65 and Over (Thousands)** 📄 **Smoking1**

Gender	Never Smoked (N)	Former Smoker (R)	Current Smoker (S)	Total
Male (M)	3,160	5,087	2,320	10,567
Female (F)	10,437	2,861	2,007	15,305
Total	13,597	7,948	4,327	25,872

Source: U.S. Department of Commerce, *Statistical Abstract of the United States, 1986*, p. 119.

Conditional probabilities may be found from Table 5.12 by restricting ourselves to a single row or column (the *condition*). For example, for males we get:

$P(N \mid M) = 3,160/10,567 = .2990$ There is a 29.9% probability that a person never smoked *given* that the person is male.

$P(R \mid M) = 5,087/10,567 = .4814$ There is a 48.1% probability that a person is a former smoker *given* that the person is male.

$P(S \mid M) = 2,320/10,567 = .2196$ There is a 22.0% probability that a person currently smokes *given* that the person is male.

On the other hand, for females we get:

$P(N \mid F) = 10{,}437/15{,}305 = .6819$ There is a 68.2% probability that a person never smoked *given* that the person is female.

$P(R \mid F) = 2{,}861/15{,}305 = .1869$ There is an 18.7% probability that a person is a former smoker *given* that the person is female.

$P(S \mid F) = 2{,}007/15{,}305 = .1311$ There is a 13.1% probability that a person currently smokes *given* that the person is female.

These conditional probabilities show that a female is over twice as likely as a male never to have smoked. However, the number of *former* smokers is higher among males (you can't be a former smoker unless you once smoked).

Table 5.13 shows the *relative frequencies* obtained by dividing each table frequency by the sample size ($n = 25{,}872$).

TABLE 5.13	Smoking and Gender for Persons Age 65 and Over			
Gender	Never Smoked (N)	Former Smoker (R)	Current Smoker (S)	Total
Male (M)	.1221	.1966	.0897	0.4084
Female (F)	.4034	.1106	.0776	0.5916
Total	.5255	.3072	.1673	1.0000

For example, the joint probability $P(M \cap N)$ is .1221 (i.e., about 12.2 percent of the males had never smoked). The six joint probabilities sum to 1.0000, as they should.

SECTION EXERCISES

connect

5.30 The contingency table below shows the results of a survey of online video viewing by age. Find the following probabilities or percentages:

a. Probability that a viewer is aged 18–34.
b. Probability that a viewer prefers watching TV videos.
c. Percentage of viewers who are 18–34 and prefer watching user-created videos.
d. Percentage of viewers aged 18–34 who prefer watching user-created videos.
e. Percentage of viewers who are 35–54 or prefer user created-videos.

	Type of Videos Preferred		
Viewer Age	User Created	TV	Row Total
18–34	39	30	69
35–54	10	10	20
55+	3	8	11
Column Total	52	48	100

5.31 The contingency table below summarizes a survey of 1,000 bottled beverage consumers. Find the following probabilities or percentages:

a. Probability that a consumer recycles beverage bottles.
b. Probability that a consumer who lives in a state with a deposit law does not recycle.
c. Percentage of consumers who recycle and live in a state with a deposit law.
d. Percentage of consumers in states with a deposit law who recycle.

	Lives in a state with a deposit law	Lives in a state with no deposit law	Row Total
Recycles beverage bottles	154	186	340
Does not recycle beverage bottles	66	594	660
Column Total	220	780	1000

5.32 A survey of 158 introductory statistics students showed the following contingency table. Find each event probability. 📂 **WebSurvey**

a. $P(V)$ b. $P(A)$ c. $P(A \cap V)$
d. $P(A \cup V)$ e. $P(A \mid V)$ f. $P(V \mid A)$

Cell Phone Provider	Visa Card (V)	No Visa Card (V')	Row Total
AT&T (A)	32	15	47
Other (A')	84	27	111
Column Total	116	42	158

5.33 A survey of 156 introductory statistics students showed the following contingency table. Find each event probability. 📂 **WebSurvey**

a. $P(D)$ b. $P(R)$ c. $P(D \cap R)$
d. $P(D \cup R)$ e. $P(R \mid D)$ f. $P(R \mid P)$

Newspaper Read	Living Where?			Row Total
	Dorm (D)	Parents (P)	Apt (A)	
Never (N)	13	6	6	25
Occasionally (O)	58	30	21	109
Regularly (R)	8	7	7	22
Column Total	79	43	34	156

5.34 This contingency table describes 200 business students. Find each probability and interpret it in words. 📂 **GenderMajor**

a. $P(A)$ b. $P(M)$ c. $P(A \cap M)$ d. $P(F \cap S)$
e. $P(A \mid M)$ f. $P(A \mid F)$ g. $P(F \mid S)$ h. $P(E \cup F)$

Gender	Major			Row Total
	Accounting (A)	Economics (E)	Statistics (S)	
Female (F)	44	30	24	98
Male (M)	56	30	16	102
Column Total	100	60	40	200

5.35 Based on the previous problem, is major independent of gender? Explain the basis for your conclusion.

5.36 The following contingency table shows average yield (rows) and average duration (columns) for 38 bond funds. For a randomly chosen bond fund, find the probability that:

a. The bond fund is long duration.
b. The bond fund has high yield.
c. The bond fund has high yield given that it is of short duration.
d. The bond fund is of short duration given that it has high yield.

Yield	Average Portfolio Duration			Row Total
	Short (D_1)	Intermediate (D_2)	Long (D_3)	
Small (Y_1)	8	2	0	10
Medium (Y_2)	1	6	6	13
High (Y_3)	2	4	9	15
Column Total	11	12	15	38

Source: Data are from *Forbes* 173, no. 2 (February 2, 2004). **BondFunds**

5.6 TREE DIAGRAMS

What Is a Tree?

LO 5-7

Interpret a tree diagram.

Events and probabilities can be displayed in the form of a **tree diagram** or *decision tree* to help visualize all possible outcomes. This is a common business planning activity. We begin with a contingency table. Table 5.14 shows a cross-tabulation of expense ratios (low, medium, high) by fund type (bond, stock) for a sample of 21 bond funds and 23 stock funds. For purposes of this analysis, a fund's expense ratio is defined as "low" if it is in the lowest ⅓ of the sample, "medium" if it is in the middle ⅓ of the sample, and "high" if it is in the upper ⅓ of the sample.

TABLE 5.14

Frequency Tabulation of Expense Ratios by Fund Type **BondFund**

Source: *Money* 32, no. 2 (February 2003).

Expense Ratio	Fund Type		Row Total
	Bond Fund (B)	Stock Fund (S)	
Low (L)	11	3	14
Medium (M)	7	9	16
High (H)	3	11	14
Column Total	21	23	44

To label the tree, we need to calculate *conditional probabilities*. Table 5.15 shows conditional probabilities by fund type (i.e., dividing each cell frequency by its column total). For example, $P(L \mid B) = 11/21 = .5238$. This says there is about a 52 percent chance that a fund has a low expense ratio if it is a bond fund. In contrast, $P(L \mid S) = 3/23 = .1304$. This says there is about a 13 percent chance that a fund has a low expense ratio if it is a stock fund.

TABLE 5.15

Conditional Probabilities by Fund Type **BondFund**

Expense Ratio	Fund Type	
	Bond Fund (B)	Stock Fund (S)
Low (L)	$= P(L \mid B) = 11/21 = .5238$	$= P(L \mid S) = 3/23 = .1304$
Medium (M)	$= P(M \mid B) = 7/21 = .3333$	$= P(M \mid S) = 9/23 = .3913$
High (H)	$= P(H \mid B) = 3/21 = .1429$	$= P(H \mid S) = 11/23 = .4783$
Column Total	1.0000	1.0000

The tree diagram in Figure 5.8 shows all events along with their marginal, conditional, and joint probabilities. To illustrate the calculation of joint probabilities, we make a slight modification of the formula for conditional probability for events A and B:

$$P(A \mid B) = \frac{P(A \cap B)}{P(B)} \quad \text{or} \quad P(A \cap B) = P(B)P(A \mid B)$$

FIGURE 5.8

Tree Diagram for Fund Type and Expense Ratios **BondFund**

Thus, the joint probability of each terminal event on the tree can be obtained by multiplying the probabilities along its branches. For example, following the top branch of the tree, the joint probability of a bond fund (*B*) with low expenses (*L*) is

$$P(B \cap L) = P(B)P(L \mid B) = (.4773)(.5238) = .2500$$

The conditional probabilities sum to 1 *within* each branch, and the joint probabilities also sum to 1 *for all six terminal events.*

SECTION EXERCISES

connect

5.37   Of grocery shoppers who have a shopping cart, 70 percent pay by credit/debit card (event C_1), 20 percent pay cash (event C_2), and 10 percent pay by check (event C_3). Of shoppers without a grocery cart, 50 percent pay by credit/debit card (event C_1), 40 percent pay cash (event C_2), and 10 percent pay by check (event C_3). On Saturday morning, 80 percent of the shoppers take a shopping cart (event S_1) and 20 percent do not (event S_2). (a) Sketch a tree based on these data. (b) Calculate the probability of all joint probabilities (e.g., $S_1 \cap C_1$). (c) Verify that the joint probabilities sum to 1.

5.38   A study showed that 60 percent of *The Wall Street Journal* subscribers watch CNBC every day. Of these, 70 percent watch it outside the home. Only 20 percent of those who don't watch CNBC every day watch it outside the home. Let *D* be the event "watches CNBC daily" and *O* be the event "watches CNBC outside the home." (a) Sketch a tree based on these data. (b) Calculate the probability of all joint probabilities (e.g., $D \cap O$). (c) Verify that the joint probabilities sum to 1.

Mini Case   5.2

Can Amazon Read Your Mind?

You go to Amazon.com to purchase a copy of *Eugenie Grandet* by Honore de Balzac. Amazon offers you 714 online choices (new, used, various vendors). But Amazon also recommends that you consider buying a copy of *Hedda Gabler* by Henrik Ibsen or *Madame Bovary* by Gustave Flaubert. How did they decide on these suggestions? The answer is that Amazon has a matrix (like an Excel pivot table) that keeps track of the frequency of *copurchased* items (e.g., books, music, DVDs) for web shoppers. Probabilities derived from the cells in this contingency table are used to recommend products that are likely to be of interest to you, assuming that you are "like" other buyers. While such predictions of your behavior are only probabilistic, even a modest chance of landing extra sales can make a difference in bottom-line profit. There are even more sophisticated logic engines that can track your web clicks. Is this an invasion of your privacy? Does it bother you to think that you may be predictable? Interestingly, many consumers don't seem to mind, and actually find value in this kind of statistical information system.

5.7 BAYES' THEOREM

LO 5-8

Use Bayes' Theorem to calculate revised probabilities.

An important theorem published by Thomas Bayes (1702–1761) provides a method of revising probabilities to reflect new information. The **prior** (unconditional) **probability** of an event B is revised after event A has occurred to yield a **posterior** (conditional) **probability**. We begin with a formula slightly different from the standard definition of conditional probability:

(5.14)
$$P(B \mid A) = \frac{P(A \mid B)P(B)}{P(A)}$$

Unfortunately, in some situations $P(A)$ is not given. The most useful and common form of **Bayes' Theorem** replaces $P(A)$ with an expanded formula:

(5.15)
$$P(B \mid A) = \frac{P(A \mid B)P(B)}{P(A \mid B)P(B) + P(A \mid B')P(B')}$$

How Bayes' Theorem Works

Bayes' Theorem is best understood by example. Suppose that 10 percent of the women who purchase over-the-counter pregnancy testing kits are actually pregnant. For a particular brand of kit, if a woman is pregnant, the test will yield a positive result 96 percent of the time and a negative result 4 percent of the time (called a "false negative"). If she is not pregnant, the test will yield a positive result 5 percent of the time (called a "false positive") and a negative result 95 percent of the time. Suppose the test comes up positive. What is the probability that she is really pregnant?

We can solve this problem intuitively. If 1,000 women use this test, the results should look like Figure 5.9. Of the 1,000 women, 100 will actually be pregnant and 900 will not. The test yields 4 percent false negatives (.04 × 100 = 4) and 5 percent false positives (.05 × 900 = 45). Therefore, of the 141 women who will test positive (96 + 45), only 96 will actually be pregnant, so P(pregnant | positive test) = 96/141 = .6809.

If the test is positive, there is a 68.09 percent chance that a woman is actually pregnant. A common error is to think that the probability should be 96 percent. But that is the probability of a positive test *if* the woman is pregnant, while many of the women who take the test are *not* pregnant. This intuitive calculation (assuming a large number of individuals) can also be arranged in a contingency like Table 5.16.

TABLE 5.16		Positive Test	Negative Test	Row Total
Bayes' Theorem—Intuitive Method for 1,000 Women	Pregnant	96	4	100
	Not Pregnant	45	855	900
	Column Total	141	859	1,000

FIGURE 5.9

Bayes' Theorem—
Intuitive Method for
1,000 Women

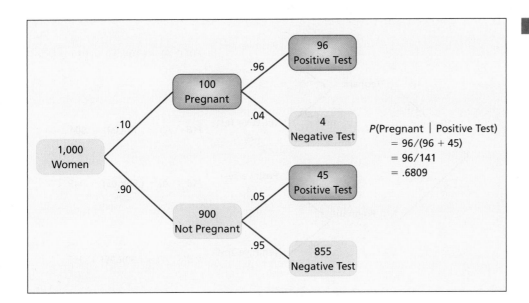

$P(\text{Pregnant} \mid \text{Positive Test})$
$= 96/(96 + 45)$
$= 96/141$
$= .6809$

Bayes' Theorem allows us to derive this result more formally. We define these events:

A = positive test B = pregnant
A' = negative test B' = not pregnant

The given facts may be stated as follows:

$$P(A \mid B) = .96 \qquad P(A \mid B') = .05 \qquad P(B) = .10$$

The complement of each event is found by subtracting from 1:

$$P(A' \mid B) = .04 \qquad P(A' \mid B') = .95 \qquad P(B') = .90$$

Applying Bayes' Theorem:

$$P(B \mid A) = \frac{P(A \mid B)P(B)}{P(A \mid B)P(B) + P(A \mid B')P(B')} = \frac{(.96)(.10)}{(.96)(.10) + (.05)(.90)}$$

$$= \frac{.096}{.096 + .045} = \frac{.096}{.141} = .6809$$

There is a 68.09 percent chance that a woman is pregnant, given that the test is positive. This is the same result that we obtained using the intuitive method.

What Bayes' Theorem does is to show us how to revise our *prior* probability of pregnancy (10 percent) to get the *posterior* probability (68.09 percent) after the results of the pregnancy test are known:

Prior (before the test)   *Posterior (after positive test result)*
$P(B) = .10$ $P(B \mid A) = .6809$

The given information did not permit a direct calculation of $P(B \mid A)$ since we only knew the conditional probabilities $P(A \mid B)$ and $P(A \mid B')$. Bayes' Theorem is useful in situations like this.

A probability tree diagram (Figure 5.10) is helpful in visualizing the situation. Only branches 1 and 3 have a positive test, and only in branch 1 is the woman actually pregnant, so $P(B \mid A) = (.096)/(.096 + .045) = .6809$. The conditional probabilities for each branch sum to 1.

The result is the same using either method. While the formal method is somewhat less intuitive, the intuitive method has the drawback that a large number of individuals must be assumed if the resulting frequencies are to be integers. Use whichever method makes sense for the problem at hand.

FIGURE 5.10

Tree Diagram for Home Pregnancy Test

🗂 Pregnancy

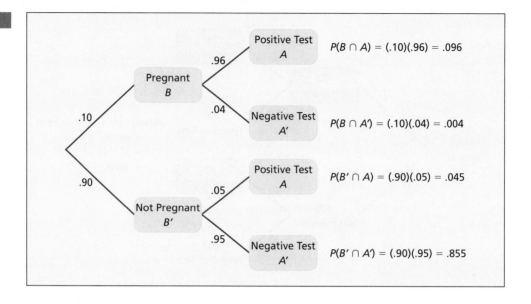

General Form of Bayes' Theorem

A generalization of Bayes' Theorem allows event B to have as many mutually exclusive and collectively exhaustive categories as we wish ($B_1, B_2, \ldots, B_n$) rather than just the two dichotomous categories B and B':

(5.16)
$$P(B_i \mid A) = \frac{P(A \mid B_i)P(B_i)}{P(A \mid B_1)P(B_1) + P(A \mid B_2)P(B_2) + \ldots + P(A \mid B_n)P(B_n)}$$

EXAMPLE 5.8

Hospital Trauma Centers

Based on historical data, three hospital trauma centers have 50, 30, and 20 percent of the cases, respectively. The probability of a case resulting in a malpractice suit in each of the three hospitals is .001, .005, and .008, respectively. If a malpractice suit is filed, what is the probability that it originated in hospital 1? This problem is solved as follows. We define:

Event A = event that a malpractice suit is filed by patient

Event B_i = event that the patient was treated at trauma center i ($i = 1, 2, 3$)

The given information can be presented in a table like Table 5.17.

TABLE 5.17	Given Information for Hospital Trauma Centers 🗂 Malpractice	
Hospital	*Marginal*	*Conditional: Suit Filed*
1	$P(B_1) = .50$	$P(A \mid B_1) = .001$
2	$P(B_2) = .30$	$P(A \mid B_2) = .005$
3	$P(B_3) = .20$	$P(A \mid B_3) = .008$

Applying formula 5.16, we can find $P(B_1 \mid A)$ as follows:

$$P(B_1 \mid A) = \frac{P(A \mid B_1)P(B_1)}{P(A \mid B_1)P(B_1) + P(A \mid B_2)P(B_2) + P(A \mid B_3)P(B_3)}$$

$$= \frac{(.001)(.50)}{(.001)(.50) + (.005)(.30) + (.008)(.20)}$$

$$= \frac{.0005}{.0005 + .0015 + .0016} = \frac{.0005}{.0036} = .1389$$

The probability that the malpractice suit was filed in hospital 1 is .1389, or 13.89 percent. Although hospital 1 sees 50 percent of the trauma patients, it is expected to generate less than half the malpractice suits, since the other two hospitals have a much higher incidence of malpractice suits.

There is nothing special about $P(B_1 \mid A)$. In fact, it is easy to calculate *all* the posterior probabilities at once by using a worksheet, as shown in Table 5.18:

$P(B_1 \mid A) = .1389$ (probability that a malpractice lawsuit originated in hospital 1)

$P(B_2 \mid A) = .4167$ (probability that a malpractice lawsuit originated in hospital 2)

$P(B_3 \mid A) = .4444$ (probability that a malpractice lawsuit originated in hospital 3)

TABLE 5.18	**Worksheet for Bayesian Probability of Malpractice Suit** Malpractice			
	Prior (Given)	**Given**		**Posterior (Revised)**
Hospital	$P(B_i)$	$P(A \mid B_i)$	$P(B_i \cap A) = P(A \mid B_i) P(B_i)$	$P(B_i \mid A) = P(B_i \cap A)/P(A)$
1	.50	.001	(.001)(.50) = .0005	.0005/.0036 = .1389
2	.30	.005	(.005)(.30) = .0015	.0015/.0036 = .4167
3	.20	.008	(.008)(.20) = .0016	.0016/.0036 = .4444
Total	1.00		$P(A) = .0036$	1.0000

We could also approach the problem intuitively by imagining 10,000 patients, as shown in Table 5.19. First, calculate each hospital's expected number of patients (50, 30, and 20 percent of 10,000). Next, find each hospital's expected number of malpractice suits by multiplying its malpractice rate by its expected number of patients:

TABLE 5.19	**Malpractice Frequencies for 10,000 Hypothetical Patients** Malpractice		
Hospital	**Malpractice Suit Filed**	**No Malpractice Suit Filed**	**Total**
1	5	4,995	5,000
2	15	2,985	3,000
3	16	1,984	2,000
Total	36	9,964	10,000

Hospital 1: .001 × 5,000 = 5   (expected malpractice suits at hospital 1)

Hospital 2: .005 × 3,000 = 15   (expected malpractice suits at hospital 2)

Hospital 3: .008 × 2,000 = 16   (expected malpractice suits at hospital 3)

Refer to Table 5.19. Adding down, the total number of malpractice suits filed is 36. Hence, $P(B_1 \mid A) = 5/36 = .1389$, $P(B_2 \mid A) = 15/36 = .4167$, and $P(B_3 \mid A) = 16/36 = .4444$. These three probabilities add to 1. Overall, there are 36 malpractice suits, so we can also calculate $P(A) = 36/10,000 = .0036$. Many people find the table method easier to understand than the formulas. Do you agree?

We could visualize this situation as shown in Figure 5.11. The initial sample space consists of three mutually exclusive and collectively exhaustive events (hospitals B_1, B_2, B_3). As indicated by their relative areas, B_1 is 50 percent of the sample space, B_2 is 30 percent of the sample space, and B_3 is 20 percent of the sample space. But *given* that a malpractice case has been filed (event A), then the relevant sample space is *reduced* to that of event A.

FIGURE 5.11

Illustration of Hospital Trauma Center Example

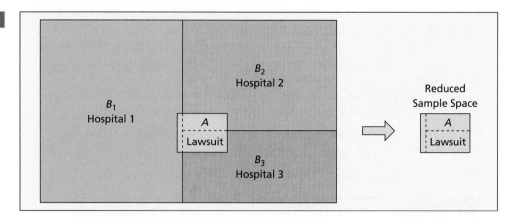

The revised (posterior) probabilities are the relative areas *within* event A:

$P(B_1 \mid A)$ is the proportion of A that lies within $B_1 = 13.89\%$

$P(B_2 \mid A)$ is the proportion of A that lies within $B_2 = 41.67\%$

$P(B_3 \mid A)$ is the proportion of A that lies within $B_3 = 44.44\%$

These percentages were calculated in Table 5.18. A worksheet is still needed to calculate $P(A)$ for the denominator.

SECTION EXERCISES

connect

5.39   A drug test for athletes has a 5 percent false positive rate and a 10 percent false negative rate. Of the athletes tested, 4 percent have actually been using the prohibited drug. If an athlete tests positive, what is the probability that the athlete has actually been using the prohibited drug? Explain your reasoning clearly.

5.40   Half of a set of the parts are manufactured by machine A and half by machine B. Four percent of all the parts are defective. Six percent of the parts manufactured on machine A are defective. Find the probability that a part was manufactured on machine A, given that the part is defective. Explain your reasoning clearly.

5.41   An airport gamma ray luggage scanner coupled with a neural net artificial intelligence program can detect a weapon in suitcases with a false positive rate of 2 percent and a false negative rate of 2 percent. Assume a .001 probability that a suitcase contains a weapon. If a suitcase triggers the alarm, what is the probability that the suitcase contains a weapon? Explain your reasoning.

Mini Case   5.3

Smoking and Gender Again

Table 5.20 shows that the proportion of women over age 65 who have never smoked is much higher than for men, that a higher proportion of men than women used to smoke but have quit, and that the number of current smokers over 65 is about the same for men and women.

TABLE 5.20	**Smoking and Gender for Persons Age 65 and Over (Thousands)** 🗁 **Smoking1**			
Gender	*Never Smoked (N)*	*Former Smoker (R)*	*Current Smoker (S)*	*Total*
Male (M)	3,160	5,087	2,320	10,567
Female (F)	10,437	2,861	2,007	15,305
Total	13,597	7,948	4,327	25,872

FIGURE 5.12

Tree Diagram for Smoking and Gender **Smoking1**

Calculation of Joint Probabilities

Never Smoked
$P(N \mid M) = .2990$

Male
$P(M) = .4084$

Former Smoker
$P(R \mid M) = .4814$

Sum is
1.0000

Current Smoker
$P(S \mid M) = .2196$

Male and Never Smoked
$P(M \cap N) = (.4084)(.2990) = .1221$

Male and Former Smoker
$P(M \cap R) = (.4084)(.4814) = .1966$

Male and Current Smoker
$P(M \cap S) = (.4084)(.2196) = .0897$

Sum is
1.0000

Never Smoked
$P(N \mid F) = .6819$

Female
$P(F) = .5916$

Former Smoker
$P(R \mid F) = .1869$

Sum is
1.0000

Current Smoker
$P(S \mid F) = .1311$

Female and Never Smoked
$P(F \cap N) = (.5916)(.6819) = .4034$

Female and Former Smoker
$P(F \cap R) = (.5916)(.1869) = .1106$

Female and Current Smoker
$P(F \cap S) = (.5916)(.1311) = .0776$

We see from Table 5.20 that $P(M) = 10,567/25,872 = .4084$ and $P(F) = 15,305/25,872 = .5916$. We also have these conditional probabilities:

$P(N \mid M) = 3,160/10,567 = .2990$ There is a 29.9 percent chance that a person never smoked *given* that the person is male.

$P(R \mid M) = 5,087/10,567 = .4814$ There is a 48.1 percent chance that a person is a former smoker *given* that the person is male.

$P(S \mid M) = 2,320/10,567 = .2196$ There is a 22.0 percent chance that a person currently smokes *given* that the person is male.

$P(N \mid F) = 10,437/15,305 = .6819$ There is a 68.2 percent chance that a person never smoked *given* that the person is female.

$P(R \mid F) = 2,861/15,305 = .1869$ There is an 18.7 percent chance that a person is a former smoker *given* that the person is female.

$P(S \mid F) = 2,007/15,305 = .1311$ There is a 13.1 percent chance that a person currently smokes *given* that the person is female.

The tree is shown in Figure 5.12.

Applying Bayes' Theorem, the probability that a 65-year-old person is male, given that a person is a smoker, is 53.62 percent (even though only 40.84 percent of 65 year olds are males):

$$P(M \mid S) = \frac{P(S \mid M) \, P(M)}{P(S \mid M)P(M) + P(S \mid M')P(M')}$$

$$= \frac{(.2196)(.4084)}{(.2196)(.4084) + (.1311)(.5916)}$$

$$= \frac{.0897}{.0897 + .0776} = \frac{.0897}{.1673} = .5362$$

5.8 COUNTING RULES

Fundamental Rule of Counting

If event A can occur in n_1 ways and event B can occur in n_2 ways, then events A and B can occur in $n_1 \times n_2$ ways. In general, the number of ways that m events can occur is $n_1 \times n_2 \times \cdots \times n_m$.

EXAMPLE 5.9

Stock-Keeping Labels

LO 5-9

Apply counting rules to calculate possible event arrangements.

How many unique stock-keeping unit (SKU) labels can a chain of hardware stores create by using two letters (ranging from *AA* to *ZZ*) followed by four numbers (digits 0 through 9)? For example:

AF1078: hex-head 6 cm bolts—box of 12

RT4855: Lime-A-Way cleaner—16 ounce

LL3119: Rust-Oleum Professional primer—gray 15 ounce

This problem may be viewed as filling six empty boxes, as shown in Figure 5.13.

FIGURE 5.13   Creating SKU Labels

There are 26 ways (letters A through Z) to fill either the first or second box. There are 10 ways (digits 0 through 9) to fill the third through sixth boxes. The number of unique inventory labels is therefore $26 \times 26 \times 10 \times 10 \times 10 \times 10 = 6{,}760{,}000$. Such a system should suffice for a moderately large retail store.

EXAMPLE 5.10

Shirt Inventory

The number of possibilities can be large, even for a very simple counting problem. For example, the L.L. Bean men's cotton chambray shirt comes in six colors (blue, stone, rust, green, plum, indigo), five sizes (*S, M, L, XL, XXL*), and two styles (short sleeve, long sleeve). Their stock, therefore, might include $6 \times 5 \times 2 = 60$ possible shirts. The number of shirts of each type to be stocked will depend on prior demand experience. Counting the outcomes is easy with the counting formula, but even for this simple problem, a tree diagram would be impossible to fit on one page, and the enumeration of them all would be tedious (but necessary for L.L. Bean).

Factorials

The number of unique ways that n items can be arranged in a particular order is *n factorial*, the product of all integers from 1 to n.

(5.17)
$$n! = n(n-1)(n-2) \cdots 1$$

This rule is useful for counting the possible arrangements of any n items. There are n ways to choose the first item, $n - 1$ ways to choose the second item, and so on until we reach the last item, as illustrated in Figure 5.14. By definition, $0! = 1$.

FIGURE 5.14

Choosing *n* Items

In very small problems we can actually count the possibilities. For example, a home appliance service truck must make three stops (*A*, *B*, *C*). In how many ways could the three stops be arranged? There are six possible arrangements: {*ABC*, *ACB*, *BAC*, *BCA*, *CAB*, *CBA*}. But if all we want is the *number of possibilities* without listing them all:

$$3! = 3 \times 2 \times 1 = 6$$

EXAMPLE 5.11

Truck Routing

Even in moderate-sized problems, listing all the possibilities is not feasible. For example, the number of possible arrangements of nine baseball players in a batting order rotation is:

$$9! = 9 \times 8 \times 7 \times 6 \times 5 \times 4 \times 3 \times 2 \times 1 = 362{,}880$$

You can calculate factorials with your calculator using the key labeled n!. Alternatively, if you have Excel, use the Excel function =FACT(n). If you have Internet access, you can enter n! in the Google search window. For example, 38! would be:

Excel Function	***Google Search Window***
=FACT(38) = 5.23023E+44	$38! = 5.23022617 \times 10^{44}$

Permutations

Choose *r* items at random without replacement from a group of *n* items. In how many ways can the *r* items be arranged, treating each arrangement as a different event (i.e., treating the three-letter sequence *XYZ* as different from the three-letter sequence *ZYX*)? A **permutation** is an arrangement of the *r* sample items *in a particular order*. The number of possible permutations of *n* items taken *r* at a time is denoted $_nP_r$.

$$_nP_r = \frac{n!}{(n-r)!} \tag{5.18}$$

Permutations are used when we are interested in finding how many possible arrangements there are when we select *r* items from *n* items, when each possible arrangement of items is a distinct event.

Five home appliance customers (*A*, *B*, *C*, *D*, *E*) need service calls, but the field technician can service only three of them before noon. The order in which they are serviced is important (to the customers, anyway) so each possible arrangement of three service calls is different. The dispatcher must assign the sequence. The number of possible permutations is

EXAMPLE 5.12

Appliance Service Calls

$$_nP_r = \frac{n!}{(n-r)!} = \frac{5!}{(5-3)!} = \frac{5 \cdot 4 \cdot 3 \cdot 2 \cdot 1}{2!} = \frac{120}{2} = 60$$

This may seem a surprisingly large number, but it can be enumerated. There are 10 distinct groups of three customers (two customers must be omitted):

ABC   ABD   ABE   ACD   ACE   ADE   BCD   BCE   BDE   CDE

> In turn, each group of three customers can be arranged in six possible orders. For example, the first distinct set of customers {A, B, C} could be arranged in six distinct ways:
>
>   ABC ACB CAB CBA BAC BCA
>
> We could do the same for each of the other nine groups of three customers. Since there are 10 distinct groups of three customers and six possible arrangements per group, there are $10 \times 6 = 60$ permutations. Clearly, we would prefer not to enumerate sequences like this very often.

As long as n and r are not too large, you can use your calculator's permutation key labeled $_nP_r$. The equivalent Excel function is =PERMUT(n,r). For example, the number of permutations of 49 things taken 9 at a time is:

Excel Function	**Calculator**
=PERMUT(49,9) = 7.45521E+14	$_{49}P_9 = 7.455208604^{14}$

Combinations

A **combination** is a collection of r items chosen at random without replacement from n items where the order of the selected items is *not* important (i.e., treating the three-letter sequence XYZ as being the same as the three-letter sequence ZYX). The number of possible combinations of r items chosen from n items is denoted $_nC_r$.

(5.19)
$$_nC_r = \frac{n!}{r!(n-r)!}$$

We use combinations when the only thing that matters is which r items are chosen, regardless of how they are arranged.

EXAMPLE 5.13

Appliance Service Calls Revised

> Suppose that five customers (A, B, C, D, E) need service calls and the maintenance worker can only service three of them this morning. The customers don't care when they are serviced as long as it's before noon, so the dispatcher does not care who is serviced first, second, or third. In other words, the dispatcher regards ABC, ACB, BAC, BCA, CAB, or CBA as being the same event because the same three customers (A, B, C) get serviced. The number of combinations is:
>
> $$_nC_r = \frac{n!}{r!(n-r)!} = \frac{5!}{3!(5-3)!} = \frac{5 \cdot 4 \cdot 3 \cdot 2 \cdot 1}{(3 \cdot 2 \cdot 1)(2 \cdot 1)} = \frac{120}{12} = 10$$
>
> This is much smaller than the number of permutations in the previous example where order was important. In fact, the possible combinations can be enumerated easily since there are only 10 distinct groups of three customers:
>
>   ABC ABD ABE ACD ACE ADE BCD BCE BDE CDE

For combinations, you can try your calculator's permutation key labeled $_nC_r$. Alternatively, use the Excel function =COMBIN(n,r) or enter n choose r in the Google search window. For example, the number of combinations of 52 things taken 24 at a time is:

Excel Function	**Calculator**	**Google Search Window**
=COMBIN(52,24) = 4.26385E+14	$_{52}C_{24} = 4.26384982^{14}$	52 choose 24 = 4.26384982 × 10^{14}

Permutations or Combinations?

Permutations and combinations both calculate the number of ways we could choose *r* items from *n* items. But in permutations *order is important* while in combinations *order does not matter*. The number of permutations $_nP_r$ always is at least as great as the number of combinations $_nC_r$ in a sample of *r* items chosen at random from *n* items.

MegaStat offers computational assistance with factorials, permutations, and combinations. It is exceptionally fast and accurate, even for very large factorials.

SECTION EXERCISES

connect

5.42 (a) Find 8! without a calculator. Show your work. (b) Use your calculator to find 32!. (c) Find 32! by typing "32!" in the Google search window. (d) Which method would you use most often? Why?

5.43 (a) Find $_{20}C_5$ without a calculator. Show your work. (b) Use your calculator to find $_{20}C_5$. (c) Find $_{20}C_5$ by entering "20 choose 5" in the Google search window. (d) Which method would you use most often? Why?

5.44 In the Minnesota Northstar Cash Drawing you pick five different numbers between 1 and 31. What is the probability of picking the winning combination (order does not matter)? *Hint:* Count how many ways you could pick the first number, the second number, and so on, and then divide by the number of permuations of the five numbers.

5.45 American Express Business Travel uses a six-letter record locator number (RLN) for each client's trip (e.g., KEZLFS). (a) How many different RLNs can be created using capital letters (A–Z)? (b) What if they allow any mixture of capital letters (A–Z) and digits (0–9)? (c) What if they allow capital letters and digits but exclude the digits 0 and 1 and the letters O and I because they look too much alike?

5.46 At Oxnard University, a student ID consists of two letters (26 possibilities) followed by four digits (10 possibilities). (a) How many unique student IDs can be created? (b) Would one letter followed by three digits suffice for a university with 40,000 students? (c) Why is extra capacity in student IDs a good idea?

5.47 Until 2005, the UPC bar code had 12 digits (0–9). The first six digits represent the manufacturer, the next five represent the product, and the last is a check digit. (a) How many different manufacturers could be encoded? (b) How many different products could be encoded? (c) In 2005, the EAN bar code replaced the UPC bar code, adding a 13th digit. If this new digit is used for product identification, how many different products could now be encoded?

5.48 Bob has to study for four final exams: accounting (*A*), biology (*B*), communications (*C*), and drama (*D*). (a) If he studies one subject at a time, in how many different ways could he arrange them? (b) List the possible arrangements in the sample space.

5.49 (a) In how many ways could you arrange seven books on a shelf? (b) Would it be feasible to list the possible arrangements?

5.50 Find the following permutations $_nP_r$:

    a. *n* = 8 and *r* = 3.
    b. *n* = 8 and *r* = 5.
    c. *n* = 8 and *r* = 1.
    d. *n* = 8 and *r* = 8.

5.51 Find the following combinations $_nC_r$:

    a. *n* = 8 and *r* = 3.
    b. *n* = 8 and *r* = 5.
    c. *n* = 8 and *r* = 1.
    d. *n* = 8 and *r* = 8.

5.52 A real estate office has 10 sales agents. Each of four new customers must be assigned an agent. (a) Find the number of agent arrangements where order *is* important. (b) Find the number of agent arrangements where order is *not* important. (c) Why is the number of combinations smaller than the number of permutations?

CHAPTER SUMMARY

The **sample space** for a **random experiment** describes all possible outcomes. **Simple events** in a **discrete** sample space can be enumerated, while outcomes of a **continuous** sample space can only be described by a rule. An **empirical** probability is based on relative frequencies, a **classical** probability can be deduced from the nature of the experiment, and a **subjective** probability is based on judgment. An event's **complement** is every outcome except the event. The **odds** are the ratio of an event's probability to the probability of its complement. The **union** of two events is all outcomes in either or both, while the intersection is only those events in both. **Mutually exclusive** events cannot both occur, and **collectively exhaustive** events cover all possibilities. The **conditional probability** of an event is its probability given that another event has occurred. Two events are **independent** if the conditional probability of one is the same as its **unconditional** probability. The **joint probability** of independent events is the product of their probabilities. A **contingency table** is a cross-tabulation of frequencies for two variables with categorical outcomes and can be used to calculate probabilities. A **tree** visualizes events in a sequential diagram. **Bayes' Theorem** shows how to revise a **prior probability** to obtain a **conditional** or **posterior probability** when another event's occurrence is known. The number of arrangements of sampled items drawn from a population is found with the formula for **permutations** (if order is important) or **combinations** (if order does not matter).

KEY TERMS

actuarial science, *176*
Bayes' Theorem, *198*
binary events, *181*
classical approach, *178*
collectively exhaustive, *181*
combination, *206*
complement, *179*
compound event, *174*
conditional probability, *182*
contingency table, *189*
dependent, *184*
disjoint, *181*
empirical approach, *176*
empty set, *181*

event, *174*
factorial, *204*
general law of addition, *180*
general law of
   multiplication, *182*
independent, *184*
intersection, *180*
joint probability, *180*
law of large numbers, *176*
marginal probability, *189*
mutually exclusive, *181*
odds, *183*
permutation, *205*
posterior probability, *198*

prior probability, *198*
probability, *175*
random experiment, *173*
redundancy, *186*
relative frequency approach, *176*
sample space, *173*
simple event, *174*
special law of addition, *181*
special law of
   multiplication, *185*
subjective approach, *178*
tree diagram, *196*
union, *179*
Venn diagram, *179*

Commonly Used Formulas in Probability

	Odds for A	Odds against A
Odds:	$\dfrac{P(A)}{1-P(A)}$	$\dfrac{1-P(A)}{P(A)}$

General Law of Addition: $P(A \cup B) = P(A) + P(B) - P(A \cap B)$

Special Law of Addition: $P(A \cup B) = P(A) + P(B)$

Conditional probability: $P(A \mid B) = \dfrac{P(A \cap B)}{P(B)}$

General Law of Multiplication: $P(A \cap B) = P(A \mid B)P(B)$

Special Law of Multiplication: $P(A \cap B) = P(A)P(B)$

Bayes' Theorem: $P(B \mid A) = \dfrac{P(A \mid B)P(B)}{P(A \mid B)P(B) + P(A \mid B')P(B')}$

Permutation: $_nP_r = \dfrac{n!}{(n-r)!}$

Combination: $_nC_r = \dfrac{n!}{r!(n-r)!}$

CHAPTER REVIEW

1. Define (a) random experiment, (b) sample space, (c) simple event, and (d) compound event.
2. What are the three approaches to determining probability? Explain the differences among them.
3. Sketch a Venn diagram to illustrate (a) complement of an event, (b) union of two events, (c) intersection of two events, (d) mutually exclusive events, and (e) dichotomous events.

4. Define *odds*. What does it mean to say that odds are usually quoted against an event?

5. (a) State the general addition law. (b) Why do we subtract the intersection?

6. (a) Write the formula for conditional probability. (b) When are two events independent?

7. (a) What is a contingency table? (b) How do we convert a contingency table into a table of relative frequencies?

8. In a contingency table, explain the concepts of (a) marginal probability and (b) joint probability.

9. Why are tree diagrams useful? Why are they not always practical?

10. What is the main point of Bayes' Theorem?

11. Define (a) fundamental rule of counting, (b) factorial, (c) permutation, and (d) combination.

Note: Explain answers and show your work clearly. Problems marked * are more difficult.

EMPIRICAL PROBABILITY EXPERIMENTS

5.53 (a) Make your own empirical estimate of the probability that a car is parked "nose first" (as opposed to "backed in"). Choose a local parking lot, such as a grocery store. Let A be the event that a car is parked nose first. Out of n cars examined, let f be the number of cars parked nose first. Then $P(A) = f/n$. (b) Do you feel your sample is large enough to have a reliable empirical probability? (c) If you had chosen a different parking lot (such as a church or a police station), would you expect the estimate of $P(A)$ to be similar? That is, would $P(A \mid \text{church}) = P(A \mid \text{police station})$? Explain.

5.54 (a) Make your own empirical estimate of the probability that a page in this book contains a figure. For n pages sampled (chosen using random numbers or some other random method), let f be the number of pages with a figure. Then $P(A) = f/n$. (b) Do you feel your sample is large enough to have a reliable empirical probability? (c) If you had chosen a different textbook (such as a biology book or an art history book), would you expect $P(A)$ to be similar? That is, would $P(A \mid \text{biology}) = P(A \mid \text{art history})$? Explain.

5.55 (a) Make your own empirical estimate of the probability that a DVD movie from your collection is longer than 2 hours (120 minutes). For the n DVDs in your sample, let f be the number that exceed 2 hours. Then $P(A) = f/n$. (b) Do you feel your sample is large enough to have a reliable empirical probability? (c) If you had chosen a different DVD collection (say, your best friend's), would you expect $P(A)$ to be similar? Explain.

5.56 M&Ms are blended in a ratio of 13 percent brown, 14 percent yellow, 13 percent red, 24 percent blue, 20 percent orange, and 16 percent green. Suppose you choose a sample of two M&Ms at random from a large bag. (a) Show the sample space. (b) What is the probability that both are brown? (c) Both blue? (d) Both green? (e) Find the probability of one brown and one green M&M. (f) Actually take 100 samples of two M&Ms (with replacement) and record the frequency of each outcome listed in (b) and (c) above. How close did your empirical results come to your predictions? (g) Which definition of probability applies in this situation? (Data are from www.mmmars.com.)

PROBLEMS

5.57 For male high school athletes, a news article reported that the probability of receiving a college scholarship is .0139 for basketball players, .0324 for swimmers/divers, and .0489 for lacrosse players. Which type of probabilities (classical, empirical, subjective) do you think these are?

5.58 A judge concludes that there is a 20 percent chance that a certain defendant will fail to appear in court if he is released after paying a full cash bail deposit. Which type of probability (classical, empirical, subjective) do you think this is?

5.59 A survey showed that 44 percent of online Internet shoppers experience some kind of technical failure at checkout (e.g., when submitting a credit card) after loading their shopping cart. Which type of probability (classical, empirical, subjective) do you think this is?

5.60 Bob says he is 50 percent sure he could swim across the Thames River. Which type of probability (classical, empirical, subjective) do you think this is?

5.61 In the first year after its release, 83 percent of emergency room doctors were estimated to have tried Dermabond glue (an alternative to sutures in some situations). Which type of probability (classical, empirical, subjective) do you think this is?

5.62   The U.S. Cesarean section delivery rate in a recent year was estimated at 20.6 percent. Which type of probability (classical, empirical, subjective) do you think this is?

5.63   A recent article states that there is a 2 percent chance that an asteroid 100 meters or more in diameter will strike the earth before 2100. Which type of probability (classical, empirical, subjective) do you think this is?

5.64   If Punxsutawney Phil sees his shadow on February 2, then legend says that winter will last 6 more weeks. In 118 years, Phil has seen his shadow 104 times. (a) What is the probability that Phil will see his shadow on a randomly chosen Groundhog Day? (b) Which type of probability (classical, empirical, subjective) do you think this is?

5.65   On Los Angeles freeways during the rush hour, there is an 18 percent probability that a driver is using a hand-held cell phone. Which type of probability (classical, empirical, subjective) do you think this is?

5.66   Bob owns two stocks. There is an 80 percent probability that stock *A* will rise in price, while there is a 60 percent chance that stock *B* will rise in price. There is a 40 percent chance that both stocks will rise in price. Are the stock prices independent?

5.67   To run its network, the Ramjac Corporation wants to install a system with dual independent servers. Employee Bob grumbled, "But that will double the chance of system failure." Is Bob right? Explain your reasoning with an example.

5.68   A study showed that trained police officers can detect a lie 65 percent of the time, based on controlled studies of videotapes with real-life lies and truths. What are the odds in favor of a lie being detected?

5.69   The probability that a 2004 Audi A4 is stolen is 1.2645 percent. Find the odds *against* the theft of a 2004 Audi A4. Round your answer to the nearest whole number. (www.nhtsa.gov/theft)

5.70   The probability of being struck by lightning is .00016. Find the odds *against* being struck by lightning. Round your answer to the nearest whole number. (www.lightningsafety.noaa.gov)

5.71   Prior to the start of the 2011 NCAA Men's Basketball playoffs, the reported odds that Butler University would *not* make it to the final game was 200 to 1. What was the implied probability that Butler would make it to the finals in 2011?

5.72   A certain model of remote-control Stanley garage door opener has nine binary (off/on) switches. The homeowner can set any code sequence. (a) How many separate codes can be programmed? (b) If you try to use your door opener on 1,000 other garages, how many times would you expect to succeed?

5.73   (a) In a certain state, license plates consist of three letters (A–Z) followed by three digits (0–9). How many different plates can be issued? (b) If the state allows any six-character mix (in any order) of 26 letters and 10 digits, how many unique plates are possible? (c) Why might some combinations of digits and letters be disallowed? *(d) Would the system described in (b) permit a unique license number for every car in the United States? For every car in the world? Explain your assumptions. *(e) If the letters O and I are not used because they look too much like the numerals 0 and 1, how many different plates can be issued?

5.74   Bob, Mary, and Jen go to dinner. Each orders a different meal. The waiter forgets who ordered which meal, so he randomly places the meals before the three diners. Let *C* be the event that a diner gets the correct meal and let *N* be the event that a diner gets an incorrect meal. Enumerate the sample space and then find the probability that:

   a. No diner gets the correct meal.
   b. Exactly one diner gets the correct meal.
   c. Exactly two diners get the correct meal.
   d. All three diners get the correct meal.

5.75   An MBA program offers seven concentrations: accounting (*A*), finance (*F*), human resources (*H*), information systems (*I*), international business (*B*), marketing (*M*), and operations management (*O*). Students in the capstone business policy class are assigned to teams of three. In how many different ways could a team contain exactly one student from each concentration?

5.76   A poker hand (5 cards) is drawn from an ordinary deck of 52 cards. Find the probability of each event, showing your reasoning carefully.

   a. The first four cards are the four aces.
   b. Any four cards are the four aces.

5.77   Two cards are drawn from an ordinary deck of 52 cards. Find the probability of each event, showing your reasoning carefully.

   a. Two aces.
   b. Two red cards.
   c. Two red aces.
   d. Two honor cards (A, K, Q, J, 10).

5.78   A certain airplane has two independent alternators to provide electrical power. The probability that a given alternator will fail on a one-hour flight is .02. What is the probability that (a) both will fail? (b) Neither will fail? (c) One or the other will fail? Show all steps carefully.

5.79   There is a 30 percent chance that a bidding firm will get contract A and a 40 percent chance they will get contract B. There is a 5 percent chance that they will get both. Are the events independent?

5.80   A couple has two children. What is the probability that both are boys, given that the first is a boy?

5.81   A turboprop aircraft has two attitude gyros, driven from independent electrical sources. On a six-hour flight, assume the probability of failure of each attitude gyroscope is 0.0008. Does this achieve "five-nines" reliability (i.e., a probability of at least 0.99999 that not all gyros will fail)?

5.82   Which are likely to be independent events? For those you think are not, suggest reasons why.

   a. Gender of two babies born consecutively in a hospital.
   b. Car accident rates and the driver's gender.
   c. Phone call arrival rates at a university admissions office and time of day.

5.83   In child-custody cases, about 70 percent of the fathers win the case if they contest it. In the next three custody cases, what is the probability that all three win? What assumption(s) are you making?

*5.84   A web server hosting company advertises 99.999 percent guaranteed network uptime. (a) How many independent network servers would be needed if each has 99 percent reliability? (b) If each has 90 percent reliability?

*5.85   Fifty-six percent of American adults eat at a table-service restaurant at least once a week. Suppose that four American adults are asked if they ate at table-service restaurants last week. What is the probability that all of them say yes?

*5.86   The probability is 1 in 4,000,000 that a single auto trip in the United States will result in a fatality. Over a lifetime, an average U.S. driver takes 50,000 trips. (a) What is the probability of a fatal accident over a lifetime? Explain your reasoning carefully. *Hint:* Assume independent events. (b) Why might the assumption of independence be violated? (c) Why might a driver be tempted not to use a seat belt "just on this trip"?

*5.87   If there are two riders on a city bus, what is the probability that no two have the same birthday? What if there are 10 riders? 20 riders? 50 riders? Hint: Use *LearningStats* from the OLC.

*5.88   How many riders would there have to be on a bus to yield (a) a 50 percent probability that at least two will have the same birthday? (b) A 75 percent probability? Hint: Use the *LearningStats* demonstration from the OLC.

5.89   Four students divided the task of surveying the types of vehicles in parking lots of four different shopping malls. Each student examined 100 cars in each of three large suburban Detroit malls and one suburban Jamestown, New York, mall, resulting in the 5×4 contingency table shown below. (a) Calculate each probability (i–vi) and explain in words what it means. (b) Do you see evidence that vehicle type is not independent of mall location? Explain. (Data are from an independent project by MBA students Steve Bennett, Alicia Morais, Steve Olson, and Greg Corda.) 🖰 **Malls**

   i. $P(C)$ ii. $P(G)$ iii. $P(V \mid S)$
   iv. $P(C \mid J)$ v. $P(C \text{ and } G)$ vi. $P(T \text{ and } O)$

Number of Vehicles of Each Type in Four Shopping Malls

Vehicle Type	Somerset (S)	Oakland (O)	Great Lakes (G)	Jamestown, NY (J)	Row Total
Car (C)	44	49	36	64	193
Minivan (M)	21	15	18	13	67
Full-size van (F)	2	3	3	2	10
SUV (V)	19	27	26	12	84
Truck (T)	14	6	17	9	46
Column Total	100	100	100	100	400

5.90 Refer to the contingency table shown below. (a) Calculate each probability (i–vi) and explain in words what it means. (b) Do you see evidence that smoking and race are *not* independent? Explain. (c) Do the smoking rates shown here correspond to your experience? (d) Why might public health officials be interested in this type of data? (Data are from *Statistical Abstract of the United States, 2001*, pp. 12 and 16. Note: Actual statistics are applied to a hypothetical sample of 1,000.) ⬚ **Smoking2**

   i. $P(S)$ ii. $P(W)$ iii. $P(S \mid W)$
  iv. $P(S \mid B)$ v. $P(S \text{ and } W)$ vi. $P(N \text{ and } B)$

Smoking by Race for Males Aged 18–24

	Smoker (S)	Nonsmoker (N)	Row Total
White (W)	290	560	850
Black (B)	30	120	150
Column Total	320	680	1,000

5.91 Analysis of forecasters' interest rate predictions over the period 1982–1990 was intended to see whether the predictions corresponded to what actually happened. The 2 × 2 contingency table below shows the frequencies of actual and predicted interest rate movements. (a) Calculate each probability (i–vi) and explain in words what it means. (b*) Do you think that the forecasters' predictions were accurate? Explain. (Data are from R. A. Kolb and H. O. Steckler, "How Well Do Analysts Forecast Interest Rates?" *Journal of Forecasting* 15, no. 15 [1996], pp. 385–394.) ⬚ **Forecasts**

   i. $P(F-)$ ii. $P(A+)$ iii. $P(A- \mid F-)$
  iv. $P(A+ \mid F+)$ v. $P(A+ \text{ and } F+)$ vi. $P(A- \text{ and } F-)$

Interest Rate Forecast Accuracy

	Actual Change		
Forecast Change	Decline (A−)	Rise (A+)	Row Total
Decline (F−)	7	12	19
Rise (F+)	9	6	15
Column Total	16	18	34

5.92 High levels of cockpit noise in an aircraft can damage the hearing of pilots who are exposed to this hazard for many hours. Cockpit noise in a jet aircraft is mostly due to airflow at hundreds of miles per hour. This 3 × 3 contingency table shows 61 observations of data collected by an airline pilot using a handheld sound meter in a Boeing 727 cockpit. Noise level is defined as "low" (under 88 decibels), "medium" (88 to 91 decibels), or "high" (92 decibels or more). There are three flight phases (climb, cruise, descent). (a) Calculate each probability (i–vi) and explain in words what it means. (b) Do you see evidence that noise level depends on flight phase? Explain. (c) Where else might ambient noise be an ergonomic issue? (*Hint:* search the web.) (Data are from Capt. Robert E. Hartl, retired.) 🖥 **Cockpit**

   i. $P(B)$ ii. $P(L)$ iii. $P(H \mid C)$
 iv. $P(H \mid D)$ v. $P(L \text{ and } B)$ vi. $P(L \text{ and } C)$

Cockpit Noise

Noise Level	Flight Phase			Row Total
	Climb (B)	Cruise (C)	Descent (D)	
Low (L)	6	2	6	14
Medium (M)	18	3	8	29
High (H)	1	3	14	18
Column Total	25	8	28	61

BAYES' THEOREM

*5.93 A test for ovarian cancer has a 5 percent rate of false positives and a 0 percent rate of false negatives. On average, 1 in every 2,500 American women over age 35 actually has ovarian cancer. If a woman over 35 tests positive, what is the probability that she actually has cancer? *Hint:* Make a contingency table for a hypothetical sample of 100,000 women. Explain your reasoning.

*5.94 A biometric security device using fingerprints erroneously refuses to admit 1 in 1,000 authorized persons from a facility containing classified information. The device will erroneously admit 1 in 1,000,000 unauthorized persons. Assume that 95 percent of those who seek access are authorized. If the alarm goes off and a person is refused admission, what is the probability that the person was really authorized?

*5.95 Dolon Web Security Consultants requires all job applicants to submit to a test for illegal drugs. If the applicant has used illegal drugs, the test has a 90 percent chance of a positive result. If the applicant has not used illegal drugs, the test has an 85 percent chance of a negative result. Actually, 4 percent of the job applicants have used illegal drugs. If an applicant has a positive test, what is the probability that he or she has actually used illegal drugs? *Hint:* Make a 2 × 2 contingency table of frequencies, assuming 500 job applicants.

Albert, James H. "College Students' Conceptions of Probability." *The American Statistician* 57, no. 1 (February 2001), pp. 37–45.

RELATED READING

CHAPTER 5 Online Learning Resources

The Online Learning Center (OLC) at www.mhhe.com/doane4e has several *LearningStats* demonstrations to help you understand probability. Your instructor may assign one or more of them, or you may decide to download the ones that sound interesting.

Topic	LearningStats Demonstrations
Contingency tables	▨ Contingency Tables ▨ Cross-Tabulations ▨ Independent Events
Probability	▨ Birthday Problem ▨ System Reliability
Random processes	▨ Law of Large Numbers ▨ Dice Rolls ▨ Pick a Card ▨ Random Names
Bayes' Theorem	▨ Bayes' Theorem

Key: ▨ = Excel

Discrete Probability Distributions

CHAPTER CONTENTS

CHAPTER LEARNING OBJECTIVES

LO

When you finish this chapter you should be able to

LO 6-1 Define a discrete random variable.

LO 6-2 Solve problems using expected value and variance.

LO 6-3 Define probability distribution, PDF, and CDF.

LO 6-4 Know the mean and variance of a uniform discrete model.

LO 6-5 Find binomial probabilities using tables, formulas, or Excel.

LO 6-6 Find Poisson probabilities using tables, formulas, or Excel.

LO 6-7 Use the Poisson approximation to the binomial (optional).

LO 6-8 Find hypergeometric probabilities using Excel.

LO 6-9 Calculate geometric probabilities (optional).

LO 6-10 Select an appropriate discrete probability distribution from problem context.

LO 6-11 Apply rules for transformations of random variables (optional).

This chapter shows how probability can be used to analyze business activities or processes that generate random data. Many business processes create data that can be thought of as random. For example, consider cars being serviced in a quick oil change shop or calls arriving at the L.L. Bean order center. Each car or call can be thought of as an experiment with random outcomes. The variable of interest for the car might be service time. The variable of interest for the call might be amount of the order. Service time and amount of order will vary randomly for each car or call.

A **probability model** assigns a probability to each outcome in the sample space defined by a random process. We use probability models to depict the essential characteristics of a stochastic process, to guide decisions or make predictions. How many service technicians do we need from noon to 1 p.m. on Friday afternoon? To answer this we need to model the process of servicing cars during the lunch hour. Can L.L. Bean predict its total order amount from the next 50 callers? To answer this question L.L. Bean needs to model the process of call orders to its call center. Probability models must be reasonably realistic yet simple enough to be analyzed.

Many random processes can be described by using common probability models whose properties are well known. To correctly use these probability models, it is important that you understand their development. In the following sections we will explain how probability models are developed and describe several commonly used models.

6.1 DISCRETE DISTRIBUTIONS

Random Variables

A **random variable** is a function or rule that assigns a numerical value to each outcome in the sample space of a random experiment. We use X when referring to a random variable in general, while specific values of X are shown in lowercase (e.g., x_1). The random variable often is a direct result of an observational experiment (e.g., counting the number of takeoffs in a given hour at O'Hare International Airport). A **discrete random variable** has a countable number of distinct values. Some random variables have a clear upper limit (e.g., number of absences in a class of 40 students) while others do not (e.g., number of text messages you receive in a given hour). Here are some examples of decision problems involving discrete random variables.

> **LO 6-1**
>
> Define a discrete random variable.

Decision Problem

- Oxnard University has space in its MBA program for 65 new students. In the past, 75 percent of those who are admitted actually enroll. The decision is made to admit 80 students. What is the probability that more than 65 admitted students will actually enroll?

- On the late morning (9 to 12) work shift, L.L. Bean's order processing center staff can handle up to 5 orders per minute. The mean arrival rate is 3.5 orders per minute. What is the probability that more than 5 orders will arrive in a given minute?

- Rolled steel from a certain supplier averages 0.01 defect per linear meter. Toyota will reject a shipment of 500 linear meters if inspection reveals more than 10 defects. What is the probability that the order will be rejected?

Discrete Random Variable

- X = number of admitted MBA students who actually enroll ($X = 0, 1, 2, \ldots, 80$)

- X = number of phone calls that arrive in a given minute at the L.L. Bean order processing center ($X = 0, 1, 2, \ldots$)

- X = number of defects in 500 meters of rolled steel ($X = 0, 1, 2, \ldots$)

Probability Distributions

A **discrete probability distribution** assigns a probability to each value of a discrete random variable X. The distribution must follow the rules of probability defined in Chapter 5. If X has n distinct values $x_1, x_2, \ldots, x_n$, then:

(6.1) $0 \le P(x_i) \le 1$ (the probability for any given value of X)

(6.2) $\sum_{i=1}^{n} P(x_i) = 1$ (the sum over all values of X)

Discrete probability distributions follow the rules of functions. More than one sample space outcome can be assigned to the same number, but you cannot assign one outcome to two different numbers. Likewise, more than one random variable value can be assigned to the same probability, but one random variable value cannot have two different probabilities. The probabilities must sum to 1. Figure 6.1 illustrates the relationship between the sample space, the random variable, and the probability distribution function for a simple experiment of rolling a die.

FIGURE 6.1

Random Experiment: Rolling a Die

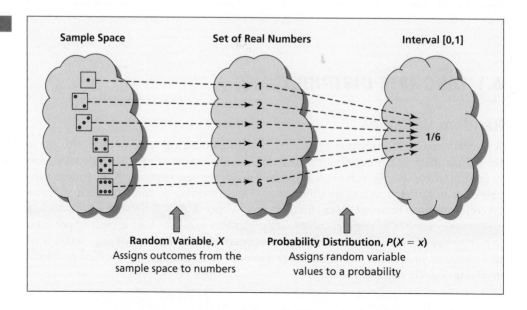

Sample Space   **Set of Real Numbers**   **Interval [0,1]**

1
2
3
4   1/6
5
6

Random Variable, X
Assigns outcomes from the sample space to numbers

Probability Distribution, $P(X = x)$
Assigns random variable values to a probability

When you flip a fair coin three times, the sample space has eight equally likely simple events: {HHH, HHT, HTH, THH, HTT, THT, TTH, TTT}. If X is the number of heads, then X is a random variable whose probability distribution is shown in Table 6.1 and Figure 6.2.

EXAMPLE 6.1

Coin Flips

ThreeCoins

TABLE 6.1	Probability Distribution for Three Coin Flips		
Possible Events		**x**	**P(x)**
TTT		0	1/8
HTT, THT, TTH		1	3/8
HHT, HTH, THH		2	3/8
HHH		3	1/8
Total			1

The values of X need not be equally likely. In this example, $X = 1$ and $X = 2$ are more likely than $X = 0$ or $X = 3$. However, the probabilities sum to 1, as in any probability distribution.

FIGURE 6.2	Probability Distribution for Three Coin Flips

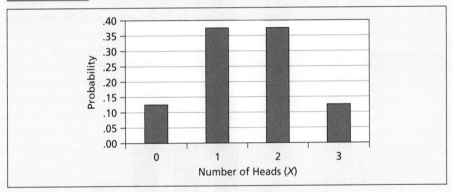

Expected Value

As shown in Figure 6.2, a discrete probability distribution is defined only at specific points on the X-axis. The **expected value** $E(X)$ of a discrete random variable is the sum of all X-values weighted by their respective probabilities. It is a measure of *center*. If there are N distinct values of $X (x_1, x_2, \ldots, x_N)$, the expected value is

$$E(X) = \mu = \sum_{i=1}^{N} x_i P(x_i) \qquad (6.3)$$

The expected value is a *weighted* average because outcomes can have different probabilities. Because it is an average, we usually call $E(X)$ the *mean* and use the symbol μ.

The distribution of Sunday emergency service calls by Ace Appliance Repair is shown in Table 6.2. The probabilities sum to 1, as must be true for any probability distribution.

The mode (most likely value of X) is 2, but the *expected* number of service calls $E(X)$ is 2.75, that is, $\mu = 2.75$. In other words, the "average" number of service calls is 2.75 on Sunday:

$$E(X) = \mu = \sum_{i=1}^{N} x_i P(x_i) = 0P(0) + 1P(1) + 2P(2) + 3P(3) + 4P(4) + 5P(5)$$

$$= 0(.05) + 1(.10) + 2(.30) + 3(.25) + 4(.20) + 5(.10) = 2.75$$

EXAMPLE 6.2

Service Calls

ServiceCalls

TABLE 6.2	Probability Distribution of Service Calls		
x		**P(x)**	**xP(x)**
0		.05	0.00
1		.10	0.10
2		.30	0.60
3		.25	0.75
4		.20	0.80
5		.10	0.50
Total		1.00	2.75

In Figure 6.3, we see that this particular probability distribution is not symmetric around the mean $\mu = 2.75$. However, the mean $\mu = 2.75$ is still the balancing point, or fulcrum.

Note that $E(X)$ need not be an observable event. For example, you could have 2 service calls or 3 service calls, but not 2.75 service calls. This makes sense because $E(X)$ is an *average*. It is like saying that "the average American family has 2.1 children" (even though families come only in integer sizes) or "Albert Pujols's batting average is .312" (even though the number of hits by Pujols in a particular game must be an integer).

FIGURE 6.3	Probability Distribution for Service Calls

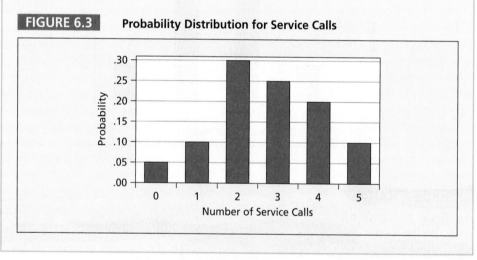

Application: Life Insurance   Expected value is the basis of life insurance, a purchase that almost everyone makes. For example, based on U.S. mortality statistics, the probability that a 30-year-old white female will die within the next year is .000642, so the probability of living another year is $1 - .000642 = .999358$. What premium should a life insurance company charge to break even on a $500,000 one-year term insurance policy (that is, to achieve zero expected payout)? This situation is shown in Table 6.3. Let X be the amount paid by the company to settle the policy. The expected payout is $321, so the premium should be $321 plus whatever return the company needs to cover its administrative overhead and profit.

TABLE 6.3

Expected Payout for a One-Year Term Life Policy

Source: Centers for Disease Control and Prevention, *National Vital Statistics Reports* 58, no. 19 (2010).

Event	x	P(x)	xP(x)
Live	0	.999358	.00
Die	500,000	.000642	321.00
Total		1.000000	321.00

The mortality rate shown here is for *all* 30-year-old women. An insurance quote (e.g., from the web) is likely to yield a lower premium, as long as you are a healthy, educated nonsmoker in a nonrisky occupation. Insurance companies make money by knowing the actuarial probabilities and using them to set their premiums. The task is difficult because actuarial probabilities must be revised as life expectancies change over time.

Application: Raffle Tickets   Expected value can be applied to raffles and lotteries. If it costs $2 to buy a ticket in a raffle to win a new luxury automobile worth $55,000 and 29,346 raffle tickets are sold, the expected value of a lottery ticket is

$$E(X) = \text{(value if you win)}P(\text{win}) + \text{(value if you lose)}P(\text{lose})$$

$$= (55,000)\left(\frac{1}{29,346}\right) + (0)\left(\frac{29,345}{29,346}\right)$$

$$= (55,000)(.000034076) + (0)(.999965924) = \$1.87$$

The raffle ticket is actually worth $1.87. So why would you pay $2.00 for it? Partly because you hope to beat the odds, but also because you know that your ticket purchase helps the charity. Since the idea of a raffle is to raise money, the sponsor tries to sell enough tickets to push the expected value of the ticket below its price (otherwise, the charity would lose money on the raffle). If the raffle prize is donated (or partially donated) by a well-wisher, the break-even point may be much less than the full value of the prize.

Like a lottery, an **actuarially fair** insurance program must collect as much in overall revenue as it pays out in claims. This is accomplished by setting the premiums to reflect empirical experience with the insured group. Individuals may gain or lose, but if the pool of insured persons is large enough, the total payout is predictable. Of course, many insurance policies have exclusionary clauses for war and natural disaster (e.g., Hurricane Katrina), to deal with cases where the events are not independent. Actuarial analysis is critical for corporate pension fund planning. Group health insurance is another major application.

Variance and Standard Deviation

The **variance** Var(X) of a discrete random variable is the sum of the squared deviations about its expected value, weighted by the probability of each X-value. If there are N distinct values of X, the variance is

$$\text{Var}(X) = \sigma^2 = \sum_{i=1}^{N}[x_i - \mu]^2 P(x_i) \qquad (6.4)$$

Just as the expected value $E(X)$ is a weighted average that measures *center,* the variance Var(X) is a weighted average that measures variability about the mean. And just as we interchangeably use μ or $E(X)$ to denote the mean of a distribution, we use either σ^2 or Var(X) to denote its variance.

The *standard deviation* is the square root of the variance and is denoted σ:

$$\sigma = \sqrt{\sigma^2} = \sqrt{\text{Var}(X)} \qquad (6.5)$$

The Bay Street Inn is a seven-room bed-and-breakfast in the sunny California coastal city of Santa Theresa. Demand for rooms generally is strong during February, a prime month for tourists. However, experience shows that demand is quite variable. The probability distribution of room rentals during February is shown in Table 6.4 where X = the number of rooms rented (X = 0, 1, 2, 3, 4, 5, 6, 7). The worksheet shows the calculation of $E(X)$ and Var(X).

EXAMPLE 6.3

Bed and Breakfast
  RoomRent

TABLE 6.4		Worksheet for $E(X)$ and $Var(X)$ for February Room Rentals			
x	$P(x)$	$xP(x)$	$x - \mu$	$[x - \mu]^2$	$[x - \mu]^2 P(x)$
0	.05	0.00	−4.71	22.1841	1.109205
1	.05	0.05	−3.71	13.7641	0.688205
2	.06	0.12	−2.71	7.3441	0.440646
3	.10	0.30	−1.71	2.9241	0.292410
4	.13	0.52	−0.71	0.5041	0.065533
5	.20	1.00	+0.29	0.0841	0.016820
6	.15	0.90	+1.29	1.6641	0.249615
7	.26	1.82	+2.29	5.2441	1.363466
Total	1.00	$\mu = 4.71$			$\sigma^2 = 4.225900$

The formulas are:

$$E(X) = \mu = \sum_{i=1}^{N} x_i \, P(x_i) = 4.71$$

$$\text{Var}(X) = \sigma^2 = \sum_{i=1}^{N} [x_i - \mu]^2 P(x_i) = 4.2259$$

$$\sigma = \sqrt{4.2259} = 2.0557$$

This distribution is skewed to the left and bimodal. The mode (most likely value) is 7 rooms rented, but the average is only 4.71 room rentals in February. The standard deviation of 2.06 indicates that there is considerable variation around the mean, as seen in Figure 6.4.

FIGURE 6.4   **Probability Distribution of Room Rentals**

What Is a PDF or a CDF?

A known distribution can be described either by its **probability distribution function** (PDF) or by its **cumulative distribution function** (CDF). The PDF and CDF are defined either by a list of X–values and their probabilities or by mathematical equations. A discrete PDF shows the probability of each X–value, while the CDF shows the cumulative sum of probabilities, adding from the smallest to the largest X–value. Figure 6.5 illustrates a discrete PDF and the corresponding CDF. Notice that the CDF approaches 1, and the PDF values of X will sum to 1.

Random variables and their distributions are described by their **parameters**. The equations for the PDF, the CDF, and the characteristics of the distribution (such as the mean and standard deviation) will depend on the parameters of the process. The rest of this chapter explains several well-known discrete distributions and their applications. Many random business processes can be described by these common distributions.

FIGURE 6.5

Illustration of PDF and CDF

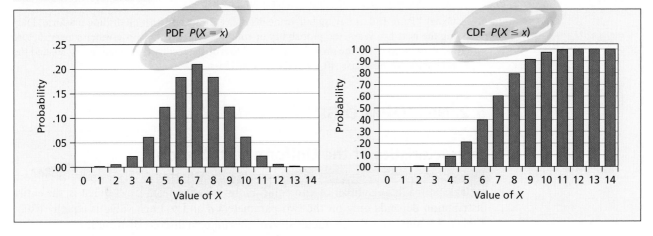

6.1   Which of the following could *not* be probability distributions? Explain.

Example A		Example B		Example C	
x	**P(x)**	**x**	**P(x)**	**x**	**P(x)**
0	.80	1	.05	50	.30
1	.20	2	.15	60	.60
		3	.25	70	.40
		4	.40		
		5	.10		

6.2   On hot, sunny, summer days, Jane rents inner tubes by the river that runs through her town. Based on her past experience, she has assigned the following probability distribution to the number of tubes she will rent on a randomly selected day. (a) Calculate the expected value and standard deviation of this random variable X by using the PDF shown. (b) Describe the shape of this distribution.

x	25	50	75	100	Total
P(x)	.20	.40	.30	.10	1.00

6.3   On the midnight shift, the number of patients with head trauma in an emergency room has the probability distribution shown below. (a) Calculate the mean and standard deviation. (b) Describe the shape of this distribution.

x	0	1	2	3	4	5	Total
P(x)	.05	.30	.25	.20	.15	.05	1.00

6.4   Pepsi and Mountain Dew products sponsored a contest giving away a Lamborghini sports car worth $215,000. The probability of winning from a single bottle purchase was .00000884. Find the expected value. Show your calculations clearly. (Data are from J. Paul Peter and Jerry C. Olson, *Consumer Behavior and Marketing Strategy,* 7th ed. [McGraw-Hill/Irwin, 2005], p. 226.)

6.5   Student Life Insurance Company wants to offer an insurance plan with a maximum claim amount of $5,000 for dorm students to cover theft of certain items. Past experience suggests that the probability of a maximum claim is .01. What premium should be charged if the company wants to make a profit of $25 per policy? Assume any student who files a claim files for the maximum amount and there is no deductible. Show your calculations clearly.

6.6   A lottery ticket has a grand prize of $28 million. The probability of winning the grand prize is .000000023. Based on the expected value of the lottery ticket, would you pay $1 for a ticket? Show your calculations and reasoning clearly.

6.7   Oxnard Petro Ltd. is buying hurricane insurance for its off-coast oil drilling platform. During the next five years, the probability of total loss of only the above-water superstructure ($250 million) is .30, the probability of total loss of the facility ($950 million) is .30, and the probability of no loss is .40. Find the expected loss.

6.2 UNIFORM DISTRIBUTION

Characteristics of the Uniform Distribution

The **uniform distribution** is one of the simplest discrete models. It describes a random variable with a finite number of consecutive integer values from *a* to *b*. That is, the entire distribution depends only on the two parameters *a* and *b*. Each value is equally likely. Table 6.5 summarizes the characteristics of the uniform discrete distribution.

TABLE 6.5	
Uniform Discrete Distribution	

Parameters	a = lower limit
	b = upper limit
PDF	$P(X = x) = \dfrac{1}{b - a + 1}$
CDF	$P(X \leq x) = \dfrac{x - a + 1}{b - a + 1}$
Domain	$x = a, a + 1, a + 2, \ldots, b$
Mean	$\dfrac{a + b}{2}$
Standard deviation	$\sqrt{\dfrac{[(b - a) + 1]^2 - 1}{12}}$
Random data generation in Excel	=RANDBETWEEN(a, b)
Comments	Useful as a benchmark, to generate random integers for sampling, or in simulation models.

LO 6-4

Know the mean and variance of a uniform discrete model.

When you roll one die, the number of dots forms a uniform discrete random variable with six equally likely integer values 1, 2, 3, 4, 5, 6, shown in the PDF and CDF in Figure 6.6. You can see that the mean (3.5) must be halfway between 1 and 6, but there is no way you could anticipate the standard deviation without using a formula.

FIGURE 6.6

PDF and CDF for Rolling a Die

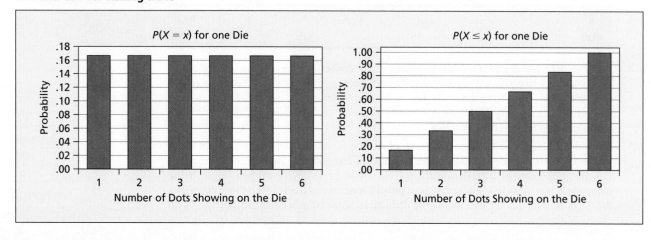

For this example, the mean and standard deviation are:

Mean $\qquad\qquad \mu = \dfrac{a+b}{2} = \dfrac{1+6}{2} = 3.5$

Std. Dev. $\qquad\quad \sigma = \sqrt{\dfrac{[(b-a)+1]^2 - 1}{12}} = \sqrt{\dfrac{[(6-1)+1]^2 - 1}{12}} = 1.708$

Consider another example of the discrete uniform distribution. When filling your car with gas, the last two digits (pennies) showing on the display of gallons dispensed will be a uniform random integer (assuming you don't "top off" but just let the pump stop automatically) ranging from $a = 00$ to $b = 99$. You could verify the predicted mean and standard deviation shown here by looking at a large sample of fill-ups on your own car:

PDF $\qquad P(X = x) = \dfrac{1}{b-a+1} = \dfrac{1}{99-0+1} = \dfrac{1}{100} = .010 \quad$ for all x

Mean $\qquad\qquad \mu = \dfrac{a+b}{2} = \dfrac{0+99}{2} = 49.5$

Std. Dev. $\qquad\quad \sigma = \sqrt{\dfrac{[(b-a)+1]^2 - 1}{12}} = \sqrt{\dfrac{[(99-0)+1]^2 - 1}{12}} = 28.87$

The discrete uniform distribution is often used to generate random integers that are then used to randomly sample from a population. To accomplish this, we can use the Excel function =RANDBETWEEN(a, b). For example, to generate a random integer from 5 through 10, the Excel function would be =RANDBETWEEN(5, 10). The same integer may come up more than once, so to obtain n distinct random integers you would have to generate a few extras and then eliminate the duplicates if you are sampling without replacement (see Chapter 2). This method is useful in accounting and auditing (e.g., to allow the auditor to choose numbered invoices at random).

Mini Case 6.1

The "Daily 3" Lottery

Many states have a "daily 3" lottery. The daily 3 is a uniformly distributed discrete random variable whose values range from 000 through 999. There are 1,000 equally likely outcomes, so the probability of any given three-digit number is 1/1,000. The theoretical characteristics of this lottery are:

$$P(X = x) = \dfrac{1}{b-a+1} = \dfrac{1}{999-0+1} = \dfrac{1}{1,000} = .001$$

$$\mu = \dfrac{a+b}{2} = \dfrac{0+999}{2} = 499.5$$

$$\sigma = \sqrt{\dfrac{(b-a+1)^2 - 1}{12}} = \sqrt{\dfrac{(999-0+1)^2 - 1}{12}} = 288.67$$

In a large sample of three-digit lottery numbers, you would expect the sample mean and standard deviation to be very close to 499.5 and 288.67, respectively. For example, in Michigan's daily three-digit lottery, from January 1, 2010, through December 31, 2010, there were 364 evening drawings. The mean of all the three-digit numbers drawn over that period was 497.1 with a standard deviation of 289.5. These sample results are extremely close to what would be expected. It is the nature of random samples to vary, so no sample is expected to yield statistics identical with the population parameters.

In Michigan, randomization is achieved by drawing a numbered ping-pong ball from each of three bins. Within each bin, the balls are agitated using air flow. Each bin contains 10 ping-pong balls. Each ball has a single digit (0, 1, 2, 3, 4, 5, 6, 7, 8, 9). The drawing is televised, so there is no possibility of bias or manipulation. Lotteries are studied frequently to make sure that they are truly random, using statistical comparisons like these, as well as tests for overall shape and patterns over time.

SECTION EXERCISES

connect

6.8 Find the mean and standard deviation of four-digit uniformly distributed lottery numbers (0000 through 9999).

6.9 The ages of Java programmers at SynFlex Corp. range from 20 to 60. (a) If their ages are uniformly distributed, what would be the mean and standard deviation? (b) What is the probability that a randomly selected programmer's age is at least 40? At least 30? *Hint:* Treat employee ages as integers.

6.10 Use Excel to generate 100 random integers from (a) 1 through 2, inclusive; (b) 1 through 5, inclusive; and (c) 0 through 99, inclusive. (d) In each case, write the Excel formula. (e) In each case, calculate the mean and standard deviation of the sample of 100 integers you generated, and compare them with their theoretical values.

6.3 BERNOULLI DISTRIBUTION

Bernoulli Experiments

A random experiment that has only two outcomes is called a **Bernoulli experiment**, named after Jakob Bernoulli (1654–1705). To create a random variable, we arbitrarily call one outcome a "success" (denoted $X = 1$) and the other a "failure" (denoted $X = 0$). The probability of success is denoted π (the Greek letter "pi," *not* to be confused with the mathematical constant 3.14159).* The probability of failure is $1 - \pi$, so the probabilities sum to 1, that is, $P(0) + P(1) = (1 - \pi) + \pi = 1$. The probability of success, π, remains the same for each trial.

The examples in Table 6.6 show that a success ($X = 1$) may in fact represent something undesirable. Metallurgists look for signs of metal fatigue. Auditors look for expense voucher errors. Bank loan officers look for loan defaults. A success, then, is merely an event of interest.

TABLE 6.6	**Bernoulli Experiment**	**Possible Outcomes**	**Probability of "Success"**
Examples of Bernoulli Experiments	Flip a coin	1 = heads 0 = tails	$\pi = .50$
	Inspect a jet turbine blade	1 = crack found 0 = no crack found	$\pi = .001$
	Purchase a tank of gas	1 = pay by credit card 0 = do not pay by credit card	$\pi = .78$
	Do a mammogram test	1 = positive test 0 = negative test	$\pi = .0004$

The probability of success π can be any value between 0 and 1. In flipping a fair coin, π is .50. But in other applications π could be close to 1 (e.g., the probability that a customer's Visa purchase will be approved) or close to 0 (e.g., the probability that an adult male is HIV positive). Table 6.6 is only intended to suggest that π depends on the situation. The definitions of success and failure are arbitrary and can be switched, although we usually define success as the less likely outcome so that π is less than .50.

The only parameter needed to define a Bernoulli process is π. A Bernoulli experiment has mean π and variance $\pi(1 - \pi)$ as we see from the definitions of $E(X)$ and $\text{Var}(X)$:

$$(6.6) \qquad E(X) = \sum_{i=1}^{2} x_i P(x_i) = (0)(1 - \pi) + (1)(\pi) = \pi \qquad \text{(Bernoulli mean)}$$

---

*Some textbooks denote the probability of success p. However, in this textbook, we prefer to use Greek letters for population parameters. In Chapters 8 and 9, the symbol p will be used to denote a *sample* estimate of π.

$$\text{Var}(X) = \sum_{i=1}^{2} [x_i - E(X)]^2 \, P(x_i)$$

$$= (0 - \pi)^2(1 - \pi) + (1 - \pi)^2(\pi) = \pi(1 - \pi) \quad \text{(Bernoulli variance)} \quad \textbf{(6.7)}$$

There are many business applications that can be described by the Bernoulli model and it is an important building block for more complex models. We will use the Bernoulli distribution to develop the next model.

6.11 Define a Bernoulli variable for (a) guessing on a true-false exam question; (b) checking to see whether an ER patient has health insurance; (c) dialing a talkative friend's cell phone; (d) going on a 10-day diet.

6.12 (a) In the previous exercise, suggest the approximate probability of success in each scenario.
(b) Is success a desirable or undesirable thing in each of these scenarios?

6.4 BINOMIAL DISTRIBUTION

Characteristics of the Binomial Distribution

LO 6-5

Find binomial probabilities using tables, formulas, or Excel.

Bernoulli experiments lead to an important and more interesting model. The **binomial distribution** arises when a Bernoulli experiment is repeated n times. Each Bernoulli trial is independent so that the probability of success π remains constant on each trial. In a binomial experiment, we are interested in X = the number of success in n trials, so the binomial random variable X is the sum of n independent Bernoulli random variables:

$$X = X_1 + X_2 + \cdots + X_n$$

We can add the n identical Bernoulli means ($\pi + \pi + \cdots + \pi$) to get the binomial mean $n\pi$. Since the n Bernoulli trials are independent, we can add* the n identical Bernoulli variances $\pi(1 - \pi) + \pi(1 - \pi) + \cdots + \pi(1 - \pi)$ to obtain the binomial variance $n\pi(1 - \pi)$ and hence its standard deviation $\sqrt{n\pi(1 - \pi)}$. The domain of the binomial is $x = 0, 1, 2, \ldots, n$. The binomial probability of a particular number of successes $P(X = x)$ is determined by the two parameters n and π. The characteristics of the binomial distribution are summarized in Table 6.7. The binomial probability function is:

$$P(X = x) = \frac{n!}{x!(n - x)!} \, \pi^x(1 - \pi)^{n-x}, \quad \text{for } X = 0, 1, 2, 3, 4, \ldots, n. \quad \textbf{(6.8)}$$

Application: Uninsured Patients Uninsured   On average, 20 percent of the emergency room patients at Greenwood General Hospital lack health insurance. In a random sample of four patients, what is the probability that two will be uninsured? Define X = number of uninsured patients and set $\pi = .20$ (i.e., a 20 percent chance that a given patient will be uninsured) and $1 - \pi = .80$ (i.e., an 80 percent chance that a patient will be insured). The domain is $X = 0, 1, 2, 3, 4$ patients. Applying the binomial formulas, the mean and standard deviation are:

$$\text{Mean} = \mu = n\pi = (4)(.20) = 0.8 \text{ patient}$$

$$\text{Standard deviation} = \sigma = \sqrt{n\pi(1 - \pi)} = \sqrt{(4)(.20)(1 - .20)} = 0.8 \text{ patient}$$

---

*The last section in this chapter (optional) explains the rules for transforming and summing random variables.

TABLE 6.7		
Binomial Distribution	Parameters	n = number of trials π = probability of success
	PDF	$P(X = x) = \dfrac{n!}{x!(n - x)!}\,\pi^x(1 - \pi)^{n-x}$
	Excel* PDF	=BINOM.DIST(x, n, π, 0)
	Excel* CDF	=BINOM.DIST(x, n, π, 1)
	Domain	$x = 0, 1, 2, \ldots, n$
	Mean	$n\pi$
	Standard deviation	$\sqrt{n\pi(1 - \pi)}$
	Random data generation in Excel	=BINOM.INV(n, π, RAND()) or use Excel's **Data Analysis Tools**
	Comments	Skewed right if $\pi < .50$, skewed left if $\pi > .50$, and symmetric if $\pi = .50$.

*Excel 2010's new function =BINOM.DIST(x, n, π, cumulative) gives the same result as the previous function =BINOMDIST(x, n, π, cumulative). This new function will not work in previous versions of Excel, but the old functions work in all versions of Excel as of the publication date of this textbook.

EXAMPLE 6.4

Servicing Cars at a Quick Oil Change Shop

Consider a shop that specializes in quick oil changes. It is important to this type of business to ensure that a car's service time is not considered "late" by the customer. Therefore, to study this process, we can define service times as being either *late* or *not late* and define the random variable X to be the number of cars that are late out of the total number of cars serviced. We further assume that cars are independent of each other and the chance of a car being late stays the same for each car. Based on our knowledge of the process we know that $P(\text{car is late}) = \pi = .10$.

Now, think of each car as a Bernoulli experiment and let's apply the binomial distribution. Suppose we would like to know the probability that exactly 2 of the next 12 cars serviced are late. In this case, $n = 12$, and we want to know $P(X = 2)$:

$$P(X = 2) = \frac{12!}{2!(12 - 2)!}\,(.10)^2(1 - .10)^{12-2} = .2301$$

Alternatively, we could calculate this by using the Excel function =BINOM.DIST (2, 12, .1, 0). The fourth parameter, 0, means that we want Excel to calculate $P(X = 2)$ rather than $P(X \leq 2)$.

Binomial Shape

A binomial distribution is skewed right if $\pi < .50$, skewed left if $\pi > .50$, and symmetric only if $\pi = .50$. However, skewness decreases as n increases, regardless of the value of π, as illustrated in Figure 6.7. Notice that $\pi = .20$ and $\pi = .80$ have the same shape, except reversed from left to right. This is true for any values of π and $1 - \pi$.

Binomial Shape

$\pi < .50$	skewed right
$\pi = .50$	symmetric
$\pi > .50$	skewed left

Using the Binomial Formula

The PDF is shown in Table 6.8. We can calculate binomial probabilities by using Excel's binomial formula =BINOM.DIST(x, n, π, cumulative) where cumulative is 0 (if you want a PDF)

FIGURE 6.7
Binomial Distributions

x	PDF P(X = x)	CDF P(X ≤ x)
0	.4096	.4096
1	.4096	.8192
2	.1536	.9728
3	.0256	.9984
4	.0016	1.0000

TABLE 6.8

Binomial Distribution for $n = 4$, $\pi = .20$

or 1 (if you want a CDF). We can also use a calculator to work it out from the mathematical formula with $n = 4$ and $\pi = .20$. For example, the PDF is:

Excel Function

$$P(X = 0) = \frac{4!}{0!(4-0)!}(.20)^0(1-.20)^{4-0} = 1 \times .20^0 \times .80^4 = .4096 \quad \text{=BINOM.DIST(0, 4, .20, 0)}$$

$$P(X = 1) = \frac{4!}{1!(4-1)!}(.20)^1(1-.20)^{4-1} = 4 \times .20^1 \times .80^3 = .4096 \quad \text{=BINOM.DIST(1, 4, .20, 0)}$$

$$P(X = 2) = \frac{4!}{2!(4-2)!}(.20)^2(1-.20)^{4-2} = 6 \times .20^2 \times .80^2 = .1536 \quad \text{=BINOM.DIST(2, 4, .20, 0)}$$

$$P(X = 3) = \frac{4!}{3!(4-3)!}(.20)^3(1-.20)^{4-3} = 4 \times .20^3 \times .80^1 = .0256 \quad \text{=BINOM.DIST(3, 4, .20, 0)}$$

$$P(X = 4) = \frac{4!}{4!(4-4)!}(.20)^4(1-.20)^{4-4} = 1 \times .20^4 \times .80^0 = .0016 \quad \text{=BINOM.DIST(4, 4, .20, 0)}$$

As for any discrete probability distribution, the probabilities sum to unity. That is, $P(0) + P(1) + P(2) + P(3) + P(4) = .4096 + .4096 + .1536 + .0256 + .0016 = 1.0000$. Figure 6.8 shows the PDF and CDF. Since $\pi < .50$, the distribution is right-skewed. The mean $\mu = n\pi = 0.8$ would be the balancing point or fulcrum of the PDF.

Compound Events

A compound event is expressed using an inequality. Consider the event that the sample of four patients will contain *at most* two uninsured patients. The probability of this event would be expressed as $P(X \le 2)$. We can add the PDF values shown above:

$$P(X \le 2) = P(X = 0) + P(X = 1) + P(X = 2) = .4096 + .4096 + .1536 = .9728$$

Alternatively, we can calculate this probability using Excel's CDF function:

$$P(X \le 2) = \text{BINOM.DIST(2, 4, .2, 1)} = .9728$$

FIGURE 6.8

Binomial Distribution for $n = 4$, $\pi = .20$

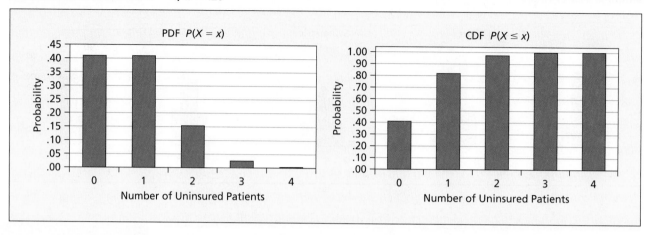

The probability that *fewer than* two patients have insurance is the same as *at most* one patient is uninsured:

$$P(X < 2) = P(X \leq 1) = \text{BINOM.DIST}(1, 4, .2, 1) = .8192$$

Suppose we want to calculate the probability that *at least* two patients are uninsured: $P(X \geq 2)$. Because $P(X \geq 2)$ and $P(X \leq 1)$ are complementary events, we can obtain $P(X \geq 2)$ using our result from above:

$$P(X \geq 2) = 1 - P(X \leq 1) = 1 - \text{BINOM.DIST}(1, 4, .2, 1) = 1 - .8192 = .1808$$

To interpret phrases such as "more than," "at most," or "at least," it is helpful to sketch a diagram, as illustrated in Figure 6.9.

FIGURE 6.9

Diagrams to Illustrate Events

				$P(X \geq 2)$		
"At least two"	0	1	2	3	4	

	$P(X < 2)$				
"Fewer than two"	0	1	2	3	4

	$P(X < 2)$			$P(X > 2)$	
"Fewer than 2 or more than 2"	0	1	2	3	4

Using Tables: Appendix A

The binomial formula is cumbersome, even for small n, so we prefer to use a computer program (Excel, MINITAB, MegaStat, Visual Statistics, or *LearningStats*) or a calculator with a built-in binomial function. When you have no access to a computer (e.g., taking an exam), you can use Appendix A to look up binomial probabilities for selected values of n and π. An abbreviated portion of Appendix A is shown in Figure 6.10. The probabilities for $n = 4$ and $\pi = .20$ are highlighted. Probabilities in Appendix A are rounded to 4 decimal places so the values may differ slightly from Excel.

FIGURE 6.10

Binomial Probabilities from Appendix A

n	X	.01	.02	.05	.10	.15	.20	.30	.40	.50	.60	.70	.80	.85	.90	.95	.98	.99
2	0	.9801	.9604	.9025	.8100	.7225	.6400	.4900	.3600	.2500	.1600	.0900	.0400	.0225	.0100	.0025	.0004	.0001
	1	.0198	.0392	.0950	.1800	.2550	.3200	.4200	.4800	.5000	.4800	.4200	.3200	.2550	.1800	.0950	.0392	.0198
	2	.0001	.0004	.0025	.0100	.0225	.0400	.0900	.1600	.2500	.3600	.4900	.6400	.7225	.8100	.9025	.9604	.9801
3	0	.9703	.9412	.8574	.7290	.6141	.5120	.3430	.2160	.1250	.0640	.0270	.0080	.0034	.0010	.0001	—	—
	1	.0294	.0576	.1354	.2430	.3251	.3840	.4410	.4320	.3750	.2880	.1890	.0960	.0574	.0270	.0071	.0012	.0003
	2	.0003	.0012	.0071	.0270	.0574	.0960	.1890	.2880	.3750	.4320	.4410	.3840	.3251	.2430	.1354	.0576	.0294
	3	—	—	.0001	.0010	.0034	.0080	.0270	.0640	.1250	.2160	.3430	.5120	.6141	.7290	.8574	.9412	.9703
4	0	.9606	.9224	.8145	.6561	.5220	.4096	.2401	.1296	.0625	.0256	.0081	.0016	.0005	.0001	—	—	—
	1	.0388	.0753	.1715	.2916	.3685	.4096	.4116	.3456	.2500	.1536	.0756	.0256	.0115	.0036	.0005	—	—
	2	.0006	.0023	.0135	.0486	.0975	.1536	.2646	.3456	.3750	.3456	.2646	.1536	.0975	.0486	.0135	.0023	.0006
	3	—	—	.0005	.0036	.0115	.0256	.0756	.1536	.2500	.3456	.4116	.4096	.3685	.2916	.1715	.0753	.0388
	4	—	—	—	.0001	.0005	.0016	.0081	.0256	.0625	.1296	.2401	.4096	.5220	.6561	.8145	.9224	.9606

Using Software

Figure 6.11 shows Excel's Formulas > Insert Function menu to calculate the probability of $x = 67$ successes in $n = 1,024$ trials with success probability $\pi = .048$. Alternatively, you could just enter the formula =BINOM.DIST(67, 1024, 0.048, 0) in the spreadsheet cell.

MegaStat will compute an entire binomial PDF (not just a single point probability) for any n and π that you specify, and also show you a graph of the PDF. This is even easier than entering your own Excel functions.

If you need binomial random data, Excel's Data Analysis or MegaStat will generate random binomial values. A third option is to use the function =BINOM.INV(4, .20, RAND()) to create a binomial random variable value.

FIGURE 6.11

Excel Binomial Probability Function

Recognizing Binomial Applications

Can you recognize a binomial situation? The binomial distribution has five main characteristics.

- There are a fixed number of trials (n).
- There are only two outcomes for each trial: *success* or *failure*.
- The probability of success for each trial (π) remains constant.
- The trials are independent of each other.
- The random variable (X) is the number of successes.

LO 6-10

Select an appropriate discrete probability distribution from problem context.

Ask yourself if the five characteristics above make sense in the following examples.

In a sample of 20 friends, how many are left-handed?

In a sample of 50 cars in a parking lot, how many have hybrid engines?

In a sample of 10 emergency patients with chest pain, how many will be uninsured?

Even if you don't know π, you may have a binomial experiment. In practice, the value of π would be estimated from experience, but in this chapter it will be given.

SECTION EXERCISES

connect

6.13 List the X values that are included in each italicized event.

a. You can miss *at most 2* quizzes out of 16 quizzes (X = number of missed quizzes).
b. You go to Starbuck's *at least 4* days a week (X = number of Starbuck's visits).
c. You are penalized if you have *more than 3* absences out of 10 lectures (X = number of absences).

6.14 Write the probability of each italicized event in symbols (e.g., $P(X \geq 5)$).

a. *At least* 7 correct answers on a 10-question quiz (X = number of correct answers).
b. *Fewer than* 4 "phishing" e-mails out of 20 e-mails (X = number of phishing e-mails).
c. *At most* 2 no-shows at a party where 15 guests were invited (X = number of no-shows).

6.15 Find the mean and standard deviation for each binomial random variable:

a. $n = 8$, $\pi = .10$ b. $n = 10$, $\pi = .40$ c. $n = 12$, $\pi = .50$

6.16 Find the mean and standard deviation for each binomial random variable:

a. $n = 30$, $\pi = .90$ b. $n = 80$, $\pi = .70$ c. $n = 20$, $\pi = .80$

6.17 Calculate each binomial probability:

a. $X = 5$, $n = 9$, $\pi = .90$ b. $X = 0$, $n = 6$, $\pi = .20$ c. $X = 9$, $n = 9$, $\pi = .80$

6.18 Calculate each binomial probability:

a. $X = 2$, $n = 8$, $\pi = .10$
b. $X = 1$, $n = 10$, $\pi = .40$
c. $X = 3$, $n = 12$, $\pi = .70$

6.19 Calculate each compound event probability:

a. $X \leq 3$, $n = 8$, $\pi = .20$
b. $X > 7$, $n = 10$, $\pi = .50$
c. $X < 3$, $n = 6$, $\pi = .70$

6.20 Calculate each compound event probability:

a. $X \leq 10$, $n = 14$, $\pi = .95$
b. $X > 2$, $n = 5$, $\pi = .45$
c. $X \leq 1$, $n = 10$, $\pi = .15$

6.21 Calculate each binomial probability:

a. More than 10 successes in 16 trials with an 80 percent chance of success.
b. At least 4 successes in 8 trials with a 40 percent chance of success.
c. No more than 2 successes in 6 trials with a 20 percent chance of success.

6.22 Calculate each binomial probability:

a. Fewer than 4 successes in 12 trials with a 10 percent chance of success.
b. At least 3 successes in 7 trials with a 40 percent chance of success.
c. At most 9 successes in 14 trials with a 60 percent chance of success.

6.23 In the Ardmore Hotel, 20 percent of the customers pay by American Express credit card. (a) Of the next 10 customers, what is the probability that none pay by American Express? (b) At least two? (c) Fewer than three? (d) What is the expected number who pay by American Express? (e) Find the standard deviation. (f) Construct the probability distribution (using Excel or Appendix A). (g) Make a graph of its PDF, and describe its shape.

6.24 Historically, 5 percent of a mail-order firm's repeat charge-account customers have an incorrect current address in the firm's computer database. (a) What is the probability that none of the next 12 repeat customers who call will have an incorrect address? (b) One customer?

(c) Two customers? (d) Fewer than three? (e) Construct the probability distribution (using Excel or Appendix A), make a graph of its PDF, and describe its shape.

6.25 At a Noodles & Company restaurant, the probability that a customer will order a nonalcoholic beverage is .38. Use Excel to find the probability that in a sample of 5 customers (a) none of the 5 will order a nonalcoholic beverage, (b) at least 2 will, (c) fewer than 4 will, (d) all 5 will order a nonalcoholic beverage.

6.26 J.D. Power and Associates says that 60 percent of car buyers now use the Internet for research and price comparisons. (a) Find the probability that in a sample of 8 car buyers, all 8 will use the Internet; (b) at least 5; (c) more than 4. (d) Find the mean and standard deviation of the probability distribution. (e) Sketch the PDF (using Excel or Appendix A) and describe its appearance (e.g., skewness). (Data are from J. Paul Peter and Jerry C. Olson, *Consumer Behavior and Marketing Strategy,* 7th ed. [McGraw-Hill/Irwin, 2005], p. 188.)

6.27 There is a 70 percent chance that an airline passenger will check bags. In the next 16 passengers that check in for their flight at Denver International Airport, find the probability that (a) all will check bags; (b) fewer than 10 will check bags; (c) at least 10 will check bags.

6.28 Police records in the town of Saratoga show that 15 percent of the drivers stopped for speeding have invalid licenses. If 12 drivers are stopped for speeding, find the probability that (a) none will have an invalid license; (b) exactly one will have an invalid license; (c) at least 2 will have invalid licenses.

6.5 POISSON DISTRIBUTION

Poisson Processes

Named for the French mathematician Siméon-Denis Poisson (1781–1840), the **Poisson distribution** describes the number of occurrences within a randomly chosen unit of time (e.g., minute, hour) or space (e.g., square foot, linear mile). For the Poisson distribution to apply, the events must occur randomly and independently over a continuum of time or space, as illustrated in Figure 6.12. We will call the continuum "time" since the most common Poisson application is modeling **arrivals** *per unit of time*. Each dot (•) is an occurrence of the event of interest.

FIGURE 6.12

Poisson Events Distributed over Time

Let X = the number of events per unit of time. The value of X is a random variable that depends on when the unit of time is observed. Figure 6.12 shows that we could get $X = 3$ or $X = 1$ or $X = 5$ events, depending on where the randomly chosen unit of time happens to fall.

We often call the Poisson distribution the *model of arrivals* (customers, defects, accidents). Arrivals can reasonably be regarded as Poisson events if each event is **independent** (i.e., each event's occurrence has no effect on the probability of other events occurring). Some situations lack this characteristic. For example, computer users know that a power interruption often presages another within seconds or minutes. But, as a practical matter, the Poisson assumptions often are met sufficiently to make it a useful model of reality. For example:

- X = number of customers arriving at a bank ATM in a given minute.
- X = number of file server virus infections at a data center during a 24-hour period.
- X = number of asthma patient arrivals in a given hour at a walk-in clinic.

- X = number of Airbus 330 aircraft engine shutdowns per 100,000 flight hours.
- X = number of blemishes per sheet of white bond paper.

The Poisson model has only one parameter denoted λ (the lowercase Greek letter "lambda") representing the *mean number of events per unit of time or space*. The unit of time usually is chosen to be short enough that the mean arrival rate is not large (typically $\lambda < 20$). For this reason, the Poisson distribution is sometimes called the *model of* **rare events**. If the mean is large, we can reformulate the time units to yield a smaller mean. For example, $\lambda = 90$ events per hour is the same as $\lambda = 1.5$ events per minute. However, the Poisson model works for any λ as long as its assumptions are met.

Characteristics of the Poisson Distribution

All characteristics of the Poisson model are determined by its mean λ, as shown in Table 6.9. The constant e (the base of the natural logarithm system) is approximately 2.71828 (to see a more precise value of e, use your calculator's e^x function with $x = 1$). The mean of the Poisson distribution is λ, and its standard deviation is the square root of the mean. The simplicity of the Poisson formulas makes it an attractive model (easier than the binomial, for example). Unlike the binomial, X has no obvious limit, that is, the number of events that can occur in a given unit of time is not bounded. However, Poisson probabilities taper off toward zero as X increases, so the effective range is usually small.

TABLE 6.9		
Poisson Distribution	Parameter	λ = mean arrivals per unit of time or space
	PDF	$P(X = x) = \dfrac{\lambda^x e^{-\lambda}}{x!}$
	Excel* PDF	=POISSON.DIST(x, λ, 0)
	Excel* CDF	=POISSON.DIST(x, λ, 1)
	Domain	$x = 0, 1, 2, \ldots$ (no obvious upper limit)
	Mean	λ
	Standard deviation	$\sqrt{\lambda}$
	Comments	Always right-skewed, but less so for larger λ.

*Excel 2010's new function =POISSON.DIST(x, λ, cumulative) gives the same result as the old function =POISSONDIST(x, λ, cumulative).

Table 6.10 shows some Poisson PDFs. Going down each column, the probabilities must sum to 1.0000 (except for rounding, since these probabilities are only accurate to four decimals). The Poisson probability function is:

$$(6.9) \qquad P(X = x) = \frac{\lambda^x e^{-\lambda}}{x!}, \quad \text{for } X = 1, 2, 3, 4, \ldots$$

TABLE 6.10					
Poisson Probabilities for Various Values of λ					

x	$\lambda = 0.1$	$\lambda = 0.5$	$\lambda = 0.8$	$\lambda = 1.6$	$\lambda = 2.0$
0	.9048	.6065	.4493	.2019	.1353
1	.0905	.3033	.3595	.3230	.2707
2	.0045	.0758	.1438	.2584	.2707
3	.0002	.0126	.0383	.1378	.1804
4	—	.0016	.0077	.0551	.0902
5	—	.0002	.0012	.0176	.0361
6	—	—	.0002	.0047	.0120
7	—	—	—	.0011	.0034
8	—	—	—	.0002	.0009
9	—	—	—	—	.0002
Sum	1.0000	1.0000	1.0000	1.0000	1.0000

Note: Probabilities less than .0001 have been omitted. Columns may not sum to 1 due to rounding.

Poisson distributions are always right-skewed (long right tail) but become less skewed and more bell-shaped as λ increases, as illustrated in Figure 6.13.

FIGURE 6.13

Poisson Becomes Less Skewed for Larger λ

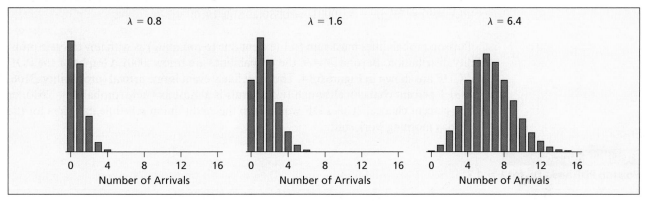

On Thursday morning between 9 a.m. and 10 a.m customers arrive at a mean rate of 1.7 customers per minute at the Oxnard University Credit Union and enter the queue (if any) for the teller windows. Using the Poisson formulas with $\lambda = 1.7$, the equations for the PDF, mean, and standard deviation are:

$$\text{PDF: } P(X = x) = \frac{\lambda^x e^{-\lambda}}{x!} = \frac{(1.7)^x e^{-1.7}}{x!}$$

$$\text{Mean: } \lambda = 1.7$$

$$\text{Standard deviation: } \sigma = \sqrt{\lambda} = \sqrt{1.7} = 1.304$$

EXAMPLE 6.5

Credit Union Customers

CreditUnion

x	P(X = x)	P(X ≤ x)
0	.1827	.1827
1	.3106	.4932
2	.2640	.7572
3	.1496	.9068
4	.0636	.9704
5	.0216	.9920
6	.0061	.9981
7	.0015	.9996
8	.0003	.9999
9	.0001	1.0000

TABLE 6.11

Probability Distribution for λ = 1.7

LO 6-6

Find Poisson probabilities using tables, formulas, or Excel.

Using the Poisson Formula

Table 6.11 shows the probabilities for each value of X. The probabilities for individual X-values can be calculated by inserting $\lambda = 1.7$ into the Poisson PDF or by using Excel's Poisson function =POISSON.DIST(x, λ, cumulative) where cumulative is 0 (if you want a PDF) or 1 (if you want a CDF).

PDF Formula   *Excel Function*

$$P(X = 0) = \frac{1.7^0 e^{-1.7}}{0!} = .1827$$ =POISSON.DIST(0, 1.7, 0)

$$P(X = 1) = \frac{1.7^1 e^{-1.7}}{1!} = .3106$$ =POISSON.DIST(1, 1.7, 0)

$$P(X = 2) = \frac{1.7^2 e^{-1.7}}{2!} = .2640$$ =POISSON.DIST(2, 1.7, 0)

$\vdots$ $\vdots$

$$P(X = 8) = \frac{1.7^8 e^{-1.7}}{8!} = .0003 \quad \text{=POISSON.DIST(8, 1.7, 0)}$$

$$P(X = 9) = \frac{1.7^9 e^{-1.7}}{9!} = .0001 \quad \text{=POISSON.DIST(9, 1.7, 0)}$$

Poisson probabilities must sum to 1 (except due to rounding) as with any discrete probability distribution. Beyond $X = 9$, the probabilities are below .0001. Graphs of the PDF and CDF are shown in Figure 6.14. The most likely event is one arrival (probability .3106, or a 31.1 percent chance), although two arrivals is almost as likely (probability .2640, or a 26.4 percent chance). This PDF would help the credit union schedule its tellers for the Thursday morning work shift.

FIGURE 6.14

Poisson PDF and CDF for $\lambda = 1.7$

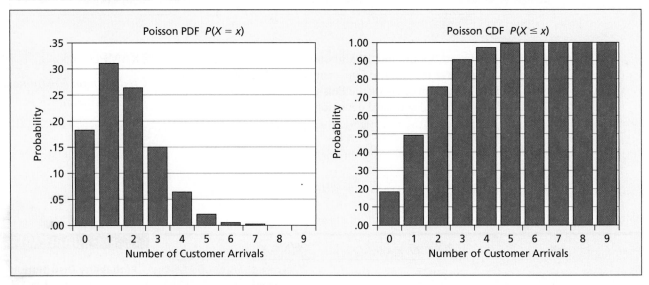

Compound Events

Cumulative probabilities can be evaluated by summing individual X probabilities. For example, the probability that *at most* two customers will arrive in a given minute is the sum of probabilities for several events:

$$P(X \le 2) = P(X = 0) + P(X = 1) + P(X = 2) = .1827 + .3106 + .2640 = .7572$$

Alternatively, we could calculate this probability using Excel's CDF function:

$$P(X \le 2) = \text{POISSON.DIST(2, 1.7, 1)} = .7572$$

We could then calculate the probability of *at least* three customers (the complementary event):

$$P(X \ge 3) = 1 - P(X \le 2) = 1 - \text{POISSON.DIST(2, 1.7, 1)} = 1 - .7572 = .2428$$

Using Tables (Appendix B)

Appendix B facilitates Poisson calculations, as illustrated in Figure 6.15 with highlighted probabilities for the terms in the sum for $P(X \ge 3)$. Appendix B doesn't go beyond $\lambda = 20$, partly because the table would become huge, but mainly because we have Excel.

Using Software

Tables are helpful for taking statistics exams (when you may not have access to Excel). However, tables contain only selected λ values, and in real-world problems, we cannot

FIGURE 6.15

Poisson Probabilities for $P(X \geq 3)$ from Appendix B

			λ			
X	**1.6**	**1.7**	**1.8**	**1.9**	**2.0**	**2.1**
0	.2019	.1827	.1653	.1496	.1353	.1225
1	.3230	.3106	.2975	.2842	.2707	.2572
2	.2584	.2640	.2678	.2700	.2707	.2700
3	.1378	.1496	.1607	.1710	.1804	.1890
4	.0551	.0636	.0723	.0812	.0902	.0992
5	.0176	.0216	.0260	.0309	.0361	.0417
6	.0047	.0061	.0078	.0098	.0120	.0146
7	.0011	.0015	.0020	.0027	.0034	.0044
8	.0002	.0003	.0005	.0006	.0009	.0011
9	—	.0001	.0001	.0001	.0002	.0003
10	—	—	—	—	—	.0001
11	—	—	—	—	—	—

FIGURE 6.16

Excel Poisson Probability Function

expect λ always to be a nice round number. Excel's menus are illustrated in Figure 6.16. In this example, Excel calculates =POISSON.DIST(11, 17, 0) as .035544812, which is more accurate than Appendix B.

Recognizing Poisson Applications

Can you recognize a Poisson situation? The Poisson distribution has four main characteristics.

- An event of interest occurs randomly over time or space.
- The average arrival rate (λ) remains constant.
- The arrivals are independent of each other.
- The random variable (X) is the number of events within an observed time interval.

Ask yourself if the four characteristics above make sense in the following examples.

In the last week, how many credit card applications did you receive by mail?

In the last week, how many checks did you write?

In the last week, how many e-mail viruses did your firewall deflect?

It may be a Poisson process, even if you don't know the mean (λ). In business applications, the value of λ would have to be estimated from experience, but in this chapter λ will be given.

LO 6-10

Select an appropriate discrete probability distribution from problem context.

6.29 Find the mean and standard deviation for each Poisson:

    a. $\lambda = 1.0$
    b. $\lambda = 2.0$
    c. $\lambda = 4.0$

6.30 Find the mean and standard deviation for each Poisson:

    a. $\lambda = 9.0$
    b. $\lambda = 12.0$
    c. $\lambda = 7.0$

6.31 Calculate each Poisson probability:

    a. $P(X = 6), \lambda = 4.0$
    b. $P(X = 10), \lambda = 12.0$
    c. $P(X = 4), \lambda = 7.0$

6.32 Calculate each Poisson probability:

    a. $P(X = 2), \lambda = 0.1$
    b. $P(X = 1), \lambda = 2.2$
    c. $P(X = 3), \lambda = 1.6$

6.33 Calculate each compound event probability:

    a. $P(X \leq 3), \lambda = 4.3$
    b. $P(X > 7), \lambda = 5.2$
    c. $P(X < 3), \lambda = 2.7$

6.34 Calculate each compound event probability:

    a. $P(X \leq 10), \lambda = 11.0$
    b. $P(X > 3), \lambda = 5.2$
    c. $P(X < 2), \lambda = 3.7$

6.35 Calculate each Poisson probability:

    a. More than 10 arrivals with $\lambda = 8.0$.
    b. No more than 5 arrivals with $\lambda = 4.0$.
    c. At least 2 arrivals with $\lambda = 5.0$

6.36 Calculate each Poisson probability:

    a. Fewer than 4 arrivals with $\lambda = 5.8$.
    b. At least 3 arrivals with $\lambda = 4.8$.
    c. At most 9 arrivals with $\lambda = 7.0$.

6.37 According to J.D. Power and Associates' 2006 Initial Quality Study, consumers reported on average 1.7 problems per vehicle with new 2006 Volkswagens. In a randomly selected new Volkswagen, find the probability of (a) at least one problem; (b) no problems; (c) more than three problems. (d) Construct the probability distribution using Excel or Appendix B, make a graph of its PDF, and describe its shape. (Data are from J.D. Power and Associates 2006 Initial Quality Study[SM].)

6.38 At an outpatient mental health clinic, appointment cancellations occur at a mean rate of 1.5 per day on a typical Wednesday. Let X be the number of cancellations on a particular Wednesday. (a) Justify the use of the Poisson model. (b) What is the probability that no cancellations will occur on a particular Wednesday? (c) One? (d) More than two? (e) Five or more?

6.39 The average number of items (such as a drink or dessert) ordered by a Noodles & Company customer in addition to the meal is 1.4. These items are called *add-ons*. Define X to be the number of add-ons ordered by a randomly selected customer. (a) Justify the use of the Poisson model. (b) What is the probability that a randomly selected customer orders at least 2 add-ons? (c) No add-ons? (d) Construct the probability distribution using Excel or Appendix B, make a graph of its PDF, and describe its shape.

6.40 (a) Why might the number of yawns per minute by students in a warm classroom not be a Poisson event? (b) Give two additional examples of events per unit of time that might violate the assumptions of the Poisson model, and explain why.

Poisson Approximation to Binomial (Optional)

The binomial and Poisson are close cousins. The Poisson distribution may be used to approximate a binomial by setting $\lambda = n\pi$. This approximation is helpful when the binomial calculation is difficult (e.g., when n is large) and when Excel is not available. For example, suppose 1,000 women are screened for a rare type of cancer that has a nationwide incidence of 6 cases per 10,000 (i.e., $\pi = .0006$). What is the probability of finding two or fewer cases? The number of cancer cases would follow a binomial distribution with $n = 1,000$ and $\pi = .0006$. However, the binomial formula would involve awkward factorials. To use a Poisson approximation, we set the Poisson mean (λ) equal to the binomial mean ($n\pi$):

$$\lambda = n\pi = (1000)(.0006) = 0.6$$

To calculate the probability of x successes, we can then use Appendix B or the Poisson PDF $P(X = x) = \lambda^x e^{-\lambda}/x!$, which is simpler than the binomial PDF $P(X = x) = \frac{n!}{x!(n-x)!}\pi^x(1-\pi)^{n-x}$. The Poisson approximation of the desired probability is $P(X \le 2) = P(0) + P(1) + P(2) = .5488 + .3293 + .0988 = .9769$.

Poisson Approximation

$P(X = 0) = 0.6^0 e^{-0.6}/0! = .5488$

$P(X = 1) = 0.6^1 e^{-0.6}/1! = .3293$

$P(X = 2) = 0.6^2 e^{-0.6}/2! = .0988$

Actual Binomial Probability

$P(X = 0) = \dfrac{1000!}{0!(1000 - 0)!} .0006^0 (1 - .0006)^{1000-0} = .5487$

$P(X = 1) = \dfrac{1000!}{1!(1000 - 1)!} .0006^1 (1 - .0006)^{1000-1} = .3294$

$P(X = 2) = \dfrac{1000!}{2!(1000 - 2)!} .0006^2 (1 - .0006)^{1000-2} = .0988$

The Poisson calculations are easy and (at least in this example) the Poisson approximation is accurate. The Poisson approximation does a good job in this example, but when is it "good enough" in other situations? The general rule for a good approximation is that n should be "large" and π should be "small." A common rule of thumb says the approximation is adequate if $n \ge 20$ and $\pi \le .05$.

LO 6-7

Use the Poisson approximation to the binomial (optional).

SECTION EXERCISES

connect

6.41 An experienced order taker at the L.L. Bean call center has a .003 chance of error on each keystroke (i.e., $\pi = .003$). In 500 keystrokes, find the approximate probability of (a) at least two errors and (b) fewer than four errors. (c) Is the Poisson approximation justified?

6.42 The probability of a manufacturing defect in an aluminum beverage can is .00002. If 100,000 cans are produced, find the approximate probability of (a) at least one defective can and (b) two or more defective cans. (c) Is the Poisson approximation justified?

6.43 Three percent of the letters placed in a certain postal drop box have incorrect postage. Suppose 200 letters are mailed. (a) For this binomial, what is the expected number with incorrect postage? (b) For this binomial, what is the standard deviation? (c) What is the approximate probability that at least 10 letters will have incorrect postage? (d) Fewer than five? (e) Is the Poisson approximation justified?

6.44 In a string of 100 Christmas lights, there is a .01 chance that a given bulb will fail within the first year of use (if one bulb fails, it does not affect the others). Find the approximate probability that two or more bulbs will fail within the first year.

6.45 The probability that a passenger's bag will be mishandled on a U.S. airline is .0046. During spring break, suppose that 500 students fly from Minnesota to various southern destinations. (a) What is the expected number of mishandled bags? (b) What is the approximate probability of no mishandled bags? More than two? (c) Would you expect the approximation to be accurate (cite a rule of thumb)?

6.6 HYPERGEOMETRIC DISTRIBUTION

Characteristics of the Hypergeometric Distribution

The **hypergeometric distribution** is similar to the binomial except that sampling is *without replacement* from a finite population of N items. Therefore, the trials are not independent and the probability of success is *not* constant from trial to trial. The hypergeometric distribution has three parameters: N (the number of items in the population), n (the number of items in the sample), and s (the number of successes in the population). The distribution of X (the number of successes in the sample) is hypergeometric, with the characteristics shown in Table 6.12. The hypergeometric distribution may be skewed right or left, and is symmetric only if $s/N = .50$ (i.e., if the proportion of successes in the population is 50 percent).

TABLE 6.12

Hypergeometric Distribution

LO 6-8

Find hypergeometric probabilities using Excel.

Parameters	N = number of items in the population n = sample size s = number of successes in population
PDF	$P(X = x) = \dfrac{_sC_x \, _{N-s}C_{n-x}}{_NC_n}$
Excel* PDF	=HYPGEOM.DIST($x, n, s, N, 0$)
Domain	$\max(0, n - N + s) \leq X \leq \min(s, n)$
Mean	$n\pi$ where $\pi = s/N$
Standard deviation	$\sqrt{n\pi(1 - \pi)} \sqrt{\dfrac{N - n}{N - 1}}$
Comments	Similar to binomial, but sampling is without replacement from a finite population. It can be approximated by a binomial with $\pi = s/N$ if $n/N < 0.05$, and is symmetric if $s/N = 0.50$.

*Excel 2010's new function =HYPGEOM.DIST(x, n, s, N, cumulative) gives the same result as the old function =HYPGEOMDIST(x, n, s, N) when *cumulative* = 0. The CDF value is returned when *cumulative* = 1.

The hypergeometric PDF, shown in formula 6.10, uses the formula for combinations:

(6.10)
$$P(X = x) = \frac{_sC_x \, _{N-s}C_{n-x}}{_NC_n}$$

where

$$_sC_x = \text{the number of ways to choose } x \\ \text{successes from } s \text{ successes in the population}$$

$$_{N-s}C_{n-x} = \text{the number of ways to choose } n - x \\ \text{failures from } N - s \text{ failures in the population}$$

$$_NC_n = \text{the number of ways to choose } n \text{ items} \\ \text{from } N \text{ items in the population}$$

and $N - s$ is the number of failures in the population, x is the number of successes in the sample, and $n - x$ is the number of failures in the sample. For a review of combinations see Chapter 5.

EXAMPLE 6.6

Damaged iPods

In a shipment of 10 iPods, 2 are damaged and 8 are good. The receiving department at Best Buy tests a sample of 3 iPods at random to see if they are defective. The number of damaged iPods in the sample is a random variable X. The problem description is:

$N = 10$ (number of iPods in the shipment)

$n = 3$ (sample size drawn from the shipment)

$s = 2$ (number of damaged iPods in the shipment, i.e., successes in population)

$N - s = 8$ (number of nondamaged iPods in the shipment)

$x = ?$ (number of damaged iPods in the sample, i.e., successes in sample)

$n - x = ?$ (number of nondamaged iPods in the sample)

It is tempting to think of this as a binomial problem with $n = 3$ and $\pi = s/N = 2/10 = .20$. But π is not constant. On the first draw, the probability of a damaged iPod is indeed $\pi_1 = 2/10$. But on the second draw, the probability of a damaged iPod could be $\pi_2 = 1/9$ (if the first draw contained a damaged iPod) or $\pi_2 = 2/9$ (if the first draw did not contain a damaged iPod). On the third draw, the probability of a damaged iPod could be $\pi_3 = 0/8$, $\pi_3 = 1/8$, or $\pi_3 = 2/8$ depending on what happened in the first two draws.

Using the Hypergeometric Formula

For the iPod example, the only possible values of x are 0, 1, and 2 since there are only 2 damaged iPods in the population. The probabilities are:

PDF Formula   *Excel Function*

$$P(X = 0) = \frac{{_2}C_0\, {_8}C_3}{{_{10}}C_3} = \frac{\left(\frac{2!}{0!2!}\right)\left(\frac{8!}{3!5!}\right)}{\left(\frac{10!}{3!7!}\right)} = \frac{56}{120} = \frac{7}{15} = .4667 \qquad =\text{HYPGEOM.DIST}(0, 3, 2, 10, 0)$$

$$P(X = 1) = \frac{{_2}C_1\, {_8}C_2}{{_{10}}C_3} = \frac{\left(\frac{2!}{1!1!}\right)\left(\frac{8!}{2!6!}\right)}{\left(\frac{10!}{3!7!}\right)} = \frac{56}{120} = \frac{7}{15} = .4667 \qquad =\text{HYPGEOM.DIST}(1, 3, 2, 10, 0)$$

$$P(X = 2) = \frac{{_2}C_2\, {_8}C_1}{{_{10}}C_3} = \frac{\left(\frac{2!}{2!0!}\right)\left(\frac{8!}{1!7!}\right)}{\left(\frac{10!}{3!7!}\right)} = \frac{8}{120} = \frac{1}{15} = .0667 \qquad =\text{HYPGEOM.DIST}(2, 3, 2, 10, 0)$$

The values of $P(X)$ sum to 1, as they should: $P(0) + P(1) + P(2) = 7/15 + 7/15 + 1/15 = 1$. We can also find the probability of compound events. For example, the probability of at least one damaged iPod is $P(X \geq 1) = P(1) + P(2) = 7/15 + 1/15 = 8/15 = .533$, or 53.3 percent. The PDF and CDF are illustrated in Figure 6.17.

FIGURE 6.17

Hypergeometric PDF and CDF Illustrated with $N = 10$, $n = 3$, and $S = 2$

Using Software

Excel   The hypergeometric formula is tedious and tables are impractical because there are three parameters, so we prefer Excel's hypergeometric function =HYPGEOM.DIST $(x, n, s, N, 0)$. For example, using $X = 5$, $n = 10$, $s = 82$, $N = 194$, the formula =HYPGEOM. DIST(5, 10, 82, 194, 0) gives .222690589, as illustrated in Figure 6.18. You can also get hypergeometric probabilities from MegaStat or Minitab (menus not shown).

FIGURE 6.18

**Excel Hypergeometric
Probability Function**

Recognizing Hypergeometric Applications

LO 6-10

Select an appropriate
discrete probability
distribution from
problem context.

Look for a finite population (*N*) containing a known number of successes (*s*) and *sampling without replacement* (*n* items in the sample) where the probability of success is not constant for each sample item drawn. For example:

- Forty automobiles are to be inspected for California emissions compliance. Thirty-two are compliant but 8 are not. A sample of 7 cars is chosen at random. What is the probability that all are compliant? At least 5?

- A law enforcement agency must process 500 background checks for firearms purchasers. Fifty applicants are convicted felons. Through a computer error, 10 applicants are approved without a background check. What is the probability that none is a felon? At least two are?

- A medical laboratory receives 40 blood specimens to check for HIV. Eight actually contain HIV. A worker is accidentally exposed to 5 specimens. What is the probability that none contained HIV?

SECTION EXERCISES

connect

6.46   (a) State the values that *X* can assume in each hypergeometric scenario. (b) Use the hypergeometric PDF formula to find the probability requested. (c) Check your answer by using Excel.

　　i. $N = 10$, $n = 3$, $s = 4$, $P(X = 3)$
　　ii. $N = 20$, $n = 5$, $s = 3$, $P(X = 2)$
　　iii. $N = 36$, $n = 4$, $s = 9$, $P(X = 1)$
　　iv. $N = 50$, $n = 7$, $s = 10$, $P(X = 3)$

6.47   ABC Warehouse has eight refrigerators in stock. Two are side-by-side models and six are top-freezer models. (a) Using Excel, calculate the entire hypergeometric probability distribution for the number of top-freezer models in a sample of four refrigerators chosen at random. (b) Make an Excel graph of the PDF for this probability distribution and describe its appearance.

6.48   A statistics textbook chapter contains 60 exercises, 6 of which are essay questions. A student is assigned 10 problems. Define *X* to be the number of essay questions the student receives. (a) Use Excel to calculate the entire hypergeometric probability distribution for *X*. (b) What is the probability that none of the questions are essay? (c) That at least one is essay? (d) That two or more are essay? (e) Make an Excel graph of the PDF of the hypergeometric distribution and describe its appearance.

6.49   Fifty employee travel expense reimbursement vouchers were filed last quarter in the finance department at Ramjac Corporation. Of these, 20 contained errors. A corporate auditor inspects five vouchers at random. Let *X* be the number of incorrect vouchers in the sample. (a) Use Excel to calculate the entire hypergeometric probability distribution. (b) Find $P(X = 0)$. (c) Find $P(X = 1)$. (d) Find $P(X \geq 3)$. (e) Make an Excel graph of the PDF of the hypergeometric distribution and describe its appearance.

6.50 A medical laboratory receives 40 blood specimens to check for HIV. Eight actually contain HIV. A worker is accidentally exposed to five specimens. (a) Use Excel to calculate the entire hypergeometric probability distribution. (b) What is the probability that none contained HIV? (c) Fewer than three? (d) At least two? (e) Make an Excel graph of the PDF of the hypergeometric distribution and describe its appearance.

Binomial Approximation to the Hypergeometric (Optional)

There is a strong similarity between the binomial and hypergeometric models. Both involve samples of size n and both treat X as the number of successes in the sample. If you replaced each item after it was selected, then you would have a binomial distribution instead of a hypergeometric distribution. If the size of the sample (n) is small in relation to the population (N), then the probability of success is nearly constant on each draw, so the two models are almost the same if we set $\pi = s/N$. A common *rule of thumb* is that the binomial is a safe approximation to the hypergeometric whenever $n/N < 0.05$. In other words, if we sample less than 5 percent of the population, π will remain essentially constant, even if we sample without replacement. For example, suppose we want $P(X = 6)$ for a hypergeometric with $N = 400$, $n = 10$, and $s = 200$. Since $n/N = 10/400 = .025$, the binomial approximation would be acceptable. Set $\pi = s/N = 200/400 = .50$ and use Appendix A to obtain $P(X = 6) = .2051$. But in the iPod example, the binomial approximation would be unacceptable because we sampled more than 5 percent of the population (i.e., $n/N = 3/10 = .30$ for the iPod problem).

Rule of Thumb

If $n/N < .05$, it is safe to use the binomial approximation to the hypergeometric, using sample size n and success probability $\pi = s/N$.

SECTION EXERCISES

connect

6.51 (a) Check whether the binomial approximation is acceptable in each of the following hypergeometric situations. (b) Find the binomial approximation (using Appendix A) for each probability requested. (c) Check the accuracy of your approximation by using Excel to find the actual hypergeometric probability.

    a. $N = 100$, $n = 3$, $s = 40$, $P(X = 3)$
    b. $N = 200$, $n = 10$, $s = 60$, $P(X = 2)$
    c. $N = 160$, $n = 12$, $s = 16$, $P(X = 1)$
    d. $N = 500$, $n = 7$, $s = 350$, $P(X = 5)$

6.52 Two hundred employee travel expense reimbursement vouchers were filed last year in the finance department at Ramjac Corporation. Of these, 20 contained errors. A corporate auditor audits a sample of five vouchers. Let X be the number of incorrect vouchers in the sample. (a) Justify the use of the binomial approximation. (b) Find the probability that the sample contains no erroneous vouchers. (c) Find the probability that the sample contains at least two erroneous vouchers.

6.53 A law enforcement agency processes 500 background checks for firearms purchasers. Fifty applicants are convicted felons. Through a clerk's error, 10 applicants are approved without checking for felony convictions. (a) Justify the use of the binomial approximation. (b) What is the probability that none of the 10 is a felon? (c) That at least two of the 10 are convicted felons? (d) That fewer than 4 of the 10 are convicted felons?

6.54 Four hundred automobiles are to be inspected for California emissions compliance. Of these, 320 actually are compliant but 80 are not. A random sample of 6 cars is chosen. (a) Justify the use of the binomial approximation. (b) What is the probability that all are compliant? (c) At least 4?

6.7 GEOMETRIC DISTRIBUTION (OPTIONAL)

Characteristics of the Geometric Distribution

The **geometric distribution** is related to the binomial. It describes the number of Bernoulli trials until the first success is observed. But the number of trials is not fixed. We define X as the number of trials until the first success, and π as the constant *probability* of a success on each trial. The geometric distribution depends only on the parameter π (i.e., it is a one-parameter model). The domain of X is $\{1, 2, \ldots\}$ since we must have at least one trial to obtain our first success, but there is no limit on how many trials may be necessary. The characteristics of the geometric distribution are shown in Table 6.13. It is always skewed to the right. It can be shown that the geometric probabilities sum to 1 and that the mean and standard deviation are nearly the same when π is small. Probabilities diminish as X increases, but not rapidly.

TABLE 6.13

Geometric Distribution

Parameter	π = probability of success
PDF	$P(X = x) = \pi(1 - \pi)^{x-1}$
CDF	$P(X \leq x) = 1 - (1 - \pi)^x$
Domain	$x = 1, 2, \ldots$
Mean	$1/\pi$
Standard deviation	$\sqrt{\dfrac{1 - \pi}{\pi^2}}$
Random data in Excel	=1+INT(LN(1−RAND())/LN(1 − π))
Comments	Describes the number of trials before the first success. Highly skewed.

EXAMPLE 6.7

Telefund Calling

Calculate geometric probabilities (optional).

At Faber University, 15 percent of the alumni (the historical percentage) make a donation or pledge during the annual telefund. What is the probability that the first donation will come within the first five calls? To calculate this geometric probability, we would set $\pi = .15$, apply the PDF formula $P(X = x) = \pi(1 - \pi)^{x-1}$, and then sum the probabilities:

$$P(1) = (.15)(1 - .15)^{1-1} = (.15)(.85)^0 = .1500$$

$$P(2) = (.15)(1 - .15)^{2-1} = (.15)(.85)^1 = .1275$$

$$P(3) = (.15)(1 - .15)^{3-1} = (.15)(.85)^2 = .1084$$

$$P(4) = (.15)(1 - .15)^{4-1} = (.15)(.85)^3 = .0921$$

$$P(5) = (.15)(1 - .15)^{5-1} = (.15)(.85)^4 = .0783$$

Then $P(X \leq 5) = P(1) + P(2) + P(3) + P(4) + P(5) = .5563$. Alternately, we can use the CDF to get $P(X \leq 5) = 1 - (1 - .15)^5 = 1 - .4437 = .5563$. The CDF is a much easier method when sums are required. The PDF and CDF are illustrated in Figure 6.19.

The expected number of phone calls until the first donation is

$$\mu = 1/\pi = 1/(.15) = 6.67 \text{ calls}$$

On the average, we expect to call between 6 and 7 alumni until the first donation. However, the standard deviation is rather large:

$$\sigma = [(1 - \pi)/\pi^2]^{1/2} = [(1 - .15)/(.15)^2]^{1/2} = 6.15 \text{ calls}$$

The large standard deviation is a signal that it would be unwise to regard the mean as a good prediction of how many trials will be needed until the first donation.

FIGURE 6.19

Geometric PDF and CDF for $\pi = .15$

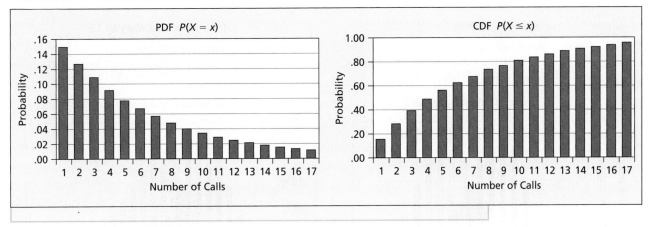

6.55 Find each geometric probability.

a. $P(X = 5)$ when $\pi = .50$
b. $P(X = 3)$ when $\pi = .25$
c. $P(X = 4)$ when $\pi = .60$

6.56 In the Ardmore Hotel, 20 percent of the guests (the historical percentage) pay by American Express credit card. (a) What is the expected number of guests until the next one pays by American Express credit card? (b) What is the probability that the first guest to use an American Express is within the first 10 to checkout?

6.57 In a certain Kentucky Fried Chicken franchise, half of the customers request "crispy" instead of "original," on average. (a) What is the expected number of customers before the next customer requests "crispy"? (b) What is the probability of serving more than 10 customers before the first request for "crispy"?

6.8 TRANSFORMATIONS OF RANDOM VARIABLES (OPTIONAL)

Linear Transformation

A **linear transformation** of a random variable X is performed by adding a constant, multiplying by a constant, or both. Below are two useful rules about the mean and variance of a transformed random variable $aX + b$, where a and b are any constants ($a \geq 0$). Adding a constant shifts the mean but does not affect the standard deviation. Multiplying by a constant affects both the mean and the standard deviation.

> **Rule 1:** $\mu_{aX+b} = a\mu_X + b$ (mean of a transformed variable)
> **Rule 2:** $\sigma_{aX+b} = a\sigma_X$ (standard deviation of a transformed variable)

LO 6-11

Apply rules for transformations of random variables (optional).

Application: Exam Scores Professor Hardtack gave a tough exam whose raw scores had $\mu = 40$ and $\sigma = 10$, so he decided to raise the mean by 20 points. One way to increase the mean to 60 is to shift the curve by adding 20 points to every student's score. Rule 1 says that adding a constant to all X-values will *shift the mean* but will leave the standard deviation unchanged, as illustrated in the left-side graph in Figure 6.20 using $a = 1$ and $b = 20$.

Alternatively, Professor Hardtack could multiply every exam score by 1.5, which would also accomplish the goal of raising the mean from 40 to 60. However, Rule 2 says that the standard deviation would rise from 10 to 15, thereby also *increasing the dispersion*. In other words, this policy would "spread out" the students' exam scores. Some scores might even exceed 100, as illustrated in the right-side graph in Figure 6.20.

FIGURE 6.20

Effect of Adding a Constant to X

Application: Total Cost   A linear transformation useful in business is the calculation of total cost as a function of quantity produced: $C = vQ + F$, where C is total cost, v is variable cost per unit, Q is the number of units produced, and F is fixed cost. Sonoro Ltd. is a small firm that manufactures kortholts. Its variable cost per unit is $v = \$35$, its annual fixed cost is $F = \$24,000$, and its monthly order quantity Q is a random variable with mean $\mu_Q = 500$ units and standard deviation $\sigma_Q = 40$. Total cost C is a random variable $C = vQ + F$, so we can apply Rules 1 and 2:

$$\text{Mean of total cost: } \mu_{vQ+F} = v\mu_Q + F = (35)(500) + 24,000 = \$41,500$$

$$\text{Std. Dev. of total cost: } \sigma_{vQ+F} = v\sigma_Q = (35)(40) = \$1,400$$

Sums of Random Variables

Below are two useful rules that apply to **sums of random variables**. Rule 3 says that the means can be added. Rule 4 says that the variances can be added *if* the variables are independent. These rules apply to the sum of any number of variables and are useful for analyzing situations where we must combine random variables. For example, if a firm has k different products, each with a known stochastic demand, then total revenue R is the sum of the revenue for each of the k product: $R = R_1 + R_2 + R_3 + \cdots + R_k$.

Rule 3: $\mu_{X+Y} = \mu_X + \mu_Y$ (mean of sum of two random variables X and Y)

Rule 4: $\sigma_{X+Y} = \sqrt{\sigma_X^2 + \sigma_Y^2}$ (standard deviation of sum if X and Y are independent)

Application: Gasoline Expenses   The daily gasoline expense of Apex Movers, Inc., is a random variable with mean $\mu = \$125$ and standard deviation $\sigma = \$35$ ($\sigma^2 = 1225$). If we define Y to be the gasoline expense *per year,* and there are 250 working days per year at Apex Movers, then

$$\mu_Y = \underbrace{\mu + \cdots + \mu}_{250 \text{ times}} = \$125 + \cdots + \$125 = \$31,250$$

$$\sigma_Y = \underbrace{\sqrt{\sigma^2 + \cdots + \sigma^2}}_{250 \text{ times}} = \sqrt{1225 + \cdots + 1225} = \$553$$

This assumes that daily gasoline expenses are independent of each other.

Application: Project Scheduling   The initial phase of a construction project entails three activities that must be undertaken sequentially (that is, the second activity cannot begin until the first is complete, and so on) and the time (in days) to complete each activity is a random variable with a known mean and standard deviation:

Excavation	*Foundations*	*Structural Steel*
$\mu_1 = 25$ days	$\mu_2 = 14$ days	$\mu_3 = 58$ days
$\sigma_1 = 3$ days	$\sigma_2 = 2$ days	$\sigma_3 = 7$ days

By Rule 3, the mean time to complete the whole project is the sum of the task means (even if the task times are not independent):

$$\mu = \mu_1 + \mu_2 + \mu_3 = 25 + 14 + 58 = 97 \text{ days}$$

By Rule 4, if the times to complete each activity are *independent,* the overall variance for the project is the sum of the task variances, so the standard deviation for the entire project is:

$$\sigma = \sqrt{\sigma_1^2 + \sigma_2^2 + \sigma_3^2} = \sqrt{3^2 + 2^2 + 7^2} = \sqrt{62} = 7.874 \text{ days}$$

From this information, we can construct $\mu \pm 1\sigma$ or $\mu \pm 2\sigma$ intervals for the entire project:

97 ± (1)(7.874), or between 89.1 and 104.9 days

97 ± (2)(7.874), or between 81.3 and 112.8 days

So the *Empirical Rule* would imply that there is about a 95 percent chance that the project will take between 81.3 and 112.8 days. This calculation could help the construction firm estimate upper and lower bounds for the project completion time. Of course, if the distribution is not normal, the Empirical Rule may not apply.

Covariance

If X and Y are *not* independent (i.e., if X and Y are *correlated*), then we cannot use Rule 4 to find the standard deviation of their sum. Recall from Chapter 4 that the **covariance** of two random variables, denoted $\text{Cov}(X, Y)$ or σ_{XY}, describes how the variables vary in relation to each other. A positive covariance indicates that the two variables tend to move in the same direction while a negative covariance indicates that the two variables move in opposite directions. We use both the covariance and the variances of X and Y to calculate the standard deviation of the sum of X and Y, as shown in formula 6.11.

$$\sigma_{X+Y} = \sqrt{\sigma_X^2 + \sigma_Y^2 + 2\sigma_{XY}} \tag{6.11}$$

Finance is one area where the covariance measure has important applications because a portfolio's income is the sum of the incomes of the assets in the portfolio. If two asset returns have a positive covariance, the variance in total return will be *greater* than the sum of the two variances (i.e., risk is increased) while if the two asset returns have a negative covariance, the variance in total return will be *less* (i.e., risk is decreased). If the asset returns are uncorrelated, then their variances can just be summed (Rule 4). The point is that investors can reduce portfolio risk (i.e., smaller variance) by choosing assets appropriately.

Application: Centralized vs. Decentralized Warehousing   The design of an optimal distribution network is critical for the operations of a firm. High demand variation means there will be a high need for inventory safety stock. Lower demand variation decreases the amount of safety stock needed at a distribution center. A firm can centralize their distribution centers (DC) so that one DC services all markets, or they can decentralize their network so each market has its own DC. The demand patterns will dictate whether a centralized or decentralized network is best. Suppose a firm has two markets to service. The parameters of the two distributions on demand for each market are given below as well as their covariance.

Market X Demand	Market Y Demand
$\mu_X = 500$ units/day	$\mu_Y = 250$ units/day
$\sigma_X = 45$ units	$\sigma_Y = 35$ units

$$\sigma_{XY} = -882 \text{ units}$$

The average *aggregate* demand for both markets combined would be

$$\mu_D = \mu_X + \mu_Y = 500 + 250 = 750 \text{ units}$$

Given that the two markets have a negative covariance, the standard deviation in aggregate demand would be

$$\sigma_D = \sqrt{\sigma_X^2 + \sigma_Y^2 + 2\sigma_{XY}} = \sqrt{45^2 + 35^2 + 2(-882)} = \sqrt{1486} = 38.55 \text{ units}$$

Note that the variation in aggregate demand is less than the variation for market X demand and close to the variation for market Y demand. This means a centralized DC could be the best solution because the firm would need less safety inventory on hand. (Of course the cost savings would need to be compared to possibly increased transportation costs.)

SECTION EXERCISES

connect

6.58 The height of a Los Angeles Lakers basketball player averages 6 feet 7.6 inches (i.e., 79.6 inches) with a standard deviation of 3.24 inches. To convert from inches to centimeters, we multiply by 2.54. (a) In centimeters, what is the mean? (b) In centimeters, what is the standard deviation? (c) Which rules did you use? (Data are from www.cnnsi.com/basketball/nba/rosters.)

6.59 July sales for Melodic Kortholt, Ltd., average $\mu_1 = \$9,500$ with $\sigma_1^2 = \$1,250$. August sales average $\mu_2 = \$7,400$ with $\sigma_2^2 = \$1,425$. September sales average $\mu_3 = \$8,600$ with $\sigma_3^2 = \$1,610$. (a) Find the mean and standard deviation of total sales for the third quarter. (b) What assumptions are you making?

6.60 The mean January temperature in Fort Collins, CO, is 37.1° F with a standard deviation of 10.3° F. Express these Fahrenheit parameters in degrees Celsius using the transformation C = 5/9F − 17.78.

6.61 There are five accounting exams. Bob's typical score on each exam is a random variable with a mean of 80 and a standard deviation of 5. His final grade is based on the sum of his exam scores. (a) Find the mean and standard deviation of Bob's point total assuming his performances on exams are independent of each other. (b) By the Empirical Rule (see Chapter 4), would you expect that Bob would earn at least 450 points (the required total for an "A")?

CHAPTER SUMMARY

A **random variable** assigns a numerical value to each outcome in the sample space of a random process. A **discrete random variable** has a countable number of distinct values. Probabilities in a **discrete probability distribution** must be between zero and one, and must sum to one. The **expected value** is the mean of the distribution, measuring center, and its **variance** is a measure of variability. A known distribution is described by its **parameters**, which imply its **probability distribution function** (PDF) and its **cumulative distribution function** (CDF).

As summarized in Table 6.14 the **uniform distribution** has two parameters (a, b) that define its domain. The **Bernoulli distribution** has one parameter (π, the probability of success) and two outcomes (0 or 1). The **binomial distribution** has two parameters (n, π). It describes the sum of n independent Bernoulli random experiments with constant probability of success. It may be skewed left ($\pi > .50$) or right ($\pi < .50$) or be symmetric ($\pi = .50$) but becomes less skewed as n increases. The **Poisson distribution** has one parameter (λ, the mean arrival rate). It describes arrivals of independent events per unit of time or space. It is always right-skewed, becoming less so as λ increases. The

TABLE 6.14			Comparison of Models	
Model	*Parameters*	*Mean*	*Variance*	*Characteristics*
Bernoulli	π	π	$\pi(1 - \pi)$	Used to generate the binomial.
Binomial	n, π	$n\pi$	$n\pi(1 - \pi)$	Skewed right if $\pi < .50$, left if $\pi > .50$.
Geometric	π	$1/\pi$	$(1 - \pi)/\pi^2$	Always skewed right and leptokurtic.
Hypergeometric	N, n, s	$n\pi$ where $\pi = s/N$	$n\pi(1 - \pi)[(N - n)/(N - 1)]$	Like binomial except sampling without replacement from a finite population.
Poisson	λ	λ	λ	Always skewed right and leptokurtic.
Uniform	a, b	$(a + b)/2$	$[(b - a + 1)^2 - 1]/12$	Always symmetric and platykurtic.

FIGURE 6.21

Relationships among Discrete Models

hypergeometric distribution has three parameters (N, n, s). It is like a binomial, except that sampling of n items is without replacement from a finite population of N items containing s successes. The **geometric distribution** is a one-parameter model (π, the probability of success) that describes the number of trials until the first success. Figure 6.21 shows the relationships among these five discrete models.

Rules for **linear transformations** of random variables say that adding a constant to a random variable shifts the distribution but does not change its variance, while multiplying a random variable by a constant changes both its mean and its variance. Rules for summing random variables permit adding of their means, but their variances can be summed only if the random variables are independent.

Commonly Used Formulas in Discrete Distributions

Total probability: $\displaystyle\sum_{i=1}^{N} P(x_i) = 1$

Expected value: $\displaystyle E(X) = \mu = \sum_{i=1}^{N} x_i P(x_i)$ if there are N distinct values $x_1, x_2, \ldots, x_N$

Variance: $\displaystyle \text{Var}(X) = \sigma^2 = \sum_{i=1}^{N} [x_i - \mu]^2 P(x_i)$

Uniform PDF: $\displaystyle P(X = x) = \frac{1}{b - a + 1}$ $x = a, a + 1, \ldots, b$

Binomial PDF: $\displaystyle P(X = x) = \frac{n!}{x!(n - x)!}\, \pi^x (1 - \pi)^{n-x}$ $x = 0, 1, 2, \ldots, n$

Poisson PDF: $\displaystyle P(X = x) = \frac{\lambda^x e^{-\lambda}}{x!}$ $x = 0, 1, 2, \ldots$

Hypergeometric PDF: $\displaystyle P(X = x) = \frac{{}_sC_x\,{}_{N-s}C_{n-x}}{{}_NC_n}$ $\max(0, n - N + s) \leq x \leq \min(s, n)$

Geometric PDF: $\displaystyle P(X = x) = \pi\,(1 - \pi)^{x-1}$ $x = 1, 2, \ldots$

CHAPTER REVIEW

1. Define (a) random process; (b) random variable; (c) discrete random variable; and (d) probability distribution.

2. Without using formulas, explain the meaning of (a) expected value of a random variable; (b) actuarial fairness; and (c) variance of a random variable.

3. What is the difference between a PDF and a CDF? Sketch a picture of each.

4. (a) What are the two parameters of a uniform distribution? (b) Why is the uniform distribution the first one considered in this chapter?

5. (a) Describe a Bernoulli experiment and give two examples. (b) What is the connection between a Bernoulli experiment and a binomial distribution?

6. (a) What are the parameters of a binomial distribution? (b) What is the mean of a binomial distribution? The standard deviation? (c) When is a binomial skewed right? Skewed left? Symmetric? (d) Suggest a data-generating situation that might be binomial.

7. (a) What are the parameters of a Poisson distribution? (b) What is the mean of a Poisson distribution? The standard deviation? (c) Is a Poisson ever symmetric? (d) Suggest a data-generating situation that might be Poisson.

8. In the binomial and Poisson models, why is the assumption of independent events important?

*9. (a) When are we justified in using the Poisson approximation to the binomial? (b) Why would we want to do this approximation?

10. (a) Explain a situation when we would need the hypergeometric distribution. (b) What are the three parameters of the hypergeometric distribution? (c) How does it differ from a binomial distribution?

*11. When are we justified in using (a) the Poisson approximation to the binomial? (b) The binomial approximation to the hypergeometric?

12. (a) Name a situation when we would need the (a) hypergeometric distribution; (b)* geometric distribution; (c) uniform distribution.

*13. What do Rules 1 and 2 say about transforming a random variable?

*14. What do Rules 3 and 4 say about sums of several random variables?

*15. What does the covariance measure? What happens to the variance of the sum of two random variables when the covariance is (a) positive? (b) negative? (c) zero?

CHAPTER EXERCISES

Note: Show your work clearly. Problems marked * are harder or rely on optional material from this chapter.

connect

6.62 The probability that a 30-year-old white male will live another year is .99863. What premium would an insurance company charge to break even on a one-year $1 million term life insurance policy? (Data are from National Center for Health Statistics, *National Vital Statistics Reports* 59, no. 4 [March 16, 2011], p. 33.)

6.63 As a birthday gift, you are mailing a new personal digital assistant (PDA) to your cousin in Toledo. The PDA cost $250. There is a 2 percent chance it will be lost or damaged in the mail. Is it worth $4 to insure the mailing? Explain, using the concept of expected value.

6.64 Use Excel to generate 1,000 random integers in the range 1 through 5. (a) What are the expected mean and standard deviation? (b) What are your sample mean and standard deviation? (c) Is your sample consistent with the uniform model? Discuss. (d) Show the Excel formula you used.

6.65 Consider the Bernoulli model. What would be a typical probability of success (π) for (a) free throw shooting by a good college basketball player? (b) Hits by a good baseball batter? (c) Passes completed by a good college football quarterback? (d) Incorrect answers on a five-part multiple choice exam if you are guessing? (e) Can you suggest reasons why independent events might not be assumed in some of these situations? Explain.

6.66 There is a 14 percent chance that a Noodles & Company customer will order bread with the meal. Use Excel to find the probability that in a sample of 10 customers (a) more than five will order bread; (b) no more than two will; (c) none of the 10 will order bread. (d) Is the distribution skewed left or right?

6.67 In a certain year, on average 10 percent of the vehicles tested for emissions failed the test. Suppose that five vehicles are tested. (a) What is the probability that all pass? (b) All but one pass? (c) Sketch the probability distribution and discuss its shape.

6.68 The probability that an American CEO can transact business in a foreign language is .20. Ten American CEOs are chosen at random. (a) What is the probability that none can transact business in a foreign language? (b) That at least two can? (c) That all 10 can?

6.69 In a certain Kentucky Fried Chicken franchise, half of the customers typically request "crispy" instead of "original." (a) What is the probability that none of the next four customers will request "crispy"? (b) At least two? (c) At most two? (d) Construct the probability distribution (Excel or Appendix A), make a graph of its PDF, and describe its shape.

6.70 On average, 40 percent of U.S. beer drinkers order light beer. (a) What is the probability that none of the next eight customers who order beer will order light beer? (b) That one customer will? (c) Two customers? (d) Fewer than three? (e) Construct the probability distribution (Excel or Appendix A), make a graph of its PDF, and describe its shape. (See George E. Belch and Michael A. Belch, *Advertising & Promotion,* 6th ed. [McGraw-Hill, 2004], p. 43.)

6.71 Write the Excel binomial formula for each probability.

    a. Three successes in 20 trials with a 30 percent chance of success.
    b. Seven successes in 50 trials with a 10 percent chance of success.
    c. Six or fewer successes in 80 trials with a 5 percent chance of success.
    d. At least 30 successes in 120 trials with a 20 percent chance of success.

6.72 Tired of careless spelling and grammar, a company decides to administer a test to all job applicants. The test consists of 20 sentences. Applicants must state whether each sentence contains any grammar or spelling errors. Half the sentences contain errors. The company requires a score of 14 or more. (a) If an applicant guesses randomly, what is the probability of passing? (b) What minimum score would be required to reduce the probability of "passing by guessing" to 5 percent or less?

6.73 The default rate on government-guaranteed student loans at a certain private 4-year institution is 7 percent. The college extends 10 such loans. (a) What is the probability that none of them will default? (b) That at least three will default? (c) What is the expected number of defaults?

6.74 Experience indicates that 8 percent of the pairs of men's trousers dropped off for dry cleaning will have an object in the pocket that should be removed before cleaning. Suppose that 14 pairs of pants are dropped off and the cleaner forgets to check the pockets. What is the probability that no pair has an object in the pocket?

6.75 A study by the Parents' Television Council showed that 80 percent of movie commercials aired on network television between 8 and 9 p.m. (the prime family viewing hour) were for R-rated films. (a) Find the probability that in 16 commercials during this time slot at least 10 will be for R-rated films. (b) Find the probability of fewer than 8 R-rated films.

6.76 Write the Excel formula for each Poisson probability, using a mean arrival rate of 10 arrivals per hour.

    a. Seven arrivals.   b. Three arrivals.   c. Fewer than five arrivals.   d. At least 11 arrivals.

6.77   A small feeder airline knows that the probability is .10 that a reservation holder will not show up for its daily 7:15 a.m. flight into a hub airport. The flight carries 10 passengers. (a) If the flight is fully booked, what is the probability that all those with reservations will show up? (b) If the airline overbooks by selling 11 seats, what is the probability that no one will have to be bumped? (c) That more than one passenger will be bumped? *(d) The airline wants to overbook the flight by enough seats to ensure a 95 percent chance that the flight will be full, even if some passengers may be bumped. How many seats would it sell?

6.78   Although television HDTV converters are tested before they are placed in the installer's truck, the installer knows that 20 percent of them still won't work properly. The driver must install eight converters today in an apartment building. (a) Ten converters are placed in the truck. What is the probability that the driver will have enough working converters? *(b) How many boxes should the driver load to ensure a 95 percent probability of having enough working converters?

6.79   (a) Why might the number of calls received per minute at a fire station not be a Poisson event? (b) Name two other events per unit of time that might violate the assumptions of the Poisson model.

6.80   Software filters rely heavily on "blacklists" (lists of known "phishing" URLs) to detect fraudulent e-mails. But such filters typically catch only 20 percent of phishing URLs. Jason receives 16 phishing e-mails. (a) What is the expected number that would be caught by such a filter? (b) What is the chance that such a filter would detect none of them?

6.81   Lunch customers arrive at a Noodles & Company restaurant at an average rate of 2.8 per minute. Define X to be the number of customers to arrive during a randomly selected minute during the lunch hour and assume X has a Poisson distribution. (a) Calculate the probability that exactly five customers will arrive in a minute during the lunch hour. (b) Calculate the probability that no more than five customers will arrive in a minute. (c) What is the average customer arrival rate for a 5-minute interval? (d) What property of the Poisson distribution did you use to find this arrival rate?

6.82   In a major league baseball game, the average is 1.0 broken bat per game. Find the probability of (a) no broken bats in a game; (b) at least 2 broken bats.

6.83   In the last 50 years, the average number of deaths due to alligators in Florida is 0.3 death per year. Assuming no change in this average, in a given year find the probability of (a) no alligator deaths; (b) at least 2 alligator deaths.

6.84   In a recent year, potentially dangerous commercial aircraft incidents (e.g., near collisions) averaged 1.2 per 100,000 flying hours. Let X be the number of incidents in a 100,000-hour period. (a) Justify the use of the Poisson model. (b) What is the probability of at least one incident? (c) More than three incidents? (d) Construct the probability distribution (Excel or Appendix B) and make a graph of its PDF.

6.85   At an outpatient mental health clinic, appointment cancellations occur at a mean rate of 1.5 per day on a typical Wednesday. Let X be the number of cancellations on a particular Wednesday. (a) Justify the use of the Poisson model. (b) What is the probability that no cancellations will occur on a particular Wednesday? (c) That one will? (d) More than two? (e) Five or more?

6.86   Car security alarms go off at a mean rate of 3.8 per hour in a large Costco parking lot. Find the probability that in an hour there will be (a) no alarms; (b) fewer than four alarms; and (c) more than five alarms.

6.87   In a certain automobile manufacturing paint shop, paint defects on the hood occur at a mean rate of 0.8 defect per square meter. A hood on a certain car has an area of 3 square meters. (a) Justify the use of the Poisson model. (b) If a customer inspects a hood at random, what is the probability that there will be no defects? (c) One defect? (d) Fewer than two defects?

6.88   Past insurance company audits have found that 2 percent of dependents claimed on an employee's health insurance actually are ineligible for health benefits. An auditor examines a random sample of 7 claimed dependents. (a) What is the probability that all are eligible? (b) That at least one is ineligible?

*6.89   A "rogue wave" (one far larger than others surrounding a ship) can be a threat to ocean-going vessels (e.g., naval vessels, container ships, oil tankers). The European Centre for Medium-Range Weather Forecasts issues a warning when such waves are likely. The average for this rare event is estimated to be .0377 rogue wave per hour in the South Atlantic. Find the probability that a ship will encounter at least one rogue wave in a 5-day South Atlantic voyage (120 hours).

6.90 In Northern Yellowstone Lake, earthquakes occur at a mean rate of 1.2 quakes per year. Let X be the number of quakes in a given year. (a) Justify the use of the Poisson model. (b) What is the probability of fewer than three quakes? (c) More than five quakes? (d) Construct the probability distribution (Excel or Appendix B) and make a graph of its PDF.

6.91 On New York's Verrazano Narrows bridge, traffic accidents occur at a mean rate of 2.0 crashes per day. Let X be the number of crashes in a given day. (a) Justify the use of the Poisson model. (b) What is the probability of at least one crash? (c) Fewer than five crashes? (d) Construct the probability distribution (Excel or Appendix B), make a graph of its PDF, and describe its shape.

APPROXIMATIONS

*6.92 Leaks occur in a pipeline at a mean rate of 1 leak per 1,000 meters. In a 2,500-meter section of pipe, what is the probability of (a) no leaks? (b) Three or more leaks? (c) What is the expected number of leaks?

*6.93 Among live deliveries, the probability of a twin birth is .02. (a) In 200 live deliveries, how many would be expected to have twin births? (b) What is the probability of no twin births? (c) One twin birth? (d) Calculate these probabilities both with and without an approximation. (e) Is the approximation justified? Discuss fully.

*6.94 The probability is .03 that a passenger on United Airlines flight 9841 is a Platinum flyer (50,000 miles per year). If 200 passengers take this flight, use Excel to find the binomial probability of (a) no Platinum flyers, (b) one Platinum flyer, and (c) two Platinum flyers. (d) Calculate the same probabilities using a Poisson approximation. (e) Is the Poisson approximation justified? Explain.

*6.95 The probability of being "bumped" (voluntarily or involuntarily) on a U.S. airline was .00128. The average number of passengers traveling through Denver International Airport each hour is 5,708. (a) What is the expected number of bumped passengers per hour? (b) What is the approximate Poisson probability of fewer than 10 bumped passengers? More than 5? (c) Would you expect the approximation likely to be accurate (cite a rule of thumb)?

*6.96 On average, 2 percent of all persons who are given a breathalyzer test by the state police pass the test (blood alcohol under .08 percent). Suppose that 500 breathalyzer tests are given. (a) What is the expected number who pass the test? (b) What is the approximate Poisson probability that 5 or fewer will pass the test?

*6.97 The probability of an incorrect call by an NFL referee is .025 (e.g., calling a pass complete, but the decision reversed on instant replays). In a certain game, there are 150 plays. (a) What is the probability of at least 4 incorrect calls by the referees? (b) Justify any assumptions that you made.

*6.98 In CABG surgery, there is a .00014 probability of a retained foreign body (e.g., a sponge or a surgical instrument) left inside the patient. (a) In 100,000 CABG surgeries, what is the expected number of retained foreign bodies? (b) What is the Poisson approximation to the binomial probability of five or fewer retained foreign bodies in 100,000 CABG surgeries? (c) Look up CABG on the Internet if you are unfamiliar with the acronym. (See *AHRQ News*, No. 335, July 2008, p. 3.)

GEOMETRIC

*6.99 The probability of a job offer in a given interview is .25. (a) What is the expected number of interviews until the first job offer? (b) What is the probability the first job offer occurs within the first six interviews?

*6.100 The probability that a bakery customer will order a birthday cake is .04. (a) What is the expected number of customers until the first birthday cake is ordered? (b) What is the probability the first cake order occurs within the first 20 customers?

*6.101 In a certain city, 8 percent of the cars have a burned-out headlight. (a) What is the expected number that must be inspected before the first one with a burned-out headlight is found? (b) What is the probability of finding the first one within the first five cars? *Hint:* Use the CDF.

*6.102 For patients aged 81 to 90, the probability is .07 that a coronary bypass patient will die soon after the surgery. (a) What is the expected number of operations until the first fatality? (b) What is the probability of conducting 20 or more operations before the first fatality? *Hint:* Use the CDF.

*6.103 Historically, 5 percent of a mail-order firm's regular charge-account customers have an incorrect current address in the firm's computer database. (a) What is the expected number of customer orders until the first one with an incorrect current address places an order? (b) What is the probability of mailing 30 bills or more until the first one is returned with a wrong address? *Hint:* Use the CDF.

*6.104 At a certain clinic, 2 percent of all pap smears show signs of abnormality. What is the expected number of pap smears that must be inspected before the first abnormal one is found?

TRANSFORMATIONS AND COVARIANCE

*6.105 The weight of a Los Angeles Lakers basketball player averages 233.1 pounds with a standard deviation of 34.95 pounds. To express these measurements in terms a European would understand, we could convert from pounds to kilograms by multiplying by .4536. (a) In kilograms, what is the mean? (b) In kilograms, what is the standard deviation? (Data are from www.cnnsi.com/basketball/nba/rosters.)

*6.106 The Rejuvo Corp. manufactures granite countertop cleaner and polish. Quarterly sales Q is a random variable with a mean of 25,000 bottles and a standard deviation of 2,000 bottles. Variable cost is $8 per unit and fixed cost is $150,000. (a) Find the mean and standard deviation of Rejuvo's total cost. (b) If all bottles are sold, what would the selling price have to be to break even, on average? To make a profit of $20,000?

*6.107 A manufacturer fills one-gallon cans (3,785 ml) on an assembly line in two independent steps. First, a high-volume spigot injects most of the paint rapidly. Next, a more precise but slower spigot tops off the can. The fill amount in each step is a normally distributed random variable. For step one, $\mu_1 = 3{,}420$ ml and $\sigma_2 = 10$ ml, while for step two $\mu_2 = 390$ ml and $\sigma_2 = 2$ ml. Find the mean and standard deviation of the total fill $X_1 + X_2$.

*6.108 A manufacturing project has five independent phases whose completion must be sequential. The time to complete each phase is a random variable. The mean and standard deviation of the time for each phase are shown below. (a) Find the expected completion time. (b) Make a 2-sigma interval around the mean completion time ($\mu \pm 2\sigma$).

Phase	Mean (hours)	Std. Dev. (hours)
Set up dies and other tools	20	4
Milling and machining	10	2
Finishing and painting	14	3
Packing and crating	6	2
Shipping	48	6

*6.109 In September, demand for industrial furnace boilers at a large plumbing supply warehouse has a mean of 7 boilers with a standard deviation of 2 boilers. The warehouse pays a unit cost of $2,225 per boiler plus a fee of $500 per month to act as dealer for these boilers. Boilers are sold for $2,850 each. (a) Find the mean and standard deviation of September profit (revenue minus cost). (b) Which rules did you use?

*6.110 A certain outpatient medical procedure has five steps that must be performed in sequence. (a) Assuming that the time (in minutes) required for each step is an independent random variable, find the mean and standard deviation for the total time. (b) Why might the assumption of independence be doubtful?

Step	Mean (minutes)	Standard Deviation (minutes)
Patient check-in	15	4
Pre-op preparation	30	6
Medical procedure	25	5
Recovery	45	10
Check-out and discharge	20	5

*6.111 Malaprop Ltd. sells two products. Daily sales of product A have a mean of $70 with a standard deviation of $10, while sales of product B have a mean of $200 with a standard deviation of $30. Sales of the products tend to rise and fall at the same time, having a positive covariance of 400. (a) Find the mean daily sales for both products together. (b) Find the standard deviation of total sales of both products. (c) Is the variance of the total sales greater than or less than the sum of the variances for the two products?

Forbes, Catherine; Merran Evans; Nicholas Hastings; and Brian Peacock. *Statistical Distributions.* 4th ed. John Wiley & Sons, 2011.

RELATED READING

CHAPTER 6   Online Learning Resources

The Online Learning Center (OLC) at www.mhhe.com/doane4e has several *LearningStats* demonstrations to help you understand discrete probability distributions. Your instructor may assign one or more of them, or you may decide to download the ones that sound interesting.

Topic	LearningStats Demonstrations
Discrete distributions	Probability Calculator Random Discrete Data Binomial/Poisson Approximation
Tables	Table A—Binomial Probabilities Table B—Poisson Probabilities
Applications	Covariance in Asset Portfolios: A Simulation

Key: = Excel

CHAPTER 7

Continuous Probability Distributions

CHAPTER CONTENTS

CHAPTER LEARNING OBJECTIVES

LO

When you finish this chapter you should be able to

LO 7-1 Define a continuous random variable.

LO 7-2 Calculate uniform probabilities.

LO 7-3 Know the form and parameters of the normal distribution.

LO 7-4 Find the normal probability for given z or x using tables or Excel.

LO 7-5 Solve for z or x for a given normal probability using tables or Excel.

LO 7-6 Use the normal approximation to a binomial or a Poisson.

LO 7-7 Find the exponential probability for a given x.

LO 7-8 Solve for x for a given exponential probability.

LO 7-9 Use the triangular distribution for "what-if" analysis (optional).

In Chapter 6, you learned about probability models and discrete random variables. We will now expand our discussion of probability models to include models that describe **continuous random variables**. Recall that a discrete random variable usually arises from *counting* something such as the number of customer arrivals in the next minute. In contrast, a continuous random variable usually arises from *measuring* something such as the waiting time until the next customer arrives. Unlike a discrete variable, a continuous random variable can have noninteger (decimal) values.

Probability for a discrete variable is defined at a point such as $P(X = 3)$ or as a sum over a series of points such as $P(X \leq 2) = P(0) + P(1) + P(2)$. But when X is a continuous variable (e.g., waiting time), it does not make sense to speak of probability "at" a particular X value (e.g., $X = 54$ seconds) because the values of X are not a set of discrete points. Rather, probabilities are defined as *areas under a curve* called the *probability density function* (PDF). Probabilities for a continuous random variable are defined on intervals such as $P(53.5 \leq X \leq 54.5)$ or $P(X < 54)$ or $P(X \geq 53)$. Figure 7.1 illustrates the differences between discrete and continuous random variables. This chapter explains how to recognize data-generating situations that produce continuous random variables, how to calculate event probabilities, and how to interpret the results.

LO 7-1

Define a continuous random variable.

FIGURE 7.1

Discrete and Continuous Events

7.1 DESCRIBING A CONTINUOUS DISTRIBUTION

PDFs and CDFs

A probability distribution can be described either by its **probability density function (PDF)** or by its **cumulative distribution function (CDF)**. For a continuous random variable, the PDF is an equation that shows the height of the curve $f(x)$ at each possible value of X. Any continuous PDF must be nonnegative and the area under the entire PDF must be 1.

The mean, variance, and shape of the distribution depend on the PDF and its *parameters*. The CDF is denoted $F(x)$ and shows $P(X \leq x)$, the cumulative *area* to the left of a given value of X. The CDF is useful for probabilities, while the PDF reveals the *shape* of the distribution. There are Excel functions for many common PDFs or CDFs.

For example, Figure 7.2 shows a hypothetical PDF and CDF for a distribution of freeway speeds. The random variable *miles per hour* is a continuous variable that can be expressed with any level of precision we choose. The curves are smooth, with the PDF showing the probability density at points along the X-axis. The CDF shows the *cumulative* probability of speeds, gradually approaching 1 as X approaches 90. In this illustration, the distribution is symmetric and bell-shaped (normal or Gaussian) with a mean of 75 and a standard deviation of 5.

FIGURE 7.2

Freeway Speed Examples

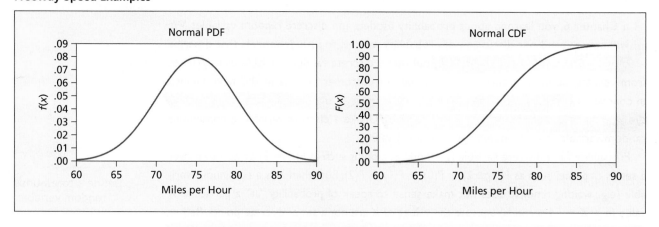

Probabilities as Areas

With discrete random variables, we take sums of probabilities over groups of points. But continuous probability functions are smooth curves, so the area *at* any point would be zero. Instead of taking sums of probabilities, we speak of *areas under curves*. In calculus terms, we would say that $P(a < X < b)$ is the **integral** of the probability density function $f(x)$ over the interval from a to b. Because $P(X = a) = 0$ the expression $P(a < X < b)$ is equal to $P(a \leq X \leq b)$. Figure 7.3 shows the area under a continuous PDF. The entire area under any PDF must be 1.

FIGURE 7.3

Probability as an Area

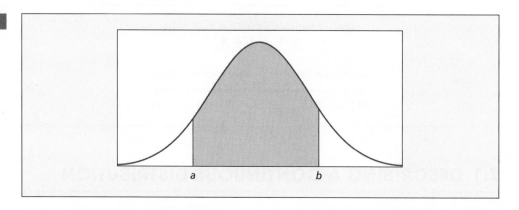

Expected Value and Variance

The mean and variance of a continuous random variable are analogous to $E(X)$ and $\text{Var}(X)$ for a discrete random variable, except that the integral sign $\int$ replaces the summation sign Σ. Integrals are taken over all X-values. The mean is still the balancing point or fulcrum for the entire distribution, and the variance is still a measure of dispersion about the mean. The mean is still the average of all X-values weighted by their probabilities, and the variance is still the weighted average of all squared deviations around the mean. The standard deviation is still the square root of the variance.

	Continuous Random Variable	*Discrete Random Variable*	
Mean	$E(X) = \mu = \int_{-\infty}^{+\infty} x f(x)\, dx$	$E(X) = \mu = \sum_{\text{all } x} x\, P(x)$	**(7.1)**
Variance	$\text{Var}(X) = \sigma^2 = \int_{-\infty}^{+\infty} (x - \mu)^2 f(x)\, dx$	$\text{Var}(X) = \sigma^2 = \sum_{\text{all } x} [x - \mu]^2 P(x)$	**(7.2)**

Calculus notation is used here for the benefit of those who have studied it. But statistics can be learned without calculus, if you are willing to accept that others have worked out the details by using calculus. If you decide to become an actuary, you *will* use calculus (so don't sell your calculus book). However, in this chapter, the means and variances are presented *without* proof for the distributions that you are most likely to see applied to business situations.

SECTION EXERCISES

connect

7.1 Flight 202 is departing Los Angeles. Is each random variable discrete (D) or continuous (C)?

 a. Number of airline passengers traveling with children under age 3.
 b. Proportion of passengers traveling without checked luggage.
 c. Weight of a randomly chosen passenger on Flight 202.

7.2 It is Saturday morning at Starbucks. Is each random variable discrete (D) or continuous (C)?

 a. Temperature of the coffee served to a randomly chosen customer.
 b. Number of customers who order only coffee with no food.
 c. Waiting time before a randomly chosen customer is handed the order.

7.3 Which of the following could *not* be probability density functions for a continuous random variable? Explain. *Hint:* Find the area under the function $f(x)$.

 a. $f(x) = .25$ for $0 \le x \le 1$
 b. $f(x) = .25$ for $0 \le x \le 4$
 c. $f(x) = x$ for $0 \le x \le 2$

7.4 For a continuous PDF, why can't we sum the probabilities of all x-values to get the total area under the curve?

7.2 UNIFORM CONTINUOUS DISTRIBUTION

Characteristics of the Uniform Distribution

The **uniform continuous distribution** is perhaps the simplest model one can imagine. If X is a random variable that is uniformly distributed between a and b, its PDF has constant height, as shown in Figure 7.4. The uniform continuous distribution is sometimes denoted $U(a, b)$ for short. Its mean and standard deviation are shown in Table 7.1.

Since the PDF is rectangular, you can easily verify that the area under the curve is 1 by multiplying its base $(b - a)$ by its height $1/(b - a)$. Its CDF increases linearly to 1, as shown in Figure 7.4. Since events can easily be shown as rectangular areas, we rarely need to refer to the CDF, whose formula is just $P(X \le x) = (x - a)/(b - a)$.

The continuous uniform distribution is similar to the discrete uniform distribution if the x values cover a wide range. For example, three-digit lottery numbers ranging from 000 to 999 would closely resemble a continuous uniform with $a = 0$ and $b = 999$.

LO 7-2

Calculate uniform probabilities.

FIGURE 7.4

Uniform Distribution

TABLE 7.1

Uniform Continuous Distribution

Parameters	a = lower limit b = upper limit
PDF	$f(x) = \dfrac{1}{b - a}$
CDF	$P(X \le x) = \dfrac{x - a}{b - a}$
Domain	$a \le x \le b$
Mean	$\dfrac{a + b}{2}$
Standard deviation	$\sqrt{\dfrac{(b - a)^2}{12}}$
Shape	Symmetric with no mode.
Random data in Excel	=a+(b–a)*RAND()
Comments	Used as a conservative what-if benchmark and in simulation.

EXAMPLE 7.1

Anesthesia Effectiveness

An oral surgeon injects a painkiller prior to extracting a tooth. Given the varying characteristics of patients, the dentist views the time for anesthesia effectiveness as a uniform random variable that takes between 15 minutes and 30 minutes. In short notation, we could say that X is $U(15, 30)$. Setting $a = 15$ and $b = 30$, we obtain the mean and standard deviation:

$$\mu = \frac{a + b}{2} = \frac{15 + 30}{2} = 22.5 \text{ minutes}$$

$$\sigma = \sqrt{\frac{(b - a)^2}{12}} = \sqrt{\frac{(30 - 15)^2}{12}} = 4.33 \text{ minutes}$$

An event probability is simply an interval width expressed as a proportion of the total. Thus, the probability of taking between c and d minutes is

(7.3) $P(c < X < d) = (d - c)/(b - a)$ (area between c and d in a uniform model)

For example, the probability that the anesthetic takes between 20 and 25 minutes is

$$P(20 < X < 25) = (25 - 20)/(30 - 15) = 5/15 = 0.3333, \text{ or } 33.3\%.$$

This situation is illustrated in Figure 7.5.

FIGURE 7.5   **Uniform Probability $P(20 < X < 25)$**

A special case of the continuous uniform distribution, denoted $U(0, 1)$, has limits $a = 0$ and $b = 1$, is shown in Figure 7.6. Using the formulas for the mean and standard deviation, you can easily show that this distribution has $\mu = 0.5000$ and $\sigma = 0.2887$. This special case is important because Excel's function =RAND() uses this distribution. If you create random numbers by using =RAND(), you know what their mean and standard deviation should be. This important distribution is discussed in more detail in later chapters on simulation and goodness-of-fit tests.

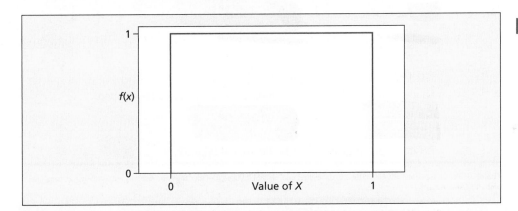

FIGURE 7.6

Unit $U(0, 1)$ Distribution

Uses of the Uniform Model

The uniform model $U(a, b)$ is used only when you have no reason to imagine that any X values are more likely than others. The uniform distribution can be useful in business for what-if analysis, in situations where you know the "worst" and "best" range, but don't want to make any assumptions about the distribution in between. That may sound like a conservative approach. But bear in mind that if the data-generating situation has any central tendency at all, the assumption of a uniform distribution would lead to a higher standard deviation than might be appropriate.

SECTION EXERCISES

7.5   Find the mean and standard deviation for each uniform continuous model.

  a. $U(0, 10)$ b. $U(100, 200)$ c. $U(1, 99)$

connect

7.6   Find each uniform continuous probability and sketch a graph showing it as a shaded area.

  a. $P(X < 10)$ for $U(0, 50)$
  b. $P(X > 500)$ for $U(0, 1,000)$
  c. $P(25 < X < 45)$ for $U(15, 65)$

7.7   For a continuous uniform distribution, why is $P(25 < X < 45)$ the same as $P(25 \leq X \leq 45)$?

7.8   Assume the weight of a randomly chosen American passenger car is a uniformly distributed random variable ranging from 2,500 pounds to 4,500 pounds. (a) What is the mean weight of a randomly chosen vehicle? (b) The standard deviation? (c) What is the probability that a vehicle will weigh less than 3,000 pounds? (d) More than 4,000 pounds? (e) Between 3,000 and 4,000 pounds?

7.3 NORMAL DISTRIBUTION

Characteristics of the Normal Distribution

LO 7-3

Know the form and parameters of the normal distribution.

The **normal** or **Gaussian distribution**, named for German mathematician Karl Gauss (1777–1855), has already been mentioned several times. Its importance gives it a major role in our discussion of continuous models. A normal probability distribution is defined by two parameters, μ and σ. It is often denoted $N(\mu, \sigma)$. The domain of a normal random variable is $-\infty < x < +\infty$. However, as a practical matter, the interval $[\mu - 3\sigma, \mu + 3\sigma]$ includes almost all the area (as you know from the Empirical Rule in Chapter 4). Besides μ and σ, the normal probability density function $f(x)$ depends on the constants e (approximately 2.71828) and π (approximately 3.14159). The expected value of a normal random variable is μ and its variance is σ^2. The normal distribution is always symmetric. Table 7.2 summarizes its main characteristics.

TABLE 7.2

Normal Distribution

Parameters	μ = population mean σ = population standard deviation
PDF	$f(x) = \dfrac{1}{\sigma\sqrt{2\pi}} e^{-\frac{1}{2}\left(\frac{x-\mu}{\sigma}\right)^2}$
Domain	$-\infty < x < +\infty$
Mean	μ
Std. Dev.	σ
Shape	Symmetric, mesokurtic, and bell-shaped.
PDF in Excel*	=NORM.DIST(x,μ,σ,0)
CDF in Excel*	=NORM.DIST(x,μ,σ,1)
Random data in Excel	=NORM.INV(RAND(),μ,σ)

*Excel 2010's new functions =NORM.DIST(x,μ,σ, cumulative) and =NORM.INV(area,μ,σ) give the same result as =NORMDIST(x,μ,σ, cumulative) and =NORMINV(area,μ,σ).

The normal probability density function $f(x)$ reaches a maximum at μ and has points of inflection at $\mu \pm \sigma$ as shown in the left chart in Figure 7.7. Despite its appearance, $f(x)$ does not reach the X-axis beyond $\mu \pm 3\sigma$, but is merely asymptotic to it. Its single peak and symmetry cause some observers to call it "mound-shaped" or "bell-shaped." Its CDF has a "lazy-S" shape, as shown in the right chart in Figure 7.7. It approaches, but never reaches, 1.

FIGURE 7.7

Normal PDF and CDF

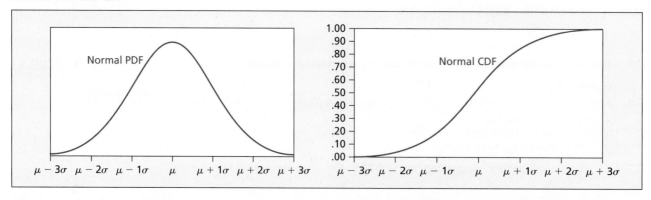

A normal distribution with mean μ and standard deviation σ is sometimes denoted $N(\mu, \sigma)$ for short. All normal distributions have the same general shape, differing only in the axis scales. For example, the left chart in Figure 7.8 shows the distribution of diameters of golf balls from a manufacturing process that produces normally distributed diameters with a mean diameter of $\mu = 42.70$ mm and a standard deviation $\sigma = 0.01$ mm, or $N(42.70, 0.01)$ in short notation. The right chart in Figure 7.8 shows the distribution of scores on the CPA theory exam, assumed to be normal with a mean of $\mu = 70$ and a standard deviation $\sigma = 10$, or $N(70, 10)$ in short notation. Although the shape of each PDF is the same, notice that the horizontal and vertical axis scales differ.

FIGURE 7.8

All Normal Distributions Look Alike Except for Scaling

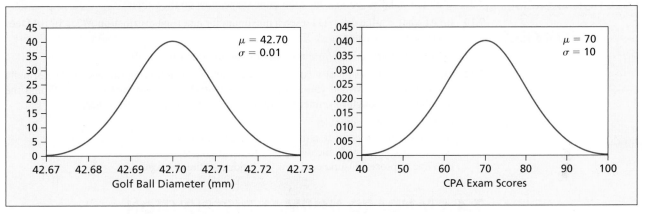

It is a common misconception that $f(x)$ must be smaller than 1, but in the left chart in Figure 7.8 you can see that this is not the case. Because the area under the entire curve must be 1, when X has a small range (e.g., the golf ball diameter range is about 0.06 mm), the height of $f(x)$ is large (about 40 for the golf ball diameters). Conversely, as shown in the right chart in Figure 7.8, when X has a large range (e.g., the CPA exam range is about 60 points), the height of $f(x)$ is small (about 0.40 for the exam scores).

What Is Normal?

Many physical measurements in engineering and the sciences resemble normal distributions. Normal random variables also can be found in economic and financial data, behavioral measurement scales, marketing research, and operations analysis. The normal distribution is especially important as a sampling distribution for estimation and hypothesis testing. To be regarded as a candidate for normality, a random variable should:

- Be measured on a continuous scale.
- Possess a clear center.
- Have only one peak (unimodal).
- Exhibit tapering tails.
- Be symmetric about the mean (equal tails).

When the range is large, we often treat a discrete variable as continuous. For example, exam scores are discrete (range from 0 to 100) but are often treated as continuous data. Here are some random variables that *might* be expected to be approximately normally distributed:

- $X =$ quantity of beverage in a 2-liter bottle of Diet Pepsi.
- $X =$ cockpit noise level in a Boeing 777 at the captain's left ear during cruise.
- $X =$ diameter in millimeters of a manufactured steel ball bearing.

Each of these variables would tend toward a certain mean but would exhibit random variation. For example, even with excellent quality control, not every bottle of a soft drink will have exactly the same fill (even if the variation is only a few milliliters). The mean and standard deviation depend on the nature of the data-generating process. Precision manufacturing can achieve very small σ in relation to μ (e.g., steel ball bearing diameter), while other data-generating situations produce relatively large σ in relation to μ (e.g., your driving fuel mileage). Thus, each normally distributed random variable may have a different coefficient of variation, even though they may share a common shape.

There are statistical tests to see whether a sample came from a normal population. In Chapter 4, for example, you saw that a histogram can be used to assess normality in a general way. More precise tests will be discussed in Chapter 15. For now, our task is to learn more about the normal distribution and its applications.

SECTION EXERCISES

connect

7.9   If all normal distributions have the same shape, how do they differ?

7.10   (a) At what x value does $f(x)$ reach a maximum for a normal distribution $N(75, 5)$? (b) Does $f(x)$ touch the X-axis at $\mu \pm 3\sigma$?

7.11   State the Empirical Rule for a normal distribution (see Chapter 4).

7.12   Discuss why you would or would not expect each of the following variables to be normally distributed. *Hint:* Would you expect a single central mode and tapering tails? Would the distribution be roughly symmetric? Would one tail be longer than the other?

   a. Shoe sizes of adult males.
   b. Years of higher education of 30-year-old employed women.
   c. Days from mailing home utility bills to receipt of payment.
   d. Time to process insurance claims for residential fire damage.

7.4 STANDARD NORMAL DISTRIBUTION

Characteristics of the Standard Normal

LO 7-3

Know the form and parameters of the normal distribution.

Since there is a different normal distribution for every pair of values of μ and σ, we often transform the variable by subtracting the mean and dividing by the standard deviation to produce a *standardized variable*, just as in Chapter 4, except that now we are talking about a population distribution instead of sample data. This important transformation is shown in formula 7.4.

(7.4) $z = \dfrac{x - \mu}{\sigma}$ (transformation of each x-value to a z-value)

If X is normally distributed $N(\mu, \sigma)$, the standardized variable Z has a **standard normal distribution**. Its mean is 0 and its standard deviation is 1, denoted $N(0, 1)$. The maximum height of $f(z)$ is at 0 (the mean) and its points of inflection are at ± 1 (the standard deviation). The shape of the distribution is unaffected by the z transformation. Table 7.3 summarizes the main characteristics of the standard normal distribution.

TABLE 7.3

Standard Normal Distribution

Parameters	μ = population mean
	σ = population standard deviation
PDF	$f(z) = \dfrac{1}{\sqrt{2\pi}}\, e^{-z^2/2}$ where $z = \dfrac{x - \mu}{\sigma}$
Domain	$-\infty < z < +\infty$
Mean	0
Standard deviation	1
Shape	Symmetric, mesokurtic, and bell-shaped.
CDF in Excel*	=NORM.S.DIST(z, 1)
Random data in Excel	=NORM.S.INV(RAND())
Comment	There is no simple formula for a normal CDF, so we need normal tables or Excel to find areas.

*Excel 2010's new functions =NORM.S.DIST(z) and =NORM.S.INV(*area*) give the same result as =NORMSDIST(z) and =NORMSINV(*area*).

Notation

Use an uppercase variable name like Z or X when speaking in general, and a lowercase variable name like z or x to denote a particular value of Z or X.

Since every transformed normal distribution will look the same, we can use a common scale, usually labeled from -3 to $+3$, as shown in Figure 7.9. Since $f(z)$ is a probability density function, the entire area under the curve is 1, as you can approximately verify by treating it as a triangle (area $= \frac{1}{2}$ base $\times$ height). As a rule, we are not interested in the height of the function $f(z)$ but rather in areas under the curve (although Excel will provide either). The probability of an event $P(z_1 < z < z_2)$ is a definite integral of $f(z)$. Although there is no simple integral for $f(z)$, a normal area can be approximated to any desired degree of accuracy using various methods (e.g., covering the area from 0 to $f(z)$ with many narrow rectangles and summing their areas). You do not need to worry about this because tables or Excel functions are available.

FIGURE 7.9
Standard Normal PDF and CDF

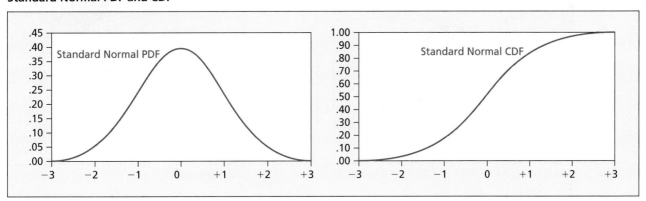

Normal Areas from Appendix C-1

Tables of normal probabilities have been prepared so you can look up any desired normal area. Such tables have many forms. Table 7.4 illustrates Appendix C-1, which shows areas from 0 to z using increments of 0.01 from $z = 0$ to $z = 3.69$ (beyond this range, areas are very small). For example, to calculate $P(0 < Z < 1.96)$, you select the row for $z = 1.9$ and the column for 0.06 (since $1.96 = 1.90 + 0.06$). This row and column are shaded in Table 7.4. At the intersection of the shaded row and column, we see $P(0 < Z < 1.96) = .4750$. This area is illustrated in Figure 7.10. Since half the total area under the curve lies to the right of the mean, we can find a right-tail area by subtraction. For example, $P(Z > 1.96) = .5000 - P(0 < Z < 1.96) = .5000 - .4750 = .0250$.

Suppose we want a middle area such as $P(-1.96 < Z < +1.96)$. Because the normal distribution is symmetric, we also know that $P(-1.96 < Z < 0) = .4750$. Adding these areas, we get

$$P(-1.96 < Z < +1.96) = P(-1.96 < Z < 0) + P(0 < Z < 1.96)$$
$$= .4750 + .4750 = .9500$$

So the interval $-1.96 < Z < 1.96$ encloses 95 percent of the area under the normal curve. Figure 7.11 illustrates this calculation. Since a point has no area in a continuous distribution, the probability $P(-1.96 \le Z \le +1.96)$ is the same as $P(-1.96 < Z < +1.96)$, so, for simplicity, we omit the equality.

TABLE 7.4	z	0.00	0.01	0.02	0.03	0.04	0.05	0.06	0.07	0.08	0.09
Normal Area from 0 to z (from Appendix C-1)	0.0	.0000	.0040	.0080	.0120	.0160	.0199	.0239	.0279	.0319	.0359
	0.1	.0398	.0438	.0478	.0517	.0557	.0596	.0636	.0675	.0714	.0753
	0.2	.0793	.0832	.0871	.0910	.0948	.0987	.1026	.1064	.1103	.1141
	⋮	⋮	⋮	⋮	⋮	⋮	⋮	⋮	⋮	⋮	⋮
	1.6	.4452	.4463	.4474	.4484	.4495	.4505	.4515	.4525	.4535	.4545
	1.7	.4554	.4564	.4573	.4582	.4591	.4599	.4608	.4616	.4625	.4633
	1.8	.4641	.4649	.4656	.4664	.4671	.4678	.4686	.4693	.4699	.4706
	1.9	.4713	.4719	.4726	.4732	.4738	.4744	.4750	.4756	.4761	.4767
	2.0	.4772	.4778	.4783	.4788	.4793	.4798	.4803	.4808	.4812	.4817
	2.1	.4821	.4826	.4830	.4834	.4838	.4842	.4846	.4850	.4854	.4857
	2.2	.4861	.4864	.4868	.4871	.4875	.4878	.4881	.4884	.4887	.4890
	2.3	.4893	.4896	.4898	.4901	.4904	.4906	.4909	.4911	.4913	.4916
	⋮	⋮	⋮	⋮	⋮	⋮	⋮	⋮	⋮	⋮	⋮
	3.6	.49984	.49985	.49985	.49986	.49986	.49987	.49987	.49988	.49988	.49989
	3.7	.49989	.49990	.49990	.49990	.49991	.49991	.49992	.49992	.49992	.49992

FIGURE 7.10

Finding Areas Using Appendix C-1

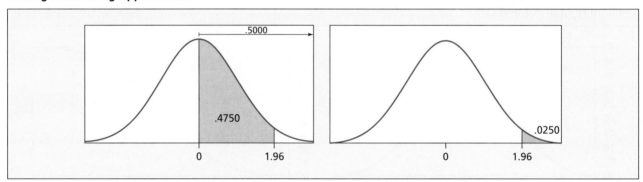

FIGURE 7.11

Finding Areas by Using Appendix C-1

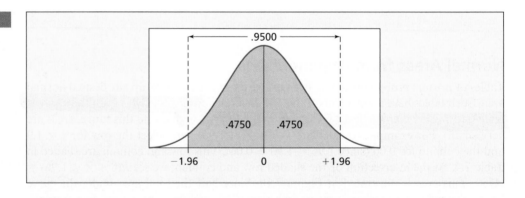

From Appendix C-1 we can see the basis for the Empirical Rule, illustrated in Figure 7.12. These are the "*k*-sigma" intervals mentioned in Chapter 4 and used by statisticians for quick reference to the normal distribution. Thus, it is *approximately* correct to say that a "2-sigma interval" contains 95 percent of the area (actually $z = 1.96$ would yield a 95 percent area):

$$P(-1.00 < Z < +1.00) = 2 \times P(0 < Z < 1.00) = 2 \times .3413 = .6826, \text{ or } 68.26\%$$

$$P(-2.00 < Z < +2.00) = 2 \times P(0 < Z < 2.00) = 2 \times .4772 = .9544, \text{ or } 95.44\%$$

$$P(-3.00 < Z < +3.00) = 2 \times P(0 < Z < 3.00) = 2 \times .49865 = .9973, \text{ or } 99.73\%$$

FIGURE 7.12
Normal Areas within $\mu \pm k\sigma$

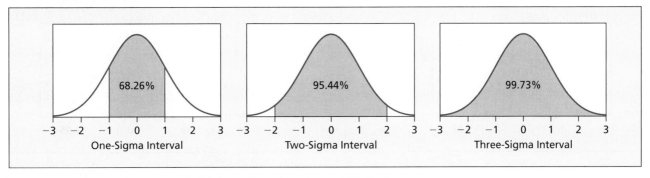

One-Sigma Interval	Two-Sigma Interval	Three-Sigma Interval
68.26%	95.44%	99.73%

Normal Areas from Appendix C-2

Table 7.5 illustrates another kind of table. Appendix C-2 shows cumulative normal areas from the left to z. This second table corresponds to the way Excel calculates normal areas. Using this approach, we see that $P(Z < -1.96) = .0250$ and $P(Z < +1.96) = .9750$. By subtraction, we get

$$P(-1.96 < Z < +1.96) = P(Z < +1.96) - P(Z < -1.96) = .9750 - .0250 = .9500$$

The result is identical to that obtained previously. The interval $-1.96 < Z < 1.96$ encloses 95 percent of the area under the normal curve. This calculation is illustrated in Figure 7.13.

LO 7-4

Find the normal probability for given z or x using tables or Excel.

TABLE 7.5

Cumulative Normal Area from Left to z (from Appendix C-2)

z	0.00	0.01	0.02	0.03	0.04	0.05	0.06	0.07	0.08	0.09
−3.7	.00011	.00010	.00010	.00010	.00009	.00009	.00008	.00008	.00008	.00008
−3.6	.00016	.00015	.00015	.00014	.00014	.00013	.00013	.00012	.00012	.00011
⋮	⋮	⋮	⋮	⋮	⋮	⋮	⋮	⋮	⋮	⋮
−2.3	.0107	.0104	.0102	.0099	.0096	.0094	.0091	.0089	.0087	.0084
−2.2	.0139	.0136	.0132	.0129	.0125	.0122	.0119	.0116	.0113	.0110
−2.1	.0179	.0174	.0170	.0166	.0162	.0158	.0154	.0150	.0146	.0143
−2.0	.0228	.0222	.0217	.0212	.0207	.0202	.0197	.0192	.0188	.0183
−1.9	.0287	.0281	.0274	.0268	.0262	.0256	**.0250**	.0244	.0239	.0233
−1.8	.0359	.0351	.0344	.0336	.0329	.0322	.0314	.0307	.0301	.0294
−1.7	.0446	.0436	.0427	.0418	.0409	.0401	.0392	.0384	.0375	.0367
−1.6	.0548	.0537	.0526	.0516	.0505	.0495	.0485	.0475	.0465	.0455
⋮	⋮	⋮	⋮	⋮	⋮	⋮	⋮	⋮	⋮	⋮
0.0	.5000	.5040	.5080	.5120	.5160	.5199	.5239	.5279	.5319	.5359
0.1	.5398	.5438	.5478	.5517	.5557	.5596	.5636	.5675	.5714	.5753
0.2	.5793	.5832	.5871	.5910	.5948	.5987	.6026	.6064	.6103	.6141
⋮	⋮	⋮	⋮	⋮	⋮	⋮	⋮	⋮	⋮	⋮
1.6	.9452	.9463	.9474	.9484	.9495	.9505	.9515	.9525	.9535	.9545
1.7	.9554	.9564	.9573	.9582	.9591	.9599	.9608	.9616	.9625	.9633
1.8	.9641	.9649	.9656	.9664	.9671	.9678	.9686	.9693	.9699	.9706
1.9	.9713	.9719	.9726	.9732	.9738	.9744	**.9750**	.9756	.9761	.9767
2.0	.9772	.9778	.9783	.9788	.9793	.9798	.9803	.9808	.9812	.9817
2.1	.9821	.9826	.9830	.9834	.9838	.9842	.9846	.9850	.9854	.9857
2.2	.9861	.9864	.9868	.9871	.9875	.9878	.9881	.9884	.9887	.9890
2.3	.9893	.9896	.9898	.9901	.9904	.9906	.9909	.9911	.9913	.9916
⋮	⋮	⋮	⋮	⋮	⋮	⋮	⋮	⋮	⋮	⋮
3.6	.99984	.99985	.99985	.99986	.99986	.99987	.99987	.99988	.99988	.99989
3.7	.99989	.99990	.99990	.99990	.99991	.99991	.99992	.99992	.99992	.99992

FIGURE 7.13

Finding Areas by Using Appendix C-2

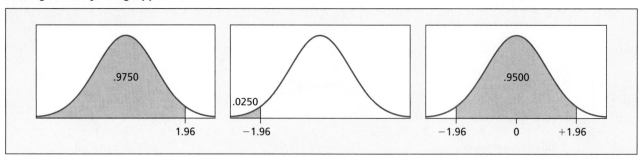

Since Appendix C-1 and Appendix C-2 yield identical results, you should use whichever table is easier for the area you are trying to find. Appendix C-1 is often easier for "middle areas." It also has the advantage of being more compact (it fits on one page), which is one reason why it has traditionally been used for statistics exams and in other textbooks (e.g., marketing). But Appendix C-2 is easier for left-tail areas and some complex areas. Further, Appendix C-2 corresponds to the way Excel calculates normal areas. When subtraction is required for a right-tail or middle area, either table is equally convenient.

SECTION EXERCISES

connect

Note: Use Appendix C-1 or C-2 for these exercises.

7.13 Find the standard normal area for each of the following, showing your reasoning clearly and indicating which table you used.

   a. $P(0 < Z < 0.50)$ b. $P(-0.50 < Z < 0)$ c. $P(Z > 0)$ d. $P(Z = 0)$

7.14 Find the standard normal area for each of the following, showing your reasoning clearly and indicating which table you used.

   a. $P(1.22 < Z < 2.15)$ b. $P(2.00 < Z < 3.00)$ c. $P(-2.00 < Z < 2.00)$ d. $P(Z > 0.50)$

7.15 Find the standard normal area for each of the following, showing your reasoning clearly and indicating which table you used.

   a. $P(-1.22 < Z < 2.15)$ b. $P(-3.00 < Z < 2.00)$ c. $P(Z < 2.00)$ d. $P(Z = 0)$

7.16 Find the standard normal area for each of the following. Sketch the normal curve and shade in the area represented below.

   a. $P(Z < -1.96)$ b. $P(Z > 1.96)$ c. $P(Z < 1.65)$ d. $P(Z > -1.65)$

7.17 Find the standard normal area for each of the following. Sketch the normal curve and shade in the area represented below.

   a. $P(Z < -1.28)$ b. $P(Z > 1.28)$ c. $P(-1.96 < Z < 1.96)$ d. $P(-1.65 < Z < 1.65)$

7.18 Bob's exam score was 2.17 standard deviations above the mean. The exam was taken by 200 students. Assuming a normal distribution, how many scores were higher than Bob's?

7.19 Joan's finishing time for the Bolder Boulder 10K race was 1.75 standard deviations faster than the women's average for her age group. There were 405 women who ran in her age group. Assuming a normal distribution, how many women ran faster than Joan?

Finding *z* for a Given Area

We can also use the tables to find the *z*-value that corresponds to a given area. For example, what *z*-value defines the top 1 percent of a normal distribution? Since half the area lies above the mean, an upper area of 1 percent implies that 49 percent of the area must lie between 0 and *z*. Searching Appendix C-1 for an area of .4900 we see that *z* = 2.33 yields an area of .4901. Without interpolation, that is as close as we can get to 49 percent. This is illustrated in Table 7.6 and Figure 7.14.

We can find other important areas in the same way. Since we are often interested in the top 25 percent, 10 percent, 5 percent, 1 percent, etc., or the middle 50 percent, 90 percent,

TABLE 7.6

**Normal Area from 0 to *z*
(from Appendix C-1)**

z	0.00	0.01	0.02	0.03	0.04	0.05	0.06	0.07	0.08	0.09
0.0	.0000	.0040	.0080	.0120	.0160	.0199	.0239	.0279	.0319	.0359
0.1	.0398	.0438	.0478	.0517	.0557	.0596	.0636	.0675	.0714	.0753
0.2	.0793	.0832	.0871	.0910	.0948	.0987	.1026	.1064	.1103	.1141
⋮	⋮	⋮	⋮	⋮	⋮	⋮	⋮	⋮	⋮	⋮
1.6	.4452	.4463	.4474	.4484	.4495	.4505	.4515	.4525	.4535	.4545
1.7	.4554	.4564	.4573	.4582	.4591	.4599	.4608	.4616	.4625	.4633
1.8	.4641	.4649	.4656	.4664	.4671	.4678	.4686	.4693	.4699	.4706
1.9	.4713	.4719	.4726	.4732	.4738	.4744	.4750	.4756	.4761	.4767
2.0	.4772	.4778	.4783	.4788	.4793	.4798	.4803	.4808	.4812	.4817
2.1	.4821	.4826	.4830	.4834	.4838	.4842	.4846	.4850	.4854	.4857
2.2	.4861	.4864	.4868	.4871	.4875	.4878	.4881	.4884	.4887	.4890
2.3	.4893	.4896	.4898	.4901	.4904	.4906	.4909	.4911	.4913	.4916
⋮	⋮	⋮	⋮	⋮	⋮	⋮	⋮	⋮	⋮	⋮
3.6	.49984	.49985	.49985	.49986	.49986	.49987	.49987	.49988	.49988	.49989
3.7	.49989	.49990	.49990	.49990	.49991	.49991	.49992	.49992	.49992	.49992

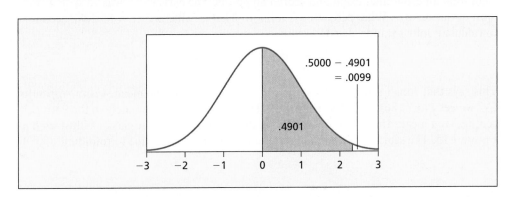

FIGURE 7.14

**Finding Areas by Using
Appendix C-1**

.5000 − .4901
= .0099

.4901

TABLE 7.7

**Important Normal
Areas**

z	Right Tail Area	Middle Area
0.675	.25	.50
1.282	.10	.80
1.645	.05	.90
1.960	.025	.95
2.326	.01	.98
2.576	.005	.99

95 percent, 99 percent, and so forth, it is convenient to record these important *z*-values for quick reference. Table 7.7 summarizes some important normal areas. For greater accuracy, these *z*-values are shown to three decimals (they were obtained from Excel).

SECTION EXERCISES

connect

Note: For each problem below, without interpolating you may only be able to approximate the actual area.

7.20 Find the associated *z*-score for each of the following standard normal areas.

  a. Highest 10 percent   b. Lowest 50 percent   c. Highest 7 percent

7.21 Find the associated z-score for each of the following standard normal areas.

a. Lowest 6 percent   b. Highest 40 percent   c. Lowest 7 percent

7.22 Find the associated z-score or scores that represent the following standard normal areas.

a. Middle 50 percent   b. Lowest 5 percent   c. Middle 90 percent

7.23 Find the associated z-score or scores that represent the following standard normal areas.

a. Middle 60 percent   b. Highest 2 percent   c. Middle 95 percent

7.24 High school students across the nation compete in a financial capability challenge each year by taking a National Financial Capability Challenge Exam. Students who score in the top 20 percent are recognized publicly for their achievement by the Department of the Treasury. Assuming a normal distribution, how many standard deviations above the mean does a student have to score to be publicly recognized?

7.25 The fastest 10 percent of runners who complete the Nosy Neighbor 5K race win a gift certificate to a local running store. Assuming a normal distribution, how many standard deviations below the mean must a runner's time be in order to win the gift certificate?

Finding Areas by Using Standardized Variables

John took an economics exam and scored 86 points. The class mean was 75 with a standard deviation of 7. What percentile is John in? That is, what is $P(X < 86)$? We need first to calculate John's standardized Z-score:

$$z_{John} = \frac{x_{John} - \mu}{\sigma} = \frac{86 - 75}{7} = \frac{11}{7} = 1.57$$

This says that John's score is 1.57 standard deviations above the mean. From Appendix C-2 we get $P(X < 86) = P(Z < 1.57) = .9418$, so John is approximately in the 94th percentile. That means that his score was better than 94 percent of the class, as illustrated in Figure 7.15. The table gives a slightly different value from Excel due to rounding.

FIGURE 7.15

Two Equivalent Areas

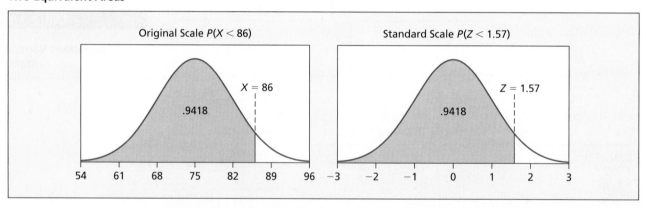

On this exam, what is the probability that a randomly chosen test-taker would have a score of at least 65? We begin by standardizing:

$$z = \frac{x - \mu}{\sigma} = \frac{65 - 75}{7} = \frac{-10}{7} = -1.43$$

Using Appendix C-1 we can calculate $P(X \geq 65) = P(Z \geq -1.43)$ as

$$P(Z \geq -1.43) = P(-1.43 < Z < 0) + .5000$$
$$= .4236 + .5000 = .9236, \text{ or } 92.4\%$$

Using Appendix C-2 we can calculate $P(X \geq 65) = P(Z \geq -1.43)$ as

$$P(Z \geq -1.43) = 1 - P(Z < -1.43) = 1 - .0764 = .9236, \text{ or } 92.4\%$$

FIGURE 7.16

Two Ways to Find an Area

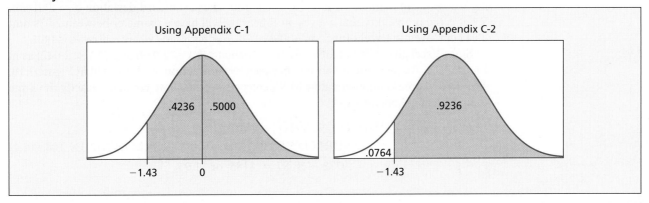

Using either method, there is a 92.4 percent chance that a student scores 65 or above on this exam. These calculations are illustrated in Figure 7.16.

Finding Normal Areas with Excel

Excel offers several functions for the normal and standard normal distributions, as shown in Figure 7.17.

FIGURE 7.17

Inserting Excel Normal Functions

Table 7.8 illustrates Excel functions that return left-tail normal areas for a given value of x or z. Excel is more accurate than a table; however, you must be careful of syntax. It is a good idea to sketch a normal curve and shade the desired area to help you *visualize* the answer you expect, so that you will recognize if you are getting an unreasonable answer from Excel. In Table 7.8, note that the cumulative argument is set to 1 (or TRUE) because we want the CDF (left-tail area) rather than the PDF (height of the normal curve).

TABLE 7.8

Excel Normal CDF Functions

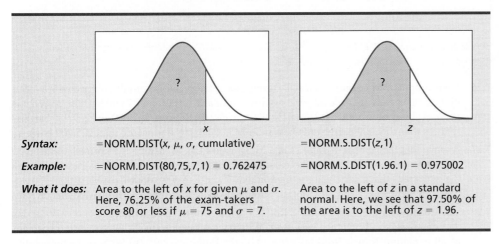

Syntax:	=NORM.DIST(x, μ, σ, cumulative)	=NORM.S.DIST(z,1)
Example:	=NORM.DIST(80,75,7,1) = 0.762475	=NORM.S.DIST(1.96.1) = 0.975002
What it does:	Area to the left of x for given μ and σ. Here, 76.25% of the exam-takers score 80 or less if $\mu = 75$ and $\sigma = 7$.	Area to the left of z in a standard normal. Here, we see that 97.50% of the area is to the left of $z = 1.96$.

Excel's NORM.DIST and NORM.INV functions let us evaluate areas and inverse areas *without* standardizing. For example, let X be the diameter of a manufactured steel ball bearing whose mean diameter is $\mu = 2.040$ cm and whose standard deviation $\sigma = .001$ cm. What is the probability that a given steel bearing will have a diameter between 2.039 and 2.042 cm? We use Excel's function =NORM.DIST(x,μ,σ,cumulative) where cumulative is TRUE.

Since Excel gives left-tail areas, we first calculate $P(X < 2.039)$ and $P(X < 2.042)$ as in Figure 7.18. We then obtain the area between by subtraction, as illustrated in Figure 7.19. The desired area is approximately 81.9 percent. Of course, we could do exactly the same thing by using Appendix C-2:

$$P(2.039 < X < 2.042) = P(X < 2.042) - P(X < 2.039)$$
$$= \text{NORM.DIST}(2.042,2.04,.001,1) - \text{NORM.DIST}(2.039,2.04,.001,1)$$
$$= .9772 - .1587 = .8185, \text{ or } 81.9\%$$

FIGURE 7.18

Left-Tail Areas Using Excel Normal CDF

FIGURE 7.19

Cumulative Areas from Excel's NORM.DIST

SECTION EXERCISES

connect

7.26 Daily output of Marathon's Garyville, Lousiana, refinery is normally distributed with a mean of 232,000 barrels of crude oil per day with a standard deviation of 7,000 barrels. (a) What is the probability of producing at least 232,000 barrels? (b) Between 232,000 and 239,000 barrels? (c) Less than 239,000 barrels? (d) Less than 245,000 barrels? (e) More than 225,000 barrels?

7.27 Assume that the number of calories in a McDonald's Egg McMuffin is a normally distributed random variable with a mean of 290 calories and a standard deviation of 14 calories. (a) What is the probability that a particular serving contains fewer than 300 calories? (b) More than 250 calories? (c) Between 275 and 310 calories? Show all work clearly. (Data are from McDonalds.com)

7.28 The weight of a miniature Tootsie Roll is normally distributed with a mean of 3.30 grams and standard deviation of 0.13 gram. (a) Within what weight range will the middle 95 percent of all miniature Tootsie Rolls fall? *Hint:* Use the Empirical rule. (b) What is the probability that a randomly chosen miniature Tootsie Roll will weigh more than 3.50 grams? (Data are from a project by MBA student Henry Scussel.)

7.29 The pediatrics unit at Carver Hospital has 24 beds. The number of patients needing a bed at any point in time is $N(19.2, 2.5)$. What is the probability that the number of patients needing a bed will exceed the pediatric unit's bed capacity?

7.30 The cabin of a business jet has a cabin height 5 feet 9 inches high. If a business traveler's height is $N(5'10'', 2.7'')$, what percentage of the business travelers will have to stoop?

7.31 On January 1, 2011, a new standard for baseball bat "liveliness" called BBCOR (Ball-Bat Coefficient of Restitution) was adopted for teams playing under NCAA rules. A higher BBCOR allows the ball to travel farther when hit, so bat manufacturers want a high BBCOR. The maximum allowable BBCOR is 0.500. BigBash Inc. produces bats whose BBCOR is $N(0.480, 0.008)$. What percentage of their bats will exceed the BBCOR standard? (See http://batrollingblog.com.)

7.32 Last year's freshman class at Big State University totaled 5,324 students. Of those, 1,254 received a merit scholarship to help offset tuition costs their freshman year (although the amount varied per student). The amount a student received was $N(\$3,456, \$478)$. If the cost of tuition was \$4,200 last year, what percentage of students did *not* receive enough to cover their full tuition?

Inverse Normal

How can we find the various normal percentiles (5th, 10th, 25th, 75th, 90th, 95th, etc.) known as the **inverse normal**? That is, how can we find X for a given area? We simply turn the standardizing transformation around:

$$x = \mu + z\sigma \qquad \left(\text{solving for } x \text{ in } z = \frac{x - \mu}{\sigma}\right) \tag{7.5}$$

Using Table 7.7 (or looking up the areas in Excel) we obtain the results shown in Table 7.9. Note that to find a lower tail area (such as the lowest 5 percent), we must use negative Z-values.

Percentile	z	$x = \mu + z\sigma$	x (to nearest integer)
95th (highest 5%)	1.645	$x = 75 + (1.645)(7)$	86.52, or 87 (rounded)
90th (highest 10%)	1.282	$x = 75 + (1.282)(7)$	83.97, or 84 (rounded)
75th (highest 25%)	0.675	$x = 75 + (0.675)(7)$	79.73, or 80 (rounded)
25th (lowest 25%)	−0.675	$x = 75 - (0.675)(7)$	70.28, or 70 (rounded)
10th (lowest 10%)	−1.282	$x = 75 - (1.282)(7)$	66.03, or 66 (rounded)
5th (lowest 5%)	−1.645	$x = 75 - (1.645)(7)$	63.49, or 63 (rounded)

TABLE 7.9

Percentiles for Desired Normal Area

Using the two Excel functions =NORM.INV() and =NORM.S.INV() shown in Table 7.10, we can solve for the value of x or z that corresponds to a given normal area. Also, for a given area and x, we might want to solve for μ or σ.

TABLE 7.10

Excel Inverse Normal Functions

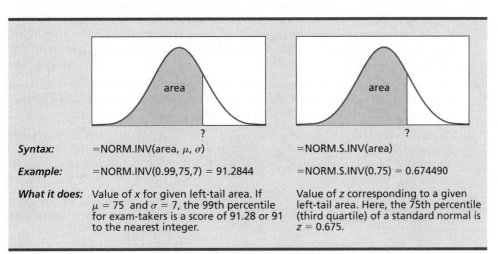

Syntax:	=NORM.INV(area, μ, σ)	=NORM.S.INV(area)
Example:	=NORM.INV(0.99,75,7) = 91.2844	=NORM.S.INV(0.75) = 0.674490
What it does:	Value of *x* for given left-tail area. If $\mu = 75$ and $\sigma = 7$, the 99th percentile for exam-takers is a score of 91.28 or 91 to the nearest integer.	Value of *z* corresponding to a given left-tail area. Here, the 75th percentile (third quartile) of a standard normal is $z = 0.675$.

For example, suppose that John's economics professor has decided that any student who scores below the 10th percentile must retake the exam. The exam scores are normal with $\mu = 75$ and $\sigma = 7$. What is the score that would require a student to retake the exam? We need to find the value of x that satisfies $P(X < x) = .10$. The approximate z-score for the 10th percentile is $z = -1.28$. The steps to solve the problem are:

- Use Appendix C or Excel to find $z = -1.28$ to satisfy $P(Z < -1.28) = .10$.
- Substitute the given information into $z = \dfrac{x - \mu}{\sigma}$ to get $-1.28 = \dfrac{x - 75}{7}$.
- Solve for x to get $x = 75 - (1.28)(7) = 66.04$ (or 66 after rounding)

Students who score below 66 points on the economics exam will be required to retake the exam.

SECTION EXERCISES

connect

7.33 The time required to verify and fill a common prescription at a neighborhood pharmacy is normally distributed with a mean of 10 minutes and a standard deviation of 3 minutes. Find the time for each event. Show your work.

a. Highest 10 percent   b. Middle 50 percent
c. Highest 80 percent   d. Lowest 10 percent

7.34 The time required to cook a pizza at a neighborhood pizza joint is normally distributed with a mean of 12 minutes and a standard deviation of 2 minutes. Find the time for each event. Show your work.

a. Highest 5 percent   b. Lowest 50 percent
c. Middle 95 percent   d. Lowest 80 percent

7.35 The weight of a McDonald's cheeseburger is normally distributed with a mean of 114 ounces and a standard deviation of 7 ounces. Find the weight that corresponds to each event. Show your work.

a. Highest 5 percent   b. Lowest 50 percent
c. Middle 95 percent   d. Lowest 80 percent

7.36 The weight of a small Starbucks coffee is a normally distributed random variable with a mean of 360 grams and a standard deviation of 9 grams. Find the weight that corresponds to each event. Show your work.

a. Highest 10 percent   b. Middle 50 percent
c. Highest 80 percent   d. Lowest 10 percent

7.37 The weights of newborn babies in Foxboro Hospital are normally distributed with a mean of 6.9 pounds and a standard deviation of 1.2 pounds. (a) How unusual is a baby weighing 8.0 pounds or more? (b) What would be the 90th percentile for birth weight? (c) Within what range would the middle 95 percent of birth weights lie?

7.38 The credit scores of 35-year-olds applying for a mortgage at Ulysses Mortgage Associates are normally distributed with a mean of 600 and a standard deviation of 100. (a) Find the credit score that defines the upper 5 percent. (b) Seventy-five percent of the customers will have a credit score higher than what value? (c) Within what range would the middle 80 percent of credit scores lie?

7.39 The number of patients needing a bed at any point in time in the pediatrics unit at Carver Hospital is $N(19.2, 2.5)$. Find the middle 50 percent of the number of beds needed (round to the next higher integer since a "bed" is indivisible).

VAILRESORTS **7.40** Vail Resorts pays part-time seasonal employees at ski resorts on an hourly basis. At a certain mountain, the hourly rates have a normal distribution with $\sigma = \$3.00$. If 20 percent of all part-time seasonal employees make more than $13.16 an hour, what is the average hourly pay rate at this mountain?

7.41 The average cost of an IRS Form 1040 tax filing at Thetis Tax Service is $157.00. Assuming a normal distribution, if 70 percent of the filings cost less than $171.00, what is the standard deviation?

After studying the process of changing oil, the shop's manager has found that the distribution of service times, *X*, is normal with a mean $\mu = 28$ minutes and a standard deviation $\sigma = 5$ minutes, that is, $X \sim N(28, 5)$. This information can now be used to answer questions about normal probabilities.

To answer these types of questions it is helpful to follow a few basic steps. (1) Draw a picture and label the picture with the information you know. (2) Shade in the area that will answer your question. (3) Standardize the random variable. (4) Find the area by using one of the tables or Excel.

EXAMPLE 7.2

Service Times in a Quick Oil Change Shop: Four Worked Problems

Worked Problem #1   *What proportion of cars will be finished in less than half an hour?*

- **Steps 1 and 2:**   Draw a picture and shade the area to the left of 30 minutes.

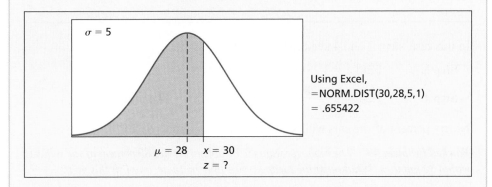

Using Excel,
=NORM.DIST(30,28,5,1)
= .655422

- **Step 3:** $z = \dfrac{30 - 28}{5} = 0.40$

- **Step 4:**   Using Appendix C-2 or Excel we find that $P(Z < 0.40) = .6554$.

Approximately 66 percent of the cars will be finished in less than half an hour.

Worked Problem #2   *What is the chance that a randomly selected car will take longer than 40 minutes to complete?*

- **Steps 1 and 2:**   Draw a picture and shade the area to the right of 40 minutes.

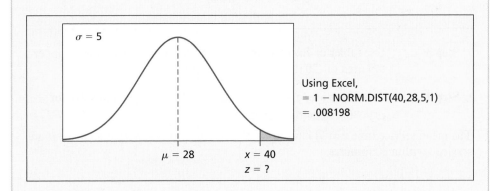

Using Excel,
= 1 − NORM.DIST(40,28,5,1)
= .008198

- **Step 3:** $z = \dfrac{40 - 28}{5} = 2.4$

- **Step 4:**   Using Appendix C-2 or Excel we find that $P(Z > 2.4) = 1 - P(Z \le 2.4) = 1 - .9918 = .0082$.

There is less than a 1 percent chance that a car will take longer than 40 minutes to complete.

Worked Problem #3 *What service time corresponds to the 90th percentile?*

- **Steps 1 and 2:** Draw a picture and shade the desired area.

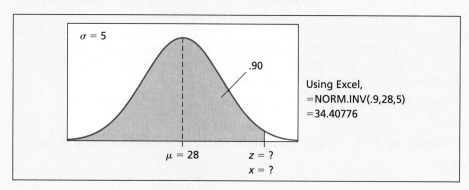

In this case, steps 3 and 4 need to be reversed.

- **Step 3:** Find $z = 1.28$ by using the tables or Excel.
- **Step 4:** $1.28 = \dfrac{x - 28}{5}$, so $x = 28 + 5(1.28) = 34.4$ minutes.

Ninety percent of the cars will be finished in 34.4 minutes or less.

Worked Problem #4 *The manager wants to be able to service 80 percent of the vehicles within 30 minutes. What must the mean service time be to accomplish this goal?*

- **Steps 1 and 2:** Draw a curve and shade the desired area.

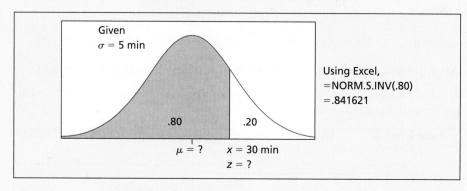

- **Step 3:** Use tables or Excel to find $z = 0.84$ (approximately) for an upper tail area of .20 (lower tail area of .80).
- **Step 4:** Substitute into $z = \dfrac{x - \mu}{\sigma}$ to get $0.84 = \dfrac{30 - \mu}{5}$ and solve for $\mu = 30 - 0.84(5) = 25.8$.

The mean service time would have to be 25.8 minutes to ensure that 80 percent are serviced within 30 minutes.

SECTION EXERCISES

connect

7.42 Use Excel to find each probability.
   a. $P(X < 110)$ for $N(100, 15)$
   b. $P(X < 2.00)$ for $N(0, 1)$
   c. $P(X < 5,000)$ for $N(6000, 1000)$
   d. $P(X < 450)$ for $N(600, 100)$

7.43 Use Excel to find each probability.
   a. $P(80 < X < 110)$ for $N(100, 15)$
   b. $P(1.50 < X < 2.00)$ for $N(0, 1)$
   c. $P(4,500 < X < 7,000)$ for $N(6000, 1000)$
   d. $P(225 < X < 450)$ for $N(600, 100)$

7.44   The weight of a small Starbucks coffee is a normal random variable with a mean of 360 g and a standard deviation of 9 g. Use Excel to find the weight corresponding to each percentile of weight.

    a. 10th percentile   b. 32nd percentile   c. 75th percentile
    d. 90th percentile   e. 99.9th percentile   f. 99.99th percentile

7.45   A study found that the mean waiting time to see a physician at an outpatient clinic was 40 minutes with a standard deviation of 28 minutes. Use Excel to find each probability. (a) What is the probability of more than an hour's wait? (b) Less than 20 minutes? (c) At least 10 minutes.

7.46   High-strength concrete is supposed to have a compressive strength greater than 6,000 pounds per square inch (psi). A certain type of concrete has a mean compressive strength of 7,000 psi, but due to variability in the mixing process it has a standard deviation of 420 psi. Assume a normal distribution. What is the probability that a given pour of concrete from this mixture will fail to meet the high-strength criterion? In your judgment, does this mixture provide an adequate margin of safety?

7.5 NORMAL APPROXIMATIONS

Normal Approximation to the Binomial

We have seen that (unless we are using Excel) binomial probabilities may be difficult to calculate when *n* is large, particularly when many terms must be summed. Instead, we can use a normal approximation. The logic of this approximation is that as *n* becomes large, the discrete binomial bars become more like a smooth, continuous, normal curve. Figure 7.20 illustrates this idea for 4, 16, and 64 flips of a fair coin with *X* defined as the number of heads in *n* tries. As sample size increases, it becomes easier to visualize a smooth, bell-shaped curve overlaid on the bars.

> **LO 7-6**
>
> Use the normal approximation to a binomial or a Poisson.

As a rule of thumb, when $n\pi \geq 10$ and $n(1 - \pi) \geq 10$, it is safe to use the normal approximation to the binomial, setting the normal μ and σ equal to the binomial mean and standard deviation:

$$\mu = n\pi \qquad\qquad (7.6)$$

$$\sigma = \sqrt{n\pi(1 - \pi)} \qquad\qquad (7.7)$$

FIGURE 7.20

Binomial Approaches Normal as *n* Increases

What is the probability of more than 17 heads in 32 flips of a fair coin? In binomial terms, this would be $P(X \geq 18) = P(18) + P(19) + \cdots + P(32)$, which would be a tedious sum even if we had a table. Could the normal approximation be used? With $n = 32$ and $\pi = .50$, we clearly meet the requirement that $n\pi \geq 10$ and $n(1 - \pi) \geq 10$. However, when translating a discrete scale into a continuous scale we must be careful about individual points. The event "more than 17" actually falls halfway *between* 17 and 18 on a discrete scale, as shown in Figure 7.21.

EXAMPLE 7.3

Coin Flips

You don't need to draw the entire distribution. All you need is a little diagram (ignoring the low and high ends of the scale since they are not relevant) to show the event "more than 17" visually:

... 14   15   16   17   *18   19   20   21   22   23* ...

FIGURE 7.21   Normal Approximation to $P(X \geq 18)$

If you make a diagram like this, you can *see* the correct cutoff point. Since the cut-off point for "more than 17" is halfway between 17 and 18, the normal approximation is $P(X > 17.5)$. The 0.5 is an adjustment called the **continuity correction**. The normal parameters are

$$\mu = n\pi = (32)(0.5) = 16$$

$$\sigma = \sqrt{n\pi(1 - \pi)} = \sqrt{(32)(0.5)(1 - 0.5)} = 2.82843$$

We then perform the usual standardizing transformation with the continuity-corrected X-value:

$$z = \frac{x - \mu}{\sigma} = \frac{17.5 - 16}{2.82843} = .53$$

From Appendix C-1 we find $P(Z > .53) = .5000 - P(0 < Z < .53) = .5000 - .2019 = .2981$. Alternately, we could use Appendix C-2 to get $P(Z > .53)$ which, by the symmetry of the normal distribution, is the same as $P(Z < -.53) = .2981$. The calculations are illustrated in Figure 7.22.

FIGURE 7.22   Normal Area for $P(Z > .53)$

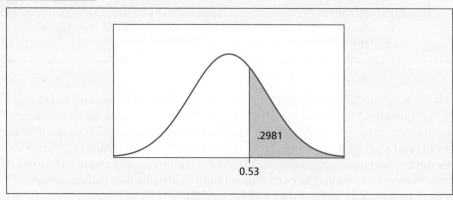

How accurate is this normal approximation to the binomial $P(X \geq 18)$ in our coin flip example? We can check it by using Excel. Since Excel's function is cumulative to the left, we find $P(X \leq 17)$ with the Excel function =BINOM.DIST(17,32,0.5,1) and then subtract from 1:

$$P(X \geq 18) = 1 - P(X \leq 17) = 1 - .7017 = .2983$$

In this case, the normal approximation (.2981) is very close to the binomial probability (.2983), partly because this binomial is roughly symmetric (π is near .50). The rule of thumb results in an error of less than .01 in the approximation. (See *LearningStats* on the OLC for a demonstration of this result.)

When a binomial distribution is badly skewed (π near 0 or 1), the normal approximation is less accurate, *ceteris paribus*. But when n is large, the normal approximation improves, regardless of π. In a *right-skewed* binomial (when $\pi < .50$), the rule $n\pi \geq 10$ ensures that the mean $\mu = n\pi$ is far enough above 0 to prevent severe truncation. In a *left-skewed* binomial distribution (when $\pi > .50$), the rule that $n(1 - \pi) \geq 10$ guards against severe truncation at the upper end of the scale by making sure that the mean is well below n. That is why both rules are needed.

To be sure you understand the continuity correction, consider the events in the table below. We sketch a diagram to find the correct cutoff point to approximate a discrete model with a continuous one.

Event	Relevant Values of X	Normal Cutoff
At least 17	. . . 14 15 16 *17 18 19 20* . . .	Use $x = 16.5$
More than 15	. . . 14 15 *16 17 18 19 20* . . .	Use $x = 15.5$
Fewer than 19	. . . *14 15 16 17 18* 19 20 . . .	Use $x = 18.5$

Note: Use Appendix C-2 for these exercises.

SECTION EXERCISES

connect

7.47 The default rate on government-guaranteed student loans at a certain public four-year institution is 7 percent. (a) If 1,000 student loans are made, what is the probability of fewer than 50 defaults? (b) More than 100? Show your work carefully.

7.48 In a certain store, there is a .03 probability that the scanned price in the bar code scanner will not match the advertised price. The cashier scans 800 items. (a) What is the expected number of mismatches? The standard deviation? (b) What is the probability of at least 20 mismatches? (c) What is the probability of more than 30 mismatches? Show your calculations clearly.

7.49 The probability is .90 that a vending machine in the Oxnard University Student Center will dispense the desired item when correct change is inserted. If 200 customers try the machine, find the probability that (a) at least 175 will receive the desired item and (b) that fewer than 190 will receive the desired item. Explain.

7.50 When confronted with an in-flight medical emergency, pilots and crew can consult staff physicians at a global response center located in Arizona. If the global response center is called, there is a 4.8 percent chance that the flight will be diverted for an immediate landing. Suppose the response center is called 8,465 times in a given year. (a) What is the expected number of diversions? (b) What is the probability of at least 400 diversions? (c) Fewer than 450 diversions? Show your work carefully.

Normal Approximation to the Poisson

The normal approximation for the Poisson works best when λ is fairly large. If you can't find λ in Appendix B (which only goes up to $\lambda = 20$), you are reasonably safe in using the normal approximation. Some textbooks allow the approximation when $\lambda \geq 10$, which is comparable to the rule that the binomial mean must be at least 10. To use the normal approximation to the Poisson we set the normal μ and σ equal to the Poisson mean and standard deviation:

$$\mu = \lambda \tag{7.8}$$

$$\sigma = \sqrt{\lambda} \tag{7.9}$$

EXAMPLE 7.4

Utility Bills

On Wednesday between 10 a.m. and noon, customer billing inquiries arrive at a mean rate of 42 inquiries per hour at Consumers Energy. What is the probability of receiving more than 50 calls? Call arrivals presumably follow a Poisson model, but the mean $\lambda = 42$ is too large to use Appendix B. The formula would entail an infinite sum $P(51) + P(52) + \cdots$ whose terms gradually become negligible (recall that the Poisson has no upper limit), but the calculation would be tedious at best. However, the normal approximation is simple. We set

$$\mu = \lambda = 42$$
$$\sigma = \sqrt{\lambda} = \sqrt{42} = 6.48074$$

The continuity-corrected cutoff point for $X \geq 51$ is $X = 50.5$ (halfway between 50 and 51):

$$\ldots 46 \ 47 \ 48 \ 49 \ 50 \ | \ \textit{51 52 53} \ldots \longrightarrow$$

The standardized Z-value for the event "more than 50" is $P(X > 50.5) = P(Z > 1.31)$ since

$$z = \frac{x - \mu}{\sigma} = \frac{50.5 - 42}{6.48074} \cong 1.31$$

Using Appendix C-2 we look up $P(Z < -1.31) = .0951$, which is the same as $P(Z > 1.31)$ because the normal distribution is symmetric. We can check the actual Poisson probability by using Excel's cumulative function =POISSON.DIST(50,42,1) and subtracting from 1:

$$P(X \geq 51) = 1 - P(X \leq 50) = 1 - .9025 = .0975$$

In this case, the normal approximation (.0951) comes fairly close to the Poisson result (.0975). Of course, if you have access to Excel, you don't need the approximation at all.

SECTION EXERCISES

connect

Note: Use Appendix C-2 for these exercises.

7.51 On average, 28 patients per hour arrive in the Foxboro 24-Hour Walk-in Clinic on Friday between 6 p.m. and midnight. (a) What is the approximate probability of more than 35 arrivals? (b) What is the approximate probability of fewer than 25 arrivals? (c) Is the normal approximation justified? Show all calculations. (d) Use Excel to calculate the actual Poisson probabilities. How close were your approximations?

7.52 For a large Internet service provider (ISP), web virus attacks occur at a mean rate of 150 per day. (a) Estimate the probability of at least 175 attacks in a given day. (b) Estimate the probability of fewer than 125 attacks. (c) Is the normal approximation justified? Show all calculations. (d) Use Excel to calculate the actual Poisson probabilities. How close were your approximations?

7.6 EXPONENTIAL DISTRIBUTION

LO 7-7

Find the exponential probability for a given *x*.

Characteristics of the Exponential Distribution

In Chapter 6 we introduced the idea of a *random process*. For example, consider the process of customers arriving at a Noodles & Company restaurant, illustrated in Figure 7.23. There are two different variables that could be used to describe this process. We could count the number of customers who arrive in a randomly selected minute, or we could

FIGURE 7.23

Customer Arrival Process at a Noodles & Company Restaurant

measure the time between two customer arrivals. As you learned in Chapter 6, the *count* of customer arrivals is a discrete random variable and typically has a Poisson distribution. When the count of customer arrivals has a Poisson distribution, the distribution of the time between two customer arrivals will have an **exponential distribution**, detailed in Table 7.11. In the exponential model, the focus is on the waiting time until the next

TABLE 7.11

Exponential Distribution

Parameter	λ = mean arrival rate per unit of time or space (same as Poisson mean)
PDF	$f(x) = \lambda e^{-\lambda x}$
CDF	$P(X \leq x) = 1 - e^{-\lambda x}$
Domain	$x \geq 0$
Mean	$1/\lambda$
Standard deviation	$1/\lambda$
Shape	Always right-skewed.
CDF in Excel	=EXPON.DIST(x,λ,1)
Random data in Excel	=−LN(RAND())/λ
Comments	Waiting time is exponential when arrivals follow a Poisson model. Often $1/\lambda$ is given (mean time between events) rather than λ. The value of e is approximately 2.71828.

event, a continuous variable. The exponential probability density function approaches zero as x increases, and is very skewed, as shown in Figure 7.24.

We are usually not interested in the height of the function $f(x)$ but rather in areas under the curve. Fortunately, the CDF is simple; no tables are needed, just a calculator

FIGURE 7.24
Exponential Areas

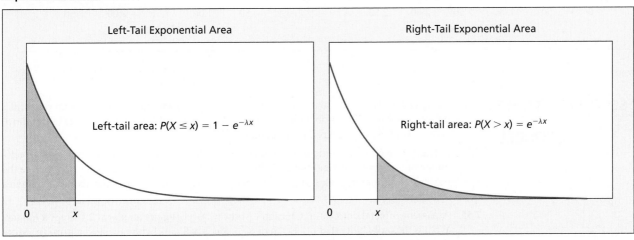

that has the e^x function key. The probability of waiting more than x units of time until the next arrival is $e^{-\lambda x}$, while the probability of waiting x units of time or less is $1 - e^{-\lambda x}$.

$$P(X \le x) = 1 - e^{-\lambda x} \quad \text{(probability of waiting } x \text{ or less)} \qquad \textbf{(7.10)}$$

$$P(X > x) = e^{-\lambda x} \qquad \text{(probability of waiting } \textit{more} \text{ than } x) \qquad \textbf{(7.11)}$$

Recall that $P(X \le x)$ is the same as $P(X < x)$ since the point x has no area. For this reason, we could use either $<$ or $\le$ in formula 7.10.

EXAMPLE 7.5

Customer Waiting Time

Between 2 p.m. and 4 p.m. on Wednesday, patient insurance inquiries arrive at Blue Choice insurance at a mean rate of 2.2 calls per minute. What is the probability of waiting more than 30 seconds for the next call? We set $\lambda = 2.2$ events per minute and $x = 0.50$ minute. Note that we must convert 30 seconds to 0.50 minute since λ is expressed in minutes, and the units of measurement must be the same. We have

$$P(X > 0.50) = e^{-\lambda x} = e^{-(2.2)(0.50)} = .3329, \text{ or } 33.29\%$$

There is about a 33 percent chance of waiting more than 30 seconds before the next call arrives. Since $x = 0.50$ is a *point* that has no area in a continuous model, $P(X \ge 0.50)$ and $P(X > 0.50)$ refer to the same event (unlike, say, a binomial model, in which a point *does* have a probability). The probability that 30 seconds or less (0.50 minute) will be needed before the next call arrives is

$$P(X \le 0.50) = 1 - e^{-(2.2)(0.50)} = 1 - .3329 = .6671$$

These calculations are illustrated in Figure 7.25.

FIGURE 7.25

Exponential Tail Areas for λ = 2.2

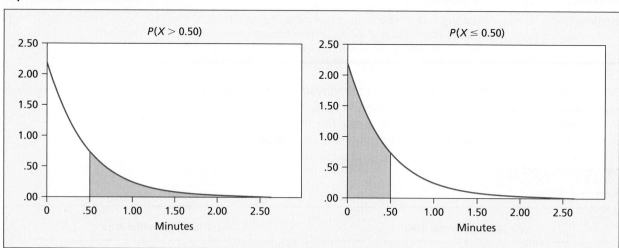

SECTION EXERCISES

connect

7.53 In Santa Theresa, false alarms are received at the downtown fire station at a mean rate of 0.3 per day. (a) What is the probability that more than 7 days will pass before the next false alarm arrives? (b) Less than 2 days? (c) Explain fully.

7.54 Between 11 p.m. and midnight on Thursday night, Mystery Pizza gets an average of 4.2 telephone orders per hour. Find the probability that (a) at least 30 minutes will elapse before the next telephone order; (b) less than 15 minutes will elapse; and (c) between 15 and 30 minutes will elapse.

7.55 A passenger metal detector at Chicago's Midway Airport gives an alarm 2.1 times a minute. What is the probability that (a) less than 60 seconds will pass before the next alarm? (b) More than 30 seconds? (c) At least 45 seconds?

7.56 The Johnson family uses a propane gas grill for cooking outdoors. During the summer they need to replace their tank on average every 30 days. At a randomly chosen moment, what is the probability that they can grill out (a) at least 40 days before they need to replace their tank; (b) no more than 20 days?

7.57 At a certain Noodles & Company restaurant, customers arrive during the lunch hour at a rate of 2.8 per minute. What is the probability that (a) at least 30 seconds will pass before the next customer walks in; (b) no more than 15 seconds; (c) more than 1 minute?

Inverse Exponential

Solve for *x* for a given exponential probability.

We can use the exponential area formula in reverse. If the mean arrival rate is 2.2 calls per minute, we want the 90th percentile for waiting time (the top 10 percent of waiting time) as illustrated in Figure 7.26. We want to find the *x*-value that defines the upper 10 percent.

FIGURE 7.26

Finding *x* for the Upper 10 Percent

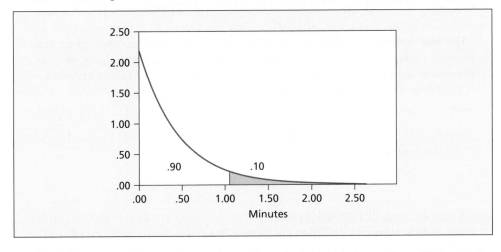

Minutes

Call the unknown time *x*. Since $P(X \le x) = .90$ implies $P(X > x) = .10$, we set the right-tail area to .10, take the natural logarithm of both sides, and solve for *x*:

$$P(X \le x) = 1 - e^{-\lambda x} = .90$$
$$\text{so} \quad e^{-\lambda x} = .10$$
$$-\lambda x = \ln(.10)$$
$$-(2.2)x = -2.302585$$
$$x = 2.302585/2.2$$
$$x = 1.0466 \text{ minutes}$$

So 90 percent of the calls will arrive within 1.0466 minutes (or 62.8 seconds). We can find any percentile in the same way. For example, Table 7.12 illustrates similar calculations to find the quartiles (25 percent, 50 percent, 75 percent) of waiting time.

TABLE 7.12	**Quartiles for Exponential with λ = 2.2**	
First Quartile Q₁	*Second Quartile Q₂ (median)*	*Third Quartile Q₃*
$P(X \le x) = 1 - e^{-\lambda x} = .25$	$P(X \le x) = 1 - e^{-\lambda x} = .50$	$P(X \le x) = 1 - e^{-\lambda x} = .75$
so $e^{-\lambda x} = .75$	so $e^{-\lambda x} = .50$	so $e^{-\lambda x} = .25$
$-\lambda x = \ln(.75)$	$-\lambda x = \ln(.50)$	$-\lambda x = \ln(.25)$
$-(2.2)x = -0.2876821$	$-(2.2)x = -0.6931472$	$-(2.2)x = -1.386294$
$x = 0.2876821/2.2$	$x = 0.6931472/2.2$	$x = 1.386294/2.2$
$x = 0.1308$ minute,	$x = 0.3151$ minute,	$x = 0.6301$ minute,
or 7.9 seconds	or 18.9 seconds	or 37.8 seconds

The calculations in Table 7.12 show that the mean waiting time is $1/\lambda = 1/2.2 = 0.4545$ minute, or 27 seconds. It is instructive to note that the median waiting time (18.9 seconds) is less than the mean. Since the exponential distribution is highly right-skewed, we would expect the mean waiting time to be above the median, which it is.

Mean Time between Events

Exponential waiting times are often described in terms of the **mean time between events** (MTBE) rather than in terms of Poisson arrivals per unit of time. In other words, we might be given $1/\lambda$ instead of λ.

$$\text{MTBE} = 1/\lambda = \textit{mean time between events (units of time per event)}$$

$$1/\text{MTBE} = \lambda = \text{mean } \textit{events per unit of time (events per unit of time)}$$

For example, if the mean time between patient arrivals in an emergency room is 20 minutes, then $\lambda = 1/20 = 0.05$ arrival per minute (or $\lambda = 3.0$ arrivals per hour). We could work a problem using either hours or minutes, as long as we are careful to make sure that x and λ are expressed in the same units when we calculate $e^{-\lambda x}$. For example, $P(X > 12 \text{ minutes}) = e^{-(0.05)(12)} = e^{-0.60}$ is the same as $P(X > 0.20 \text{ hour}) = e^{-(3)(0.20)} = e^{-0.60}$.

EXAMPLE 7.6

Flat-Panel Displays

The NexGenCo color flat-panel display in an aircraft cockpit has a mean time between failures (MTBF) of 22,500 flight hours. What is the probability of a failure within the next 10,000 flight hours? Since 22,500 hours per failure implies $\lambda = 1/22,500$ failures per hour, we calculate:

$$P(X < 10,000) = 1 - e^{-\lambda x} = 1 - e^{-(1/22,500)(10,000)} = 1 - e^{-0.4444} = 1 - .6412 = .3588$$

There is a 35.88 percent chance of failure within the next 10,000 hours of flight. This assumes that failures follow the Poisson model.

EXAMPLE 7.7

Warranty Period

A manufacturer of GPS navigation receivers for boats knows that their mean life under typical maritime conditions is 7 years. What warranty should be offered in order that not more than 30 percent of the GPS units will fail before the warranty expires? The situation is illustrated in Figure 7.27.

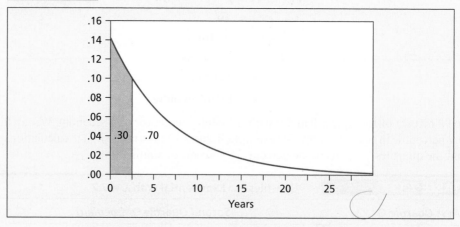

FIGURE 7.27   **Finding x for the Lower 30 Percent**

Let x be the length of the warranty. To solve this problem, we note that if 30 percent fail before the warranty expires, 70 percent will fail afterward. That is, $P(X > x) = 1 - P(X \le x) = 1 - 0.30 = .70$.

We set $P(X > x) = e^{-\lambda x} = .70$ and solve for x by taking the natural log of both sides of the equation:

$$e^{-\lambda x} = .70$$

$$-\lambda x = \ln(.70)$$

$$-\lambda x = -0.356675$$

$$x = (0.356675)/\lambda$$

But in this case, we are not given λ but rather its reciprocal MTBF $= 1/\lambda$. Seven years *mean time between failures* is the same as saying $\lambda = 1/7$ *failures per year*. So we plug in $\lambda = 1/7 = 0.1428571$ to finish solving for x:

$$x = (0.356675)/(0.142857) = 2.497 \text{ years}$$

Thus, the firm would offer a 30-month warranty.

It may seem paradoxical that such a short warranty would be offered for something that lasts 7 years. However, the right tail is very long. A few long-lived GPS units will pull up the mean. This is typical of electronic equipment, which helps explain why your laptop computer may have only a 1-year warranty when we know that laptops often last for many years. Similarly, automobiles typically outlast their warranty period (although competitive pressures have recently led to warranties of 5 years or more, even though it may result in a loss on a few warranties). In general, warranty periods are a policy tool used by business to balance costs of expected claims against the competitive need to offer contract protection to consumers.

Using Excel

The Excel function =EXPON.DIST(x,Lambda,1) will return the left-tail area $P(X \leq x)$. The "1" indicates a cumulative area. If you enter 0 instead of 1, you will get the height of the PDF instead of the left-tail area for the CDF.

Every situation with Poisson arrivals over time is associated with an exponential waiting time. Both models depend solely on the parameter λ = mean arrival rate per unit of time. These two closely related distributions are summarized in Table 7.13.

TABLE 7.13	Relation between Exponential and Poisson Models			
Model	**Random Variable**	**Parameter**	**Domain**	**Variable Type**
Poisson	X = number of arrivals per unit of time	$\lambda = \dfrac{\text{(mean arrivals)}}{\text{(unit of time)}}$	$x = 0, 1, 2, \ldots$	Discrete
Exponential	X = waiting time until next arrival	$\lambda = \dfrac{\text{(mean arrivals)}}{\text{(unit of time)}}$	$x \geq 0$	Continuous

The exponential model may also remind you of the geometric model, which describes the number of items that must be sampled until the first success. In spirit, they are similar. However, the models are different because the geometric model tells us the number of *discrete* events until the next success, while the exponential model tells the *continuous* waiting time until the next arrival of an event.

7.58 The time it takes a ski patroller to respond to an accident call has an exponential distribution with an average equal to 5 minutes. (a) In what time will 90 percent of all ski accident calls be responded to? (b) If the ski patrol would like to be able to respond to 90 percent of the accident calls within 10 minutes, what does the average response time need to be?

7.59 Between 11 p.m. and midnight on Thursday night, Mystery Pizza gets an average of 4.2 telephone orders per hour. (a) Find the median waiting time until the next telephone order. (b) Find the upper quartile of waiting time before the next telephone order. (c) What is the upper 10 percent of waiting time until the next telephone order? Show all calculations clearly.

7.60 A passenger metal detector at Chicago's Midway Airport gives an alarm 0.5 time a minute. (a) Find the median waiting time until the next alarm. (b) Find the first quartile of waiting time before the next alarm. (c) Find the 30th percentile waiting time until the next alarm. Show all calculations clearly.

SECTION EXERCISES

connect

7.61 Between 2 a.m. and 4 a.m. at an all-night pizza parlor, the mean time between arrival of telephone pizza orders is 20 minutes. (a) Find the median wait for pizza order arrivals. (b) Explain why the median is not equal to the mean. (c) Find the upper quartile.

7.62 The mean life of a certain computer hard disk in continual use is 8 years. (a) How long a warranty should be offered if the vendor wants to ensure that not more than 10 percent of the hard disks will fail within the warranty period? (b) Not more than 20 percent?

7.7 TRIANGULAR DISTRIBUTION (OPTIONAL)

Characteristics of the Triangular Distribution

Table 7.14 shows the characteristics of the **triangular distribution**. Visually, it is a simple distribution, as you can see in Figure 7.28. It can be symmetric or skewed. Its X values must lie within the interval $[a, c]$. But unlike the uniform, it has a mode or "peak." The peak is reminiscent of a normal, which also has a single maximum. But unlike the normal, the triangular does not go on forever, since its X values are confined by a and c. The triangular distribution is sometimes denoted $T(a, b, c)$ or T(min, mode, max).

TABLE 7.14

Triangular Distribution

LO 7-9

Use the triangular distribution for "what-if" analysis (optional).

Parameters	a = lower limit b = mode c = upper limit
PDF	$f(x) = \dfrac{2(x - a)}{(b - a)(c - a)}$ for $a \leq x \leq b$ $f(x) = \dfrac{2(c - x)}{(c - a)(c - b)}$ for $b \leq x \leq c$
CDF	$P(X \leq x) = \dfrac{(x - a)^2}{(b - a)(c - a)}$ for $a \leq x \leq b$ $P(X \leq x) = 1 - \dfrac{(c - x)^2}{(c - a)(c - b)}$ for $b \leq x \leq c$
Domain	$a \leq x \leq c$
Mean	$\dfrac{a + b + c}{3}$
Standard deviation	$\sqrt{\dfrac{a^2 + b^2 + c^2 - ab - ac - bc}{18}}$
Shape	Positively skewed if $b < (a + c)/2$. Negatively skewed if $b > (a + c)/2$.
Comments	Practical model, useful in business what-if analysis. A symmetric triangular is the sum of two identically distributed uniform variates.

FIGURE 7.28

Triangular PDFs

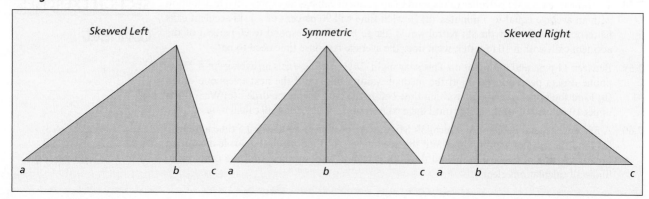

Skewed Left   *Symmetric*   *Skewed Right*

a b c a b c a b c

EXAMPLE 7.8

Anesthetic Effectiveness Using Triangular Distribution

An oral surgeon injects a painkiller prior to extracting a tooth. Given the varying characteristics of patients, the dentist views the time for anesthesia effectiveness as a triangular random variable that takes between 15 minutes and 30 minutes, with 20 minutes as the most likely time. Setting $a = 15$, $b = 20$, and $c = 30$, we obtain

$$\mu = \frac{a + b + c}{3} = \frac{15 + 20 + 30}{3} = 21.7 \text{ minutes}$$

$$\sigma = \sqrt{\frac{a^2 + b^2 + c^2 - ab - ac - bc}{18}}$$

$$= \sqrt{\frac{15^2 + 20^2 + 30^2 - (15)(20) - (15)(30) - (20)(30)}{18}}$$

$$= 3.12 \text{ minutes}$$

Using the cumulative distribution function or CDF, we can calculate the probability of taking less than x minutes:

$$P(X \leq x) = \frac{(x - a)^2}{(b - a)(c - a)} \quad \text{for } a \leq x \leq b \qquad \textbf{(7.12)}$$

$$P(X \leq x) = 1 - \frac{(c - x)^2}{(c - a)(c - b)} \quad \text{for } b \leq x \leq c \qquad \textbf{(7.13)}$$

For example, the probability that the anesthetic takes less than 25 minutes is

$$P(X \leq 25) = 1 - \frac{(30 - 25)^2}{(30 - 15)(30 - 20)} = .8333$$

Basically, we are finding the small triangle's area ($\frac{1}{2}$ base $\times$ height) and then subtracting from 1. This situation is illustrated in Figure 7.29. In contrast, assuming a uniform distribution with parameters $a = 15$ and $b = 30$ would yield $P(X \leq 25) = .6667$. Why is it different? Because the triangular, with mode 20, has more probability on the low end, making it more likely that a patient will be fully anesthetized within 25 minutes. Assuming a uniform distribution may seem conservative, but it could lead to patients sitting around longer waiting to be sure the anesthetic has taken effect. Only experience could tell us which model is more realistic.

FIGURE 7.29 Triangular $P(X \leq 25)$

Special Case: Symmetric Triangular

An interesting special case is a **symmetric triangular distribution** centered at 0, whose lower limit is identical to its upper limit except for sign (e.g., from $-c$ to $+c$) with mode 0 (halfway between $-c$ and $+c$). If you set $c = 2.45$, the distribution $T(-2.45, 0, +2.45)$ closely resembles a standard normal distribution $N(0, 1)$.

Figure 7.30 compares these two distributions. Unlike the normal $N(0, 1)$, the triangular distribution $T(-2.45, 0, +2.45)$ always has values within the range $-2.45 \leq X \leq +2.45$. Yet over much of the range, the distributions are alike, and random samples from

FIGURE 7.30

Symmetric Triangular Is Approximately Normal

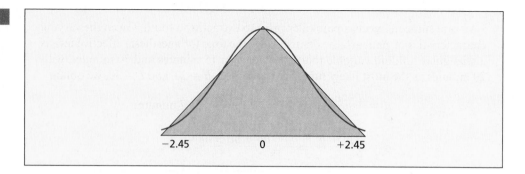

$T(-2.45, 0, +2.45)$ are surprisingly similar to samples from a normal $N(0, 1)$ distribution. It is easy to generate symmetric triangular random data in Excel by summing two $U(0, 1)$ random variables using the function =2.45 *(RAND()+RAND()-1).

Uses of the Triangular

The triangular distribution is a way of thinking about variation that corresponds rather well to what-if analysis in business. It is not surprising that business analysts are attracted to the triangular model. Its finite range and simple form are more understandable than a normal distribution. It is more versatile than a normal because it can be skewed in either direction. Yet it has some of the nice properties of a normal, such as a distinct mode. The triangular model is especially handy for what-if analysis when the business case depends on predicting a stochastic variable (e.g., the price of a raw material, an interest rate, a sales volume). If the analyst can anticipate the range (a to c) and most likely value (b), it will be possible to calculate probabilities of various outcomes. Many times, such distributions will be skewed, so a normal wouldn't be much help. The triangular distribution is often used in simulation modeling software such as Arena. In Chapter 18, we will explore what-if analysis using the triangular $T(a, b, c)$ model in simulations.

SECTION EXERCISES

connect

7.63   Suppose that the distribution of order sizes (in dollars) at L.L. Bean has a distribution that is $T(0, 25, 75)$. (a) Find the mean. (b) Find the standard deviation. (c) Find the probability that an order will be less than $25. (d) Sketch the distribution and shade the area for the event in part (c).

7.64   Suppose that the distribution of oil prices ($/bbl) is forecast to be $T(50, 65, 105)$. (a) Find the mean. (b) Find the standard deviation. (c) Find the probability that the price will be greater than $75. (d) Sketch the distribution and shade the area for the event in part (c).

CHAPTER SUMMARY

The **probability density function (PDF)** of a **continuous random variable** is a smooth curve, and probabilities are *areas* under the curve. The area under the entire PDF is 1. The **cumulative distribution function (CDF)** shows the area under the PDF to the left of X, approaching 1 as X increases. The mean $E(X)$ and variance $Var(X)$ are integrals, rather than sums, as for a discrete random variable. The **uniform continuous distribution,** denoted $U(a, b)$, has two parameters a and b that enclose the range. It is a simple what-if model with applications in simulation. The **normal distribution,** denoted $N(\mu, \sigma)$, is symmetric and bell-shaped. It has two parameters, the mean μ and standard deviation σ. It serves as a benchmark. Because there is a different normal distribution for every possible μ and σ, we apply the transformation $z = (x - \mu)/\sigma$ to get a new random variable that follows a **standard normal distribution,** denoted $N(0, 1)$, with mean 0 and standard deviation 1. There is no simple formula for normal areas, but tables or Excel functions are available to find an area under the curve for given z-values or to find z-values that give a specified area (the "inverse normal"). As shown in Figure 7.31, a **normal approximation** for a binomial or Poisson probability is acceptable when the mean is at least 10. The **exponential distribution** describes *waiting time* until the next Poisson arrival. Its one parameter is λ (the mean arrival rate) and its right tail area is $e^{-\lambda x}$ (the probability of waiting at least x time units for the next arrival). It is strongly right-skewed and is used to predict warranty claims or to schedule facilities. The **triangular distribution** $T(a, b, c)$ has three parameters (a and c enclose the range, and b is the mode). It may be symmetric or skewed in either direction. It is easy to visualize and is a useful model for what-if simulation. Table 7.15 compares these five models.

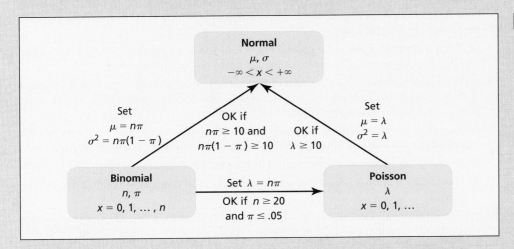

FIGURE 7.31

Relationships among Three Models

TABLE 7.15 — **Comparison of Models**

Model	Parameters	Mean	Variance	Characteristics
Uniform	a, b	$(a + b)/2$	$(b - a)^2/12$	Always symmetric
Normal	μ, σ	μ	σ^2	Symmetric. Useful as reference benchmark.
Standard normal	μ, σ	0	1	Special case of the normal with $z = (x - \mu)/\sigma$
Exponential	λ	$1/\lambda$	$1/\lambda^2$	Always skewed right. Right-tail area is $e^{-\lambda x}$ for waiting times.
Triangular	a, b, c	$(a + b + c)/3$	$(a^2 + b^2 + c^2 - ab - ac - bc)/18$	Useful for what-if business modeling.

KEY TERMS

Commonly Used Formulas in Continuous Distributions

$$\text{Uniform CDF: } P(X \le x) = \frac{x - a}{b - a} \quad \text{for } a \le x \le b$$

$$\text{Standard Normal Random Variable: } \quad z = \frac{x - \mu}{\sigma} \quad \text{for } -\infty < x < +\infty$$

$$\text{Normal Approximation to Binomial: } \quad \mu = n\pi \quad \sigma = \sqrt{n\pi(1 - \pi)}$$
$$\text{for } n\pi \ge 10 \text{ and } n(1 - \pi) \ge 10$$

$$\text{Normal Approximation to Poisson: } \quad \mu = \lambda \quad \sigma = \sqrt{\lambda} \quad \text{for } \lambda \ge 10$$

$$\text{Exponential CDF: } P(X \le x) = 1 - e^{-\lambda x} \quad \text{for } x \ge 0$$

CHAPTER REVIEW

1. (a) Why does a point have zero probability in a continuous distribution? (b) Why are probabilities areas under curves in a continuous distribution?

2. Define (a) parameter, (b) PDF, and (c) CDF.

3. For the uniform distribution: (a) tell how many parameters it has; (b) indicate what the parameters represent; (c) describe its shape; and (d) explain when it would be used.

4. For the normal distribution: (a) tell how many parameters it has; (b) indicate what the parameters represent; (c) describe its shape; and (d) explain why all normal distributions are alike despite having different μ and σ.

5. (a) What features of a stochastic process might lead you to anticipate a normal distribution? (b) Give two examples of random variables that might be considered normal.

6. (a) What is the transformation to standardize a normal random variable? (b) Why do we standardize a variable to find normal areas? (c) How does a standard normal distribution differ from any other normal distribution, and how is it similar?

7. (a) Explain the difference between Appendix C-1 and Appendix C-2. (b) List advantages of each type of table. (c) Which table do you expect to use, and why? (d) Why not always use Excel?

8. Write an example of each of the four normal functions in Excel and tell what each function does.

9. List the standard normal z-values for several common areas (tail and/or middle). *You will use them often.*

10. For the exponential distribution: (a) tell how many parameters it has; (b) indicate what the parameters represent; (c) describe its shape; and (d) explain when it would be used.

11. When does the normal give an acceptable approximation (a) to a binomial and (b) to a Poisson? (c) Why might you never need these approximations? (d) When might you need them?

12. For the triangular distribution: (a) tell how many parameters it has; (b) indicate what the parameters represent; (c) describe its shape in a general way (e.g., skewness); and (d) explain when it would be used.

CHAPTER EXERCISES

Note: Show your work clearly. Problems with * are harder or based on optional material.

7.65 Which of the following is a continuous random variable?

a. Number of Honda Civics sold in a given day at a car dealership.
b. Amount of gasoline used for a 200-mile trip in a Honda Civic.
c. Distance driven on a particular Thursday by the owner of a Honda Civic.

7.66 Which of the following could be probability density functions for a continuous random variable? Explain.

a. $f(x) = .50$ for $0 \le x \le 2$
b. $f(x) = 2 - x$ for $0 \le x \le 2$
c. $f(x) = .5x$ for $0 \le x \le 2$

7.67 Applicants for a night caretaker position are uniformly distributed in age between 25 and 65. (a) What is the mean age of an applicant? (b) The standard deviation? (c) What is the probability that an applicant will be over 45? (d) Over 55? (e) Between 30 and 60?

7.68 Passengers using New York's MetroCard system must swipe the card at a rate between 10 and 40 inches per second, or else the card must be re-swiped through the card reader. Research shows that actual swipe rates by subway riders are uniformly distributed between 5 and 50 inches per second. (a) What is the mean swipe rate? (b) What is the standard deviation of the swipe rate? (c) What are the quartiles? (d) What percentage of subway riders must re-swipe the card because they were outside the acceptable range? (Data are from *The New York Times,* July 18, 2004, p. 23.)

7.69 Discuss why you would or would not expect each of the following variables to be normally distributed. *Hint:* Would you expect a single central mode and tapering tails? Would the distribution be roughly symmetric? Would one tail be longer than the other?

a. Time for households to complete the U.S. Census short form.
b. Size of automobile collision damage claims.
c. Diameters of randomly chosen circulated quarters.
d. Weight of contents of 16-ounce boxes of elbow macaroni.

7.70 Why might the following *not* be normally distributed? (a) The time it takes you to drive to the airport. (b) The annual income for a randomly chosen Major League Baseball player. (c) The annual hurricane losses suffered by homeowners in Florida.

7.71 Scores on a certain accounting exam were normally distributed with a mean of 75 and a standard deviation of 7. Find the percentile for each individual using Excel's =NORM.S.DIST function. (a) Bob's score was 82; (b) Phyllis's score was 93; (c) Tom's score was 63.

7.72 Chlorine concentration in a municipal water supply is a uniformly distributed random variable that ranges between 0.74 ppm and 0.98 ppm. (a) What is the mean chlorine concentration? (b) The standard deviation? (c) What is the probability that the chlorine concentration will exceed 0.80 ppm on a given day? (d) Will be under 0.85 ppm? (e) Will be between 0.80 ppm and 0.90 ppm?

7.73 The weekly demand for Baked Lay's potato chips at a certain Subway sandwich shop is a random variable with mean 450 and standard deviation 80. Find the value(s) of X for each event. Show your work.

   a. Highest 50 percent   b. Lowest 25 percent
   c. Middle 80 percent   d. 5th percentile

7.74 The weekly demand for Papa Chubby's pizzas on a Friday night is a random variable with mean 235 and standard deviation 10. Find the value(s) of X for each event. Show your work.

   a. Lowest 50 percent   b. Highest 25 percent
   c. 90th percentile   d. Middle 80 percent

7.75 The amounts spent by customers at a Noodles & Company restaurant during lunch are normally distributed with a mean equal to $7.00 and a standard deviation equal to $0.35. (a) What amount is the first quartile? (b) The second quartile? (c) The 90th percentile?

7.76 The length of a Colorado brook trout is normally distributed. (a) What is the probability that a brook trout's length exceeds the mean? (b) Exceeds the mean by at least 1 standard deviation? (c) Exceeds the mean by at least 2 standard deviations? (d) Is within 2 standard deviations?

7.77 The caffeine content of a cup of home-brewed coffee is a normally distributed random variable with a mean of 115 mg with a standard deviation of 20 mg. (a) What is the probability that a randomly chosen cup of home-brewed coffee will have more than 130 mg of caffeine? (b) Less than 100 mg? (c) A very strong cup of tea has a caffeine content of 91 mg. What is the probability that a cup of coffee will have less caffeine than a very strong cup of tea?

7.78 The fracture strength of a certain type of manufactured glass is normally distributed with a mean of 579 MPa with a standard deviation of 14 MPa. (a) What is the probability that a randomly chosen sample of glass will break at less than 579 MPa? (b) More than 590 MPa? (c) Less than 600 MPa?

7.79 Tire pressure in a certain car is a normally distributed random variable with mean 30 psi (pounds per square inch) and standard deviation 2 psi. The manufacturer's recommended correct inflation range is 28 psi to 32 psi. A motorist's tire is inspected at random. (a) What is the probability that the tire's inflation is within the recommended range? (b) What is the probability that the tire is underinflated? *(c) A company has developed a microchip that will warn when a tire is 25 percent below the recommended mean, to warn of dangerously low tire pressure. How often would such an alarm be triggered?

7.80 In a certain microwave oven on the high power setting, the time it takes a randomly chosen kernel of popcorn to pop is normally distributed with a mean of 140 seconds and a standard deviation of 25 seconds. What percentage of the kernels will fail to pop if the popcorn is cooked for (a) 2 minutes? (b) Three minutes? (c) If you wanted 95 percent of the kernels to pop, what time would you allow? (d) If you wanted 99 percent to pop?

7.81 Procyon Manufacturing produces tennis balls. Their manufacturing process has a mean ball weight of 2.035 ounces with a standard deviation of 0.03 ounce. Regulation tennis balls are required to have a weight between 1.975 ounces and 2.095 ounces. What proportion of Procyon's production will fail to meet these specifications?

7.82 Shower temperature at the Oxnard Health Club showers is regulated automatically. The heater kicks in when the temperature falls to 99°F and shuts off when the temperature reaches 107°F. Water temperature then falls slowly until the heater kicks in again. At a given moment, the water temperature is a uniformly distributed random variable $U(99,107)$. (a) Find the mean temperature. (b) Find the standard deviation of the temperature. (c) Find the 75th percentile for water temperature.

7.83 Tests show that, on average, the Li-ion Hitachi stick driver can drive 207 drywall screws on a single charge. Bob needs to drive 230 drywall screws. If the standard deviation is 14 screws, find the probability that Bob can finish his job without recharging. *Hint:* Assume a normal distribution and treat the data as continuous.

7.84 The time it takes to give a man a shampoo and haircut is normally distributed with mean 22 minutes and standard deviation 3 minutes. Customers are scheduled every 30 minutes. (a) What is the probability that a male customer will take longer than the allotted time? *(b) If three male customers are scheduled sequentially on the half-hour, what is the probability that all three will be finished within their allotted half-hour times?

7.85 The length of a time-out during a televised professional football game is normally distributed with a mean of 84 seconds and a standard deviation of 10 seconds. If the network runs consecutive commercials totaling 90 seconds, what is the probability that play will resume before the commercials are over?

7.86 If the weight (in grams) of cereal in a box of Lucky Charms is $N(470,5)$, what is the probability that the box will contain less than the advertised weight of 453 g?

7.87 Demand for residential electricity at 6:00 p.m. on the first Monday in October in Santa Theresa County is normally distributed with a mean of 4,905 MW (megawatts) and a standard deviation of 355 MW. Due to scheduled maintenance and unexpected system failures in a generating station, the utility can supply a maximum of 5,200 MW at that time. What is the probability that the utility will have to purchase electricity from other utilities or allow brownouts?

7.88 Jim's systolic blood pressure is a random variable with a mean of 145 mmHg and a standard deviation of 20 mmHg. For Jim's age group, 140 is the threshold for high blood pressure. (a) If Jim's systolic blood pressure is taken at a randomly chosen moment, what is the probability that it will be 135 or less? (b) 175 or more? (c) Between 125 and 165? (d) Discuss the implications of variability for physicians who are trying to identify patients with high blood pressure.

7.89 A statistics exam was given. Calculate the percentile for each of the following four students.

a. John's z-score was -1.62.
b. Mary's z-score was 0.50.
c. Zak's z-score was 1.79.
d. Frieda's z-score was 2.48.

7.90 Are the following statements true or false? Explain your reasoning.

a. "If we see a standardized z-value beyond ± 3, the variable cannot be normally distributed."
b. "If X and Y are two normally distributed random variables measured in different units (e.g., X is in pounds and Y is in kilograms), then it is not meaningful to compare the standardized z-values."
c. "Two machines fill 2-liter soft drink bottles by using a similar process. Machine A has $\mu = 1,990$ ml and $\sigma = 5$ ml while Machine B has $\mu = 1,995$ ml and $\sigma = 3$ ml. The variables cannot both be normally distributed since they have different standard deviations."

*7.91 John can take either of two routes (A or B) to LAX airport. At midday on a typical Wednesday the travel time on either route is normally distributed with parameters $\mu_A = 54$ minutes, $\sigma_A = 6$ minutes, $\mu_B = 60$ minutes, and $\sigma_B = 3$ minutes. (a) Which route should he choose if he must be at the airport in 54 minutes to pick up his spouse? (b) Sixty minutes? (c) Sixty-six minutes? Explain carefully.

7.92 The amount of fill in a half-liter (500 ml) soft drink bottle is normally distributed. The process has a standard deviation of 5 ml. The mean is adjustable. (a) Where should the mean be set to ensure a 95 percent probability that a half-liter bottle will not be underfilled? (b) A 99 percent probability? (c) A 99.9 percent probability? Explain.

7.93 The length of a certain kind of Colorado brook trout is normally distributed with a mean of 12.5 inches and a standard deviation of 1.2 inches. What minimum size limit should the Department of Natural Resources set if it wishes to allow people to keep 80 percent of the trout they catch?

7.94 Times for a surgical procedure are normally distributed. There are two methods. Method A has a mean of 28 minutes and a standard deviation of 4 minutes, while method B has a mean of 32 minutes and a standard deviation of 2 minutes. (a) Which procedure is preferred if the procedure must be completed within 28 minutes? (b) Thirty-eight minutes? (c) Thirty-six minutes? Explain your reasoning fully.

7.95 The length of a brook trout is normally distributed. Two brook trout are caught. (a) What is the probability that both exceed the mean? (b) Neither exceeds the mean? (c) One is above the mean and one is below? (d) Both are equal to the mean?

APPROXIMATIONS

7.96 Among live deliveries, the probability of a twin birth is .02. (a) In 2,000 live deliveries, what is the probability of at least 50 twin births? (b) Fewer than 35?

7.97 Nationwide, the probability that a rental car is from Hertz is 25 percent. In a sample of 100 rental cars, what is the probability that fewer than 20 are from Hertz?

7.98 The probability of being in a car accident when driving more than 10 miles over the speed limit in a residential neighborhood is .06. Of the next 1,000 cars that pass through a particular neighborhood, what are the first and third quartiles for the number of car accidents in this neighborhood?

7.99 A multiple-choice exam has 100 questions. Each question has four choices. (a) What minimum score should be required to reduce the chance of passing by random guessing to 5 percent? (b) To 1 percent? (c) Find the quartiles for a guesser.

7.100 The probability that a certain kind of flower seed will germinate is .80. (a) If 200 seeds are planted, what is the probability that fewer than 150 will germinate? (b) That at least 150 will germinate?

7.101 On a cold morning the probability is .02 that a given car will not start in the small town of Eureka. Assume that 1,500 cars are started each cold morning. (a) What is the probability that at least 25 cars will not start? (b) More than 40?

7.102 At a certain fire station, false alarms are received at a mean rate of 0.2 per day. In a year, what is the probability that fewer than 60 false alarms are received?

EXPONENTIAL DISTRIBUTION

7.103 The HP dvd1040i 20X Multiformat DVD Writer has an MTBF of 70,000 hours. (a) Assuming continuous operation, what is the probability that the DVD writer will last more than 100,000 hours? (b) Less than 50,000 hours? (c) At least 50,000 hours but not more than 80,000 hours? (Product specifications are from www.hp.com.)

7.104 Automobile warranty claims for engine mount failure in a Troppo Malo 2000 SE are rare at a certain dealership, occurring at a mean rate of 0.1 claim per month. (a) What is the probability that the dealership will wait at least 6 months until the next claim? (b) At least a year? (c) At least 2 years? (d) At least 6 months but not more than 1 year?

7.105 Suppose the average time to service a Noodles & Company customer at a certain restaurant is 3 minutes and the service time follows an exponential distribution. (a) What is the probability that a customer will be serviced in less than 3 minutes? (b) Why is your answer more than 50 percent? Shouldn't exactly half the area be below the mean?

7.106 Systron Donner Inertial manufactures inertial subsystems for automotive, commercial/industrial, and aerospace and defense applications. The sensors use a one-piece, micromachined inertial sensing element to measure angular rotational velocity or linear acceleration. The MTBF for a single axis sensor is 400,000 hours. (a) Find the probability that a sensor lasts at least 30 years, assuming continuous operation. (b) Would you be surprised if a sensor has failed within the first 3 years? Explain. (Product specifications are from www.systron.com/techsupp_A.asp.)

TRIANGULAR DISTRIBUTION

*7.107 The price (dollars per 1,000 board feet) of Douglas fir from western Washington and Oregon varies according to a triangular distribution $T(300, 350, 490)$. (a) Find the mean. (b) Find the standard deviation. (c) What is the probability that the price will exceed 400?

*7.108 The distribution of scores on a statistics exam is $T(50, 60, 95)$. (a) Find the mean. (b) Find the standard deviation. (c) Find the probability that a score will be less than 75. (d) Sketch the distribution and shade the area for the event in part (c).

*7.109 The distribution of beach condominium prices in Santa Theresa ($ thousands) is $T(500, 700, 2,100)$. (a) Find the mean. (b) Find the standard deviation. (c) Find the probability that a condo price will be greater than $750K. (d) Sketch the distribution and shade the area for the event in part (c).

PROJECTS AND DISCUSSION

7.110 (a) Write an Excel formula to generate a random normal deviate from $N(0, 1)$ and copy the formula into 10 cells. (b) Find the mean and standard deviation of your sample of 10 random data values. Are you satisfied that the random data have the desired mean and standard deviation? (c) Press F9 to generate 10 more data values and repeat question (b).

7.111 (a) Write an Excel formula to generate a random normal deviate from $N(4000, 200)$ and copy the formula into 100 cells. (b) Find the mean and standard deviation of your sample of 100 random data values. Are you satisfied that the random data have the desired mean and standard deviation? (c) Make a histogram of your sample. Does it appear normal?

7.112 On a police sergeant's examination, the historical mean score was 80 with a standard deviation of 20. Four officers who were alleged to be cronies of the police chief scored 195, 171, 191, and 189, respectively, on the test. This led to allegations of irregularity in the exam. (a) Convert these four officers' scores to standardized z-values. (b) Do you think there was sufficient reason to question these four exam scores? What assumptions are you making? (Data are from *Detroit Free Press,* March 19, 1999, p. 10A.)

RELATED READING

Balakrishnan, N., and V. B. Nevzorov. *A Primer on Statistical Distributions*. Wiley, 2003.

Forbes, Catherine; Merran Evans; Nicholas Hastings; and Brian Peacock. *Statistical Distributions.* 4th ed. Wiley, 2011.

CHAPTER 7   Online Learning Resources

The Online Learning Center (OLC) at www.mhhe.com/doane4e has several *LearningStats* demonstrations to help you understand continuous probability distributions. Your instructor may assign one or more of them, or you may decide to download the ones that sound interesting.

Topic	LearningStats Demonstrations
Calculations	☒ Normal Areas ☒ Probability Calculator
Normal approximations	☒ Evaluating Rules of Thumb ▣ Why the Rule of 10?
Random data	☒ Random Continuous Data ☒ Visualizing Random Normal Data
Tables	☒ Table C—Normal Probabilities

Key: ☒ = Excel   ▣ = Word

EXAM REVIEW QUESTIONS FOR CHAPTERS 5–7

1. Which type of probability (empirical, classical, subjective) is each of the following?

   a. On a given Friday, the probability that Flight 277 to Chicago is on time is 23.7%.
   b. Your chance of going to Disney World next year is 10%.
   c. The chance of rolling a 3 on two dice is 1/8.

2. For the following contingency table, find (a) $P(H \cap T)$; (b) $P(S \mid G)$; (c) $P(S)$

	R	S	T	Row Total
G	10	50	30	90
H	20	50	40	110
Col Total	30	100	70	200

3. If $P(A) = .30$, $P(B) = .70$, and $P(A \cap B) = .25$, are A and B independent events? Explain.

4. Which statement is *false*? Explain.

   a. If $P(A) = .05$, then the odds against event A's occurrence are 19 to 1.
   b. If A and B are mutually exclusive events, then $P(A \cup B) = 0$.
   c. The number of permutations of 5 things taken 2 at a time is 20.

5. Which statement is *true*? Why not the others?

   a. The Poisson distribution has two parameters.
   b. The binomial distribution assumes dependent random trials.
   c. The uniform distribution has two parameters.

6. If the payoff of a risky investment has three possible outcomes ($1,000, $2,000, $5,000) with probabilities .60, .30, and .10 respectively, find the expected value.

   a. $1,500   b. $2,300   c. $1,700

7. Assuming independent arrivals with a mean of 2.5 arrivals per minute, find the probability that in a given minute there will be (a) exactly 2 arrivals; (b) at least 3 arrivals; (c) fewer than 4 arrivals. (d) Which probability distribution did you use and why?

8. If a random experiment whose success probability is .20 is repeated 8 times, find the probability of (a) exactly 3 successes; (b) more than 3 successes; (c) at most 2 successes. (d) Which probability distribution did you use and why?

9. In a random experiment with 50 independent trials with constant probability of success .30, find the mean and standard deviation of the number of successes.

10. Which probability distribution (uniform, binomial, Poisson) is most nearly appropriate to describe each situation (assuming you knew the relevant parameters)?

   a. The number of dimes older than 10 years in a random sample of 8 dimes.
   b. The number of hospital patients admitted during a given minute on Tuesday morning.
   c. The last digit of a randomly chosen student's Social Security number.

11. Which statement is *false*? Explain.

   a. In the hypergeometric distribution, sampling is done without replacement.
   b. The mean of the uniform distribution is always $(a + b)/2$.
   c. We use the geometric distribution to find probabilities of arrivals per unit of time.

12. Which statement is *false*? Explain.

   a. To find probabilities in a continuous distribution, we add up the probabilities at each point.
   b. A uniform continuous model $U(5,21)$ has mean 13 and standard deviation 4.619.
   c. A uniform PDF is constant for all values within the interval $a \leq X \leq b$.

13. Which statement is *true* for a normal distribution? Why not the others?

   a. The shape of the PDF is always symmetric regardless of μ and σ.
   b. The shape of the CDF resembles a bell-shaped curve.
   c. When no tables are available, areas may be found by a simple formula.

14. If freeway speeds are normally distributed with a mean of $\mu = 70$ mph and $\sigma = 7$ mph, find the probability that the speed of a randomly chosen vehicle (a) exceeds 78 mph; (b) is between 65 and 75 mph; (c) is less than 70 mph.

15. In the previous problem, calculate (a) the 95th percentile of vehicle speeds (i.e., 95 percent below); (b) the lowest 10 percent of speeds; (c) the highest 25 percent of speeds (3rd quartile).

16. Which of the following Excel formulas would be a correct way to calculate $P(X < 450)$ given that X is $N(500, 60)$?

   a. =NORM.DIST(450, 500, 60, 1)   b. =NORM.S.DIST(450, 60)   c. =1−NORM.DIST(450, 500, 60, 0)

17. If arrivals follow a Poisson distribution with mean 1.2 arrivals per minute, find the probability that the waiting time until the next arrival will be (a) less than 1.5 minutes; (b) more than 30 seconds; (c) between 1 and 2 minutes.

18. In the previous problem, find (a) the 95th percentile of waiting times (i.e., 95 percent below); (b) the first quartile of waiting times; (c) the mean time between arrivals.

19. Which statement is *correct* concerning the normal approximation? Why not the others?

   a. The normal Poisson approximation is acceptable when $\lambda \geq 10$.
   b. The normal binomial approximation is better when n is small and π is large.
   c. Normal approximations are needed since Excel lacks discrete probability functions.

20. Which statement is *incorrect*? Explain.

   a. The triangular always has a single mode.
   b. The mean of the triangular is $(a + b + c)/3$.
   c. The triangular cannot be skewed left or right.

CHAPTER 8

Sampling Distributions and Estimation

CHAPTER LEARNING OBJECTIVES

LO

When you finish this chapter you should be able to

LO 8-1 Define sampling error, parameter, and estimator.

LO 8-2 Explain the desirable properties of estimators.

LO 8-3 State the Central Limit Theorem for a mean.

LO 8-4 Explain how sample size affects the standard error.

LO 8-5 Construct a 90, 95, or 99 percent confidence interval for μ.

LO 8-6 Know when to use Student's t instead of z to estimate μ.

LO 8-7 Construct a 90, 95, or 99 percent confidence interval for π.

LO 8-8 Construct confidence intervals for finite populations.

LO 8-9 Calculate sample size to estimate a mean or proportion.

LO 8-10 Construct a confidence interval for a variance (optional).

8.1 SAMPLING VARIATION

A sample statistic is a *random variable* whose value depends on which population items happen to be included in the *random sample*. Some samples may represent the population well, while other samples could differ greatly from the population (particularly if the sample size is small). To illustrate **sampling variation**, let's draw some random samples from a large population of GMAT scores for MBA applicants. The population *parameters* are $\mu = 520.78$ and $\sigma = 86.80$. Figure 8.1 shows a dot plot of the entire population ($N = 2{,}637$), which resembles a normal distribution.

Population Parameters
$\mu = 520.78$
$\sigma = 86.80$

Population of 2,637 GMAT Scores

FIGURE 8.1

Dot Plot of GMAT Population 📷 GMAT

Source: Data for 2,637 MBA applicants at a medium-sized public university located in the Midwest.

The table on the next page shows eight random samples of $n = 5$ from this population. The items that happen to be included in the samples vary. Sampling variation is inevitable, yet there is a tendency for the sample *means* to be close to the population mean ($\mu = 520.78$) shown as a dashed line in Figure 8.2. In larger samples, the sample means would tend to be even closer to μ. This fact is the basis for **statistical estimation**.

Random Samples from the GMAT Score Population ⎙ MBASamples							
Sample 1	**Sample 2**	**Sample 3**	**Sample 4**	**Sample 5**	**Sample 6**	**Sample 7**	**Sample 8**
490	310	500	450	420	450	490	670
580	590	450	590	640	670	450	610
440	730	510	710	470	390	590	550
580	710	570	240	530	500	640	540
430	540	610	510	640	470	650	540
$\bar{x}_1 = 504.0$	$\bar{x}_2 = 576.0$	$\bar{x}_3 = 528.0$	$\bar{x}_4 = 500.0$	$\bar{x}_5 = 540.0$	$\bar{x}_6 = 496.0$	$\bar{x}_7 = 564.0$	$\bar{x}_8 = 582.0$

FIGURE 8.2

Dot Plots of Eight Sample Means

From Figure 8.2 we see that the sample *means* (red markers) have much less variation than the *individual* sample items. This is because the mean is an *average*. This chapter describes the behavior of the sample mean and other statistical estimators of population parameters, and explains how to make *inferences* about a population that take into account four factors:

- Sampling variation (uncontrollable).
- Population variation (uncontrollable).
- Sample size (controllable).
- Desired *confidence* in the estimate (controllable).

8.2 ESTIMATORS AND SAMPLING ERROR

Estimators

An **estimator** is a statistic derived from a sample to infer the value of a population **parameter**. An **estimate** is the value of the estimator in a particular sample. Table 8.1 and Figure 8.3 show some common estimators. We usually denote a population parameter by a lowercase Greek letter (e.g., μ, σ, or π). The corresponding sample estimator is usually a Roman letter (e.g., $\bar{x}$, s, or p) or a Greek letter with a "hat" (e.g., $\hat{\mu}$, $\hat{\sigma}$, or $\hat{\pi}$). Statistics books may use different symbols for these things. That's because the science of statistics developed over many decades and its founders had various ways of expressing their ideas.

TABLE 8.1

Examples of Estimators

Estimator	Formula	Parameter
Sample mean	$\bar{x} = \dfrac{1}{n}\sum_{i=1}^{n} x_i$ where x_i is the *i*th data value and *n* is the sample size	μ
Sample proportion	$p = x/n$ where x is the number of successes in the sample and n is the sample size	π
Sample standard deviation	$s = \sqrt{\dfrac{\sum_{i=1}^{n}(x_i - \bar{x})^2}{n - 1}}$ where x_i is the *i*th data value and *n* is the sample size	σ

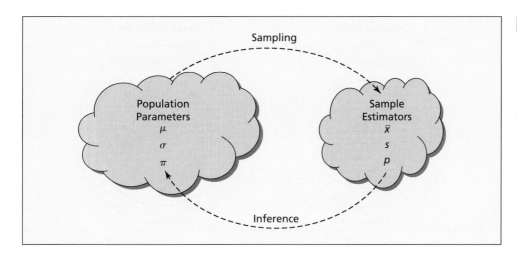

Sampling Error

Random samples vary, so an estimator is a *random variable*. The **sampling error** is the difference between an estimate and the corresponding population parameter. For example, for the population mean:

$$\text{Sampling Error} = \bar{x} - \mu \qquad \textbf{(8.1)}$$

Sampling error exists because different samples will yield different values for $\bar{x}$, depending on which population items happen to be included in the sample. For example, we happen to know the true mean GMAT score, so we could calculate the sampling error for any given sample on the previous page. For Sample 1, the sample mean ($\bar{x} = 504.00$) is less than the population mean ($\mu = 520.78$) and its sampling error is $\bar{x} - \mu = 504.00 - 520.78 = -16.78$. For Sample 2, the sample mean ($\bar{x} = 576.00$) is greater than the population mean ($\mu = 520.78$) and its sampling error is $\bar{x} - \mu = 576.00 - 520.78 = +55.22$. Usually the parameter we are estimating is unknown, so we cannot calculate the sampling error. What we do know is that the sample mean $\bar{X}$ is a random variable that correctly estimates μ on average because the sample means that overestimate μ will tend to be offset by those that underestimate μ.

Bias

The **bias** is the difference between the expected value (i.e., the average value) of the estimator and the true parameter. For the mean:

$$\text{Bias} = E(\bar{X}) - \mu \qquad \textbf{(8.2)}$$

An estimator is *unbiased* if its expected value is the parameter being estimated. We say $\bar{X}$ is an unbiased estimate of μ because $E(\bar{X}) = \mu$. There can be sampling error in a particular sample, but an **unbiased estimator** neither overstates nor understates the true parameter *on average*.

Sampling error is *random* whereas bias is *systematic*. Consider an analogy with target shooting, illustrated in Figure 8.4. An expert whose rifle sights are correctly aligned will produce a target pattern like the one on the left. The same expert shooting a rifle with misaligned sights might produce the pattern on the right. Both targets show sampling variation, but the unbiased estimator is correctly *aimed*. Some samples may happen to hit closer to the bull's-eye than others, but at least an unbiased estimator avoids *systematic* error. You cannot observe bias in a sample because you do not know the true population parameter, but bias can be studied mathematically or by simulation experiments.

The sample mean ($\bar{x}$) and sample proportion (p) are unbiased estimators of μ and π, respectively. But we can find examples of biased estimators. For example, if you use Excel's population standard deviation formula =STDEV.P(Data) instead of its sample standard deviation formula =STDEV.S(Data) to estimate σ, you will get a biased estimate. By using the population formula we will tend to underestimate the true value of σ *on average*. Sampling

FIGURE 8.4

Illustration of Bias

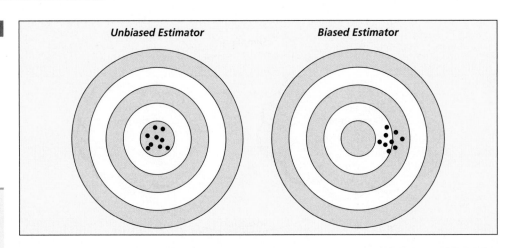

Explain the desirable properties of estimators.

error is an inevitable risk in statistical sampling. You cannot *know* whether you have sampling error without knowing the population parameter (and if you knew it, you wouldn't be taking a sample). It is more important to understand that a large sample will yield a more reliable estimate and to take the sample scientifically (see Chapter 2, "Data Collection").

Efficiency

Efficiency refers to the variance of the estimator's sampling distribution. Smaller variance means a more efficient estimator. Among all unbiased estimators, we prefer the **minimum variance estimator**, referred to as MVUE (minimum variance unbiased estimator). Figure 8.5 shows two unbiased estimators. Both patterns are centered on the bull's-eye, but the estimator on the left has less variation. A more efficient estimator is closer *on average* to the true value of the parameter. You cannot assess efficiency from one sample, but it can be studied either mathematically or by simulation. While an MVUE does not exist for every parameter of every distribution, statisticians have proved that, for a normal distribution, $\bar{x}$ and s^2 are minimum variance estimators of μ and σ^2, respectively (i.e., no other estimators can have smaller variance). Similarly, the sample proportion p is an MVUE of the population proportion π. That is one reason these statistics are widely used.

FIGURE 8.5

Illustration of Efficiency

Consistency

A **consistent estimator** converges toward the parameter being estimated as the sample size increases. That is, the sampling distribution collapses on the true parameter, as illustrated in Figure 8.6. It seems logical that in larger samples $\bar{x}$ ought to be closer to μ, p ought to be closer to π, and s ought to be closer to σ. In fact, it can be shown that the variances of these three estimators diminish as n increases, so all are consistent estimators. Figure 8.6 illustrates the importance of a large sample because in a large sample your estimated mean is likely to be closer to μ.

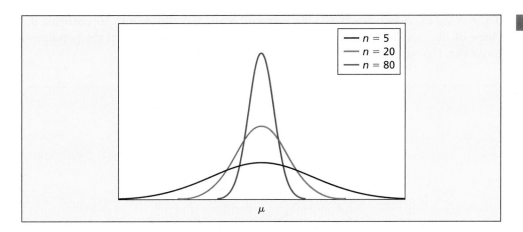

FIGURE 8.6

Illustration of Consistency

8.3 SAMPLE MEAN AND THE CENTRAL LIMIT THEOREM

The **sampling distribution** of an estimator is the probability distribution of all possible values the statistic may assume when a random sample of size n is taken. An estimator has a probability distribution with a mean and variance.

Consider the sample mean $\overline{X}$ used to estimate the population mean μ. Our objective is to use the sampling distribution of $\overline{X}$ to say something about the population that we are studying. To describe the sampling distribution, we need to know the mean, variance, and shape of the distribution. As we've already learned, the sample mean is an unbiased estimator for μ; therefore,

$$E(\overline{X}) = \mu \quad \text{(expected value of the mean)} \quad (8.3)$$

We've also learned that $\overline{X}$ is a *random variable* whose value will change whenever we take a different sample. And as long as our samples are *random samples,* the only type of error we will have in our estimating process is *sampling error.* The sampling error of the sample mean is described by its standard deviation. This value has a special name, the **standard error of the mean**. Notice that the standard error of the mean decreases as the sample size increases:

$$\sigma_{\overline{x}} = \frac{\sigma}{\sqrt{n}} \quad \text{(standard error of the mean)} \quad (8.4)$$

Suppose the average price, μ, of a 2 GB MP3 player is \$80.00 with a standard deviation, σ, equal to \$10.00. What will be the mean and standard error of $\overline{x}$ from a sample of 20 MP3 players?

$$\mu_{\overline{x}} = \$80.00, \qquad \sigma_{\overline{x}} = \frac{\$10.00}{\sqrt{20}} = \$2.236$$

Furthermore, if the population is normal, then the sample mean follows a normal distribution for any sample size. Unfortunately, the population may not have a normal distribution, or we may simply not know *what* the population distribution looks like. What can we do in these circumstances? We can use one of the most fundamental laws of statistics, the Central Limit Theorem.

Central Limit Theorem for a Mean

Central Limit Theorem for a Mean

If a random sample of size n is drawn from a population with mean μ and standard deviation σ, the distribution of the sample mean $\overline{X}$ approaches a normal distribution with mean μ and standard deviation $\sigma_{\overline{x}} = \sigma/\sqrt{n}$ as the sample size increases.

LO 8-3

State the Central Limit Theorem for a mean.

The **Central Limit Theorem** (CLT) is a powerful result that allows us to approximate the shape of the sampling distribution of $\bar{X}$ even when we don't know what the population looks like. Here are three important facts about the sample mean.

1. If the population is normal, the sample mean has a normal distribution centered at μ, with a standard error equal to $\sigma/\sqrt{n}$.

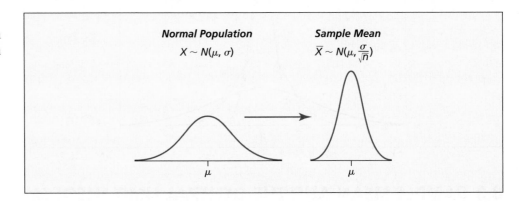

2. As sample size n increases, the distribution of sample means converges to the population mean μ (i.e., the *standard error of the mean* $\sigma_{\bar{x}} = \sigma/\sqrt{n}$ gets smaller).

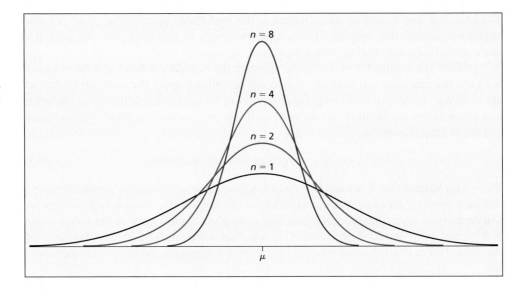

3. Even if your population is *not* normal, by the Central Limit Theorem, if the sample size is large enough, the sample means will have approximately a normal distribution.

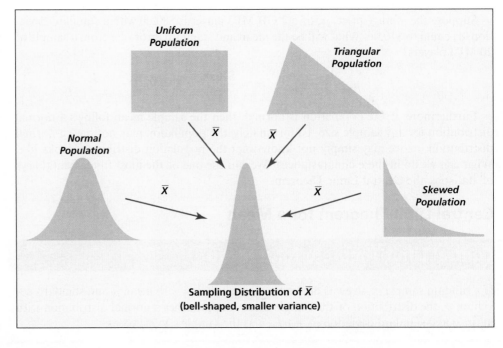

Illustration: Uniform Population   You may have heard the rule of thumb that $n \geq 30$ is required to ensure a normal distribution for the sample mean, but actually a much smaller n will suffice if the population is symmetric. You can demonstrate this by performing your own simulations in *LearningStats* (see OLC resources at the end of this chapter). For example, consider a uniform population $U(0,1000)$ with mean $\mu = 500$ and standard deviation $\sigma = 288.7$. The Central Limit Theorem predicts that the distribution of sample means drawn from the population will be approximately normal. Also, the standard error of the sample mean will decrease as sample size increases. $\bar{\bar{x}}$ is the notation used to represent the average of many $\bar{x}$'s and $s_{\bar{x}}$ represents the standard deviation of many $\bar{x}$'s. This is illustrated in Table 8.2.

TABLE 8.2	Samples from a Uniform Population ☞ CLTPopulations			
	Sampling Distribution Parameters		Simulation Results for 2,000 Sample Means	
Sample Size	Mean of $\bar{X}$	Standard Error of $\bar{X}$	Mean of $\bar{X}$'s	Standard Deviation of $\bar{X}$'s
$n = 1$	$\mu = 500$	$\sigma_{\bar{x}} = \sigma/\sqrt{n} = 288.7/\sqrt{1} = 288.7$	$\bar{\bar{x}} = 508.7$	$s_{\bar{x}} = 290.7$
$n = 2$	$\mu = 500$	$\sigma_{\bar{x}} = \sigma/\sqrt{n} = 288.7/\sqrt{2} = 204.1$	$\bar{\bar{x}} = 497.9$	$s_{\bar{x}} = 202.6$
$n = 4$	$\mu = 500$	$\sigma_{\bar{x}} = \sigma/\sqrt{n} = 288.7/\sqrt{4} = 144.3$	$\bar{\bar{x}} = 498.4$	$s_{\bar{x}} = 145.2$
$n = 8$	$\mu = 500$	$\sigma_{\bar{x}} = \sigma/\sqrt{n} = 288.7/\sqrt{8} = 102.1$	$\bar{\bar{x}} = 498.8$	$s_{\bar{x}} = 100.2$

Figure 8.7 shows histograms of the actual means of many samples drawn from this uniform population. There is sampling variation, but the means and standard deviations of

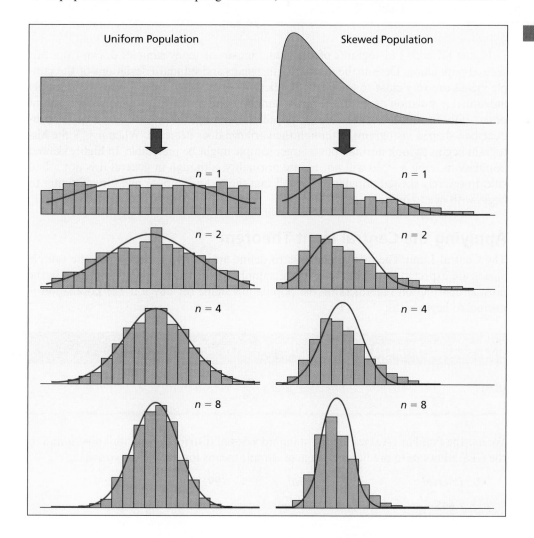

FIGURE 8.7

Illustrations of Central Limit Theorem

the sample means are very close to the predictions in Table 8.2. When $n = 1$, the "means" are simply individual population items, so the histogram looks like the population, and is not normal. For $n = 2$, the histogram of means is triangular, while for $n = 4$ and $n = 8$ we clearly see the approach to a bell-shaped histogram and decreasing variance of the sample mean as sample size increases.

Illustration: Skewed Population   A symmetric, uniform population does not pose much of a challenge for the Central Limit Theorem. But what if the population is severely skewed? For example, consider a strongly skewed population (e.g., waiting times at airport security screening). The Central Limit Theorem predicts that *for any population* the distribution of sample means drawn from this population will approach normality. The standard error of the sample mean will diminish as sample size increases, as illustrated in Table 8.3.

TABLE 8.3	Samples from a Skewed Population CLTPopulations			
	Sampling Distribution Parameters		**Simulation Results for 2,000 Sample Means**	
Sample Size	**Mean of** $\overline{X}$	**Standard Error of** $\overline{X}$	**Mean of** $\overline{X}$'s	**Standard Deviation of** $\overline{X}$'s
$n = 1$	$\mu = 3.000$	$\sigma_{\bar{x}} = \sigma/\sqrt{n} = 2.449/\sqrt{1} = 2.449$	$\bar{\bar{x}} = 3.050$	$s_{\bar{x}} = 2.517$
$n = 2$	$\mu = 3.000$	$\sigma_{\bar{x}} = \sigma/\sqrt{n} = 2.449/\sqrt{2} = 1.732$	$\bar{\bar{x}} = 2.982$	$s_{\bar{x}} = 1.704$
$n = 4$	$\mu = 3.000$	$\sigma_{\bar{x}} = \sigma/\sqrt{n} = 2.449/\sqrt{4} = 1.225$	$\bar{\bar{x}} = 2.973$	$s_{\bar{x}} = 1.196$
$n = 8$	$\mu = 3.000$	$\sigma_{\bar{x}} = \sigma/\sqrt{n} = 2.449/\sqrt{8} = 0.866$	$\bar{\bar{x}} = 3.005$	$s_{\bar{x}} = 0.868$

Figure 8.7 shows histograms of the actual means of many samples drawn from this skewed population. Despite the skewness, the means and standard deviations of the sample means are very close to the CLT's predictions. When $n = 1$, the "means" are simply individual population items, so the histogram of means looks just like the skewed parent population. In contrast to the uniform population example, $n = 2$ and $n = 4$ do *not* produce bell-shaped histograms, although the variance does decrease. When $n = 8$ the histogram begins to look normal, but a larger sample might be preferable. In highly skewed populations, even $n \geq 30$ will not ensure normality, although in general it is not a bad rule. In severely skewed populations, recall that the mean is a poor measure of center to begin with due to outliers.

Applying the Central Limit Theorem

The Central Limit Theorem permits us to define an interval within which the sample means are expected to fall. As long as the sample size n is large enough, we can use the normal distribution regardless of the population shape (or any n if the population is normal to begin with):

Expected Range of Sample Means

(8.5)
$$\mu \pm z\frac{\sigma}{\sqrt{n}}$$

We use the familiar z-values for the standard normal distribution. If we know μ and σ, the CLT allows us to predict the range of sample means for samples of size n:

90% Interval	*95% Interval*	*99% Interval*
$\mu \pm 1.645 \dfrac{\sigma}{\sqrt{n}}$	$\mu \pm 1.960 \dfrac{\sigma}{\sqrt{n}}$	$\mu \pm 2.576 \dfrac{\sigma}{\sqrt{n}}$

For example, within what interval would we expect GMAT sample means to fall for samples of $n = 5$ applicants (see Figure 8.1)? The population is approximately normal with parameters $\mu = 520.78$ and $\sigma = 86.80$, so the predicted range for 95 percent of the sample means is

$$520.78 \pm 1.960\frac{86.80}{\sqrt{5}} \quad \text{or} \quad 520.78 \pm 76.08 \quad \text{or} \quad [444.70, 596.86]$$

Our eight sample means for $n = 5$ (see Figure 8.2) drawn from this population fall within this interval (roughly 444 to 597), as predicted by the Central Limit Theorem.

EXAMPLE 8.1

Bottle Filling: Variation in $\overline{X}$

The amount of liquid in a half-liter (500 ml) bottle of Diet Coke is normally distributed with mean $\mu = 505$ ml and standard deviation $\sigma = 1.2$ ml. Since the population is normal, the sample mean $\overline{X}$ will be a normally distributed random variable for any sample size. If we sample a single bottle (i.e., $n = 1$) and measure its fill, the sample "mean" is just X, which should lie within the ranges shown in Table 8.4. It appears that the company has set the mean far enough above 500 ml that essentially all bottles contain at least the advertised half-liter quantity. If we increase the sample size to $n = 4$ bottles, we expect the sample means to lie within a narrower range, as shown in Table 8.4, because when we average 4 items, we *reduce the variability* in the sample mean.

TABLE 8.4	Expected 95 Percent Range of the Sample Mean	
$n = 1$		**$n = 4$**
$\mu \pm 1.960\,\dfrac{\sigma}{\sqrt{n}}$		$\mu \pm 1.960\,\dfrac{\sigma}{\sqrt{n}}$
$505 \pm 1.960\dfrac{1.2}{\sqrt{1}}$		$505 \pm 1.960\dfrac{1.2}{\sqrt{4}}$
505 ± 2.352		505 ± 1.176
$[502.6, 507.4]$		$[503.8, 506.2]$

If this experiment were repeated a large number of times, we would expect that the sample means would lie within the limits shown above. For example, if we took 1,000 samples and computed the mean fill for each sample, we would expect that approximately 950 of the sample means would lie within the 95 percent limits. But we don't really take 1,000 samples (except in a computer simulation). We actually take only *one* sample. The importance of the CLT is that it *predicts* what will likely happen with that *one* sample.

Sample Size and Standard Error

Even if the population standard deviation σ is large, the sample means will fall within a narrow interval as long as n is large. The key is the *standard error of the mean:* $\sigma_{\overline{x}} = \sigma/\sqrt{n}$. The standard error decreases as n increases. Figure 8.8 illustrates how increasing n reduces the standard error (expressed in this diagram as a fraction of σ). For example, when $n = 4$ the standard error is halved. To halve it again requires $n = 16$, and to halve it again requires $n = 64$. To *halve* the standard error, you must *quadruple* the sample size (the law of diminishing returns).

Sample Size	*Standard Error*
$n = 4$	$\sigma_{\overline{x}} = \sigma/\sqrt{4} = \sigma/2$
$n = 16$	$\sigma_{\overline{x}} = \sigma/\sqrt{16} = \sigma/4$
$n = 64$	$\sigma_{\overline{x}} = \sigma/\sqrt{64} = \sigma/8$

You can make the interval $\mu \pm z\sigma/\sqrt{n}$ as small as you want by increasing n. Thus, the mean of sample means converges to the true population mean μ as n increases.

FIGURE 8.8

**Standard Error Declines
as *n* Increases**

Illustration: All Possible Samples from a Uniform Population

To help visualize the meaning of the Central Limit Theorem, consider a discrete uniform population consisting of the integers $\{0, 1, 2, 3\}$. The population parameters are $\mu = 1.5$ and $\sigma = 1.118$ (using the population definition of σ).

$$\mu = \frac{1}{N}\sum_{i=1}^{N}x_i = \frac{0 + 1 + 2 + 3}{4} = 1.5$$

$$\sigma = \sqrt{\frac{\sum_{i=1}^{n}(x_i - \mu)^2}{N}} = \sqrt{\frac{(0 - 1.5)^2 + (1 - 1.5)^2 + (2 - 1.5)^2 + (3 - 1.5)^2}{4}} = 1.118$$

Take all possible random samples of $n = 2$ items *with replacement*. There are 16 equally likely outcomes (x_1, x_2). Each sample mean is $\bar{x} = (x_1 + x_2)/2$:

$\bar{x} = (0 + 0)/2 = 0.0 \quad \bar{x} = (1 + 0)/2 = 0.5 \quad \bar{x} = (2 + 0)/2 = 1.0 \quad \bar{x} = (3 + 0)/2 = 1.5$

$\bar{x} = (0 + 1)/2 = 0.5 \quad \bar{x} = (1 + 1)/2 = 1.0 \quad \bar{x} = (2 + 1)/2 = 1.5 \quad \bar{x} = (3 + 1)/2 = 2.0$

$\bar{x} = (0 + 2)/2 = 1.0 \quad \bar{x} = (1 + 2)/2 = 1.5 \quad \bar{x} = (2 + 2)/2 = 2.0 \quad \bar{x} = (3 + 2)/2 = 2.5$

$\bar{x} = (0 + 3)/2 = 1.5 \quad \bar{x} = (1 + 3)/2 = 2.0 \quad \bar{x} = (2 + 3)/2 = 2.5 \quad \bar{x} = (3 + 3)/2 = 3.0$

The population is uniform (0, 1, 2, 3 are equally likely) yet the distribution of all possible sample means has a peaked triangular shape, as shown in Table 8.5 and Figure 8.9. The distribution of sample means is approaching a bell shape or normal distribution, as predicted by the Central Limit Theorem.

The predictions for the mean and standard error are

$$\mu_{\bar{x}} = \mu = 1.5 \quad \text{and} \quad \sigma_{\bar{x}} = \frac{\sigma}{\sqrt{n}} = \frac{1.118}{\sqrt{2}} = 0.7905$$

These theoretical predictions are borne out exactly for all 16 possible sample means. The mean of *means* $\bar{\bar{x}}$ is

$$\bar{\bar{x}} = \frac{1(0.0) + 2(0.5) + 3(1.0) + 4(1.5) + 3(2.0) + 2(2.5) + 1(3.0)}{16} = 1.5$$

Sample Mean ($\bar{x}$)	Frequency	Relative Frequency	
0.0	1	0.0625	**TABLE 8.5**
0.5	2	0.1250	
1.0	3	0.1875	**Sampling Distribution**
1.5	4	0.2500	**of $\bar{X}$ for $n = 2$**
2.0	3	0.1875	
2.5	2	0.1250	
3.0	1	0.0625	
Total	16	1.0000	

FIGURE 8.9

Population and Sampling Distribution of $\bar{X}$ for $n = 2$

The standard deviation of *all possible sample means* is

$$\sigma_{\bar{x}} = \sqrt{\frac{\left[\begin{array}{c} 1(0.0 - 1.5)^2 + 2(0.5 - 1.5)^2 + 3(1.0 - 1.5)^2 + 4(1.5 - 1.5)^2 \\ + 3(2.0 - 1.5)^2 + 2(2.5 - 1.5)^2 + 1(3.0 - 1.5)^2 \end{array}\right]}{16}} = 0.7906$$

8.1 Find the standard error of the mean for each sampling situation (assuming a normal population). What happens to the standard error each time you quadruple the sample size?

  a. $\sigma = 32, n = 4$
  b. $\sigma = 32, n = 16$
  c. $\sigma = 32, n = 64$

8.2 Find the standard error of the mean for each sampling situation (assuming a normal population). What happens to the standard error each time you quadruple the sample size?

  a. $\sigma = 24, n = 9$
  b. $\sigma = 24, n = 36$
  c. $\sigma = 24, n = 144$

8.3 Find the interval $\left[\mu - z\dfrac{\sigma}{\sqrt{n}}, \mu + z\dfrac{\sigma}{\sqrt{n}} \right]$ within which 90 percent of the sample means would be expected to fall, assuming that each sample is from a normal population.

  a. $\mu = 100, \sigma = 12, n = 36$
  b. $\mu = 2{,}000, \sigma = 150, n = 9$
  c. $\mu = 500, \sigma = 10, n = 25$

8.4 Find the interval $\left[\mu - z\dfrac{\sigma}{\sqrt{n}}, \mu + z\dfrac{\sigma}{\sqrt{n}} \right]$ within which 95 percent of the sample means would be expected to fall, assuming that each sample is from a normal population.

  a. $\mu = 200, \sigma = 12, n = 36$
  b. $\mu = 1{,}000, \sigma = 15, n = 9$
  c. $\mu = 50, \sigma = 1, n = 25$

SECTION EXERCISES

connect

8.5 The diameter of bushings turned out by a manufacturing process is a normally distributed random variable with a mean of 4.035 mm and a standard deviation of 0.005 mm. A sample of 25 bushings is taken once an hour. (a) Within what interval should 95 percent of the bushing diameters fall? (b) Within what interval should 95 percent of the sample *means* fall? (c) What conclusion would you reach if you saw a sample mean of 4.020? A sample mean of 4.055?

8.6 The fuel economy of a 2011 Lexus RX 350 2WD 6 cylinder 3.5 L automatic 5-speed using premium fuel is a normally distributed random variable with a mean of $\mu = 25.0$ MPG and a standard deviation of $\sigma = 1.25$ MPG. (a) What is the standard error of $\bar{X}$, the mean from a random sample of 16 fill-ups by one driver? (b) Within what interval would you expect the sample mean to fall, with 90 percent probability? (Source: www .fueleconomy.gov.)

8.7 The fat content of a pouch of Keebler Right Bites© Fudge Shoppe© Mini-Fudge Stripes is normally distributed with a mean of 3.50 grams. Assume a known standard deviation of 0.25 gram. (a) What is the standard error of $\bar{X}$, the mean weight from a random sample of 10 pouches of cookies? (b) Within what interval would you expect the sample mean to fall, with 95 percent probability? (Source: http://www.keebler.com.)

8.8 Concerns about climate change and CO_2 reduction have initiated the commercial production of blends of biodiesel (e.g., from renewable sources) and petrodiesel (from fossil fuel). Random samples of 35 blended fuels are tested in a lab to ascertain the bio/total carbon ratio. (a) If the true mean is .9480 with a standard deviation of 0.0060, within what interval will 95 percent of the sample means fall? (b) What is the sampling distribution of $\bar{X}$? In other words, state the shape, center, and variability of the distribution of $\bar{X}$. (c) What theorem did you use to answer part (b)?

8.4 CONFIDENCE INTERVAL FOR A MEAN (μ) WITH KNOWN σ

What Is a Confidence Interval?

A sample mean $\bar{x}$ calculated from a random sample $x_1, x_2, \ldots, x_n$ is a **point estimate** of the unknown population mean μ. Because samples vary, we need to indicate our uncertainty about the true value of μ. Based on our knowledge of the sampling distribution of $\bar{X}$, we can create an **interval estimate** for μ. We construct a **confidence interval** for the unknown mean μ by adding and subtracting a **margin of error** from $\bar{x}$, the mean of our random sample. The **confidence level** for this interval is expressed as a percentage such as 90, 95, or 99 percent.

LO 8-5	Confidence Interval for a Mean μ with Known σ
Construct a 90, 95, or 99 percent confidence interval for μ.	**(8.6)** $\quad \bar{x} \pm z_{\alpha/2} \dfrac{\sigma}{\sqrt{n}} \quad$ where $\dfrac{\sigma}{\sqrt{n}}$ is the standard error of the mean

If samples are drawn from a normal population (or if the sample is large enough that $\bar{X}$ is approximately normal by the Central Limit Theorem) and σ is known, then the margin of error is calculated using the standard normal distribution. The value $z_{\alpha/2}$ is determined by the desired level of confidence, which we call $1 - \alpha$. Because the sampling distribution is symmetric, $\alpha/2$ is the area in each tail of the normal distribution as shown in Figure 8.10.

The middle area shows the confidence level. The remaining area is divided into two symmetrical tails, each having area equal to $\alpha/2$. The value of $z_{\alpha/2}$ will depend on the level

FIGURE 8.10

Confidence Interval for μ

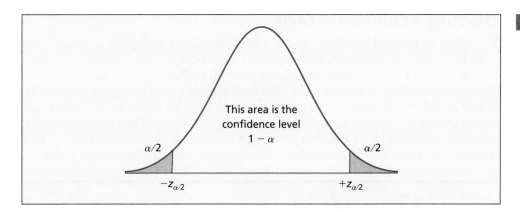

of confidence desired. For example, if the chosen confidence level is 90 percent ($1 - \alpha = .90$ and $\alpha = .10$), we would use $z_{\alpha/2} = z_{.10/2} = z_{.05} = 1.645$ for an upper tail area of .05. Similarly, for a 95 percent confidence level ($1 - \alpha = .95$ and $\alpha = .05$), we would use $z_{\alpha/2} = z_{.05/2} = z_{.025} = 1.960$ for an upper tail area of .025, as illustrated in Figure 8.11. Notice that the 95 percent confidence interval is *wider* than the 90 percent confidence interval.

FIGURE 8.11

90 Percent and 95 Percent Confidence Intervals Compared

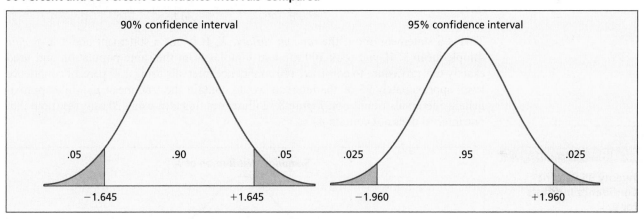

The volume of liquid in a half-liter bottle of Diet Coke is a normally distributed random variable. The standard deviation of volume is known to be $\sigma = 1.20$ ml. A sample of 10 bottles gives a sample mean volume $\bar{x} = 503.4$ ml. Since the population is normal, the sample mean is a normally distributed random variable for any sample size, so we can use the z distribution to construct a confidence interval for μ.

For a 90 percent confidence interval, we insert $z_{\alpha/2} = 1.645$ in formula 8.6.

90% confidence interval: $\bar{x} \pm z_{\alpha/2}\dfrac{\sigma}{\sqrt{n}}$ or $503.4 \pm 1.645\dfrac{1.20}{\sqrt{10}}$ or $[502.78, 504.02]$

For a 95 percent confidence interval, we would use $z_{\alpha/2} = 1.960$:

95% confidence interval: $\bar{x} \pm z_{\alpha/2}\dfrac{\sigma}{\sqrt{n}}$ or $503.4 \pm 1.96\dfrac{1.20}{\sqrt{10}}$ or $[502.66, 504.14]$

For a 99 percent confidence interval, we would use $z_{\alpha/2} = 2.576$ in the formula:

99% confidence interval: $\bar{x} \pm z_{\alpha/2}\dfrac{\sigma}{\sqrt{n}}$ or $503.4 \pm 2.576\dfrac{1.2}{\sqrt{10}}$ or $[502.42, 504.38]$

Notice that lower bounds for all three of the confidence intervals are well above 500, indicating that the mean of the bottle-filling process is safely above the required minimum half liter (500 ml).

EXAMPLE 8.2

*Bottle Filling:
Confidence Intervals
for μ*

Choosing a Confidence Level

You might be tempted to assume that a higher confidence level gives a "better" estimate. However, confidence is not free—there is a trade-off that must be made. A higher confidence level leads to a wider confidence interval, as illustrated in Example 8.2. The 95 percent confidence interval is *wider* than the 90 percent confidence interval. In order to gain confidence, we must accept a wider range of possible values for μ. Greater confidence implies loss of precision (i.e., a greater margin of error). Table 8.6 shows several common confidence levels and their associated z-values. A 95 percent confidence level is often used because it is a reasonable compromise between confidence and precision.

TABLE 8.6

Common Confidence Levels and z-Values

Confidence Level	$1 - \alpha$	α	$\alpha/2$	$z_{\alpha/2}$
90%	.90	.10	.05	$z_{.05} = 1.645$
95%	.95	.05	.025	$z_{.025} = 1.960$
99%	.99	.01	.005	$z_{.005} = 2.576$

Interpretation

Before actually taking a random sample we can think of the confidence level $1 - \alpha$ as a *probability on the procedure* used to calculate the confidence interval.

(8.7)
$$P\left(\overline{X} - z_{\alpha/2}\frac{\sigma}{\sqrt{n}} < \mu < \overline{X} + z_{\alpha/2}\frac{\sigma}{\sqrt{n}}\right) = 1 - \alpha$$

This is a statement about the *random variable* $\overline{X}$. It is not a statement about a *specific* sample mean $\bar{x}$. If you took 100 random samples from the same population and used exactly this procedure to construct 100 confidence intervals using a 95 percent confidence level, approximately 95 of the intervals would contain the true mean μ, while approximately 5 intervals would not. Figure 8.12 illustrates this idea using 20 samples (note that one interval does not contain μ).

FIGURE 8.12

Twenty 95 Percent Confidence Intervals for μ

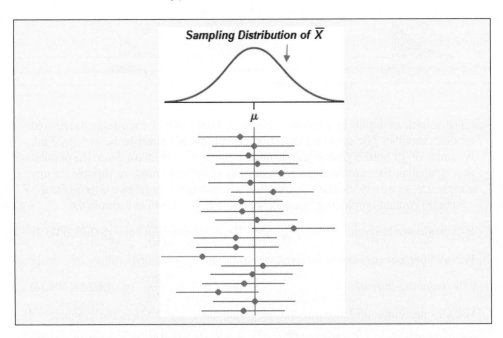

Once you've taken a random sample and have calculated $\bar{x}$ and the corresponding confidence interval, the confidence level $1 - \alpha$ no longer is thought of as a probability. The confidence interval you've calculated either does or does not contain μ. Because you only do it once, you won't know if your specific interval contains the true mean μ or not. You can only say that $1 - \alpha$ is now your level of *confidence* that the interval contains μ.

When Can We Assume Normality?

If σ is known and the population is normal, then we can safely use formula 8.6 to construct the confidence interval for μ. If σ is known but we do not know whether the population is normal, a common rule of thumb is that $n \geq 30$ is sufficient to assume a normal distribution for $\overline{X}$ (by the CLT) as long as the population is reasonably symmetric and has no outliers. However, a larger n may be needed to assume normality if you are sampling from a strongly skewed population or one with outliers. When σ is *unknown*, a different approach is used, as described in the next section.

Is σ Ever Known?

Yes, but not very often. In quality control applications with ongoing manufacturing processes, it may be reasonable to assume that σ stays the same over time. The type of confidence interval just seen is therefore important because it is used to construct *control charts* to track the mean of a process (such as bottle filling) over time. However, the case of unknown σ is more typical, and will be examined in the next section.

SECTION EXERCISES

connect

8.9 Find a confidence interval for μ assuming that each sample is from a normal population.

  a. $\bar{x} = 14$, $\sigma = 4$, $n = 5$, 90 percent confidence
  b. $\bar{x} = 37$, $\sigma = 5$, $n = 15$, 99 percent confidence
  c. $\bar{x} = 121$, $\sigma = 15$, $n = 25$, 95 percent confidence

8.10 Calculate a confidence interval for μ assuming that each sample is from a normal population.

  a. $\bar{x} = 24$, $\sigma = 3$, $n = 10$, 90 percent confidence
  b. $\bar{x} = 125$, $\sigma = 8$, $n = 25$, 99 percent confidence
  c. $\bar{x} = 12.5$, $\sigma = 1.2$, $n = 50$, 95 percent confidence

8.11 Use the sample information $\bar{x} = 2.4$, $\sigma = 0.15$, $n = 9$ to calculate the following confidence intervals for μ assuming the sample is from a normal population: (a) 90 percent confidence; (b) 95 percent confidence; (c) 99 percent confidence. (d) Describe how the intervals change as you increase the confidence level.

8.12 Use the sample information $\bar{x} = 37$, $\sigma = 5$, $n = 15$ to calculate the following confidence intervals for μ assuming the sample is from a normal population: (a) 90 percent confidence; (b) 95 percent confidence; (c) 99 percent confidence. (d) Describe how the intervals change as you increase the confidence level.

8.13 A random sample of 25 items is drawn from a population whose standard deviation is known to be $\sigma = 40$. The sample mean is $\bar{x} = 270$.

  a. Construct an interval estimate for μ with 95 percent confidence.
  b. Repeat part a assuming that $n = 50$.
  c. Repeat part a assuming that $n = 100$.
  d. Describe how the confidence interval changes as n increases.

8.14 A random sample of 100 items is drawn from a population whose standard deviation is known to be $\sigma = 50$. The sample mean is $\bar{x} = 850$.

  a. Construct an interval estimate for μ with 95 percent confidence.
  b. Repeat part a assuming that $\sigma = 100$.
  c. Repeat part a assuming that $\sigma = 200$.
  d. Describe how the confidence interval changes as σ increases.

8.15 The fuel economy of a 2011 Lexus RX 350 2WD 6 cylinder 3.5 L automatic 5-speed using premium fuel is normally distributed with a known standard deviation of 1.25 MPG. If a random sample of 10 tanks of gas yields a mean of 21.0 MPG, find the 95 percent confidence interval for the true mean MPG. (Source: www.fueleconomy.gov.)

8.16 Guest ages at a Vail Resorts ski mountain typically have a right-skewed distribution. Assume the standard deviation (σ) of *age* is 14.5 years. (a) Even though the population distribution of age is right-skewed, what will be the shape of the distribution of $\overline{X}$, the average age, in a random sample of 40 guests? (b) From a random sample of 40 guests, the sample mean is 36.4 years. Calculate a 99 percent confidence interval for μ, the true mean age of Vail Resorts ski mountain guests.   VAILRESORTS

8.17 The Ball Corporation's beverage can manufacturing plant in Fort Atkinson, Wisconsin, uses a metal supplier that provides metal with a known thickness standard deviation $\sigma = .000959$ mm. If a random sample of 58 sheets of metal resulted in an $\bar{x} = 0.2731$ mm, calculate the 99 percent confidence interval for the true mean metal thickness.

8.5 CONFIDENCE INTERVAL FOR A MEAN (μ) WITH UNKNOWN σ

Student's *t* Distribution

In situations where the population is normal but its standard deviation σ is unknown, the **Student's *t* distribution** should be used instead of the normal z distribution. This is particularly important when the sample size is small. When σ is unknown, the formula for a confidence interval resembles the formula for known σ except that t replaces z and s replaces σ.

Confidence Interval for a Mean μ with Unknown σ

(8.8) $\bar{x} \pm t_{\alpha/2}\dfrac{s}{\sqrt{n}}$ where $\dfrac{s}{\sqrt{n}}$ is the *estimated* standard error of the mean

---

LO 8-6

Know when to use Student's *t* instead of *z* to estimate μ.

The interpretation of the confidence interval is the same as when σ is known, as illustrated in Figure 8.13. However, the confidence intervals will be wider (other things being the same) because $t_{\alpha/2}$ is always greater than $z_{\alpha/2}$. Intuitively, our confidence interval will be wider because we face added uncertainty when we use the sample standard deviation s to estimate the unknown population standard deviation σ.

FIGURE 8.13

Confidence Interval Format for Known *s*

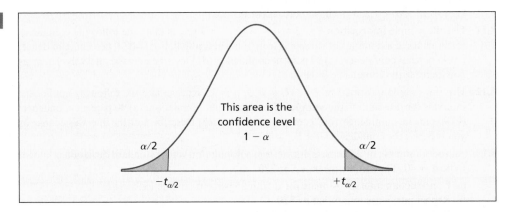

The Student's *t* distributions were proposed by a Dublin brewer named W. S. Gossett (1876–1937) who published his research under the name "Student" because his employer did not approve of publishing research based on company data. The *t* distributions are symmetric and shaped very much like the standard normal distribution, except they are somewhat less peaked and have thicker tails. Note that the *t* distributions are a class of distributions, each of which is dependent on the size of the sample we are using. Figure 8.14 shows how the

FIGURE 8.14

Comparison of Normal and Student's *t*

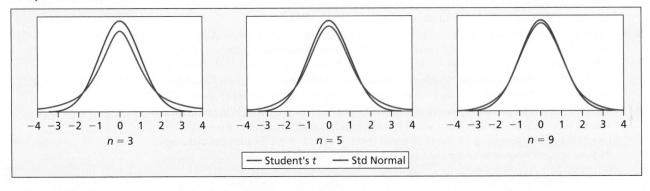

tails of the distributions change as the sample size increases. A closer look reveals that the *t* distribution's tails lie *above* the normal (i.e., the *t* distribution always has longer tails).

Degrees of Freedom

Knowing the sample size allows us to calculate a parameter called **degrees of freedom** (sometimes abbreviated *d.f.*). This parameter is used to determine the value of the *t* statistic used in the confidence interval formula. The degrees of freedom tell us how many observations we used to calculate *s*, the sample standard deviation, less the number of intermediate estimates we used in our calculation. Recall that the formula for *s* uses all *n* individual values from the sample and also $\bar{x}$, the sample mean. Therefore, the degrees of freedom are equal to the sample size minus 1.

$$d.f. = n - 1 \quad \text{(degrees of freedom for a confidence interval for } \mu) \quad \textbf{(8.9)}$$

For large degrees of freedom, the *t* distribution approaches the shape of the normal distribution, as illustrated in Figure 8.14. However, in small samples, the difference is important. For example, in Figure 8.14 the lower axis scale range extends out to ±4, while a range of ±3 would cover most of the area for a standard normal distribution. We have to go out further into the tails of the *t* distribution to enclose a given area, so for a given confidence level, *t is always larger than z* so the confidence interval is always *wider* than if *z* were used.

Comparison of *z* and *t*

Table 8.7 (taken from Appendix D) shows that for very small samples the *t*-values differ substantially from the normal *z* values. But for a given confidence level, as degrees of freedom increase, the *t*-values approach the familiar normal *z*-values (shown at the bottom of each column corresponding to an infinitely large sample). For example, for *n* = 31, we would have degrees of freedom *d.f.* = 31 − 1 = 30, so for a 90 percent confidence interval, we would use *t* = 1.697, which is only slightly larger than *z* = 1.645. It might seem tempting to use the *z*-values to avoid having to look up the correct degrees of freedom, but this would not be conservative (because the resulting confidence interval would be too narrow).

TABLE 8.7

Student's *t*-values for Selected Degrees of Freedom

d.f.	Confidence Level 80%	90%	95%	98%	99%
1	3.078	6.314	12.706	31.821	63.656
2	1.886	2.920	4.303	6.965	9.925
3	1.638	2.353	3.182	4.541	5.841
4	1.533	2.132	2.776	3.747	4.604
5	1.476	2.015	2.571	3.365	4.032
10	1.372	1.812	2.228	2.764	3.169
20	1.325	1.725	2.086	2.528	2.845
30	1.310	1.697	2.042	2.457	2.750
40	1.303	1.684	2.021	2.423	2.704
60	1.296	1.671	2.000	2.390	2.660
100	1.290	1.660	1.984	2.364	2.626
∞	1.282	1.645	1.960	2.326	2.576

Note: The bottom row shows the *z*-values for each confidence level.

EXAMPLE 8.3

GMAT Scores

📁 GMATScores

Consider a random sample of GMAT scores submitted by 20 applicants to an MBA program. A dot plot of this sample is shown in Figure 8.15.

530	450	600	570	360
550	640	490	460	550
480	440	530	470	560
500	430	640	420	530

FIGURE 8.15   Dot Plot and 90 Percent Confidence Interval (*n* = 20 Scores)
GMATScores

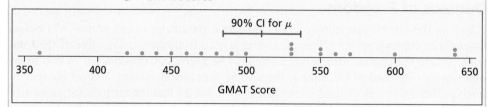

We will construct a 90 percent confidence interval for the mean GMAT score of all MBA applicants. The sample mean is $\bar{x} = 510$ and the sample standard deviation is $s = 73.77$. Since the population standard deviation σ is unknown, we will use the Student's t for our confidence interval with 19 degrees of freedom:

$$d.f. = n - 1 = 20 - 1 = 19 \quad \text{(degrees of freedom for } n = 20\text{)}$$

For a 90 percent confidence interval, we consult Appendix D and find $t_{\alpha/2} = t_{.05} = 1.729$:

	Confidence Level (1 − α)				
	0.80	0.90	0.95	0.98	0.99
	Upper Tail Area (α/2)				
d.f.	0.10	0.05	0.025	0.01	0.005
1	3.078	6.314	12.706	31.821	63.656
2	1.886	2.920	4.303	6.965	9.925
⋮	⋮	⋮	⋮	⋮	⋮
18	1.330	1.734	2.101	2.552	2.878
19	1.328	**1.729**	2.093	2.539	2.861
20	1.325	1.725	2.086	2.528	2.845

The 90 percent confidence interval is

$$\bar{x} \pm t_{\alpha/2}\frac{s}{\sqrt{n}} \quad \text{or} \quad 510 \pm (1.729)\frac{73.77}{\sqrt{20}} \quad \text{or} \quad 510 \pm 28.52$$

We are 90 percent confident that the true mean GMAT score is within the interval [481.48, 538.52] as shown in Figure 8.15. If we wanted a narrower interval with the same level of confidence, we would need a larger sample size to reduce the right-hand side of $\bar{x} \pm t_{\alpha/2}\frac{s}{\sqrt{n}}$.

EXAMPLE 8.4

Hospital Stays
Maternity

During a certain period of time, Balzac Hospital had 8,261 maternity cases. Hospital management needs to know the mean length of stay (LOS) so they can plan the maternity unit bed capacity and schedule the nursing staff. Each case is assigned a code called a DRG (which stands for "Diagnostic Related Group"). The most common DRG was 373 (simple delivery without complicating diagnoses), accounting for 4,409 cases during the study period. For DRG 373, a random sample of hospital records for $n = 25$ births, the mean length of stay was $\bar{x} = 39.144$ hours with a standard deviation of $s = 16.204$ hours. What is the 95 percent confidence interval for the true mean?

To justify using the Student's t distribution, we will assume that the population is normal (we will examine this assumption later). Since the population standard deviation is unknown, we use the Student's t for our confidence interval with 24 degrees of freedom:

$$d.f. = n - 1 = 25 - 1 = 24 \qquad \text{(degrees of freedom for } n = 25\text{)}$$

For a 95 percent confidence interval, we consult Appendix D and find $t_{\alpha/2} = t_{.025} = 2.064$:

	Confidence Level $(1 - \alpha)$				
	0.80	0.90	0.95	0.98	0.99
	Upper Tail Area $(\alpha/2)$				
d.f.	0.10	0.05	0.025	0.01	0.005
1	3.078	6.314	12.706	31.821	63.656
2	1.886	2.920	4.303	6.965	9.925
⋮	⋮	⋮	⋮	⋮	⋮
23	1.319	1.714	2.069	2.500	2.807
24	1.318	1.711	2.064	2.492	2.797
25	1.316	1.708	2.060	2.485	2.787

The 95 percent confidence interval is

$$\bar{x} \pm t_{\alpha/2}\frac{s}{\sqrt{n}} \quad \text{or} \quad 39.144 \pm (2.064)\frac{16.204}{\sqrt{25}} \quad \text{or} \quad 39.144 \pm 6.689$$

With 95 percent confidence, the true mean LOS is within the interval [32.455, 45.833] so our estimate is that a simple maternity stay averages between 32.5 hours and 45.8 hours. A dot plot of this sample and confidence interval are shown in Figure 8.16.

FIGURE 8.16   **Dot Plot and 95 Percent Confidence Interval ($n = 25$ Births)**   📝 **Maternity**

Our confidence interval width reflects the sample size, the confidence level, and the standard deviation. If we wanted a narrower interval (i.e., more precision), we could either increase the sample size or lower the confidence level (e.g., to 90 percent or even 80 percent). But we cannot do anything about the standard deviation because it is an aspect of the sample. In fact, some samples could have larger standard deviations than this one.

Outliers and Messy Data

Outliers and messy data are common. Managers often encounter large databases containing unruly data and they must decide how to treat atypical observations. What if we had a patient in our LOS example that stayed in the hospital for 254 hours? If a handful of maternity patients stay 10 days (240 hours) instead of 2 days (48 hours), real resources will be required to treat them. Would this be common or an outlier? Even if we decide that 10 days is unusual or an outlier, we cannot simply ignore it. We should investigate what might have happened to make this patient's stay longer than usual. It's possible that the diagnostic code DRG 373 (simple delivery without complicating diagnoses) was assigned incorrectly. We should ask if there are multiple outliers that might invalidate the assumption of normality. If the data are highly skewed, we might consider taking a sample larger than 25 so that the Central Limit Theorem is more applicable. Health care managers in hospitals, clinics, insurers, and state and federal agencies all spend significant time working with messy data just like this. In the United States, health care spending is more than one-sixth of the GDP, suggesting that one job out of every six (perhaps yours) is tied directly or indirectly to health care, so examples like this are not unusual. You need to be ready to deal with messy data.

Must the Population Be Normal?

The t distribution assumes a normal population. While this assumption is often in doubt, simulation studies have shown that confidence intervals using Student's t are reliable as long as the population is not badly skewed and if the sample size is not too small (see Chapter 8 Online Learning Center supplements for simulation demonstrations).

Using Appendix D

Beyond $d.f. = 50$, Appendix D shows $d.f.$ in steps of 5 or 10. If Appendix D does not show the exact degrees of freedom that you want, use the t-value for the *next lower d.f.* For example, if $d.f. = 54$, you would use $d.f. = 50$. Using the next lower degrees of freedom is a conservative procedure because it overestimates the margin of error. Since t-values change very slowly as $d.f.$ rises beyond $d.f. = 50$, rounding down will make little difference.

Can I Ever Use *z* Instead of *t*?

In large samples, z and t give similar results. But a conservative statistician always uses the t distribution for confidence intervals when σ is unknown because using z would underestimate the margin of error. Since t tables are easy to use (or we can get t-values from Excel), there isn't much justification for using z when σ is unknown.

Using Excel

If you have access to Excel, you don't need tables. Excel* 2010's function =T.INV.2T (probability,degrees of freedom) gives the value of $t_{\alpha/2}$, where probability is α. For example, for a 95 percent confidence interval with 60 degrees of freedom, the function =T.INV.2T(0.05,60) yields $t_{.025} = 2.000298$. So we would use 0.05 for 95 percent, 0.01 for 99 percent, etc. The output from Excel's Data Analysis > Descriptive Statistics does not give the confidence interval limits, but it does give the standard error and width of the confidence interval $t_{\alpha/2}s/\sqrt{n}$ (the oddly labeled last line in the table). Figure 8.17 shows Excel's results for sample 1 (maternity LOS).

---

*Note that previous versions of Excel used the function =TINV(probability, degrees of freedom) to calculate the value of $t_{\alpha/2}$. Please see Appendix J for a complete description of Excel functions from both 2010 and previous versions.

FIGURE 8.17

Excel's Confidence Interval for μ

Using MegaStat

If you really want to make the calculations easy, MegaStat gives you a choice of z or t, and does all the calculations for you, as illustrated in Figure 8.18 for sample 1 (maternity LOS). Notice the Preview button. If you click OK you will also see the t-value and other details.

FIGURE 8.18

MegaStat's Confidence Interval for μ

Using MINITAB

Use MINITAB's Stat > Basic Statistics > Graphical Summary to get confidence intervals, as well as a histogram and box plot. MINITAB uses the Student's t for the confidence interval for the mean. It also gives confidence intervals for the median and standard deviation. Figure 8.19 shows the MINITAB Graphical Summary for sample 1 (maternity LOS).

FIGURE 8.19

MINITAB's Confidence Interval and Graphical Summary

SECTION EXERCISES

connect

8.18   Find a confidence interval for μ assuming that each sample is from a normal population.

  a. $\bar{x} = 24$, $s = 3$, $n = 7$, 90 percent confidence
  b. $\bar{x} = 42$, $s = 6$, $n = 18$, 99 percent confidence
  c. $\bar{x} = 119$, $s = 14$, $n = 28$, 95 percent confidence

8.19   For each value of $d.f.$ (degrees of freedom), look up the value of Student's t in Appendix D for the stated level of confidence. Then use Excel to find the value of Student's t to four decimal places. Which method (Appendix D or Excel) do you prefer, and why?

  a. $d.f. = 9$, 95 percent confidence
  b. $d.f. = 15$, 98 percent confidence
  c. $d.f. = 47$, 90 percent confidence

8.20   For each value of $d.f.$ look up the value of Student's t in Appendix D for the stated level of confidence. How close is the t-value to the corresponding z-value (at the bottom of the column for $d.f. = \infty$)?

  a. $d.f. = 40$, 95 percent confidence
  b. $d.f. = 80$, 95 percent confidence
  c. $d.f. = 100$, 95 percent confidence

8.21   A random sample of 10 items is drawn from a population whose standard deviation is unknown. The sample mean is $\bar{x} = 270$ and the sample standard deviation is $s = 20$. Use Appendix D to find the values of Student's t.

  a. Construct an interval estimate for μ with 95 percent confidence.
  b. Repeat part a assuming that $n = 20$.
  c. Repeat part a assuming that $n = 40$.
  d. Describe how the confidence interval changes as n increases.

8.22   A random sample of 25 items is drawn from a population whose standard deviation is unknown. The sample mean is $\bar{x} = 850$ and the sample standard deviation is $s = 15$. Use Appendix D to find the values of Student's t.

  a. Construct an interval estimate of μ with 95 percent confidence.
  b. Repeat part a assuming that $s = 30$.
  c. Repeat part a assuming that $s = 60$.
  d. Describe how the confidence interval changes as s increases.

8.23   A sample of 21 minivan electrical warranty repairs for "loose, not attached" wires (one of several electrical failure categories the dealership mechanic can select) showed a mean repair cost of $45.66 with a standard deviation of $27.79. (a) Construct a 95 percent confidence interval for the true mean repair cost. (b) How could the confidence interval be made narrower? (Data are from a project by MBA student Tim Polulak.)

8.24   A random sample of 16 pharmacy customers showed the waiting times below (in minutes). Find a 90 percent confidence interval for μ, assuming that the sample is from a normal population. 📄 **Pharmacy**

21	22	22	17	21	17	23	20
20	24	9	22	16	21	22	21

8.25   A random sample of monthly rent paid by 12 college seniors living off campus gave the results below (in dollars). Find a 99 percent confidence interval for μ, assuming that the sample is from a normal population. 📄 **Rent1**

900	810	770	860	850	790
810	800	890	720	910	640

8.26   A random sample of 10 shipments of stick-on labels showed the following order sizes. (a) Construct a 95 percent confidence interval for the true mean order size. (b) How could the confidence interval be made narrower? (Data are from a project by MBA student Henry Olthof Jr.) 📄 **OrderSize**

12,000	18,000	30,000	60,000	14,000	10,500	52,000	14,000	15,700	19,000

8.27   Prof. Green gave three exams last semester. Scores were normally distributed on each exam. Below are scores for 10 randomly chosen students on each exam. (a) Find the 95 percent confidence interval for the mean score on each exam. (b) Do the confidence intervals overlap? What inference might you draw by comparing the three confidence intervals? 📄 **Exams2**

Exam 1: 81, 79, 88, 90, 82, 86, 80, 92, 86, 86
Exam 2: 87, 76, 81, 83, 100, 95, 93, 82, 99, 90
Exam 3: 77, 79, 74, 75, 82, 69, 74, 80, 74, 76

8.6 CONFIDENCE INTERVAL FOR A PROPORTION (π)

The Central Limit Theorem (CLT) also applies to a sample proportion, since a proportion is just a mean of data whose only values are 0 or 1. For a proportion, the CLT says that the distribution of a sample proportion $p = x/n$ tends toward normality as n increases. The distribution is centered at the population proportion π. Its standard error σ_p will decrease as n increases just as in the case of the standard error for $\bar{X}$. We say that $p = x/n$ is a *consistent* estimator of π.

Central Limit Theorem for a Proportion

As sample size increases, the distribution of the sample proportion $p = x/n$ approaches a normal distribution with mean π and standard error $\sigma_p = \sqrt{\dfrac{\pi(1 - \pi)}{n}}$.

Illustration: Internet Hotel Reservations 🖾 Hotel

Management of the Pan-Asian Hotel System tracks the percent of hotel reservations made over the Internet to adjust its advertising and web reservation system. Such data are binary: either a reservation is made on the Internet (x) or not (o). Last week (2,000 reservations) the proportion of Internet reservations was 20 percent ($\pi = .20$) as you can verify if you have the time. We can visualize the week's data like this:

LO 8-7

Construct a 90, 95, or 99 percent confidence interval for π.

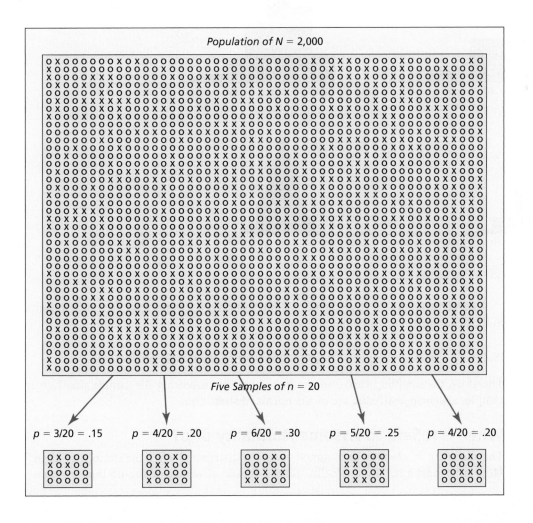

Population of N = 2,000

Five Samples of n = 20

$p = 3/20 = .15$ $p = 4/20 = .20$ $p = 6/20 = .30$ $p = 5/20 = .25$ $p = 4/20 = .20$

Five random samples of $n = 20$ hotel reservations are shown. Some sample proportions (p) are close to $\pi = .20$ while others are not, due to sampling variation. But each sample proportion p is a valid *point estimate* of the population proportion π:

$$p = \frac{x}{n} = \frac{\text{number of Internet reservations}}{\text{number of items in the sample}}$$

If we took many such samples, we could empirically study the *sampling distribution* of p. But even for a single sample, we can apply the CLT to *predict* the behavior of p. In Chapter 6, you learned that the binomial model describes the number of successes in a sample of n items from a population with constant probability of success π. A binomial distribution is symmetric if $\pi = .50$, and as n increases approaches symmetry even if $\pi \neq .50$. The same is true for the distribution of the sample proportion $p = x/n$. Figure 8.20 shows histograms of $p = x/n$ for 1,000 samples of various sizes with $\pi = .20$. For small n, the distribution is quite discrete. For example:

Sample Size	Possible Values of $p = x/n$
$n = 5$	0/5, 1/5, 2/5, 3/5, 4/5, 5/5
$n = 10$	0/10, 1/10, 2/10, 3/10, 4/10, 5/10, 6/10, 7/10, 8/10, 9/10, 10/10

As n increases, the statistic $p = x/n$ more closely resembles a continuous random variable and its distribution becomes more symmetric and bell-shaped.

FIGURE 8.20

Histograms of $p = x/n$ When $\pi = .20$ 🖥 **Hotel**

As n increases, the range of the sample proportion $p = x/n$ narrows because n appears in the denominator of the *standard error*:

(8.10) $\sigma_p = \sqrt{\dfrac{\pi(1 - \pi)}{n}}$ (standard error of the sample proportion)

Therefore, the sampling variation can be reduced by increasing the sample size. Larger samples also help justify the use of the normal distribution.

When Is It Safe to Assume Normality of *p*?

The statistic $p = x/n$ may be assumed normally distributed when the sample is "large." How large must n be? Table 8.8 illustrates a conservative rule of thumb that normality

π	n
.50	20
.40 or .60	25
.30 or .70	33
.20 or .80	50
.10 or .90	100
.05 or .95	200
.02 or .98	500
.01 or .99	1,000
.005 or .995	2,000
.002 or .998	5,000
.001 or .999	10,000

TABLE 8.8

Minimum Sample Size to Assume Normality of $p = x/n$

may be assumed whenever $n\pi \geq 10$ and $n(1 - \pi) \geq 10$. By this rule, a very large sample may be needed to assume normality of the sample proportion when π differs greatly from .50.*

Rule of Thumb

The sample proportion $p = x/n$ may be assumed normal if both $n\pi \geq 10$ and $n(1 - \pi) \geq 10$.

Standard Error of the Proportion

The **standard error of the proportion** is denoted σ_p. It depends on π, as well as on n, being largest when the population proportion is near $\pi = .50$ and becoming smaller when π is near 0 or 1. For example:

If $\pi = .50$, then for $n = 50$ $\sigma_p = \sqrt{\dfrac{\pi(1 - \pi)}{n}} = \sqrt{\dfrac{.50(1 - .50)}{50}} = \sqrt{\dfrac{.25}{50}} = .0707$

for $n = 200$ $\sigma_p = \sqrt{\dfrac{\pi(1 - \pi)}{n}} = \sqrt{\dfrac{.50(1 - .50)}{200}} = \sqrt{\dfrac{.25}{200}} = .0354$

If $\pi = .10$, then for $n = 50$ $\sigma_p = \sqrt{\dfrac{\pi(1 - \pi)}{n}} = \sqrt{\dfrac{.10(1 - .10)}{50}} = \sqrt{\dfrac{.09}{50}} = .0424$

for $n = 200$ $\sigma_p = \sqrt{\dfrac{\pi(1 - \pi)}{n}} = \sqrt{\dfrac{.10(1 - .10)}{200}} = \sqrt{\dfrac{.09}{200}} = .0212$

The formula is symmetric (i.e., $\pi = .10$ gives the same standard error as $\pi = .90$). Notice also that even if the sample size is quadrupled, the standard error is only halved. Figure 8.21 shows that as n increases, the standard error σ_p decreases, but at a slower rate.

Confidence Interval for π

By the Central Limit Theorem, we can state the probability that a sample proportion will fall within a given interval. For example, there is a 95 percent chance that p will fall within the interval $\pi \pm z_{.025}\sqrt{\dfrac{\pi(1 - \pi)}{n}}$ where $z_{.025} = 1.96$ and similarly for other values of z.

---

*A good alternative rule is to require $n > 9(1 - \pi)/\pi$ and $n > 9\pi/(1 - \pi)$. See Catherine Forbes, Merran Evans, Nicholas Hastings, and Brian Peacock, *Statistical Distributions,* 4th ed. (Wiley, 2011). Later on, we will discuss what to do when normality cannot be assumed.

FIGURE 8.21

Effect of _n_ on σ_p

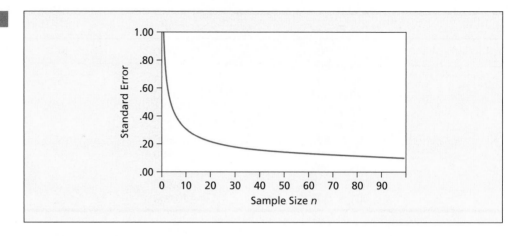

This is the basis for a confidence interval estimate of π. Replacing π with $p = x/n$ (since π is unknown) and assuming a large sample (to justify the assumption of normality) we obtain the formula for the confidence interval for π.

Confidence Interval for π

(8.11)
$$p \pm z_{\alpha/2}\sqrt{\frac{p(1-p)}{n}}$$

Table 8.9 shows $z_{\alpha/2}$ values for common confidence levels.

TABLE 8.9

Common Confidence Levels and z-Values

Confidence level	1 − α	α	α/2	$z_{\alpha/2}$
90%	.90	.10	.05	$z_{.05} = 1.645$
95%	.95	.05	.025	$z_{.025} = 1.960$
99%	.99	.01	.005	$z_{.005} = 2.576$

EXAMPLE 8.5

Auditing

A sample of 75 retail in-store purchases showed that 24 were paid in cash. We will construct a 95 percent confidence interval for the proportion of all retail in-store purchases that are paid in cash. The sample proportion is

$p = x/n = 24/75 = .32$ (proportion of in-store cash transactions)

We can assume that p is normally distributed* since np and $n(1 - p)$ exceed 10. That is, $np = (75)(.32) = 24$ and $n(1 - p) = (75)(.68) = 51$. The 95 percent confidence interval is

$$p \pm z_{\alpha/2}\sqrt{\frac{p(1-p)}{n}} \quad \text{or} \quad .32 \pm 1.960\sqrt{\frac{.32(1-.32)}{75}} \quad \text{or} \quad .32 \pm .106 \quad \text{or} \quad [.214 , .426]$$

We cannot know with certainty whether or not the true proportion lies within the interval [.214, .426]. Either it does, or it does not. And it is true that different samples could yield different intervals. But we can say that, on average, 95 percent of the intervals constructed in this way would contain the true population proportion π. Therefore, we are 95 percent confident that the true proportion π is between .214 and .426.

*When constructing a confidence interval, we use p instead of π in our rule of thumb to test whether n is large enough to assure normality because π is unknown. The test is therefore equivalent to asking if $x \geq 10$ and $n - x \geq 10$.

Narrowing the Interval?

In this example, the confidence interval is fairly wide. The width of the confidence interval for π depends on

- Sample size
- Confidence level
- Sample proportion p

We cannot do anything about p because it is calculated from the sample. If we want a narrower interval (i.e., more precision), we could either increase the sample size or reduce the confidence level (e.g., from 95 percent to 90 percent). Once the confidence level is chosen, our only choice is to increase n. Of course, larger samples are more costly (or even impossible). The next example illustrates how the width of the interval becomes narrower when using a larger sample and a lower confidence level.

> A random sample of 200 pages from the *Ameritech Pages Plus Yellow Pages* telephone directory revealed that 30 of the pages contained at least one multicolored display ad. What is the 90 percent confidence interval for the proportion of all pages with at least one multicolored display ad? The sample proportion is
>
> $$p = x/n = 30/200 = .15 \qquad \text{(proportion of pages with at least one display ad)}$$
>
> The normality test is easily met because $np = (200)(.15) = 30$ and $n(1 - p) = (200)(.85) = 170$. The 90 percent confidence interval requires $z = 1.645$:
>
> $$p \pm z_{\alpha/2}\sqrt{\frac{p(1 - p)}{n}} \quad \text{or} \quad .15 \pm 1.645\sqrt{\frac{.15(1 - .15)}{200}} \quad \text{or} \quad .15 \pm .042 \quad \text{or} \quad [.108, .192].$$
>
> We are 90 percent confident that between 10.8 percent and 19.2 percent of the pages have multicolor display ads. This confidence interval is narrower than the previous example because the sample size is larger, this sample proportion is farther from .5, and the confidence level is lower.
>
> To illustrate the trade-off between *confidence* and *precision* (the interval half-width), here are some alternatives that could have been used in the display ad example:
>
> | Confidence Level | z | Interval Width |
> |---|---|---|
> | 90% | $z = 1.645$ | $.15 \pm .042$ |
> | 95% | $z = 1.960$ | $.15 \pm .049$ |
> | 99% | $z = 2.576$ | $.15 \pm .065$ |

EXAMPLE 8.6

Display Ads

Using Excel and MegaStat

Excel's Data Analysis does not offer a confidence interval for a proportion, presumably because the calculations are easy. For example:

```
=0.15–NORM.S.INV(.95)*SQRT(0.15*(1-0.15)/200) = .108   for the lower 90% confidence limit
=0.15+NORM.S.INV(.95)*SQRT(0.15*(1-0.15)/200) = .192   for the upper 90% confidence limit
```

MegaStat does offer a confidence interval for a proportion, as shown in Figure 8.22. You only need to enter p and n. A convenient feature is that, if you enter p larger than 1, MegaStat assumes that it is the x-value in $p = x/n$ so you don't even have to calculate p. Click the Preview button to see the confidence interval. This example verifies the Ameritech calculations shown previously (click OK for additional details). MegaStat always assumes normality, even when it is not justified, so you need to check this assumption for yourself.

FIGURE 8.22

MegaStat's 90 Percent Confidence Interval for π

Small Samples: MINITAB

If the sample is small (i.e., if we cannot meet the requirement that $n\pi \geq 10$ and $n(1 - \pi) \geq 10$), the distribution of p may not be well approximated by the normal. Instead of assuming a continuous normal model, confidence limits around p can be constructed by using the binomial distribution. MINITAB uses this method by default, since it works for any n (you have to press the Options button to assume normality). Although the underlying calculations are a bit complex, MINITAB does all the work and the resulting interval is correct for any n and p.

FIGURE 8.23

Minitab's 95 Percent Confidence Interval for π

For example, in a sample of 14 purchasers of the 2011 movie *Thor* DVD, 11 watched only the film and never even looked at the "extras." The sample proportion is $p = 11/14$. What is the 95 percent confidence interval for the proportion of purchasers who never viewed the "extras"? We have $np = 11$, but $n(1 - p) = 3$, which is less than 10, so we should not assume normality. Figure 8.23 shows a sample of MINITAB's confidence interval using the binomial distribution with Stat > Basic Statistics > One Proportion. MINITAB's binomial confidence interval [.492, .953] is quite different from the normal confidence interval [.571, 1.000]. MINITAB includes a warning about the normal confidence interval.

Polls and Margin of Error

In polls and survey research, the margin of error is typically based on a 95 percent confidence level and the initial assumption that $\pi = .50$. This is a conservative assumption since σ_p is at its maximum when $\pi = .50$. Table 8.10 shows the margin of error for various sample sizes. The law of diminishing returns is apparent. Greater accuracy is possible, but each reduction in the margin of error requires a disproportionately larger sample size.

TABLE 8.10

Margin of Error for 95 Percent Confidence Interval Assuming $\pi = .50$

$n = 100$	$n = 200$	$n = 400$	$n = 800$	$n = 1,200$	$n = 1,600$
±9.8%	±6.9%	±4.9%	±3.5%	±2.8%	±2.5%

> A hotly contested race for a Colorado senate seat took place in November 2010 between Michael Bennet and Ken Buck. A poll by Public Policy Polling on November 1, 2010, showed Buck leading Bennet 49 percent to 48 percent. The sample size was 1,059 likely adult voters, and the reported accuracy was ±3 percent. On the same day, a FOX News poll, conducted by Pulse Opinion Research, showed Buck leading Bennet 50 percent to 46 percent, based on 1,000 likely voters, with a reported accuracy of ±3 percent. These are typical sample sizes for opinion polls on major issues such as state and national elections, foreign policy, or a Supreme Court decision. Tracking polls do vary, but if several different independent polls show the same candidate ahead, and if the margin is stable over time, they usually get it right. In this case, the margins of error for both polls made the outcome too close to call before all votes were tallied. Bennet ended up winning with 48 percent of the vote while Buck garnered 47 percent of the vote.
>
> The margin of error is sometimes referred to as the *sample accuracy*. Popular media sometimes use statistical terminology loosely, but the idea is the same. Statewide political polls, such as a gubernatorial race, typically have 800 respondents (margin of error ±3.5 percent) while a mayoral or local political poll might have 400 respondents (margin of error ±4.9 percent). Private market research or customer mail surveys may rely on even smaller samples, while Internet surveys can yield very large samples. In spite of the large samples possible from an Internet survey, it is important to consider *nonresponse bias* (see Chapter 2).

EXAMPLE 8.7

Election Polls

Rule of Three

A useful quick rule is the *Rule of Three*. If in *n* independent trials no events occur, the upper 95 percent confidence bound is approximately $3/n$. For example, if no medical complications arise in 17 prenatal fetal surgeries, the upper bound on such complications is roughly $3/17 = .18$, or about 18 percent. This rule is sometimes used by health care practitioners when limited data are available. This rule is especially useful because the formula for the standard error σ_p breaks down when $p = 0$. The rule of three is a conservative approach with an interesting history.*

Proportions Are Important in Business

Proportions are easy to work with, and they occur frequently in business (most often expressed as percents). In many ways, estimating π is simpler than estimating μ because you are just counting things. Using surveys, businesses study many aspects of their customers' satisfaction to determine where they are doing well and where they need to improve. Of particular importance is the proportion of customers who say they are extremely likely to recommend the company to a friend or colleague. The higher this percentage is, the larger the group of "promoters" a company has among its customers.

8.28 Calculate the standard error of the sample proportion.

    a. $n = 30, \pi = .50$ b. $n = 50, \pi = .20$ c. $n = 100, \pi = .10$ d. $n = 500, \pi = .005$

8.29 Should *p* be assumed normal?

    a. $n = 25, \pi = .50$ b. $n = 60, \pi = .20$ c. $n = 100, \pi = .08$

8.30 Find the margin of error for a poll, assuming that $\pi = .50$.

    a. $n = 50$ b. $n = 200$ c. $n = 500$ d. $n = 2,000$

8.31 A car dealer is taking a customer satisfaction survey. Find the margin of error (i.e., assuming 95% confidence and $\pi = .50$) for (a) 250 respondents, (b) 125 respondents, and (c) 65 respondents.

SECTION EXERCISES

connect

---

*For further details, see B. D. Jovanovic and P. S. Levy, "A Look at the Rule of Three," *The American Statistician* 51, no. 2 (May 1997), pp. 137–139.

8.32 In a sample of 500 new websites registered on the Internet, 24 were anonymous (i.e., they shielded their name and contact information). (a) Construct a 95 percent confidence interval for the proportion of all new websites that were anonymous. (b) May normality of p be assumed? Explain.

8.33 From a list of stock mutual funds, 52 funds were selected at random. Of the funds chosen, it was found that 19 required a minimum initial investment under $1,000. (a) Construct a 90 percent confidence interval for the true proportion requiring an initial investment under $1,000. (b) May normality of p be assumed? Explain.

8.34 Of 43 bank customers depositing a check, 18 received some cash back. (a) Construct a 90 percent confidence interval for the proportion of all depositors who ask for cash back. (b) Check the normality assumption of p.

8.35 A survey showed that 4.8 percent of the 250 Americans surveyed had suffered some kind of identity theft in the past 12 months. (a) Construct a 99 percent confidence interval for the true proportion of Americans who had suffered identity theft in the past 12 months. (b) May normality of p be assumed? Explain.

8.36 A sample of 50 homes in a subdivision revealed that 24 were ranch style (as opposed to colonial, tri-level, or Cape Cod). (a) Construct a 95 percent confidence interval for the true proportion of ranch style homes. (b) Check the normality assumption of p.

8.37 In a grocery parking lot, 32 of 136 cars selected at random were white. (a) Construct a 99 percent confidence interval for the true proportion of white cars. (b) May normality of p be assumed? Explain.

Mini Case 8.1

Airline Water Quality

Is the water on your airline flight safe to drink? It isn't feasible to analyze the water on every flight, so sampling is necessary. In August and September 2004, the Environmental Protection Agency (EPA) found bacterial contamination in water samples from the lavatories and galley water taps on 20 of 158 randomly selected U.S. flights (12.7 percent of the flights). Alarmed by the data, the EPA ordered sanitation improvements and then tested water samples again in November and December 2004. In the second sample, bacterial contamination was found in 29 of 169 randomly sampled flights (17.2 percent of the flights).

Aug./Sep. sample: $p = 20/158 = .12658$, or 12.7% contaminated

Nov./Dec. sample: $p = 29/169 = .17160$, or 17.2% contaminated

Is the problem getting worse instead of better? From these samples, we can construct confidence intervals for the true proportion of flights with contaminated water. We begin with the 95 percent confidence interval for π based on the August/September water sample:

$$p \pm z_{\alpha/2}\sqrt{\frac{p(1-p)}{n}} \text{ or } .12658 \pm 1.96\sqrt{\frac{.12658(1-.12658)}{158}}$$

$$\text{or } .12658 \pm .05185, \text{ or } 7.5\% \text{ to } 17.8\%$$

Next we determine the 95 percent confidence interval for π based on the November/December water sample:

$$p \pm z_{\alpha/2}\sqrt{\frac{p(1-p)}{n}} = .17160 \pm 1.96\sqrt{\frac{.17160(1-.17160)}{169}}$$

$$= .17160 \pm .05684, \text{ or } 11.5\% \text{ to } 22.8\%$$

Although the sample percentage (a point estimate of π) did rise, the margin of error is a little over 5 percent in each sample. Since the confidence intervals overlap, we cannot rule out the possibility that there has been no change in water contamination on airline flights; that is, the difference could be due to sampling variation. Nonetheless, the EPA is taking further steps to encourage airlines to improve water quality.

The Wall Street Journal, November 10, 2004, and January 20, 2005.

8.7 ESTIMATING FROM FINITE POPULATIONS

In Chapter 2 we discussed infinite and finite populations and the implication of a finite population when sampling without replacement. If the sample size n is less than 5 percent of the population, and we are sampling without replacement, then we consider the size of the population to be effectively infinite. However, on occasion we will take samples without replacement where n is greater than 5 percent of the population. When this happens, our margin of error on the interval estimate is actually less than when the sample size is "small" relative to the population size. As we sample more of the population, we get more precise estimates. We need to account for the fact that we are sampling a larger percentage of the population.

The **finite population correction factor** (FPCF) $\sqrt{\frac{N-n}{N-1}}$ reduces the margin of error and provides a more precise interval estimate, shown in formulas 8.12–8.15 in the box below. The FPCF can be omitted when the population is infinite (e.g., sampling from an ongoing production process) or effectively infinite (population at least 20 times as large as the sample, i.e., $n/N < .05$). When $n/N < .05$, the FPCF is almost equal to 1, so it will have a negligible effect on the confidence interval. See Chapters 2 and 6 for further discussion of finite populations.

Confidence Intervals for Finite Populations

$$\bar{x} \pm z_{\alpha/2} \frac{\sigma}{\sqrt{n}} \sqrt{\frac{N-n}{N-1}} \qquad \text{estimating } \mu \text{ with known } \sigma \qquad (8.12)$$

$$\bar{x} \pm t_{\alpha/2} \frac{s}{\sqrt{n}} \sqrt{\frac{N-n}{N-1}} \qquad \text{estimating } \mu \text{ with unknown } \sigma \qquad (8.13)$$

$$p \pm z_{\alpha/2} \sqrt{\frac{p(1-p)}{n}} \sqrt{\frac{N-n}{N-1}} \qquad \text{estimating } \pi \qquad (8.14)$$

where

$$\sqrt{\frac{N-n}{N-1}} \quad \text{is the finite population correction factor (FPCF)} \qquad (8.15)$$

> **LO 8-8**
>
> Construct confidence intervals for finite populations.

Consider a population of 1,000 employees at an organization. The human resources department sent a survey to a sample of employees to estimate the average number of hours per week employees use the company's onsite exercise facility. The sample results showed an $\bar{x} = 3.5$ hours with an $s = 0.75$ hour. If they randomly surveyed 75 employees, the FPCF would be

$$\sqrt{\frac{N-n}{N-1}} = \sqrt{\frac{1,000-75}{1,000-1}} = \sqrt{.9259} = .9623$$

The 95 percent confidence interval estimate, with $t_{.025} = 1.993$ (*d.f.* = 74), would be

$$\bar{x} \pm t_{\alpha/2} \sqrt{\frac{N-n}{N-1}} \frac{s}{\sqrt{n}} \quad \text{or} \quad 3.5 \pm 1.993(.9623)\left(\frac{0.75}{\sqrt{75}}\right) \quad \text{or} \quad 3.5 \pm 0.166$$

If, however, they had sampled 200 employees, the FPCF would be

$$\sqrt{\frac{N-n}{N-1}} = \sqrt{\frac{1{,}000-200}{1{,}000-1}} = \sqrt{.8008} = .8949$$

The 95 percent confidence interval estimate, with $t_{.025} = 1.972$ ($d.f. = 199$), would be

$$\bar{x} \pm t_{\alpha/2} \sqrt{\frac{N-n}{N-1}} \frac{s}{\sqrt{n}} \quad \text{or} \quad 3.5 \pm 1.972(.8949)\left(\frac{0.75}{\sqrt{200}}\right) \quad \text{or} \quad 3.5 \pm 0.094$$

The sample of 200 gives a more precise estimate for the population.

SECTION EXERCISES

connect

8.38   Calculate the FPCF for each sample and population size. Can the population be considered effectively infinite in each case?
a. $N = 450$, $n = 10$
b. $N = 300$, $n = 25$
c. $N = 1800$, $n = 280$

8.39   Use the following information—$\bar{x} = 50$, $\sigma = 15$, $n = 90$, $N = 1{,}000$—to calculate confidence intervals for μ assuming the sample is from a normal population: (a) 90 percent confidence; (b) 95 percent confidence; (c) 99 percent confidence.

8.40   Use the following information—$\bar{x} = 3.7$, $s = 0.2$, $n = 1{,}200$, $N = 5{,}800$—to calculate confidence intervals for μ assuming the sample is from a normal population: (a) 90 percent confidence; (b) 95 percent confidence; (c) 99 percent confidence.

8.41   A random survey of 500 students was conducted from a population of 2,300 students to estimate the proportion who had part-time jobs. The sample showed that 245 had part-time jobs. Calculate the 90 percent confidence interval for the true proportion of students who had part-time jobs.

8.8 SAMPLE SIZE DETERMINATION FOR A MEAN

Sample Size to Estimate μ

LO 8-9

Calculate sample size to estimate a mean or proportion.

Suppose we wish to estimate a population mean with a maximum allowable margin of error of $\pm E$. What sample size is required? We start with the general form of the confidence interval:

General Form	*What We Want*
$\bar{x} \pm z \dfrac{\sigma}{\sqrt{n}}$	$\bar{x} \pm E$

In this confidence interval, we use z instead of t because we are going to solve for n, and degrees of freedom cannot be determined unless we know n. Equating the maximum error E to half of the confidence interval width and solving for n,

$$E = z\frac{\sigma}{\sqrt{n}} \quad \rightarrow \quad E^2 = z^2\frac{\sigma^2}{n} \quad \rightarrow \quad n = z^2\frac{\sigma^2}{E^2}$$

Thus, the formula for the sample size can be written:

(8.16) $$n = \left(\frac{z\sigma}{E}\right)^2 \quad \text{(sample size to estimate } \mu\text{)}$$

Always round n to the next higher integer to be conservative.

A Myth

Many people believe that when the population is large, you need a larger sample to obtain a given level of precision in the estimate. This is incorrect. For a given level of precision, it is only the sample size that matters, even if the population is a million or a billion. This is apparent from the confidence interval formula, which includes n but not N.

How to Estimate σ?

We can plug our desired precision E and the appropriate z for the desired confidence level into formula 8.11. However, σ poses a problem since it is usually unknown. Table 8.11 shows several ways to approximate the value of σ. You can always try more than one method and see how much difference it makes. But until you take the sample, you will not know for sure if you have achieved your goal (i.e., the desired precision E).

TABLE 8.11

Four Ways to Estimate σ

Method 1: Take a Preliminary Sample
Take a small preliminary sample and use the sample estimate s in place of σ. This method is the most common, though its logic is somewhat circular (i.e., take a sample to plan a sample).

Method 2: Assume Uniform Population
Estimate upper and lower limits a and b and set $\sigma = [(b - a)^2/12]^{1/2}$. For example, we might guess the weight of a light-duty truck to range from 1,500 pounds to 3,500 pounds, implying a standard deviation of $\sigma = [(3,500 - 1,500)^2/12]^{1/2} = 577$ pounds. Since a uniform distribution has no central tendency, the actual σ is probably smaller than our guess, so we get a larger n than necessary (a conservative result).

Method 3: Assume Normal Population
Estimate upper and lower bounds a and b, and set $\sigma = (b - a)/6$. This assumes normality with most of the data within $\mu + 3\sigma$ and $\mu - 3\sigma$ so the range is 6σ. For example, we might guess the weight of a light truck to range from 1,500 pounds to 3,500 pounds, implying $\sigma = (3,500 - 1,500)/6 = 333$ pounds. This estimate of σ is based on the Empirical Rule. Recent research suggests that this method may not be conservative enough (see Related Reading).

Method 4: Poisson Arrivals
In the special case when λ is a Poisson arrival rate, then $\sigma = \sqrt{\lambda}$. For example, if you think the arrival rate is about 20 customers per hour, then you would estimate $\sigma = \sqrt{20} = 4.47$.

EXAMPLE 8.8

Onion Weight

A produce manager wants to estimate the mean weight of Spanish onions being delivered by a supplier, with 95 percent confidence and an error of ± 1 ounce. A preliminary sample of 12 onions shows a sample standard deviation of 3.60 ounces. For a 95 percent confidence interval, we will set $z = 1.96$. We use $s = 3.60$ in place of σ and set the desired error $E = 1$ to obtain the required sample size:

$$n = [(1.96)(3.60)/(1)]^2 = 49.79, \text{ or } 50 \text{ onions}$$

We would round to the next higher integer and take a sample of 50 Spanish onions. This should ensure an estimate of the true mean weight with an error not exceeding ± 1 ounce.

A seemingly modest change in E can have a major effect on the sample size because E is squared. Suppose we reduce the maximum error to $E = 0.5$ ounce to obtain a more precise estimate. The required sample size would then be

$$n = [(1.96)(3.60)/(0.5)]^2 = 199.1, \text{ or } 200 \text{ onions}$$

Using MegaStat

There is also a sample size calculator in MegaStat, as illustrated in Figure 8.24. The Preview button lets you change the setup and see the result immediately.

Practical Advice

When estimating a mean, the maximum error E is expressed in the same units as X and σ. For example, E would be expressed in dollars when estimating the mean order size for mail-order customers (e.g., $E = \$2$) or in minutes to estimate the mean wait time for patients at a clinic (e.g., $E = 10$ minutes). To estimate last year's starting salaries for MBA graduates from a university, the maximum error could be large (e.g., $E = \$2,000$) because a $2,000 error in estimating μ might still be a reasonably accurate estimate.

Using z in the sample size formula for a mean is necessary but not conservative. Because t always exceeds z for a given confidence level, your actual interval may be wider than $\pm E$ as intended. As long as the required sample size is large (say 30 or more), the difference will be acceptable.

The sample size formulas for a mean are not conservative, that is, they tend to underestimate the required sample size (see Kupper and Hafner article in the end-of-chapter references). Therefore, the sample size formulas for a mean should be regarded only as a minimum guideline. Whenever possible, samples should exceed this minimum.

If you are sampling a finite population without replacement and your required sample size (n) exceeds 5 percent of the population size (N), you can adjust the sample size by using $n' = \frac{nN}{n + (N - 1)}$. This adjustment allows you to meet the desired confidence level with a smaller sample and will also guarantee that the sample size never exceeds the population size. See *LearningStats* for details.

SECTION EXERCISES

connect

8.42 For each level of precision, find the required sample size to estimate the mean starting salary for a new CPA with 95 percent confidence, assuming a population standard deviation of $7,500 (same as last year).

    a. $E = \$2,000$ b. $E = \$1,000$ c. $E = \$500$

8.43 Last year, a study showed that the average ATM cash withdrawal took 65 seconds with a standard deviation of 10 seconds. The study is to be repeated this year. How large a sample would be needed to estimate this year's mean with 95 percent confidence and an error of ± 4 seconds?

8.44 The EPA city/hwy mpg range for a Saturn Vue FWD automatic 5-speed transmission is 20 to 28 mpg. (a) Estimate σ using Method 3 from Table 8.11. (b) If you owned this vehicle, how large a sample (e.g., how many tanks of gas) would be required to estimate your mean mpg with an error of ± 1 mpg and 90 percent confidence? (Source: www.fueleconomy.gov.).

8.45 Popcorn kernels are believed to take between 100 and 200 seconds to pop in a certain microwave. (a) Estimate σ using Method 3 from Table 8.11. (b) What sample size (number of kernels) would be needed to estimate the true mean seconds to pop with an error of ± 5 seconds and 95 percent confidence?

8.46 Analysis showed that the mean arrival rate for vehicles at a certain Shell station on Friday afternoon last year was 4.5 vehicles per minute. How large a sample would be needed to estimate this year's mean arrival rate with 98 percent confidence and an error of ± 0.5?

8.47 Noodles & Company wants to estimate the mean spending per customer at a certain restaurant with 95 percent confidence and an error of $\pm \$0.25$. What is the required sample size, assuming a standard deviation of $2.50 (based on similar restaurants elsewhere)?

8.48 In an intra-squad swim competition, men's freestyle 100 swim times at a certain university ranged from 43.89 seconds to 51.96 seconds. (a) Estimate the standard deviation using Method 3 (the Empirical Rule for a normal distribution). (b) What sample size is needed to estimate the mean for all swimmers with 95 percent confidence and an error of ± 0.50 second?

8.49 The city fuel economy of a 2009 Toyota 4Runner 2WD 6 cylinder 4 L automatic 5-speed using regular gas is a normally distributed random variable with a range 16 MPG to 21 MPG. (a) Estimate the standard deviation using Method 3 (the Empirical Rule for a normal distribution). (b) What sample size is needed to estimate the mean with 90 percent confidence and an error of ± 0.25 MPG? (Source: www.fueleconomy.gov.)

8.9 SAMPLE SIZE DETERMINATION FOR A PROPORTION

Suppose we wish to estimate a population proportion with a precision (maximum error) of $\pm E$. What sample size is required? We start with the general form of the confidence interval:

LO 8-9

Calculate sample size to estimate a mean or proportion.

General Form   *What We Want*

$$p \pm z\sqrt{\frac{\pi(1-\pi)}{n}} \qquad\qquad p \pm E$$

We equate the maximum error E to half of the confidence interval width and solve for n:

$$E = z\sqrt{\frac{\pi(1-\pi)}{n}} \quad \rightarrow \quad E^2 = z^2\frac{\pi(1-\pi)}{n} \quad \rightarrow \quad n = z^2\frac{\pi(1-\pi)}{E^2}$$

Thus, the formula for the sample size for a proportion can be written:

$$n = \left(\frac{z}{E}\right)^2 \pi(1-\pi) \qquad \text{(sample size to estimate } \pi\text{)} \qquad\qquad \textbf{(8.17)}$$

Always round n to the next higher integer.

Because a proportion is a number between 0 and 1, the maximum error E is also between 0 and 1. For example, if we want an error of ± 7 percent, we would specify $E = 0.07$.

Because π is unknown (that's why we are taking the sample) we need to make an assumption about π to plan our sample size. If we have a prior estimate of π (e.g., from last year or a comparable application), we can plug p into the formula. Or we could take a small preliminary sample to obtain an initial value of p. Some experts recommend using $\pi = .50$ because the resulting sample size will guarantee the desired precision for any π. However, this conservative assumption may lead to a larger sample than necessary because π is not always equal to .5. Sampling costs money, so if a prior estimate of π is available, it might be advisable to use it, especially if you think that π differs greatly from .50. For example, in estimating the proportion of home equity loans that result in default, we would expect π to be much smaller than .50, while in estimating the proportion of motorists who use seat belts, we would hope that π would be much larger than .50. Table 8.12 details three ways to estimate π.

TABLE 8.12

Three Ways to Estimate π

Method 1: Assume That $\pi = .50$
This method is conservative and ensures the desired precision. It is therefore a sound choice and is often used. However, the sample may end up being larger than necessary.

Method 2: Take a Preliminary Sample
Take a small preliminary sample and insert p into the sample size formula in place of π. This method is appropriate if π is believed to differ greatly from .50, as is often the case, though its logic is somewhat circular (i.e., we must take a sample to plan our sample).

Method 3: Use a Prior Sample or Historical Data
A reasonable approach, but how often are such data available? And might π have changed enough to make it a questionable assumption?

EXAMPLE 8.9

ATM Withdrawals

A university credit union wants to know the proportion of cash withdrawals that exceed \$50 at its ATM located in the student union building. With an error of ± 2 percent and a confidence level of 95 percent, how large a sample is needed to estimate the proportion of withdrawals exceeding \$50? The z-value for 95 percent confidence is $z = 1.960$. Using $E = 0.02$ and assuming conservatively that $\pi = .50$, the required sample size is

$$n = \left(\frac{z}{E}\right)^2 \pi(1 - \pi) = \left(\frac{1.960}{0.02}\right)^2(.50)(1 - .50) = 2,401$$

We would need to examine $n = 2,401$ withdrawals to estimate π within ± 2 percent and with 95 percent confidence. In this case, last year's proportion of ATM withdrawals over \$50 was 27 percent. If we had used this estimate in our calculation, the required sample size would be

$$n = \left(\frac{z}{E}\right)^2 p(1 - p) = \left(\frac{1.960}{0.02}\right)^2(.27)(1 - .27) = 1,893 \quad \text{(rounded to next higher integer)}$$

We would need to examine $n = 1,893$ withdrawals to estimate π within ± 0.02. The required sample size is smaller than when we make the conservative assumption $\pi = .50$.

Alternatives

Suppose that our research budget will not permit a large sample. In the previous example, we could reduce the confidence interval level from 95 to 90 percent and increase the maximum error to ± 4 percent. Assuming $\pi = .50$, the required sample size is

$$n = \left(\frac{z}{E}\right)^2 \pi(1 - \pi) = \left(\frac{1.645}{0.04}\right)^2(.50)(1 - .50) = 423 \quad \text{(rounded to next higher integer)}$$

These seemingly modest changes make a huge difference in the sample size.

Practical Advice

Choosing a sample size is a common problem. Clients who take samples are constrained by time and money. Naturally, they prefer the highest possible confidence level and the lowest possible error. But when a statistical consultant shows them the required sample size, they may find it infeasible. A better way to look at it is that the formula for sample size provides a structure for a dialogue between statistician and client. A good consultant can propose several possible confidence levels and errors, and let the client choose the combination that best balances the need for accuracy against the available time and budget. The statistician can offer advice about these trade-offs, so the client's objectives are met. Other issues include nonresponse rates, dropout rates from ongoing studies, and possibly incorrect assumptions used in the calculation.

A common error is to insert $E = 2$ in the formula when you want an error of ± 2 percent. Because we are dealing with a *proportion*, a 2% error is $E = 0.02$. In other words, when estimating a proportion, E is always between 0 and 1.

8.50 What sample size would be required to estimate the true proportion of American female business executives who prefer the title "Ms.," with an error of ± 0.025 and 98 percent confidence?

8.51 What sample size would be needed to estimate the true proportion of American households that own more than one DVD player, with 90 percent confidence and an error of ± 0.02?

8.52 What sample size would be needed to estimate the true proportion of students at your college (if you are a student) who are wearing backpacks, with 95 percent confidence and an error of ± 0.04?

8.53 What sample size would be needed to estimate the true proportion of American adults who know their cholesterol level, using 95 percent confidence and an error of ± 0.02?

8.54 How large a sample size would be needed to estimate the percentage of wireless routers in San Francisco that use data encryption, with an error of ± 2 percent and 95 percent confidence?

8.55 Inspection of a random sample of 19 aircraft showed that 15 needed repairs to fix a wiring problem that might compromise safety. How large a sample would be needed to estimate the true proportion of jets with the wiring problem, with 90 percent confidence and an error of ± 6 percent?

8.10 CONFIDENCE INTERVAL FOR A POPULATION VARIANCE, σ^2 (OPTIONAL)

Chi-Square Distribution

In our previous discussions of means and differences in means, we have indicated that many times we do not know the population variance, σ^2. A variance estimate can be useful information for many business applications. If the population is normal, we can construct a confidence interval for the population variance σ^2 using the **chi-square distribution** (the Greek letter χ is pronounced "kye") with degrees of freedom equal to $d.f. = n - 1$. Lower-tail and upper-tail percentiles for the chi-square distribution (denoted χ_L^2 and χ_U^2, respectively) can be found in Appendix E. Alternatively, we can use the Excel functions =CHISQ.INV($\alpha/2$,df) and =CHISQ.INV.RT($\alpha/2$,df) to find χ_L^2 and χ_U^2, respectively. Using the sample variance s^2, the confidence interval is

$$\frac{(n-1)s^2}{\chi_U^2} \le \sigma^2 \le \frac{(n-1)s^2}{\chi_L^2} \qquad \text{(confidence interval for } \sigma^2 \text{ from sample variance } s^2) \qquad \textbf{(8.18)}$$

> **LO 8-10**
>
> Construct a confidence interval for a variance (optional).

> **EXAMPLE 8.10**
>
> *Pizza Delivery*
> 📁 **PIZZA**

On a particular Friday night, the charges for 40 pizza delivery orders from Mama Frida's Pizza showed a mean of $\bar{x} = 24.76$ with a sample variance $s^2 = 12.77$.

29.51	21.09	29.98	29.95	21.07	29.52	21.07	24.95	21.07	24.95
24.98	29.95	24.95	21.07	25.30	25.30	29.95	29.99	29.95	24.95
24.95	21.07	24.98	21.09	21.07	24.98	21.07	25.30	29.95	25.30
25.30	24.98	16.86	25.30	25.30	16.86	24.95	24.98	25.30	21.07

The sample data were nearly symmetric (median $24.98) with no outliers. Normality of the prices will be assumed. From Appendix E, using 39 degrees of freedom ($d.f. = n - 1 = 40 - 1 = 39$) we obtain bounds for the 95 percent middle area, as illustrated in Figures 8.25 and 8.26.

$\chi_L^2 = 23.65$ (lower 2.5 percent)   or χ_L^2 =CHISQ.INV(.025,39)

$\chi_U^2 = 58.12$ (upper 2.5 percent)   or χ_U^2 =CHISQ.INV.RT(.025,39)

The 95 percent confidence interval for the population variance σ^2 is

Lower bound: $\dfrac{(n-1)s^2}{\chi_U^2} = \dfrac{(40-1)(12.77)}{58.12} = 8.569$

Upper bound: $\dfrac{(n-1)s^2}{\chi_L^2} = \dfrac{(40-1)(12.77)}{23.65} = 21.058$

With 95 percent confidence, we believe that $8.569 \le \sigma^2 \le 21.058$.

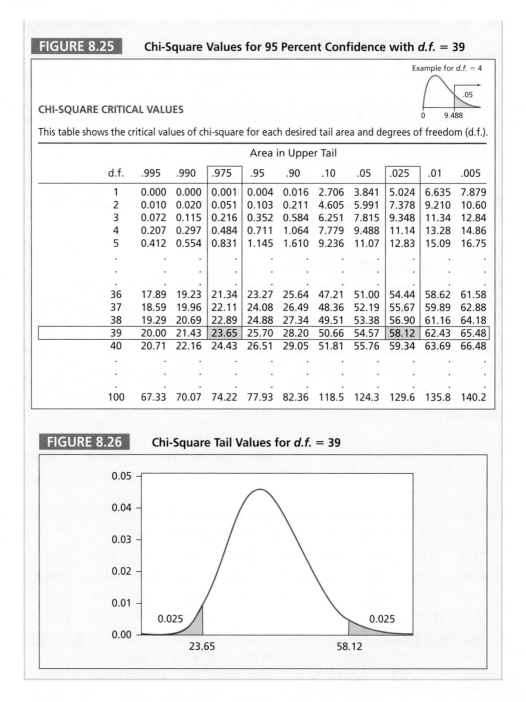

FIGURE 8.25 Chi-Square Values for 95 Percent Confidence with *d.f.* = 39

Example for *d.f.* = 4

.05

0   9.488

CHI-SQUARE CRITICAL VALUES

This table shows the critical values of chi-square for each desired tail area and degrees of freedom (d.f.).

					Area in Upper Tail					
d.f.	.995	.990	.975	.95	.90	.10	.05	.025	.01	.005
1	0.000	0.000	0.001	0.004	0.016	2.706	3.841	5.024	6.635	7.879
2	0.010	0.020	0.051	0.103	0.211	4.605	5.991	7.378	9.210	10.60
3	0.072	0.115	0.216	0.352	0.584	6.251	7.815	9.348	11.34	12.84
4	0.207	0.297	0.484	0.711	1.064	7.779	9.488	11.14	13.28	14.86
5	0.412	0.554	0.831	1.145	1.610	9.236	11.07	12.83	15.09	16.75
·	·	·	·	·	·	·	·	·	·	·
36	17.89	19.23	21.34	23.27	25.64	47.21	51.00	54.44	58.62	61.58
37	18.59	19.96	22.11	24.08	26.49	48.36	52.19	55.67	59.89	62.88
38	19.29	20.69	22.89	24.88	27.34	49.51	53.38	56.90	61.16	64.18
39	20.00	21.43	23.65	25.70	28.20	50.66	54.57	58.12	62.43	65.48
40	20.71	22.16	24.43	26.51	29.05	51.81	55.76	59.34	63.69	66.48
·	·	·	·	·	·	·	·	·	·	·
100	67.33	70.07	74.22	77.93	82.36	118.5	124.3	129.6	135.8	140.2

FIGURE 8.26 Chi-Square Tail Values for *d.f.* = 39

0.025   0.025
23.65   58.12

Confidence Interval for σ

If you want a confidence interval for the standard deviation, just take the square root of the interval bounds. In the pizza delivery example, we get $2.93 \le \sigma \le 4.59$. If you have raw data, MINITAB's Stat > Basic Statistics > Graphical Summary gives nice confidence intervals for the mean, median, and standard deviation for a column of raw data, as well as a histogram and box plot. MINITAB uses Student's *t* for the confidence interval for the mean and calculates the confidence interval for σ, as illustrated in Figure 8.27.

Caution: Assumption of Normality

The methods just described for confidence interval estimation of the variance and standard deviation are highly dependent on the population having a normal distribution. There is not a CLT that can be used for the statistic s^2. If the population does not have a

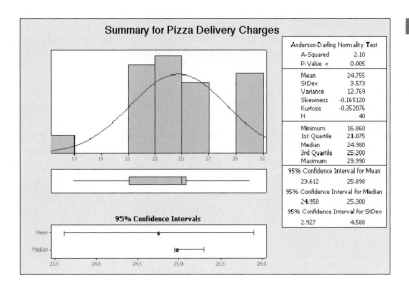

FIGURE 8.27

MINITAB's Confidence Intervals

normal distribution, then the confidence interval for the variance should not be considered accurate.

8.56 Find the 95 percent confidence interval for the population variance from these samples.

   a. $n = 15$ commuters, $s = 10$ miles driven
   b. $n = 18$ students, $s = 12$ study hours

SECTION EXERCISES

connect

8.57 The weights of 20 oranges (in ounces) are shown below. Construct a 95 percent confidence interval for the population standard deviation. *Note:* Scale was only accurate to the nearest ¼ ounce. (Data are from a project by statistics student Julie Gillman.) **Oranges**

5.50	6.25	6.25	6.50	6.50	7.00	7.00	7.00	7.50	7.50
7.75	8.00	8.00	8.50	8.50	9.00	9.00	9.25	10.00	10.50

8.58 A pediatrician's records showed the mean height of a random sample of 25 girls at age 12 months to be 29.530 inches with a standard deviation of 1.0953 inches. Construct a 95 percent confidence interval for the population variance. (Data are from a project by statistics students Lori Bossardet, Shannon Wegner, and Stephanie Rader.)

8.59 Find the 90 percent confidence interval for the standard deviation of gasoline mileage mpg for these 16 San Francisco commuters driving hybrid gas-electric vehicles. **Hybrid**

38.8	48.9	28.5	40.0	38.8	29.2	29.1	38.5
34.4	46.1	51.8	30.7	36.9	25.6	42.7	38.3

CHAPTER SUMMARY

An **estimator** is a sample statistic ($\bar{x}$, s, p) that is used to estimate an unknown population **parameter** (μ, σ, π). A desirable estimator is **unbiased** (correctly centered), **efficient** (minimum variance), and **consistent** (variance goes to zero as n increases). **Sampling error** (the difference between an estimator and its parameter) is inevitable, but a larger sample size yields estimates that are closer to the unknown parameter. The **Central Limit Theorem** (CLT) states that the sample mean $\bar{x}$ is centered at μ and follows a normal distribution if n is large, regardless of the population shape. A **confidence interval** for μ consists of lower and upper bounds that have a specified **confidence level** of enclosing μ. Any confidence level may be used, but 90, 95, and 99 percent are common. If the population variance is unknown, we replace z in the confidence interval formula for μ with **Student's** t using $n - 1$ degrees of freedom. The CLT also applies to the sample proportion (p) as an estimator of π, using a rule of thumb to decide if normality may be assumed. The **margin of error** is the half-width of the confidence interval. The **finite population correction factor** adjusts the margin of error to reflect better estimation precision when sample size is close to the population size. Formulas exist for the required **sample size** for a given level of precision in a confidence interval for μ or π, although they entail assumptions and are only approximate. Confidence intervals and sample sizes may be adjusted for finite populations, but often the adjustments are not material. Confidence intervals may be created for a variance using the **chi-square distribution**.

KEY TERMS

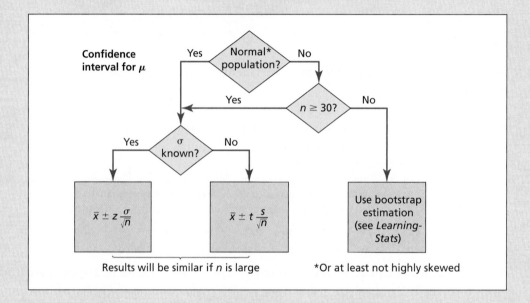

Commonly Used Formulas in Sampling Distributions and Estimation

Sample proportion: $p = \dfrac{x}{n}$

Standard error of the sample mean: $\sigma_{\bar{x}} = \dfrac{\sigma}{\sqrt{n}}$

Confidence interval for μ, known σ: $\bar{x} \pm z_{\alpha/2}\dfrac{\sigma}{\sqrt{n}}$

Confidence interval for μ, unknown σ: $\bar{x} \pm t_{\alpha/2}\dfrac{s}{\sqrt{n}}$ with $d.f. = n - 1$

Standard error of the sample proportion: $\sigma_p = \sqrt{\dfrac{\pi(1 - \pi)}{n}}$

Confidence interval for π: $p \pm z_{\alpha/2}\sqrt{\dfrac{p(1 - p)}{n}}$

Finite population correction factor (FPCF): $\sqrt{\dfrac{N - n}{N - 1}}$

Confidence interval for μ, known σ, finite population: $\bar{x} \pm z_{\alpha/2}\dfrac{\sigma}{\sqrt{n}}\sqrt{\dfrac{N - n}{N - 1}}$

Confidence interval for μ, unknown σ, finite population: $\bar{x} \pm t_{\alpha/2}\dfrac{s}{\sqrt{n}}\sqrt{\dfrac{N - n}{N - 1}}$

Confidence interval for π, finite population:

$$p \pm z_{\alpha/2} \sqrt{\frac{p(1-p)}{n}} \sqrt{\frac{N-n}{N-1}}$$

Sample size to estimate μ:

$$n = \left(\frac{z\sigma}{E}\right)^2$$

Sample size to estimate π:

$$n = \left(\frac{z}{E}\right)^2 \pi(1-\pi)$$

CHAPTER REVIEW

1. Define (a) parameter, (b) estimator, (c) sampling error, and (d) sampling distribution.

2. Explain the difference between sampling error and bias. Can they be controlled?

3. Name three estimators. Which ones are unbiased?

4. Explain what it means to say an estimator is (a) unbiased, (b) efficient, and (c) consistent.

5. State the main points of the Central Limit Theorem for a mean.

6. Why is population shape of concern when estimating a mean? What does sample size have to do with it?

7. (a) Define the standard error of the mean. (b) What happens to the standard error as sample size increases? (c) How does the law of diminishing returns apply to the standard error?

8. Define (a) point estimate, (b) margin of error, (c) confidence interval, and (d) confidence level.

9. List some common confidence levels. What happens to the margin of error as you increase the confidence level, all other things being equal?

10. List differences and similarities between Student's t and the standard normal distribution.

11. Give an example to show that (a) for a given confidence level, the Student's t confidence interval for the mean is wider than if we use a z-value; and (b) it makes little difference in a large sample whether we use Student's t or z.

12. Why do outliers and skewed populations pose a problem for estimating a sample mean?

13. (a) State the Central Limit Theorem for a proportion. (b) When is it safe to assume normality for a sample proportion?

14. (a) Define the standard error of the proportion. (b) What happens to the standard error as sample size increases? (c) Why does a larger sample improve a confidence interval?

15. When would you use the FPCF and what does it do to the margin of error?

16. (a) Why does σ pose a problem for sample size calculation for a mean? (b) How can σ be approximated when it is unknown?

17. When calculating a sample size for a proportion, why is it conservative to assume that $\pi = .50$?

18. Why would we be interested in a confidence interval for a variance? Give an example.

CHAPTER EXERCISES

Note: Explain answers and show your work clearly. Problems marked * rely on optional material from this chapter.

8.60 A random sample of 30 lunch orders at Noodles and Company showed a mean bill of $10.36 with a standard deviation of $5.31. Find the 95 percent confidence interval for the mean bill of all lunch orders. 🖼 **NoodlesOrderSize**

8.61 A random sample of 21 nickels measured with a very accurate micrometer showed a mean diameter of 0.834343 inch with a standard deviation of 0.001886 inch. (a) Why would nickel diameters vary? (b) Construct a 99 percent confidence interval for the true mean diameter of a nickel. (c) Discuss any assumptions that are needed. (d) What sample size would ensure an error of ± 0.0005 inch with 99 percent confidence? (Data are from a project by MBA student Bob Tindall.)

8.62 A random sample of 10 miniature Tootsie Rolls was taken from a bag. Each piece was weighed on a very accurate scale. The results in grams were

3.087	3.131	3.241	3.241	3.270	3.353	3.400	3.411	3.437	3.477

(a) Construct a 90 percent confidence interval for the true mean weight. (b) What sample size would be necessary to estimate the true weight with an error of ± 0.03 gram with 90 percent confidence? (Data are from a project by MBA student Henry Scussel.) 🖼 **Tootsie**

8.63 Statistics students were asked to go home and fill a 1-cup measure with raisin bran, tap the cup lightly on the counter three times to settle the contents, if necessary add more raisin bran to bring the contents exactly up to the 1-cup line, spread the contents on a large plate, and count the raisins. For the 13 students who chose Kellogg's brand, the reported results were

23	33	44	36	29	42	31	33	61	36	34	23	24

Construct a 90 percent confidence interval for the mean number of raisins per cup. Show your work clearly. 🗔 **Raisins**

8.64 A sample of 20 pages was taken without replacement from a Yellow Pages directory that has 1,591 pages. (a) Calculate the FPCF for this sample. (b) Should the population be considered effectively infinite?

8.65 Twenty-five blood samples were selected by taking every seventh blood sample from racks holding 187 blood samples from the morning draw at a medical center. (a) Calculate the FPCF for this sample. (b) Should the population be considered effectively infinite?

8.66 A sample of 20 pages was taken from a Yellow Pages directory. On each page, the mean area devoted to display ads was measured (a display ad is a large block of multicolored illustrations, maps, and text). The data (in square millimeters) are shown below:

0	260	356	403	536	0	268	369	428	536
268	396	469	536	162	338	403	536	536	130

(a) Construct a 95 percent confidence interval for the true mean. (b) What sample size would be needed to obtain an error of ± 20 square millimeters with 95 percent confidence? (Data are based on a project by MBA student Daniel R. Dalach.) 🗔 **DisplayAds**

8.67 Sixteen owners of 2010 Audi A4 sedans kept track of their average fuel economy for a month. The results are shown below. (a) Construct a 95 percent confidence interval for the mean. (b) What factor(s) limit the conclusions that can be drawn about the true mean? (Data are from www.fueleconomy.gov.) 🗔 **MPG**

20.8	20.0	19.4	19.7	21.1	22.6	18.3	20.1
20.5	19.5	17.4	22.4	18.9	20.2	19.6	19.0

8.68 Twenty-five blood samples were selected by taking every seventh blood sample from racks holding 187 blood samples from the morning draw at a medical center. The white blood count (WBC) was measured using a Coulter Counter Model S. The mean WBC was 8.636 with a standard deviation of 3.9265. (a) Construct a 90 percent confidence interval for the true mean using the FPCF. (b) What sample size would be needed for an error of ± 1.5 with 90 percent confidence? (Data are from a project by MBA student Wendy Blomquist.)

8.69 Twenty-one warranty repairs were selected from a population of 126 by selecting every sixth item. The population consisted of "loose, not attached" minivan electrical wires (one of several electrical failure categories the dealership mechanic can select). The mean repair cost was $45.664 with a standard deviation of $27.793. (a) Construct a 95 percent confidence interval for the true mean repair cost. (b) What sample size would be needed to obtain an error of $\pm\$5$ with 95 percent confidence? *(c) Construct a 95 percent confidence interval for the true standard deviation. (Data are from a project by MBA student Tim Polulak.)

8.70 Dave the jogger runs the same route every day (about 2.2 miles). On 18 consecutive days, he recorded the number of steps using a pedometer. The results were

3,450	3,363	3,228	3,360	3,304	3,407	3,324	3,365	3,290
3,289	3,346	3,252	3,237	3,210	3,140	3,220	3,103	3,129

(a) Construct a 95 percent confidence interval for the true mean number of steps Dave takes on his run. (b) What sample size would be needed to obtain an error of ± 20 steps with 95 percent confidence? (c) Using Excel, plot a line chart of the data. What do the data suggest about the pattern over time? 🗔 **DaveSteps**

8.71 A pediatrician's records showed the mean height of a random sample of 25 girls at age 12 months to be 29.530 inches with a standard deviation of 1.0953 inches. (a) Construct a 95 percent confidence interval for the true mean height. (b) What sample size would be needed for 95 percent confidence and an error of $\pm.20$ inch? (Data are from a project by statistics students Lori Bossardet, Shannon Wegner, and Stephanie Rader.)

*8.72 A random sample of 10 exam scores showed a standard deviation of 7.2 points. Find the 95 percent confidence interval for the population standard deviation. Use Appendix E to obtain the values of χ_L^2 and χ_U^2.

*8.73 A random sample of 30 lunch orders at Noodles and Company showed a standard deviation of \$5.31. Find the 90 percent confidence interval for the population standard deviation. Use Excel to obtain $\chi_L^2 =$ CHISQ.INV($\alpha/2,d.f.$) and $\chi_U^2 =$ CHISQ.INV.RT($\alpha/2,d.f.$)

8.74 During the Rose Bowl, the length (in seconds) of 12 randomly chosen commercial breaks during timeouts (following touchdown, turnover, field goal, or punt) were

| 65 | 75 | 85 | 95 | 80 | 100 | 90 | 80 | 85 | 85 | 60 | 65 |

Assuming a normal population, construct a 90 percent confidence interval for the mean length of a commercial break during the Rose Bowl. **TimeOuts**

8.75 A sample of 40 CDs from a student's collection showed a mean length of 52.74 minutes with a standard deviation of 13.21 minutes. (a) Construct a 95 percent confidence interval for the mean. (b) Why might the normality assumption be an issue here? (c) What sample size would be needed to estimate μ with 95 percent confidence and an error of ± 3 minutes? (Data are from a project by statistics students Michael Evatz, Nancy Petack, and Jennifer Skladanowski.)

8.76 The Environmental Protection Agency (EPA) requires that cities monitor over 80 contaminants in their drinking water. Samples from the Lake Huron Water Treatment Plant gave the results shown here. Only the range is reported, not the mean. For each substance, estimate the *standard deviation σ* by using one of the methods shown in Table 8.11 in Section 8.8.

Substance	MCLG Range Detected	Allowable MCLG	Origin of Substance
Chromium	0.47 to 0.69	100	Discharge from steel and pulp mills, natural erosion
Barium	0.004 to 0.019	2	Discharge from drilling wastes, metal refineries, natural erosion
Fluoride	1.07 to 1.17	4.0	Natural erosion, water additive, discharge from fertilizer and aluminum factories

MCLG = Maximum contaminant level goal

8.77 In a sample of 100 Planter's Mixed Nuts, 19 were found to be almonds. (a) Construct a 90 percent confidence interval for the true proportion of almonds. (b) May normality be assumed? Explain. (c) What sample size would be needed for 90 percent confidence and an error of ± 0.03? (d) Why would a quality control manager at Planter's need to understand sampling?

8.78 A study showed that fourteen of 180 publicly traded business services companies failed a test for compliance with Sarbanes-Oxley requirements for financial records and fraud protection. Assuming that these are a random sample of all publicly traded companies, construct a 95 percent confidence interval for the overall noncompliance proportion.

8.79 How "decaffeinated" is decaffeinated coffee? If a researcher wants to estimate the mean caffeine content of a cup of Starbucks' decaffeinated espresso with 98 percent confidence and an error of ± 0.1 mg, what is the required number of cups that must be tested? Assume a standard deviation of 0.5 mg, based on a small preliminary sample of 12 cups.

8.80 Noodles & Company wants to estimate the percent of customers who order dessert, with 95 percent confidence and an error of $\pm 10\%$. What is the required sample size?

8.81 Junior Achievement and Deloitte commissioned a "teen ethics poll" of 787 students aged 13–18, finding that 29 percent felt inadequately prepared to make ethical judgments. (a) Assuming that this was a random sample, find the 95 percent confidence interval for the true proportion of U.S. teens who feel inadequately prepared to make ethical judgments. (b) Is the sample size large enough to assume normality? (See http://ja.org/.)

8.82 A certain brand of dry noodles contains a mixture of beet, spinach, carrot, and plain. A random sample of 200 dry noodles contained 47 beet noodles. (a) Construct a 95 percent confidence interval for the true proportion of beet noodles. (b) Check the normality assumption for p. Show your work. (c) What sample size would be needed to obtain an error of ± 0.04 with 95 percent confidence?

8.83 CBS asked a sample of DVR owners to record *Late Night with David Letterman* on their DVRs. Of the 125 DVR owners surveyed, 83 either "gave up or screwed up" because they did not understand how to program the DVR. Construct a 90 percent confidence interval for the true proportion of DVR owners who cannot program their DVRs.

8.84 A survey of 4,581 U.S. households that owned a mobile phone found that 58 percent are satisfied with the coverage of their cellular phone provider. Assuming that this was a random sample, construct a 90 percent confidence interval for the true proportion of satisfied U.S. mobile phone owners.

8.85 A "teen ethics poll" was commissioned by Junior Achievement and Deloitte. The survey by Harris Interactive surveyed 787 students aged 13–18. (a) Assuming that this was a random sample of all students in this age group, find the margin of error of the poll. (b) Would the margin of error be greater or smaller for the subgroup consisting only of male students? Explain. (See http://ja.org/.)

8.86 Biting an unpopped kernel of popcorn hurts! As an experiment, a self-confessed connoisseur of cheap popcorn carefully counted 773 kernels and put them in a popper. After popping, the unpopped kernels were counted. There were 86. (a) Construct a 90 percent confidence interval for the proportion of all kernels that would not pop. (b) Check the normality assumption for p.

8.87 A sample of 213 newspaper tire ads from several Sunday papers showed that 98 contained a low-price guarantee (offer to "meet or beat any price"). (a) Assuming that this was a random sample, construct a 95 percent confidence interval for the proportion of all Sunday newspaper tire ads that contain a low-price guarantee. (b) Is the criterion for normality of p met?

8.88 A physician's billing office conducted a random check of patient records and found that 36 of 50 patients had changed insurance plans within the past year. Construct a 90 percent confidence interval for the true proportion.

8.89 Of 250 college students taking a statistics class, 4 reported an allergy to peanuts. (a) Is the criterion for normality of p met? (b) Assuming that this was a random sample, use MINITAB to construct a 95 percent confidence interval for the proportion of all college statistics students with a peanut allergy.

8.90 (a) A poll of 2,277 likely voters was conducted on the president's performance. Approximately what margin of error would the approval rating estimate have? (b) The poll showed that 44 percent approved the president's performance. Construct a 90 percent confidence interval for the true proportion. (c) Would you say that the percentage of all voters who approve of the president's performance could be 50 percent?

8.91 To determine the proportion of taxpayers who prefer filing tax returns electronically, a survey of 600 taxpayers was conducted. Calculate the margin of error used to estimate this proportion. What assumptions are required to find the margin of error?

8.92 A sample of 40 CDs from a student's collection showed a mean length of 52.74 minutes with a standard deviation of 13.21 minutes. Construct a 95 percent confidence interval for the population standard deviation. (Data are from a project by statistics students Michael Evatz, Nancy Petack, and Jennifer Skladanowski.)

VAIL RESORTS **8.93** Vail Resorts would like to send a survey to their guests asking about their satisfaction with the new 2009 website design. They would like to have a margin of error of ± 5 percent on responses with 95 percent confidence. (a) Using the conservative approach, what sample size is needed to ensure this level of confidence and margin of error? (b) If Vail Resorts wanted the margin of error to be only ± 2.5 percent, what would happen to the required sample size?

MINI-PROJECTS

8.94 This is an exercise using Excel. (a) Use =RANDBETWEEN(0,99) to create 20 samples of size $n = 4$ by choosing two-digit random numbers between 00 and 99. (b) For each sample, calculate the mean. (c) Make a histogram of the 80 *individual X-values* using bins 10 units wide (i.e., 0, 10, 20, . . . , 100). Describe the shape of the histogram. (d) Make a histogram of your 20 *sample means* using bins 10 units wide. (e) Discuss the histogram shape. Does the Central Limit Theorem seem to be working? (f) Find the mean of your 20 sample means. Was it what you would expect? Explain. (g) Find the standard deviation of your 20 sample means. Was it what you would expect?

8.95 For 10 tanks of gas for your car, calculate the miles per gallon. (a) Construct a 95 percent confidence interval for the true mean mpg for your car. (b) How many tanks of gas would you need to obtain an error of ± 0.2 mpg with 95 percent confidence? Use the value of s from your sample.

8.96 (a) Look at 50 vehicles in a parking lot near you. Count the number that are SUVs (state your definition of SUV). Use any sampling method you like (e.g., the first 50 you see). (b) Construct a 95 percent confidence interval for the true population proportion of SUVs. (c) What sample size would be needed to ensure an error of ± 0.025 with 98 percent confidence? (d) Would the proportion be the same if this experiment were repeated in a university parking lot?

8.97 (a) From the New York Stock Exchange website, take a random sample of 30 companies that are on the IPO (Initial Public Offering) Showcase list for last year. (b) Calculate a 90 percent confidence interval for the average closing stock price on the day of the IPO.

RELATED READING

Boos, Dennis D.; and Jacqueline M. Hughes-Oliver. "How Large Does n Have to be for z and t Intervals?" *The American Statistician* 54, no. 2 (May 2000), pp. 121–28.

Browne, Richard H. "Using the Sample Range as a Basis for Calculating Sample Size in Power Calculations." *The American Statistician* 55, no. 4 (November 2001), pp. 293–98.

Kupper, Lawrence L.; and Kerry B. Hafner. "How Appropriate Are Popular Sample Size Formulas?" *The American Statistician* 43, no. 2 (May 1989), pp. 101–105.

Lenth, Russell V. "Some Practical Guidelines for Effective Sample Size Determination." *The American Statistician* 55, no. 3 (August 2001), pp. 187–93.

Parker, Robert A. "Sample Size: More Than Calculations." *The American Statistician* 57, no. 3 (August 2003), pp. 166–70.

van Belle, Gerald. *Statistical Rules of Thumb*. Wiley, 2002.

CHAPTER 8 Online Learning Resources

The Online Learning Center (OLC) at www.mhhe.com/doane4e has several *LearningStats* demonstrations to help you understand sampling distributions and confidence intervals. Your instructor may assign one or more of them, or you may decide to download the ones that sound interesting.

Topic	*LearningStats Demonstrations*
Central Limit Theorem	▨ CLT Demonstration: Simulation ▨ CLT Demonstration: Finite Population
Sampling distributions	▨ Sampling Distributions ▨ Critical Values (z, t, χ^2) ▨ Sample Proportion Demonstration
Confidence intervals	▨ Confidence Interval: Means ▨ Confidence Interval: Proportions ▨ Confidence Interval: Variances ▨ Confidence Interval: Simulation ▨ Confidence Interval: Bootstrap ▧ Finite Populations ▧ Bootstrap Explained
Sample size	▨ Sample Size Calculator
Tables	▨ Appendix D—Student's t ▨ Appendix E—Chi-Square

Key: ▧ = Word ▨ = Excel

CHAPTER

9

One-Sample Hypothesis Tests

CHAPTER CONTENTS

CHAPTER LEARNING OBJECTIVES

LO

When you finish this chapter you should be able to

LO 9-1   List the steps in testing hypotheses.

LO 9-2   Explain the difference between H_0 and H_1.

LO 9-3   Define Type I error, Type II error, and power.

LO 9-4   Formulate a null and alternative hypothesis for μ or π.

LO 9-5   Find critical values of z or t in tables or by using Excel.

LO 9-6   Perform a hypothesis test for a mean with known σ using z.

LO 9-7   Perform a hypothesis test for a mean with unknown σ using t.

LO 9-8   Use tables or Excel to find the p-value in tests of μ.

LO 9-9   Perform a hypothesis test for a proportion and find the p-value.

LO 9-10 Interpret a power curve or OC curve (optional).

LO 9-11 Perform a hypothesis test for a variance (optional).

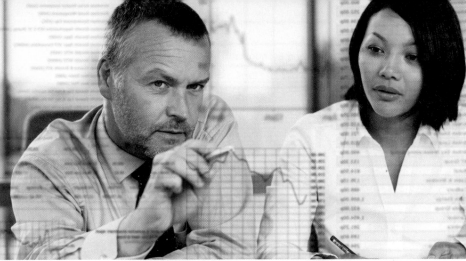

Data are used in business every day to support marketing claims, help managers make decisions, and measure business improvement. Whether the business is small or large, profit or nonprofit, the use of data allows businesses to find the best answers to their questions.

- Should Ball Corporation's aluminum can division change suppliers of metal?
- Did the proportion of defective products decrease after a new manufacturing process was introduced?
- Has the average service time at a Noodles & Company restaurant decreased since last year?
- Has a ski resort decreased its average response time to accidents?
- Did the proportion of satisfied car repair customers increase after providing more training for the employees?

Savvy businesspeople use data and many of the statistical tools that you've already learned to answer these types of questions. We will build on these tools in this chapter and learn about one of the most widely used statistical tools—**hypothesis testing**. Hypothesis testing is used in science and business to test assumptions and theories and guide managers when facing decisions. First we will explain the logic behind hypothesis testing and then show how *statistical hypothesis testing* helps businesses make decisions.

9.1 LOGIC OF HYPOTHESIS TESTING

The business analyst asks questions, makes assumptions, and proposes testable theories about the values of key parameters of the business operating environment. Each assumption is tested against observed data. If an assumption has not been disproved, in spite of rigorous efforts to do so, the business may operate under the belief that the statement is true. The analyst states the assumption, called a **hypothesis**, in a format that can be tested using well-known statistical procedures. The hypothesis is compared with sample data to determine if the data are consistent or inconsistent with the hypothesis. When the data are found to be inconsistent (i.e., in conflict) with the hypothesis, the hypothesis is either discarded or reformulated. The process of **hypothesis testing** can be an iterative process, as illustrated in Figure 9.1.

Not every hypothesis has to be retested continuously. Some questions are relevant only at a point in time, such as asking whether or not consumers under age 25 prefer a new Coke flavor to an existing flavor. If a carefully designed marketing study provides a clear-cut answer, no more testing is required. On the other hand, clinical testing of new drugs may

FIGURE 9.1

Hypothesis Testing as an Ongoing Process

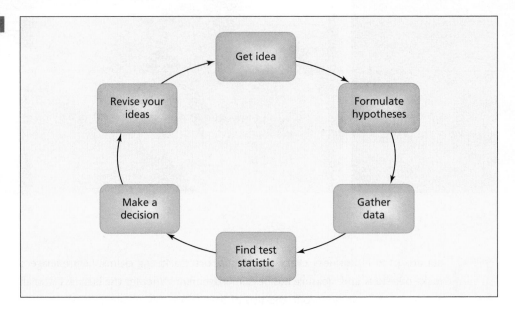

go on for years, at different hospitals and with different types of patients. The efficacy and side effects of new drugs may involve subtle effects that only show up in very large samples and over longer periods of time, sometimes with profound financial implications for the company. Automobile safety testing is ongoing because of changes in car technology and driver habits. There is plenty of work for data analysts who continually look for changes in customer satisfaction, shifts in buying patterns, and trends in warranty claims.

Who Uses Hypothesis Testing?

The innovative vigor of our economy is largely based on technology: new materials, new manufacturing methods, new distribution systems, new information strategies. All business managers need at least a basic understanding of hypothesis testing because managers often interact with specialists, read technical reports, and then make recommendations on key financial or strategic decisions based on statistical evidence. A confidence interval sometimes gives enough information to make a decision. Knowing the 95 percent range of likely values for a key decision parameter (e.g., the proportion of repeat customers under age 30) may be all you need. This chapter extends the idea of confidence intervals by showing how to test a sample against a benchmark, and how to assess the risk of incorrect decisions.

Steps in Hypothesis Testing

LO 9-1

List the steps in testing hypotheses.

Step 1: State the hypothesis to be tested.

Step 2: Specify what level of inconsistency with the data will lead to rejection of the hypothesis. This is called a *decision rule*.

Step 3: Collect data and calculate necessary statistics to test the hypothesis.

Step 4: Make a decision. Should the hypothesis be rejected or not?

Step 5: Take action based on the decision.

LO 9-2

Explain the difference between H_0 and H_1.

Step 1: State the Hypotheses Formulate a pair of mutually exclusive, collectively exhaustive statements about the world. One statement or the other must be true, but they cannot both be true.

H_0: Null Hypothesis

H_1: Alternative Hypothesis

The two statements are *hypotheses* because the truth is unknown. Efforts will be made to reject the **null hypothesis** (sometimes called the *maintained hypothesis* or the *research hypothesis*). H_0 must be stated in a precise way, so that it can be tested against empirical evidence from a sample. If H_0 happens to be an established theory, we might not really expect to reject it, but we try anyway. If we reject H_0, we tentatively conclude that the **alternative hypothesis** H_1 is the case. H_0 represents the *status quo* (e.g., the current state of affairs), while H_1 is sometimes called the *action alternative* because action may be required if we reject H_0 in favor of H_1. For example:

Criminal Trial   In a criminal trial, the hypotheses are:

  H_0: The defendant is innocent

  H_1: The defendant is guilty

Our legal system assumes a defendant is innocent *unless the evidence gathered by the prosecutor is sufficient to reject this assumption.*

Drug Testing   When an Olympic athlete is tested for performance-enhancing drugs such as steroids, the presumption is that the athlete is in compliance with the rules. The hypotheses are:

  H_0: No illegal steroid use

  H_1: Illegal steroid use

Samples of urine or blood are taken as evidence and *used only to disprove the null hypothesis because we assume the athlete is free of illegal steroids.*

Biometric Security   To identify authorized and unauthorized persons for computer access, ATM withdrawals, and entry into secure facilities, there is increasing interest in using the person's physical characteristics (e.g., fingerprints, facial structure, or iris patterns) instead of paper and plastic IDs, which can be forged. The hypotheses are:

  H_0: User is legitimate

  H_1: User is not legitimate

The system assumes the user is legitimate *unless the physical characteristic being presented is inconsistent with the biometric profile of that individual.*

Step 2: Specify the Decision Rule   Before collecting data to compare against the hypothesis, the researcher must specify *how* the evidence will be used to reach a decision about the null hypothesis. In our legal system, the evidence presented by the prosecutor must convince a jury "beyond a reasonable doubt" that the defendant is not innocent. In steroid testing, the lab that analyzes the urine or blood sample must conduct tests to decide whether the sample exceeds the agreed-upon benchmark or threshhold. With biometric screening, the designer of the security system determines how many discrepancies on a fingerprint would indicate an unauthorized user.

Steps 3 and 4: Data Collection and Decision Making   Much of the critical work in hypothesis testing takes place during steps 1 and 2. Once the hypotheses and decision rule have been clearly articulated, the process of data collection, while occasionally time-consuming, is straightforward. We compare the data with the hypothesis, using the decision rule, and decide to reject or not reject the null hypothesis.

Step 5: Take Action Based on Decision   This last step—taking action—requires experience and expertise on the part of the decision maker. Suppose the evidence presented at a trial convinces a jury that the defendant is not innocent. What punishment should the judge impose? Or suppose the blood sample of an athlete shows steroid use. What fine should the athletic commission impose? Should the athlete be banned from competing? If the fingerprint presented for authentication has been rejected, should an alarm go off? Should a security breach be recorded in the system? Appropriate action for the decision should relate back to the purpose of conducting the hypothesis test in the first place.

Can a Null Hypothesis Be Proved?

No, we cannot prove a null hypothesis—we can only *fail to reject* it. A null hypothesis that survives repeated tests without rejection is "true" only in the limited sense that it has been thoroughly scrutinized and tested. Today's "true" hypothesis could be disproved tomorrow if new data are found. If we fail to reject H_0, the same hypothesis may be retested. That is how scientific inquiry works. Einstein's theories, for example, are over 100 years old but are still being subjected to rigorous tests. Few scientists really think that Einstein's theories are "wrong." Yet it's in the nature of science to keep trying to refute accepted theories, especially when a new test is possible or when new data become available. Similarly, the safety of commonly used prescription drugs is continually being studied. Sometimes, "safe" drugs are revealed to have serious side effects only after large-scale, long-term use by consumers (e.g., the Vioxx arthritis drug that was at first shown to be safe in clinical trials, but later showed a dangerous association with heart attack after years of use by millions of people).

Two Types of Error

Because our ability to collect evidence can be limited by our tools and by time and financial resources, we recognize that on occasion we will be making a decision about the null hypothesis that could be wrong. Consequently, our decision rule will be based on the levels of risk of making a wrong decision. We can allow more risk or less risk by changing the threshold of the decision rule.

It is possible to make an incorrect decision regarding the null hypothesis. As illustrated in the table below, either the null hypothesis is true or it is false. We have only two possible choices concerning the null hypothesis. We either reject H_0 or fail to reject H_0.

	H_0 *is true*	H_0 *is false*
Reject H_0	Type I error	Correct decision
Fail to reject H_0	Correct decision	Type II error

The true situation determines whether our decision was correct. If the decision about the null hypothesis matches the true situation, the decision was correct. Rejecting the null hypothesis when it is true is a **Type I error**. Failure to reject the null hypothesis when it is false is a **Type II error**. In either case, an incorrect decision was made.

Because we rarely have perfect information about the true situation, we can't always know whether we have committed a Type I or Type II error. But by using statistics, we can calculate the *probability* of making an incorrect decision. We can minimize the chance of error by collecting as much sample evidence as our resources allow, and by choosing proper testing procedures.

Consequences of Type I and Type II Errors

The consequences of these two errors are quite different, and the costs are borne by different parties. Depending on the situation, decision makers may fear one error more than the other. It would be nice if both types of error could be avoided. Unfortunately, when making a decision based on a fixed body of sample evidence, reducing the risk of one type of error often increases the risk of the other. Consider our examples of a criminal trial, drug testing, and biometric security.

H_0: Defendant is innocent
H_1: Defendant is guilty

Criminal Trial   Type I error is convicting an innocent defendant, so the costs are borne by the defendant. Type II error is failing to convict a guilty defendant, so the costs are borne by society if the guilty person returns to the streets. Concern for the rights of the accused and stricter rules of evidence may suggest rules that would reduce the risk of Type I error. But concern over the social costs of crime and victims' rights could lead to rules that would reduce Type II error, presumably at the expense of Type I error. Both risks can be reduced only by devoting more effort to gathering evidence and strengthening the legal process (expediting trials, improving jury quality, increasing investigative work).

Drug Testing   Type I error is unfairly disqualifying an athlete who is "clean." Type II error is letting the drug user get away with it and have an unfair competitive advantage. The costs of Type I error are hard feelings, unnecessary embarrassment, and possible loss of lifetime earnings for professional athletes. The costs of Type II error are tarnishing the Olympic image and rewarding those who break the rules. Over time, improved tests have reduced the risk of both types of error. However, for a given technology, the threshold can be set lower or higher, balancing Type I and Type II error.

H_0: No illegal steroid use

H_1: Illegal steroid use

Biometric Security   Type I error means denying a legitimate user access to a facility or funds. Type II error is letting an unauthorized user have access to facilities or a financial account. Technology has progressed to the point where Type II errors have become very rare, though Type I errors remain a problem. The error rates depend, among other things, on how much is spent on the equipment and software.

H_0: User is legitimate

H_1: User is not legitimate

Probability of Type I and Type II Errors

The *probability* of a Type I error (rejecting a true null hypothesis) is denoted α (the lowercase Greek letter "alpha"). Statisticians refer to α as the **level of significance**. The probability of a Type II error (not rejecting a false hypothesis) is denoted β (the lowercase Greek letter "beta"), as shown in Table 9.1.

Key Term	What Is It?	Symbol	Definition	Also Called
Type I error	Reject a true hypothesis	α	$P(\text{reject } H_0 \mid H_0 \text{ is true})$	False positive
Type II error	Fail to reject a false hypothesis	β	$P(\text{fail to reject } H_0 \mid H_0 \text{ is false})$	False negative
Power	Correctly reject a false hypothesis	$1 - \beta$	$P(\text{reject } H_0 \mid H_0 \text{ is false})$	Sensitivity

TABLE 9.1

Key Terms in Hypothesis Testing

The **power** of a test is the probability that a false hypothesis *will* be rejected (as it should be). Power equals $1 - \beta$ and is the complement of Type II error. Reducing β would correspondingly increase power (usually accomplished by increasing the sample size).

More powerful tests are more likely to detect false hypotheses. For example, if a new weight-loss drug actually is effective, we would want to reject the null hypothesis that the drug has no effect. We prefer the most powerful test possible. Larger samples lead to increased power, which is why clinical trials often involve thousands of people.

LO 9-3

Define Type I error, Type II error, and power.

Relationship between α and β

We desire tests that avoid false negatives (small β) yet we also want to avoid false positives (small α). Given two equivalent tests, we will choose the more powerful test (smaller β). But for a given type of test and fixed sample size, there is a trade-off between α and β. The larger critical value needed to reduce α makes it harder to reject H_0, thereby increasing β. The proper balance between α and β can be elusive. Consider these examples:

- If your household carbon monoxide detector's sensitivity threshold is increased to reduce the risk of overlooking danger (reduced β), there will be more false alarms (increased α).

- A doctor who is conservative about admitting patients with symptoms of heart attack to the ICU (reduced β) will admit more patients with no heart attack (increased α).

- More sensitive airport weapons detectors (reduced β) will inconvenience more safe passengers (increased α).

Both α and β can be reduced simultaneously only by increasing the sample size (gathering more evidence), which is not always feasible or cost-effective.

Mini Case 9.1

BIOMETRIC SECURITY

If your ATM could recognize your physical characteristics (e.g., fingerprint, face, palm, iris), you wouldn't need an ATM card or a PIN. A reliable biometric ID system could also reduce the risk of ID theft, eliminate computer passwords, and speed airport security screening. The hypotheses are

H_0: User is legitimate

H_1: User is not legitimate

Fujitsu Laboratories has tested a palm ID system on 700 people, ranging from children to seniors. It achieved a false rejection rate of 1 percent and a false acceptance rate of 0.5 percent. Bank of Tokyo-Mitsubishi introduced palm-scanning at its ATM machines in 2004. DigitalPersona of Redwood City, California, has developed a fingerprint scanner (called *U.Are.U*) that is able to recognize fingerprints in 200 milliseconds with a 1 percent false rejection rate and a 0.002 percent false acceptance rate. In some high-end devices, false acceptance rates as low as 25 per million have been achieved. These low rates of false acceptance (Type II error) are encouraging, since they mean that others cannot easily impersonate you. Fingerprint scanning is popular (e.g., at the entrance gates of Disney World or Universal Studios) because it is cheaper and easier to implement, though some experts believe that iris scanning or several combined tests have better long-run potential to reduce both error rates. Any such system requires a stored database of biometric data.

Sources: *BusinessWeek,* November 22, 2004, p. 127; *Scientific American* 290, no. 6 (June 2004), p. 108, and 289, no. 4 (April 2003), p. 74; and *PC Magazine,* April 22, 2003, p. 74.

PRODUCT SAFETY

Firms are increasingly wary of Type II error (failing to recall a product as soon as sample evidence begins to indicate potential problems):

H_0: Product is performing safely

H_1: Product is not performing safely

They may even order a precautionary product recall before the statistical evidence has become convincing (e.g., Verizon's 2004 recall of 50,000 cell phone batteries after one exploded and another caused a car fire) or even *before* anything bad happens (e.g., Intel's 2004 recall of its 915 G/P and 925X chip sets from OEMs (original equipment manufacturers), before the chips actually reached any consumers). Failure to act swiftly can generate liability and adverse publicity as with the spate of Ford Explorer rollover accidents and eventual recall of certain 15-inch Firestone radial tires. Ford and Firestone believed they had found an engineering work-around to make the tire design safe, until accumulating accident data, lawsuits, and NHTSA pressure forced recognition that there was a problem. In 2004, certain COX_2 inhibitor drugs that had previously been thought effective and safe, based on extensive clinical trials, were found to be associated with increased risk of heart attack. The makers' stock price plunged (e.g., Merck). The courts often must use statistical evidence to adjudicate product liability claims.

SECTION EXERCISES

connect

9.1 If you repeated a hypothesis test 1,000 times (in other words, 1,000 different samples from the same population), how many times would you expect to commit a Type I error, assuming the null hypothesis were true, if (a) $\alpha = .05$; (b) $\alpha = .01$; or (c) $\alpha = .001$?

9.2 Define Type I and Type II error for each scenario, and identify the cost(s) of each type of error.

    a. A 25-year-old ER patient in Minneapolis complains of chest pain. Heart attacks in 25-year-olds are rare, and beds are scarce in the hospital. The null hypothesis is that there is no heart attack (perhaps muscle pain due to shoveling snow).

b. Approaching O'Hare for landing, a British Air flight from London has been in a holding pattern for 45 minutes due to bad weather. Landing is expected within 15 minutes. The flight crew could declare an emergency and land immediately, but an FAA investigation would be launched and other flights might be endangered. The null hypothesis is that there is enough fuel to stay aloft for 15 more minutes.

c. You are trying to finish a lengthy statistics report and print it for your evening class. Your color printer is very low on ink, and you just have time to get to Staples for a new cartridge. But it is snowing and you need every minute to finish the report. The null hypothesis is that you have enough ink.

9.3 A firm decides to test its employees for illegal drugs. (a) State the null and alternative hypotheses. (b) Define Type I and II errors. (c) What are the consequences of each type of error, and to whom?

9.4 A hotel installs smoke detectors with adjustable sensitivity in all public guest rooms. (a) State the null and alternative hypotheses. (b) Define Type I and II errors. (c) What are the consequences of each type of error, and to whom?

9.5 What is the consequence of a false negative in an inspection of your car's brakes? *Hint:* The null hypothesis is the status quo (things are OK).

9.6 What is the consequence of a false positive in a weekly inspection of a nuclear plant's cooling system? *Hint:* The null hypothesis is the status quo (things are OK).

9.2 STATISTICAL HYPOTHESIS TESTING

A **statistical hypothesis** is a statement about the value of a population parameter that we are interested in. For example, the parameter could be a mean, a proportion, or a variance. A **hypothesis test** is a decision between two competing, mutually exclusive, and collectively exhaustive hypotheses about the value of the parameter.

The hypothesized value of the parameter is the center of interest. For example, if the true value of μ is 5, then the sample mean should not differ greatly from 5. We rely on our knowledge of the *sampling distribution* and the *standard error of the estimate* to decide if the sample estimate is far enough away from 5 to contradict the assumption that $\mu = 5$. We can calculate the likelihood of an observed sample outcome. If the sample outcome is very unlikely, we would reject the claimed mean $\mu = 5$.

The null hypothesis states a benchmark value that we denote with the subscript "0" as in μ_0 or π_0. The hypothesized value μ_0 or π_0 does not come from a sample but is based on past performance, an industry standard, a target, or a product specification.

Where Do We Get μ_0 (or π_0)?

For a mean (or proportion), the value of μ_0 (or π_0) that we are testing is a *benchmark* based on past experience, an industry standard, a target, or a product specification. The value of μ_0 (or π_0) does *not* come from a sample.

For a mean, the null hypothesis H_0 states the value(s) of μ_0 that we will try to reject. There are three possible alternative hypotheses:

Left-Tailed Test	*Two-Tailed Test*	*Right-Tailed Test*
$H_0: \mu \geq \mu_0$	$H_0: \mu = \mu_0$	$H_0: \mu \leq \mu_0$
$H_1: \mu < \mu_0$	$H_1: \mu \neq \mu_0$	$H_1: \mu > \mu_0$

LO 9-4

Formulate a null and alternative hypothesis for μ or π.

The application will dictate which of the three alternatives is appropriate. The *direction of the test* is indicated by which way the inequality symbol points in H_1:

$<$ indicates a **left-tailed test**

$\neq$ indicates a **two-tailed test**

$>$ indicates a **right-tailed test**

EXAMPLE 9.1

Right-Tailed Test for μ

EPA guidelines for the maximum safe level of radon (a naturally occurring radioactive gas) in a home is 4.0 pCi/L (picocuries per liter of air). When a home is tested, a number of measurements are taken and averaged. A homeowner would be concerned if the average radon level is too high. In this case, the homeowner would choose a *right-tailed test*. The inequality in H_1 indicates the tail of the test.

H_0: $\mu \le 4.0$ pCiL $\Leftarrow$ Assume H_0 is true unless evidence says otherwise
H_1: $\mu > 4.0$ pCiL $\Leftarrow$ The $>$ inequality in H_1 points right (right-tailed test)

The mean radon level is assumed safe (i.e., H_0 is assumed to be true) unless the sample mean indicates an average radon level too far *above* 4.0 to be due to chance variation.

EXAMPLE 9.2

Left-Tailed Test for μ

The Diehard Platinum automobile battery has a claimed CCA (cold cranking amperes) of 880 amps. A consumer testing agency chooses a sample of several batteries and finds the average CCA for the batteries tested. The consumer testing agency would only be concerned if the battery delivers less than the claimed CCA, so they would choose a *left-tailed test.* The inequality in H_1 indicates the tail of the test.

H_0: $\mu \ge 880$ CCA $\Leftarrow$ Assume H_0 is true unless evidence says otherwise
H_1: $\mu < 880$ CCA $\Leftarrow$ The $<$ inequality in H_1 points left (left-tailed test)

The CCA mean is assumed at or above 880 amps (i.e., H_0 is assumed to be true) unless the sample mean indicates that CCA is too far *below* 880 to be due to chance variation.

EXAMPLE 9.3

Two-Tailed Test for μ

The width of a sheet of standard size copier paper should be $\mu = 216$ mm (i.e., 8.5 inches). There is variation in paper width due to the nature of the production process, so the width of a sheet of paper is a random variable. Samples are taken from the production process and the mean width is calculated. If the paper is too narrow, the pages might not be well-centered in the sheet feeder. If the pages are too wide, sheets could jam in the feeder or paper trays. Either violation poses a quality problem, so the manufacturer might choose a *two-tailed test.*

H_0: $\mu = 216$ mm $\Leftarrow$ Assume H_0 is true unless evidence says otherwise
H_1: $\mu \ne 216$ mm $\Leftarrow$ The $\ne$ in H_1 points to both tails (two-tailed test)

If the null hypothesis is rejected, action is required to adjust the manufacturing process. The action depends on the severity of the departure from H_0.

Decision Rule

When performing a statistical hypothesis test, we compare a sample statistic to the hypothesized value of the population parameter stated in the null hypothesis. Extreme outcomes occurring in the left tail would cause us to reject the null hypothesis in a left-tailed test; extreme outcomes occurring in the right tail would cause us to reject the null hypothesis in a right-tailed test. Extreme values in *either* the left or right tail would cause us to reject the null hypothesis in a two-tailed test.

We specify our decision rule by defining an "extreme" outcome. We rely on our knowledge of the *sampling distribution* and the *standard error of the estimate* to decide if the sample statistic is far enough away from μ_0 to contradict the assumption that $\mu = \mu_0$. The area under the sampling distribution curve that defines an extreme outcome is called the **rejection region**. You may visualize the level of significance (α) as an area in the tail(s) of a distribution (e.g., normal) far enough from the center that it represents an unlikely outcome if our null hypothesis is true. We will calculate a **test statistic** that measures the difference between the sample statistic and the hypothesized parameter. A test statistic that falls in the shaded region will cause rejection of H_0, as illustrated in Figure 9.2. The area of the nonrejection region (white area) is $1 - \alpha$.

FIGURE 9.2

Tests for H_0: $\mu = \mu_0$

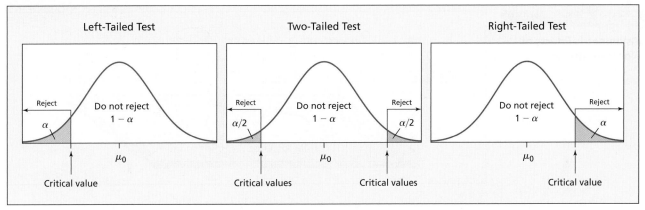

The **critical value** is the boundary between the two regions (reject H_0, do not reject H_0). The **decision rule** states what the critical value of the test statistic would have to be in order to reject H_0 at the chosen level of significance (α). For example, if we are dealing with a normal sampling distribution for a mean, we might reject H_0 if the sample mean $\bar{x}$ differs from μ_0 by more than 1.96 times the standard error of the mean (outside the 95 percent confidence interval for μ).

The decision maker specifies the value of α for the test (common choices for α are .10, .05, or .01). The level of significance is usually expressed as a percent (e.g., 10 percent, 5 percent, or 1 percent). A small value of α is desirable, to ensure a low probability of Type I error. For example, if we specify a decision rule based on $\alpha = .05$, we would expect to commit a Type I error about 5 times in 100 samples. In a two-tailed test, the risk is split with $\alpha/2$ in each tail, since there are two ways to reject H_0. For example, in a two-tailed test using $\alpha = .10$ we would put $\alpha/2 = .05$ in each tail. We can look up the critical value from a table or from Excel (e.g., z or t).

By choosing a small α (say $\alpha = .01$), the decision maker can make it harder to reject the null hypothesis. By choosing a larger α (say $\alpha = .05$), it is easier to reject the null hypothesis. This raises the possibility of manipulating the decision. For this reason, the choice of α should precede the calculation of the test statistic, thereby minimizing the temptation to select α so as to favor one conclusion over the other.

In a left-tailed or right-tailed test, the inequality in H_0 comprises an *infinite* number of hypotheses. We can only test *one* value of the hypothesized parameter at a time, so we test the null hypothesis (H_0: $\mu \le \mu_0$ or H_0: $\mu \ge \mu_0$) *only* at the point of equality $\mu = \mu_0$. If we reject $\mu = \mu_0$ in favor of the alternative, we implicitly reject the *entire class* of H_0 possibilities. For example, suppose the sample mean in the radon test is far enough above 4.0 to cause us to reject the null hypothesis H_0: $\mu = 4.0$ in favor of the alternative hypothesis H_1: $\mu > 4.0$. The same sample would also permit rejection of any value of μ *less than* $\mu = 4.0$, so we actually can reject H_0: $\mu \le 4.0$.

In quality control, any deviation from specifications indicates that something may be wrong, so a two-tailed test is common. If the decision maker has no *a priori* reason to expect rejection in one direction, it is reasonable to use a two-tailed test. Rejection in a two-tailed test guarantees rejection in a one-tailed test, other things being equal.

When the consequences of rejecting H_0 are asymmetric, or where one tail is of special importance to the researcher, we might perform a one-tailed test. For example, suppose that a machine is supposed to bore holes with a 3.5-mm diameter in a piece of sheet metal. Although any deviation from 3.5 mm is a violation of the specification, the consequences of rejecting H_0 may be different. Suppose an attachment pin is to be inserted into the hole. If the hole is too small, the pin cannot be inserted, but the metal piece might be reworked to enlarge the hole so the pin does fit. On the other hand, if the hole is too large, the pin will fit too loosely and may fall out. The piece may have to be discarded since an oversized hole cannot be made smaller. This is illustrated in Figure 9.3.

FIGURE 9.3

Asymmetric Effects of Nonconformance

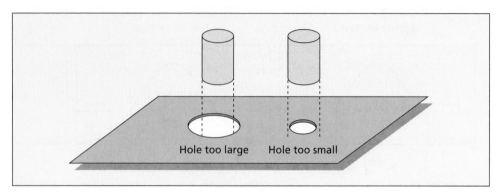

Hole too large   Hole too small

SECTION EXERCISES

9.7 A manufacturer claims that its compact fluorescent bulbs contain an average of 2.5 mg of mercury. Write the hypotheses for a two-tailed test, using the manufacturer's claim about the mean as the null hypothesis.

9.8 Noodles & Company is interested in testing whether their new menu design helps reduce the average order time for their customers. Suppose that the average order time prior to the introduction of their new menu was 1.2 minutes. Write the hypotheses for a left-tailed test, using their previous average order time as the claim about the mean for the null hypothesis.

9.9 The Scottsdale fire department aims to respond to fire calls in 4 minutes or less, on average. State the hypotheses you would use if you had reason to believe that the fire department's claim is not being met. *Hint:* Remember that sample data are used as evidence *against* the null, not to prove the null is true.

VAILRESORTS **9.10** The average age of a part-time seasonal employee at a Vail Resorts ski mountain has historically been 37 years. State the hypotheses one would use to test if this average has decreased since the last season.

9.11 Sketch a diagram of the decision rule for each pair of hypotheses.

    a. $H_0: \mu \geq 80$ versus $H_1: \mu < 80$
    b. $H_0: \mu = 80$ versus $H_1: \mu \neq 80$
    c. $H_0: \mu \leq 80$ versus $H_1: \mu > 80$

9.12 The Ball Corporation's aluminum can manufacturing facility in Ft. Atkinson, Wisconsin, wants to use a sample to perform a two-tailed test to see whether the mean incoming metal thickness is at the target of 0.2731 mm. A deviation in either direction would pose a quality concern. State the hypotheses they should test.

9.3 TESTING A MEAN: KNOWN POPULATION VARIANCE

We will first explain how to test a population mean, μ. The sample statistic used to estimate μ is the random variable $\overline{X}$. The sampling distribution for $\overline{X}$ depends on whether or not the population variance σ^2 is known. We begin with the case of known σ^2. We learned in Chapter 8 that the sampling distribution of $\overline{X}$ will be a normal distribution provided that we have a normal population (or, by the Central Limit Theorem, if the sample size is large). In Section 9.4 we will turn to the more common case when σ^2 is unknown.

Test Statistic

A *test statistic* measures the difference between a given sample mean $\bar{x}$ and a benchmark μ_0 in terms of the standard error of the mean. The test statistic is the "standardized score" of the sample statistic. When testing μ with a known σ, the test statistic is a z score. Once we have collected our sample, we calculate a value of the test statistic using the sample mean and then compare it against the critical value of z. We will refer to the calculated value of the test statistic as z_{calc}.

Test Statistic for a Mean: Known σ

Sample mean →   ← Hypothesized mean

$$z_{calc} = \frac{\bar{x} - \mu_0}{\sigma_{\bar{x}}} = \frac{\bar{x} - \mu_0}{\dfrac{\sigma}{\sqrt{n}}} \tag{9.1}$$

↑ Standard error of the sample mean

If the true mean of the population is μ_0, then the value of a particular sample mean $\bar{x}$ calculated from our sample should be near μ_0 and therefore the test statistic should be near zero.

Critical Value

The test statistic is compared with a *critical value* from a table. The critical value is the boundary between two regions (reject H_0, do not reject H_0) in the decision rule. For a two-tailed test (but *not* for a one-tailed test), the hypothesis test is equivalent to asking whether the confidence interval for μ includes zero. In a two-tailed test, half the risk of Type I error (i.e., $\alpha/2$) goes in each tail, as shown in Table 9.2, so the z-values are the same as for a confidence interval. You can verify these z-values from Excel.

> **LO 9-5**
>
> Find critical values of z or t in tables or by using Excel.

> **TABLE 9.2**
>
> **Some Common z-Values**

Level of Significance (α)	Left-Tailed Test	Two-Tailed Test	Right-Tailed Test
.10	−1.282	±1.645	+1.282
.05	−1.645	±1.960	+1.645
.01	−2.326	±2.576	+2.326

EXAMPLE 9.4

Paper Manufacturing

The Hammermill Company produces paper for laser printers. Standard paper width is 216 mm, or 8.5 inches. Suppose that the actual width is a random variable that is normally distributed with a known standard deviation of .0230 based on the manufacturing technology currently in use. Variation arises during manufacturing because of slight differences in the paper stock, vibration in the rollers and cutting tools, and wear and tear on the equipment. The cutters can be adjusted if the paper width drifts from the correct mean. Suppose that a quality control inspector chooses 50 sheets at random and measures them with a precise instrument, obtaining a mean width of 216.0070 mm. Using a 5 percent level of significance ($\alpha = .05$), does this sample show that the product mean exceeds the specification? 📄 **Paper**

LO 9-6

Perform a hypothesis test for a mean with known σ using z.

Step 1: State the Hypotheses   The question indicates a right-tailed test, so the hypotheses would be

H_0: $\mu \leq 216$ mm (product mean does not exceed the specification)

H_1: $\mu > 216$ mm (product mean has risen above the specification)

From the null hypothesis we see that $\mu_0 = 216$ mm, which is the product specification.

Step 2: Specify the Decision Rule   We use the *level of significance* to find the *critical value* of the z statistic that determines the threshold for rejecting the null hypothesis to be $\alpha = .05$. The critical value of z that accomplishes this is $z_{.05} = 1.645$. As illustrated in Figure 9.4, the decision rule is

Reject H_0 if $z_{\text{calc}} > 1.645$

Otherwise do not reject H_0

FIGURE 9.4

Right-Tailed z Test for $\alpha = .05$

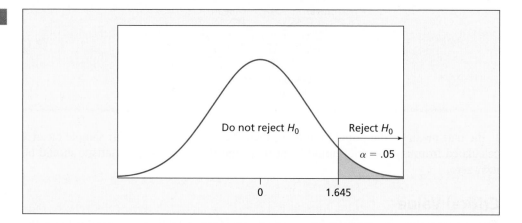

Step 3: Collect Sample Data and Calculate the Test Statistic   If H_0 is true, then the test statistic should be near 0 because $\bar{x}$ should be near μ_0. The value of the test statistic is

$$z_{\text{calc}} = \frac{\bar{x} - \mu_0}{\frac{\sigma}{\sqrt{n}}} = \frac{216.0070 - 216.0000}{\frac{.0230}{\sqrt{50}}} = \frac{0.0070}{0.00325269} = 2.152$$

Step 4: Make the Decision   The test statistic falls in the right rejection region, so we reject the null hypothesis H_0: $\mu \leq 216$ and conclude the alternative hypothesis H_1: $\mu > 216$ at the 5 percent level of significance. Although the difference is slight, it is statistically significant.

Step 5: Take Action   Now that we have concluded that the process is producing paper with an average width *greater* than the specification, it is time to adjust the manufacturing process to bring the average width back to specification. Our course of action could be to readjust the machine settings or it could be time to resharpen the cutting tools. At this point it is the responsibility of the process engineers to determine the best course of action.

p-Value Method

The critical value method described above requires that you specify your rejection criterion in terms of the test statistic before you take a sample. The **p-value method** is a more flexible approach that is often preferred by statisticians over the critical value method. It requires that you express the strength of your evidence (i.e., your sample) against the null hypothesis in terms of a probability. The *p*-value is a direct measure of the likelihood of the observed sample under H_0. The *p*-value answers the following question: If the null hypothesis is true, what is the probability that we would observe our particular sample mean (or one even farther away from μ_0)? The *p*-value gives us more information than a test using one particular value of α because the observer can choose any α that is appropriate for the problem.

We compare the *p*-value with the level of significance. If the *p*-value is smaller than α, the sample contradicts the null hypothesis, and so we reject H_0. For a right-tailed test, the decision rule using the *p*-value approach is stated as:

Reject H_0 if $P(Z > z_{calc}) < \alpha$, otherwise fail to reject H_0.

Whether we use the critical value approach or the *p*-value approach, our decision about the null hypothesis will be the same.

What Is a *p*-Value?

A sample statistic is a random variable that may differ from the hypothesized value merely by chance, so we do not expect the sample to agree *exactly* with H_0. The *p*-value is the probability of obtaining a test statistic as extreme as the one observed, assuming that the null hypothesis is true. A large *p*-value (near 1.00) tends to support H_0, while a small *p*-value (near 0.00) tends to contradict H_0. If the *p*-value is less than the chosen level of significance (α), then we conclude that the null hypothesis is false.

In order to calculate the *p*-value, we first need to find z_{calc}. The *p*-value for this right-tailed test is $P(Z > 2.152)$. The direction of the inequality in the *p*-value is the same as in the alternative hypothesis: H_1: $\mu > 216$ mm.

To find the *p*-value, we can use Excel's function =NORM.S.DIST(2.152,1) to obtain the left-tail area for the cumulative Z distribution (see Figure 9.5). Since $P(Z < 2.152) = .9843$, the right-tail area is $P(Z > 2.152) = 1 - .9843 = .0157$. This is the *p*-value for the right-tailed test, as illustrated in Figure 9.5. The *p*-value diagram does not show α. The *p*-value of .0157 indicates that in a right-tailed test, a test statistic of $z_{calc} = 2.152$ (or a more extreme test statistic) would happen by chance about 1.57 percent of the time if the null hypothesis were true.

FIGURE 9.5

p-Value for a Right-Tailed Test with $z_{calc} = 2.152$, Using Excel

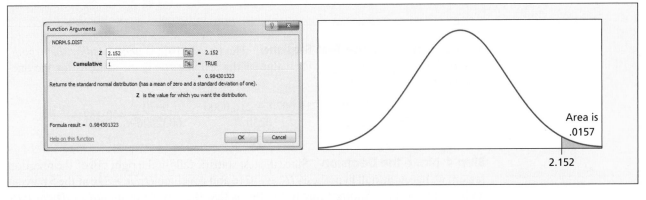

We could also obtain the *p*-value from Appendix C-2, which shows cumulative standard normal areas less than *z*, as illustrated in Table 9.3. The cumulative area is not exactly the same as Excel because Appendix C-2 requires that we round the test statistic to two decimals ($z = 2.15$).

TABLE 9.3

Finding the *p*-Value for $z = 2.15$ in Appendix C-2

z	.00	.01	.02	.03	.04	.05	.06	.07	.08	.09
−3.7	.00011	.00010	.00010	.00010	.00009	.00009	.00008	.00008	.00008	.00008
−3.6	.00016	.00015	.00015	.00014	.00014	.00013	.00013	.00012	.00012	.00011
−3.5	.00023	.00022	.00022	.00021	.00020	.00019	.00019	.00018	.00017	.00017
⋮	⋮	⋮	⋮	⋮	⋮	⋮	⋮	⋮	⋮	⋮
2.0	.97725	.97778	.97831	.97882	.97932	.97982	.98030	.98077	.98124	.98169
2.1	.98214	.98257	.98300	.98341	.98382	*.98422*	.98461	.98500	.98537	.98574
2.2	.98610	.98645	.98679	.98713	.98745	.98778	.98809	.98840	.98870	.98899

Two-Tailed Test

In this case, the manufacturer decided that a two-tailed test would be more appropriate, since the objective is to detect a deviation from the desired mean in *either* direction.

Step 1: State the Hypotheses　For a two-tailed test, the hypotheses are

H_0: $\mu = 216$ mm (product mean is what it is supposed to be)

H_1: $\mu \neq 216$ mm (product mean is not what it is supposed to be)

Step 2: Specify the Decision Rule　We will use the same $\alpha = .05$ as in the right-tailed test. But for a two-tailed test, we split the risk of Type I error by putting $\alpha/2 = .05/2 = .025$ in each tail. For $\alpha = .05$ in a two-tailed test, the critical value is $z_{.025} = \pm 1.96$ so the decision rule is

Reject H_0 if $z_{\text{calc}} > +1.96$ or if $z_{\text{calc}} < -1.96$

Otherwise do not reject H_0

The decision rule is illustrated in Figure 9.6.

FIGURE 9.6

Two-Tailed *z* Test for $\alpha = .05$

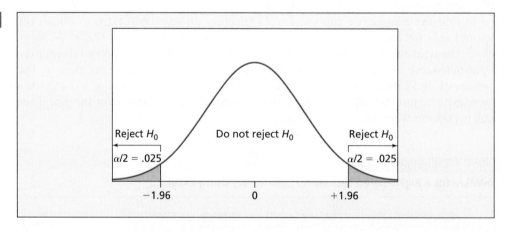

Step 3: Calculate the Test Statistic　The test statistic is *unaffected by the hypotheses or the level of significance.* The value of the test statistic is the same as for the one-tailed test:

$$z_{\text{calc}} = \frac{\bar{x} - \mu_0}{\frac{\sigma}{\sqrt{n}}} = \frac{216.0070 - 216.0000}{\frac{.0230}{\sqrt{50}}} = \frac{.0070}{.00325269} = 2.152$$

Step 4: Make the Decision　Since the test statistic falls in the right tail of the rejection region, we reject the null hypothesis H_0: $\mu = 216$ and conclude H_1: $\mu \neq 216$ at the 5 percent level of significance. Another way to say this is that the sample mean *differs significantly* from the desired specification at $\alpha = .05$ in a two-tailed test. Note that this decision is rather a close one, since the test statistic just barely falls into the rejection region.

Step 5: Take Action An adjustment is needed, such as changing the cutting tool settings. Now it is up to the process engineers to choose the best course of action.

Using the *p*-Value Approach

LO 9-8

Use tables or Excel to find the *p*-value in tests of μ.

In a two-tailed test, the decision rule using the *p*-value is the same as in a one-tailed test.

Reject H_0 if *p*-value $< \alpha$. Otherwise, do not reject H_0.

The difference between a one-tailed and a two-tailed test is how we obtain the *p*-value. Because we allow rejection in either the left or the right tail in a two-tailed test, the level of significance, α, is divided equally between the two tails to establish the rejection region. In order to fairly evaluate the *p*-value against α, we must now double the tail area. The *p*-value in this two-tailed test is $2 \times P(z_{calc} > 2.152) = 2 \times .0157 = .0314$. See Figure 9.7. This says that in a two-tailed test a result as extreme as 2.152 would arise about 3.14 percent of the time by chance alone *if the null hypothesis were true*.

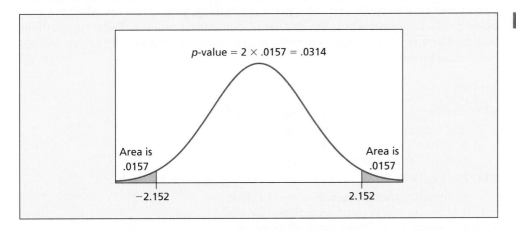

FIGURE 9.7

Two-Tailed *p*-Value for $z = 2.152$

p-value = 2 × .0157 = .0314

Area is .0157

Area is .0157

−2.152   2.152

Interpretation Although the sample mean 216.007 might seem very close to 216, it is more than two standard deviations from the desired mean. This example shows that even a small difference can be significant. It all depends on σ and n, that is, on the standard error of the mean in the denominator of the test statistic. In this case, there is a high degree of precision in the manufacturing process ($\sigma = .023$ is very small) so the standard error (and hence the allowable variation) is extremely small. Such a tiny difference in means would not be noticeable to consumers, but stringent quality control standards are applied to ensure that no shipment goes out with any noticeable nonconformance.

Our statistical tests show that there is a statistically *significant* departure from the desired mean for paper width at $\alpha = .05$. But is the difference *important*? Is 216.007 so close to 216 that nobody could tell the difference? The question of whether to adjust the process is up to the engineers or business managers, not statisticians.

Analogy to Confidence Intervals

A two-tailed hypothesis test at the 5 percent level of significance ($\alpha = .05$) is exactly equivalent to asking whether the 95 percent confidence interval for the mean includes the hypothesized mean. If the confidence interval includes the hypothesized mean H_0: $\mu = 216$, then we cannot reject the null hypothesis. In this case the 95 percent confidence interval would be

$$\bar{x} \pm z_{\alpha/2} \frac{\sigma}{\sqrt{n}} \quad \text{or} \quad 216.0070 \pm 1.960 \frac{.0230}{\sqrt{50}} \quad \text{or} \quad [216.001, 216.013]$$

Because this confidence interval does not include 216, we reject the null hypothesis H_0: $\mu = 216$. However, the decision is rather a close one as it was with the two-tailed hypothesis test, as the lower limit of the confidence interval almost includes 216.

Statistical Significance versus Practical Importance

Suppose that a redesigned engine could improve a truck's mpg rating by 0.5 mpg, but requires spending $1.2 billion on new plant and equipment. Is it worth doing? Such a decision requires understanding not only statistical **significance**, but also the **importance** of the potential improvement: the magnitude of the effect and its implications for product durability, customer satisfaction, budgets, cash flow, and staffing.

Because the standard error of most sample estimators approaches zero as sample size increases (if they are consistent estimators), even a small difference between the sample statistic and the hypothesized parameter may be significant if the sample size is large enough. Researchers who deal with large samples must expect "significant" effects, even when an effect is too slight to have practical importance. Is an improvement of 0.2 mpg in fuel economy *important* to Toyota buyers? Is a 0.2 percent loss of market share *important* to Hertz? Is a 15-minute increase in laptop battery life *important* to Dell customers?

Such questions require a cost/benefit calculation. Because resources are always scarce, a dollar spent on a quality improvement always has an opportunity cost (the forgone alternative). If we spend money to make a certain product improvement, then some other project may have to be shelved. We can't do everything, so we must ask whether a proposed product improvement is the best use of our scarce resources. These are questions that must be answered by experts in medicine, marketing, product safety, or engineering, rather than by statisticians.

SECTION EXERCISES

connect

9.13 Find the z_{calc} test statistic for each hypothesis test.

   a. $\bar{x} = 242$, $\mu_0 = 230$, $\sigma = 18$, $n = 20$
   b. $\bar{x} = 3.44$, $\mu_0 = 3.50$, $\sigma = 0.24$, $n = 40$
   c. $\bar{x} = 21.02$, $\mu_0 = 20.00$, $\sigma = 2.52$, $n = 30$

9.14 Use Excel to find the critical value of z for each hypothesis test.

   a. 10 percent level of significance, two-tailed test
   b. 1 percent level of significance, right-tailed test
   c. 5 percent level of significance, left-tailed test

9.15 Use Excel to find the critical value of z for each hypothesis test.

   a. $\alpha = .05$, two-tailed test
   b. $\alpha = .10$, right-tailed test
   c. $\alpha = .01$, left-tailed test

9.16 Find the z_{calc} test statistic for each hypothesis test.

   a. $\bar{x} = 423$, $\mu_0 = 420$, $\sigma = 6$, $n = 9$
   b. $\bar{x} = 8330$, $\mu_0 = 8,344$, $\sigma = 48$, $n = 36$
   c. $\bar{x} = 3.102$, $\mu_0 = 3.110$, $\sigma = .250$, $n = 25$

9.17 GreenBeam Ltd. claims that its compact fluorescent bulbs average no more than 3.50 mg of mercury. A sample of 25 bulbs shows a mean of 3.59 mg of mercury. (a) Write the hypotheses for a right-tailed test, using GreenBeam's claim as the null hypothesis about the mean. (b) Assuming a known standard deviation of 0.18 mg, calculate the z test statistic to test the manufacturer's claim. (c) At the 1 percent level of significance ($\alpha = .01$) does the sample exceed the manufacturer's claim? (d) Find the *p*-value.

9.18 The mean potassium content of a popular sports drink is listed as 140 mg in a 32-oz bottle. Analysis of 20 bottles indicates a sample mean of 139.4 mg. (a) Write the hypotheses for a two-tailed test of the claimed potassium content. (b) Assuming a known standard deviation of 2.00 mg, calculate the z test statistic to test the manufacturer's claim. (c) At the 10 percent level of significance ($\alpha = .10$), does the sample contradict the manufacturer's claim? (d) Find the *p*-value.

9.19 Calculate the test statistic and *p*-value for each sample.

   a. H_0: $\mu = 60$ versus H_1: $\mu \neq 60$, $\alpha = .025$, $\bar{x} = 63$, $\sigma = 8$, $n = 16$
   b. H_0: $\mu \geq 60$ versus H_1: $\mu < 60$, $\alpha = .05$, $\bar{x} = 58$, $\sigma = 5$, $n = 25$
   c. H_0: $\mu \leq 60$ versus H_1: $\mu > 60$, $\alpha = .05$, $\bar{x} = 65$, $\sigma = 8$, $n = 36$

9.20 Determine the *p*-value for each test statistic.

  a. Right-tailed test, $z = +1.34$
  b. Left-tailed test, $z = -2.07$
  c. Two-tailed test, $z = -1.69$

9.21 Procyon Mfg. produces tennis balls. Weights are supposed to be normally distributed with a mean of 2.035 ounces and a standard deviation of 0.002 ounce. A sample of 25 tennis balls shows a mean weight of 2.036 ounces. At $\alpha = .025$ in a right-tailed test, is the mean weight heavier than it is supposed to be?

9.22 The mean arrival rate of flights at O'Hare Airport in marginal weather is 195 flights per hour with a historical standard deviation of 13 flights. To increase arrivals, a new air traffic control procedure is implemented. In the next 30 days of marginal weather, the mean arrival rate is 200 flights per hour. (a) Set up a right-tailed decision rule at $\alpha = .025$ to decide whether there has been a significant increase in the mean number of arrivals per hour. (b) Carry out the test and make the decision. Is it close? Would the decision be different if you used $\alpha = .01$? (c) What assumptions are you making, if any? ☞ **Flights**

210	215	200	189	200	213	202	181	197	199
193	209	215	192	179	196	225	199	196	210
199	188	174	176	202	195	195	208	222	221

9.23 An airline serves bottles of Galena Spring Water that are supposed to contain an average of 10 ounces. The filling process follows a normal distribution with process standard deviation 0.07 ounce. Twelve randomly chosen bottles had the weights shown below (in ounces). (a) Set up a two-tailed decision rule to detect quality control violations using the 5 percent level of significance. (b) Carry out the test. (c) What assumptions are you making, if any? ☞ **BottleFill**

| 10.02 | 9.95 | 10.11 | 10.10 | 10.08 | 10.04 | 10.06 | 10.03 | 9.98 | 10.01 | 9.92 | 9.89 |

9.24 The Scottsdale fire department aims to respond to fire calls in 4 minutes or less, on average. Response times are normally distributed with a standard deviation of 1 minute. Would a sample of 18 fire calls with a mean response time of 4 minutes 30 seconds provide sufficient evidence to show that the goal is not being met at $\alpha = .01$? What is the *p*-value? (See *Arizona Republic,* November 23, 2006, p. A10.)

9.25 The lifespan of xenon metal halide arc-discharge bulbs for aircraft landing lights is normally distributed with a mean of 3,000 hours and a standard deviation of 500 hours. If a new ballast system shows a mean life of 3,515 hours in a test on a sample of 10 prototype new bulbs, would you conclude that the new lamp's mean life exceeds the current mean life at $\alpha = .01$? What is the *p*-value? (For more information, see www.xevision.com.)

9.26 Discuss the issues of *statistical significance* and *practical importance* in each scenario.

  a. A process for producing I-beams of oriented strand board used as main support beams in new houses has a mean breaking strength of 2,000 lbs./ft. A sample of boards from a new process has a mean breaking strength of 2,150 lbs./ft. The improvement is statistically significant, but the per-unit cost is higher.
  b. Under continuous use, the mean battery life in a certain cell phone is 45 hours. In tests of a new type of battery, the sample mean battery life is 46 hours. The improvement is statistically significant, but the new battery costs more to produce.
  c. For a wide-screen HDTV LCD unit, the mean half-life (i.e., to lose 50 percent of its brightness) is 32,000 hours. A new process is developed. In tests of the new display, the sample mean half-life is 35,000 hours. The improvement is statistically significant, though the new process is more costly.

9.27 The target activation force of the buttons on a keyless entry clicker is 1.967 newtons. Variation exists in activation force due to the nature of the manufacturing process. A sample of 9 clickers showed a mean activation force of 1.88 newtons. The standard deviation is known to be 0.145 newton. Too much force makes the keys hard to click, while too little force means the keys might be clicked accidentally. Therefore, the manufacturer's quality control engineers use a two-tailed hypothesis test for samples taken from each production batch, to detect excessive deviations in either direction. At $\alpha = .05$, does the sample indicate a significant deviation from the target?

9.4 TESTING A MEAN: UNKNOWN POPULATION VARIANCE

If the population variance σ^2 must be estimated from the sample, the hypothesis testing procedure is modified. There is a loss of information when s replaces σ in the formulas, and it is no longer appropriate to use the normal distribution. However, the basic hypothesis testing steps are the same.

Using Student's *t*

When the population standard deviation σ is unknown (as it usually is) and the population may be assumed normal (or generally symmetric with no outliers), the test statistic follows the Student's t distribution with $n - 1$ degrees of freedom. Since σ is rarely known, we generally expect to use Student's t instead of z, as you saw for confidence intervals in the previous chapter.

Test Statistic for a Mean: σ Unknown

$$t_{\text{calc}} = \frac{\bar{x} - \mu_0}{\dfrac{s}{\sqrt{n}}} \quad \text{if } \sigma \text{ is unknown} \tag{9.2}$$

Sample mean $\rightarrow \bar{x}$
Hypothesized mean $\rightarrow \mu_0$
Sample st. dev. $\rightarrow s / \sqrt{n}$

EXAMPLE 9.5

Hot Chocolate

LO 9-7

Perform a hypothesis test for a mean with unknown σ using t.

In addition to its core business of bagels and coffee, Bruegger's Bagels also sells hot chocolate for the noncoffee crowd. Customer research shows that the ideal temperature for hot chocolate is 142°F ("hot" but not "too hot"). A random sample of 24 cups of hot chocolate is taken at various times, and the temperature of each cup is measured using an ordinary kitchen thermometer that is accurate to the nearest whole degree. 📁 **HotChoc**

140	140	141	145	143	144	142	140
145	143	140	140	141	141	137	142
143	141	142	142	143	141	138	139

The sample mean is 141.375 with a sample standard deviation of 1.99592. At $\alpha = .10$, does this sample evidence show that the true mean differs from 142?

Step 1: State the Hypotheses
We use a two-tailed test. The null hypothesis is in conformance with the desired standard.

H_0: $\mu = 142$ (mean temperature is correct)

H_1: $\mu \neq 142$ (mean temperature is incorrect)

Step 2: Specify the Decision Rule
For $\alpha = .10$, using the Excel function =T.INV.2T(α, d.f.) =T.INV.2T(0.10,23) = 1.714 gives the two-tailed critical value for $d.f. = n - 1 = 24 - 1 = 23$ degrees of freedom. The same value can be obtained from Appendix D, shown here in abbreviated form:

		Upper Tail Area		
d.f.	*.10*	*.05*	*.025*	*.01*	*.005*
1	3.078	6.314	12.706	31.821	63.657
2	1.886	2.920	4.303	6.965	9.925
3	1.638	2.353	3.182	4.541	5.841
:	:	:	:	:	:
21	1.323	1.721	2.080	2.518	2.831
22	1.321	1.717	2.074	2.508	2.819
23	1.319	*1.714*	2.069	2.500	2.807
24	1.318	1.711	2.064	2.492	2.797
25	1.316	1.708	2.060	2.485	2.787

We will reject H_0 if $t_{calc} > 1.714$ or if $t_{calc} < -1.714$, as illustrated in Figure 9.8.

FIGURE 9.8   **Two-Tailed Test for a Mean Using *t* for *d.f.* = 23**

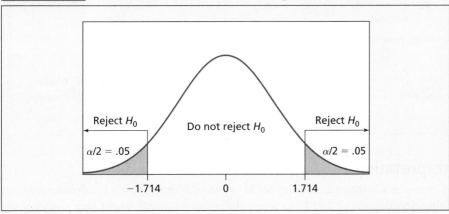

Step 3: Calculate the Test Statistic
Inserting the sample information, the test statistic is

$$t_{calc} = \frac{\bar{x} - \mu_0}{\frac{s}{\sqrt{n}}} = \frac{141.375 - 142}{\frac{1.99592}{\sqrt{24}}} = \frac{-.6250}{.40742} = -1.534$$

Step 4: Make the Decision
Since the test statistic lies within the range of chance variation, we cannot reject the null hypothesis H_0: $\mu = 142$.

Sensitivity to α   How sensitive is our conclusion to the choice of level of significance? Table 9.4 shows several critical values of Student's *t*. At $\alpha = .20$ we could reject H_0, but not at the other α values shown. This table is not to suggest that experimenting with various α values is desirable, but merely to illustrate that our decision is affected by our choice of α.

	$\alpha = .20$	$\alpha = .10$	$\alpha = .05$	$\alpha = .01$
Critical value	$t_{.10} = \pm1.319$	$t_{.05} = \pm1.714$	$t_{.025} = \pm2.069$	$t_{.005} = \pm2.807$
Decision	Reject H_0	Don't reject H_0	Don't reject H_0	Don't reject H_0

TABLE 9.4

Effect of α on the Decision (Two-Tailed *t* Test with *d.f.* = 23)

Using the *p*-Value

LO 9-8

Use tables or Excel
to find the *p*-value in
tests of μ.

A more general approach favored by researchers is to find the *p*-value. After the *p*-value is calculated, different analysts can compare it to the level of significance (α) that is appropriate for the task. We want to determine the tail area less than $t = -1.534$ or greater than $t = +1.534$. However, from Appendix D we can only get a range for the *p*-value. From Appendix D, we see that the two-tail *p*-value must lie between .20 and .10 (it's a two-tailed test, so we double the right-tail area). It is easier and more precise to use Excel's function =T.DIST.2T(t test statistic, degrees of freedom) =T.DIST.2T(1.534,23) to get the two-tailed *p*-value of .13867. The area of each tail is half that, or .06934, as shown in Figure 9.9. A sample mean as extreme in either tail would occur by chance about 139 times in 1,000 two-tailed tests if H_0 were true. Since the *p*-value $> \alpha$, we cannot reject H_0.

FIGURE 9.9

Two-Tailed *p*-Value for *t* = 1.534

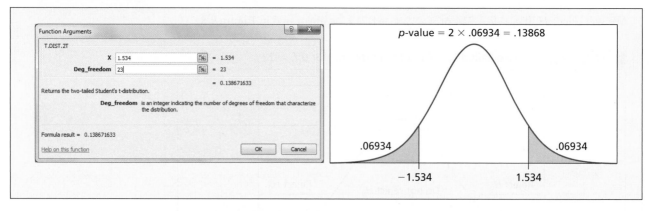

Interpretation

It is doubtful whether a consumer could tell the difference in hot chocolate temperature within a few degrees of 142°F, so a tiny difference in means might lack *practical importance* even if it were *statistically significant*. Importance must be judged by management, not by the statistician.

In the hot chocolate example, there are no outliers and something of a bell-shape, as shown in the dot plot below. The *t* test is reasonably robust to mild non-normality. However, outliers or extreme skewness can affect the test, just as when we construct confidence intervals.

Who Uses *p*-Values?

"Executives at Noodles & Company may not perform a statistical analysis themselves, but they do understand the *p*-value associated with the results of an analysis. The *p*-value allows us to objectively consider the data and statistical results when we make an important strategic decision."

Dave Boennighausen, VP of Finance at Noodles & Company

Confidence Interval versus Hypothesis Test

The two-tailed test at the 10 percent level of significance is equivalent to a two-tailed 90 percent confidence interval. If the confidence interval does not contain μ_0, we reject H_0. For the hot chocolate, the sample mean is 141.375 with a sample standard deviation of 1.99592. Using Appendix D we find $t_{.05} = 1.714$ so the 90 percent confidence interval for μ is

$$\bar{x} \pm t_{\alpha/2} \frac{s}{\sqrt{n}} \quad \text{or} \quad 141.375 \pm (1.714)\frac{1.99592}{\sqrt{24}} \quad \text{or} \quad 141.375 \pm .6983$$

Since $\mu = 142$ lies within the 90 percent confidence interval [140.677, 142.073], we cannot reject the hypothesis H_0: $\mu = 142$ at $\alpha = .10$ in a two-tailed test. Many decisions can be handled either as hypothesis tests or using confidence intervals. The confidence interval has the appeal of providing a graphic feeling for the location of the hypothesized mean within the confidence interval, as shown in Figure 9.10. We can see that 142 is near the upper end of the confidence interval, nearly leading to a rejection of H_0: $\mu = 142$.

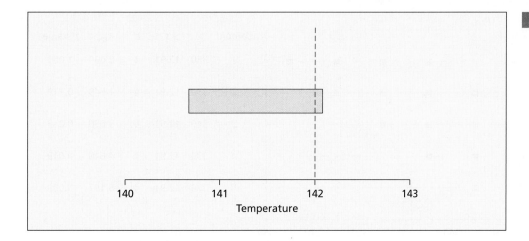

FIGURE 9.10

90 Percent Confidence Interval for μ

Using MegaStat

Excel does not offer a one-sample *t*-test, but you can get tests for one mean, including a confidence interval, using MegaStat. Figure 9.11 shows its setup screen and output for the test of one mean for the hot chocolate data. You enter the data range and everything else is automatic. You have a choice of *z* or *t*, but to use *z* you must know σ.

FIGURE 9.11

MegaStat Test for One Mean

Large Samples

From Appendix D you can verify that when *n* is large, there is little difference between critical values of *t* and *z* (the last line in Appendix D, for *d.f.* $= \infty$). For this reason, it is unlikely that harm will result if you use *z* instead of *t*, as long as the sample size is not small. The test statistic is

$$z_{\text{calc}} = \frac{\bar{x} - \mu_0}{\frac{s}{\sqrt{n}}} \qquad \text{(large sample, unknown } \sigma\text{)} \qquad \textbf{(9.3)}$$

However, using z instead of t is not conservative because it will increase Type I error somewhat. Therefore, statisticians recommend that we always apply t when σ is unknown. We then can use Excel or Appendix D to get the critical value.

How's Your Intuition?

A laptop manufacturer claims an average battery life of 6 hours (360 minutes). Four laptops are operated until the battery is exhausted. Which samples in the illustration below would make you doubt that $\mu = 360$? Sample 1's mean agrees perfectly with H_0: $\mu = 360$, and its p-value is 1.000, so the sample gives no evidence to contradict H_0. The other four samples give progressively stronger evidence against H_0. If you choose $\alpha = .05$, then samples 4 and 5 would lead to rejection of H_0: $\mu = 360$, while sample 3 would be near the borderline.

Sample	$\bar{x}$	s	n	t_{calc}	p-value
1	360	12.91	4	0.000	1.000
2	350	12.91	4	−1.549	0.219
3	340	12.91	4	−3.098	0.053
4	330	12.91	4	−4.648	0.019
5	320	12.91	4	−6.197	0.009

SECTION EXERCISES

connect

9.28 Find the t_{calc} test statistic for each hypothesis test.

  a. $\bar{x} = 14.7$, $\mu_0 = 13.0$, $s = 1.8$, $n = 12$
  b. $\bar{x} = 241$, $\mu_0 = 250$, $s = 12$, $n = 8$
  c. $\bar{x} = 2{,}102$, $\mu_0 = 2{,}000$, $s = 242$, $n = 17$

9.29 Find the critical value of Student's t for each hypothesis test.

  a. 10 percent level of significance, two-tailed test, $n = 21$
  b. 1 percent level of significance, right-tailed test, $n = 9$
  c. 5 percent level of significance, left-tailed test, $n = 28$

9.30 Find the critical value of Student's t for each hypothesis test.

  a. Two-tailed test, $n = 18$, $a = .05$
  b. Right-tailed test, $n = 15$, $a = .10$
  c. Left-tailed test, $n = 31$, $a = .01$

9.31 Find the t_{calc} test statistic for each hypothesis test.

  a. $\bar{x} = 347$, $\mu_0 = 349$, $s = 1.8$, $n = 9$
  b. $\bar{x} = 45$, $\mu_0 = 50$, $s = 12$, $n = 16$
  c. $\bar{x} = 4.103$, $\mu_0 = 4.004$, $s = 0.245$, $n = 25$

9.32 Estimate the p-value *as a range* using Appendix D (*not* Excel):

  a. $t = 1.457$, $d.f. = 14$, right-tailed test
  b. $t = 2.601$, $d.f. = 8$, two-tailed test
  c. $t = -1.847$, $d.f. = 22$, left-tailed test

9.33 Find the *p*-value using Excel (*not* Appendix D):

  a. $t = 1.457$, *d.f.* = 14, right-tailed test
  b. $t = 2.601$, *d.f.* = 8, two-tailed test
  c. $t = -1.847$, *d.f.* = 22, left-tailed test

9.34 Use Excel to find the *p*-value for each test statistic.

  a. Right-tailed test, $t = +1.677$, $n = 13$
  b. Left-tailed test, $t = -2.107$, $n = 5$
  c. Two-tailed test, $t = -1.865$, $n = 34$

9.35 Calculate the test statistic and *p*-value for each sample. State the conclusion for the specified α.

  a. $H_0: \mu = 200$ versus $H_1: \mu \neq 200$, $\alpha = .025$, $\bar{x} = 203$, $s = 8$, $n = 16$
  b. $H_0: \mu \geq 200$ versus $H_1: \mu < 200$, $\alpha = .05$, $\bar{x} = 198$, $s = 5$, $n = 25$
  c. $H_0: \mu \leq 200$ versus $H_1: \mu > 200$, $\alpha = .05$, $\bar{x} = 205$, $s = 8$, $n = 36$

9.36 The manufacturer of an airport baggage scanning machine claims it can handle an average of 530 bags per hour. At $\alpha = .05$ in a left-tailed test, would a sample of 16 randomly chosen hours with a mean of 510 and a standard deviation of 50 indicate that the manufacturer's claim is overstated?

9.37 The manufacturer of Glo-More flat white interior latex paint claims one-coat coverage of 400 square feet per gallon on interior walls. A painter keeps careful track of 6 gallons and finds coverage (in square feet) of 360, 410, 380, 360, 390, 400. (a) At $\alpha = .10$ does this evidence contradict the claim? State your hypotheses and decision rule. (b) Is this conclusion sensitive to the choice of α? (c) Use Excel to find the *p*-value. Interpret it. (d) Discuss the distinction between importance and significance in this example. 📁 **Paint**

9.38 The average weight of a package of rolled oats is supposed to be at least 18 ounces. A sample of 18 packages shows a mean of 17.78 ounces with a standard deviation of 0.41 ounce. (a) At the 5 percent level of significance, is the true mean smaller than the specification? Clearly state your hypotheses and decision rule. (b) Is this conclusion sensitive to the choice of α? (c) Use Excel to find the *p*-value. Interpret it.

9.39 According to J.D. Power & Associates, the mean purchase price of a smartphone device (such as an iPhone or Blackberry) in 2008 was $216. In 2009, a random sample of 20 business managers who owned a smartphone device showed a mean purchase price of $209 with a sample standard deviation of $13. (a) At $\alpha = .05$, has the mean purchase price decreased? State the hypotheses and decision rule clearly. (b) Use Excel to find the *p*-value and interpret it.

9.40 The average age of a part-time seasonal employee at a Vail Resorts ski mountain has historically been 37 years. A random sample of 50 part-time seasonal employees in 2010 had a sample mean age of 38.5 years with a sample standard deviation equal to 16 years. At the 10 percent level of significance, does this sample show that the average age was different in 2010? **VAIL**RESORTS

9.41 The number of entrees purchased in a single order at a Noodles & Company restaurant has had an historical average of 1.60 entrees per order. On a particular Saturday afternoon, a random sample of 40 Noodles orders had a mean number of entrees equal to 1.80 with a standard deviation equal to 1.11. At the 5 percent level of significance, does this sample show that the average number of entrees per order was greater than expected?

9.42 In 2008, a small dealership leased 21 Suburu Outbacks on 2-year leases. When the cars were returned in 2010, the mileage was recorded (see below). Is the dealer's mean significantly greater than the national average of 30,000 miles for 2-year leased vehicles, using the 10 percent level of significance? 📁 **Mileage**

40,060	24,960	14,310	17,370	44,740	44,550	20,250
33,380	24,270	41,740	58,630	35,830	25,750	28,910
25,090	43,380	23,940	43,510	53,680	31,810	36,780

9.43 At Oxnard University, a sample of 18 senior accounting majors showed a mean cumulative GPA of 3.35 with a standard deviation of 0.25. (a) At $\alpha = .05$ in a two-tailed test, does this differ significantly from 3.25 (the mean GPA for all business school seniors at the university)? (b) Use the sample to construct a 95 percent confidence interval for the mean. Does the confidence interval include 3.25? (c) Explain how the hypothesis test and confidence interval are equivalent.

Mini Case 9.2

Beauty Products and Small Business

Lisa has been working at a beauty counter in a department store for 5 years. In her spare time she's also been creating lotions and fragrances using all natural products. After receiving positive feedback from her friends and family about her beauty products, Lisa decides to open her own store. Lisa knows that convincing a bank to help fund her new business will require more than a few positive testimonials from family. Based on her experience working at the department store, Lisa believes women in her area spend more than the national average on fragrance products. This fact could help make her business successful.

Lisa would like to be able to support her belief with data to include in a business plan proposal that she would then use to obtain a small business loan. Lisa took a business statistics course while in college and decides to use the hypothesis testing tool she learned. After conducting research she learns that the national average spending by women on fragrance products is $59 every 3 months.

The hypothesis test is based on this survey result:

$H_0: \mu \leq \$59$
$H_1: \mu > \$59$

In other words, she will assume the average spending in her town is the same as the national average *unless she has strong evidence that says otherwise*. Lisa takes a random sample of 25 women and finds that the sample mean $\bar{x}$ is $68 and the sample standard deviation s is $15. Lisa uses a t statistic because she doesn't know the population standard deviation. Her calculated t statistic is

$$t_{calc} = \frac{68 - 59}{\frac{15}{\sqrt{25}}} = 3.00 \qquad \text{with 24 degrees of freedom}$$

Using the Excel formula =T.DIST.RT(3,24), Lisa finds that the right-tail p-value is .003103. This p-value is quite small and she can safely reject her null hypothesis. Lisa now has strong evidence to conclude that over a 3-month period women in her area spend more than $59 on average.

Lisa would also like to include an estimate for the average amount women in her area *do* spend. Calculating a confidence interval would be her next step. Lisa chooses a 95 percent confidence level and finds the t value to use in her calculations by using the Excel formula =T.INV(0.05,24). The result is $t_{.025} = 2.0639$. Her 95 percent confidence interval for μ is

$$\bar{x} \pm t_{\alpha/2} \frac{s}{\sqrt{n}} \quad \text{or} \quad \$68 \pm 2.0639 \frac{15}{\sqrt{25}} \quad \text{or} \quad \$68 \pm \$6.19 \quad \text{or} \quad [61.81, 74.19].$$

Lisa's business plan proposal can confidently claim that women in her town spend more than the national average on fragrance products and that she estimates the average spending is between $62 and $74 every 3 months. Hopefully the bank will see not only that Lisa creates excellent beauty products, but she also is a smart businessperson!

Source: For national average spending see The NPD Group press release, "New NPD Beauty Study Identifies Key Consumer Differences and Preferences," March 28, 2005.

9.5 TESTING A PROPORTION

Proportions are used frequently in business situations and collecting proportion data is straightforward. It is easier for customers to say whether they like or dislike this year's new automobile color than it is for customers to quantify their degree of satisfaction with the new color. Also, many business performance indicators such as market share, employee retention rates, and employee accident rates are expressed as proportions.

EXAMPLE 9.6

Testing a Proportion

In 2006, U.S. airlines mishandled 6 out of every 1,000 bags checked for air travel. One airline, FlyFast, found that 54 percent of their mishandled bag incidents were related to transferring baggage to a connecting flight. FlyFast recently installed an RFID (Radio Frequency Identification) system with the goal of decreasing the proportion of mistakes caused during transfer and ultimately reducing the overall proportion of lost bags. After operating their new system for several months, FlyFast would like to know if the wireless system has been effective. FlyFast could use a hypothesis test to answer this question. The benchmark for the null hypothesis is their proportion of transfer mistakes using their old system ($\pi_0 = .54$.) The possible set of statistical hypotheses would be:

Left-Tailed Test	*Two-Tailed Test*	*Right-Tailed Test*
$H_0: \pi \geq .54$	$H_0: \pi = .54$	$H_0: \pi \leq .54$
$H_1: \pi < .54$	$H_1: \pi \neq .54$	$H_1: \pi > .54$

Which set of hypotheses would be most logical for FlyFast to use? Since FlyFast believes the RFID system will reduce the proportion of transfer errors, they might use a left-tailed test. They would assume there has been no improvement, unless their evidence shows otherwise. If they can reject H_0 in favor of H_1 in a left-tailed test FlyFast would be able to say that their data provide evidence that the proportion of transfer errors has decreased since the RFID tagging system was implemented.

The steps we follow for testing a hypothesis about a population proportion, π, are the same as the ones we follow for testing a mean. The difference is that we now calculate a sample proportion, p, to calculate the test statistic. We know from Chapter 8 that for a sufficiently large sample the sample proportion can be assumed to follow a normal distribution. Our rule is to assume normality if $n\pi_0 \geq 10$ and $n(1 - \pi_0) \geq 10$. If we can assume a normal sampling distribution, then the test statistic would be the z-score. Recall that the sample proportion is

LO 9-9

Perform a hypothesis test for a proportion and find the *p*-value.

$$p = \frac{x}{n} = \frac{\text{number of successes}}{\text{sample size}} \qquad (9.4)$$

The test statistic, calculated from sample data, is the difference between the sample proportion p and the hypothesized proportion π_0 divided by the *standard error of the proportion* (sometimes denoted σ_p):

Test Statistic for a Proportion

$$z_{\text{calc}} = \frac{p - \pi_0}{\sigma_p} = \frac{p - \pi_0}{\sqrt{\dfrac{\pi_0(1 - \pi_0)}{n}}} \qquad (9.5)$$

The value of π_0 we are testing is a **benchmark**, such as past performance, an industry standard, or a product specification. The value of π_0 does *not* come from a sample.

EXAMPLE 9.7

Return Policy

Retailers such as Guess, Staples, Sports Authority, and Limited Brands are employing new technology to crack down on "serial exchangers"—customers who abuse their return and exchange policies (*The Wall Street Journal*, November 29, 2004). For example, some customers buy an outfit, wear it once or twice, and then return it. Software called *Verify-1*, a product of a California-based company Return Exchange, tracks a shopper's record of bringing back items. The historical return rate for merchandise at department stores is 13.0 percent. At one department store, after implementing the new software, there were 22 returns in a sample of 250 purchases. At $\alpha = .05$, does this sample indicate that the true return rate has fallen?

Step 1: State the Hypotheses
The hypotheses are

$H_0: \pi \geq .13$ (return rate is the same or greater than the historical rate)

$H_1: \pi < .13$ (return rate has fallen below the historical rate)

Step 2: Specify the Decision Rule
For $\alpha = .05$ in a left-tailed test, the critical value is $z_{.05} = -1.645$, so the decision rule is

Reject H_0 if $z_{calc} < -1.645$
Otherwise do not reject H_0

This decision rule is illustrated in Figure 9.12.

FIGURE 9.12   **Left-Tailed z Test Using $\alpha = .05$**

Before using z we should check the normality assumption. To assume normality we require that $n\pi_0 \geq 10$ and $n(1 - \pi_0) \geq 10$. Note that we use the hypothesized proportion π_0 (not p) to check normality because we are assuming H_0 to be the truth about the population. Inserting $\pi_0 = .13$ and $n = 250$, we see that these conditions are easily met: $(250)(.13) = 32.5$ and $(250)(1 - .13) = 217.5$.

Step 3: Calculate the Test Statistic
Since $p = x/n = 22/250 = .088$, the sample seems to favor H_1. But we will assume that H_0 is true and see if the test statistic contradicts this assumption. We test the hypothesis at $\pi = .13$. If we can reject $\pi = .13$ in favor of $\pi < .13$, then we implicitly reject the class of hypotheses $\pi \geq .13$. The test statistic is the difference between the sample proportion $p = x/n$ and the hypothesized parameter π_0 divided by the standard error of p:

$$z_{calc} = \frac{p - \pi_0}{\sqrt{\dfrac{\pi_0(1 - \pi_0)}{n}}} = \frac{.088 - .13}{\sqrt{\dfrac{.13(1 - .13)}{250}}} = \frac{-.042}{.02127} = -1.975$$

Step 4: Make the Decision
Because the test statistic falls in the left-tail rejection region, we reject H_0. We conclude that the return rate is less than .13 after implementing the new software.

Step 5: Take Action
The rate of returns seems to be reduced, so the store might want to try using the software at its other locations.

Calculating the *p*-Value

For our test statistic $z_{calc} = -1.975$, the *p*-value (.02413) can be obtained from Excel's cumulative standard normal =NORM.S.DIST(−1.975). Alternatively, if we round the test statistic to two decimals, we can use the cumulative normal table in Appendix C-2. Depending on how we round the test statistic, we might obtain two possible *p*-values, as shown in Table 9.5. Using the *p*-value, we reject H_0 at $\alpha = .05$, but the decision would be very close if we had used $\alpha = .025$. Figure 9.13 illustrates the *p*-value.

TABLE 9.5			Finding the *p*-Value for *z* = 1.975 in Appendix C-2							
z	.00	.01	.02	.03	.04	.05	.06	.07	.08	.09
−3.7	.00011	.00010	.00010	.00010	.00009	.00009	.00008	.00008	.00008	.00008
−3.6	.00016	.00015	.00015	.00014	.00014	.00013	.00013	.00012	.00012	.00011
−3.5	.00023	.00022	.00022	.00021	.00020	.00019	.00019	.00018	.00017	.00017
⋮	⋮	⋮	⋮	⋮	⋮	⋮	⋮	⋮	⋮	⋮
−2.0	.02275	.02222	.02169	.02118	.02068	.02018	.01970	.01923	.01876	.01831
−1.9	.02872	.02807	.02743	.02680	.02619	.02559	.02500	*.02442*	*.02385*	.02330
−1.8	.03593	.03515	.03438	.03362	.03288	.03216	.03144	.03074	.03005	.02938

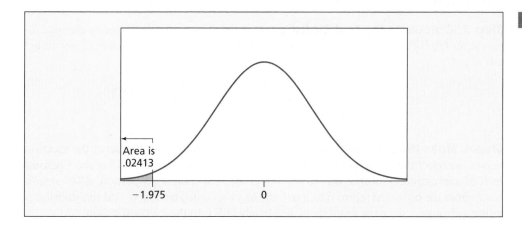

FIGURE 9.13

p-Value for a Left-Tailed Test with $z_{calc} = -1.975$

The *smaller* the *p*-value, the more we are inclined to *reject* H_0. Does this seem backward? You might think a large *p*-value would be "more significant" than a small one. But the *p*-value is the likelihood of the sample if H_0 is true, so a small *p*-value makes us doubt H_0. The *p*-value is a direct measure of the level of significance at which we could reject H_0, so *a smaller p-value is more convincing*. For the left-tailed test, the *p*-value tells us that there is a .02413 probability of getting a sample proportion of .088 or less if the true proportion is .13; that is, such a sample would arise by chance only about 24 times in 1,000 tests if the null hypothesis is true. In our left-tailed test, we would reject H_0 because the *p*-value (.02413) is smaller than α (.05). In fact, we could reject H_0 at *any* α greater than .02413.

Two-Tailed Test

What if we used a two-tailed test? This might be appropriate if the objective is to detect a change in the return rate in *either* direction. In fact, two-tailed tests are used more often, because rejection in a two-tailed test always implies rejection in a one-tailed test, other things being equal. The same sample can be used for either a one-tailed or two-tailed test. The type of hypothesis test is up to the statistician.

Step 1: State the Hypotheses The hypotheses are

H_0: $\pi = .13$ (return rate is the same as the historical rate)

H_1: $\pi \neq .13$ (return rate is different from the historical rate)

Step 2: Specify the Decision Rule For a two-tailed test, we split the risk of Type I error by putting $\alpha/2 = .05/2 = .025$ in each tail (as we would for a confidence interval). For $\alpha = .05$ in a two-tailed test, the critical value is $z_{.025} = 1.96$, so the decision rule is

Reject H_0 if $z_{calc} > +1.96$ or if $z_{calc} < -1.96$

Otherwise do not reject H_0

The decision rule is illustrated in Figure 9.14.

Two-Tailed z Test for $\alpha = .05$

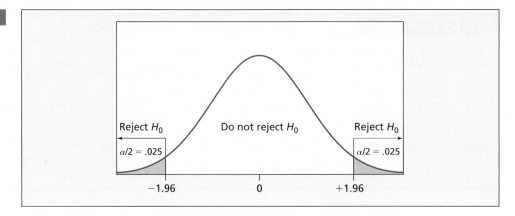

Step 3: Calculate the Test Statistic The test statistic is *unaffected by the hypotheses or the level of significance.* The value of the test statistic is the same as for the one-tailed test:

$$z_{calc} = \frac{p - \pi_0}{\sqrt{\dfrac{\pi_0(1 - \pi_0)}{n}}} = \frac{.088 - .13}{\sqrt{\dfrac{.13(1 - .13)}{250}}} = \frac{-.042}{.02127} = -1.975$$

Step 4: Make the Decision Because the test statistic falls in the left tail of the rejection region, we reject the null hypothesis H_0: $\pi = .13$ and conclude H_1: $\pi \neq .13$ at the 5 percent level of significance. Another way to say this is that the sample proportion *differs significantly* from the historical return rate at $\alpha = .05$ in a two-tailed test. Note that this decision is rather a close one, since the test statistic just barely falls into the rejection region.

The rejection was stronger in a one-tailed test, that is, the test statistic is farther from the critical value. *Holding α constant, rejection in a two-tailed test always implies rejection in a one-tailed test.* This reinforces the logic of choosing a two-tailed test unless there is a specific reason to prefer a one-tailed test.

Calculating a *p*-Value for a Two-Tailed Test

In a two-tailed test, we divide the risk into equal tails, one on the left and one on the right, to allow for the possibility that we will reject H_0 whenever the sample statistic is very small or very large. With the *p*-value approach in a two-tailed test, we find the tail area associated with our sample test statistic, multiply this by two, and then compare that probability to α. Our z statistic was calculated to be -1.975. The *p*-value would then be

$$2 \times P(Z < -1.975) = 2 \times .02413 = .04826$$

We would reject the null hypothesis because the *p*-value .04826 is less than α (.05).

Effect of α

Would the decision be the same if we had used a different level of significance? Table 9.6 shows some possibilities. *The test statistic is the same regardless of α.* While we can reject the null hypothesis at $\alpha = .10$ or $\alpha = .05$, we cannot reject at $\alpha = .01$. Therefore, we would say that the current return rate differs from the historical return rate at the 10 percent and 5 percent levels of significance, but not at the 1 percent level of significance.

α	*Test Statistic*	*Two-Tailed Critical Values*	*Decision*
.10	$z_{calc} = -1.975$	$z_{.05} = \pm 1.645$	Reject H_0
.05	$z_{calc} = -1.975$	$z_{.025} = \pm 1.960$	Reject H_0
.01	$z_{calc} = -1.975$	$z_{.005} = \pm 2.576$	Don't reject H_0

TABLE 9.6

Effect of Varying α

Which level of significance is the "right" one? They all are. It depends on how much Type I error we are willing to allow. Before concluding that $\alpha = .01$ is "better" than the others because it allows less Type I error, you should remember that smaller Type I error leads to increased Type II error. In this case, Type I error would imply that there has been a change in return rates when in reality nothing has changed, while Type II error implies that the software had no effect on the return rate, when in reality the software did decrease the return rate.

EXAMPLE 9.8

Length of Hospital Stay

A hospital is comparing its performance against an industry benchmark that no more than 50 percent of normal births should result in a hospital stay exceeding 2 days (48 hours). Thirty-one births in a sample of 50 normal births had a length of stay (LOS) greater than 48 hours. At $\alpha = .025$, does this sample prove that the hospital exceeds the benchmark? This question requires a right-tailed test.

Step 1: State the Hypotheses
The hypotheses are

H_0: $\pi \leq .50$ (the hospital is compliant with the benchmark)

H_1: $\pi > .50$ (the hospital is exceeding the benchmark)

Step 2: Specify the Decision Rule
For $\alpha = .025$ in a right-tailed test, the critical value is $z_{.025} = 1.96$, so the decision rule is

Reject H_0 if $z > 1.960$

Otherwise do not reject H_0

This decision rule is illustrated in Figure 9.15.

FIGURE 9.15   **Right-Tailed *z* Test Using $\alpha = .025$**

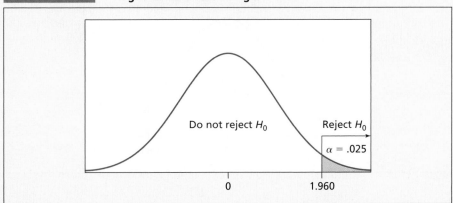

To assume normality of the sample proportion p, we require that $n\pi_0 \geq 10$ and $n(1 - \pi_0) \geq 10$. Inserting $\pi_0 = .50$ and $n = 50$, we see that the normality conditions are easily met: $(50)(.50) = 25$ and $(50)(1 - .50) = 25$.

Step 3: Calculate the Test Statistic
Since $p = x/n = 31/50 = .62$, the sample seems to favor H_1. But we will assume that H_0 is true and see if the test statistic contradicts this assumption. We test the

hypothesis at $\pi = .50$. If we can reject $\pi = .50$ in favor of $\pi > .50$, then we can reject the class of hypotheses $\pi \leq .50$. The test statistic is the difference between the sample proportion $p = x/n$ and the hypothesized parameter π_0 divided by the standard error of p:

$$z_{calc} = \frac{p - \pi_0}{\sqrt{\dfrac{\pi_0(1 - \pi_0)}{n}}} = \frac{.62 - .50}{\sqrt{\dfrac{.50(1 - .50)}{50}}} = \frac{.12}{.07071068} = 1.697$$

Step 4: Make the Decision
The test statistic does not fall in the right-tail rejection region, so we cannot reject the hypothesis that $\pi \leq .50$ at the 2.5 percent level of significance. In other words, the test statistic is within the realm of chance at $\alpha = .025$.

Step 5: Take Action
The hospital appears compliant with the benchmark, so no action is required at this time.

Calculating the p-Value

In this case, the p-value can be obtained from Excel's cumulative standard normal function =1−NORM.S.DIST(1.697) = .04485 or from Appendix C-2 (using $z = 1.70$ we get $p = 1 - .9554 = .0446$). Excel's accuracy is greater because $z = 1.697$ is not rounded to $z = 1.70$. Since we want a right-tail area, we must subtract the cumulative distribution function from 1. The p-value is greater than .025 so we fail to reject the null hypothesis in a right-tailed test. We could (barely) reject at $\alpha = .05$. This demonstrates that the level of significance can affect our decision. The advantage of the p-value is that it tells you exactly the point of indifference between rejecting or not rejecting H_0. The p-value is illustrated in Figure 9.16.

FIGURE 9.16

p-Value for a Right-Tailed Test with $z_{calc} = 1.697$

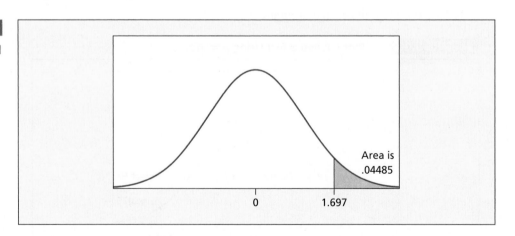

SECTION EXERCISES

connect

9.44 Interpret each p-value in your own words:

    a. p-value = .387, H_0: $\pi \geq .20$, H_1: $\pi < .20$, $\alpha = .10$
    b. p-value = .043, H_0: $\pi \leq .90$, H_1: $\pi > .90$, $\alpha = .05$
    c. p-value = .0012, H_0: $\pi = .50$, H_1: $\pi \neq .50$, $\alpha = .01$

9.45 Calculate the test statistic and p-value for each sample.

    a. H_0: $\pi = .20$ versus H_1: $\pi \neq .20$, $\alpha = .025$, $p = .28$, $n = 100$
    b. H_0: $\pi \leq .50$ versus H_1: $\pi > .50$, $\alpha = .025$, $p = .60$, $n = 90$
    c. H_0: $\pi \leq .75$ versus H_1: $\pi > .75$, $\alpha = .10$, $p = .82$, $n = 50$

9.46 Calculate the test statistic and *p*-value for each sample.

    a. H_0: $\pi \leq .60$ versus H_1: $\pi > .60$, $\alpha = .05$, $x = 56$, $n = 80$
    b. H_0: $\pi = .30$ versus H_1: $\pi \neq .30$, $\alpha = .05$, $x = 18$, $n = 40$
    c. H_0: $\pi \geq .10$ versus H_1: $\pi < .10$, $\alpha = .01$, $x = 3$, $n = 100$

9.47 May normality of the sample proportion *p* be assumed? Show your work.

    a. H_0: $\pi = .30$ versus H_1: $\pi \neq .30$, $n = 20$
    b. H_0: $\pi = .05$ versus H_1: $\pi \neq .05$, $n = 50$
    c. H_0: $\pi = .10$ versus H_1: $\pi \neq .10$, $n = 400$

9.48 In a recent survey, 10 percent of the participants rated Pepsi as being "concerned with my health." PepsiCo's response included a new "Smart Spot" symbol on its products that meet certain nutrition criteria, to help consumers who seek more healthful eating options. At $\alpha = .05$, would a follow-up survey showing that 18 of 100 persons now rate Pepsi as being "concerned with my health" provide sufficient evidence that the percentage has increased? (Data are from *The Wall Street Journal*, July 30, 2004.)

9.49 In a hospital's shipment of 3,500 insulin syringes, 14 were unusable due to defects. (a) At $\alpha = .05$, is this sufficient evidence to reject future shipments from this supplier if the hospital's quality standard requires 99.7 percent of the syringes to be acceptable? State the hypotheses and decision rule. (b) May normality of the sample proportion *p* be assumed? (c) Explain the effects of Type I error and Type II error. (d) Find the *p*-value.

9.50 To combat antibiotic resistance, the Quality Improvement Consortium recommends a throat swab to confirm strep throat before a physician prescribes antibiotics to children under age 5. In a random sample of 60 children who received antibiotics for throat infections, 18 did not have a throat swab. (a) At $\alpha = .05$, is this a statistically significant reduction over last year's national rate of 40 percent? (b) Is it safe to assume normality of the sample proportion *p*? Explain.

9.51 To encourage telephone efficiency, a catalog call center issues a guideline that at least half of all telephone orders should be completed within 2 minutes. Subsequently, a random sample of 64 telephone calls showed that only 24 calls lasted 2 minutes or less. (a) At $\alpha = .05$ is this a significant departure from the guideline in a left-tailed test? State your hypotheses and decision rule. (b) Find the *p*-value. (c) Is the difference important (as opposed to significant)?

9.52 The recent default rate on all student loans is 5.2 percent. In a recent random sample of 300 loans at private universities, there were 9 defaults. (a) Does this sample show sufficient evidence that the private university loan default rate is below the rate for all universities, using a left-tailed test at $\alpha = .01$? (b) Calculate the *p*-value. (c) Verify that the assumption of normality of the sample proportion *p* is justified.

9.53 A poll of 702 frequent and occasional fliers found that 442 respondents favored a ban on cell phones in flight, even if technology permits it. At $\alpha = .05$, can we conclude that more than half the sampled population supports a ban?

Small Samples and Non-Normality

In random tests by the FAA, 12.5 percent of all passenger flights failed the agency's test for bacterial count in water served to passengers (*The Wall Street Journal*, November 10, 2004, p. D1). Airlines now are trying to improve their compliance with water quality standards. Random inspection of 16 recent flights showed that only 1 flight failed the water quality test. Has overall compliance improved?

H_0: $\pi \geq .125$ (failure rate has not improved)

H_1: $\pi < .125$ (failure rate has declined)

The sample is clearly too small to assume normality since $n\pi_0 = (16)(.125) = 2$. Instead, we use MINITAB to test the hypotheses by finding the exact binomial left-tail probability of a sample proportion $p = 1/16 = .0625$ under the assumption that $\pi = .125$, as shown in Figure 9.17.

The *p*-value of .388 does not permit rejection of H_0 at any of the usual levels of significance (e.g., 5 percent). The binomial test is easy and is always correct since no assumption of normality is required. Lacking MINITAB, you could do the same thing by using Excel to calculate the cumulative binomial probability of the observed sample result under the null hypothesis as $P(X \leq 1 \mid n = 16, \pi = .125) =$ BINOM.DIST(1,16,.125,1) $= .38793$.

FIGURE 9.17

MINITAB Small-Sample Test of a Proportion

Test and CI for One Proportion

Test of p = 0.125 vs p < 0.125

				95%	
				Upper	Exact
Sample	X	N	Sample p	Bound	P-Value
1	1	16	0.062500	0.263957	0.388

Mini Case 9.3

Every Minute Counts

As more company business is transacted by telephone or Internet, there is a considerable premium to reduce customer time spent with human operators. Verizon recently installed a new speech recognition system for its repair calls. In the old system, the user had to press keys on the numeric keypad to answer questions, which led many callers to opt to talk to an operator instead. Under the old system, 94 percent of the customers had to talk to an operator to get their needs met. Suppose that, using the new system, a sample of 150 calls showed that 120 required an operator. The hypotheses are

H_0: $\pi \geq .94$ (the new system is no better than the old system)

H_1: $\pi < .94$ (the new system has reduced the proportion of operator calls)

These hypotheses call for a left-tailed test. Using $\alpha = .01$, the left-tail critical value is $z_{.01} = -2.326$, as illustrated in Figure 9.18.

FIGURE 9.18 **Decision Rule for Left-Tailed Test**

Reject H_0

$\alpha = .01$

-2.326 0

For normality of the sample proportion p, we want $n\pi_0 \geq 10$ and $n(1 - \pi_0) \geq 10$. The condition for normality is not quite met, since $(150)(.94) = 141$ but $(150)(.06) = 9$. We will proceed, bearing in mind this possible concern. The sample proportion is $p = 120/150 = .80$, so the test statistic is

$$z_{calc} = \frac{p - \pi_0}{\sqrt{\dfrac{\pi_0(1 - \pi_0)}{n}}} = \frac{.80 - .94}{\sqrt{\dfrac{.94(1 - .94)}{150}}} = \frac{-.14}{.01939} = -7.22$$

The test statistic is far below the critical value, so we conclude that the percentage of customers who require an operator has declined. MINITAB verifies this calculation and also gives the *p*-value (.000) as shown in Figure 9.19.

Besides being significant, such savings are important. For example, Boston Financial Data Services, a company that provides record-keeping services for mutual funds, shaved a minute off the mean time to process a customer request. Its call centers process 1.7 million calls a year, so the savings are very large. See *The Wall Street Journal,* July 26, 2004.

FIGURE 9.19

MINITAB Results for One-Sample Proportion

```
Test and CI for One Proportion

Test of p = 0.94 vs p < 0.94
99%

                                Upper
Sample   X    N  Sample p     Bound   Z-Value  P-Value
1      120  150  0.800000  0.875978    -7.22    0.000
```

SECTION EXERCISES

connect

9.54 A coin was flipped 12 times and came up heads 10 times. (a) Would we be justified in assuming that the sample proportion *p* is normally distributed? Explain. (b) Calculate a *p*-value for the observed sample outcome, using the normal distribution. At the .05 level of significance in a right-tailed test, is the coin biased toward heads? (c) Use Excel to calculate the binomial probability $P(X \geq 10 \mid n = 12, \pi = .50) = 1 - P(X \leq 9 \mid n = 12, \pi = .50)$.

9.55 BriteScreen, a manufacturer of 19-inch LCD computer screens, requires that on average 99.9 percent of all LCDs conform to its quality standard. In a day's production of 2,000 units, 4 are defective. (a) Assuming this is a random sample, is the standard being met, using the 10 percent level of significance? *Hint:* Use Excel to find the binomial probability $P(X \geq 4 \mid n = 2000, \pi = .001) = 1 - P(X \leq 3 \mid n = 2000, \pi = .001)$. Alternatively, use MINITAB. (b) Show that normality of the sample proportion *p* should not be assumed.

9.56 Perfect pitch is the ability to identify musical notes correctly without hearing another note as a reference. The probability that a randomly chosen person has perfect pitch is .0005. (a) If 20 students at Julliard School of Music are tested, and 2 are found to have perfect pitch, would you conclude at the .01 level of significance that Julliard students are more likely than the general population to have perfect pitch? *Hint:* Use Excel to find the right-tailed binomial probability $P(X \geq 2 \mid n = 20, \pi = .0005)$. Alternatively, use MINITAB. (b) Show that normality of the sample proportion *p* should not be assumed.

9.6 POWER CURVES AND OC CURVES (OPTIONAL)

Recall that *power* is the probability of correctly rejecting a false null hypothesis. While we cannot always attain the power we desire in a statistical test, we can at least calculate what the power would be in various possible situations. We will show step by step how to calculate power for tests of a mean or proportion, and how to draw *power curves* that show how power depends on the true value of the parameter we are estimating.

LO 9-10

Interpret a power curve or OC curve (optional).

Power Curve for a Mean: An Example

Power depends on how far the true value of the parameter is from the null hypothesis value. The further away the true population value is from the assumed value, the easier it is for your hypothesis test to detect and the more power it has. To illustrate the calculation of β risk and power, consider a utility that is installing underground PVC pipe as a cable conduit. The specifications call for a mean strength of 12,000 psi (pounds per square inch). A sample of 25 pieces of pipe is tested under laboratory conditions to ascertain the compressive pressure that causes the pipe to collapse. The standard deviation is known from past experience to be $\sigma = 500$ psi. If the pipe proves stronger than the specification, there is no problem, so the utility requires a left-tailed test:

$H_0: \mu \geq 12,000$

$H_1: \mu < 12,000$

If the true mean strength is 11,900 psi, what is the probability that the utility will fail to reject the null hypothesis and mistakenly conclude that $\mu = 12,000$? At $\alpha = .05$, what is the power of the test? Recall that β is the risk of Type II error, the probability of incorrectly accepting a false hypothesis. Type II error is bad, so we want β to be small.

(9.6) $$\beta = P(\text{accept } H_0 \mid H_0 \text{ is false})$$

In this example, $\beta = P(\text{conclude } \mu = 12,000 \mid \mu = 11,900)$.

Conversely, power is the probability that we correctly reject a false hypothesis. More power is better, so we want power to be as close to 1 as possible:

(9.7) $$\text{Power} = P(\text{reject } H_0 \mid H_0 \text{ is false}) = 1 - \beta$$

The values of β and power will vary, depending on the difference between the true mean μ and the hypothesized mean μ_0, the standard deviation σ, the sample size n, and the level of significance α.

(9.8) $$\text{Power} = f(\mu - \mu_0, \sigma, n, \alpha) \quad \text{(determinants of power for a mean)}$$

Table 9.7 summarizes their effects. While we cannot change μ and σ, the sample size and level of significance often are under our control. We can get more power by increasing α, but would we really want to increase Type I error in order to reduce Type II error? Probably not, so the way we usually increase power is by choosing a larger sample size. We will discuss each of these effects in turn.

	Parameter	If . . .	then . . .
TABLE 9.7	True mean (μ)	$\lvert \mu - \mu_0 \rvert \uparrow$	Power $\uparrow$
Determinants of Power in Testing One Mean	True standard deviation (σ)	$\sigma \uparrow$	Power $\downarrow$
	Sample size (n)	$n \uparrow$	Power $\uparrow$
	Level of significance (α)	$\alpha \uparrow$	Power $\uparrow$

Calculating Power

To calculate β and power, we follow a simple sequence of steps for any given values of μ, σ, n, and α. We assume a normal population (or a large sample) so that the sample mean $\bar{X}$ may be assumed normally distributed.

Step 1 Find the left-tail *critical value* for the sample mean. At $\alpha = .05$ in a left-tailed test, we know that $z_{.05} = -1.645$. Using the formula for a z-score,

$$z_{\text{critical}} = \frac{\bar{x}_{\text{critical}} - \mu_0}{\frac{\sigma}{\sqrt{n}}}$$

we can solve algebraically for $\bar{x}_{\text{critical}}$:

$$\bar{x}_{\text{critical}} = \mu_0 + z_{\text{critical}} \frac{\sigma}{\sqrt{n}} = 12,000 - 1.645 \left(\frac{500}{\sqrt{25}} \right) = 11,835.5$$

In terms of the data units of measurement (pounds per square inch), the decision rule is

Reject $H_0: \mu \geq 12,000$ if $\bar{X} < 11,835.5$ psi

Otherwise do not reject H_0

Now suppose that the true mean is $\mu = 11{,}900$. Then the sampling distribution of $\overline{X}$ would be centered at 11,900 instead of 12,000 as we hypothesized. The probability of β error is the area to the right of the critical value $\overline{x}_{\text{critical}} = 11{,}835.5$ (the nonrejection region) representing $P(\overline{X} > \overline{x}_{\text{critical}} \mid \mu = 11{,}900)$. Figure 9.20 illustrates this situation.

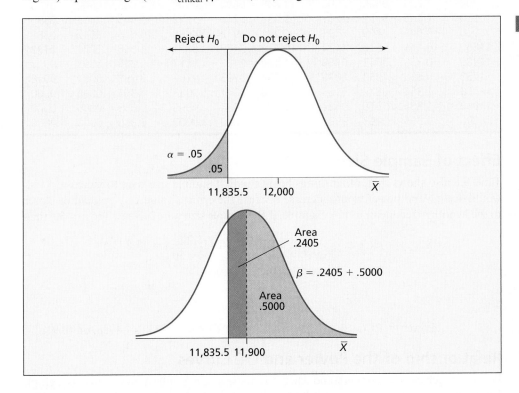

FIGURE 9.20

Finding β When $\mu = 11{,}900$

Step 2 Express the difference between the critical value $\overline{x}_{\text{critical}}$ and the true mean μ as a z-value:

$$z = \frac{\overline{x}_{\text{critical}} - \mu}{\dfrac{\sigma}{\sqrt{n}}} = \frac{11{,}835.5 - 11{,}900}{\dfrac{500}{\sqrt{25}}} = -0.645$$

Step 3 Find the β risk and power as areas under the normal curve, using Appendix C-2 or Excel:

Calculation of β

$\beta = P(\overline{X} > \overline{x}_{\text{critical}} \mid \mu = 11{,}900)$

$\quad = P(Z > -0.645)$

$\quad = 0.2405 + 0.5000$

$\quad = 0.7405$, or 74.1%

Calculation of Power

$\text{Power} = P(\overline{X} < \overline{x}_{\text{critical}} \mid \mu = 11{,}900)$

$\quad = 1 - \beta$

$\quad = 1 - 0.7405$

$\quad = 0.2595$, or 26.0%

This calculation shows that if the true mean is $\mu = 11{,}900$, then there is a 74.05 percent chance that we will commit β error by failing to reject $\mu = 12{,}000$. Since 11,900 is not very far from 12,000 in terms of the standard error, our test has relatively low power. Although our test may not be sensitive enough to reject the null hypothesis reliably if μ is only *slightly* less than 12,000, we would expect that if μ is *far* below 12,000 our test would be more likely to lead to rejection of H_0. Although we cannot know the true mean, we *can* repeat our power calculation for as many values of μ and n as we wish. These calculations may appear tedious, but they are straightforward in a spreadsheet. Table 9.8 shows β and power for samples of $n = 25$, 50, and 100 over a range of μ values from 12,000 down to 11,600.

Notice that β drops toward 0 and power approaches 1 when the true value μ is far from the hypothesized mean $\mu_0 = 12{,}000$. When $\mu = 12{,}000$ there can be no β error, since β error can only occur if H_0 is false. Power is then equal to $\alpha = .05$, the lowest power possible.

TABLE 9.8

β and Power for
$\mu_0 = 12{,}000$

True μ	n = 25			n = 50			n = 100		
	z	β	Power	z	β	Power	z	β	Power
12000	−1.645	.9500	.0500	−1.645	.9500	.0500	−1.645	.9500	.0500
11950	−1.145	.8739	.1261	−0.938	.8258	.1742	−0.645	.7405	.2595
11900	−0.645	.7405	.2595	−0.231	.5912	.4088	0.355	.3612	.6388
11850	−0.145	.5576	.4424	0.476	.3169	.6831	1.355	.0877	.9123
11800	0.355	.3612	.6388	1.184	.1183	.8817	2.355	.0093	.9907
11750	0.855	.1962	.8038	1.891	.0293	.9707	3.355	.0004	.9996
11700	1.355	.0877	.9123	2.598	.0047	.9953	4.355	.0000	1.0000
11650	1.855	.0318	.9682	3.305	.0005	.9995	5.355	.0000	1.0000
11600	2.355	.0093	.9907	4.012	.0000	1.0000	6.355	.0000	1.0000

Effect of Sample Size

Table 9.8 also shows that, other things being equal, if sample size were to increase, β risk would decline and power would increase because the critical value $\bar{x}_{\text{critical}}$ would be closer to the hypothesized mean μ. For example, if the sample size were increased to $n = 50$, then

$$\bar{x}_{\text{critical}} = \mu_0 + z_{\text{critical}} \frac{\sigma}{\sqrt{n}} = 12{,}000 - 1.645\left(\frac{500}{\sqrt{50}}\right) = 11{,}883.68$$

$$z = \frac{\bar{x}_{\text{critical}} - \mu}{\frac{\sigma}{\sqrt{n}}} = \frac{11{,}883.68 - 11{,}900}{\frac{500}{\sqrt{25}}} = -0.231$$

$$\text{Power} = P(\bar{X} < \bar{x}_{\text{critical}} \mid \mu = 11{,}900) = P(Z < -.231) = .4088, \text{ or } 40.9\%$$

Relationship of the Power and OC Curves

Power is much easier to understand when it is made into a graph. A **power curve** is a graph whose Y-axis shows the power of the test $(1 - \beta)$ and whose X-axis shows the various possible true values of the parameter while holding the sample size constant. Figure 9.21 shows the power curve for this example, using three different sample sizes. You can see that power increases as the departure of μ from 12,000 becomes greater and that each larger sample size creates a higher power curve. In other words, larger samples have more power. Since the power curve approaches $\alpha = .05$ as the true mean approaches the hypothesized mean of 12,000, we can see that α also affects the power curve. If we increase α, the power curve will shift up. Although it is not illustrated here, power also rises if the standard deviation is smaller because a small σ gives the test more precision.

FIGURE 9.21

Power Curves for
$H_0: \mu \geq 12{,}000$
$H_1: \mu < 12{,}000$

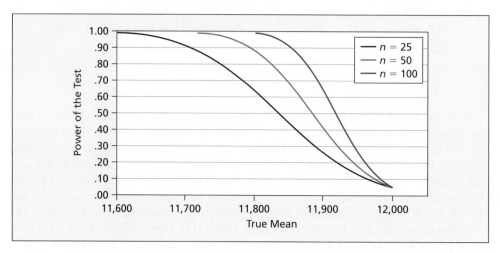

The graph of β risk against this same X-axis is called the operating characteristic or **OC curve**. Figure 9.22 shows the OC curve for this example. It is simply the converse of the power curve, so it is redundant if you already have the power curve.

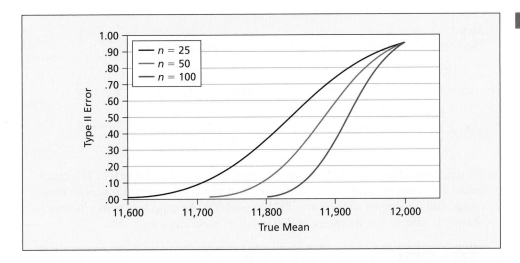

FIGURE 9.22

OC Curves for
H_0: $\mu \geq$ **12,000**
H_1: $\mu <$ **12,000**

Power Curve for Tests of a Proportion

For tests of a proportion, power depends on the true proportion π, the hypothesized proportion π_0, the sample size n, and the level of significance α. Table 9.9 summarizes their effects on power. As with a mean, enlarging the sample size is the most common method of increasing power, unless we are willing to raise the level of significance (that is, trade off Type I error against Type II error).

TABLE 9.9

Determinants of Power in Testing a Proportion

Parameter	If . . .	then . . .
True proportion π	$\lvert \pi - \pi_0 \rvert \uparrow$	Power $\uparrow$
Sample size n	$n \uparrow$	Power $\uparrow$
Level of significance α	$\alpha \uparrow$	Power $\uparrow$

EXAMPLE 9.9

Length of Hospital Stay: Power Curve

A sample is taken of 50 births in a major hospital. We are interested in knowing whether at least half of all mothers have a length of stay (LOS) less than 48 hours. We will do a right-tailed test using $\alpha = .10$. The hypotheses are

H_0: $\pi \leq .50$
H_1: $\pi > .50$

To find the power curve, we follow the same procedure as for a mean—actually, it is easier than a mean because we don't have to worry about σ. For example, what would be the power of the test if the true proportion were $\pi = .60$ and the sample size were $n = 50$?

Step 1
Find the right-tail *critical value* for the sample proportion. At $\alpha = .10$ in a right-tailed test, we would use $z_{.10} = 1.282$ (actually, $z_{.10} = 1.28155$ if we use Excel) so

$$p_{\text{critical}} = \pi_0 + 1.28155\sqrt{\frac{\pi_0(1 - \pi_0)}{n}} = .50 + 1.28155\sqrt{\frac{(.50)(1 - .50)}{50}} = .590619$$

Step 2
Express the difference between the critical value p_{critical} and the true proportion π as a z-value:

$$z = \frac{p_{\text{critical}} - \pi}{\sqrt{\frac{\pi(1 - \pi)}{n}}} = \frac{.590619 - .600000}{\sqrt{\frac{(.60)(1 - .60)}{50}}} = -0.1354$$

Step 3

Find the β risk and power as areas under the normal curve:

Calculation of β

$$\beta = P(p < p_{\text{critical}} \mid \pi = .60)$$
$$= P(Z < -0.1354)$$
$$= .4461, \text{ or } 44.61\%$$

Calculation of Power

$$\text{Power} = P(p > p_{\text{critical}} \mid \pi = .60)$$
$$= 1 - \beta$$
$$= 1 - 0.4461$$
$$= .5539, \text{ or } 55.39\%$$

We can repeat these calculations for any values of π and n. Table 9.10 illustrates power for values of π ranging from .50 to .70, at which point power is near its maximum, and for sample sizes of $n = 50$, 100, and 200. As expected, power increases sharply as sample size increases, and as π differs more from $\pi_0 = .50$.

TABLE 9.10			β and Power for $\pi_0 = .50$							
		$n = 50$			$n = 100$			$n = 200$		
π	z	β	*Power*	z	β	*Power*	z	β	*Power*
.50	1.282	.9000	.1000	1.282	.9000	.1000	1.282	.9000	.1000
.52	1.000	.8412	.1588	0.882	.8112	.1888	0.716	.7631	.2369
.54	0.718	.7637	.2363	0.483	.6855	.3145	0.151	.5599	.4401
.56	0.436	.6686	.3314	0.082	.5327	.4673	−0.419	.3378	.6622
.58	0.152	.5605	.4395	−0.323	.3735	.6265	−0.994	.1601	.8399
.60	−0.135	.4461	.5539	−0.733	.2317	.7683	−1.579	.0572	.9428
.62	−0.428	.3343	.6657	−1.152	.1246	.8754	−2.176	.0148	.9852
.64	−0.727	.2335	.7665	−1.582	.0569	.9431	−2.790	.0026	.9974
.66	−1.036	.1502	.8498	−2.025	.0214	.9786	−3.424	.0003	.9997
.68	−1.355	.0877	.9123	−2.485	.0065	.9935	−4.083	.0000	1.0000
.70	−1.688	.0457	.9543	−2.966	.0015	.9985	−4.774	.0000	1.0000

Interpretation   Figure 9.23 presents the results for our LOS example visually. As would be expected, the power curves for the larger sample sizes are higher, and the power of each curve is lowest when π is near the hypothesized value of $\pi_0 = .50$. The lowest point on the curve has power equal to $\alpha = .10$. Thus, if we increase α, the power curve would shift up. Otherwise, we can only decrease β (and thereby raise power) by increasing the chance of Type I error, a trade-off we might not wish to make.

FIGURE 9.23

Power Curve Families for
$H_0: \pi \le .50$
$H_1: \pi > .50$

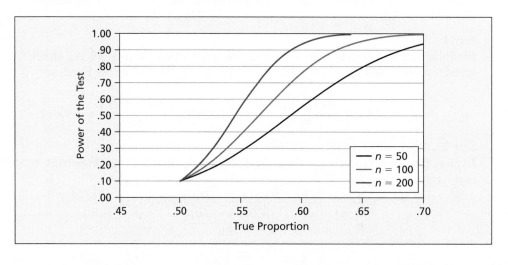

Two-Tailed Power Curves and OC Curves

Both previous examples used one-tailed tests. But if we choose a two-tailed hypothesis test, we will see both sides of the power curve and/or OC curve. Figure 9.24 shows the two-tailed power and OC curves for the previous two examples (H_0: $\mu = 12,000$ and H_0: $\pi = .50$). Each power curve resembles an inverted normal curve, reaching its minimum value when $\mu = \mu_0$ (for a mean) or at $\pi = \pi_0$ (for a proportion). The minimum power is equal to the value of α that we select. In our examples, we chose $\alpha = .05$ for testing μ and $\alpha = .10$ for testing π. If we change α, we will raise or lower the entire power curve. You can download power curve spreadsheet demonstrations for μ and π (see OLC resources at the end of this chapter) if you want to try your own experiments with power curves (with automatic calculations).

FIGURE 9.24

Two-Tailed Power and OC Curves

Hint: Check your answers using *LearningStats* (from the OLC downloads at the end of this chapter).

SECTION EXERCISES

connect

9.57 A quality expert inspects 400 items to test whether the population proportion of defectives exceeds .03, using a right-tailed test at $\alpha = .10$. (a) What is the power of this test if the true proportion of defectives is $\pi = .04$? (b) If the true proportion is $\pi = .05$? (c) If the true proportion of defectives is $\pi = .06$?

9.58 Repeat the previous exercise, using $\alpha = .05$. For each true value of π, is the power higher or lower?

9.59 For a certain wine, the mean pH (a measure of acidity) is supposed to be 3.50 with a known standard deviation of $\sigma = .10$. The quality inspector examines 25 bottles at random to test whether the pH is too low, using a left-tailed test at $\alpha = .01$. (a) What is the power of this test if the true mean is $\mu = 3.48$? (b) If the true mean is $\mu = 3.46$? (c) If the true mean is $\mu = 3.44$?

9.60 Repeat the previous exercise, using $\alpha = .05$. For each true value of μ, is the power higher or lower?

9.7 TESTS FOR ONE VARIANCE (OPTIONAL)

Not all business hypothesis tests involve proportions or means. In quality control, for example, it is important to compare the variance of a process with a historical benchmark, σ_0^2, to see whether variance reduction has been achieved, or to compare a process standard deviation with an engineering specification.

EXAMPLE 9.10

Attachment Times

LO 9-11

Perform a hypothesis test for a variance (optional).

Historical statistics show that the standard deviation of attachment times for an instrument panel in an automotive assembly line is $\sigma = 7$ seconds. Observations on 20 randomly chosen attachment times are shown in Table 9.11. At $\alpha = .05$, does the variance in attachment times differ from the historical variance ($\sigma^2 = 7^2 = 49$)?

TABLE 9.11	Panel Attachment Times (seconds)		Attachment	
120	143	136	126	122
140	133	133	131	131
129	128	131	123	119
135	137	134	115	122

The sample mean is $\bar{x} = 129.400$ with a standard deviation of $s = 7.44382$. We ignore the sample mean since it is irrelevant to this test. For a two-tailed test, the hypotheses are

$$H_0: \sigma^2 = 49$$
$$H_1: \sigma^2 \neq 49$$

For a test of one variance, assuming a normal population, the test statistic follows the **chi-square distribution** with degrees of freedom equal to $d.f. = n - 1 = 20 - 1 = 19$. Denoting the hypothesized variance as σ_0^2, the test statistic is

(9.9) $$\chi_{calc}^2 = \frac{(n-1)s^2}{\sigma_0^2} \qquad \text{(test for one variance)}$$

For a two-tailed test, the decision rule based on the upper and lower critical values of chi-square is

Reject H_0 if $\chi_{calc}^2 < \chi_{lower}^2$ or if $\chi_{calc}^2 > \chi_{upper}^2$
Otherwise do not reject H_0

We can use the Excel function =CHISQ.INV to get the critical values:

$$\chi_{lower}^2 = \text{CHISQ.INV}(\alpha/2, d.f.) = \text{CHISQ.INV}(0.025, 19) = 8.907$$
$$\chi_{upper}^2 = \text{CHISQ.INV}(1 - \alpha/2, d.f.) = \text{CHISQ.INV}(0.975, 19) = 32.852$$

The decision rule is illustrated in Figure 9.25. The value of the test statistic is

$$\chi_{calc}^2 = \frac{(n-1)s^2}{\sigma^2} = \frac{(20-1)(7.44382)^2}{7^2} = 21.49$$

| FIGURE 9.25 | **Decision Rule for Chi-Square Test** |

Because the test statistic is within the middle range, we conclude that the population variance does not differ significantly from 49; that is, the assembly process variance is unchanged.

If Excel is unavailable, we can obtain upper and lower critical values of chi-square to define the rejection region from Appendix E, as illustrated in Figure 9.26.

| FIGURE 9.26 | **Two-Tail Chi-Square Values for *d.f.* = 19 and σ = .05** |

Example for d.f. = 4

CHI-SQUARE CRITICAL VALUES

This table shows the critical value of chi-square for each desired tail area and degrees of freedom (d.f.).

	Area in Upper Tail									
d.f.	.995	.990	.975	.95	.90	.10	.05	.025	.01	.005
1	0.000	0.000	0.001	0.004	0.016	2.706	3.841	5.024	6.635	7.879
2	0.010	0.020	0.051	0.103	0.211	4.605	5.991	7.378	9.210	10.60
3	0.072	0.115	0.216	0.352	0.584	6.251	7.815	9.348	11.34	12.84
4	0.207	0.297	0.484	0.711	1.064	7.779	9.488	11.14	13.28	14.86
5	0.412	0.554	0.831	1.145	1.610	9.236	11.07	12.83	15.09	16.75
.	.	.	.	.	.	.	.	.	.	.
.	.	.	.	.	.	.	.	.	.	.
.	.	.	.	.	.	.	.	.	.	.
16	5.142	5.812	6.908	7.962	9.312	23.54	26.30	28.85	32.00	34.27
17	5.697	6.408	7.564	8.672	10.09	24.77	27.59	30.19	33.41	35.72
18	6.265	7.015	8.231	9.390	10.86	25.99	28.87	31.53	34.81	37.16
19	6.844	7.633	8.907	10.12	11.65	27.20	30.14	32.85	36.19	38.58
20	7.434	8.260	9.591	10.85	12.44	28.41	31.41	34.17	37.57	40.00
.	.	.	.	.	.	.	.	.	.	.
.	.	.	.	.	.	.	.	.	.	.
100	67.33	70.06	74.22	77.93	82.36	118.5	124.3	129.6	135.8	140.2

Using MegaStat

Excel has no test for a variance, but you can use Minitab or MegaStat. Figure 9.27 shows MegaStat's setup screen and output for the variance test, including a confidence interval for σ^2.

FIGURE 9.27

MegaStat Test for One Variance

Chi-square Variance Test

49.000000	hypothesized variance
55.410456	observed variance of Blood Pressure
20	n
19	df
21.49	chi-square
.6212	p-value (two-tailed)
32.046386	confidence interval 95% lower
118.205464	confidence interval 95% upper

When to Use Tests for One Variance

In general, we would be interested in a test of variances when it is not the *center* of the distribution, but rather the *variability* of the process, that matters. More variation implies a more erratic data-generating process. For example, variance tests are important in manufacturing processes because increased variation around the mean can be a sign of wear and tear on equipment or other problems that would require attention.

Caution The chi-square test for a variance is not robust to non-normality of the population. If normality cannot be assumed (e.g., if the data set has outliers or severe skewness), you might need to use a bootstrap method (see *LearningStats* Unit 08) to test the hypothesis, using specialized software. In such a situation, it is best to consult a statistician.

Mini Case   9.4

Ball Corporation Metal Thickness

Ball Corporation is the largest supplier of beverage cans in the world. Metal beverage containers are lightweight, fully recyclable, quickly chilled, and easy to store. For these reasons, the metal beverage container is the package of choice in homes, vending machines, and coolers around the world. Ball's many manufacturing sites throughout the world turn out more than 100 million cans each day.

At its Ft. Atkinson, Wisconsin, manufacturing facility, Ball's quality group must evaluate the metal of potential new suppliers. Because of the large quantity of cans produced each day, Ball has established very precise specifications on the metal characteristics. One characteristic that is critical to production is the variation in metal thickness. Inconsistent thickness across a sheet of metal can create serious problems for Ball's manufacturing process. Ball's current supplier has a known thickness standard deviation $\sigma = 0.000959$ mm. To qualify a potential new metal supplier, Ball conducted a two-tailed hypothesis test to determine if the potential supplier's thickness variance was consistent with that of the current supplier. The null and alternative hypotheses are

$$H_0: \sigma^2 = (0.000959)^2$$
$$H_1: \sigma^2 \neq (0.000959)^2$$

Ball received a sample of 168 sheets of metal from the potential supplier. Therefore, the degrees of freedom for the chi-square test statistic are 167. Using $\alpha = .10$, the decision rule states:

If $\chi^2_{\text{calc}} < 138.1$ or $\chi^2_{\text{calc}} > 198.2$, reject H_0

The sample standard deviation was calculated to be $s = 0.00106$ mm. The calculated test statistic was then found to be

$$\chi^2_{calc} = \frac{(n-1)s^2}{\sigma^2} = \frac{(168-1)(0.00106)^2}{(0.000959)^2} = 204.03$$

Because $\chi^2_{calc} > 198.2$, the decision was to reject H_0. Ball concluded that the variation in metal thickness for the potential supplier was not equivalent to that of their primary supplier. The potential supplier was not a candidate for supplying metal to Ball.

SECTION EXERCISES

connect

9.61   A sample of size $n = 15$ has variance $s^2 = 35$. At $\alpha = .01$ in a left-tailed test, does this sample contradict the hypothesis that $\sigma^2 = 50$?

9.62   A sample of size $n = 10$ has variance $s^2 = 16$. At $\alpha = .10$ in a two-tailed test, does this sample contradict the hypothesis that $\sigma^2 = 24$?

9.63   A sample of size $n = 19$ has variance $s^2 = 1.96$. At $\alpha = .05$ in a right-tailed test, does this sample contradict the hypothesis that $\sigma^2 = 1.21$?

9.64   pH is a measure of acidity that winemakers must watch. A "healthy wine" should have a pH in the range 3.1 to 3.7. The target standard deviation is $\sigma = 0.10$ (i.e., $\sigma^2 = 0.01$). The pH measurements for a sample of 16 bottles of wine are shown below. At $\alpha = .05$ in a two-tailed test, is the sample variance either too high or too low? Show all steps, including the hypotheses and critical values from Appendix E. *Hint:* Ignore the mean. (See www.winemakermag.com.) 📷 **WinePH**

3.49	3.54	3.58	3.57	3.54	3.34	3.48	3.60
3.48	3.27	3.46	3.32	3.51	3.43	3.56	3.39

9.65   In U.S. hospitals, the average length of stay (LOS) for a diagnosis of pneumonia is 137 hours with a standard deviation of 25 hours. The LOS (in hours) for a sample of 12 pneumonia patients at Santa Theresa Memorial Hospital is shown below. In a two-tailed test at $\alpha = .05$, is this sample variance consistent with the national norms? Show all steps, including the hypotheses and critical values from Appendix E. *Hint:* Ignore the mean. (See National Center for Health Statistics, *Advance Data from Vital and Health Statistics,* no. 332 [April 9, 2003], p. 13.) 📷 **Pneumonia**

132	143	143	120	124	116
130	165	100	83	115	141

CHAPTER SUMMARY

The **null hypothesis (H_0)** represents the status quo or a benchmark. We try to reject H_0 in favor of the **alternative hypothesis (H_1)** on the basis of the sample evidence. The alternative hypothesis points to the tail of the test ($<$ for a left-tailed test, $>$ for a right-tailed test, $\neq$ for a two-tailed test). Rejecting a true H_0 is **Type I error,** while failing to reject a false H_0 is **Type II error.** The **power** of the test is the probability of correctly rejecting a false H_0. The probability of Type I error is denoted α (often called **the level of significance**) and can be set by the researcher. The probability of Type II error is denoted β and is dependent on the true parameter value, sample size, and α. In general, lowering α increases β, and vice versa. The **test statistic** compares the sample statistic with the hypothesized parameter. For a mean, the **decision rule** tells us whether to reject H_0 by comparing the test statistic with the **critical value** of z (known σ) or t (unknown σ) from a table or from Excel. Tests of a proportion are based on the normal distribution (if the sample is large enough, according to a rule of thumb), although in small samples the binomial is required. In any hypothesis test, the **p-value** shows the probability that the test statistic (or one more extreme) would be observed by chance, assuming that H_0 is true. If the p-value is smaller than α, we reject H_0 (i.e., a small p-value indicates a **significant** departure from H_0). A two-tailed test is analogous to a confidence interval seen in the last chapter. Power is greater when the true parameter is farther from the null hypothesis value. A **power curve** is a graph that plots the power of the test $(1 - \beta)$ against possible values of the true parameter, while the **OC curve** is a plot of the probability of a false negative (β). Tests of a variance use the **chi-square distribution** and suffer if the data are badly skewed.

KEY TERMS

alternative hypothesis, *343*	importance, *356*	rejection region, *349*
benchmark, *365*	left-tailed test, *347*	right-tailed test, *347*
chi-square distribution, *380*	level of significance, *345*	significance, *356*
critical value, *349*	null hypothesis, *343*	statistical hypothesis, *347*
decision rule, *349*	OC curve, *376*	test statistic, *349*
hypothesis, *341*	power, *345*	two-tailed test, *347*
hypothesis test, *347*	power curve, *376*	Type I error, *344*
hypothesis testing, *341*	*p*-value method, *352*	Type II error, *344*

Commonly Used Formulas in One-Sample Hypothesis Tests

Type I error: $\quad \alpha = P(\text{reject } H_0 \mid H_0 \text{ is true})$

Type II error: $\quad \beta = P(\text{fail to reject } H_0 \mid H_0 \text{ is false})$

Power: $\quad 1 - \beta = P(\text{reject } H_0 \mid H_0 \text{ is false})$

Test statistic for sample mean, σ known: $\quad z_{\text{calc}} = \dfrac{\bar{x} - \mu_0}{\dfrac{\sigma}{\sqrt{n}}}$

Test statistic for sample mean, σ unknown: $\quad t_{\text{calc}} = \dfrac{\bar{x} - \mu_0}{\dfrac{s}{\sqrt{n}}}$ with $d.f. = n - 1$

Test statistic for sample proportion: $\quad z_{\text{calc}} = \dfrac{p - \pi_0}{\sqrt{\dfrac{\pi_0(1 - \pi_0)}{n}}}$

CHAPTER REVIEW

Note: Questions labeled * are based on optional material from this chapter.

1. (a) List the steps in testing a hypothesis. (b) Why can't a hypothesis ever be proven?

2. (a) Explain the difference between the null hypothesis and the alternative hypothesis. (b) How is the null hypothesis chosen (why is it "null")?

3. (a) Why do we say "fail to reject H_0" instead of "accept H_0"? (b) What does it mean to "provisionally accept a hypothesis"?

4. (a) Define Type I error and Type II error. (b) Give an example to illustrate.

5. (a) Explain the difference between a left-tailed test, two-tailed test, and right-tailed test. (b) When would we choose a two-tailed test? (c) How can we tell the direction of the test by looking at a pair of hypotheses?

6. (a) What is a test statistic? (b) Explain the meaning of the rejection region in a decision rule. (c) Why do we need to know the sampling distribution of a statistic before we can do a hypothesis test?

7. (a) Define level of significance. (b) Define power.

8. (a) Why do we prefer low values for α and β? (b) For a given sample size, why is there a trade-off between α and β? (c) How could we decrease both α and β?

9. (a) Why is a "statistically significant difference" not necessarily a "practically important difference"? Give an illustration. (b) Why do statisticians play only a limited role in deciding whether a significant difference requires action?

10. (a) In a hypothesis test for a proportion, when can normality be assumed? *Optional* (b) If the sample is too small to assume normality, what can we do?

11. (a) In a hypothesis test of one mean, when do we use t instead of z? (b) When is the difference between z and t small?

12. (a) Explain what a p-value means. Give an example and interpret it. (b) Why is the p-value method an attractive alternative to specifying α in advance?

13. Why is a confidence interval similar to a two-tailed test?

*14. (a) What does a power curve show? (b) What factors affect power for a test of a mean? (c) What factors affect power for a proportion? (d) What is the most commonly used method of increasing power?

*15. (a) In testing a hypothesis about a variance, what distribution do we use? (b) When would a test of a variance be needed? (c) If the population is not normal, what can we do?

Note: Explain answers and show your work clearly. Problems marked * rely on optional material from this chapter.

CHAPTER EXERCISES

connect

HYPOTHESIS FORMULATION AND TYPE I AND II ERROR

9.66 Suppose you always reject the null hypothesis, regardless of any sample evidence. (a) What is the probability of Type II error? (b) Why is this a bad policy?

9.67 Suppose the judge decides to acquit all defendants, regardless of the evidence. (a) What is the probability of Type I error? (b) Why is this a bad policy?

9.68 High blood pressure, if untreated, can lead to increased risk of stroke and heart attack. A common definition of hypertension is diastolic blood pressure of 90 or more. (a) State the null and alternative hypotheses for a physician who checks your blood pressure. (b) Define Type I and II error. What are the consequences of each?

9.69 A nuclear power plant replaces its ID card facility access system cards with a biometric security system that scans the iris pattern of the employee and compares it with a data bank. Users are classified as authorized or unauthorized. (a) State the null and alternative hypotheses. (b) Define Type I and II error. What are the consequences of each?

9.70 A test-preparation company advertises that its training program raises SAT scores by an average of at least 30 points. A random sample of test-takers who had completed the training showed a mean increase smaller than 30 points. (a) Write the hypotheses for a left-tailed test of the mean. (b) Explain the consequences of a Type I error in this context.

9.71 Telemarketers use a predictive dialing system to decide whether a person actually answers a call (as opposed to an answering machine). If so, the call is routed to a telemarketer. If no telemarketer is free, the software must automatically hang up the phone within two seconds, to comply with FAA regulations against tying up the line. The SmartWay company says that its new system is smart enough to hang up on no more than 2 percent of the answered calls. Write the hypotheses for a right-tailed test, using SmartWay's claim about the proportion as the null hypothesis.

9.72 If the true mean is 50 and we reject the hypothesis that $\mu = 50$, what is the probability of Type II error? *Hint:* This is a trick question.

9.73 If we fail to reject the null hypothesis that $\pi = .50$ even though the true proportion is .60, what is the probability of Type I error? *Hint:* This is a trick question.

9.74 Pap smears are a test for abnormal cancerous and precancerous cells taken from the cervix. (a) State a pair of hypotheses and then explain the meaning of a false negative and a false positive. (b) Why is the null hypothesis "null"? (c) Who bears the cost of each type of error?

9.75 In a commercially available fingerprint scanner (e.g., for your home or office PC), false acceptances are 1 in 25 million, with false rejection rates of 3 percent. (a) Define Type I and II error. (b) Why do you suppose the false rejection rate is so high compared with the false acceptance rate?

9.76 When told that over a 10-year period a mammogram test has a false positive rate of 50 percent, Bob said, "That means that about half the women tested actually have no cancer." Correct Bob's mistaken interpretation.

TESTS OF MEANS AND PROPORTIONS

9.77 Malcheon Health Clinic claims that the average waiting time for a patient is 20 minutes or less. A random sample of 15 patients shows a mean wait time of 24.77 minutes with a standard deviation of 7.26 minutes. (a) Write the hypotheses for a right-tailed test, using the clinic's claim as the null hypothesis. (b) Calculate the t test statistic to test the claim. (c) At the 5 percent level of significance ($\alpha = .05$), does the sample contradict the clinic's claim? (d) Use Excel to find the p-value and compare it to the level of significance. Did you come to the same conclusion as you did in part (c)?

9.78 The sodium content of a popular sports drink is listed as 220 mg in a 32-oz bottle. Analysis of 10 bottles indicates a sample mean of 228.2 mg with a sample standard deviation of 18.2 mg. (a) Write the hypotheses for a two-tailed test of the claimed sodium content. (b) Calculate the t test statistic to test the manufacturer's claim. (c) At the 5 percent level of significance ($\alpha = .05$), does the sample contradict the manufacturer's claim? (d) Use Excel to find the p-value and compare it to the level of significance. Did you come to the same conclusion as you did in part (c)?

9.79 A can of peeled whole tomatoes is supposed to contain an average of 19 ounces of tomatoes (excluding the juice). The actual weight is a normally distributed random variable whose standard deviation is known to be 0.25 ounce. (a) In quality control, would a one-tailed or two-tailed test be used? Why? (b) Explain the consequences of departure from the mean in either direction. (c) Which sampling distribution would you use if samples of four cans are weighed? Why? (d) Set up a two-tailed decision rule for $\alpha = .01$.

9.80 At Ajax Spring Water, a half-liter bottle of soft drink is supposed to contain a mean of 520 ml. The filling process follows a normal distribution with a known process standard deviation of 4 ml. (a) Which sampling distribution would you use if random samples of 10 bottles are to be weighed? Why? (b) Set up hypotheses and a two-tailed decision rule for the correct mean using the 5 percent level of significance. (c) If a sample of 16 bottles shows a mean fill of 515 ml, does this contradict the hypothesis that the true mean is 520 ml?

9.81 On eight Friday quizzes, Bob received scores of 80, 85, 95, 92, 89, 84, 90, 92. He tells Prof. Hardtack that he is really a 90+ performer, but this sample just happened to fall below his true performance level. (a) State an appropriate pair of hypotheses. (b) State the formula for the test statistic and show your decision rule using the 1 percent level of significance. (c) Carry out the test. Show your work. (d) What assumptions are required? (e) Use Excel to find the p-value and interpret it. 📄 **BobQuiz**

9.82 Faced with rising fax costs, a firm issued a guideline that transmissions of 10 pages or more should be sent by 2-day mail instead. Exceptions are allowed, but they want the average to be 10 or below. The firm examined 35 randomly chosen fax transmissions during the next year, yielding a sample mean of 14.44 with a standard deviation of 4.45 pages. (a) At the .01 level of significance, is the true mean greater than 10? (b) Use Excel to find the right-tail p-value.

9.83 A U.S. dime weighs 2.268 grams when minted. A random sample of 15 circulated dimes showed a mean weight of 2.256 grams with a standard deviation of .026 gram. (a) Using $\alpha = .05$, is the mean weight of all circulated dimes lower than the mint weight? State your hypotheses and decision rule. (b) Why might circulated dimes weigh less than the mint specification?

9.84 A coin was flipped 60 times and came up heads 38 times. (a) At the .10 level of significance, is the coin biased toward heads? Show your decision rule and calculations. (b) Calculate a p-value and interpret it.

9.85 A sample of 100 one-dollar bills from the Subway cash register revealed that 16 had something written on them besides the normal printing (e.g., "Bob ♥ Mary"). (a) At $\alpha = .05$, is this sample evidence consistent with the hypothesis that 10 percent or fewer of all dollar bills have anything written on them besides the normal printing? Include a sketch of your decision rule and show all calculations. (b) Is your decision sensitive to the choice of α? (c) Find the p-value.

9.86 A sample of 100 mortgages approved during the current year showed that 31 were issued to a single-earner family or individual. The historical percentage is 25 percent. (a) At the .05 level of significance in a right-tailed test, has the percentage of single-earner or individual mortgages risen? Include a sketch of your decision rule and show all work. (b) Is this a close decision? (c) State any assumptions that are required.

9.87 A state weights-and-measures standard requires that no more than 5 percent of bags of Halloween candy be underweight. A random sample of 200 bags showed that 16 were underweight. (a) At $\alpha = .025$, is the standard being violated? Use a right-tailed test and show your work. (b) Find the *p*-value.

9.88 Ages for the 2009 Boston Red Sox pitchers are shown below. (a) Assuming this is a random sample of major league pitchers, at the 5 percent level of significance does this sample show that the true mean age of all American League pitchers is over 30 years? State your hypotheses and decision rule and show all work. (b) If there is a difference, is it important? (c) Find the *p*-value and interpret it. (Data are from http://boston.redsox.mlb.com.) 📁 **RedSox**

Ages of Boston Red Sox Pitchers, May 2009							
Bard	24	Lester	25	Okajima	34	Ramirez	28
Beckett	29	Masterson	24	Papelbon	29	Saito	39
Delcarmen	27	Matsuzaka	29	Penny	31	Wakefield	43

9.89 The EPA is concerned about the quality of drinking water served on airline flights. A sample of 112 flights found unacceptable bacterial contamination on 14 flights. (a) At $\alpha = .05$, does this sample show that more than 10 percent of all flights have contaminated water? (b) Find the *p*-value.

9.90 A web-based company has a goal of processing 95 percent of its orders on the same day they are received. If 485 out of the next 500 orders are processed on the same day, would this prove that they are exceeding their goal, using $\alpha = .025$?

9.91 In the Big Ten (the NCAA sports league), a sample showed that only 267 out of 584 freshmen football players graduated within 6 years. (a) At $\alpha = .05$, does this sample contradict the claim that at least half graduate within 6 years? State your hypotheses and decision rule. (b) Calculate the *p*-value and interpret it. (c) Do you think the difference is important, as opposed to significant?

9.92 An auditor reviewed 25 oral surgery insurance claims from a particular surgical office, determining that the mean out-of-pocket patient billing above the reimbursed amount was $275.66 with a standard deviation of $78.11. (a) At the 5 percent level of significance, does this sample prove a violation of the guideline that the average patient should pay no more than $250 out-of-pocket? State your hypotheses and decision rule. (b) Is this a close decision?

9.93 The average service time at a Noodles & Company restaurant was 3.5 minutes in the previous year. Noodles implemented some time-saving measures and would like to know if they have been effective. They sample 20 service times and find the sample average is 3.2 minutes with a sample standard deviation of .4 minute. Using $\alpha = .05$, were the measures effective?

9.94 A digital camcorder repair service has set a goal not to exceed an average of 5 working days from the time the unit is brought in to the time repairs are completed. A random sample of 12 repair records showed the following repair times (in days): 9, 2, 5, 1, 5, 4, 7, 5, 11, 3, 7, 2. At $\alpha = .05$, is the goal being met? 📁 **Repair**

9.95 A recent study by the Government Accountability Office found that consumers got correct answers about Medicare only 67 percent of the time when they called 1-800-MEDICARE. (a) At $\alpha = .05$, would a subsequent audit of 50 randomly chosen calls with 40 correct answers suffice to show that the percentage had risen? What is the *p*-value? (b) Is the normality criterion for the sample proportion met? (See *The New York Times,* November 7, 2006.)

9.96 Beer shelf life is a problem for brewers and distributors because when beer is stored at room temperature, its flavor deteriorates. When the average furfuryl ether content reaches 6 μg per liter, a typical consumer begins to taste an unpleasant chemical flavor. (a) At $\alpha = .05$, would the following sample of 12 randomly chosen bottles stored for a month convince you that the mean furfuryl ether content exceeds the taste threshhold? (b) What is the *p*-value? 📁 **BeerTaste**

6.53, 5.68, 8.10, 7.50, 6.32, 8.75, 5.98, 7.50, 5.01, 5.95, 6.40, 7.02

9.97   (a) A statistical study reported that a drug was effective with a *p*-value of .042. Explain in words what this tells you. (b) How would that compare to a drug that had a *p*-value of .087?

9.98   Bob said, "Why is a small *p*-value significant, when a large one isn't? That seems backwards." Try to explain it to Bob, giving an example to make your point.

PROPORTIONS: SMALL SAMPLES

9.99   An automaker states that its cars equipped with electronic fuel injection and computerized engine controls will start on the first try (hot or cold) 99 percent of the time. A survey of 100 new car owners revealed that 3 had not started on the first try during a recent cold snap. (a) At $\alpha = .025$, does this demonstrate that the automaker's claim is incorrect? (b) Calculate the *p*-value and interpret it. *Hint:* Use MINITAB, or use Excel to calculate the cumulative binomial probability $P(X \geq 3 \mid n = 100, \pi = .01) = 1 - P(X \leq 2 \mid n = 100, \pi = .01)$.

9.100   A quality standard says that no more than 2 percent of the eggs sold in a store may be cracked (not broken, just cracked). In 3 cartons (12 eggs each carton), 2 eggs are cracked. (a) At the .10 level of significance, does this prove that the standard is exceeded? (b) Calculate a *p*-value for the observed sample result. *Hint:* Use Excel to calculate the binomial probability $P(X \geq 2 \mid n = 36, \pi = .02) = 1 - P(X \leq 1 \mid n = 36, \pi = .02)$.

9.101   An experimental medication is administered to 16 people who suffer from migraines. After an hour, 10 say they feel better. Is the medication effective (i.e., is the percent who feel better greater than 50 percent)? Use $\alpha = .10$, explain fully, and show all steps.

9.102   The historical on-time percentage for Amtrak's Sunset Limited is 10 percent. In July, the train was on time 0 times in 31 runs. At the .10 level of significance, has the on-time percentage fallen? Explain clearly. *Hint:* Use Excel to calculate the cumulative binomial probability $P(X \leq 0 \mid n = 31, \pi = .10)$.

9.103   After 7 months, none of 238 angioplasty patients who received a drug-coated stent to keep their arteries open had experienced restenosis (re-blocking of the arteries). (a) Use MINITAB to construct a 95 percent binomial confidence interval for the proportion of all angioplasty patients who experience restenosis. (b) Why is it necessary to use a binomial in this case? (c) If the goal is to reduce the occurrence of restenosis to 5 percent or less, does this sample show that the goal is being achieved?

POWER

Hint: In the power problems, use *LearningStats* (from the OLC downloads) to check your answers.

9.104   A certain brand of flat white interior latex paint claims one-coat coverage of 400 square feet per gallon. The standard deviation is known to be 20. A sample of 16 gallons is tested. (a) At $\alpha = .05$ in a left-tailed test, find the β risk and power assuming that the true mean is really 380 square feet per gallon. (b) Construct a left-tailed power curve, using increments of 5 square feet (400, 395, 390, 385, 380).

9.105   A process is normally distributed with standard deviation 12. Samples of size 4 are taken. Suppose that you wish to test the hypothesis that $\mu = 500$ at $\alpha = .05$ in a left-tailed test. (a) What is the β risk if the true mean is 495? If the true mean is 490? If the true mean is 485? If the true mean is 480? (b) Calculate the power for each of the preceding values of μ and sketch a power curve. (c) Repeat the previous exercises using $n = 16$.

TESTS OF VARIANCES

Hint: Use MegaStat to check your work.

9.106   Is this sample of 25 exam scores inconsistent with the hypothesis that the true variance is 64 (i.e., $\sigma = 8$)? Use the 5 percent level of significance in a two-tailed test. Show all steps, including the hypotheses and critical values from Appendix E.   Exams

80	79	69	71	74
73	77	75	65	52
81	84	84	79	70
78	62	77	68	77
88	70	75	85	84

9.107 Hammermill Premium Inkjet 24 lb. paper has a specified brightness of 106. (a) At $\alpha =$ .005, does this sample of 24 randomly chosen test sheets from a day's production run show that the mean brightness exceeds the specification? (b) Does the sample show that $\sigma^2 <$ 0.0025? State the hypotheses and critical value for the left-tailed test from Appendix E. 🗁 **Brightness**

106.98	107.02	106.99	106.98	107.06	107.05	107.03	107.04
107.01	107.00	107.02	107.04	107.00	106.98	106.91	106.93
107.01	106.98	106.97	106.99	106.94	106.98	107.03	106.98

Vickers, Andrew J. *What Is a p-Value Anyway? 34 Stories to Help You Actually Understand Statistics.* Addison-Wesley, 2010.

RELATED READING

CHAPTER 9   Online Learning Resources

The Online Learning Center (OLC) at www.mhhe.com/doane4e has several *LearningStats* demonstrations to help you understand one-sample hypothesis tests. Your instructor may assign one or more of them, or you may decide to download the ones that sound interesting.

LearningCenter

Topic	LearningStats Demonstrations
Common hypothesis tests	🆇 Do-It-Yourself Simulation 🆇 Sampling Distribution Examples
Type I error and power	🆇 Type I Error 🆇 p-Value Illustration 🆇 Power Curves: Examples 🆇 Power Curves: Do-It-Yourself 🆇 Power Curve Families: μ 🆇 Power Curve Families: π
Tables	🆇 Appendix C—Normal 🆇 Appendix D—Student's t 🆇 Appendix E—Chi-Square

Key: 🆇 = Excel

10

Two-Sample Hypothesis Tests

CHAPTER CONTENTS

CHAPTER LEARNING OBJECTIVES

LO

When you finish this chapter you should be able to

LO 10-1 Recognize and perform a test for two means with known σ_1 and σ_2.

LO 10-2 Recognize and perform a test for two means with unknown σ_1 and σ_2.

LO 10-3 Recognize paired data and be able to perform a paired t test.

LO 10-4 Explain the assumptions underlying the two-sample test of means.

LO 10-5 Perform a test to compare two proportions using z.

LO 10-6 Check whether normality may be assumed for two proportions.

LO 10-7 Use Excel to determine p-values for two-sample tests using z or t.

LO 10-8 Carry out a test of two variances using the F distribution.

LO 10-9 Construct a confidence interval for $\mu_1 - \mu_2$ or $\pi_1 - \pi_2$.

10.1 TWO-SAMPLE TESTS

The logic and applications of hypothesis testing that you learned in Chapter 9 will continue here, but now we consider two-sample tests. The two-sample test is used to make inferences about the two populations from which the samples were drawn. The use of these techniques is widespread in science and engineering as well as social sciences. For example, drug companies use clinical trials to determine the effectiveness of new drugs, agricultural science uses these methods to compare crop yields, and marketing firms use them to contrast purchase patterns in different demographic groups.

What Is a Two-Sample Test?

Two-sample tests compare two sample estimates *with each other,* whereas one-sample tests compare a sample estimate with a nonsample benchmark (a claim or prior belief about a population parameter). Here are some actual two-sample tests from this chapter:

Automotive   A new bumper is installed on selected vehicles in a corporate fleet. During a 1-year test period, 12 vehicles with the new bumper were involved in accidents, incurring mean damage of $1,101 with a standard deviation of $696. During the same year, 9 vehicles with the old bumpers were involved in accidents, incurring mean damage of $1,766 with a standard deviation of $838. Did the new bumper significantly reduce damage? Did it significantly reduce variation?

Marketing   At a University of Colorado women's home basketball game, a random sample of 25 concession purchases showed a mean of $7.12 with a standard deviation of $2.14. For the next week's home game, the admission ticket had a discount coupon for popcorn printed on the back. A random sample of 25 purchases from that week showed a mean of $8.29 with a standard deviation of $3.02. Was there a statistically significant increase in the average concession stand purchases with the coupon?

Environment   Samples of methane gas emissions (in standard cubic feet per day) from two different manufacturers of low-bleed pneumatic controllers were analyzed. Manufacturer A's sample mean was 510.5 with a standard deviation of 147.2 in 18 tests, compared with Manufacturer B's mean of 628.9 with a standard deviation of 237.9 in 17 tests. Is the difference statistically significant?

Safety   In Dallas, some fire trucks were painted yellow (instead of red) to heighten their visibility. During a test period, the fleet of red fire trucks made 153,348 runs and had 20 accidents, while the fleet of yellow fire trucks made 135,035 runs and had 4 accidents. Is the difference in accident rates significant?

Education   In a certain college class, 20 randomly chosen students were given a tutorial, while 20 others used a self-study computer simulation. On the same 20-point quiz, the tutorial students' mean score was 16.7 with a standard deviation of 2.5, compared with a mean of 14.5 and a standard deviation of 3.2 for the simulation students. Did the tutorial students do better, or is it just due to chance? Is there any significant difference in the degree of variation in the two groups?

Mini Case   10.1

Early Intervention Saves Lives

Statistics is helping U.S. hospitals prove the value of innovative organizational changes to deal with medical crisis situations. At the Pittsburgh Medical Center, "SWAT teams" were shown to reduce patient mortality by cutting red tape for critically ill patients. They formed a Rapid Response Team (RRT) consisting of a critical care nurse, intensive care therapist, and a respiratory therapist, empowered to make decisions without waiting until the patient's doctor could be paged. Statistics were collected on cardiac arrests for two months before and after the RRT concept was implemented. The sample data revealed more than a 50 percent reduction in total cardiac deaths and a 46 percent decline in average ICU days after cardiac arrest from 2.59 days to only 1.50 days after RRT. These improvements were both *statistically significant* and of *practical importance* because of the medical benefits and the large cost savings in hospital care. Statistics played a similar role at the University of California San Francisco Medical Center in demonstrating the value of a new method of expediting treatment of heart attack emergency patients. (See *The Wall Street Journal*, December 1, 2004, p. D1; and "How Statistics Can Save Failing Hearts," *The New York Times*, March 7, 2007, p. C1.)

Basis of Two-Sample Tests

Two-sample tests are especially useful because they possess a built-in point of comparison. You can think of many situations where two groups are to be compared:

- Before *versus* after
- Old *versus* new
- Experimental *versus* control

Sometimes we don't really care about the actual value of the population parameter, but only whether the parameter is the same for both populations. Usually, the null hypothesis is that both samples were drawn from populations with the same parameter value, but we can also test for a given degree of difference.

The logic of two-sample tests is based on the fact that two samples drawn from the *same population* may yield *different estimates* of a parameter due to chance. For example, exhaust emission tests could yield different results for two vehicles of the same type. Only if the two sample statistics differ by more than the amount attributable to chance can we conclude that the samples came from populations with different parameter values, as illustrated in Figure 10.1.

Test Procedure

The testing procedure is like that of one-sample tests. We state our hypotheses, set up a decision rule, insert the sample statistics, and make a decision. Because the true parameters are unknown, we rely on statistical theory to help us reach a defensible conclusion about our hypotheses. Our decision could be wrong—we could commit a **Type I** or **Type II error**—but at least we can specify our risk of making an error. Larger samples are always

FIGURE 10.1

Same Population or Different?

$\theta_1 = \theta_2$

$\hat{\theta}_1$ $\hat{\theta}_2$

θ_1 θ_2

$\hat{\theta}_1$ $\hat{\theta}_2$

Samples came from the same population. Any differences are due to sampling variation.

Samples came from populations with different parameter values.

desirable because they permit us to reduce the chance of making either a Type I error or Type II error (i.e., increase the power of the test). However, larger samples take time and cost money, so we often must work with the available data.

10.2 COMPARING TWO MEANS: INDEPENDENT SAMPLES

Comparing two population means is a common business problem. Is there a difference between the average customer purchase at Starbucks on Saturday and Sunday mornings? Is there a difference between the average satisfaction scores from a taste test for two versions of a new menu item at Noodles & Company? Is there a difference between the average age of full-time and part-time seasonal employees at a Vail Resorts ski mountain?

Format of Hypotheses

The process of comparing two means starts by stating null and alternative hypotheses, just as we did in Chapter 9. To test for a difference in means of magnitude D_0, the possible pairs of null and alternative hypotheses are:

Left-Tailed Test	*Two-Tailed Test*	*Right-Tailed Test*
$H_0: \mu_1 - \mu_2 \geq D_0$	$H_0: \mu_1 - \mu_2 = D_0$	$H_0: \mu_1 - \mu_2 \leq D_0$
$H_1: \mu_1 - \mu_2 < D_0$	$H_1: \mu_1 - \mu_2 \neq D_0$	$H_1: \mu_1 - \mu_2 > D_0$

For example, we might ask if the difference between the average number of years worked at a Vail Resorts ski mountain for full-time and part-time seasonal employees is greater than two years. In this situation we would formulate the null hypothesis as: $H_0: \mu_1 - \mu_2 \leq 2$ where $D_0 = 2$ years. If a company is simply interested in knowing whether or not a difference exists between two populations, they would want to test the null hypothesis $H_0: \mu_1 - \mu_2 = 0$ where $D_0 = 0$.

Test Statistic

The **sample statistic** used to test the parameter $\mu_1 - \mu_2$ is $\bar{X}_1 - \bar{X}_2$ where both $\bar{X}_1$ and $\bar{X}_2$ are calculated from independent random samples taken from normal populations. The **test statistic** will follow the same general format as the z- and t-scores we calculated in Chapter 9. The test statistic is the difference between the sample statistic and the parameter divided by the standard error of the sample statistic. The formula for the test statistic is determined by the sampling distribution of the sample statistic and whether or not we know the population variances. There are three cases to consider.

Recognize and perform a test for two means with known σ_1 and σ_2.

Case 1: Known Variances

(10.1)
$$z_{calc} = \frac{(\bar{x}_1 - \bar{x}_2) - (\mu_1 - \mu_2)}{\sqrt{\dfrac{\sigma_1^2}{n_1} + \dfrac{\sigma_2^2}{n_2}}}$$

For the case where we know the values of the population variances, σ_1^2 and σ_2^2, the test statistic is a z-score. We would use the standard normal distribution to find *p-values* or critical values of z_α.

Recognize and perform a test for two means with unknown σ_1 and σ_2.

Case 2: Unknown Variances Assumed Equal

(10.2)
$$t_{calc} = \frac{(\bar{x}_1 - \bar{x}_2) - (\mu_1 - \mu_2)}{\sqrt{\dfrac{s_p^2}{n_1} + \dfrac{s_p^2}{n_2}}} \quad \text{where the pooled variance is}$$

$$s_p^2 = \frac{(n_1 - 1)s_1^2 + (n_2 - 1)s_2^2}{n_1 + n_2 - 2} \quad \text{and } d.f. = n_1 + n_2 - 2$$

For the more common case where we *don't* know the values of the population variances but we have reason to believe they are equal, we would use the Student's t distribution. We would need to rely on sample estimates s_1^2 and s_2^2 for the population variances, σ_1^2 and σ_2^2. By assuming that the population variances are equal, we are allowed to *pool* the sample variances by taking a weighted average of s_1^2 and s_2^2 to calculate an estimate of the common population variance. Weights are assigned to s_1^2 and s_2^2 based on their respective degrees of freedom $(n_1 - 1)$ and $(n_2 - 1)$. Because we are pooling the sample variances, the common variance estimate is called the **pooled variance** and is denoted s_p^2. Case 2 is often called the *pooled* t *test*. Degrees of freedom for the pooled t test will be the sum of the degrees of freedom for each individual sample.

Case 3: Unknown Variances Assumed Unequal

(10.3)
$$t_{calc} = \frac{(\bar{x}_1 - \bar{x}_2) - (\mu_1 - \mu_2)}{\sqrt{\dfrac{s_1^2}{n_1} + \dfrac{s_2^2}{n_2}}} \quad \text{with } d.f. = \frac{\left(\dfrac{s_1^2}{n_1} + \dfrac{s_2^2}{n_2}\right)^2}{\dfrac{\left(\dfrac{s_1^2}{n_1}\right)^2}{n_1 - 1} + \dfrac{\left(\dfrac{s_2^2}{n_2}\right)^2}{n_2 - 1}}$$

If the unknown variances σ_1^2 and σ_2^2 are assumed *unequal,* we do not pool the variances. Instead, we replace σ_1^2 and σ_2^2 with the sample variances s_1^2 and s_2^2. This is a more conservative assumption than Case 2. Under these conditions the distribution of the random variable $\bar{X}_1 - \bar{X}_2$ is no longer certain, a difficulty known as the **Behrens-Fisher problem**. However, the comparison of means can reliably be performed using a Student's t test with **Welch's adjusted degrees of freedom**.

Finding Welch's degrees of freedom requires a tedious calculation, but this is easily handled by Excel, MegaStat, or MINITAB. When computer software is not available, a conservative quick rule for degrees of freedom is to use $d.f. = \min(n_1 - 1, n_2 - 1)$. The formulas for Case 2 and Case 3 will usually yield the same decision about the hypotheses unless the sample sizes and variances differ greatly.

For the common situation of testing for a zero difference ($D_0 = 0$) in two population means the possible pairs of null and alternative hypotheses are

Left-Tailed Test

$H_0: \mu_1 - \mu_2 \geq 0$

$H_1: \mu_1 - \mu_2 < 0$

Two-Tailed Test

$H_0: \mu_1 - \mu_2 = 0$

$H_1: \mu_1 - \mu_2 \neq 0$

Right-Tailed Test

$H_0: \mu_1 - \mu_2 \leq 0$

$H_1: \mu_1 - \mu_2 > 0$

Table 10.1 summarizes the formulas for the test statistic in each of the three cases described above when we assume that $\mu_1 - \mu_2 = 0$. We have simplified the formulas based on the assumption that we will usually be testing for equal population means. We have left off the expression $\mu_1 - \mu_2$ because we are assuming that $\mu_1 - \mu_2 = 0$. All of these test statistics presume independent random samples from normal populations, although in practice they are robust to non-normality as long as the samples are not too small and the populations are not too skewed.

Case 1	Case 2	Case 3
Known Variances	Unknown Variances, Assumed Equal	Unknown Variances, Assumed Unequal
$z_{calc} = \dfrac{\bar{x}_1 - \bar{x}_2}{\sqrt{\dfrac{\sigma_1^2}{n_1} + \dfrac{\sigma_2^2}{n_2}}}$	$t_{calc} = \dfrac{(\bar{x}_1 - \bar{x}_2)}{\sqrt{\dfrac{s_p^2}{n_1} + \dfrac{s_p^2}{n_2}}}$ where $s_p^2 = \dfrac{(n_1 - 1)s_1^2 + (n_2 - 1)s_2^2}{n_1 + n_2 - 2}$	$t_{calc} = \dfrac{(\bar{x}_1 - \bar{x}_2)}{\sqrt{\dfrac{s_1^2}{n_1} + \dfrac{s_2^2}{n_2}}}$
For critical value, use standard normal distribution	For critical value, use Student's t with $d.f. = n_1 + n_2 - 2$	For critical value, use Student's t with Welch's adjusted degrees of freedom or $\min(n_1 - 1, n_2 - 1)$

TABLE 10.1

Test Statistic for Zero Difference of Means

Most of the time you will be using a computer. As long as you have raw data (i.e., the original samples of n_1 and n_2 observations), Excel's Data Analysis menu handles all three cases, as shown in Figure 10.2. Both MegaStat and MINITAB also perform these tests and will do so for summarized data as well (i.e., when you have $\bar{x}_1$, $\bar{x}_2$, s_1, s_2 instead of the n_1 and n_2 data columns).

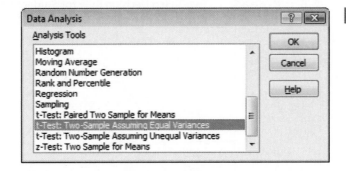

FIGURE 10.2

Excel's Data Analysis Menu

EXAMPLE 10.1

Drug Prices in Two States

The price of prescription drugs is an ongoing national issue in the United States. Zocor is a common prescription cholesterol-reducing drug prescribed for people who are at risk for heart disease. Table 10.2 shows Zocor prices from randomly selected pharmacies in two states. At $\alpha = .05$, is there a difference in the mean for all pharmacies in Colorado and Texas?

TABLE 10.2   Zocor Prices (30-Day Supply) in Two States   Zocor

Colorado Pharmacies		Texas Pharmacies	
City	Price ($)	City	Price ($)
Alamosa	125.05	Austin	145.32
Avon	137.56	Austin	131.19
Broomfield	142.50	Austin	151.65
Buena Vista	145.95	Austin	141.55
Colorado Springs	117.49	Austin	125.99
Colorado Springs	142.75	Dallas	126.29
Denver	121.99	Dallas	139.19
Denver	117.49	Dallas	156.00
Eaton	141.64	Dallas	137.56
Fort Collins	128.69	Houston	154.10
Gunnison	130.29	Houston	126.41
Pueblo	142.39	Houston	114.00
Pueblo	121.99	Houston	144.99
Pueblo	141.30		
Sterling	153.43		
Walsenburg	133.39		
$\bar{x}_1 = \$133.994$		$\bar{x}_2 = \$138.018$	
$s_1 = \$11.015$		$s_2 = \$12.663$	
$n_1 = 16$ pharmacies		$n_2 = 13$ pharmacies	

Source: Public Research Interest Group (www.pirg.org). Surveyed pharmacies were chosen from the telephone directory in 2004. Data used with permission.

Step 1: State the Hypotheses

To check for a significant difference without regard for its direction, we choose a two-tailed test. The hypotheses to be tested are

$H_0: \mu_1 - \mu_2 = 0$

$H_1: \mu_1 - \mu_2 \neq 0$

LO 10-2

Recognize and perform a test for two means with unknown σ_1 and σ_2.

Step 2: Specify the Decision Rule

We will assume equal variances. For the pooled-variance t test, degrees of freedom are $d.f. = n_1 + n_2 - 2 = 16 + 13 - 2 = 27$. From Appendix D we get the two-tail critical value $t = \pm 2.052$. The decision rule is illustrated in Figure 10.3.

FIGURE 10.3   Two-Tailed Decision Rule for Student's t with $\alpha = .05$ and $d.f. = 27$

Step 3: Calculate the Test Statistic

The sample statistics are

$\bar{x}_1 = 133.994$ $\bar{x}_2 = 138.018$

$s_1 = 11.015$ $s_2 = 12.663$

$n_1 = 16$ $n_2 = 13$

Because we are assuming equal variances, we use the formulas for Case 2. The pooled variance s_p^2 is

$$s_p^2 = \frac{(n_1 - 1)s_1^2 + (n_2 - 1)s_2^2}{n_1 + n_2 - 2} = \frac{(16 - 1)(11.015)^2 + (13 - 1)(12.663)^2}{16 + 13 - 2} = 138.6737$$

Using s_p^2 the test statistic is

$$t_{calc} = \frac{\bar{x}_1 - \bar{x}_2}{\sqrt{\frac{s_p^2}{n_1} + \frac{s_p^2}{n_2}}} = \frac{133.994 - 138.018}{\sqrt{\frac{138.6737}{16} + \frac{138.6737}{13}}} = \frac{-4.024}{4.39708} = -0.915$$

The pooled standard deviation is $s_p = \sqrt{138.6737} = 11.776$. Notice that s_p always lies between s_1 and s_2 (if not, you made an arithmetic error). This is because s_p^2 is a weighted average of s_1^2 and s_2^2.

Step 4: Make the Decision
The test statistic $t_{calc} = -0.915$ does not fall in the rejection region so we cannot reject the hypothesis of equal means. Excel's menu and output are shown in Figure 10.4. Both one-tailed and two-tailed tests are shown.

Step 5: Take Action
Because the difference in sample means is within the realm of chance assuming that H_0 is true, no further investigation is required.

FIGURE 10.4   **Excel's Data Analysis with Unknown but Equal Variances**

The *p*-value can be verified using the two-tailed Excel function =T.DIST.2T(.915,27) = .3681. This large *p*-value says that a difference of sample means of this magnitude would happen by chance about 37 percent of the time if $\mu_1 = \mu_2$. The observed difference in sample means seems to be well within the realm of chance.

The sample variances in this example are similar, so the assumption of equal variances is reasonable. But if we did use the formulas for Case 3 (assuming *unequal* variances), the test statistic would be

$$t_{calc} = \frac{\bar{x}_1 - \bar{x}_2}{\sqrt{\frac{s_1^2}{n_1} + \frac{s_2^2}{n_2}}} = \frac{133.994 - 138.018}{\sqrt{\frac{(11.015)^2}{16} + \frac{(12.663)^2}{13}}} = \frac{-4.024}{4.4629} = -0.902$$

Welch's adjusted degrees of freedom will be smaller than in Case 2 (24 instead of 27):

$$d.f. = \frac{\left[\frac{s_1^2}{n_1} + \frac{s_2^2}{n_2}\right]^2}{\frac{\left(\frac{s_1^2}{n_1}\right)^2}{n_1 - 1} + \frac{\left(\frac{s_2^2}{n_2}\right)^2}{n_2 - 1}} = \frac{\left[\frac{(11.015)^2}{16} + \frac{(12.663)^2}{13}\right]^2}{\frac{\left(\frac{(11.015)^2}{16}\right)^2}{16 - 1} + \frac{\left(\frac{(12.663)^2}{13}\right)^2}{13 - 1}} = 24$$

The degrees of freedom are truncated to the next lower integer, to be conservative.

LO 10-7

Use Excel to determine *p*-values for two-sample tests using *z* or *t*.

For the unequal-variance t test with $d.f. = 24$, Appendix D or Excel gives the two-tail critical value $t_{.025} = \pm 2.064$. The decision rule is illustrated in Figure 10.5.

FIGURE 10.5 **Two-Tail Decision Rule for Student's t with $\alpha = .05$ and $d.f. = 24$**

The calculations are best done by computer. Excel's menu and output are shown in Figure 10.6. Excel shows one-tailed and two-tailed tests.

FIGURE 10.6 **Excel's Data Analysis with Unknown and Unequal Variances**

For the Zocor data, either assumption about the variances would lead to the same conclusion:

Case 2 (equal variances) $t_{.025} = \pm 2.052 \ (d.f. = 27)$ $t_{calc} = -0.915 \ (p = .3681)$
                                                                      Do not reject at $\alpha = .05$

Case 3 (unequal variances) $t_{.025} = \pm 2.064 \ (d.f. = 24)$ $t_{calc} = -0.902 \ (p = .3761)$
                                                                      Do not reject at $\alpha = .05$

Which Assumption Is Best?

If the *sample sizes are equal,* the Case 2 and Case 3 test statistics will always be identical, but the degrees of freedom (and hence the critical values) may differ. If you have no information about the population variances, then the best choice is Case 3. The fewer assumptions you make about your populations, the less likely you are to make a mistake in your conclusions. Case 1 (known population variances) is not explored further here because it is uncommon in business.

Must Sample Sizes Be Equal?

Unequal sample sizes are common, and the formulas still apply. However, there are advantages to equal sample sizes. We avoid unbalanced sample sizes when possible to increase the *power* of the test. But many times, we have to take the samples as they come.

Large Samples

For unknown variances, if both samples are large ($n_1 \geq 30$ and $n_2 \geq 30$) and you have reason to think the population isn't badly skewed (look at the histograms or dot plots of the samples), it is common to use formula 10.4 with Appendix C. Although it usually gives results very close to the "proper" *t* tests, this approach is not conservative (i.e., it may increase Type I risk).

$$z_{\text{calc}} = \frac{\bar{x}_1 - \bar{x}_2}{\sqrt{\dfrac{s_1^2}{n_1} + \dfrac{s_2^2}{n_2}}} \qquad \text{(large samples, symmetric populations)} \qquad \textbf{(10.4)}$$

Caution: Three Issues

Bear in mind three questions when you are comparing two sample means:

- Are the populations skewed? Are there outliers?
- Are the sample sizes large ($n \geq 30$)?
- Is the difference *important* as well as significant?

The first two questions refer to the assumption of normal populations, upon which the tests are based. Fortunately, the *t* test is robust to non-normality as long as the samples are not too small and the populations are not too skewed. Skewness or outliers can usually be seen in a histogram or dot plot of each sample. The *t* tests (Case 2 and Case 3) are probably OK in the face of moderate skewness, especially if the samples are large (e.g., sample sizes of at least 30). Outliers are more serious and might require consultation with a statistician. In such cases, you might ask yourself whether a test of means is appropriate. With small samples or skewed data, the mean may not be a very reliable indicator of central tendency, and your test may lack power. In such situations, it may be better merely to describe the samples and skip the formal *t* tests.

A small difference in means or proportions could be *statistically* significant if the sample size is large because the standard error gets smaller as the sample size gets larger. So, we must separately ask if the difference is *important*. The answer depends on the data magnitude and the consequences to the decision maker. For example, individuals who took an experimental weight-loss drug called Lorcaserin lost 5.8 percent of their weight after a year, compared to 2.5 percent for those who took a placebo. The difference was statistically significant. However, in rejecting the obesity drug, the FDA said that the 3.3 percent difference was below the 5 percent efficacy criterion set by the FDA. Although *significant,* the difference was not *important* enough to approve the new medication, given the possibility of additional health risks. (See *The New York Times,* September 17, 2010, p. B1).

> **LO 10-4**
>
> Explain the assumptions underlying the two-sample test of means.

Mini Case | 10.2

Methane Gas Emissions of Pneumatic Controllers

Certain types of equipment can be controlled pneumatically through the use of pressurized gas such as natural gas. Such equipment is often used in the oil and gas production industry because electricity is not always available in remote locations. As part of normal operations, pneumatic controllers release methane gas to the atmosphere. Older technology controllers, called high-bleed controllers, typically release more methane gas than newer technology controllers, called low-bleed controllers. Measuring the amount of gas emissions reduction is a critical factor when evaluating the benefits of switching out the high-bleed for the low-bleed controllers.

The American Carbon Registry, www.americancarbonregistry.org, provides approved measurement methodologies for energy companies who wish to show greenhouse gas emission reduction through retrofitting high-bleed pneumatic controllers with low-bleed controllers. One step is determining whether different manufacturers of high-bleed controllers have different baseline gas emissions. Independent samples of gas emissions from two different manufacturers were analyzed using a two-tailed two-sample hypothesis test. Summary sample data from the two manufacturers are shown in Table 10.3.

TABLE 10.3	Pneumatic Controller Methane Gas Emission (scfd)	
	Cemco	**Invalco**
	$\bar{x}_1 = 510.5$	$\bar{x}_2 = 628.9$
	$s_1 = 147.2$	$s_2 = 237.9$
	$n_1 = 18$	$n_2 = 17$

Note: scfd: standard cubic foot per day.
Source: www.americancarbonregistry.org/carbonaccounting/.

We will do a two-tailed test at $\alpha = .10$. The hypotheses are

$$H_0: \mu_1 - \mu_2 = 0$$
$$H_1: \mu_1 - \mu_2 \neq 0$$

Because the variances are unknown and the sample standard deviations appear very different, we will assume the population variances are unequal, using formula 10.3 for the t statistic. (Later on, in Section 10.7, we will learn how to actually test the equality of variances.)

$$t_{calc} = \frac{\bar{x}_1 - \bar{x}_2}{\sqrt{\frac{s_1^2}{n_1} + \frac{s_2^2}{n_2}}} = \frac{510.5 - 628.9}{\sqrt{\frac{147.2^2}{18} + \frac{237.9^2}{17}}} = -1.759$$

Welch's adjusted degrees of freedom are

$$d.f. = \frac{\left[\frac{s_1^2}{n_1} + \frac{s_2^2}{n_2}\right]^2}{\frac{\left(\frac{s_1^2}{n_1}\right)^2}{n_1 - 1} + \frac{\left(\frac{s_2^2}{n_2}\right)^2}{n_2 - 1}} = \frac{\left[\frac{147.2^2}{18} + \frac{237.9^2}{17}\right]^2}{\frac{\left(\frac{147.2^2}{18}\right)^2}{18 - 1} + \frac{\left(\frac{237.9^2}{17}\right)^2}{17 - 1}} = 26$$

The critical value is $=$T.INV.2T$(.10,26) = t_{.05} = 1.706$. If we use the quick rule for degrees of freedom instead of wading through this tedious calculation, we would get $d.f. = \min(n_1 - 1, n_2 - 1) = \min(18 - 1, 17 - 1) = 16$ or $t_{.05} = 1.746$. In either case we arrive at the same decision, which is to reject H_0 and conclude that the average emissions from the two manufacturers' controllers are not equal. The p-value for this test is found using Excel: $=$T.DIST.2T$(1.759,26) = .0903$. Because $.0903 < .10$, our decision is to reject the assumption that the means are equal and conclude that the means are not equal. The implication is that baseline emissions must be calculated separately for each manufacturer in order to accurately measure emissions reductions when retrofitting high-bleed controllers with low-bleed controllers.

SECTION EXERCISES

connect

Hint: Calculate the p-values using Excel, and show each Excel formula you used. Excel has no t test for summarized data (i.e., given $\bar{x}_1, s_1, n_1, \bar{x}_2, s_2, n_2$), but from the OLC (www.mhhe.com/doane4e) you can download a spreadsheet calculator for summarized data, or you can use MegaStat.

10.1 Do a two-sample test for equality of means assuming equal variances. Calculate the p-value.

    a. Comparison of GPA for randomly chosen college juniors and seniors: $\bar{x}_1 = 3.05$, $s_1 = .20$, $n_1 = 15$, $\bar{x}_2 = 3.25$, $s_2 = .30$, $n_2 = 15$, $\alpha = .025$, left-tailed test.

    b. Comparison of average commute miles for randomly chosen students at two community colleges: $\bar{x}_1 = 15$, $s_1 = 5$, $n_1 = 22$, $\bar{x}_2 = 18$, $s_2 = 7$, $n_2 = 19$, $\alpha = .05$, two-tailed test.

    c. Comparison of credits at time of graduation for randomly chosen accounting and economics students: $\bar{x}_1 = 139$, $s_1 = 2.8$, $n_1 = 12$, $\bar{x}_2 = 137$, $s_2 = 2.7$, $n_2 = 17$, $\alpha = .05$, right-tailed test.

10.2   Repeat the previous exercise, assuming unequal variances. Calculate the *p*-value using Excel, and show the Excel formula you used.

10.3   Is there a difference in the average number of years' seniority between returning part-time seasonal employees and returning full-time seasonal employees at a Vail Resorts' ski mountain? From a random sample of 191 returning part-time employees, the average seniority, $\bar{x}_1$, was 4.9 years with a standard deviation, s_1, equal to 5.4 years. From a random sample of 833 returning full-time employees, the average seniority, $\bar{x}_2$, was 7.9 years with a standard deviation, s_2, equal to 8.3 years. Assume the population variances are not equal. (a) Test the hypothesis of equal means using $\alpha = .01$. (b) Calculate the *p*-value using Excel.

VAILRESORTS

10.4   The average mpg usage for a 2009 Toyota Prius for a sample of 10 tanks of gas was 45.5 with a standard deviation of 1.8. For a 2009 Honda Insight, the average mpg usage for a sample of 10 tanks of gas was 42.0 with a standard deviation of 2.3. (a) Assuming equal variances, at $\alpha = .01$, is the true mean mpg lower for the Honda Insight? (b) Calculate the *p*-value using Excel.

10.5   When the background music tempo was slow, the mean amount of bar purchases for a sample of 17 restaurant patrons was $30.47 with a standard deviation of $15.10. When the background music tempo was fast, the mean amount of bar purchases for a sample of 14 patrons in the same restaurant was $21.62 with a standard deviation of $9.50. (a) Assuming equal variances, at $\alpha = .01$, is the true mean higher when the music is slow? (b) Calculate the *p*-value using Excel.

10.6   Are women's feet getting bigger? Retailers in the last 20 years have had to increase their stock of larger sizes. Wal-Mart Stores, Inc., and Payless ShoeSource, Inc., have been aggressive in stocking larger sizes, and Nordstrom's reports that its larger sizes typically sell out first. Assuming equal variances, at $\alpha = .025$, do these random shoe size samples of 12 randomly chosen women in each age group show that women's shoe sizes have increased? 📷 **ShoeSize1**

Born in 1980:	8	7.5	8.5	8.5	8	7.5	9.5	7.5	8	8	8.5	9
Born in 1960:	8.5	7.5	8	8	7.5	7.5	7.5	8	7	8	7	8

10.7   Researchers analyzed 12 samples of two kinds of Stella's decaffeinated coffee. The caffeine in a cup of decaffeinated espresso had a mean of 9.4 mg with a standard deviation of 3.2 mg, while brewed decaffeinated coffee had a mean of 12.7 mg with a standard deviation of 0.35 mg. Assuming unequal population variances, is there a significant difference in caffeine content between these two beverages at $\alpha = .01$?

10.8   On a random basis, Bob buys a small take-out coffee from one of two restaurants. As a statistics project in the month of May, he measured the temperature of each cup immediately after purchase, using an analog cooking thermometer. Assuming equal variances, is the mean temperature higher at Panera than at Bruegger's at $\alpha = .01$? *Note:* Ideal coffee temperature is a matter of individual preference (see www.coffeedetective.com). 📷 **Coffee**

Panera	171	161	169	179	171	166	169	178	171	165	172	172
Bruegger's	168	165	172	151	162	158	157	160	158	160	158	164

10.9   For a marketing class term project, Bob is investigating whether college seniors eat less frequently in fast-food chains than college freshmen. He asked 11 freshmen and 11 seniors to keep track of how many times they ate in a fast-food restaurant during the month of October. Assuming equal variances, can you conclude that the mean is significantly smaller for college seniors at the 5 percent level of significance? 📷 **FastFood**

Seniors	10	5	15	13	5	7	18	8	19	9	8
Freshmen	16	9	17	14	15	11	18	12	7	16	20

10.3 CONFIDENCE INTERVAL FOR THE DIFFERENCE OF TWO MEANS, $\mu_1 - \mu_2$

There may be occasions when we want to estimate the difference between two unknown population means. The point estimate for $\mu_1 - \mu_2$ is $\bar{X}_1 - \bar{X}_2$, where $\bar{X}_1$ and $\bar{X}_2$ are calculated from independent random samples. We can use a confidence interval estimate to find a range within which the true difference might fall. If the confidence interval for the **difference of two means** includes zero, we could conclude that there is no significant difference in means.

When the population variances are unknown (the usual situation), the procedure for constructing a confidence interval for $\mu_1 - \mu_2$ depends on our assumption about the

LO 10-9

Construct a confidence interval for $\mu_1 - \mu_2$ or $\pi_1 - \pi_2$.

unknown variances. If both populations are normal and the population variances can be assumed equal, the difference of means follows a Student's t distribution with $(n_1 - 1) + (n_2 - 1)$ degrees of freedom. Assuming *equal variances*, the **pooled variance** is a weighted average of the sample variances with weights $n_1 - 1$ and $n_2 - 1$ (the respective degrees of freedom for each sample):

(10.5)
$$(\bar{x}_1 - \bar{x}_2) \pm t_{\alpha/2} \sqrt{\frac{(n_1 - 1)s_1^2 + (n_2 - 1)s_2^2}{n_1 + n_2 - 2}} \sqrt{\frac{1}{n_1} + \frac{1}{n_2}}$$

with $d.f. = (n_1 - 1) + (n_2 - 1)$

If the population variances are unknown and are assumed to be unequal, we should not pool the variances. For *unequal variances*, a practical alternative is to use the t distribution, adding the variances and using Welch's formula for the degrees of freedom:

(10.6)
$$(\bar{x}_1 - \bar{x}_2) \pm t_{\alpha/2} \sqrt{\frac{s_1^2}{n_1} + \frac{s_2^2}{n_2}} \quad \text{with} \quad d.f. = \frac{\left[s_1^2/n_1 + s_2^2/n_2 \right]^2}{\dfrac{(s_1^2/n_1)^2}{n_1 - 1} + \dfrac{(s_2^2/n_2)^2}{n_2 - 1}}$$

If you wish to avoid the algebra of Welch's formula, you can just use degrees of freedom equal to $d.f. = \min(n_1 - 1, n_2 - 1)$. This quick rule is conservative because it allows fewer degrees of freedom than Welch's formula.

EXAMPLE 10.2

Marketing Teams

Senior marketing majors were randomly assigned to a virtual team that met only electronically or to a face-to-face team that met in person. Both teams were presented with the task of analyzing eight complex marketing cases. After completing the project, they were asked to respond on a $1-5$ Likert scale to this question:

"As compared to other teams, the members got along together."

TABLE 10.4	Means and Standard Deviations for the Two Marketing Teams	
Statistic	**Virtual Team**	**Face-to-Face Team**
Sample Mean	$\bar{x}_1 = 2.48$	$\bar{x}_2 = 1.83$
Sample Std. Dev.	$s_1 = 0.76$	$s_2 = 0.82$
Sample Size	$n_1 = 44$	$n_2 = 42$

Source: Roger W. Berry, "The Efficacy of Electronic Communication in the Business School: Marketing Students' Perception of Virtual Teams," *Marketing Education Review* 12, no. 2 (Summer 2002), pp. 73–78. Copyright © 2002. Reprinted with permission, CTC press. All rights reserved.

Table 10.4 shows the means and standard deviations for the two groups. The population variances are unknown but will be assumed equal (note the similar standard deviations). For a confidence level of 90 percent we use Student's t with $d.f. = 44 + 42 - 2 = 84$. From Appendix D we obtain $t_{.05} = 1.664$ (using 80 degrees of freedom, the next lower value). The confidence interval is

$$(\bar{x}_1 - \bar{x}_2) \pm t \sqrt{\frac{(n_1 - 1)s_1^2 + (n_2 - 1)s_2^2}{n_1 + n_2 - 2}} \sqrt{\frac{1}{n_1} + \frac{1}{n_2}}$$

$$= (2.48 - 1.83) \pm (1.664) \sqrt{\frac{(44 - 1)(0.76)^2 + (42 - 1)(0.82)^2}{44 + 42 - 2}} \sqrt{\frac{1}{44} + \frac{1}{42}}$$

$$= 0.65 \pm 0.284 \quad \text{or} \quad [0.366, 0.934]$$

Since this confidence interval does not include zero, we can say with 90 percent confidence that there is a difference between the means (i.e., the virtual team's mean differs from the face-to-face team's mean).

Because the calculations for the comparison of two sample means are time-consuming, it is helpful to use software. Figure 10.7 shows a MINITAB menu that gives the option to assume equal variances or not. If we had not assumed equal variances, the results would be the same in this case because the samples are large and of similar size, and the variances do not differ greatly. But when you have small, unequal sample sizes or unequal variances, the methods can yield different conclusions.

FIGURE 10.7

MINITAB's Menu for Comparing Two Sample Means

Should Sample Sizes Be Equal?

Many people instinctively try to choose equal sample sizes for tests of means. It is preferable to avoid unbalanced sample sizes to increase the power of the test, but it is not necessary. Unequal sample sizes are common, and the formulas still apply.

SECTION EXERCISES

connect

10.10 A special bumper was installed on selected vehicles in a large fleet. The dollar cost of body repairs was recorded for all vehicles that were involved in accidents over a 1-year period. Those with the special bumper are the test group and the other vehicles are the control group, shown below. Each "repair incident" is defined as an invoice (which might include more than one separate type of damage).

Statistic	Test Group	Control Group
Mean Damage	$\bar{x}_1 = \$1,101$	$\bar{x}_2 = \$1,766$
Sample Std. Dev.	$s_1 = \$696$	$s_2 = \$838$
Repair Incidents	$n_1 = 12$	$n_2 = 9$

Source: Unpublished study by Thomas W. Lauer and Floyd G. Willoughby.

(a) Construct a 90 percent confidence interval for the true difference of the means assuming equal variances. Show all work clearly. (b) Repeat, using the assumption of unequal variances with either Welch's formula for *d.f.* or the quick rule for degrees of freedom. (c) Did the assumption about variances change the conclusion? (d) Construct separate confidence intervals for each mean. Do they overlap?

10.11 In trials of an experimental Internet-based method of learning statistics, pre-tests and post-tests were given to two groups: traditional instruction (22 students) and Internet-based (17 students). Pre-test scores were not significantly different. On the post-test, the first group (traditional instruction) had a mean score of 8.64 with a standard deviation of 1.88, while the second group (experimental instruction) had a mean score of 8.82 with a standard deviation of 1.70. (a) Construct a 90 percent confidence interval for the true difference of the means assuming equal variances. Show all work clearly. (b) Repeat, using the assumption of unequal variances with either Welch's formula for *d.f.* or the quick rule for degrees of freedom. (c) Did the assumption about variances change the conclusion? (d) Construct separate confidence intervals for each mean. Do they overlap?

10.12 Construct a 95 percent confidence interval for the difference of mean monthly rent paid by undergraduates and graduate students. What do you conclude?   📁 **Rent2**

Undergraduate Student Rents ($n = 10$)

820	780	870	670	800
790	810	680	1,000	730

Graduate Student Rents ($n = 12$)

1,130	920	930	880	780	910
790	840	930	910	860	850

10.4 COMPARING TWO MEANS: PAIRED SAMPLES

Paired Data

LO 10-3

Recognize paired data and be able to perform a paired *t* test.

When sample data consist of n matched pairs, a different approach is required. If the *same* individuals are observed twice but under different circumstances, we have a **paired comparison**. For example:

- Fifteen retirees with diagnosed hypertension are assigned a program of diet, exercise, and meditation. A baseline measurement of blood pressure is taken *before* the program begins and again *after* 2 months. Was the program effective in reducing blood pressure?

- Ten cutting tools use lubricant A for 10 minutes. The blade temperatures are taken. When the machine has cooled, it is run with lubricant B for 10 minutes and the blade temperatures are again measured. Which lubricant makes the blades run cooler?

- Weekly sales of Snapple at 12 Walmart stores are compared *before* and *after* installing a new eye-catching display. Did the new display increase sales?

Paired data typically come from a *before-after* experiment, but not always. For example, paired data might also arise in marketing studies that use one focus group to rate two different products. When we use *one* focus group of n individuals to compare two products, we have *paired* ratings. If we treat the data as two independent samples, ignoring the *dependence* between the data pairs, the test is less powerful.

Paired *t* Test

In the **paired *t* test** we define a new variable $d = X_1 - X_2$ as the *difference* between X_1 and X_2. The *two* samples are reduced to *one* sample of n differences $d_1, d_2, \ldots, d_n$. We usually present the n observed differences in column form:

Obs	Sample 1	Sample 2	Differences
1	x_{11}	x_{12}	$d_1 = x_{11} - x_{12}$
2	x_{21}	x_{22}	$d_2 = x_{21} - x_{22}$
3	x_{31}	x_{32}	$d_3 = x_{31} - x_{32}$
...	...	...	...
n	x_{n1}	x_{n2}	$d_n = x_{n1} - x_{n2}$

The same sample data could also be presented in row form:

Obs	1	2	3	...	n
Sample 1	x_{11}	x_{21}	x_{31}	...	x_{n1}
Sample 2	x_{12}	x_{22}	x_{32}	...	x_{n2}
Difference	$d_1 = x_{11} - x_{12}$	$d_2 = x_{21} - x_{22}$	$d_3 = x_{31} - x_{32}$	...	$d_n = x_{n1} - x_{n2}$

We calculate the mean $\bar{d}$ and standard deviation s_d of the sample of n differences $d_1, d_2, \ldots,$ d_n with the usual formulas for a mean and standard deviation. We call the mean $\bar{d}$ instead of $\bar{x}$ merely to remind ourselves that we are dealing with *differences*.

$$\bar{d} = \frac{\sum\limits_{i=1}^{n} d_i}{n} \qquad \text{(mean of } n \text{ differences)} \qquad \textbf{(10.7)}$$

$$s_d = \sqrt{\sum_{i=1}^{n} \frac{(d_i - \bar{d})^2}{n-1}} \qquad \text{(Std. Dev. of } n \text{ differences)} \qquad \textbf{(10.8)}$$

Since the population variance of d is unknown, we will do a paired t test using Student's t with $n - 1$ degrees of freedom to compare the sample mean difference $\bar{d}$ with a hypothesized difference μ_d (usually $\mu_d = 0$). The test statistic is really a one-sample t test, just like those in Chapter 9.

$$t_{\text{calc}} = \frac{\bar{d} - \mu_d}{\dfrac{s_d}{\sqrt{n}}} \qquad \text{(test statistic for \textbf{paired samples})} \qquad \textbf{(10.9)}$$

EXAMPLE 10.3

Repair Estimates

📂 Repair

An insurance company's procedure in settling a claim under $10,000 for fire or water damage to a home owner is to require two estimates for cleanup and repair of structural damage before allowing the insured to proceed with the work. The insurance company compares estimates from two contractors who most frequently handle this type of work in this geographical area. Table 10.5 shows the 10 most recent claims for which damage estimates were provided by both contractors. At the .05 level of significance, is there a difference between the two contractors?

TABLE 10.5	Damage Repair Estimates ($) for 10 Claims 📂 Repair		
	X_1	X_2	$d = X_1 - X_2$
Claim	Contractor A	Contractor B	Difference
1. Jones, C.	5,500	6,000	−500
2. Smith, R.	1,000	900	100
3. Xia, Y.	2,500	2,500	0
4. Gallo, J.	7,800	8,300	−500
5. Carson, R.	6,400	6,200	200
6. Petty, M.	8,800	9,400	−600
7. Tracy, L.	600	500	100
8. Barnes, J.	3,300	3,500	−200
9. Rodriguez, J.	4,500	5,200	−700
10. Van Dyke, P.	6,500	6,800	−300
			$\bar{d} = -240.00$
			$s_d = 327.28$
			$n = 10$

Step 1: State the Hypotheses
We will choose a two-tailed test using these hypotheses:

$H_0: \mu_d = 0$

$H_1: \mu_d \neq 0$

Step 2: Specify the Decision Rule

Our test statistic will follow a Student's t distribution with $d.f. = n - 1 = 10 - 1 = 9$, so from Appendix D with $\alpha = .05$ the two-tail critical value is $t_{.025} = \pm 2.262$, as illustrated in Figure 10.8. The decision rule is

Reject H_0 if $t_{calc} < -2.262$ or if $t_{calc} > +2.262$

Otherwise do not reject H_0

FIGURE 10.8   **Decision Rule for Two-Tailed Paired t Test at $\alpha = .05$**

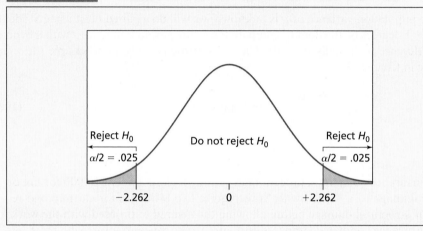

Step 3: Calculate the Test Statistic

The mean and standard deviation are calculated in the usual way, as shown in Table 10.5, so the test statistic is

$$ t_{calc} = \frac{\bar{d} - \mu_d}{\dfrac{s_d}{\sqrt{n}}} = \frac{-240 - 0}{\left(\dfrac{327.28}{\sqrt{10}} \right)} = \frac{-240}{103.495} = -2.319 $$

Step 4: Make the Decision

Since $t_{calc} = -2.319$ falls in the left-tail critical region (below -2.262), we reject the null hypothesis and conclude that there is a significant difference between the two contractors. However, it is a *very* close decision.

Step 5: Take Action

Because the difference is significant in a two-tailed test, it would also be significant in a left-tailed test. The insurance company might talk to Contractor B to see why their estimates are higher.

Excel's Paired Difference Test

The calculations for our repair estimates example are easy in Excel, as illustrated in Figure 10.9. Excel gives you the option of choosing either a one-tailed or two-tailed test, and also shows the p-value. For a two-tailed test, the p-value is $p = .0456$, which would barely lead to rejection of the hypothesis of zero difference of means at $\alpha = .05$. The borderline p-value reinforces our conclusion that the decision is sensitive to our choice of α. MegaStat and MINITAB also provide a paired t test.

FIGURE 10.9

**Results of Excel's Paired
t Test at $\alpha = .05$**

Analogy to Confidence Interval

A two-tailed test for a zero difference is equivalent to asking whether the confidence interval for the true mean difference μ_d includes zero.

$$\bar{d} \pm t_{\alpha/2}\frac{s_d}{\sqrt{n}} \qquad \text{(confidence interval for difference of paired means)} \qquad \textbf{(10.10)}$$

It depends on the confidence level:

90% confidence ($t_{\alpha/2} = 1.833$): $[-429.72, -50.28]$

95% confidence ($t_{\alpha/2} = 2.262$): $[-474.12, -5.88]$

99% confidence ($t_{\alpha/2} = 3.250$): $[-576.34, +96.34]$

As Figure 10.10 shows, the 99 percent confidence interval includes zero, but the 90 percent and 95 percent confidence intervals do not.

FIGURE 10.10

**Confidence Intervals for
Difference of Means**

Why Not Treat Paired Data as
Independent Samples?

When observations are matched pairs, the paired *t* test is more powerful because it utilizes information that is ignored if we treat the samples separately. To show this, let's treat each data column as an **independent sample**. The summary statistics are:

$$\bar{x}_1 = 4,690.00 \qquad \bar{x}_2 = 4,930.00$$
$$s_1 = 2,799.38 \qquad s_2 = 3,008.89$$
$$n_1 = 10 \qquad n_2 = 10$$

Assuming equal variances, we get the results shown in Figure 10.11. The *p*-values (one-tail or two-tail) are not even close to being significant at the usual α levels. By ignoring the dependence between the samples, we unnecessarily *sacrifice the power of the test*. Therefore, if the two data columns are paired, we should not treat them independently.

FIGURE 10.11

Excel's Paired Sample and Independent Sample *t* Tests

	Best Test : Paired Samples			Less Power : Independent Samples	

t-Test: Paired Two Sample for Means

	Contractor A	Contractor B
Mean	4690	4930
Variance	7836555.556	9053444.444
Observations	10	10
Pearson Correlation	0.996247386	
Hypothesized Mean Diff	0	
df	9	
t Stat	-2.318963855	
P(T<=t) one-tail	0.022781515	
t Critical one-tail	1.833112923	
P(T<=t) two-tail	0.045563029	
t Critical two-tail	2.262157158	

t-Test: Two-Sample Assuming Equal Variances

	Contractor A	Contractor B
Mean	4690	4930
Variance	7836555.556	9053444.444
Observations	10	10
Pooled Variance	8445000	
Hypothesized Mean Differe	0	
df	18	
t Stat	-0.184670029	
P(T<=t) one-tail	0.427776285	
t Critical one-tail	1.734063592	
P(T<=t) two-tail	0.855552569	
t Critical two-tail	2.100922037	

SECTION EXERCISES

connect

10.13 (a) At $\alpha = .05$, does the following sample show that daughters are taller than their mothers? (b) Is the decision close? (c) Why might daughters tend to be taller than their mothers? Why might they not? 📆 **Height**

Family	Daughter's Height (cm)	Mother's Height (cm)
1	167	172
2	166	162
3	176	157
4	171	159
5	165	157
6	181	177
7	173	174

10.14 An experimental surgical procedure is being studied as an alternative to the old method. Both methods are considered safe. Five surgeons perform the operation on two patients matched by age, sex, and other relevant factors, with the results shown. The time to complete the surgery (in minutes) is recorded. (a) At the 5 percent significance level, is the new way faster? State your hypotheses and show all steps clearly. (b) Is the decision close? 📆 **Surgery**

	Surgeon 1	Surgeon 2	Surgeon 3	Surgeon 4	Surgeon 5
Old way	36	55	28	40	62
New way	29	42	30	32	56

10.15 Blue Box is testing a new "half price on Tuesday" policy on DVD rentals at a sample of 10 locations. (a) At $\alpha = .10$, do the data show that the mean number of Tuesday rentals has increased? (b) Is the decision close? (c) Are you convinced? 📆 **DVDRental**

Location	New Price	Old Price
1	14	10
2	12	7
3	14	10
4	13	13
5	10	9
6	13	14
7	12	12
8	10	7
9	13	13
10	13	9

10.16 The U.S. government's "Cash for Clunkers" program encouraged individuals to trade in their old gas-guzzlers for new, more efficient vehicles. At $\alpha = .05$, do the data below support the hypothesis that the gain in mpg was more than 5 mpg? *Hint:* The null hypothesis is $H_0: \mu_d \leq 5$ mpg. 📁 **Guzzlers**

Buyer	New Car	Old Car	Buyer	New Car	Old Car
Buyer 1	23.0	20.1	Buyer 8	26.3	16.1
Buyer 2	20.3	15.8	Buyer 9	27.2	19.2
Buyer 3	24.6	19.1	Buyer 10	28.0	19.8
Buyer 4	25.3	17.4	Buyer 11	18.9	17.7
Buyer 5	20.6	13.9	Buyer 12	23.8	21.8
Buyer 6	26.8	15.6	Buyer 13	27.8	18.5
Buyer 7	22.9	17.1	Buyer 14	27.1	19.4

10.17 The coach told the high school swim team that times in the 200-yard individual medley in the Division I-AA Swim Championships typically are more than 1/2 second faster than their seed times going into the meet. At $\alpha = .05$, do these times (in seconds) for 26 male competitors (actual data with altered names) contradict the coach's assertion? *Hint:* The null hypothesis is $H_0: \mu_d \leq 0.5$ second. 📁 **Swimmers**

Swimmer	Seed	Prelims	Swimmer	Seed	Prelims
Jason	122.06	117.49	Wolfgang	122.33	122.35
Walter	116.23	116.62	Jin	120.68	117.56
Fred	122.88	121.93	Li	121.81	121.70
Tom	123.33	123.81	Brian	121.08	120.58
Andy	122.33	122.52	Pete	122.38	123.16
David	120.41	118.75	Otto	120.87	120.64
Jon	122.44	123.57	Joon	122.46	124.82
Bruce	120.42	123.27	Jeffrey	115.16	110.88
Victor	118.19	117.15	Roger	119.68	114.16
Karl	123.27	121.28	Bill	115.94	113.30
Kurt	120.23	119.21	John	122.98	119.93
Frank	117.66	113.10	Preston	123.28	120.70
Cedric	122.61	122.40	Steve	116.50	113.15

10.18 Below is a random sample of shoe sizes for 12 mothers and their daughters. (a) At $\alpha = .01$, does this sample show that women's shoe sizes have increased? State your hypotheses and show all steps clearly. (b) Is the decision close? (c) Are you convinced? (d) Why might shoe sizes change over time? 📁 **ShoeSize2**

	1	2	3	4	5	6	7	8	9	10	11	12
Daughter	8	8	7.5	8	9	9	8.5	9	9	8	7	8
Mother	7	7	7.5	8	8.5	8.5	7.5	7.5	6	8	7	7

10.19 A newly installed automatic gate system was being tested to see if the number of failures in 1,000 entry attempts was the same as the number of failures in 1,000 exit attempts. A random sample of eight delivery trucks was selected for data collection. Do these sample results show that there is a significant difference between entry and exit gate failures? Use $\alpha = .01$. 📁 **Gates**

	Truck 1	Truck 2	Truck 3	Truck 4	Truck 5	Truck 6	Truck 7	Truck 8
Entry failures	43	45	53	56	61	51	48	44
Exit failures	48	51	60	58	58	45	55	50

Mini Case   10.3

Weight-Loss Contest

Table 10.6 shows the results of a weight-loss contest sponsored by a city's local news-paper. Participants came from all over the city, and were encouraged to compete over a 1-month period. At $\alpha = .01$, was there a significant weight loss? The hypotheses are $H_0: \mu_d \geq 0$ and $H_1: \mu_d < 0$.

TABLE 10.6	Results of Weight-Loss Contest	Weightloss		
Obs	Name	After	Before	Difference
1	Mickey	203.8	218.3	−14.5
2	Teresa	179.3	189.3	−10.0
3	Gary	211.3	226.3	−15.0
4	Bradford	158.3	169.3	−11.0
5	Diane	170.3	179.3	−9.0
6	Elaine	174.8	183.3	−8.5
7	Kim	164.8	175.8	−11.0
8	Cathy	154.3	162.8	−8.5
9	Abby	171.8	178.8	−7.0
10	William	337.3	359.8	−22.5
11	Margaret	175.3	182.3	−7.0
12	Tom	198.8	211.3	−12.5

$$\bar{d} = -11.375$$
$$s_d = 4.37516$$

The test statistic is over nine standard errors from zero, a highly significant difference:

$$t_{\text{calc}} = \frac{\bar{d} - 0}{\dfrac{s_d}{\sqrt{n}}} = \frac{-11.375 - 0}{\dfrac{4.37516}{\sqrt{12}}} = -9.006$$

Excel's p-value for the paired t test is p-value = .0000 for a one-tailed test (a significant result at any α). Therefore, the mean weight loss of 11.375 pounds was *significant* at $\alpha = .01$. Moreover, to most people, a weight loss of 11.375 pounds would also be *important*.

10.5 COMPARING TWO PROPORTIONS

The test for two proportions is perhaps the most commonly used two-sample test, because percents are ubiquitous. Is the president's approval rating greater, lower, or the same as last month? Is the proportion of satisfied Dell customers greater than Gateway's? Is the annual nursing turnover percentage at Mayo Clinic higher, lower, or the same as that at Johns Hopkins? To answer such questions, we would compare two sample proportions.

LO 10-5

Perform a test
to compare two
proportions using z.

Testing for Zero Difference: $\pi_1 - \pi_2 = 0$

Let the true proportions in the two populations be denoted π_1 and π_2. When testing the difference between two proportions, we typically assume the population proportions are equal and set up our hypotheses using the null hypothesis $H_0: \pi_1 - \pi_2 = 0$. This is similar to our approach when testing the difference between two means. The research question will determine the format of our alternative hypothesis. The three possible pairs of hypotheses are

Left-Tailed Test	*Two-Tailed Test*	*Right-Tailed Test*
$H_0: \pi_1 - \pi_2 \geq 0$	$H_0: \pi_1 - \pi_2 = 0$	$H_0: \pi_1 - \pi_2 \leq 0$
$H_1: \pi_1 - \pi_2 < 0$	$H_1: \pi_1 - \pi_2 \neq 0$	$H_1: \pi_1 - \pi_2 > 0$

Sample Proportions

The sample proportion p_1 is a point estimate of π_1, and the sample proportion p_2 is a point estimate of π_2. A "success" is any event of interest (not necessarily something desirable).

$$p_1 = \frac{x_1}{n_1} = \frac{\text{number of "successes" in sample 1}}{\text{number of items in sample 1}} \tag{10.11}$$

$$p_2 = \frac{x_2}{n_2} = \frac{\text{number of "successes" in sample 2}}{\text{number of items in sample 2}} \tag{10.12}$$

Pooled Proportion

If H_0 is true, there is no difference between π_1 and π_2, so the samples can logically be *pooled* into one "big" sample to estimate the common population proportion:

$$\bar{p} = \frac{x_1 + x_2}{n_1 + n_2} = \frac{\text{number of successes in combined samples}}{\text{combined sample sizes}} \quad \text{(pooled proportion)} \tag{10.13}$$

Test Statistic

If the samples are large, the difference of proportions $p_1 - p_2$ may be assumed normally distributed. The *test statistic* is the difference of the sample proportions $p_1 - p_2$ minus the parameter $\pi_1 - \pi_2$ divided by the standard error of the difference $p_1 - p_2$. The standard error is calculated by using the pooled proportion. The general form of the test statistic for testing the difference between two proportions is

$$z_{\text{calc}} = \frac{(p_1 - p_2) - (\pi_1 - \pi_2)}{\sqrt{\dfrac{\bar{p}(1 - \bar{p})}{n_1} + \dfrac{\bar{p}(1 - \bar{p})}{n_2}}} \tag{10.14}$$

If we are testing the hypothesis that $\pi_1 - \pi_2 = 0$, we can simplify formula 10.14 as shown in formula 10.15.

Test Statistic for Equality of Proportions

$$z_{\text{calc}} = \frac{p_1 - p_2}{\sqrt{\bar{p}(1 - \bar{p})\left[\dfrac{1}{n_1} + \dfrac{1}{n_2}\right]}} \tag{10.15}$$

In order to measure the level of satisfaction with Vail Resorts' websites, the Vail Resorts marketing team periodically surveys a random sample of guests and asks them to rate their likelihood of recommending the website to a friend or colleague. An *active promoter* is a guest who responds that they are highly likely to recommend the website. From a random sample of 2,386 Vail ski mountain guests in last year's ski season, there were 2,014 active promoters and from a random sample of 2,309 Vail ski mountain guests in this year's ski season, there were 2,048 active promoters. Results from the survey are shown in Table 10.7. At the .01 level of significance, did the proportion of active promoters increase?

EXAMPLE 10.4

Active Promoters Vail Resorts

VAILRESORTS

TABLE 10.7	Website Satisfaction Survey	
Statistic	**This Year**	**Last Year**
Number of active promoters	$x_1 = 2048$	$x_2 = 2014$
Number of guests surveyed	$n_1 = 2309$	$n_2 = 2386$
Active promoter proportion	$p_1 = \dfrac{2048}{2309} = .8870$	$p_2 = \dfrac{2014}{2386} = .8441$

Step 1: State the Hypotheses

Because Vail Resorts had redesigned their ski mountain websites for this year's season, they were interested in seeing if the proportion of active promoters had increased. Therefore we will do a right-tailed test for equality of proportions.

$H_0: \pi_1 - \pi_2 \leq 0$
$H_1: \pi_1 - \pi_2 > 0$

Step 2: Specify the Decision Rule

Using $\alpha = .01$ the right-tail critical value is $z_{.01} = 2.326$, which yields the decision rule

Reject H_0 if $z_{calc} > 2.326$

Otherwise do not reject H_0

The decision rule is illustrated in Figure 10.12. Since Excel uses cumulative left-tail areas, the right-tail critical value $z_{.01} = 2.326$ is obtained using =NORM.S.INV(.99).

FIGURE 10.12   **Right-Tailed Test for Two Proportions**

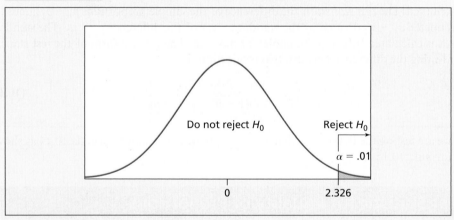

Step 3: Calculate the Test Statistic

The sample proportions indicate that this year's season had a higher proportion of active promoters than last year's season. We assume that $\pi_1 - \pi_2 = 0$ and see if a contradiction stems from this assumption. Assuming that the proportions are equal, we can pool the two samples to obtain a **pooled estimate** of the common proportion by dividing the combined number of active promoters by the combined sample size.

$$\bar{p} = \frac{\bar{x}_1 + \bar{x}_2}{n_1 + n_2} = \frac{2048 + 2014}{2309 + 2386} = \frac{4062}{4695} = .8652, \text{ or } 86.52\%$$

Assuming normality (i.e., large samples), the test statistic is

$$z_{calc} = \frac{p_1 - p_2}{\sqrt{\bar{p}(1 - \bar{p})\left[\dfrac{1}{n_1} + \dfrac{1}{n_2}\right]}} = \frac{.8870 - .8441}{\sqrt{.8652(1 - .8652)\left[\dfrac{1}{2309} + \dfrac{1}{2386}\right]}} = 4.313$$

Step 4: Make the Decision

If H_0 were true, the test statistic should be near zero. Since the test statistic ($z_{calc} = 4.313$) exceeds the critical value ($z_{.01} = 2.326$), we reject the null hypothesis and conclude that $\pi_1 - \pi_2 > 0$. If we were to use the *p*-value approach, we would find the *p*-value by using the function =1–NORM.S.DIST(4.313,1) in Excel. This function returns a value so small (.00000807) it is, for all practical purposes, equal to zero. Because the *p*-value is less than .01, we would reject the null hypothesis.

Whether we use the critical value approach or the *p*-value approach, we would reject the null hypothesis of equal proportions. In other words, the proportion of active promoters this year is significantly greater than in the previous year. The new website design appeared to be attractive to Vail Resorts' guests.

Step 5: Take Action

Keep the new website design because it appears to increase the number of promoters.

Checking Normality

We have assumed a normal distribution for the statistic $p_1 - p_2$. This assumption can be checked. For a test of two proportions, the criterion for normality is $n\pi \geq 10$ and $n(1 - \pi) \geq 10$ for *each* sample, using each sample proportion in place of π:

$$n_1 p_1 = (2309)(2048/2309) = 2048 \quad n_1(1 - p_1) = (2309)(1 - 2048/2309) = 261$$
$$n_2 p_2 = (2386)(2014/2386) = 2014 \quad n_2(1 - p_2) = (2386)(1 - 2014/2386) = 372$$

The normality requirement is comfortably fulfilled in this case. Ideally, these numbers should exceed 10 by a comfortable margin, as they do in this example. Since the samples are pooled, this guarantees that the pooled proportion $(n_1 + n_2)\bar{p} \geq 10$. Note that when using sample data, the sample size rule of thumb is equivalent to requiring that each sample contains at least 10 "successes" and at least 10 "failures." In this example, this requirement is easily met (there are 2,048 and 2,014 promoters, and 261 and 372 nonpromoters).

If sample sizes do not justify the normality assumption, each sample should be treated as a binomial experiment. Unless you have good computational software, this may not be worthwhile. If the samples are small, the test is likely to have low power.

Must Sample Sizes Be Equal? No. Balanced sample sizes are not necessary. Unequal sample sizes are common, and the formulas still apply.

LO 10-6

Check whether normality may be assumed for two proportions.

Mini Case   10.4

How Does Noodles & Company Provide Value to Customers?

Value perception is an important concept for all companies, but is especially relevant for consumer-oriented industries such as retail and restaurants. Most retailers and restaurant concepts periodically make price increases to reflect changes in inflationary items such as cost of goods and labor costs. In 2006, however, Noodles & Company took the opposite approach when it evaluated its value perception through its consumers.

Through rigorous statistical analysis, Noodles recognized that a significant percentage of current customers would increase their frequency of visits if the menu items were priced slightly lower. The company evaluated the trade-offs that a price decrease would represent and determined that they should be able to increase revenue by reducing price. Despite not advertising this price decrease, the company did in fact see an increase in frequency of visits after the change. To measure the impact, the company statistically evaluated both the increase in frequency as well as customer evaluations of Noodles & Company's value perception. Within a few months, the statistical analysis showed that not only had customer frequency increased by 2–3%, but also that improved value perception led to an increase in average party size of 2%. They concluded that the price decrease of roughly 2% led to a total revenue increase of 4–5%.

10.20 Calculate the test statistic and p-value for a test of equal population proportions. What is your conclusion?

   a. Right-tailed test, $\alpha = .10$, $x_1 = 228$, $n_1 = 240$, $x_2 = 703$, $n_2 = 760$
   b. Left-tailed test, $\alpha = .05$, $x_1 = 36$, $n_1 = 80$, $x_2 = 66$, $n_2 = 120$
   c. Two-tailed test, $\alpha = .05$, $x_1 = 52$, $n_1 = 80$, $x_2 = 56$, $n_2 = 70$

10.21 Calculate the test statistic and p-value for a test of equal population proportions. What is your conclusion?

   a. Left-tailed test, $\alpha = .10$, $x_1 = 28$, $n_1 = 336$, $x_2 = 14$, $n_2 = 112$
   b. Right-tailed test, $\alpha = .05$, $x_1 = 276$, $n_1 = 300$, $x_2 = 440$, $n_2 = 500$
   c. Two-tailed test, $\alpha = .10$, $x_1 = 35$, $n_1 = 50$, $x_2 = 42$, $n_2 = 75$

10.22 Find the sample proportions and test statistic for equal proportions. Find the p-value.

   a. Dissatisfied workers in two companies: $x_1 = 40$, $n_1 = 100$, $x_2 = 30$, $n_2 = 100$, $\alpha = .05$, two-tailed test.
   b. Rooms rented at least a week in advance at two hotels: $x_1 = 24$, $n_1 = 200$, $x_2 = 12$, $n_2 = 50$, $\alpha = .01$, left-tailed test.
   c. Home equity loan default rates in two banks: $x_1 = 36$, $n_1 = 480$, $x_2 = 26$, $n_2 = 520$, $\alpha = .05$, right-tailed test.

10.23 Find the test statistic and do the two-sample test for equality of proportions.

   a. Repeat buyers at two car dealerships: $p_1 = .30$, $n_1 = 50$, $p_2 = .54$, $n_2 = 50$, $\alpha = .01$, left-tailed test.
   b. Honor roll students in two sororities: $p_1 = .45$, $n_1 = 80$, $p_2 = .25$, $n_2 = 48$, $\alpha = .10$, two-tailed test.
   c. First-time Hawaii visitors at two hotels: $p_1 = .20$, $n_1 = 80$, $p_2 = .32$, $n_2 = 75$, $\alpha = .05$, left-tailed test.

10.24 During the period 1990−1998 there were 46 Atlantic hurricanes, of which 19 struck the United States. During the period 1999−2006 there were 70 hurricanes, of which 45 struck the United States. (a) State the hypotheses to test whether the percentage of hurricanes that strike the United States is increasing. (b) Calculate the test statistic. (c) State the critical value at $\alpha = .01$. (d) What is your conclusion? (e) Can normality of $p_1 - p_2$ be assumed?

10.25 In 2006, a sample of 200 in-store shoppers showed that 42 paid by debit card. In 2009, a sample of the same size showed that 62 paid by debit card. (a) Formulate appropriate hypotheses to test whether the percentage of debit card shoppers increased. (b) Carry out the test at $\alpha = .01$. (c) Find the p-value. (d) Test whether normality of $p_1 - p_2$ may be assumed.

10.26 A survey of 100 mayonnaise purchasers showed that 65 were loyal to one brand. For 100 bath soap purchasers, only 53 were loyal to one brand. Perform a two-tailed test comparing the proportion of brand-loyal customers at $\alpha = .05$.

10.27 A 20-minute consumer survey mailed to 500 adults aged 25−34 included a $5 Starbucks gift certificate. The same survey was mailed to 500 adults aged 25−34 without the gift certificate. There were 65 responses from the first group and 45 from the second group. Perform a two-tailed test comparing the response rates (proportions) at $\alpha = .05$.

10.28 Is the water on your airline flight safe to drink? It is not feasible to analyze the water on every flight, so sampling is necessary. The Environmental Protection Agency (EPA) found bacterial contamination in water samples from the lavatories and galley water taps on 20 of 158 randomly selected U.S. flights. Alarmed by the data, the EPA ordered sanitation improvements, and then tested water samples again. In the second sample, bacterial contamination was found in 29 of 169 randomly sampled flights. (a) Use a left-tailed test at $\alpha = .05$ to check whether the percent of all flights with contaminated water was lower in the first sample. (b) Find the *p*-value. (c) Discuss the question of significance versus importance in this specific application. (d) Test whether normality of $p_1 - p_2$ may be assumed.

10.29 When tested for compliance with Sarbanes-Oxley requirements for financial records and fraud protection, 14 of 180 publicly traded business services companies failed, compared with 7 of 67 computer hardware, software, and telecommunications companies. (a) Is this a statistically significant difference at $\alpha = .05$? (b) Can normality of $p_1 - p_2$ be assumed?

Testing for Nonzero Difference (Optional)

Testing for equality of π_1 and π_2 is a special case of testing for a specified difference D_0 between the two proportions:

Left-Tailed Test	Two-Tailed Test	Right-Tailed Test
$H_0: \pi_1 - \pi_2 \geq D_0$	$H_0: \pi_1 - \pi_2 = D_0$	$H_0: \pi_1 - \pi_2 \leq D_0$
$H_1: \pi_1 - \pi_2 < D_0$	$H_1: \pi_1 - \pi_2 \neq D_0$	$H_1: \pi_1 - \pi_2 > D_0$

We have shown how to test for $D_0 = 0$, that is, $\pi_1 = \pi_2$. If the hypothesized difference D_0 is nonzero, we do not pool the sample proportions, but instead use the test statistic shown in formula 10.16.

$$z_{calc} = \frac{p_1 - p_2 - D_0}{\sqrt{\dfrac{p_1(1 - p_1)}{n_1} + \dfrac{p_2(1 - p_2)}{n_2}}} \qquad \text{(test statistic for nonzero difference } D_0\text{)} \qquad \textbf{(10.16)}$$

A sample of 111 magazine advertisements in *Good Housekeeping* showed 70 that listed a website. In *Fortune,* a sample of 145 advertisements showed 131 that listed a website. At $\alpha = .025$, does the *Fortune* proportion differ from the *Good Housekeeping* proportion by at least 20 percent? Table 10.8 shows the data.

EXAMPLE 10.5

Magazine Ads

TABLE 10.8	Magazine Ads with Websites	
Statistic	**Fortune**	**Good Housekeeping**
Number with websites	$x_1 = 131$ with website	$x_2 = 70$ with website
Number of ads examined	$n_1 = 145$ ads	$n_2 = 111$ ads
Proportion	$p_1 = \dfrac{131}{145} = .90345$	$p_2 = \dfrac{70}{111} = .63063$

Source: Project by MBA students Frank George, Karen Orso, and Lincy Zachariah.

Test Statistic

We will do a right-tailed test for $D_0 = .20$. The hypotheses are

$H_0: \pi_1 - \pi_2 \leq .20$

$H_1: \pi_1 - \pi_2 > .20$

The test statistic is

$$z_{calc} = \frac{p_1 - p_2 - D_0}{\sqrt{\dfrac{p_1(1 - p_1)}{n_1} + \dfrac{p_2(1 - p_2)}{n_2}}}$$

$$= \frac{.90345 - .63063 - .20}{\sqrt{\dfrac{.90345(1 - .90345)}{145} + \dfrac{.63063(1 - .63063)}{111}}} = 1.401$$

At $\alpha = .025$ the right-tail critical value is $z_{.025} = 1.960$, so the difference of proportions is insufficient to reject the hypothesis that the difference is .20 or less. The decision rule is illustrated in Figure 10.13.

FIGURE 10.13

Right-Tailed Test for Magazine Ads at $\alpha = .025$

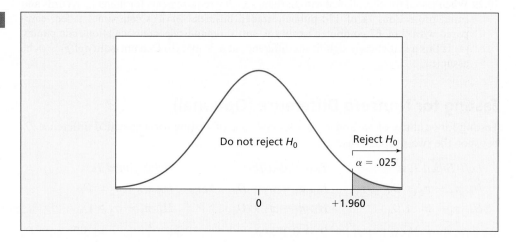

Calculating the *p*-Value

Using the *p*-value approach, we would insert the test statistic $z_{calc} = 1.401$ into Excel's cumulative normal =1-NORM.S.DIST(1.401,1) to obtain a right-tail area of .0806 as shown in Figure 10.14. Since the *p*-value $> .025$, we would not reject H_0. The conclusion is that the difference in proportions is not greater than .20.

FIGURE 10.14

***p*-Value for Magazine Proportions Differing by $D_0 = .20$**

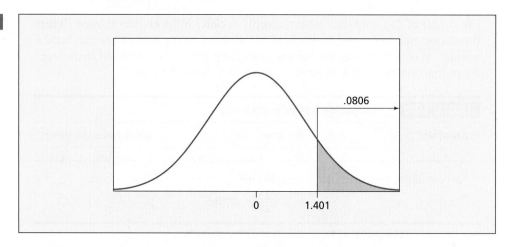

SECTION EXERCISES

connect

Note: Use MINITAB or MegaStat for calculations.

10.30 In 2009, a sample of 200 in-store shoppers showed that 42 paid by debit card. In 2012, a sample of the same size showed that 62 paid by debit card. (a) Formulate appropriate hypotheses to test whether the percentage of debit card shoppers increased by more than 5 percent, using $\alpha = .10$. (b) Find the *p*-value.

10.31 From a telephone log, an executive finds that 36 of 128 incoming telephone calls last week lasted at least 5 minutes. She vows to make an effort to reduce the length of time spent on calls. The phone log for the next week shows that 14 of 96 incoming calls lasted at least 5 minutes. (a) At $\alpha = .05$, has the proportion of 5-minute phone calls declined by more than 10 percent? (b) Find the *p*-value.

10.32 A 30-minute consumer survey mailed to 500 adults aged 25−34 included a $10 gift certificate to Borders. The same survey was mailed to 500 adults aged 25−34 without the gift certificate. There were 185 responses from the first group and 45 from the second group. (a) At $\alpha = .025$, did the gift certificate increase the response rate by more than 20 percent? (b) Find the *p*-value.

Mini Case   10.5

Automated Parking Lot Entry/Exit Gate System

Large universities have many different parking lots. Delivery trucks travel between various buildings all day long to deliver food, mail, and other items. Automated entry/exit gates make travel time much faster for the trucks and cars entering and exiting the different parking lots because the drivers do not have to stop to activate the gate manually. The gate is electronically activated as the truck or car approaches the parking lot.

One large university with two campuses recently negotiated with a company to install a new automated system. One requirement of the contract stated that the proportion of failed gate activations on one campus would be no different from the proportion of failed gate activations on the second campus. (A failed activation was one in which the driver had to manually activate the gate.) The university facilities operations manager designed and conducted a test to establish whether the gate company had violated this requirement of the contract. The university could renegotiate the contract if there was significant evidence showing that the two proportions were different.

The test was set up as a two-tailed test and the hypotheses tested were

$H_0: \pi_1 - \pi_2 = 0$

$H_1: \pi_1 - \pi_2 \neq 0$

Both the university and the gate company agreed on a 5 percent level of significance. Random samples from each campus were collected. The data are shown in Table 10.9.

TABLE 10.9	**Proportion of Failed Gate Activations**	
Statistic	*Campus 1*	*Campus 2*
Number of failed activations	$x_1 = 52$	$x_2 = 63$
Sample size (number of entry/exit attempts)	$n_1 = 1{,}000$	$n_2 = 1{,}000$
Proportion	$p_1 = \dfrac{52}{1{,}000} = .052$	$p_2 = \dfrac{63}{1{,}000} = .063$

The pooled proportion is

$$\bar{p} = \frac{x_1 + x_2}{n_1 + n_2} = \frac{52 + 63}{1{,}000 + 1{,}000} = \frac{115}{2{,}000} = .0575$$

The test statistic is

$$z_{calc} = \frac{p_1 - p_2}{\sqrt{\bar{p}(1 - \bar{p})\left[\dfrac{1}{n_1} + \dfrac{1}{n_2}\right]}} = \frac{.052 - .063}{\sqrt{.0575(1 - .0575)\left[\dfrac{1}{1{,}000} + \dfrac{1}{1{,}000}\right]}} = -1.057$$

Using the 5 percent level of significance the critical value is $Z_{.025} = 1.96$, so it is clear that there is no significant difference between these two proportions. This conclusion is reinforced by Excel's cumulative normal function =NORM.S.DIST(−1.057,1), which gives the area to the left of −1.057 as .1453. Because this is a two-tailed test, the *p*-value is .2906.

Was it reasonable to assume normality of the test statistic? Yes, because we have at least 10 successes and 10 failures in each sample:

$n_1 p_1 = 1{,}000(52/1{,}000) = 52$ $\qquad$ $n_1(1 - p_1) = 1{,}000(1 - 52/1{,}000) = 948$

$n_2 p_2 = 1{,}000(63/1{,}000) = 63$ $\qquad$ $n_2(1 - p_2) = 1{,}000(1 - 63/1{,}000) = 937$

Based on this sample, the university had no evidence to refute the gate company's claim that the failed activation proportions were the same for each campus.

Source: This case was based on a real contract negotiation between a large western university and a private company. The contract was still being negotiated as of the publication of this text.

10.6 CONFIDENCE INTERVAL FOR THE DIFFERENCE OF TWO PROPORTIONS, $\pi_1 - \pi_2$

A confidence interval for the **difference of two population proportions**, $\pi_1 - \pi_2$, is given by

(10.17)
$$(p_1 - p_2) \pm z_{\alpha/2}\sqrt{\frac{p_1(1 - p_1)}{n_1} + \frac{p_2(1 - p_2)}{n_2}}$$

This formula assumes that both samples are large enough to assume normality. The rule of thumb for assuming normality is that $np \geq 10$ and $n(1 - p) \geq 10$ for each sample.

EXAMPLE 10.6

Fire Truck Color

Compared to a traditional red fire truck, does a bright yellow fire truck have a lower accident rate? Proponents of the brighter yellow color argued that its enhanced visibility allowed other traffic to see the trucks and avoid them during fire runs. A frequently cited 4-year study in Dallas, Texas, produced the statistics shown in Table 10.10.

TABLE 10.10	Accident Rate for Dallas Fire Trucks	
Statistic	**Red Fire Trucks**	**Yellow Fire Trucks**
Number of accidents	$x_1 = 20$ accidents	$x_2 = 4$ accidents
Number of fire runs	$n_1 = 153{,}348$ runs	$n_2 = 135{,}035$ runs
Accident rate	$p_1 = \dfrac{20}{153{,}348}$ $= .000130422$	$p_2 = \dfrac{4}{135{,}035}$ $= .000029622$

Source: *The Wall Street Journal*, June 26, 1995, p. B1.

The 95 percent confidence interval for the difference between the proportions is

$$(p_1 - p_2) \pm z_{\alpha/2}\sqrt{\frac{p_1(1 - p_1)}{n_1} + \frac{p_2(1 - p_2)}{n_2}}$$

$$= (.000130422 - .000029622)$$

$$\pm (1.960)\sqrt{\frac{(.000130422)(.999869578)}{153{,}348} + \frac{(.000029622)(.999970378)}{135{,}035}}$$

$$= .0001008 \pm .000064106 \text{ or } [0.0000366959, 0.000164905].$$

Since the confidence interval for $\pi_1 - \pi_2$ does not include zero, it appears that the accident rates are significantly different. Should all fire trucks be painted yellow? Because $n_2 p_2 < 10$ for the second sample, our margin of error might be underestimated. However, both accident rates are quite small to begin with, an argument used by those who favor the traditional red color. A greater problem, the critics say, is that the public has become inured to sirens and flashing lights. As often happens, statistics may play only a small part in the policy decision.

SECTION EXERCISES

connect

10.33 The American Bankers Association reported that, in a sample of 120 consumer purchases in France, 60 were made with cash, compared with 26 in a sample of 50 consumer purchases in the United States. Construct a 90 percent confidence interval for the difference in proportions.

10.34 A study showed that 36 of 72 cell phone users with a headset missed their exit, compared with 12 of 72 talking to a passenger. Construct a 95 percent confidence interval for the difference in proportions.

10.35 A survey of 100 cigarette smokers showed that 71 were loyal to one brand, compared to 122 of 200 toothpaste users. Construct a 90 percent confidence interval for the difference in proportions.

10.7 COMPARING TWO VARIANCES

LO 10-8

Carry out a test of two variances using the F distribution.

Comparing the *variances* may be as important as comparing the *means* of two populations. In manufacturing, smaller variation around the mean would indicate a more reliable product. In finance, smaller variation around the mean would indicate less volatility in asset returns. In services, smaller variation around the mean would indicate more consistency in customer treatment. For example, is the *variance* in Ford Mustang assembly times the same this month as last month? Is the *variability* in customer waiting times the same at two Tim Horton's franchises? Is the *variation* the same for customer concession purchases at a movie theater on Friday and Saturday nights?

Format of Hypotheses

We may test the null hypothesis against a left-tailed, two-tailed, or right-tailed alternative:

Left-Tailed Test	*Two-Tailed Test*	*Right-Tailed Test*
$H_0: \sigma_1^2 \geq \sigma_2^2$	$H_0: \sigma_1^2 = \sigma_2^2$	$H_0: \sigma_1^2 \leq \sigma_2^2$
$H_1: \sigma_1^2 < \sigma_2^2$	$H_1: \sigma_1^2 \neq \sigma_2^2$	$H_1: \sigma_1^2 > \sigma_2^2$

An equivalent way to state these hypotheses is to look at the *ratio* of the two variances. A ratio near 1 would indicate equal variances.

Left-Tailed Test	*Two-Tailed Test*	*Right-Tailed Test*
$H_0: \dfrac{\sigma_1^2}{\sigma_2^2} \geq 1$	$H_0: \dfrac{\sigma_1^2}{\sigma_2^2} = 1$	$H_0: \dfrac{\sigma_1^2}{\sigma_2^2} \leq 1$
$H_1: \dfrac{\sigma_1^2}{\sigma_2^2} < 1$	$H_1: \dfrac{\sigma_1^2}{\sigma_2^2} \neq 1$	$H_1: \dfrac{\sigma_1^2}{\sigma_2^2} > 1$

The *F* Test

In a left-tailed or right-tailed test, we actually test only at the equality, with the understanding that rejection of H_0 would imply rejecting values more extreme. The test statistic is the ratio of the sample variances. Assuming the populations are normal, the test statistic follows the **F distribution**, named for Ronald A. Fisher (1890−1962), one of the most famous statisticians of all time.

$$F_{\text{calc}} = \frac{s_1^2 \quad\longleftarrow\; df_1 = n_1 - 1}{s_2^2 \quad\longleftarrow\; df_2 = n_2 - 1}$$

$$(10.18)$$

If the null hypothesis of equal variances is true, this ratio should be near 1:

$$F_{\text{calc}} \cong 1 \qquad (\text{if } H_0 \text{ is true})$$

If the test statistic F is much less than 1 or much greater than 1, we would reject the hypothesis of equal population variances. The numerator s_1^2 has degrees of freedom $df_1 = n_1 - 1$, while the denominator s_2^2 has degrees of freedom $df_2 = n_2 - 1$. The F distribution is skewed. Its mean is always greater than 1 and its mode (the "peak" of the distribution) is always less than 1, but both the mean and mode tend to be near 1 for large samples. F cannot be negative, since s_1^2 and s_2^2 cannot be negative.

Two-Tailed *F* Test

Critical values for the **F test** are denoted F_L (left tail) and F_R (right tail). The form of the two-tailed *F* test is shown in Figure 10.15. Notice that the rejection regions are asymmetric.

FIGURE 10.15

Critical Values for Two-Tailed *F* Test for Equal Variances

A right-tail critical value F_R may be found from Appendix F using df_1 and df_2 degrees of freedom. It is written

(10.19) $F_R = F_{df_1, df_2}$ (right-tail critical *F*)

To obtain a left-tail critical value F_L we reverse the numerator and denominator degrees of freedom, find the critical value from Appendix F, and take its reciprocal:

(10.20) $F_L = \dfrac{1}{F_{df_2, df_1}}$ (left-tail critical *F* with switched df_1 and df_2)

Illustration: Collision Damage

An experimental bumper was designed to reduce damage in low-speed collisions. This bumper was installed on an experimental group of vans in a large fleet, but not on a control group. At the end of a trial period, accident data showed 12 repair incidents (a "repair incident" is a repair invoice) for the experimental vehicles and 9 repair incidents for the control group vehicles. Table 10.11 shows the dollar cost of the repair incidents.

TABLE 10.11

Repair Cost ($) for Accident Damage
📄 **Damage**

Source: Unpublished study by Floyd G. Willoughby and Thomas W. Lauer, Oakland University.

Experimental Vehicles	Control Vehicles
1,973	1,185
403	885
509	2,955
2,103	815
1,153	2,852
292	1,217
1,916	1,762
1,602	2,592
1,559	1,632
547	
801	
359	
$\bar{x}_1 = \$1,101.42$	$\bar{x}_2 = \$1,766.11$
$s_1 = \$696.20$	$s_2 = \$837.62$
$n_1 = 12$ incidents	$n_2 = 9$ incidents

A dot plot of the two samples, shown in Figure 10.16, suggests that the new bumper may have reduced the *mean* damage. However, the firm was also interested in whether the *variance* in damage had changed. We use the *F* test to test the hypothesis of equal variances.

FIGURE 10.16

Dot Plots for Collision Repair Costs
📁 **Damage**

Comparison of Variances: Two-Tailed Test

Do the sample variances support the idea of equal variances in the population? We will perform a two-tailed test.

Step 1: State the Hypotheses For a two-tailed test for equality of variances, the hypotheses are

$$H_0: \sigma_1^2 = \sigma_2^2 \quad \text{or} \quad H_0: \sigma_1^2 / \sigma_2^2 = 1$$
$$H_1: \sigma_1^2 \neq \sigma_2^2 \qquad\quad H_1: \sigma_1^2 / \sigma_2^2 \neq 1$$

Step 2: Specify the Decision Rule Degrees of freedom for the *F* test are

Numerator: $df_1 = n_1 - 1 = 12 - 1 = 11$
Denominator: $df_2 = n_2 - 1 = 9 - 1 = 8$

For a two-tailed test, we split the α risk and put $\alpha/2$ in each tail. Using Excel, the left-tail critical value for $\alpha/2 = .025$ is F_L =F.INV(.025,11,8) = 0.273, and the right-tail critical value is F_R =F.INV(.975,11,8) = 4.243. Alternatively, we could use Appendix F. To avoid interpolating, we use the next lower degrees of freedom when the required entry is not found in Appendix F. This conservative practice will not increase the probability of Type I error. For example, since $F_{11,8}$ is not in the table, we use $F_{10,8}$, as shown in Figure 10.17.

$$F_R = F_{df_1, df_2} = F_{11,8} \approx F_{10,8} = 4.30 \qquad \text{(right-tail critical value)}$$

To find the left-tail critical value, we reverse the numerator and denominator degrees of freedom, find the critical value from Appendix F, and take its reciprocal:

$$F_L = \frac{1}{F_{df_2, df_1}} = \frac{1}{F_{8,11}} = \frac{1}{3.66} = 0.273 \qquad \text{(left-tail critical value)}$$

CRITICAL VALUES OF $F_{.025}$

FIGURE 10.17

Critical Values of *F* for $\alpha/2 = .025$

This table shows the 2.5 percent right-tail critical values of *F* for the stated degrees of freedom.

Denominator Degrees of Freedom (df_2)	Numerator Degrees of Freedom (df_1)										
	1	2	3	4	5	6	7	8	9	10	12
1	647.8	799.5	864.2	899.6	921.8	937.1	948.2	956.6	963.3	968.6	976.7
2	38.51	39.00	39.17	39.25	39.30	39.33	39.36	39.37	39.39	39.40	39.41
3	17.44	16.04	15.44	15.10	14.88	14.73	14.62	14.54	14.47	14.42	14.34
4	12.22	10.65	9.98	9.60	9.36	9.20	9.07	8.98	8.90	8.84	8.75
5	10.01	8.43	7.76	7.39	7.15	6.98	6.85	6.76	6.68	6.62	6.52
6	8.81	7.26	6.60	6.23	5.99	5.82	5.70	5.60	5.52	5.46	5.37
7	8.07	6.54	5.89	5.52	5.29	5.12	4.99	4.90	4.82	4.76	4.67
8	7.57	6.06	5.42	5.05	4.82	4.65	4.53	4.43	4.36	4.30	4.20
9	7.21	5.71	5.08	4.72	4.48	4.32	4.20	4.10	4.03	3.96	3.87
10	6.94	5.46	4.83	4.47	4.24	4.07	3.95	3.85	3.78	3.72	3.62
11	6.72	5.26	4.63	4.28	4.04	3.88	3.76	3.66	3.59	3.53	3.43
12	6.55	5.10	4.47	4.12	3.89	3.73	3.61	3.51	3.44	3.37	3.28
13	6.41	4.97	4.35	4.00	3.77	3.60	3.48	3.39	3.31	3.25	3.15
14	6.30	4.86	4.24	3.89	3.66	3.50	3.38	3.29	3.21	3.15	3.05
15	6.20	4.77	4.15	3.80	3.58	3.41	3.29	3.20	3.12	3.06	2.96

As shown in Figure 10.18, the two-tailed decision rule is

Reject H_0 if $F_{calc} < 0.273$ or if $F_{calc} > 4.30$

Otherwise do not reject H_0

FIGURE 10.18

Two-Tailed F Test at
$\alpha = .05$

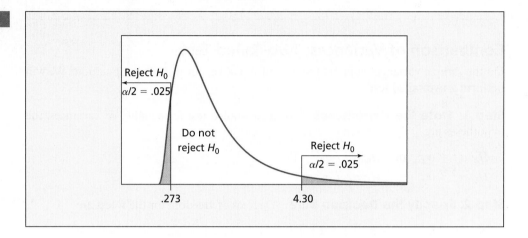

Step 3: Calculate the Test Statistic   The test statistic is

$$F_{calc} = \frac{s_1^2}{s_2^2} = \frac{(696.20)^2}{(837.62)^2} = 0.691$$

Step 4: Make the Decision   Since $F_{calc} = 0.691$, we cannot reject the hypothesis of equal variances in a two-tailed test at $\alpha = .05$. In other words, the ratio of the sample variances does not differ significantly from 1. The p-value will depend on the value of F_{calc}:

If $F_{calc} > 1$ Two-tailed p-value is $=2*F.DIST.RT(F_{calc}, df_1, df_2)$

If $F_{calc} < 1$ Two-tailed p-value is $=2*F.DIST(F_{calc}, df_1, df_2, 1)$

For the bumper data, $F_{calc} = 0.691$, so Excel's two-tailed p-value is $=2*F.DIST(0.691, 11, 8, 1) = .5575$.

Folded F Test

We can make the two-tailed test for equal variances into a right-tailed test, so it is easier to look up the critical values in Appendix F. This method requires that we put the *larger observed variance* in the numerator, and then look up the critical value for $\alpha/2$ instead of the chosen α. The test statistic for the folded F test is

(10.21)
$$F_{calc} = \frac{s_{larger}^2}{s_{smaller}^2}$$

The larger variance goes in the numerator and the smaller variance in the denominator. *"Larger" refers to the variance (not to the sample size)*. But the hypotheses are the same as for a two-tailed test:

H_0: $\sigma_1^2/\sigma_2^2 = 1$

H_1: $\sigma_1^2/\sigma_2^2 \neq 1$

For the bumper data, the second sample variance ($s_2^2 = 837.62$) is larger than the first sample variance ($s_1^2 = 696.20$), so the folded F test statistic is

$$F_{calc} = \frac{s_{larger}^2}{s_{smaller}^2} = \frac{s_2^2}{s_1^2} = \frac{(837.62)^2}{(696.20)^2} = 1.448$$

We must be careful that the degrees of freedom match the variances in the modified F statistic. In this case, the second sample variance is larger (it goes in the numerator), so we must reverse the degrees of freedom:

Numerator: $n_2 - 1 = 9 - 1 = 8$

Denominator: $n_1 - 1 = 12 - 1 = 11$

Now we look up the critical value for $F_{8, 11}$ in Appendix F using $\alpha/2 = .05/2 = .025$:

$$F_{.025} = 3.66$$

Alternatively, we can use the Excel function =F.INV.RT(0.025,8,11) = 3.66. Since the test statistic $F_{calc} = 1.448$ does not exceed the critical value $F_{.025} = 3.66$, we cannot reject the hypothesis of equal variances. This is the same conclusion that we reached in the two-tailed test. Since $F_{calc} > 1$, Excel's two-tailed p-value is =2*F.DIST.RT(1.448,8,11) = .5569, which is the same as in the previous result except for rounding. Anytime you want a two-tailed F test, you may use the folded F test if you think it is easier.

One-Tailed *F* Test

In this case, the firm was interested in knowing whether the new bumper had *reduced* the variance in collision damage cost, so the consultant was asked to do a left-tailed test.

Step 1: State the Hypotheses   The hypotheses for a left-tailed test are

$H_0: \sigma_1^2/\sigma_2^2 \geq 1$

$H_1: \sigma_1^2/\sigma_2^2 < 1$

Step 2: Specify the Decision Rule   Degrees of freedom for the F test are the same as for a two-tailed test (the hypothesis doesn't affect the degrees of freedom):

Numerator: $df_1 = n_1 - 1 = 12 - 1 = 11$

Denominator: $df_2 = n_2 - 1 = 9 - 1 = 8$

However, now the entire $\alpha = .05$ goes in the left tail. Using Excel, the left-tail critical value is F_L =F.INV(.05,11,8) = 0.339. Alternatively, we can find the left-tail critical value from Appendix F by reversing the degrees of freedom and calculating the reciprocal of the table value, as illustrated in Figures 10.19 and 10.20. Notice that the asymmetry of the F distribution causes the left-tail area to be compressed in the horizontal direction.

$$F_L = \frac{1}{F_{df_2, df_1}} = \frac{1}{F_{8,11}} = \frac{1}{2.95} = 0.339 \qquad \text{(left-tail critical value)}$$

The decision rule is

Reject H_0 if $F_{calc} < 0.339$

Otherwise do not reject H_0

Step 3: Calculate the Test Statistic   The test statistic is the same as for a two-tailed test (the hypothesis doesn't affect the test statistic):

$$F_{calc} = \frac{s_1^2}{s_2^2} = \frac{(696.20)^2}{(837.62)^2} = 0.691$$

FIGURE 10.19

Right-Tail F_R for $\alpha = .05$

CRITICAL VALUES OF $F_{.05}$

This table shows the 5 percent right-tail critical values of F for the stated degrees of freedom.

Denominator Degrees of Freedom (df_2)	Numerator Degrees of Freedom (df_1)										
	1	2	3	4	5	6	7	8	9	10	12
1	161.4	199.5	215.7	224.6	230.2	234.0	236.8	238.9	240.5	241.9	243.9
2	18.51	19.00	19.16	19.25	19.30	19.33	19.35	19.37	19.38	19.40	19.41
3	10.13	9.55	9.28	9.12	9.01	8.94	8.89	8.85	8.81	8.79	8.74
4	7.71	6.94	6.59	6.39	6.26	6.16	6.09	6.04	6.00	5.96	5.91
5	6.61	5.79	5.41	5.19	5.05	4.95	4.88	4.82	4.77	4.74	4.68
6	5.99	5.14	4.76	4.53	4.39	4.28	4.21	4.15	4.10	4.06	4.00
7	5.59	4.74	4.35	4.12	3.97	3.87	3.79	3.73	3.68	3.64	3.57
8	5.32	4.46	4.07	3.84	3.69	3.58	3.50	3.44	3.39	3.35	3.28
9	5.12	4.26	3.86	3.63	3.48	3.37	3.29	3.23	3.18	3.14	3.07
10	4.96	4.10	3.71	3.48	3.33	3.22	3.14	3.07	3.02	2.98	2.91
11	4.84	3.98	3.59	3.36	3.20	3.09	3.01	2.95	2.90	2.85	2.79
12	4.75	3.89	3.49	3.26	3.11	3.00	2.91	2.85	2.80	2.75	2.69
13	4.67	3.81	3.41	3.18	3.03	2.92	2.83	2.77	2.71	2.67	2.60
14	4.60	3.74	3.34	3.11	2.96	2.85	2.76	2.70	2.65	2.60	2.53
15	4.54	3.68	3.29	3.06	2.90	2.79	2.71	2.64	2.59	2.54	2.48

FIGURE 10.20

Left-Tail F_L for $\alpha = .05$

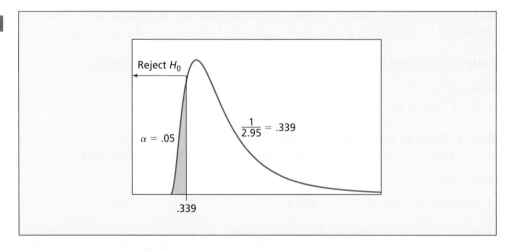

Step 4: Make the Decision Since the test statistic $F = 0.691$ is not in the critical region, we cannot reject the hypothesis of equal variances in a one-tailed test. The bumpers did not significantly decrease the variance in collision repair cost.

Excel's *F* Test

Figure 10.21 shows Excel's left-tailed test. One advantage of using Excel is that you also get a *p*-value. For the bumper data, the *p*-value of .279 indicates that we would face a Type I error risk of about 28 percent if we were to reject H_0. In other words, a sample variance ratio as extreme as $F = 0.691$ would occur by chance about 28 percent of the time if the population variances were in fact equal. The sample evidence does not indicate that the variances differ.

Assumptions of the *F* Test

The *F* test assumes that the populations being sampled are normal. Unfortunately, the test is rather sensitive to non-normality of the sampled populations. To test for equal variances, MINITAB reports both the *F* test and a more robust alternative known as

FIGURE 10.21

Excel's *F* Test of Variances

F-Test Two-Sample for Variances		
	Experimental	*Control*
Mean	1101.416667	1766.111111
Variance	484700.8106	701611.1111
Observations	12	9
df	11	8
F	0.690839702	
P(F<=f) one-tail	0.278623089	
F Critical one-tail	0.33921414	

Levene's test along with their *p*-values. As long as you know how to interpret a *p*-value, you really don't need to know the details of Levene's test. An attractive feature of MINITAB's *F* test is its graphical display of a confidence interval for each population standard deviation, shown in Figure 10.22.

FIGURE 10.22

MINITAB's Test for Variances

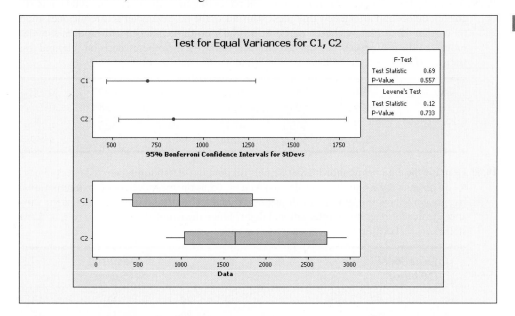

Significance versus Importance

The test of means showed a mean difference of $665 per repair incident. That is large enough that it might be important. The incremental cost per vehicle of the new bumper would have to be compared with the discounted present value of the expected annual savings per vehicle over its useful life. In a large fleet of vehicles, the payback period could be calculated. Most firms require that a change pay for itself in a fairly short period of time. *Importance* is a question to be answered ultimately by financial experts, not statisticians.

Hint: Use Excel or MegaStat.

SECTION EXERCISES

connect

10.36 Which samples show unequal variances? Use $\alpha = .10$ in all tests. Show the critical values and degrees of freedom clearly and illustrate the decision rule.

    a. $s_1 = 10.2$, $n_1 = 22$, $s_2 = 6.4$, $n_2 = 16$, two-tailed test

    b. $s_1 = 0.89$, $n_1 = 25$, $s_2 = 0.67$, $n_2 = 18$, right-tailed test

    c. $s_1 = 124$, $n_1 = 12$, $s_2 = 260$, $n_2 = 10$, left-tailed test

10.37 Which samples show unequal variances? Use $\alpha = .05$ in all tests. Show the critical values and degrees of freedom clearly and illustrate the decision rule.

    a. $s_1 = 5.1$, $n_1 = 11$, $s_2 = 3.2$, $n_2 = 8$, two-tailed test

    b. $s_1 = 221$, $n_1 = 8$, $s_2 = 445$, $n_2 = 8$, left-tailed test

    c. $s_1 = 67$, $n_1 = 10$, $s_2 = 15$, $n_2 = 13$, right-tailed test

10.38 Researchers at the Mayo Clinic have studied the effect of sound levels on patient healing and have found a significant association (louder hospital ambient sound level is associated with slower postsurgical healing). Based on the Mayo Clinic's experience, Ardmore Hospital installed a new vinyl flooring that is supposed to reduce the mean sound level (decibels) in the hospital corridors. The sound level is measured at five randomly selected times in the main corridor. (a) At $\alpha = .05$, has the mean been reduced? Show the hypotheses, decision rule, and test statistic. (b) At $\alpha = .05$, has the variance changed? Show the hypotheses, decision rule, and test statistic. 📁 **Decibels**

New Flooring	Old Flooring
42	48
41	51
40	44
37	48
44	52

10.39 A manufacturing process drills holes in sheet metal that are supposed to be .5000 cm in diameter. Before and after a new drill press is installed, the hole diameter is carefully measured (in cm) for 12 randomly chosen parts. At $\alpha = .05$, do these independent random samples prove that the new process has smaller variance? Show the hypotheses, decision rule, and test statistic. *Hint:* Use Excel =F.INV(α, n_1-1, n_2-1) to get F_L. 📁 **Diameter**

New drill:	.5005	.5010	.5024	.4988	.4997	.4995
	.4976	.5042	.5014	.4995	.4988	.4992
Old drill:	.5052	.5053	.4947	.4907	.5031	.4923
	.5040	.5035	.5061	.4956	.5035	.4962

10.40 Examine the data below showing the weights (in pounds) of randomly selected checked bags for an airline's flights on the same day. (a) At $\alpha = .05$, is the mean weight of an international bag greater? Show the hypotheses, decision rule, and test statistic. (b) At $\alpha = .05$, is the variance greater for bags on an international flight? Show the hypotheses, decision rule, and test statistic. 📁 **Luggage**

International (10 bags)		Domestic (15 bags)		
39	47	29	37	43
54	48	36	33	42
46	28	33	29	32
39	54	34	43	35
69	62	38	39	39

CHAPTER SUMMARY

A **two-sample test** compares samples with each other rather than comparing with a benchmark, as in a one-sample test. For **independent samples,** the comparison of means generally utilizes the Student's t distribution because the population variances are almost always unknown. If the unknown variances are **assumed equal,** we use a **pooled variance** estimate and **add the degrees of freedom.** If the unknown variances are **assumed unequal,** we do not pool the variances and we reduce the degrees of freedom by using **Welch's formula.** The test statistic is the difference of means divided by their standard error. For tests of means or proportions, **equal sample sizes** are desirable, but not necessary. The t **test for paired samples** uses the differences of n paired observations, thereby being a **one-sample** t **test.** For two proportions, the samples may be **pooled** if the population proportions are assumed equal, and the test statistic is the difference of proportions divided by the standard error, the square root of the sum of the sample variances. For proportions, **normality** of $p_1 - p_2$ may be assumed if both samples are large, that is, if each contains at least 10 successes and 10 failures. The F **test** for equality of **two variances** is named after Sir Ronald Fisher. Its test statistic is the **ratio** of the sample variances. We want to see if the ratio differs significantly from 1. The F table shows critical values based on both **numerator** and **denominator** degrees of freedom.

Commonly Used Formulas in Two-Sample Hypothesis Tests

Test Statistic (Difference of Means, Assuming Equal Variances):

$$t_{calc} = \frac{\bar{x}_1 - \bar{x}_2}{\sqrt{\dfrac{s_p^{\,2}}{n_1} + \dfrac{s_p^{\,2}}{n_1}}}, \text{ with } d.f. = n_1 + n_2 - 2 \text{ and } s_p^{\,2} = \frac{(n_1 - 1)s_1^{\,2} + (n_2 - 1)s_2^{\,2}}{n_1 + n_2 - 2}$$

Test Statistic (Difference of Means, Assuming Unequal Variances):

$$t_{calc} = \frac{\bar{x}_1 - \bar{x}_2}{\sqrt{\dfrac{s_1^{\,2}}{n_1} + \dfrac{s_2^{\,2}}{n_2}}}, \text{ with } d.f. = \frac{[s_1^{\,2}/n_1 + s_2^{\,2}/n_2]^2}{\dfrac{(s_1^{\,2}/n_1)^2}{n_1 - 1} + \dfrac{(s_2^{\,2}/n_2)^2}{n_2 - 1}}$$

Confidence Interval for $\mu_1 - \mu_2$:

$$(\bar{x}_1 - \bar{x}_2) \pm t_{\alpha/2}\sqrt{\dfrac{s_1^{\,2}}{n_1} + \dfrac{s_2^{\,2}}{n_2}}, \text{ with } d.f. = \frac{\left(\dfrac{s_1^{\,2}}{n_1} + \dfrac{s_2^{\,2}}{n_2}\right)^2}{\dfrac{\left(\dfrac{s_1^{\,2}}{n_1}\right)^2}{n_1 - 1} + \dfrac{\left(\dfrac{s_2^{\,2}}{n_2}\right)^2}{n_2 - 1}}$$

Test Statistic (Paired Differences): $t_{calc} = \dfrac{\bar{d} - \mu_d}{\dfrac{s_d}{\sqrt{n}}}$, with $d.f. = n - 1$

Test Statistic (Equality of Proportions): $z_{calc} = \dfrac{p_1 - p_2}{\sqrt{\bar{p}(1 - \bar{p})\left[\dfrac{1}{n_1} + \dfrac{1}{n_2}\right]}}$, with $\bar{p} = \dfrac{x_1 + x_2}{n_1 + n_2}$

Confidence Interval for $\pi_1 - \pi_2$: $(p_1 - p_2) \pm z_{\alpha/2}\sqrt{\dfrac{p_1(1 - p_1)}{n_1} + \dfrac{p_2(1 - p_2)}{n_2}}$

Test Statistic (Two Variances): $F_{calc} = \dfrac{s_1^{\,2}}{s_2^{\,2}}$, with $df_1 = n_1 - 1$, $df_2 = n_2 - 1$

CHAPTER REVIEW

1. (a) Explain why two samples from the same population could differ. (b) Why do we say that two-sample tests have a built-in point of reference?

2. (a) In a two-sample test of proportions, what is a pooled proportion? (b) Why is the test for normality important for a two-sample test of proportions? (c) What is the criterion for assuming normality of the test statistic?

3. (a) Is it necessary that sample sizes be equal for a two-sample test of proportions? Is it desirable? (b) Explain the analogy between overlapping confidence intervals and testing for equality of two proportions.

4. List the three cases for a test comparing two means. Explain how they differ.

5. Consider *Case 1* (known variances) in the test comparing two means. (a) Why is *Case 1* unusual and not used very often? (b) What distribution is used for the test statistic? (c) Write the formula for the test statistic.

6. Consider *Case 2* (unknown but equal variances) in the test comparing two means. (a) What distribution is used for the test statistic? (b) State the degrees of freedom used in this test. (c) Write the formula for the pooled variance and interpret it. (d) Write the formula for the test statistic.

7. Consider *Case 3* (unknown and unequal variances) in the test comparing two means. (a) What complication arises in degrees of freedom for *Case 3*? (b) What distribution is used for the test statistic? (c) Write the formula for the test statistic.

8. (a) Is it ever acceptable to use a normal distribution in a test of means with unknown variances? (b) If we assume normality, what is gained? What is lost?

9. Why is it a good idea to use a computer program like Excel to do tests of means?

10. (a) Explain why the paired *t* test for dependent samples is really a one-sample test. (b) State the degrees of freedom for the paired *t* test. (c) Why not treat two paired samples as if they were independent?

11. Explain how a difference in means could be statistically *significant* but not *important*.

12. (a) Why do we use an *F* test? (b) When two population variances are equal, what value would you expect of the *F* test statistic?

13. (a) In an *F* test for two variances, explain how to obtain left- and right-tail critical values. (b) What are the assumptions underlying the *F* test?

CHAPTER EXERCISES

connect

Note: For tests on two proportions, two means, or two variances, it is a good idea to check your work by using MINITAB, MegaStat, or the *LearningStats* two-sample calculators in Unit 10.

10.41 The top food snacks consumed by adults aged 18–54 are gum, chocolate candy, fresh fruit, potato chips, breath mints/candy, ice cream, nuts, cookies, bars, yogurt, and crackers. Out of a random sample of 25 men, 15 ranked fresh fruit in their top five snack choices. Out of a random sample of 32 women, 22 ranked fresh fruit in their top five snack choices. Is there a difference in the proportion of men and women who rank fresh fruit in their top five list of snacks? (a) State the hypotheses and a decision rule for $\alpha = .10$. (b) Calculate the sample proportions. (c) Find the test statistic and its *p*-value. What is your conclusion? (d) Is normality of $p_1 - p_2$ assured? (Data are from The NPD Group press release, "Fruit #1 Snack Food Consumed by Kids," June 16, 2005.)

10.42 In an early home game, an NBA team made 66 of their 94 free throw attempts. In one of their last home games, the team made 68 of 89 attempts. (a) At $\alpha = .10$, did the team significantly improve its free throw percentage (left-tailed test)? (b) Use Excel to calculate the *p*-value and interpret it.

10.43 Do a larger proportion of college students than young children eat cereal? Researchers surveyed both age groups to find the answer. The results are shown in the table below. (a) State the hypotheses used to answer the question. (b) Using $\alpha = .05$, state the decision rule and sketch it. (c) Find the sample proportions and *z* statistic. (d) Make a decision. (e) Find the *p*-value and interpret it. (f) Is the normality assumption fulfilled? Explain.

Statistic	College Students (ages 18–25)	Young Children (ages 6–11)
Number who eat cereal	$x_1 = 833$	$x_2 = 692$
Number surveyed	$n_1 = 850$	$n_2 = 740$

10.44 A 2005 study found that 202 women held board seats out of a total of 1,195 seats in the Fortune 100 companies. A 2003 study found that 779 women held board seats out of a total of 5,727 seats in the Fortune 500 companies. Treating these as random samples (board seat assignments change often), can we conclude that Fortune 100 companies have a greater proportion of women board members than the Fortune 500? (a) State the hypotheses. (b) Calculate the sample proportions. (c) Find the test statistic and its *p*-value. What is your conclusion at $\alpha = .05$? (d) If statistically significant, can you suggest factors that might explain the increase? (Data are from *The 2003 Catalyst Census of Women Board Directors of the Fortune 500,* and "Women and Minorities on Fortune 100 Boards," *The Alliance for Board Diversity,* May 17, 2005.)

10.45 A study of the Fortune 100 board of director members showed that there were 36 minority women holding board seats out of 202 total female board members. There were 142 minority men holding board seats out of 993 total male board members. (a) Treating the findings from this study as samples, calculate the sample proportions. (b) Find the test statistic and its *p*-value. (c) At the 5 percent level of significance, is there a difference in the percentage of minority women board directors and minority men board directors? (Data are from "Women and Minorities on Fortune 100 Boards," *The Alliance for Board Diversity,* May 17, 2005.)

10.46 To test his hypothesis that students who finish an exam first get better grades, a professor kept track of the order in which papers were handed in. Of the first 25 papers, 10 received a B or better compared with 8 of the last 24 papers handed in. Is the first group better, at $\alpha = .10$? (a) State your hypotheses and obtain a test statistic and *p*-value. Interpret the results. (b) Are the samples large enough to assure normality of $p_1 - p_2$? (c) Make an argument that early-finishers should do better. Then make the opposite argument. Which is more convincing?

10.47 How many full-page advertisements are found in a magazine? In an October issue of *Muscle and Fitness,* there were 252 ads, of which 97 were full-page. For the same month, the magazine *Glamour* had 342 ads, of which 167 were full-page. (a) Is the difference significant at $\alpha = .01$? (b) Find the *p*-value. (c) Is normality assured? (d) Based on what you know of these magazines, why might the proportions of full-page ads differ? (Data are from a project by MBA students Amy DeGuire and Don Finney.)

10.48 Male and female students in a personal finance class were asked to count how much cash they carried. (a) At $\alpha = .01$, can you conclude that the males carry more cash on average? Assume unequal population variances. (b) Is it reasonable to assume unequal variances? 🖼 **Cash**

Male	18.34	18.16	22.87	19.50	25.52	15.18	34.87	16.62	12.13	40.18	27.77
Female	21.66	15.39	15.23	15.81	15.64	21.78	16.37	17.60	16.54		

10.49 After John F. Kennedy Jr. was killed in an airplane crash at night, a survey was taken, asking whether a noninstrument-rated pilot should be allowed to fly at night. Of 409 New York State residents, 61 said yes. Of 70 aviation experts who were asked the same question, 40 said yes. (a) At $\alpha = .01$, did a larger proportion of experts say yes compared with the general public, or is the difference within the realm of chance? (b) Find the *p*-value and interpret it. (c) Is normality of $p_1 - p_2$ assured? (Data are from www.siena.edu/sri.)

10.50 A ski company in Vail owns two ski shops, one on the east side and one on the west side. Sales data showed that at the eastern location there were 56 pairs of large gloves sold out of 304 total pairs sold. At the western location there were 145 pairs of large gloves sold out of 562 total pairs sold. (a) Calculate the sample proportion of large gloves for each location. (b) At $\alpha = .05$, is there a significant difference in the proportion of large gloves sold? (c) Can you suggest any reasons why a difference might exist? (*Note:* Problem is based on actual sales data).

10.51 At a University of Colorado woman's home basketball game, a random sample of 25 concession purchases showed a mean of $7.12 with a standard deviation of $2.14. For the next week's home game, the admission ticket had a discount coupon for popcorn printed on the back. A random sample of 25 purchases from that week showed a mean of $8.29 with a standard deviation of $3.02. Was there an increase in the average concession stand purchases with the coupon? Assume unequal variances and use $\alpha = .05$.

10.52 Vail Resorts tracks the proportion of seasonal employees who are rehired each season. Rehiring a seasonal employee is beneficial in many ways, including lowering the costs incurred during the hiring process such as training costs. A random sample of 833 full-time and 386 part-time seasonal employees from 2009 showed that 434 full-time employees were rehired compared with 189 part-time employees. (a) Is there a significant difference in the proportion of rehires between the full-time and part-time seasonal employees? Use $\alpha = .10$ for the level of significance. (b) Use Excel to calculate the *p*-value.

VAILRESORTS

10.53 Does a "follow-up reminder" increase the renewal rate on a magazine subscription? A magazine sent out 760 subscription renewal notices (without a reminder) and got 703 renewals. As an experiment, they sent out 240 subscription renewal notices (with a reminder) and got 228 renewals. (a) At $\alpha = .05$, was the renewal rate higher in the experimental group? (b) Can normality be assumed?

10.54 A study revealed that the 30-day readmission rate was 31.4 percent for 370 patients who received after-hospital care instructions (e.g., how to take their medications) compared to a readmission rate of 45.1 percent for 368 patients who did not receive such information. (a) Set up the hypotheses to see whether the admissions rate was lower for those who received the information. (b) Find the *p*-value for the test. (c) What is your conclusion at $\alpha = .05$? At $\alpha = .01$? (Source: U.S. Department of Health and Human Services, *AHRQ Research Activities,* no. 343, March 2009, pp. 1–2.)

10.55 In a marketing class, 44 student members of virtual (Internet) project teams (group 1) and 42 members of face-to-face project teams (group 2) were asked to respond on a 1–5 scale to the question: "As compared to other teams, the members helped each other." For group 1 the mean was 2.73 with a standard deviation of 0.97, while for group 2 the mean was 1.90 with a standard deviation of 0.91. At $\alpha = .01$, is the virtual team mean significantly higher? (Data are from Roger W. Berry, *Marketing Education Review* 12, no. 2 [2002], pp. 73–78.)

10.56 In San Francisco, a sample of 3,106 wireless routers showed that 40.12 percent used encryption (to prevent hackers from intercepting information). In Seattle, a sample of 3,013 wireless routers showed that 25.99 percent used encryption. (a) Set up hypotheses to test whether or not the population proportion of encryption is higher in San Francisco than Seattle. (b) Test the hypotheses at $\alpha = .05$. (Source: *PNAS* 106, no. 5 [February 3, 2009], pp. 1318–23, www.pnas.org/cgi/doi/10.1073/pnas.081197310.)

10.57 Former U.S. Vice President Dick Cheney received a lot of publicity after his fourth heart attack. A portable defibrillator was surgically implanted in his chest to deliver an electric shock to restore his heart rhythm whenever another attack was threatening. Researchers at the University of Rochester (NY) Medical Center implanted defibrillators in 742 patients after a heart attack and compared them with 490 similar patients without the implant. Over the next 2 years, 98 of those without defibrillators had died, compared with 104 of those with defibrillators. (a) State the hypotheses for a one-tailed test to see if the defibrillators reduced the death rate. (b) Obtain a test statistic and *p*-value. (c) Is normality assured? (d) Why might such devices not be widely implanted in heart attack patients? (Data are from *Science News* 161 [April 27, 2002], p. 270.)

10.58 In 2009 Noodles & Company introduced spaghetti and meatballs to their menu. Before putting it on the menu, they performed taste tests to determine the best-tasting spaghetti sauce. In a paired comparison, 70 tasters were asked to rate their satisfaction with two different sauces on a scale of 1–10 with 10 being the highest. The mean difference in ratings was $\bar{d} = -0.385714$ with a standard deviation of $s_d = 1.37570$. (a) State the hypotheses for a two-tailed test. (b) Calculate the test statistic. (c) Calculate the critical value for $\alpha = .025$. (d) Calculate the *p*-value. (e) State your conclusion.

10.59 Has the cost to outsource a standard employee background check changed? A random sample of 10 companies in spring 2010 showed a sample average of $105 with a sample standard deviation equal to $32. A random sample of 10 different companies in spring 2012 resulted in a sample average of $75 with a sample standard deviation equal to $45. (a) Conduct a hypothesis test to test the difference in sample means with a level of significance equal to .05. Assume the population variances are not equal. (b) Discuss why a paired sample design might have made more sense in this case.

10.60 From her firm's computer telephone log, an executive found that the mean length of 64 telephone calls during July was 4.48 minutes with a standard deviation of 5.87 minutes. She vowed to make an effort to reduce the length of calls. The August phone log showed 48 telephone calls whose mean was 2.396 minutes with a standard deviation of 2.018 minutes. (a) State the hypotheses for a right-tailed test. (b) Obtain a test statistic and *p*-value assuming unequal variances. Interpret these results using $\alpha = .01$. (c) Why might the sample data *not* resemble a normal, bell-shaped curve? If not, how might this affect your conclusions?

10.61 An experimental bumper was designed to reduce damage in low-speed collisions. This bumper was installed on an experimental group of vans in a large fleet, but not on a control group. At the end of a trial period, accident data showed 12 repair incidents for the experimental group and 9 repair incidents for the control group. Vehicle downtime (in days per repair incident) is shown below. At $\alpha = .05$, did the new bumper reduce downtime? (a) Make stacked dot plots of the data (a sketch is OK). (b) State the hypotheses. (c) State the decision rule and sketch it. (d) Find the test statistic. (e) Make a decision. (f) Find the *p*-value and interpret it. (g) Do you think the difference is large enough to be important? Explain. (Data are from an unpublished study by Floyd G. Willoughby and Thomas W. Lauer, Oakland University). ☒ **DownTime**

New bumper (12 repair incidents): 9, 2, 5, 12, 5, 4, 7, 5, 11, 3, 7, 1

Control group (9 repair incidents): 7, 5, 7, 4, 18, 4, 8, 14, 13

10.62 Based on the sample data below, is the average Medicare spending in the northern region significantly less than the average spending in the southern region at the 1 percent level?

(a) State the hypotheses and decision rule. (b) Find the test statistic assuming unequal variances. (c) State your conclusion. Is this a strong conclusion? (d) Can you suggest reasons why a difference might exist?

Medicare Spending per Patient (adjusted for age, sex, and race)

Statistic	Northern Region	Southern Region
Sample mean	$3,123	$8,456
Sample standard deviation	$1,546	$3,678
Sample size	14 patients	16 patients

10.63 In a 15-day survey of air pollution in two European capitals, the mean particulate count (micrograms per cubic meter) in Athens was 39.5 with a standard deviation of 3.75, while in London the mean was 31.5 with a standard deviation of 2.25. (a) Assuming equal population variances, does this evidence convince you that the mean particulate count is higher in Athens, at $\alpha = .05$? (b) Are the variances equal or not, at $\alpha = .05$?

10.64 One group of accounting students took a distance learning class, while another group took the same course in a traditional classroom. At $\alpha = .10$, is there a significant difference in the mean scores listed below? (a) State the hypotheses. (b) State the decision rule and sketch it. (c) Find the test statistic. (d) Make a decision. (e) Use Excel to find the p-value and interpret it.

Exam Scores for Accounting Students

Statistic	Distance	Classroom
Mean scores	$\bar{x}_1 = 9.1$	$\bar{x}_2 = 10.3$
Sample std. dev.	$s_1 = 2.4$	$s_2 = 2.5$
Number of students	$n_1 = 20$	$n_2 = 20$

10.65 Do male and female school superintendents earn the same pay? Salaries for 20 males and 17 females in a certain metropolitan area are shown below. At $\alpha = .01$, were the mean superintendent salaries greater for men than for women? (a) State the hypotheses. (b) State the decision rule and sketch it. (c) Find the test statistic. (d) Make a decision. (e) Estimate the p-value and interpret it. 📷 **Paycheck**

School Superintendent Pay

Men (n = 20)		Women (n = 17)	
114,000	121,421	94,675	96,000
115,024	112,187	123,484	112,455
115,598	110,160	99,703	120,118
108,400	128,322	86,000	124,163
109,900	128,041	108,000	76,340
120,352	125,462	94,940	89,600
118,000	113,611	83,933	91,993
108,209	123,814	102,181	
110,000	111,280	86,840	
151,008	112,280	85,000	

10.66 The average take-out order size for Ashoka Curry House restaurant is shown. Assuming equal variances, at $\alpha = .05$, is there a significant difference in the order sizes? (a) State the hypotheses. (b) State the decision rule and sketch it. (c) Find the test statistic. (d) Make a decision. (e) Use Excel to find the p-value and interpret it.

Customer Order Size (dollars)

Statistic	Friday Night	Saturday Night
Mean order size	$\bar{x}_1 = 22.32$	$\bar{x}_2 = 25.56$
Standard deviation	$s_1 = 4.35$	$s_2 = 6.16$
Number of orders	$n_1 = 13$	$n_2 = 18$

10.67 Cash withdrawals from a college credit union for a random sample of 30 Fridays and 30 Mondays are shown. At $\alpha = .01$, is there a difference in the mean withdrawal on Monday and Friday? (a) Make stacked dot plots of the data (a sketch is OK). (b) State the hypotheses. (c) State the decision rule and sketch it. (d) Find the test statistic. (e) Make a decision. (f) Find the p-value and interpret it. ATM

Randomly Chosen Cash Withdrawals ($)

Friday			Monday		
250	10	10	40	30	10
20	10	30	100	70	370
110	20	10	20	20	10
40	20	40	30	50	30
70	10	10	200	20	40
20	20	400	20	30	20
10	20	10	10	20	100
50	20	10	30	40	20
100	20	20	50	10	20
20	60	70	60	10	20

10.68 In MiniCase 10.2, we found that the mean methane gas emissions for the two pneumatic controller manufacturers were not equal. When choosing formula 10.3 to calculate the t statistic, we assumed that their variances were not equal. Was this a valid assumption? Use Cemco's sample $s_1 = 147.2$ scfd ($n_1 = 18$) and Invalco's sample $s_2 = 237.9$ scfd ($n_2 = 17$) to find out. (a) State the hypotheses for a two-tailed test. (b) Calculate the critical value for $\alpha = .10$. (c) Calculate the test statistic. (d) What is your conclusion?

10.69 A ski company in Vail owns two ski shops, one on the west side and one on the east side of Vail. Is there a difference in daily average goggle sales between the two stores? Assume equal variances. (a) State the hypotheses for a two-tailed test. (b) State the decision rule for a level of significance equal to 5 percent and sketch it. (c) Find the test statistic and state your conclusion.

Sales Data for Ski Goggles

Statistic	East Side Shop	West Side Shop
Mean sales	$328	$435
Sample std. dev.	$104	$147
Sample size	28 days	29 days

10.70 A ski company in Vail owns two ski shops, one on the west side and one on the east side of Vail. Ski hat sales data (in dollars) for a random sample of 5 Saturdays during the 2004 season showed the following results. Is there a significant difference in sales dollars of hats between the west side and east side stores at the 5 percent level of significance? (a) State the hypotheses. (b) State the decision rule and sketch it. (c) Find the test statistic and state your conclusion. Hats

Saturday Sales Data ($) for Ski Hats

Saturday	East Side Shop	West Side Shop
1	548	523
2	493	721
3	609	695
4	567	510
5	432	532

10.71 Emergency room arrivals in a large hospital showed the statistics below for 2 months. At $\alpha = .05$, has the variance changed? Show all steps clearly, including an illustration of the decision rule.

Statistic	October	November
Mean arrivals	177.0323	171.7333
Standard deviation	13.48205	15.4271
Days	31	30

10.72 Concerned about graffiti, mayors of nine suburban communities instituted a citizen Community Watch program. (a) State the hypotheses to see whether the number of graffiti incidents declined. (b) Find the test statistic. (c) State the critical value for $\alpha = .05$. (d) Find the *p*-value. (e) State your conclusion. **Graffiti**

Community	Monthly Incidents After	Monthly Incidents Before
Burr Oak	8	12
Elgin Corners	3	6
Elm Grove	7	8
Greenburg	0	1
Huntley	4	2
North Lyman	0	4
South Lyman	4	4
Pin Oak	4	3
Victorville	0	3

10.73 A certain company will purchase the house of any employee who is transferred out of state and will handle all details of reselling the house. The purchase price is based on two assessments, one assessor being chosen by the employee and one by the company. Based on the sample of eight assessments shown, do the two assessors agree? Use the .01 level of significance, state hypotheses clearly, and show all steps. **HomeValue**

Assessments of Eight Homes ($ thousands)

Assessed by	Home 1	Home 2	Home 3	Home 4	Home 5	Home 6	Home 7	Home 8
Company	328	350	455	278	290	285	535	745
Employee	318	345	470	285	310	280	525	765

10.74 Nine homes are chosen at random from real estate listings in two suburban neighborhoods, and the square footage of each home is noted in the following table. At the .10 level of significance, is there a difference between the average sizes of homes in the two neighborhoods? State your hypotheses and show all steps clearly. **HomeSize**

Size of Homes in Two Subdivisions

Subdivision	Square Footage								
Greenwood	2,320	2,450	2,270	2,200	2,850	2,150	2,400	2,800	2,430
Pinewood	2,850	2,560	2,300	2,100	2,750	2,450	2,550	2,750	3,150

10.75 Two labs produce 1280 × 1024 LCD displays. At random, records are examined for 12 independently chosen hours of production in each lab, and the number of bad pixels per thousand displays is recorded. (a) Assuming equal variances, at the .01 level of significance, is there a difference in the defect rate between the two labs? State your hypotheses and show all steps clearly. (b) At the .01 level of significance, can you reject the hypothesis of equal variances? State your hypotheses and show all steps clearly. ☞ **LCDDefects**

Defects in Randomly Inspected LCD Displays

Lab A   422, 319, 326, 410, 393, 368, 497, 381, 515, 472, 423, 355

Lab B   497, 421, 408, 375, 410, 489, 389, 418, 447, 429, 404, 477

10.76 A cognitive retraining clinic assists outpatient victims of head injury, anoxia, or other conditions that result in cognitive impairment. Each incoming patient is evaluated to establish an appropriate treatment program and estimated length of stay. To see if the evaluation teams are consistent, 12 randomly chosen patients are separately evaluated by two expert teams (*A* and *B*) as shown. At the .10 level of significance, are the evaluator teams consistent in their estimates? State your hypotheses and show all steps clearly. ☞ **LengthStay**

Estimated Length of Stay in Weeks

Team	Patient											
	1	2	3	4	5	6	7	8	9	10	11	12
A	24	24	52	30	40	30	18	30	18	40	24	12
B	24	20	52	36	36	36	24	36	16	52	24	16

10.77 Rates of return (annualized) in two investment portfolios are compared over the last 12 quarters. They are considered similar in safety, but portfolio *B* is advertised as being "less volatile." (a) At $\alpha = .025$, does the sample show that portfolio *A* has significantly greater variance in rates of return than portfolio *B*? (b) At $\alpha = .025$, is there a significant difference in the means? ☞ **Portfolio**

Portfolio A	Portfolio B	Portfolio A	Portfolio B
5.23	8.96	7.89	7.68
10.91	8.60	9.82	7.62
12.49	7.61	9.62	8.71
4.17	6.60	4.93	8.97
5.54	7.77	11.66	7.71
8.68	7.06	11.49	9.91

VAILRESORTS   **10.78** Is there a difference between the variance in ages for full-time seasonal employees and part-time seasonal employees at Vail Resorts? A sample of 62 full-time employees had an $s_1^2 = 265.69$. A sample of 78 part-time employees had an $s_2^2 = 190.44$. (a) Test for equal variances with $\alpha = .05$. (b) If you were to then test for equal mean ages between the two groups, would you use the pooled *t* statistic for the test statistic? Why or why not?

10.79 A survey of 100 mayonnaise purchasers showed that 65 were loyal to one brand. For 100 bath soap purchasers, only 53 were loyal to one brand. Form a 95 percent confidence interval for the difference of proportions. Does it include zero?

10.80 A 20-minute consumer survey mailed to 500 adults aged 25–34 included a $5 Starbucks gift certificate. The same survey was mailed to 500 adults aged 25–34 without the gift certificate. There were 65 responses from the first group and 45 from the second group. Form a 95 percent confidence interval for the difference of proportions. Does it include zero?

10.81 One group of accounting students used simulation programs, while another group received a tutorial. Scores on an exam were compared. (a) Construct a 90 percent confidence interval for the true difference in mean scores, explaining any assumptions that are necessary. (b) Do you think the learning methods have significantly different results? Explain.

Statistic	Simulation	Tutorial
Mean score	$\bar{x}_1 = 9.1$	$\bar{x}_2 = 10.3$
Sample std. dev.	$s_1 = 2.4$	$s_2 = 2.5$
Number of students	$n_1 = 20$	$n_2 = 20$

10.82 Advertisers fear that users of DVD recorders will "fast forward" past commercials when they watch a recorded program. A leading British pay television company told their advertisers that this effect might be offset because DVD users watch more TV. A sample of 15 DVD users showed a daily mean screen time of 2 hours and 26 minutes with a standard deviation of 14 minutes, compared with a daily mean of 2 hours and 7 minutes with a standard deviation of 12 minutes for a sample of 15 non-DVD users. (a) Construct a 95 percent confidence interval for the difference in mean TV watching. Would this sample support the company's claim (i.e., is zero within the confidence interval for the mean difference)? (b) Discuss any assumptions that are needed.

10.83 In preliminary tests of a vaccine that may help smokers quit by reducing the "rush" from tobacco, 64 subjects who wanted to quit smoking were given either a placebo or the vaccine. Of the 32 in the placebo group, only 3 quit smoking for 30 days (the U.S. Food and Drug Administration's criterion for smoking cessation) compared with 11 of the vaccine group. (a) Assuming equal sample sizes, find the 95 percent confidence interval for the difference in proportions. What does it suggest? (b) Why is the sample size a problem here?

10.84 Do positive emotions reduce susceptibility to colds? Healthy volunteers were divided into two groups based on their emotional profiles and each group was exposed to rhinovirus (the common cold). Of those who reported mostly positive emotions, 14 of 50 developed cold symptoms, compared with 23 of 56 who reported mostly negative emotions. (a) Find the 95 percent confidence interval for the difference in proportions. What does it suggest? (b) Is the criterion for normality met?

10.85 Male and female students in a finance class were asked how much their last tank of gas cost. Can you conclude that on average males spent more on gas than females? (a) State the hypotheses for this test. (b) Show the calculation of the test statistic, assuming unequal population variances. (c) State the decision rule, using $\alpha = .01$ and the quick rule for degrees of freedom. (d) Draw the conclusion. (e) Is it reasonable to assume unequal variances? Explain.

Males	Females
$\bar{x}_1 = \$43.20$	$\bar{x}_2 = \$36.60$
$s_1 = \$8.30$	$s_2 = \$3.10$
$n_1 = 13$	$n_2 = 9$

10.86 Students in nutrition classes at two high schools were asked to keep track of the number of times during the past month that they ordered from a fast-food chain restaurant. (a) The research hypothesis is that Sonando High School students choose fast-food restaurants more often. State the hypotheses for this test. (b) Show the calculation of the test statistic, using $\alpha = .01$ and assuming equal population variances. (c) State the decision rule. (d) Draw the conclusion. (e) Is it reasonable to assume equal variances? Explain.

Sonando High School	Gedacht High School
$\bar{x}_1 = 14.51$	$\bar{x}_2 = 11.88$
$s_1 = 2.69$	$s_2 = 2.66$
$n_1 = 11$	$n_2 = 16$

DO-IT-YOURSELF

10.87 Count the number of two-door vehicles among 50 vehicles from a college or university student parking lot. Use any sampling method you like (e.g., the first 50 you see). Do the same for a grocery store that is not very close to the college or university. At $\alpha = .10$, is there a significant difference in the proportion of two-door vehicles in these two locations? (a) State the hypotheses. (b) State the decision rule and sketch it. (c) Find the sample proportions and z test statistic. (d) Make a decision. (e) Find the p-value and interpret it. (f) Is the normality assumption fulfilled? Explain.

RELATED READING

Best, D. J., and J. C. W. Rayner. "Welch's Approximate Solution for the Behrens-Fisher Problem." *Technometrics* 29 (1987), pp. 205–10.

Payton, Mark E.; Matthew H. Greenstone; and Nathan Schenker. "Overlapping Confidence Intervals or Standard Error Intervals: What Do They Mean in terms of Statistical Significance?" *Journal of Insect Science* 3, no. 34 (October 2003), pp. 1–6.

Posten, H. O. "Robustness of the Two-Sample t-Test under Violations of the Homogeneity of Variance Assumption, Part II." *Communications in Statistics—Theory and Methods* 21 (1995), pp. 2169–84.

Scheffé, H. "Practical Solutions of the Behrens-Fisher Problem." *Journal of the American Statistical Association* 65 (1970), pp. 1501–08.

Shoemaker, Lewis F. "Fixing the F Test for Equal Variances." *The American Statistician* 57, no. 2 (May 2003), pp. 105–14.

CHAPTER 10   Online Learning Resources

The Online Learning Center (OLC) at www.mhhe.com/doane4e has several *LearningStats* demonstrations to help you understand two-sample hypothesis tests. Your instructor may assign one or more of them, or you may decide to download the ones that sound interesting.

Topic	LearningStats Demonstrations
Common hypothesis tests	⊠ Calculator for Two Means ⊠ Calculator for Two Proportions
Simulations	⊠ Two-Sample Bootstrap
	⊠ Appendix F—F Distribution

Key: ⊠ = Excel

EXAM REVIEW QUESTIONS FOR CHAPTERS 8–10

1. Which statement is *not* correct? Explain.
   a. The sample data $x_1, x_2, \ldots, x_n$ will be approximately normal if the sample size n is large.
   b. For a skewed population, the distribution of $\bar{X}$ is approximately normal if n is large.
   c. The expected value of $\bar{X}$ is equal to the true mean μ even if the population is skewed.

2. Match each statement to the correct property of an estimator (unbiased, consistent, efficient):
   a. The estimator "collapses" on the true parameter as n increases.
   b. The estimator has a relatively small variance.
   c. The expected value of the estimator is the true parameter.

3. Concerning confidence intervals, which statement is *most nearly* correct? Why not the others?
   a. We should use z instead of t when n is large.
   b. We use the Student's t distribution when σ is unknown.
   c. Using the Student's t distribution instead of z narrows the confidence interval.

4. A sample of 9 customers in the "quick" lane in a supermarket showed a mean purchase of $14.75 with a standard deviation of $2.10. (a) Find the 95 percent confidence interval for the true mean. (b) Why should you use t instead of z in this case?

5. A sample of 200 customers at a supermarket showed that 28 used a debit card to pay for their purchases. (a) Find the 95 percent confidence interval for the population proportion. (b) Why

is it OK to assume normality in this case? (c) What sample size would be needed to estimate the population proportion with 90 percent confidence and an error of $\pm .03$?

6. Which statement is *incorrect*? Explain.

   a. If $p = .50$ and $n = 100$, the estimated standard error of the sample proportion is .05.
   b. In a sample size calculation for estimating π, it is conservative to assume $\pi = .50$.
   c. If $n = 250$ and $p = .07$ it is not safe to assume normality in a confidence interval for π.

7. Given $H_0: \mu \geq 18$ and $H_1: \mu < 18$, we would commit Type I error if we

   a. conclude that $\mu \geq 18$ when the truth is that $\mu < 18$.
   b. conclude that $\mu < 18$ when the truth is that $\mu \geq 18$.
   c. fail to reject $\mu \geq 18$ when the truth is that $\mu < 18$.

8. Which is the correct z value for a two-tailed test at $\alpha = .05$?

   a. $z = \pm 1.645$ b. $z = \pm 1.960$ c. $z = \pm 2.326$

9. The process that produces Sonora Bars (a type of candy) is intended to produce bars with a mean weight of 56 grams (g). The process standard deviation is known to be 0.77g. A random sample of 49 candy bars yields a mean weight of 55.82 g. (a) State the hypotheses to test whether the mean is smaller than it is supposed to be. (b) What is the test statistic? (c) At $\alpha = .05$, what is the critical value for this test? (d) What is your conclusion?

10. A sample of 16 ATM transactions shows a mean transaction time of 67 seconds with a standard deviation of 12 seconds. (a) State the hypotheses to test whether the mean transaction time exceeds 60 seconds. (b) Find the test statistic. (c) At $\alpha = .025$, what is the critical value for this test? (d) What is your conclusion?

11. Which statement is *correct*? Why not the others?

   a. The level of significance α is the probability of committing Type I error.
   b. As the sample size increases, critical values of $t_{.05}$ increase, gradually approaching $z_{.05}$.
   c. When σ is unknown, it is conservative to use $z_{.05}$ instead of $t_{.05}$ in a hypothesis test for μ.

12. Last month, 85 percent of the visitors to the Sonora Candy Factory made a purchase in the on-site candy shop after taking the factory tour. This month, a random sample of 500 such visitors showed that 435 purchased candy after the tour. The manager said, "Good, the percentage of candy-buyers has risen significantly." (a) At $\alpha = .05$, do you agree? (b) Why is it reasonable to assume normality in this test?

13. Weights of 12 randomly chosen Sonora Bars (a type of candy) from assembly line 1 had a mean weight of 56.25 grams (g) with a standard deviation of 0.65 g, while the weights of 12 randomly chosen Sonora Bars from assembly line 2 had a mean weight of 56.75 g with a standard deviation of 0.55 g. (a) Find the test statistic to test whether or not the mean population weights are the same for both assembly lines (i.e., that the difference is due to random variation). (b) State the critical value for $\alpha = .05$ and degrees of freedom that you are using. (c) State your conclusion.

14. In a random sample of 200 Colorado residents, 150 had skied at least once last winter. A similar sample of 200 Utah residents revealed that 140 had skied at least once last winter. At $\alpha = .025$, is the percentage significantly greater in Colorado? Explain fully and show calculations.

15. Five students in a large lecture class compared their scores on two exams. "Looks like the class mean was higher on the second exam," Bob said. (a) What kind of test would you use? (b) At $\alpha = .10$, what is the critical value? (c) Do you agree with Bob? Explain.

	Bill	Mary	Sam	Sarah	Megan
Exam 1	75	85	90	65	86
Exam 2	86	81	90	71	89

16. Which statement is *not* correct concerning a *p*-value? Explain.

   a. *Ceteris paribus,* a larger *p*-value makes it more likely that H_0 will be rejected.
   b. The *p*-value shows the risk of Type I error if we reject H_0 when H_0 is true.
   c. In making a decision, we compare the *p*-value with the desired level of significance α.

17. Given $n_1 = 8$, $s_1 = 14$, $n_2 = 12$, $s_2 = 7$. (a) Find the test statistic for a test for equal population variances. (b) At $\alpha = .05$ in a two-tailed test, state the critical value and degrees of freedom.

CHAPTER CONTENTS

CHAPTER LEARNING OBJECTIVES

LO

When you finish this chapter you should be able to

LO 11-1   Use basic ANOVA terminology correctly.

LO 11-2   Recognize from data format when one-factor ANOVA is appropriate.

LO 11-3   Interpret sums of squares and calculations in an ANOVA table.

LO 11-4   Use Excel or other software for ANOVA calculations.

LO 11-5   Use a table or Excel to find critical values for the F distribution.

LO 11-6   Explain the assumptions of ANOVA and why they are important.

LO 11-7   Understand and perform Tukey's test for paired means.

LO 11-8   Use Hartley's test for equal variances in c treatment groups.

LO 11-9   Recognize from data format when two-factor ANOVA is needed.

LO 11-10 Interpret main effects and interaction effects in two-factor ANOVA.

LO 11-11 Recognize the need for experimental design and GLM (optional).

11.1 OVERVIEW OF ANOVA

You have already learned to compare the means of two samples. In this chapter, you will learn to compare more than two means *simultaneously* and how to trace sources of variation to potential explanatory factors by using **analysis of variance** (commonly referred to as **ANOVA**). Proper *experimental design* can make efficient use of limited data to draw the strongest possible inferences. Although analysis of variance has a relatively short history, it is one of the richest and most thoroughly explored fields of statistics. Originally developed by the English statistician Ronald A. Fisher (1890–1962) in connection with agricultural research (factors affecting crop growth), it was quickly applied in biology and medicine. Because of its versatility, it is now used in engineering, psychology, marketing, and many other areas. In this chapter, we will only illustrate a few kinds of problems where ANOVA may be utilized (see Related Reading if you need to go further).

The Goal: Explaining Variation

Analysis of variance seeks to identify *sources of variation* in a numerical *dependent* variable Y (the **response variable**). Variation in the response variable about its mean either is **explained** by one or more categorical *independent* variables (the **factors**) or is **unexplained** (random error):

LO 11-1

Use basic ANOVA terminology correctly.

Variation in Y	=	Explained Variation	+	Unexplained Variation
(around its mean)		(due to factors)		(random error)

ANOVA is a *comparison of means.* Each possible value of a factor or combination of factors is a **treatment**. Sample observations within each treatment are viewed as coming from populations with possibly different means. We test whether each factor has a significant effect on Y, and sometimes we test for interaction between factors. The test uses the F distribution, which was introduced in Chapter 10. ANOVA can handle any number of factors, but the researcher often is interested only in a few. Also, data collection costs may impose practical limits on the number of factors or treatments we can choose. This chapter concentrates on ANOVA models with one or two factors, although more complex models are briefly mentioned at the end of the chapter. We will begin with some illustrations of **one-factor ANOVA**.

Illustration: Manufacturing Defect Rates

Figure 11.1 shows a dot plot of daily defect rates for automotive computer chips manufactured at four plant locations. Samples of 10 days' production were taken at each plant. Are the observed differences in the plants' sample mean defect rates merely due to

FIGURE 11.1

Chip defect rates at four plants. The treatment means are significantly different ($p = .02$). Note that the confidence interval for Lee's Bluff falls to the right of the dotted vertical line, which represents the overall mean.

random variation? Or are the observed differences between the plants' defect rates too great to be attributed to chance? This is the kind of question that one-factor ANOVA is designed to answer.

A simple way to state the one-factor ANOVA hypothesis is

H_0: $\mu_1 = \mu_2 = \mu_3 = \mu_4$ (mean defect rates are the same at all four plants)

H_1: Not all the means are equal (at least one mean differs from the others)

If we cannot reject H_0, then we conclude that the observations within each treatment or group actually have a common mean μ (represented by a dashed line in Figure 11.1). This one-factor ANOVA model may be visualized as in Figure 11.2.

FIGURE 11.2

ANOVA Model for Chip Defect Rates

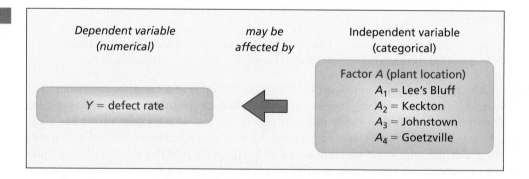

Illustration: Hospital Length of Stay

To allocate resources and fixed costs correctly, hospital management needs to test whether a patient's length of a stay (LOS) depends on the diagnostic-related group (DRG) code. Consider the case of a bone fracture. LOS is a *numerical* response variable (measured in hours). The hospital organizes the data by using five diagnostic codes for type of fracture (facial, radius or ulna, hip or femur, other lower extremity, all other), as illustrated in Figure 11.3. Type of fracture is a *categorical* variable.

Illustration: Automobile Painting

Paint quality is a major concern of car makers. A key characteristic of paint is its viscosity, a continuous *numerical* variable. Viscosity is to be tested for dependence on application temperature (low, medium, high), as illustrated in Figure 11.3. Although temperature is a numerical variable, it has been coded into *categories* that represent the test conditions of the experiment because the car maker did not want to assume that viscosity was linearly related to temperature.

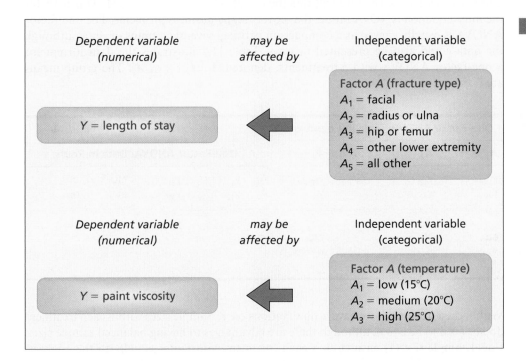

FIGURE 11.3

ANOVA Models for Hospital Length of Stay and Paint Viscosity

ANOVA Assumptions

Analysis of variance assumes that the

Explain the assumptions of ANOVA and why they are important.

- Observations on Y are independent.
- Populations being sampled are normal.
- Populations being sampled have equal variances.

Fortunately, ANOVA is somewhat robust to departures from the normality and equal variance assumptions. Later in this chapter, you will see tests for equal variances and normality.

ANOVA Calculations

ANOVA calculations usually are too tedious to do by calculator, so after we choose an ANOVA model and collect the data, we rely on software (e.g., Excel, MegaStat, MINITAB, SPSS) to do the calculations. In some applications (accounting, finance, human resources, marketing), large samples can easily be taken from existing records, while in others (engineering, manufacturing, computer systems), experimental data collection is so expensive that small samples are used. Large samples increase the power of the test, but power also depends on the degree of variation in Y. Lowest power would be in small samples with high variation in Y, and conversely. Specialized software is needed to calculate power for more complex multifactor ANOVA experiments.

11.2 ONE-FACTOR ANOVA (COMPLETELY RANDOMIZED MODEL)

Data Format

If we are only interested in comparing the means of c groups (*treatments* or *factor levels*), we have a one-factor ANOVA. If subjects (or individuals) are assigned randomly to treatments, then we call this the **completely randomized model**. This is by far the most common ANOVA model that covers many business problems. The one-factor ANOVA is usually viewed as a comparison between several columns of data, although the data could also be presented in rows. Table 11.1 illustrates the data format for a one-factor ANOVA with c treatments, denoted $A_1, A_2, \ldots, A_c$. The group means are $\bar{y}_1, \bar{y}_2, \ldots, \bar{y}_c$.

TABLE 11.1

Format of One-Factor ANOVA Data

LO 11-2

Recognize from data format when one-factor ANOVA is appropriate.

One-Factor ANOVA: Data in Columns					One-Factor ANOVA: Data in Rows						
A_1	A_2	$\cdots$	A_c								
y_{11}	y_{12}	$\cdots$	y_{1c}	A_1	y_{11}	y_{21}	y_{31}	$\cdots$	etc.	n_1 obs.	$\bar{y}_1$
y_{21}	y_{22}	$\cdots$	y_{2c}	A_2	y_{12}	y_{22}	y_{32}	$\cdots$	etc.	n_2 obs.	$\bar{y}_2$
y_{31}	y_{32}	$\cdots$	y_{3c}	$\cdots$					$\cdots$	$\cdots$	$\cdots$
$\cdots$	$\cdots$	$\cdots$	$\cdots$	A_c	y_{1c}	y_{2c}	y_{3c}	$\cdots$	etc.	n_c obs.	$\bar{y}_c$
etc.	etc.	$\cdots$	etc.								
n_1 obs.	n_2 obs.	$\cdots$	n_c obs.								
$\bar{y}_1$	$\bar{y}_2$	$\cdots$	$\bar{y}_c$								

Within each treatment j we have n_j observations on Y. Sample sizes within each treatment do *not* need to be equal, although there are advantages to having balanced sample sizes. Equal sample size (1) ensures that each treatment contributes equally to the analysis; (2) reduces problems arising from violations of the assumptions (e.g., nonindependent Y values, unequal variances or nonidentical distributions within treatments, or nonnormality of Y); and (3) increases the power of the test (i.e., the ability of the test to detect differences in treatment means). The total number of observations is the sum of the sample sizes for each treatment:

(11.1) $$n = n_1 + n_2 + \cdots + n_c$$

Hypotheses to Be Tested

The question of interest is whether the mean of Y varies from treatment to treatment. The hypotheses to be tested are

H_0: $\mu_1 = \mu_2 = \cdots = \mu_c$ (all the treatment means are equal)

H_1: Not all the means are equal (at least one pair of treatment means differs)

Since one-factor ANOVA is a generalization of the test for equality of two means, why not just compare all possible pairs of means by using repeated two-sample t tests (as in Chapter 10)? Consider our experiment comparing the four manufacturing plant average defect rates. To compare pairs of plant averages, we would have to perform six different t tests. If each t test has a Type I error probability equal to .05, then the probability that at least one of those tests results in a Type I error is $1 - (.95)^6 = .2649$. ANOVA tests all the means *simultaneously* and therefore does not inflate our Type I error.

One-Factor ANOVA as a Linear Model

An equivalent way to express the one-factor model is to say that observations in treatment j came from a population with a common mean (μ) plus a treatment effect (A_j) plus random error (ε_{ij}):

$$y_{ij} = \mu + A_j + \varepsilon_{ij} \qquad j = 1, 2, \ldots, c \quad \text{and} \quad i = 1, 2, \ldots, n_j \qquad \text{(11.2)}$$

The random error is assumed to be normally distributed with zero mean and the same variance for all treatments. If we are interested only in what happens to the response for the particular *levels* of the factor that were selected (a **fixed-effects model**), then the hypotheses to be tested are

H_0: $A_1 = A_2 = \cdots = A_c = 0$ (all treatment effects are zero)

H_1: Not all A_j are zero (some treatment effects are nonzero)

If the null hypothesis is true ($A_j = 0$ for all j), then knowing that an observation x came from treatment j does not help explain the variation in Y and the ANOVA model collapses to

$$y_{ij} = \mu + \varepsilon_{ij} \qquad \text{(11.3)}$$

If the null hypothesis is false, then at least some of the A_j must be nonzero. The A_j that are negative (below μ) must be offset by the A_j that are positive (above μ) when weighted by sample size.

Group Means

The *mean of each group* is calculated in the usual way by summing the observations in the treatment and dividing by the sample size:

$$\bar{y}_j = \frac{1}{n_j} \sum_{i=1}^{n_j} y_{ij} \qquad \text{(11.4)}$$

The *overall sample mean* or *grand mean* $\bar{y}$ can be calculated either by summing *all* the observations and dividing by n or by taking a weighted average of the c sample means:

$$\bar{y} = \frac{1}{n} \sum_{j=1}^{c} \sum_{i=1}^{n_j} y_{ij} = \frac{1}{n} \sum_{j=1}^{c} n_j \bar{y}_j \qquad \text{(11.5)}$$

Partitioned Sum of Squares

To understand the logic of ANOVA, consider that for a given observation y_{ij} the following relationship must hold (on the right-hand side we just add and subtract $\bar{y}_j$):

$$(y_{ij} - \bar{y}) = (\bar{y}_j - \bar{y}) + (y_{ij} - \bar{y}_j) \qquad \text{(11.6)}$$

This says that any deviation of an observation from the grand mean $\bar{y}$ may be expressed in two parts: the deviation of the column mean ($\bar{y}_j$) from the grand mean ($\bar{y}$), or *between* treatments, and the deviation of the observation (y_{ij}) from its own column mean ($\bar{y}_j$), or *within* treatments. We can show that this relationship also holds for *sums* of squared deviations, yielding the **partitioned sum of squares**:

$$\sum_{j=1}^{c} \sum_{i=1}^{n_j} (y_{ij} - \bar{y})^2 = \sum_{j=1}^{c} n_j (\bar{y}_j - \bar{y})^2 + \sum_{j=1}^{c} \sum_{i=1}^{n_j} (y_{ij} - \bar{y}_j)^2 \qquad \text{(11.7)}$$

This important relationship may be expressed simply as

$$SST = SSA + SSE \qquad \text{(partitioned sum of squares)} \qquad \text{(11.8)}$$

Partitioned Sum of Squares

Sum of Squares Total (SST)	=	Sum of Squares between Treatments (SSA)	+	Sum of Squares within Treatments (SSE)
		↑ Explained by Factor A		↑ Unexplained Random Error

If the treatment means do not differ greatly from the grand mean, *SSA* will be small and *SSE* will be large (and conversely). The sums *SSA* and *SSE* may be used to test the hypothesis that the treatment means differ from the grand mean. However, we first divide each sum of squares by its *degrees of freedom* (to adjust for group sizes). The *F test statistic* is the ratio of the resulting **mean squares**. These calculations can be arranged in a worksheet like Table 11.2.

TABLE 11.2

One-Factor ANOVA Table

LO 11-3

Interpret sums of squares and calculations in an ANOVA table.

Source of Variation	Sum of Squares	Degrees of Freedom	Mean Square	F Statistic
Treatment (between groups)	$SSA = \sum_{j=1}^{c} n_j(\bar{y}_j - \bar{y})^2$	$c - 1$	$MSA = \dfrac{SSA}{c - 1}$	$F = \dfrac{MSA}{MSE}$
Error (within groups)	$SSE = \sum_{j=1}^{c}\sum_{i=1}^{n_j}(y_{ij} - \bar{y}_j)^2$	$n - c$	$MSE = \dfrac{SSE}{n - c}$	
Total	$SST = \sum_{j=1}^{c}\sum_{i=1}^{n_j}(y_{ij} - \bar{y})^2$	$n - 1$		

The ANOVA calculations are mathematically simple but involve tedious sums. These calculations are almost always done on a computer.* For example, Excel's one-factor ANOVA menu using Data Analysis is shown in Figure 11.4. MegaStat uses a similar menu.

FIGURE 11.4

Excel's ANOVA Menu

Test Statistic

At the beginning of this chapter we described the variation in *Y* as consisting of explained variation and unexplained variation. To test whether the independent variable explains a significant proportion of the variation in *Y*, we need to compare the

---

*Detailed step-by-step examples of all ANOVA calculations can be downloaded from the OLC case studies in *LearningStats* Unit 11.

explained (due to treatments) and unexplained (due to error) variation. Recall that the F distribution describes the *ratio of two variances.* Therefore it makes sense that the ANOVA test statistic is the *F test statistic.* The F statistic is the ratio of the variance due to treatments to the variance due to error. *MSA* is the mean square due to treatments and *MSE* is the mean square within treatments. Formula 11.9 shows the F statistic and its degrees of freedom.

$$\begin{matrix} \textit{Between } \text{groups} \\ \text{(explained)} \\ \\ \textit{Within } \text{groups} \\ \text{(unexplained)} \end{matrix} \qquad F = \frac{MSA}{MSE} = \frac{\left(\dfrac{SSA}{c-1}\right)}{\left(\dfrac{SSE}{n-c}\right)} \qquad \begin{matrix} df_1 = c - 1 \text{ (numerator)} \\ \\ \\ df_2 = n - c \text{ (denominator)} \end{matrix} \qquad (11.9)$$

The test statistic $F = MSA/MSE$ cannot be negative (it's based on sums of squares—see Table 11.2). The F test for equal treatment means is always a right-tailed test because it is the ratio of explained to unexplained variance. If there is little difference among treatments, we would expect *MSA* to be near zero because the treatment means $\bar{y}_j$ would be near the overall mean $\bar{y}$. Thus, when F is near zero, we would not expect to reject the hypothesis of equal group means. The larger the F statistic, the more we are inclined to reject the hypothesis of equal means. But how large must F be to convince us that the means differ? Just as with a z test or a t test, we need a *decision rule.*

Decision Rule

The F distribution is a right-skewed distribution that starts at zero (F cannot be negative since variances are sums of squares) and has no upper limit (since the variances could be of any magnitude). For ANOVA, the F test is a right-tailed test. For a given level of significance α, we can use Appendix F to obtain the right-tail critical value of F. Alternatively, we can use Excel's function =F.INV.RT(α, df_1, df_2). The decision rule is illustrated in Figure 11.5. This critical value is denoted F_{df_1, df_2} or $F_{c-1, n-c}$.

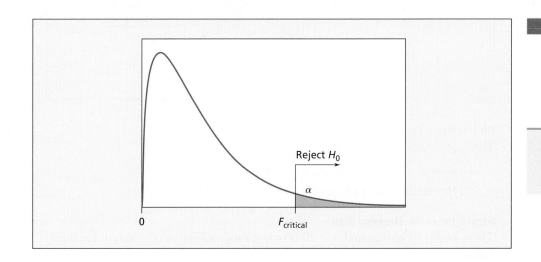

FIGURE 11.5

Decision Rule for an *F* Test

LO 11-5

Use a table or Excel to find critical values for the *F* distribution.

EXAMPLE 11.1

Carton Packing

A cosmetics manufacturer's regional distribution center has four workstations that are responsible for packing cartons for shipment to small retailers. Each workstation is staffed by two workers. The task involves assembling each order, placing it in a shipping carton, inserting packing material, taping the carton, and placing a computer-generated shipping label on each carton. Generally, each station can pack 200 cartons a day, and often more. However, there is variability, due to differences in orders, labels, and cartons. Table 11.3 shows the number of cartons packed per day during a recent week. Is the variation among stations within the range attributable to chance, or do these samples indicate actual differences in the means?

TABLE 11.3	Number of Cartons Packed	Cartons		
	Station 1	*Station 2*	*Station 3*	*Station 4*
	236	238	220	241
	250	239	236	233
	252	262	232	212
	233	247	243	231
	239	246	213	213
Sum	1,210	1,232	1,144	1,130
Mean	242.0	246.4	228.8	226.0
St. Dev.	8.515	9.607	12.153	12.884
n	5	5	5	5

As a preliminary step, we plot the data (Figure 11.6) to check for any time pattern and just to visualize the data. We see some potential differences in means, but no obvious time pattern (otherwise we would have to consider observation order as a second factor). We proceed with the hypothesis test.

FIGURE 11.6	Plot of the Data

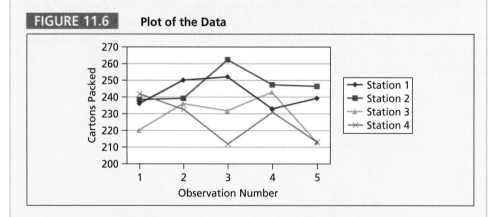

Step 1: State the Hypotheses
The hypotheses to be tested are

H_0: $\mu_1 = \mu_2 = \mu_3 = \mu_4$ (the means are the same)

H_1: Not all the means are equal (at least one mean is different)

Step 2: State the Decision Rule
There are $c = 4$ groups and $n = 20$ observations, so degrees of freedom for the F test are

Numerator: $df_1 = c - 1 = 4 - 1 = 3$ (between treatments, factor)

Denominator: $df_2 = n - c = 20 - 4 = 16$ (within treatments, error)

We will use $\alpha = .05$ for the test. The 5 percent right-tail critical value from Appendix F is $F_{3,16} = 3.24$. Instead of Appendix F we could use Excel's function =F.INV.RT(0.05,3,16), which yields $F_{.05} = 3.238872$. This decision rule is illustrated in Figure 11.7.

FIGURE 11.7	*F* Test Using $\alpha = .05$ with $F_{3,16}$

Appendix F: Critical Values for F$_{.05}$

This table shows the critical value that defines the 5% right-tail area for the stated degrees of freedom.

	Numerator Degrees of Freedom (v_1)										
	1	2	3	4	5	6	7	8	9	10	12
1	161.4	199.5	215.7	224.6	230.2	234.0	236.8	238.9	240.5	241.9	243.9
2	18.51	19.00	19.16	19.25	19.30	19.33	19.35	19.37	19.38	19.40	19.41
3	10.13	9.55	9.28	9.12	9.01	8.94	8.89	8.85	8.81	8.79	8.74
4	7.71	6.94	6.59	6.39	6.26	6.16	6.09	6.04	6.00	5.96	5.91
5	6.61	5.79	5.41	5.19	5.05	4.95	4.88	4.82	4.77	4.74	4.68
6	5.99	5.14	4.76	4.53	4.39	4.28	4.21	4.15	4.10	4.06	4.00
7	5.59	4.74	4.35	4.12	3.97	3.87	3.79	3.73	3.68	3.64	3.57
8	5.32	4.46	4.07	3.84	3.69	3.58	3.50	3.44	3.39	3.35	3.28
9	5.12	4.26	3.86	3.63	3.48	3.37	3.29	3.23	3.18	3.14	3.07
10	4.96	4.10	3.71	3.48	3.33	3.22	3.14	3.07	3.02	2.98	2.91
11	4.84	3.98	3.59	3.36	3.20	3.09	3.01	2.95	2.90	2.85	2.79
12	4.75	3.89	3.49	3.26	3.11	3.00	2.91	2.85	2.80	2.75	2.69
13	4.67	3.81	3.41	3.18	3.03	2.92	2.83	2.77	2.71	2.67	2.60
14	4.60	3.74	3.34	3.11	2.96	2.85	2.76	2.70	2.65	2.60	2.53
15	4.54	3.68	3.29	3.06	2.90	2.79	2.71	2.64	2.59	2.54	2.48
16	4.49	3.63	3.24	3.01	2.85	2.74	2.66	2.59	2.54	2.49	2.42
17	4.45	3.59	3.20	2.96	2.81	2.70	2.61	2.55	2.49	2.45	2.38
18	4.41	3.55	3.16	2.93	2.77	2.66	2.58	2.51	2.46	2.41	2.34
19	4.38	3.52	3.13	2.90	2.74	2.63	2.54	2.48	2.42	2.38	2.31
20	4.35	3.49	3.10	2.87	2.71	2.60	2.51	2.45	2.39	2.35	2.28

Reject H_0

$\alpha = .05$

0   3.24

Step 3: Perform the Calculations

Using Excel for the calculations, we obtain the results shown in Figure 11.8. You can specify the desired level of significance (Excel's default is $\alpha = .05$). Note that Excel labels *SSA* "between groups" and *SSE* "within groups." This is an intuitive and attractive way to describe the variation.

LO 11-5

Use a table or Excel to find critical values for the *F* distribution.

FIGURE 11.8	Excel's One-Factor ANOVA Results 🗇 Cartons

Anova: Single Factor

SUMMARY

Groups	Count	Sum	Average	Variance
Station 1	5	1210	242	72.5
Station 2	5	1232	246.4	92.3
Station 3	5	1144	228.8	147.7
Station 4	5	1130	226	166

ANOVA

Source of Variation	SS	df	MS	F	P-value	F crit
Between Groups	1479.2	3	493.0667	4.121769	0.024124	3.238872
Within Groups	1914	16	119.625			
Total	3393.2	19				

LO 11-4

Use Excel or other software for ANOVA calculations.

Step 4: Make the Decision

Since the test statistic $F = 4.12$ exceeds the critical value $F_{.05} = 3.24$, we can reject the hypothesis of equal means. Since Excel gives the *p*-value, you don't actually need Excel's critical value. The *p*-value ($p = .024124$) is less than the level of significance ($\alpha = .05$), which confirms that we should reject the hypothesis of equal treatment means. The Excel function for the *p*-value is =F.DIST.RT(4.121769,3,16). For comparison, Figure 11.9 shows MegaStat's ANOVA table for the same data. The results are the same, although MegaStat rounds things off, highlights significant *p*-values, and gives standard deviations instead of variances for each treatment.

FIGURE 11.9   **MegaStat's One-Factor ANOVA Results**   🗁 **Cartons**

One factor ANOVA

Mean	n	Std. Dev	
242.0	5	8.51	Station 1
246.4	5	9.61	Station 2
228.8	5	12.15	Station 3
226.0	5	12.88	Station 4
235.8	20	13.36	Total

ANOVA table

Source	SS	df	MS	F	p-value
Treatment	1,479.20	3	493.067	4.12	.0241
Error	1,914.00	16	119.625		
Total	3,393.20	19			

Step 5: Take Action

As there is a significant difference in means, the distributor will undertake further analysis to see which stations are most efficient and identify possible reasons.

MegaStat provides additional insights by showing a dot plot of observations by group, shown in Figure 11.10. The display includes group means (shown as short horizontal tick marks) and the overall mean (shown as a dashed line). The dot plot suggests that stations 3 and 4 have means below the overall mean, while stations 1 and 2 are above the overall mean.

FIGURE 11.10   **Dot Plot of Four Samples**   🗁 **Cartons**

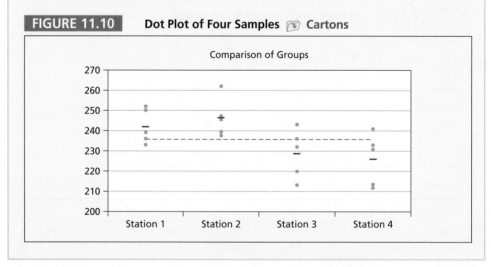

Using MINITAB

MINITAB's output, shown in Figure 11.11, is the same as Excel's except that MINITAB rounds off the results and displays a confidence interval for each group mean, an attractive feature.* In our carton example, the confidence intervals overlap, except possibly stations 2 and 4. But comparing pairs of confidence intervals is not quite the same as what an ANOVA test does, since ANOVA seeks to compare *all* the group means *simultaneously.*

---

*MINITAB and most other statistical packages prefer the data in *stacked* format. Each variable has its own column (e.g., column one contains all the *Y* values, while column two contains group labels like "Station 1"). MINITAB will convert *unstacked* data to *stacked* data for one-factor ANOVA, but not for other ANOVA models.

FIGURE 11.11

MINITAB's One-Factor ANOVA

11.1 Using the following Excel results: (a) What was the overall sample size? (b) How many groups were there? (c) Write the hypotheses. (d) Find the critical value of F for $\alpha = .05$. (e) Calculate the test statistic. (f) Do the population means differ at $\alpha = .05$?

SECTION EXERCISES

connect

ANOVA

Source of Variation	SS	df	MS	F
Between Groups	119.9816	4	29.9954	
Within Groups	583.2201	35	16.6634	
Total	703.2016	39		

11.2 Using the following Excel results: (a) What was the overall sample size? (b) How many groups were there? (c) Write the hypotheses. (d) Find the critical value of F for $\alpha = .10$. (e) Calculate the test statistic. (f) Do the population means differ at $\alpha = .10$?

ANOVA

Source of Variation	SS	df	MS	F
Between Groups	120.8706	3	40.29018	
Within Groups	325.0202	20	16.25101	
Total	445.8907	23		

11.3 In a one-factor ANOVA with sample sizes $n_1 = 5$, $n_2 = 7$, $n_3 = 6$, $n_4 = 7$, $n_5 = 5$, the test statistic was $F_{calc} = 2.447$. (a) State the hypotheses. (b) State the degrees of freedom for the test. (c) What is the critical value of F for $\alpha = .10$? (d) What is your conclusion? (e) Write the Excel function for the p-value.

11.4 In a one-factor ANOVA with sample sizes $n_1 = 8$, $n_2 = 5$, $n_3 = 6$, $n_4 = 6$, the test statistic was $F_{calc} = 3.251$. (a) State the hypotheses. (b) State the degrees of freedom for the test. (c) What is the critical value of F for $\alpha = .05$? (d) What is your conclusion? (e) Write the Excel function for the p-value.

Instructions for exercises 11.5 through 11.8: For each data set: (a) State the hypotheses. (b) Use Excel's Data Analysis (or MegaStat or MINITAB) to perform the one-factor ANOVA, using $\alpha = .05$. (c) State your conclusion about the population means. (d) Interpret the *p*-value. *Optional challenge:* (e) Include a plot of the data for each group (if you are using MegaStat), or confidence intervals for the group means (if you are using MINITAB). What do the plots show?

11.5   Scrap rates per thousand (parts whose defects cannot be reworked) are compared for 5 randomly selected days at three plants. Do the data show a significant difference in mean scrap rates?   ScrapRate

Scrap Rate (Per Thousand Units)		
Plant A	*Plant B*	*Plant C*
11.4	11.1	10.2
12.5	14.1	9.5
10.1	16.8	9.0
13.8	13.2	13.3
13.7	14.6	5.9

11.6   One particular morning, the length of time spent in the examination rooms is recorded for each patient seen by each physician at an orthopedic clinic. Do the data show a significant difference in mean times?   Physicians

Time in Examination Rooms (minutes)			
Physician 1	*Physician 2*	*Physician 3*	*Physician 4*
34	33	17	28
25	35	30	33
27	31	30	31
31	31	26	27
26	42	32	32
34	33	28	33
21		26	40
		29	

11.7   Semester GPAs are compared for seven randomly chosen students in each class level at Oxnard University. Do the data show a significant difference in mean GPAs?   GPA1

GPA for Randomly Selected Students in Four Business Majors			
Accounting	*Finance*	*Human Resources*	*Marketing*
2.48	3.16	2.93	3.54
2.19	3.01	2.89	3.71
2.62	3.07	3.48	2.94
3.15	2.88	3.33	3.46
3.56	3.33	3.53	3.50
2.53	2.87	2.95	3.25
3.31	2.85	3.58	3.20

11.8   Sales of *People* magazine are compared over a 5-week period at four Borders outlets in Chicago. Do the data show a significant difference in mean weekly sales?   Magazines

Weekly Sales			
Store 1	**Store 2**	**Store 3**	**Store 4**
102	97	89	100
106	77	91	116
105	82	75	87
115	80	106	102
112	101	94	100

11.3 MULTIPLE COMPARISONS

Tukey's Test

Besides performing an *F* test to compare the *c* means *simultaneously,* we also could ask whether *pairs* of means differ. You might expect to do a *t* test for two independent means (Chapter 10), or check whether there is overlap in the confidence intervals for each group's mean. But the null hypothesis in ANOVA is that *all* the means are the same, so to maintain the desired overall probability of Type I error, we need to create a *simultaneous confidence interval* for the difference of means based on the *pooled* variances for all *c* groups at once and then see which pairs exclude zero. For *c* groups, there are $c(c-1)/2$ distinct pairs of means to be compared.

Several **multiple comparison** tests are available. Their logic is similar. We will discuss only one, called **Tukey's studentized range test** (sometimes called the *HSD* or "honestly significant difference" test). It has good power and is widely used. We will refer to it as *Tukey's test,* named for statistician John Wilder Tukey (1915–2000). This test is available in most statistical packages (but not in Excel's Data Analysis). It is a two-tailed test for equality of paired means from *c* groups compared simultaneously and is a natural follow-up when the results of the one-factor ANOVA test show a significant difference in at least one mean. The hypotheses to compare group *j* with group *k* are

$H_0: \mu_j = \mu_k$

$H_1: \mu_j \neq \mu_k$

The decision rule is

$$\text{Reject } H_0 \text{ if } T_{\text{calc}} = \frac{|\bar{y}_j - \bar{y}_k|}{\sqrt{MSE\left[\dfrac{1}{n_j} + \dfrac{1}{n_k}\right]}} > T_{c,n-c} \qquad \textbf{(11.10)}$$

where $T_{c,n-c}$ is a critical value of the *Tukey test statistic* T_{calc} for the desired level of significance. Table 11.4 shows 5 percent critical values of $T_{c,n-c}$. If the desired degrees of freedom cannot be found, we could interpolate or rely on a computer package like MegaStat to provide the exact critical value. We take *MSE* directly from the ANOVA calculations (see Table 11.2). The MSE is the *pooled variance* for all *c* samples combined (rather than pooling just two sample variances as in Chapter 10). Therefore, Tukey's test statistic could also be written as

$$T_{\text{calc}} = \frac{|\bar{x}_j - \bar{x}_k|}{\sqrt{\dfrac{s_p^2}{n_j} + \dfrac{s_p^2}{n_k}}} \quad \text{where } s_p^2 = \frac{(n_1-1)s_1^2 + (n_2-1)s_2^2 + \cdots + (n_c-1)s_c^2}{(n_1-1) + (n_2-1) + \cdots + (n_c-1)} \quad \textbf{(11.10a)}$$

This alternative formula reveals similarities to the two-sample *t*-test (e.g., pooled variance) yet also reveals dissimilarities (e.g., pooling of *c* variances instead of just two variances). *MSE* is available from the ANOVA, so we will use the first formula.

$n - c$	Number of Groups (c)								
	2	**3**	**4**	**5**	**6**	**7**	**8**	**9**	**10**
5	2.57	3.26	3.69	4.01	4.27	4.48	4.66	4.81	4.95
6	2.45	3.07	3.46	3.75	3.98	4.17	4.33	4.47	4.59
7	2.37	2.95	3.31	3.58	3.79	3.96	4.11	4.24	4.36
8	2.31	2.86	3.20	3.46	3.66	3.82	3.96	4.08	4.19
9	2.26	2.79	3.12	3.36	3.55	3.71	3.84	3.96	4.06
10	2.23	2.74	3.06	3.29	3.47	3.62	3.75	3.86	3.96
15	2.13	2.60	2.88	3.09	3.25	3.38	3.49	3.59	3.68
20	2.09	2.53	2.80	2.99	3.14	3.27	3.37	3.46	3.54
30	2.04	2.47	2.72	2.90	3.04	3.16	3.25	3.34	3.41
40	2.02	2.43	2.68	2.86	2.99	3.10	3.20	3.28	3.35
60	2.00	2.40	2.64	2.81	2.94	3.05	3.14	3.22	3.29
120	1.98	2.37	2.61	2.77	2.90	3.00	3.09	3.16	3.22
∞	1.96	2.34	2.57	2.73	2.85	2.95	3.03	3.10	3.16

We will illustrate the Tukey test for the carton-packing data. We assume that a one-factor ANOVA has already been performed and the results showed that at least one mean was significantly different. We will use the *MSE* from the ANOVA. For the carton-packing data there are 4 groups and 20 observations, so $c = 4$ and $n - c = 20 - 4 = 16$. From Table 11.4 we must interpolate between $T_{4,15} = 2.88$ and $T_{4,20} = 2.80$ to get $T_{4,16} = 2.86$. The decision rule for any pair of means is therefore

$$\text{Reject } H_0 \text{ if } T_{calc} = \frac{|\bar{y}_j - \bar{y}_k|}{\sqrt{MSE\left[\dfrac{1}{n_j} + \dfrac{1}{n_k}\right]}} > 2.86$$

There may be a different decision rule for every pair of stations unless the sample sizes n_j and n_k are identical (in our example, the group sizes are the same). For example, to compare groups 2 and 4, the test statistic is

$$T_{calc} = \frac{|\bar{y}_2 - \bar{y}_4|}{\sqrt{MSE\left[\dfrac{1}{n_2} + \dfrac{1}{n_4}\right]}} = \frac{|246.4 - 226.0|}{\sqrt{119.625\left[\dfrac{1}{5} + \dfrac{1}{5}\right]}} = 2.95$$

Since $T_{calc} = 2.95$ exceeds 2.86, we reject the hypothesis of equal means for station 2 and station 4. We conclude that there is a significant difference between the mean output of stations 2 and 4. MegaStat shows the critical values $T_{.05} = 2.86$ and $T_{.01} = 3.67$ for the experimentwise error rate in the Tukey test, so you do not need to refer to Table 11.4.

Tukey simultaneous comparison *t* values (d.f. = 16)

		Station 4 226.0	Station 3 228.8	Station 1 242.0	Station 2 246.4
Station 4	226.0				
Station 3	228.8	0.40			
Station 1	242.0	2.31	1.91		
Station 2	246.4	2.95	2.54	0.64	

critical values for experimentwise error rate:

0.05	2.86
0.01	3.67

A similar test must be performed for every possible pair of means. All six possible comparisons of means are shown in Figure 11.12. Only stations 2 and 4 differ at $\alpha = .05$. An attractive feature of MegaStat's Tukey test is that it highlights significant results using color-coding for $\alpha = .05$ and $\alpha = .01$, as seen in Figure 11.12. Note that a *simultaneous* Tukey's *T* test is not the same as comparing individual pairs of means using the independent *t* test discussed in Chapter 10. If enough independent hypotheses are tested from the same data set, eventually we might find a statistically significant result even if none existed in the population. Tukey's *T* test prevents this buildup of the Type I error probability that was explained previously in section 11.2.

SECTION EXERCISES

connect

11.9 Consider a one-factor ANOVA with $n_1 = 9$, $n_2 = 10$, $n_3 = 7$, $n_4 = 8$. (a) How many possible comparisons of means are there? (b) State the degrees of freedom for Tukey's *T*. (c) Find the critical value of Tukey's *T* for $\alpha = .05$.

11.10 Consider a one-factor ANOVA with $n_1 = 6$, $n_2 = 5$, $n_3 = 4$, $n_4 = 6$, $n_5 = 4$. (a) How many possible comparisons of means are there? (b) State the degrees of freedom for Tukey's *T*. (c) Find the critical value of Tukey's *T* for $\alpha = .05$.

Instructions for exercises 11.11 through 11.14: Use MegaStat, MINITAB, or another software package to perform Tukey's test for significant pairwise differences. Perform the test using both the 5 percent and 1 percent levels of significance.

11.11 Refer to Exercise 11.5. Which pairs of mean scrap rates differ significantly (3 plants)? 📁 **ScrapRate**

11.12 Refer to Exercise 11.6. Which pairs of mean examination times differ significantly (4 physicians)? 📁 **Physicians**

11.13 Refer to Exercise 11.7. Which pairs of mean GPAs differ significantly (4 majors)? 📁 **GPA1**

11.14 Refer to Exercise 11.8. Which pairs of mean weekly sales differ significantly (4 stores)? 📁 **Magazines**

11.4 TESTS FOR HOMOGENEITY OF VARIANCES

ANOVA Assumptions

Analysis of variance assumes that observations on the response variable are from normally distributed populations that have the same variance. We have noted that few populations meet these requirements perfectly and unless the sample is quite large, a test for normality is impractical. However, we can easily test the assumption of **homogeneous** (equal) **variances**. Although the one-factor ANOVA test is only slightly affected by inequality of variance when group sizes are equal or nearly so, it is still a good idea to test this assumption. In general, surprisingly large differences in variances must exist to conclude that the population variances are unequal.

Hartley's Test

If we had only two groups, we could use the *F* test you learned in Chapter 10 to compare the variances. But for *c* groups, a more general test is required. One such test is **Hartley's test**, named for statistician H. O. Hartley (1912–1980). The hypotheses are

$H_0: \sigma_1^2 = \sigma_2^2 = \cdots = \sigma_c^2$ (equal variances)

$H_1:$ The σ_j^2 are not all equal (unequal variances)

Hartley's test statistic is the ratio of the largest sample variance to the smallest sample variance:

$$H_{calc} = \frac{s_{max}^2}{s_{min}^2}$$

(11.11)

LO 11-8

Use Hartley's test for equal variances in *c* treatment groups.

The decision rule is:

Reject H_0 if $H_{calc} > H_{critical}$

Critical values of $H_{critical}$ may be found in Table 11.5 using degrees of freedom given by

Numerator: $df_1 = c$

Denominator: $df_2 = \dfrac{n}{c} - 1$

where n is the total number of observations. This test assumes equal group sizes, so df_2 would be an integer. For group sizes that are not drastically unequal, this procedure will still be approximately correct, using the next lower integer if df_2 is not an integer.

TABLE 11.5

Critical 5 Percent Values of Hartley's $H = s^2_{max}/s^2_{min}$

Source: E. S. Pearson and H. O. Hartley, *Biometrika Tables for Statisticians,* 3rd ed. (Oxford University Press, 1970), p. 202. Copyright © 1970 Oxford University Press. Used with permission.

Denominator df_2	Numerator df_1								
	2	3	4	5	6	7	8	9	10
2	39.0	87.5	142	202	266	333	403	475	550
3	15.4	27.8	39.2	50.7	62.0	72.9	83.5	93.9	104
4	9.60	15.5	20.6	25.2	29.5	33.6	37.5	41.1	44.6
5	7.15	10.8	13.7	16.3	18.7	20.8	22.9	24.7	26.5
6	5.82	8.38	10.4	12.1	13.7	15.0	16.3	17.5	18.6
7	4.99	6.94	8.44	9.7	10.8	11.8	12.7	13.5	14.3
8	4.43	6.00	7.18	8.12	9.03	9.78	10.5	11.1	11.7
9	4.03	5.34	6.31	7.11	7.80	8.41	8.95	9.45	9.91
10	3.72	4.85	5.67	6.34	6.92	7.42	7.87	8.28	8.66
12	3.28	4.16	4.79	5.30	5.72	6.09	6.42	6.72	7.00
15	2.86	3.54	4.01	4.37	4.68	4.95	5.19	5.40	5.59
20	2.46	2.95	3.29	3.54	3.76	3.94	4.10	4.24	4.37
30	2.07	2.40	2.61	2.78	2.91	3.02	3.12	3.21	3.29
60	1.67	1.85	1.96	2.04	2.11	2.17	2.22	2.26	2.30
∞	1.00	1.00	1.00	1.00	1.00	1.00	1.00	1.00	1.00

EXAMPLE 11.2

Carton Packing: Tukey Test 📁 **Cartons**

Using the carton-packing data in Table 11.3, there are 4 groups and 20 total observations, so we have

Numerator: $df_1 = c = 4$

Denominator: $df_2 = n/c - 1 = 20/4 - 1 = 5 - 1 = 4$

From Table 11.5 we choose the critical value $H_{critical} = 20.6$ using $df_1 = 4$ and $df_2 = 4$. The sample statistics (from Excel) for our workstations are

Work Station	n	Mean	Variance
Station 1	15	242.0	72.5
Station 2	17	246.4	92.3
Station 3	15	228.8	147.7
Station 4	12	226.0	166.0

The test statistic is

$$H_{calc} = \frac{s^2_{max}}{s^2_{min}} = \frac{166.0}{72.5} = 2.29$$

In this case, we cannot reject the hypothesis of equal variances. Indeed, Table 11.5 makes it clear that unless the sample size is very large, the variance ratio would have to be quite large to reject the hypothesis of equal population variances.

Levene's Test

Hartley's test relies on the assumption of normality in the populations from which the sample observations are drawn. A more robust alternative is **Levene's test**, which does not assume a normal distribution. This test requires a computer package. It is not necessary to discuss the computational procedure except to say that Levene's test is based on the distances of the observations from their sample *medians* rather than their sample *means*. As long as you know how to interpret a *p*-value, Levene's test is easy to use. Figure 11.13 shows MINITAB's output for the test of homogeneity of variance for the carton-packing data using Levene's test, with the added attraction of confidence intervals for each population standard deviation. Since the confidence intervals overlap and the *p*-value (.823) is large, we cannot reject the hypothesis of equal population variances. This confirms that the one-factor ANOVA procedure was appropriate for the carton-packing data.

LO 11-6

Explain the assumptions of ANOVA and why they are important.

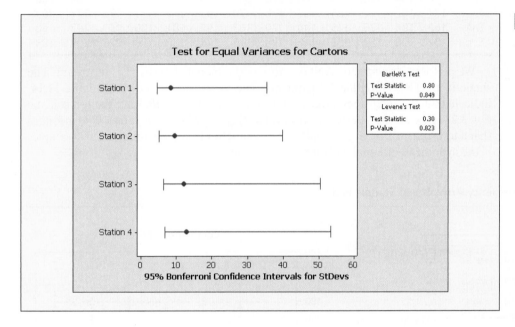

FIGURE 11.13

MINITAB's Equal-Variance Test Cartons

11.15 In a one-factor ANOVA with $n_1 = 6$, $n_2 = 4$, and $n_3 = 5$, the sample variances were $s_1^2 = 121$, $s_2^2 = 929$, and $s_3^2 = 456$. For Hartley's test: (a) State the hypotheses. (b) Calculate the degrees of freedom. (c) Find the critical value at the 5 percent level of significance. (d) Calculate Hartley's test statistic. (e) What is your conclusion?

11.16 In a one-factor ANOVA with $n_1 = 7$, $n_2 = 6$, $n_3 = 5$, $n_4 = 5$, and $n_5 = 7$, the sample standard deviations were $s_1 = 12$, $s_2 = 24$, $s_3 = 16$, $s_4 = 46$, and $s_5 = 27$. For Hartley's test: (a) State the hypotheses. (b) Calculate the degrees of freedom. (c) Find the critical value at the 5 percent level of significance. (d) Calculate Hartley's test statistic. (e) What is your conclusion?

Instructions for exercises 11.17 through 11.20: For each data set, use Hartley's test to test the hypothesis of equal variances, using the 5 percent table of critical values from Table 11.5 and the largest and smallest sample variances from your previous ANOVA. *Optional challenge:* If you have access to MINITAB or another software package, perform Levene's test for equal group variances, discuss the *p*-value, and interpret the graphical display of confidence intervals for standard deviations.

11.17 Refer to Exercise 11.5. Are the population variances the same for scrap rates (3 plants)? **ScrapRate**

11.18 Refer to Exercise 11.6. Are the population variances the same for examination times (4 physicians)? **Physicians**

11.19 Refer to Exercise 11.7. Are the population variances the same for the GPAs (4 majors)? **GPA1**

11.20 Refer to Exercise 11.8. Are the population variances the same for weekly sales (4 stores)? **Magazines**

SECTION EXERCISES

connect

Mini Case   11.1

Hospital Emergency Arrivals

To plan its staffing schedule, a large urban hospital examined the number of arrivals per day over a 13-week period, as shown in Table 11.6. Data are shown in rows rather than in columns to make a more compact table.

TABLE 11.6	Number of Emergency Arrivals by Day of the Week											Emergency
Mon	188	175	208	176	179	184	191	194	174	191	198	213	217
Tue	174	167	165	164	169	164	150	175	178	164	202	175	191
Wed	177	169	180	173	182	181	168	165	174	175	174	177	182
Thu	170	164	190	169	164	170	153	150	156	173	177	183	208
Fri	177	167	172	185	185	170	170	193	212	171	175	177	209
Sat	162	184	173	175	144	170	163	157	181	185	199	203	198
Sun	182	176	183	228	148	178	175	174	188	179	220	207	193

We perform a one-factor ANOVA to test the model *Arrivals = f(Weekday)*. The single factor (*Weekday*) has 7 treatments. The Excel results, shown in Figure 11.14, indicate that *Weekday* does have a significant effect on *Arrivals,* since the test statistic $F = 3.270$ exceeds the 5 percent critical value $F_{6,84} = 2.209$. The *p*-value (.006) indicates that a test statistic this large would arise by chance only about 6 times in 1,000 samples if the hypothesis of equal daily means were true.

FIGURE 11.14

One-Factor ANOVA for Emergency Arrivals and Sample Plot

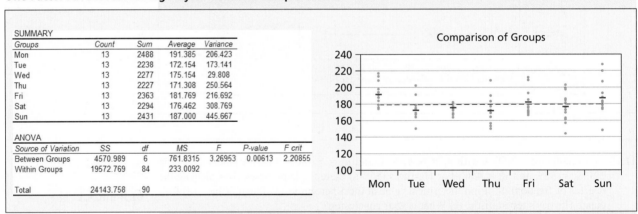

The Tukey multiple comparison test (Figure 11.15) shows that the only pairs of *significantly* different means at $\alpha = .05$ are (*Mon, Tue*) and (*Mon, Thu*). In testing

FIGURE 11.15   MegaStat's Tukey Test for $\mu_j - \mu_k$

Tukey simultaneous comparison *t*-values (d.f. = 84)

		Thu	Tue	Wed	Sat	Fri	Sun	Mon
		171.3	172.2	175.2	176.5	181.8	187.0	191.4
Thu	171.3							
Tue	172.2	0.14						
Wed	175.2	0.64	0.50					
Sat	176.5	0.86	0.72	0.22				
Fri	181.8	1.75	1.61	1.10	0.89			
Sun	187.0	2.62	2.48	1.98	1.76	0.87		
Mon	191.4	3.35	3.21	2.71	2.49	1.61	0.73	

critical values for experimentwise error rate:

0.05	3.03
0.01	3.59

for equal variances, we get conflicting conclusions, depending on which test we use. Hartley's test gives $H_{calc} = (445.667)/(29.808) = 14.95$, which exceeds the critical value $H_{7,12} = 6.09$ (note that *Wed* has a *very* small variance). But Levene's test for homogeneity of variances (Figure 11.16) has a *p*-value of .221, which at $\alpha = .05$ does not allow us to reject the equal-variance assumption that underlies the ANOVA test. When it is available, we prefer Levene's test because it does not depend on the assumption of normality.

FIGURE 11.16   **MINITAB Test for Equal Variances** **Emergency**

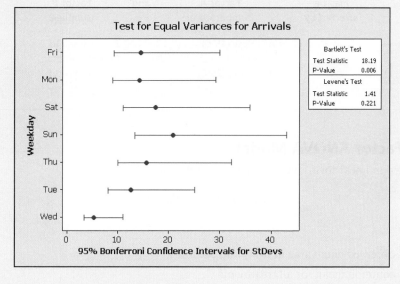

11.5 TWO-FACTOR ANOVA WITHOUT REPLICATION (RANDOMIZED BLOCK MODEL)

Data Format

Suppose that two factors A and B may affect Y. One way to visualize this is to imagine a data matrix with r rows and c columns. Each row is a level of factor A, while each column is a level of factor B. Initially, we will consider the case where all levels of both factors occur, and each cell contains only one observation. In this **two-factor ANOVA without replication** (or *nonrepeated measures design*), each factor combination is observed exactly once. The mean of Y can be computed either across the rows or down the columns, as shown in Table 11.7. The grand mean $\bar{y}$ is the sum of all data values divided by the sample size rc.

TABLE 11.7

Format of Two-Factor ANOVA Data Set without Replication

Levels of Factor A	Levels of Factor B				Row Mean
	B_1	B_2	...	B_c	
A_1	y_{11}	y_{12}	...	y_{1c}	$\bar{y}_{1.}$
A_2	y_{21}	y_{22}	...	y_{2c}	$\bar{y}_{2.}$
...	...	...	...	...	...
A_r	y_{r1}	y_{r2}	...	y_{rc}	$\bar{y}_{r.}$
Col Mean	$\bar{y}_{.1}$	$\bar{y}_{.2}$	...	$\bar{y}_{.c}$	$\bar{y}$

LO 11-9

Recognize from data format when two-factor ANOVA is needed.

Figure 11.17 illustrates a two-factor ANOVA model in which a numerical response variable (paint viscosity) may vary both by temperature (*Factor A*) and by paint supplier (*Factor B*). Three different temperature settings (A_1, A_2, A_3) were tested on shipments from three different suppliers (B_1, B_2, B_3) yielding a table with $3 \times 3 = 9$ cells. Each factor combination is a *treatment*. With only one observation per treatment, no interaction between the two factors is included.*

FIGURE 11.17

Two Factor Model of Paint Viscosity

Two-Factor ANOVA Model

Expressed in linear form, the two-factor ANOVA model is

(11.12)
$$y_{jk} = \mu + A_j + B_k + \varepsilon_{jk}$$

where

y_{jk} = observed data value in row j and column k

μ = common mean for all treatments

A_j = effect of row factor A ($j = 1, 2, \ldots, r$)

B_k = effect of column factor B ($k = 1, 2, \ldots, c$)

ε_{jk} = random error

The random error is assumed to be normally distributed with zero mean and the same variance for all treatments.

Hypotheses to Be Tested

If we are interested only in what happens to the response for the particular levels of the factors that were selected (a *fixed-effects model*), then the hypotheses to be tested are

LO 11-10

Interpret main effects and interaction effects in two-factor ANOVA.

Factor A

H_0: $A_1 = A_2 = \cdots = A_r = 0$ (row means are the same)

H_1: Not all the A_j are equal to zero (row means differ)

Factor B

H_0: $B_1 = B_2 = \cdots = B_c = 0$ (column means are the same)

H_1: Not all the B_k are equal to zero (column means differ)

If we are unable to reject either null hypothesis, all variation in Y is just a random disturbance around the mean μ:

(11.13)
$$y_{jk} = \mu + \varepsilon_{jk}$$

---

*There are not enough degrees of freedom to estimate an interaction unless the experiment is replicated.

Randomized Block Model

A special terminology is used when only one factor is of research interest and the other factor is merely used to control for potential confounding influences. In this case, the two-factor ANOVA model with one observation per cell is sometimes called the **randomized block model**. In the randomized block model, it is customary to call the column effects *treatments* (as in one-factor ANOVA to signify that they are the effect of interest) while the row effects are called *blocks*.* For example, a North Dakota agribusiness might want to study the effect of four kinds of fertilizer (F_1, F_2, F_3, F_4) in promoting wheat growth (Y) on three soil types (S_1, S_2, S_3). To control for the effects of soil type, we could define three blocks (rows) each containing one soil type, as shown in Table 11.8. Subjects within each block (soil type) would be randomly assigned to the treatments (fertilizer).

LO 11-9

Recognize from data format when two-factor ANOVA is needed.

Block (Soil Type)	Treatment (Fertilizer)			
	F_1	F_2	F_3	F_4
S_1				
S_2				
S_3				

TABLE 11.8

Format of Randomized Block Experiment: Two Factors

A randomized block model looks like a two-factor ANOVA and is computed exactly like a two-factor ANOVA. However, its interpretation by the researcher may resemble a one-factor ANOVA since only the column effects (treatments) are of interest. The blocks exist only to reduce variance. The effect of the blocks will show up in the hypothesis test, but is of no interest to the researcher as a separate factor. In short, the difference between a randomized block model and a standard two-way ANOVA model lies in the mind of the researcher. Since calculations for a randomized block design are identical to the two-factor ANOVA with one observation per cell, we will not call the row factor a "block" and the column factor a "treatment." Instead, we just call them *factor A* and *factor B*. Interpretation of the factors is not a mathematical issue. If only the column effect is of interest, you may call the column effect the "treatment."

Format of Calculation of Nonreplicated Two-Factor ANOVA

Calculations for the unreplicated two-factor ANOVA may be arranged as in Table 11.9. Degrees of freedom sum to $n - 1$. For a data set with r rows and c columns, notice that $n = rc$. The total sum of squares shown in Table 11.9 has three components:

$$SST = SSA + SSB + SSE \qquad (11.14)$$

where

SST = total sum of squared deviations about the mean

SSA = between rows sum of squares (effect of factor A)

SSB = between columns sum of squares (effect of factor B)

SSE = error sum of squares (residual variation)

SSE is a measure of unexplained variation. If SSE is relatively high, we would fail to reject the null hypothesis that the factor effects do not differ significantly from zero. Conversely, if SSE is relatively small, it is a sign that at least one factor is a relevant predictor of Y, and we would expect either SSA or SSB (or both) to be relatively large. Before doing the F test, each sum of squares must be divided by its degrees of freedom to obtain the *mean square*.

LO 11-3

Interpret sums of squares and calculations in an ANOVA table.

---

*In principle, either rows or columns could be the blocking factor, but it is customary to put the blocking factor in rows.

TABLE 11.9	Format of Two-Factor ANOVA with One Observation per Cell			
Source of Variation	**Sum of Squares**	**Degrees of Freedom**	**Mean Square**	**F Ratio**
Factor A (row effect)	$SSA = c\sum_{j=1}^{r}(\bar{y}_{j.} - \bar{y})^2$	$r - 1$	$MSA = \dfrac{SSA}{r-1}$	$F_A = \dfrac{MSA}{MSE}$
Factor B (column effect)	$SSB = r\sum_{k=1}^{c}(\bar{y}_{.k} - \bar{y})^2$	$c - 1$	$MSB = \dfrac{SSB}{c-1}$	$F_B = \dfrac{MSA}{MSE}$
Error	$SSE = \sum_{j=1}^{r}\sum_{k=1}^{r}(y_{jk} - \bar{y}_{j.} - \bar{y}_{.k} + \bar{y})^2$	$(r-1)(c-1)$	$MSE = \dfrac{SSE}{(c-1)(r-1)}$	
Total	$SST = \sum_{j=1}^{c}\sum_{k=1}^{r}(y_{jk} - \bar{y})^2$	$rc - 1$		

Calculations are almost always done by a computer. For details of two-factor calculation methods, see *LearningStats* Unit 11. There are case studies for each ANOVA.

EXAMPLE 11.3

Vehicle Acceleration

Drivers expect a car to have good acceleration. A driver is coasting on the highway, with his foot off the accelerator. He steps on the gas to speed up. What is the peak acceleration to a final speed of 80 mph? Tests were carried out on one vehicle at 4 different initial speeds (10, 25, 40, 55 mph) and three different levels of rotation of accelerator pedal (5, 8, 10 degrees). The acceleration results are shown in Table 11.10. Does this sample show that the two experimental factors (pedal rotation, initial speed) are significant predictors of acceleration? Bear in mind that a different sample could yield different results; this is an *unreplicated* experiment.

TABLE 11.10	Maximum Acceleration under Test Conditions Acceleration			
	Initial Speed			
Pedal Rotation	**10 mph**	**25 mph**	**40 mph**	**55 mph**
5 degrees	0.35	0.19	0.14	0.10
8 degrees	0.37	0.28	0.19	0.19
10 degrees	0.42	0.30	0.29	0.23

Note: Maximum acceleration is measured as a fraction of acceleration due to gravity (32 ft./sec.^{2}).

Step 1: State the Hypotheses
It is helpful to assign short, descriptive variable names to each factor. The general form of the model is

$$Acceleration = f(PedalRotation, InitialSpeed)$$

Stated as a linear model:

$$y_{jk} = \mu + A_j + B_k + \varepsilon_{jk}$$

The hypotheses are

Factor A (PedalRotation)

$H_0: A_1 = A_2 = A_3 = 0$ (pedal rotation has no effect)
$H_1:$ Not all the A_j are equal to zero

Factor B (InitialSpeed)

$H_0: B_1 = B_2 = B_3 = B_4 = 0$ (initial speed has no effect)
$H_1:$ Not all the B_k are equal to zero

Step 2: State the Decision Rule

Each F test may require a different right-tail critical value because the numerator degrees of freedom depend on the number of factor levels, while denominator degrees of freedom (error SSE) are the same for all three tests:

Factor A: $df_1 = r - 1 = 3 - 1 = 2$ ($r = 3$ pedal rotations)

Factor B: $df_1 = c - 1 = 4 - 1 = 3$ ($c = 4$ initial speeds)

Error: $df_2 = (r - 1)(c - 1) = (3 - 1)(4 - 1) = 6$

From Appendix F, the 5 percent critical values in a right-tailed test (all ANOVA tests are right-tailed tests) are

$F_{2,6} = 5.14$ for factor A

$F_{3,6} = 4.76$ for factor B

We will reject the null hypothesis (no factor effect) if the F test statistic exceeds the critical value.

Step 3: Perform the Calculations

Calculations are done by using Excel's Data Analysis. The menu and results are shown in Figure 11.18. There is a table of means and variances, followed by the ANOVA table.

LO 11-4

Use Excel or other software for ANOVA calculations.

FIGURE 11.18

Excel's ANOVA: Two-Factor without Replication Acceleration

Anova: Two-Factor Without Replication

SUMMARY	Count	Sum	Average	Variance
5 degrees	4	0.78	0.1950	0.0120
8 degrees	4	1.03	0.2575	0.0074
10 degrees	4	1.24	0.3100	0.0063
10 mph	3	1.14	0.3800	0.0013
25 mph	3	0.77	0.2567	0.0034
40 mph	3	0.62	0.2067	0.0058
55 mph	3	0.52	0.1733	0.0044

ANOVA						
Source of Variation	SS	df	MS	F	P-value	F crit
Rows	0.026517	2	0.013258	22.83732	0.001565	5.143253
Columns	0.073892	3	0.024631	42.42584	0.000196	4.757063
Error	0.003483	6	0.000581			
Total	0.103892	11				

Step 4: Make the Decision

Since $F_A = 22.84$ (rows) exceeds $F_{2,6} = 5.14$, we see that factor A (pedal rotation) has a significant effect on acceleration. The p-value for pedal rotation is very small ($p = .001565$), which says that the F statistic is not due to chance. Similarly, $F_B = 42.43$ exceeds $F_{3,6} = 4.76$, so we see that factor B (initial speed) also has a significant effect on acceleration. Its tiny p-value ($.000196$) is unlikely to be a chance result. In short, we conclude that

• Acceleration is significantly affected by pedal rotation ($p = .001565$).

• Acceleration is significantly affected by initial speed ($p = .000196$).

Step 5: Take Action

The p-values suggest that initial speed is a more significant predictor than pedal rotation, although both are highly significant. These results conform to your own experience. Maximum acceleration ("pushing you back in your seat") from a low speed or standing stop is greater than when you are driving down the freeway, and, of course, the harder you press the accelerator pedal, the faster you will accelerate. In fact, you might think of the pedal rotation as a blocking factor since its relationship to acceleration is tautological and of little research interest. Nonetheless, omitting pedal rotation and using a one-factor model would not be a correct model specification. Further, the engineers who did this experiment were actually interested in both effects.

Visual Display of Data

Figure 11.19 shows MegaStat's dot plot and ANOVA table. The dot plot shows the column factor (presumed to be the factor of research interest) on the horizontal axis, while the row factor (presumed to be a blocking factor) is only used to define the line graphs. MegaStat rounds its ANOVA results more than Excel and highlights significant *p*-values. MegaStat does not provide critical *F* values, which are basically redundant since you have the *p*-values.

FIGURE 11.19

MegaStat's Two-Factor ANOVA (Randomized Block Model) Acceleration

Multiple Comparisons

Figure 11.20 shows MegaStat's Tukey simultaneous comparisons of the treatment pairs using a pooled variance. MegaStat presents Tukey comparisons *only for the column factor* (the row factor is presumed merely to be a blocking factor). MegaStat's Tukey test highlights significant results using color-coding for $\alpha = .05$ and $\alpha = .01$. Three of the comparisons are significant at $\alpha = .01$ ($T_{calc} > 4.97$) and one is significant at $\alpha = .01$ ($T_{calc} > 3.46$). Only two comparisons (45 mph *vs* 40 mph, 40 mph *vs* 55 mph) show no significant difference in mean acceleration.

FIGURE 11.20

MegaStat's Tukey and Independent Sample *t* Tests Acceleration

Tukey simultaneous comparison *t* values (d.f. = 6)

		55 mph	40 mph	25 mph	10 mph
		0.17333	0.20667	0.25667	0.38000
55 mph	0.17333				
40 mph	0.20667	1.69			
25 mph	0.25667	4.24	2.54		
10 mph	0.38000	10.50	8.81	6.27	

critical values for experimentwise error rate:

0.05	3.46
0.01	4.97

LO 11-7

Understand and perform Tukey's test for paired means.

Limitations of Two-Factor ANOVA without Replication

When replication is impossible or extremely expensive, two-factor ANOVA without replication must suffice. For example, crash-testing of automobiles to estimate collision damage is very costly. However, whenever possible, there is a strong incentive to replicate the experiment to add power to the tests. Would different results have been obtained if the car had been tested not once but several times at each speed? Or if several different cars had been tested? For testing acceleration, there would seem to be no major cost impediment to replication except the time and effort required to take the measurements. Of course, it could be argued that if the measurements of acceleration were careful and precise the first time, replication would be a waste of time. And yet, some random variation is found in any experiment. These are matters to ponder. But two-factor ANOVA *with replication* does offer advantages, as you will see.

SECTION EXERCISES

connect

Instructions: For each data set: (a) State the hypotheses. If you are viewing this data set as a randomized block, which is the blocking factor, and why? (b) Use Excel's Data Analysis (or MegaStat or MINITAB) to perform the two-factor ANOVA without replication, using $\alpha = .05$. (c) State your conclusions about the treatment means. (d) Interpret the *p*-values carefully. (e) Include a plot of the data for each group if you are using MegaStat, or individual value plots if you are using MINITAB. What do the plots show?

11.21 Concerned about Friday absenteeism, management examined absenteeism rates for the last three Fridays in four assembly plants. Does this sample provide sufficient evidence to conclude that there is a significant difference in treatment means? **Absences**

	Plant 1	Plant 2	Plant 3	Plant 4
March 4	19	18	27	22
March 11	22	20	32	27
March 18	20	16	28	26

11.22 Engineers are testing company fleet vehicle fuel economy (miles per gallon) performance by using different types of fuel. One vehicle of each size is tested. Does this sample provide sufficient evidence to conclude that there is a significant difference in treatment means? **MPG2**

	87 Octane	89 Octane	91 Octane	Ethanol 5%	Ethanol 10%
Compact	27.2	30.0	30.3	26.8	25.8
Mid-Size	23.0	25.6	28.6	26.6	23.3
Full-Size	21.4	22.5	22.2	18.9	20.8
SUV	18.7	24.1	22.1	18.7	17.4

11.23 Five statistics professors are using the same textbook with the same syllabus and common exams. At the end of the semester, the department committee on instruction looked at average exam scores. Does this sample provide sufficient evidence to conclude that there is a significant difference in treatment means? **ExamScores**

	Prof. Argand	Prof. Blague	Prof. Clagmire	Prof. Dross	Prof. Ennuyeux
Exam 1	80.9	72.3	84.9	81.2	70.9
Exam 2	75.5	74.6	78.7	76.5	70.3
Exam 3	79.0	76.0	79.6	75.0	73.7
Final	69.9	78.0	77.8	74.1	73.9

11.24 A beer distributor is comparing quarterly sales of Coors Light (number of six-packs sold) at three convenience stores. Does this sample provide sufficient evidence to conclude that there is a significant difference in treatment means? **BeerSales**

	Store 1	Store 2	Store 3
Qtr 1	1,521	1,298	1,708
Qtr 2	1,396	1,492	1,382
Qtr 3	1,178	1,052	1,132
Qtr 4	1,730	1,659	1,851

Mini Case   11.2

Automobile Interior Noise Level

Most consumers prefer quieter cars. Table 11.11 shows interior noise level for five vehicles selected from tests performed by a popular magazine. Noise level (in decibels) was measured at idle, at 60 miles per hour, and under hard acceleration from 0 to 60 mph. For reference, 60 dB is a normal conversation, 75 dB is a typical vacuum cleaner, 85 dB is city traffic, 90 dB is a typical hair dryer, and 110 dB is a chain saw. Two questions may be asked: (1) Does noise level vary significantly among the vehicles? (2) Does noise level vary significantly with speed? If you wish to think of this as a randomized block experiment, the column variable (*vehicle type*) is the research question, while the row variable (*speed*) is the blocking factor.

TABLE 11.11   **Interior Noise Levels in Five Randomly Selected Vehicles**
NoiseLevel

Speed	Chrysler 300M	BMW 528i Sport Wagon	Ford Explorer Sport Trac	Chevy Malibu LS	Subaru Outback H6-3.0
Idle	41	45	44	45	46
60 mph	65	67	66	66	76
0–60 mph	76	72	76	77	64

Source: *Popular Science* 254–258 (selected issues).

Note: Data are a random sample to be used for educational purposes only and should not be viewed as a guide to vehicle performance.

The general form of the model is *NoiseLevel* $= f(CarSpeed, CarType)$. Degrees of freedom for *CarSpeed* (rows) will be $r - 1 = 3 - 1 = 2$, while degrees of freedom for *CarType* (columns) will be $c - 1 = 5 - 1 = 4$. Denominator degrees of freedom will be the same for both factors since *SSE* has degrees of freedom $(r - 1)(c - 1) = (3 - 1)(5 - 1) = 8$. Excel's ANOVA results and MegaStat's dot plot are shown in Figure 11.21.

FIGURE 11.21

Results of Two-Factor ANOVA without Replication for Car Noise

SUMMARY	Count	Sum	Average	Variance
Idle	5	221	44.200	3.700
60 mph	5	340	68.000	20.500
0-60 mph	5	365	73.000	29.000
Chrysler 300M	3	182	60.667	320.333
BMW 528i Sport Wagon	3	184	61.333	206.333
Ford Explorer Sport Trac	3	186	62.000	268.000
Chevy Malibu LS	3	188	62.667	264.333
Subaru Outback H6-3.0	3	186	62.000	228.000

ANOVA: Two-Factor Without Replication

Source of Variation	SS	df	MS	F	P-value	F crit
Rows	2368.133	2	1184.067	46.01295	0.00004	4.45897
Columns	6.933333	4	1.733333	0.06736	0.99006	3.83785
Error	205.8667	8	25.73333			
Total	2580.933	14				

Comparison of Groups

Since $F = 46.01$ exceeds $F_{2,8} = 4.46$, we see that *CarSpeed* (row factor) does have a highly significant effect on noise level. Its very small p-value ($p = .00004$) is unlikely to be a chance result. But *CarType* (column factor) has no significant effect on noise level since $F = 0.07$ does not exceed $F_{4,8} = 3.84$. The p-value for *CarType* ($p = .99006$) says that its F statistic could easily have arisen by chance. In short, we conclude that

- Interior noise *is* significantly affected by car speed ($p = .00004$).

- Interior noise *is not* significantly affected by car type ($p = .9901$).

We do not bother with Tukey multiple comparisons of means since we know that car type has no significant effect on noise level (the research hypothesis) and the effect of initial speed is of less research interest (a blocking factor).

11.6 TWO-FACTOR ANOVA WITH REPLICATION (FULL FACTORIAL MODEL)

What Does Replication Accomplish?

In a two-factor model, suppose that each factor combination is observed m times. With multiple observations within each cell, we can do more detailed statistical tests. With an equal number of observations in each cell (*balanced data*), we have a two-factor ANOVA model *with* **replication**. Replication allows us to test not only the factors' **main effects** but also an **interaction effect**. This model is often called the **full factorial** model. In linear model format it may be written

$$y_{ijk} = \mu + A_j + B_k + AB_{jk} + \varepsilon_{ijk} \qquad (11.15)$$

where

y_{ijk} = observation i for row j and column k ($i = 1, 2, \ldots, m$)

μ = common mean for all treatments

A_j = effect attributed to factor A in row j ($j = 1, 2, \ldots, r$)

B_k = effect attributed to factor B in column k ($k = 1, 2, \ldots, c$)

AB_{jk} = effect attributed to interaction between factors A and B

ε_{ijk} = random error (normally distributed, zero mean, same variance for all treatments)

Interaction effects can be important. For example, an agribusiness researcher might postulate that corn yield is related to seed type (A), soil type (B), interaction between seed type and soil type (AB), or all three. An interaction effect can be significant even if the main effects are not. In the absence of any factor effects, all variation about the mean μ is purely random.

Format of Hypotheses

For a fixed-effects ANOVA model, the hypotheses that could be tested in the two-factor ANOVA model with replicated observations are

Factor A: Row Effect

H_0: $A_1 = A_2 = \cdots = A_r = 0$ (row means are the same)

H_1: Not all the A_j are equal to zero (row means differ)

Factor B: Column Effect

H_0: $B_1 = B_2 = \cdots = B_c = 0$ (column means are the same)

H_1: Not all the B_k are equal to zero (column means differ)

LO 11-1

Use basic ANOVA terminology correctly.

LO 11-10

Interpret main effects and interaction effects in two-factor ANOVA.

Interaction Effect

H_0: All the AB_{jk} are equal to zero (there is no interaction effect)

H_1: Not all AB_{jk} are equal to zero (there is an interaction effect)

If none of the proposed factors has anything to do with Y, then the model collapses to

(11.16)
$$y_{ijk} = \mu + \varepsilon_{ijk}$$

Format of Data

Table 11.12 shows the format of a data set with two factors and a balanced (equal) number of observations per treatment (each row/column intersection is a treatment). To avoid needless subscripts, the m observations in each treatment are represented simply as yyy. Except for the replication within cells, the format is the same as the unreplicated two-factor ANOVA.

TABLE 11.12

Data Format of Replicated Two-Factor ANOVA

Levels of Factor A	Levels of Factor B				Row Mean
	B_1	B_2	...	B_c	
A_1	yyy yyy ... yyy	yyy yyy ... yyy	... ...	yyy yyy ... yyy	$\bar{y}_{1.}$
A_2	yyy yyy ... yyy	yyy yyy ... yyy	... ...	yyy yyy ... yyy	$\bar{y}_{2.}$
...	...	...	...	...	...
A_r	yyy yyy ... yyy	yyy yyy ... yyy	... ...	yyy yyy ... yyy	$\bar{y}_{r.}$
Col Mean	$\bar{y}_{.1}$	$\bar{y}_{.2}$	...	$\bar{y}_{.c}$	$\bar{y}$

LO 11-9

Recognize from data format when two-factor ANOVA is needed.

Sources of Variation

There are now three F tests that could be performed: one for each main effect (factors A and B) and a third F test for interaction. The total sum of squares is partitioned into four components:

(11.17)
$$SST = SSA + SSB + SSI + SSE$$

where

SST = total sum of squared deviations about the mean

SSA = between rows sum of squares (effect of factor A)

SSB = between columns sum of squares (effect of factor B)

SSI = interaction sum of squares (effect of AB)

SSE = error sum of squares (residual variation)

For an experiment with r rows, c columns, and m replications per treatment, the sums of squares and ANOVA calculations may be presented in a table, shown in Table 11.13.

If SSE is relatively high, we expect that we would fail to reject H_0 for the various hypotheses. Conversely, if SSE is relatively small, it is likely that at least one of the factors (row effect, column effect, or interaction) is a relevant predictor of Y. Before doing the F test, each sum of squares must be divided by its degrees of freedom to obtain its *mean square*. Degrees of freedom sum to $n - 1$ (note that $n = rcm$).

TABLE 11.13 ▌ **Two-Factor ANOVA with Replication**

Source of Variation	Sum of Squares	Degrees of Freedom	Mean Square	F Ratio
Factor A (row effect)	$SSA = cm\sum_{j=1}^{r}(\bar{y}_{j.} - \bar{y})^2$	$r - 1$	$MSA = \dfrac{SSA}{r-1}$	$F_A = \dfrac{MSA}{MSE}$
Factor B (column effect)	$SSB = rm\sum_{k=1}^{c}(\bar{y}_{.k} - \bar{y})^2$	$c - 1$	$MSB = \dfrac{SSB}{c-1}$	$F_B = \dfrac{MSA}{MSE}$
Interaction (A × B)	$SSI = m\sum_{j=1}^{r}\sum_{k=1}^{c}(\bar{y}_{jk} - \bar{y}_{j.} - \bar{y}_{.k} + \bar{y})^2$	$(r-1)(c-1)$	$MSI = \dfrac{SSI}{(r-1)(c-1)}$	$F_I = \dfrac{MSI}{MSE}$
Error	$SSE = \sum_{i=1}^{m}\sum_{j=1}^{r}\sum_{k=1}^{c}(\bar{y}_{ijk} - \bar{y}_{jk})^2$	$rc(m-1)$	$MSE = \dfrac{SSE}{rc(m-1)}$	
Total	$SST = \sum_{i=1}^{m}\sum_{j=1}^{r}\sum_{k=1}^{c}(y_{ijk} - \bar{y})^2$	$rcm - 1$		

A health maintenance organization orders weekly medical supplies for its four clinics from five different suppliers. Delivery times (in days) for 4 recent weeks are shown in Table 11.14.

EXAMPLE 11.4

Delivery Time

LO 11-3

Interpret sums of squares and calculations in an ANOVA table.

TABLE 11.14 **Delivery Times (in days)** 📨 **Deliveries**

	Supplier 1	Supplier 2	Supplier 3	Supplier 4	Supplier 5
Clinic A	8	14	10	8	17
	8	9	15	7	12
	10	14	10	13	9
	13	11	7	10	10
Clinic B	13	9	12	6	15
	14	9	10	10	12
	12	7	10	12	12
	13	8	11	8	10
Clinic C	11	8	12	10	14
	10	9	10	11	13
	12	11	13	7	10
	14	12	10	10	12
Clinic D	7	8	7	8	14
	10	13	5	5	13
	10	9	6	11	8
	13	12	5	4	11

Using short variable names, the two-factor ANOVA model has the general form

$$DeliveryTime = f(Clinic, Supplier, Clinic \times Supplier)$$

The effects are assumed additive. The linear model is

$$y_{ijk} = \mu + A_j + B_k + AB_{jk} + \varepsilon_{ijk}$$

Step 1: State the Hypotheses
The hypotheses are

Factor A: Row Effect (*Clinic*)

$H_0: A_1 = A_2 = \cdots = A_r = 0$ (clinic means are the same)

H_1: Not all the A_j are equal to zero (clinic means differ)

Factor *B*: Column Effect (*Supplier*)

H_0: $B_1 = B_2 = \cdots = B_c = 0$ (supplier means are the same)

H_1: Not all the B_k are equal to zero (supplier means differ)

Interaction Effect (*Clinic × Supplier*)

H_0: All the AB_{jk} are equal to zero (there is no interaction effect)

H_1: Not all AB_{jk} are equal to zero (there is an interaction effect)

Step 2: State the Decision Rule

Each *F* test may require a different right-tail critical value because the numerator degrees of freedom depend on the number of factor levels, while denominator degrees of freedom (error *SSE*) are the same for all three tests:

Factor A: $df_1 = r - 1 = 4 - 1 = 3$ ($r = 4$ clinics)

Factor B: $df_1 = c - 1 = 5 - 1 = 4$ ($c = 5$ suppliers)

Interaction (AB): $df_1 = (r - 1)(c - 1) = (4 - 1)(5 - 1) = 12$

Error $df_2 = rc(m - 1) = 4 \times 5 \times (4 - 1) = 60$

Excel provides the right-tail *F* critical values for $\alpha = .05$, which we can verify using Appendix F:

$F_{3,60} = 2.76$ for Factor *A*

$F_{4,60} = 2.53$ for Factor *B*

$F_{12,60} = 1.92$ for Factor *AB*

We reject the null hypothesis if an *F* test statistic exceeds its critical value.

Step 3: Perform the Calculations

Excel provides tables of row and column sums and means (not shown here because they are lengthy). The ANOVA table in Figure 11.22 summarizes the partitioning of variation into its component sums of squares, degrees of freedom, mean squares, *F* test statistics, *p*-values, and critical *F*-values for $\alpha = .05$.

FIGURE 11.22

Excel's Two-Factor ANOVA with Replication 📂 **Deliveries**

ANOVA						
Source of Variation	SS	df	MS	F	P-value	F crit
Sample	51.350	3	17.1167	3.434783	0.022424	2.758078
Columns	104.425	4	26.1063	5.238712	0.001097	2.525215
Interaction	102.775	12	8.5646	1.718645	0.085176	1.917396
Within	299.000	60	4.9833			
Total	557.550	79				

Step 4: Make the Decision

For the row variable (*Clinic*), the test statistic $F = 3.435$ and its *p*-value ($p = .0224$) lead us to conclude that the mean delivery times among clinics are not the same at $\alpha = .05$. For the column variable (*Supplier*), the test statistic $F = 5.239$ and its *p*-value ($p = .0011$) lead us to conclude that the mean delivery times from suppliers are not the same at $\alpha = .05$. For the interaction effect, the test statistic $F = 1.719$

and its *p*-value ($p = .0852$) lack significance at $\alpha = .05$. The *p*-values permit a more flexible interpretation since α need not be specified in advance. In summary:

Variable	p-Value	Interpretation
Clinic	.0224	Clinic means differ (significant at $\alpha = .05$)
Supplier	.0011	Supplier means differ (significant at $\alpha = .01$)
Clinic×Supplier	.0852	Weak interaction effect (significant at $\alpha = .10$)

Using MegaStat

MegaStat's two-factor ANOVA results, shown in Figure 11.23, are similar to Excel's except that the table of treatment means is more compact, the results are rounded, and significant *p*-values are highlighted (bright yellow for $\alpha = .01$, light green for $\alpha = .05$).

FIGURE 11.23

MegaStat's Two-Factor ANOVA Deliveries

Two factor ANOVA

Means: Factor 2

Factor 1		Supplier 1	Supplier 2	Supplier 3	Supplier 4	Supplier 5	
	Clinic A	9.8	12.0	10.5	9.5	12.0	10.8
	Clinic B	13.0	8.3	10.8	9.0	12.3	10.7
	Clinic C	11.8	10.0	11.3	9.5	12.3	11.0
	Clinic D	10.0	10.5	5.8	7.0	11.5	9.0
		11.1	10.2	9.6	8.8	12.0	10.3

ANOVA table

Source	SS	df	MS	F	p-value
Factor 1	51.35	3	17.117	3.43	.0224
Factor 2	104.43	4	26.106	5.24	.0011
Interaction	102.78	12	8.565	1.72	.0852
Error	299.00	60	4.983		
Total	557.56	79			

Interaction Effect

The statistical test for interaction is just like any other *F* test. But you might still wonder, What *is* an interaction, anyway? You may be familiar with the idea of drug interaction. If you consume a few ounces of vodka, it has an effect on you. If you take an allergy pill, it has an effect on you. But if you combine the two, the effect may be different (and possibly dangerous) compared with using either drug by itself. That is why many medications carry a warning like "Avoid alcohol while using this medication."

To visualize an interaction, we plot the treatment means for one factor against the levels of the other factor. Within each factor level, we connect the means. In the absence of an interaction, the lines will be roughly parallel or will tend to move in the same direction at the same time. If there is a strong interaction, the lines will have differing slopes and will tend to cross one another.

Figure 11.24 illustrates several possible situations, using a hypothetical two-factor ANOVA model in which factor *A* has three levels and factor *B* has two levels. For the delivery time example, a significant *interaction effect* would mean that suppliers have different mean delivery times for different clinics. However, Figure 11.25 shows that, while the interaction plot lines do cross, there is no consistent pattern, and the lines tend to be parallel more than crossing. The visual indications of interaction are, therefore, weak for the delivery time data. This conclusion is consistent with the interaction *p*-value ($p = .085$) for the *F* test of $A \times B$.

FIGURE 11.24
Possible Interaction Patterns

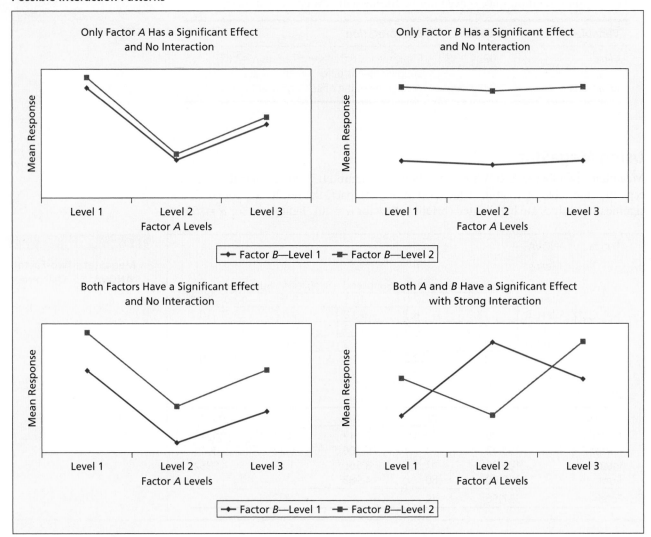

FIGURE 11.25
Interaction Plots from MegaStat 📁 **Deliveries**

Tukey Tests of Pairs of Means

LO 11-7

Understand and perform Tukey's test for paired means.

MegaStat's Tukey comparisons, shown in Figure 11.26, reveal significant differences at $\alpha = .05$ between clinics C, D and between suppliers (1, 4) and (3, 5). At $\alpha = .01$ there is also a significant difference in means between one pair of suppliers (4, 5).

FIGURE 11.26

MegaStat Table of Tukey Comparisons 🖘 **Deliveries**

Tukey simultaneous comparison *t*-values (d.f. = 60)

		Clinic D 9.0	Clinic B 10.7	Clinic A 10.8	Clinic C 11.0
Clinic D	9.0				
Clinic B	10.7	2.41			
Clinic A	10.8	2.55	0.14		
Clinic C	11.0	2.83	0.42	0.28	

critical values for experimentwise error rate:
0.05   2.64
0.01   3.25

Tukey simultaneous comparison *t*-values (d.f. = 60)

		Supplier 4 8.8	Supplier 3 9.6	Supplier 2 10.2	Supplier 1 11.1	Supplier 5 12.0
Supplier 4	8.8					
Supplier 3	9.6	1.03				
Supplier 2	10.2	1.82	0.79			
Supplier 1	11.1	3.01	1.98	1.19		
Supplier 5	12.0	4.12	3.09	2.30	1.11	

critical values for experimentwise error rate:
0.05   2.81
0.01   3.41

Significance versus Importance

MegaStat's table of means (Figure 11.23) allows us to explore these differences further and to assess the question of *importance* as well as *significance*. The largest differences in means between clinics or suppliers are about 2 days. Such a small difference might be unimportant most of the time. However, if their inventory is low, a 2-day difference could be important.

Instructions: For each data set: (a) State the hypotheses. (b) Use Excel's Data Analysis (or MegaStat or MINITAB) to perform the two-factor ANOVA with replication, using $\alpha = .05$. (c) State your conclusions about the main effects and interaction effects. (d) Interpret the *p*-values carefully. (e) Create interaction plots and interpret them.

SECTION EXERCISES

connect

11.25 A small independent stock broker has created four sector portfolios for her clients. Each portfolio always has five stocks that may change from year to year. The volatility (coefficient of variation) of each stock is recorded for each year. Are the main effects significant? Is there an interaction? 🖘 **Volatility**

Year	Stock Portfolio Type			
	Health	**Energy**	**Retail**	**Leisure**
2007	14.5	23.0	19.4	17.6
	18.4	19.9	20.7	18.1
	13.7	24.5	18.5	16.1
	15.9	24.2	15.5	23.2
	16.2	19.4	17.7	17.6
2009	21.6	22.1	21.4	25.5
	25.6	31.6	26.5	24.1
	21.4	22.4	21.5	25.9
	26.6	31.3	22.8	25.5
	19.0	32.5	27.4	26.3
2011	12.6	12.8	22.0	12.9
	13.5	14.4	17.1	11.1
	13.5	13.1	24.8	4.9
	13.0	8.1	13.4	13.3
	13.6	14.7	22.2	12.7

11.26 Oxnard Petro, Ltd., has three interdisciplinary project development teams that function on an ongoing basis. Team members rotate from time to time. Every 4 months (three times a year) each department head rates the performance of each project team (using a 0 to 100 scale, where 100 is the best rating). Are the main effects significant? Is there an interaction? **Ratings**

Year	Marketing	Engineering	Finance
2007	90	69	96
	84	72	86
	80	78	86
2009	72	73	89
	83	77	87
	82	81	93
2011	92	84	91
	87	75	85
	87	80	78

11.27 A market research firm is testing consumer reaction to a new shampoo on four age groups in four regions. There are five consumers in each test panel. Each consumer completes a 10-question product satisfaction instrument with a 5-point scale (5 is the highest rating) and the average score is recorded. Are the main effects significant? Is there an interaction? **Satisfaction**

	Northeast	Southeast	Midwest	West
Youth (under 18)	3.9	3.9	3.6	3.9
	4.0	4.2	3.9	4.4
	3.7	4.4	3.9	4.0
	4.1	4.1	3.7	4.1
	4.3	4.0	3.3	3.9
College (18–25)	4.0	3.8	3.6	3.8
	4.0	3.7	4.1	3.8
	3.7	3.7	3.8	3.6
	3.8	3.6	3.9	3.6
	3.8	3.7	4.0	4.1
Adult (26–64)	3.2	3.5	3.5	3.8
	3.8	3.3	3.8	3.6
	3.7	3.4	3.8	3.4
	3.4	3.5	4.0	3.7
	3.4	3.4	3.7	3.1
Senior (65+)	3.4	3.6	3.3	3.4
	2.9	3.4	3.3	3.2
	3.6	3.6	3.1	3.5
	3.7	3.6	3.1	3.3
	3.5	3.4	3.1	3.4

11.28 Oxnard Petro, Ltd., has three suppliers of catalysts. Orders are placed with each supplier every 15 working days, or about once every 3 weeks. The delivery time (days) is recorded for each order over 1 year. Are the main effects significant? Is there an interaction? **Deliveries2**

	Supplier 1	Supplier 2	Supplier 3
Qtr 1	12	10	16
	15	13	13
	11	11	14
	11	9	14
Qtr 2	13	10	14
	11	10	11
	13	13	12
	12	11	12
Qtr 3	12	11	13
	8	9	8
	8	8	13
	13	6	6
Qtr 4	8	8	11
	10	10	11
	13	10	10
	11	10	11

Mini Case   11.3

Turbine Engine Thrust

Engineers testing turbofan aircraft engines wanted to know if oil pressure and turbine temperature are related to engine thrust (pounds). They chose four levels for each factor and observed each combination five times, using the two-factor replicated ANOVA model *Thrust = f(OilPres, TurbTemp, OilPres×TurbTemp)*. The test data are shown in Table 11.15.

TABLE 11.15   **Turbofan Engine Thrust Test Results**   Turbines

Oil Pressure	Turbine Temperature			
	T1	**T2**	**T3**	**T4**
P1	1,945.0	1,942.3	1,934.2	1,916.7
	1,933.0	1,931.7	1,930.0	1,943.0
	1,942.4	1,946.0	1,944.0	1,948.8
	1,948.0	1,959.0	1,941.0	1,928.0
	1,930.0	1,939.9	1,942.0	1,946.0
P2	1,939.4	1,922.0	1,950.6	1,929.6
	1,952.8	1,936.8	1,947.9	1,930.0
	1,940.0	1,928.0	1,950.0	1,934.0
	1,948.0	1,930.7	1,922.0	1,923.0
	1,925.0	1,939.0	1,918.0	1,914.0
P3	1,932.0	1,939.0	1,952.0	1,960.4
	1,955.0	1,932.0	1,963.0	1,946.0
	1,949.7	1,933.1	1,923.0	1,931.0
	1,933.0	1,952.0	1,965.0	1,949.0
	1,936.5	1,943.0	1,944.0	1,906.0
P4	1,960.2	1,937.0	1,940.0	1,924.0
	1,909.3	1,941.0	1,984.0	1,906.0
	1,950.0	1,928.2	1,971.0	1,925.8
	1,920.0	1,938.9	1,930.0	1,923.0
	1,964.9	1,919.0	1,944.0	1,916.7

Source: Research project by three engineering students enrolled in an MBA program. Data are disguised.

The ANOVA results in Figure 11.27 indicate that only turbine temperature is significantly related to thrust. The table of means suggests that, because mean thrust varies only over a tiny range, the effect may not be very important. The lack of interaction is revealed by the nearly parallel **interaction plots**. Levene's test for equal variances (not shown) shows a *p*-value of $p = .42$ indicating that variances may be assumed equal, as is desirable for an ANOVA test.

FIGURE 11.27   **MegaStat Two-Factor ANOVA Results**

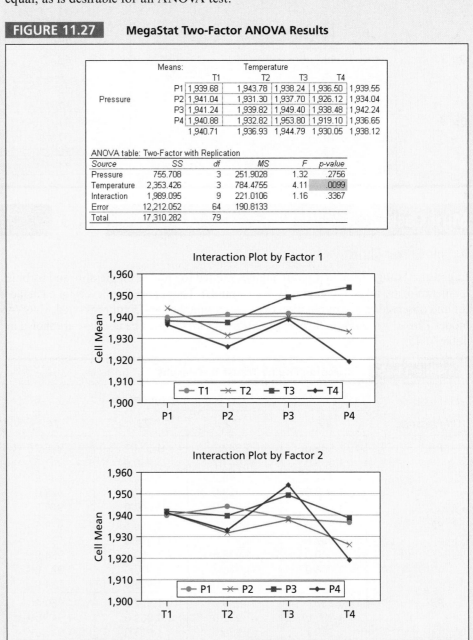

11.7 HIGHER-ORDER ANOVA MODELS (OPTIONAL)

Higher-Order ANOVA Models

Why limit ourselves to two factors? Although a three-factor data set cannot be shown in a two-dimensional table, the idea of a three-factor ANOVA is not difficult to grasp. Consider the paint viscosity problem introduced at the beginning of this chapter. Figure 11.28 adds a third factor (solvent ratio) to the paint viscosity model.

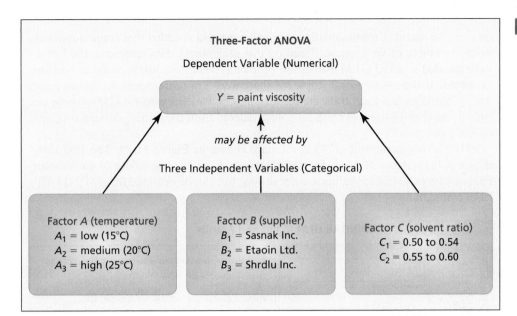

FIGURE 11.28

Three-Factor ANOVA Model for Paint Viscosity

A three-factor ANOVA allows more two-factor interactions ($A \times B$, $A \times C$, $B \times C$) and even a three-factor interaction ($A \times B \times C$). However, since the computations are already done by computer, the analysis would be no harder than a two-factor ANOVA. The "catch" is that higher-order ANOVA models are beyond Excel's capabilities, so you will need fancier software. Fortunately, any general-purpose statistical package (e.g., MINITAB, SPSS, SAS) can handle ANOVA with *any* number of factors with *any* number of levels (subject to computer software limitations).

What Is GLM?

The **general linear model** (GLM) is a versatile tool for estimating large and complex ANOVA models. Besides allowing more than two factors, GLM permits unbalanced data (unequal sample size within treatments) and any desired subset of interactions among factors (including three-way interactions or higher) as long as you have enough observations (i.e., enough degrees of freedom) to compute the effects. GLM can also provide predictions and identify unusual observations. GLM does not require equal variances, although care must be taken to avoid sparse or empty cells in the data matrix. Data are expected to be in stacked format (one column for Y and one column for each factor A, B, C, etc.). The output of GLM is easily understood by anyone who is familiar with ANOVA, as you can see in Mini Case 11.4.

Mini Case   11.4

Hospital Maternity Stay 🖻 **MaternityLOS**

The data set consists of 4,409 maternity hospital visits whose DRG (diagnostic-related group) code is 373 (simple delivery without complicating diagnoses). The dependent variable of interest is the length of stay (LOS) in the hospital. The model contains one discrete numerical factor and two categorical factors: the number of surgical stops (*NumStops*), the CCS diagnostic code (*CCSDiag*), and the CCS procedure code (*CCSProc*). CCS codes are a medical classification scheme developed by the American Hospital Research Council to help hospitals and researchers organize medical information. The proposed model has three factors and one interaction:

$$LOS = f(NumStops, CCSDiag, CCSProc, CCSDiag \times CCSProc)$$

Before starting the GLM analysis, a frequency tabulation was prepared for each factor. The tabulation (not shown) revealed that some factor levels were observed too rarely to be useful. Cross-tabulations (not shown) also revealed that some treatments would be empty or very sparse. Based on this preliminary data screening, the factors were recoded to avoid GLM estimation problems. *NumStops* was recoded as a binary variable (2 if there were 1 or 2 stops, 3 if there were 3 or more stops). *CCSDiag* codes with a frequency less than 100 were recoded as 999. Patients whose *CCSProc* code occurred less than 10 times (19 patients) were deleted from the sample, leaving a sample of 4,390 patients.

MINITAB's menu and GLM results are shown in Figure 11.29. The first thing shown is the number of levels for each factor and the discrete values of each factor. Frequencies of the factor values are not shown, but can be obtained from MINITAB's Tables command.

FIGURE 11.29   MINITAB GLM Menu and Results

The *p*-values from the ANOVA table suggest that *NumStops* is significant at $\alpha = .10$ ($p = .072$) while the other two main effects, *CCSDiag* and *CCSProc* ($p = .000$ and $p = .001$), are highly significant (such small *p*-values would arise less than once in 1,000 samples if there were no relationship). The interaction *CCSDiag*$\times$*CCSProc* is also highly significant ($p = .000$). Because the sample size is large, even slight effects could be *significant*, so further analysis may be needed to see if the effects are also *important*.

LO 11-11

Recognize the need for experimental design and GLM (optional).

What Is Experimental Design?

Experimental design refers to the number of factors under investigation, the number of levels assigned to each factor, the way factor levels are defined, and the way observations are obtained. *Fully crossed* or *full factorial* designs include all possible combinations of factor levels. **Fractional factorial designs**, for reasons of economy, limit data collection to a subset of possible factor combinations. If all levels of one factor are fully contained in another, the design is **nested** or **hierarchical**. **Balanced designs** are characterized by an equal number of observations for each factor combination. In a *fixed-effects model*, the levels of each factor are predetermined, which implies that our inferences are valid only for the specified factor levels. For example, if a firm has only three paint suppliers (S_1, S_2, S_3), these would be our factor levels. In a *random effects model*, the factor levels would be chosen randomly from a population of potential factor levels. For example, if a firm has 20 paint suppliers (S_1 through S_{20}) but we only want to study three of them, we might choose three at random (say S_7, S_{11}, and S_{18}) from the 6,840 possible ways to choose 3 items from 20. Fixed effects are by far the most common models used in business analysis, where randomization and controlled experiments are not practical.

Experimental design is a specialized topic that goes far beyond this textbook. However, you may need to interact professionally with engineers or quality improvement teams that are working on product design, reliability, and product performance. It is therefore helpful to have a general idea of what experimental design is all about and to learn some of the basic terminology. If you become more deeply involved, you can ask your employer to send you to a 3-day training class in experimental design to boost your skills.

2^k Models

When there are k factors, each with two levels, we have a *2^k factorial design*. Reducing a factor to two levels is a useful simplification that reduces the data requirements in a replicated experiment because the data matrix will have fewer cells. Even a continuous factor (e.g., *Pressure*) can be "binarized" into roughly equal groups (*Low, High*) by cutting the data array at the median. The 2^k design is especially useful when the number of factors is very large. In automotive engineering, for example, it is not uncommon to study more than a dozen factors that are predictive of exhaust emissions. Even when each factor is limited to only two levels, full factorial 2^k experiments with replication can require substantial data-collection effort.

Fractional Factorial Designs

Unlike a full factorial design, a *fractional factorial* design, for reasons of economy, limits data collection to a subset of the possible factor combinations. Fractional factorial designs are important in real-life situations where many factors exist. For example, suppose that automobile combustion engineers are investigating 10 factors, each with two levels, to determine their effect on emissions. This would yield $2^{10} = 1,024$ possible factor combinations. It would be impractical and uneconomical to gather data for all 1,024 factor combinations.

By excluding some factor combinations, a fractional factorial model necessarily sacrifices some of the interaction effects. But if the most important objective is to study the *main effects* (which is frequently the case, or is at least an acceptable compromise), it is possible to get by with a much smaller number of observations. It often is possible to estimate some, though not all, interaction effects in a fractional factorial experiment. Templates are published to guide experimenters in choosing the correct design and sample size for the desired number of factors (see Related Reading) to make efficient use of available data.

Nested or Hierarchical Design

If all levels of one factor are fully contained within another, the design is *nested* or *hierarchical*. Using most computer packages, nested designs can be represented using simple notation like

$$Defects = f\,(Experience,\ Method\,(Machine))$$

In this model, *Machine* is nested within *Method* so the effect of *Machine* cannot appear as a main effect. Presumably the nature of the manufacturing process dictates that *Machine* depends on *Method*. Although the model is easy to state, this example is not intended to suggest that estimates of nested models are easy to interpret.

Random Effects Models

In a *fixed-effects model* the levels of each factor are predetermined, which implies that our inferences are valid only for the specified factor levels. In a *random effects model* the factor levels are chosen randomly from a population of potential factor levels. Computation and interpretation of random effects are more complicated, and not all tests may be feasible. Novices are advised that estimation of random effects models should be preceded by further study (see Related Reading).

CHAPTER SUMMARY

ANOVA tests whether a numerical dependent variable (**response variable**) is associated with one or more categorical independent variables (**factors**) with several **levels.** Each level or combination of levels is a treatment. A **one-factor ANOVA** compares means in c columns of data. It is a generalization of a two-tailed t test for two independent sample means. Fisher's F **statistic** is a ratio of two variances (treatment versus error). It is compared with a right-tailed critical value from an F table or from Excel for appropriate numerator and denominator degrees of freedom. Alternatively, we can compare the p-value for the F test statistic with the desired level of significance (any p-value less than α is significant). An **unreplicated two-factor ANOVA** can be viewed as a **randomized block model** if only one factor is of research interest. A **replicated two-factor ANOVA** (or full factorial model) has more than one observation per treatment, permitting inclusion of an interaction test in addition to tests for the **main effects. Interaction effects** can be seen as crossing lines on plots of factor means. The **Tukey test** compares individual treatment means. We test for homogeneous variances (an assumption of ANOVA) using **Hartley's test** or **Levene's test.** The **general linear model** (GLM) can be used when there are more than two factors. **Experimental design** helps make efficient use of limited data. Other general advice:

- ANOVA may be helpful even if those who collected the data did not utilize a formal experimental design (often the case in real-world business situations).

- ANOVA calculations are tedious because of the sums required, so computers are generally used.

- One-factor ANOVA is the most common and suffices for many business situations.

- ANOVA is an overall test. To tell which specific pairs of treatment means differ, use the Tukey test.

- Although real-life data may not perfectly meet the normality and equal-variance assumptions, ANOVA is reasonably robust (and alternative tests do exist).

KEY TERMS

analysis of variance (ANOVA), *439*	general linear model, *475*	partitioned sum of squares, *443*
balanced designs, *476*	Hartley's test, *453*	randomized block model, *459*
completely randomized model, *442*	hierarchical design, *476*	replication, *465*
experimental design, *476*	homogeneous variances, *453*	response variable, *439*
explained variance, *439*	interaction effect, *465*	treatment, *439*
factors, *439*	interaction plots, *474*	Tukey's studentized range test, *451*
fixed-effects model, *443*	Levene's test, *455*	two-factor ANOVA without replication, *457*
fractional factorial designs, *476*	main effects, *465*	unexplained variance, *439*
full factorial, *465*	mean squares, *444*	
	multiple comparison, *451*	
	nested design, *476*	
	one-factor ANOVA, *439*	

CHAPTER REVIEW

Note: Questions labeled * are based on optional material from this chapter.

1. Explain each term: (a) explained variation; (b) unexplained variation; (c) factor; (d) treatment.

2. (a) Explain the difference between one-factor and two-factor ANOVA. (b) Write the linear model form of one-factor ANOVA. (c) State the hypotheses for a one-factor ANOVA in two different ways. (d) Why is one-factor ANOVA used a lot?

3. (a) State three assumptions of ANOVA. (b) What do we mean when we say that ANOVA is fairly robust to violations of these assumptions?

4. (a) Sketch the format of a one-factor ANOVA data set (completely randomized model). (b) Must group sizes be the same for one-factor ANOVA? Is it better if they are? (c) Explain the concepts of variation *between treatments* and variation *within treatments*. (d) What is the F statistic? (e) State the degrees of freedom for the F test in one-factor ANOVA.

5. (a) Sketch the format of a two-factor ANOVA data set without replication. (b) State the hypotheses for a two-factor ANOVA without replication. (c) What is the difference between a randomized block model and a two-factor ANOVA without replication? (d) What do the two F statistics represent in a two-factor ANOVA without replication? (e) What are their degrees of freedom?

6. (a) Sketch the format of a two-factor ANOVA data set with replication. (b) What is gained by replication? (c) State the hypotheses for a two-factor ANOVA with replication. (d) What do the three F statistics represent in a two-factor ANOVA with replication? (e) What are their degrees of freedom?

7. (a) What is the purpose of the Tukey test? (b) Why can't we just compare all possible pairs of group means using the two-sample t test?

8. (a) What does a test for homogeneity of variances tell us? (b) Why should we test for homogeneity of variances? (c) Explain what Hartley's test measures. (d) Why might we use Levene's test instead of Hartley's test?

*9. What is the general linear model and why is it useful?

*10. (a) What is a 2^k design, and what are its advantages? (b) What is a fractional factorial design, and what are its advantages? (c) What is a nested or hierarchical design? (d) How is a random effects model different than a fixed-effects model?

CHAPTER EXERCISES

connect

Instructions: You may use Excel, MegaStat, MINITAB, or another computer package of your choice. Attach appropriate copies of the output or capture the screens, tables, and relevant graphs and include them in a written report. Try to state your conclusions succinctly in language that would be clear to a decision maker who is a nonstatistician. Exercises marked * are based on optional material. Answer the following questions, or those your instructor assigns.

a. Choose an appropriate ANOVA model. State the hypotheses to be tested.

b. Display the data visually (e.g., dot plots or MegaStat's line plots). What do the displays show?

c. Do the ANOVA calculations using the computer.

d. State the decision rule for $\alpha = .05$ and make the decision. Interpret the p-value.

e. In your judgment, are the observed differences in treatment means (if any) large enough to be of practical importance?

f. Given the nature of the data, would more data collection be practical?

g. Perform Tukey multiple comparison tests and discuss the results.

h. Perform a test for homogeneity of variances. Explain fully.

11.29 Below are grade point averages for 25 randomly chosen university business students during a recent semester. *Research question:* Are the mean grade point averages the same for students in these four class levels? 📄 **GPA2**

Grade Point Averages of 25 Business Students			
Freshman (5 students)	*Sophomore* (7 students)	*Junior* (7 students)	*Senior* (6 students)
1.91	3.89	3.01	3.32
2.14	2.02	2.89	2.45
3.47	2.96	3.45	3.81
2.19	3.32	3.67	3.02
2.71	2.29	3.33	3.01
	2.82	2.98	3.17
	3.11	3.26	

11.30 The XYZ Corporation is interested in possible differences in days worked by salaried employees in three departments in the financial area. A survey of 23 randomly chosen employees reveals the data shown below. Because of the casual sampling methodology in this survey, the sample sizes are unequal. *Research question:* Are the mean annual attendance rates the same for employees in these three departments? 📄 **DaysWorked**

Days Worked Last Year by 23 Employees									
Department	**Days Worked**								
Budgets (5 workers)	278	260	265	245	258				
Payables (10 workers)	205	270	220	240	255	217	266	239	240	228
Pricing (8 workers)	240	258	233	256	233	242	244	249	

11.31 Mean output of solar cells of three types are measured six times under random light intensity over a period of 5 minutes, yielding the results shown. *Research question:* Is the mean solar cell output the same for all cell types? 📖 **SolarWatts**

Solar Cell Output (watts)

Cell Type			Output (watts)			
A	123	121	123	124	125	127
B	125	122	122	121	122	126
C	126	128	125	129	131	128

11.32 In a bumper test, three types of autos were deliberately crashed into a barrier at 5 mph, and the resulting damage (in dollars) was estimated. Five test vehicles of each type were crashed, with the results shown below. *Research question:* Are the mean crash damages the same for these three vehicles? 📖 **Crash1**

Crash Damage ($)

Goliath	Varmint	Weasel
1,600	1,290	1,090
760	1,400	2,100
880	1,390	1,830
1,950	1,850	1,250
1,220	950	1,920

11.33 The waiting time (in minutes) for emergency room patients with non-life-threatening injuries was measured at four hospitals for all patients who arrived between 6:00 and 6:30 p.m. on a certain Wednesday. The results are shown below. *Research question:* Are the mean waiting times the same for emergency patients in these four hospitals? 📖 **ERWait**

Emergency Room Waiting Time (minutes)

Hospital A (5 patients)	Hospital B (4 patients)	Hospital C (7 patients)	Hospital D (6 patients)
10	8	5	0
19	25	11	20
5	17	24	9
26	36	16	5
11		18	10
		29	12
		15	

11.34 The results shown below are mean productivity measurements (average number of assemblies completed per hour) for a random sample of workers at each of three plants. *Research question:* Are the mean hourly productivity levels the same for workers in these three plants? 📖 **Productivity**

Hourly Productivity of Assemblers in Plants

Plant			Finished Units Produced per Hour						
A (9 workers)	3.6	5.1	2.8	4.6	4.7	4.1	3.4	2.9	4.5
B (6 workers)	2.7	3.1	5.0	1.9	2.2	3.2			
C (10 workers)	6.8	2.5	5.4	6.7	4.6	3.9	5.4	4.9	7.1	8.4

11.35 Below are results of braking tests of the Ford Explorer on glare ice, packed snow, and split traction (one set of wheels on ice, the other on dry pavement), using three braking methods. *Research question:* Is the mean stopping distance affected by braking method and/or by surface type? 📖 **Braking**

Stopping Distance from 40 mph to 0 mph

Method	Ice	Split Traction	Packed Snow
Pumping	441	223	149
Locked	455	148	146
ABS	460	183	167

Source: *Popular Science* 252, no. 6 (June 1998), p. 78.

11.36 An MBA director examined GMAT scores for the first 10 MBA applicants (assumed to be a random sample of early applicants) for four academic quarters. *Research question:* Do the mean GMAT scores for early applicants differ by quarter? 📁 **GMAT**

GMAT Scores of First Ten Applicants

Fall	490	580	440	580	430	420	640	470	530	640
Winter	310	590	730	710	540	450	670	390	500	470
Spring	500	450	510	570	610	490	450	590	640	650
Summer	450	590	710	240	510	670	610	550	540	540

11.37 An ANOVA study was conducted to compare dental offices in five small towns. The response variable was the number of days each dental office was open last year. *Research question:* Is there a difference in the means among these five towns? 📁 **DaysOpen**

Dental Clinic Days Open during the Last Year in Five Towns

Chalmers	Greenburg	Villa Nueve	Ulysses	Hazeltown
230	194	206	198	214
215	193	200	186	196
221	208	208	206	194
205	198	206	189	190
232		232	181	203
210		208		

11.38 The Environmental Protection Agency (EPA) advocates a maximum arsenic level in water of 10 micrograms per liter. Below are results of EPA tests on randomly chosen wells in a suburban Michigan county. *Research question:* Is the mean arsenic level affected by well depth and/or age of well? 📁 **Arsenic**

Arsenic Level in Wells (micrograms per liter)

Well Depth	Under 10	Age of Well (years) 10 to 19	20 and Over
Shallow	5.4	6.1	6.8
	4.3	4.1	5.4
	6.1	5.8	5.7
Medium	3.4	5.1	4.5
	3.7	3.7	5.5
	4.3	4.4	4.6
Deep	2.4	3.8	3.9
	2.9	2.7	2.9
	2.7	3.4	4.0

11.39 Is a state's income related to its high school dropout rate? *Research question:* Do the high school dropout rates differ among the five income quintiles? 📁 **Dropout**

State High School Dropout Rates by Income Groups

Lowest Income Quintile		2nd Income Quintile		3rd Income Quintile		4th Income Quintile		Highest Income Quintile	
State	Dropout %	State	Dropout %	State	Dropout %	State	Dropout %	State	Dropout %
Mississippi	40.0	Kentucky	34.3	N. Carolina	39.5	Oregon	26.0	Minnesota	15.3
W. Virginia	24.2	S. Carolina	44.5	Wyoming	23.3	Ohio	30.5	Illinois	24.6
New Mexico	39.8	N. Dakota	15.5	Missouri	27.6	Pennsylvania	25.1	California	31.7
Arkansas	27.3	Arizona	39.2	Kansas	25.5	Michigan	27.2	Colorado	28.0
Montana	21.5	Maine	24.4	Nebraska	12.1	Rhode Island	31.3	N. Hampshire	27.0
Louisiana	43.0	S. Dakota	28.1	Texas	39.4	Alaska	33.2	Maryland	27.4
Alabama	39.0	Tennessee	40.1	Georgia	44.2	Nevada	26.3	New York	39.0
Oklahoma	26.9	Iowa	16.8	Florida	42.2	Virginia	25.7	New Jersey	20.4
Utah	16.3	Vermont	19.5	Hawaii	36.0	Delaware	35.9	Massachusetts	25.0
Idaho	22.0	Indiana	28.8	Wisconsin	21.9	Washington	25.9	Connecticut	28.2

Source: *Statistical Abstract of the United States, 2002.*

11.40 In a bumper test, three test vehicles of each of three types of autos were crashed into a barrier at 5 mph, and the resulting damage was estimated. Crashes were from three angles: head-on, slanted, and rear-end. The results are shown below. *Research questions:* Is the mean repair cost affected by crash type and/or vehicle type? Are the observed effects (if any) large enough to be of practical importance (as opposed to statistical significance)? 📄 **Crash2**

5 mph Collision Damage ($)

Crash Type	Goliath	Varmint	Weasel
Head-on	700	1,700	2,280
	1,400	1,650	1,670
	850	1,630	1,740
Slant	1,430	1,850	2,000
	1,740	1,700	1,510
	1,240	1,650	2,480
Rear-end	700	860	1,650
	1,250	1,550	1,650
	970	1,250	1,240

11.41 As a volunteer for a consumer research group, LaShonda was assigned to analyze the freshness of three brands of tortilla chips. She examined four randomly chosen bags of chips for four brands of chips from three different stores. She recorded the number of days from the current date until the "fresh until" expiration date printed on the package. *Research question:* Do mean days until the expiration date differ by brand or store? *Note:* Some data values are negative. 📄 **Freshness**

Days Until Expiration Date on Package

	Store 1	Store 2	Store 3
Brand A	−1	25	17
	−1	24	18
	20	10	21
	22	27	6
Brand B	−7	15	29
	30	−8	40
	24	6	24
	23	31	50
Brand C	16	11	41
	7	16	17
	16	30	27
	19	21	18
Brand D	21	42	31
	11	32	30
	10	38	39
	19	28	45

11.42 Three samples of each of three types of PVC pipe of equal wall thickness are tested to failure under three temperature conditions, yielding the results shown below. *Research questions:* Is mean burst strength affected by temperature and/or by pipe type? Is there a "best" brand of PVC pipe? Explain. 📄 **PVCPipe**

Burst Strength of PVC Pipes (psi)

Temperature	*PVC1*	*PVC2*	*PVC3*
Hot (70° C)	250	301	235
	273	285	260
	281	275	279
Warm (40° C)	321	342	302
	322	322	315
	299	339	301
Cool (10° C)	358	375	328
	363	355	336
	341	354	342

11.43 Below are data on truck production (number of vehicles completed) during the second shift at five truck plants for each day in a randomly chosen week. *Research question:* Are the mean production rates the same by plant and by day? 📄 **Trucks**

Trucks Produced during Second Shift

	Mon	*Tue*	*Wed*	*Thu*	*Fri*
Plant A	130	157	208	227	216
Plant B	204	230	252	250	196
Plant C	147	208	234	213	179
Plant D	141	200	288	260	188

11.44 To check pain-relieving medications for potential side effects on blood pressure, it is decided to give equal doses of each of four medications to test subjects. To control for the potential effect of weight, subjects are classified by weight groups. Subjects are approximately the same age and are in general good health. Two subjects in each category are chosen at random from a large group of male prison volunteers. Subjects' blood pressures 15 minutes after the dose are shown below. *Research question:* Is mean blood pressure affected by body weight and/or by medication type? 📄 **Systolic**

Systolic Blood Pressure of Subjects (mmHg)

Ratio of Subject's Weight to Normal Weight	*Medication M1*	*Medication M2*	*Medication M3*	*Medication M4*
Under 1.1	131	146	140	130
	135	136	132	125
1.1 to 1.3	136	138	134	131
	145	145	147	133
1.3 to 1.5	145	149	146	139
	152	157	151	141

11.45 To assess the effects of instructor and student gender on student course scores, an experiment was conducted in 11 sections of managerial accounting classes ranging in size from 25 to 66 students. The factors were instructor gender (*M*, *F*) and student gender (*M*, *F*). There were 11 instructors (7 male, 4 female). Steps were taken to eliminate subjectivity in grading, such as common exams and sharing exam grading responsibility among all instructors so no one instructor could influence exam grades unduly. (a) What type of ANOVA is this? (b) What conclusions can you draw? (c) Discuss sample size and raise any questions you think may be important.

Analysis of Variance for Students' Course Scores

Source of Variation	Sum of Squares	Degrees of Freedom	Mean Square	F Ratio	p-Value
Instructor gender (*I*)	97.84	1	97.84	0.61	0.43
Student gender (*S*)	218.23	1	218.23	1.37	0.24
Interaction (*I* × *S*)	743.84	1	743.84	4.66	0.03
Error	63,358.90	397	159.59		
Total	64,418.81	400			

Source: Marlys Gascho Lipe, "Further Evidence on the Performance of Female versus Male Accounting Students," *Issues in Accounting Education* 4, no. 1 (Spring 1989), pp. 144–50.

11.46 In a market research study, members of a consumer test panel are asked to rate the visual appeal (on a 1 to 10 scale) of the texture of dashboard plastic trim in a mockup of a new fuel cell car. The manufacturer is testing four finish textures. Panelists are assigned randomly to evaluate each texture. The test results are shown below. Each cell shows the average rating by panelists who evaluated each texture. *Research question:* Is mean rating affected by age group and/or by surface type? **Texture**

Mean Ratings of Dashboard Surface Texture

Age Group	Shiny	Satin	Pebbled	Pattern
Youth (under 21)	6.7	6.6	5.5	4.3
Adult (21 to 39)	5.5	5.3	6.2	5.9
Middle-Age (40 to 61)	4.5	5.1	6.7	5.5
Senior (62 and over)	3.9	4.5	6.1	4.1

11.47 This table shows partial results for a one-factor ANOVA, (a) Calculate the *F* test statistic. (b) Calculate the *p*-value using Excel's function =F.DIST.RT(F,DF1,DF2). (c) Find the critical value $F_{.05}$ from Appendix F or using Excel's function =F.INV.RT(.05,DF1,DF2). (d) Interpret the results.

ANOVA Source of Variation	SS	df	MS	F	p-value	$F_{.05}$
Between groups	3207.5	3	1069.17			
Within groups	441730	36	12270.28			
Total	444937.5	39				

11.48 (a) What kind of ANOVA is this (one-factor, two-factor, or two-factor with replication)? (b) Calculate each *F* test statistic. (b) Calculate the *p*-value for each *F* test using Excel's function =F.DIST.RT(F,DF1,DF2). (c) Interpret the results.

ANOVA Source of Variation	SS	df	MS	F	p-value
Factor A	36,598.56	3	12,199.52		
Factor B	22,710.29	2	11,355.15		
Interaction	177,015.38	6	29,502.56		
Error	107,561.25	36	2,987.81		
Total	343,885.48	47			

11.49 Here is an Excel ANOVA table for an experiment to assess the effects of ambient noise level and plant location on worker productivity. (a) What kind of ANOVA is this (one-factor, two-factor, two-factor replicated)? (b) Describe the original data format (i.e., how many rows, columns, and observations per cell). (c) At $\alpha = 0.05$ what are your conclusions?

ANOVA						
Source of Variation	SS	df	MS	F	p-value	$F_{.05}$
Plant location	3.0075	3	1.0025	2.561	0.1200	3.863
Noise level	8.4075	3	2.8025	7.16	0.0093	3.863
Error	3.5225	9	0.3914			
Total	14.9375					

11.50 Several friends go bowling several times per month. They keep track of their scores over several months. An ANOVA was performed. (a) What kind of ANOVA is this (one-factor, two-factor, etc.)? (b) How many friends were there? How many months were observed? How many observations per bowler per month? Explain how you know. (c) At $\alpha = .01$, what are your conclusions about bowling scores? Explain, referring either to the F tests or p-values.

ANOVA						
Source of Variation	SS	df	MS	F	p-value	F crit
Month	1702.389	2	851.194	11.9793	0.0002	3.4028
Bowler	4674.000	3	1558.000	21.9265	0.0000	3.0088
Interaction	937.167	6	156.194	2.1982	0.0786	2.5082
Within	1705.333	24	71.056			
Total	9018.889	35				

11.51 Air pollution (micrograms of particulate per ml of air) was measured along four freeways at each of five different times of day, with the results shown below. (a) What kind of ANOVA is this (one-factor, two-factor, etc.)? (b) What is your conclusion about air pollution? Explain, referring either to the F tests or p-values. (c) Do you think the variances can be assumed equal? Explain your reasoning. Why does it matter? (d) Perform Hartley's test to test for unequal variances.

SUMMARY	Count	Sum	Average	Variance
Chrysler	5	1584	316.8	14333.7
Davidson	5	1047	209.4	3908.8
Reuther	5	714	142.8	2926.7
Lodge	5	1514	302.8	11947.2
12:00A-6:00A	4	505	126.25	872.9
6:00A-10:00A	4	1065	266.25	11060.3
10:00A-3:00P	4	959	239.75	5080.3
3:00P-7:00P	4	1451	362.75	14333.6
7:00P-12:00A	4	879	219.75	7710.9

ANOVA						
Source of Variation	SS	df	MS	F	p-value	F crit
Freeway	100957.4	3	33652.45	24.903	0.000	3.490
Time of Day	116249.2	4	29062.3	21.506	0.000	3.259
Error	16216.4	12	1351.367			
Total	233423	19				

11.52 A company has several suppliers of office supplies. It receives several shipments each quarter from each supplier. The time (days) between order and delivery was recorded for several randomly chosen shipments from each supplier in each quarter, and an ANOVA was performed. (a) What kind of ANOVA is this (one-factor, two-factor, etc.)? (b) How many suppliers were there? How many quarters? How many observations per supplier per quarter? Explain how you know. (c) At $\alpha = .01$, what are your conclusions about shipment time? Explain, referring either to the F tests or p-values.

ANOVA

Source of Variation	SS	df	MS	F	p-value	F crit
Quarter	148.04	3	49.34667	6.0326	0.0009	2.7188
Supplier	410.14	4	102.535	12.5348	0.0000	2.4859
Interaction	247.06	12	20.5883	2.5169	0.0073	1.8753
Within	654.40	80	8.180			
Total	1459.64	99				

11.53 Several friends go bowling several times per month. They keep track of their scores over several months. An ANOVA was performed. (a) What kind of ANOVA is this (one-factor, two-factor, etc.)? (b) How could you tell how many friends there were in the sample just from the ANOVA table? Explain. (c) What are your conclusions about bowling scores? Explain, referring either to the F test or p-value. (d) Do you think the variances can be assumed equal? Explain your reasoning.

SUMMARY

Bowler	Count	Sum	Average	Variance
Mary	15	1856	123.733	77.067
Bill	14	1599	114.214	200.797
Sally	12	1763	146.917	160.083
Robert	15	2211	147.400	83.686
Tom	11	1267	115.182	90.164

ANOVA

Source of Variation	SS	df	MS	F	p-value	F crit
Between Groups	14465.63	4	3616.408	29.8025	0.0000	2.5201
Within Groups	7523.444	62	121.3459			
Total	21989.07	66				

11.54 Are large companies more profitable *per dollar of assets*? The largest 500 companies in the world were ranked according to their number of employees, with groups defined as follows: Small = Under 25,000 employees, Medium = 25,000 to 49,999 employees, Large = 50,000 to 99,000 employees, Huge = 100,000 employees or more. An ANOVA was performed using the company's profit-to-assets ratio (percent) as the dependent variable. (a) What kind of ANOVA is this (one-factor, two-factor, etc.)? (b) What is your conclusion about the research question? Explain, referring either to the F test or p-value. (c) What can you learn from the plots that compare the groups? (d) Do you think the variances can be assumed equal? Explain your reasoning. (e) Perform Hartley's test to test for unequal variances. (f) Which groups of companies have significantly different means? Explain.

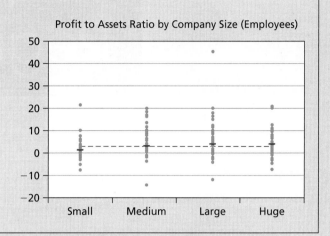

Mean	n	Std. Dev	
1.054	119	2.8475	Small
3.058	113	4.8265	Medium
3.855	147	5.8610	Large
3.843	120	4.3125	Huge
3.004	499	4.7925	Total

ANOVA table

Source	SS	df	MS	F	p-value
Treatment	643.9030	3	214.63433	9.84	2.58E-06
Error	10,794.2720	495	21.80661		
Total	11,438.1750	498			

Post hoc analysis
Tukey simultaneous comparison t-values (d.f. = 495)

		Small 1.054	Medium 3.058	Huge 3.843	Large 3.855
Small	1.054				
Medium	3.058	3.27			
Huge	3.843	4.62	1.28		
Large	3.855	4.86	1.37	0.02	

critical values for experimentwise error rate:

0.05	2.60
0.01	3.18

Profit to Assets Ratio by Company Size (Employees)

RELATED READING

Box, George E.; J. Stuart Hunter; and William G. Hunter. *Statistics for Experimenters.* 2nd ed. John Wiley & Sons, 2005.

Hilbe, Joseph M. "Generalized Linear Models." *The American Statistician* 48, no. 3 (August 1994), pp. 255–65.

Kutner, Michael H.; Christopher Nachtsheim; John Neter; and William Li. *Applied Linear Statistical Models.* 5th ed. McGraw-Hill, 2005.

Montgomery, Douglas C. *Design and Analysis of Experiments.* 5th ed. John Wiley & Sons, 2000.

CHAPTER 11   Online Learning Resources

The Online Learning Center (OLC) at www.mhhe.com/doane4e has several *LearningStats* demonstrations to help you understand analysis of variance. Your instructor may assign one or more of them, or you may decide to download the ones that sound interesting.

Topic	*LearningStats Demonstrations*
Excel examples	⊠ Examples: ANOVA Tests ⊠ ANOVA Simulation
Tables	⊠ Appendix F—Critical Values of *F*

Key: ⊠ = Excel

Simple Regression

CHAPTER CONTENTS

CHAPTER LEARNING OBJECTIVES

LO   **When you finish this chapter you should be able to**

LO 12-1   Calculate and test a correlation coefficient for significance.

LO 12-2   Interpret the slope and intercept of a regression equation.

LO 12-3   Make a prediction for a given x value using a regression equation.

LO 12-4   Fit a simple regression on an Excel scatter plot.

LO 12-5   Calculate and interpret confidence intervals for regression coefficients.

LO 12-6   Test hypotheses about the slope and intercept by using t tests.

LO 12-7   Perform regression analysis with Excel or other software.

LO 12-8   Interpret the standard error, R^2, ANOVA table, and F test.

LO 12-9   Distinguish between confidence and prediction intervals for Y.

LO 12-10 Test residuals for violations of regression assumptions.

LO 12-11 Identify unusual residuals and high-leverage observations.

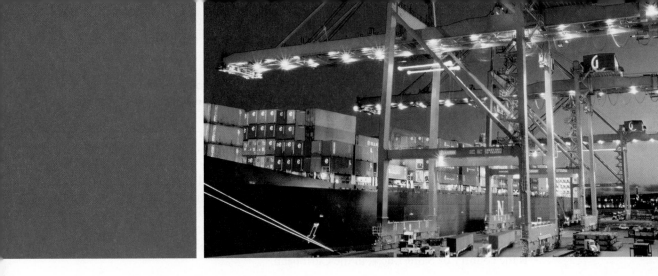

12.1 VISUAL DISPLAYS AND CORRELATION ANALYSIS

Up to this point, our study of the discipline of statistical analysis has primarily focused on learning how to describe and make inferences about single variables. It is now time to learn how to describe and summarize relationships *between* variables. Businesses of all types can be quite complex. Understanding how different variables in our business processes are related to each other helps us predict and, hopefully, improve our business performance.

Examples of quantitative variables that might be related to each other include: spending on advertising and sales revenue, produce delivery time and percentage of spoiled produce, premium and regular gas prices, preventive maintenance spending and manufacturing productivity rates. It may be that with some of these pairs there is one variable that we would like to be able to *predict* such as sales revenue, percentage of spoiled produce, and productivity rates. But first we must learn how to *visualize, describe,* and *quantify* the relationships between variables such as these.

Visual Displays

Analysis of **bivariate data** (i.e., two variables) typically begins with a **scatter plot** that displays each observed data pair (x_i, y_i) as a dot on an *X-Y* grid. This diagram provides a visual indication of the strength of the relationship or association between the two random variables. This simple display requires no assumptions or computation. A scatter plot is typically the precursor to more complex analytical techniques. Figure 12.1 shows a scatter plot comparing the average price per gallon of regular unleaded gasoline to the average price per gallon of premium gasoline for all 50 states.

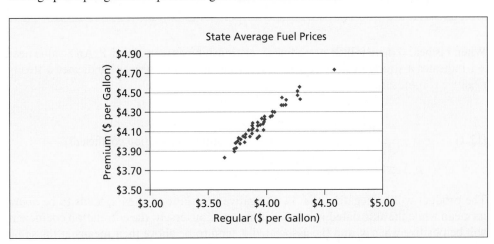

FIGURE 12.1

**Fuel Prices
(*n* = 50 states)**
FuelPrices

Source: AAA Fuel Gauge Report, May 8, 2011, www.fuelgaugereport.aaa.com

We look at scatter plots to get an initial idea of the relationship between two random variables. Is there an evident pattern to the data? Is the pattern linear or nonlinear? Are there data points that are not part of the overall pattern? We would characterize the fuel price relationship as linear (although not perfectly linear) and positive (as premium prices increase, so do regular unleaded prices). We see one pair of values set slightly apart from the rest, above and to the right. This happens to be the state of Hawaii.

In contrast to the positive relationship seen in Figure 12.1, Figure 12.2 shows a negative relationship. This scatter plot compares the incidence of infectious disease to average IQ scores for 184 different countries. We would characterize this relationship as fairly linear and negative (as the incidence of infectious disease decreases, the average IQ score increases). We see one pair of unusual values near the bottom of the scatter plot, which is the country of Saint Lucia, in the Caribbean.

FIGURE 12.2

IQ Scores (n = 184 countries)

📁 **IQScores**

Source: Christopher Eppig, Corey L. Fincher, and Randy Thornhill, "Parasite Prevalence and the Worldwide Distribution of Cognitive Ability," *Proceedings of the Royal Society of Biological Sciences* (published online June 30, 2010). Used with permission.

Correlation Coefficient

A visual display is a good first step in analysis, but we would also like to quantify the strength of the association between two variables. Therefore, accompanying the scatter plot is the **sample correlation coefficient** (also called the Pearson correlation coefficient.) This statistic measures the degree of linearity in the relationship between two random variables X and Y and is denoted r. Its value will fall in the interval $[-1, 1]$.

Strong Negative Correlation   *No Correlation*   *Strong Positive Correlation*

−1.00   0.00   +1.00

LO 12-1

Calculate and test a correlation coefficient for significance.

When r is near 0 there is little or no linear relationship between X and Y. An r-value near +1 indicates a strong positive relationship, while an r-value near −1 indicates a strong negative relationship.

$$(12.1) \qquad r = \frac{\sum\limits_{i=1}^{n}(x_i - \bar{x})(y_i - \bar{y})}{\sqrt{\sum\limits_{i=1}^{n}(x_i - \bar{x})^2}\sqrt{\sum\limits_{i=1}^{n}(y_i - \bar{y})^2}} \qquad \text{(sample correlation coefficient)}$$

The product will be negative, that is, a negative correlation, when x_i tends to be *above* its mean while the associated y_i is *below* its mean. Conversely, the correlation coefficient will be positive when x_i and the associated y_i tend to be above their means at the same time or below their means at the same time. To simplify the notation here and elsewhere in this chapter, we define three terms called **sums of squares**:

$$SS_{xx} = \sum_{i=1}^{n}(x_i - \bar{x})^2 \qquad SS_{yy} = \sum_{i=1}^{n}(y_i - \bar{y})^2 \qquad SS_{xy} = \sum_{i=1}^{n}(x_i - \bar{x})(y_i - \bar{y}) \quad \textbf{(12.2)}$$

Using this notation, the formula for the sample correlation coefficient can be written

$$r = \frac{SS_{xy}}{\sqrt{SS_{xx}}\sqrt{SS_{yy}}} \qquad \text{(sample correlation coefficient)} \qquad \textbf{(12.3)}$$

Excel Tip

To calculate a sample correlation coefficient, use Excel's function =CORREL(array1,array2) where array1 is the range for X and array2 is the range for Y. Data may be in rows or columns. Arrays must be the same length.

The correlation coefficient for the variables shown in Figure 12.1 is $r = .970$, which is not surprising. We would expect to see a strong linear positive relationship between state regular unleaded gasoline prices and premium gasoline prices. The correlation coefficient for the variables shown in Figure 12.2 is $r = -.822$. We observed a fairly linear negative relationship between infectious disease incidence and average IQ scores. Figure 12.3 shows prototype scatter plots. We see that a correlation of .500 implies a great deal of random variation, and even a correlation of .900 is far from "perfect" linearity. The last scatter plot shows $r = .00$ despite an obvious *curvilinear* relationship between X and Y. This illustrates the fact that a correlation coefficient only measures the degree of *linear* relationship between X and Y.

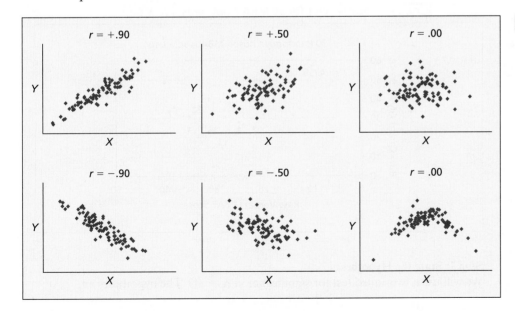

FIGURE 12.3

Scatter Plots Showing Various Correlation Coefficient Values $(n = 100)$

Correlation analysis has many business applications. For example:

- Financial planners study correlations between asset classes over time, in order to help their clients diversify their portfolios.
- Marketing analysts study correlations between customer online purchases in order to develop new web advertising strategies.
- Human resources experts study correlations between measures of employee performance in order to devise new job-training programs.

Tests for Significance Using Student's *t*

The sample correlation coefficient r is an estimate of the **population correlation coefficient** ρ (the Greek letter *rho*). There is no flat rule for a "high" correlation because sample size must be taken into consideration. To test the hypothesis $H_0\colon \rho = 0$, the test statistic is

(12.4)
$$t_{\text{calc}} = r\sqrt{\frac{n-2}{1-r^2}}\qquad\text{(test for zero correlation)}$$

We compare this t test statistic with a critical value of t for a one-tailed or two-tailed test from Appendix D using $d.f. = n - 2$ degrees of freedom and any desired α. Recall that we lose a degree of freedom for each parameter that we estimate when we calculate a statistic. Because both $\bar{x}$ and $\bar{y}$ are used to calculate r, we lose 2 degrees of freedom and so $d.f. = n - 2$. After calculating the t **statistic**, we can find its p-value by using Excel's function =T.DIST.2T(t,deg_freedom). MINITAB directly calculates the p-value for a two-tailed test without displaying the t statistic.

EXAMPLE 12.1

MBA Applicants

📁 **MBA**

In its admission decision process, a university's MBA program examines an applicant's score on the GMAT (Graduate Management Aptitude Test), which has both verbal and quantitative components. Figure 12.4 shows the scatter plot with the sample correlation coefficient for 30 MBA applicants randomly chosen from 1,961 MBA applicant records at a public university in the Midwest. Is the correlation ($r = .4356$) between verbal and quantitative GMAT scores statistically significant? It is not clear from the scatter plot shown in Figure 12.4 that there is a statistically significant linear relationship.

FIGURE 12.4   **Scatter Plot for 30 MBA Applicants** 📁 **MBA**

Step 1: State the Hypotheses
We will use a two-tailed test for significance at $\alpha = .05$. The hypotheses are

$H_0\colon \rho = 0$
$H_0\colon \rho \neq 0$

Step 2: Specify the Decision Rule
For a two-tailed test using $d.f. = n - 2 = 30 - 2 = 28$ degrees of freedom, Appendix D gives $t_{.025} = 2.048$. The decision rule is

Reject H_0 if $t_{\text{calc}} > 2.048$ or if $t_{\text{calc}} < -2.048$.

Step 3: Calculate the Test Statistic
To calculate the test statistic, we first need to calculate the value for r. Using Excel's function =CORREL(array1,array2), we find $r = .4356$ for the variables *Quant GMAT* and *Verbal GMAT*. We must then calculate t_{calc}.

$$t_{calc} = r\sqrt{\frac{n-2}{1-r^2}} = .4356\sqrt{\frac{30-2}{1-(.4356)^2}} = 2.561$$

Step 4: Make a Decision
The test statistic value ($t_{calc} = 2.561$) exceeds the critical value $t_{.025} = 2.048$, so we reject the hypothesis of zero correlation at $\alpha = .05$. We can also find the *p*-value using the Excel function =T.DIST.2T(t,deg_freedom). The two-tailed *p*-value for GMAT score is =T.DIST.2T(2.561,28) = .0161. We would reject $\rho = 0$ since the *p*-value < .05.

Step 5: Take Action
The admissions officers recognize that these scores tend to vary together for applicants.

Critical Value for Correlation Coefficient

An equivalent approach is to calculate a critical value for the correlation coefficient. First, look up the critical value of t from Appendix D with $d.f. = n - 2$ degrees of freedom for either a one-tailed or two-tailed test, with the α you choose. Then, the critical value of the correlation coefficient, $r_{critical}$, is

$$r_{critical} = \frac{t}{\sqrt{t^2 + n - 2}} \qquad \text{(critical value for a correlation coefficient)} \qquad \textbf{(12.5)}$$

An advantage of this method is that you get a benchmark for the correlation coefficient. Its disadvantage is that there is no *p*-value and it is inflexible if you change your mind about α. MegaStat uses this method, giving two-tail critical values for $\alpha = .05$ and $\alpha = .01$.

Table 12.1 shows that, as sample size increases, the critical value of r becomes smaller. Thus, in very large samples, even very small correlations could be "significant." In a larger sample, smaller values of the sample correlation coefficient can be considered "significant." While a larger sample does give a better estimate of the true value of ρ, a larger sample does *not* mean that the correlation is stronger nor does its increased *significance* imply increased *importance*.

Sample Size	$r_{.05}$	$r_{.01}$
$n = 25$	.395	.504
$n = 50$	.279	.361
$n = 100$	.197	.256
$n = 200$	.139	.182

TABLE 12.1

Values for $r_{critical}$ for Different Sample Sizes

Tip

In large samples, small correlations may be significant, even if the scatter plot shows little evidence of linearity. Thus, a *significant* correlation may lack practical *importance*.

SECTION EXERCISES

connect

12.1   For each sample, do a test for zero correlation. (a) Use Appendix D to find the critical value of t_α. (b) State the hypotheses about ρ. (c) Perform the t test and report your decision.

a. $r = +.45, n = 20, \alpha = .05$, two-tailed test
b. $r = -.35, n = 30, \alpha = .10$, two-tailed test
c. $r = +.60, n = 7, \alpha = .05$, right-tailed test
d. $r = -.30, n = 61, \alpha = .01$, left-tailed test

Instructions for exercises 12.2 and 12.3: (a) Make an Excel scatter plot. What does it suggest about the population correlation between X and Y? (b) Make an Excel worksheet to calculate SS_{xx}, SS_{yy}, and SS_{xy}. Use these sums to calculate the sample correlation coefficient. Check your work by using Excel's function =CORREL(array1,array2). (c) Use Appendix D to find $t_{.025}$ for a two-tailed test for zero correlation at $\alpha = .05$. (d) Calculate the t test statistic. Can you reject $\rho = 0$? (e) Use Excel's function =T.DIST.2T(t,deg_freedom) to calculate the two-tail p-value.

12.2   College Student Weekly Earnings in Dollars ($n = 5$) 🖫 WeekPay

Hours Worked (X)	Weekly Pay (Y)
10	93
15	171
20	204
20	156
35	261

12.3   Phone Hold Time for Concert Tickets in Seconds ($n = 5$) 🖫 CallWait

Operators (X)	Wait Time (Y)
4	385
5	335
6	383
7	344
8	288

Instructions for exercises 12.4–12.6: (a) Make a scatter plot of the data. What does it suggest about the correlation between X and Y? (b) Use Excel, MegaStat, or MINITAB to calculate the correlation coefficient. (c) Use Excel or Appendix D to find $t_{.025}$ for a two-tailed test at $\alpha = .05$. (d) Calculate the t test statistic. (e) Can you reject $\rho = 0$?

12.4   Moviegoer Snack Spending ($n = 10$) 🖫 Movies

Age (X)	Spent (Y)	Age (X)	Spent (Y)
30	2.85	33	6.75
50	6.50	36	3.60
34	1.50	26	6.10
12	6.35	18	8.35
37	6.20	46	4.35

12.5   Annual Percent Return on Mutual Funds ($n = 17$) 🖫 Portfolio

Last Year (X)	This Year (Y)
11.9	15.4
19.5	26.7
11.2	18.2
14.1	16.7
14.2	13.2
5.2	16.4
20.7	21.1
11.3	12.0
−1.1	12.1
3.9	7.4
12.9	11.5
12.4	23.0
12.5	12.7
2.7	15.1
8.8	18.7
7.2	9.9
5.9	18.9

12.6   Order Size and Shipping Cost ($n = 12$) 🖫 ShipCost

Orders (X)	Ship Cost (Y)
1,068	4,489
1,026	5,611
767	3,290
885	4,113
1,156	4,883
1,146	5,425
892	4,414
938	5,506
769	3,346
677	3,673
1,174	6,542
1,009	5,088

Mini Case   12.1

Do Loyalty Cards Promote Sales Growth?

A business can achieve sales growth by increasing the number of new customers. Another way is by increasing business from existing customers. Loyal customers visit more often, thus contributing to sales growth. Loyalty cards are used by many companies to foster positive relationships with their customers. Customers carry a card that records the number of purchases or visits they make. They are rewarded with a free item or discount after so many visits. But do these loyalty cards provide incentive to repeat customers to visit more often? Surprisingly, Noodles & Company found out that this wasn't happening in some markets. After several years of running a loyalty card program without truly measuring its impact on the business, in 2005, Noodles performed a correlation analysis on the variables "Sales Growth Percentage" and "Loyalty Card Sales Percentage." The results showed that in some markets there was no significant correlation, meaning the loyalty cards weren't associated with increased sales revenue. However, in other markets there was actually *a statistically significant negative correlation*. In other words, loyalty cards were associated with a decrease in sales growth. Why? Ultimately, the free visits that customers had earned were replacing visits that they would have otherwise paid full price for. Moreover, the resources the company was devoting to the program were taking away from more proven sales-building techniques, such as holding nonprofit fundraisers or tastings for local businesses. Based on this analysis, Noodles & Company made the decision to discontinue their loyalty card program and focused on other approaches to building loyal customers. See Chapter Exercise 12.64.

12.2 SIMPLE REGRESSION

What Is Simple Regression?

Correlation coefficients and scatter plots provide clues about relationships among variables and may suffice for some purposes. But often, the analyst would like to mathematically model the relationship for prediction purposes. For example, a business might hypothesize that

- Advertising expenditures predict quarterly sales revenue.
- Number of dependents predicts employee prescription drug expenses.
- Apartment size predicts monthly rent.
- Engine horsepower predicts miles per gallon.

The hypothesized relationship may be linear, quadratic, or some other form. For now we will focus on the simple linear model in slope-intercept form: $Y = \text{slope} \times X + y\text{-intercept}$. In statistics this straight-line model is often referred to as a **simple regression equation**. The slope and intercept of the simple regression equation are used to describe the relationship between the two variables.

We define the Y variable as the **response variable** (the *dependent variable*) and the X variable as the **predictor variable** (the *independent variable*). If the relationship can be estimated, a business can explore policy questions such as

- How much extra sales will be generated, on average, by a $1 million increase in advertising expenditures? What would expected sales be with no advertising?
- How much do prescription drug costs per employee rise, on average, with each extra dependent? What would be the expected cost if the employee had no dependents?
- How much extra rent, on average, is paid per extra square foot?
- How much fuel efficiency, on average, is lost when the engine horsepower is increased?

Terms You Should Know

The *response* variable is the *dependent* variable. This is the Y variable. The *predictor* variable is the *independent* variable. This is the X variable. Only the dependent variable (not the independent variable) is treated as a random variable.

Interpreting an Estimated Regression Equation

LO 12-2

Interpret the slope and intercept of a regression equation.

The intercept and slope of an estimated regression can provide useful information. For example:

$Sales = 268 + 7.37\,Ads$

Each extra $1 million of advertising will generate $7.37 million of sales on average. The firm would average $268 million of sales with zero advertising. However, the intercept may not be meaningful because $Ads = 0$ may be outside the range of observed data.

$DrugCost = 410 + 550\,Dependents$

Each extra dependent raises the mean annual prescription drug cost by $550. An employee with zero dependents averages $410 in prescription drugs.

$Rent = 150 + 1.05\,SqFt$

Each extra square foot adds $1.05 to monthly apartment rent. The intercept is not meaningful because no apartment can have $SqFt = 0$.

$MPG = 49.22 - 0.079\,Horsepower$

Each unit increase in engine horsepower decreases the fuel efficiency by 0.079 mile per gallon. The intercept is not meaningful because a zero horsepower engine does not exist.

Cause and Effect?

When we propose a regression model, we might have a causal mechanism in mind, but cause and effect is not proven by a simple regression. We cannot assume that the explanatory variable is "causing" the variation we see in the response variable.

Prediction Using Regression

LO 12-3

Make a prediction for a given *x* value using a regression equation.

One of the main uses of regression is to make predictions. Once we have a fitted regression equation that shows the estimated relationship between X (the independent variable) and Y (the dependent variable), we can plug in any value of X to obtain the prediction for Y. For example:

$Sales = 268 + 7.37\,Ads$

If the firm spends $10 million on advertising, its predicted sales would be $341.7 million, that is, $Sales = 268 + 7.37\,(10) = 341.7$.

$DrugCost = 410 + 550\,Dependents$

If an employee has four dependents, the predicted annual drug cost would be $2,610, that is, $DrugCost = 410 + 550(4) = 2,610$.

$Rent = 150 + 1.05\,SqFt$

The predicted rent on an 800-square-foot apartment is $990, that is, $Rent = 150 + 1.05\,(800) = 990$.

$MPG = 49.22 - 0.079\,Horsepower$

If an engine has 200 horsepower, the predicted fuel efficiency is 33.42 mpg, that is, $MPG = 49.22 - 0.079(200) = 33.42$.

Range of *X*

Predictions from our fitted regression model are stronger within the range of our observed *x* values. The relationship seen in the scatter plot may not be true for values far outside our observation window. *Extrapolation* outside the observed range of *x* is always tempting but should be approached with caution.

12.7 (a) Interpret the slope of the fitted regression *HomePrice* = 125,000 + 150 *SquareFeet*. (b) What is the prediction for *HomePrice* if *SquareFeet* = 2,000? (c) Would the intercept be meaningful if this regression applies to home sales in a certain subdivision?

12.8 (a) Interpret the slope of the fitted regression *Sales* = 842 − 37.5 *Price*. (b) If *Price* = 20, what is the prediction for *Sales*? (c) Would the intercept be meaningful if this regression represents DVD sales at Blockbuster?

12.9 (a) Interpret the slope of the fitted regression *CarTheft* = 1,667 − 35.3 *MedianAge*, where *CarTheft* is the number of car thefts per 100,000 people by state, and *MedianAge* is the median age of the population. (b) What is the prediction for *CarTheft* if *MedianAge* is 40? (c) Would the intercept be meaningful if this regression applies to car thefts per 100,000 people by state?

12.10 (a) Interpret the slope of the fitted regression *Computer power dissipation* = 15.73 + 0.032 *Microprocessor speed*, where *Power dissipation* is measured in watts and *Microprocessor speed* is measured in MHz. (b) What is the prediction for *Power dissipation* if *Microprocessor speed* is 3,000 MHz? (c) Is this intercept meaningful?

12.11 (a) Interpret the slope of the fitted regression *Number of International Franchises* = −47.5 + 1.75 *PowerDistanceIndex*. The *PowerDistanceIndex* is a measure on a scale of 0–100 of the wealth gap between the richest and poorest in a country. (b) What is the prediction for number of international franchises in a country that has a *PowerDistanceIndex* of 85? (c) Is this intercept meaningful?

SECTION EXERCISES

12.3 REGRESSION TERMINOLOGY

Model and Parameters

The regression model's *unknown population parameters* are denoted by Greek letters β_0 (the **intercept**) and β_1 (the **slope**). The *population model* for a linear relationship is

$$y = \beta_0 + \beta_1 x + \varepsilon \quad \text{(population regression model)} \quad \textbf{(12.6)}$$

This relationship is assumed to be true for all (x_i, y_i) pairs in the population. Inclusion of a random error ε is necessary because other unspecified variables also may affect *Y* and because there may be measurement error in *Y*.

Each value of *X* may be paired with many different values of *Y* (e.g., there are many 800-square-foot apartments near a university, but each may rent for a different amount). The regression model without the error term represents the *expected value* of *Y* for a given *x* value. This is called the *simple regression equation*:

$$E(Y|x) = \beta_0 + \beta_1 x \quad \text{(simple regression equation)} \quad \textbf{(12.7)}$$

Even though the error term ε is not observable, we assume that the error is a normally distributed random variable with mean 0 and standard deviation σ. We also assume that σ is the same for each *x* and that the errors are independent of each other. These are called the **regression assumptions**. Figure 12.5 illustrates the regression assumptions.

- Assumption 1: The errors are normally distributed.
- Assumption 2: The errors have constant variance, σ^2.
- Assumption 3: The errors are independent of each other.

FIGURE 12.5

Regression Parameters and Error Assumptions

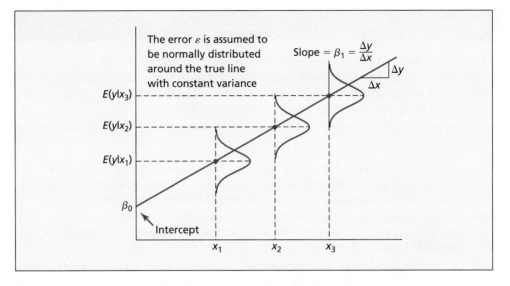

From the sample, we estimate the regression equation and use it to *predict* the expected value of Y for a given value of X:

(12.8) $\qquad\qquad \hat{y} = b_0 + b_1 x \qquad$ (estimated regression equation)

Roman letters denote the *coefficients* b_0 (the estimated intercept) and b_1 (the estimated slope). For a given value x_i, the estimated value of the dependent variable is $\hat{y}_i$. (You can read this as "y-hat.") The difference between the observed value y_i and its estimated value $\hat{y}_i$ is called a **residual** and is denoted e_i. The residual is the vertical distance between each y_i and the estimated regression line on a scatter plot of (x_i, y_i) values.

What Is a Residual?

A residual is calculated as the observed value of y minus the estimated value of y:

(12.9) $\qquad\qquad\qquad\qquad e_i = y_i - \hat{y}_i \qquad$ (residual)

The n residuals $e_1, e_2, \ldots, e_n$ are used to estimate σ, the standard deviation of the errors.

Fitting a Regression on a Scatter Plot

LO 12-4

Fit a simple regression on an Excel scatter plot.

From a scatter plot, we could visually estimate the slope and intercept. Although this method is inexact, experiments suggest that people are pretty good at "eyeball" line fitting. We instinctively try to adjust the line to ensure that the line passes through the "center" of the scatter of data points, to match the data as closely as possible. In other words, we try to minimize the vertical distances between the *fitted* line and the observed y values.

A more precise method is to let Excel calculate the estimates. We enter observations on the independent variable $x_1, x_2, \ldots, x_n$ and the dependent variable $y_1, y_2, \ldots, y_n$ into separate columns, and let Excel fit the regression equation, as illustrated in Figure 12.6.* Excel will choose the regression coefficients so as to produce a good fit.

Follow these steps to use Excel to fit a regression line to the scatter plot. Figure 12.7 illustrates steps 4 and 5.

- Step 1:   Highlight the data columns.
- Step 2:   Click on Insert and choose Scatter to create a graph.
- Step 3:   Click on the scatter plot points to select the data.

---

*Excel calls its regression equation a "trendline," although actually that would refer to a time-series trend.

FIGURE 12.6

Excel's Trendline

FIGURE 12.7

Excel's Trendline Menus

- Step 4: Right-click and choose Add Trendline.
- Step 5: Choose Options and check Display equation on chart.

Illustration: Miles per Gallon and Horsepower

Figure 12.6 shows a sample of miles per gallon and horsepower for 15 engines. The Excel graph and its fitted regression equation are also shown.

Slope Interpretation   The fitted regression is $\hat{y} = 49.216 - 0.0785x$. The slope ($b_1 = -0.0785$) says that for each additional unit of engine horsepower, the miles per gallon decreases by 0.0785 mile. This estimated slope is a *statistic* because a different sample might yield a different estimate of the slope.

Intercept Interpretation   The intercept ($b_0 = 49.216$) suggests that when the engine has no horsepower ($x = 0$), the fuel efficiency would be quite high. However, the intercept has little meaning in this case, not only because zero horsepower makes no logical sense, but also because extrapolating to $x = 0$ is beyond the range of the observed data.

Regression Caveats

- The "fit" of the regression does *not* depend on the sign of its slope. The sign of the fitted slope merely tells whether X has a positive or negative association with Y.
- View the intercept with skepticism unless $x = 0$ is logically possible and is within the observed range of X.
- Regression does not demonstrate cause and effect between X and Y. A good fit only shows that X and Y vary together. Both could be affected by another variable or by the way the data are defined.

SECTION EXERCISES

connect

12.12 The regression equation *NetIncome* = 2,277 + .0307 *Revenue* was estimated from a sample of 100 leading world companies (variables are in millions of dollars). (a) Interpret the slope. (b) Is the intercept meaningful? Explain. (c) Make a prediction of *NetIncome* when *Revenue* = 20,000. 📂 **Global100**

12.13 The regression equation *HomePrice* = 51.3 + 2.61 *Income* was estimated from a sample of 34 cities in the eastern United States. Both variables are in thousands of dollars. *HomePrice* is the median selling price of homes in the city, and *Income* is median family income for the city. (a) Interpret the slope. (b) Is the intercept meaningful? Explain. (c) Make a prediction of *HomePrice* when *Income* = 50 and also when *Income* = 100. 📂 **HomePrice1**

12.14 The regression equation *Credits* = 15.4 − .07 *Work* was estimated from a sample of 21 statistics students. *Credits* is the number of college credits taken and *Work* is the number of hours worked per week at an outside job. (a) Interpret the slope. (b) Is the intercept meaningful? Explain. (c) Make a prediction of *Credits* when *Work* = 0 and when *Work* = 40. What do these predictions tell you? 📂 **Credits**

12.15 Below are fitted regressions for Y = asking price of a used vehicle and X = the age of the vehicle. The observed range of X was 1 to 8 years. The sample consisted of all vehicles listed for sale in a particular week. (a) Interpret the slope of each fitted regression. (b) Interpret the intercept of each fitted regression. Does the intercept have meaning? (c) Predict the price of a 5-year-old Chevy Blazer. (d) Predict the price of a 5-year-old Chevy Silverado. 📂 **CarPrices**

Chevy Blazer: *Price* = 16,189 − 1,050 *Age* (n = 21 vehicles, observed X range was 1 to 8 years).
Chevy Silverado: *Price* = 22,591 − 1,339 *Age* (n = 24 vehicles, observed X range was 1 to 10 years).

12.16 Refer back to the regression equation in exercise 12.12: *NetIncome* = 2,277 + .0307 *Revenue*. Recall that the variables are both in millions of dollars. (a) Calculate the residual for the x, y pair ($41,078, $8,301). Did the regression equation underestimate or overestimate the net income? (b) Calculate the residual for the x, y pair ($61,768, $893). Did the regression equation underestimate or overestimate the net income?

12.17 Refer back to the regression equation in exercise 12.14: *Credits* = 15.4 − .07 *Work*. (a) Calculate the residual for the x, y pair (14, 18). Did the regression equation underestimate or overestimate the credits? (b) Calculate the residual for the x, y pair (30, 6). Did the regression equation underestimate or overestimate the credits?

12.4 ORDINARY LEAST SQUARES FORMULAS

Slope and Intercept

The **ordinary least squares** method (or **OLS** method for short) is used to estimate a regression so as to ensure the best fit. "Best" fit in this case means that we have selected the slope and intercept so that our residuals are as small as possible. Recall that a residual $e_i = y_i - \hat{y}_i$ is the difference between the observed y and the estimated y. Residuals can be either positive or negative. It is a characteristic of the OLS estimation method that the residuals around the regression line always sum to zero. That is, the positive residuals exactly cancel the negative ones:

$$\sum_{i=1}^{n} e_i = \sum_{i=1}^{n}(y_i - \hat{y}_i) = 0 \qquad \text{(OLS residuals always sum to zero)} \qquad \textbf{(12.10)}$$

Therefore to work with an equation that has a nonzero sum, we square the residuals, just as we squared the deviations from the mean when we developed the equation for variance back in Chapter 4. The fitted coefficients b_0 and b_1 are chosen so that the fitted linear model $\hat{y} = b_0 + b_1 x$ has the smallest possible sum of squared residuals (*SSE*):

$$SSE = \sum_{i=1}^{n} e_i^2 = \sum_{i=1}^{n}(y_i - \hat{y}_i)^2 = \sum_{i=1}^{n}(y_i - b_0 - b_1 x_i)^2 \qquad \text{(sum to be minimized)} \qquad \textbf{(12.11)}$$

This is an optimization problem that can be solved for b_0 and b_1 by using Excel's Solver Add-In. However, we can also use calculus to solve for b_0 and b_1.

$$b_1 = \frac{\sum_{i=1}^{n}(x_i - \bar{x})(y_i - \bar{y})}{\sum_{i=1}^{n}(x_i - \bar{x})^2} \qquad \text{(OLS estimator for slope)} \qquad \textbf{(12.12)}$$

$$b_0 = \bar{y} - b_1 \bar{x} \qquad \text{(OLS estimator for intercept)} \qquad \textbf{(12.13)}$$

If we use the notation for sums of squares (see formula 12.2), then the OLS formula for the slope can be written

$$b_1 = \frac{SS_{xy}}{SS_{xx}} \qquad \text{(OLS estimator for slope)} \qquad \textbf{(12.14)}$$

These formulas require only a few spreadsheet operations to find the means, deviations around the means, and their products and sums. They are built into Excel and many calculators. Their Excel formulas are

$$b_0 = \text{INTERCEPT(YData, XData)}$$
$$b_1 = \text{SLOPE(YData, XData)}$$

The OLS formulas give unbiased and consistent estimates* of β_0 and β_1. *The OLS regression line always passes through the point $(\bar{x}, \bar{y})$ for any data, as illustrated in Figure 12.8.*

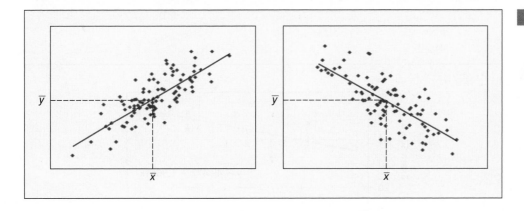

FIGURE 12.8

OLS Regression Line Always Passes Through $(\bar{x}, \bar{y})$.

---

*Recall from Chapter 8 that an unbiased estimator's expected value is the true parameter and that a consistent estimator approaches ever closer to the true parameter as the sample size increases.

Illustration: Exam Scores and Study Time

What is the relationship between the number of hours a student studies and his or her exam score? We can estimate the regression line for these two variables using a sample of 10 students. The worksheet in Table 12.2 shows the calculations of the sums needed for the slope and intercept. Figure 12.9 shows a fitted regression line. The vertical line segments in the scatter plot show the differences between the actual and fitted exam scores (i.e., residuals). The OLS residuals always sum to zero. We have:

$$b_1 = \frac{SS_{xy}}{SS_{xx}} = \frac{519.50}{264.50} = 1.9641 \qquad \text{(fitted slope)}$$

$$b_0 = \bar{y} - b_1\bar{x} = 70.1 - (1.9641)(10.5) = 49.477 \qquad \text{(fitted intercept)}$$

The fitted regression *Score* = 49.477 + 1.9641 *Study* says that, on average, each additional hour of study yields a little less than 2 additional exam points (the slope). A student who did not study (*Study* = 0) would expect a score of about 49 (the intercept). In this example, the intercept is meaningful because zero study time not only is possible (though hopefully uncommon) but also was almost within the range of observed data. The scatter plot shows an imperfect fit, since not all of the variation in exam scores can be explained by study time. The remaining *unexplained* variation in exam scores reflects other factors (e.g., previous night's sleep, class attendance, test anxiety). We can use the fitted regression equation $\hat{y} = 1.9641x + 49.477$ to find each student's *expected* exam score. Each

TABLE 12.2

Worksheet for Slope and Intercept Calculations
🗂 **ExamScores**

Student	Hours x_i	Score y_i	$x_i - \bar{x}$	$y_i - \bar{y}$	$(x_i - \bar{x})(y_i - \bar{y})$	$(x_i - \bar{x})^2$
Tom	1	53	−9.5	−17.1	162.45	90.25
Mary	5	74	−5.5	3.9	−21.45	30.25
Sarah	7	59	−3.5	−11.1	38.85	12.25
Oscar	8	43	−2.5	−27.1	67.75	6.25
Cullyn	10	56	−0.5	−14.1	7.05	0.25
Jaime	11	84	0.5	13.9	6.95	0.25
Theresa	14	96	3.5	25.9	90.65	12.25
Knut	15	69	4.5	−1.1	−4.95	20.25
Jin-Mae	15	84	4.5	13.9	62.55	20.25
Courtney	19	83	8.5	12.9	109.65	72.25
Sum	105	701	0	0	$SS_{xy} = 519.50$	$SS_{xx} = 264.50$
Mean	$\bar{x} = 10.5$	$\bar{y} = 70.1$				

FIGURE 12.9

Scatter Plot with Fitted Line and Residuals Shown as Vertical Line Segments

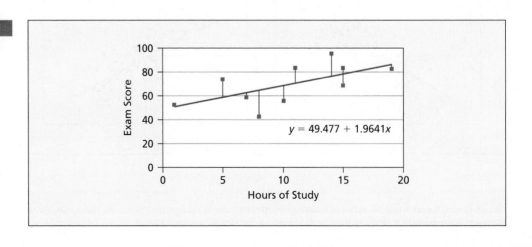

$y = 49.477 + 1.9641x$

prediction is a *conditional mean,* given the student's study hours. For example:

Student and Study Time	Expected Exam Score
Oscar, $x = 8$ hours	$\hat{y} = 49.48 + 1.964(8) = 65.19$ (65 to nearest integer)
Theresa, $x = 14$ hours	$\hat{y} = 49.48 + 1.964(14) = 76.98$ (77 to nearest integer)
Courtney, $x = 19$ hours	$\hat{y} = 49.48 + 1.964(19) = 86.79$ (87 to nearest integer)

Oscar's actual exam score was only 43, so he did worse than his predicted score of 65. Theresa scored 96, far above her predicted score of 77. Courtney, who studied the longest (19 hours), scored 83, fairly close to her predicted score of 87. These examples show that study time is not a perfect predictor of exam scores.

Sources of Variation in *Y*

In a regression, we seek to explain the variation in the dependent variable around its mean. We express the *total variation* as a sum of squares (denoted *SST*):

$$SST = \sum_{i=1}^{n}(y_i - \bar{y})^2 \qquad \text{(total sum of squares)} \qquad \textbf{(12.15)}$$

We can split the total variation into two parts:

SST	=	*SSR*	+	*SSE*
(*total* variation around the mean)		(variation explained by the *regression*)		(unexplained or *error* variation)

The *explained variation* in *Y* (denoted *SSR*) is the sum of the squared differences between the conditional mean $\hat{y}_i$ (conditioned on a given value x_i) and the unconditional mean $\bar{y}$ (same for all x_i):

$$SSR = \sum_{i=1}^{n}(\hat{y}_i - \bar{y})^2 \qquad \text{(\textit{regression} sum of squares, explained)} \qquad \textbf{(12.16)}$$

The *unexplained variation* in *Y* (denoted *SSE*) is the sum of *squared* residuals, sometimes referred to as the **error sum of squares.***

$$SSE = \sum_{i=1}^{n}(y_i - \hat{y}_i)^2 \qquad \text{(\textit{error} sum of squares, unexplained)} \qquad \textbf{(12.17)}$$

If the fit is good, *SSE* will be relatively small compared to *SST*. If each observed data value y_i is exactly the same as its estimate $\hat{y}_i$ (i.e., a perfect fit), then *SSE* will be zero. There is no upper limit on *SSE*. Table 12.3 shows the calculation of *SSE* for the exam scores.

TABLE 12.3			Calculations of Sums of Squares ExamScores				
Student	**Hours** x_i	**Score** y_i	**Estimated Score** $\hat{y}_i = 1.9641x_i + 49.477$	**Residual** $y_i - \hat{y}_i$	$(y_i - \hat{y}_i)^2$	$(\hat{y}_i - \bar{y})^2$	$(y_i - \bar{y})^2$
Tom	1	53	51.441	1.559	2.43	348.15	292.41
Mary	5	74	59.298	14.702	216.15	116.68	15.21
Sarah	7	59	63.226	−4.226	17.86	47.25	123.21
Oscar	8	43	65.190	−22.190	492.40	24.11	734.41
Cullyn	10	56	69.118	−13.118	172.08	0.96	198.81
Jaime	11	84	71.082	12.918	166.87	0.96	193.21
Theresa	14	96	76.974	19.026	361.99	47.25	670.81
Knut	15	69	78.939	−9.939	98.78	78.13	1.21
Jin-Mae	15	84	78.939	5.061	25.61	78.13	193.21
Courtney	19	83	86.795	−3.795	14.40	278.72	166.41
					SSE	*SSR*	*SST*
					= 1,568.57	= 1,020.34	= 2,588.90

---

*But bear in mind that the residual e_i (observable) is not the same as the true error ε_i (unobservable).

Assessing Fit: Coefficient of Determination

Because the magnitude of SSE is dependent on sample size and on the units of measurement (e.g., dollars, kilograms, ounces), we want a *unit-free* benchmark to assess the fit of the regression equation. We can obtain a measure of *relative fit* by comparing SST to SSR. Recall that total variation in Y can be expressed as

$$SST = SSR + SSE$$

By dividing both sides by SST we now have the sum of two proportions on the right-hand side.

$$\frac{SST}{SST} = \frac{SSR}{SST} + \frac{SSE}{SST} \quad \text{or} \quad 1 = \frac{SSR}{SST} + \frac{SSE}{SST}$$

The first proportion SSR/SST has a special name: **coefficient of determination or R^2.** You can calculate this statistic in two ways.

(12.18) $$R^2 = \frac{SSR}{SST} \quad \text{or} \quad R^2 = 1 - \frac{SSE}{SST}$$

The range of the coefficient of determination is $0 \leq R^2 \leq 1$. The highest possible R^2 is 1 because, if the regression gives a perfect fit, then $SSE = 0$:

$$R^2 = 1 - \frac{SSE}{SST} = 1 - \frac{0}{SST} = 1 - 0 = 1 \quad \text{if } SSE = 0 \text{ (perfect fit)}$$

The lowest possible R^2 is 0 because, if knowing the value of X does not help predict the value of Y, then $SSE = SST$:

$$R^2 = 1 - \frac{SSE}{SST} = 1 - \frac{SST}{SST} = 1 - 1 = 0 \quad \text{if } SSE = SST \text{ (worst fit)}$$

For the exam scores, the coefficient of determination is

$$R^2 = 1 - \frac{SSE}{SST} = 1 - \frac{1{,}568.57}{2{,}588.90} = 1 - .6059 = .3941$$

Because a coefficient of determination always lies in the range $0 \leq R^2 \leq 1$, it is often expressed as a *percent of variation explained*. Since the exam score regression yields $R^2 = .3941$, we could say that X (hours of study) "explains" 39.41 percent of the variation in Y (exam scores). On the other hand, 60.59 percent of the variation in exam scores is *not* explained by study time. The *unexplained variation* reflects factors not included in our model (e.g., reading skills, hours of sleep, hours of work at a job, physical health, etc.) or just plain random variation. Although the word "explained" does not necessarily imply causation, in this case we have *a priori* reason to believe that causation exists, that is, that increased study time improves exam scores.

Tip

In a bivariate regression, R^2 is the square of the correlation coefficient r. Thus, if $r = .50$, then $R^2 = .25$. For this reason, MegaStat (and some textbooks) denotes the coefficient of determination as r^2 instead of R^2. In this textbook, the uppercase notation R^2 is used to indicate the difference in their definitions. It is tempting to think that a low R^2 indicates that the model is not useful. Yet in some applications (e.g., predicting crude oil future prices) even a slight improvement in predictive power can translate into millions of dollars.

SECTION EXERCISES

connect

Instructions for exercises 12.18 and 12.19: (a) Make an Excel worksheet to calculate SS_{xx}, SS_{yy}, and SS_{xy} (the same worksheet you used in exercises 12.2 and 12.3). (b) Use the formulas to calculate the slope and intercept. (c) Use your estimated slope and intercept to make a worksheet to calculate SSE, SSR, and SST. (d) Use these sums to calculate the R^2. (e) To check your answers, make an

Excel scatter plot of X and Y, select the data points, right-click, select Add Trendline, select the Options tab, and choose Display equation on chart and Display R-squared value on chart.

12.18	College Student Weekly Earnings in Dollars ($n = 5$) WeekPay		12.19	Phone Hold Time for Concert Tickets in Seconds ($n = 5$) CallWait

Hours Worked (X)	Weekly Pay (Y)	Operators (X)	Wait Time (Y)
10	93	4	385
15	171	5	335
20	204	6	383
20	156	7	344
35	261	8	288

Instructions for exercises 12.20–12.22: (a) Use Excel to make a scatter plot of the data. (b) Select the data points, right-click, select Add Trendline, select the Options tab, and choose Display equation on chart and Display R-squared value on chart. (c) Interpret the fitted slope. (d) Is the intercept meaningful? Explain. (e) Interpret the R^2.

12.20	Moviegoer Snack Spending ($n = 10$) Movies	12.21	Annual Percent Return on Mutual Funds ($n = 17$) Portfolio	12.22	Order Size and Shipping Cost ($n = 12$) ShipCost

Age (X)	Spent (Y)	Last Year (X)	This Year (Y)	Orders (X)	Ship Cost (Y)
30	2.85	11.9	15.4	1,068	4,489
50	6.50	19.5	26.7	1,026	5,611
34	1.50	11.2	18.2	767	3,290
12	6.35	14.1	16.7	885	4,113
37	6.20	14.2	13.2	1,156	4,883
33	6.75	5.2	16.4	1,146	5,425
36	3.60	20.7	21.1	892	4,414
26	6.10	11.3	12.0	938	5,506
18	8.35	−1.1	12.1	769	3,346
46	4.35	3.9	7.4	677	3,673
		12.9	11.5	1,174	6,542
		12.4	23.0	1,009	5,088
		12.5	12.7		
		2.7	15.1		
		8.8	18.7		
		7.2	9.9		
		5.9	18.9		

12.5 TESTS FOR SIGNIFICANCE

Standard Error of Regression

A measure of overall fit is the **standard error** of the estimate, denoted s_e:

$$s_e = \sqrt{\frac{SSE}{n-2}} \qquad \text{(standard error)} \qquad \textbf{(12.19)}$$

If the fitted model's predictions are perfect ($SSE = 0$), the standard error s_e will be zero. In general, a smaller value of s_e indicates a better fit. For the exam scores, we can use SSE from Table 12.3 to find s_e:

$$s_e = \sqrt{\frac{SSE}{n-2}} = \sqrt{\frac{1,568.57}{10-2}} = \sqrt{\frac{1,568.57}{8}} = 14.002$$

LO 12-5

Calculate and interpret confidence intervals for regression coefficients.

The standard error s_e is an estimate of σ (the standard deviation of the unobservable errors). Because it measures overall fit, the standard error s_e serves somewhat the same function as the coefficient of determination. However, unlike R^2, the magnitude of s_e depends on the units of measurement of the dependent variable (e.g., dollars, kilograms, ounces) and on the data magnitude. For this reason, R^2 is often the preferred measure of overall fit because its scale is always 0 to 1. The main use of the standard error s_e is to construct confidence intervals.

Confidence Intervals for Slope and Intercept

Once we have the standard error s_e, we construct confidence intervals for the coefficients from the formulas shown below. Excel, MegaStat, and MINITAB find them automatically.

(12.20)
$$s_{b_1} = \frac{s_e}{\sqrt{\sum_{i=1}^{n}(x_i - \bar{x})^2}} \qquad \text{(standard error of slope)}$$

(12.21)
$$s_{b_0} = s_e \sqrt{\frac{1}{n} + \frac{\bar{x}^2}{\sum_{i=1}^{n}(x_i - \bar{x})^2}} \qquad \text{(standard error of intercept)}$$

For the exam score data, plugging in the sums from Table 12.2, we get

$$s_{b_1} = \frac{s_e}{\sqrt{\sum_{i=1}^{n}(x_i - \bar{x})^2}} = \frac{14.002}{\sqrt{264.50}} = 0.86095$$

$$s_{b_0} = s_e \sqrt{\frac{1}{n} + \frac{\bar{x}^2}{\sum_{i=1}^{n}(x_i - \bar{x})^2}} = 14.002\sqrt{\frac{1}{10} + \frac{(10.5)^2}{264.50}} = 10.066$$

These standard errors are used to construct confidence intervals for the true slope and intercept, using Student's t with $d.f. = n - 2$ degrees of freedom and any desired confidence level. Some software packages (e.g., Excel and MegaStat) provide confidence intervals automatically, while others do not (e.g., MINITAB).

(12.22) $\quad b_1 - t_{\alpha/2}s_{b_1} \leq \beta_1 \leq b_1 + t_{\alpha/2}s_{b_1} \qquad$ (CI for true slope)

(12.23) $\quad b_0 - t_{\alpha/2}s_{b_0} \leq \beta_0 \leq b_0 + t_{\alpha/2}s_{b_0} \qquad$ (CI for true intercept)

For the exam scores, degrees of freedom are $n - 2 = 10 - 2 = 8$, so from Appendix D we get $t_{.025} = 2.306$ for 95 percent confidence. The 95 percent confidence intervals for the coefficients are

Slope

$$b_1 - t_{.025}s_{b_1} \leq \beta_1 \leq b_1 + t_{.025}s_{b_1}$$
$$1.9641 - (2.306)(0.86101) \leq \beta_1 \leq 1.9641 + (2.306)(0.86101)$$
$$-0.0213 \leq \beta_1 \leq 3.9495$$

Intercept

$$b_0 - t_{\alpha/2}s_{b_0} \leq \beta_0 \leq b_0 + t_{\alpha/2}s_{b_0}$$
$$49.477 - (2.306)(10.066) \leq \beta_0 \leq 49.477 + (2.306)(10.066)$$
$$26.26 \leq \beta_0 \leq 72.69$$

These confidence intervals are fairly wide. The width of any confidence interval can be reduced by obtaining a larger sample, partly because the t-value would shrink (toward the normal z-value) but mainly because the standard errors shrink as n increases. For the exam scores, the confidence interval for the slope includes zero, suggesting that the true slope could be zero.

Hypothesis Tests

Is the true slope different from zero? This is an important question because if $\beta_1 = 0$, then X does not influence Y and the regression model collapses to a constant β_0 plus a random error term:

Initial Model	*If $\beta_1 = 0$*	*Then*
$y = \beta_0 + \beta_1 x + \varepsilon$	$y = \beta_0 + (0)x + \varepsilon$	$y = \beta_0 + \varepsilon$

We could also test for a zero intercept. For either coefficient, we use a t test with $d.f. = n - 2$ degrees of freedom. The hypotheses and their test statistics are:

Coefficient	Hypotheses	Test Statistic	
Slope	$H_0: \beta_1 = 0$ $H_1: \beta_1 \neq 0$	$t_{calc} = \dfrac{\text{estimated slope} - \text{hypothesized slope}}{\text{standard error of the slope}} = \dfrac{b_1 - 0}{s_{b_1}}$	**(12.24)**
Intercept	$H_0: \beta_0 = 0$ $H_1: \beta_0 \neq 0$	$t_{calc} = \dfrac{\text{estimated intercept} - \text{hypothesized intercept}}{\text{standard error of the intercept}} = \dfrac{b_0 - 0}{s_{b_0}}$	**(12.25)**

LO 12-6

Test hypotheses about the slope and intercept by using t tests.

Usually we are interested in testing whether the parameter is equal to zero as shown here, but you may substitute another value in place of 0 if you wish. The critical value of t is obtained from Appendix D or from Excel's function =T.INV.2T(α, d.f.). Often, the researcher uses a two-tailed test as the starting point because rejection in a two-tailed test always implies rejection in a one-tailed test (but not vice versa).

Useful Fact

The test for zero slope is the same as the test for zero correlation. That is, the t test for zero slope (formula 12.24) will always yield *exactly* the same t_{calc} as the t test for zero correlation (formula 12.4).

Test for Zero Slope: Exam Scores ExamScores

For the exam scores, we would anticipate a positive slope (i.e., more study hours should improve exam scores) so we will use a right-tailed test.

Step 1: State the Hypotheses

$$H_0: \beta_1 = 0$$
$$H_1: \beta_1 > 0$$

Step 2: Specify the Decision Rule

For a right-tailed test with $\alpha = .05$ and $d.f. = 10 - 2 = 8$, $t_{.05} = 1.860$. Our decision rule states:

$$\text{Reject } H_0 \text{ if } t_{calc} > 1.860$$

Step 3: Calculate the Test Statistic

To calculate the test statistic, we use the slope estimate ($b_1 = 1.9641$) and the standard error ($s_{b_1} = 0.86095$) we calculated previously:

$$t_{calc} = \frac{b_1 - 0}{s_{b_1}} = \frac{1.9641 - 0}{0.86095} = 2.281$$

Step 4: Make a Decision

Because $t_{calc} > t_{.05}$ (2.281 > 1.860), we can reject the hypothesis of a zero slope in a right-tailed test. (We would be unable to do so in a two-tailed test because the critical value of our t statistic would be 2.306.) Once we calculate the test statistic for the slope or intercept, we can find the *p*-value by using Excel's function =T.DIST.RT(2.281, 8) = .025995. Because .02995 < .05, we would reject H_0. We conclude the slope is positive.

LO 12-7

Perform regression analysis with Excel or other software.

Using Excel: Exam Scores 📁 ExamScores

These calculations are normally done by computer (we have demonstrated the calculations only to illustrate the formulas). The Excel menu to accomplish these tasks is shown in Figure 12.10. The resulting output, shown in Figure 12.11, can be used to verify our calculations. Excel always does two-tailed tests, so you must halve the *p*-value if you need a one-tailed test. You may specify the confidence level, but Excel's default is 95 percent confidence.

FIGURE 12.10

Excel's Regression Menus

FIGURE 12.11

Excel's Regression Output

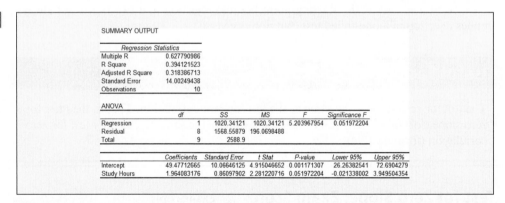

Tip

Avoid checking the Constant is Zero box in Excel's menu. This would force the intercept through the origin, changing the model drastically. Leave this option to the experts.

Using MegaStat: Exam Scores 📁 ExamScores

Figure 12.12 shows MegaStat's menu. The output format is similar to Excel's, except that MegaStat highlights coefficients that differ significantly from zero at $\alpha = .05$ in a two-tailed test.

Using MINITAB: Exam Scores 📁 ExamScores

Figure 12.13 shows MINITAB's regression menus. MINITAB gives you the same general output as Excel, but with strongly rounded results.*

---

*You may have noticed that both Excel and MINITAB calculated something called "adjusted R-Square." For a bivariate regression, this statistic is of little interest, but in the next chapter it becomes important.

FIGURE 12.12

MegaStat's Regression Menus

FIGURE 12.13

MINITAB's Regression Menus

Application: Retail Sales RetailSales

Is there a positive association between gross leasable area (X) and retail sales (Y) in shopping malls? We will assume a linear relationship between X and Y:

$$Sales = \beta_0 + \beta_1 \, Area + \varepsilon$$

We anticipate a positive slope (more leasable area permits more retail sales) and an intercept near zero (zero leasable space would imply no retail sales). Since retail sales do not depend solely on leasable area, the random error term will reflect all other factors that influence retail sales as well as possible measurement error. The regression line is estimated using a sample of $n = 24$ shopping malls randomly chosen from 24 different U.S. states.

Based on the scatter plot and Excel's fitted linear regression, displayed in Figure 12.14, the linear model seems justified. The very high R^2 says that *Area* "explains" about 98 percent of the variation in *Sales*. Although it is reasonable to assume causation between *Area* and *Sales* in this model, the high R^2 alone does not prove cause and effect.

FIGURE 12.14

Leasable Area and Retail Sales RetailSales

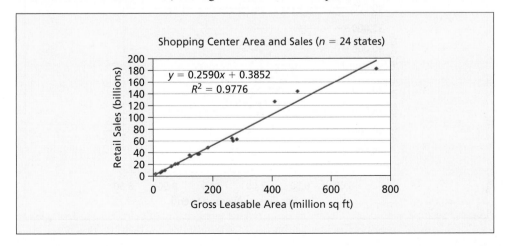

Using MegaStat   For a more detailed look, we examine MegaStat's regression output for these data, shown in Figure 12.15. On average, each extra million square feet of leasable space yields an extra \$259.4 billion in retail sales ($b_1 = .2590$). The slope is nonzero in MegaStat's two-tail test ($t = 30.972$) as indicated by its tiny p-value (1.22×10^{-19}). Mega-Stat's yellow highlight indicates that the slope differs significantly from zero at $\alpha = .01$, and the narrow confidence interval for the slope [0.2417 to 0.2764] does not enclose zero. We conclude that this sample result (nonzero slope) did not arise by chance—rarely will you see such small p-values (except perhaps in time series data). But the intercept ($b_0 = 0.3852$) does not differ significantly from zero (p-value $= .8479$, $t = 0.194$) and the confidence interval for the intercept [-3.7320, 4.5023] includes zero. These conclusions are in line with our prior expectations.

FIGURE 12.15

MegaStat Regression Results for Retail Sales
 RetailSales

Regression Output					Confidence Interval	
Variables	Coefficients	Std. Error	t (df = 26)	p-value	95% lower	95% upper
Intercept	0.3852	1.9853	0.194	.8479	−3.7320	4.5023
Area	0.2590	0.0084	30.972	1.22E-19	0.2417	0.2764

Tip

The test for zero slope always yields a t statistic that is identical to the test for zero correlation coefficient. Therefore, it is not necessary to do both tests. Since regression output always includes a t test for the slope, that is the test we usually use.

Mini Case   12.2

Does Per Person Spending Predict Weekly Sales?   **NoodlesRevenue**

Can Noodles & Company predict their average weekly sales at a restaurant from the average amount a person spends when visiting their restaurant? A random sample of data from 74 restaurants was used to answer this question. The scatter plot in Figure 12.16 below shows the relationship between *average spending per person* and *average weekly sales.*

FIGURE 12.16   **Noodles Weekly Sales**

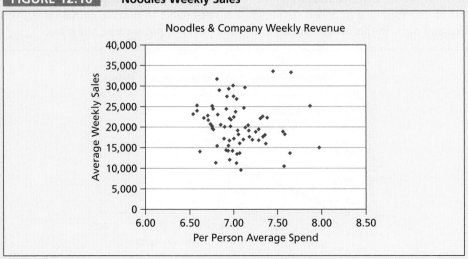

Regression Output					Confidence Interval	
Variables	*Coefficients*	*Std. Error*	*t(d.f. = 72)*	*p-value*	*95% lower*	*95% upper*
Intercept	32,710.5607	14,987.2764	2.183	.0323	2,833.9717	62,587.1497
Per Person Spend	−1,751.4472	2,125.6830	−0.824	.4127	−5,988.9187	2,486.0243

FIGURE 12.17

MegaStat Regression Results for Weekly Sales

The scatter plot shows almost no relationship between the two variables. This observation is also supported by the regression results shown in Figure 12.17.

The regression results show that b_1, the estimate for the slope β_1, is −$1,751.45. It would appear that on average for each additional dollar an individual spends in a restaurant, weekly sales would decrease by $1,751.45—seemingly a large number. But notice that the confidence interval for the slope [−$5,988.92, $2,486.02] contains zero and the standard error ($2,125.68) is larger than the estimated coefficient. When we perform a two-tailed test for zero slope with $H_0: \beta_1 = 0$ and $H_1: \beta_1 \neq 0$, the p-value for this test is .4127. Because this p-value is much greater than any value of α we might choose, we *fail to reject* the null hypothesis of zero slope. Both the hypothesis for zero slope and the confidence interval show that the slope is not significantly different from zero. Our conclusion is that average weekly sales *should not be* predicted by per person average spending. Based on the information we have here, our best prediction of average weekly sales at a Noodles & Company restaurant is simply the mean ($\bar{y} = \$20,373$).

Instructions for exercises 12.23 and 12.24: (a) Perform a regression using MegaStat or Excel. (b) State the null and alternative hypotheses for a two-tailed test for a zero slope. (c) Report the p-value and the 95 percent confidence interval for the slope shown in the regression results. (d) Is the slope significantly different from zero? Explain your conclusion.

SECTION EXERCISES

connect

12.23   College Student Weekly Earnings in Dollars ($n = 5$) 📁 WeekPay

Hours Worked (X)	Weekly Pay (Y)
10	93
15	171
20	204
20	156
35	261

12.24   Phone Hold Time for Concert Tickets in Seconds ($n = 5$) 📁 CallWait

Operators (X)	Wait Time (Y)
4	385
5	335
6	383
7	344
8	288

12.25 A regression was performed using data on 32 NFL teams in 2003. The variables were $Y =$ current value of team (millions of dollars) and $X =$ total debt held by the team owners (millions of dollars). (a) Write the fitted regression equation. (b) Construct a 95 percent confidence interval for the slope. (c) Perform a right-tailed t test for zero slope at $\alpha = .05$. State the hypotheses clearly. (d) Use Excel to find the p-value for the t statistic for the slope. (Data are from *Forbes* 172, no. 5, pp. 82−83.) 📁 NFL

variables	coefficients	std. error
Intercept	557.4511	25.3385
Debt	3.0047	0.8820

12.26 A regression was performed using data on 16 randomly selected charities. The variables were Y = expenses (millions of dollars) and X = revenue (millions of dollars). (a) Write the fitted regression equation. (b) Construct a 95 percent confidence interval for the slope. (c) Perform a right-tailed t test for zero slope at $\alpha = .05$. State the hypotheses clearly. (d) Use Excel to find the p-value for the t statistic for the slope. 🖾 **Charities**

variables	coefficients	std. error
Intercept	7.6425	10.0403
Revenue	0.9467	0.0936

12.6 ANALYSIS OF VARIANCE: OVERALL FIT

Decomposition of Variance

LO 12-8

Interpret the standard error, R^2, ANOVA table, and F test.

A regression seeks to explain variation in the dependent variable around its mean. A simple way to see this is to express the deviation of y_i from its mean $\bar{y}$ as the sum of the deviation of y_i from the regression estimate $\hat{y}_i$ plus the deviation of the regression estimate $\hat{y}_i$ from the mean $\bar{y}$:

(12.26) $$y_i - \bar{y} = (y_i - \hat{y}_i) + (\hat{y}_i - \bar{y})$$ (adding and subtracting $\hat{y}_i$)

It can be shown that this same decomposition also holds for the *sums of squares:*

(12.27) $$\sum_{i=1}^{n}(y_i - \bar{y})^2 = \sum_{i=1}^{n}(y_i - \hat{y}_i)^2 + \sum_{i=1}^{n}(\hat{y}_i - \bar{y})^2$$ (sums of squares)

As we have already seen, this *decomposition of variance* may be written as

$$\begin{array}{ccccc} SST & = & SSE & + & SSR \\ (\textit{total}\ \text{variation} & & (\text{unexplained} & & (\text{variation explained} \\ \text{around the mean)} & & \text{or } \textit{error} \text{ variation)} & & \text{by the } \textit{regression}) \end{array}$$

F Statistic for Overall Fit

To test a regression for overall significance, we use an F test to compare the explained (SSR) and unexplained (SSE) sums of squares. We divide each sum by its respective degrees of freedom to obtain *mean squares* (MSR and MSE). The F *statistic* is the ratio of these two mean squares. Calculations of the F statistic are arranged in a table called the *analysis of variance* or ANOVA table (see Table 12.4). The ANOVA table also contains

TABLE 12.4

ANOVA Table for a Simple Regression

Source of Variation	Sum of Squares	df	Mean Square	F	Excel p-value
Regression (explained)	$SSR = \sum_{i=1}^{n}(\hat{y}_i - \bar{y})^2$	1	$MSR = \dfrac{SSR}{1}$	$F_{calc} = \dfrac{MSR}{MSE}$	=F.DIST(F_{calc},1, n−2)
Residual (unexplained)	$SSE = \sum_{i=1}^{n}(y_i - \hat{y}_i)^2$	n − 2	$MSE = \dfrac{SSE}{n-2}$		
Total	$SST = \sum_{i=1}^{n}(y_i - \bar{y})^2$	n − 1			

the sums required to calculate $R^2 = SSR/SST$. An ANOVA table is provided automatically by any regression software (e.g., Excel, MegaStat).

The formula for the F test statistic is:

$$F_{calc} = \frac{MSR}{MSE} = \frac{SSR/1}{SSE/(n-2)} = (n-2)\frac{SSR}{SSE} \quad (F \text{ statistic for simple regression}) \quad (12.28)$$

The F statistic reflects both the sample size and the ratio of SSR to SSE. For a given sample size, a larger F statistic indicates a better fit (larger SSR relative to SSE), while F close to zero indicates a poor fit (small SSR relative to SSE). The F statistic must be compared with a critical value $F_{1,n-2}$ from Appendix F for whatever level of significance is desired, and we can find the p-value by using Excel's function =F.DIST(F_{calc},1,n−2). Software packages provide the p-value automatically.

EXAMPLE 12.2

Exam Scores: F Statistic

📰 **ExamScores**

Figure 12.18 shows an ANOVA table for the exam scores. The F statistic is

$$F_{calc} = \frac{MSR}{MSE} = \frac{1020.3412}{196.0698} = 5.20$$

From Appendix F the critical value of $F_{1,8}$ at the 5 percent level of significance would be 5.32, so the exam score regression is not quite significant at $\alpha = .05$. The p-value of .052 says a sample such as ours would be expected about 52 times in 1,000 samples if X and Y were unrelated. In other words, if we reject the hypothesis of no relationship between X and Y, we face a Type I error risk of 5.2 percent. This p-value might be called *marginally significant*.

FIGURE 12.18 **ANOVA Table for Exam Data**

ANOVA table

Source	SS	df	MS	F	p-value
Regression	1,020.3412	1	1,020.3412	5.20	.0520
Residual	1,568.5588	8	196.0698		
Total	2,588.9000	9			

From the ANOVA table, we can calculate the standard error from the mean square for the residuals:

$$s_e = \sqrt{MSE} = \sqrt{196.0698} = 14.002 \quad \text{(standard error for exam scores)}$$

Tip

In a simple regression, the F test always yields the same p-value as a two-tailed t test for zero slope, which in turn always gives the same p-value as a two-tailed test for zero correlation. The relationship between the test statistics is $F_{calc} = t^2_{calc}$.

12.27 Below is a regression using X = home price (000), Y = annual taxes (000), n = 20 homes. (a) Write the fitted regression equation. (b) Write the formula for each t statistic and verify the t statistics shown below. (c) State the degrees of freedom for the t tests and find the two-tail critical value for t by using Appendix D. (d) Use Excel's function =T.DIST.2T(t, d.f.) to verify the p-value shown for each t statistic (slope, intercept). (e) Verify that $F = t^2$ for the slope. (f) In your own words, describe the fit of this regression.

SECTION EXERCISES

connect

R²	0.452
Std. Error	0.454
n	12

ANOVA table

Source	SS	df	MS	F	p-value
Regression	1.6941	1	1.6941	8.23	.0167
Residual	2.0578	10	0.2058		
Total	3.7519	11			

Regression output   confidence interval

variables	coefficients	std. error	t (df = 10)	p-value	95% lower	95% upper
Intercept	1.8064	0.6116	2.954	.0144	0.4438	3.1691
Slope	0.0039	0.0014	2.869	.0167	0.0009	0.0070

12.28 Below is a regression using X = average price, Y = units sold, n = 20 stores. (a) Write the fitted regression equation. (b) Write the formula for each t statistic and verify the t statistics shown below. (c) State the degrees of freedom for the t tests and find the two-tail critical value for t by using Appendix D. (d) Use Excel's function =T.DIST.2T(t, *d.f.*) to verify the p-value shown for each t statistic (slope, intercept). (e) Verify that $F = t^2$ for the slope. (f) In your own words, describe the fit of this regression.

R²	0.200
Std. Error	26.128
n	20

ANOVA table

Source	SS	df	MS	F	p-value
Regression	3,080.89	1	3,080.89	4.51	.0478
Residual	12,288.31	18	682.68		
Total	15,369.20	19			

Regression output   confidence interval

variables	coefficients	std. error	t (df = 18)	p-value	95% lower	95% upper
Intercept	614.9300	51.2343	12.002	.0000	507.2908	722.5692
Slope	−109.1120	51.3623	−2.124	.0478	−217.0202	−1.2038

Instructions for exercises 12.29–12.31: (a) Use Excel's **Data Analysis > Regression** (or MegaStat or MINITAB) to obtain regression estimates. (b) Interpret the 95 percent confidence interval for the slope. Does it contain zero? (c) Interpret the t test for the slope and its p-value. (d) Interpret the F statistic. (e) Verify that the p-value for F is the same as for the slope's t statistic, and show that $t^2 = F$. (f) Describe the fit of the regression.

12.29   Moviegoer Snack Spending (n = 10) Movies

Age (X)	Spent (Y)	Age (X)	Spent (Y)
30	2.85	33	6.75
50	6.50	36	3.60
34	1.50	26	6.10
12	6.35	18	8.35
37	6.20	46	4.35

12.30	Annual Percent Return on Mutual Funds (*n* = 17) Portfolio
Last Year (X)	**This Year (Y)**
11.9	15.4
19.5	26.7
11.2	18.2
14.1	16.7
14.2	13.2
5.2	16.4
20.7	21.1
11.3	12.0
−1.1	12.1
3.9	7.4
12.9	11.5
12.4	23.0
12.5	12.7
2.7	15.1
8.8	18.7
7.2	9.9
5.9	18.9

12.31	Order Size and Shipping Cost (*n* = 12) ShipCost
Orders (X)	**Ship Cost (Y)**
1,068	4,489
1,026	5,611
767	3,290
885	4,113
1,156	4,883
1,146	5,425
892	4,414
938	5,506
769	3,346
677	3,673
1,174	6,542
1,009	5,088

Mini Case 12.3

Airplane Cockpit Noise Cockpit

Career airline pilots face the risk of progressive hearing loss, due to the noisy cockpits of most jet aircraft. Much of the noise comes not from engines but from air roar, which increases at high speeds. To assess this workplace hazard, a pilot measured cockpit noise at randomly selected points during the flight by using a handheld meter. Noise level (in decibels) was measured in seven different aircraft at the first officer's left ear position using a handheld meter. For reference, 60 dB is a normal conversation, 75 is a typical vacuum cleaner, 85 is city traffic, 90 is a typical hair dryer, and 110 is a chain saw. Table 12.5 shows 61 observations on cockpit noise (decibels) and airspeed (knots indicated air speed, KIAS) for a Boeing 727, an older type of aircraft lacking design improvements in newer planes.

The scatter plot in Figure 12.19 suggests that a linear model provides a reasonable description of the data. The fitted regression shows that each additional knot of airspeed increases the noise level by 0.0765 dB. Thus, a 100-knot increase in airspeed would add about 7.65 dB of noise. The intercept of 64.229 suggests that if the plane were not flying (*KIAS* = 0), the noise level would be only slightly greater than a normal conversation.

TABLE 12.5									Cockpit Noise Level and Airspeed for B-727 (*n* = 61) Cockpit		
Speed	*Noise*	*Speed*	*Noise*	*Speed*	*Noise*	*Speed*	*Noise*	*Speed*	*Noise*	*Speed*	*Noise*
250	83	380	93	340	90	330	91	350	90	272	84.5
340	89	380	91	340	91	360	94	380	92	310	88
320	88	390	94	380	96	370	94.5	310	88	350	90
330	89	400	95	385	96	380	95	295	87	370	91
346	92	400	96	420	97	395	96	280	86	405	93
260	85	405	97	230	82	365	91	320	88	250	82
280	84	320	89	340	91	320	88	330	90		
395	92	310	88.5	250	86	250	85	320	88		
380	92	250	82	320	89	250	82	340	89		
400	93	280	87	340	90	320	88	350	90		
335	91	320	89	320	90	305	88	270	84		

FIGURE 12.19   **Scatter Plot of Cockpit Noise Data**

Cockpit Noise in B-727 ($n = 61$)

$y = 0.0765x + 64.229$
$R^2 = .8947$

The regression results in Figure 12.20 show that the fit is very good ($R^2 = .895$) and that the regression is highly significant ($F = 501.16$, p-value $< .001$). Both the slope and intercept have p-values below .001, indicating that the true parameters are non-zero. Thus, the regression is significant, as well as having practical value.

FIGURE 12.20   **Regression Results of Cockpit Noise**

Regression Analysis

r^2	0.895	n	61
r	0.946	k	1
Std. Error	1.292	Dep. Var.	**Noise**

ANOVA table

Source	SS	df	MS	F	p-value
Regression	836.9817	1	836.9817	501.16	1.60E-30
Residual	98.5347	59	1.6701		
Total	935.5164	60			

Regression output   confidence interval

variables	coefficients	std. error	t (df = 59)	p-value	95% lower	95% upper
Intercept	64.2294	1.1489	55.907	8.29E-53	61.9306	66.5283
Speed	0.0765	0.0034	22.387	1.60E-30	0.0697	0.0834

12.7 CONFIDENCE AND PREDICTION INTERVALS FOR *Y*

How to Construct an Interval Estimate for *Y*

The regression line is an estimate of the *conditional mean* of *Y*, that is, the expected value of *Y* for a given value of *X*, *denoted* $E(Y|x_i)$. But the estimate may be too high or too low. To make this *point estimate* more useful, we need an *interval estimate* to show a range of likely values. To do this, we insert the x_i value into the fitted regression equation, calculate the estimated $\hat{y}_i$, and use the formulas shown on the next page. The first formula gives a

confidence interval for the conditional mean of Y, while the second is a **prediction interval** for individual values of Y. The formulas are similar, except that prediction intervals are wider because *individual Y* values vary more than the *mean* of Y.

LO 12-9

Distinguish between confidence and prediction intervals for Y.

$$\hat{y}_i \pm t_{\alpha/2} s_e \sqrt{\frac{1}{n} + \frac{(x_i - \bar{x})^2}{\sum\limits_{i=1}^{n}(x_i - \bar{x})^2}} \quad \text{(confidence interval for mean of } Y) \quad \textbf{(12.29)}$$

$$\hat{y}_i \pm t_{\alpha/2} s_e \sqrt{1 + \frac{1}{n} + \frac{(x_i - \bar{x})^2}{\sum\limits_{i=1}^{n}(x_i - \bar{x})^2}} \quad \text{(prediction interval for individual } Y) \textbf{(12.30)}$$

Let's use formula 12.30 to predict the exam score for a student who studies 4 hours, using the regression model developed in Section 12.4. What is the 95 percent prediction interval? The student's predicted exam score (see Table 12.4) would be $\hat{y} = 1.9641(4) + 49.477 = 57.333$. For 95 percent confidence with $d.f. = n - 2 = 10 - 2 = 8$, we use $t_{.025} = 2.306$. Using the sums from Table 12.3, the 95 percent prediction interval is:

$$57.333 \pm (2.306)(14.002)\sqrt{1 + \frac{1}{10} + \frac{(4 - 10.5)^2}{264.5}} \quad \text{or} \quad 57.33 \pm 36.24$$

This very wide interval says that we cannot make precise predictions of the exam score for a student who studies 4 hours. This is not surprising since the fit for the exam score data ($R^2 = .3941$) was not very high. Prediction intervals are more precise when R^2 is high.

Interval width varies with the value of x_i, being narrowest when x_i is near its mean (note that when $x_i = \bar{x}$, the last term under the square root disappears completely). For some data sets, the degree of narrowing near $\bar{x}$ is almost indiscernible, while for other data sets it is quite pronounced. These calculations are usually done by computer (see Figure 12.21). Both MegaStat and MINITAB, for example, will let you type in the x_i values and will give both confidence and prediction intervals *only* for that x_i value, but you must make your own graphs.

FIGURE 12.21

MegaStat's Confidence and Prediction Intervals

Two Illustrations: Exam Scores and Retail Sales

ExamScores **RetailSales**

Since there will be a different interval for every X value, it is helpful to see confidence and prediction intervals over the entire range of X. Figure 12.22 shows confidence and prediction intervals for exam scores and retail sales. The contrast between the two graphs is striking. Confidence and prediction intervals for exam scores are wide and clearly narrower for X values near the mean. The prediction bands for exam scores for large X values (e.g., $x = 20$ hours of study) even extend above 100 points (presumably the upper limit for an exam score). In contrast, the intervals for retail sales appear narrow and only slightly wider for X values below or above the mean. While the prediction bands for retail

FIGURE 12.22

Confidence and Prediction Intervals Illustrated

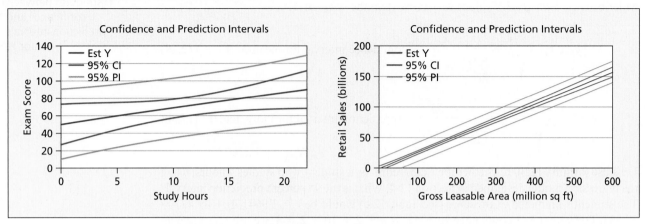

sales seem narrow, they still represent billions of dollars (e.g., for $x = 500$, the retail sales prediction interval has a width of about $33 billion). This shows that a high R^2 does not guarantee precise predictions.

Quick Rules for Confidence and Prediction Intervals

Because the confidence interval formulas are complex enough to discourage their use, we are motivated to consider approximations. When x_i is not too far from $\bar{x}$, the last term under the square root is small and might be ignored. As a further simplification, we might ignore $1/n$ in the individual Y formula (if n is large, then $1/n$ will be small). These simplifications yield the quick confidence and prediction intervals shown below. If you want a *really* quick 95 percent interval, you can plug in $t = 2$ (since most 95 percent t-values are not far from 2).

(12.31) $\qquad \hat{y}_i \pm t_{\alpha/2} \dfrac{s_e}{\sqrt{n}} \quad$ (quick confidence interval for mean of Y)

(12.32) $\qquad \hat{y}_i \pm t_{\alpha/2} s_e \quad$ (quick prediction interval for individual Y)

These quick rules lead to constant width intervals and are *not* conservative (i.e., the resulting intervals will be somewhat too narrow). They work best for large samples and when X is near its mean. They are questionable when X is near either extreme of its range. Yet they often are close enough to convey a general idea of the accuracy of your predictions. Their purpose is to give a quick answer without getting lost in unwieldy formulas.

SECTION EXERCISES

connect

12.32 Refer to the Weekly Earnings data set below. (a) Use MegaStat or MINITAB to find confidence and prediction intervals for Y using the following set of x values: 12, 17, 21, 25, and 30. (b) Report the 95 percent confidence interval and prediction interval for $x = 17$. (c) Calculate the 95 percent confidence interval for μ_y using the appropriate method from Chapter 8. (d) Compare the result from part (c) to the confidence interval you reported in part (b). How are they different?

College Student Weekly Earnings ($n = 5$) 📄 WeekPay	
Hours Worked (X)	**Weekly Pay (Y)**
10	93
15	171
20	204
20	156
35	261

12.33 Refer to the Revenue and Profit data set below. Data are in billions of dollars. (a) Use Mega-Stat or MINITAB to find confidence and prediction intervals for Y using the following set of x values: 1.8, 15, and 30. (b) Report the 95 percent confidence interval and prediction interval for $x = 15$. (c) Calculate the 95 percent confidence interval for μ_y using the appropriate method from Chapter 8. (d) Compare the result from part (c) to the confidence interval you reported in part (b). How are they different?

Revenue and Profit of Entertainment Companies ($n = 9$) 📽 Entertainment	
Revenue (X)	**Profit (Y)**
1.792	−0.020
8.931	1.146
2.446	−0.978
1.883	−0.162
2.490	0.185
43.877	2.639
1.311	0.155
26.585	1.417
27.061	1.267

12.8 RESIDUAL TESTS

Three Important Assumptions

Recall that the dependent variable is a random variable that has an error component, ε. In Section 12.3 we discussed three assumptions that the OLS method makes about the random error term ε. The regression assumptions are restated here:

- Assumption 1: The errors are *normally* distributed.
- Assumption 2: The errors have *constant* variance.
- Assumption 3: The errors are *independent*.

Because we cannot observe the error ε, we must rely on the residuals $e_1, e_2, \ldots, e_n$ from the estimated regression for clues about possible violations of these assumptions. While formal tests exist for identifying assumption violations, many analysts rely on simple visual tools to help them determine when an assumption has not been met and how serious the violation is.

In this chapter we will discuss the consequences of violating each assumption and explain the visual tools used for examining the residuals. In Chapter 13 we will discuss in more detail how to remedy an assumption violation and demonstrate a more formal method for examining assumption 3.

Violation of Assumption 1: Non-normal Errors

The main consequence of non-normality of errors is that confidence intervals for the parameters may be untrustworthy because the normality assumption is used to justify using Student's t to construct confidence intervals. However, if the sample size is large (say, $n > 30$), the confidence intervals should be OK. An exception would be if outliers exist, posing a serious problem that may be cured by large sample size. Non-normality of errors is usually considered a mild violation because the regression parameter estimates b_0 and b_1 and their variances remain unbiased and consistent.

A simple way to check for non-normality is to make a histogram of the residuals. You can use either plain residuals or **standardized residuals**. A *standardized residual* is obtained by dividing each residual by its standard error. Histogram shapes will be the same, but standardized residuals offer the advantage of a predictable scale (between −3 and +3 unless there are outliers). A simple "eyeball test" can usually reveal outliers or serious asymmetry. Figure 12.23 shows a standardized residual histogram for Mini Case 12.3

FIGURE 12.23

Cockpit Noise Residuals (Histogram) Cockpit

(cockpit noise). There are no outliers and the histogram is roughly symmetric, albeit possibly platykurtic (i.e., flatter than normal).

Another visual test for normality is the **normal probability plot**. It is produced as an option by all three software packages we've discussed. The hypotheses are

H_0: Errors are normally distributed

H_1: Errors are not normally distributed

If the null hypothesis is true, the residual normal probability plot should be linear. For example, in Figure 12.24 we see slight deviations from linearity at the lower and upper ends of the residual probability plot for Mini Case 12.3 (cockpit noise). The residuals seem to be consistent with the null hypothesis of normality. There are more precise tests for normality, but the histogram and normal probability plot suffice for most purposes.

FIGURE 12.24

Cockpit Noise Residuals (Normal Probability Plot)

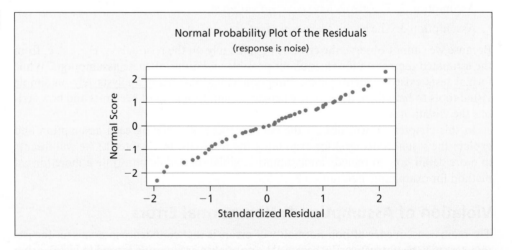

Tip

Non-normality is not considered a major violation because the parameter estimates remain unbiased and consistent. Don't worry too much about it *unless* you have major outliers.

Violation of Assumption 2: Nonconstant Variance

The regression should fit equally well for all values of X. If the error magnitude is constant for all X, the errors are **homoscedastic** (the ideal condition). If the error magnitudes increase or decrease as X changes, they are **heteroscedastic**. Although the OLS regression parameter estimates b_0 and b_1 are still unbiased and consistent, their estimated variances are biased and are neither efficient nor asymptotically efficient. In the most common form of heteroscedasticity, the variances of the estimators are likely to be understated, resulting in overstated t statistics and artificially narrow confidence intervals. Your regression estimates may thus seem more significant than is warranted.

For a simple regression, you can see heteroscedasticity on the XY scatter plot, but a more general visual test is to plot the residuals against X or against $\hat{Y}$. Ideally, there is no pattern in the residuals as we move from left to right, as shown in the illustration below. Notice that residuals *always* have a mean of zero.

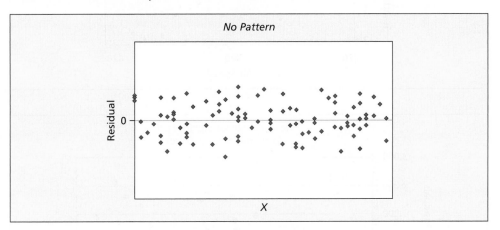

Although many patterns of nonconstant variance might exist, the "fan-out" pattern (increasing residual variance) is most common. Less frequently we might see a "funnel-in" pattern, which shows decreasing residual variance.

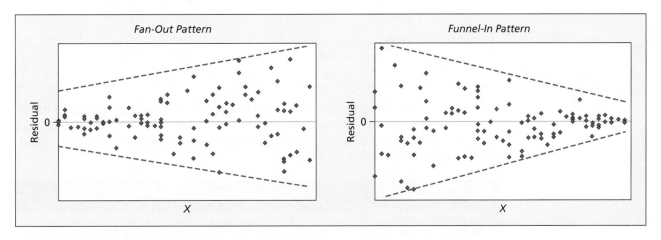

Residual plots provide a fairly sensitive "eyeball test" for heteroscedasticity. The residual plot is therefore considered an important tool in the statistician's diagnostic kit. The hypotheses are

H_0: Errors have constant variance (homoscedastic)

H_1: Errors have nonconstant variance (heteroscedastic)

Figure 12.25 shows a residual plot for Mini Case 12.3 (cockpit noise). In this residual plot, the magnitude of the residuals does not increase or decrease as we look from left to right. A pattern like this is consistent with the null hypothesis of homoscedasticity (constant variance).

Figure 12.26 shows a heteroscedastic residual plot from a regression of home prices versus square feet. The magnitude of the residuals increases as the home size increases. A pattern like this is consistent with heteroscedasticity (nonconstant variance). In Chapter 13 you will learn how we might remedy the violation of constant error variance.

FIGURE 12.25

Cockpit Noise Residual Plot (Homoscedastic)

FIGURE 12.26

Home Price Residual Plot (Heteroscedastic)

Caution: When using visual tools, we are looking for *obvious* departures from the assumptions of normality and constant variance. Consider the overall shape of the plot and don't focus on one or two residuals that might be considered outliers. We will discuss how to spot outliers in Section 12.9.

Tip

Although it can widen the confidence intervals for the coefficients, heteroscedasticity does not bias the estimates. At this stage of your training, it is sufficient just to recognize its existence.

Violation of Assumption 3: Autocorrelated Errors

Autocorrelation is a pattern of nonindependent errors, mainly found in time-series data. When variable observations are collected in a specific order such as in a time series, it is possible that the errors $e_1, e_2, \ldots, e_n$ are related to each other. In a regression, each residual e_t should be independent of its predecessors $e_{t-1}, e_{t-2}, \ldots, e_1$. Violations of this assumption can show up in different ways. In the simple model of *first-order autocorrelation,* we would find that e_t is correlated with the prior residual e_{t-1}. The OLS estimators b_0 and b_1 are still unbiased and consistent, but their estimated variances are biased in a way that typically leads to confidence intervals that are too narrow and t statistics that are too large. Thus, the model's fit may be overstated.

Positive autocorrelation is indicated by runs of residuals with the *same* sign, while *negative autocorrelation* is indicated by runs of residuals with *alternating* signs. Such patterns can sometimes be seen in a plot of the residuals against the order of data entry. In the *runs test,* we count the number of sign reversals (i.e., how often does the residual plot cross the zero centerline?). If the pattern is random, the number of sign changes should be approximately $n/2$. Fewer than $n/2$ centerline crossings would suggest positive autocorrelation, while more than $n/2$ centerline crossings would suggest negative autocorrelation. For example, if $n = 50$, we would expect about 25 centerline crossings. In the first illustration, there are only 11 crossings (positive autocorrelation), while in the second illustration there are 36 crossings (negative autocorrelation). Positive autocorrelation is common in economic time-series regressions due to the cyclical nature of the economy. It is harder to envision logical reasons for negative autocorrelation, and in fact it is rarely observed.

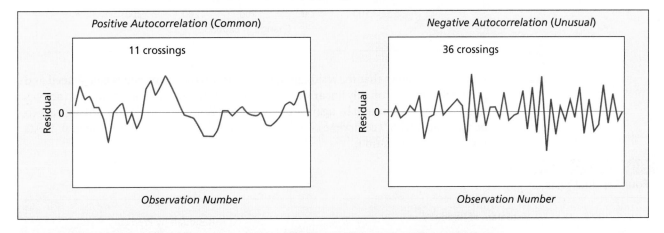

Tip

Autocorrelation is a concern with time-series data. Although it can widen the confidence intervals for the coefficients, autocorrelation does not bias the estimates. At this stage of your training, it is sufficient just to recognize when you have autocorrelation.

Mini Case   12.4

Exports and Imports 📂 **Exports**

We often see headlines about the persistent imbalance in U.S. foreign trade (e.g., "U.S. Trade Deficit Sets Record," *International Herald Tribune,* March 14, 2007). But when U.S. imports increase, other nations acquire dollar balances that economists predict will lead to increased purchases of U.S. goods and services, thereby increasing U.S. exports (i.e., trade imbalances are supposed to be self-correcting). Figure 12.27 shows a regression based on U.S. exports and imports for 1959−2005. To reduce autocorrelation (these are time-series data), the model regresses the *change* in exports (denoted $\triangle Exports$) against the *change* in imports (denoted $\triangle Imports$) for each period. The fitted model is $\triangle Exports = 5.2849 + 0.5193\ \triangle Imports$. As expected, the slope is positive and significant ($t = 10.277$, p-value $< .0001$) and the fit is fairly good ($R^2 = .7059$) despite the first-differences data transformation. But the slope ($b_1 = 0.5193$) indicates that the change in exports is only about half the change in imports, so the trade imbalance remains a puzzle. An economist would perhaps want to examine the role of exchange rate inflexibility, vis-à-vis China or other factors, in constructing a more complex model.

FIGURE 12.27   **Excel Scatter Plot and Regression**

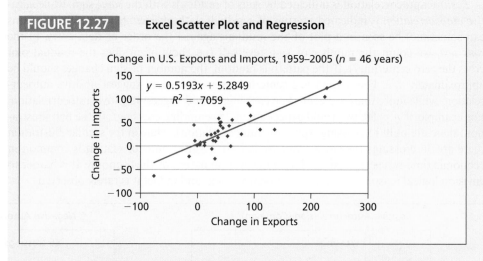

Change in U.S. Exports and Imports, 1959–2005 ($n = 46$ years)

$y = 0.5193x + 5.2849$
$R^2 = .7059$

Figure 12.28 shows that the residuals appear normal (the histogram is bell-shaped and probability plot is roughly linear with no obvious outliers) and homoscedastic (no pattern in the plot of residuals against predicted Y). But autocorrelation still appears to be a problem with 9 centerline crossings in the residual plot over time, which suggests positive autocorrelation.

FIGURE 12.28

Four Residual Tests

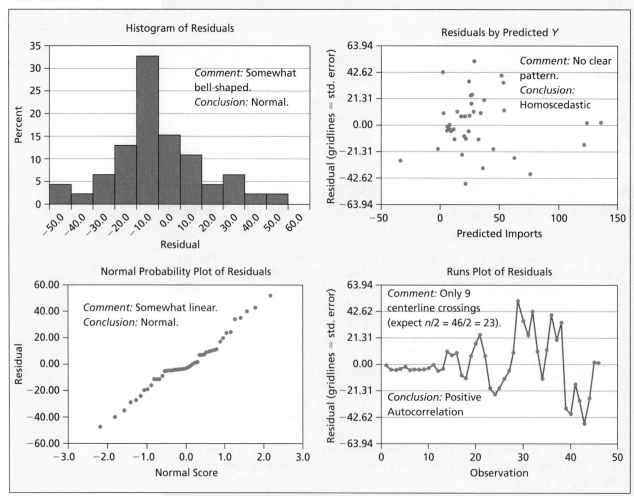

12.34 Review the two residual plots below. Do either of these show evidence that the regression error assumptions of normality and constant variation have been violated? Explain.

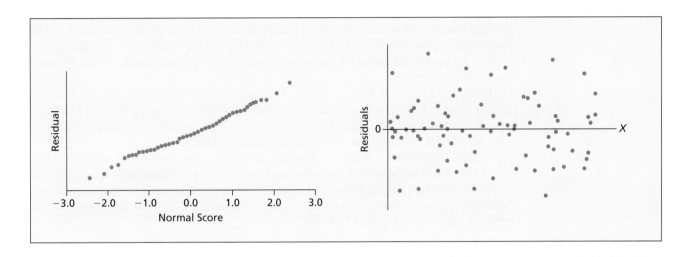

12.35 Review the two residual plots below. Do either of these show evidence that the regression error assumptions of normality and constant variation have been violated? Explain.

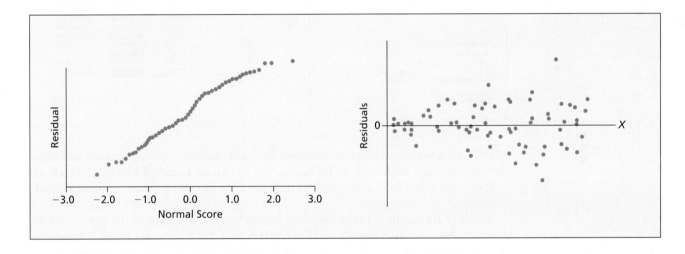

12.9 UNUSUAL OBSERVATIONS

In a regression, we look for observations that are unusual. An observation could be unusual because its *Y*-value is poorly predicted by the regression model (*unusual residual*) or because its unusual *X*-value greatly affects the regression line (*high leverage*). Tests for unusual residuals and high leverage are important diagnostic tools in evaluating the fitted regression.

Unusual Residuals

Because every regression may have different *Y* units (e.g., stock price in dollars, shipping time in days), it is helpful to *standardize* the residuals by dividing each residual, e_i, by its individual standard error, s_{e_i}.

(12.33) $$e_i^* = \frac{e_i}{s_{e_i}} \quad \text{(standardized residual for observation } i\text{)}$$

LO 12-11

Identify unusual residuals and high-leverage observations.

where

$$s_{e_i} = s_e\sqrt{1 - h_i} \quad \text{and} \quad h_i = \frac{1}{n} + \frac{(x_i - \bar{x})^2}{\sum (x_i - \bar{x})^2}$$

Notice that this calculation requires a unique adjustment for each residual based on the observation's distance from the mean. We will refer to this value e_i^* as a *standardized residual*. An equivalent name for this value is **studentized residual**, which is used by many software packages.

Using the Empirical Rule as a rule of thumb, any standardized residual whose absolute value is 2 or more is unusual, and any residual whose absolute value is 3 or more would be considered an outlier. There are subtle differences in the way Excel, MegaStat, and MINITAB calculate and display standardized residuals.

Excel's Data Analysis > Regression provides residuals as an option, as shown in Figure 12.29. Excel calculates its "standardized residuals" by dividing each residual by the standard deviation of the column of residuals. This procedure is not quite correct, but generally suffices to identify unusual residuals. Using the Empirical Rule, there are no unusual residuals in Figure 12.29.

FIGURE 12.29

Excel's Exam Score Residuals

MINITAB gives the same general output as Excel, but with rounded results and more detailed residual information. Its menus are shown in Figure 12.30. MINITAB reports standardized residuals, which usually are close in value to Excel's "standardized" residuals.

MINITAB's results confirm that there are no unusual residuals in the exam score regression. An attractive feature of MINITAB is that the actual and fitted Y-values are displayed (Excel shows only the fitted Y-values). MINITAB also gives the standard error for the mean of Y (the column labeled SE Fit), which you can multiply by $t_{\alpha/2}$ to get the confidence interval width.

FIGURE 12.30

MINITAB's Exam Score Residuals

MegaStat gives the same general output as Excel and MINITAB. Its regression menu is shown in Figure 12.31. Like MINITAB, it offers studentized residuals, but MegaStat also shows *studentized deleted residuals*. This is yet another way to identify unusual residuals. The calculation is equivalent to rerunning the regression n times, with each observation omitted in turn, and recalculating the studentized residuals. Further calculation details are reserved for an advanced statistics class, but interpretation is simple. A studentized deleted residual whose absolute value is 2 or more is unusual and one whose absolute value is 3 or more is typically considered an outlier. To make the output more readable, MegaStat rounds off the values (like MINITAB) and highlights unusual and outlier standardized residuals.

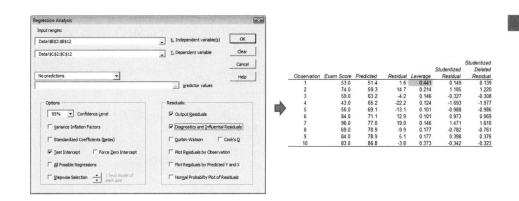

FIGURE 12.31

MegaStat's Exam Score Residuals

Observation	Exam Score	Predicted	Residual	Leverage	Studentized Residual	Studentized Deleted Residual
1	53.0	51.4	1.6	0.441	0.149	0.139
2	74.0	59.3	14.7	0.214	1.185	1.220
3	59.0	63.2	-4.2	0.146	-0.327	-0.308
4	43.0	65.2	-22.2	0.124	-1.693	-1.977
5	56.0	69.1	-13.1	0.101	-0.988	-0.986
6	84.0	71.1	12.9	0.101	0.973	0.969
7	96.0	77.0	19.0	0.146	1.471	1.610
8	69.0	78.9	-9.9	0.177	-0.782	-0.761
9	84.0	78.9	5.1	0.177	0.398	0.376
10	83.0	86.8	-3.8	0.373	-0.342	-0.323

High Leverage

A high **leverage** statistic indicates that the observation is far from the mean of X. Such observations have great influence on the regression estimates because they are at the "end of the lever." Figure 12.32 illustrates this concept. One individual worked 65 hours, while the others worked between 12 and 42 hours. This individual will have a big effect on the slope estimate because he is so far above the mean of X.

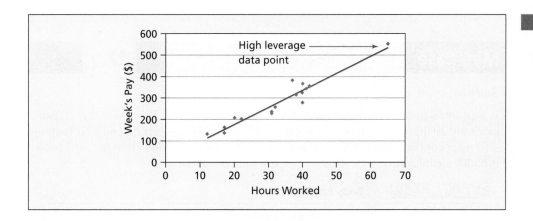

FIGURE 12.32

Illustration of High Leverage Leverage

The leverage for observation i is denoted h_i and is calculated as

$$h_i = \frac{1}{n} + \frac{(x_i - \bar{x})^2}{\sum\limits_{i=1}^{n} (x_i - \bar{x})^2} \qquad (12.34)$$

High Leverage

As a rule of thumb for a simple regression, a leverage statistic that exceeds $4/n$ is unusual (if $x_i = \bar{x}$, the leverage statistic h_i is $1/n$ so the rule of thumb is just four times this value).

EXAMPLE 12.3

Exam Scores: Leverage and Influence

📁 **ExamScores**

We see from Figure 12.33 that two data points (Tom and Courtney) are likely to have high leverage because Tom studied for only 1 hour (far below the mean) while Courtney studied for 19 hours (far above the mean). Using the sums from Table 12.3, we can calculate their leverages:

$$h_{\text{Tom}} = \frac{1}{10} + \frac{(1 - 10.5)^2}{264.50} = .441 \quad \text{(Tom's leverage)}$$

$$h_{\text{Courtney}} = \frac{1}{10} + \frac{(19 - 10.5)^2}{264.50} = .373 \quad \text{(Courtney's leverage)}$$

FIGURE 12.33   **Scatter Plot for Exam Data** 📁 **ExamScores**

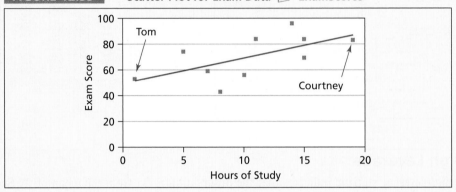

By the quick rule, Tom's leverage exceeds $4/n = 4/10 = .400$, so it appears that his observation is *influential*. Yet, despite his high leverage, the regression fits Tom's actual exam score well, so his residual is not unusual. This illustrates that *high leverage* and *unusual residuals* are two different concepts.

Mini Case   12.5

Body Fat 📁 **BodyFat**

Is waistline a good predictor of body fat? A random sample of 50 men's body fat (percent) and girths (centimeters) was collected. Figure 12.34 suggests that a linear regression is appropriate, and the MegaStat output in Figure 12.35 shows that the regression is highly significant ($F = 97.68$, $t = 9.883$, p-value = .0000).

FIGURE 12.34   **Body Fat Regression**

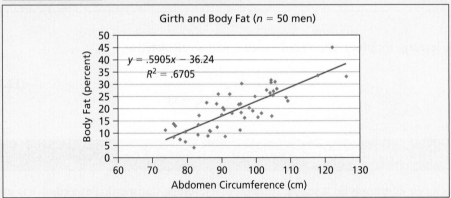

The table of residuals, shown in Figure 12.36, highlights four unusual observations. Observations 5, 45, and 50 have high leverage values (exceeding $4/n = 4/50 = .08$)

FIGURE 12.35	**Body Fat Scatter Plot**

Regression Analysis

r^2	0.671	n	50	
r	0.819	k	1	
Std. Error	5.086	Dep. Var.	Fat% 1	

ANOVA table

Source	SS	df	MS	F	p-value
Regression	2,527.1190	1	2,527.1190	97.68	3.71E-13
Residual	1,241.8162	48	25.8712		
Total	3,768.9352	49			

Regression output   *confidence interval*

variables	coefficients	std. error	t (df= 48)	p-value	95% lower	95% upper
Intercept	−36.2397	5.6690	−6.393	6.28E-08	−47.6379	−24.8415
Abdomen	0.5905	0.0597	9.883	3.71E-13	0.4704	0.7107

because their abdomen measurements are far from the mean. Observation 37 has a large studentized deleted residual (actual body fat of 30.20 percent is much greater than the predicted 20.33 percent). "Well-behaved" observations are omitted because they are not unusual according to any of the diagnostic criteria (leverage, studentized residual, or studentized deleted residual).

FIGURE 12.36	**Unusual Body Fat Residuals**

Observation	Fat%	Predicted	Residual	Leverage	Studentized Residual	Studentized Deleted Residual
5	33.60	33.44	0.16	0.099	0.033	0.032
37	30.20	20.33	9.87	0.020	1.960	2.022
45	33.10	38.28	−5.18	0.162	−1.114	−1.116
50	45.10	35.86	9.24	0.128	1.945	2.005

SECTION EXERCISES

connect

12.36 An estimated regression for a random sample of observations on an assembly line is *Defects* = 3.2 + 0.045 *Speed*, where *Defects* is the number of defects per million parts and *Speed* is the number of units produced per hour. The estimated standard error is s_e = 1.07. Suppose that 100 units per hour are produced and the actual (observed) defect rate is *Defects* = 4.4. (a) Calculate the predicted *Defects*. (b) Calculate the residual. (c) Standardize the residual using s_e. (d) Is this observation an outlier?

12.37 An estimated regression for a random sample of vehicles is *MPG* = 49.22 − 0.081 *Horsepower*, where *MPG* is miles per gallon and *Horsepower* is the engine's horsepower. The standard error is s_e = 2.03. Suppose an engine has 200 horsepower and its actual (observed) fuel efficiency is *MPG* = 38.15. (a) Calculate the predicted *MPG*. (b) Calculate the residual. (c) Standardize the residual using s_e. (d) Is this engine an outlier?

12.38 A sample of season performance measures for 29 NBA teams was collected for a season. A regression analysis was performed on two of the variables with *Y* = *total number of free throws made* and *X* = *total number of free throws attempted*. Calculate the leverage statistic for the following three teams and state whether or not the leverage would be considered high. Given: $SS_{xx} = 999{,}603$ and $\bar{x} = 2004$.

a. The Golden State Warriors attempted 2,382 free throws.
b. The New Jersey Nets attempted 2,125 free throws.
c. The New York Knicks attempted 1,620 free throws.

12.39 A sample of 74 Noodles & Company restaurants was used to perform a regression analysis with $Y = \%$ *Annual Revenue Growth* and $X = \%$ *Revenue Due to Loyalty Card Use*. Calculate the leverage statistic for the following three restaurants and state whether or not the leverage would be considered high. Given: $SS_{xx} = 22.285$ and $\bar{x} = 2.027$ percent.

a. Restaurant 21 earned .072 percent of revenue from loyalty card use.
b. Restaurant 29 earned 1.413 percent of revenue from loyalty card use.
c. Restaurant 64 earned 3.376 percent of revenue from loyalty card use.

12.10 OTHER REGRESSION PROBLEMS (OPTIONAL)

Outliers

We have mentioned outliers under the discussion of non-normal residuals. However, outliers are the source of many other woes, including loss of fit. What causes outliers? An outlier may be an error in recording the data. If so, the observation should be deleted. But how can you tell? Impossible or bizarre data values are *prima facie* reasons to discard a data value. For example, in a sample of body fat data, one adult man's weight was reported as 205 pounds and his height as 29.5 inches (probably a typographical error that should have been 69.5 inches). It is reasonable to discard the observation on grounds that it represents a population different from the other men. An outlier may be an observation that has been influenced by an unspecified "lurking" variable that should have been controlled but wasn't. If so, we should try to identify the lurking variable and formulate a *multiple* regression model that includes the lurking variable(s) as predictors.

Model Misspecification

If a relevant predictor has been omitted, then the model is *misspecified*. Instead of simple regression, you should use *multiple regression*. Such a situation is so common that it is almost a warning against relying on bivariate regression, since we usually can think of more than one explanatory variable. As you will see in the next chapter, multiple regression is computationally easy because the computer does all the work. In fact, most computer packages just call it "regression" regardless of the number of predictors.

Ill-Conditioned Data

Variables in the regression should be of the same general order of magnitude, and most people take steps intuitively to make sure this is the case (**well-conditioned data**). Unusually large or small data (called **ill-conditioned**) can cause loss of regression accuracy or can create awkward estimates with exponential notation. Consider the data in Table 12.6 for 30 randomly selected large companies (only a few of the 30 selected are shown in this table).

TABLE 12.6				
	Company	*Net Income in Thousands*	*Revenue in Thousands*	*Net Income in Millions*	*Revenue in Millions*
Net Income and Revenue for Selected Global 100 Companies	Allstate	1,714,000	30,142,000	1,714	30,142
Global30	American Int'l Group	5,493,000	70,272,000	5,493	70,272
	Barclays	3,348,000	26,565,000	3,348	26,565
Source: www.forbes.com and *Forbes* 172, no. 2 (July 21, 2003), pp. 108–110.	⋮	⋮	⋮	⋮	⋮
	Volkswagen Group	2,432,000	84,707,000	2,432	84,707
	Wachovia	3,693,000	23,455,000	3,693	23,455
	Walt Disney	1,024,000	26,255,000	1,024	26,255

The table shows two ways of displaying the same data, but with the decimal point changed. Figures 12.37 and 12.38 show Excel scatter plots with regression lines. Their appearance is the same, but the first graph has disastrously crowded axis labels. The graphs have the same slope and R^2, but the first regression has an unintelligible intercept (4E+07).

FIGURE 12.37

Ill-Conditioned Data

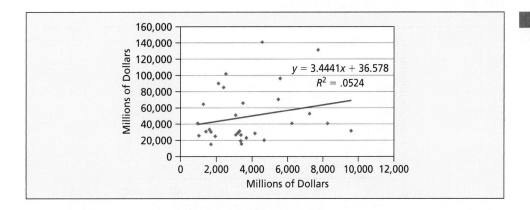

FIGURE 12.38

Well-Conditioned Data

Awkwardly small numbers may also require adjustment. For example, the number of automobile thefts per capita in the United States in 2009 was 0.002588. However, this statistic is easier to work with if it is reported "per 100,000 population" as 258.8. Worst of all would be to mix very large data with very small data. For example, in 2009 the per capita income in New York was $46,957 and the number of active physicians per capita was 0.00391. To avoid mixing magnitudes, we can redefine the variables as per capita income in thousands of dollars (46.957) and the number of active physicians per 10,000 population (39.1).

Tip

Adjust the magnitude of your data *before* running the regression.

Spurious Correlation Prisoners

In a **spurious correlation**, two variables appear related because of the way they are defined. For example, consider the hypothesis that a state's spending on education is a linear function of its prison population. Such a hypothesis seems absurd, and we would expect the regression to be insignificant. But if the variables are defined as *totals* without adjusting for population, we will observe significant correlation. This phenomenon is called the *size effect* or the *problem of totals*. Table 12.7 shows selected data, first with the variables as *totals* and then as adjusted for population.

TABLE 12.7

State Spending on
Education and State
and Federal Prisoners
📁 Prisoners

Source: *Statistical Abstract of the
United States, 2001* .

State	Total Population (millions)	Using Totals		Using Per Capita Data	
		K–12 Spending ($ billions)	No. of Prisoners (thousands)	K–12 Spending per Capita ($)	Prisoners per 1,000 Pop.
Alabama	4.447	4.52	24.66	1,016	5.54
Alaska	0.627	1.33	3.95	2,129	6.30
⋮	⋮	⋮	⋮	⋮	⋮
Wisconsin	5.364	8.48	20.42	1,580	3.81
Wyoming	0.494	0.76	1.71	1,543	3.47

Figure 12.39 shows that, contrary to expectation, the regression on totals gives a very strong fit to the data. Yet Figure 12.40 shows that if we divide by population and adjust the decimals, the fit is nonexistent and the slope is indistinguishable from zero. The spurious correlation arose merely because both variables reflect the size of a state's population. For example, New York and California lie far to the upper right on the first scatter plot because they are populous states, while less populous states like South Dakota and Delaware are near the origin.

FIGURE 12.39

Spurious Model Using
Totals

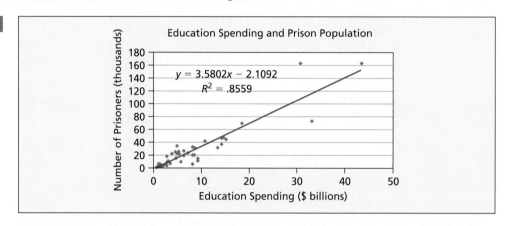

FIGURE 12.40

Better Model: Per Capita
Data

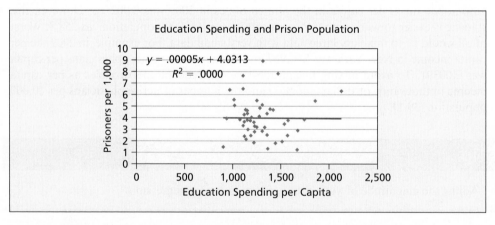

Model Form and Variable Transforms 📁 MPG 1

Sometimes a relationship cannot be modeled using a linear regression. For example, Figure 12.41 shows fuel efficiency (city MPG) and engine size (horsepower) for a sample of 93 vehicles with a nonlinear model form fitted by Excel. This is one of several nonlinear forms offered by Excel (there are also logarithmic and exponential functions). Figure 12.42 shows an alternative, which is a linear regression after taking *logarithms* of each variable. These logarithms are in base 10, but any base will do (scientists prefer base *e*). This is an example of a **variable transform**. An advantage of the **log transformation** is that

FIGURE 12.41

Nonlinear Regression

Source: Robin H. Lock, *Journal of Statistics Education* 1, no. 1 (1993).

FIGURE 12.42

After Log Transformation

it reduces heteroscedasticity and improves the normality of the residuals, especially when dealing with totals (the *size problem* mentioned earlier). But log transforms will not work if any data values are zero or negative.

Excel makes it easy to fit all sorts of regression models. But fit is only one criterion for evaluating a regression model. Since nonlinear or transformed models might be hard to justify or explain to others, the principle of *Occam's Razor* (choosing the simplest explanation that fits the facts) favors linear regression, unless there are other compelling factors.

Mini Case 12.6

CEO Compensation 📂 CEO

Do highly compensated executives lead their corporations to outperform other firms? Statistics student Greg Burks examined 1-year total shareholder returns in 2001 less the S&P 500 average (i.e., percentage points above or below the S&P average) as a function of total CEO compensation in 2001 for the top 200 U.S. corporations. A scatter plot is shown in Figure 12.43. There appears to be little relationship, but a dozen or so hugely compensated CEOs (e.g., those earning over 50 million) stretch the X-axis scale while many others are clustered near the origin. A log transformation of X (using base 10) is shown in Figure 12.44. Neither fitted regression is significant. That is, there is little relationship between CEO compensation and stockholder returns (if anything, the slope is negative). However, the transformed data give a clearer picture. An advantage of the log transformation is that it improves the scatter of the residuals, producing a more homoscedastic distribution. In short, a log transformation with skewed data is an excellent option to consider.

FIGURE 12.43   **CEO Compensation and Stock Returns**

2001 CEO Compensation ($n = 200$)

$y = -.0003x + 19.393$
$R^2 = .0419$

Source: *The New York Times,* Apr. 4, 2004, pp. 8–9.

FIGURE 12.44   **After Log Transformation**

2001 CEO Compensation ($n = 200$)

$y = -17.027x + 82.737$
$R^2 = .0595$

CHAPTER SUMMARY

The **sample correlation coefficient** r measures linear association between X and Y, with values near 0 indicating a lack of linearity while values near -1 (negative correlation) or $+1$ (positive correlation) suggest linearity. The **t test** is used to test hypotheses about the **population correlation** ρ. In **simple regression** there is an assumed linear relationship between the independent variable X (the **predictor**) and the dependent variable Y (the **response**). The slope (β_1) and intercept (β_0) are unknown **parameters** that are estimated from a sample. **Residuals** are the differences between **observed** and **fitted** Y-values. The **ordinary least squares** (OLS) method yields **regression coefficients** for the slope (b_1) and intercept (b_0) that minimize the sum of squared residuals. The **coefficient of determination** (R^2) measures the overall fit of the regression, with R^2 near 1 signifying a good fit and R^2 near 0 indicating a poor fit. The **F statistic** in the **ANOVA table** is used to test for significant overall regression, while the **t statistics** (and their p-values) are used to test hypotheses about the slope and intercept. The **standard error** of the regression is used to create **confidence intervals** or **prediction intervals** for Y. Regression assumes that the errors are normally distributed, independent random variables with constant variance σ^2. **Residual tests** identify possible **violations** of assumptions (**nonnormality, autocorrelation, heteroscedasticity**). Data values with high **leverage** (unusual X-values) have strong influence on the regression. Unusual **standardized residuals** indicate cases where the regression gives a poor fit. **Ill-conditioned** data may lead to **spurious** correlation or other problems. **Data transforms** may help, but they also change the **model specification**.

Commonly Used Formulas in Simple Regression

Sample correlation coefficient:
$$r = \frac{\sum_{i=1}^{n} (x_i - \bar{x})(y_i - \bar{y})}{\sqrt{\sum_{i=1}^{n} (x_i - \bar{x})^2}\sqrt{\sum_{i=1}^{n} (y_i - \bar{y})^2}}$$

Test statistic for zero correlation:
$$t_{\text{calc}} = r\sqrt{\frac{n-2}{1-r^2}} \text{ with } d.f. = n - 2$$

True regression line:
$$y = \beta_0 + \beta_1 x + \varepsilon$$

Fitted regression line:
$$\hat{y} = b_0 + b_1 x$$

Slope of fitted regression:
$$b_1 = \frac{\sum_{i=1}^{n} (x_i - \bar{x})(y_i - \bar{y})}{\sum_{i=1}^{n} (x_i - \bar{x})^2}$$

Intercept of fitted regression d:
$$b_0 = \bar{y} - b_1\bar{x}$$

Sum of squared residuals:
$$SSE = \sum_{i=1}^{n} (y_i - \hat{y}_i)^2 = \sum_{i=1}^{n} (y_i - b_0 - b_1 x_i)^2$$

Coefficient of determination:
$$R^2 = 1 - \frac{\sum_{i=1}^{n} (y_i - \hat{y}_i)^2}{\sum_{i=1}^{n} (y_i - \bar{y})^2} = 1 - \frac{SSE}{SST}$$

Standard error of the estimate:
$$s_e = \sqrt{\frac{\sum_{i=1}^{n} (y_i - \hat{y}_i)^2}{n-2}} = \sqrt{\frac{SSE}{n-2}}$$

Standard error of the slope:
$$s_{b_1} = \frac{s_e}{\sqrt{\sum_{i=1}^{n} (x_i - \bar{x})^2}} \text{ with } d.f. = n - 2$$

t test for zero slope:
$$t_{\text{calc}} = \frac{b_1 - 0}{s_{b_1}}$$

Confidence interval for true slope:
$$b_1 - t_{\alpha/2}\, s_{b_1} \le \beta_1 \le b_1 + t_{\alpha/2}\, s_{b_1}$$

Confidence interval for conditional mean of Y: $\quad \hat{y}_i \pm t_{\alpha/2} s_e \sqrt{\dfrac{1}{n} + \dfrac{(x_i - \bar{x})^2}{\displaystyle\sum_{i=1}^{n} (x_i - \bar{x})^2}}$

Prediction interval for Y: $\quad \hat{y}_i \pm t_{\alpha/2} s_e \sqrt{1 + \dfrac{1}{n} + \dfrac{(x_i - \bar{x})^2}{\displaystyle\sum_{i=1}^{n} (x_i - \bar{x})^2}}$

CHAPTER REVIEW

1. (a) How does correlation analysis differ from regression analysis? (b) What does a correlation coefficient reveal? (c) State the quick rule for a significant correlation and explain its limitations. (d) What sums are needed to calculate a correlation coefficient? (e) What are the two ways of testing a correlation coefficient for significance?

2. (a) What is a simple regression model? (b) State three caveats about regression. (c) What does the random error component in a regression model represent? (d) What is the difference between a regression residual and the true random error?

3. (a) Explain how you fit a regression to an Excel scatter plot. (b) What are the limitations of Excel's scatter plot fitted regression?

4. (a) Explain the logic of the ordinary least squares (OLS) method. (b) How are the least squares formulas for the slope and intercept derived? (c) What sums are needed to calculate the least squares estimates?

5. (a) Why can't we use the sum of the residuals to assess fit? (b) What sums are needed to calculate R^2? (c) Name an advantage of using the R^2 statistic instead of the standard error s_{yx} to measure fit. (d) Why do we need the standard error s_{yx}?

6. (a) Explain why a confidence interval for the slope or intercept would be equivalent to a two-tailed hypothesis test. (b) Why is it especially important to test for a zero slope?

7. (a) What does the F statistic show? (b) What is its range? (c) What is the relationship between the F test and the t tests for the slope and correlation coefficient?

8. (a) For a given X, explain the distinction between a confidence interval for the conditional mean of Y and a prediction interval for an individual Y-value. (b) Why is the individual prediction interval wider? (c) Why are these intervals narrowest when X is near its mean? (d) When can quick rules for these intervals give acceptable results, and when not?

9. (a) What is a residual? (b) What is a standardized residual and why is it useful? (c) Name two alternative ways to identify unusual residuals.

10. (a) When does a data point have high leverage (refer to the scatter plot)? (b) Name one test for unusual leverage.

11. (a) Name three assumptions about the random error term in the regression model. (b) Why are the residuals important in testing these assumptions?

12. (a) What are the consequences of non-normal errors? (b) Explain two tests for non-normality.

13. (a) What is heteroscedasticity? Identify its two common forms. (b) What are its consequences? (c) How do we test for it?

14. (a) What is autocorrelation? Identify two main forms of it. (b) What are its consequences? (c) How do we test for it?

15. (a) Why might there be outliers in the residuals? (b) What actions could be taken?

16. (a) What is ill-conditioned data? How can it be avoided? (b) What is spurious correlation? How can it be avoided?

17. (a) What is a log transform? (b) What are its advantages and disadvantages?

CHAPTER EXERCISES

connect

Instructions: Choose one or more of the data sets *A–J* below, or as assigned by your instructor. The first column is the *X*, or independent, variable and the second column is the *Y*, or dependent, variable. Use a spreadsheet or a statistical package (e.g., MegaStat or MINITAB) to obtain the simple regression and required graphs. Write your answers to exercises 12.40 through 12.55

(or those assigned by your instructor) in a concise report, labeling your answers to each question. Insert tables and graphs in your report as appropriate. You may work with a partner if your instructor allows it.

12.40 Are the variables cross-sectional data or time-series data?

12.41 How do you imagine the data were collected?

12.42 Is the sample size sufficient to yield a good estimate? If not, do you think more data could easily be obtained, given the nature of the problem?

12.43 State your *a priori* hypothesis about the sign of the slope. Is it reasonable to suppose a cause-and-effect relationship?

12.44 Make a scatter plot of *Y* against *X*. Discuss what it tells you.

12.45 Use Excel's Add Trendline feature to fit a linear regression to the scatter plot. Is a linear model credible?

12.46 Interpret the slope. Does the intercept have meaning, given the range of the data?

12.47 Use Excel, MegaStat, or MINITAB to fit the regression model, including residuals and standardized residuals.

12.48 (a) Does the 95 percent confidence interval for the slope include zero? If so, what does this tell you? If not, what does it mean? (b) Do a two-tailed *t* test for zero slope at $\alpha = .05$. State the hypotheses, degrees of freedom, and critical value for your test. (c) Interpret the *p*-value for the slope. (d) Did the sample support your hypothesis about the sign of the slope?

12.49 (a) Based on the R^2 and ANOVA table for your model, how would you assess the fit? (b) Interpret the *p*-value for the *F* statistic. (c) Would you say that your model's fit is good enough to be of practical value?

12.50 Study the table of residuals. Identify as *outliers* any standardized residuals that exceed 3 and as *unusual* any that exceed 2. Can you suggest any reasons for these unusual residuals?

12.51 (a) Make a histogram (or normal probability plot) of the residuals and discuss its appearance. (b) Do you see evidence that your regression may violate the assumption of normal errors?

12.52 Inspect the residual plot to check for heteroscedasticity and report your conclusions.

12.53 Is an autocorrelation test appropriate for your data? If so, perform an eyeball inspection of residual plot against observation order or a runs test.

12.54 Use MegaStat or MINITAB to generate 95 percent confidence and prediction intervals for various *X*-values.

12.55 Use MegaStat or MINITAB to identify observations with high leverage.

DATA SET A	Median Income and Median Home Prices in Selected Eastern Cities ($n = 34$ cities) 📂 HomePrice1	
City	**Income**	**Home**
Alexandria, VA	59.976	290.000
Bernards Twp., NJ	112.435	279.900
Brentwood, TN	107.866	338.250
⋮	⋮	⋮
Sugarland Run, VA	103.350	278.250
Sully, VA	92.942	290.000
Wellington, FL	76.076	230.000

Source: *Money Magazine* 32, no. 1 (January 2004), pp. 102–103.

Note: Values are in thousands of dollars. Data are for educational purposes only.

DATA SET B	Midterm and Final Exam Scores for Business Statistics Students Fall Semester 2011 ($n = 58$ students) 📂 ExamScores2
Midterm Exam Score	**Final Exam Score**
80	78
87	85
72	81
⋮	⋮
80	82
68	70
73	69

DATA SET C   Estimated and Actual Length of Stay in Months (n = 16 patients) 📁 Hospital

Patient	ELOS	ALOS
1	10.5	10
2	4.5	2
3	7.5	4
⋮	⋮	⋮
14	6	10
15	7.5	7
16	3	5.5

Source: Records of a hospital outpatient cognitive retraining clinic.

Note: ELOS used a 42-item assessment instrument combined with expert team judgment. Patients had suffered head trauma, stroke, or other medical conditions affecting cognitive function.

DATA SET D   Single-Engine Aircraft Performance (n = 52 airplanes) 📁 Airplanes

Mfgr/Model	TotalHP	Cruise
AMD CH 2000	116	100
Beech Baron 58	600	200
Beech Baron 58P	650	241
⋮	⋮	⋮
Sky Arrow 650 TC	81	98
Socata TB20 Trinidad	250	163
Tiger AG-5B	180	143

Source: New and used airplane reports in *Flying* (various issues).

Note: Cruise is in knots (nautical miles per hour). Data are for educational purposes only and should not be used as a guide to aircraft performance. *TotalHP* is total horse power.

DATA SET E   Microprocessor Speed (MHz) and Power Dissipation (watts) (n = 14 chips) 📁 Microprocessors

Chip	Speed (MHz)	Power (watts)
1989 Intel 80486	20	3
1993 Pentium	100	10
1997 Pentium II	233	35
1998 Intel Celeron	300	20
1999 Pentium III	600	42
1999 AMD Athlon	600	50
2000 Pentium 4	1300	51
2004 Celeron D	2100	73
2004 Pentium 4	3800	115
2005 Pentium D	3200	130
2007 AMD Phenom	2300	95
2008 Intel Core 2	3200	136
2009 Intel Core i7	2900	95
2009 AMD Phenom II	3200	125

Source: *New Scientist*, 208, no. 2780 (October 2, 2010), p. 41.

DATA SET F   Restaurant Weekly Revenue and Weekly Website Hits (n = 10 restaurants) 📁 WebSiteHits

Restaurant	Weekly Revenue	Website Hits
John's Café	$12,113	1,213
Buccan	11,409	1,490
New City Diner	14,579	1,365
Black Pearl	11,605	1,455
Saratoga	12,308	1,269
Burnt Toast	12,320	1,632
University Seat	13,225	1,323
Jimmy's	13,652	1,865
Maroon and Orange	13,893	1,590
Burger Palace	13,896	1,878

DATA SET G   Mileage and Vehicle Weight (n = 43 vehicles) 📁 MPG2

Vehicle	Weight	City MPG
Acura CL	3450	20
Accura TSX	3320	23
BMW 3-Series	3390	19
⋮	⋮	⋮
Toyota Sienna	4120	19
Volkswagen Jetta	3045	34
Volvo C70	3690	20

Source: *Consumer Reports New Car Buying Guide 2003–2004* (Consumers Union, 2003).

Note: Sample is the first vehicle on every 5th page starting at page 40. Data are for statistical education only and should not be viewed as a guide to vehicle performance.

DATA SET H   Pasta Sauce per Gram Total Calories and Fat Calories (n = 20 products) 📁 Pasta

Product	Fat Cal/gm	Cal/gm
Barilla Roasted Garlic & Onion	0.20	0.64
Barilla Tomato & Basil	0.12	0.56
Classico Tomato & Basil	0.08	0.40
⋮	⋮	⋮
Ragu Roasted Garlic	0.19	0.70
Ragu Traditional	0.20	0.56
Sutter Home Tomato & Garlic	0.16	0.64

Source: Independent project by statistics students Donna Bennett, Nicole Cook, Latrice Haywood, and Robert Malcolm.

Note: Data are intended for educational purposes only and should not be viewed as a nutrition guide.

DATA SET I	Temperature and Energy Usage for a Residence (*n* = 24 months) 🖭 Electric	
Month	Avg Temp (F°)	Usage (kWh)
1	62	436
2	71	464
3	76	446
⋮	⋮	⋮
22	25	840
23	38	867
24	48	606

Source: Electric bills for a residence and NOAA weather data.

DATA SET J	U.S. Annual Percent Inflation in Prices of Commodities and Services (*n* = 47 years) 🖭 Inflation	
Year	Commodities%	Services%
1960	0.9	3.4
1961	0.6	1.7
1962	0.9	2.0
⋮	⋮	⋮
2004	2.3	2.9
2005	3.6	3.3
2006	2.4	3.8

Source: *Economic Report of the President, 2007.*

Note: Data are year-to-year percent changes in the Consumer Price Index (CPI) in these two categories.

12.56 Researchers found a correlation coefficient of $r = .50$ on personality measures for identical twins. A reporter interpreted this to mean that "the environment orchestrated one-half of their personality differences." Do you agree with this interpretation? Discuss.

12.57 A study of the role of spreadsheets in planning in 55 small firms defined Y = "satisfaction with sales growth" and X = "executive commitment to planning." Analysis yielded an overall correlation of $r = .3043$. Do a two-tailed test for zero correlation at $\alpha = .025$.

12.58 In a study of stock prices from 1970 to 1994, the correlation between Nasdaq closing prices on successive days (i.e., with a 1-day lag) was $r = .13$ with a t statistic of 5.47. Interpret this result. (See David Nawrocki, "The Problems with Monte Carlo Simulation," *Journal of Financial Planning* 14, no. 11 [November 2001], p. 96.)

12.59 Regression analysis of free throws by 29 NBA teams during the 2002–2003 season revealed the fitted regression $Y = 55.2 + .73X$ ($R^2 = .874$, $s_{yx} = 53.2$), where Y = total free throws made and X = total free throws attempted. The observed range of X was from 1,620 (New York Knicks) to 2,382 (Golden State Warriors). (a) Find the expected number of free throws made for a team that shoots 2,000 free throws. (b) Do you think that the intercept is meaningful? *Hint:* Make a scatter plot and let Excel fit the line. (c) Use the quick rule to make a 95 percent prediction interval for Y when $X = 2,000$. 🖭 **FreeThrows**

12.60 In the following regression, X = weekly pay, Y = income tax withheld, and $n = 35$ McDonald's employees. (a) Write the fitted regression equation. (b) State the degrees of freedom for a two-tailed test for zero slope, and use Appendix D to find the critical value at $\alpha = .05$. (c) What is your conclusion about the slope? (d) Interpret the 95 percent confidence limits for the slope. (e) Verify that $F = t^2$ for the slope. (f) In your own words, describe the fit of this regression.

R^2	0.202
Std. Error	6.816
n	35

ANOVA table

Source	SS	df	MS	F	p-value
Regression	387.6959	1	387.6959	8.35	.0068
Residual	1,533.0614	33	46.4564		
Total	1,920.7573	34			

Regression output					confidence interval	
variables	coefficients	std. error	t (df = 33)	p-value	95% lower	95% upper
Intercept	30.7963	6.4078	4.806	.0000	17.7595	43.8331
Slope	0.0343	0.0119	2.889	.0068	0.0101	0.0584

12.61 In the following regression, X = monthly maintenance spending (dollars), Y = monthly machine downtime (hours), and n = 15 copy machines. (a) Write the fitted regression equation. (b) State the degrees of freedom for a two-tailed test for zero slope, and use Appendix D to find the critical value at α = .05. (c) What is your conclusion about the slope? (d) Interpret the 95 percent confidence limits for the slope. (e) Verify that $F = t^2$ for the slope. (f) In your own words, describe the fit of this regression.

R^2	0.370
Std. Error	286.793
n	15

ANOVA table

Source	SS	df	MS	F	p-value
Regression	628,298.2	1	628,298.2	7.64	.0161
Residual	1,069,251.8	13	82,250.1		
Total	1,697,550.0	14			

Regression output					confidence interval		
variables	coefficients	std. error	t (df = 13)	p-value	95% lower	95% upper
Intercept	1,743.57	288.82	6.037	.0000	1,119.61	2,367.53
Slope	−1.2163	0.4401	−2.764	.0161	−2.1671	−0.2656

12.62 In the following regression, X = total assets ($ billions), Y = total revenue ($ billions), and n = 64 large banks. (a) Write the fitted regression equation. (b) State the degrees of freedom for a two-tailed test for zero slope, and use Appendix D to find the critical value at α = .05. (c) What is your conclusion about the slope? (d) Interpret the 95 percent confidence limits for the slope. (e) Verify that $F = t^2$ for the slope. (f) In your own words, describe the fit of this regression.

R^2	0.519
Std. Error	6.977
n	64

ANOVA table

Source	SS	df	MS	F	p-value
Regression	3,260.0981	1	3,260.0981	66.97	1.90E-11
Residual	3,018.3339	62	48.6828		
Total	6,278.4320	63			

Regression output					confidence interval		
variables	coefficients	std. error	t (df = 62)	p-value	95% lower	95% upper
Intercept	6.5763	1.9254	3.416	.0011	2.7275	10.4252
X1	0.0452	0.0055	8.183	1.90E-11	0.0342	0.0563

12.63 Do stock prices of competing companies move together? Below are daily closing prices of two computer services firms (IBM = International Business Machines Corporation, HPQ = Hewlett-Packard Company. (a) Calculate the sample correlation coefficient (e.g., using Excel or MegaStat). (b) At α = .01 can you conclude that the true correlation coefficient is not equal to zero? (c) Make a scatter plot of the data. What does it say? (*Source:* finance.yahoo .com.) 📂 **StockPrices**

Daily Closing Price ($) of Two Stocks in March and April 2011 (*n* = 43 days)		
Date	*IBM*	*HPQ*
3/1/11	159.26	42.83
3/2/11	159.45	43.16
3/3/11	162.75	43.12
⋮	⋮	⋮
4/27/11	169.61	41.04
4/28/11	170.02	40.53
4/29/11	169.82	40.37

12.64 Below are percentages for *annual sales growth* and *net sales attributed to loyalty card usage* at 74 Noodles & Company restaurants. (a) Make a scatter plot. (b) Find the correlation coefficient and interpret it. (c) Test the correlation coefficient for significance, clearly stating the degrees of freedom. (d) Does it appear that loyalty card usage is associated with increased sales growth? **LoyaltyCard**

Annual Sales Growth (%) and Loyalty Card Usage (% of Net Sales) (*n* = 74 restaurants)		
Store	*Growth%*	*Loyalty%*
1	−8.3	2.1
2	−4.0	2.5
3	−3.9	1.7
⋮	⋮	⋮
72	20.8	1.1
73	25.5	0.6
74	28.8	1.8

Source: Noodles & Company

12.65 Below are fertility rates (average children born per woman) in 15 EU nations for 2 years. (a) Make a scatter plot. (b) Find the correlation coefficient and interpret it. (c) Test the correlation coefficient for significance, clearly stating the degrees of freedom. (Data are from the World Health Organization.) **Fertility**

Fertility Rates for EU Nations (*n* = 15)		
Nation	*1990*	*2000*
Austria	1.5	1.3
Belgium	1.6	1.5
Denmark	1.6	1.7
⋮	⋮	⋮
Spain	1.4	1.1
Sweden	2.0	1.4
U.K.	1.8	1.7

12.66 Consider the following prices and accuracy ratings for 27 stereo speakers. (a) Make a scatter plot of accuracy rating as a function of price. (b) Calculate the correlation coefficient. At $\alpha = .05$, does the correlation differ from zero? (c) In your own words, describe the scatter plot. (Data are from *Consumer Reports* 68, no. 11 [November 2003], p. 31. Data are intended for statistical education and not as a guide to speaker performance.) **Speakers**

Price and Accuracy of Selected Stereo Speakers (n = 27)

Brand and Model	Type	Price ($)	Accuracy
BIC America Venturi DV62si	Shelf	200	91
Bose 141	Shelf	100	86
Bose 201 Series V	Shelf	220	89
⋮	⋮	⋮	⋮
Sony SS-MB350H	Shelf	100	92
Sony SS-MF750H	Floor	280	91
Sony SS-X30ED	Shelf	500	83

12.67 Choose *one* of these three data sets. (a) Make a scatter plot. (b) Let Excel estimate the regression line, with fitted equation and R^2. (c) Describe the fit of the regression. (d) Write the fitted regression equation and interpret the slope. (e) Do you think that the estimated intercept is meaningful? Explain.

Commercial Real Estate (Y = assessed value, $000; X = floor space, sq. ft.) (n = 15)
Assessed

Size	Assessed
4,790	1,796
4,720	1,544
5,940	2,094
⋮	⋮
4,880	1,678
1,620	710
1,820	678

Sasnak Co. Salaries (X = employee age; Y = employee salary, $000) (n = 23)
Salaries

Employee	Age	Salary
Mary	23	28.6
Frieda	31	53.3
Alicia	44	73.8
⋮	⋮	⋮
Marcia	54	75.8
Ellen	44	79.8
Iggy	36	70.2

Poway Big Homes, Ltd. (X = home size, sq. ft.; Y = selling price, $000) (n = 20)
HomePrice2

SqFt	Price
3,570	861
3,410	740
2,690	563
⋮	⋮
3,020	720
2,320	575
3,130	785

12.68 Simple regression was employed to establish the effects of childhood exposure to lead. The effective sample size was about 122 subjects. The independent variable was the level of dentin lead (parts per million). Below are regressions using various dependent variables. (a) Calculate the t statistic for each slope. (b) From the p-values, which slopes differ from zero at $\alpha = .01$? (c) Do you feel that cause and effect can be assumed? *Hint:* Do a web search for information about effects of childhood lead exposure. (Data are from H. L. Needleman et al., *The New England Journal of Medicine* 322, no. 2 [January 1990], p. 86.)

Dependent Variable	R^2	Estimated Slope	Std. Error	p-value
Highest grade achieved	.061	−0.027	0.009	.008
Reading grade equivalent	.121	−0.070	0.018	.000
Class standing	.039	−0.006	0.003	.048
Absence from school	.071	4.8	1.7	.006
Grammatical reasoning	.051	0.159	0.062	.012
Vocabulary	.108	−0.124	0.032	.000
Hand-eye coordination	.043	0.041	0.018	.020
Reaction time	.025	11.8	6.66	.080
Minor antisocial behavior	.025	−0.639	0.36	.082

12.69 Below are recent financial ratios for a random sample of 20 integrated health care systems. *Operating Margin* is total revenue minus total expenses divided by total revenue plus net operating profits. *Equity Financing* is fund balance divided by total assets. (a) Make a scatter plot of $Y =$ operating margin and $X =$ equity financing (both variables are in percent). (b) Use Excel to fit the regression, with fitted equation and R^2. (c) In your own words, describe the fit. (Data are from *Hospitals & Health Networks* 71, no. 6 [March 20, 1997], pp. 48–49. Copyright © 1997 by Health Forum, Inc. Used with permission. Data are intended for statistical education and not as a guide to financial performance.) 🖰 **HealthCare**

Financial Ratios for Selected Health Care Systems (*n* = 20)

Name of Health Care System	Operating Margin	Equity Financing
Albert Einstein Healthcare Network	3.89	35.58
Alliant Health Systems	8.23	59.68
Baptist Memorial Health Care System	2.56	40.48
⋮	⋮	⋮
OSF Healthcare Network	4.75	54.21
Samaritan Health System	0.00	59.73
Scottsdale Memorial Health System	10.79	46.21

12.70 Consider the following data on 20 chemical reactions, with $Y =$ chromatographic retention time (seconds) and $X =$ molecular weight (gm/mole). (a) Make a scatter plot. (b) Use Excel to fit the regression, with fitted equation and R^2. (c) In your own words, describe the fit. (Data provided by John Seeley of Oakland University.) 🖰 **Chemicals**

Retention Time and Molecular Weight (*n* = 20)

Name	Retention Time	Molecular Weight
alpha-pinene	234.50	136.24
cyclopentene	95.27	68.12
p-diethylbenzene	284.00	134.22
⋮	⋮	⋮
pentane	78.00	72.15
isooctane	136.90	114.23
hexane	106.00	86.18

12.71 A common belief among faculty is that teaching ratings are lower in large classes. Below are MINITAB results from a regression using $Y =$ mean student evaluation of the professor and X = class size for 364 business school classes taught during the 2002–2003 academic year. Ratings are on a scale of 1 (lowest) to 5 (highest). (a) What do these regression results tell you about the relationship between class size and faculty ratings? (b) Is a bivariate model adequate? If not, suggest additional predictors to be considered.

Predictor	Coef	SE Coef	T	P
Constant	4.18378	0.07226	57.90	0.000
Enroll	0.000578	0.002014	0.29	0.774

S = 0.5688   R-Sq = 0.0%   R-Sq(adj) = 0.0%

12.72 Below are revenue and profit (both in $ billions) for nine large entertainment companies. (a) Make a scatter plot of profit as a function of revenue. (b) Use Excel to fit the regression, with fitted equation and R^2. (c) In your own words, describe the fit. (Data are from *Fortune* 149, no. 7 [April 5, 2005], p. F-50.) ⧅ **Entertainment**

Revenue and Profit of Entertainment Companies ($n = 9$)

Company	Revenue	Profit
AMC Entertainment	1.792	−0.020
Clear Channel Communication	8.931	1.146
Liberty Media	2.446	−0.978
⋮	⋮	⋮
Univision Communications	1.311	0.155
Viacom	26.585	1.417
Walt Disney	27.061	1.267

12.73 Below are fitted regressions based on used vehicle ads. Observed ranges of X are shown. The assumed regression model is *AskingPrice* = f(*VehicleAge*). (a) Interpret the slopes. (b) Are the intercepts meaningful? Explain. (c) Assess the fit of each model. (d) Is a bivariate model adequate to explain vehicle prices? If not, what other predictors might be considered? (Data are from *Detroit's AutoFocus* 4, Issue 38 [September 17–23, 2004]. Data are for educational purposes only and should not be viewed as a guide to vehicle prices.)

Vehicle	n	Intercept	Slope	R^2	Min Age	Max Age
Ford Explorer	31	22,252	−2,452	.643	2	6
Ford F-150 Pickup	43	26,164	−2,239	.713	1	37
Ford Mustang	33	21,308	−1,691	.328	1	10
Ford Taurus	32	13,160	−906	.679	1	14

12.74 Below are results of a regression of Y = average stock returns (in percent) as a function of X = average price/earnings ratios for the period 1949–1997 (49 years). Separate regressions were done for various holding periods (sample sizes are therefore variable). (a) Summarize what the regression results tell you. (b) Would you anticipate autocorrelation in this type of data? Explain. (Data are from Ruben Trevino and Fiona Robertson, "P/E Ratios and Stock Market Returns," *Journal of Financial Planning* 15, no. 2 [February 2002], p. 78.)

Holding Period	Intercept	Slope	t	R^2	p
1-Year	28.10	−0.92	1.86	.0688	.0686
2-Year	26.11	−0.86	2.57	.1252	.0136
5-Year	20.67	−0.57	2.99	.1720	.0046
8-Year	24.73	−0.94	6.93	.5459	.0000
10-Year	24.51	−0.95	8.43	.6516	.0000

12.75 Adult height is somewhat predictable from average height of both parents. For females, a commonly used equation is *YourHeight = ParentHeight* − 2.5 while for males the equation is *YourHeight = ParentHeight* + 2.5. (a) Test these equations on yourself (or on somebody else). (b) How well did the equations predict your height? (c) How do you suppose these equations were derived?

CHAPTER 12   Online Learning Resources

The Online Learning Center (OLC) at www.mhhe.com/doane4e has several *LearningStats* demonstrations to help you understand simple regression. Your instructor may assign one or more of them, or you may decide to download the ones that sound interesting.

Topic	LearningStats Demonstrations
Correlation	Overview of Correlation Scatter Plot Simulation
Regression	Overview of Simple Regression Using Excel for Regression
Ordinary least squares estimators	Least Squares Method Demonstration Derivation of OLS Estimators Effect of Model Form Effect of *X* Range
Confidence and prediction intervals	Confidence and Prediction Intervals Superimposing Many Fitted Regressions
Violations of assumptions	Non-Normal Errors Heteroscedastic Errors Autocorrelated Errors

Key: = PowerPoint = Word = Excel

Multiple Regression

CHAPTER CONTENTS

CHAPTER LEARNING OBJECTIVES

LO

When you finish this chapter you should be able to

LO 13-1   Use a fitted multiple regression equation to make predictions.

LO 13-2   Interpret the R^2 and perform an F test for overall significance.

LO 13-3   Test individual predictors for significance.

LO 13-4   Interpret confidence intervals for regression coefficients.

LO 13-5   Incorporate a categorical variable into a multiple regression model.

LO 13-6   Detect multicollinearity and assess its effects.

LO 13-7   Analyze residuals to check for violations of residual assumptions.

LO 13-8   Identify unusual residuals and high leverage observations.

LO 13-9   Explain the role of data conditioning and data transformations.

13.1 MULTIPLE REGRESSION

LO 13-1

Use a fitted multiple regression equation to make predictions.

Suppose you own a home and need to sell. How do you predict the selling price? It would be naïve to use a *simple regression* model based on one independent variable (e.g., square footage) to predict your home's value. Home values are affected by economic conditions as well as the physical characteristics of your house. Economic conditions might include mortgage interest rates and job opportunities in your city. Lower interest rates tend to be associated with higher home prices because buyers can afford to borrow more to purchase a house. Better job opportunities can increase the demand for homes in your area, which can increase home prices. Physical characteristics such as the size of your home, the number of bathrooms and bedrooms, and the age of the home also are used to determine the price of your home. Because *multiple* variables affect your home's value, we need a model that uses multiple independent variables for predicting.

Multiple regression extends simple regression to include several independent variables (called *predictors*). Multiple regression is required when a single-predictor model is inadequate to describe the true relationship between the dependent variable Y (the response variable) and its potential predictors ($X_1, X_2, X_3, \ldots$). The interpretation of multiple regression is similar to simple regression because simple regression is a special case of multiple regression. In fact, statisticians make no distinction between simple and multiple regression—they just call it *regression*.

Figure 13.1 illustrates the idea of a multiple regression model. Some of the proposed predictors may be useful, while others may not. The regression analysis will tell us whether or not each variable is useful. One of our objectives in regression modeling is to know whether or not we have a *parsimonious* model. A parsimonious regression model is a *lean* model, that is, one that has only useful predictors. If an estimated coefficient has a positive ($+$) sign, then higher X values are associated with higher Y values, and conversely if an estimated coefficient has a negative sign.

FIGURE 13.1

Visualizing a Multiple Regression

Objective:
To explain variation in Y

X_k X_1

Y

X_4 X_2

X_3

Potential explanatory variables (predictors) $X_1, X_2, X_3, \ldots, X_k$

Calculations are done by computer; therefore, there is no extra computational burden. However, there are additional interpretations to consider when analyzing a multiple regression. Using multiple predictors is more than a matter of "improving the fit." Rather, it is a question of specifying a correct model. A low R^2 in a simple regression model does not necessarily mean that X and Y are unrelated, but may simply indicate that the model is incorrectly specified. Omission of relevant predictors (*model misspecification*) can cause biased estimates and misleading results.

Limitations of Simple Regression

- Multiple relationships usually exist.
- Biased estimates if relevant predictors are omitted.
- Lack of fit does not show that X is unrelated to Y if the true model is multivariate.

Because multiple predictors usually are relevant, simple regression is only used when there is a compelling need for a simple model, or when other predictors have only modest effects and a single logical predictor "stands out" as doing a very good job all by itself.

Regression Terminology

The **response variable** (Y) is assumed to be related to the k **predictors** ($X_1, X_2, \ldots, X_k$) by a linear equation called the *population regression model:*

(13.1) $$y = \beta_0 + \beta_1 x_1 + \beta_2 x_2 + \cdots + \beta_k x_k + \varepsilon$$

A *random error* ε represents everything that is not part of the model. The unknown regression coefficients $\beta_0, \beta_1, \beta_2, \ldots, \beta_k$ are *parameters* and are denoted by Greek letters. Each coefficient β_j shows the change in the expected value of Y for a unit change in X_j while holding everything else constant (*ceteris paribus*). The errors are assumed to be unobservable, independent random disturbances that are normally distributed with zero mean and constant variance, that is, $\varepsilon \sim N(0, \sigma^2)$. Under these assumptions, the ordinary least squares (OLS) estimation method yields unbiased, consistent, efficient estimates of the unknown parameters.

The *sample estimates* of the regression coefficients are denoted by Roman letters $b_0, b_1, b_2, \ldots, b_k$. The *predicted* value of the response variable is denoted $\hat{y}$ and is calculated by inserting the values of the predictors into the *estimated regression equation:*

(13.2) $$\hat{y} = b_0 + b_1 x_1 + b_2 x_2 + \cdots + b_k x_k \quad \text{(predicted value of } Y)$$

In this chapter, we will not show formulas for the estimated coefficients $b_0, b_1, b_2, \ldots, b_k$ because they entail matrix algebra. All regression equations are estimated by computer software (Excel, MegaStat, MINITAB, etc.) utilizing the appropriate formulas.

In a simple regression (one predictor), the fitted regression is a *line,* while in multiple regression (more than one predictor), the fitted regression is a *surface* or *plane* as illustrated in Figure 13.2. If there are more than two predictors, no diagram can be drawn, and the fitted regression is represented by a hyperplane.

Data Format

To obtain a fitted regression, we need n observed values of the response variable Y and its proposed predictors $X_1, X_2, \ldots, X_k$. A multivariate data set is a single column of Y-values and k columns of X-values. The form of this $n \times k$ matrix of observations is shown in Figure 13.3.

In Excel's Data Analysis > Regression, you are required to have the X data in contiguous columns. However, MegaStat and MINITAB permit nonadjacent columns of X data. Flexibility in choosing data columns is useful if you decide to omit one or more X data columns and rerun the regression (e.g., to seek parsimony).

FIGURE 13.2

Fitted Regression: Bivariate versus Multivariate

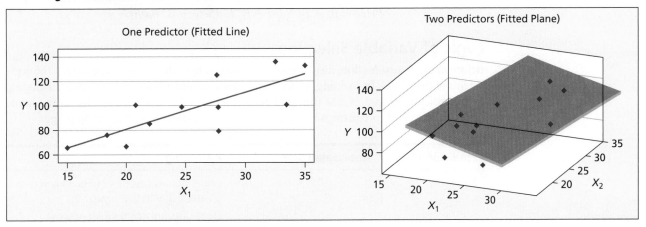

FIGURE 13.3

Data for a Multiple Regression

	Response	Predictors			
	Y	X_1	X_2	...	X_k
	y_1	x_{11}	x_{12}	...	x_{1k}
	y_2	x_{21}	x_{22}	...	x_{2k}
	$\vdots$	$\vdots$	$\vdots$	$\vdots$	$\vdots$
	y_n	x_{n1}	x_{n2}	...	x_{nk}

Illustration: Home Prices

Table 13.1 shows sales of 30 new homes in an upscale development. Although the selling price of a home (the *response variable*) may depend on many factors, we will examine three potential *explanatory variables*.

Definition of Variable	*Short Name*
Y = selling price of a home (thousands of dollars)	*Price*
X_1 = home size (square feet)	*SqFt*
X_2 = lot size (thousand square feet)	*LotSize*
X_3 = number of bathrooms	*Baths*

TABLE 13.1				Characteristics of 30 New Homes 🖅 NewHomes					
Home	*Price*	*SqFt*	*LotSize*	*Baths*	*Home*	*Price*	*SqFt*	*LotSize*	*Baths*
1	505.5	2,192	16.4	2.5	16	675.1	3,076	19.8	3.0
2	784.1	3,429	24.7	3.5	17	710.4	3,259	20.8	3.5
3	649.0	2,842	17.7	3.5	18	674.7	3,162	19.4	4.0
4	689.8	2,987	20.3	3.5	19	663.6	2,885	23.2	3.0
5	709.8	3,029	22.2	3.0	20	606.6	2,550	20.2	3.0
6	590.2	2,616	20.8	2.5	21	758.9	3,380	19.6	4.5
7	643.3	2,978	17.3	3.0	22	723.7	3,131	22.5	3.5
8	789.7	3,595	22.4	3.5	23	621.8	2,754	19.2	2.5
9	683.0	2,838	27.4	3.0	24	622.4	2,710	21.6	3.0
10	544.3	2,591	19.2	2.0	25	631.3	2,616	20.8	2.5
11	822.8	3,633	26.9	4.0	26	574.0	2,608	17.3	3.5
12	637.7	2,822	23.1	3.0	27	863.8	3,572	29.0	4.0
13	618.7	2,994	20.4	3.0	28	652.7	2,924	21.8	2.5
14	619.3	2,696	22.7	3.5	29	844.2	3,614	25.5	3.5
15	490.5	2,134	13.4	2.5	30	629.9	2,600	24.1	3.5

Using short variable names instead of Y and X, we may write the regression model in an intuitive form:

$$Price = \beta_0 + \beta_1 \, SqFt + \beta_2 \, LotSize + \beta_3 \, Baths + \varepsilon$$

Logic of Variable Selection

Before doing the estimation, it is desirable to state our hypotheses about the sign of the coefficients in the model. In so doing, we force ourselves to think about our motives for including each predictor, instead of just throwing predictors into the model willy-nilly. In the home price example, each predictor is expected to contribute positively to the selling price.

Predictor	Anticipated Sign	Reasoning
SqFt	>0	Larger homes cost more to build and give greater utility to the buyer.
LotSize	>0	Larger lots are desirable for privacy, gardening, and play.
Baths	>0	Additional baths give more utility to the purchaser with a family.

Explicit *a priori* reasoning about cause and effect permits us to compare the regression estimates with our expectation and to recognize any surprising results that may occur.

Estimated Regression

A regression equation can be estimated by using Excel, MegaStat, MINITAB, or any other statistical package. Using the sample of $n = 30$ home sales, we obtain the fitted regression and its statistics of fit (R^2 is the coefficient of determination, SE is the standard error):

$$Price = -28.85 + 0.171 \, SqFt + 6.78 \, LotSize + 15.53 \, Baths \ (R^2 = .956, \, SE = 20.31)$$

The intercept is not meaningful, since there can be no home with $SqFt = 0$, $LotSize = 0$, and $Baths = 0$. Each additional square foot seems to add about 0.171 (i.e., $171, since *Price* is measured in thousands of dollars) to the average selling price, *ceteris paribus*. The coefficient of *LotSize* implies that, on average, each additional thousand square feet of lot size adds 6.78 (i.e., $6,780) to the selling price. The coefficient of *Baths* says that, on average, each additional bathroom adds 15.53 (i.e., $15,530) to the selling price. Although the three-predictor model's fit ($R^2 = .956$) is good, its standard error (20.31 or $20,310) suggests that prediction intervals will be rather wide.

Predictions from a Fitted Regression

We can use the fitted regression model to make predictions for various assumed predictor values. For example, what would be the expected selling price of a 2,800-square-foot home with 2½ baths on a lot with 18,500 square feet? In the fitted regression equation, we simply plug in $SqFt = 2800$, $LotSize = 18.5$, and $Baths = 2.5$ to get the predicted selling price:

$$SqFt = 2800 \qquad LotSize = 18.5 \qquad Baths = 2.5$$

$$Price = -28.85 + 0.171 \, (2800) + 6.78 \, (18.5) + 15.53 \, (2.5) = 614.23, \text{ or } \$614,230$$

Although we could plug in any desired values of the predictors (*SqFt, LotSize, Baths*), it is risky to use predictor values outside the predictor value ranges in the data set used to estimate the fitted regression. For example, it would be risky to choose $SqFt = 4000$ since no home this large was seen in the original data set. Although the prediction might turn out to be reasonable, we would be extrapolating beyond the range of observed data.

Common Misconceptions about Fit

A common mistake is to assume that the equation that best fits our observed data is preferred. Sometimes a model with a low R^2 may give useful predictions, while a model with a high R^2 may conceal problems. Fit is only one criterion for assessing a regression. For example, a bivariate model using only *SqFt* as a predictor does a pretty good job of predicting *Price* and has an attractive simplicity:

$$Price = 15.47 + 0.222 \, SqFt \, (R^2 = .914, \, s = 27.28)$$

Should we perhaps prefer the simpler model? The principle of **Occam's Razor** says that a complex model that is only slightly better may not be preferred if a simpler model will do the job. However, in this case, the three-predictor model is not very complex and is based on solid *a priori* logic.

Principle of Occam's Razor

When two explanations are otherwise equivalent, we prefer the simpler, more parsimonious one.

Also, a high R^2 only indicates a good fit for the observed data set ($i = 1, 2, \ldots, n$). If we wanted to use the fitted regression equation to predict Y from a different set of X's, the fit might not be the same. For this reason, if the sample is large enough, a statistician likes to use half the data to *estimate* the model and the other half to *test* the model's predictions.

Regression Modeling

The choices of predictors and model form (e.g., linear or nonlinear) are tasks of *regression modeling*. To begin with, we restrict our attention to predictors that meet the test of *a priori* logic, to avoid endless "data shopping." Naturally, we want predictors that are significant in "explaining" the variation in Y (i.e., predictors that improve the "fit"). But we also prefer predictors that add new information, rather than mirroring one another.

For example, we would expect that *LotSize* and *SqFt* are related (a bigger house may require a bigger lot) and likewise *SqFt* and *Baths* (a bigger house is likely to require more baths). If so, there may be overlap in their contributions to explaining *Price*. Closely related predictors can introduce instability in the regression estimates. If we include too many predictors, we violate the principle of Occam's Razor, which favors simple models, *ceteris paribus*. In this chapter, you will see how these criteria can be used to develop and assess regression models.

Four Criteria for Regression Assessment

- **Logic**   Is there an *a priori* reason to expect a causal relationship between the predictors and the response variable?

- **Fit**   Does the *overall* regression show a significant relationship between the predictors and the response variable?

- **Parsimony**   Does *each predictor* contribute significantly to the explanation? Are some predictors not worth the trouble?

- **Stability**   Are the predictors related to one another so strongly that regression estimates become erratic?

13.1 Observations are taken on net revenue from sales of a certain LCD TV at 50 retail outlets. The regression model was Y = net revenue (thousands of dollars), X_1 = shipping cost (dollars per unit), X_2 = expenditures on print advertising (thousands of dollars), X_3 = expenditure on electronic media ads (thousands), X_4 = rebate rate (percent of retail price). (a) Write the fitted regression equation. (b) Interpret each coefficient. (c) Would the intercept be likely to have

SECTION EXERCISES

connect

meaning in this regression? (d) Use the fitted equation to make a prediction for *NetRevenue* when *ShipCost* = 10, *PrintAds* = 50, *WebAds* = 40, and *Rebate%* = 15. 📄 **LCDTV**

Predictor	Coefficient
Intercept	4.306
ShipCost	−0.082
PrintAds	2.265
WebAds	2.498
Rebate%	16.697

13.2 Observations are taken on sales of a certain mountain bike in 30 sporting goods stores. The regression model was Y = total sales (thousands of dollars), X_1 = display floor space (square meters), X_2 = competitors' advertising expenditures (thousands of dollars), X_3 = advertised price (dollars per unit). (a) Write the fitted regression equation. (b) Interpret each coefficient. (c) Would the intercept seem to have meaning in this regression? (d) Make a prediction for *Sales* when *FloorSpace* = 80, *CompetingAds* = 100, and *Price* = 1,200. 📄 **Bikes**

Predictor	Coefficient
Intercept	1225.44
FloorSpace	11.52
CompetingAds	−6.935
Price	−0.1496

VAILRESORTS·

13.3 Vail Resorts asked a random sample of guests to rate their satisfaction on various attributes of their visit on a scale of 1–5 with 1 = very unsatisfied and 5 = very satisfied. The estimated regression model was Y = overall satisfaction score, X_1 = lift line wait, X_2 = amount of ski trail grooming, X_3 = safety patrol visibility, and X_4 = friendliness of guest services. (a) Write the fitted regression equation. (b) Interpret each coefficient. (c) Would the intercept seem to have meaning in this regression? (d) Make a prediction for *Overall Satisfaction* when a guest's satisfaction in all four areas is rated a 5. 📄 **VailGuestSat2**

Predictor	Coefficient
Intercept	2.8931
LiftWait	0.1542
AmountGroomed	0.2495
SkiPatrolVisibility	0.0539
FriendlinessHosts	−0.1196

13.4 A regression model to predict Y, the state-by-state 2005 burglary crime rate per 100,000 people, used the following four state predictors: X_1 = median age in 2005, X_2 = number of 2005 bankruptcies per 1,000 people, X_3 = 2004 federal expenditures per capita, and X_4 = 2005 high school graduation percentage. (a) Write the fitted regression equation. (b) Interpret each coefficient. (c) Would the intercept seem to have meaning in this regression? (d) Make a prediction for *Burglary* when X_1 = 35 years, X_2 = 7.0 bankruptcies per 1,000, X_3 = $6,000, and X_4 = 80 percent. 📄 **Burglary**

Predictor	Coefficient
Intercept	4,198.5808
AgeMed	−27.3540
Bankrupt	17.4893
FedSpend	−0.0124
HSGrad%	−29.0314

13.2 ASSESSING OVERALL FIT

As in simple regression, there is one residual for every observation in a multiple regression:

$$e_i = y_i - \hat{y}_i \quad \text{for } i = 1, 2, \ldots, n$$

Figure 13.4 illustrates the residual for one data value in a two-predictor regression. Each expected value of Y is a point on the fitted regression plane for a given pair of X-values (x_1, x_2). The residual is the vertical distance from the actual y_i value for those particular X-values (x_1, x_2) to $\hat{y}_i$. Just as in simple regression, we use the sum of squared residuals (SSE) as a measure of "fit" of the model.

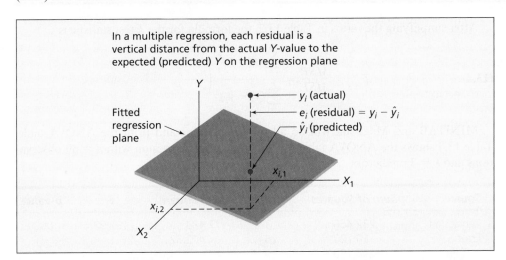

In a multiple regression, each residual is a vertical distance from the actual Y-value to the expected (predicted) Y on the regression plane

FIGURE 13.4

Residual in Two-Predictor Model

LO 13-2

Interpret the R^2 and perform an F test for overall significance.

F Test for Significance

Before determining which, if any, of the individual predictors are significant, we perform a *global test* for overall fit using the ***F* test**. For a regression with k predictors, the hypotheses to be tested are

H_0: All the true coefficients are zero ($\beta_1 = \beta_2 = \cdots = \beta_k = 0$)

H_1: At least one of the coefficients is nonzero

Recall from Chapters 10 and 11 that the F statistic is the ratio of two variances. The basis for the regression F test is the **ANOVA table**, which decomposes variation of the response variable around its mean into two parts:

$$
\begin{array}{ccccc}
SST & = & SSR & + & SSE \\
\text{Total} & & \text{Explained by} & & \text{Unexplained} \\
\text{variation} & & \text{regression} & & \text{error} \\
\displaystyle\sum_{i=1}^{n}(y_i - \bar{y})^2 & = & \displaystyle\sum_{i=1}^{n}(\hat{y}_i - \bar{y})^2 & + & \displaystyle\sum_{i=1}^{n}(y_i - \hat{y}_i)^2
\end{array}
\quad \textbf{(13.3)}
$$

The OLS method of estimation will minimize the sum of the squared residuals represented by the SSE term, in formula 13.3 above, where SSE is the *unexplained* variation in Y. Each predicted value $\hat{y}_i$ is based on a fitted regression equation with k predictors. The ANOVA calculations for a k-predictor model can be summarized in a table like Table 13.2.

When F_{calc} is close to 1, the values of MSR and MSE are close in magnitude. This suggests that *none* of the predictors provides a good predictive model for Y (i.e., all β_j are equal to 0). When the value of MSR is much greater than MSE, this suggests that at least one of the predictors in the regression model is significant (i.e., at least one β_j is not equal to 0).

TABLE 13.2		ANOVA Table Format				
Source of Variation	**Sum of Squares**	**df**	**Mean Square**	**F**	**Excel p-Value**	
Regression (explained)	$SSR = \sum_{i=1}^{n}(\hat{y}_i - \bar{y})^2$	k	$MSR = \dfrac{SSR}{k}$	$F_{calc} = \dfrac{MSR}{MSE}$	=F.DIST.RT(F_{calc}, k, n − k−1)	
Residual (unexplained)	$SSE = \sum_{i=1}^{n}(y_i - \hat{y})^2$	$n - k - 1$	$MSE = \dfrac{SSE}{n-k-1}$			
Total	$SST = \sum_{i=1}^{n}(y_i - \bar{y})^2$	$n - 1$				

After simplifying the ratios in Table 13.2, the formula for the F test statistic is:

$$(13.4) \qquad F_{calc} = \frac{MSR}{MSE} = \frac{\sum_{i=1}^{n}(\hat{y}_i - \bar{y})^2}{\sum_{i=1}^{n}(y_i - \hat{y}_i)^2}\left(\frac{n-k-1}{k}\right)$$

MINITAB and MegaStat will do all the calculations and print the ANOVA table. Table 13.3 shows the ANOVA table for the home price regression with $n = 30$ observations and $k = 3$ predictors.

TABLE 13.3					
Source	**Sum of Squares**	**d.f.**	**Mean Square**	**F**	**p-value**
Regression	232,450	3	77,483	187.92	.0000
Error	10,720	26	412.32		
Total	243,170	29			

ANOVA Results for Three-Predictor Home Price Regression

The hypotheses to be tested are

H_0: All the coefficients are zero ($\beta_1 = \beta_2 = \beta_3 = 0$)

H_1: At least one coefficient is nonzero

Calculation of the sums SSR, SSE, and SST would be tedious without the computer. The F test statistic is $F_{calc} = MSR/MSE = 77{,}483/412.32 = 187.92$. Degrees of freedom are $k = 3$ for the numerator and $n - k - 1 = 30 - 3 - 1 = 26$ for the denominator. For $\alpha = .05$, Appendix F gives a critical value of $F_{3,26} = 2.98$, so the regression clearly is significant overall. MINITAB and MegaStat calculate the p-value (.000) for the F statistic. Alternatively, we can also use Excel's function =F.DIST.RT(187.92,3,26) to verify the p-value (.000).

Coefficient of Determination (R^2)

The most common measure of overall fit is the **coefficient of determination** or R^2, which is based on the ANOVA table's sums of squares. It can be calculated in two ways by using the error sum of squares (SSE), regression sum of squares (SSR), and total sum of squares (SST). The formulas are illustrated using the three-predictor regression of home prices.

$$(13.5) \qquad R^2 = 1 - \frac{SSE}{SST} = 1 - \frac{\sum_{i=1}^{n}(y_i - \hat{y}_i)^2}{\sum_{i=1}^{n}(y_i - \bar{y}_i)^2} = 1 - \frac{10{,}720}{243{,}170} = 1 - .044 = .956$$

or equivalently

$$(13.6) \qquad R^2 = \frac{SSR}{SST} = \frac{\sum_{i=1}^{n}(\hat{y}_i - \bar{y}_i)^2}{\sum_{i=1}^{n}(y_i - \bar{y}_i)^2} = \frac{232{,}450}{243{,}170} = .956$$

For the home price data, the R^2 statistic indicates that 95.6 percent of the variation in selling price is "explained" by our three predictors. While this indicates a very good fit, there is still some unexplained variation. Adding more predictors can *never* decrease the R^2. However, when R^2 already is high, there is not a lot of room for improvement.

Adjusted R^2

In multiple regression, it is possible to raise the coefficient of determination R^2 by including additional predictors. This may tempt you to imagine that we should always include many predictors to get a "better fit." To discourage this tactic (called *overfitting the model*), an adjustment can be made to the R^2 statistic to penalize the inclusion of useless predictors. The **adjusted coefficient of determination** using n observations and k predictors is

$$R^2_{adj} = 1 - \frac{\left(\dfrac{SSE}{n-k-1}\right)}{\left(\dfrac{SST}{n-1}\right)} \qquad \text{(adjusted } R^2) \qquad (13.7)$$

R^2_{adj} is always less than R^2. As you add predictors, R^2 will not decrease. But R^2_{adj} may increase, remain the same, or decrease, depending on whether the added predictors increase R^2 sufficiently to offset the penalty. If R^2_{adj} is substantially smaller than R^2, it suggests that the model contains useless predictors. For the home price data with three predictors, both statistics are similar ($R^2 = .956$ and $R^2_{adj} = .951$), which suggests that the model does not contain useless predictors.

$$R^2_{adj} = 1 - \frac{\left(\dfrac{10,720}{26}\right)}{\left(\dfrac{243,170}{29}\right)} = .951$$

There is no fixed rule of thumb for comparing R^2 and R^2_{adj}. A smaller gap between R^2 and R^2_{adj} indicates a more parsimonious model. A large gap would suggest that if some weak predictors were deleted, a leaner model would be obtained without losing very much predictive power.

How Many Predictors?

One way to prevent overfitting the model is to limit the number of predictors based on the sample size. A conservative rule (**Evans' Rule**) suggests that n/k should be at least 10 (i.e., at least 10 observations per predictor). A more relaxed rule (**Doane's Rule**) suggests that n/k be only at least 5 (i.e., at least 5 observations per predictor). For the home price regression with $n = 30$ and $k = 3$ example, $n/k = 30/3 = 10$, so either guideline is met.

Evans' Rule (conservative): $n/k \geq 10$ (at least 10 observations per predictor)

Doane's Rule (relaxed): $n/k \geq 5$ (at least 5 observations per predictor)

These rules are merely suggestions. Technically, a regression is possible as long as the sample size exceeds the number of predictors. But when n/k is small, the R^2 no longer gives a reliable indication of fit. Sometimes, researchers must work with small samples that cannot be enlarged. For example, a start-up business selling health food might have only 12 observations on quarterly sales. Should they attempt a regression model to predict sales using four predictors (advertising, product price, competitor prices, and population density)? Although $n = 12$ and $k = 3$ would violate even the lax guideline ($n/k = 12/4 = 3$), the firm might feel that an imperfect analysis is better than none at all.

13.5 Refer to the ANOVA table below. (a) State the degrees of freedom for the F test for overall significance. (b) Use Appendix F to look up the critical value of F for $\alpha = .05$. (c) Calculate the F statistic. Is the regression significant overall? (d) Calculate R^2 and R^2_{adj}, showing your formulas clearly. ⊞ **LCDTV**

Source	d.f.	SS	MS
Regression	4	259,412	64,853
Error	45	224,539	4,990
Total	49	483,951	

13.6 Refer to the ANOVA table below. (a) State the degrees of freedom for the F test for overall significance. (b) Use Appendix F to look up the critical value of F for $\alpha = .05$. (c) Calculate the F statistic. Is the regression significant overall? (d) Calculate R^2 and R^2_{adj}, showing your formulas clearly. ⊞ **Bikes**

Source	d.f.	SS	MS
Regression	3	1,196,410	398,803
Error	26	379,332	14,590
Total	29	1,575,742	

VAILRESORTS **13.7** Refer to the ANOVA table below. (a) State the degrees of freedom for the F test for overall significance. (b) Use Appendix F to look up the critical value of F for $\alpha = .05$. (c) Calculate the F statistic. Is the regression significant overall? (d) Calculate R^2 and R^2_{adj}, showing your formulas clearly. ⊞ **VailResortsSat2**

Source	SS	df	MS
Regression	33.0730	4	8.2682
Residual	317.9868	497	0.6398
Total	351.0598	501	

13.8 Refer to the ANOVA table below. (a) State the degrees of freedom for the F test for overall significance. (b) Use Appendix F to look up the critical value of F for $\alpha = .05$. (c) Calculate the F statistic. Is the regression significant overall? (d) Calculate R^2 and R^2_{adj}, showing your formulas clearly. ⊞ **Burglary**

Source	SS	df	MS
Regression	1,182,733	4	295,683
Residual	1,584,952	45	35,221
Total	2,767,685	49	

13.3 PREDICTOR SIGNIFICANCE

Hypothesis Tests

Each estimated coefficient shows the change in the conditional mean of Y associated with a one-unit change in an explanatory variable, holding the other explanatory variables constant. If a predictor coefficient β_j is equal to zero, it means that the explanatory variable X_j does not help explain variation in the response variable Y. We are usually interested in testing each fitted coefficient to see whether it is significantly different from zero. If there is an *a priori* reason to anticipate a particular direction of association, we could choose a right-tailed or left-tailed test. For example, we would expect *SqFt* to have a positive effect on *Price,* so a right-tailed test might be used. However, the default choice is a two-tailed test because, if the null hypothesis can be rejected in a two-tailed test, it can also be rejected in a one-tailed test at the same level of significance.

Hypothesis Tests for Coefficient of Predictor X_j

Left-Tailed Test	*Two-Tailed Test*	*Right-Tailed Test*
H_0: $\beta_j = 0$	H_0: $\beta_j = 0$	H_0: $\beta_j = 0$
H_1: $\beta_j < 0$	H_1: $\beta_j \neq 0$	H_1: $\beta_j > 0$

Tip

Software packages like Excel, MegaStat, or MINITAB report only two-tail *p*-values because, if you can reject H_0 in a two-tailed test, you can also reject H_0 in a one-tailed test at the same α.

If we cannot reject the hypothesis that a coefficient is zero, then the corresponding predictor does not significantly contribute to the prediction of Y. For example, consider a three-predictor model:

$$y = \beta_0 + \beta_1 x_1 + \beta_2 x_2 + \beta_3 x_3 + \varepsilon$$

Does X_2 help us to predict Y? To find out, we might choose a two-tailed test:

H_0: $\beta_2 = 0$ (X_2 is *not* related to Y)

H_1: $\beta_2 \neq 0$ (X_2 *is* related to Y)

If we are unable to reject H_0, the term involving x_2 will drop out:

$$y = \beta_0 + \beta_1 x_1 + \boxed{0x_2} + \beta_3 x_3 + \varepsilon \quad (x_2 \text{ term drops out if } \beta_2 = 0)$$

and the regression will collapse to a *two-variable* model:

$$y = \beta_0 + \beta_1 x_1 + \beta_3 x_3 + \varepsilon$$

Test Statistic

Rarely would a fitted coefficient be *exactly* zero, so we use a *t* test to test whether the difference from zero* is *significant*. For predictor X_j the test statistic for k predictors is Student's t with $n - k - 1$ degrees of freedom. To test for a zero coefficient, we take the ratio of the fitted coefficient b_j to its standard error s_j:

$$t_{\text{calc}} = \frac{b_j - 0}{s_j} \quad \text{(test statistic for coefficient of predictor } X_j) \tag{13.8}$$

where

$$s_j = \sqrt{\frac{MSE}{SS_{X_j}(1 - R_j^2)}} \tag{13.9}$$

The value of s_j is usually not calculated by the analyst but rather taken from the regression output because the calculation is tedious. The value of *MSE* comes from the *ANOVA* table on the regression output (see Table 13.2). SS_{X_j} is the sum of the squared deviations of X_j about its mean and R_j^2 is the coefficient of determination when predictor j is regressed against *all* the other predictors (excluding Y).

We can use Appendix D to find a critical value of t for a chosen level of significance α, or we could find the *p*-value for the t statistic using Excel's function =T.DIST.2T (t, deg_freedom). All computer packages report the t statistic and the *p*-value for each

---

*You needn't use 0 in the t test. For example, if you want to know whether an extra square foot adds at least $200 to a home's selling price, you would use 200 instead of 0 in the formula for the test statistic. However, $\beta = 0$ is the default hypothesis in Excel and other statistical packages.

predictor, so we actually do not need tables. To test for a zero coefficient, we could alternatively construct a confidence interval for the true coefficient β_j and see whether the interval includes zero. Excel and MegaStat show a confidence interval for each coefficient, using this form:

(13.10)　　$b_j - t_{\alpha/2} s_j \leq \beta_j \leq b_j + t_{\alpha/2} s_j$　　(95% confidence interval for coefficient β_j)

MegaStat allows 99, 95, or 90 percent confidence intervals, while in Excel you can enter any confidence level you wish. All calculations are provided by Excel, so you only have to know how to interpret the results.

Tip

Checking to see whether the confidence interval includes zero is equivalent to a two-tailed test of H_0: $\beta_j = 0$.

Regression output contains many statistics, but some of them are especially important in getting the "big picture." Figure 13.5 shows a typical regression printout (Y = car theft rate in the 50 states) with certain key features circled and comments that a statistician might make.

FIGURE 13.5

Typical Regression Output

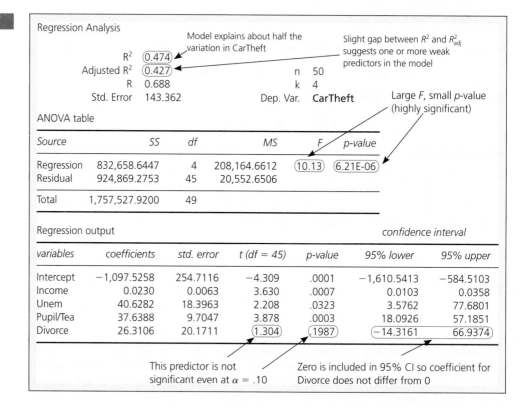

EXAMPLE 13.1

Home Prices

Figure 13.6 shows MegaStat's fitted regression for the three-predictor model of home prices, including a table of estimated coefficients, standard errors, t statistics, and p-values. MegaStat computes two-tail p-values, as do most statistical packages. Notice that 0 is within the 95 percent confidence interval for *Baths,* while the confidence intervals for *SqFt* and *LotSize* do not include 0. This suggests that the hypothesis of a zero coefficient can be rejected for *SqFt* and *LotSize* but not for *Baths.*

FIGURE 13.6   MegaStat's Regression for Home Prices (three predictors)

| Regression output | | | | | confidence interval | |
variables	coefficients	std. error	t(df = 26)	p-value	95% lower	95% upper
Intercept	−28.8477	29.7115	−0.971	0.3405	−89.9206	32.2251
SqFt	0.1709	0.0154	11.064	0.0000	0.1392	0.2027
LotSize	6.7777	1.4213	4.769	0.0001	3.8562	9.6992
Baths	15.5347	9.2083	1.687	0.1036	−3.3932	34.4626

There are four estimated coefficients (counting the intercept). For reasons stated previously, the intercept is of no interest. For the three predictors, each t test uses $n − k − 1$ degrees of freedom. Since we have $n = 30$ observations and $k = 3$ predictors, we have $n − k − 1 = 30 − 3 − 1 = 26$ degrees of freedom. From Appendix D we can obtain two-tailed critical values of t for α equal to .10, .05, or .01 ($t_{.05} = 1.706$, $t_{.025} = 2.056$, and $t_{.005} = 2.779$). However, since p-values are provided, we do not really need these critical values.

$$SqFt: t_{calc} = 0.1709/0.01545 = 11.06 \ (p\text{-value} = .0000)$$
$$LotSize: t_{calc} = 6.778/1.421 = 4.77 \ (p\text{-value} = .0001)$$
$$Baths: t_{calc} = 15.535/9.208 = 1.69 \ (p\text{-value} = .1036)$$

The coefficients of *SqFt* and *LotSize* differ significantly from zero at any common α because their p-values are practically zero. The coefficient of *Baths* is not quite significant at $\alpha = .10$. Based on the t-values, we conclude that *SqFt* is a very strong predictor of *Price*, followed closely by *LotSize*, while *Baths* is of marginal significance.

SECTION EXERCISES

connect

13.9 Observations are taken on net revenue from sales of a certain LCD TV at 50 retail outlets. The regression model was $Y =$ net revenue (thousands of dollars), $X_1 =$ shipping cost (dollars per unit), $X_2 =$ expenditures on print advertising (thousands of dollars), $X_3 =$ expenditure on electronic media ads (thousands), $X_4 =$ rebate rate (percent of retail price). (a) Calculate the t statistic for each coefficient to test for $\beta = 0$. (b) Look up the critical value of Student's t in Appendix D for a two-tailed test at $\alpha = .01$. Which coefficients differ significantly from zero? (c) Use Excel to find the p-value for each coefficient. **LCDTV**

Predictor	Coefficient	SE
Intercept	4.310	70.82
ShipCost	−0.0820	4.678
PrintAds	2.265	1.050
WebAds	2.498	0.8457
Rebate%	16.697	3.570

13.10 Observations are taken on sales of a certain mountain bike in 30 sporting goods stores. The regression model was $Y =$ total sales (thousands of dollars), $X_1 =$ display floor space (square meters), $X_2 =$ competitors' advertising expenditures (thousands of dollars), $X_3 =$ advertised price (dollars per unit). (a) Calculate the t statistic for each coefficient to test for $\beta = 0$. (b) Look up the critical value of Student's t in Appendix D for a two-tailed test at $\alpha = .01$. Which coefficients differ significantly from zero? (c) Use Excel to find the p-value for each coefficient. **Bikes**

Predictor	Coefficient	SE
Intercept	1225.4	397.3
FloorSpace	11.522	1.330
CompetingAds	−6.935	3.905
Price	−0.14955	0.08927

VAILRESORTS˙ **13.11** A random sample of 502 Vail Resorts' guests were asked to rate their satisfaction on various attributes of their visit on a scale of 1–5 with 1 = very unsatisfied and 5 = very satisfied. The regression model was Y = overall satisfaction score, X_1 = lift line wait, X_2 = amount of ski trail grooming, X_3 = ski patrol visibility, and X_4 = friendliness of guest services. (a) Calculate the t statistic for each coefficient to test for $\beta_j = 0$. (b) Look up the critical value of Student's t in Appendix D for a two-tailed test at $\alpha = .01$. Which coefficients differ significantly from zero? (c) Use Excel to find a p-value for each coefficient. **VailGuestSat2**

Predictor	Coefficient	SE
Intercept	2.8931	0.3680
LiftWait	0.1542	0.0440
AmountGroomed	0.2495	0.0529
SkiPatrolVisibility	0.0539	0.0443
FriendlinessHosts	−0.1196	0.0623

13.12 A regression model to predict Y, the state burglary rate per 100,000 people for 2005, used the following four state predictors: X_1 = median age in 2005, X_2 = number of 2005 bankruptcies, X_3 = 2004 federal expenditures per capita (a *leading* predictor), and X_4 = 2005 high school graduation percentage. (a) Calculate the t statistic for each coefficient to test for $\beta_j = 0$. (b) Look up the critical value of Student's t in Appendix D for a two-tailed test at $\alpha = .01$. Which coefficients differ significantly from zero? (c) Use Excel to find a p-value for each coefficient. **Burglary**

Predictor	Coefficient	SE
Intercept	4,198.5808	799.3395
AgeMed	−27.3540	12.5687
Bankrupt	17.4893	12.4033
FedSpend	−0.0124	0.0176
HSGrad%	−29.0314	7.1268

13.4 CONFIDENCE INTERVALS FOR *Y*

Standard Error

LO 13-4

Interpret confidence intervals for regression coefficients.

Another important measure of fit is the **standard error (s_e) of the regression**, derived from the sum of squared residuals (SSE) for n observations and k predictors:

$$(13.11) \quad s_e = \sqrt{\frac{\sum_{i=1}^{n}(y_i - \hat{y}_i)^2}{n - k - 1}} = \sqrt{\frac{SSE}{n - k - 1}} \quad \text{(standard error of the regression)}$$

The standard error is measured in the same units as the response variable Y (dollars, square feet, etc.). A smaller s_e indicates a better fit. If all predictions were perfect (i.e., if $y_i = \hat{y}_i$ for all observations), then s_e would be zero. However, perfect predictions are unlikely.

EXAMPLE 13.2

Home Prices II

From the ANOVA table for the three-predictor home price model we obtain $SSE = 10,720$, so

$$s_e = \sqrt{\frac{SSE}{n - k - 1}} = \sqrt{\frac{10,720}{30 - 3 - 1}} = 20.31$$

$s_e = 20.31$ (i.e., $20,310 since Y is measured in thousands of dollars) suggests that the model has room for improvement, despite its good fit ($R^2 = .956$). Forecasters find the standard error more useful than R^2 because s_e tells more about the *practical utility* of the forecasts, especially when it is used to make confidence or prediction intervals.

Approximate Confidence and Prediction Intervals for *Y*

We can use the standard error to create approximate confidence or prediction intervals for values of $X_1, X_2, \ldots, X_k$ that are not far from their respective means.* Although these approximate intervals somewhat understate the interval widths, they are helpful when you only need a general idea of the accuracy of your model's predictions.

$$\hat{y}_i \pm t_{\alpha/2} \frac{s_e}{\sqrt{n}} \quad \text{(approximate confidence interval for conditional mean of } Y) \quad \textbf{(13.12)}$$

$$\hat{y}_i \pm t_{\alpha/2} s_e \quad \text{(approximate prediction interval for individual } Y\text{-value)} \quad \textbf{(13.13)}$$

> For home prices using the three-predictor model ($s_e = 20.31$), the 95 percent confidence interval would require $n - k - 1 = 30 - 3 - 1 = 26$ degrees of freedom. From Appendix D we obtain $t_{.025} = 2.056$, so the *approximate* intervals are
>
> $$\hat{y}_i \pm (2.056)\frac{20.31}{\sqrt{30}} \text{ or } \hat{y}_i \pm 7.62 \quad \text{(95\% confidence interval for conditional mean)}$$
>
> $$\hat{y}_i \pm (2.056)(20.31) \text{ or } \hat{y}_i \pm 41.76 \quad \text{(95\% prediction interval for individual home price)}$$
>
> Exact 95 percent confidence and prediction intervals for a home with *SqFt* = 2,950, *LotSize* = 21, and *Baths* = 3 (these values are very near the predictor means for our sample) are $\hat{y}_i \pm 8.55$ and $\hat{y}_i \pm 42.61$, respectively. Thus, our *approximate* intervals are not conservative (i.e., slightly too narrow). Nonetheless, the approximate intervals provide a ballpark idea of the accuracy of the model's predictions. Despite its good fit ($R^2 = .956$), we see that the three-predictor model's predictions are far from perfect. For example, the 95 percent prediction interval for an individual home price is $\hat{y}_i \pm \$41,760$.

EXAMPLE 13.3

Home Prices III

Quick 95 Percent Confidence and Prediction Interval for *Y*

The *t*-values for a 95 percent confidence level are typically near 2 (as long as *n* is not too small). This suggests a quick interval, without using a *t* table:

$$\hat{y}_i \pm 2\frac{s_e}{\sqrt{n}} \quad \text{(quick 95\% confidence interval for conditional mean of } Y) \quad \textbf{(13.14)}$$

$$\hat{y}_i \pm 2s_e \quad \text{(quick 95\% prediction interval for individual } Y\text{-value)} \quad \textbf{(13.15)}$$

These quick formulas are suitable only for rough calculations when you lack access to regression software or *t* tables (e.g., when taking a statistics exam).

13.13 A regression of accountants' starting salaries in a large firm was estimated using 40 new hires and five predictors (college GPA, gender, score on CPA exam, years' prior experience, size of graduating class). The standard error was $3,620. Find the approximate width of a 95 percent prediction interval for an employee's salary, assuming that the predictor values for the individual are near the means of the sample predictors. Would the quick rule give similar results?

13.14 An agribusiness performed a regression of wheat yield (bushels per acre) using observations on 25 test plots with four predictors (rainfall, fertilizer, soil acidity, hours of sun). The standard error was 1.17 bushels. Find the approximate width of a 95 percent prediction interval for wheat yield, assuming that the predictor values for a test plot are near the means of the sample predictors. Would the quick rule give similar results?

SECTION EXERCISES

connect

---

*The exact formulas for a confidence or prediction interval for $\mu_{Y|X}$ or *Y* require matrix algebra. If you need exact intervals, you should use MINITAB or a similar computer package. You must specify the value of *each predictor* for which the confidence interval or prediction is desired.

Mini Case   13.1

Birth Rates and Life Expectancy 🗁 BirthRates1

Table 13.4 shows the birth rate (Y = births per 1,000 population), life expectancy (X_1 = life expectancy at birth), and literacy (X_2 = percent of population that can read and write) for a random sample of 49 world nations.

TABLE 13.4	Birth Rates, Life Expectancy, and Literacy in Selected World Nations		
Nation	**BirthRate**	**LifeExp**	**Literate**
Albania	18.59	72.1	93
Algeria	22.34	70.2	62
Australia	12.71	80.0	100
⋮	⋮	⋮	⋮
Yemen	43.30	60.6	38
Zambia	41.01	37.4	79
Zimbabwe	24.59	36.5	85

FIGURE 13.7	MegaStat's Output for Birth Rate Data

Regression Analysis: Birth Rates

R^2	0.743	n	49
Adjusted R^2	0.732	k	2
Std. Error	5.190	Dep. Var.	**BirthRate**

ANOVA table

Source	SS	df	MS	F	p-value
Regression	3,578.2364	2	1,789.1182	66.42	0.0000
Residual	1,239.1479	46	26.9380		
Total	4,817.3843	48			

Regression output   confidence interval

variables	coefficients	std. error	t(df = 46)	p-value	95% lower	95% upper
Intercept	65.8790	3.8513	17.106	0.0000	58.1268	73.6312
LifeExp	−0.3618	0.0666	−5.431	0.0000	−0.4960	−0.2277
Literate	−0.2330	0.0415	−5.610	0.0000	−0.3166	−0.1494

From Figure 13.7, the fitted regression equation is *BirthRate* = 65.9 − 0.362*LifeExp* − 0.233*Literate,* which says, *ceteris paribus,* that one year's increase in *LifeExp* is associated with 0.362 fewer babies per 1,000 persons, while one extra percent of *Literate* is associated with 0.233 fewer babies per 1,000 persons. The coefficient of determination is fairly high (R^2 = .743) and the overall regression is significant (F_{calc} = 66.42, p-value = .000). Since both predictors are significant (t_{calc} = −5.431 and t_{calc} = −5.610, p-values near .000), the evidence favors the hypothesis that birth rates tend to fall as nations achieve higher life expectancy and greater literacy. Although cause and effect are unproven, the conclusions are consistent with what we know about nutrition, health, and education.

Source: Central Intelligence Agency, *The World Factbook, 2003.*

13.5 CATEGORICAL PREDICTORS

LO 13-5

Incorporate a categorical variable into a multiple regression model.

We cannot directly include a *categorical* variable (qualitative data) as a predictor in a regression because regression requires *numerical* data (quantitative data). But through simple data coding, we can convert categorical data into useful predictors. We will begin our discussion with categorical variables that have only two levels, for which coding is quite simple. We achieve this by defining a binary variable. Recall that a binary variable has two values, denoting the presence or absence of a condition (usually coded 0 and 1). By coding each category as a binary variable we have created a **binary** or **categorical predictor**. Statisticians like to use intuitive names for the binary predictor variable. For example:

For *n* Graduates from an MBA Program

Employed = 1   (if the individual is currently employed)
Employed = 0   (otherwise)

For *n* Quarters of Sales Data

Recession = 1   (if the sales data are for a recession year)
Recession = 0   (otherwise)

For *n* Business Schools

AACSB = 1   (if the school is accredited by the AACSB)
AACSB = 0   (otherwise)

For *n* States

West = 1   (if the state is west of the Mississippi)
West = 0   (otherwise)

Binary predictors are easy to create and are extremely important because they allow us to capture the effects of nonquantitative (categorical) variables such as gender (female, male) or stock fund type (load, no-load). Such variables are also called **dummy**, **dichotomous**, or **indicator variables**.

Tip

Name the binary variable for the characteristic that is present when the variable is 1 (e.g., *Male*) so that others can immediately see what the "1" stands for.

Testing a Binary for Significance

The binary predictor variable's coefficient is tested for equality to zero by using a *t* test, just as we test the coefficient on a quantitative predictor variable. If the binary coefficient is found to be significantly different from zero, then we conclude that the binary predictor is a significant predictor for *Y*. Its coefficient contributes to the predicted value of *Y* when the binary variable value is 1, but has no effect on *Y* when the binary is 0.

Effects of a Binary Predictor

A binary predictor is sometimes called a **shift variable** because it shifts the regression plane up or down. Suppose that we have a two-predictor fitted regression $y = b_0 + b_1 x_1 + b_2 x_2$ where x_1 is a binary predictor. Since the only values that x_1 can take on are either 0 or 1, its contribution to the regression is either b_1 or nothing, as seen in this example:

If $x_1 = 0$, then $y = b_0 + b_1(0) + b_2 x_2$, so $y = b_0 + b_2 x_2$.
If $x_1 = 1$, then $y = b_0 + b_1(1) + b_2 x_2$, so $y = (b_0 + b_1) + b_2 x_2$.

The coefficient b_2 is the same, regardless of the value of x_1, but the intercept either is b_0 (when $x_1 = 0$) or $b_0 + b_1$ (when $x_1 = 1$).

For example, suppose we have a fitted regression of fuel economy based on a sample of 43 cars:

$$MPG = 39.5 - 0.00463 \ Weight + 1.51 \ Manual$$

where

> $Weight$ = vehicle curb weight as tested (pounds)
> $Manual$ = 1 if manual transmission, 0 if automatic

If $Manual = 0$, then

$$MPG = 39.5 - 0.00463 \ Weight + 1.51(0)$$
$$= 39.5 - 0.00463 \ Weight$$

If $Manual = 1$, then

$$MPG = 39.5 - 0.00463 \ Weight + 1.51(1)$$
$$= 41.01 - 0.00463 \ Weight$$

Thus, the binary variable shifts the intercept, leaving the slope unchanged. The situation is illustrated in Figure 13.8. In this case, we see that, although a manual transmission raises *MPG* slightly (by 1.51 miles per gallon, on average), the change in the intercept is rather small (i.e., manual transmission did not have a very large effect). Many experts feel that the choice of automatic versus manual transmission makes very little difference in fuel economy today.

FIGURE 13.8

Binary Shift Variable Illustrated

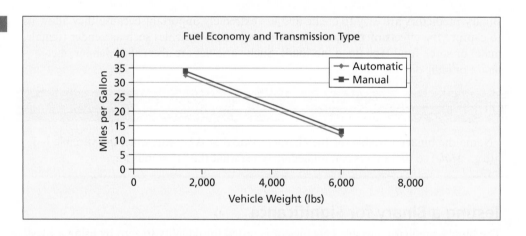

EXAMPLE 13.4

Subdivision Home Prices

🖼 **OakKnoll**

We know that location is an important determinant of home price. But how can we include "location" in a regression? The answer is to code it as a binary predictor. Table 13.5 shows 20 home sales in two different subdivisions, Oak Knoll and Hidden Hills. We create a binary predictor, arbitrarily designating *OakKnoll* = 1 if the home is in the Oak Knoll subdivision, and *OakKnoll* = 0 otherwise. We then do an ordinary regression, shown in Figure 13.9.

The model has a rather good fit ($R^2 = .922$) and is significant overall ($F_{calc} = 100.94$, *p*-value = .0000). Both predictors have a significant effect on *Price* at $\alpha = .05$, although *SqFt* ($t_{calc} = 14.008$, *p*-value = .0000) is a much stronger predictor than *OakKnoll* ($t_{calc} = 2.340$, *p*-value = .0317). The fitted coefficient of *OakKnoll* tells us that, on average, a home in the Oak Knoll subdivision sells for 33.538 more

TABLE 13.5   Home Prices with Binary Predictor ☞ OakKnoll

Obs	Price ($000)	SqFt	OakKnoll	Subdivision
1	615.6	3,055	0	Hidden Hills
2	557.4	2,731	0	Hidden Hills
3	472.6	2,515	0	Hidden Hills
4	595.3	3,011	0	Hidden Hills
5	696.9	3,267	1	Oak Knoll
6	409.2	2,061	1	Oak Knoll
7	814.2	3,842	1	Oak Knoll
8	592.4	2,777	1	Oak Knoll
9	695.5	3,514	0	Hidden Hills
10	495.3	2,145	1	Oak Knoll
11	488.4	2,277	1	Oak Knoll
12	605.4	3,200	0	Hidden Hills
13	635.7	3,065	0	Hidden Hills
14	654.8	2,998	0	Hidden Hills
15	565.6	2,875	0	Hidden Hills
16	642.2	3,000	0	Hidden Hills
17	568.9	2,374	1	Oak Knoll
18	686.5	3,393	1	Oak Knoll
19	724.5	3,457	0	Hidden Hills
20	749.7	3,754	0	Hidden Hills

than a home in Hidden Hills (i.e., $33,538 since *Price* is in thousands of dollars). Rounded off a bit, the fitted regression equation is *Price* = 10.6 + 0.199 *SqFt* + 33.5 *OakKnoll*. The intercept (t_{calc} = 0.237, *p*-value = .8154) does not differ significantly from zero, as can also be seen from the 95 percent confidence interval for the intercept (which includes zero).

FIGURE 13.9   Oak Knoll Regression for 20 Home Sales

Regression Analysis: Subdivision Binary (n = 20)

R²	0.922			
Adjusted R²	0.913		n	20
R	0.960		k	2
Std. Error	29.670		Dep. Var.	**Price (000)**

ANOVA table

Source	SS	df	MS	F	p-value
Regression	177,706.7957	2	88,853.3979	100.94	.0000
Residual	14,964.9538	17	880.2914		
Total	192,671.7495	19			

Regression output   confidence interval

variables	coefficients	std. error	t (df = 17)	p-value	95% lower	95% upper
Intercept	10.6185	44.7725	0.237	.8154	−83.8433	105.0803
SqFt	0.1987	0.0142	14.008	0.0000	0.1688	0.2286
OakKnoll	33.5383	14.3328	2.340	.0317	3.2986	63.7780

More Than One Binary

A variable like gender (male, female) requires only one binary predictor (e.g., *Male*) because *Male* = 0 would indicate the individual is a female. But what if we need several binary predictors to code the data? This occurs when the number of categories to be coded exceeds two. For example, we might have home sales in five subdivisions, or quarterly Walmart profits, or student GPA by class level:

> Home sales by subdivision: *OakKnoll, HiddenHills, RockDale, Lochmoor, KingsRidge*
> Walmart profit by quarter: *Qtr1, Qtr2, Qtr3, Qtr4*
> GPA by class level: *Freshman, Sophomore, Junior, Senior, Master's, Doctoral*

Each category is a binary variable denoting the presence (1) or absence (0) of the characteristic of interest. For example:

> *Freshman* = 1 if the student is a freshman, 0 otherwise
> *Sophomore* = 1 if the student is a sophomore, 0 otherwise
> *Junior* = 1 if the student is a junior, 0 otherwise
> *Senior* = 1 if the student is a senior, 0 otherwise
> *Master's* = 1 if the student is a master's candidate, 0 otherwise
> *Doctoral* = 1 if the student is a PhD candidate, 0 otherwise

But if there are *c* categories (assuming they are mutually exclusive and collectively exhaustive), we need only *c* − 1 binaries to code each observation. This is equivalent to omitting any *one* of the categories. This is possible because *c* − 1 binary values uniquely determine the omitted binary. For example, Table 13.6 shows that we could omit the last binary column without losing any information. Since only one column can be 1 and the other columns must be 0, the following relation holds:

$$Freshman + Sophomore + Junior + Senior + Master's + Doctoral = 1$$

that is,

$$Doctoral = 1 - Freshman - Sophomore - Junior - Senior - Master's$$

TABLE 13.6						
Why We Need Only c − 1 Binaries to Code c Categories	*Name*	*Freshman*	*Sophomore*	*Junior*	*Senior*	*Master's*	**Doctoral (Omitted)**

Name	*Freshman*	*Sophomore*	*Junior*	*Senior*	*Master's*	**Doctoral (Omitted)**
Jaime	0	0	1	0	0	0
Fritz	0	1	0	0	0	0
Mary	0	0	0	0	0	1
Jean	0	0	0	1	0	0
Otto	0	0	0	0	1	0
Gail	1	0	0	0	0	0
etc.	...	...	...	...	...	...

That Mary is a doctoral student can be inferred from the fact that 0 appears in all the other columns. Since Mary is *not* in any of the other five categories, she must be in the sixth category:

$$Doctoral = 1 - 0 - 0 - 0 - 0 - 0 = 1$$

There is nothing special about the last column; we could have omitted any other column instead. Similarly, we might omit the *KingsRidge* data column from home sales data, since a home that is not in one of the first four subdivisions must be *KingsRidge*. We could omit the *Qtr4* column from the Walmart time series, since if an observation is not from the first, second, or third quarter, it must be from *Qtr4*:

> Home sales: *OakKnoll, HiddenHills, RockDale, Lochmoor, ~~KingsRidge~~*
> Walmart profit: *Qtr1, Qtr2, Qtr3, ~~Qtr4~~*

Again, there is nothing special about omitting the last category. We can omit any single binary instead. The omitted binary becomes the base reference point for the regression; that is, it is part of the intercept. No information is lost.

What If I Forget to Exclude One Binary?

If you include all *c* binaries for *c* categories, you will have a redundant independent variable that we say is *collinear* with the other binary categories. When the value of one independent variable can be determined from the values of the other independent variables, this creates a serious problem for the regression estimation because one column in the *X* data matrix will then be a perfect linear combination of the other column(s). The least squares estimation would then fail because the data matrix would be singular (i.e., would have no inverse). MINITAB automatically checks for such a situation and omits one of the offending predictors, while Excel merely gives an error. It is safer to decide for yourself which binary to exclude.

Mini Case 13.2

Age or Gender Bias? Oxnard

We can't use simple *t* tests to compare employee groups based on gender or age or job classification because they fail to take into account relevant factors such as education and experience. A simplistic salary equity study that fails to account for such control variables would be subject to criticism. Instead, we can use binary variables to study the effects of age, experience, gender, and education on salaries within a corporation. Gender and education can be coded as binary variables, and age can be forced into a binary variable that defines older employees explicitly, rather than assuming that age has a linear effect on salary.

Table 13.7 shows salaries for 25 employees in the advertising department at Oxnard Petro, Ltd. As an initial step in a salary equity study, the human resources consultant performed a linear regression using the proposed model $Salary = \beta_0 + \beta_1\ Male + \beta_2\ Exper + \beta_3\ Ovr50 + \beta_4\ MBA$. *Exper* is the employee's experience in years; *Salary* is in thousands of dollars. Binaries are used for gender (*Male* = 0, 1), age (*Ovr50* = 0, 1), and

TABLE 13.7 Salaries of Advertising Staff of Oxnard Petro, Ltd.

Obs	Employee	Salary	Male	Exper	Ovr50	MBA
1	Mary	28.6	0	0	0	1
2	Frieda	53.3	0	4	0	1
3	Alicia	73.8	0	12	0	0
4	Tom	26.0	1	0	0	0
5	Nicole	77.5	0	19	0	0
6	Xihong	95.1	1	17	0	0
7	Ellen	34.3	0	1	0	1
8	Bob	63.5	1	9	0	0
9	Vivian	96.4	0	19	0	0
10	Cecil	122.9	1	31	0	0
11	Barry	63.8	1	12	0	0
12	Jaime	111.1	1	29	1	0
13	Wanda	82.5	0	12	0	1
14	Sam	80.4	1	19	1	0
15	Saundra	69.3	0	10	0	0
16	Pete	52.8	1	8	0	0
17	Steve	54.0	1	2	0	1
18	Juan	58.7	1	11	0	0
19	Dick	72.3	1	14	0	0
20	Lee	88.6	1	21	0	0
21	Judd	60.2	1	10	0	0
22	Sunil	61.0	1	7	0	0
23	Marcia	75.8	0	18	0	0
24	Vivian	79.8	0	19	0	0
25	Igor	70.2	1	12	0	0

MBA degree ($MBA = 0, 1$). Can we reject the hypothesis that the coefficients of *Male* and *Ovr50* are zero? If so, it would suggest salary inequity based on gender and/or age.

The coefficients in Figure 13.10 suggest that, *ceteris paribus,* a male ($Male = 1$) makes $3,013 more on average than a female. However, the coefficient of *Male* does not differ significantly from zero even at $\alpha = .10$ ($t_{calc} = 0.86$, *p*-value $= .399$). The evidence for age discrimination is a little stronger. Although an older employee ($Ovr50 = 1$) makes $8,598 less than others, on average, the *p*-value for *Ovr50* ($t_{calc} = -1.36$, *p*-value $= .189$) is not convincing at $\alpha = .10$. The coefficient of MBA indicates that, *ceteris paribus,* MBA degree holders earn $9,587 more than others, and the coefficient differs from zero at $\alpha = .10$ ($t_{calc} = 1.92$, *p*-value $= .070$). Salaries at Oxnard Petro are dominated by *Exper* ($t_{calc} = 12.08$, *p*-value $= .000$). Each additional year of experience adds $3,019, on average, to an employee's salary. The regression is significant overall ($F_{calc} = 52.62$, $p = .000$) and has a good fit ($R^2 = .913$). Although the sample fails Evans' 10:1 ratio test for n/k, it passes Doane's 5:1 ratio test. A more complete salary equity study might consider additional predictors.

FIGURE 13.10   **MINITAB Results for Oxnard Salary Equity Study**

```
The regression equation is
Salary = 28.9 + 3.01 Male − 8.60 Ovr50 + 3.02 Exper + 9.59 MBA
```

Predictor	Coef	SE Coef	T	P
Constant	28.878	4.925	5.86	0.000
Male	3.013	3.496	0.86	0.399
Ovr50	−8.598	6.324	−1.36	0.189
Exper	3.0190	0.2499	12.08	0.000
MBA	9.587	5.003	1.92	0.070

$S = 7.44388$ R-Sq $= 91.3\%$ R-Sq(adj) $= 89.6\%$

Regional Binaries

One very common use of binaries is to code regions. Figure 13.11 shows how the 50 states of the United States could be divided into four regions by using these binaries:

$Midwest = 1$ if state is in the Midwest, 0 otherwise

$Neast = 1$ if state is in the Northeast, 0 otherwise

$Seast = 1$ if state is in the Southeast, 0 otherwise

$West = 1$ if state is in the West, 0 otherwise

For example, we can use regression to analyze the U.S. voting patterns in the 2000 U.S. presidential election. Binary predictors could permit us to analyze the effects of region (a qualitative variable) on voting patterns.

FIGURE 13.11

Four Regional Binaries

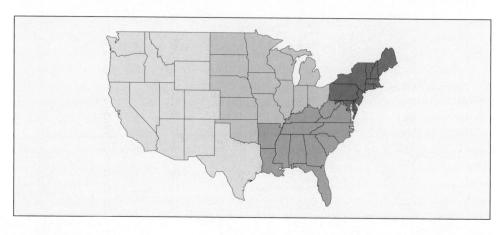

Mini Case 13.3

Regional Voting Patterns 📄 Election2008

Table 13.8 shows an abbreviated data set for the 50 U.S. states. There are four regional binaries, but we only need to include three in our model. Arbitrarily, we omit the *Seast* column, which becomes the baseline for the regression to examine a hypothesis about the effects of population age, college graduation rates, home ownership, unemployment rates, and region on voting patterns in the 2008 U.S. presidential election. The dependent variable (*Obama%*) is the percentage vote for Barack Obama, and the proffered hypothesis to be investigated is

$$Obama\% = \beta_0 + \beta_1\, Age65\% + \beta_2\, ColGrad\% + \beta_3\, HomeOwn\% + \beta_4\, UnEmp\%$$
$$+ \beta_5\, Midwest + \beta_6\, Neast + \beta_7\, West$$

TABLE 13.8 **Characteristics of U.S. States in 2008 Election**

State	Obama%	Age65%	ColGrad%	HomeOwn%	Unemp%	MidWest	Neast	West	Seast (Omitted)
AL	38.8	13.8	22.0	73.0	5.0	0	0	0	1
AK	37.9	7.3	27.3	66.4	6.7	0	0	1	0
AZ	44.9	13.3	25.1	69.1	5.5	0	0	1	0
AR	38.9	14.3	18.8	68.9	5.1	0	0	0	1
CA	60.9	11.2	29.6	57.5	7.2	0	0	1	0
CO	53.7	10.3	35.6	69.0	4.9	0	0	1	0
CT	60.6	13.7	35.6	70.7	5.7	0	1	0	0
⋮	⋮	⋮	⋮	⋮	⋮	⋮	⋮	⋮	⋮
etc.	etc.	etc.	etc.	etc.	etc.	etc.	etc.	etc.	etc.

The fitted regression shown in Figure 13.12 has four quantitative predictors and three binaries. The regression is significant overall ($F_{calc} = 12.27$, *p*-value $= 2.04E{-}08$).

FIGURE 13.12 **Regression Output for Voting Patterns**

Regression Analysis

R^2	0.672			
Adjusted R^2	0.617		n	50
R	0.819		k	7
Std. Error	5.883		Dep. Var.	**Obama%**

ANOVA table

Source	SS	df	MS	F	p-value
Regression	2,971.6423	7	424.5203	12.27	2.04E-08
Residual	1,453.6465	42	34.6106		
Total	4,425.2888	49			

Regression output — *confidence interval*

variables	coefficients	std. error	t (df = 42)	p-value	95% lower	95% upper
Intercept	0.4988	23.5964	0.021	.9832	−47.1207	48.1184
Age65%	2.2891	0.6195	3.695	.0006	1.0389	3.5393
ColGrad%	0.9787	0.2608	3.752	.0005	0.4523	1.5050
HomeOwn%	−0.3377	0.2120	−1.593	.1187	−0.7655	0.0902
Unemp%	2.6293	0.7262	3.621	.0008	1.1637	4.0949
MidWest	3.2490	2.5005	1.299	.2009	−1.7971	8.2951
Neast	6.7259	3.3019	2.037	.0480	0.0624	13.3893
West	4.6094	2.7555	1.673	.1018	−0.9514	10.1702

The *p*-values suggest that, *ceteris paribus,* the percent of voters choosing Obama was higher in states with older citizens, a higher percentage of college graduates, and higher unemployment. Home ownership was not a highly significant predictor with t_{calc}= -1.593 (*p*-value = .1187). The Obama vote was, *ceteris paribus,* significantly higher in the Northeast as compared to the Southeast (t_{calc}= 2.037, *p*-value = .048). The difference between the Western and Southeastern states was marginally significant (t_{calc}= 1.673, *p*-value = .1018), but there was *not* a significant difference in the Obama vote between the Midwestern states and the Southeastern states (t_{calc}= 1.299, *p*-value = .2009). Using regional binaries allows us to analyze the effects of these qualitative factors.

SECTION EXERCISES

connect™

13.15 A regression model to predict the price of a condominium for a weekend getaway in a resort community included the following predictor variables: number of nights needed, number of bedrooms, whether the condominium complex had a swimming pool or not, and whether or not a parking garage was available. (a) Identify the quantitative predictor variable(s). (b) How many binary variables would be included in the model? (c) Write the proposed model form for predicting condominium price.

13.16 A regression model to predict the price of diamonds included the following predictor variables: the weight of the stone (in carats where 1 carat = 0.2 gram), the color rating (D, E, F, G, H, or I), and the clarity rating (IF, VVS1, VVS2, VS1, or VS2). (a) Identify the quantitative predictor variable(s). (b) How many indicator variables would be included in the model in order to prevent the least squares estimation from failing? (c) Write the proposed model form for predicting a diamond price.

13.17 Refrigerator prices are affected by characteristics such as whether or not the refrigerator is on sale, whether or not it is listed as a Sub-Zero brand, the number of doors (one door or two doors), and the placement of the freezer compartment (top, side, or bottom). The table below shows the regression output from a regression model using the natural log of price as the dependent variable. The model was developed by the Bureau of Labor Statistics. (a) Write the regression model, being careful to exclude the base indicator variable. (b) Find the *p*-value for each coefficient, using 319 degrees of freedom. Using an $\alpha = .01$, which predictor variable(s) are *not* significant predictors? (c) By how much does the natural log of refrigerator price decrease from a *two-door, side freezer model* to a *two-door, top freezer model*? (d) Which model demands a higher price: the side freezer or the one door with freezer model?

Variable	Coefficient	Standard Error	t Statistic
Intercept	5.484092	0.13081309	41.923
Sale price	−0.0733	0.02338826	−3.134
Sub-Zero brand	1.11962	0.14615699	7.660
Total capacity (in cubic ft)	0.06956	0.00535103	12.999
Two-door, freezer on bottom	0.046569	0.0808569	0.576
Two-door, side freezer	Base		
Two-door, freezer on top	−0.343246	0.03595873	−9.546
One door with freezer	−0.709558	0.13097047	−5.418
One door, no freezer	−0.881981	0.14913992	−5.914

Source: www.bls.gov/cpi/cpirfr.htm

13.18 A model was developed to predict the length of a sentence (the response variable) for a male convicted of assault using the following predictor variables: age (in years), number of prior felony convictions, whether the criminal was married or not (1 = married), and whether the criminal was employed or not (1 = employed). The table below shows the regression output. (a) Write the regression model. (b) Using 45 degrees of freedom, find the *p*-value for each coefficient. Using an $\alpha = .01$, which predictor variable(s) are *not* significant predictors of length of sentence? (c) Interpret the coefficient of Married. (d) How much shorter is the sentence if the criminal is employed? (e) Predict the length of sentence for an unmarried, unemployed, 25-year old male with one prior conviction. Show your calculations. 🖼 **Sentencing**

Variable	Coefficient	Standard Error	t Statistic
Intercept	3.2563	4.3376	0.751
Age	0.5219	0.1046	4.989
Convictions	7.7412	1.0358	7.474
Married?	−6.0852	2.5809	−2.358
Employed?	−14.3402	2.5356	−5.656

13.6 TESTS FOR NONLINEARITY AND INTERACTION

Tests for Nonlinearity

Sometimes the effect of a predictor is nonlinear. A simple example would be estimating the volume of lumber to be obtained from a tree before cutting. This is a practical problem facing a timber farm. The manager can inventory the trees and measure their heights and diameters then use this information to estimate the lumber volume. In addition to improving the accuracy of asset valuation on the balance sheet, the manager can decide the best time to cut the trees, based on their expected growth rates.

The volume of lumber that can be milled from a tree depends on the height of the tree and its radius, that is, *Volume* = f(*Height, Radius*). But what is the appropriate model form? Figure 13.13 shows a scatter plot of tree *radius* versus tree *volume*. You'll see that the quadratic model actually fits the data better than the linear model.

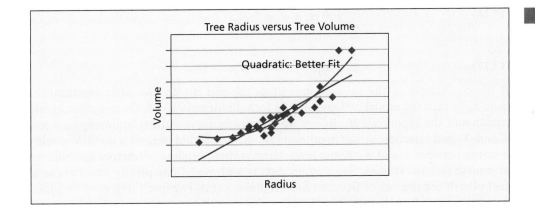

FIGURE 13.13

Scatter Plot Tree Radius versus Volume

Figure 13.14 shows the MINITAB regression output for two regressions of *Volume* on *Height* and *Radius*:

Model 1: Volume = −58.0 + 0.3393 *Height* + 9.4163 *Radius* (R^2 = .948, s = 3.88)

Model 2: Volume = −27.5 + 0.3488 *Height* + 0.6738 *Radius²* (R^2 = .973, s = 2.78)

If we regard a log as a cylinder, we would prefer the second regression because the usable volume of a cylinder is proportional to the square of its radius.* The *t* statistics for both *Height* and *Radius* are improved in model 2, and the higher R^2 and reduced standard errors indicate a better fit. Although we introduced a squared term for the radius predictor variable, the model still is said to be linear because none of the parameters (i.e., β_0, β_1, or β_2) shows up as exponents nor do we divide any parameter by another.

---

* $V = \pi h r^2$ would describe the relationship between the tree's radius (r), height (h), and volume (V). A logarithmic model $ln(Volume) = \beta_0 + \beta_1 ln(Height) + \beta_2 ln(Radius)$ might be more appropriate, although the resulting R^2 and s_e would not be comparable to the models shown above because the response variable would be in different units.

FIGURE 13.14

Regression Results for Tree Data

Model 1: The regression equation is
Volume = −58.0 + 0.339 Height + 9.42 Radius

Predictor	Coef	SE Coef	T	P
Constant	−57.988	8.638	−6.71	0.000
Height	0.3393	0.1302	2.61	0.014
Radius	9.4163	0.5285	17.82	0.000

S = 3.88183   R-Sq = 94.8%   R-Sq(adj) = 94.4%

Model 2: The regression equation is
Volume = −27.5 + 0.349 Height + 0.674 Radius2

Predictor	Coef	SE Coef	T	P
Constant	−27.512	6.558	−4.20	0.000
Height	0.34881	0.09315	3.74	0.001
Radius2	0.67383	0.02672	25.22	0.000

S = 2.79946   R-Sq = 97.3%   R-Sq(adj) = 97.1%

To test for suspected nonlinearity of any *predictor*, we can include its square in the regression. For example, instead of

(13.16)
$$y = \beta_0 + \beta_1 x_1 + \beta_2 x_2 + \varepsilon$$

we would use

(13.17)
$$y = \beta_0 + \beta_1 x_1 + \beta_2 x_1^2 + \beta_3 x_2 + \beta_4 x_2^2 + \varepsilon$$

If the coefficients of the squared predictors (β_2 and β_4) do not differ significantly from zero, then the model collapses to the form in formula 13.16. On the other hand, rejection of the hypothesis $H_0: \beta_2 = 0$ would suggest a quadratic relationship between Y and X_1 and rejection of the hypothesis $H_0: \beta_4 = 0$ would suggest a quadratic relationship between Y and X_2. Some researchers include squared predictors as a matter of course in large studies. Squared predictors add model complexity and impose a cost of reduced degrees of freedom for significance tests (we lose 1 degree of freedom for each squared predictor), but the potential reward is a more appropriate model specification.

For example, rising total U.S. petroleum consumption from 1980 through 2004 can be fairly well described by a linear time trend model ($R^2 = .8691$). Yet, adding a squared predictor (making it a quadratic model) gives an even better fit ($R^2 = .9183$) and the x_t^2 term is significant ($t_{calc} = 3.640$). This suggests a nonlinear trend, using $x_t = 1, 2, \ldots, 25$ to represent the year.

Linear: $\hat{y}_t = 0.2012 \, x_t + 15.029 \, (R^2 = 0.8691)$

Quadratic: $\hat{y}_t = 0.0074 \, x_t^2 + 0.0078 \, x_t + 15.899 \, (R^2 = 0.9183)$

Tests for Interaction

We can test for **interaction** between two predictors by including their product in the regression. For example, we might hypothesize that Y depends on X_1 and X_2, and $X_1 X_2$. To test for interaction, we estimate the model:

(13.18)
$$y = \beta_0 + \beta_1 x_1 + \beta_2 x_2 + \beta_3 \, x_1 x_2 + \varepsilon$$

If the *t* test for β_3 allows us to reject the hypothesis H_0: $\beta_3 = 0$, then we conclude that there is a significant interaction effect that transcends the roles of X_1 and X_2 separately (similar to the two-factor ANOVA tests for interaction in Chapter 11). Interaction effects require careful interpretation and cost 1 degree of freedom per interaction. However, if the interaction term improves the model specification, it is well worth the cost. For example, a bank's lost revenue (*Loss*) due to loan defaults depends on the loan size (*Size*) and the degree of risk (*Risk*). Small loans may be risky but may not contribute much to the total losses. Large loans may be less risky but potentially represent a large loss. An interaction term (*Size* × *Risk*) would be large if either predictor is large, thereby capturing the effect of both predictors. Thus, the interaction term might be a significant predictor in the model:

$$Loss = b_0 + b_1\ Size + b_2\ Risk + b_3\ Size \times Risk$$

Mini Case — 13.4

Cockpit Noise 🖾 **CockpitNoise**

Cockpit sound level was measured 61 times at various flight phases for seven different B-727 aircraft (an older model) at the first officer's left ear position using a handheld meter. Sound level was measured in decibels. For reference, 60 dB is a normal conversation, 75 is a typical vacuum cleaner, 85 is city traffic, 90 is a typical hair dryer, and 110 is a chain saw. The proposed regression model is *Noise* = β_0 + β_1 *Climb* + β_2 *Descent* + β_3 *Speed* + β_4 *Speed*^{2} + β_5 *Alt* + β_6 *Alt*^{2}. The airspeed (*Speed*) is in KIAS (knots indicated air speed) or nautical miles per hour. Altitude (*Alt*) is in thousands of feet above MSL (mean sea level). Squared predictors (*SpeedSqr* and *AltSqr*) are included for tests of nonlinearity (*SpeedSqr* is divided by 1,000 to improve data conditioning). There are three flight phases, represented by binaries (*Climb, Cruise, Descent*), but *Cruise* is omitted from the regression since it is implied by the other two binaries (i.e., if *Climb* = 0 and *Descent* = 0, then necessarily *Cruise* = 1). Table 13.9 shows a partial data list.

TABLE 13.9 **Cockpit Noise in B-727 Aircraft** 🖾 **CockpitNoise**

Obs	Noise	Climb	Cruise	Descent	Speed	Alt	SpeedSqr	AltSqr
1	83	1	0	0	250	10	62.50	100
2	89	1	0	0	340	15	115.60	225
3	88	1	0	0	320	18	102.40	324
4	89	0	1	0	330	24	108.90	576
5	92	0	1	0	346	27	119.72	729
⋮	⋮	⋮	⋮	⋮	⋮	⋮	⋮	⋮
61	82	0	0	1	250	4.5	62.50	20.25

Regression results are shown in Figure 13.15. The coefficient of *Climb* indicates a slight average reduction in *Noise* of 0.814 decibel during the climb flight phase (relative to the baseline of *Cruise*). The coefficient of *Descent* indicates a significant reduction of 1.66 decibels during the descent flight phase. *Speed* and *Alt* have nonlinear effects, as indicated by the significance of *SpeedSqr* (t_{calc} = 2.336, *p*-value = .0232) and *AltSqr* (t_{calc} = −2.348, *p*-value = .0226).

FIGURE 13.15   **MegaStat's Regression Results for Cockpit Noise**

Regression Analysis: Cockpit Noise ($n = 61$ flights)

R^2	0.920		
Adjusted R^2	0.911	n	61
R	0.959	k	6
Std. Error	1.179	Dep. Var.	**Noise**

ANOVA table

Source	SS	df	MS	F	p-value
Regression	860.4680	6	143.4113	103.19	0.0000
Residual	75.0484	54	1.3898		
Total	935.5164	60			

Regression output   confidence interval

variables	coefficients	std. error	t(df = 54)	p-value	95% lower	95% upper
Intercept	83.0833	8.0747	10.289	0.0000	66.8946	99.2721
Climb	−0.8140	0.5649	−1.441	0.1553	−1.9465	0.3185
Descent	−1.6612	0.5557	−2.989	0.0042	−2.7754	−0.5471
Speed	−0.0492	0.0525	−0.936	0.3533	−0.1545	0.0561
Alt	0.3134	0.1328	2.361	0.0219	0.0472	0.5796
SpeedSqr	0.1867	0.0799	2.336	0.0232	0.0265	0.3470
AltSqr	−0.0074	0.0031	−2.348	0.0226	−0.0137	−0.0011

SECTION EXERCISES

connect

13.19 The data set below shows a sample of salaries for 39 engineers employed by the Solnar Company along with each engineer's years of experience. (a) Construct a scatter plot using *Salary* as the response variable and *Years* as the explanatory variable. Describe the shape of the scatter plot. Does it appear that a nonlinear model would be appropriate? Explain. (b) Run the regression with *Salary* as the response variable and *Years* and *YearsSq* as the explanatory variables. Report the R^2, F_{calc} statistic, and p-value. Is the nonlinear model significant? (c) Report the p-values for both *Years* and *YearsSq*. Are these variables significant predictors? Use $\alpha = .10$.

Engineer Salaries and Years of Experience at Solnar Company ($n = 39$)
 Salaries

Salaries ($)	Years	YearsSq
50,000	1	1
54,000	1	1
52,000	1	1
.	.	.
.	.	.
.	.	.
134,000	32	1,023
118,000	34	1,156
134,000	35	1,225

13.20 The same data set from exercise 13.19 also has gender information for each engineer. The binary variable *Male* = 1 indicates the engineer is male and *Male* = 0 indicates the engineer is female. Run the regression with *Salary* as the response variable and *Years*, *YearsSq*, *Male*, and *Years* × *Male* as the explanatory variables. Report the p-values for the binary variable *Male* and the interaction term *Years* × *Male*. Are these two variables significant? Use $\alpha = .10$.

Engineer Salaries, Years of Experience, and Gender at Solnar Company (*n* = 39)				
📁 Salaries				
Salaries ($)	Years	YearsSq	Male	Years × Male
48,000	1	1	0	0
50,000	1	1	0	0
52,000	1	1	1	1
.	.	.	.	.
.	.	.	.	.
.	.	.	.	.
131,000	20	400	1	20
134,000	32	1,023	1	32
134,000	35	1,225	1	35

13.7 MULTICOLLINEARITY

What Is Multicollinearity?

When the independent variables $X_1, X_2, \ldots, X_m$ are related to each other instead of being independent, we have a condition known as **multicollinearity**. If only two predictors are correlated, we have **collinearity**. Almost any data set will have some degree of correlation among the predictors. The depth of our concern would depend on the *degree* of multicollinearity.

LO 13-6

Detect multicollinearity and assess its effects.

Variance Inflation

Multicollinearity does not bias the least squares estimates or the predictions for Y, but it does induce *variance inflation*. When predictors are strongly intercorrelated, the variances of their estimated coefficients tend to become inflated, widening the confidence intervals for the true coefficients $\beta_1, \beta_2, \ldots, \beta_k$ and making the t statistics less reliable. It can thus be difficult to identify the separate contribution of each predictor to "explaining" the response variable, due to the entanglement of their roles. Consequences of variance inflation can range from trivial to severe. In the most extreme case, when one X data column is an exact linear function of one or more other X data columns, the least squares estimation will fail.* That could happen, for example, if you inadvertently included the same predictor twice, or if you forgot to omit one of the c binaries used to code c attribute categories. Some software packages (e.g., MINITAB) will check for perfect multicollinearity and will remove one of the offending predictors, but don't count on it.

Variance inflation generally does not cause major problems, and some researchers suggest that it is best ignored except in extreme cases. However, it is a good idea to investigate the degree of multicollinearity in the regression model. There are several ways to do this.

Correlation Matrix

To check whether two predictors are correlated (*collinearity*), we can inspect the **correlation matrix** for the predictors using Excel's function =CORREL(Data) or MegaStat's Correlation Matrix or MINITAB's Stat > Basic Statistics > Correlation. The correlation matrix for Mini Case 13.4 (cockpit noise) is shown in Table 13.10. The response variable (*Noise*) is not included, since collinearity *among the predictors* is the condition we are investigating. Cells above the diagonal are redundant and hence are not shown. Correlations that differ from zero at $\alpha = .05$ in a two-tailed test are highlighted in blue in Table 13.10. In this example, a majority of the predictors are significantly correlated, which is not an unusual situation in regression modeling. The very high correlations between *Speed* and *SpeedSqr* and between *Alt* and *AltSqr* are highlighted in yellow. These are an artifact of the model specification (i.e., using squared predictors as tests for nonlinearity) and are not necessarily a cause for removal of either predictor.

---

*If the X data matrix has no inverse, we cannot solve for the OLS estimates.

TABLE 13.10

Correlation Matrix for Cockpit Noise Data
CockpitNoise

	Climb	Cruise	Descent	Speed	Alt	SpeedSqr
Cruise	−0.391					
Descent	−0.694	−0.391				
Speed	−0.319	−0.044	0.353			
Alt	−0.175	0.584	−0.282	0.063		
SpeedSqr	−0.351	−0.055	0.393	0.997	0.040	
AltSqr	−0.214	0.624	−0.274	−0.087	0.972	−0.103

Significant predictor correlations do not *per se* indicate a serious problem. **Klein's Rule** (see Related Reading) suggests that we should worry about the stability of the regression coefficient estimates only when a pairwise predictor correlation exceeds the multiple correlation coefficient R (i.e., the square root of R^2). In Mini Case 13.4 (cockpit noise), the correlations between *Speed* and *SpeedSqr* ($r = .997$) and between *Alt* and *AltSqr* ($r = .972$) do exceed the multiple correlation coefficient ($R = .959$), which suggests that the confidence intervals and t tests may be affected.

Variance Inflation Factor (VIF)

Although the matrix scatter plots and correlation matrix are easy to understand, they only show correlations between *pairs* of predictors (e.g., X_1 and X_2). A general test for multicollinearity should reveal more complex relationships *among* predictors. For example, X_2 might be a linear function of X_1, X_3, and X_4 even though its pairwise correlation with each is not very large.

The **variance inflation factor (VIF)** for each predictor provides a more comprehensive test. For a given predictor X_j, the VIF is defined as

(13.19)
$$VIF_j = \frac{1}{1 - R_j^2}$$

where R_j^2 is the coefficient of determination when predictor j is regressed against *all* the other predictors (excluding Y).

Response Variable	Explanatory Variables	R^2
X_1	$X_2, X_3, \ldots, X_k$	R_1^2
X_2	$X_1, X_3, \ldots, X_k$	R_2^2
⋮	⋮	⋮
X_k	$X_1, X_2, \ldots, X_{k-1}$	R_k^2

If predictor j is unrelated to the other predictors, its R_j^2 will be 0 and its VIF will be 1 (an ideal situation that will rarely be seen with actual data). Some possible situations are:

R_j^2	VIF_j	Interpretation
0.00	$\dfrac{1}{1 - R_j^2} = \dfrac{1}{1 - 0.00} = 1.0$	No variance inflation
0.50	$\dfrac{1}{1 - R_j^2} = \dfrac{1}{1 - 0.50} = 2.0$	Mild variance inflation
0.90	$\dfrac{1}{1 - R_j^2} = \dfrac{1}{1 - 0.90} = 10.0$	Strong variance inflation
0.99	$\dfrac{1}{1 - R_j^2} = \dfrac{1}{1 - 0.99} = 100.0$	Severe variance inflation

There is no limit on the magnitude of a VIF. Some researchers suggest that when a VIF exceeds 10, there is cause for concern, or even removal of predictor *j* from the model. But that rule of thumb is perhaps too conservative. A VIF of 10 says that the other predictors "explain" 90 percent of the variation in predictor *j*. While a VIF of 10 shows that predictor *j* is strongly related to the other predictors, it is not necessarily indicative of instability in the least squares estimates. Removing a relevant predictor is a step that should not be taken lightly, for it could result in misspecification of the model. A better way to think of it is that a large VIF is a warning to consider whether predictor *j* really belongs in the model.

Are Coefficients Stable?

Evidence of instability would be when X_1 and X_2 have a high pairwise correlation with Y, yet one or both predictors have insignificant t statistics in the fitted multiple regression. Another symptom would be if X_1 and X_2 are positively correlated with Y, yet one of them has a negative slope in the multiple regression. As a general test, you can try dropping a collinear predictor from the regression and watch what happens to the fitted coefficients in the re-estimated model. If they do not change very much, multicollinearity was probably not a concern. If dropping one collinear predictor causes sharp changes in one or more of the remaining coefficients in the model, then your multicollinearity may be causing instability. Keep in mind that a predictor must be significantly different from zero in order to say that it "changed" in the reestimation.

Both MegaStat and MINITAB will calculate variance inflation factors, but you must request it as an option. Their VIF menu options are shown in Figure 13.16.

FIGURE 13.16

MegaStat and Minitab VIF Menu Options

Mini Case   13.5

Regional Voting Patterns Election2008

Mini Case 13.3 investigated a hypothesis about predictors for the percentage vote for Barack Obama in each of the 50 states. The proffered model was $Obama\% = \beta_0 + \beta_1 Age65\% + \beta_2 ColGrad\% + \beta_3 HomeOwn\% + \beta_4 UnEmp\% + \beta_5 Midwest + \beta_6 Neast + \beta_7 West$. Table 13.11 shows the correlation matrix for the predictors. A quick rule says that a correlation is significant if it exceeds $2/\sqrt{n} = 2/\sqrt{50} = 0.28$. By this rule, 11 of the predictor correlations are significant at $\alpha = .05$ (shaded cells in table). However, none is close to the multiple correlation coefficient ($R = .819$), so by Klein's Rule we should not worry. It should also be mentioned that correlations between the binary variables may exist by design. For example, it is understood that if a state is in the Midwest, it *cannot* be in any of the other three regions.

TABLE 13.11	Correlation Matrix for 2008 Election Predictors 📁 Election2008						
	Age65%	**ColGrad%**	**HomeOwn%**	**Unemp%**	**MidWest**	**Neast**	**West**
ColGrad%	−0.194						
HomeOwn%	0.153	−0.357					
Unemp%	−0.122	−0.091	−0.147				
MidWest	0.161	−0.109	0.137	−0.118			
Neast	0.227	0.548	−0.067	0.013	−0.315		
West	−0.476	0.038	−0.318	−0.078	−0.370	−0.331	
Seast	0.114	−0.460	0.259	0.191	−0.333	−0.298	−0.350

Despite the significant correlations between certain predictors, Figure 13.17 shows that for the election data no VIF exceeds 10 and the overall mean VIF is small. Thus, the confidence intervals should be reliable.

FIGURE 13.17	MegaStat's VIFs for Election Study

Regression output						confidence interval		
variables	*coefficients*	*std. error*	*t (df=42)*	*p-value*	*95% lower*	*95% upper*	*VIF*
Intercept	0.4988	23.5964	0.021	.9832	−47.1207	48.1184	
Age65%	2.2891	0.6195	3.695	.0006	1.0389	3.5393	1.563
ColGrad%	0.9787	0.2608	3.752	.0005	0.4523	1.5050	2.183
HomeOwn%	−0.3377	0.2120	−1.593	.1187	−0.7655	0.0902	1.390
Unemp%	2.6293	0.7262	3.621	.0008	1.1637	4.0949	1.174
MidWest	3.2490	2.5005	1.299	.2009	−1.7971	8.2951	1.738
Neast	6.7259	3.3019	2.037	.0480	0.0624	13.3893	2.703
West	4.6094	2.7555	1.673	.1018	−0.9514	10.1702	2.211

SECTION EXERCISES

connect

VAILRESORTS

13.21 Using the "Vail Guest Satisfaction Survey" data, construct a correlation matrix of the 11 independent variables. The response variable is *ovalue*. (a) Identify the four pairs of independent variables that have the highest pairwise correlation values. Do they show significant correlation? (b) Using MegaStat or MINITAB, run the regression with all 11 predictor variables, calculating the VIF for each predictor. (c) Did you see any cause for concern based on the VIF values? Why or why not? 📁 **VailGuestSat2**

13.22 Using the "Metals" data, construct a correlation matrix of the six independent variables. The response variable is *Price/lb.* (a) Identify any pairs of independent variables that have a significant pairwise correlation. (b) Using MegaStat or MINITAB, run the regression with all six predictor variables, calculating the VIF for each predictor. (c) Did you see any cause for concern based on the VIF values? Why or why not? 📁 **Metals**

13.8 VIOLATIONS OF ASSUMPTIONS

Recall that the least squares method makes several assumptions about the random error ε. Although ε is unobservable, clues may be found in the residuals e_i. We routinely test three important assumptions:

- *Assumption* 1: The errors are normally distributed.
- *Assumption* 2: The errors have constant variance (i.e., they are homoscedastic).
- *Assumption* 3: The errors are independent (i.e., they are nonautocorrelated).

Regression residuals often violate one or more of these assumptions. The consequences may be mild, moderate, or severe, depending on various factors. **Residual tests** for violations of regression assumptions are routinely provided by regression software. Visual tools for testing these assumptions were presented in Sections 12.8 and 12.9. We will review each assumption and provide suggestions for possible remedies of assumption violations.

LO 13-7

Analyze residuals to check for violations of residual assumptions.

Non-Normal Errors

Except when there are major outliers, non-normal residuals are usually considered a mild violation. The regression coefficients and their variances remain unbiased and consistent. The main ill consequence is that confidence intervals for the parameters may be unreliable because the normality assumption is used to construct them. However, if the sample size is large (say, $n > 30$), the confidence intervals generally are OK unless serious outliers exist. The hypotheses are:

H_0: Errors are normally distributed

H_1: Errors are not normally distributed

A simple "eyeball test" of the *histogram of residuals* can usually reveal outliers or serious asymmetry. You can use either plain residuals or standardized (i.e., studentized) residuals. Standardized residuals offer the advantage of a predictable scale (between -3 and $+3$ unless there are outliers). Another visual test for normality is the *probability plot,* which is produced as an option by MINITAB and MegaStat. If the null hypothesis is true, the probability plot should be approximately linear.

What can we do about non-normality? First, consider trimming outliers—but only if they clearly are mistakes. Second, can you increase the sample size? If so, it will help assure asymptotic normality of the estimates. Third, you could try a logarithmic transformation of the variables. However, this is a new model specification that may require advice from a professional statistician. Fourth, you could do nothing—just be aware of the problem.

Nonconstant Variance (Heteroscedasticity)

The regression should fit equally well for all values of X. If the error variance is constant, the errors are *homoscedastic.* If the error variance is nonconstant, the errors are *heteroscedastic.* This violation is potentially serious. Although the least squares regression parameter estimates are still unbiased and consistent, their estimated variances are biased and are neither efficient nor asymptotically efficient. In the most common form of heteroscedasticity, the variances of the estimators are likely to be understated, resulting in overstated t statistics and artificially narrow confidence intervals. In a multiple regression, a visual test for constant variance can be performed by examining scatter plots of the residuals against each predictor or against the fitted Y-values. Ideally, there will be no pattern and the vertical spread (residual variance) will be similar regardless of the X-values. The hypotheses are:

H_0: Errors have constant variance (homoscedastic)

H_1: Errors have nonconstant variance (heteroscedastic)

In a multiple regression, to avoid looking at all k residual plots (one for each predictor), we usually just examine the plot of residuals against the predicted Y-values. Although many patterns of nonconstant variance might exist, the "fan-out" pattern of increasing variance is most common (see Figure 13.18). The zero line appears more or less in the center of the residual plot, since the residuals always sum to zero.

FIGURE 13.18

Heteroscedastic Residual Plots

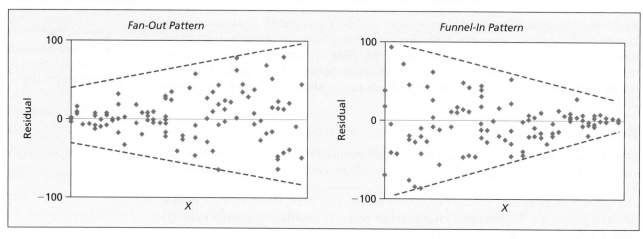

What can we do about heteroscedasticity? Heteroscedasticity may arise in economic time-series data if X and Y increase in magnitude over time, causing the errors also to increase. In financial data (e.g., GDP), heteroscedasticity can sometimes be reduced by expressing the data in constant dollars (dividing by a price index). In cross-sectional data (e.g., total crimes in a state), heteroscedasticity may be mitigated by expressing the data in relative terms (e.g., per capita crime). A more general approach to reducing heteroscedasticity is to transform the variables (e.g., by taking logs). However, this is a new model specification, which requires a reverse transformation when making predictions of Y.

EXAMPLE 13.5

The foreclosure rate by state for 2007 was regressed against that state's share of all new mortgages issued in 2005 that were subprime (i.e., loans that fall into risky categories based on the borrower's credit rating or the high amount of the loan). The explanatory variable explained approximately 25 percent ($R^2 = .251$) of the variation in state foreclosure rates; however, the plot of residuals against predicted foreclosure rate shows a clear heteroscedastic pattern, shown in Figure 13.19.

The presence of nonconstant error variance can cause the confidence interval for the regression coefficient to be narrower than it should be because the standard error of the slope estimate is possibly underestimated. In this example, the 95 percent confidence interval for the slope of the estimated regression equation is [43.8599, 131.9923]. It is possible that the true confidence interval should be wider than this. Techniques for reducing the effect of heteroscedasticity include transforming either the X or Y variable and or expressing the variables in relative terms. It is also important to consider other explanatory variables that might better explain variation in Y than our chosen X variable. You will have a chance to examine these data in more detail in the end-of-chapter exercises.

📁 **Foreclosures**

FIGURE 13.19   **Heteroscedastic Residual Plot**

Mini Case   13.6

Non-Normality and Heteroscedasticity 📁 HeartDeaths

Figure 13.20 shows MINITAB regression diagnostics for a regression model of heart deaths in all 50 U.S. states for the year 2000. The dependent variable is *Heart* = heart deaths per 100,000 population and the three predictors are *Age65%* = percent of

FIGURE 13.20

MINITAB Diagnostics for Heart Death Regression

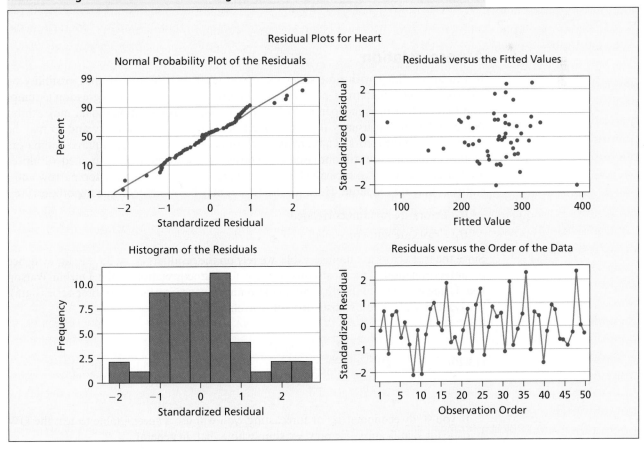

population age 65 and over, *Income* = per capita income in thousands of dollars, and *Black%* = percent of population that is African American.

The histogram is arguably bell-shaped. Since the residuals have been standardized, we can see that there are no outliers (more than 3 standard errors from zero). The probability plot reveals slight deviations from linearity at the lower and upper ends, but overall the plot is consistent with the hypothesis of normality. For an overall test for heteroscedasticity, we can look at the plot of residuals against the fitted *Y*-values in Figure 13.20. It shows no clear pattern, so we are disinclined to suspect heteroscedasticity. But we should also examine residual plots against each predictor. The residual plots for the three predictors (Figure 13.21) show no pronounced consistent "fan-out" or "funnel-in" pattern, thereby favoring the hypothesis of homoscedasticity (constant variance).

FIGURE 13.21

MINITAB Residual Plots for Heart Death Regression

Autocorrelation

If you are working with time-series data, you need to be aware of the possibility of *autocorrelation,* a pattern of nonindependent errors that violates the regression assumption that each error is independent of its predecessor. Cross-sectional data may exhibit autocorrelation, but usually it is an artifact of the order of data entry and so may be ignored. When the errors in a regression are autocorrelated, the least squares estimators of the coefficients are still unbiased and consistent. However, their estimated variances are biased in a way that typically leads to confidence intervals that are too narrow and *t* statistics that are too large. Thus, the model's fit may be overstated. The hypotheses are:

H_0: Errors are nonautocorrelated

H_1: Errors are autocorrelated

Since the true errors are unobservable, we rely on the residuals $e_1, e_2, \ldots, e_n$ for evidence of autocorrelation. The most common test for autocorrelation is the Durbin-Watson test. Using e_t to denote the *t*th residual (assuming you are working with time-series data), the Durbin-Watson test statistic for autocorrelation is

(13.20)
$$DW = \frac{\sum\limits_{t=2}^{n} (e_t - e_{t-1})^2}{\sum\limits_{t=1}^{n} e_t^2}$$
(Durbin-Watson test statistic)

If you study econometrics or forecasting, you will use a special table to test the DW statistic for significance. For now, we simply note that, in general,

$DW < 2$ suggests positive autocorrelation (common).

$DW \approx 2$ suggests no autocorrelation (ideal).

$DW > 2$ suggests negative autocorrelation (rare).

What can we do about autocorrelation? First-order time-series autocorrelation can be reduced by transforming the variables. A very simple transformation is the *method of first differences* in which the variables are redefined as *changes:*

$$\Delta x_t = x_t - x_{t-1} \qquad \text{(change in } X \text{ from period } t - 1 \text{ to period } t)$$

$$\Delta y_t = y_t - y_{t-1} \qquad \text{(change in } Y \text{ from period } t - 1 \text{ to period } t)$$

Then we regress ΔY against ΔX. This transformation can easily be done in a spreadsheet by subtracting each cell from its predecessor and then rerunning the regression. One observation is lost, since the first observation has no predecessor. The method of first differences has logical appeal, since there is little conceptual difference between regressing taxes against income and regressing the *change in taxes* against the *change in income*. The new slope should be the same as in the original model, but the new intercept should be zero. You will learn about more general transformations, favored by researchers, if you study econometrics.

Unusual Observations

Several tests for unusual observations are routinely provided by regression software. An observation may be unusual for two reasons: (1) because the fitted model's prediction is poor (*unusual residuals*) or (2) because one or more observations may be having a large influence on the regression estimates (*high leverage*). Unusual observations may be highlighted (MegaStat), displayed separately and marked (MINITAB), or not indicated at all (Excel).

> **LO 13-8**
>
> Identify unusual residuals and high leverage observations.

Unusual Residuals   To check for unusual residuals, we can inspect the standardized residuals to find instances where the model does not predict well.

Unusual Residuals

We apply the Empirical Rule. Standardized residuals more than $2s_e$ from zero are *unusual*, while residuals more than $3s_e$ from zero are outliers.

As explained in Chapter 12, different software packages may use different definitions for "standardized" or "studentized" residuals, but usually they give similar indications of "unusual" residuals. For example, in Figure 13.22 the last two columns of the printout can be interpreted the same even though there are slight differences in the values.

High Leverage   To check for high leverage, we look at the *leverage statistic* for each observation. It shows how far the predictors are from their means. As you saw in Chapter 12 (Section 12.8), such observations potentially have great influence on the regression estimates because they are at the "end of the lever."

High Leverage

For n observations and k predictors, an observation is considered to be a high leverage observation if the leverage statistic exceeds

$$\frac{2(k + 1)}{n}.$$

FIGURE 13.22

MegaStat Output for Heart Death Regression

Regression Analysis: Heart Deaths per 100,000

R^2	0.779		
Adjusted R^2	0.764	n	50
R	0.883	k	3
Std. Error	27.422	Dep. Var.	**Heart**

ANOVA table

Source	SS	df	MS	F	p-value
Regression	121,809.5684	3	40,603.1895	54.00	0.0000
Residual	34,590.3558	46	751.9643		
Total	156,399.9242	49			

Regression output   confidence interval

variables	coefficients	std. error	t (df = 46)	p-value	95% lower	95% upper	VIF
Intercept	−37.0813	39.2007	−0.946	0.3491	−115.9882	41.8256	
Age65%	24.2509	2.0753	11.686	0.0000	20.0736	28.4282	1.018
Income	−1.0800	0.9151	−1.180	0.2440	−2.9220	0.7620	1.012
Black%	2.2682	0.4116	5.511	0.0000	1.4398	3.0967	1.013

Unusual Observations

Observation	Heart	Predicted	Residual	Leverage	Studentized Residual	Studentized Deleted Residual
AK	90.90	76.62	14.28	0.304	0.624	0.620
CT	278.10	274.33	3.77	0.208	0.154	0.153
FL	340.40	392.45	−52.05	0.177	−2.092	−2.176
HI	203.30	259.06	−55.76	0.037	−2.072	−2.152
MS	337.20	316.02	21.18	0.223	0.876	0.874
OK	335.40	274.87	60.53	0.047	2.261	2.372
UT	130.80	145.05	−14.25	0.172	−0.571	−0.567
WV	377.50	317.55	59.95	0.108	2.315	2.436

Mini Case   13.7

Unusual Observations   HeartDeaths

Figure 13.22 shows MegaStat's regression results for a regression model of heart deaths in the 50 U.S. states for the year 2000 (variables are drawn from the *LearningStats* state database). The response variable is *Heart* = heart deaths per 100,000 population, with predictors *Age65%* = percent of population age 65 and over, *Income* = per capita income in thousands of dollars, and *Black%* = percent of population classified as African American. The fitted regression is

$$Heart = -37.1 + 24.3\ Age65\% - 1.08\ Income + 2.27\ Black\%$$

Age65% has the anticipated positive sign and is highly significant, and similarly for *Black%*. Income has a negative sign but is not significant even at $\alpha = .10$. The regression overall is significant ($F_{calc} = 54.00$, *p*-value = .0000). The R^2 shows that the predictors explain 77.9 percent of the variation in *Heart* among the states. The adjusted R^2 is 76.4 percent, indicating that no unhelpful predictors are present. Since this is cross-sectional data, the DW statistic was not requested.

Figure 13.22 lists eight unusual observations (the other 42 states are not unusual). Five states (AK, CT, FL, MS, UT) are highlighted because they have unusual *leverage*—a leverage statistic that exceeds $2(k + 1)/n = (2)(3 + 1)/50 = 0.16$. One or more predictors for these states must differ greatly from the mean of that predictor, but only by inspecting the *X* data columns (*Age65%, Income,* or *Black%*) could we identify their unusual *X*-values. Four states are highlighted because they have unusual *residuals*—a gap of at least two standard deviations (studentized residuals) between actual and predicted *Heart* values. FL and HI are more than 2 standard deviations lower than predicted, while OK and WV are more than 2 standard deviations higher than predicted. One state, FL, is unusual with respect to both residual and leverage.

SECTION EXERCISES

connect

13.23 Which would be "high leverage" observations?

    a. Leverage $h_i = .15$ in a regression with 5 predictors and 72 observations.

    b. Leverage $h_i = .18$ in a regression with 4 predictors and 100 observations.

    c. Leverage $h_i = .08$ in a regression with 7 predictors and 240 observations.

13.24 Which violations of regression assumptions, if any, do you see in these residual diagnostics? Explain.

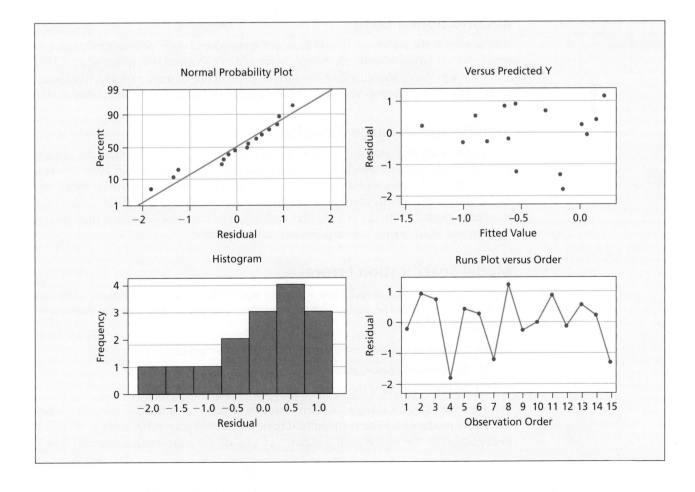

13.9 OTHER REGRESSION TOPICS

Outliers

An outlier may be due to an error in recording the data. If so, the observation should be deleted. But how can you tell? Impossible or truly bizarre data values are apparent reasons to discard an observation. For example, a Realtor's database of recent home sales in a million-dollar neighborhood contained this observation:

Price	BR	Bath	Basement	Built	SqFeet	Garage
95,000	4	3	Y	2001	4,335	Y

LO 13-9

Explain the role of data conditioning and data transformations.

The 95,000 price is probably a typographical error. Even if the price were correct, it would be reasonable to discard the observation on grounds that it represents a different population than the other homes (e.g., a "gift" sale by a wealthy parent to a newlywed couple).

Missing Predictors

An outlier may also be an observation that has been influenced by an unspecified "lurking" variable that should have been controlled but wasn't. In this case, we should try to identify the lurking variable and formulate a multiple regression model that includes both predictors. For example, a reasonable model such as Y = home price, X_1 = square feet, and X_2 = lot size might give poor predictions unless we add a neighborhood binary predictor (you can probably think of areas where a large house on a large lot might still command a poor price). If there are unspecified "lurking" variables, our fitted regression model will not give accurate predictions.

Ill-Conditioned Data

All variables in the regression should be of the same general order of magnitude (not too small, not too large). If your coefficients come out in exponential notation (e.g., 7.3154 E+06), you probably should adjust the decimal point in one or more variables to a convenient magnitude, as long as you treat all the values in the same data column consistently.

Significance in Large Samples

Statistical significance may not imply *practical importance*. In a large sample, we can obtain very large t statistics with low p-values for our predictors when, in fact, their effect on Y is very slight. There is an old saying in statistics that you can make anything significant if you get a large enough sample. In medical research, where thousands of patients are enrolled in clinical trials, this is a familiar problem. It can become difficult in such models to figure out which *significant* variables are really *important*.

Model Specification Errors

If you estimate a linear model when actually a nonlinear model is required, or when you omit a relevant predictor, then you have a *misspecified model*. How can you detect misspecification? You can:

- Plot the residuals against estimated Y (should be no discernable pattern).
- Plot the residuals against actual Y (should be no discernable pattern).
- Plot the fitted Y against the actual Y (should be a 45-degree line).

What are the cures for misspecification? Start by looking for a missing relevant predictor, seek a model with a better theoretical basis, or redefine your variables (e.g., assume a multiplicative model of the form $y = \beta_0 x_1^{\beta_1} x_2^{\beta_2} \ldots x_m^{\beta_m}$ for a production function, which becomes linear if you take logarithms). Model specification is a topic that will be covered in considerable depth if you study econometrics. For now, just remember that *residual patterns* are clues that the model may be incorrectly specified.

Missing Data

If many values in a data column are missing, we might want to discard that variable. If a Y data value is missing, we must discard the entire observation. If any X data values are missing, the conservative action is to discard the entire observation. However, since discarding an entire observation would mean losing other good information, statisticians have developed procedures for imputing missing values, such as using the mean of the X data column or by a regression procedure to "fit" the missing X-value from the complete observations. Imputing missing values requires specialized software and expert statistical advice.

Logistic Regression

Sometimes we need to predict something that has only two possible values (a binary *dependent* variable). For example, will a Chase bank customer choose online banking, or not? Will a Verizon customer switch cell phone providers when the current contract expires, or remain with Verizon? Will an Amazon customer make another purchase within the next six months, or not? Such research questions would seem to be candidates for regression modeling because firms would have many possible predictors (such as a customer's age, gender, length of time as an existing customer, past transaction history, and so on). You would expect the predicted value of Y to be a number between 0 and 1, denoting the *probability* of the event of interest.

Unfortunately, if you perform an ordinary least-squares regression with a binary (0 or 1) response variable, there will be complications. Your predicted Y-values could be greater than one or less than zero, which would be illogical. Another issue is that your regression errors will violate the assumptions of homoscedasticity (constant variance). As the predicted Y-values vary from .50 (in either direction), the variance of the errors will decrease and approach zero. Further, significance tests assume that errors are normally distributed, which cannot be the case when Y has only two values (0 or 1). Therefore, tests for significance of regression coefficients are in doubt if you use linear regression with a binary response variable.

The solution is to use **logistic regression.** A full discussion of logistic regression is beyond the scope of this textbook. However, any major statistical package (e.g., SPSS, SAS, or MINITAB) will safely perform logistic regression (sometimes called *logit* for short) and will provide p-values for the estimated coefficients and predictions for Y.

The estimated logistic regression equation is the *nonlinear* regression model shown below. This equation predicts the *probability* that $y = 1$ for specific values of the independent variables $x_1, x_2, \ldots, x_k$.

$$y = \frac{e^{b_0 + b_1 x_1 + b_2 x_2 + \cdots + b_k x_k}}{1 + e^{b_0 + b_1 x_1 + b_2 x_2 + \cdots + b_k x_k}} \qquad (13.21)$$

You will no longer see the familiar statistics such as R^2, but equivalent measures of fit and significance (with p-values) will be provided. What is important at this stage of training is for you to recognize the need for a specialized tool when Y is a binary (yes/no) variable.

Stepwise and Best Subsets Regression

It may have occurred to you that there ought to be a way to automate the task of fitting the "best" regression using k predictors. The *stepwise regression* procedure uses the power of the computer to fit the best model using 1, 2, 3, . . . , k predictors. For example, aerospace engineers had a large data set of 469 observations on *Thrust* (takeoff thrust of a jet turbine) along with seven potential predictors (*TurbTemp, AirFlow, TurbSpeed, OilTemp, OilPres, RunTime, ThermCyc*). In the absence of a theoretical model, a stepwise regression was run, with the results shown in Figure 13.23. Only *p*-values are shown for each predictor, along with R^2, R^2_{adj}, and standard error. You can easily assess the effect of adding more predictors. In this example, most *p*-values are tiny due to the large *n*. While stepwise regression is an efficient way to identify the "best" model for each number of predictors (1, 2, . . . , *k*), it is appropriate only when there is no theoretical model that specifies which predictors *should* be used. A further degree of automation of the regression task is to perform *best subsets* regression using all possible combinations of predictors. This option is offered by many computer packages, but is not recommended because it yields too much output and too little additional insight.

FIGURE 13.23

MegaStat's Stepwise Regression of Turbine Data   Turbines

Regression Analysis—Stepwise Selection displaying the best model of each size

469 observations
Thrust is the dependent variable

p-values for the coefficients

Nvar	TurbTemp	Airflow	TurbSpeed	OilTemp	OilPres	RunTime	ThermCyc	s	Adj R²	R²
1		.0000						12.370	.252	.254
2		.0000			.0004			12.219	.270	.273
3	.0003	.0000					.0005	12.113	.283	.287
4		.0000		.0081	.0000		.0039	12.041	.291	.297
5	.0010	.0000		.0009	.0003		.0006	11.914	.306	.314
6	.0010	.0000	.1440	.0037	.0005		.0010	11.899	.308	.317
7	.0008	.0000	.1624	.0031	.0007	.2049	.0006	11.891	.309	.319

CHAPTER SUMMARY

Multivariate regression extends simple regression to include multiple **predictors** of the **response variable.** Criteria to judge a fitted regression model include **logic, fit, parsimony,** and **stability.** Using too many predictors violates the principle of **Occam's Razor,** which favors a simpler model if it is adequate. If the R^2 differs greatly from R^2_{adj}, the model may contain unhelpful predictors. The ANOVA table and **F test** measure overall significance, while the **t test** is used to test hypotheses about individual predictors. A **confidence interval** for each unknown **parameter** is equivalent to a two-tailed hypothesis test for $\beta = 0$. The **standard error** of the regression is used to create **confidence intervals** or **prediction intervals** for *Y*. A **categorical predictor** (also called a **dummy variable** or an **indicator**) has value 1 if the condition of interest is present, 0 otherwise. For *c* categories, we only include $c - 1$ binaries or the regression will fail. Including a squared predictor provides a test for **nonlinearity** of the predictors. Including the product of two predictors is a test for **interaction.** Collinearity (correlation between *two* predictors) is detected in the **correlation matrix,** while **multicollinearity** (when a predictor depends on *several* other predictors) is identified from the **variance inflation factor** (VIF) for each predictor. Regression assumes that the errors are normally distributed, independent random variables with constant variance. **Residual tests** identify possible **non-normality, autocorrelation,** or **heteroscedasticity.**

KEY TERMS

adjusted coefficient of
   determination R^2_{adj}, *555*
ANOVA table, *553*
binary predictor, *563*
categorical predictor, *563*
coefficient of determination
   (R^2), *554*
collinearity, *575*
correlation matrix, *575*
dichotomous variable, *563*
Doane's Rule, *555*

dummy variable, *563*
Evans' Rule, *555*
fit, *551*
F test, *553*
indicator variable, *563*
interaction, *572*
Klein's Rule, *576*
logic, *551*
logistic regression, *587*
multicollinearity, *575*
multiple regression, *547*

Occam's Razor, *551*
parsimony, *551*
predictors, *548*
residual tests, *579*
response variable, *548*
shift variable, *563*
stability, *551*
standard error (s_e) of the
   regression, *560*
variance inflation factor
   (VIF), *576*

Commonly Used Formulas

Population regression model for k predictors: $y = \beta_0 + \beta_1 x_1 + \beta_2 x_2 + \cdots + \beta_k x_k + \varepsilon$

Fitted regression equation for k predictors: $\hat{y} = b_0 + b_1 x_1 + b_2 x_2 + \cdots + b_k x_k$

Residual for ith observation: $e_i = y_i - \hat{y}_i$ (for $i = 1, 2, \ldots, n$)

ANOVA sums: $SST = SSR + SSE$

SST (total sum of squares): $\displaystyle\sum_{i=1}^{n} (y_i - \bar{y})^2$

SSR (regression sum of squares): $\displaystyle\sum_{i=1}^{n} (\hat{y}_i - \bar{y})^2$

SSE (error sum of squares): $\displaystyle\sum_{i=1}^{n} (y_i - \hat{y}_i)^2$

MSR (regression mean square): $MSR = SSR/k$

MSE (error mean square): $MSE = SSE/(n - k - 1)$

F test statistic for overall significance: $F_{calc} = MSR/MSE$

Coefficient of determination: $R^2 = 1 - \dfrac{SSE}{SST}$ or $R^2 = \dfrac{SSR}{SST}$

Adjusted R^2: $R_{adj}^2 = 1 - \dfrac{\left(\dfrac{SSE}{n - k - 1}\right)}{\left(\dfrac{SST}{n - 1}\right)}$

Test statistic for coefficient of predictor X_j: $t_{calc} = \dfrac{b_j - 0}{s_j}$ where s_j is the standard error of b_j

Confidence interval for coefficient β_j: $b_j - t_{\alpha/2} s_j \le \beta_j \le b_j + t_{\alpha/2} s_j$

Estimated standard error of the regression: $s_e = \sqrt{\dfrac{\displaystyle\sum_{i=1}^{n} (y_i - \hat{y}_i)^2}{n - k - 1}} = \sqrt{\dfrac{SSE}{n - k - 1}}$

Approximate confidence interval for $E(Y/X)$: $\hat{y}_i \pm t_{\alpha/2} \dfrac{s_e}{\sqrt{n}}$

Approximate prediction interval for Y: $\hat{y}_i \pm t_{n-k-1} s_e$

Variance inflation factor for predictor j: $VIF_j = \dfrac{1}{1 - R_j^2}$

Evans' Rule (conservative): $n/k \ge 10$ (10 observations per predictor)

Doane's Rule (relaxed): $n/k \ge 5$ (5 observations per predictor)

CHAPTER REVIEW

1. (a) List two limitations of simple regression. (b) Why is estimating a multiple regression model just as easy as simple regression?

2. (a) What does ε represent in the regression model? (b) What assumptions do we make about ε? What is the distinction between Greek letters (β) and Roman letters (b) in representing a regression equation?

3. (a) Describe the format of a multiple regression data set. (b) Why is it a good idea to write down our *a priori* reasoning about a proposed regression?

4. (a) Why does a higher R^2 not always indicate a good model? (b) State the principle of Occam's Razor. (c) List four criteria for assessing a regression model.

5. (a) What is the role of the F test in multiple regression? (b) How is the F statistic calculated from the ANOVA table? (c) Why are tables rarely needed for the F test?

6. (a) Why is testing H_0: $\beta = 0$ a very common test for a predictor? (b) How many degrees of freedom do we use in a t test for an individual predictor's significance?

7. (a) Explain why a confidence interval for a predictor coefficient is equivalent to a two-tailed test of significance. (b) Why are t tables rarely needed in performing significance tests?

8. (a) What does a coefficient of determination (R^2) measure? (b) When R^2 and R^2_{adj} differ considerably, what does it indicate?

9. State some guidelines to prevent inclusion of too many predictors in a regression.

10. (a) State the formula for the standard error of the regression. (b) Why is it sometimes preferred to R^2 as a measure of "fit"? (c) What is the formula for a quick prediction interval for individual Y-values? (d) When you need an exact prediction, what must you do?

11. (a) What is a categorical predictor? (b) Why is a binary predictor sometimes called a "shift variable"? (c) How do we test a binary predictor for significance?

12. If we have c categories for an attribute, why do we only use $c - 1$ binaries to represent them in a fitted regression?

13. (a) Explain why it might be useful to include a quadratic term in a regression. (b) Explain why it might be useful to include an interaction term between two predictors in a regression. (c) Name a drawback to including quadratic or interaction terms in a regression.

14. (a) What is multicollinearity? (b) What are its potential consequences? (c) Why is it a matter of degree? (d) Why might it be ignored?

15. (a) How does multicollinearity differ from collinearity? (b) Explain how we can use the correlation matrix to test for collinearity. (c) State a quick rule to test for significant collinearity in a correlation matrix. (d) What is Klein's Rule?

16. (a) State the formula for a variance inflation factor (VIF) for a predictor. (b) Why does the VIF provide a more general test for multicollinearity than a correlation matrix or a matrix plot? (c) State a rule of thumb for detecting strong variance inflation.

17. If multicollinearity is severe, what might its symptoms be?

18. (a) How can we detect an unusual residual? An outlier? (b) How can we identify an influential observation?

19. (a) Name two ways to detect non-normality of the residuals. (b) What are the potential consequences of this violation? (c) What remedies might be appropriate?

20. (a) Name two ways to detect heteroscedastic residuals. (b) What are the potential consequences of this violation? (c) What remedies might be appropriate?

21. (a) Name two ways to detect autocorrelated residuals. (b) What are the potential consequences of this violation? (c) What remedies might be appropriate?

22. (a) What is a lurking variable? How might it be inferred? (b) What are ill-conditioned data?

CHAPTER EXERCISES

connect

Instructions for Data Sets: Choose one of the data sets $A-K$ below or as assigned by your instructor. Only the first three and last three observations are shown for each data set (files are on the CD). In each data set, the dependent variable (*response*) is the first variable. Choose the independent variables (*predictors*) as you judge appropriate. Use a spreadsheet or a statistical package (e.g., MegaStat or MINITAB) to perform the necessary regression calculations and to obtain the required graphs. Write a concise report answering questions 13.25 through 13.41 (or a subset of these questions assigned by your instructor). Label sections of your report to correspond to the questions. Insert tables and graphs in your report as appropriate. You may work with a partner if your instructor allows it.

13.25 Are these cross-sectional data or time-series data? What is the unit of observation (e.g., firm, individual, year)?

13.26 Are the X and Y data well-conditioned? If not, make any transformations that may be necessary and explain.

13.27 State your *a priori* hypotheses about the sign (+ or −) of each predictor and your reasoning about cause and effect. Would the intercept have meaning in this problem? Explain.

13.28 Does your sample size fulfill Evans' Rule ($n/k \geq 10$) or at least Doane's Rule ($n/k \geq 5$)?

13.29 Perform the regression and write the estimated regression equation (round off to 3 or 4 significant digits for clarity). Do the coefficient signs agree with your *a priori* expectations?

13.30 Does the 95 percent confidence interval for each predictor coefficient include zero? What conclusion can you draw? *Note:* Skip this question if you are using MINITAB, since predictor confidence intervals are not shown.

13.31 Do a two-tailed t test for zero slope for each predictor coefficient at $\alpha = .05$. State the degrees of freedom and look up the critical value in Appendix D (or from Excel).

13.32 (a) Which *p*-values indicate predictor significance at $\alpha = .05$? (b) Do the *p*-values support the conclusions you reached from the *t* tests? (c) Do you prefer the *t* test or the *p*-value approach? Why?

13.33 Based on the R^2 and ANOVA table for your model, how would you describe the fit?

13.34 Use the standard error to construct an *approximate* prediction interval for *Y*. Based on the width of this prediction interval, would you say the predictions are good enough to have practical value?

13.35 (a) Generate a correlation matrix for your predictors. Round the results to three decimal places. (b) Based on the correlation matrix, is collinearity a problem? What rules of thumb (if any) are you using?

13.36 (a) If you did not already do so, rerun the regression requesting variance inflation factors (VIFs) for your predictors. (b) Do the VIFs suggest that multicollinearity is a problem? Explain.

13.37 (a) If you did not already do so, request a table of standardized residuals. (b) Are any residuals *outliers* (three standard errors) or *unusual* (two standard errors)?

13.38 If you did not already do so, request leverage statistics. Are any observations influential? Explain.

13.39 If you did not already do so, request a histogram of standardized residuals and/or a normal probability plot. Do the residuals suggest non-normal errors? Explain.

13.40 If you did not already do so, request a plot of residuals versus the fitted *Y*. Is heteroscedasticity a concern?

13.41 If you are using time-series data, perform one or more tests for autocorrelation (visual inspection of residuals plotted against observation order, runs test, Durbin-Watson test). Is autocorrelation a concern?

DATA SET A **Mileage and Other Characteristics of Randomly Selected Vehicles ($n = 43$, $k = 4$)** Mileage

Obs	Vehicle	City	Length	Width	Weight	Japan
1	Acura CL	20	192	69	3,450	1
2	Accura TSX	23	183	59	3,320	1
3	BMW 3-Series	19	176	69	3,390	0
⋮	⋮	⋮	⋮	⋮	⋮	⋮
41	Toyota Sienna	19	200	77	4,120	1
42	Volkswagen Jetta	34	172	68	3,045	0
43	Volvo C70	20	186	72	3,690	0

City = EPA miles per gallon in city driving, *Length* = vehicle length (inches), *Width* = vehicle width (inches), *Weight* = weight (pounds), *Japan* = 1 if carmaker is Japanese, 0 otherwise.

Source: *Consumer Reports New Car Buying Guide 2003–2004* (Consumers Union, 2003). Sampling methodology was to select the vehicle on every fifth page starting at page 40. Data are intended for purposes of statistical education and should not be viewed as a guide to vehicle performance.

DATA SET B **Noodles & Company Sales, Seating, and Demographic Data ($n = 74$, $k = 5$)** Noodles2

Obs	Sales/SqFt	Seats-Inside	Seats-Patio	MedIncome	MedAge	BachDeg%
1	702	66	18	45.2	34.4	31
2	210	69	16	51.9	41.2	20
3	365	67	10	51.4	40.3	24
⋮	⋮	⋮	⋮	⋮	⋮	⋮
72	340	63	28	60.9	43.5	21
73	401	72	15	73.8	41.6	29
74	327	76	24	64.2	31.4	15

Sales/SqFt = sales per square foot of floor space, *Seats-Inside* = number of interior seats, *Seats-Patio* = number of outside seats. The three demographic variables refer to a three-mile radius of the restaurant: *MedIncome* = median family income, *MedAge* = median age, and *BachDeg%* = percentage of population with at least a bachelor's degree.

Source: Noodles & Company.

DATA SET C   Assessed Value of Small Medical Office Buildings ($n = 32$, $k = 5$) 📁 Assessed

Obs	Assessed	Floor	Offices	Entrances	Age	Freeway
1	1796	4790	4	2	8	0
2	1544	4720	3	2	12	0
3	2094	5940	4	2	2	0
⋮	⋮	⋮	⋮	⋮	⋮	⋮
30	1264	3580	3	2	27	0
31	1162	3610	2	1	8	1
32	1447	3960	3	2	17	0

Assessed = assessed value (thousands of dollars), *Floor* = square feet of floor space, *Offices* = number of offices in the building, *Entrances* = number of customer entrances (excluding service doors), *Age* = age of the building (years), *Freeway* = 1 if within one mile of freeway, 0 otherwise.

DATA SET D   Changes in Consumer Price Index, Capacity Utilization, Changes in Money Supply Components, and Unemployment ($n = 41$, $k = 4$) 📁 Money

Year	ChgCPI	CapUtil	ChgM1	ChgM2	Unem
1966	2.9	91.1	2.5	4.6	3.8
1967	3.1	87.2	6.6	9.3	3.8
1968	4.2	87.1	7.7	8.0	3.6
⋮	⋮	⋮	⋮	⋮	⋮
2004	2.7	76.6	5.3	5.8	5.5
2005	3.4	78.8	−0.2	4.0	5.1
2006	3.2	80.4	−0.5	5.3	4.6

ChCPI = percent change in the Consumer Price Index (CPI) over previous year, *CapUtil* = percent utilization of manufacturing capacity in current year, *ChgM1* = percent change in currency and demand deposits (M1) over previous year, *ChgM2* = percent change in small time deposits and other near-money (M2) over previous year, *Unem* = civilian unemployment rate in percent.

Source: *Economic Report of the President, 2007*.

DATA SET E   College Graduation Rate and Selected Characteristics of U.S. States ($n = 50$, $k = 8$) 📁 ColGrads

State	ColGrad%	Dropout	EdSpend	Metro%	Age	LPRFem	Neast	Seast	West
AL	19.8	19.1	1221	89.2	37.4	55.8	0	1	0
AK	28.7	8.3	2187	74.7	33.9	65.6	0	0	1
AZ	27.9	14.3	1137	96.7	34.5	57.4	0	0	1
⋮	⋮	⋮	⋮	⋮	⋮	⋮	⋮	⋮	⋮
WV	15.1	17.6	1538	75.0	40.7	49.1	0	1	0
WI	25.1	9.5	1792	85.9	37.9	66.6	0	0	0
WY	22.0	9.1	1896	71.5	39.1	65.3	0	0	1

ColGrad% = percent of state population with a college degree, *Dropout* = percent of high school students who do not graduate, *EdSpend* = per capita spending on K–12 education, *Metro%* = 2005 percent of population living in metropolitan and micropolitan statistical areas, *Age* = median age of state's population, *LPRFem* = percent of adult females who are in the labor force, *Neast* = 1 if state is in the Northeast, 0 otherwise, *Seast* = 1 if state is in the Southeast, 0 otherwise, *West* = 1 if state is in the West, 0 otherwise. *Midwest* is the omitted fourth binary.

Source: *Statistical Abstract of the United States, 2007*.

DATA SET F Characteristics of Selected Piston Aircraft ($n = 55$ m, $k = 4$)
CruiseSpeed

Obs	Mfgr/Model	Cruise	Year	TotalHP	NumBlades	Turbo
1	Cessna Turbo Stationair TU206	148	1981	310	3	1
2	Cessna 310 R	194	1975	570	3	0
3	Piper 125 Tri Pacer	107	1951	125	2	0
⋮		⋮	⋮	⋮	⋮	⋮
53	OMF Aircraft Symphony	128	2002	160	2	0
54	Liberty XL-2	132	2003	125	2	0
55	Piper 6X	148	2004	300	3	0

Cruise = best cruise speed (knots indicated air speed) at 65–75 percent power, *Year* = year of manufacture, *TotalHP* = total horsepower (both engines if twin), *NumBlades* = number of propeller blades, *Turbo* = 1 if turbocharged, 0 otherwise.

Source: *Flying Magazine* (various issues). Data are for educational purposes only and not as a guide to performance.

DATA SET G Characteristics of Randomly Chosen Hydrocarbons ($n = 35$, $k = 7$) Retention

Obs	Name	Ret	MW	BP	RI	H1	H2	H3	H4
1	2,4,4-trimethyl-2-pentene	153.57	112.215	105.06	1.4135	0	1	0	0
2	1,5-cyclooctadiene	237.56	108.183	150.27	1.4905	0	0	0	1
3	methylcyclohexane	153.57	98.188	101.08	1.4206	0	0	1	0
⋮		⋮	⋮	⋮	⋮	⋮	⋮	⋮	⋮
33	ethylbenzene	209.700	106.170	136.000	1.4950	0	0	0	0
34	m-ethyl toluene	247.800	120.194	161.480	1.4941	0	0	0	0
35	3-methylhexane	132.320	100.204	92.000	1.3861	1	0	0	0

Ret = chromatographic retention time (seconds), *MW* = molecular weight (gm/mole), *BP* = boiling point in °C, *RI* = refractive index (dimensionless), *Class* = hydrocarbon class (*H1* = acyclic saturated, *H2* = acyclic unsaturated, *H3* = cyclic saturated, *H4* = cyclic unsaturated, *H5* = aromatic is the omitted fifth binary).

Source: Data are courtesy of John Seeley of Oakland University.

DATA SET H 2007 Foreclosure Rates ($n = 50$, $k = 7$) Foreclosures2

State	Foreclosure	MassLayoff	SubprimeShare	PriceIncomeRatio	Ownership	5YrApp	UnempChange	%HousMoved
Alabama	2.70	5.96	28%	4.04	76.6	32.51	0.00%	0.448
Alaska	4.90	2.78	18%	5.54	66.0	53.91	−4.62%	0.426
Arizona	15.20	1.56	26%	6.79	71.1	96.55	−7.32%	0.383
⋮	⋮	⋮	⋮	⋮	⋮	⋮	⋮	⋮
West Virginia	0.50	1.05	21%	4.34	81.3	35.82	−2.13%	0.502
Wisconsin	4.90	12.50	21%	4.83	71.1	36.37	4.26%	0.428
Wyoming	1.50	0.96	23%	5.06	72.8	62.56	−9.09%	0.498

Each observation shows the 2007 state foreclosure rate, *MassLayoff* = mass layoff events per 100,000 people, *SubprimeShare* = share of new mortgages that were subprime in 2005, *PriceIncomeRatio* = average home prices to median household income ratio, *Ownership* = home ownership rates (%) in 2005, *5YrApp* = period ended December 2006 average 5-year home price appreciation, *UnempChange* = 2007 unemployment rate percent change, *%HousMoved* = % of housing that was moved into in 2000–2005.

Source: MBA Project by Steve Rohlwing and Rediate Eshetu.

DATA SET I   Body Fat and Personal Measurements for Males ($n = 50$, $k = 8$) 🖫 BodyFat2

Obs	Fat%	Age	Weight	Height	Neck	Chest	Abdomen	Hip	Thigh
1	12.6	23	154.25	67.75	36.2	93.1	85.2	94.5	59.0
2	6.9	22	173.25	72.25	38.5	93.6	83.0	98.7	58.7
3	24.6	22	154.00	66.25	34.0	95.8	87.9	99.2	59.6
⋮	⋮	⋮	⋮	⋮	⋮	⋮	⋮	⋮	⋮
48	6.4	39	148.50	71.25	34.6	89.8	79.5	92.7	52.7
49	13.4	45	135.75	68.50	32.8	92.3	83.4	90.4	52.0
50	5.0	47	127.50	66.75	34.0	83.4	70.4	87.2	50.6

Fat% = percent body fat, *Age* = age (yrs.), *Weight* = weight (lbs.), *Height* = height (in.), *Neck* = neck circumference (cm), *Chest* = chest circumference (cm), *Abdomen* = abdomen circumference (cm), *Hip* = hip circumference (cm), *Thigh* = thigh circumference (cm).

Data are a subsample of 252 males analyzed in Roger W. Johnson, "Fitting Percentage of Body Fat to Simple Body Measurements," *Journal of Statistics Education* 4, no. 1(1996).

DATA SET J   Used Vehicle Prices ($n = 637$, $k = 4$) 🖫 Vehicles

Obs	Model	Price	Age	Car	Truck	SUV
1	Astro GulfStream Conversion	12,988	3	0	0	0
2	Astro LS 4.3L V6	5,950	9	0	0	0
3	Astro LS V6	19,995	4	0	0	0
⋮	⋮	⋮	⋮	⋮	⋮	⋮
635	DC 300M Autostick	10,995	6	1	0	0
636	DC 300M Special Edition	22,995	1	1	0	0
637	GM 3500 4×4 w/8ft bed and plow	17,995	5	0	1	0

Price = asking price ($), *Age* = vehicle age (yrs), *Car* = 1 if passenger car, 0 otherwise, *Truck* = 1 if truck, 0 otherwise, *SUV* = 1 if sport utility vehicle, 0 otherwise (*Van* is the omitted fourth binary).

Source: *Detroit AutoFocus* 4, no. 38 (Sept. 17–23, 2004). Data are for educational purposes only and should not be used as a guide to depreciation.

DATA SET K   2009 Summer National Senior Games—500-Yard Freestyle ($n = 198$, $k = 3$) 🖫 Olympics

Swim Time	Seed	Gender	Age
371.20	446.29	1	51
372.28	390.56	1	52
380.10	391.20	1	50
⋮	⋮	⋮	⋮
789.29	795.30	0	85
883.70	1021.20	0	87
1027.22	1074.70	0	86

Times courtesy of FastLane Tek, Inc., www.fastlanetek.com, Contractor License. Participant names have been omitted.

GENERAL EXERCISES

13.42 In a model of Ford's quarterly revenue *TotalRevenue* $= \beta_0 + \beta_1$ *CarSales* $+ \beta_2$ *TruckSales* $+ \beta_3$ *SUVSales* $+ \varepsilon$, the three predictors are measured in number of units sold (not dollars). (a) Interpret each slope. (b) Would the intercept be meaningful? (c) What factors might be reflected in the error term? Explain.

13.43 In a study of paint peel problems, a regression was suggested to predict defects per million (the response variable). The intended predictors were supplier (four suppliers, coded as binaries) and substrate (four materials, coded as binaries). There were 11 observations. Explain why regression is impractical in this case, and suggest a remedy.

13.44 A hospital emergency room analyzed $n = 17,664$ hourly observations on its average occupancy rates using six binary predictors representing days of the week and two binary predictors representing the 8-hour work shift (12 a.m.–8 a.m., 8 a.m.–4 p.m., 4 p.m.–12 a.m.) when the ER census was taken. The fitted regression equation was $AvgOccupancy = 11.2 + 1.19\ Mon - 0.187\ Tue - 0.785\ Wed - 0.580\ Thu - 0.451\ Fri - 0.267\ Sat - 4.58\ Shift1 - 1.65\ Shift2$ ($SE = 6.18$, $R^2 = .094$, $R^2_{adj} = .093$). (a) Why did the analyst use only six binaries for days when there are 7 days in a week? (b) Why did the analyst use only two work shift binaries when there are three work shifts? (c) Which is the busiest day? (d) Which is the busiest shift? (e) Interpret the intercept. (f) Assess the regression's fit.

13.45 Using test data on 20 types of laundry detergent, an analyst fitted a regression to predict *CostPerLoad* (average cost per load in cents per load) using binary predictors *TopLoad* (1 if washer is a top-loading model, 0 otherwise) and *Powder* (if detergent was in powder form, 0 otherwise). Interpret the results. (Data are from *Consumer Reports* 68, no. 8 [November 2003], p. 42.) ⌨ **Laundry**

R^2	0.117			
Adjusted R^2	0.006	n	19	
R	0.341	k	2	
Std. Error	5.915	Dep. Var.	**Cost Per Load**	

ANOVA table

Source	SS	df	MS	F	p-value
Regression	73.8699	2	36.9350	1.06	.3710
Residual	559.8143	16	34.9884		
Total	633.6842	18			

Regression output					confidence interval	
variables	coefficients	std. error	t (df = 16)	p-value	95% lower	95% upper
Intercept	26.0000	4.1826	6.216	1.23E-05	17.1333	34.8667
Top-Load	−6.3000	4.5818	−1.375	.1881	−16.0130	3.4130
Powder	−0.2714	2.9150	−0.093	.9270	−6.4509	5.9081

13.46 A researcher used stepwise regression to create regression models to predict *BirthRate* (births per 1,000) using five predictors: *LifeExp* (life expectancy in years), *InfMort* (infant mortality rate), *Density* (population density per square kilometer), *GDPCap* (Gross Domestic Product per capita), and *Literate* (literacy percent). Interpret these results. ⌨ **BirthRates2**

Regression Analysis—Stepwise Selection (best model of each size)

153   observations
BirthRate is the dependent variable

		p-values for the coefficients						
Nvar	LifeExp	InfMort	Density	GDPCap	Literate	s	Adj R²	R²
1		.0000				6.318	.722	.724
2		.0000			.0000	5.334	.802	.805
3		.0000		.0242	.0000	5.261	.807	.811
4	.5764	.0000		.0311	.0000	5.273	.806	.812
5	.5937	.0000	.6289	.0440	.0000	5.287	.805	.812

13.47 A sports enthusiast created an equation to predict *Victories* (the team's number of victories in the National Basketball Association regular season play) using predictors *FGP* (team field goal percentage), *FTP* (team free throw percentage), *Points* (team average points per game), *Fouls* (team average number of fouls per game), *TrnOvr* (team average number of turnovers per game), and *Rbnds* (team average number of rebounds per game). The fitted regression was $Victories = -281 + 523\ FGP + 3.12\ FTP + 0.781\ Points - 2.90\ Fouls + 1.60\ TrnOvr + 0.649\ Rbnds$ ($R^2 = .802$, $F = 10.80$, $SE = 6.87$). The strongest predictors were *FGP* ($t = 4.35$) and *Fouls* ($t = -2.146$). The other predictors were only marginally significant and *FTP* and *Rbnds* were not significant. The matrix of correlations is shown below. At the time of this analysis, there were 23 NBA teams. (a) Do the regression coefficients make sense? (b) Is the intercept meaningful? Explain. (c) Is the sample size a problem (using Evans' Rule or Doane's Rule)? (d) Why might collinearity account for the lack of significance of some predictors? (Data are from a research project by MBA student Michael S. Malloy.)

	FGP	FTP	Points	Fouls	TrnOvr	Rbnds
FGP	1.000					
FTP	−0.039	1.000				
Points	0.475	0.242	1.000			
Fouls	−0.014	0.211	0.054	1.000		
TrnOvr	0.276	0.028	0.033	0.340	1.000	
Rbnds	0.436	0.137	0.767	−0.032	0.202	1.000

13.48 An expert witness in a case of alleged racial discrimination in a state university school of nursing introduced a regression of the determinants of *Salary* of each professor for each year during an 8-year period ($n = 423$) with the following results, with dependent variable *Salary* and predictors *Year* (year in which the salary was observed), *YearHire* (year when the individual was hired), *Race* (1 if individual is black, 0 otherwise), and *Rank* (1 if individual is an assistant professor, 0 otherwise). Interpret these results.

Variable	Coefficient	t	p
Intercept	−3,816,521	−29.4	.000
Year	1,948	29.8	.000
YearHire	−826	−5.5	.000
Race	−2,093	−4.3	.000
Rank	−6,438	−22.3	.000
$R^2 = 0.811$		$R^2_{adj} = 0.809$	$s = 3,318$

13.49 Analysis of a Detroit Marathon ($n = 1{,}015$ men, $n = 150$ women) produced the regression results shown below, with dependent variable *Time* (the marathon time in minutes) and predictors *Age* (runner's age), *Weight* (runner's weight in pounds), *Height* (runner's height in inches), and *Exp* (1 if runner had prior marathon experience, 0 otherwise). (a) Interpret the coefficient of *Exp*. (b) Does the intercept have any meaning? (c) Why do you suppose squared predictors were included? (d) Plug in your own *Age, Height, Weight,* and *Exp* to predict your own running time. Do you believe it? (Data courtesy of Detroit Striders.)

	Men ($n = 1{,}015$)		Women ($n = 150$)	
Variable	Coefficient	t	Coefficient	t
Intercept	−366		−2,820	
Age	−4.827	−6.1	−3.593	−2.5
Age^2	0.07671	7.1	0.05240	2.6
Weight	−1.598	−1.9	3.000	0.7
$Weight^2$	0.008961	3.4	−0.004041	−2.0
Height	24.65	1.5	96.13	1.6
$Height^2$	−0.2074	−1.7	−0.8040	−1.8
Exp	−41.74	−17.0	−28.65	−4.3
	$R^2 = 0.423$		$R^2 = 0.334$	

13.50 Using test data on 43 vehicles, an analyst fitted a regression to predict *CityMPG* (miles per gallon in city driving) using as predictors *Length* (length of car in inches), *Width* (width of car in inches), and *Weight* (weight of car in pounds). Interpret the results. Do you see evidence that some predictors were unhelpful? 🖼 **CityMPG**

R^2	0.682		
Adjusted R^2	0.658	n	43
R	0.826	k	3
Std. Error	2.558	Dep. Var.	**CityMPG**

ANOVA table

Source	SS	df	MS	F	p-value
Regression	547.3722	3	182.4574	27.90	8.35E-10
Residual	255.0929	39	6.5408		
Total	802.4651	42			

Regression output   *confidence interval*

variables	coefficients	std. error	t (df = 39)	p-value	95% lower	95% upper	VIF
Intercept	39.4492	8.1678	4.830	.0000	22.9283	55.9701	
Length (in)	−0.0016	0.0454	−0.035	.9725	−0.0934	0.0902	2.669
Width (in)	−0.0463	0.1373	−0.337	.7379	−0.3239	0.2314	2.552
Weight (lbs)	−0.0043	0.0008	−5.166	.0000	−0.0060	−0.0026	2.836

13.51 A researcher used stepwise regression to create regression models to predict *CarTheft* (thefts per 1,000) using four predictors: *Income* (per capita income), *Unem* (unemployment percent), *Pupil/Tea* (pupil-to-teacher ratio), and *Divorce* (divorces per 1,000 population) for the 50 U.S. states. Interpret these results.   **CarTheft**

Regression Analysis—Stepwise Selection (best model of each size)

50   observations
CarTheft is the dependent variable

p-values for the coefficients

Nvar	Income	Unem	Pupil/Tea	Divorce	Std. Err	Adj R^2	R^2
1			.0004		167.482	.218	.234
2	.0018		.0000		152.362	.353	.379
3	.0013	.0157	.0001		144.451	.418	.454
4	.0007	.0323	.0003	.1987	143.362	.427	.474

Kennedy, Peter. *A Guide to Econometrics.* 5th ed. MIT Press, 2003, p. 132 (Klein's Rule).

Kutner, Michael H.; Christopher J. Nachtsheim; and John Neter. *Applied Linear Regression Models.* 4th ed. McGraw-Hill/Irwin, 2004.

Wooldridge, Jeff. *Introductory Econometrics,* 3e (Southwestern, 2005).

RELATED READING

CHAPTER 13   Online Learning Resources

The Online Learning Center (OLC) at www.mhhe.com/doane4e has several *LearningStats* demonstrations to help you understand multiple regression. Your instructor may assign one or more of them, or you may decide to download the ones that sound interesting.

Online *Learning*Center

Topic	LearningStats Demonstrations
Multiple regression overview	Multiple Regression Overview Violations of Assumptions
Simulation	Effects of Collinearity Effects of Multicollinearity
Logistic regression	Logistic Regression Binary Logistic Regression
Other supplements	Partial *F* Test Durbin-Watson Test

Key: = PowerPoint   = Excel   = Adobe PDF

EXAM REVIEW QUESTIONS FOR CHAPTERS 11–13

1. Which statement is *correct* concerning one-factor ANOVA? Why not the others?

   a. The ANOVA is a test to see whether the variances of c groups are the same.
   b. In ANOVA, the k groups are compared two at a time, not simultaneously.
   c. ANOVA depends on the assumption of normality of the populations sampled.

2. Which statement is *incorrect?* Explain.

   a. We need a Tukey test because ANOVA doesn't tell *which* group means differ.
   b. Hartley's test is needed to determine whether the means of the groups differ.
   c. ANOVA assumes equal variances in the k groups being compared.

3. Given the following ANOVA table, find the F statistic and the critical value of $F_{.05}$.

Source	Sum of Squares	df	Mean Square	F
Treatment	744.00	4		
Error	751.50	15		
Total	1,495.50	19		

4. Given the following ANOVA: (a) How many ATM locations were there? (b) What was the sample size? (c) At $\alpha = .05$, is there a significant effect due to **Day of Week?** (d) At $\alpha = .05$, is there a significant interaction?

Source of Variation	SS	df	MS	F	P-Value	F Crit
ATM Location	41926.67	2	20963.33	9.133	0.0002	3.044
Day of Week	4909.52	6	818.25	0.356	0.9055	2.147
Interaction	29913.33	12	2492.78	1.086	0.3740	1.804
Error	433820.00	189	2295.34			
Total	510569.52	209				

5. Given a sample correlation coefficient $r = .373$ with $n = 30$, can you reject the hypothesis $\rho = 0$ for the population at $\alpha = .01$? Explain, stating the critical value you are using in the test.

6. Which statement is *incorrect?* Explain.

   a. Correlation uses a t-test with $n - 2$ degrees of freedom.
   b. Correlation analysis assumes that X is independent and Y is dependent.
   c. Correlation analysis is a test for the degree of linearity between X and Y.

7. Based on the information in this ANOVA table, the coefficient of determination R^2 is

   a. 0.499   b. 0.501   c. 0.382

ANOVA Table

Source	Sum of Squares	df	Mean Square	F	p-Value
Regression	158.3268	1	158.3268	24.88	0.00004
Residual	159.0806	25	6.3632		
Total	317.4074	26			

8. In a test of the regression model $Y = \beta_0 + \beta_1 X$ with 27 observations, what is the critical value of t to test the hypothesis that $\beta_1 = 0$ using $\alpha = .05$ in a two-tailed test?

   a. 1.960   b. 2.060   c. 1.708

9. Which statement is *correct* for a simple regression? Why not the others?

   a. A 95% confidence interval (CI) for the mean of Y is wider than the 95% CI for the predicted Y.
   b. A confidence interval for the predicted Y is widest when $X = \bar{x}$.
   c. The t test for zero slope always gives the same t_{calc} as the correlation test for $\rho = 0$.

10. Tell if each statement is *true* or *false* for a simple regression. If false, explain.

    a. If the standard error is $s_{yx} = 3,207$, then a residual $e_i = 4,327$ would be an outlier.
    b. In a regression with $n = 50$, then a leverage statistic $h_i = .10$ indicates unusual leverage.
    c. A decimal change is often used to improve data conditioning.

11. For a multiple regression, which statement is *true*? Why not the others?

    a. Evans' Rule suggests at least 10 observations for each predictor.
    b. The t_{calc} in a test for significance of a binary predictor can have only two values.
    c. Occam's Razor says we must prefer simple regression because it is simple.

12. For a multiple regression, which statement is *false*? Explain.

    a. If $R^2 = .752$ and $R^2_{adj} = .578$, the model probably has at least one weak predictor.
    b. R^2_{adj} can exceed R^2 if the model contains some very strong predictors.
    c. Deleting a predictor could increase the R^2_{adj} but will not increase R^2.

13. Which *predictor coefficients* differ significantly from zero at $\alpha = .05$?

    a. X3 and X5   b. X5 only   c. all but X1 and X3

	Coefficients	Std. Error	Lower 95%	Upper 95%
Intercept	22.47427	6.43282	9.40122	35.54733
X1	−0.243035	0.162983	−0.574256	0.088186
X2	0.187555	0.278185	−0.377784	0.752895
X3	−0.339730	0.063168	−0.468102	−0.211358
X4	0.001902	0.008016	−0.014389	0.018193
X5	1.602511	0.723290	0.132609	3.072413

14. Which predictors differ significantly from zero at $\alpha = .05$?

    a. X3 only   b. X4 only   c. both X3 and X4

	Coefficients	Std. Error	p-Value
Intercept	23.3015	4.1948	0.0000
X1	−0.227977	0.178227	0.2100
X2	0.218970	0.300784	0.4719
X3	−0.343658	0.059742	0.0000
X4	1.588353	0.742737	0.0402

15. In this regression with $n = 40$, which *predictor* differs significantly from zero at $\alpha = .01$?

    a. X2   b. X3   c. X5

	Coefficients	Std. Error
Intercept	3.210610	0.918974
X1	−0.034719	0.023283
X2	0.026794	0.039741
X3	−0.048533	0.009024
X4	0.000272	0.001145
X5	0.228930	0.103327

CHAPTER CONTENTS

CHAPTER LEARNING OBJECTIVES

LO

When you finish this chapter you should be able to

LO 14-1 Define time-series data and their components.

LO 14-2 Interpret a linear, exponential, or quadratic trend model.

LO 14-3 Fit any common trend model and use it to make forecasts.

LO 14-4 Know the definitions of common fit measures.

LO 14-5 Interpret a moving average and use Excel to create it.

LO 14-6 Use exponential smoothing to forecast trendless data.

LO 14-7 Use software to deseasonalize a time series.

LO 14-8 Use regression with seasonal binaries to make forecasts.

LO 14-9 Interpret index numbers.

14.1 TIME-SERIES COMPONENTS

Time-Series Data

Businesses must track their performance. By looking at their sales, costs, or profits over time, businesses can tell where they've been, whether they are performing poorly or satisfactorily, and how much improvement is needed, in both the short term and the long term. A **time-series variable** (denoted Y) consists of data observed over n periods of time. Consider a clothing retailer that specializes in blue jeans. Examples of time-series data this company might be interested in tracking would be the number of jeans sold and the company's market share. Or, from the manufacturing perspective, the company might track cost of raw materials over time.

Businesses also use time-series data to monitor whether a particular process is stable or unstable. And they use time-series data to help predict the future, a process we call *forecasting.* In addition to business time-series data, we see economic time-series data in *The Wall Street Journal* or *Bloomberg Businessweek,* and also in *USA Today* or *Time,* or even when we browse the web. Although business and economic time-series data are most common, we can see time-series data for population, health, crime, sports, and social problems. Usually, time-series data are presented in a graph, like Figures 14.1 and 14.2.

LO 14-1

Define time-series data and their components.

FIGURE 14.1

U.S. Employment (monthly, not seasonally adjusted) 📁 **Labor**

Source: www.bls.gov.

Percent   Percent

U.S. LABOR MARKET INDICATORS

Employment-to-population ratio

Civilian unemployment rate

2001 2002 2003 2004 2005 2006 2007 2008 2009 2010 2011

FIGURE 14.2

**Exchange Rates
(daily)** 🖾 **Exchange**

Source: www.federalreserve.gov.

It is customary to plot time-series data either as a line graph or as a bar graph, with time on the horizontal X-axis and the variable of interest on the vertical Y-axis to reveal how the variable changes over time. In a line graph, the X-Y data points are connected with line segments to make it easier to see fluctuations. While anyone can understand time-series graphs in a general way, this chapter explains how to interpret time-series data *statistically* and to make defensible forecasts. Our analysis begins with sample observations $y_1, y_2, \ldots, y_n$ covering n time periods. The following notation is used:

- y_t is the value of the time series in period t.
- t is an index denoting the time period ($t = 1, 2, \ldots, n$).
- n is the number of time periods.
- $y_1, y_2, \ldots, y_n$ is the data set for analysis.

To distinguish time-series data from cross-sectional data, we use y_t for an individual observation, with a subscript t instead of i.

Time-series data may be measured *at a point in time* or *over an interval of time.* For example, in accounting, balance sheet data are measured at the end of the fiscal year, while income statement data are measured over an entire fiscal year. The Gross Domestic Product (GDP) is a flow of goods and services measured *over an interval of time,* while the prime rate of interest is measured *at a point in time.* Your GPA is measured *at a point in time* while your weekly pay is measured *over an interval of time.* The distinction is sometimes vague in reported data, but a little thought will usually clarify matters. For example, Canada's 2010 unemployment rate (7.8 percent) would be measured at a point in time (e.g., at year's end) while Canada's 2010 hydroelectric production (355 terawatt-hours) would be measured over the entire year (see www.statcan.gc.ca).

Periodicity

The **periodicity** is the time interval over which data are collected (decade, year, quarter, month, week, day, hour). For example, the U.S. population is measured each *decade,* your personal income tax is calculated *annually,* GDP is reported *quarterly,* the unemployment rate is estimated *monthly,* and *The Wall Street Journal* reports the closing price of General Motors stock *daily* (although stock prices are also monitored continuously on the web). Firms typically report profits by quarter, but pension liabilities only at year's end.

Any periodicity is possible, but the principles of time-series modeling can be understood with these three common data types:

- Annual data (1 observation per year)
- Quarterly data (4 observations per year)
- Monthly data (12 observations per year)

Time Series Components

Time-series *decomposition* seeks to separate a time-series Y into four components: trend (T), cycle (C), seasonal (S), and irregular (I).

Figure 14.3 illustrates these four components in a hypothetical time series. The four components may be thought of as layering atop one another to produce the actual time series. In this example, the irregular component (I) is large enough to obscure the cycle (C) and seasonal (S) components, but not the trend (T). However, we can usually extract the original components from the time series by using statistical methods. These components are assumed to follow either an additive or a multiplicative model, as shown in Table 14.1.

FIGURE 14.3

Four Components of a Time-Series

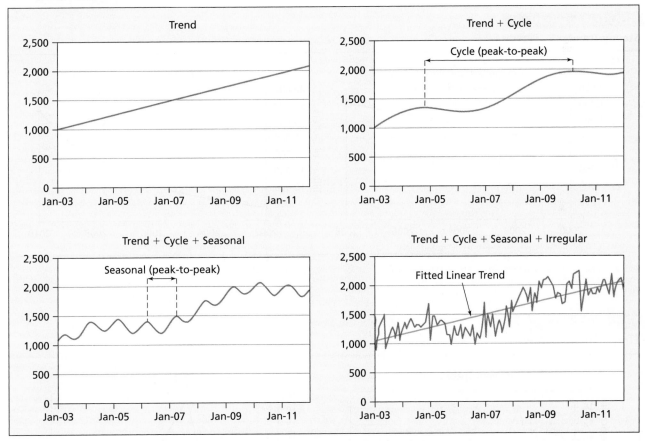

TABLE 14.1

Components of a Time-Series

Model	Components	Used For
Additive	$Y = T + C + S + I$	Data of similar magnitude (short-run or trend-free data) with constant *absolute* growth or decline.
Multiplicative	$Y = T \times C \times S \times I$	Data of increasing or decreasing magnitude (long-run or trended data) with constant *percent* growth or decline.

LO 14-1

Define time-series data and their components.

The additive form is attractive for its simplicity, but the multiplicative model is often more useful for forecasting financial data, particularly when the data vary over a range of magnitudes. Especially in the short run, it may not matter greatly which form is assumed. In fact, the model forms are fundamentally equivalent because the multiplicative model becomes additive if logarithms are taken (as long as the data are nonnegative):

$$\log(Y) = \log(T \times C \times S \times I) = \log(T) + \log(C) + \log(S) + \log(I)$$

Trend

Trend (*T*) is a general movement over all years (*t* = 1, 2, . . . , *n*). Change over a few years is not a trend. Some trends are steady and predictable. For example, the data may be steadily growing (e.g., total U.S. population), neither growing nor declining (e.g., your current car's mpg), or steadily declining (infant mortality rates in a developing nation). A mathematical trend can be fitted to any data, but its predictive value depends on the situation. For example, to predict average daily cost at community hospitals or Amazon's net sales (Figure 14.4), a mathematical trend might be useful, but a mathematical model might not be very helpful for predicting space launches or Fargo, ND, snowfall (Figure 14.5).

FIGURE 14.4

Steady Trend 📁 **Steady**

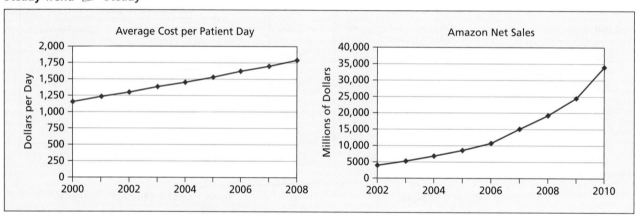

Sources: *Statistical Abstract of the U.S, 2011*, p. 118; and Mergent Online.

FIGURE 14.5

Erratic Pattern 📁 **Erratic**

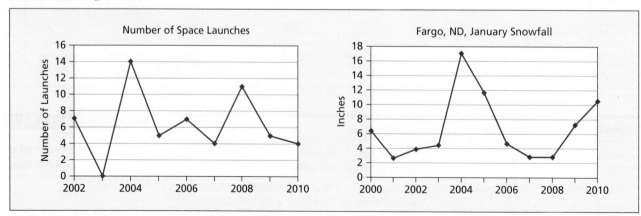

Sources: www.faa.gov and www.noaa.gov.

Most of us think of three general patterns: growth, stability, or decline. But there are subtler trends within each category. A time series can increase at a steady *linear* rate (e.g., the number of books you have read in your lifetime), at an *increasing* rate (e.g., Medicare costs for an aging population), or at a *decreasing* rate (e.g., live attendance at NFL football games). It can grow for awhile and then level off (e.g., sales of HDTV) or grow toward an asymptote (e.g., percent of adults owning a camera phone).

Cycle

Cycle (*C*) is a repetitive up-and-down movement around the trend that covers *several years*. For example, industry analysts have studied cycles for sales of new automobiles, new home construction, inventories, and business investment. These cycles are based primarily on product life and replacement cycles. In any market economy, there are broad business cycles that affect employment and production. After we have extracted the trend and seasonal components of a time series, a cycle may be detected as autocorrelation in the residuals (see Chapter 12, Section 12.8). Although cycles are important, there is no general theory of cycles, and even those cycles that have been identified in specific industries have erratic timing and complex causes that defy generalization. Over a small number of time periods (a typical forecasting situation), cycles are undetectable or may resemble a trend. For this reason cycles are not discussed further in this chapter.

Seasonal

Seasonal (*S*) is a repetitive cyclical pattern *within a year*.* For example, many retail businesses experience strong sales during the fourth quarter because of Christmas. Automobile sales rise when new models are released. Peak demand for airline flights to Europe occurs during summer vacation travel. Although often imagined as sine waves, seasonal patterns may not be smooth. Peaks and valleys can occur in any month or quarter, and each industry may face its own unique seasonal pattern. For example, June weddings tend to create a "spike" in bridal sales, but there is no "sine wave" pattern in bridal sales. By definition, annual data have no seasonality.

Irregular

Irregular (*I*) is a random disturbance that follows no apparent pattern. It is also called the *error* component or *random noise* reflecting all factors other than trend, cycle, and seasonality. Large error components are not unusual. For example, daily prices of many common stocks fluctuate greatly. When the irregular component is large, it may be difficult to isolate other individual model components. Some data are pure *I* (lacking meaningful *T* or *S* or *C* components). In such cases, we use special techniques (e.g., **moving average** or **exponential smoothing**) to make short-run forecasts. Faced with erratic data, experts may use their own knowledge of a particular industry to make *judgment forecasts*. For example, monthly sales forecasts of a particular automobile may combine judgment forecasts from dealers, financial staff, and economists.

14.2 TREND FORECASTING

There are many forecasting methods designed for specific situations. Much of this chapter deals with *trend models* because they are so common in business. You will also learn to use *decomposition* to make adjustments for *seasonality,* and how to use *smoothing models*. The important topics of *ARIMA models* and *causal models* are reserved for a more specialized class in forecasting. Figure 14.6 summarizes the main categories of forecasting models.

---

*Repetitive patterns within a week, day, or other time period also may be considered seasonal. For example, mail volume in the U.S. Postal Service is higher on Monday. Emergency arrivals at hospitals are lower during the first shift (between midnight and 6:00 a.m.). In this chapter, we will discuss only *monthly* and *quarterly* seasonal patterns because these are most typical of business data.

FIGURE 14.6

Overview of Forecasting

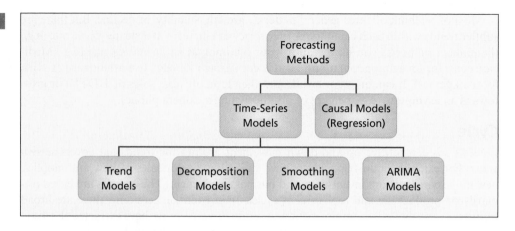

Three Trend Models

There are many possible trend models, but three of them are especially useful in business:

(14.1)	$y_t = a + bt$	for $t = 1, 2, \ldots, n$ (linear trend)
(14.2)	$y_t = ae^{bt}$	for $t = 1, 2, \ldots, n$ (exponential trend)
(14.3)	$y_t = a + bt + ct^2$	for $t = 1, 2, \ldots, n$ (quadratic trend)

The linear and exponential models are widely used because they have only two parameters and are familiar to most business audiences. The quadratic model may be useful when the data have a turning point. All three can be fitted by Excel, MegaStat, or MINITAB. Each model will be examined in turn.

Linear Trend Model

The **linear trend** model has the form $y_t = a + bt$. It is useful for a time-series that grows or declines by the same amount (b) in each period, as shown in Figure 14.7. It is the simplest model and may suffice for short-run forecasting. It is generally preferred in business as a baseline forecasting model unless there are compelling reasons to consider a more complex model.

FIGURE 14.7

Linear Trend Models

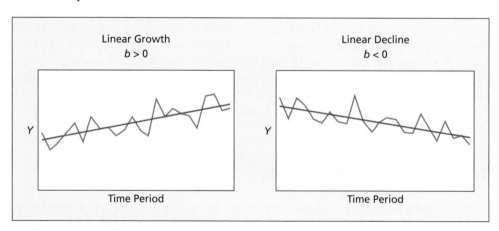

Illustration: Linear Trend

Following the population "echo boom," some U.S. states (especially in the Northeast and Midwest) began to see declines in the number of high school graduates. Concerned about its potential loss of traditional student populations aged 18–25, a midwestern university wanted to extrapolate the recent trend in enrollments. The slope of Excel's fitted trend, shown in Figure 14.8, indicates that, on average, the university has lost 235 students per year.

FIGURE 14.8

Excel's Linear Trend
📁 **Enrollment**

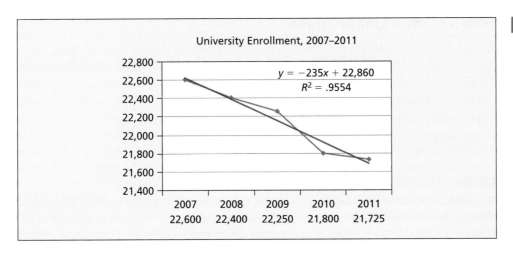

Linear Trend Calculations

The linear trend is fitted in the usual way by using the ordinary least squares formulas, as illustrated in Table 14.2. Because you are already familiar with regression, we will only point out the use of the index $t = 1, 2, 3, 4, 5$ as the independent variable (instead of using the years 2007, 2008, 2009, 2010, 2011). We use this time index to simplify the calculations and keep the data magnitudes under control (Excel uses this method too).

$$\text{Slope:} \quad b = \frac{\sum_{t=1}^{n}(t - \bar{t})(y_t - \bar{y})}{\sum_{t=1}^{n}(t - \bar{t})^2} = \frac{-2{,}350}{10} = -235$$

$$\text{Intercept:} \quad a = \bar{y} - b\bar{t} = 22{,}155 - (-235)(3) = 22{,}860$$

LO 14-3

Fit any common trend model and use it to make forecasts.

The *slope* of the fitted trend $y_t = 22{,}860 - 235t$ says that, unless the university takes steps to recruit new, non-traditional student populations, it can expect to lose 235 students each year ($dy_t/dt = -235$). The *intercept* is the "starting point" for the time series in period $t = 0$; that is, $y_0 = 22{,}860 - 235(0) = 22{,}860$.

TABLE 14.2

Sums for Least Squares Calculations

Year	t	y_t	$t - \bar{t}$	$y_t - \bar{y}$	$(t - \bar{t})^2$	$(t - \bar{t})(y_t - \bar{y})$
2007	1	22,600	−2	445	4	−890
2008	2	22,400	−1	245	1	−245
2009	3	22,250	0	95	0	0
2010	4	21,800	1	−355	1	−355
2011	5	21,725	2	−430	4	−860
Sum	15	110,775	0	0	10	−2,350
Mean	3	22,155	0	0	2	−470

Fitting and Interpreting an Annual Trend

In fitting a trend to annual data, the years (2007, 2008, 2009, 2010, 2011) are merely used as labels for the *X*-axis. The yearly labels should *not* be used in fitting the trend or calculating the forecast. To fit a trend to annual data, convert the labels to a time index ($t = 1, 2, \ldots$, etc.). To make a forecast, insert a value for the time index ($t = 1, 2, \ldots$, etc.) into Excel's fitted trend.

Forecasting a Linear Trend

We can make a forecast for any future year by using the fitted model $y_t = 22{,}860 - 235t$. In the enrollment example, the fitted trend equation is based on only 5 years' data, so we should be wary of extrapolating very far ahead:

For 2012 ($t = 6$): $y_6 = 22{,}860 - 235(6) = 21{,}450$

For 2013 ($t = 7$): $y_7 = 22{,}860 - 235(7) = 21{,}215$

For 2014 ($t = 8$): $y_8 = 22{,}860 - 235(8) = 20{,}980$

Linear Trend: Calculating R^2

The worksheet shown in Table 14.3 shows the calculation of the coefficient of determination. In this illustration, the linear model gives a good fit ($R^2 = .9554$) to the *past* data. However, a good fit to the past data does not guarantee good *future* forecasts. A deeper analysis of underlying causes of enrollment declines is needed. Are the causal forces likely to remain the same in subsequent years? Could the current demographic decline continue indefinitely, or will enrollments approach an asymptote, or even start to grow again? These are questions that forecasters must ask. The forecast is simply a projection of current trend assuming that nothing changes.

$$\text{Coefficient of determination:} \quad R^2 = 1 - \frac{\sum_{t=1}^{n}(y_t - \hat{y}_t)^2}{\sum_{t=1}^{n}(y_t - \bar{y})^2} = 1 - \frac{25{,}750}{578{,}000} = .9554$$

TABLE 14.3

Sums for R^2 Calculations

Year	t	y_t	$\hat{y}_t = 22{,}860 - 235t$	$y_t - \hat{y}_t$	$(y_t - \hat{y}_t)^2$	$(y_t - \bar{y})^2$
2007	1	22,600	22,625	−25	625	198,025
2008	2	22,400	22,390	10	100	60,025
2009	3	22,250	22,155	95	9,025	9,025
2010	4	21,800	21,920	−120	14,400	126,025
2011	5	21,725	21,685	40	1,600	184,900
Sum	15		110,775	0	25,750	578,000

Exponential Trend Model

The **exponential trend** model has the form $y_t = ae^{bt}$. It is useful for a time series that grows or declines at the same *rate* (b) in each period, as shown in Figure 14.9. When the growth rate is positive ($b > 0$), then Y grows by an *increasing* amount each period (unlike the linear model, which assumes a *constant* increment each period). If the growth rate is negative ($b < 0$), then Y declines by a *decreasing* amount each period (unlike the linear model, which assumes a *constant* decrement each period).

FIGURE 14.9

Exponential Trend Models

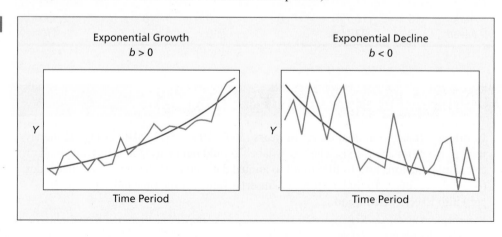

When to Use the Exponential Model

The exponential model is often preferred for financial data or data that cover a longer period of time. When you invest money in a commercial bank savings account, interest accrues at a given percent. Your savings grow faster than a linear rate because you earn interest on the accumulated interest. Banks use the exponential formula to calculate interest on CDs. Financial analysts often find the exponential model attractive because costs, revenue, and salaries are best projected under assumed *percent* growth rates.

Another nice feature of the exponential model is that you can compare two growth rates in two time-series variables with dissimilar data units (i.e., a percent growth rate is *unit-free*). For example, between 2000 and 2010 the number of Medicare enrollees grew from 39.6 million persons to 46.6 million persons (1.63 percent compound annual growth rate), while Medicare payments to hospitals grew from \$125.7 billion to \$230.5 billion (6.25 percent compound annual growth rate). Comparing the percents, we see that Medicare insurance payments have been growing more than four times as fast as the Medicare head count (see Research and Data at www.cms.gov). These facts underlie the ongoing debate about Medicare spending in the United States.

There may not be much difference between a linear and exponential model when the growth rate is small and the data set covers only a few time periods. For example, suppose your starting salary is \$50,000. Table 14.4 compares salary increases of \$2,500 each year ($y_t = 50,000 + 2,500t$) with a continuously compounded 4.879 percent salary growth ($y_t = 50,000e^{.04879t}$). Over the first few years, there is little difference. But after 20 years, the difference is obvious, as shown in Figure 14.10. Despite its attractive simplicity,* the linear model's assumptions may be inappropriate for some financial variables.

t	$y_t = 50,000 + 2,500t$ *Linear*	$y_t = 50,000e^{.04879t}$ *Exponential*
0	50,000	50,000
5	62,500	63,814
10	75,000	81,445
15	87,500	103,946
20	100,000	132,665

TABLE 14.4

Two Models of Salary Growth

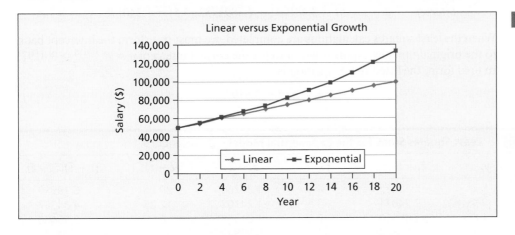

FIGURE 14.10

Linear and Exponential Growth Compared

Illustration: Exponential Trend

Spending on Internet security in the United States has shown explosive growth, as indicated in Figure 14.11. Clearly, a linear trend (constant *dollar* growth) would be inadequate. It is more reasonable to assume a constant *percent* rate of growth and fit

---

*In a sense, the linear model ($y_t = a + bt$) and the exponential model ($y_t = ae^{bt}$) are equally simple because they are two-parameter models, and a log-transformed exponential model $\ln(y_t) = \ln(a) + bt$ is actually linear.

FIGURE 14.11

Excel's Exponential Trend
📁 DolonCorp

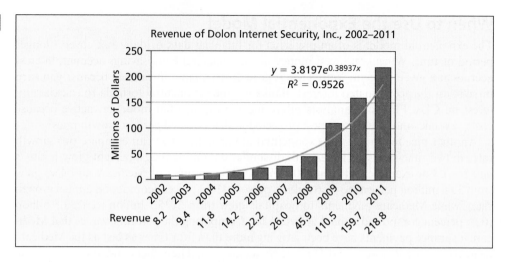

an exponential model. For the Dolon company's revenue, the fitted exponential trend is $y_t = 3.8197e^{.3894t}$. The value of b in the exponential model $y_t = ae^{bt}$ is the continuously compounded growth rate, so we can say that Dolon's revenue is growing at an astonishing rate of 38.94 percent per year. A negative value of b in the equation $y_t = ae^{bt}$ would indicate *decline* instead of growth. The intercept a is the "starting point" in period $t = 0$. For example, $y_0 = 3.8197e^{.3894(0)} = 3.8197$.

Exponential Trend Calculations

LO 14-3

Fit any common trend model and use it to make forecasts.

Table 14.5 shows the worksheet for the required sums. Calculations of the exponential trend are done by using a transformed variable $z_t = \ln(y_t)$ instead of y_t, to produce a linear equation so that we can use the least squares formulas.

$$\text{Slope:} \qquad b = \frac{\sum_{t=1}^{n}(t - \bar{t})(z_t - \bar{z})}{\sum_{t=1}^{n}(t - \bar{t})^2} = \frac{32.12329}{82.5} = .3893732$$

$$\text{Intercept:} \qquad a = \bar{z} - \bar{b}t = 3.481731 - (.3893732)(5.5) = 1.340178$$

When the least squares calculations are completed, we must transform the intercept back to the original units by exponentiation to get the correct intercept $a = e^{1.340178} = 3.8197$. In final form, the fitted trend equation is

$$y_t = ae^{bt} = 3.8197\ e^{.38937t}$$

TABLE 14.5			Least Squares Sums for the Exponential Model 📁 DolonCorp				
Year	t	y_t	$z_t = \ln(y_t)$	$t - \bar{t}$	$z_t - \bar{z}$	$(t - \bar{t})^2$	$(t - \bar{t})(z_t - \bar{z})$
2002	1	8.2	2.10413	−4.5	−1.37760	20.25	6.19919
2003	2	9.4	2.24071	−3.5	−1.24102	12.25	4.34357
2004	3	11.8	2.46810	−2.5	−1.01363	6.25	2.53408
2005	4	14.2	2.65324	−1.5	−0.82849	2.25	1.24273
2006	5	22.2	3.10009	−0.5	−0.38164	0.25	0.19082
2007	6	26.0	3.25810	0.5	−0.22363	0.25	−0.11182
2008	7	45.9	3.82647	1.5	0.34473	2.25	0.51710
2009	8	110.5	4.70502	2.5	1.22328	6.25	3.05821
2010	9	159.7	5.07330	3.5	1.59157	12.25	5.57048
2011	10	218.8	5.38816	4.5	1.90643	20.25	8.57892
Sum	55	626.7	34.81731	0.0	0.00000	82.5	32.12329
Mean	5.5	62.67	3.481731				

Forecasting an Exponential Trend

We can make a forecast of debit card usage for any future year by using the fitted model*:

For 2012 ($t = 11$): $y_{11} = 3.8197e^{.38937\,(11)} = 276.8$

For 2013 ($t = 12$): $y_{12} = 3.8197e^{.38937\,(12)} = 408.5$

For 2014 ($t = 13$): $y_{13} = 3.8197e^{.38937\,(13)} = 603.0$

Can Dolon's revenue actually continue to grow at a rate of 38.937 percent? It seems unlikely. Typically, when a new product is introduced, its growth rate at first is very strong, but eventually slows down as the market becomes saturated and/or as competitors arise.

Exponential Trend: Calculating R^2

As shown in Table 14.6, we calculate R^2 the same way as for the linear trend, except that we replace the dependent variable y_t with $z_t = \ln(y_t)$ and the fitted value with $\hat{z}_t = 1.340178 + .389373t$. This is necessary because Excel's trend-fitting calculations are done in logarithms in an exponential model:

$$\text{Coefficient of determination:} \quad R^2 = 1 - \frac{\sum_{t=1}^{n}(z_t - \hat{z}_t)^2}{\sum_{t=1}^{n}(z_t - \bar{z})^2} = 1 - \frac{0.62228}{13.13021} = .9526$$

In this example, the exponential trend gives a very good fit ($R^2 = .9526$) to the past data. Although a high R^2 does not guarantee good forecasts, Internet security protection is expected to reach a wider consumer audience in the future, so the high growth rate could continue if the firm is able to manage its expansion.

TABLE 14.6		Sums for R^2 Calculations in Exponential Model DolonCorp			
t	$z_t = \ln(y_t)$	$\hat{z}_t = 1.340178 + .389373t$	$z_t - \hat{z}_t$	$(z_t - \hat{z}_t)^2$	$(z_t - \bar{z})^2$
1	2.10413	1.72955	0.37458	0.14031	1.89777
2	2.24071	2.11892	0.12178	0.01483	1.54013
3	2.46810	2.50830	−0.04020	0.00162	1.02745
4	2.65324	2.89767	−0.24443	0.05975	0.68639
5	3.10009	3.28704	−0.18695	0.03495	0.14565
6	3.25810	3.67642	−0.41832	0.17499	0.05001
7	3.82647	4.06579	−0.23933	0.05728	0.11884
8	4.70502	4.45516	0.24985	0.06243	1.49643
9	5.07330	4.84454	0.22876	0.05233	2.53308
10	5.38816	5.23391	0.15425	0.02379	3.63446
Sum	34.81731	34.81731	0	0.62228	13.13021
Mean	3.48173				

Quadratic Trend Model

The **quadratic trend** model has the form $y_t = a + bt + ct^2$. The t^2 term allows a nonlinear shape. It is useful for a time series that has a turning point or that is not captured by

---

*Excel uses the exponential formula $y_t = ae^{bt}$ in which the coefficient b is the *continuously compounded* growth rate. But MINITAB uses an equivalent formula $y_t = y_0(1 + r)^t$, which you may recognize as the formula for compound interest. Although the formulas appear different, they give identical forecasts. For example, for the debit card data, MINITAB's fitted trend is $y_t = 3.81972(1.47606)^t$ so the forecasts are

For 2012 ($t = 11$): $y_{11} = 3.81972(1.47606)^{11} = 276.8$

For 2013 ($t = 12$): $y_{12} = 3.81972(1.47606)^{12} = 408.5$

For 2014 ($t = 13$): $y_{13} = 3.81972(1.47606)^{13} = 603.0$

To convert MINITAB's fitted equation to Excel's, set $a = y_0$ and $b = \ln(1 + r)$. To convert Excel's fitted equation to MINITAB's, set $y_0 = a$ and $r = e^b - 1$.

the exponential model. If $c = 0$, the quadratic model $y_t = a + bt + ct^2$ becomes a linear model because the term ct^2 drops out of the equation (i.e., the linear model is a special case of the quadratic model). Some forecasters fit a quadratic model as a way of checking for nonlinearity. If the coefficient c does not differ significantly from zero, then the linear model would suffice. Depending on the values of b and c, the quadratic model can assume any of four shapes, as shown in Figure 14.12.

FIGURE 14.12

Four Quadratic Trend Models

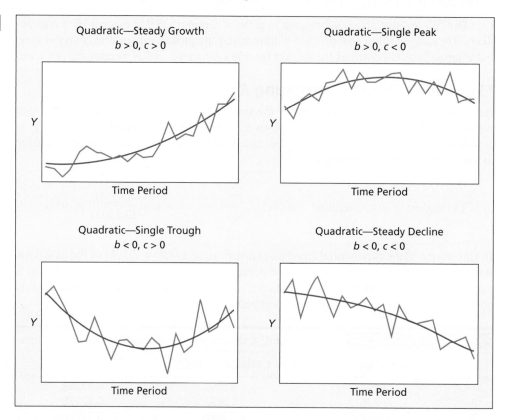

Illustration: Quadratic Trend

The number of hospital beds (Table 14.7) in the United States declined during the late 1990s, showed signs of leveling out, and then declined again. What trend would we choose if the objective is to make a realistic 1-year forecast?

TABLE 14.7

U.S. Hospital Beds (thousands), 1995–2004
📷 HospitalBeds

Source: *Statistical Abstract of the United States, 2007,* p. 114.

Year	Beds	Year	Beds
1995	1,081	2000	984
1996	1,062	2001	987
1997	1,035	2002	976
1998	1,013	2003	965
1999	994	2004	956

Figure 14.13 shows 1-year projections using the linear and quadratic models. Many observers would think that the quadratic model offers a more believable prediction because the quadratic model is able to capture the slight curvature in the data pattern. But this gain in forecast credibility must be weighed against the added complexity of the quadratic model. It appears that the forecasts would turn upward if projected more than 1 year ahead. We should be especially skeptical of any polynomial model that is projected more than one or two periods into the future.

Because the quadratic trend model $y_t = a + bt + ct^2$ is a multiple regression with two predictors (t and t^2), the least squares calculations are not shown. However, Figure 14.14 shows the MINITAB fitted regression. Note that both t and t^2 are significant predictors (large t, small p).

FIGURE 14.13

Two Trend Models for U.S. Hospital Beds HospitalBeds

Linear Trend
U.S. Hospital Beds, 1995–2004

$y = -13.255x + 1078.2$
$R^2 = 0.9222$

Quadratic Trend
U.S. Hospital Beds, 1995–2004

$y = 1.3371x^2 - 27.963x + 1107.6$
$R^2 = 0.9823$

The regression equation is
Beds = $1108 - 28.0$ Time + 1.34 Time2

Predictor	Coef	SE Coef	T	P
Constant	1107.62	7.42	149.37	0.000
Time	−27.963	3.097	−9.03	0.000
Time2	1.3371	0.2744	4.87	0.002

S = 6.30473   R-Sq = 98.2%   R-Sq(adj) = 97.7%

FIGURE 14.14

MINITAB's Quadratic Regression
 HospitalBeds

Using Excel for Trend Fitting

Plot the data, right-click on the data, and choose a trend. Figure 14.15 shows Excel's menu of six trend options. The menu includes a sketch of each trend type. Click the Options tab if you want to display the R^2 and fitted equation on the graph, or if you want to plot forecasts (trend extrapolations) on the graph. The quadratic model is a **polynomial model** of order 2. Despite the many choices, some patterns cannot be captured by any of the common trend models. By default, Excel only reports four decimal accuracy. However, you can click on Excel's fitted trend equation, choose Format Data Labels, choose Number, and set the number of decimal places you want to see.

LO 14-3

Fit any common trend model and use it to make forecasts.

FIGURE 14.15

Excel's Trend-Fitting Menus WomenPilots

Principle of Occam's Razor

Given two *sufficient* explanations, we prefer the simpler one.
—*William of Occam (1285–1347)*

Trend-Fitting Criteria

It is so easy to fit a trend in Excel that it is tempting to "shop around" for the best fit. But forecasters prefer the simplest trend model that adequately matches the trend. Simple models are easier to interpret and explain to others. Criteria for selecting a trend model for forecasting include:

Criterion	Ask Yourself
• Occam's Razor	Would a simpler model suffice?
• Overall fit	How does the trend fit the past data?
• Believability	Does the extrapolated trend "look right"?
• Fit to recent data	Does the fitted trend match the last few data points?

EXAMPLE 14.1

Comparing Trends

You can usually increase the R^2 by choosing a more complex model. But if you are making a *forecast,* this is not the only relevant issue because R^2 measures the fit to the *past* data. Figure 14.16 shows four fitted trends using the same data, with

FIGURE 14.16

Four Fitted Trends Using the Same Data

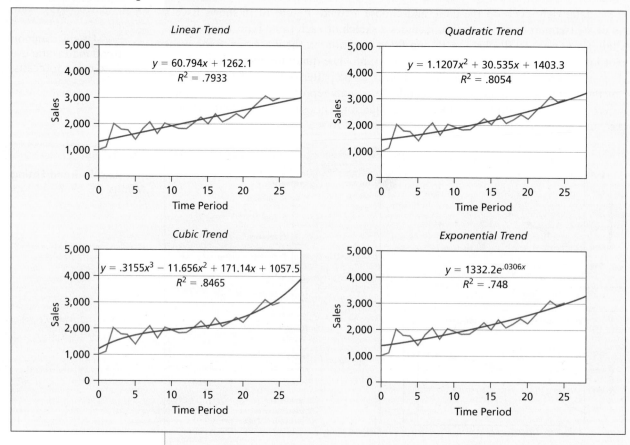

Linear Trend
$y = 60.794x + 1262.1$
$R^2 = .7933$

Quadratic Trend
$y = 1.1207x^2 + 30.535x + 1403.3$
$R^2 = .8054$

Cubic Trend
$y = .3155x^3 - 11.656x^2 + 171.14x + 1057.5$
$R^2 = .8465$

Exponential Trend
$y = 1332.2e^{.0306x}$
$R^2 = .748$

three-period forecasts. For this data set, the linear model may be inadequate because its fit to recent periods is marginal (we prefer the simplest model *only if* it "does the job"). Here, the cubic trend yields the highest R^2, but the fitted equation is nonintuitive and would be hard to explain or defend. Also, its forecasts appear to be increasing too rapidly. In this example, the exponential model has the lowest R^2, yet matches the recent data fairly well and its forecasts appear credible when projected a few periods ahead.

Any trend model's forecasts become less reliable as they are extrapolated farther into the future. The quadratic trend, the simplest of Excel's polynomial models, is sometimes acceptable for short-term forecasting. However, forecasters avoid higher-order polynomial models (cubic and higher) not only because they are complex, but also because they can give bizarre forecasts when extrapolated more than one period ahead. Table 14.8 compares the features of the three most common trend models.

TABLE 14.8   **Comparison of Three Trend Models**

Model	Pro	Con
Linear	1. Simple, familiar to everyone. 2. May suffice for short-run data.	1. Assumes constant slope. 2. Cannot capture nonlinear change.
Exponential	1. Familiar to financial analysts. 2. Shows compound percent growth rate.	1. Some managers are unfamiliar with e^x. 2. Data values must be positive.
Quadratic	1. Useful for data with a turning point. 2. Useful test for nonlinearity.	1. Complex and no intuitive interpretation. 2. Can give untrustworthy forecasts if extrapolated too far.

LO 14-2

Interpret a linear, exponential, or quadratic trend model.

SECTION EXERCISES

connect

14.1 In 2009, US Airways Flight 1549 made a successful emergency landing in the Hudson River, after striking birds shortly after takeoff. Are bird strikes an increasing threat to planes? (a) Make an Excel graph of the data on bird strikes. (b) Discuss the underlying causes that might explain the trend. (c) Use Excel, MegaStat, or MINITAB to fit three trends (linear, quadratic, and exponential) to the time series. (d) Which trend model do you think is best to make forecasts for the next 3 years? Why? (e) Use *each* of the three fitted trend equations to make numerical forecasts for 2008, 2009, and 2010. How much difference does the choice of model make? Which forecasts do you trust the most, and why? (f) If you have access to the web, check your forecasts. How accurate were they? 📂 **BirdStrikes**

Number of Reported Bird Strikes to Civil Aircraft in U.S., 1997–2007
📂 BirdStrikes

Year	Strikes	Year	Strikes
1990	1,738	1999	5,002
1991	2,252	2000	5,872
1992	2,351	2001	5,644
1993	2,395	2002	6,044
1994	2,459	2003	5,854
1995	2,643	2004	6,398
1996	2,840	2005	7,036
1997	3,351	2006	6,996
1998	3,658	2007	7,439

Source: http://wildlife-mitigation.tc.faa.gov.

14.2 (a) Make an Excel graph of the data on the number of certified organic farms in the United States. (b) Discuss the underlying causes that might explain the trend or pattern. (c) Use Excel, MegaStat, or MINITAB to fit three trends (linear, quadratic, exponential) to the time series. (d) Which trend model do you think is best to make forecasts for the next 3 years? Why? (e) Use *each* of the three fitted trend equations to make numerical forecasts for the next 3 years. How similar are the three models' forecasts? 📄 **Organic**

Number of Certified Organic Farms in the United States, 2001–2008	
Year	**Farms**
2001	6,949
2002	7,323
2003	8,035
2004	8,021
2005	8,493
2006	9,469
2007	11,352
2008	12,941

Source: *Statistical Abstract of the United States, 2011,* p. 537.

14.3 (a) Make an Excel line graph of the data on employee work stoppages. (b) Discuss the underlying causes that might explain the trend or pattern. (c) Fit three trends (linear, exponential, quadratic). (d) Which trend model is best, and why? If none is satisfactory, explain. (e) Make numerical forecasts for the next 3 years using a trend model of your choice or a judgment forecast. 📄 **Strikers**

U.S. Workers Involved in Work Stoppages, 2000–2010 (thousands)			
Year	**Strikers**	**Year**	**Strikers**
2000	394	2006	70
2001	99	2007	189
2002	46	2008	72
2003	129	2009	13
2004	171	2010	45
2005	100		

Source: http://data.bls.gov.

14.4 (a) Make an Excel line graph of the car dealership data. (b) Discuss the underlying causes that might explain the trend or pattern. (c) Fit three trends (linear, exponential, quadratic). (d) Would any of the three trend models yield adequate forecasts? Explain. 📄 **Dealerships**

Number of U.S. New Car Dealerships, 2003–2009 📄 Dealerships	
Year	**Dealerships**
2003	21,725
2004	21,650
2005	21,640
2006	21,495
2007	20,770
2008	20,010
2009	18,460

Source: *Statistical Abstract of the United States, 2011,* p. 663.

14.5 (a) Plot the data on fruit and vegetable consumption. (b) Discuss the underlying causes that might explain the trend or pattern. (c) Fit a linear trend to the data. (d) Interpret the trend equation. What are its implications for producers? (e) Make a forecast for 2010. *Note:* Time increments are 5 years, so use $t = 6$ for your 2010 forecast. 📄 **Fruits**

U.S. Per Capita Consumption of Commercially Produced Fruits and Vegetables (pounds)

Year	Total
1980	608.8
1985	632.2
1990	660.2
1995	692.5
2000	711.7
2005	694.3

Source: *Statistical Abstract of the United States, 2007,* p. 134.

Mini Case   14.1

U.S. Trade Deficit

The imbalance between imports and exports has been a vexing policy problem for U.S. policymakers for decades. The last time the United States had a trade surplus was in 1975, partly due to reduced dependency on foreign oil through conservation measures enacted after the oil crisis (shortages and gas lines) in the early 1970s. However, the trade deficit has become more acute over time, due partly to continued oil imports, and, more recently, to availability of cheaper goods from China and other emerging economies.

Prior to the recent recession, imports had been growing faster than exports. Yet over the past decade, the fitted trend equations show that exports have grown at a slightly higher compound annual rate of 6.63 percent, compared with 5.92 percent for imports (see Figure 14.17). Possible reasons would include reduced industrial production due to the recession, improved vehicle fuel economy, rising import prices, and the impact of exchange rates.

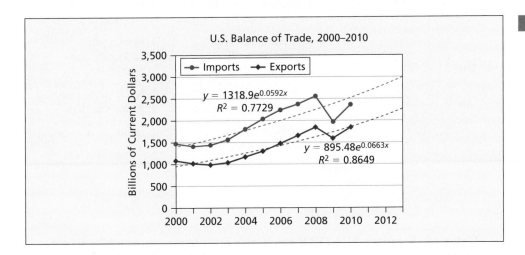

FIGURE 14.17

U.S. Trade, 2000–2010
 TradeDeficit

Although the trade deficit is projected to widen in *absolute* terms (calculations shown below using Excel functions), it should grow smaller in *percent* terms. Perhaps the U.S. can achieve trade balance—but only far in the future, given the tiny difference in growth rates. Further, the assumption of *ceteris paribus* may not hold. Much depends on the world's recovery from the recent financial crisis and slowdown, how the U.S. and other nations handle their internal finances, and international conflicts.

LO 14-2

Interpret a linear, exponential, or quadratic trend model.

Year	t	Exports (projection)	Imports (projection)
2011	$t = 12$	$y_{12} = 895.48 * \text{EXP}(0.0663 * 12) = 1{,}984$	$y_{12} = 1318.9 * \text{EXP}(0.0592 * 12) = 2{,}684$
2012	$t = 13$	$y_{13} = 895.48 * \text{EXP}(0.0663 * 13) = 2{,}120$	$y_{13} = 1318.9 * \text{EXP}(0.0592 * 13) = 2{,}847$
2013	$t = 14$	$y_{14} = 895.48 * \text{EXP}(0.0663 * 14) = 2{,}266$	$y_{14} = 1318.9 * \text{EXP}(0.0592 * 14) = 3{,}021$

Forecasts are less a way of predicting the future than of showing where we are heading *if* nothing changes. A paradox of forecasting is that, as soon as decision makers see the implications of a distasteful forecast, they may try to take steps to ensure that the forecast is wrong!

14.3 ASSESSING FIT

LO 14-4

Know the definitions of common fit measures.

Five Measures of Fit

In time-series analysis, you are likely to encounter several different measures of "fit" that show how well the estimated trend model matches the observed time series. "Fit" refers to historical data, and you should bear in mind that a good fit is no guarantee of good forecasts—the usual goal. Five common measures of fit are shown in Table 14.9.

TABLE 14.9   Five Measures of Fit

Statistic	Description	Pro	Con
(14.4) $R^2 = 1 - \dfrac{\sum\limits_{t=1}^{n}(y_t - \hat{y}_t)^2}{\sum\limits_{t=1}^{n}(y_t - \bar{y}_t)^2}$	Coefficient of Determination	1. Unit-free measure. 2. Very common.	1. Often interpreted incorrectly (e.g., "percent of correct predictions").
(14.5) $MAPE = \dfrac{100}{n}\sum\limits_{t=1}^{n}\dfrac{|y_t - \hat{y}_t|}{y_t}$	Mean Absolute Percent Error (MAPE)	1. Unit-free measure (%). 2. Intuitive meaning.	1. Requires $y_t > 0$. 2. Lacks nice math properties.
(14.6) $MAD = \dfrac{1}{n}\sum\limits_{t=1}^{n}|y_t - \hat{y}_t|$	Mean Absolute Deviation (MAD)	1. Intuitive meaning. 2. Same units as y_t.	1. Not unit-free. 2. Lacks nice math properties.
(14.7) $MSD = \dfrac{1}{n}\sum\limits_{t=1}^{n}(y_t - \hat{y}_t)^2$	Mean Squared Deviation (MSD)	1. Nice math properties. 2. Penalizes big errors more.	1. Nonintuitive meaning. 2. Rarely reported.
(14.8) $SE = \sqrt{\sum\limits_{t=1}^{n}\dfrac{(y_t - \hat{y}_t)^2}{n - 2}}$	Standard Error (SE)	1. Same units as y_t. 2. For confidence intervals.	1. Nonintuitive meaning.

EXAMPLE 14.2

Fire Losses

Figure 14.18 shows a MINITAB graph with fitted linear trend and 3-year forecasts for aggregate U.S. fire losses between 1997 and 2007. Notice that, instead of R^2, MINITAB displays *MAPE*, *MAD*, and *MSD* statistics. Table 14.10 shows the calculations for these statistics of fit. Because the residuals $y_t - \hat{y}_t$ sum to zero, we see why it's necessary to sum either their absolute values or their squares to obtain a measure of fit. *MAPE*, *MAD*, *MSD*, and *SE* would be zero if the trend provided a perfect fit to the time series.

| FIGURE 14.18 | MINITAB's Time-Series Trend—Linear Model | FireLosses |

| TABLE 14.10 | Sums for *MAD, MAPE, MSD*, and Standard Error | FireLosses |

Period	Year	Losses	$\hat{y}_t = 9.8034 + 1.2949t$	$y_t - \hat{y}_t$	$|y_t - \hat{y}_t|$	$|y_t - \hat{y}_t|/y_t$	$(y_t - \hat{y}_t)^2$
1	1997	12.940	11.0983	1.8417	1.8417	0.1423	3.3919
2	1998	11.510	12.3932	−0.8832	0.8832	0.0767	0.7800
3	1999	12.428	13.6881	−1.2601	1.2601	0.1014	1.5879
4	2000	13.457	14.9830	−1.5260	1.5260	0.1134	2.3287
5	2001	17.118	16.2779	0.8401	0.8401	0.0491	0.7058
6	2002	17.586	17.5728	0.0132	0.0132	0.0008	0.0002
7	2003	21.129	18.8677	2.2613	2.2613	0.1070	5.1135
8	2004	18.874	20.1626	−1.2886	1.2886	0.0683	1.6605
			Sum	0.00	9.9142	0.6590	15.5683
			Mean	0.00	1.2393	0.0824	1.9460

Source: *Statistical Abstract of the United States, 2007*, p. 212. Losses are in billions of dollars.

Calculations

Using the sums in Table 14.10, we can apply the formulas for each fit statistic:

$$MAPE = \frac{100}{n} \sum_{t=1}^{n} \frac{|y_t - \hat{y}_t|}{y_t} = \frac{100}{8}(0.6590) = 8.24\%$$

$$MAD = \frac{1}{n} \sum_{t=1}^{n} |y_t - \hat{y}_t| = \frac{1}{8}(9.9142) = 1.239$$

$$MSD = \frac{1}{n} \sum_{t=1}^{n} (y_t - \hat{y}_t)^2 = \frac{1}{8}(15.5683) = 1.946$$

$$SE = \sqrt{\sum_{t=1}^{n} \frac{(y_t - \hat{y}_t)^2}{n - 2}} = \sqrt{\frac{15.5683}{8 - 2}} = 1.611$$

Interpretation

The *MAPE* says that our fitted trend has a mean absolute error of 8.24 percent. The *MAD* says that the average error is 1.239 billion dollars (ignoring the sign). The *MSD* lacks a simple interpretation. These fit statistics are most useful in comparing different trend models for the same data. All the statistics (especially the *MSD*) are affected by the unusual residual in 1997, when fire losses greatly exceeded the trend. The standard error is useful if we want to make a prediction interval for a forecast, using formula 14.9. It is the same formula you saw in Chapter 12.

$$
(14.9) \quad \hat{y}_t \pm t_{n-2} \, SE \sqrt{1 + \frac{1}{n} + \frac{(t - \bar{t})^2}{\displaystyle\sum_{t=1}^{n}(t - \bar{t})^2}} \quad \text{(prediction interval for future } y_t)
$$

You may recall from Chapter 12 that you can get a "quick" approximate 95 percent prediction interval by using $\hat{y}_t \pm 2 \, SE$. However, for forecasts beyond the range of the observed data, you should use formula 14.9, which widens the confidence intervals when the time index is far from its historic mean.

14.4 MOVING AVERAGES

Trendless or Erratic Data

LO 14-5

Interpret a moving average and use Excel to create it.

What if the time series $y_1, y_2, \ldots, y_n$ is erratic or has no consistent trend? In such cases, there may be little point in fitting a trend, and if the mean is changing over time, we cannot just "take the average" over the entire data set. Instead, a conservative approach is to calculate a *moving average*. There are two main types of moving averages: trailing or centered. We will illustrate each.

Trailing Moving Average (*TMA*)

The simplest kind of moving average is the **trailing moving average (TMA)** over the last m periods.

$$
(14.10) \quad \hat{y}_t = \frac{y_t + y_{t-1} + \cdots + y_{t-m+1}}{m} \quad \text{(trailing moving average over } m \text{ periods)}
$$

The *TMA* smoothes the past fluctuations in the time series, helping us see the pattern more clearly. The choice of m depends on the situation. A larger m yields a "smoother" *TMA* but requires more data. The value of $\hat{y}_t$ may also be used as a forecast for period $t + 1$. Beyond the range of the observed data $y_1, y_2, \ldots, y_n$ there is no way to update the moving average, so it is best regarded as a *one-period-ahead forecast*.

EXAMPLE 14.3

Fuel Economy

Many drivers keep track of their fuel economy. For a given vehicle, there is likely to be little trend over time, but there is always random fluctuation. Also, current driving conditions (e.g., snow, hot weather, road trips) could temporarily affect mileage over several consecutive time periods. In this situation, a moving average might be considered. Table 14.11 shows Andrew's fuel economy data set. Column five shows a three-period *TMA*. For example, for period 6 (yellow-shaded cells), the *TMA* is

$$
\hat{y}_6 = \frac{24.392 + 21.458 + 24.128}{3} = 23.326
$$

It is easiest to appreciate the moving average's "smoothing" of the data when it is displayed on a graph, as in Figure 14.19. It is clear that Andrew's mean is around 23 mpg, though the moving average fluctuates over a range of approximately ±2 mpg.

TABLE 14.11		Andrew's Miles Per Gallon (*n* = 20) AndrewsMPG				
Obs	**Date**	**Miles Driven**	**Gallons**	**MPG**	**TMA**	**CMA**
1	5-Jan	285	11.324	25.168		
2	7-Jan	185	8.731	21.189		23.074
3	11-Jan	250	10.934	22.864	23.074	22.815
4	15-Jan	296	12.135	*24.392*	22.815	22.905
5	19-Jan	232	10.812	*21.458*	22.905	23.326
6	25-Jan	301	12.475	*24.128*	*23.326*	22.158
7	30-Jan	285	13.645	20.887	22.158	22.581
8	3-Feb	263	11.572	22.727	22.581	22.747
9	7-Feb	250	10.152	24.626	22.747	23.856
10	14-Feb	307	12.678	24.215	23.856	23.283
11	22-Feb	242	11.520	21.007	23.283	22.942
12	29-Feb	288	12.201	23.605	22.942	22.937
13	5-Mar	285	11.778	*24.198*	22.937	24.103
14	8-Mar	313	12.773	*24.505*	24.103	*22.638*
15	13-Mar	283	14.732	*19.210*	22.638	23.330
16	18-Mar	318	12.103	26.274	23.330	21.620
17	22-Mar	195	10.064	19.376	21.620	23.746
18	28-Mar	320	12.506	25.588	23.746	22.904
19	2-Apr	270	11.369	23.749	22.904	23.910
20	12-Apr	259	11.566	22.393	23.910	

Example:
TMA

Example:
CMA

Source: Data were collected by statistics student Andrew Fincher for his 11-year-old Pontiac Bonneville 3.8L V6.

FIGURE 14.19	Three-Period Moving Average of MPG

Centered Moving Average (*CMA*)

Another moving average is the **centered moving average** (*CMA*). Formula 14.11 shows a *CMA* for *m* = 3 periods. The formula looks both forward *and* backward in time, to express the current "forecast" as the mean of the current observation *and* observations on either side of the current data.

$$\hat{y}_t = \frac{y_{t-1} + y_t + y_{t+1}}{3} \qquad \text{(centered moving average over } m \text{ periods)} \qquad (14.11)$$

This is not really a forecast at all, but merely a way of smoothing the data. In Table 14.11, column seven shows the *CMA* for Andrew's MPG data. For example, for period 14 (blue-shaded cells), the *CMA* is

$$\hat{y}_t = \frac{24.198 + 24.505 + 19.210}{3} = 22.638$$

When n is odd ($m = 3$, 5, etc.), the CMA is easy to calculate. When m is even, the formula is more complex because the mean of an even number of data points would lie *between* two data points and would not be correctly centered. Instead, we take a double moving average (yipe!) to get the resulting CMA centered properly. For example, for $m = 4$, we would average y_{t-2} through y_{t+1}, then average y_{t-1} through y_{t+2}, and finally average the two averages! You need not worry about this formula for now. It will be illustrated shortly in the context of seasonal data.

Using Excel for a TMA

Excel offers a TMA in its Add Trendline option when you click on a time-series line graph or bar chart. Its menus are displayed in Figure 14.20. The TMA is a conservative choice whenever you doubt that one of Excel's five other trend models (linear, logarithmic, polynomial, power, exponential) would be appropriate. However, Excel does *not* give you the option of making any forecasts with its moving average model.

FIGURE 14.20

Excel's Moving Average Menus

SECTION EXERCISE

connect

14.6 (a) Make an Excel line graph of the exchange rate data. Describe the pattern. (b) Click on the data and choose Add Trendline > Moving Average. Describe the effect of increasing m (e.g., $m = 2$, 4, 6, etc.). Include a copy of each graph with your answer. (c) Discuss how this moving average might help a currency speculator. **DollarEuro**

Daily Dollar/Euro Exchange Rate for First 3 Months of 2005 ($n = 64$ days)							
Date	Rate	Date	Rate	Date	Rate	Date	Rate
3-Jan	1.3476	25-Jan	1.2954	16-Feb	1.2994	10-Mar	1.3409
4-Jan	1.3295	26-Jan	1.3081	17-Feb	1.3083	11-Mar	1.3465
5-Jan	1.3292	27-Jan	1.3032	18-Feb	1.3075	14-Mar	1.3346
6-Jan	1.3187	28-Jan	1.3033	21-Feb	1.3153	15-Mar	1.3315
7-Jan	1.3062	31-Jan	1.3049	22-Feb	1.3230	16-Mar	1.3423
10-Jan	1.3109	1-Feb	1.3017	23-Feb	1.3208	17-Mar	1.3373
11-Jan	1.3161	2-Feb	1.3015	24-Feb	1.3205	18-Mar	1.3311
12-Jan	1.3281	3-Feb	1.2959	25-Feb	1.3195	21-Mar	1.3165
13-Jan	1.3207	4-Feb	1.2927	28-Feb	1.3274	22-Mar	1.3210
14-Jan	1.3106	7-Feb	1.2773	1-Mar	1.3189	23-Mar	1.3005
17-Jan	1.3075	8-Feb	1.2783	2-Mar	1.3127	24-Mar	1.2957
18-Jan	1.3043	9-Feb	1.2797	3-Mar	1.3130	25-Mar	1.2954
19-Jan	1.3036	10-Feb	1.2882	4-Mar	1.3244	28-Mar	1.2877
20-Jan	1.2959	11-Feb	1.2864	7-Mar	1.3203	29-Mar	1.2913
21-Jan	1.3049	14-Feb	1.2981	8-Mar	1.3342	30-Mar	1.2944
24-Jan	1.3041	15-Feb	1.2986	9-Mar	1.3384	31-Mar	1.2969

Source: www.federalreserve.gov.

14.5 EXPONENTIAL SMOOTHING

Forecast Updating

The *exponential smoothing* model is a special kind of moving average. It is used for on-going one-period-ahead forecasting for data that has up-and-down movements but no consistent trend. For example, a retail outlet may place orders for thousands of different stock-keeping units (SKUs) each week, so as to maintain its inventory of each item at the desired level (to avoid emergency calls to warehouses or suppliers). For such forecasts, many firms choose exponential smoothing, a simple forecasting model with only two inputs and one constant. The updating formula for the forecasts is

$$F_{t+1} = \alpha y_t + (1 - \alpha)F_t \quad \text{(smoothing update)} \qquad (14.12)$$

where

F_{t+1} = the forecast for the next period

α = the "smoothing constant" $(0 \leq \alpha \leq 1)$

y_t = the actual data value in period t

F_t = the previous forecast for period t

Smoothing Constant (α)

The next forecast F_{t+1} is a weighted average of y_t (the current data) and F_t (the previous forecast). The value of α, called the **smoothing constant**, is the weight given to the latest data. A small value of α would give low weight to the most recent observation and heavy weight $1 - \alpha$ to the previous forecast (a "heavily smoothed" series). The larger the value of α, the more quickly the forecasts adapt to recent data. For example,

If $\alpha = .05$, then $F_{t+1} = .05y_t + .95F_t$ (heavy smoothing, slow adaptation)

If $\alpha = .20$, then $F_{t+1} = .20y_t + .80F_t$ (moderate smoothing, moderate adaptation)

If $\alpha = .50$, then $F_{t+1} = .50y_t + .50F_t$ (little smoothing, quick adaptation)

Choosing the Value of α

If $\alpha = 1$, there is no smoothing at all, and the forecast for next period is the same as the latest data point, which basically defeats the purpose of exponential smoothing. MINITAB uses $\alpha = .20$ (i.e., moderate smoothing) as its default, which is a fairly common choice of α. The fit of the forecasts to the data will change as you try different values of α. Most computer packages can, as an option, solve for the "best" α using a criterion such as minimum *SSE*.

Over time, earlier data values have less effect on the exponential smoothing forecasts than more recent y-values. To see this, we can replace F_t in formula 14.12 with the prior forecast F_{t-1}, and repeat this type of substitution indefinitely to obtain this result:

$$F_{t+1} = \alpha y_t + \alpha(1 - \alpha)y_{t-1} + \alpha(1 - \alpha)^2 y_{t-2} + \alpha(1 - \alpha)^3 y_{t-3} + \cdots \qquad (14.13)$$

We see that the next forecast F_{t+1} depends on *all* the prior data (y_{t-1}, y_{t-2}, etc). As long as $\alpha < 1$, as we go farther into the past, each prior data value has less and less impact on the current forecast.

Initializing the Process

From formula 14.12, we see that F_{t+1} depends on F_t, which in turn depends on F_{t-1}, and so on, all the way back to F_1. But where do we get F_1 (the initial forecast)? There are many ways to initialize the forecasting process. For example, Excel simply sets the initial forecast equal to the first actual data value:

Method *A*

Set $F_1 = y_1$ (use the first data value)

This method has the advantage of simplicity, but if y_1 happens to be unusual, it could take a few iterations for the forecasts to stabilize. Another approach is to set the initial forecast equal to the average of the first several observed data values. For example, MINITAB uses the first six data values:

Method *B*

Set $F_1 = \dfrac{y_1 + y_2 + y_3 + y_4 + y_5 + y_6}{n}$ (average of first 6 data values)

This method tends to iron out the effects of unusual *y*-values, but it consumes more data and is still vulnerable to unusual *y*-values.

Method *C*

Set F_1 = prediction from *backcasting* (backward extrapolation)

You may think of this method as fitting a trend to the data *in reverse time order* and extrapolating the trend to "predict" the initial value in the series. This method is common because it tends to generate a more appropriate initial forecast F_1. However, backcasting requires special software, so it will not be discussed here.

EXAMPLE 14.4

Weekly Sales Data

Table 14.12 shows weekly sales of deck sealer (a paint product sold in gallon containers) at a large do-it-yourself warehouse-style retailer. For exponential smoothing forecasts, the company uses $\alpha = .10$. Its choice of α is based on experience. Because α is fairly small, it will provide strong smoothing. The last two columns compare the two methods of initializing the forecasts. Unusually high sales in week 5 have a strong effect on method *B*'s starting point. At first, the difference in forecasts is striking, but over time the methods converge.

TABLE 14.12   **Deck Sealer Sales: Exponential Smoothing ($n = 18$ weeks)**
  🖅 DeckSealer

Week	Sales in Gallons	Method A: $F_1 = y_1$	Method B: F_1 = Average (1st 6)
1	106	106.000	127.833
2	110	106.000	125.650
3	108	106.400	124.085
4	97	106.560	122.477
5	210	105.604	119.929
6	136	116.044	128.936
7	128	118.039	129.642
8	134	119.035	129.478
9	107	120.532	129.930
10	123	119.179	127.637
11	139	119.561	127.174
12	140	121.505	128.356
13	144	123.354	129.521
14	94	125.419	130.969
15	108	122.277	127.272
16	168	120.849	125.344
17	179	125.564	129.610
18	120	130.908	134.549

Smoothed forecasts using $\alpha = .10$.

Using Method A:

$F_2 = \alpha y_1 + (1 - \alpha)F_1 = (.10)(106) + (.90)(106) = 106$
$F_3 = \alpha y_2 + (1 - \alpha)F_2 = (.10)(110) + (.90)(106) = 106.4$
$F_4 = \alpha y_3 + (1 - \alpha)F_3 = (.10)(108) + (.90)(106.4) = 106.56$

$\vdots$

$F_{19} = \alpha y_{18} + (1 - \alpha)F_{18} = (.10)(120) + (.90)(130.908) = 129.82$

Using Method B:

$$F_2 = \alpha y_1 + (1-\alpha)F_1 = (.10)(106) + (.90)(127.833) = 125.650$$
$$F_3 = \alpha y_2 + (1-\alpha)F_2 = (.10)(110) + (.90)(125.650) = 124.085$$
$$F_4 = \alpha y_3 + (1-\alpha)F_3 = (.10)(108) + (.90)(124.085) = 122.477$$
$$\vdots$$
$$F_{19} = \alpha y_{18} + (1-\alpha)F_{18} = (.10)(120) + (.90)(134.549) = 133.094$$

Despite their different starting points, the forecasts for period 19 do not differ greatly. Rounding to the next higher integer, for week 19, the firm would order 130 gallons (using method *A*) or 134 gallons (using method *B*). Figures 14.21 and 14.22 show the similarity in *patterns* of the forecasts, although the *level* of forecasts is always higher in method *B* because of its higher initial value. This demonstrates that the choice of starting values *does* affect the forecasts.

FIGURE 14.21   **Using the First *y*-Value**

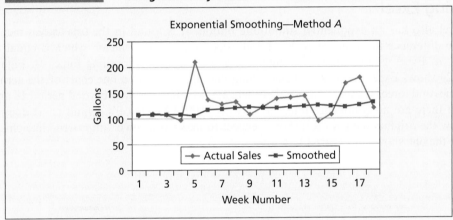

FIGURE 14.22   **Averaging the First Six *y*-Values**

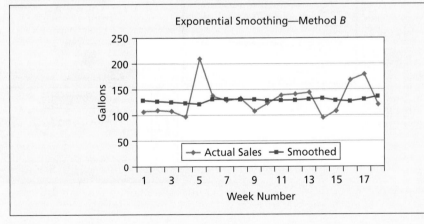

Using MINITAB

Figure 14.23 shows MINITAB's single exponential smoothing and 4 weeks' forecasts. After week 18, the exponential smoothing method cannot be updated with actual data, so the forecasts are constant. The wide 95 percent confidence intervals reflect the rather erratic past sales pattern.

FIGURE 14.23

MINITAB's Exponential Smoothing

Using Excel

Excel also has an exponential smoothing option. It is found in the Data Analysis menu. One difference to be noted is that Excel asks for a *damping factor,* which is equal to $1 - \alpha$. Excel uses method A to initialize the exponential smoothing forecasts. Figure 14.24 shows Excel's exponential smoothing dialogue box and a line chart of the actual values and forecast values. Notice that there are no forecast values beyond period 18 and that there are no confidence intervals as with MINITAB. Excel's default chart doesn't show the original data, so you should expect to make your own "improved" line chart, like the one shown in Figure 14.24.

FIGURE 14.24

Excel's Exponential Smoothing

Smoothing with Trend and Seasonality

Single exponential smoothing is intended for *trendless* data. If your data have a trend, you can try *Holt's method* with *two* smoothing constants (one for *trend,* one for *level*). If you have both trend and seasonality, you can try *Winters's method* with *three* smoothing constants (one for *trend,* one for *level,* one for *seasonality*). These advanced methods are similar to single smoothing in that they use simple formulas to update the forecasts, and you may use them without special caution. These topics are usually reserved for a class in forecasting, so they will not be explained here.

Mini Case   14.2

Exchange Rates

We have data for March 1 to March 30 and want to forecast 1 day ahead to March 31 by using exponential smoothing. We choose a smoothing constant value of $\alpha = .20$ and set the initial forecast F_1 to the average of the first six data values. Table 14.13 shows the actual data (y_t) and MINITAB's forecasts (F_t) for each date. The March 31 forecast is $F_{23} = \alpha y_{22} + (1 - \alpha)F_{22} = (.20)(1.2164) + (.80)(1.21395) = 1.2144.$

TABLE 14.13		Exchange Rate Canada/U.S. Dollar 🐃 Canada		
t	**Date**	**Actual** y_t	**Forecast** F_t	**Error** $e_t = y_t - F_t$
1	1-Mar-05	1.2425	1.23450	0.0080
2	2-Mar-05	1.2395	1.23610	0.0034
3	3-Mar-05	1.2463	1.23678	0.0095
4	4-Mar-05	1.2324	1.23868	−0.0063
5	7-Mar-05	1.2300	1.23743	−0.0074
6	8-Mar-05	1.2163	1.23594	−0.0196
7	9-Mar-05	1.2064	1.23201	−0.0256
8	10-Mar-05	1.2050	1.22689	−0.0219
9	11-Mar-05	1.2041	1.22251	−0.0184
10	14-Mar-05	1.2087	1.21883	−0.0101
11	15-Mar-05	1.2064	1.21680	−0.0104
12	16-Mar-05	1.2038	1.21472	−0.0109
13	17-Mar-05	1.2028	1.21254	−0.0097
14	18-Mar-05	1.2027	1.21059	−0.0079
15	21-Mar-05	1.2110	1.20901	0.0020
16	22-Mar-05	1.2017	1.20941	−0.0077
17	23-Mar-05	1.2133	1.20787	0.0054
18	24-Mar-05	1.2150	1.20895	0.0061
19	25-Mar-05	1.2180	1.21016	0.0078
20	28-Mar-05	1.2234	1.21173	0.0117
21	29-Mar-05	1.2135	1.21406	−0.0006
22	30-Mar-05	1.2164	1.21395	0.0024
23	31-Mar-05		1.21444	

Source: Data from www.federalreserve.gov.

The column of errors (e_t) shown in Table 14.13 is used to calculate the measures of fit (e.g., *MAPE, MAD, MSE*) as shown on the spreadsheet 🐃 **Canada**. The resulting measures of fit are displayed in Figure 14.25 along with the MINITAB plot of the data and forecasts. The forecasts adapt, but always with a lag. The actual exchange rate on March 31 was 1.2094, slightly lower than the forecast, but well within the 95 percent prediction limits.

FIGURE 14.25   MINITAB's Exponential Smoothing ($\alpha = .20$)

SECTION EXERCISE

14.7 (a) Make an Excel line graph of the following bond yield data. Describe the pattern. Is there a consistent trend? (b) Use exponential smoothing (MegaStat, MINITAB, or Excel) with $\alpha = .20$. Use both methods A and B to initialize the forecast (the default in both MegaStat and MINITAB). (c) Record the statistics of fit. (MegaStat uses MSE and MSD; MINITAB uses MSD and $MAPE$. With Excel you will have to calculate these by creating cell formulas.) (d) Do the smoothing again with $\alpha = .10$ and then with $\alpha = .30$, recording the statistics of fit. (e) Compare the statistics of fit for the three values of α. (f) Make a one-period forecast (i.e., $t = 53$) using each of the three α values. How did α affect your forecasts? 📄 **BondYield**

U.S. Treasury 10-Year Bond Yields at Week's End ($n = 52$ weeks)							
Week	**Yield**	**Week**	**Yield**	**Week**	**Yield**	**Week**	**Yield**
4/2/04	3.95	7/2/04	4.63	10/1/04	4.10	12/31/04	4.29
4/9/04	4.21	7/9/04	4.49	10/8/04	4.20	1/7/05	4.28
4/16/04	4.36	7/16/04	4.47	10/15/04	4.08	1/14/05	4.25
4/23/04	4.43	7/23/04	4.46	10/22/04	4.03	1/21/05	4.19
4/30/04	4.49	7/30/04	4.56	10/29/04	4.05	1/28/05	4.19
5/7/04	4.62	8/6/04	4.41	11/5/04	4.12	2/4/05	4.14
5/14/04	4.81	8/13/04	4.28	11/12/04	4.22	2/11/05	4.06
5/21/04	4.74	8/20/04	4.23	11/19/04	4.17	2/18/05	4.16
5/28/04	4.68	8/27/04	4.25	11/26/04	4.20	2/25/05	4.28
6/4/04	4.74	9/3/04	4.19	12/3/04	4.35	3/4/05	4.37
6/11/04	4.80	9/10/04	4.21	12/10/04	4.19	3/11/05	4.45
6/18/04	4.75	9/17/04	4.14	12/17/04	4.16	3/18/05	4.51
6/25/04	4.69	9/24/04	4.04	12/24/04	4.21	3/25/05	4.59

Source: www.federalreserve.gov.

14.6 SEASONALITY

When and How to Deseasonalize

LO 14-7

Use software to deseasonalize a time series.

When the data periodicity is monthly or quarterly, we should calculate a seasonal index and use it to **deseasonalize** the data (annual data have no seasonality). For a multiplicative model (the usual assumption), a seasonal index is a *ratio*. For example, if the seasonal index for July is 1.25, it means that July is 125 percent of the monthly average. If the seasonal index for January is 0.84, it means that January is 84 percent of the monthly average. If the seasonal index for October is 1.00, it means that October is an average month. The seasonal indexes must sum to 12 for monthly data or 4 for quarterly data. The following steps are used to deseasonalize data for time-series observations:

- Step 1   Calculate a centered moving average (CMA) for each month (quarter).
- Step 2   Divide each observed y_t value by the CMA to obtain seasonal ratios.
- Step 3   Average the seasonal ratios by month (quarter) to get raw seasonal indexes.
- Step 4   Adjust the raw seasonal indexes so they sum to 12 (monthly) or 4 (quarterly).
- Step 5   Divide each y_t by its seasonal index to get deseasonalized data.

In step 1, we lose 12 observations (monthly data) or 4 observations (quarterly data) because of the centering process. We will illustrate this technique for quarterly data.

Illustration of Calculations

Table 14.14 shows 6 years' data on quarterly revenue from sales of carpeting, tile, wood, and vinyl flooring by a floor-covering retailer. The data have an upward trend (see Figure 14.26), perhaps due to a boom in consumer spending on home improvement and new homes. There also appears to be seasonality, with lower sales in the third quarter (summer) and higher sales in the first quarter (winter).

The seasonal decomposition of these data is shown in Table 14.15 and Figure 14.26. Calculations are handled automatically by MegaStat so it's actually easy to perform the

Quarter	2006	2007	2008	2009	2010	2011
1	259	306	379	369	515	626
2	236	300	262	373	373	535
3	164	189	242	255	339	397
4	222	275	296	374	519	488

TABLE 14.14

Sales of Floor Covering Materials ($ thousands)
📁 **FloorSales**

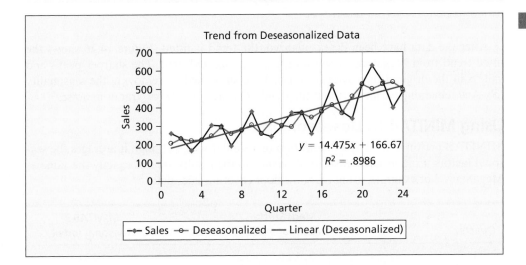

FIGURE 14.26

MegaStat's Deseasonalized Trend

decomposition. Because the number of subperiods (quarters) is even ($m = 4$), each value of the *CMA* is the average of two averages. For example, the first *CMA* value 226.125 is the average of $(259 + 236 + 164 + 222)/4$ and $(236 + 164 + 222 + 306)/4$. Table 14.16 shows how the indexes are averaged. The *CMA* loses two quarters at the beginning and two quarters at the end, so each seasonal index is an average of only five quarters (instead of six). Each mean is then adjusted to force the sum to be 4.000, and these become the seasonal indexes. If we had monthly data, the indexes would be adjusted so that their sum would be 12.000.

Obs	Year	Quarter	Sales	CMA	Sales/CMA	Seasonal Index	Deseasonalized
1	2006	1	259			1.252	206.9
2		2	236			1.021	231.1
3		3	164	*226.125*	0.725	0.740	221.7
4		4	222	240.000	0.925	0.987	224.9
5	2007	1	306	251.125	1.219	1.252	244.4
6		2	300	260.875	1.150	1.021	293.8
7		3	189	276.625	0.683	0.740	255.5
8		4	275	281.000	0.979	0.987	278.6
9	2008	1	379	282.875	1.340	1.252	302.7
10		2	262	292.125	0.897	1.021	256.6
11		3	242	293.500	0.825	0.740	327.2
12		4	296	306.125	0.967	0.987	299.8
13	2009	1	369	321.625	1.147	1.252	294.7
14		2	373	333.000	1.120	1.021	365.3
15		3	255	361.000	0.706	0.740	344.7
16		4	374	379.250	0.986	0.987	378.8
17	2010	1	515	389.750	1.321	1.252	411.3
18		2	373	418.375	0.892	1.021	365.3
19		3	339	450.375	0.753	0.740	458.3
20		4	519	484.500	1.071	0.987	525.7
21	2011	1	626	512.000	1.223	1.252	500.0
22		2	535	515.375	1.038	1.021	524.0
23		3	397			0.740	536.7
24		4	488			0.987	494.3

TABLE 14.15

Calculation of Deseasonalized Sales ($n = 24$ quarters)
📁 **FloorSales**

TABLE 14.16

Calculation of Seasonal Indexes
🖫 **FloorSales**

Quarter	2006	2007	2008	2009	2010	2011	Mean	Adjusted
1		1.219	1.340	1.147	1.321	1.223	1.250	1.252
2		1.150	0.897	1.120	0.892	1.038	1.019	1.021
3	0.725	0.683	0.825	0.706	0.753		0.738	0.740
4	0.925	0.979	0.967	0.986	1.071		0.986	0.987
							3.993	4.000

Due to rounding, details may not yield the result shown.

After the data have been deseasonalized, the trend is fitted. Figure 14.26 shows the fitted trend from MegaStat, based on the deseasonalized data. The sharper peaks and valleys in the original time series (Y) have been smoothed by removing the seasonality (S). Any remaining variation about the trend (T) is irregular (I) or "random noise."

Using MINITAB to Deseasonalize

LO 14-7

Use software to deseasonalize a time series.

MINITAB performs its deseasonalization in a similar way, although it averages the seasonal factors using *medians* instead of *means,* so the results are not exactly the same as MegaStat's. For example, using the same floor covering sales data:

Quarter	MegaStat's Seasonal Index	MINITAB's Seasonal Index
1	1.252	1.234
2	1.021	1.047
3	0.740	0.732
4	0.987	0.987
Sum	4.000	4.000
Fitted trend	$y_t = 166.67 + 14.475t$	$y_t = 166.62 + 14.483t$

MINITAB offers nice graphical displays for decomposition, as well as forecasts, as shown in Figure 14.27. MINITAB also offers additive as well as multiplicative seasonality. In an additive model, the *CMA* is calculated in the same way, but the raw seasonals are *differences* (instead of ratios) and the seasonal indexes are forced to sum to *zero* (e.g., months with higher sales must exactly balance months with lower sales). Most analysts prefer multiplicative models (assuming trended data), so the additive model is not discussed in detail here.

FIGURE 14.27

MINITAB's Graphs for Floor Covering Sales

Seasonal Forecasts Using Binary Predictors

Another way to address seasonality is to estimate a regression model using **seasonal binaries** as predictors. For quarterly data, for example, the data set would look as shown in Table 14.17. When we have four binaries (i.e., four quarters), we must exclude one binary to prevent perfect multicollinearity (see Chapter 13, Section 13.5). Arbitrarily, we exclude the fourth quarter binary *Qtr4* (it will be a portion of the intercept when $Qtr1 = 0$ and $Qtr2 = 0$ and $Qtr3 = 0$).

Year	Quarter	Sales	Time	Qtr1	Qtr2	Qtr3
2006	1	259	1	1	0	0
	2	236	2	0	1	0
	3	164	3	0	0	1
	4	222	4	0	0	0
2007	1	306	5	1	0	0
	2	300	6	0	1	0
	3	189	7	0	0	1
	4	275	8	0	0	0
2008	1	379	9	1	0	0
	2	262	10	0	1	0
	3	242	11	0	0	1
	4	296	12	0	0	0
2009	1	369	13	1	0	0
	2	373	14	0	1	0
	3	255	15	0	0	1
	4	374	16	0	0	0
2010	1	515	17	1	0	0
	2	373	18	0	1	0
	3	339	19	0	0	1
	4	519	20	0	0	0
2011	1	626	21	1	0	0
	2	535	22	0	1	0
	3	397	23	0	0	1
	4	488	24	0	0	0

TABLE 14.17

Sales Data with Seasonal Binaries
📁 **FloorSales**

LO 14-8

Use regression with seasonal binaries to make forecasts.

We assume a linear trend, and specify the regression model *Sales* = *f*(*Time, Qtr1, Qtr2, Qtr3*). MINITAB's estimated regression is shown in Figure 14.28. This is an additive model of the form $Y = T + S + I$ (recall that we omit the cycle C in practice). The fitted equation is

$$Sales = 161 + 14.4 \ Time + 89.8 \ Qtr1 + 12.9 \ Qtr2 - 83.6 \ Qtr3$$

FIGURE 14.28

MINITAB's Fitted Regression for Seasonal Binaries

```
The regression equation is
Sales = 161 + 14.4 Time + 89.8 Qtr1 + 12.9 Qtr2 − 83.6 Qtr3

Predictor        Coef        SE Coef          T           P
Constant        161.21        24.33         6.62       0.000
Time             14.366        1.244        11.55       0.000
Qtr1             89.76        24.32         3.69        0.002
Qtr2             12.90        24.16         0.53        0.600
Qtr3            −83.63        24.07        −3.47        0.003

S = 41.6313        R-Sq = 90.0%          R-Sq(adj) = 87.9%
```

Time is a significant predictor ($p = .000$), indicating significant linear trend. Two of the binaries are significant: *Qtr1* ($p = .002$) and *Qtr3* ($p = .003$). The second quarter binary *Qtr2* ($p = .600$) is not significant. The model gives a good overall fit ($R^2 = .90$). The main virtue of the seasonal regression model is its versatility. We can plug in future values of *Time* and the seasonal binaries to create forecasts as far ahead as we wish. For example, the forecasts for 2006 are

Period 25: Sales = $161 + 14.4(25) + 89.8(1) + 12.9(0) - 83.6(0) = 610.8$

Period 26: Sales = $161 + 14.4(26) + 89.8(0) + 12.9(1) - 83.6(0) = 548.3$

Period 27: Sales = $161 + 14.4(27) + 89.8(0) + 12.9(0) - 83.6(1) = 466.2$

Period 28: Sales = $161 + 14.4(28) + 89.8(0) + 12.9(0) - 83.6(0) = 564.2$

SECTION EXERCISES

connect

14.8 (a) Use MegaStat or MINITAB to deseasonalize the quarterly data on PepsiCo's revenues and fit a trend. Interpret the results. (b) Use MegaStat or MINITAB to perform a regression using seasonal binaries. Interpret the results. (c) Use the regression equation to make a prediction for each quarter in 2011. (d) If you have access to http://finance.yahoo.com, check your forecasts. How accurate were they? ☞ **PepsiCo**

PepsiCo Revenues ($ millions), 2005–2010

Quarter	2005	2006	2007	2008	2009	2010
Qtr1	6,585	7,205	7,350	8,333	8,263	9,368
Qtr2	7,697	8,599	9,607	10,945	10,592	14,801
Qtr3	8,184	8,950	10,171	11,244	11,080	15,514
Qtr4	10,096	10,383	12,346	12,729	13,297	18,155

Source: *Standard & Poor's Stock Reports,* March 2007, http://finance.yahoo.com, and mergentonline.com.

14.9 (a) Use MegaStat or MINITAB to deseasonalize the monthly Corvette sales data and fit a trend. Interpret the results. (b) Use MegaStat or MINITAB to perform a regression using seasonal binaries. Interpret the results. (c) Use the regression equation to make a prediction for each month in 2008. (d) If you have access to *Ward's Automotive Yearbook,* check your forecasts. How accurate were they? ☞ **Corvette**

U.S. Corvette Sales, 2004–2007 (number of cars sold)

Month	2004	2005	2006	2007
Jan	2,986	2,382	2,579	2,234
Feb	2,382	2,365	3,058	2,784
Mar	3,033	3,215	3,655	3,158
Apr	3,169	3,177	3,516	3,227
May	3,420	3,078	3,317	3,300
Jun	3,398	2,417	2,938	3,055
Jul	3,492	1,872	2,794	2,377
Aug	2,067	2,202	2,990	2,877
Sep	3,705	2,372	3,056	2,837
Oct	2,607	2,981	2,761	2,484
Nov	2,120	3,157	2,773	2,438
Dec	2,897	3,271	3,081	2,914
Total	35,276	32,489	36,518	33,685

Source: *Ward's Automotive Yearbook, 2005–2008.*

Mini Case

Using Seasonal Binaries 📁 Beer

Figure 14.29 shows monthly U.S. shipments of bottled beer for 2001–2006. A strong seasonal pattern is evident, presumably because people drink more beer in the warmer months. How can we describe the pattern statistically?

FIGURE 14.29   **U.S. Bottled Beer Shipments, 2001–2006**

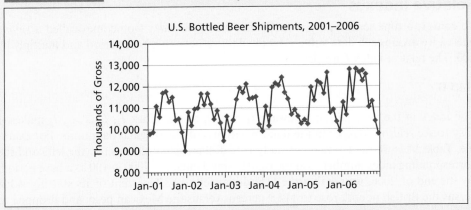

Source: www.census.gov.

We create a regression data set with linear trend (Time = 1, 2, . . . , 72) and 11 seasonal binaries (Feb–Dec). The January binary is omitted to prevent perfect multicollinearity. The regression results, shown in Figure 14.30, indicate a good fit (R^2 = .857), significant upward trend (p = 0.000 for Time), and several seasonal binaries that differ significantly from zero (p-values near zero). Binary predictor coefficients indicate that shipments are above the January average during the spring and summer (Mar–Aug), below the January average in the winter (Nov–Feb), and near the January average in the fall (Sep–Oct). The fitted regression equation can be used to forecast any future months' shipments.

FIGURE 14.30   **MINITAB's Fitted Regression for Seasonal Binaries**

The regression equation is
Beer = 10164 + 16.9 Time − 484 Feb + 768 Mar + 579 Apr
   + 1311 May + 1182 Jun + 975 Jul + 892 Aug − 99 Sep
   + 107 Oct − 644 Nov − 1089 Dec

Predictor	Coef	SE Coef	T	P
Constant	10163.7	161.4	62.97	0.000
Time	16.9	2.1	8.11	0.000
Feb	−483.9	209.2	−2.31	0.024
Mar	767.5	209.2	3.67	0.001
Apr	579.0	209.3	2.77	0.008
May	1310.7	209.3	6.26	0.000
Jun	1182.0	209.4	5.64	0.000
Jul	975.3	209.5	4.65	0.000
Aug	892.2	209.7	4.26	0.000
Sep	−99.3	209.8	−0.47	0.638
Oct	106.9	210.0	0.51	0.613
Nov	−644.1	210.2	−3.06	0.003
Dec	−1089.0	210.4	−5.18	0.000

S = 362.302 R-Sq = 85.7%   R-Sq (adj) = 82.8%

LO 14-8

Use regression with seasonal binaries to make forecasts.

14.7 INDEX NUMBERS

A simple way to measure changes over time (and especially to compare two or more variables) is to convert time-series data into **index numbers**. The idea is to create an index that starts at 100 in a *base period,* so we can see *relative changes* in the data regardless of the original data units. Indexes are most often used for financial data (e.g., prices, wages, costs) but can be used with any numerical data (e.g., number of units sold, warranty claims, computer spam).

Relative Indexes

LO 14-9

Interpret index numbers.

To convert a time series $y_1, y_2, \ldots, y_n$ into a *relative index* (sometimes called a *simple index*), we divide each data value y_t by the data value y_1 in a base period and multiply by 100. The relative index I_t for period t is

(14.14)
$$I_t = 100 \times \frac{y_t}{y_1}$$

The index in the base period is always $I_1 = 100$, so the index $I_1, I_2, \ldots, I_n$ makes it easy to see *relative changes* in the data, regardless of the original data units. For example, Table 14.18 shows six-years of daily U.S. dollar exchange rates (on the left) and the corresponding index numbers (on the right) using January 3, 2000 = 100 as a base period. By the end of 2006, we see that the U.S. dollar fell to 83.1 percent of its starting value versus the British pound, rose to 114.9 percent versus the Mexican peso, and dropped to 80.6 percent versus the Canadian dollar.

TABLE 14.18

U.S. Foreign Exchange Rates, 2000–2006
📄 Currency

Date	Foreign Currency per Dollar			Index Numbers (Jan 3, 2000 = 100)		
	U.K.	Mexico	Canada	U.K.	Mexico	Canada
3-Jan-00	0.61463	9.4015	1.4465	100.0	100.0	100.0
4-Jan-00	0.61087	9.4570	1.4518	99.4	100.6	100.4
5-Jan-00	0.60920	9.5350	1.4518	99.1	101.4	100.4
⋮	⋮	⋮	⋮	⋮	⋮	⋮
27-Dec-06	0.51109	10.8820	1.1610	83.2	115.7	80.3
28-Dec-06	0.50966	10.8740	1.1599	82.9	115.7	80.2
29-Dec-06	0.51057	10.7995	1.1652	83.1	114.9	80.6

Source: www.federalreserve.gov.

A graph like Figure 14.31 allows us to display seven years (1,759 days) of data. Since each index starts at the same point (100), we can easily see the fluctuations and trends. We could fit a moving average, if we wanted to smooth the data. Speculators who engage in currency arbitrage would use even more-sophisticated tools to analyze movements in currency indexes.

FIGURE 14.31

U.S. Foreign Exchange Rates, 2000–2006
📄 Currency

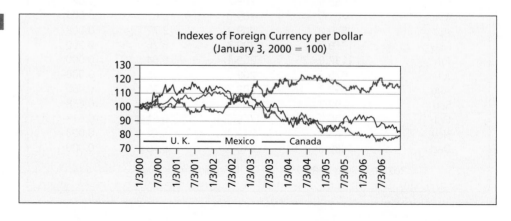

Weighted Indexes

A different calculation is required for a *weighted index* such as the Consumer Price Index for all urban consumers (CPI-U). The CPI-U is a measure of the relative prices paid by urban consumers for a market basket of goods and services, based on prices of hundreds of goods and services in eight major groups. The goal is to make the CPI-U representative of the prices paid for all goods and services purchased by all urban consumers. This requires assigning weights to each consumer good or service to reflect its importance relative to all the other goods and services in the market basket (e.g., housing gets a higher weight because it is a larger proportion of total spending). The basic formula for a simple weighted price index is

$$I_t = 100 \times \frac{\sum_{i=1}^{m} p_{it}q_i}{\sum_{i=1}^{m} p_{i1}q_i} = 100 \times \frac{p_{1t}q_1 + p_{2t}q_2 + \cdots + p_{mt}q_m}{p_{11}q_1 + p_{21}q_2 + \cdots + p_{m1}q_m} \qquad \textbf{(14.15)}$$

where
I_t = weighted index for period t ($t = 1, 2, \ldots, n$)
p_{it} = price of good i in period t ($t = 1, 2, \ldots, n$)
q_i = weight assigned to good i ($i = 1, 2, \ldots m$)

The numerator is the cost of buying a given market basket of goods and services at today's prices (period t) relative to the cost of the same market basket in the base period (period 1). The weight q_i represents the relative quantity of the item in the consumer's budget. For example, suppose there is a price increase of 5 percent for food and beverages and a 10 percent increase for medical care costs, with no price changes for the other expenditure categories. This would result in an increase of 1.4 percent in the CPI, as shown in Table 14.19.

TABLE 14.19	**Illustrative Calculation of Price Index**						
	Base Year ($t = 1$)			**Current Year ($t = 2$)**			
Expenditure Category	**Weight (q_i)**	**Relative Price (p_{i1})**	**Relative Spending ($p_{i1}q_i$)**	**Weight (q_i)**	**Relative Price (p_{i2})**	**Relative Spending ($p_{i2}q_i$)**	
Food and beverages	15.7 ×	1.00 =	15.7	15.7 ×	1.05 =	16.5	
Housing	40.9 ×	1.00 =	40.9	40.9 ×	1.00 =	40.9	
Apparel	4.4 ×	1.00 =	4.4	4.4 ×	1.00 =	4.4	
Transportation	17.1 ×	1.00 =	17.1	17.1 ×	1.00 =	17.1	
Medical care	5.8 ×	1.00 =	5.8	5.8 ×	1.10 =	6.4	
Recreation	6.0 ×	1.00 =	6.0	6.0 ×	1.00 =	6.0	
Education/communication	5.8 ×	1.00 =	5.8	5.8 ×	1.00 =	5.8	
Other goods and services	4.3 ×	1.00 =	4.3	4.3 ×	1.00 =	4.3	
Sum	100.0	$\sum_{i=1}^{n} p_{i1}q_i$ =	100.0	100.0	$\sum_{i=1}^{n} p_{i2}q_i$ =	101.4	

From Table 14.19, the price index rose from 100.0 to 101.4, or a 1.4 percent increase:

$$I_2 = 100 \times \frac{\sum_{i=1}^{n} p_{i2}q_i}{\sum_{i=1}^{n} p_{i1}q_i} = 100 \times \frac{101.4}{100.0} = 101.4$$

Formula (14.15) is called a *Laspeyres index.* It treats the base year quantity weights as constant. Weights are based on the *Survey of Consumer Expenditures.* In your economics classes, you may learn more sophisticated methods that take into account the fact that expenditure weights do change over time. One such method is the *Paasche index,* which uses a formula similar to the Laspeyres index, except that quantity weights are adjusted for each period.

Importance of Index Numbers

The CPI affects nearly all Americans because it is used to adjust things like retirement benefits, food stamps, school lunch benefits, alimony, and tax brackets. The CPI-U could be compared with an index of salary growth for workers, or to measure current-dollar salaries in "real dollars." The Bureau of Labor Statistics (www.bls.gov) publishes CPI historical statistics for each of the eight categories shown in Table 14.19. The most widely used CPI-U uses 1982–84 as a reference. That is, the Bureau of Labor Statistics sets the CPI-U (the average price level) for the 36-month period covering the years 1982, 1983, and 1984 equal to 100, and then measures changes in relation to that figure. As of May 2007, for example, the CPI-U was 207.9, meaning that, on average, prices had slightly more than doubled over the previous 25 years (about a 3.1 percent annual increase, applying the geometric mean formula 4.6 with $n = 25$). The CPI is based on the buying habits of the "average" consumer, so it may not be a perfect reflection of anyone's individual price experience.

Other familiar price indexes, such as the Dow Jones Industrial Average (DJIA), have their own unique methodologies. Originally a simple arithmetic mean of stock prices, the DJIA now is the sum of the 30 stock prices divided by a "divisor" to compensate for stock splits and other changes over time. The divisor is revised periodically. Because high-priced stocks comprise a larger proportion of the sum, the DJIA is more strongly affected by changes in high-priced stocks. A little web research can tell you a lot about how stock price indexes are calculated, their strengths and weaknesses, and some alternative indexes that finance experts have invented.

14.8 FORECASTING: FINAL THOUGHTS

Role of Forecasting

In many ways, forecasting resembles planning. *Forecasting* is an analytical way to describe a "what-if" future that might confront the organization. *Planning* is the organization's attempt to determine actions it will take under each foreseeable contingency. Forecasts help decision makers become aware of trends or patterns that require a response. Actions taken by the decision makers may actually head off the contingency envisioned in the forecast. Thus, forecasts tend to be self-defeating because they trigger homeostatic organizational responses.

Behavioral Aspects of Forecasting

Forecasts can facilitate organizational communication. The forecast (or even just a nicely prepared time-series chart) lets everyone examine the same facts concurrently, and perhaps argue with the data or the assumptions that underlie the forecast or its relevance to the organization. A quantitative forecast helps *make assumptions explicit*. Those who prepare the forecast must explain and defend their assumptions, while others must challenge them. In the process, everyone gains understanding of the data, the underlying realities, and the imperfections in the data. Forecasts *focus the dialogue* and can make it more productive.

Of course, this assumes a certain maturity among the individuals around the table. Strong leaders (or possibly meeting facilitators) can play a role in guiding the discourse to produce a positive result. The danger is that people may try to find scapegoats (yes, they do tend to blame the forecaster), deny facts, or avoid responsibility for tough decisions. But one premise of this book is that statistics, when done well, can strengthen any dialogue and lead to better decisions.

Forecasts Are Always Wrong

We discussed several measures to use to determine if a forecast model fits the time series. Successful forecasters understand that a forecast is never precise. There is always some error, but we can *use* the error measures to track forecast error. Many companies use several different forecasting models and rely on the model that has had the least error over some time period.

We have described simple models in this chapter. You may take a class specifically focusing on forecasting in which you will learn about other time-series models including AR (autoregressive) and ARIMA (autoregressive integrated moving average) models. Such models take advantage of the dependency that might exist between values in the time series. To ensure good forecast outcomes

- Maintain up-to-date databases of *relevant* data.
- Allow sufficient lead time to analyze the data.
- State several alternative forecasts or scenarios.
- Track forecast errors over time.
- State your assumptions and qualifications and consider your time horizon.
- Don't underestimate the power of a good graph.

Mini Case 14.4

How Does Noodles & Company Ensure Its Ingredients Are as Fresh as Possible?

Using only fresh ingredients is key for great food and success for restaurants like Noodles & Company. To be sure that the restaurants are serving only the freshest ingredients, while also reducing food waste, Noodles & Company turned to statistical forecasting for ordering ingredients and daily food preparation. The challenge was to create a forecast that is sophisticated enough to be accurate, yet simple enough for new restaurant employees to understand.

Noodles & Company uses a food management software system to forecast the demand for its menu items based on the moving average of the previous four weeks' sales. This simple forecasting technique has been very accurate. The automated process also uses the forecast of each item to estimate how many ingredients to order as well as how much to prepare each day. For example, the system might forecast that during next Wednesday's lunch, the location in Longmont, Colorado, will sell 55 Pesto Cavatappi's. After forecasting the demand for each menu item, the system then specifies exactly how much of each ingredient to prepare for that lunch period.

For the restaurant teams, the old manual process of estimating and guessing how much of each ingredient to prepare is now replaced with an automated prep sheet. Noodles & Company has reduced food waste because restaurants are less likely to overorder ingredients and overprepare menu items. The restaurant teams are more efficient and customers are served meals made with the freshest ingredients possible.

CHAPTER SUMMARY

A **time series** is assumed to have four components. For most business data, **trend** is the general pattern of change over all years observed while **cycle** is a repetitive pattern of change around the trend over several years and **seasonality** is a repetitive pattern within a year. The **irregular** component is a random disturbance that follows no pattern. The **additive model** is adequate in the short run because the four components' magnitude does not change much, but for observations over longer periods of time, the **multiplicative model** is preferred. Common trend models include **linear** (constant slope and no turning point), **quadratic** (one turning point), and **exponential** (constant percent growth or decline). Higher polynomial models are untrustworthy and liable to give strange forecasts, though any trend model is less reliable the farther out it is projected. In forecasting, forecasters use fit measures besides R^2, such as mean absolute percent error (*MAPE*), mean absolute deviation (*MAD*), and mean squared deviation (*MSD*). For trendless or erratic data, we use a **moving average** over m periods or **exponential smoothing**. Forecasts adapt rapidly to changing data when the **smoothing constant** α is large (near 1) and conversely for a small α (near 0). For monthly or quarterly data, a **seasonal adjustment** is required before extracting the trend. Alternatively, regression with **seasonal binaries** can be used to capture seasonality and make forecasts. **Index numbers** are used to show changes relative to a base period.

KEY TERMS

centered moving average
  (*CMA*), *621*
coefficient of
  determination, *618*
cycle, *605*
deseasonalize, *628*
exponential smoothing, *605*
exponential trend, *608*
index numbers, *634*
irregular, *605*

linear trend, *606*
Mean Absolute Deviation
  (*MAD*), *618*
Mean Absolute Percent Error
  (*MAPE*), *618*
Mean Squared Deviation
  (*MSD*), *618*
moving average, *605*
Occam's Razor, *614*
periodicity, *602*

polynomial model, *613*
quadratic trend, *611*
seasonal, *605*
seasonal binaries, *631*
smoothing constant, *623*
standard error (SE), *618*
time-series variable, *601*
trailing moving average
  (*TMA*), *620*
trend, *604*

Commonly Used Formulas

Additive time-series model: $Y = T + C + S + I$

Multiplicative time-series model: $Y = T \times C \times S \times I$

Linear trend model: $y_t = a + bt$

Exponential trend model: $y_t = ae^{bt}$

Quadratic trend model: $y_t = a + bt + ct^2$

Coefficient of determination: $R^2 = 1 - \dfrac{\sum\limits_{t=1}^{n}(y_t - \hat{y}_t)^2}{\sum\limits_{t=1}^{n}(y_t - \bar{y})^2}$

Mean absolute percent error: $MAPE = \dfrac{100}{n}\sum\limits_{t=1}^{n}\dfrac{|y_t - \hat{y}_t|}{y_t}$

Mean absolute deviation: $MAD = \dfrac{1}{n}\sum\limits_{t=1}^{n}|y_t - \hat{y}_t|$

Mean squared deviation: $MSD = \dfrac{1}{n}\sum\limits_{t=1}^{n}(y_t - \hat{y}_t)^2$

Standard error: $SE = \sqrt{\sum\limits_{t=1}^{n}\dfrac{(y_t - \hat{y}_t)^2}{n - 2}}$

Forecast updating equation for exponential smoothing: $F_{t+1} = \alpha y_t + (1 - \alpha)F_t$

CHAPTER REVIEW

1. Explain the difference between (a) stocks and flows; (b) cross-sectional and time-series data; (c) additive and multiplicative models.

2. (a) What is periodicity? (b) Give original examples of data with different periodicity.

3. (a) What are the distinguishing features of each component of a time series (trend, cycle, seasonal, irregular)? (b) Why is cycle usually ignored in time-series modeling?

4. Name four criteria for assessing a trend forecast.

5. Name two advantages and two disadvantages of each of the common trend models (linear, exponential, quadratic).

6. When would the exponential trend model be preferred to a linear trend model?

7. Explain how to obtain the compound percent growth rate from a fitted exponential model.

8. (a) When might a quadratic model be useful? (b) What precautions must be taken when forecasting with a quadratic model? (c) Why are higher-order polynomial models dangerous?

9. Name five measures of fit for a trend, and state their advantages and disadvantages.

10. (a) When do we use a moving average? (b) Name two types of moving averages. (c) When is a centered moving average harder to calculate?

11. (a) When is exponential smoothing most useful? (b) Interpret the smoothing constant α. What is its range? (c) What does a small α say about the degree of smoothing? A large α?

12. (a) Explain two ways to initialize the forecasts in an exponential smoothing process. (b) Name an advantage and a disadvantage of each method.

13. (a) Why is seasonality irrelevant for annual data? (b) List the steps in deseasonalizing a monthly time series. (c) What is the sum of a monthly seasonal index? A quarterly index?

14. (a) How can forecasting improve communication within an organization? (b) List five tips for ensuring effective forecasting outcomes.

15. (a) Explain how seasonal binaries can be used to model seasonal data. (b) What is the advantage of using seasonal binaries?

16. Explain the equivalency between the two forms of an exponential trend model.

17. What is the purpose of index numbers?

CHAPTER EXERCISES

connect

Instructions: For each exercise, use Excel, MegaStat, or MINITAB to make an attractive, well-labeled time-series line chart. Adjust the Y-axis scale if necessary to show more detail (because Excel usually starts the scale at zero). If a fitted trend is called for, use Excel's option to display the equation and R^2 statistic (or *MAPE, MAD,* and *MSD* in MINITAB). Include printed copies of all relevant graphs with your answers to each exercise. Exercises marked with * are based on harder material.

14.10 (a) Make a line chart for JetBlue's revenue. (b) Describe the trend (if any) and discuss possible causes. (c) Fit both a linear and an exponential trend to the data. (d) Which model is preferred? Why? (e) Make annual forecasts for 2011–2013, using a trend model of your choice (or a judgment forecast). 📁 **JetBlue**

JetBlue Airlines Revenue, 2003–2010 (millions)

Year	Revenue	Year	Revenue
2003	998	2007	2,843
2004	1,265	2008	3,392
2005	1,701	2009	3,292
2006	2,361	2010	3,779

Sources: *Standard & Poor's Stock Reports,* February 2007; http://finance.yahoo.com; and http://money.msn.com. Data are for December 31 of each year.

14.11 (a) Plot both Swiss watch time series on the same graph. (b) Describe the trend (if any) and discuss possible causes. (c) Fit an exponential trend to each time series. (d) Interpret each fitted trend carefully. What conclusion do you draw? (e) Make forecasts for the next 3 years, using the linear trend model. Why might 2009 have been unusual? Explain. 📁 **Swiss**

Swiss Watch Exports (thousands of units), 2005–2010

Year	Mechanical	Electronic
2005	3,368	20,996
2006	3,757	21,109
2007	4,213	21,679
2008	4,316	21,784
2009	3,737	17,956
2010	4,938	21,177

Source: Fédération de L'Industrie Horlogère Suisse, Swiss Watch Exports, www.fhs.ch/en/statistics.php.

14.12 (a) Plot the total minutes of TV viewing time per household. (b) Describe the trend (if any) and discuss possible causes. (c) Fit a linear trend to the data. (d) Would this model give reasonable forecasts? Would another trend model be better? Explain. (e) Make a forecast for 2015. Show the forecast calculations. (f) Would these data ever approach an asymptote? Explain. *Note:* Time is in 5-year increments, so use $t = 14$ for the 2015 forecast. 📁 **Television**

Average Daily TV Viewing Time Per U.S. Household

Year	Hours	Min	Total Min
1950	4	35	275
1955	4	51	291
1960	5	6	306
1965	5	29	329
1970	5	56	356
1975	6	7	367
1980	6	36	396
1985	7	10	430
1990	6	53	413
1995	7	17	437
2000	7	35	455
2005	8	11	491
2010	8	21	501

Source: As published by the TVB based on Nielsen Media Research data. Used with permission. Latest year is preliminary from http://blog.nielsen.com.

14.13 (a) Plot the voter participation rate. (b) Describe the trend (if any) and discuss possible causes. (c) Fit both a linear and a quadratic trend to the data. (d) Which model is preferred? Why? (e) Make a forecast for 2012, using a trend model of your choice (or a judgment forecast). (f) If possible, check the web for the actual 2012 voter participation rate. How close was your forecast? *Note:* Time is in 4-year increments, so use $t = 16$ for the 2012 forecast. 🗗 **Voters**

U.S. Presidential Election Voter Participation, 1952–2008

Year	Voting Age Population	Voted for President	% Voting Pres
1952	99,929	61,551	61.6
1956	104,515	62,027	59.3
1960	109,672	68,838	62.8
1964	114,090	70,645	61.9
1968	120,285	73,212	60.9
1972	140,777	77,719	55.2
1976	152,308	81,556	53.5
1980	163,945	86,515	52.8
1984	173,995	92,653	53.3
1988	181,956	91,595	50.3
1992	189,524	104,425	55.1
1996	196,928	96,278	49.0
2000	207,884	105,397	50.7
2004	220,377	122,349	55.5
2008	229,945	131,407	57.1

Source: *Statistical Abstract of the United States, 2011,* www.census.gov. Voters are in thousands.

14.14 For each of the following fitted trends, make a prediction for period $t = 17$:

a. $y_t = 2286 \, e^{.076t}$

b. $y_t = 1149 + 12.78t$

c. $y_t = 501 + 18.2t - 7.1t^2$

14.15 (a) Choose *one* category of consumer credit and plot it. (b) Describe the trend (if any) and discuss possible causes. (c) Fit a trend model of your choice. (d) Make forecasts for 3 years (2011–2013), using a trend model of your choice. *Note:* Revolving credit is mostly credit card and home equity loans, while nonrevolving credit is for a specific purchase such as a car. 🗗 **Consumer**

Consumer Credit Outstanding, 2000–2010 ($ billions)

Year	Total	Revolving	Nonrevolving
2000	1,722	683	1,039
2001	1,872	716	1,155
2002	1,984	749	1,235
2003	2,088	771	1,317
2004	2,202	801	1,401
2005	2,296	827	1,469
2006	2,385	871	1,514
2007	2,522	942	1,580
2008	2,561	958	1,604
2009	2,449	866	1,584
2010	2,403	796	1,607

Source: *Economic Report of the President,* 2011.

14.16 (a) Plot the data on U.S. general aviation shipments. (b) Describe the pattern and discuss possible causes. (c) Would a fitted trend be helpful? Explain. (d) Make a similar graph for 1993–2008 only. Would a fitted trend be helpful in making a prediction for 2009? (e) Fit a trend model of your choice to the 1993–2008 data. (f) Make a forecast for 2009, using either a fitted trend model or a judgment forecast. (g) Might it be best to ignore earlier years in this data set? 📄 **Airplanes**

U.S. Manufactured General Aviation Shipments, 1977–2008

Year	Planes	Year	Planes	Year	Planes	Year	Planes
1977	16,904	1985	2,029	1993	964	2001	2,634
1978	17,811	1986	1,495	1994	928	2002	2,207
1979	17,048	1987	1,085	1995	1,077	2003	2,137
1980	11,877	1988	1,212	1996	1,115	2004	2,355
1981	9,457	1989	1,535	1997	1,549	2005	2,857
1982	4,266	1990	1,144	1998	2,200	2006	3,147
1983	2,691	1991	1,021	1999	2,504	2007	3,279
1984	2,431	1992	941	2000	2,816	2008	3,079

Source: U.S. Manufactured General Aviation Shipments, *Statistical Databook 2008,* General Aviation Manufacturers Association, used with permission.

14.17 (a) Choose *one* beverage category and plot the data. (b) Describe the trend (if any) and discuss possible causes. (c) Would a fitted trend be helpful? Explain. (d) Fit several trend models. Which is best, and why? If none is satisfactory, explain. (e) Make forecasts for 2010 and 2015, using a trend model of your choice or a judgment forecast. Discuss. *Note:* Time increments are 5 years, so use $t = 7$ and $t = 8$ for your forecasts. 📄 **Beverages**

U.S. Per Capita Annual Consumption of Selected Beverages (gallons)

Beverage	1980	1985	1990	1995	2000	2005
Milk	27.6	26.7	25.7	23.9	22.5	21.0
Whole	17.0	14.3	10.5	8.6	8.1	7.0
Reduced-fat	10.5	12.3	15.2	15.3	14.4	14.1
Fruit juices	7.4	7.8	7.8	8.3	8.7	8.1
Alcoholic	28.3	28.0	27.5	24.7	24.9	25.2
Beer	24.3	23.8	23.9	21.8	21.7	21.5
Wine	2.1	2.4	2.0	1.7	2.0	2.3
Distilled spirits	2.0	1.8	1.5	1.2	1.3	1.4

Source: *Statistical Abstract of the United States, 2011.*

14.18 (a) Plot *either* receipts and outlays *or* federal debt and GDP (plot both time series on the same graph). (b) Describe the trend (if any) and discuss possible causes. (c) Fit a trend of your choice to each. (d) Interpret each fitted trend equation, explaining its implications. (e) To whom is this issue relevant? ☞ **FedBudget**

U.S. Federal Finances, 2000–2011 ($ billions current)

Year	Receipts	Outlays	Federal Debt	GDP
2000	2,025	1,789	5,629	9,821
2001	1,991	1,863	5,770	10,225
2002	1,853	2,011	6,198	10,544
2003	1,782	2,160	6,760	10,980
2004	1,880	2,293	7,355	11,686
2005	2,154	2,472	7,905	12,446
2006	2,407	2,655	8,451	13,225
2007	2,568	2,729	8,951	13,892
2008	2,524	2,983	9,986	14,394
2009	2,105	3,518	11,876	14,098
2010	2,163	3,456	13,529	14,508
2011	2,174	3,819	15,476	15,080

Source: *Economic Report of the President, 2011.*

14.19 (a) Plot both men's and women's winning times on the same graph. (b) Fit a linear trend model to each series. From the fitted trends, will the times eventually converge? *Hint:* Ask Excel for forecasts (e.g., 20 years ahead). (c) Make a copy of your graph, and click each fitted trend and change it to a moving average trend type. (d) Would a moving average be a reasonable approach to modeling these data sets? *Note:* The data file ☞ **Boston** has the data converted to decimal minutes.

Boston Marathon Champions, 1980–2011

	Men			Women	
Year	Name of Winner	Time	Year	Name of Winner	Time
1980	Bill Rodgers	2:12:11	1980	Jacqueline Gareau	2:34:28
1981	Toshihiko Seko	2:09:26	1981	Allison Roe	2:26:46
1982	Alberto Salazar	2:08:52	1982	Charlotte Teske	2:29:33
⋮	⋮	⋮	⋮	⋮	⋮
2009	Deriba Merga	2:08:42	2009	Salina Kosgei	2:23:16
2010	Robert Cheruiyot	2:05:52	2010	Teyba Erkesso	2:26:11
2011	Geoffrey Mutai	2:03:02	2011	Caroline Kilel	2:22:36

Source: www.wikipedia.org.

14.20 (a) Plot the data on leisure and hospitality employment. (b) Describe the trend (if any) and discuss possible causes. (c) Fit the linear and exponential trends. Would these trend models give credible forecasts? Explain. (d) Make a forecast for 2008, using any method (including your own judgment). ☞ **Leisure**

Leisure and Hospitality Employment, 1998–2007 (thousands)

Year	Employees	Year	Employees	Year	Employees	Year	Employees
1998	11,232	2001	12,032	2004	12,495	2006	13,139
1999	11,544	2002	11,986	2005	12,814	2007	13,448
2000	11,860	2003	12,173				

Source: http://data.bls.gov.

14.21 (a) Plot the data on law enforcement officers killed. (b) Describe the trend (if any) and discuss possible causes or anomalies in the data. (c) Would a fitted trend be helpful? Explain. (c) Make a forecast for 2009 using any method you like (including judgment). 📄 **LawOfficers**

U.S. Law Enforcement Officers Killed, 1994–2008

Year	Killed	Year	Killed	Year	Killed	Year	Killed
1994	141	1998	142	2002	132	2006	114
1995	133	1999	107	2003	133	2007	140
1996	113	2000	134	2004	139	2008	109
1997	133	2001	218	2005	122		

Source: *Statistical Abstract of the United States, 2011*, p. 207.

14.22 (a) Plot the data on lightning deaths. (b) Describe the trend (if any) and discuss possible causes. (c) Fit an exponential trend to the data. Interpret the fitted equation. (d) Make a forecast for 2015, using a trend model of your choice (or a judgment forecast). Explain the basis for your forecast. *Note:* Time is in 5-year increments, so use $t = 16$ for your 2015 forecast. 📄 **Lightning**

U.S. Lightning Deaths, 1940–2010

Year	Deaths	Year	Deaths	Year	Deaths	Year	Deaths
1940	340	1960	129	1980	74	2000	51
1945	268	1965	149	1985	74	2005	38
1950	219	1970	122	1990	74	2010	29
1955	181	1975	91	1995	85		

Sources: *Statistical Abstract of the United States, 2011*, p. 234, and www.nws.noaa.gov.

14.23 (a) Plot the data on skier/snowboard visits. (b) Would a fitted trend be helpful? Explain. (c) Make a forecast for 2007–2008, using a trend model of your choice (or a judgment forecast). 📄 **SnowBoards**

U.S. Skier/Snowboarder Visits, 1984–2007 (millions)

Season	Visits	Season	Visits	Season	Visits
1984–1985	51.354	1992–1993	54.032	2000–2001	57.337
1985–1986	51.921	1993–1994	54.637	2001–2002	54.411
1986–1987	53.749	1994–1995	52.677	2002–2003	57.594
1987–1988	53.908	1995–1996	53.983	2003–2004	57.067
1988–1989	53.335	1996–1997	52.520	2004–2005	56.882
1989–1990	50.020	1997–1998	54.122	2005–2006	58.897
1990–1991	46.722	1998–1999	52.089	2006–2007	55.068
1991–1992	50.835	1999–2000	52.198		

Source: www.nsaa.org/nsaa/press/industryStats.asp.

14.24 (a) Plot both men's and women's winning times on the same graph. (b) Fit a linear trend model to each series (men, women). (c) Use Excel's option to forecast each trend graphically to 2040 (i.e., to period $t = 27$ periods because observations are in 4-year increments). From these projections, does it appear that the times will eventually converge? *(d) Set the fitted trends equal, solve for x (the time period when the trends will cross), and convert x to a year. Is the result plausible? Explain. (e) If possible, use the web to check your 2012 forecast. 📄 **Olympic**

Summer Olympics 100-Meter Winning Times

Year	Men's 100-Meter Winner	Seconds	Women's 100-Meter Winner	Seconds
1928	Percy Williams, Canada	10.80	Elizabeth Robinson, United States	12.20
1932	Eddie Tolan, United States	10.30	Stella Walsh, Poland	11.90
1936	Jesse Owens, United States	10.30	Helen Stephens, United States	11.50
1948	Harrison Dillard, United States	10.30	Fanny Blankers-Koen, Netherlands	11.90
1952	Lindy Remigino, United States	10.40	Marjorie Jackson, United States	11.50
1956	Bobby Morrow, United States	10.50	Betty Cuthbert, Australia	11.50
1960	Armin Hary, West Germany	10.20	Wilma Rudolph, United States	11.00
1964	Bob Hayes, United States	10.00	Wyomia Tyus, United States	11.40
1968	Jim Hines, United States	9.95	Wyomia Tyus, United States	11.00
1972	Valery Borzov, USSR	10.14	Renate Stecher, East Germany	11.07
1976	Hasely Crawford, Trinidad	10.06	Annegret Richter, West Germany	11.08
1980	Allan Wells, Great Britain	10.25	Lyudmila Kondratyeva, USSR	11.06
1984	Carl Lewis, United States	9.99	Evelyn Ashford, United States	10.97
1988	Carl Lewis, United States	9.92	Florence Griffith-Joyner, United States	10.54
1992	Linford Christie, Great Britain	9.96	Gail Devers, United States	10.82
1996	Donovan Bailey, Canada	9.84	Gail Devers, United States	10.94
2000	Maurice Greene, United States	9.87	Marion Jones, United States	10.75
2004	Justin Gatlin, United States	9.85	Yulia Nestsiarenka, Belarus	10.93
2008	Usain Bolt, Jamaica	9.69	Shelly-Ann Fraser, Jamaica	10.78

Sources: *The World Almanac, 2002*, pp. 900–904, and www.wikipedia.org.

14.25 (a) Plot U.S. petroleum imports on a graph. (b) Describe the trend (if any) and discuss possible causes. (c) Fit both a linear and an exponential trend. (c) Interpret each fitted trend equation, explaining the implications. (d) Make a projection for 2010. Do you believe it? (e) To whom is this issue relevant? *Note:* Time increments are 5 years, so use $t = 11$ for the 2010 forecast. 🖰 **Petroleum**

U.S. Annual Petroleum Imports, 1960–2005 (billions of barrels)

Year	Imports	Year	Imports
1960	664	1985	1,850
1965	901	1990	2,926
1970	1,248	1995	3,225
1975	2,210	2000	4,194
1980	2,529	2005	4,937

Source: www.eia.doe.gov.

14.26 (a) Use Excel, MegaStat, or MINITAB to fit an m-period moving average to the exchange rate data shown below with $m = 2, 3, 4,$ and 5 periods. Make a line chart. (b) Which value of m do you prefer? Why? (c) Is a moving average appropriate for this kind of data? Include a chart for each value of m. 🖰 **Sterling**

Daily Spot Exchange Rate, U.S. Dollars per Pound Sterling

Date	Rate	Date	Rate	Date	Rate
1-Apr-04	1.8564	13-Apr-04	1.8160	23-Apr-04	1.7674
2-Apr-04	1.8293	14-Apr-04	1.7902	26-Apr-04	1.7857
5-Apr-04	1.8140	15-Apr-04	1.7785	27-Apr-04	1.7925
6-Apr-04	1.8374	16-Apr-04	1.8004	28-Apr-04	1.7720
7-Apr-04	1.8410	19-Apr-04	1.8055	29-Apr-04	1.7751
8-Apr-04	1.8325	20-Apr-04	1.7914	30-Apr-04	1.7744
9-Apr-04	1.8322	21-Apr-04	1.7720	3-May-04	1.7720
12-Apr-04	1.8358	22-Apr-04	1.7684	4-May-04	1.7907

(continued)

Date	Rate	Date	Rate	Date	Rate
5-May-04	1.7932	13-May-04	1.7584	21-May-04	1.7880
6-May-04	1.7941	14-May-04	1.7572	24-May-04	1.7908
7-May-04	1.7842	17-May-04	1.7695	25-May-04	1.8135
10-May-04	1.7723	18-May-04	1.7695	26-May-04	1.8142
11-May-04	1.7544	19-May-04	1.7827	27-May-04	1.8369
12-May-04	1.7743	20-May-04	1.7710	28-May-04	1.8330

Source: Federal Reserve Board of Governors.

14.27 Refer to exercise 14.26. (a) Plot the dollar/pound exchange rate data. Make the graph nice, then copy and paste it so you have four copies. (b) Use MegaStat or MINITAB to perform a simple exponential smoothing using $\alpha = .05, .10, .20,$ and $.50$, using a different line chart for each. (c) Which value of α do you prefer? Why? (d) Is an exponential smoothing process appropriate for this kind of data? ⬚ **Sterling**

14.28 (a) Plot the data on gas bills. (b) Can you see seasonal patterns? Explain. (c) Use MegaStat or MINITAB to calculate estimated seasonal indexes and trend. (d) Which months are the most expensive? The least expensive? Can you explain this pattern? (e) Is there a trend in the deseasonalized data? *(f) Use MegaStat or MINITAB to perform a regression using seasonal binaries. Interpret the results. ⬚ **GasBills**

Natural Gas Bills for a Residence, 2000–2003

Month	2000	2001	2002	2003
Jan	78.98	118.86	101.44	155.37
Feb	84.44	111.31	122.20	148.77
Mar	65.54	75.62	99.49	115.12
Apr	62.60	77.47	55.85	85.89
May	29.24	29.23	44.94	46.84
Jun	18.10	17.10	19.57	24.93
Jul	91.57	16.59	15.98	20.84
Aug	6.48	27.64	14.97	26.94
Sep	19.35	28.86	18.03	34.17
Oct	29.02	48.21	56.98	88.58
Nov	94.09	67.15	115.27	100.63
Dec	101.65	125.18	130.95	174.63

Source: Homeowner's records.

14.29 (a) Plot the data on air travel delays. (b) Can you see seasonal patterns? Explain. (c) Use MegaStat or MINITAB to calculate estimated seasonal indexes and trend. (d) Which months have the most delays? The fewest? Is this logical? (e) Is there a trend in the deseasonalized data? ⬚ **Delays**

U.S. Airspace Total System Delays, 2002–2006

Month	2002	2003	2004	2005	2006
Jan	14,158	16,159	28,104	32,121	29,463
Feb	13,821	18,260	32,274	30,176	24,705
Mar	20,020	25,387	34,001	34,633	37,218
Apr	24,027	17,474	32,459	25,887	35,132
May	28,533	26,544	50,800	30,920	40,669
Jun	33,770	27,413	52,121	48,922	48,096
Jul	32,304	32,833	46,894	58,471	47,606
Aug	29,056	37,066	43,770	45,328	46,547
Sep	24,493	28,882	30,412	32,949	48,092
Oct	25,266	21,422	37,271	34,221	51,053
Nov	17,712	34,116	35,234	34,273	43,482
Dec	22,489	31,332	32,446	29,766	39,797

Source: www.faa.gov.

14.30 (a) Plot the data on airplane shipments. (b) Can you see seasonal patterns? Explain. (c) Use MegaStat or MINITAB to calculate estimated seasonal indexes and trend. Is there a trend in the deseasonalized data? 🖜 **AirplanesQtr**

U.S. Manufactured General Aviation Shipments, 1995–2003

Year	Qtr 1	Qtr 2	Qtr 3	Qtr 4	Total
1995	208	248	257	315	1,077
1996	229	284	230	310	1,115
1997	253	337	367	525	1,549
1998	481	486	546	602	2,200
1999	502	611	606	702	2,504
2000	613	704	685	712	2,816
2001	568	711	586	673	2,632
2002	442	576	510	641	2,207
2003	393	526	492	679	2,137

Note: Quarterly shipments may not add to annual total because some manufacturers report only annual totals.

Source: U.S. Manufactured General Aviation Shipments, *Statistical Databook 2003,* General Aviation Manufacturers Association, used with permission.

14.31 (a) Plot the data on revolving credit (credit cards and home equity lines of credit are the two major types of revolving credit). (b) Use MegaStat or MINITAB to calculate seasonal indexes and trend. Is there a trend in the deseasonalized data? (c) Which months have the most borrowing? The least? Is this logical? (d) Discuss anything unusual in the shape of the trend that might make forecasting difficult. 🖜 **Revolving**

U.S. Consumers Revolving Credit (billions)

Month	2005	2006	2007	2008	2009	2010
Jan	816	844	885	962	969	868
Feb	804	834	876	953	943	845
Mar	794	826	873	947	923	828
Apr	803	832	879	952	917	820
May	802	840	889	954	910	819
Jun	808	840	896	960	905	817
Jul	808	843	902	966	904	816
Aug	816	853	916	974	902	816
Sep	819	856	920	973	893	807
Oct	820	859	930	969	887	803
Nov	833	876	947	975	884	808
Dec	857	900	973	989	894	827

Source: www.federalreserve.gov.

14.32 (a) Use MegaStat or MINITAB to deseasonalize the quarterly data on Coca-Cola's revenues and fit a trend. Interpret the results. (b) Use MegaStat or MINITAB to perform a regression using seasonal binaries. Interpret the results. (c) Use the regression equation to make a prediction for each quarter in 2011. (d) If you have access to http://finance.yahoo.com, check your forecasts. How accurate were they? 🖜 **CocaCola**

Coca-Cola Revenues ($ millions), 2005–2010

Quarter	2005	2006	2007	2008	2009	2010
Qtr1	5,206	5,226	6,103	7,379	7,169	7,525
Qtr2	6,310	6,476	7,733	9,046	8,267	8,674
Qtr3	6,037	6,454	7,690	8,393	8,044	8,426
Qtr4	5,551	5,932	7,331	7,126	7,510	10,494

Sources: *Standard & Poor's Stock Reports,* March 2007; http://finance.yahoo.com; and mergentonline.com.

14.33 (a) Use MegaStat or MINITAB to perform a regression using seasonal binaries. Interpret the results. (b) Make monthly forecasts for 2010. If you can find data on the web, check your forecasts. 📁 **StudentPilots**

Student Pilot Certificates Issued by Month, 2004–2009

Month	2004	2005	2006	2007	2008	2009
Jan	4,747	4,248	4,489	5,343	5,628	4,466
Feb	4,317	3,824	3,951	4,701	4,752	4,347
Mar	4,853	4,687	4,605	5,523	4,944	4,414
Apr	4,616	4,486	4,375	5,162	5,061	4,402
May	4,613	4,706	5,217	6,094	5,363	4,736
Jun	5,485	5,509	6,050	6,401	5,956	5,231
Jul	6,130	5,306	5,684	6,525	6,265	5,470
Aug	6,145	6,284	7,203	7,541	6,127	5,739
Sep	5,524	4,698	6,064	5,795	5,163	4,807
Oct	4,800	3,985	5,437	5,473	4,977	4,218
Nov	4,353	3,443	4,468	4,583	3,554	3,423
Dec	2,779	2,400	3,905	3,812	3,404	3,623

Source: www.faa.gov/data_statistics/aviation_data_statistics.

RELATED READING

Diebold, Francis X. *Elements of Forecasting*. 4th ed. South-Western, 2007.

Hanke, John E., and Dean W. Wichern. *Business Forecasting*. 8th ed. Prentice-Hall, 2005.

Makridakis, Spyros; Steven C. Wheelwright; and Rob J. Hyndman. *Forecasting: Methods and Applications*. 4th ed. Wiley, 2006.

Wilson, J. Holton, and Barry Keating. *Business Forecasting*. 4th ed. Irwin, 2002.

CHAPTER 14 Online Learning Resources

The Online Learning Center (OLC) at www.mhhe.com/doane4e has several *LearningStats* demonstrations to help you understand time-series analysis. Your instructor may assign one or more of them, or you may decide to download the ones that sound interesting.

Topic	LearningStats Demonstrations
Trends and forecasting	🅖 Trend Forecasting 🅧 Measures of Fit 🅧 Exponential Trend Formula
Simulations	🅧 Time-Series Components 🅧 Trend Simulator 🅧 Seasonal Time-Series Generator
Exponential Smoothing	🅖 Advanced Forecasting Methods 🅧 Single Exponential Smoothing 🅧 Brown's Double Smoothing 🅧 Holt-Winters Seasonal Smoothing
ARIMA Models	🅟 ARIMA Terminology 🅧 ARIMA Patterns 🅧 ARIMA Calculations 🅧 Seasonal ARIMA

Key: 🅖 = PowerPoint   🅧 = Excel   🅟 = Adobe PDF

Chi-Square Tests

CHAPTER CONTENTS

CHAPTER LEARNING OBJECTIVES

LO

When you finish this chapter you should be able to

LO 15-1 Recognize a contingency table.

LO 15-2 Find degrees of freedom and use the chi-square table of critical values.

LO 15-3 Perform a chi-square test for independence on a contingency table.

LO 15-4 Perform a goodness-of-fit (GOF) test for a uniform distribution.

LO 15-5 Explain the GOF test for a Poisson distribution.

LO 15-6 Use computer software to perform a chi-square GOF test for normality.

LO 15-7 State advantages of ECDF tests as compared to chi-square GOF tests.

15.1 CHI-SQUARE TEST FOR INDEPENDENCE

Not all information pertaining to business can be summarized numerically. We are often interested in answers to questions such as: Do employees in different age groups choose different types of health plans? Do consumers prefer red, yellow, or blue package lettering on our bread bags? Does the name of our new lawn mower influence how we perceive the quality? Answers to questions such as these are not measurements on a numerical scale. Rather, the variables that we are interested in learning about may be *categorical* or *ordinal*. Health plans are categorized by the way services are paid, so the variable *health plan* might have four different categories: Catastrophic, HMO (health maintenance organization), POS (point of service), and CDHP (consumer-driven health plan). The variable *package lettering color* would have categories red, yellow, and blue, and the variable *perceived quality* might have categories excellent, satisfactory, and poor.

We can collect observations on these variables to answer the types of questions posed either by surveying our customers and employees or by conducting carefully designed experiments. Once our data have been collected, we summarize by tallying response frequencies on a table that we call a *contingency table*. A **contingency table** is a cross-tabulation of *n* paired observations into categories. Each cell shows the count of observations that fall into the category defined by its row and column heading.

As online shopping has grown, opportunity has also grown for personal data collection and invasion of privacy. Mainstream online retailers have policies known as "privacy disclaimers" that define the rules regarding their uses of information collected, the customer's right to refuse third-party promotional offers, and so on. You can access these policies through a web link, found either on the website's home page, on the order page (i.e., as you enter your credit card information), on a client web page, or on some other web page. In the United States, such links are voluntary, while in the European Union (EU) they are mandated by law. Location of the privacy disclaimer is considered to be a measure of the degree of consumer protection (the farther the link is from the home page, the less likely it is to be noticed). Marketing researchers did a survey of 291 websites in three nations (France, U.K., U.S.) and obtained the *contingency table* shown here as Table 15.1. Is location of the privacy disclaimer *independent* of the website's nationality? This question can be answered by using a test based on the frequencies in this contingency table.

EXAMPLE 15.1

Web Pages (4 × 3 Table)

| TABLE 15.1 | Privacy Disclaimer Location and Website Nationality | 🖰 WebSites |

| Location of Disclaimer | Nationality of Website | | | Row Total |
	France	U.K.	U.S.	
Home page	56	68	35	159
Order page	19	19	28	66
Client page	6	10	16	32
Other page	12	9	13	34
Col Total	93	106	92	291

Source: Calin Gurau, Ashok Ranchhod, and Claire Gauzente, "To Legislate or Not to Legislate: A Comparative Exploratory Study of Privacy/Personalisation Factors Affecting French, UK, and US Web Sites," *Journal of Consumer Marketing* 20, no. 7 (2003), p. 659. Used with permission, Emerald Group Publishing Limited.

LO 15-1

Recognize a contingency table.

Table 15.2 illustrates the terminology of a contingency table. Variable A has r levels (rows) and variable B has c levels (columns), so we call this an $r \times c$ contingency table. Each cell shows the observed frequency f_{jk} in row j and column k.

TABLE 15.2

Table of Observed Frequencies

| Variable A | Variable B | | | | Row Total |
	1	2	...	c	
1	f_{11}	f_{12}	...	f_{1c}	R_1
2	f_{21}	f_{22}	...	f_{2c}	R_2
:	:	:	:	:	:
r	f_{r1}	f_{r2}	...	f_{rc}	R_r
Col Total	C_1	C_2	...	C_c	n

LO 15-3

Perform a chi-square test for independence on a contingency table.

Chi-Square Test

In a test of independence for an $r \times c$ contingency table, the hypotheses are:

H_0: Variable A is independent of variable B

H_1: Variable A is not independent of variable B

To test these hypotheses, we use the **chi-square test** *for independence,* developed by Karl Pearson (1857–1936). It is a test based on *frequencies*. It measures the association between the two variables A and B in the contingency table. The chi-square test for independence is called a *distribution-free test* because it requires no assumptions about the shape of the populations from which the samples are drawn. The only operation performed is classifying the n data pairs into r rows (variable A) and c columns (variable B), and then comparing the **observed frequency** f_{jk} in each cell of the contingency table with the **expected frequency** e_{jk} under the assumption of independence. The chi-square test statistic measures the *relative* difference between expected and observed frequencies:

(15.1)
$$\chi^2_{calc} = \sum_{j=1}^{r} \sum_{k=1}^{c} \frac{[f_{jk} - e_{jk}]^2}{e_{jk}}$$

If the two variables are **independent**, then f_{jk} should be close to e_{jk}, leading to a chi-square test statistic near zero. Conversely, large differences between f_{jk} and e_{jk} will lead to a large chi-square test statistic. The chi-square test statistic cannot be negative (due to squaring) so it is always a right-tailed test. If the test statistic is far enough in the right tail, we will reject the hypothesis of independence. Squaring each difference removes the sign, so it doesn't matter whether e_{jk} is greater than or less than f_{jk}. Each squared difference is expressed *relative to* e_{jk}.

Chi-Square Distribution

The test statistic is compared with a critical value from the **chi-square probability distribution**. It has one parameter called **degrees of freedom**. For the $r \times c$ contingency table, the degrees of freedom are:

$$d.f. = \text{degrees of freedom} = (r - 1)(c - 1) \qquad \textbf{(15.2)}$$

where

r = the number of rows in the contingency table

c = the number of columns in the contingency table

The parameter $d.f.$ is the number of nonredundant cells in the contingency table. There is a different chi-square distribution for each value of $d.f.$ Appendix E contains critical values for right-tail areas of the chi-square distribution. Its mean is $d.f.$ and its variance is $2 d.f.$ As illustrated in Figure 15.1, all chi-square distributions are skewed to the right, but become more symmetric as $d.f.$ increases. For $d.f. = 1$, the distribution is discontinuous at the origin. As $d.f.$ increases, the shape begins to resemble a normal, bell-shaped curve. However, for any contingency table you are likely to encounter, degrees of freedom will not be large enough to assume normality.

> **LO 15-2**
>
> Find degrees of freedom and use the chi-square table of critical values.

FIGURE 15.1
Various Chi-Square Distributions

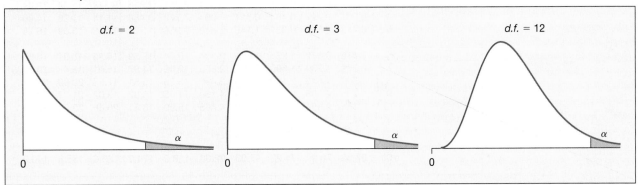

Expected Frequencies

Assuming that H_0 is true, the expected frequency of row j and column k is

$$e_{jk} = R_j C_k / n \qquad \text{(expected frequency in row } j \text{ and column } k) \qquad \textbf{(15.3)}$$

where

R_j = total for row j ($j = 1, 2, \ldots, r$)

C_k = total for column k ($k = 1, 2, \ldots, c$)

n = sample size (or number of responses)

This formula for expected frequencies stems from the definition of independent events (see Chapter 5). When two events are independent, their *joint* probability is the product of their marginal probabilities, so for a cell in row j and column k, the joint probability would be $(R_j/n)(C_k/n)$. To get the expected cell frequency, we multiply this joint probability by the sample size n to obtain $e_{jk} = R_j C_k / n$. The e_{jk} always sum to the same row and column frequencies as the observed frequencies. Expected frequencies will not, in general, be integers.

Illustration of the Chi-Square Calculations

We will illustrate the chi-square test by using the web page frequencies from the contingency table (Table 15.1). We follow the usual five-step hypothesis testing procedure:

Step 1: State the Hypotheses   For the web page example, the hypotheses are:

H_0: Privacy disclaimer location is independent of website nationality

H_1: Privacy disclaimer location is dependent on website nationality

Step 2: Specify the Decision Rule   For the web page contingency table, we have $r = 4$ rows and $c = 3$ columns, so degrees of freedom are $d.f. = (r - 1)(c - 1) = (4 - 1)(3 - 1) = 6$. We will choose $\alpha = .05$ for the test. Figure 15.2 shows that the right-tail critical value from Appendix E with $d.f. = 6$ is $\chi^2_{.05} = 12.59$. This critical value could also be obtained from Excel using =CHISQ.INV.RT(.05,6) = 12.59159.

FIGURE 15.2

Critical Value of
Chi-Square from
Appendix E for $d.f. = 6$
and $\alpha = .05$

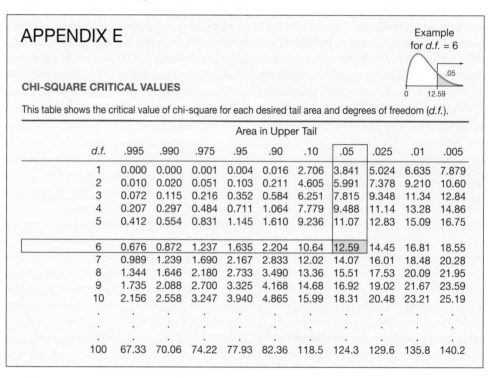

APPENDIX E

Example
for $d.f. = 6$

.05

0   12.59

CHI-SQUARE CRITICAL VALUES

This table shows the critical value of chi-square for each desired tail area and degrees of freedom ($d.f.$).

				Area in Upper Tail						
$d.f.$	.995	.990	.975	.95	.90	.10	.05	.025	.01	.005
1	0.000	0.000	0.001	0.004	0.016	2.706	3.841	5.024	6.635	7.879
2	0.010	0.020	0.051	0.103	0.211	4.605	5.991	7.378	9.210	10.60
3	0.072	0.115	0.216	0.352	0.584	6.251	7.815	9.348	11.34	12.84
4	0.207	0.297	0.484	0.711	1.064	7.779	9.488	11.14	13.28	14.86
5	0.412	0.554	0.831	1.145	1.610	9.236	11.07	12.83	15.09	16.75
6	0.676	0.872	1.237	1.635	2.204	10.64	12.59	14.45	16.81	18.55
7	0.989	1.239	1.690	2.167	2.833	12.02	14.07	16.01	18.48	20.28
8	1.344	1.646	2.180	2.733	3.490	13.36	15.51	17.53	20.09	21.95
9	1.735	2.088	2.700	3.325	4.168	14.68	16.92	19.02	21.67	23.59
10	2.156	2.558	3.247	3.940	4.865	15.99	18.31	20.48	23.21	25.19
.	.	.	.	.	.	.	.	.	.	.
.	.	.	.	.	.	.	.	.	.	.
.	.	.	.	.	.	.	.	.	.	.
100	67.33	70.06	74.22	77.93	82.36	118.5	124.3	129.6	135.8	140.2

For $\alpha = .05$ in this right-tailed test, the decision rule is:

Reject H_0 if $\chi^2_{calc} > 12.59$

Otherwise do no reject H_0

The decision rule is illustrated in Figure 15.3.

FIGURE 15.3

Right-Tailed Chi-Square
Test for $d.f. = 6$

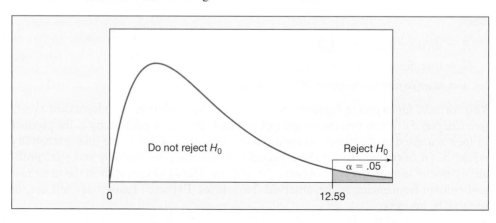

Do not reject H_0

Reject H_0

$\alpha = .05$

0   12.59

Step 3: Calculate the Test Statistic   The expected frequency in row j and column k is $e_{jk} = R_j C_k / n$. The calculations are illustrated in Table 15.3. The expected frequencies (lower part of Table 15.3) must sum to the same row and column frequencies as the observed frequencies (upper part of Table 15.3).

TABLE 15.3		Observed and Expected Frequencies 📺 WebSites		
Observed Frequencies				
Location	*France*	*UK*	*USA*	*Row Total*
Home	56	68	35	159
Order	19	19	28	66
Client	6	10	16	32
Other	12	9	13	34
Col Total	93	106	92	291
Expected Frequencies (assuming independence)				
Location	*France*	*UK*	*USA*	*Row Total*
Home	(159 × 93)/291 = 50.81	(159 × 106)/291 = 57.92	(159 × 92)/291 = 50.27	159
Order	(66 × 93)/291 = 21.09	(66 × 106)/291 = 24.04	(66 × 92)/291 = 20.87	66
Client	(32 × 93)/291 = 10.23	(32 × 106)/291 = 11.66	(32 × 92)/291 = 10.12	32
Other	(34 × 93)/291 = 10.87	(34 × 106)/291 = 12.38	(34 × 92)/291 = 10.75	34
Col Total	93	106	92	291

The chi-square test statistic is

$$\chi^2_{calc} = \sum_{j=1}^{r} \sum_{k=1}^{c} \frac{[f_{jk} - e_{jk}]^2}{e_{jk}} = \frac{(56 - 50.81)^2}{50.81} + \cdots + \frac{(13 - 10.75)^2}{10.75}$$

$$= 0.53 + \cdots + 0.47 = 17.54$$

Even for this simple problem, the calculations are too lengthy to show in full. In fact, few would choose to do the calculations of the expected frequencies and chi-square test statistic without a spreadsheet. Fortunately, any statistical package will do a chi-square test. MegaStat's setup and output are shown in Figure 15.4. As you can see, MegaStat's calculations are arranged in a tabular form.

FIGURE 15.4

MegaStat's Chi-Square Test for Web Page Data

Step 4: Make the Decision   Because the test statistic $\chi^2_{calc} = 17.54$ exceeds 12.59, we conclude that the observed differences between expected and observed frequencies differ significantly at $\alpha = .05$. The p-value (.0075) indicates that H_0 should be rejected at $\alpha = .05$. You can obtain this same p-value using Excel's function =CHISQ.DIST.RT(χ^2, d.f.) or, in this case, =CHISQ.DIST.RT(17.54,6), which gives a right-tail area of .0075. This p-value indicates that privacy disclaimer location is *not* independent of nationality at $\alpha = .05$, based on this sample of 291 websites.

Step 5: Take Action   These results suggest that in the United States, the privacy disclaimer placement is more evenly distributed between various website pages when compared to France and the UK. This may change if the Commercial Privacy Bill of Rights Act of 2011 passes in the United States.

Discussion   MegaStat rounds things off for display purposes, though it maintains full internal accuracy in the calculations (as you must, if you do these calculations by hand). Differences between observed and expected frequencies (O − E) must sum to zero across each row and down each column. If you are doing these calculations by hand, check these sums (if they are not zero, you have made an error). From Figure 15.4 we see that only three cells (column 3, rows 1, 2, and 3) contribute a majority (4.64, 2.44, 3.42) of the chi-square sum (17.54). The hypothesis of independence fails largely because of these three cells.

Using Excel   Instead of MegaStat, we could have used Excel's =CHISQ.TEST(*observed frequency range, expected frequency range*) function. After using Excel to calculate expected frequencies for each cell using formula 15.3, we would enter the cell ranges for the observed frequencies and the cell ranges for the expected frequencies into the function. Excel then returns the p-value for our chi-square statistic. In this case, Excel would return the value .0075. To see the value of χ^2_{calc}, we could use Excel's function =CHISQ.INV.RT(*probability, degrees of freedom*), =CHI.INV.RT(.0075,6) = 17.54.

EXAMPLE 15.2

Night Flying
(2 × 2 Table)

After the accident in which U.S. Senator John F. Kennedy Jr. died while piloting his airplane at night from New York to Cape Cod, a random telephone poll was taken in which 409 New Yorkers were asked, "Should private pilots be allowed to fly at night without an instrument rating?" The same question was posed to 70 aviation experts. Results are shown in Table 15.4. The totals exclude those who had "No Opinion" (1 expert and 25 general public).

TABLE 15.4	Should Noninstrument-Rated Pilots Fly at Night? 📂 Pilots		
Opinion	Experienced Pilots	General Public	Row Total
Yes	40	61	101
No	29	323	352
Col Total	69	384	453

Source: Siena College Research Institute.

The hypotheses are:

H_0: Opinion is independent of aviation expertise
H_1: Opinion is not independent of aviation expertise

The test results from MegaStat are shown in Figure 15.5. Degrees of freedom are $d.f. = (r - 1)(c - 1) = (2 - 1)(2 - 1) = 1$. Appendix E shows that the critical value of chi-square for $\alpha = .005$ is 7.879. Since the test statistic $\chi^2 = 59.80$ greatly exceeds 7.879, we firmly reject the hypothesis. The p-value (.0000) confirms that opinion is *not* independent of aviation experience.

FIGURE 15.5	**Chi-Square Test for Night-Flying Data with *d.f.* = 1**

Chi-square Contingency Table Test for Independence

	Col 1	Col 2	Total
Row 1 Observed	**40**	**61**	101
Expected	15.38	85.62	101.00
O − E	24.62	−24.62	0.00
$(O − E)^2/E$	39.39	7.08	46.47
Row 2 Observed	**29**	**323**	352
Expected	53.62	298.38	352.00
O − E	−24.62	24.62	0.00
$(O − E)^2/E$	11.30	2.03	13.33
Total Observed	69	384	453
Expected	69.00	384.00	453.00
O − E	0.00	0.00	0.00
$(O − E)^2/E$	50.69	9.11	59.80

$$59.80 \quad \text{chi-square}$$
$$1 \quad \text{df}$$
$$1.05\text{E-}14 \quad \text{p-value}$$

Test of Two Proportions

For a 2×2 contingency table, the chi-square test is equivalent to a two-tailed z test for two proportions, if the samples are large enough to ensure normality. The hypotheses are:

$$H_0: \pi_1 - \pi_2 = 0$$
$$H_1: \pi_1 - \pi_2 \neq 0$$

In the aviation survey example, the proportion of aviation experts who said yes on the survey is $p_1 = x_1/n_1 = 40/69 = .57971$, or 58.0 percent, compared to the proportion of the general public $p_2 = x_2/n_2 = 61/384 = .15885$, or 15.9 percent. The pooled proportion is $\bar{p} = (x_1 + x_2)/(n_1 + n_2) = 101/453 = .22296$. The z test statistic is then

$$z_{\text{calc}} = \frac{p_1 - p_2}{\sqrt{\bar{p}(1 - \bar{p})\left(\frac{1}{n_1} + \frac{1}{n_2}\right)}} = \frac{.57971 - .15885}{\sqrt{.22296(1 - .22296)\left(\frac{1}{69} + \frac{1}{384}\right)}} = 7.7329$$

To find the two-tailed p-value we use Excel's function =2*(1-NORM.S.DIST(7.7329,1)) = .0000. The square of the z test statistic for the two-tailed test of proportions is the same as the chi-square test statistic for the corresponding 2×2 contingency table. In the aviation example, $z^2 = 7.7329^2 = 59.80 = \chi^2$. Our conclusion is identical whether we used the chi-square test or the test for two proportions.

Small Expected Frequencies

The chi-square test is unreliable if the *expected* frequencies are too small. As you can see from the formula for the test statistic, when e_{jk} in the denominator is small, the chi-square statistic may be inflated. A commonly used rule of thumb known as **Cochran's Rule** requires that $e_{jk} > 5$ for all cells. Another rule of thumb says that up to 20 percent of the cells may have $e_{jk} < 5$. Statisticians generally become quite nervous when $e_{jk} < 2$, and there is agreement that a chi-square test is infeasible if $e_{jk} < 1$ in any cell. Computer packages may offer warnings or refuse to proceed when expected frequencies are too small. When this happens, it may be possible to salvage the test by combining adjacent rows or columns to enlarge the expected frequencies. In the web page example, all the expected frequencies are safely greater than 5.

Cross-Tabulating Raw Data

Chi-square tests for independence are quite flexible. Although most often used with nominal data such as gender (male, female), we can also analyze quantitative variables (such as salary) by coding them into categories (e.g., under $25,000; $25,000 to $50,000; $50,000 and over). Open-ended classes are acceptable. We can mix data types as required (nominal, ordinal, interval, ratio) by defining the bins appropriately. Few statistical tests are so versatile. Continuous data may be classified into any categories that make sense. To tabulate a continuous variable into two classes, we would make the cut at the median. For three bins, we would use the 33rd and 67th percentiles as cutpoints. For four bins, we would use the 25th, 50th, and 75th percentiles as cutpoints. We prefer classes that yield approximately equal frequencies for each cell to help protect against small expected frequencies (recall that Cochran's Rule requires expected frequencies be at least 5). Our bin choices are limited when we have integer data with a small range (e.g., a Likert scale with responses 1, 2, 3, 4, 5), but we can still define classes however we wish (e.g., 1 or 2, 3, 4 or 5).

EXAMPLE 15.3

Doctors and Infant Mortality 📁 **Doctors**

Let X = doctors per 100,000 residents of a state, and Y = infant deaths per 1,000 births in the state. We might reasonably hypothesize that states with more doctors relative to population would have lower infant mortality, but do they? We are reluctant to assume normality and equal variances, so we prefer to avoid a t test. Instead, we hypothesize:

H_0: Infant mortality rate is independent of doctors per 100,000 population

H_1: Infant mortality rate is not independent of doctors per 100,000 population

Depending on how we form the contingency table, we could get different results. Figure 15.6 shows 2 × 2 and 3 × 3 tables. Each table shows both actual and expected frequencies assuming the null hypothesis. Neither p-value indicates a very strong relationship. Since we cannot reject H_0 at these customary levels of significance, we conclude that doctors and infant mortality are not strongly related. A *multivariate* regression model might be the next step, to explore other predictors (e.g., per capita income, per capita Medicaid spending, percent of college graduates) that might be related to infant mortality in a state.

FIGURE 15.6

Two Cross-Tabulations of Same Raw Data

		2 × 2 Table Doctors per 100,000						**3 × 3 Table** Doctors per 100,000			
Infant Deaths per 1,000 Births		Low	High	Total		*Infant Deaths per 1,000 Births*		Low	Med	High	Total
Low	Obs	**10**	**14**	24		Low	Obs	**4**	**6**	**6**	16
	Exp	12.00	12.00				Exp	5.44	5.44	5.12	
High	Obs	**15**	**11**	26		Med	Obs	**5**	**6**	**6**	17
	Exp	13.00	13.00				Exp	5.78	5.78	5.44	
Total		25	25	50		High	Obs	**8**	**5**	**4**	17
							Exp	5.78	5.78	5.44	
						Total		17	17	16	50

1.28 chi-square (*d.f.* = 1)
.2575 p-value

2.10 chi-square (*d.f.* = 4)
.7173 p-value

Why Do a Chi-Square Test on Numerical Data?

Why would anyone convert numerical data (X, Y) into categorical data in order to make a contingency table and do a chi-square test? Why not use the (X, Y) data to calculate a correlation coefficient or fit a regression? Here are three reasons:

- The researcher may believe there is a relationship between X and Y but does not want to make an assumption about its form (linear, curvilinear, etc.) as required in a regression.

- There are outliers or other anomalies that prevent us from assuming that the data came from a normal population. Unlike correlation and regression, the chi-square test does *not* require any normality assumptions.

- The researcher has numerical data for one variable but not the other. A chi-square test can be used if we convert the numerical variable into categories.

3-Way Tables and Higher

There is no conceptual reason to limit ourselves to two-way contingency tables comparing two variables. However, such tables become rather hard to visualize, even when they are "sliced" into a series of 2-way tables. A table comparing three variables can be visualized as a *cube* or as a stack of tiled 2-way contingency tables. Major computer packages (SAS, SPSS, and others) permit 3-way contingency tables. For four or more variables, there is no physical analog to aid us, and their cumbersome nature would suggest analytical methods other than chi-square tests.

Instructions: For each exercise, include MegaStat or Excel exhibits to support your chi-square calculations. (a) State the hypotheses. (b) Show how the degrees of freedom are calculated for the contingency table. (c) Using the level of significance specified in the exercise, find the critical value of chi-square from Appendix E or from Excel's function =CHISQ.INV.RT(alpha, deg_freedom). (d) Carry out the calculations for a chi-square test for independence and draw a conclusion. (e) Which cells of the contingency table contribute the most to the chi-square test statistic? (f) Are any of the expected frequencies too small? (g) Interpret the *p*-value. If necessary, you can calculate the *p*-value using Excel's function =CHISQ.DIST.RT(test statistic, deg_freedom). *(h) If it is a 2 × 2 table, perform a two-tailed, two-sample *z* test for $\pi_1 = \pi_2$ and verify that z^2 is the same as your chi-square statistic. *Note:* Exercises marked with an asterisk (*) are more difficult.

SECTION EXERCISES

connect

15.1 In a study of how managers attempt to manage earnings, researchers analyzed a sample of 515 earnings-management attempts from a survey of experienced auditors. The frequency of effects is summarized in the table shown. *Research question:* At $\alpha = .01$, is the effect on earnings independent of the approach used? (Data are from Mark W. Nelson, John A. Elliott, and Robin L. Tarpley, "How Are Earnings Managed? Examples from Auditors," *Accounting Horizons,* Supplement, 2003, pp. 17–35.) 📂 **Earnings**

Current-Period Income Effect of Four Earnings Management Approaches				
Approach Used	*Increase*	*Decrease*	*No Clear Effect*	*Row Total*
Expenses and Other Losses	133	113	23	269
Revenue and Other Gains	86	20	8	114
Business Combinations	12	22	33	67
Other Approaches	41	4	20	65
Col Total	272	159	84	515

15.2 Teenagers make up a large percentage of the market for clothing. Below are data on running shoe ownership in four world regions (excluding China). *Research question:* At $\alpha = .01$, does this sample show that running shoe ownership depends on world region? (See J. Paul Peter and Jerry C. Olson, *Consumer Behavior and Marketing Strategy,* 9th ed. [McGraw-Hill, 2004], p. 64.) 📂 **Running**

Running Shoe Ownership in World Regions					
Owned By	*U.S.*	*Europe*	*Asia*	*Latin America*	*Row Total*
Teens	80	89	69	65	303
Adults	20	11	31	35	97
Col Total	100	100	100	100	400

15.3 Students applying for admission to an MBA program must submit scores from the GMAT test, which includes a verbal and a quantitative component. Shown here are raw scores for 100 randomly chosen MBA applicants at a Midwestern, public, AACSB-accredited business school. *Research question:* At $\alpha = .005$, is the quantitative score independent of the verbal score? 📄 **GMAT**

	Quantitative			
Verbal	Under 25	25 to 34	35 or More	Row Total
Under 25	25	9	1	35
25 to 34	4	28	18	50
35 or More	1	3	11	15
Col Total	30	40	30	100

15.4 Computer abuse by employees is an ongoing worry to businesses. A study revealed the data shown below. *Research question:* At $\alpha = .01$, is the frequency of disciplinary action independent of the abuser's level of privilege? (Data are from Detmar W. Straub and William D. Nance, "Discovering and Disciplining Computer Abuse in Organizations," *MIS Quarterly* 14, no. 1 [March 1990], pp. 45–60.) 📄 **Abuse**

Computer Abuse Incidents Cross-Tabulated by Privilege and Punishment			
Level of Privilege	Disciplined	Not Disciplined	Row Total
Low	20	11	31
Medium	42	3	45
High	33	3	36
Col Total	95	17	112

15.5 Marketing researchers sent an advance e-mail notice announcing an upcoming Internet survey and describing the purpose of their research. Half the target customers received the prenotification, followed by the survey. The other half received only the survey. The survey completion frequencies are shown below. *Research question:* At $\alpha = .025$, is completion rate independent of prenotification? 📄 **Advance**

Cross-Tabulation of Completion by Notification			
Pre-Notified?	Completed	Not Completed	Row Total
Yes	39	155	194
No	22	170	192
Col Total	61	325	386

Mini Case   15.1

Student Work and Car Age

Do students work longer hours to pay for newer cars? This hypothesis was tested using data from a survey of introductory business statistics students at a large commuter university campus. The survey contained these two fill-in-the-blank questions:

About how many hours per week do you expect to work at an outside job this semester?

What is the age (in years) of the car you usually drive?

The contingency table shown in Table 15.5 summarizes the responses of 162 students. Very few students worked less than 15 hours. Most drove cars less than 3 years old, although a few drove cars 10 years old or more. Neither variable was normally

TABLE 15.5	Frequency Classification for Work Hours and Car Age CarAge				
Hours of Outside Work per Week	Age of Car Usually Driven				Row Total
	Less than 3	3 to <6	6 to <10	10 or More	
Under 15	9	8	8	4	29
15 to <25	34	17	11	9	71
25 or More	28	20	8	6	62
Col Total	71	45	27	19	162

distributed (and there were outliers), so a chi-square test was preferable to a correlation or regression model. The hypotheses to be tested are:

H_0: Car age is independent of work hours

H_1: Car age is not independent of work hours

Figure 15.7 shows MegaStat's analysis of the 3×4 contingency table. Two expected frequencies (upper right) are below 5, so Cochran's Rule is not quite met. MegaStat has highlighted these cells to call attention to this concern. But the most striking feature of this table is that almost all of the actual frequencies are very close to the frequencies expected under the hypothesis of independence, leading to a very small chi-square test statistic (5.24). The test requires six degrees of freedom, i.e. $(r-1)(c-1) = (3-1)(4-1) = 6$. From Appendix E we obtain the right-tail critical value $\chi^2_{.10} = 10.64$ at $\alpha = .10$. Even at this rather weak level of significance, we cannot reject H_0. MegaStat's p-value (.5132) says that a test statistic of this magnitude could arise by chance more than half the time in samples from a population in which the two variables really were independent. Hence, the data lend no support to the hypothesis that work hours are related to car age.

FIGURE 15.7   **MegaStat's Analysis of Car Age Data**

Chi-square Contingency Table Test for Independence

		Less than 3	3 to <6	6 to <10	10 or More	Total
Under 15	Observed	9	8	8	4	29
	Expected	12.71	8.06	4.83	3.40	29.00
	O − E	−3.71	−0.06	3.17	0.60	0.00
	(O − E)²/E	1.08	0.00	2.07	0.11	3.26
15 to <25	Observed	34	17	11	9	71
	Expected	31.12	19.72	11.83	8.33	71.00
	O − E	2.88	−2.72	−0.83	0.67	0.00
	(O − E)²/E	0.27	0.38	0.06	0.05	0.76
25 or More	Observed	28	20	8	6	62
	Expected	27.17	17.22	10.33	7.27	62.00
	O − E	0.83	2.78	−2.33	−1.27	0.00
	(O − E)²/E	0.03	0.45	0.53	0.22	1.22
Total	Observed	71	45	27	19	162
	Expected	71.00	45.00	27.00	19.00	162.00
	O − E	0.00	0.00	0.00	0.00	0.00
	(O − E)²/E	1.38	0.82	2.66	0.38	5.24

5.24   chi-square
6   df
.5132   p-value

15.2 CHI-SQUARE TESTS FOR GOODNESS-OF-FIT

Purpose of the Test

A **goodness-of-fit test** (or GOF test) is used to help you decide whether your sample resembles a particular kind of population. The chi-square test can be used to compare sample frequencies with any probability distribution. Tests for goodness-of-fit are easy to understand, but until spreadsheets came along, the calculations were tedious. Today, computers make it easy, and tests for departure from normality or any other distribution are routine. We will first illustrate the GOF test using a general type of distribution. A **multinomial distribution** is defined by any k probabilities $\pi_1, \pi_2, \ldots, \pi_k$ that sum to one. You can apply this same technique for the three familiar distributions we have already studied (uniform, Poisson, and normal). Although there are many tests for goodness-of-fit, the chi-square test is attractive because it is versatile and easy to understand.

Multinomial GOF Test: M&M Colors

According to the "official" M&M website,* the distribution of M&M colors is:

Brown (13%)	Red (13%)	Blue (24%)
Orange (20%)	Yellow (16%)	Green (14%)

But do bags of M&Ms shipped to retailers actually follow this distribution? We will use a sample of four bags of candy and conduct a chi-square GOF test. We will assume the distribution is the same as stated on the website *unless the sample shows us otherwise.*

Hypotheses

The hypotheses are:

H_0: $\pi_{\text{brown}} = .13, \pi_{\text{red}} = .13, \pi_{\text{blue}} = .24, \pi_{\text{orange}} = .20, \pi_{\text{yellow}} = .16, \pi_{\text{green}} = .14$

H_1: At least one of the π's differs from the hypothesized value

To test these hypotheses, statistics students opened four bags of M&Ms ($n = 220$ pieces) and counted the number of each color, with the results shown in Table 15.6. We assign an index to each of the six colors ($j = 1, 2, \ldots, 6$) and define:

f_j = the actual frequency of M&Ms of color j

e_j = the expected frequency of M&Ms of color j assuming that H_0 is true

Each expected frequency (e_j) is calculated by multiplying the sample size (n) by the hypothesized proportion (π_j). We can now calculate a chi-square test statistic that compares the actual and expected frequencies:

(15.4)
$$\chi^2_{\text{calc}} = \sum_{j=1}^{c} \frac{[f_j - e_j]^2}{e_j}$$

TABLE 15.6

Hypothesis Test of M&M Proportions
📂 MM

Color	Official π_j	Observed f_j	Expected $e_j = n \times \pi_j$	$f_j - e_j$	$(f_j - e_j)^2/e_j$
Brown	0.13	38	28.6	+9.4	3.0895
Red	0.13	30	28.6	+1.4	0.0685
Blue	0.24	44	52.8	−8.8	1.4667
Orange	0.20	52	44.0	+8.0	1.4545
Yellow	0.16	30	35.2	−5.2	0.7682
Green	0.14	26	30.8	−4.8	0.7481
Sum	1.00	220	220.0	0.0	$\chi^2_{\text{calc}} = 7.5955$

*The official website for M&M candies is http://us.mms.com/. These proportions were taken from their website during June 2006.

If the proposed distribution gives a good fit to the sample, the chi-square statistic will be near zero because f_j and e_j will be approximately equal. Conversely, if f_j and e_j differ greatly, the chi-square statistic will be large. It is always a right-tail test. We will reject H_0 if the test statistic exceeds the chi-square critical value chosen from Appendix E. For any GOF test, the rule for degrees of freedom is:

$$d.f. = c - m - 1 \tag{15.5}$$

where c is the number of classes used in the test and m is the number of parameters estimated.

Results of the Test

Table 15.6 summarizes the calculations in a worksheet. No parameters were estimated ($m = 0$) and we have six classes ($c = 6$), so degrees of freedom are:

$$d.f. = c - m - 1 = 6 - 0 - 1 = 5$$

From Appendix E, the critical value of chi-square for $\alpha = .01$ is $\chi^2_{.01} = 15.09$. Since the test statistic $\chi^2_{calc} = 7.5955$ (from Table 15.6) is smaller than the critical value, we cannot reject the hypothesis that the M&M's color distribution is as stated on the M&M website. Notice that the f_j and e_j *always* sum exactly to the sample size ($n = 220$ in this example) and the differences $f_j - e_j$ must sum to zero. If not, you have made a mistake in your calculations—a useful way to check your work.

Excel can also be used to conduct a chi-square goodness-of-fit test. Enter the observed frequencies on an Excel spreadsheet and then calculate the expected frequencies. Insert the function =CHISQ.TEST(*observed frequency range, expected frequency range*) into a cell. Excel will return the *p*-value for your test. In our M&M example, Excel's =CHISQ.TEST returns the value .17998. Because .17998 > .01, our chosen value of α, we would fail to reject the null hypothesis. Using Excel's function =CHISQ.INV.RT(*probability, degrees of freedom*), we can determine the value of χ^2_{calc}. In our example χ^2_{calc} =CHISQ.INV.RT(.17998, 5) = 7.5995.

Small Expected Frequencies

Goodness-of-fit tests may lack power in small samples. Further, small expected frequencies tend to inflate the χ^2 test statistic because e_j is in the denominator of formula 15.4. The minimum necessary sample size depends on the type of test being employed. As a guideline, a chi-square goodness-of-fit test should be avoided if $n < 25$ (some experts would suggest a higher number). Cochran's Rule that expected frequencies should be at least 5 (i.e., all $e_j \geq 5$) also provides a guideline, although some experts would weaken the rule to require only $e_j \geq 2$. In the M&M example, the expected frequencies are all large, so there is no reason to doubt the test.

GOF Tests for Other Distributions

We can also use the chi-square GOF test to compare a sample of data with a familiar distribution such as the uniform, Poisson, or normal. We would state the hypotheses as below:

H_0: The population follows a _____ distribution.

H_1: The population doesn't follow a _____ distribution.

The blank may contain the name of any theoretical distribution. Assuming that we have n observations, we group the observations into c classes and then find the *chi-square test statistic* using formula 15.4. In a GOF test, if we use sample data to *estimate* the distribution's parameters, then our degrees of freedom would be as follows:

Uniform:	$d.f. = c - m - 1 = c - 0 - 1 = c - 1$ (no parameters are estimated)	**(15.6)**
Poisson:	$d.f. = c - m - 1 = c - 1 - 1 = c - 2$ (if λ is estimated)	**(15.7)**
Normal:	$d.f. = c - m - 1 = c - 2 - 1 = c - 3$ (if μ and σ are estimated)	**(15.8)**

Data-Generating Situations

"Fishing" for a good-fitting model is inappropriate. Instead, we visualize *a priori* the characteristics of the underlying *data-generating process.* It is undoubtedly true that the most common GOF test is for the normal distribution, simply because so many parametric tests assume normality, and that assumption must be tested. Also, the normal distribution may be used as a default benchmark for any mound-shaped data that have centrality and tapering tails, as long as you have reason to believe that a constant mean and variance would be reasonable (e.g., weights of circulated dimes). However, you would not consider a Poisson distribution for continuous data (e.g., gasoline price per liter) or certain integer variables (e.g., exam scores) because a Poisson model only applies to integer data on arrivals or rare, independent events (e.g., number of paint defects per square meter). We remind you of this because software makes it possible to fit inappropriate distributions all too easily.

Mixtures: A Problem

Your sample may not resemble any known distribution. One common problem is *mixtures.* A sample may have been created by more than one data-generating process superimposed on top of another. For example, adult heights of either sex would follow a normal distribution, but a combined sample of both genders will be bimodal, and its mean and standard deviation may be unrepresentative of either sex. Obtaining a good fit is not *per se* sufficient justification for assuming a particular model. Each probability distribution has its own logic about the nature of the underlying process, so we must also examine the data-generating situation and be convinced that the proposed model is both logical *and* empirically apt.

Eyeball Tests

A simple "eyeball" inspection of the histogram or dot plot may suffice to rule out a hypothesized population. For example, if the sample is strongly bimodal or skewed, or if outliers are present, we would anticipate a poor fit to a normal distribution. The shape of the histogram can give you a rough idea whether a normal distribution is a likely candidate for a good fit. You can be fairly sure that a formal test will agree with what your common sense tells you, as long as the sample size is not too small.

Yet a limitation of eyeball tests is that we may be unsure just how much variation is expected for a given sample size. If anything, the human eye is overly sensitive, causing us to commit α error (rejecting a true null hypothesis) too often. People are sometimes unduly impressed by a small departure from the hypothesized distribution, when actually it is within chance. We will see examples of this.

SECTION EXERCISES

connect

15.6 U.S. market share for smartphones with larger screens is increasing. As of the first quarter of 2011, smartphones with screens 4 inches or larger had captured 24 percent of the smartphone market. The market for smartphones with screens between 3.5 and 3.9 inches has stayed fairly steady at 40 percent, while that for smartphones with screens less than 3.5 inches has declined to 36 percent. Does smartphone ownership by college students follow this national pattern? A sample of 148 student smartphone users showed that 30 owned a smartphone with a large screen (4 inches or greater), 75 owned a smartphone with a medium-sized screen (between 3.5 and 3.9 inches), and 43 owned a smartphone with a small screen (less than 3.5 inches). Conduct a chi-square GOF test to answer this research question.

15.7 Market research has shown that Americans will continue to eat out even in a depressed economy. A market analysis during the most recent recession showed the following distribution of visits to the various types of restaurants:

Fast food (36%)   Quick casual (29%)   Casual dining (15%)

Family style (15%)   Fine dining (5%)

A new survey of 250 Americans reported the following types of visits on their last restaurant visit: 95 visited a fast food establishment, 68 visited a quick casual restaurant, 38 visited a casual dining restaurant, 30 visited a family style restaurant, and 19 visited a fine dining establishment. Does this sample indicate that the distribution of type of restaurant visited has changed since the market analysis shown above was conducted? Conduct a chi-square GOF test to answer this research question.

15.3 UNIFORM GOODNESS-OF-FIT TEST

The uniform goodness-of-fit test is a special case of the multinomial in which every value has the same chance of occurrence. Uniform data-generating situations are rare, but some data *must* be from a **uniform distribution**, such as winning lottery numbers or random digits generated by a computer for random sampling. Another use of the uniform distribution is as a worst case scenario for an unknown distribution whose range is specified in a what-if analysis.

LO 15-4

Perform a goodness-of-fit (GOF) test for a uniform distribution.

The chi-square test for a uniform distribution is a generalization of the test for equality of two proportions. The hypotheses are:

H_0: $\pi_1 = \pi_2 = \cdots = \pi_c = 1/c$
H_1: Not all the π_j are equal

The chi-square test compares all c groups *simultaneously*. Each discrete outcome should have probability $1/c$, so the test is very easy to perform. Evidence against H_0 would consist of sample frequencies that were not the same for all categories.

Classes need not represent numerical values. For example, we might compare the total number of items scanned per hour by four supermarket checkers (Bob, Frieda, Sam, and Wanda). The uniform test is quite versatile. For numerical variables, bins do not have to be of equal width and can be open-ended. For example, we might be interested in the ages of X-ray machines in a hospital (under 2 years, 2 to <5 years, 5 to <10 years, 10 years and over). In a uniform population, each category would be expected to have $e_j = n/c$ observations, so the calculation of expected frequencies is simple.

Uniform GOF Test: Grouped Data

The test is easiest if data are already tabulated into groups, which saves us the effort of defining the groups. For example, one year, a certain state had 756 traffic fatalities. Table 15.7 suggests that fatalities are not uniformly distributed by day of week, being higher on weekends. Can we reject the hypothesis of a uniform distribution, say, at $\alpha = .005$? The hypotheses are:

H_0: Traffic fatalities are uniformly distributed by day of the week
H_1: Traffic fatalities are not uniformly distributed by day of the week

Day	f_j	e_j	$f_j - e_j$	$(f_j - e_j)^2$	$(f_j - e_j)^2/e_j$
Sun	121	108	13	169	1.565
Mon	96	108	−12	144	1.333
Tue	91	108	−17	289	2.676
Wed	92	108	−16	256	2.370
Thu	96	108	−12	144	1.333
Fri	122	108	14	196	1.815
Sat	138	108	30	900	8.333
Total	756	756	0		$\chi^2_{calc} = 19.426$

TABLE 15.7

Traffic Fatalities by Day of Week 📁 **Traffic**

Source: Based on www-nrd.nhtsa.dot.gov.

Under H_0 the expected frequency for each weekday is $e_j = n/c = 756/7 = 108$. The expected frequencies happen to be integers, although this is not true in general. Since no parameters were estimated ($m = 0$) to form the seven classes ($c = 7$), the chi-square test will have $d.f. = c - m - 1 = 7 - 0 - 1 = 6$ degrees of freedom. From Appendix E the critical value of chi-square for the 1 percent level of significance is $\chi^2_{.01} = 16.81$, so the hypothesis of a rectangular or uniform population can be rejected. The *p*-value (.0035) can be obtained from the Excel function =CHISQ.DIST.RT(19.426,6). The *p*-value tells us that such a sample result would occur by chance only about 35 times in 10,000 samples. There is a believable underlying causal mechanism at work (e.g., people may drink and drive more often on weekends).

Uniform GOF Test: Raw Data

When we are using raw data, we must form c bins of equal width and create our own frequency distribution. For example, suppose an auditor is checking the fairness of a state's "Daily 3" lottery. Table 15.8 shows winning three-digit lottery numbers for 100 consecutive days. All numbers from 000 to 999 are supposed to be equally likely, so the auditor is testing these hypotheses:

H_0: Lottery numbers are uniformly distributed

H_1: Lottery numbers are not uniformly distributed

TABLE 15.8

100 Consecutive Winning Three-Digit Lottery Numbers
📁 **Lottery-A**

367	865	438	437	596	567	121	244	036	337
152	260	470	821	452	606	417	674	786	311
739	611	359	739	184	229	418	565	547	403
103	344	303	531	054	496	167	550	403	785
341	237	913	991	656	661	178	983	431	472
315	792	676	299	738	080	450	991	673	846
500	001	016	581	154	677	457	617	261	807
452	048	052	018	037	517	760	522	711	898
294	605	135	333	886	257	533	119	882	899
814	490	490	885	329	033	033	707	551	651

We know that three-digit lottery numbers must lie in the range 000 to 999, so there are many ways we could define our classes (e.g., 5 bins of width 200, 10 bins of width 100, 20 bins of width 50). We will use 10 bins, with the realization that we might get a different result if we chose different bins. The steps are:

- Step 1   Divide the range into 10 bins of equal width.
- Step 2   Calculate the observed frequency f_j for each bin.
- Step 3   Define $e_j = n/c = 100/10 = 10$.
- Step 4   Perform the chi-square calculations (see Table 15.9).
- Step 5   Make the decision.

TABLE 15.9

Uniform GOF Test for Lottery Numbers

Bin	f_j	e_j	$f_j - e_j$	$(f_j - e_j)^2$	$(f_j - e_j)^2/e_j$
0 < 100	11	10	1	1	0.100
100 < 200	9	10	−1	1	0.100
200 < 300	8	10	−2	4	0.400
300 < 400	10	10	0	0	0.000
400 < 500	16	10	6	36	3.600
500 < 600	12	10	2	4	0.400
600 < 700	11	10	1	1	0.100
700 < 800	9	10	−1	1	0.100
800 < 900	10	10	0	0	0.000
900 < 1,000	4	10	−6	36	3.600
Total	100	100	0		$\chi^2_{calc} = 8.400$

Since no parameters were estimated ($m = 0$) to form the 10 classes ($c = 10$), we have $d.f. = c - m - 1 = 10 - 0 - 1 = 9$ degrees of freedom. From Appendix E the critical value of chi-square for the 10 percent level of significance is $\chi^2_{.10} = 14.684$. Since the test statistic is 8.400, the hypothesis of a uniform distribution cannot be rejected.

If the bin limits cannot be set using *a priori* knowledge (as was possible in the lottery example), we maximize the test's power by defining bin width as the range divided by the number of classes:

(15.9)   Bin width $= \dfrac{x_{\max} - x_{\min}}{c}$ (setting bin width from sample data)

The resulting bin limits may not be aesthetically pleasing, but the expected frequencies will be as large as possible (you might be able to round the bin limits to a "nice" number without affecting the calculations very much). If the sample size is small, small expected frequencies could be a problem. Since all expected frequencies are the same in a uniform model, this problem will exist in all classes simultaneously. For example, we could not classify 25 observations into 10 classes without violating Cochran's Rule (although the more relaxed rule $e_j \geq 2$ would be satisfied).

The histograms in Figures 15.8 and 15.9 suggest too many winning lottery numbers in the middle and too few at the top. But histogram appearance is affected by the way we define our bins and the number of classes, so the chi-square test is a more reliable guide. Humans are adept at finding patterns in sample distributions that actually are within the realm of chance.

FIGURE 15.8

Ten-Bin Histogram

FIGURE 15.9

Five-Bin Histogram

As you learned in Chapter 6, a discrete uniform distribution $U(a, b)$ is symmetric with mean $\mu = (a + b)/2$ and $\sigma = \sqrt{[(b - a + 1)^2 - 1]/12}$. For the lottery, we have $a = 000$ and $b = 999$, so we expect the mean to be $\mu = (0 + 999)/2 = 499.5$ and $\sigma = \sqrt{[(999 - 0 + 1)^2 - 1]/12} = 288.7$. For the sample, Table 15.10 shows that the low (001) and high (991) are near their theoretical values, as are the sample mean (472.2), standard

Statistic	Sample	If Uniform
Minimum	001	000
Maximum	991	999
Mean	472.2	499.5
Median	471.0	499.5
Standard Deviation	271.0	288.7
Quartile 1	260.5	249.8
Quartile 3	675.5	749.3
Skewness	0.01	0.00

TABLE 15.10

Descriptive Statistics
☞ **Lottery-A**

deviation (271.0), and skewness coefficient (.01). The first quartile (260.5) is close to its expected value (.25 × 999 = 249.8), while the third quartile (675.5) is smaller than expected (.75 × 999 = 749.3).

Since the data are not skewed (mean ≈ median) and the sample size is large ($n \geq 30$), the mean is approximately normally distributed, so we can use the normal distribution to test the sample mean for a significant difference from the hypothesized uniform mean, assuming that $\sigma = 288.7$ as would be true if the data were uniform:

$$z = \frac{\bar{x} - \mu}{\frac{\sigma}{\sqrt{n}}} = \frac{472.2 - 499.5}{\frac{288.7}{\sqrt{100}}} = -0.95 \qquad (\text{two-tail } p\text{-value} = .34)$$

The difference is not significant at any common level of α. Overall, these statistics show no convincing evidence of departure from a uniform distribution, thereby confirming the chi-square test's conclusion, that is, the lottery is fair.

SECTION EXERCISES

connect

15.8 Advertisers need to know which age groups are likely to see their ads. Purchasers of 120 copies of *Cosmopolitan* are shown by age group. (a) Make a bar chart and describe it. (b) Calculate expected frequencies for each class. (c) Perform the chi-square test for a uniform distribution. At $\alpha = .01$, does this sample contradict the assumption that readership is uniformly distributed among these six age groups? (See J. Paul Peter and Jerry C. Olson, *Consumer Behavior and Marketing Strategy*, 9th ed. [McGraw-Hill, 2004], p. 300.) ☞ **Cosmo**

Purchaser Age	Units Sold
18–24	38
25–34	28
35–44	19
45–54	16
55–64	10
65+	9
Total	120

15.9 One-year sales volume of four similar 20-oz. beverages on a college campus is shown. (a) Make a bar chart and describe it. (b) Calculate expected frequencies for each class. (c) Perform the chi-square test for a uniform distribution. At $\alpha = .05$, does this sample contradict the assumption that sales are the same for each beverage? ☞ **Frapp**

Beverage	Sales (Cases)
Frappuccino Coffee	18
Frappuccino Mocha	23
Frappuccino Vanilla	23
Frappuccino Caramel	20
Total	84

15.10 In a three-digit lottery, each of the three digits is supposed to have the same probability of occurrence (counting initial blanks as zeros, e.g., 32 is treated as 032). The table shows the frequency of occurrence of each digit for 90 consecutive daily three-digit drawings. (a) Make a bar chart and describe it. (b) Calculate expected frequencies for each class. (c) Perform the chi-square test for a uniform distribution. At $\alpha = .05$, can you reject the hypothesis that the digits are from a uniform population? ☞ **Lottery3**

Digit	Frequency
0	33
1	17
2	25
3	30
4	31
5	28
6	24
7	25
8	32
9	25
Total	270

15.11 Ages of 56 attendees of a Harry Potter movie are shown. (a) Form seven age classes (10 to 20, 20 to 30, etc.). Tabulate the frequency of attendees in each class. (b) Calculate expected frequencies for each class. (c) Perform a chi-square GOF test for a uniform distribution, using the 5 percent level of significance. 📁 **Harry**

10	22	58	11	73	22	57
35	33	33	59	54	55	75
79	24	13	73	52	69	30
71	64	17	50	72	67	50
72	35	26	59	47	65	35
64	34	39	66	37	41	58
51	43	29	74	73	50	62
58	34	50	27	13	67	67

15.4 POISSON GOODNESS-OF-FIT TEST

Poisson Data-Generating Situations

In a **Poisson distribution** model, X represents the number of events per unit of time or space. By definition, X is a discrete nonnegative random variable with integer values (0, 1, 2, . . .). Event arrivals must be independent of one another. Events that tend to fit this definition might include customer arrivals per minute at an ATM, calls per minute at Ticketmaster, or alarms per hour at a fire station. In such cases, the mean arrival rate would vary by time of day, day of the week, and so on. The Poisson has been demonstrated to apply to scores in some sports events (goals scored per soccer game, goals in hockey games) and to defects in manufactured components such as LCDs, printed circuits, and automobile paint jobs. Typically X has a fairly small mean, which is why the Poisson is sometimes called a model of *rare events*. If the mean is large, we might fit a normal distribution instead. Poisson random number generators are used by researchers who model queues, an important application in dense urban cultures. The Poisson distribution is inappropriate for noninteger data or financial data such as you would find in company annual reports. Remembering these facts can spare you from wasted time trying to fit a Poisson model when it is inappropriate.

LO 15-5

Explain the GOF test for a Poisson distribution.

Poisson Goodness-of-Fit Test

A Poisson model is completely described by its one parameter, the mean λ. Assuming that λ is unknown and must be estimated from the sample, the initial steps are:

- Step 1 Tally the observed frequency f_j of each x-value.
- Step 2 Estimate the mean λ from the sample.
- Step 3 Use the estimated λ to find the Poisson probability $P(X = x)$ for each x-value.

- Step 4   Multiply $P(X = x)$ by the sample size n to get expected Poisson frequencies e_j.
- Step 5   Perform the chi-square calculations.
- Step 6   Make the decision.

If the data are already tabulated, we can skip the first step. A Poisson test always has an open-ended class on the high end, since technically X has no upper limit. Unfortunately, Poisson tail probabilities are very small, and so will be the corresponding expected frequencies. But classes can be combined from each end inward until expected frequencies become large enough for the test (at least until $e_j \geq 2$). Combining classes implies using fewer classes than you would wish, but a more detailed breakdown isn't justified unless the sample is very large.

Poisson GOF Test: Tabulated Data

The number of U.S. Supreme Court appointments in a given year might be hypothesized to be a Poisson variable, since rare events that occur independently over time are often well approximated by the Poisson model. We formulate these hypotheses:

H_0: Supreme Court appointments follow a Poisson distribution

H_1: Supreme Court appointments do not follow a Poisson distribution

The frequency of U.S. Supreme Court appointments for the period 1900 through 1999 is summarized in Table 15.11. This sample of 100 years should be large enough to obtain a valid hypothesis test. In a typical year, there are no appointments, and only twice have there been three or four appointments (1910 and 1941).

TABLE 15.11

Number of Annual U.S. Supreme Court Appointments, 1900–1999

📄 **Supreme**

Source: *The World Almanac and Book of Facts*, 2002, p. 94. Copyright © 2002 World Almanac Education Group, Inc.

x	f_j	$x_j f_j$
0	59	0
1	31	31
2	8	16
3	1	3
4	1	4
Total	100	54

The total number of appointments is

$$\sum_{j=1}^{c} x_j f_j = (0)(59) + (1)(31) + (2)(8) + (3)(1) + (4)(1) = 54$$

so the sample mean is

$$\hat{\lambda} = \frac{54}{100} = 0.54 \text{ appointment per year}$$

Using the estimated mean $\hat{\lambda} = 0.54$, we can calculate the Poisson probabilities, either by using the Poisson formula $P(X = x) = (\lambda^x e^{-\lambda})/x!$ or Excel's function =POISSON.DIST (x,mean,0). We multiply $P(X = x)$ by n to get the expected frequencies, with $n = 100$ years, as shown in Table 15.12.

TABLE 15.12

Fitted Poisson Probabilities

📄 **Supreme**

x	$P(X = x)$	$e_j = nP(X = x)$
0	0.58275	100 × 0.58275 = 58.275
1	0.31468	100 × 0.31468 = 31.468
2	0.08496	100 × 0.08496 = 8.496
3	0.01529	100 × 0.01529 = 1.529
4	0.00206	100 × 0.00206 = 0.206
5	0.00022	100 × 0.00022 = 0.022
6 or more	0.00004	100 × 0.00004 = 0.004
Sum	1.00000	100.00

The probabilities rapidly become small as X increases. To ensure that $e_j \geq 2$, it is necessary to combine the top classes to end up with only three classes, the top class being "2 or more," before doing the chi-square calculations shown in Table 15.13. Since f_j and e_j are almost identical, the Poisson distribution obviously gives an excellent fit, so we are not surprised that the test statistic (0.022) is very near zero.

x	f_j	e_j	$f_j - e_j$	$(f_j - e_j)^2$	$(f_j - e_j)^2/e_j$
0	59	58.275	0.725	0.525625	0.009
1	31	31.468	−0.468	0.219024	0.007
2 or more	10	10.257	−0.257	0.066049	0.006
Total	100	100			$\chi^2_{calc} = 0.022$

TABLE 15.13

Chi-Square Test for Supreme Court Data

Using $c = 3$ classes in the test and with $m = 1$ parameter estimated, the degrees of freedom are $c - m - 1 = 3 - 1 - 1 = 1$. From Appendix E, we see that the critical value for $\alpha = .10$ is $\chi^2_{.10} = 2.706$, so we clearly cannot reject the hypothesis of a Poisson distribution, even at a modest level of significance. Excel's function =CHISQ.DIST.RT(.022,1) gives the p-value .882, which indicates an excellent fit. Although we can never *prove* that the annual U.S. Supreme Court appointments follow a Poisson distribution, we can see that the Poisson distribution fits the sample well, as in the graph in Figure 15.10 (orange bar is actual, green line is fitted Poisson).

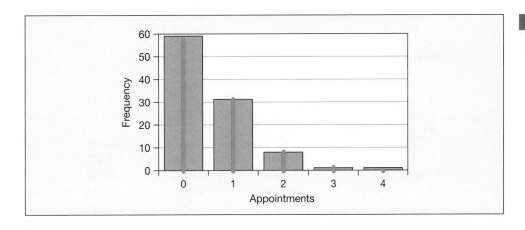

FIGURE 15.10

Supreme Court Vacancy Poisson GOF Test

Poisson GOF Test: Raw Data

Figure 15.11 shows the menu from Excel's Data Analysis > Random Number Generation, which was used to create 100 Poisson random numbers with a mean of $\lambda = 4.0$. We would like to test this generator's accuracy.

FIGURE 15.11

Excel's Poisson Random Number Generator

Table 15.14 shows 100 Excel-generated Poisson arrivals whose mean is supposed to be $\lambda = 4.0$ arrivals per minute. Is Excel's simulation algorithm working properly? A visual inspection shows two possibly unusual observations (two 11s), but beyond that it is hard to tell.

TABLE 15.14

100 Random Poisson Arrivals with $\lambda = 4$
📄 RandPoisson

5	3	11	4	5	1	7	4	4	5
3	2	5	7	4	4	6	5	5	7
2	4	9	7	5	5	4	5	4	3
4	6	3	3	3	4	6	2	6	7
6	2	7	3	6	6	4	4	2	0
4	8	4	4	4	2	5	2	5	4
3	6	7	8	4	5	4	3	7	5
2	3	2	4	3	5	2	6	5	7
2	3	7	2	1	4	2	3	4	5
0	3	3	7	3	8	5	5	6	11

The hypotheses are:

H_0: Excel's random data are from a Poisson distribution

H_1: Excel's random data are not from a Poisson distribution

Figure 15.12 shows the chi-square test for this data set. To ensure that all expected frequencies are at least 2, the 0s and 1s have been combined into one category, and all values of 9 or more have been combined.

FIGURE 15.12

Chi-Square Test

Arrivals	Obs	Exp	Obs-Exp	Chi-Square
1 or less	4	9.158	−5.158	2.905
2	13	14.653	−1.653	0.186
3	16	19.537	−3.537	0.640
4	22	19.537	2.463	0.311
5	18	15.629	2.371	0.360
6	10	10.420	−0.420	0.017
7	11	5.954	5.046	4.276
8	3	2.977	0.023	0.000
9 or more	3	2.136	0.864	0.349
Total	100	100.000	0.000	9.044
Assuming known $\lambda = 4.0$			d.f. = 8	p-value = 0.339

No parameters were estimated, since we specified *a priori* the value $\lambda = 4$. For $c = 9$ classes and $m = 0$ parameters estimated, the degrees of freedom are $c - m - 1 = c - 1 = 8$. At $\alpha = .10$, the test statistic (9.044) does not exceed the critical value from Appendix E for $d.f. = 8 (\chi^2_{.10} = 13.36)$ so we do not reject the hypothesis of a Poisson distribution despite the surfeit of 7s ($f = 11$, $e = 5.954$) and dearth of 0s or 1s ($f = 4$, $e = 9.158$). Presumably, this peculiarity of our sample would not be repeated if we took another sample of 100. The *p*-value (.339) suggests that such a result would occur about 339 times in 1,000 samples if the population we are sampling were Poisson, which suggests that any differences are within the realm of chance. Figure 15.13 shows a histogram of actual frequencies (orange bars) and expected frequencies (green lines).

In addition to a chi-square GOF test, we can examine the sample statistics to see if they resemble what would be expected for a Poisson distribution. In a Poisson distribution, the mean is λ, the standard deviation is $\sqrt{\lambda}$, and the skewness is $1/\sqrt{\lambda}$. Table 15.15 shows that the sample mean (4.46) is a little larger than expected ($\mu = \lambda = 4.0$), but the sample standard deviation (2.072) is very close to the expected Poisson standard deviation ($\sigma = \sqrt{\lambda} = \sqrt{4} = 2$). The sample skewness (0.57) is close to the expected skewness ($1/\sqrt{4} = 0.50$). All in all, the evidence is compatible with the hypothesis that Excel's data follow a Poisson distribution.

FIGURE 15.13

Histogram

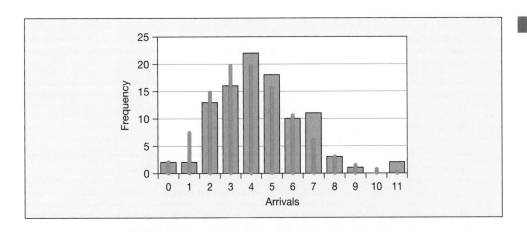

TABLE 15.15

**Statistics for
Excel Sample**
RandPoisson

Statistic	Sample	If Poisson
Mean	4.460	4.000
Standard Deviation	2.072	2.000
Skewness	0.57	0.50

As a last check, since the sample is large enough ($n \geq 30$) to assume normality of the mean, we can do a z test to see whether the sample mean equals the theoretical mean $\lambda = 4.0$. Interestingly, the z test does indicate a potentially significant difference in the sample mean from the intended mean:

$$z = \frac{\bar{x} - \mu}{\frac{\sigma}{\sqrt{n}}} = \frac{4.460 - 4.000}{\frac{2}{\sqrt{100}}} = 2.300 \qquad (p = .021 \text{ in a two-tailed test})$$

The p-value says that such a difference could occur about 21 times in 1,000 samples if the null hypothesis is true. Depending on our α, this could be a significant difference. This difference between the sample mean and the theoretical mean arises from the two outliers (at $x = 11$), which did not have much effect on the chi-square test.

15.12 Excel was asked to generate 50 Poisson random numbers with mean $\lambda = 5$. (a) Calculate the sample mean. How close is it to the desired value? (b) Calculate the expected frequencies assuming a Poisson distribution with $\lambda = 5$. Show your calculations in a spreadsheet format. (c) Carry out the chi-square test at $\alpha = .05$, combining end categories as needed to ensure that all expected frequencies are at least five. Show your degrees of freedom calculation. (d) Do you think your calculations would have been materially different if you had used the sample mean instead of $\lambda = 5.0$? Explain. **RandPois**

SECTION EXERCISES

connect

x	Frequency
0	1
1	1
2	4
3	7
4	7
5	8
6	10
7	3
8	3
9	4
10	1
11	1

15.13 During the 1973–74 hockey season, the Boston Bruins played 39 home games and scored 193 points, as shown below. (a) Estimate the mean from the sample. (b) Calculate the expected frequencies assuming a Poisson distribution. Show your calculations in a spreadsheet format. (c) Carry out the chi-square test, combining end categories as needed to ensure that all expected frequencies are at least five. Show your degrees of freedom calculation. (d) At $\alpha = .05$, can you reject the hypothesis that goals per game follow a Poisson process? (Data are from Gary M. Mullett, "Simeon Poisson and the National Hockey League," *The American Statistician* 31, no. 1 [1977], p. 9.) 📂 **Boston**

Number of Goals Scored (per game) by Boston Bruins, 1973–74

| | Number of Goals | | | | | | | | | | | |
	0	1	2	3	4	5	6	7	8	9	10	Total
Frequency	0	1	2	5	9	10	5	2	3	1	1	39

15.14 At a local supermarket receiving dock, the number of truck arrivals per day is recorded for 100 days. (a) Estimate the mean from the sample. (b) Calculate the expected frequencies assuming a Poisson distribution. Show your calculations in a spreadsheet format. (c) Carry out the chi-square test, combining end categories as needed to ensure that all expected frequencies are at least five. Show your degrees of freedom calculation. (d) At $\alpha = .05$, can you reject the hypothesis that arrivals per day follow a Poisson process? 📂 **Trucks**

Arrivals per Day at a Loading Dock

| | Number of Arrivals | | | | | | | | |
	0	1	2	3	4	5	6	7	Total
Frequency	4	23	28	22	8	9	4	2	100

15.5 NORMAL CHI-SQUARE GOODNESS-OF-FIT TEST

Normal Data-Generating Situations

LO 15-6

Use computer software to perform a chi-square GOF test for normality.

Any normal population is fully described by the two parameters μ and σ. Many data-generating situations could be compatible with a **normal distribution**, if the data possess a reasonable degree of central tendency and are not badly skewed. Measurements of continuous variables such as physical attributes (e.g., weight, size, travel time) may have a constant mean and variance if the underlying process is stable and the population is homogeneous. The normal model might apply to discrete or integer data if the range is relatively large, such as the number of successes in a large binomial sample or Poisson occurrences if the mean is large. Unless μ and σ parameters are known *a priori* (a rare circumstance), they must be estimated from a sample by using $\bar{x}$ and s. Using these statistics, we can set up the chi-square goodness-of-fit test. There are several ways this could be done.

Method 1: Standardizing the Data

There are various ways to calculate the frequencies for a chi-square test. One way is to transform the sample observations $x_1, x_2, \ldots, x_n$ into standardized values:

(15.10) $$z = \frac{x_i - \bar{x}}{s}$$ (standardized data transformation)

We could count the sample observations f_j within intervals of the form $\bar{x} \pm ks$ and compare them with the known frequencies e_j based on the normal distribution, as illustrated in Figure 15.14. We could break the intervals down into more classes if we wish. This

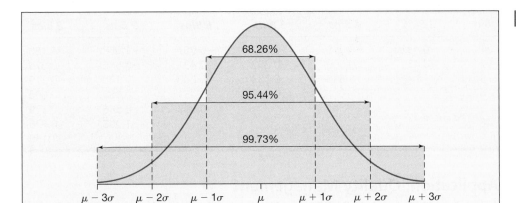

FIGURE 15.14

Normal Areas

method has the advantage of using a standardized scale, but the disadvantage that data no longer are in the original units of measurement (e.g., kilograms) plus the effort required to standardize the data.

Method 2: Equal Bin Widths

An alternative approach is to create a histogram for the original data with equal-width bins. Rather than using "nice" bin limits (as we often do for histograms), we divide the *exact data range* into *c* groups of equal width.

$$\text{Bin width} = \frac{x_{\max} - x_{\min}}{c} \quad \text{(setting bin width from sample data)} \quad \textbf{(15.11)}$$

This avoids "empty" space within histogram intervals. We then proceed as follows:

- Step 1   Count the sample observations in each bin to get observed frequencies f_j.
- Step 2   Convert the bin limits into standardized z-values by using formula 15.10.
- Step 3   Find the area within each bin assuming a normal distribution.
- Step 4   Find expected frequencies e_j by multiplying each normal area by the sample size n.

An advantage of this test is that it corresponds directly to the histogram. Its disadvantage is that, in the end classes, very few observations would be expected. Since small expected frequencies can cause trouble for a chi-square test, classes may need to be collapsed from the ends inward, to enlarge the expected frequencies.

Method 3: Equal Expected Frequencies

A third method is to define histogram bins in such a way that an equal number of observations would be *expected* within each bin under the null hypothesis. That is, define bin limits so that

$$e_j = n/c \quad \text{(define bins to get equal expected frequencies)} \quad \textbf{(15.12)}$$

We want a normal area of $1/c$ in each of the c bins. The first and last classes must be open-ended for a normal distribution, so to define c bins we need $c - 1$ cutpoints. The upper limit of bin j can be found directly by using Excel's function =NORM.INV($j/c, \bar{x}, s$). Alternatively, we can find z_j for bin j with Excel's normal function =NORM.INV($j/c,0,1$) and then calculate the upper limit for bin j as $\bar{x} + z_j s$. Table 15.16 shows some typical z-values to put an area of $1/c$ in each bin.

Once the bins are defined, we count the observations f_j within each bin and compare them with the expected frequencies $e_j = n/c$. Although the bin limits will not be "nice," the compelling advantage of this method is that it guarantees the largest possible expected frequencies, and hence the most powerful test for c bins. MegaStat uses this method (Descriptive Statistics > Normal Curve Goodness of Fit) and calculations are automatic, but you cannot vary the number of bins. MegaStat always uses the number of bins suggested by Sturges' Rule $k = 1 + 3.3 \log_{10}(n)$.

TABLE 15.16

Standard Normal Cutpoints for Equal Area Bins

Bin	3 Bins	4 Bins	5 Bins	6 Bins	7 Bins	8 Bins
1	−0.431	−0.675	−0.842	−0.967	−1.068	−1.150
2	0.431	0.000	−0.253	−0.431	−0.566	−0.675
3		0.675	0.253	0.000	−0.180	−0.319
4			0.842	0.431	0.180	0.000
5				0.967	0.566	0.319
6					1.068	0.675
						1.150

Application: Quality Management

A sample of 35 Hershey's Milk Chocolate Kisses was taken from a bag containing 84 Kisses. The population is assumed infinite. After removing the foil wrapper, each Kiss was weighed. The weights are shown in Table 15.17. Are these weights from a normal population?

TABLE 15.17

Weights of 35 Hershey's Milk Chocolate Kisses (in grams) 📂 **Kisses**

4.666	4.854	4.868	4.849	4.700	4.683	5.064
4.800	4.694	4.760	5.075	4.780	4.781	5.103
4.568	4.983	5.076	4.808	5.084	4.749	5.092
4.783	4.520	4.698	5.084	4.880	4.883	4.880
4.928	4.651	4.797	4.682	4.756	5.041	4.906

Source: An independent project by MBA student Frances Williams. Kisses were weighed on an American Scientific Model S/P 120 analytical balance accurate to 0.0001 gm.

It might be supposed *a priori* that Kiss weights would be normally distributed, since the manufacturing process should have a single, constant mean and standard deviation. Variation is inevitable in any manufacturing process. Chocolate is especially difficult to handle because liquid chocolate must be dropped in precisely measured amounts, solidified, wrapped, and bagged. Since chocolate is soft and crumbles easily, even the process of weighing the Kisses may abrade some chocolate and introduce measurement error. We will test the following hypotheses:

H_0: Kisses' weights are from a normal distribution

H_1: Kisses' weights are not from a normal distribution

Before undertaking a GOF test, consider the histograms in Figure 15.15. The graphs show fitted normal distributions, based on the estimated mean and standard deviation from the data. Although it is only a visual aid, the fitted normal gives you a clue as to the likely outcome of the test. The histograms reveal no apparent outliers, and nothing in conflict with

FIGURE 15.15

Histograms of 35 Hershey's Kiss Weights

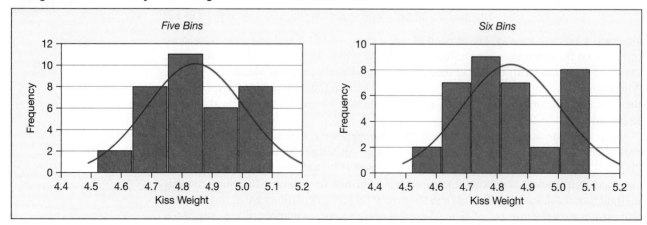

the idea of a normal population except a second mode toward the high end of the scale and perhaps a flatter appearance than normal. Since histogram appearance can vary, depending on the number of classes and the way the bin limits are specified, further tests are needed.

Table 15.18 compares the sample statistics with parameters expected for a normal distribution. Since the mean and standard deviation were fitted from the data, they tell us nothing. The median (4.808) is slightly less than the mean (4.844), but the skewness coefficient (0.14) is fairly close to the value (0.00) that would be expected in a symmetric normal distribution. The sample quartiles (4.700 and 4.983) are nearly what we expect for a normal distribution using the 25th and 75th percentiles ($\bar{x} \pm 0.675s$). There are no outliers, as the smallest Kiss (4.520 grams) is 2.01 standard deviations below the mean, while the largest Kiss (5.103 grams) is 1.61 standard deviations above the mean.

Statistic	Kiss Weight	If Normal
Mean	4.844	4.844
Standard Deviation	0.161	0.161
Quartile 1	4.700	4.735
Median	4.808	4.844
Quartile 3	4.983	4.952
Skewness	0.14	0.00

TABLE 15.18

Sample versus Normal 📁 **Kisses**

For a chi-square GOF test, degrees of freedom are $d.f. = c - m - 1$, where c is the number of classes used in the test and m is the number of parameters estimated. Since two parameters, μ and σ, are estimated from the sample, $m = 2$. We need at least four bins to ensure at least 1 degree of freedom, while Cochran's Rule (at least 5 *expected* observations per bin) suggests a maximum of 7 bins for $n = 35$ data points (since $35/7 = 5$).

Because we anticipate that the number of bins may affect the results, we will vary the number of bins from 4 to 6. We will concentrate on seeing whether the result is affected by the number of bins, and whether certain bins have a disproportionate effect on the chi-square test statistic. We will use method 3 (equal expected frequencies) because it is the most powerful.

Using four bins (Figure 15.16), the chi-square test statistic (0.086) is not significant at $\alpha = .10$ ($\chi^2_{.10} = 2.706$) and its p-value (.770) indicates that such a result would be expected about 770 times in 1,000 samples if the population were normal. Using five bins (Figure 15.17), the chi-square test statistic (4.857) is barely significant at $\alpha = .10$ ($\chi^2_{.10} = 4.605$) and its p-value (.088) indicates that such a result would be expected about 88 times in 1,000

Kiss Weight	Obs	Exp	Obs-Exp	Chi-Square
Under 4.735	9	8.75	0.25	0.007
4.735 < 4.844	9	8.75	0.25	0.007
4.844 < 4.952	8	8.75	−0.75	0.064
4.952 or more	9	8.75	0.25	0.007
Total	35	35	0	0.086
Parameters from sample			d.f. = 1	p < 0.770

FIGURE 15.16

Four Bins (c = 4)

Kiss Weight	Obs	Exp	Obs-Exp	Chi-Square
Under 4.708	9	7.00	2.00	0.571
4.708 < 4.803	8	7.00	1.00	0.143
4.803 < 4.884	7	7.00	0.00	0.000
4.884 < 4.979	2	7.00	−5.00	3.571
4.979 or more	9	7.00	2.00	0.571
Total	35	35	0	4.857
Parameters from sample			d.f. = 2	p < 0.088

FIGURE 15.17

Five Bins (c = 5)

samples if the population were normal. Bin four (highlighted) contributes heavily to the chi-square statistic. In these GOF tests, a low *p*-value indicates *less* resemblance to a normal. Using six bins (Figure 15.18), the chi-square test statistic (3.571) is not significant at $\alpha = .10$ ($\chi^2_{.10} = 6.251$) and its *p*-value (.312) indicates that such a result would be expected about 312 times in 1,000 samples if the population were normal. Bin five (highlighted) contributes heavily to the chi-square statistic.

FIGURE 15.18

Six Bins (c = 6)

Kiss Weight	Obs	Exp	Obs-Exp	Chi-Square
Under 4.688	6	5.83	0.17	0.005
4.688 < 4.774	6	5.83	0.17	0.005
4.774 < 4.844	6	5.83	0.17	0.005
4.844 < 4.913	7	5.83	1.17	0.233
4.913 < 4.999	2	5.83	−3.83	2.519
4.999 or more	8	5.83	2.17	0.805
Total	35	35	0	3.571
Parameters from sample			d.f. = 3	p < 0.312

Interpretation   Depending on the number of bins, the chi-square tests either fail to reject the hypothesis of normality or reject it at a weak level of significance. These results fail to *disprove* normality convincingly. However, the histograms do suggest a bimodal shape. This could occur if the Kisses were molded by two or more different machines. If each machine has a different μ and σ, this could lead to the "mixture of distributions" problem mentioned earlier. If so, a platykurtic distribution (flatter than normal) would be likely. This issue bears further investigation. A quality control analyst would probably take a larger sample and study the manufacturing methods to see what could be learned.

SECTION EXERCISES

connect™

Hint: Check your work using MegaStat's Descriptive Statistics > Normal curve goodness of fit test.

15.15 Exam scores of 40 students in a statistics class are shown. (a) Estimate the mean and standard deviation from the sample. (b) Assuming that the data are from a normal distribution, define bins by using method 3 (equal expected frequencies). Use 8 bins. (c) Set up an Excel worksheet for your chi-square calculations, with a column showing the expected frequency for each bin (they must add to 40). (d) Tabulate the observed frequency for each bin and record it in the next column. (e) Carry out the chi-square test, using $\alpha = .05$. Can you reject the hypothesis that the exam scores came from a normal population? 📄 **ExamScores**

79	75	77	57	81	70	83	66
81	89	59	83	75	60	96	86
78	76	71	78	78	70	54	60
71	81	79	88	77	82	75	68
77	69	83	79	79	76	78	71

15.16 One Friday night, there were 42 carry-out orders at Ashoka Curry Express. (a) Estimate the mean and standard deviation from the sample. (b) Assuming that the data are from a normal distribution, define bins by using method 3 (equal expected frequencies). Use 8 bins. (c) Set up an Excel worksheet for your chi-square calculations, with a column showing the expected frequency for each bin (they must add to 42). (d) Tabulate the observed frequency for each bin and record it in the next column. (e) Do the chi-square test at $\alpha = .025$. Can you reject the hypothesis that carry-out orders follow a normal population? 📄 **TakeOut**

18.74	21.05	31.19	23.06	20.17	25.12	24.30
46.04	33.96	45.04	34.63	35.24	30.13	29.93
52.33	26.52	19.68	19.62	32.96	42.07	47.82
38.62	31.88	44.97	36.35	21.50	41.42	33.87
26.43	35.28	21.88	24.80	27.49	18.30	44.47
28.40	36.72	26.30	47.08	34.33	13.15	15.51

15.6 ECDF TESTS (OPTIONAL)

There are many alternatives to the chi-square test for goodness of fit. These alternatives are based on the **empirical cumulative distribution function (ECDF)**.

LO 15-7

State advantages of ECDF tests as compared to chi-square GOF tests.

Anderson-Darling Test

The **Anderson-Darling test** is perhaps the most widely used test for non-normality because of its power. It is always done on a computer because it requires the inverse CDF for the hypothesized distribution. The A-D test is based on a **probability plot**. When the data fit the hypothesized distribution closely, the probability plot will be close to a straight line. The A-D test statistic measures the overall distance between the actual and the hypothesized distributions, using a weighted squared distance. It provides a *p*-value to complement the visual plot. The A-D statistic is not difficult to calculate, but its formula is rather complex, so it is omitted. Figure 15.19 shows a graph displaying the probability plot and A-D statistic for the Hershey's Kiss data using MINITAB's Stats > Basic Statistics > Normality Test. The *p*-value (.091) suggests a departure from normality at the 10 percent level of significance, but not at the 5 percent level. This result is consistent with our previous findings. The A-D test is more powerful than a chi-square test if raw data are available because it treats the observations individually. Also, the probability plot has the attraction of revealing discrepancies between the sample and the hypothesized distribution, and it is usually easy to spot outliers.

FIGURE 15.19

MINITAB's Probability Plot and Anderson-Darling Test for Kiss Weights

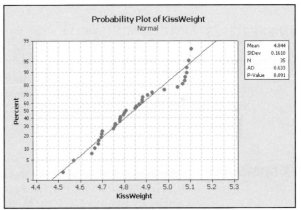

Kolmogorov-Smirnov and Lilliefors Tests

Another such test is the **Kolmogorov-Smirnov test**. The K-S test statistic D is the largest absolute difference between the actual and expected cumulative relative frequency of the n data values:

$$D = \text{Max} |F_a - F_e| \tag{15.13}$$

The K-S test is not recommended for grouped data, as it may be less powerful than the chi-square test.

F_a is the actual cumulative frequency at observation i, and F_e is the expected cumulative frequency at observation i under the assumption that the data came from the hypothesized distribution. The K-S test assumes that no parameters are estimated. If they are (e.g., the mean and variance may be estimated), we use a **Lilliefors test**, whose test statistic is the same but with a different table of critical values. Since these tests are always done by computer (F_e requires the inverse CDF for the hypothesized distribution), we will omit further details and merely illustrate the test visually. Because observations are treated individually, information is not lost by combining categories, as in a chi-square test. Thus,

ECDF tests may surpass the chi-square test in their ability to detect departures from the distribution specified in the null hypothesis, if raw data are available.

Illustrations: Lottery Numbers and Kiss Weights

The CDF under the hypothesis of normality would be *S*-shaped. Figure 15.20 shows a *normality* test for weights of Hershey's Kisses. The largest difference occurs at observation 28, but the *p*-value does not warrant rejection of the hypothesis of normality. For this data set, the K-S test lacks sufficient power to reject a normal distribution.

FIGURE 15.20

K-S Test for Normality
Kisses

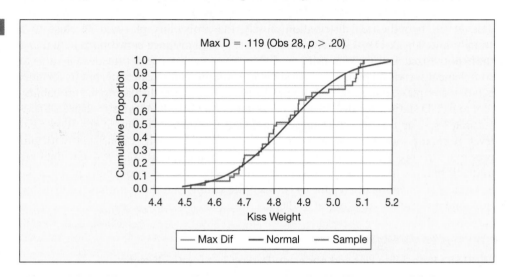

SECTION EXERCISES

connect

*15.17 Use MINITAB's Stat > Basic Statistics > Normality Test to obtain a probability plot for the exam score data (see Exercise 15.15). Interpret the probability plot and Anderson-Darling statistic. Was MINITAB easier to use than the chi-square test? **ExamScores**

*15.18 Use MINITAB's Stat > Basic Statistics > Normality Test to obtain a probability plot for the Ashoka Curry House carry-out order data (see Exercise 15.16). Interpret the probability plot and Anderson-Darling statistic. Was MINITAB easier to use than the chi-square test? **TakeOut**

CHAPTER SUMMARY

A **chi-square test of independence** requires an $r \times c$ **contingency table** that has r rows and c columns. Degrees of freedom for the chi-square test will be $(r - 1)(c - 1)$. In this test, the **observed frequencies** are compared with the **expected frequencies** under the hypothesis of independence. The test assumes categorical data (attribute data) but can also be used with numerical data grouped into classes. **Cochran's Rule** requires that expected frequencies be at least 5 in each cell, although this rule is often relaxed. A test for **goodness-of-fit (GOF)** uses the chi-square statistic to decide whether a sample is from a specified distribution (e.g., multinomial, uniform, Poisson, normal). The **parameters** of the fitted distribution (e.g., the mean) may be specified *a priori,* but more often are estimated from the sample. Degrees of freedom for the GOF test are $c - m - 1$ where c is the number of categories and m is the number of parameters estimated. The **Kolmogorov-Smirnov** and **Lilliefors** tests are **ECDF-based tests** that look at differences between the sample's empirical cumulative distribution function (ECDF) and the hypothesized distribution. They are best used with n individual observations. The **Anderson-Darling** test and the **probability plot** are the most common ECDF tests, most often used to test for normality.

KEY TERMS

Anderson-Darling test, *677*
chi-square probability
   distribution, *651*
chi-square test, *650*
Cochran's Rule, *655*
contingency table, *649*
degrees of freedom, *651*

empirical cumulative
   distribution function
   (ECDF), *677*
expected frequency, *650*
goodness-of-fit test, *660*
independent, *650*
Kolmogorov-Smirnov test, *677*

Lilliefors test, *677*
multinomial distribution, *660*
normal distribution, *672*
observed frequency, *650*
Poisson distribution, *667*
probability plot, *677*
uniform distribution, *663*

Commonly Used Formulas

Chi-Square Test for Independence

Test statistic for independence in a contingency table with r rows

and c columns: $\chi^2_{\text{calc}} = \sum_{j=1}^{r} \sum_{k=1}^{c} \frac{[f_{jk} - e_{jk}]^2}{e_{jk}}$

Degrees of freedom for a contingency table with r rows
and c columns: $d.f. = (r - 1)(c - 1)$

Expected frequency in row j and column k: $e_{jk} = R_j C_k / n$

Chi-Square Test for Goodness-of-Fit

Test statistic for observed frequencies in c classes under a hypothesized distribution

H_0 (e.g., uniform, Poisson, normal): $\chi^2_{\text{calc}} = \sum_{j=1}^{c} \frac{[f_j - e_j]^2}{e_j}$

where

f_j = the observed frequency in class j

e_j = the expected frequency in class j

Degrees of freedom for the chi-square GOF test: $d.f. = c - m - 1$

where

c = the number of classes used in the test
m = the number of parameters estimated

Estimated mean of Poisson distribution with c classes: $\lambda = \sum_{j=1}^{c} x_j f_j$

where

x_j = the value of X in class j

f_j = the observed frequency in class j

Expected frequency in class j assuming a uniform distribution with c classes: $e_j = n/c$

CHAPTER REVIEW

Note: Questions labeled * are based on optional material from this chapter.

1. (a) What are the hypotheses in a chi-square test for independence? (b) Why do we call it a test of frequencies? (c) What distribution is used in this test? (d) How do we calculate the degrees of freedom for an $r \times c$ contingency table?

2. How do we calculate the expected frequencies for each cell of the contingency table?

3. What is Cochran's Rule, and why is it needed? Why do we call it a "rule of thumb"?

4. (a) Explain why the 2×2 table is analogous to a z test for two proportions. (b) What is the relationship between z and χ^2 in the 2×2 table?

5. (a) What are the hypotheses for a GOF test? (b) Explain how a chi-square GOF test is carried out in general.

6. What is the general formula for degrees of freedom in a chi-square GOF test?

7. (a) In a uniform GOF test, how do we calculate the expected frequencies? (b) Why is the test easier if the data are already grouped?

8. (a) In a Poisson GOF test, how do we calculate the expected frequencies? (b) Why do we need the mean λ before carrying out the chi-square test?

9. (a) Very briefly describe three ways of calculating expected frequencies for a normal GOF test. (b) Name advantages and disadvantages of each way. (c) Why is a normal GOF test almost always done on a computer?

*10. What is an ECDF test? Give an example.

*11. (a) Name potential advantages of the Kolmogorov-Smirnov or Lilliefors tests. (b) Why would this type of test almost always be done on a computer?

*12. (a) What does a probability plot show? (b) If the hypothesized distribution is a good fit to the data, what would be the appearance of the probability plot? (c) What are the advantages and disadvantages of a probability plot?

*13. (a) Name two advantages of the Anderson-Darling test. (b) Why is it almost always done on a computer?

CHAPTER EXERCISES

connect

Instructions: In all exercises, include MegaStat, Excel, or MINITAB exhibits to support your calculations. State the hypotheses, show how the degrees of freedom are calculated, find the critical value of chi-square from Appendix E or from Excel's function =CHISQ.INV.RT(alpha, deg_freedom), and interpret the *p*-value. Tell whether the conclusion is sensitive to the level of significance chosen, identify cells that contribute the most to the chi-square test statistic, and check for small expected frequencies. If necessary, you can calculate the *p*-value by using Excel's function =CHISQ.DIST.RT(test statistic, deg_freedom). *Note:* Exercises marked * are harder or require optional material.

15.19 Employees of Axolotl Corporation were sampled at random from pay records and asked to complete an anonymous job satisfaction survey, yielding the tabulation shown. *Research question:* At $\alpha = .05$, is job satisfaction independent of pay category? 📄 **Employees**

Pay Type	Satisfied	Neutral	Dissatisfied	Total
Salaried	20	13	2	35
Hourly	135	127	58	320
Total	155	140	60	335

15.20 Sixty-four students in an introductory college economics class were asked how many credits they had earned in college, and how certain they were about their choice of major. *Research question:* At $\alpha = .01$, is the degree of certainty independent of credits earned? 📄 **Certainty**

Credits Earned	Very Uncertain	Somewhat Certain	Very Certain	Row Total
0–9	12	8	3	23
10–59	8	4	10	22
60 or more	1	7	11	19
Col Total	21	19	24	64

15.21 To see whether students who finish an exam first get the same grades as those who finish later, a professor kept track of the order in which papers were handed in. Of the first 25 papers, 10 received a "B" or better, compared with 8 of the last 24 papers handed in. *Research question:* At $\alpha = .10$, is the grade independent of the order handed in? Since it is a 2 × 2 table, try also a two-tailed, two-sample *z* test for $\pi_1 = \pi_2$ (see Chapter 10) and verify that z^2 is the same as your chi-square statistic. Which test do you prefer? Why? 📄 **Grades**

Grade	Earlier Hand-In	Later Hand-In	Row Total
"B" or better	10	8	18
"C" or worse	15	16	31
Col Total	25	24	49

15.22 From 74 of its restaurants, Noodles & Company managers collected data on per-person sales and the percent of sales due to "potstickers" (a popular food item). Both numerical variables failed tests for normality, so they tried a chi-square test. Each variable was converted into ordinal categories (low, medium, high) using cutoff points that produced roughly equal group sizes. *Research question:* At $\alpha = .05$, is per-person spending independent of percent of sales from potstickers? 📄 **Noodles**

	Potsticker % of Sales			
Per Person Spending	Low	Medium	High	Row Total
Low	14	6	3	23
Medium	7	16	5	28
High	3	4	16	23
Col Total	24	26	24	74

15.23 A web-based anonymous survey of students asked for a self-rating on proficiency in a language other than English and the student's frequency of newspaper reading. *Research question:* At $\alpha = .10$, is frequency of newspaper reading independent of foreign language proficiency? **WebSurvey**

Non-English Proficiency	Daily Newspaper Reading			Row Total
	Never	*Occasionally*	*Regularly*	
None	4	13	5	22
Slight	11	45	9	65
Moderate	6	33	7	46
Fluent	5	19	1	25
Col Total	26	110	22	158

15.24 A student team examined parked cars in four different suburban shopping malls. One hundred vehicles were examined in each location. *Research question:* At $\alpha = .05$, does vehicle type vary by mall location? (Data are from a project by MBA students Steve Bennett, Alicia Morais, Steve Olson, and Greg Corda.) **Vehicles**

Vehicle Type	Somerset	Oakland	Great Lakes	Jamestown	Row Total
Car	44	49	36	64	193
Minivan	21	15	18	13	67
Full-sized Van	2	3	3	2	10
SUV	19	27	26	12	84
Truck	14	6	17	9	46
Col Total	100	100	100	100	400

15.25 Choose either 2×2 contingency table shown below (males *or* females). *Research question:* At $\alpha = .005$, is smoking independent of race? (Smoking rates are from *Statistical Abstract of the United States, 2001,* pp. 16 and 12, applied to hypothetical samples of 500.) **Smoking**

Smoking by Race for Males Aged 18–24

Race	Smoker	Nonsmoker	Row Total
White	145	280	425
Black	15	60	75
Col Total	160	340	500

Smoking by Race for Females Aged 18–24

Race	Smoker	Nonsmoker	Row Total
White	116	299	415
Black	7	78	85
Col Total	123	377	500

15.26 High levels of cockpit noise in an aircraft can damage the hearing of pilots who are exposed to this hazard for many hours. A Boeing 727 co-pilot collected 61 noise observations using a handheld sound meter. Noise level is defined as "Low" (under 88 decibels), "Medium" (88 to 91 decibels), or "High" (92 decibels or more). There are three flight phases (Climb, Cruise, Descent). *Research question:* At $\alpha = .05$, is the cockpit noise level independent of flight phase? ☞ **Noise**

Noise Level	Climb	Cruise	Descent	Row Total
Low	6	2	6	14
Medium	18	3	8	29
High	1	3	14	18
Col Total	25	8	28	61

15.27 Forecasters' interest rate predictions over an eight-year period were studied to see whether the predictions corresponded to what actually happened. The 2×2 contingency table below shows the frequencies of actual and predicted interest rate movements. *Research question:* At $\alpha = .10$, is the actual change independent of the predicted change? ☞ **Forecasts**

Forecasted Change	Rates Fell	Rates Rose	Row Total
Rates would fall	7	12	19
Rates would rise	9	6	15
Col Total	16	18	34

15.28 In a study of childhood asthma, 4,317 observations were collected on education and smoking during pregnancy, shown in the 4×3 contingency table below. *Research question:* At $\alpha = .005$, is smoking during pregnancy independent of education level? ☞ **Pregnancy**

Education	No Smoking	$<\frac{1}{2}$ Pack	$\geq\frac{1}{2}$ Pack	Row Total
<High School	641	196	196	1,033
High School	1,370	290	270	1,930
Some College	635	68	53	756
College	550	30	18	598
Col Total	3,196	584	537	4,317

15.29 Two contingency tables below show return on investment (ROI) and percent of sales growth over the previous 5 years for 85 U.S. firms. ROI is defined as percentage of return on a combination of stockholders' equity (both common and preferred) plus capital from long-term debt including current maturities, minority stockholders' equity in consolidated subsidiaries, and accumulated deferred taxes and investment tax credits. *Research question:* At $\alpha = .05$, is ROI independent of sales growth? Would you expect it to be? Do the two tables (2×2 and 3×3) agree? Are small expected frequencies a problem? ☞ **ROI**

2 × 2 Cross-Tabulation of Companies

ROI	Low Growth	High Growth	Row Total
Low ROI	24	16	40
High ROI	14	31	45
Col Total	38	47	85

3 × 3 Cross-Tabulation of Companies

ROI	Low Growth	Medium Growth	High Growth	Row Total
Low ROI	9	12	7	28
Medium ROI	6	14	7	27
High ROI	1	12	17	30
Col Total	16	38	31	85

15.30 Can people really identify their favorite brand of cola? Volunteers tasted Coke, Pepsi, Diet Coke, and Diet Pepsi, with the results shown below. *Research question:* At $\alpha = .05$, is the correctness of the prediction different for regular cola and diet cola drinkers? Since it is a 2×2 table, try also a two-tailed, two-sample z test for $\pi_1 = \pi_2$ (see Chapter 10) and verify that z^2 is the same as your chi-square statistic. 📁 **Cola**

Correct?	Regular Cola	Diet Cola	Row Total
Yes, got it right	7	7	14
No, got it wrong	12	20	32
Col Total	19	27	46

15.31 A survey of randomly chosen new students at a certain university revealed the data below concerning the main reason for choosing this university instead of another. *Research question:* At $\alpha = .01$, is the main reason for choosing the university independent of student type? 📁 **Students**

New Student	Tuition	Location	Reputation	Row Total
Freshmen	50	30	35	115
Transfers	15	29	20	64
MBAs	5	20	60	85
Col Total	70	79	115	264

15.32 A survey of 189 statistics students asked the age of car usually driven and the student's political orientation. The car age was a numerical variable, which was converted into ordinal categories. *Research question:* At $\alpha = .10$, are students' political views independent of the age of car they usually drive? 📁 **Politics**

Politics	Age of Car Usually Driven			Row Total
	Under 3	3–6	7 or More	
Liberal	19	12	13	44
Middle-of-Road	33	31	28	92
Conservative	16	24	13	53
Col Total	68	67	54	189

15.33 The actual distribution of car colors for 2006 model car buyers is shown below. Based on the sample of 200 car buyers for 2012 model vehicles, use the multinomial chi-square GOF test at $\alpha = .05$ to test whether car buyers' color preferences have changed.

Car Color	2006 Percent	2012 Sample Frequencies
Silver/gray	22	52
Blue	12	24
White	16	32
Tan/beige	11	6
Black	15	48
Green	5	4
Red	13	12
Other	6	22
Total	100	200

15.34 Prof. Green's multiple-choice exam had 50 questions with the distribution of correct answers shown below. *Research question:* At $\alpha = .05$, can you reject the hypothesis that Green's exam answers came from a uniform population? 📄 **Correct**

Correct Answer	Frequency
A	8
B	8
C	9
D	11
E	14
Total	50

15.35 Oxnard Kortholt, Ltd., employs 50 workers. During the last year, the company noted the number of visits with health care professionals (doctor, emergency, home) for each of its employees. U.S. national percentages are also shown. *Research question:* At $\alpha = .05$, do Oxnard employees differ significantly from the national percent distribution? (National percentages are from *The World Almanac and Book of Facts, 2005* [World Almanac Education Group, Inc., 2005], p. 180.) 📄 **Oxnard**

Health Care Visits	National Percentage	Oxnard Employees Frequency
No visits	16.5	4
1–3 visits	45.8	20
4–9 visits	24.4	15
10 or more visits	13.3	11
Total	100.0	50

15.36 In a four-digit lottery, each of the four digits is supposed to have the same probability of occurrence. The table shows the frequency of occurrence of each digit for 89 consecutive daily four-digit drawings. *Research question:* At $\alpha = .01$, can you reject the hypothesis that the digits are from a uniform population? Why do the frequencies add to 356? 📄 **Lottery4**

Digit	Frequency
0	39
1	27
2	35
3	39
4	35
5	35
6	27
7	42
8	36
9	41
Total	356

15.37 A student rolled a supposedly fair die 60 times, resulting in the distribution of dots shown. *Research question:* At $\alpha = .10$, can you reject the hypothesis that the die is fair? 📄 **Dice**

			Number of Dots				
	1	*2*	*3*	*4*	*5*	*6*	*Total*
Frequency	7	14	9	13	7	10	60

15.38 The World Cup soccer tournament is held every 4 years, with 32 teams from various nations competing. In the World Cup tournaments between 1990 and 2002, there were 232 games with the distribution of goals shown in this worksheet. *Research question:* At $\alpha = .025$, can you reject the hypothesis that goals per game follow a Poisson process? *Hint:* You must calculate the mean and look up the Poisson probabilities in Appendix B or Excel. (Data are from Singfat Chu, "Using Soccer Goals to Motivate the Poisson Process," *INFORMS Transactions on Education* 3, no. 2 [January 2003], pp. 62–68.) 📄 **WorldCup**

Goals	f_j	$P(X)$	e_j	$f_j - e_j$	$(f_j - e_j)^2$	$(f_j - e_j)^2/e_j$
0	19					
1	49					
2	60					
3	47					
4	32					
5	18					
6 or more	7					
Total games	232					
Total goals	575					
Mean goals/game						

*15.39 The table below shows the number of ATM customer arrivals per minute in 60 randomly chosen minutes. *Research question:* At $\alpha = .025$, can you reject the hypothesis that the number of arrivals per minute follows a Poisson process? 📄 **ATM**

0	0	0	1	3	0	0	0	2	5	2	0	1	1	1	2	1	1	0	2
3	0	0	3	0	1	0	1	1	1	1	2	0	2	0	3	0	2	0	1
1	0	0	0	0	1	3	2	1	0	0	0	4	1	0	1	0	3	3	1

15.40 Pick *one* Excel data set (A through F) and investigate whether the data could have come from a normal population using $\alpha = .01$. Use any test you wish, including a histogram, or MegaStat's Descriptive Statistics > Normal curve goodness of fit test, or MINITAB's Stats > Basic Statistics > Normality Test to obtain a probability plot with the Anderson-Darling statistic. Interpret the *p*-value from your tests. For larger data sets, only the first three and last three observations are shown.

DATA SET A **Kentucky Derby Winning Time (Seconds), 1950–2011 ($n = 62$)**
📄 **Derby**

Year	Derby Winner	Time
1950	Middleground	121.6
1951	Count Turf	122.6
1952	Hill Gail	121.6
⋮	⋮	⋮
2009	Mine That Bird	122.7
2010	Super Saver	124.5
2011	Animal Kingdom	122.0

Sources: *Information Please Sports Almanac* (ESPN Books, 1998), *Facts on File, Detroit Free Press,* and *The New York Times,* selected issues.

DATA SET B   National League Runs Scored Leader, 1900–2010 ($n = 111$)
       Runs

Year	Player	Runs
1900	Roy Thomas, Phil	131
1901	Jesse Burkett, StL	139
1902	Honus Wagner, Pitt	105
⋮	⋮	⋮
2008	Hanley Ramirez, FLA	125
2009	Albert Pujols, STL	124
2010	Albert Pujols, STL	115

Sources: *Sports Illustrated 2003 Almanac*, pp. 100–113; www.baseball-almanac.com; www.hickoksports.com; and http://www .baseball-reference.com.

DATA SET C   Weight (in grams) of Pieces of Halloween Candy ($n = 78$)
       Candy

1.6931	1.8320	1.3167	0.5031	0.7097	1.4358
1.8851	1.6695	1.6101	1.6506	1.2105	1.4074
1.5836	1.1164	1.2953	1.4107	1.3212	1.6353
1.5435	1.7175	1.3489	1.1688	1.5543	1.3566
1.4844	1.4636	1.1701	1.5238	1.7346	1.1981
1.6601	1.8359	1.1334	1.7030	1.2481	1.4356
1.3756	1.3172	1.3700	1.0145	1.0002	0.9409
1.4942	1.2316	1.6505	1.7088	1.1850	1.3583
1.5188	1.3460	1.3928	1.6522	0.5303	1.6301
1.0474	1.4664	1.2902	1.9638	1.9687	1.2406
1.6759	1.6989	1.4959	1.4180	1.5218	2.1064
1.3213	1.1116	1.4535	1.4289	1.9156	1.8142
1.3676	1.7157	1.4493	1.4303	1.2912	1.7137

Source: Independent project by statistics student Frances Williams. Weighed on an American Scientific Model S/P 120 analytical balance, accurate to 0.0001 gram.

DATA SET D   Price/Earnings Ratios for Specialty Retailers ($n = 58$)
       PERatios

Company	PE Ratio
Abercrombie and Fitch	19
Advance AutoParts	16
American Eagle Outfitters	30
⋮	⋮
United Auto Group	12
Williams-Sonoma	28
Zale	15

Source: *Business Week*, November 22, 2004, pp. 95–98.

DATA SET E   U.S. Presidents' Ages at Inauguration (*n* = 43) 🖭 Presidents

President	Age
Washington	57
J. Adams	61
Jefferson	57
⋮	⋮
Clinton	46
G. W. Bush	54
Obama	47

Source: *The World Almanac and Book of Facts,* 2002, p. 545.

DATA SET F   Weights of 31 Randomly Chosen Circulated Nickels (*n* = 31) 🖭 Nickels

5.043	4.980	4.967	5.043	4.956	4.999	4.917	4.927
4.893	5.003	4.951	5.040	5.043	5.004	5.014	5.035
4.883	5.022	4.932	4.998	5.032	4.948	5.001	4.983
4.912	4.796	4.970	4.956	5.036	5.045	4.801	

Note: Weighed by statistics student Dorothy Duffy as an independent project. Nickels were weighed on a Mettler PE 360 Delta Range scale, accurate to 0.001 gram.

INTEGRATIVE PROJECTS

*15.41 In 2002, the Anaheim Angels defeated the San Francisco Giants in the World Series 4 games to 3. The table below shows the inning-by-inning breakdown of runs by each team ($\times$ indicates unnecessary last half of inning). (a) Estimate λ (the mean runs per game). (b) Use Excel's function =POISSON.DIST(x,mean,0) to fill in the $P(X = x)$ column. (c) Multiply $P(X = x)$ by 121 to obtain the expected frequencies. (d) Carry out the chi-square test at $\alpha = .05$, combining classes as needed to enlarge expected frequencies. (e) Explain how you obtained the degrees of freedom. (f) Which cells show the largest contribution to the chi-square test statistic? (g) Obtain the p-value using Excel's function =CHISQ.DIST.RT(x, degrees of freedom). (h) Why is the Poisson distribution a poor fit for baseball runs, even though it fits hockey goals pretty well? 🖭 WorldSeries

2002 World Series Runs by inning

		1	2	3	4	5	6	7	8	9	Score
1	San Fran	0	2	0	0	0	2	0	0	0	4
	Anaheim	0	1	0	0	0	2	0	0	0	3
2	San Fran	0	4	1	0	4	0	0	0	1	10
	Anaheim	5	2	0	0	1	1	0	2	×	11
3	Anaheim	0	0	4	4	0	1	0	1	0	10
	San Fran	1	0	0	0	3	0	0	0	0	4
4	Anaheim	0	1	2	0	0	0	0	0	0	3
	San Fran	0	0	0	0	3	0	0	1	×	4
5	Anaheim	0	0	0	0	3	1	0	0	0	4
	San Fran	3	3	0	0	0	2	4	4	×	16
6	San Fran	0	0	0	0	3	1	1	0	0	5
	Anaheim	0	0	0	0	0	0	3	3	×	6
7	San Fran	0	1	0	0	0	0	0	0	0	1
	Anaheim	0	1	3	0	0	0	0	0	×	4

Sources: *The Baseball Encyclopedia,* 10th ed. (Macmillan, 1996), and *Baseball Almanac,* www.cnnsi.com.

Runs (x)	f_j	$P(X = x)$	e_j	$f_j - e_j$	$(f_j - e_j)^2$	$(f_j - e_j)^2/e_j$
0	83					
1	15					
2	7					
3	9					
4	6					
5 or more	1					
Total ½ innings	121					
Total runs	85					
Mean runs/inning						

*15.42 Refer to the previous problem. In the 2002 World Series, a total of 85 runs were scored. (a) Before doing any calculations, based on your understanding of baseball, why might runs per inning *not* be uniform? (b) Complete the tabulation below, by counting the frequency of runs in each of the nine innings with all games combined. (c) Calculate the frequency of runs per inning by dividing the total number of runs by 9. (d) Perform the chi-square goodness-of-fit test and obtain a *p*-value using Excel's function =CHISQ.DIST.RT(test statistic,deg_freedom). (e) State your conclusions plainly. 🖻 **WorldSeries**

Inning	f_j	e_j	$f_j - e_j$	$(f_j - e_j)^2$	$(f_j - e_j)^2/e_j$
1					
2					
3					
4					
5					
6					
7					
8					
9					
Total					

*15.43 (a) Use either MINITAB or MegaStat or Excel's function =NORM.INV(RAND(),0,1) or Excel's Data Analysis > Random Numbers to generate 100 normally distributed random numbers with a mean of 0 and a standard deviation of 1. (b) Make a histogram of your sample and assess its shape. Are there outliers? (c) Calculate descriptive statistics. Are the sample mean and standard deviation close to their intended values? (d) See if the first and third quartiles are approximately -0.675 and $+0.675$, as they should be. (e) Use a *z* test

$$z = \frac{\bar{x} - \mu}{\sigma/\sqrt{n}} = \frac{\bar{x} - 0}{1/\sqrt{100}} = 10\bar{x}$$

to compare the sample mean to the desired mean. *Note:* Use *z* instead of *t* because the hypothesized mean $\mu = 0$ and standard deviation $\sigma = 1$ are known. (f) What would happen if 100 statistics students performed similar experiments, assuming that the random number generator is working correctly?

*15.44 (a) Use either MegaStat or Excel's function =RAND() or Excel's Data Analysis > Random Numbers to generate 100 uniformly distributed random numbers between 0 and 1. (b) Make a histogram of your sample and assess its shape. (c) Calculate descriptive statistics. Are the sample mean and standard deviation close to their intended values $\mu = (0 + 1)/2 = 0.5000$ and $\sigma = \sqrt{1/12} = 0.288675$? (d) See if the first and third quartiles are approximately 0.25 and 0.75, as they should be. (e) Use a *z* test

$$z = \frac{\bar{x} - \mu}{\sigma/\sqrt{n}} = \frac{\bar{x} - 0.5000}{(0.288675)/\sqrt{100}}$$

to compare the sample mean to the desired mean. *Note:* Use *z* instead of *t* because the hypothesized mean $\mu = 0.5000$ and standard deviation $\sigma = 0.288675$ are known. (f) What would happen if 100 statistics students performed similar experiments, assuming that the random number generator is working correctly?

*15.45 (a) Use Excel's Data Analysis > Random Numbers to generate 100 Poisson-distributed random numbers with a mean of $\lambda = 4$. (b) Make a histogram of your sample and assess its shape. (c) Calculate descriptive statistics. Are the sample mean and standard deviation close to their intended values $\lambda = 4$ and $\sigma = \sqrt{\lambda} = \sqrt{4} = 2$? (d) Use a z test

$$z = \frac{\bar{x} - \mu}{\sigma/\sqrt{n}} = \frac{\bar{x} - 4}{2/\sqrt{100}} = 5\bar{x} - 20$$

to compare the sample mean to the desired mean. *Note:* Use z instead of t because the hypothesized mean $\mu = 4$ and standard deviation $\sigma = 2$ are known. (e) What would happen if 100 statistics students performed similar experiments, assuming that Excel's random number generator is working correctly?

15.46 Refer back to Table 15.11, which shows the distribution of the number of U.S. Supreme Court appointments per year from 1900–1999. Since 1999 there have been four Supreme Court appointments with one each in the years 2005, 2006, 2009, and 2010. Redo the Poisson GOF test to determine if the assumption of a Poisson distribution is still reasonable for the years 1900–2010. (Note that the number of years in this range is 111.)

RELATED READINGS

D'Agostino, Ralph B., and Michael A. Stephens. *Goodness-of-Fit Techniques.* Marcel Dekker, 1986.

Haber, Michael. "A Comparison of Some Continuity Corrections for the Chi-Squared Test on 2×2 Tables." *Journal of the American Statistical Association* 75, no. 371 (1980), pp. 510–15.

Thode, Henry C., Jr. *Testing for Normality.* Marcel Dekker, 2002.

CHAPTER 15   Online Learning Resources

The Online Learning Center (OLC) at www.mhhe.com/doane4e has several *LearningStats* demonstrations to help you understand chi-square tests. Your instructor may assign one or more of them, or you may decide to download the ones that sound interesting.

Topic	LearningStats Demonstrations
Goodness-of-fit tests	⊠ Normal and Uniform Tests
	⊠ ECDF Plots Illustrated
	⊠ Contingency Tables: A Simulation
	⊠ Probability Plots: A Simulation
	⊠ CDF Normality Test
	⊠ Degrees of Freedom
	⊠ How Big a Sample

Key: ⊠ = Excel

CHAPTER CONTENTS

CHAPTER LEARNING OBJECTIVES

LO

When you finish this chapter you should be able to

LO 16-1 Define nonparametric tests and explain when they may be desirable.

LO 16-2 Use the one-sample runs test.

LO 16-3 Use the Wilcoxon signed-rank test.

LO 16-4 Use the Wilcoxon rank sum test for two samples.

LO 16-5 Use the Kruskal-Wallis test for c independent samples.

LO 16-6 Use the Friedman test for related samples.

LO 16-7 Use the Spearman rank correlation test.

LO 16-8 Use computer software to perform the tests and obtain p-values.

16.1 WHY USE NONPARAMETRIC TESTS?

The hypothesis tests in previous chapters require the estimation of one or more unknown parameters (for example, the population mean or variance). These tests often make unrealistic assumptions about the normality of the underlying population or require large samples to invoke the Central Limit Theorem. In contrast, **nonparametric tests** or distribution-free tests usually focus on the sign or rank of the data rather than the exact numerical value of the variable, do not specify the shape of the parent population, can often be used in smaller samples, and can be used for ordinal data (when the measurement scale is not interval or ratio). Table 16.1 highlights the advantages and disadvantages of nonparametric tests.

Advantages	Disadvantages
1. Can often be used in small samples.	1. Require special tables for small samples.
2. Generally more powerful than parametric tests when normality cannot be assumed.	2. If normality *can* be assumed, parametric tests are generally more powerful.
3. Can be used for ordinal data.	

TABLE 16.1

Advantages and Disadvantages of Nonparametric Tests

Rejection of a hypothesis using a nonparametric test is especially convincing because nonparametric tests generally make fewer assumptions about the population. If two methods are justified and have similar **power**, the principle of Occam's Razor favors the simpler method. For this reason, statisticians are attracted to nonparametric tests, particularly in applications where data are likely to be ill-behaved and when samples are small.

You might expect that nonparametric tests would primarily be used in areas of business where nominal or ordinal data are common (e.g., human resources, marketing). Yet business analysts who mostly use ratio data (e.g., accounting, finance) may encounter skewed populations that render parametric tests unreliable. These analysts might use nonparametric tests as a *complement* to their customary **parametric tests**. Figure 16.1 shows common nonparametric tests and their parametric counterparts, which you have seen in earlier chapters.

This chapter illustrates only a few of the many nonparametric techniques that are available. The selections are those you are most likely to encounter. Small-sample nonparametric tests are omitted, but references are shown at the end of the chapter for those who need them.

LO 16-1

Define nonparametric tests and explain when they may be desirable.

FIGURE 16.1
Some Common Nonparametric Tests

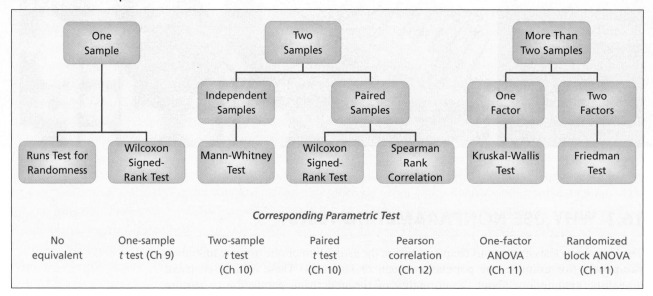

16.2 ONE-SAMPLE RUNS TEST

LO 16-2

Use the one-sample runs test.

The one-sample **runs test** is also called the **Wald-Wolfowitz test** after its inventor Abraham Wald (1902–1950) and his student Jacob Wolfowitz. Its purpose is to detect nonrandomness. A nonrandom pattern suggests that the observations are not *independent*—a fundamental assumption of many statistical tests. We are asking whether each observation in a sequence is independent of its predecessor. In a time series, a nonrandom pattern of residuals indicates *autocorrelation* (as in Chapters 12 and 13). In quality control, a nonrandom pattern of deviations from the design specification may indicate an *out-of-control* process. We will illustrate only the large-sample version of this test (defined as samples of 10 or more).

Runs Test

This test is to determine whether a sequence of binary events follows a random pattern. A nonrandom sequence suggests nonindependent observations.

The hypotheses are:

H_0: Events follow a random pattern

H_1: Events do not follow a random pattern

To test the hypothesis of randomness, we first count the number of outcomes of each type:

n_1 = number of outcomes of the first type

n_2 = number of outcomes of the second type

n = total sample size = $n_1 + n_2$

Application: Quality Inspection 📁 Defects

Inspection of 44 computer chips reveals the following sequence of defective (*D*) or acceptable (*A*) chips:

DAAAAAAADDDDDAAAAAAAADDAAAAAAAADDDDDAAAAAAAAA

Do defective chips appear at random? A pattern could indicate that the assembly process has a cyclic problem due to unknown causes. The hypotheses are:

H_0: Defects follow a random sequence

H_1: Defects follow a nonrandom sequence

A *run* is a series of consecutive outcomes of the same type, surrounded by a sequence of outcomes of the other type. We group sequences of similar outcomes and count the runs:

D	AAAAAAA	DDDD	AAAAAAAA	DD	AAAAAAAA	DDDD	AAAAAAAAAA
1	2	3	4	5	6	7	8

A run can be a single outcome if it is preceded and followed by outcomes of the other type. There are 8 runs in our sample ($R = 8$). The number of outcomes of each type is:

n_1 = number of defective chips (D) = 11

n_2 = number of acceptable chips (A) = 33

n = total sample size = $n_1 + n_2 = 11 + 33 = 44$

In a large-sample situation (when $n_1 \geq 10$ and $n_2 \geq 10$), the number of runs R may be assumed to be normally distributed with mean μ_R and standard deviation σ_R.

$$z_{calc} = \frac{R - \mu_R}{\sigma_R} \qquad \text{(test statistic comparing } R \text{ with its expected value } \mu_R) \qquad \textbf{(16.1)}$$

$$\mu_R = \frac{2n_1 n_2}{n} + 1 \qquad \text{(expected value of } R \text{ if } H_0 \text{ is true)} \qquad \textbf{(16.2)}$$

$$\sigma_R = \sqrt{\frac{2n_1 n_2(2n_1 n_2 - n)}{n^2(n - 1)}} \qquad \text{(standard error of } R \text{ if } H_0 \text{ is true)} \qquad \textbf{(16.3)}$$

For our data, the expected number of runs would be

$$\mu_R = \frac{2n_1 n_2}{n} + 1 = \frac{2(11)(33)}{44} + 1 = 17.5$$

Because the actual number of runs ($R = 8$) is far less than expected ($\mu_R = 17.5$), our sample suggests that the null hypothesis may be false, depending on the standard deviation. For our data, the standard deviation is

$$\sigma_R = \sqrt{\frac{2n_1 n_2(2n_1 n_2 - n)}{n^2(n - 1)}} = \sqrt{\frac{2(11)(33)[2(11)(33) - 44]}{44^2(44 - 1)}} = 2.438785$$

The actual number of runs is $R = 8$, so the test statistic is

$$z_{calc} = \frac{R - \mu_R}{\sigma_R} = \frac{8 - 17.5}{2.438785} = -3.90$$

Since either too many runs or too few runs would be nonrandom, we choose a two-tailed test. The critical value $z_{.005}$ for a two-tailed test at $\alpha = .01$ is ± 2.576, so the decision rule is:

Reject the hypothesis of a random pattern if $z < -2.576$ or $z > +2.576$

Otherwise the observed difference is attributable to chance

The test statistic $z = -3.90$ is well below the lower critical limit, as shown in Figure 16.2, so we can easily reject the hypothesis of randomness. The difference between the observed number of runs and the expected number of runs is too great to be due to chance ($p = .0001$).

Figure 16.3 shows the MegaStat output for this problem, which also includes the *p*-value and the entire distribution for various values of R (not shown because it is

FIGURE 16.2

Decision Rule for Large-Sample Runs Test

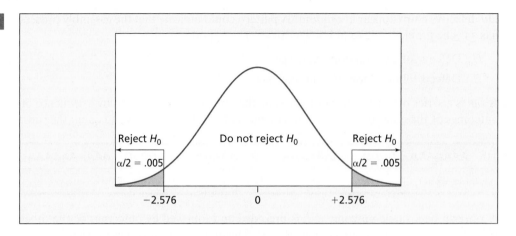

FIGURE 16.3

MegaStat's Runs Test

Runs Test for Random Sequence

Number of Defects

n	runs	
11	4	D
33	4	A
44	8	total

17.50 expected value
2.44 standard deviation
−3.895 z
.0001 p-value (two-tailed)

LO 16-8

Use computer software to perform the tests and obtain *p*-values.

lengthy). As with any hypothesis test, the smaller the *p*-value, the stronger the evidence against H_0. Here, the small *p*-value provides very strong evidence that H_0 is false (i.e., that the sequence is not random).

Small Samples

See end-of-chapter RELATED READINGS for small-sample procedures and tables of critical values that extend the test to small samples ($n < 10$). The problem with small samples is that they lack power. That is, in a small sample, it would take an extremely small or large number of runs to convince us that the sequence is nonrandom. While some re-searchers must deal with small samples, business analysts (e.g., quality control) often have hundreds of observations, so small samples rarely pose a problem.

SECTION EXERCISES

connect

16.1 Using $\alpha = .05$, perform a runs test for randomness on the sample data ($n = 27$).

$A\ A\ B\ B\ A\ A\ B\ B\ A\ B\ A\ A\ B\ B\ B\ A\ A\ B\ B\ B\ B\ A\ A\ B\ A\ B\ B$

16.2 Using $\alpha = .10$, perform a runs test for randomness on the sample data ($n = 24$).

$X\ O\ X\ X\ X\ X\ O\ O\ O\ O\ X\ O\ O\ O\ X\ O\ O\ O\ X\ O\ O\ X\ X\ O$

16.3 On a professional certifying exam, there are 25 true-false questions. The correct answers are $T\ F\ T\ T\ F\ F\ F\ T\ T\ F\ T\ F\ T\ T\ T\ F\ F\ T\ T\ F\ F\ T\ T\ F\ T$. *Research question:* At $\alpha = .05$, is the T/F pattern random? 📁 **TrueFalse**

16.4 A baseball player was at bat 33 times during preseason exhibition games. His pattern of hits (H) and nonhits (N) is shown (a nonhit is a walk or a strikeout). *Research question:* At $\alpha = .01$, is the pattern of hits random? 📁 **Hits**

$N\ N\ N\ H\ N\ H\ N\ N\ H\ N\ N\ H\ H\ N\ N\ N\ H\ N\ H\ N\ N\ N\ H\ N\ N\ H\ N\ H\ N\ N\ N\ H\ H$

16.3 WILCOXON SIGNED-RANK TEST

The **Wilcoxon signed-rank test** was developed by Frank Wilcoxon (1892–1965) to compare a single sample with a benchmark using only **ranks** of the data instead of the original observations, as in a one-sample t test. It is more often used to compare *paired* observations, as an alternative to the paired-sample t test, which is a special case of the one-sample t test. The advantages of the Wilcoxon test are its freedom from the normality assumption, its robustness to outliers, and its applicability to ordinal data. Although the test does require the population to be roughly symmetric, it has fairly good power over a range of possible non-normal population shapes. It is slightly less powerful than the one-sample t test when the population is normal.

Wilcoxon Signed-Rank Test

The Wilcoxon signed-rank test is a nonparametric test to compare a sample median with a benchmark or to test the median difference in paired samples. It does not require normality but does assume symmetric populations. It corresponds to the parametric t test for one mean.

If we denote the hypothesized benchmark median as M_0, the hypotheses about the population median M are:

LO 16-3

Use the Wilcoxon signed-rank test.

Left-Tailed Test	*Two-Tailed Test*	*Right-Tailed Test*
$H_0: M \geq M_0$	$H_0: M = M_0$	$H_0: M \leq M_0$
$H_1: M < M_0$	$H_1: M \neq M_0$	$H_1: M > M_0$

When the variable of interest is the median difference between paired observations, the test is the same, but we use the symbol M_d for the population median *difference* and (generally) use zero as the benchmark:

Left-Tailed Test	*Two-Tailed Test*	*Right-Tailed Test*
$H_0: M_d \geq 0$	$H_0: M_d = 0$	$H_0: M_d \leq 0$
$H_1: M_d < 0$	$H_1: M_d \neq 0$	$H_1: M_d > 0$

We calculate the difference between each observation and the hypothesized median (or the differences between the paired observations), rank them from smallest to largest by absolute value, and add the ranks of the *positive* differences to obtain the Wilcoxon signed-rank test statistic W. Its expected value and variance depend only on the sample size n.

$$W = \sum_{i=1}^{n} R^+ \quad \text{(the sum of all positive ranks)} \quad \textbf{(16.4)}$$

$$\mu_W = \frac{n(n+1)}{4} \quad \text{(expected value of the } W \text{ statistic)} \quad \textbf{(16.5)}$$

$$\sigma_W = \sqrt{\frac{n(n+1)(2n+1)}{24}} \quad \text{(standard deviation of the } W \text{ statistic)} \quad \textbf{(16.6)}$$

For large samples ($n \geq 20$), the test statistic is approximately normal:

$$z_{\text{calc}} = \frac{W - \dfrac{n(n+1)}{4}}{\sqrt{\dfrac{n(n+1)(2n+1)}{24}}} \quad \text{(Wilcoxon test statistic for large } n) \quad \textbf{(16.7)}$$

Application: Median versus Benchmark

Are price-earnings (P/E) ratios of stocks in *specialty* retail stores (e.g., Abercrombie & Fitch) the same as P/E ratios for stocks of *multiline* retail stores (e.g., Target)? Table 16.2 shows P/E ratios for a random sample of 21 specialty stores. The median P/E ratio for all multiline retail stores for the same date was $M_0 = 20.2$ (our benchmark). Our hypotheses are:

$H_0: M = 20.2$ (the median P/E ratio for specialty stores is 20.2)

$H_1: M \neq 20.2$ (the median P/E ratio for specialty stores is not 20.2)

TABLE 16.2		Wilcoxon Signed-Rank Test of P/E Ratios ($n = 21$ firms) 🗇 WilcoxonA				
Company	**X**	**X − 20.2**	**|X − 20.2|**	**Rank**	**R⁺**	**R⁻**
Bebe Stores Inc	19.8	−0.4	0.4	1.5		1.5
Barnes & Noble Inc	19.8	−0.4	0.4	1.5		1.5
Aeropostale Inc	20.6	0.4	0.4	3	3	
Deb Shops	18.7	−1.5	1.5	4		4
Gap Inc	22.0	1.8	1.8	5	5	
PETsMART Inc	17.9	−2.3	2.3	6		6
Payless Shoesource	17.0	−3.2	3.2	7		7
Abercrombie & Fitch Co	16.8	−3.4	3.4	8.5		8.5
AutoZone Inc	16.8	−3.4	3.4	8.5		8.5
Lithia Motors Inc A	16.3	−3.9	3.9	10		10
Genesco Inc	24.3	4.1	4.1	11	11	
Sherwin-Williams Co	16.0	−4.2	4.2	12		12
CSK Auto Corp	14.5	−5.7	5.7	13		13
Tiffany & Co	26.2	6.0	6.0	14	14	
Rex Stores	14.0	−6.2	6.2	15		15
Casual Male Retail Group	12.6	−7.6	7.6	16		16
Sally Beauty Co Inc	28.9	8.7	8.7	17	17	
Syms Corp	32.1	11.9	11.9	18	18	
Zale Corp	40.4	20.2	20.2	19	19	
Coldwater Creek Inc	41.0	20.8	20.8	20	20	
Talbots Inc	124.7	104.5	104.5	21	21	
			Sum	231.0	128.0	103.0

Source: http://investing.businessweek.com, accessed on June 19, 2007. Companies are sorted by rank of absolute differences.

To perform the test, we subtract 20.2 (the benchmark) from each specialty store's P/E ratio, take absolute values, convert to ranks, and sum the *positive* ranks. Negative ranks are shown but are not used. We assign tie ranks so that the sum of the tied values is the same as if they were not tied. For example, 3.4 occurs twice (Abercrombie & Fitch and AutoZone). If not tied, these data values would have ranks 8 and 9, so we assign a "tie" rank of 8.5 to each. Companies are shown in rank order of absolute differences.

The test statistic is:

$$z_{calc} = \frac{W - \dfrac{n(n+1)}{4}}{\sqrt{\dfrac{n(n+1)(2n+1)}{24}}} = \frac{128.0 - \dfrac{21(21+1)}{4}}{\sqrt{\dfrac{21(21+1)(42+1)}{24}}} = \frac{128.0 - 115.5}{28.770645} = 0.43447$$

Using Excel, the two-tailed *p*-value is $p = .6639$ (or $p = .6672$ if we use Appendix C with $z = 0.43$). At any customary level of significance, we cannot reject the hypothesis that specialty retail stores have the same median P/E as multiline retail stores. Although we use the z table for the *test statistic* (because $n \geq 20$), the P/E *data* do not seem to be from a normal population (for example, look at Talbot's extreme P/E ratio of 124.7). Thus, Wilcoxon's nonparametric test of the *median* is preferred to a one-sample t test of the *mean* (Chapter 9).

Application: Paired Data

Did P/E ratios decline between 2003 and 2007? We will perform a Wilcoxon test for *paired data* using a random sample of 23 common stocks. The parameter of interest is the median difference (M_d). Because the P/E ratios do not appear to be normally distributed (e.g., Rohm & Haas Co.'s 2003 P/E ratio), the Wilcoxon test of *medians* is attractive (instead of the paired t test for *means* in Chapter 10). Using $d = X_{2007} - X_{2003}$, a left-tailed test is appropriate:

H_0: $M_d \geq 0$ (the median difference is zero or positive)

H_1: $M_d < 0$ (the median difference is negative, i.e., 2007 P/E is less than 2003 P/E)

Table 16.3 shows the calculations for the Wilcoxon signed-rank statistic, with the companies in rank order of absolute differences. Because the first three have zero difference (neither positive nor negative), these three observations (highlighted) are *excluded* from the analysis.

TABLE 16.3	Wilcoxon Signed-Rank Paired Test (n = 23 firms)			WilcoxonB			
Company (Ticker Symbol)	**2007 P/E**	**2003 P/E**	**d**	**|d|**	**Rank**	**R^+**	**R^-**
FirstEnergy Corp (FE)	14	14	0	0	—		
Whirlpool Corp (WHR)	18	18	0	0	—		
Burlington/Santa (BNI)	14	14	0	0	—		
Constellation Energy (CEG)	16	15	1	1	1	1	
Mellon Financial (MEL)	17	19	−2	2	2.5		2.5
Yum! Brands Inc (YUM)	18	16	2	2	2.5	2.5	
Baxter International (BAX)	20	23	−3	3	5		5
Fluor Corp (FLR)	22	19	3	3	5	5	
Allied Waste Ind (AW)	21	18	3	3	5	5	
Ingersoll-Rand-A (IR)	12	16	−4	4	7.5		7.5
Lexmark Intl A (LXK)	17	21	−4	4	7.5		7.5
Moody's Corp (MCO)	29	24	5	5	9	9	
Electronic Data (EDS)	17	23	−6	6	10		10
Freeport-Mcmor-B (FCX)	11	18	−7	7	11		11
Family Dollar Stores (FDO)	19	27	−8	8	12.5		12.5
Leggett & Platt (LEG)	13	21	−8	8	12.5		12.5
Wendy's Intl Inc (WEN)	24	15	9	9	14	14	
Sara Lee Corp (SLE)	25	13	12	12	15	15	
Bed Bath & Beyond (BBBY)	20	37	−17	17	16		16
Ace Ltd (ACE)	8	26	−18	18	17.5		17.5
ConocoPhillips (COP)	8	26	−18	18	17.5		17.5
Baker Hughes Inc (BHI)	13	55	−42	42	19		19
Rohm & Haas Co (ROH)	15	68	−53	53	20		20
				Sum	210.0	51.5	158.5

Sources: *The Wall Street Journal*, July 31, 2003, and Standard & Poors, *Security Owner's Stock Guide*, February 2007. P/E ratios were reported as integers in these publications. Companies are sorted by rank of absolute differences.

Despite losing three observations due to zero differences, we still have $n \geq 20$ so we can use the large-sample test statistic:

$$z_{calc} = \frac{W - \frac{n(n+1)}{4}}{\sqrt{\frac{n(n+1)(2n+1)}{24}}} = \frac{51.5 - \frac{20(20+1)}{4}}{\sqrt{\frac{20(20+1)(40+1)}{24}}} = \frac{51.5 - 105.0}{26.7862} = -1.9973$$

Using Excel, we find the left-tailed *p*-value to be $p = .0229$ (or $p = .0228$ if we use Appendix C with $z = -2.00$) so at $\alpha = .05$ we conclude that P/E ratios did decline between 2003 and 2007. Figure 16.4 shows that MegaStat confirms our calculations.

FIGURE 16.4

MegaStat Signed-Rank Test for Paired Data

Wilcoxon Signed-Rank Test

variables: 2007 P/E-2003 P/E
    51.5 sum of positive ranks
    158.5 sum of negative ranks

    20 n
    105.00 expected value
    26.79 standard deviation
    −1.997 z
    .0229 p-value (one-tailed, lower)

LO 16-8

Use computer software to perform the tests and obtain *p*-values.

16.5 A sample of 28 student scores on the chemistry midterm exam is shown. (a) At $\alpha = .10$, does the population median differ from 50? Make a worksheet in Excel for your calculations. (b) Make a histogram of the data. Would you be justified in using a parametric t test that assumes normality? Explain. 📁 **Chemistry**

74	60	7	97	62	2	100
5	99	78	93	32	43	64
87	37	70	54	60	62	17
26	45	84	24	66	7	48

16.6 Final exam scores for a sample of 20 students in a managerial accounting class are shown. (a) At $\alpha = .05$, is there a difference in the population median scores on the two exams? Make an Excel worksheet for your Wilcoxon signed-rank test calculations and check your work by using MegaStat or a similar computer package. (b) Perform a two-tailed parametric t test for paired two-sample means by using Excel or MegaStat. Do you get the same decision? 📁 **Accounting**

Student	Exam 1	Exam 2	Student	Exam 1	Exam 2	Student	Exam 1	Exam 2
1	70	81	8	71	69	15	59	68
2	74	89	9	52	53	16	54	47
3	65	59	10	79	84	17	75	84
4	60	68	11	84	96	18	92	100
5	63	75	12	95	96	19	70	81
6	58	77	13	83	99	20	54	58
7	72	82	14	81	76			

16.4 WILCOXON RANK SUM TEST

The **Wilcoxon rank sum test** (also known as the **Mann-Whitney test**) is named after statisticians Frank Wilcoxon (1892–1965), Henry B. Mann (1905–2000), and D. Ransom Whitney (1915–2007). It is a nonparametric test that compares two populations whose distributions are assumed to be the same except for a shift in location (e.g., all X values shifted by a given amount). It does not assume normality. Assuming that the populations differ only in centrality (i.e., location), it is a test for equality of *medians*. It is analogous to the t test for two independent sample means.

Wilcoxon Rank Sum Test

The Wilcoxon rank sum test is a nonparametric test to compare two populations, utilizing only the ranks of the data from two independent samples. If the populations differ only in location (center), it is a test for equality of medians, corresponding to the parametric t test for two means.

Studies suggest that the Wilcoxon test has only slightly less power in distinguishing between centrality of two populations than the t test for two independent sample means, which you studied in Chapter 10. The Wilcoxon test requires independent samples from populations with equal variances, but the populations need not be normal. To avoid the use of special tables, we will illustrate only a large-sample version of this test (defined as samples of 10 or more). We will illustrate two versions of the test.

Assuming that the only difference in the populations is in location, the hypotheses for a two-tailed test of the population medians would be:

LO 16-4

Use the Wilcoxon rank sum test for two samples.

H_0: $M_1 - M_2 = 0$ (no difference in medians)

H_1: $M_1 - M_2 \neq 0$ (medians differ for the two groups)

Application: Restaurant Quality 📁 Restaurants

Does spending more at a restaurant lead to greater customer satisfaction? Readers of *Consumer Reports* rated 29 American, Italian, and Mexican chain restaurants on a scale of 0 to 100, based mainly on the taste of the food. Results are shown in Table 16.4, sorted by satisfaction rating (note that, in this test, the lowest data value is assigned a rank of 1, which is rather counterintuitive for restaurant ratings). Each restaurant is assigned to one of two price groups: *Low* (under $15 per person) and *High* ($15 or more per person). Is there a significant difference in satisfaction between the higher-priced restaurants and the lower-priced ones? The parametric *t* test for two means would require that the variable be measured on a ratio or interval level. Because the satisfaction ratings are solely based on human perception, we are unwilling to assume the strong measurement properties associated with ratio or interval data. Instead, we treat these measurements as ordinal data (i.e., ranked data).

Obs	Satisfaction	Rank	Price	Obs	Satisfaction	Rank	Price
1	73	1	Low	16	81	16.5	Low
2	76	2.5	Low	17	81	16.5	Low
3	76	2.5	High	18	82	18.5	High
4	77	4.5	Low	19	82	18.5	High
5	77	4.5	Low	20	83	20.5	Low
6	78	7	Low	21	83	20.5	Low
7	78	7	High	22	84	22.5	High
8	78	7	High	23	84	22.5	High
9	79	10	Low	24	85	25	High
10	79	10	Low	25	85	25	High
11	79	10	Low	26	85	25	High
12	80	13.5	Low	27	86	28	High
13	80	13.5	Low	28	86	28	High
14	80	13.5	Low	29	86	28	High
15	80	13.5	High				

TABLE 16.4

Satisfaction and Ranks for 29 Chain Restaurants
📁 **Restaurants**

Source: © 2003 by Consumers Union of U.S., Inc., Yonkers, NY 10703-1057, excerpted or adapted with permission from the July 2003 issue of *Consumer Reports* for educational purposes only.

In Table 16.4, we convert the customer satisfaction ratings into ranks by sorting the *combined* samples from lowest to highest satisfaction, and then assigning a rank to each satisfaction score. If values are tied, the average of the ranks is assigned to each. Restaurants are then separated into two groups based on the price category (*Low, High*), as displayed in Table 16.5.

Low-Priced Restaurants ($n_1 = 15$)		High-Priced Restaurants ($n_2 = 14$)	
Satisfaction	Rank	Satisfaction	Rank
73	1	76	2.5
76	2.5	78	7
77	4.5	78	7
77	4.5	80	13.5
78	7	82	18.5
79	10	82	18.5
79	10	84	22.5
79	10	84	22.5
80	13.5	85	25
80	13.5	85	25
80	13.5	85	25
81	16.5	86	28
81	16.5	86	28
83	20.5	86	28
83	20.5		
Rank sum:	$T_1 = 164$	Rank sum:	$T_2 = 271$
Sample size	$n_1 = 15$	Sample size	$n_2 = 14$
Mean rank:	$\bar{T}_2 = 164/15 = 10.93333$	Mean rank:	$\bar{T}_2 = 271/14 = 19.35714$

TABLE 16.5

Chain Restaurant Customer Satisfaction Score

The ranks are summed for each column to get $T_1 = 164$ and $T_2 = 271$. The sum $T_1 + T_2$ must be $n(n + 1)/2$ where $n = n_1 + n_2 = 15 + 14 = 29$. Because $n(n + 1)/2 = (29)(30)/2 = 435$ and the sample sums are $T_1 + T_2 = 164 + 271 = 435$, our calculations check.* Next, we calculate the mean rank sums $\bar{T}_1$ and $\bar{T}_2$. If there is no difference between groups, we would expect $\bar{T}_1 - \bar{T}_2$ to be near zero. For large samples ($n_1 \geq 10$, $n_2 \geq 10$) we can use a z test (see end-of-chapter RELATED READINGS for small sample tables and procedures). The test statistic is the difference in mean ranks, divided by its standard error:

$$\textbf{(16.8)} \qquad z_{calc} = \frac{\bar{T}_1 - \bar{T}_2}{(n_1 + n_2)\sqrt{\dfrac{n_1 + n_2 + 1}{12 n_1 n_2}}} \qquad \begin{matrix} \longleftarrow \text{ difference in mean ranks} \\ \\ \longleftarrow \text{ standard error of difference} \end{matrix}$$

For our restaurant data:

$$z_{calc} = \frac{10.93333 - 19.35714}{(15 + 14)\sqrt{\dfrac{15 + 14 + 1}{(12)(15)(14)}}} = -2.662$$

At $\alpha = .01$, rejection in a two-tailed test requires $z > +2.326$ or $z < -2.326$, so we would reject the hypothesis that the population medians are the same. From Appendix C the two-tail p-value is .0078, which says that a sample difference of this magnitude would be expected only about 8 times in 1,000 samples if the populations were the same.

An alternative way to perform the large-sample Wilcoxon rank sum z-test is based on the expected value and variance of the rank sum T_1. Using this alternate form, the test statistic is

$$\textbf{(16.9)} \qquad z_{calc} = \frac{T_1 - E(T_1)}{\sqrt{\text{Var}(T_1)}} = \frac{T_1 - \dfrac{n_1(n_1 + n_2 + 1)}{2}}{\sqrt{\dfrac{n_1 n_2}{12}(n_1 + n_2 + 1)}}$$

For our restaurant example, $T_1 = 164$, so the test statistic is

$$z_{calc} = \frac{T_1 - \dfrac{n_1(n_1 + n_2 + 1)}{2}}{\sqrt{\dfrac{n_1 n_2}{12}(n_1 + n_2 + 1)}} = \frac{164 - \dfrac{15(15 + 14 + 1)}{2}}{\sqrt{\dfrac{(15)(14)}{12}(15 + 14 + 1)}}$$

$$= \frac{164 - 225}{\sqrt{525}} = \frac{-61}{22.91287847} = -2.662$$

As you can see, either formula for z_{calc} will give the same result. MegaStat uses a different version of this test but obtains a similar result, as shown in Figure 16.5.

FIGURE 16.5

MegaStat's Wilcoxon Mann-Whitney Test

Wilcoxon Mann/Whitney Test		
n	sum of ranks	
15	164	Group 1
14	271	Group 2
29	435	total

225.00 expected value
22.91 standard deviation
−2.662 z
.0078 p-value (two-tailed)

---

*If the sum $T_1 + T_2$ does not check, you have made an error in calculating the ranks. Avoid Excel's functions =RANK() and =RANK.EQ(), because they do not adjust for ties. Instead, use Excel's =RANK.AVG() function, which will average tied data values.

16.7 Bob and Tom are "paper investors." They each "buy" stocks they think will rise in value and "hold" them for a year. At the end of the year, they compare their stocks' appreciation (percent). (a) At $\alpha = .05$, is there a difference in the medians (assume these are samples of Bob's and Tom's stock-picking skills)? Use MegaStat or a similar computer package for the Wilcoxon rank sum test (Mann-Whitney test) calculations. (b) Perform a two-tailed parametric *t* test for two independent sample means by using Excel or MegaStat. Do you get the same decision? 📁 **Investors**

Bob's Portfolio (10 stocks)	7.0, 2.5, 6.2, 4.4, 4.2, 8.5, 10.0, 6.4, 3.6, 7.6
Tom's Portfolio (12 stocks)	5.2, 0.4, 2.6, −0.2, 4.0, 5.2, 8.6, 4.3, 3.0, 0.0, 8.6, 7.5

16.8 An experimental bumper was designed to reduce damage in low-speed collisions. This bumper was installed on an experimental group of vans in a large fleet, but not on a control group. At the end of a trial period, there were 12 repair incidents (a "repair incident" is an accident that resulted in a repair invoice) for the experimental group and 9 repair incidents for the control group. The dollar cost per repair incident is shown below. (a) Use Mega-Stat or MINITAB to perform a two-tailed Wilcoxon rank sum test (Mann-Whitney test) at $\alpha = .05$. (b) Perform a two-tailed parametric *t* test for two independent sample means by using Excel or MegaStat. Do you get the same decision? (Data are from Floyd G. Willoughby and Thomas W. Lauer, confidential case study.) 📁 **Damage**

Old bumper: 1,185, 885, 2,955, 815, 2,852, 1,217, 1,762, 2,592, 1,632

New bumper: 1,973, 403, 509, 2,103, 1,153, 292, 1,916, 1,602, 1,559, 547, 801, 359

16.5 KRUSKAL-WALLIS TEST FOR INDEPENDENT SAMPLES

William H. Kruskal and W. Allen Wallis proposed a test to compare *c* independent samples. It may be viewed as a generalization of the Wilcoxon (Mann-Whitney) rank sum test, which compares two independent samples. Groups can be of different sizes if each has five or more observations. If we assume that the populations differ only in centrality (i.e., location), the **Kruskal-Wallis test** (K-W test) compares the medians of *c* independent samples. It is analogous to one-factor ANOVA (completely randomized model). The K-W test requires that the populations be of similar shape, but does not require normal populations as in ANOVA, making it an attractive alternative for applications in finance, engineering, and marketing.

Kruskal-Wallis Test

The K-W test compares the medians of *c* independent samples. It may be viewed as a generalization of the Mann-Whitney test and is a nonparametric alternative to one-factor ANOVA.

LO 16-5

Use the Kruskal-Wallis test for *c* independent samples.

Assuming that the populations are otherwise similar, the hypotheses to be tested are:

H_0: All *c* population medians are the same

H_1: Not all the population medians are the same

In testing for equality of location, the K-W test may be almost as powerful as one-factor ANOVA. It can even be useful for ratio or interval data when there are outliers or unequal group variances, or if the population is thought to be non-normal. For a completely randomized design with *c* groups, the test statistic is

$$H_{calc} = \frac{12}{n(n+1)} \sum_{j=1}^{c} \frac{T_j^2}{n_j} - 3(n+1) \qquad \text{(Kruskal-Wallis test statistic)} \quad \textbf{(16.10)}$$

where

$$n = n_1 + n_2 + \cdots + n_c$$

n_j = number of observations in group j

T_j = sum of ranks for group j

Application: Employee Absenteeism

The XYZ Corporation is interested in possible differences in days worked by salaried employees in three departments in the financial area. Table 16.6 shows annual days worked by 23 randomly chosen employees from these departments. Because the sampling methodology reflects the department sizes, the sample sizes are unequal.

TABLE 16.6

Annual Days Worked by Department

📁 **Days**

Department	Days Worked									
Budgets	278	260	265	245	258					
Payables	205	270	220	240	255	217	266	239	240	228
Pricing	240	258	233	256	233	242	244	249		

To get the test statistic, we combine the samples and assign a rank to each observation in each group, as shown in Table 16.7. We use a column worksheet so the calculations are easier to follow. When a tie occurs, each observation is assigned the average of the ranks.

TABLE 16.7

Merged Data Converted to Ranks

Obs	Rank	Days	Dept
1	1	205	Payables
2	2	217	Payables
3	3	220	Payables
4	4	228	Payables
5	5.5	233	Pricing
6	5.5	233	Pricing
7	7	239	Payables
8	9	240	Payables
9	9	240	Payables
10	9	240	Pricing
11	11	242	Pricing
12	12	244	Pricing
13	13	245	Budgets
14	14	249	Pricing
15	15	255	Payables
16	16	256	Pricing
17	17.5	258	Budgets
18	17.5	258	Pricing
19	19	260	Budgets
20	20	265	Budgets
21	21	266	Payables
22	22	270	Payables
23	23	278	Budgets

Next, the data are arranged by groups, as shown in Table 16.8, and the ranks are summed to give T_1, T_2, and T_3. As a check on our work, the sum of the ranks must be $n(n + 1)/2 = (23)(23 + 1)/2 = 276$. This is easily verified because $T_1 + T_2 + T_3 = 92.5 + 93.0 + 90.5 = 276$. The value of the test statistic is

$$H_{\text{calc}} = \frac{12}{n(n + 1)} \sum_{j=1}^{c} \frac{T_j^2}{n_j} - 3(n + 1)$$

$$= \frac{12}{(23)(23 + 1)} \left[\frac{92.5^2}{5} + \frac{93^2}{10} + \frac{90.5^2}{8} \right] - 3(23 + 1) = 6.259$$

Budgets	Rank	Payables	Rank	Pricing	Rank
245	13	205	1	233	5.5
258	17.5	217	2	233	5.5
260	19	220	3	240	9
265	20	228	4	242	11
278	23	239	7	244	12
		240	9	249	14
		240	9	256	16
		255	15	258	17.5
		266	21		
		270	22		
Sum of ranks	92.5	Sum of ranks	93	Sum of ranks	90.5
Sample size	$n_1 = 5$	Sample size	$n_2 = 10$	Sample size	$n_3 = 8$

TABLE 16.8

Worksheet for Rank Sums

The H test statistic follows a chi-square distribution with degrees of freedom $d.f. = c - 1 = 3 - 1 = 2$. This is a right-tailed test (i.e., we will reject the null hypothesis of equal medians if H exceeds its critical value). Using $d.f. = 2$, from Appendix E we obtain critical values for various levels of significance:

α	χ^2_α	Interpretation
.10	4.605	Reject H_0—conclude that the medians differ
.05	5.991	Reject H_0—conclude that the medians differ
.025	7.378	Do not reject H_0—conclude that the medians are not different

In this instance, our decision is sensitive to the level of significance chosen. The p-value is between .05 and .025, so it seems appropriate to conclude that the difference among the three groups is not overwhelming. MegaStat gives the exact p-value (.0437), as shown in Figure 16.6. We could also obtain this p-value from Excel's function =CHISQ.DIST.RT(6.259,2). The stacked dot plots in Figure 16.7 reveal that the three distributions overlap quite a bit, so there may be little practical difference in the distributions. The MINITAB K-W test is similar but requires unstacked data (one column for the data, one column for the group name). MINITAB warns you if the sample size is too small.

Kruskal-Wallis Test

Median	n	Avg. Rank	
260.00	5	18.50	Budgets
239.50	10	9.30	Payables
243.00	8	11.31	Pricing
244.00	23		Total
		6.259	H
		2	d.f.
		.0437	p-value

FIGURE 16.6

MegaStat's Kruskal-Wallis Test

LO 16-8

Use computer software to perform the tests and obtain p-values.

FIGURE 16.7

MINITAB's Stacked Dot Plots for Days Worked

16.9 Samples are shown of volatility (coefficient of variation) for sector stocks over a certain period of time. (a) At $\alpha = .05$, is there a difference in median volatility in these four portfolios? Use MegaStat, MINITAB, or a similar computer package for the calculations. (b) Use one-factor ANOVA to compare the means. Do you reach the same conclusion? (c) Make a histogram or other display of each sample. Would you be willing to assume normality? 📁 **Volatile**

Health	Energy	Retail	Leisure
14.5	23.0	19.4	17.6
18.4	19.9	20.7	18.1
13.7	24.5	18.5	16.1
16.9	24.2	15.5	23.2
16.2	19.4	17.7	17.6
21.6	22.1	21.4	25.5
25.6	31.6	26.5	24.1
21.4	22.4	21.5	25.9
26.6	31.3	22.8	25.5
19.0	32.5	27.4	26.3
12.6	12.8	22.0	12.9
13.5	14.4	17.1	11.1
13.5		24.8	4.9
13.0		13.4	
13.6			

16.10 The results shown below are mean productivity measurements (average number of assemblies completed per hour) for a random sample of workers at each of three work stations. (a) At $\alpha = .05$, is there a difference in median productivity? Use MegaStat, MINITAB, or a similar computer package for the calculations. (b) Use one-factor ANOVA to compare the means. Do you reach the same conclusion? (c) Make a histogram or other display of the pooled data. Does the assumption of normality seem justified? 📁 **Workers**

Hourly Productivity of Assemblers in Plants									
Work Station	**Finished Units Produced Per Hour**								
A (9 workers)	3.6	5.1	2.8	4.6	4.7	4.1	3.4	2.9	4.5
B (6 workers)	2.7	3.1	5.0	1.9	2.2	3.2			
C (10 workers)	6.8	2.5	5.4	6.7	4.6	3.9	5.4	4.9	7.1	8.4

Mini Case   16.1

Price/Earnings Ratios

Are price/earnings ratios different for firms in the five sectors shown in Table 16.9? Since the data are interval, we could try either one-factor ANOVA or a Kruskal-Wallis test. How can we decide?

Combining the samples, the histogram in Figure 16.8 and the probability plot in Figure 16.9 suggest non-normality, so instead of one-factor ANOVA we would prefer the nonparametric Kruskal-Wallis test with $d.f. = c - 1 = 5 - 1 = 4$ degrees of freedom. MINITAB's output in Figure 16.10 shows that the medians differ ($p = .000$). The test statistic ($H = 25.32$) exceeds the chi-square critical value for $\alpha = .01$ (13.28). We conclude that the P/E ratios are *not* the same for these five sectors.

TABLE 16.9   Common Stock P/E Ratios of Selected Companies   PERatios

Automotive and Components (n = 17)

9	13	14	29	10	32	16	14	9
21	17	21	10	7	20	13	17	

Energy Equipment and Services (n = 12)

31	22	39	25	46	7	29	36	42
36	49	35						

Food and Staples Retailing (n = 22)

25	22	18	24	27	21	66	30	24
22	21	9	11	16	13	32	15	25
36	29	25	18					

Hotels, Restaurants, and Leisure (n = 18)

34	26	74	24	17	19	22	34	30
22	24	19	23	19	21	31	16	19

Multiline Retail Firms (n = 18)

16	29	22	19	20	14	22	18	28
13	16	20	21	23	20	3	14	27

Source: *BusinessWeek*, November 22, 2004.

FIGURE 16.8   Histogram of Combined Samples (*n* = 87)

FIGURE 16.9   Probability Plot of Combined Samples (*n* = 87)

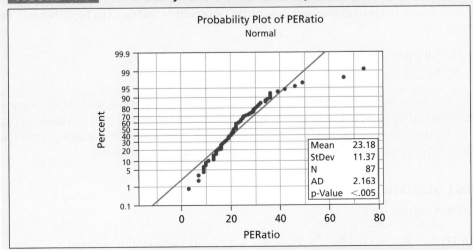

LO 16-8

Use computer software to perform the tests and obtain *p*-values.

FIGURE 16.10   **MINITAB's Kruskal-Wallis Test**

Kruskal-Wallis Test: PERatio versus Sector

Sector	N	Median	Ave Rank	z
Auto	17	14.00	24.4	−3.58
EnergyEq	12	35.50	68.5	3.62
FoodDrug	22	23.00	46.9	0.62
Leisure	18	22.50	51.1	1.34
Retail	18	20.00	35.6	−1.58
Overall	87		44.0	

H = 25.27 DF = 4 P = 0.000
H = 25.32 DF = 4 P = 0.000 (adjusted for ties)

16.6 FRIEDMAN TEST FOR RELATED SAMPLES

LO 16-6

Use the Friedman test for related samples.

The **Friedman test** is a nonparametric test that will reveal whether c treatments have the same central tendency when there is a second factor with r levels. If the populations are assumed the same except for centrality (location), the test is a comparison of medians. The test is analogous to two-factor ANOVA without replication (or randomized block design) with one observation for each cell. The groups must be of the same size, treatments should be randomly assigned within the blocks, and data should be at least interval scale.

Friedman Test

The Friedman test is a nonparametric procedure to discover whether c population medians are the same or different when classification is based on two factors. It is analogous to randomized block ANOVA (two-factor without replication) but without the normality assumption.

The Friedman test resembles the Kruskal-Wallis test except that, in addition to the c treatment levels that define the columns of the observation matrix, it also specifies r block factor levels to define each row of the observation matrix. The hypotheses to be tested are:

H_0: All c populations have the same median

H_1: Not all the populations have the same median

The Friedman test may be almost as powerful as two-way ANOVA without replication (randomized block design) and may be used with ratio or interval data when there is concern for outliers or non-normality of the underlying populations. It is a rare population that meets the normality requirement, so Friedman's test is quite useful.

Test Statistic

The test statistic is

$$(16.11) \qquad F_{calc} = \frac{12}{rc(c+1)}\sum_{j=1}^{c} T_j^2 - 3r(c+1) \qquad \text{(Friedman test statistic)}$$

where

  r = the number of blocks (rows)

  c = the number of treatments (columns)

  T_j = the sum of ranks for treatment j

Although the Friedman formula resembles the Kruskal-Wallis formula, there is a difference: the ranks are computed *within each block* rather than within a pooled sample.

Application: Braking Effectiveness

Experiments are being conducted to test the effect of brake pad composition on stopping distance. Five prototype brake pads are prepared. Each pad is installed on the same automobile, which is accelerated to 100 kph and then braked to the shortest possible stop without loss of control. This test is repeated four times in rapid succession to reveal brake fade due to heating and lining abrasion. Car weight and balance are identical in all tests, and the same expert driver performs all tests. The pavement is dry and the outside air temperature is the same for all tests. To eliminate potential bias, the driver has no information about which pad is installed for a given test. The results are shown in Table 16.10.

TABLE 16.10

Stopping Distance from 100 kph
📁 **Braking**

	Pad 1		Pad 2		Pad 3		Pad 4		Pad 5	
	Feet	*Rank*	*Feet*	*Rank*	*Feet*	*Rank*	*Feet*	*Rank*	*Feet*	*Rank*
Trial 1	166	3	176	4	152	2	198	5	148	1
Trial 2	174	4	170	3	148	1	206	5	152	2
Trial 3	184	3	186	4	160	1	212	5	168	2
Trial 4	220	5	204	3	184	1	216	4	196	2
Rank sum	$T_1 = 15$		$T_2 = 14$		$T_3 = 5$		$T_4 = 19$		$T_5 = 7$	

The Friedman test requires that either the number of blocks or the number of treatments be at least 5. Our matrix meets this requirement because $r = 4$ and $c = 5$. Ranks are computed *within each row*. As a check on our arithmetic, we may utilize the fact that the ranks must sum to $rc(c + 1)/2 = (4)(5)(5 + 1)/2 = 60$. We see that our sums are correct because $T_1 + T_2 + T_3 + T_4 + T_5 = 15 + 14 + 5 + 19 + 7 = 60$.

We now compute the test statistic:

$$F_{calc} = \frac{12}{rc(c + 1)}\sum_{j=1}^{c} T_j^2 - 3r(c + 1)$$

$$= \frac{12}{(4)(5)(5 + 1)}[15^2 + 14^2 + 5^2 + 19^2 + 7^2] - 3(4)(5 + 1) = 13.6$$

The Friedman test statistic follows a chi-square distribution with degrees of freedom $d.f. = c - 1 = 5 - 1 = 4$. Using $d.f. = 4$, from Appendix E we obtain the critical values for various α levels:

α	χ_α^2	*Interpretation*
.025	11.143	Reject H_0—conclude that the medians differ
.01	13.277	Reject H_0—conclude that the medians differ
.005	14.861	Do not reject H_0—the medians do not differ

The *p*-value is between .01 and .005, so we conclude that there is a significant difference in brake pads except at very strict Type I error levels. The results from MegaStat shown in Figure 16.11 show the exact *p*-value (.0087). We could also obtain this *p*-value by using Excel's function =CHISQ.DIST.RT(13.6,4).

FIGURE 16.11

MegaStat's Friedman Test for Brake Pads

Friedman Test

Sum of Ranks	Avg. Rank	
15.00	3.75	
14.00	3.50	
5.00	1.25	
19.00	4.75	
7.00	1.75	
60.00	3.00	Total

4 n
13.600 chi-square
4 d.f.
.0087 p-value

LO 16-8

Use computer software to perform the tests and obtain *p*-values.

SECTION EXERCISES

16.11 Consumers are asked to rate the attractiveness of four potential dashboard surface textures on an interval scale (1 = least attractive, 10 = most attractive). Use MegaStat or another software package to perform a Friedman test to see whether the median ratings of surfaces differ at $\alpha = .05$, using age as the blocking factor. 📷 **Texture**

	Shiny	Satin	Pebbled	Pattern	Embossed
Youth (Under 21)	6.7	6.6	5.5	4.3	4.4
Adult (21 to 39)	5.5	5.3	6.2	5.9	6.2
Middle-Age (40 to 61)	4.5	5.1	6.7	5.5	5.4
Senior (62 and over)	3.9	4.5	6.1	4.1	4.9

16.12 JavaMax is a neighborhood take-out coffee shop that offers three sizes. Yesterday's sales are shown. Use MegaStat or another software package to perform a Friedman test to see whether the median sales of coffee sizes differ at $\alpha = .05$, using time of day as the blocking factor. 📷 **Coffee**

	Small	Medium	Large
6 a.m. < 8 a.m.	60	77	85
8 a.m. < 11 a.m.	65	74	76
11 a.m. < 3 p.m.	70	70	70
3 p.m. < 7 p.m.	61	60	55
7 p.m. to 11 p.m.	55	50	48

16.7 SPEARMAN RANK CORRELATION TEST

LO 16-7

Use the Spearman rank correlation test.

An overall nonparametric test of association between two variables can be performed by using **Spearman's rank correlation coefficient** (sometimes called **Spearman's rho**). This statistic is useful when it is inappropriate to assume an interval scale (a requirement of the Pearson correlation coefficient you learned in Chapter 12). The statistic is named for Charles E. Spearman (1863–1945), a British behavioral psychologist who was interested in assessment of human intelligence. The research question was the extent of agreement between different I.Q. tests (e.g., Stanford-Binet and Wechsler's WAIS). However, ordinal data are also common in business. For example, Moody's bond ratings (e.g., Aaa, Aa, A, Baa, Ba, B, etc.), bank safety ratings (e.g., by Veribanc or BankRate.com), or

Morningstar's mutual fund ratings (e.g., 5/5, 5/4, 4/4, etc.) are ordinal (not interval) measurements. We could use Spearman's rank correlation to answer questions like these:

- When *n* corporate bonds are assigned a quality rating by two different agencies (e.g., Moody and Dominion), to what extent do the ratings agree?

- When creditworthiness scores are assigned to *n* individuals by different credit-rating agencies (e.g., Equifax and TransUnion), to what extent do the scores agree?

In cases like these, we would expect strong agreement, since presumably the rating agencies are trying to measure the same thing. In other cases, we may have ratio or interval data, but prefer to rely on rank-based tests because of serious non-normality or outliers. For example:

- To what extent do rankings of *n* companies based on revenues agree with their rankings based on profits?

- To what extent do rankings of *n* mutual funds based on 1-year rates of return agree with their rankings based on 5-year rates of return?

Spearman Rank Correlation

Spearman rank correlation is a nonparametric test that measures the strength of the association, if any, between two variables using only ranks. It does not assume interval measurement.

The formula for Spearman's rank correlation coefficient for a sample is

$$r_s = 1 - \frac{6\sum\limits_{i=1}^{n} d_i^2}{n(n^2 - 1)} \qquad \text{(Spearman rank correlation)} \qquad \textbf{(16.12)}$$

where

d_i = difference in ranks for case *i*

n = sample size

The sample rank correlation coefficient r_s must fall in the range $-1 \le r_s \le +1$. Its sign tells whether the relationship is direct (ranks tend to vary in the same direction) or inverse (ranks tend to vary in opposite directions). If r_s is near zero, there is little or no agreement between the rankings. If r_s is near $+1$, there is strong agreement between the ranks, while if r_s is near -1, there is strong *inverse* agreement between the ranks.

Application: Calories and Fat

Calories come from fat, but also from carbohydrates. How closely related are fat calories and total calories? As an experiment, a student team examined a sample of 20 brands of pasta sauce, obtaining the data shown in Table 16.11. The serving sizes (in grams) varied, so we divided each product's total calories and fat calories by serving size to obtain a per-gram measurement. Ranks were then calculated for each measure of calories. If more than one value was the same, they were assigned the average of the ranks. As a check, the sums of ranks within each column must always be $n(n + 1)/2$, which in our case is $(20)(20 + 1)/2 = 210$. After checking the ranks, the difference in ranks d_i is computed for each observation. As a further check on our calculations, we verify that the rank differences sum to zero (if not, we have made an error somewhere). The sample rank correlation coefficient $r_s = .9109$ indicates positive agreement:

$$r_s = 1 - \frac{6\sum\limits_{i=1}^{n} d_i^2}{n(n^2 - 1)} = 1 - \frac{(6)(118.5)}{(20)(20^2 - 1)} = .9109$$

TABLE 16.11

Calories per Gram for 20 Pasta Sauces

📁 **Pasta**

Source: This data set was created by statistics students Donna Bennett, Nicole Cook, Latrice Haywood, and Robert Malcolm. It is intended for training purposes only and should not be viewed as a nutrition guide.

Product	Total Calories		Fat Calories		d_i	d_i^2
	Per Gram	Rank	Per Gram	Rank		
Barilla Roasted Garlic & Onion	0.64	10	0.20	8	2	4
Barilla Tomato & Basil	0.56	13	0.12	13.5	−0.5	0.25
Classico Tomato & Basil	0.40	19.5	0.08	17	2.5	6.25
Del Monte Mushroom	0.48	17	0.04	19	−2	4
Five Bros. Tomato & Basil	0.64	10	0.12	13.5	−3.5	12.25
Healthy Choice Traditional	0.40	19.5	0.00	20	−0.5	0.25
Master Choice Chunky Garden Veg.	0.56	13	0.08	17	−4	16
Meijer All Natural Meatless	0.55	15	0.08	17	−2	4
Newman's Own Traditional	0.48	17	0.12	13.5	3.5	12.25
Paul Newman Venetian	0.48	17	0.12	13.5	3.5	12.25
Prego Fresh Mushrooms	1.25	1	0.38	1	0	0
Prego Hearty Meat—Pepperoni	1.00	3.5	0.33	2.5	1	1
Prego Hearty Meat—Hamburger	1.00	3.5	0.29	4	−0.5	0.25
Prego Traditional	1.17	2	0.33	2.5	−0.5	0.25
Prego Roasted Red Pepper & Garlic	0.92	5	0.25	5.5	−0.5	0.25
Ragu Old World Style w/meat	0.67	8	0.25	5.5	2.5	6.25
Ragu Roasted Red Pepper & Onion	0.86	6	0.20	8	−2	4
Ragu Roasted Garlic	0.70	7	0.19	10	−3	9
Ragu Traditional	0.56	13	0.20	8	5	25
Sutter Home Tomato & Garlic	0.64	10	0.16	11	−1	1
Column Sum		210		210	0	118.5

Our sample correlation r_s is 0.9109. For a right-tailed test the hypotheses are:

H_0: True rank correlation is zero ($\rho_s \le 0$)

H_1: True rank correlation is positive ($\rho_s > 0$)

In this case we choose a right-tailed test because *a priori* we would expect positive agreement. That is, a pasta sauce that ranks high in fat calories would be expected also to rank high in total calories. If the sample size is small, a special table is required (see end-of-chapter RELATED READINGS). If n is large (usually defined as at least 20 observations), then r_s may be assumed to follow the normal distribution using the test statistic

(16.13) $$z_{\text{calc}} = r_s \sqrt{n - 1}$$

To illustrate this formula, we will plug in our previous sample result:

$$z_{\text{calc}} = (.9109)\sqrt{20 - 1} = 3.971$$

Using Appendix C we obtain one-tail critical values of z for various levels of significance:

α	z_α	Interpretation
.025	1.960	Reject H_0
.01	2.326	Reject H_0
.005	2.576	Reject H_0

Clearly, we can reject the hypothesis of no correlation at any of the customary α levels. Using MegaStat, we can obtain equivalent results, as shown in Figure 16.12, except that the critical value of r_s is shown instead of the t statistic.

FIGURE 16.12

MegaStat's Rank Correlation Test

Spearman Coefficient of Rank Correlation

	Total Calories/gram	Fat Calories/gram
Total Calories/gram	1.000	
Fat Calories/gram	.911	1.000

20 sample size

±.444 critical value .05 (two-tail)
±.561 critical value .01 (two-tail)

Correlation versus Causation

One final word of caution: you should remember that correlation does not imply causation. Countless examples can be found of correlations that are "significant" even when there is no causal relation between the two variables. On the other hand, causation is not ruled out. More than one scientific discovery has occurred because of an unexpected correlation. Just bear in mind that if you look at 1,000 correlation coefficients in samples drawn from uncorrelated populations, approximately 50 will be "significant" at $\alpha = .05$, approximately 10 will be "significant" at $\alpha = .01$, and so on. Testing for significance is just one step in the scientific process.

Bear in mind also that multiple causes may be present. Correlation between X and Y could be caused by an unspecified third variable Z. Even more complex systems of causation may exist. Bivariate correlations of any kind must be regarded as potentially out of context if the true relationship is *multivariate* rather than *bivariate*.

16.13 Profits of 20 consumer food companies are shown. (a) Convert the data to ranks. Check the column sums. (b) Calculate Spearman's rank correlation coefficient. Show your calculations. (c) At $\alpha = .01$ can you reject the hypothesis of zero rank correlation? (d) Check your work by using MegaStat. (e) Calculate the Pearson correlation coefficient (using Excel). (f) Why might the rank correlation be preferred? **Food-B**

SECTION EXERCISES

connect

Profit of 20 Food Consumer Products Firms ($ millions)

Company	2004	2005
Campbell Soup	595	647
ConAgra Foods	775	880
Dean Foods	356	285
Del Monte Foods	134	165
Dole Food	105	134
Flowers Foods	15	51
General Mills	917	1,055
H. J. Heinz	566	804
Hershey Foods	458	591
Hormel Foods	186	232
Interstate Bakeries	27	−26
J. M. Smucker	96	111
Kellogg	787	891
Land O'Lakes	107	21
McCormick	211	215
PepsiCo	3,568	4,212
Ralcorp Holdings	7	65
Sara Lee	1,221	1,272
Smithfield Foods	26	227
Wm. Wrigley, Jr.	446	493

Source: *Fortune* 151, no. 8 (April 18, 2005), p. F-52.

16.14 Rates of return on 24 mutual funds are shown. (a) Convert the data to ranks. Check the column sums. (b) Calculate Spearman's rank correlation coefficient. Show your calculations. (c) At $\alpha = .01$ can you reject the hypothesis of zero rank correlation? (d) Check your work by using MegaStat. (e) Calculate the Pearson correlation coefficient (using Excel). (f) In this case, why might either test be used? 📷 **Funds**

Rates of Return on 24 Selected Mutual Funds (percent)

Fund	12-Mo.	5-Year	Fund	12-Mo.	5-Year
1	11.2	10.5	13	14.0	9.7
2	−2.4	5.0	14	11.6	14.7
3	8.6	8.6	15	13.2	11.8
4	3.4	3.7	16	−1.0	2.3
5	3.9	−2.9	17	6.2	10.5
6	10.3	9.6	18	21.1	9.0
7	16.1	14.1	19	−1.2	3.0
8	6.7	6.2	20	8.7	7.1
9	6.5	7.4	21	9.7	10.2
10	11.1	14.0	22	0.4	9.3
11	8.0	7.3	23	0.9	6.0
12	11.2	14.2	24	12.7	10.0

CHAPTER SUMMARY

Statisticians are attracted to **nonparametric tests** because they avoid the restrictive assumption of normality, although often there are still assumptions to be met (e.g., similar population shape). Many nonparametric tests have similar power to their parametric counterparts (and superior power when samples are small). The **runs test** (or **Wald-Wolfowitz** test) checks for random order in binary data. The **Wilcoxon signed-rank test** resembles a parametric one-sample t test, most often being used as a substitute for the parametric paired-difference t test. The **Wilcoxon rank-sum test** (also called the **Mann-Whitney test**) compares medians in independent samples, resembling a parametric two-sample t test. The **Kruskal-Wallis test** is a c-sample comparison of medians (similar to one-factor ANOVA). The **Friedman test** resembles a randomized block ANOVA except that it compares medians instead of means. **Spearman's rank correlation coefficient** is like the usual Pearson correlation coefficient except the data are ranks. Calculations of these tests are usually done by computer. Special tables are required when samples are small (see RELATED READINGS or check the Internet for small-sample procedures and tables of critical values, e.g., http://en.wikipedia.org/wiki/Mann-Whitney_U_test).

KEY TERMS

Friedman test, *706*	power, *691*	Spearman's rho, *708*
Kruskal-Wallis test, *701*	ranks, *695*	Wald-Wolfowitz test, *692*
Mann-Whitney test, *698*	runs test, *692*	Wilcoxon signed-rank
nonparametric tests, *691*	Spearman's rank correlation	test, *695*
parametric tests, *691*	coefficient, *708*	Wilcoxon rank sum test, *698*

Commonly Used Formulas

Wald-Wolfowitz one-sample runs test for randomness (for $n_1 \geq 10$, $n_2 \geq 10$):

$$z_{calc} = \frac{R - \frac{2n_1 n_2}{n} + 1}{\sqrt{\frac{2n_1 n_2 (2n_1 n_2 - n)}{n^2(n-1)}}}$$

where

R = number of runs
n = total sample size = $n_1 + n_2$

Wilcoxon signed-rank test for one sample median (for $n \geq 20$):

$$z_{\text{calc}} = \frac{W - \dfrac{n(n+1)}{4}}{\sqrt{\dfrac{n(n+1)(2n+1)}{24}}}$$

where

W = sum of positive ranks

Wilcoxon rank sum (Mann-Whitney) test for equality of two medians (for $n_1 \geq 10$, $n_2 \geq 10$):

$$z_{\text{calc}} = \frac{\bar{T}_1 - \bar{T}_2}{(n_1 + n_2)\sqrt{\dfrac{n_1 + n_2 + 1}{12 n_1 n_2}}}$$

where

T_1 = mean rank for sample 1
T_2 = mean rank for sample 2

Alternate form of Wilcoxon rank sum (Mann-Whitney) test for two medians ($n_1 \geq 10$, $n_2 \geq 10$):

$$z_{\text{calc}} = \frac{T_1 - E(T_1)}{\sqrt{\text{Var}(T_1)}} = \frac{T_1 - \dfrac{n_1(n_1 + n_2 + 1)}{2}}{\sqrt{\dfrac{n_1 n_2}{12}(n_1 + n_2 + 1)}}$$

Kruskal-Wallis test for equality of c medians: $H_{\text{calc}} = \dfrac{12}{n(n+1)} \sum_{j=1}^{c} \dfrac{T_j^2}{n_j} - 3(n+1)$ with $d.f. = c - 1$

where

n_j = number of observations in group j
T_j = sum of ranks for group j
$n = n_1 + n_2 + \cdots + n_c$

Friedman test for equality of medians in an array with r rows and c columns:

$$F_{\text{calc}} = \frac{12}{rc(c+1)} \sum_{j=1}^{c} T_j^2 - 3r(c+1) \quad \text{with } d.f. = c - 1$$

where

r = the number of blocks (rows)
c = the number of treatments (columns)
T_j = the sum of ranks for treatment j

Spearman's rank correlation coefficient for n paired observations (for $n \geq 20$):

$$r_s = 1 - \frac{6 \sum_{i=1}^{n} d_i^2}{n(n^2 - 1)} \quad \text{and} \quad z_{\text{calc}} = r_s \sqrt{n-1}$$

CHAPTER REVIEW

1. (a) Name three advantages of nonparametric tests. (b) Name two deficiencies in data that might cause us to prefer a nonparametric test. (c) Why is significance in a nonparametric test especially convincing?

2. (a) What is the purpose of a runs test? (b) How many runs of each type are needed for a large-sample runs test? (c) Give an example of a sequence containing runs and count the runs. (d) What distribution do we use for the large-sample runs test?

3. (a) What is the purpose of a Wilcoxon signed-rank test? (b) How large a sample is needed to use a normal table for the test statistic? (c) The Wilcoxon signed-rank test resembles which parametric test(s)?

4. (a) What is the purpose of a Wilcoxon rank sum (Mann-Whitney) test? (b) The Wilcoxon rank sum (Mann-Whitney) test is a test of two medians under what assumption? (c) What sample sizes are needed for the large-sample Wilcoxon rank sum (Mann-Whitney) test? (d) The Wilcoxon rank sum (Mann-Whitney) test is analogous to which parametric test?

5. (a) In the Wilcoxon rank sum (Mann-Whitney) test, how are ranks assigned when there is a tie? (b) What distribution do we use for the large-sample version of this test?

6. (a) What is the purpose of a Kruskal-Wallis test? (b) The K-W test is a test of c medians under what assumption? (c) The K-W test is analogous to which parametric test?

7. (a) In the Kruskal-Wallis test, what is the procedure for assigning ranks to observations in each group? (b) What distribution do we use for the K-W test? (c) What are the degrees of freedom for the K-W test?

8. (a) What is the purpose of a Friedman test? (b) The Friedman test is analogous to what parametric test? (c) How does the Friedman test differ from the ANOVA test in the way it handles the blocking factor?

9. (a) Describe the assignment of ranks in the Friedman test. (b) What distribution do we use for the Friedman test? (c) What are the degrees of freedom for the Friedman test?

10. (a) What is the purpose of the Spearman rank correlation test? (b) Describe the way in which ranks are assigned in calculating the Spearman rank correlation test.

11. (a) Why is a significant correlation not proof of causation? (b) When might a bivariate correlation be misleading?

CHAPTER EXERCISES

connect

Instructions: In all exercises, use a computer package (e.g., MegaStat, MINITAB) or show the calculations in a worksheet, depending on your instructor's wishes. If you use the computer, include relevant output or screen shots. If you do the calculations manually, show your work. State the hypotheses and give the test statistic and its two-tailed *p*-value. Make the decision. If the decision is close, say so. Are there issues of sample size? Is non-normality a concern?

16.15 A supplier of laptop PC power supplies uses a control chart to track the output (in watts) of each unit produced. The pattern below shows whether each unit's output was above (A) or below (B) the desired specification. *Research question:* At $\alpha = .05$, do the deviations follow a random pattern? 📂 **Watts**

B A A B B B A B A B A A B A A B B A B B A A B A B A

A A B B A A A A B B A A B A A A A B B A A B A A

16.16 A basketball player took 35 free throws during the season. Her sequence of hits (H) and misses (M) is shown. *Research question:* At $\alpha = .01$, is her hit/miss sequence random? 📂 **FreeThrows**

H M M H H M H M M H H H H H H M M H H M M M H M H H H M H H H H M M M H H

16.17 Thirty-four customers at Starbucks either ordered coffee (C) or did not order coffee (X). *Research question:* At $\alpha = .05$, is the sequence random? 📂 **Starbucks**

C X C X C C C C C X X X X C X C X C X C X C C C X C X C X C C X C X X X C C X

16.18 The price of a particular stock over a period of 60 days rises ($+$) or declines ($-$) in the following pattern. *Research question:* At $\alpha = .05$, is the pattern random? 📂 **Stock**

++ + − − − + + + + + + + − − − − + + − + − + − + − − − − + + + +

− + + + + − + + + − + − + − + + + − − − − − − − + + + + − −

16.19 A forecasting model is fitted to sales data over 24 months. Forecasting errors are tabulated to reveal whether the model provides an overestimate ($+$) or an underestimate ($-$) for each month's sales. The results are − − + + + − + − − + − − − − − − + + + + + − −. *Research question:* At $\alpha = .05$, is the pattern random? 📂 **Forecast**

16.20 A cognitive retraining clinic assists outpatient victims of head injury, anoxia, or other conditions that result in cognitive impairment. Each incoming patient is evaluated to establish an appropriate treatment program and estimated length of stay (ELOS is always a multiple of 4 weeks because treatment sessions are scheduled on a monthly basis). To see if there is any difference in ELOS between the two clinics, a sample is taken, consisting of all patients evaluated at each clinic during October, with the results shown. *Research question:* At $\alpha = .10$, do the medians differ? 📂 **Cognitive**

Clinic A (10 patients): 24, 24, 52, 30, 40, 40, 18, 30, 18, 40

Clinic B (12 patients): 20, 20, 52, 36, 36, 36, 24, 32, 16, 40, 24, 16

16.21 Two manufacturing facilities produce 1280 × 1024 LED (light-emitting diode) displays. Twelve shipments are tested at random from each lab, and the number of bad pixels per

billion is noted for each shipment. *Research question:* At $\alpha = .05$, do the medians differ?
📄 **LED**

Defects in Randomly Inspected LED Displays											
Facility	**Number of Bad Pixels per billion**										
Lab *A*	422	319	326	410	393	368	497	381	515	472	423	355
Lab *B*	497	421	408	375	410	489	389	418	447	429	404	477

16.22 Salaries of 30 randomly chosen individuals in the same occupation (only the first 3 and last 3 observations are shown). The data are from a salary equity study comparing two industries. *Research question:* Without assuming normality of the populations, is there a difference in the medians at $\alpha = .01$? 📄 **Salaries**

Industry A	Industry B
53,599	62,092
56,107	64,928
69,957	64,993
. . .	. . .
99,180	122,001
92,863	123,189
108,101	120,571

16.23 Does a class break stimulate the pulse? Here are heart rates for a sample of 30 students before and after a class break. *Research question:* At $\alpha = .05$, do the medians differ? 📄 **HeartRate**

Heart Rate before and after Class Break						
Student	**Before**	**After**	**Student**	**Before**	**After**
1	60	62	16	70	64
2	70	76	17	69	66
3	77	78	18	64	69
4	80	83	19	70	73
5	82	82	20	59	58
6	82	83	21	62	65
7	41	66	22	66	68
8	65	63	23	81	77
9	58	60	24	56	57
10	50	54	25	64	62
11	82	93	26	78	79
12	56	55	27	75	74
13	71	67	28	66	67
14	67	68	29	59	63
15	66	75	30	98	82

Thanks to colleague Gene Fliedner for having his evening students take their own pulses before and after the 10-minute class break.

16.24 An experimental bumper was designed to reduce damage in low-speed collisions. This bumper was installed on an experimental group of vans in a large fleet, but not on a control group. At the end of a trial period, accident data showed 12 repair incidents for the experimental group and 9 repair incidents for the control group. The vehicle downtime (in days) per repair incident is shown. *Research question:* At $\alpha = .05$, do the medians differ? (Data are from Floyd G. Willoughby and Thomas W. Lauer, confidential case study.) 📄 **Downtime**

New bumper: 9, 2, 5, 12, 5, 4, 7, 5, 11, 3, 7, 1

Old bumper: 7, 5, 7, 4, 18, 4, 8, 14, 13

16.25 The square footage of each of the last 11 homes sold in each of two suburban neighborhoods is noted. *Research question:* At $\alpha = .01$, do the medians differ? 📄 **SqFt**

Square Footage of Homes Sold

Grosse Hills (Built in 1985)	Haut Nez Estates (Built in 2003)	Grosse Hills (Built in 1985)	Haut Nez Estates (Built in 2003)
3,220	3,850	2,800	3,400
3,450	3,560	3,050	3,550
3,270	4,300	2,950	3,750
3,200	4,100	3,430	4,150
4,850	3,750	3,220	3,850
3,150	3,450		

16.26 Below are grade point averages for 25 randomly chosen university business students during a recent semester. *Research question:* At $\alpha = .01$, are the median grade point averages the same for students in these four class levels? 📄 **GPA**

Grade Point Averages of 25 Business Students

Freshman (5 students)	Sophomore (7 students)	Junior (7 students)	Senior (6 students)
1.91	3.89	3.01	3.32
2.14	2.02	2.89	2.45
3.47	2.96	3.45	3.81
2.19	3.32	3.67	3.02
2.71	2.29	3.33	3.01
	2.82	2.98	3.17
	3.11	3.26	

16.27 In a bumper test, three types of autos were deliberately crashed into a barrier at 5 mph, and the resulting damage (in dollars) was estimated. Five test vehicles of each type were crashed, with the results shown below. *Research question:* At $\alpha = .01$, are the median crash damages the same for these three vehicles? 📄 **Crash**

Crash Damage in Dollars

Goliath	Varmint	Weasel
1,600	1,290	1,090
760	1,400	2,100
880	1,390	1,830
1,950	1,850	1,250
1,220	950	1,920

16.28 The waiting time (in minutes) for emergency room patients with non-life-threatening injuries was measured at four hospitals for all patients who arrived between 6:00 and 6:30 p.m. on a certain Wednesday. The results are shown below. *Research question:* At $\alpha = .05$, are the median waiting times the same for emergency patients in these four hospitals? 📄 **Emergency**

Emergency Room Waiting Time (minutes)

Hospital A (5 patients)	Hospital B (4 patients)	Hospital C (7 patients)	Hospital D (6 patients)
10	8	5	0
19	25	11	20
5	17	24	9
26	36	16	5
11		18	10
		29	12
		15	

16.29 Mean output of arrays of solar cells of three types are measured four times under random light intensity over a period of 5 minutes, yielding the results shown below. *Research question:* At $\alpha = .05$, is the median solar cell output the same for all three types? Solar

Solar Cell Output (Watts)

Cell Type	Output (Watts)					
A	123	121	123	124	125	127
B	125	122	122	121	122	126
C	126	128	125	129	131	128

16.30 Below are results of braking tests of the Ford Explorer on glare ice, packed snow, and split traction (one set of wheels on ice, the other on dry pavement), using three braking methods. *Research question:* At $\alpha = .01$, is braking method related to stopping distance? Stopping

Stopping Distance from 40 mph to Zero

Road Condition	Pumping	Locked	ABS
Glare Ice	441	455	460
Split Traction	223	148	183
Packed Snow	149	146	167

Source: *Popular Science* 252, no. 6 (June 1998), p. 78.

16.31 In a call center, the average waiting time for an answer (in seconds) is shown below by time of day. *Research question:* At $\alpha = .01$, does the waiting time differ by day of the week? *Note:* Only the first 3 and last 3 observations are shown. Wait

Average Waiting Time (in Seconds) for Answer ($n = 26$)

Time	Mon	Tue	Wed	Thu	Fri
06:00	34	71	33	39	39
06:30	52	70	88	53	49
07:00	36	103	47	32	91
⋮	⋮	⋮	⋮	⋮	⋮
17:30	28	31	27	22	26
18:00	35	14	115	26	22
18:30	25	34	9	5	47

16.32 The table below shows annual financial data for a sample of 20 companies in the food consumer products sector. *Research question:* At $\alpha = .01$, is there a significant correlation between revenue and profit? Why is a rank correlation preferred? What factors might result in a less-than-perfect correlation? *Note:* Only the first 3 and last 3 companies are shown. Food-A

Food Consumer Products Companies' 2004 Revenue and Profit ($ millions)

Obs	Company	Revenue	Profit
1	Campbell Soup	7,109	647
2	ConAgra Foods	18,179	880
3	Dean Foods	10,822	285
⋮	⋮	⋮	⋮
18	Sara Lee	19,556	1,272
19	Smithfield Foods	10,107	227
20	Wm. Wrigley, Jr.	3,649	493

Source: *Fortune* 151, no. 8 (April 18, 2005), p. F-52.

16.33 Fertility rates (children born per woman) are shown for 27 EU member nations in 2 years. *Research question:* At $\alpha = .05$, is there a significant rank correlation? *Note:* Only the first 3 and last 3 nations are shown. Fertility

Fertility Rates in EU Member Nations (*n* = 27)

Nation	2000	2009
Austria	1.364	1.390
Belgium	1.667	1.840
Bulgaria	1.261	1.568
⋮	⋮	⋮
Slovenia	1.259	1.533
Sweden	1.544	1.935
United Kingdom	1.641	1.938

Source: http://epp.eurostat.ec.europa.eu/portal/page/portal/population/data/database.

16.34 A newspaper article listed nutritional facts for 56 frozen dinners. From that list, 16 frozen dinners were randomly selected by using the random number method. *Research question:* Choose any two variables. At $\alpha = .01$, based on this sample, is there a significant rank correlation between the two variables? *Note:* Only the first 3 and last 3 observations are shown. 📂 **Dinners**

Frozen Dinner Nutritional Information (*n* = 16)

Dinner/Entree	Fat (g)	Calories	Sodium (mg)
French Recipe Chicken	9	240	1,000
Chicken au Gratin	11	250	870
Stuffed Turkey Breast	6	230	520
⋮	⋮	⋮	⋮
Filet of Fish au Gratin	6	200	700
Beef Sirloin Tips	7	220	540
Lasagna with Meat Sauce	10	320	630

16.35 The table below shows ratings of 18 movies by two reviewers (on a 0 to 5 ☆ scale using half ☆ increments). *Research question:* At $\alpha = .05$, based on these data, is the rank correlation between reviewers significantly greater than zero (i.e., a right-tail test)? 📂 **Reviews**

	Reviewer			Reviewer	
Movie	A	B	Movie	A	B
Black Death	3.5	2.0	No Strings Attached	2.5	3.0
Blue Valentine	4.0	4.5	Priest	1.5	1.5
Bridesmaids	4.0	4.5	Rio The Movie	2.5	2.0
Everything Must Go	3.0	2.5	Something Borrowed	0.5	1.0
Fast Five	3.5	3.0	The Dilemma	2.0	2.5
From Prada to Nada	2.5	1.5	The Green Hornet	3.0	2.5
Hesher	2.5	3.5	The Illusionist	4.0	3.5
Jumping the Broom	3.5	3.0	Thor	3.0	2.0
Justin Bieber	2.5	2.0	Water for Elephants	3.0	3.0

16.36 Are gasoline prices a potential policy tool in controlling carbon emissions? The table below shows 2001 gasoline prices (dollars per liter) and carbon dioxide emissions per dollar of GDP. *Research question:* At $\alpha = .05$, based on these data, is there a significant rank correlation between these two variables? *Note:* Only the first 3 and last 3 observations are shown. 📂 **Emissions**

Gasoline Prices and Carbon Emissions for Selected Nations (*n* = 31)

Nation	Gas Price ($/L)	CO_2/GDP (kg/$)
Australia	0.489	0.79
Austria	0.888	0.25
Belgium	0.984	0.37
⋮	⋮	⋮
Turkey	1.003	0.99
United Kingdom	1.165	0.41
United States	0.381	0.63

Source: International Energy Agency, www.iea.org.

16.37 Below are the top 20 U.S. football teams in the seventh and eighth weeks of the 2003 season, along with the points awarded to each team by the *ESPN/USA Today* coaches poll. *Research question:* At $\alpha = .01$, based on these data, does the true rank correlation differ from zero for these two ratings?   Teams

Football Ratings in *ESPN/USA Today* Coaches Poll ($n = 20$)

Team	This Week	Last Week	Team	This Week	Last Week
Oklahoma	1575	1622	Texas	881	605
Southern Cal	1502	1470	TCU	875	727
Florida State	1412	1320	Wash State	827	1260
LSU	1337	1241	Purdue	667	487
Virginia Tech	1281	1026	Michigan State	645	1041
Miami	1263	1563	Nebraska	558	924
Ohio State	1208	1226	Tennessee	544	449
Michigan	1135	938	Minnesota	490	149
Georgia	951	1378	Florida	480	246
Iowa	932	762	Bowling Green	369	577

Source: *Detroit Free Press.*

RELATED READING

Corder, Gregory W., and Dale I. Foreman. *Nonparametric Statistics for Non-Statisticians: A Step-by-Step Approach* (Wiley, 2009).

Gibbons, Jean D. *Nonparametric Statistics: An Introduction* (Sage, 1999).

Higgins, James J. *Introduction to Modern Nonparametric Statistics* (Brooks/Cole, 2004).

Huber, Peter J. *Robust Statistics* (Wiley, 2003).

Lehmann, Erich L. *Nonparametrics: Statistical Methods Based on Ranks.* Rev. ed. (Springer, 2006).

CHAPTER 16   Online Learning Resources

The Online Learning Center (OLC) at www.mhhe.com/doane4e has several *LearningStats* demonstrations to help you understand nonparametric tests. Your instructor may assign one or more of them, or you may decide to download the ones that sound interesting.

Topic	*LearningStats* Demonstrations
Overview	What Are Nonparametric Tests?
Case studies	Runs Test: Baseball Streaks Wilcoxon Signed-Rank: Exam Scores Mann-Whitney: ATM Withdrawals Kruskal-Wallis: DVD Prices Friedman Test: Freeway Pollution Spearman's Rho: EU Nations Fertility
Tables	Chi-Square Critical Values
Supplemental Topics	Sign Test Mann-Whitney Small Sample Test

Key: = PowerPoint   = Excel   = Adobe PDF

CHAPTER

17

Quality Management

CHAPTER CONTENTS

CHAPTER LEARNING OBJECTIVES

LO

When you finish this chapter you should be able to

LO 17-1 Define quality and explain how it may be measured.

LO 17-2 Distinguish between common cause variation and special cause variation.

LO 17-3 Name key individuals and their contributions to the quality movement.

LO 17-4 List common statistical tools used in quality improvement.

LO 17-5 List steps toward continuous quality improvement and variance reduction.

LO 17-6 Make and interpret common control charts ($\bar{x}$, R, and p).

LO 17-7 Recognize abnormal patterns in control charts and their potential causes.

LO 17-8 Assess the capability of a process.

17.1 QUALITY AND VARIATION

What Is Quality?

Quality can be measured in many ways. Quality may be a *physical* metric, such as the number of bad sectors on a computer hard disk or the quietness of an air-conditioning fan. Quality may be an *aesthetic* attribute such as the ripeness of a banana or cleanliness of a clinic waiting room. (Does the fig bar turned in the wrong direction in Figure 17.1 affect the aesthetic quality of the product?) Quality may be a *functional* characteristic such as ergonomic accessibility of car radio controls or convenience of hours that a bank is open. It may be a *personal* attribute such as friendliness of service at a restaurant or diligence of follow-up by a veterinary clinic. It may be an *efficiency* attribute such as promptness in delivery of an order or the waiting time at a dentist's. Quality is generally understood to include these attributes:

- Conformance to specifications.
- Performance in the intended use.
- As near to zero defects as possible.

- Reliability and durability.
- Serviceability when needed.
- Favorable customer perceptions.

Unopened Fig Bars: Quality as an Aesthetic Attribute

Measurement of quality is specific to the organization and its products. To improve quality, we must undertake systematic data collection and careful measurement of key metrics that describe the product or service that is valued by customers. In manufacturing, the focus is likely to be on physical characteristics (e.g., defects, reliability, consistency), while in services, the focus is likely to be on customer perceptions (e.g., courtesy, responsiveness, competence). Table 17.1 lists some typical quality indicators that might be important to firms engaged in manufacturing as compared to firms that deliver services.

TABLE 17.1

Typical Quality
Indicators

Manufacturing	Services
Proportion of nonconforming output	Proportion of satisfied customers
Warranty claim costs	Average customer waiting time
Repeat purchase rate (loyalty)	Repeat client base (loyalty)

Productivity, Processes, and Quality

Productivity (ratio of output to input) is a measure of efficiency. High productivity lowers cost per unit, increases profit, and supports higher wages and salaries. Productivity, like quality, can be measured in various ways. There are single-factor ratios that compare process output to a single input such as labor. And there are multifactor ratios that compare process output to the sum of multiple inputs such as labor, energy, and materials. Measuring productivity in a manufacturing business is typically straightforward because the output and inputs are easy to quantify. Productivity in a service business is less straightforward and will depend on the type of service. For example, a professional service firm might compare number of clients serviced to billable hours. On the other hand, a restaurant might compare the number of tables serviced to operating costs for an evening.

In the past, many companies assumed an inverse relationship between quality and productivity. This view was based on a short-term perspective. The belief was that the only way to truly improve quality was to slow down and put more time into each product. While slowing or stopping an assembly line does imply less output today, defective products lead to waste, rework, and lost customers. In the modern view, quality and productivity move in the same direction because doing it right the first time saves time and money in the long run. Similarly, in services (e.g., health care), reducing delays and avoiding errors will make customers happier and will reduce the burden of follow-up to fix problems. Our focus in the 21st century is on designing and operating effective business processes to meet customer requirements consistently.

A process is a sequence of interconnected tasks that result in the creation of a product or in the delivery of a service. Manufacturing, assembly, or packaging operations usually come to mind when we hear the term "process." Yet service operations such as filling mail orders, providing customer support, handling loan applications, delivering health services, and meeting payrolls are also processes. Because a majority of workers are in the service sector, it is reasonable to say that nonmanufacturing processes are predominant in today's economy. Quality control refers to methods used by organizations to ensure that their products and services meet customer expectations and to ensure that there is improvement over time. Process control refers to methods used by organizations to ensure that their processes are predictable and produce products and services that meet customers' expectations in an efficient manner.

Common Cause versus Special Cause Variation

Where does statistics enter the quality picture? Statistics focuses on the phenomenon of *variation*. Processes that produce, package, and deliver supposedly identical products and services will always contain some degree of variation. Although variation is normal and expected, firms still strive for consistency in their products and services. Excessive variation is often a sign of poor quality because this affects real or perceived performance of the product or service. The quest for *reduced variation* is a never-ending activity for any firm or not-for-profit organization.

Statisticians define two categories of variation. Common cause variation (random "noise") comes from within the process and is normal and expected. Processes that vary only due to common cause variability are considered stable and predictable. Special cause variation is due to factors that are outside of a process, producing a process that is unpredictable. Until special cause variation is identified and eliminated, a process is considered out of control. For example, waiting time at a ski lift is a random variable that follows a

LO 17-2

Distinguish between common cause variation and special cause variation.

predictable pattern at different times of day (common cause variation, normal and expected). But when there is an equipment malfunction, waiting times may change dramatically (special cause variation).

Sources of variation in processes include human abilities, training, motivation, technology, materials, management, and organization. Some of these factors are under the control of the organization, while others cannot easily be changed. Most factors are fixed in the short run but may be changed in the long run. For example, technology can be changed through research and development and capital spending on new equipment, but such changes may take years. Human performance can change over time through education and training, but usually not in hours or days.

Role of Statisticians

Statisticians can help a company define appropriate metrics, set up a system to collect valid data, and track variation in the chosen metric(s). Trained statisticians know how to collect and analyze data to determine if processes are in control or out of control (i.e., contain only common cause variability or both common cause and special cause variability). We use statistics to measure variation, set attainable goals for variance reduction, and establish rules to decide whether processes are in control. The degree to which variation can be reduced depends on equipment, technology, and worker training.

Managers make the decisions necessary to invest in new equipment or technology and to train nonstatisticians who comprise the majority of the workforce. A manufacturing firm may require broad-based statistical training for engineers, plant managers, supervisors, and even assembly workers. But financial, purchasing, marketing, and sales managers also must understand statistics because they interact with technical experts on cost control, waste management, and quality improvement. Even in banks or health care, broad-based training in statistical methods can be helpful in increasing efficiency and improving quality.

17.1 Define (a) productivity, (b) quality control, and (c) process control.

17.2 Explain the relationship between productivity and quality from a modern perspective. How does this differ from the past perspective?

17.3 Explain the difference between common cause variation and special cause variation.

17.4 Can zero variation be achieved? Explain.

17.5 Explain the role of statisticians in quality improvement.

17.2 PIONEERS IN QUALITY MANAGEMENT

Brief History of Quality Control

LO 17-3

Name key individuals and their contributions to the quality movement.

During the early 1900s, quality control took the form of improved inspection and improvement in the methods of mass production, under the leadership of American experts. From about 1920 to just after World War II, techniques such as process control charts (Walter A. Shewhart) and acceptance sampling from lots (Harold F. Dodge and Harry G. Romig) were perfected and were widely applied in North America. But during the 1950s and 1960s, Japanese manufacturers (particularly automotive) shed their previous image as low-quality producers and began to apply American quality control techniques. The Japanese based their efforts largely on ideas and training from American statisticians W. Edwards Deming and Joseph M. Juran, as well as Japanese statisticians Genichi Taguchi and Kaoru Ishikawa. They developed new approaches that focused on customer satisfaction and costs of quality. By the 1970s, despite exhortation by Deming and others, North American firms had lost their initial leadership in quality control, while the Japanese devised and perfected new quality improvement methods, soon adopted by the Europeans.

During the 1980s, North American firms began a process of recommitment to quality improvement and Japanese production methods. In their quest for quality improvement, these firms sought training and advice by experts such as Deming, Juran, and Armand Feigenbaum. The Japanese, however, continued to push the quality frontier forward, under the teachings of Taguchi and the perfection of the Kaizen philosophy of continuous improvement. The Europeans articulated the ISO 9000 standards, now adopted by most world-class firms. North American firms have implemented their own style of total quality management. Manufacturers now seek to build *quality* into their products and services, all the way down the supply chain. Quality is best viewed as a *management system* rather than purely as an application of statistics.

W. Edwards Deming

The late **W. Edwards Deming** (1900–1993) deserves special mention as an influential thinker. He was widely honored in his lifetime. Many know him primarily for his contributions to improving productivity and quality in Japan. In 1950, at the invitation of the Union of Japanese Scientists and Engineers, Deming gave a series of lectures to 230 leading Japanese industrialists who together controlled 80 percent of Japan's capital. His message was the same as to Americans he had taught during the previous decades. The Japanese listened carefully to his message, and their success in implementing Deming's ideas is a matter of historical record.

Deming said that *profound knowledge* of a system is needed for an individual to become a good listener who can teach others. He emphasized that all people are different, that management is not about ranking people, and that anyone's performance is governed largely by the system that he/she works in. He said that fear invites presentation of bad data. If bearers of bad news fare badly, the boss will hear only good news—guaranteeing bad management decisions.

Deming believed that most employees want to do a good job. He found that most quality problems do not stem from willful disregard of quality, but from flaws in the process or system, such as

- Inadequate equipment.
- Inadequate maintenance.
- Inadequate training.
- Inadequate supervision.
- Inadequate support systems.
- Inadequate task design.

It is difficult to encapsulate Deming's many ideas succinctly, but most observers would agree that his philosophy is reflected in his widely reproduced *14 Points,* which can be found in full on the web. The 14 Points are primarily statements about management, not statistics. They ask that management take responsibility for improving quality and avoid blaming workers. Deming spent much of his long life explaining these and other of his ideas, through a series of seminars aimed initially at management, an activity that continues today through the work of his followers at The W. Edwards Deming Institute (www.deming.org).

Other Influential Thinkers

Walter A. Shewhart (1891–1967) invented the control chart and the concepts of special cause and common cause variation. Shewhart's charts were adopted by the American Society for Testing Materials (ASTM) in 1933 and were used to improve production during World War II. *Joseph M. Juran* (1904–2008) also taught quality education in Japan, contemporaneously with Deming. Like Deming, he became more influential with North American management in the 1980s. He felt that 80 percent of quality defects arise from management actions, and therefore that quality control was management's responsibility.

Juran articulated the idea of the *vital few*—a handful of causes that account for a vast majority of quality problems (the principle behind the **Pareto chart**). Effort, he said, should be concentrated on key problems, rather than diffused over many less-important problems.

Kaoru Ishikawa is a Japanese quality expert who is associated with the idea of *quality circles,* which characterize the Japanese approach. He also pioneered the idea of companywide quality control and was influential in popularizing statistical tools for quality control. He taught that elementary statistical tools (Pareto charts, histograms, scatter diagrams, and control charts) should be understood by everyone, while advanced tools (experimental design, regression) might best be left to specialists.

Armand V. Feigenbaum first used the term *total quality control* in 1951. He favored broad sharing of responsibility for quality assurance. This was at a time when many companies assumed that quality was the responsibility of the Quality Assurance Department alone. He felt that quality is an essential element of modern management, like marketing or finance. *Philip B. Crosby* was among the first to popularize the catch-phrase "zero defects." *Genichi Taguchi* is a pioneer whose contributions are discussed further at the end of this chapter.

Other quality gurus include *Claus Moller,* whose European company specializes in management training. Moller believes that people can be inspired to do their best through development of the individual's self-esteem. Moller is known for his 12 Golden Rules and 17 hallmarks of a quality company. *Shigeo Shingo* has had great impact on Japanese industry. His basic idea is to stop a process whenever a defect occurs, define the cause, and prevent future occurrences. If source inspections are used, statistical sampling becomes unnecessary because the worker is prevented from making errors in the first place.

SECTION EXERCISES

17.6 On the Internet, look up *two* influential thinkers in quality control, and briefly state their contributions.

17.7 Look up *two* of Deming's 14 points on the Internet and explain their meaning.

17.3 QUALITY IMPROVEMENT

Measuring Quality

Quality improvement begins with measurement of a *variable* (e.g., dimensions of an automobile door panel) or an *attribute* (e.g., number of emergency patients who wait more than 30 minutes). For a variable, quality improvement means reducing variation from the target specification. For an attribute, quality improvement means decreasing the rate of nonconformance. Statistical methods are used to ensure that the process is stable and in control by eliminating sources of *special cause* (nonrandom) variation, as opposed to *common cause* (random) variation that is normal and inherent in the process. We change the process whenever a way is discovered to reduce variation or to decrease nonconformance (especially if the process is incapable of meeting the target specifications).

Data collection of appropriate quality measures is essential for monitoring processes and improving quality. Employees and customers may not agree on the interpretation of quality measures, so customer input, planning, and training are essential to ensure that employees collect meaningful data that lead to improved quality and customer satisfaction. Table 17.2 gives examples of different quality measures. We may have to measure several aspects of the product or service to assess quality, while sometimes a single quality measurement may be sufficient.

Statistical quality control or **SQC** refers to a subset of quality improvement techniques that rely on statistics. A few of the descriptive tools (see Figure 17.2) have already been covered in earlier chapters, while others (e.g., control charts) will be discussed in this chapter.

LO 17-4

List common statistical tools used in quality improvement.

TABLE 17.2

Examples of Quality Measures

Process	Measurable Aspects
Payroll department in a large hospital	Percent of employees paid incorrectly or late each month.
	Percent of employees with insufficient taxes withheld each year.
	Number of weekly creditor telephone complaints.
Aluminum beverage container manufacturing plant	Monthly hours of downtime due to delayed shipments.
	Thickness and weight of alloy or number of structurally defective cans per 100,000.
	Number of worker injuries per month.
Retail pharmacy	Percent of prescriptions filled within 15 minutes.
	Average wait for phone to be answered or percent of callers getting a busy signal.
	Time (in minutes) a cashier must wait for pharmacist.

FIGURE 17.2

Descriptive SQC Tools

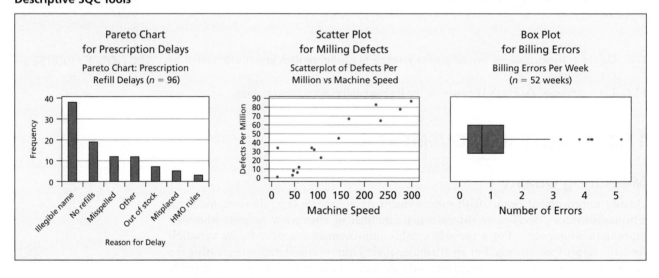

Descriptive Tools	Analytic Methods
• Pareto diagrams	• Control charts
• Scatter plots	• Lot and batch inspection plans
• Box plots	• Acceptance sampling
• Fishbone diagrams	• Experimental design
• Check sheets	• Taguchi robust design

A *check sheet* is a form for counting the frequency of sources of nonconformance. The **fishbone chart** (also called a *cause-and-effect diagram*) is a visual display that summarizes the factors that increase process variation or adversely affect achievement of the target. For example, Figure 17.3 shows a fishbone chart for factors affecting patient length of stay in a hospital. The six main categories (materials, methods, people, management, measurement, technology) are general and may apply to almost any process.

FIGURE 17.3

Fishbone (Cause-and-Effect) Chart for Patient Length of Stay

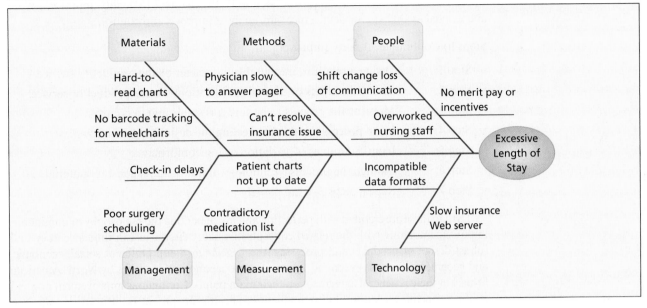

You can insert as many verbal descriptions ("fishbones") as you need to identify the causes of variation. The fishbone chart is not, strictly speaking, a statistical tool, but it is helpful in thinking about root causes. MINITAB will make fishbone charts.

Statistical process control or **SPC** refers specifically to the monitoring of ongoing repetitive processes to ensure conformance to standards by using methods of statistics. Its main tools are *capability analysis* and *control charts*. Control charts are used for monitoring both quality characteristics and process characteristics. We will discuss how to create and use control charts in the next section and then we will discuss process capability measures later in this chapter.

Quality Improvement Programs

Businesses typically follow a disciplined approach for quality improvement using the tools we've identified in this section. Quality and process improvement programs are ubiquitous in the business world. A quick Google search using the terms *quality improvement* or *process improvement* will turn up hundreds of links to consulting firms advertising their programs to help improve your business. Each of these programs is based on some combination of the philosophies taught by the quality gurus described in Section 17.2. The following are a few that you should know before you enter the workforce.

Total quality management or **TQM** requires that all business activities should be oriented toward meeting and exceeding customer needs, empowering employees, eliminating waste or rework, and ensuring the long-run viability of the enterprise through continuous quality improvement. TQM encompasses a broad spectrum of behavioral, managerial, and technical approaches. It includes diverse but complementary elements such as statistics, benchmarking, process redesign, team building, group communications, quality function deployment, and crossfunctional management.

Like TQM, **business process redesign** or **BPR** has a cross-functional orientation. But instead of focusing on incremental change and gradual improvement of processes, BPR seeks radical redesign of processes to achieve breakthrough improvement in performance measures—a lofty goal that is easier to state than to achieve. Business schools typically incorporate TQM and/or BPR concepts into a variety of nonstatistics core classes.

The concept of **continuous quality improvement** or **CQI** arises from the idea that we continue to seek ways to reduce variation and/or nonconformance to even lower levels. Many

LO 17-5

List steps toward continuous quality improvement and variance reduction.

improvement programs have defined this never-ending cycle by stating a set of iterative steps. For example, Deming used an improvement cycle he called **PDCA** or Plan-Do-Check-Act. In the **Six Sigma** school of thought (see Section 17.10), the steps to quality improvement are abbreviated as **DMAIC** or define, measure, analyze, improve, and control.

Steps to Continuous Quality Improvement

- Step 1:   Define a relevant, measurable parameter of the product or service.
- Step 2:   Establish targets or desired specifications for the product or service.
- Step 3:   Monitor the process to be sure it is stable and in control.
- Step 4:   Is the process capable of meeting the desired specifications?
- Step 5:   Identify sources of variation or nonconformance.
- Step 6:   Change the process (technology, training, management, materials).
- Step 7:   Repeat steps 3–6 indefinitely.

The Japanese are credited with perfecting and implementing the philosophy of continuous improvement, along with the related concepts of quality circles, just-in-time inventory, and robust design of products and processes (the **Taguchi method**). Different social, economic, and geographic factors prevent adoption of some Japanese approaches by North American firms, but there is general agreement on their main points. Continuous improvement now is a guiding principle for automobile manufacturers, health care providers, insurance companies, computer software designers, fast-food restaurants, and even universities, churches, entertainment, and sports teams. Permanent change and a continuous search for better ways of doing things cascade down the organizational chart and across departmental lines.

Service Quality

Service quality measures have been elusive because it is difficult to quantify intangible services. However, in 1988 a group of researchers developed a survey called **SERVQUAL** to assess customer satisfaction along five service quality dimensions. The dimensions are reliability, responsiveness, assurance, empathy, and tangibles. A *reliable* service is one that is dependable and consistent. A *responsive* service is one that meets the customers' needs. *Assurance* means that the customer can trust the service provider. *Empathy* refers to a caring service provider. *Tangibles* refer to the physical environment in which the service is delivered.

The SERVQUAL instrument measures both customer expectations and customer perceptions of the service in each of these five areas. A business uses the results of the survey to quantify the gap between customer expectations and perceptions. By identifying the largest gap, a business knows where to focus their quality improvement efforts. Quality improvement tools specific to service businesses include **service blueprints** and **service transaction analysis**. A service blueprint is a map of the service process used by a business to identify points of possible service failure. Service transaction analysis is a method of analyzing a service from the customer's perspective to determine how to close the gap between expectations and perceptions.

SECTION EXERCISES

17.8 Define a measurable aspect of quality for (a) the car dealership where you bought your car, (b) the bank or credit union where you usually make personal transactions, and (c) the movie theater where you usually go.

17.9 Explain the difference between SQC and SPC.

17.10 Identify three common quality improvement programs and give their acronyms.

17.11 Why is the quality improvement process never-ending? Identify the steps of one improvement cycle identified in the textbook.

17.12 Name the survey instrument used to measure service quality. What are the five service quality dimensions?

17.13 Describe two quality improvement tools unique to the service industry.

17.4 CONTROL CHARTS: OVERVIEW

What Is a Control Chart?

A **control chart** is a visual display used to study how a process changes over time. Data are plotted in time order. It compares the statistic with limits showing the range of expected common cause variation in the data. Control charts are tools for monitoring process stability and for alerting managers if the process changes. In some processes, inspection of every item may be possible. But random sampling is needed when measurements are costly, time-consuming, or destructive. For example, we can't test every cell phone battery's useful life, trigger every air bag to see whether it will deploy correctly, or cut open every watermelon to test for pesticide. Sample size and sampling frequency vary with the problem. In SPC the sample size *n* is referred to as the *subgroup size*.

Two Data Types

For *numerical* data (sometimes called *variable* data), the control chart displays a measure of central tendency (e.g., the sample mean) and/or a measure of variation (e.g., the sample range or standard deviation). A *variable control chart* is used for measurable quantities like weight, diameter, or time. Typically, such data are found in manufacturing (e.g., dimensions of a metal fastener) but sometimes also in services (e.g., client waiting time). The subgroup size for numerical data may be quite small (e.g., under 10) or even a single item.

For *attribute* data (sometimes called *qualitative* data), the focus is on counting nonconforming items (those that do not meet the target specification). An *attribute control chart* may show the proportion nonconforming (assumed binomial process) or the total number nonconforming (assumed binomial or Poisson process). Attribute control charts are important in service or manufacturing environments when physical measurements are not appropriate. Subgroup size for attribute data may be large (e.g., over 100) depending on the rate of nonconformance. Because modern manufacturing processes may have very low nonconformance rates (e.g., .00001 or .0000001), even larger samples are needed.

Three Common Control Charts

For a sample mean, the control chart is called an $\bar{x}$ **chart**. For a sample range, it is called an **R chart**. For a sample proportion, it is called a **p chart**. These three charts are illustrated in Figure 17.4. Each chart plots a sample statistic over time, as well as upper and lower *control limits* that define the expected range of the sample statistic. In these illustrations, all samples fall within the control limits. Control limits are based on the sampling distribution of the statistic. While there are many others, the basic concepts of SPC and setting control limits can be illustrated with these three chart types.

FIGURE 17.4

Three Common Control Charts (from MINITAB)

17.14 What is the difference between an attribute control chart and a variable control chart?

17.15 (a) What determines sampling frequency? (b) Why are variable samples often small? (c) Why are attribute samples often large?

17.5 CONTROL CHARTS FOR A MEAN

$\bar{x}$ Charts: Bottle-Filling Example

A bottling plant is filling 2-liter (2,000 ml) soft drink bottles. It is important that the equipment neither overfill nor underfill the bottle. The filling process is stable and in control with mean fill μ and standard deviation σ. The degree of variation depends on the process technology used in the plant. Every 10 minutes, n bottles are chosen at random and their fill is measured. The unit of measurement is milliliters. For a subgroup of size $n = 5$, the sample might look like this:

The mean fill for these five bottles is $\bar{x} = 1999.6$. Each time we take a sample of five bottles, we expect a different value of the sample mean due to random variation inherent in the process. From previous chapters, we know that the sample mean is an unbiased estimator of the true process mean (i.e., its expected value is μ):

(17.1) $\qquad E(\bar{X}) = \mu \qquad$ ($\bar{X}$ tends toward the true process mean)

The Central Limit Theorem says that the standard error of the sample mean is

(17.2) $\qquad \sigma_{\bar{X}} = \dfrac{\sigma}{\sqrt{n}} \qquad$ (larger n implies smaller variance of $\bar{X}$)

The sample mean follows a normal distribution if the population is normal, or if the sample is large enough to assure normality by the Central Limit Theorem.

Control Limits: Known μ and σ

Sample means from a process that is in control should be near the process mean μ, which is the *centerline* of the control chart. The **upper control limit (UCL)** and **lower control limit (LCL)** are set at ± 3 standard errors from the centerline, using the Empirical Rule, which says that almost all the sample means (actually 99.73 percent) will fall within "3-sigma" limits:

(17.3) $\qquad \text{UCL} = \mu + 3\dfrac{\sigma}{\sqrt{n}} \qquad$ (upper control limit for $\bar{X}$, known μ and σ)

(17.4) $\qquad \text{LCL} = \mu - 3\dfrac{\sigma}{\sqrt{n}} \qquad$ (lower control limit for $\bar{X}$, known μ and σ)

The $\bar{x}$ chart provides a kind of visual hypothesis test. Sample means will vary, sometimes above the centerline and sometimes below the centerline, but they should stay within the control limits and be symmetrically distributed on either side of the centerline. You will recognize the similarity between *control limits* and *confidence limits* covered in previous chapters. The idea is that if a sample mean falls outside these limits, we suspect that the sample may be from a different population from the one we have specified.

Table 17.3 shows 25 samples of size $n = 5$ from a bottling process with $\mu = 2000$ and $\sigma = 4$. For each sample, the mean and range are calculated. The control limits are:

$$UCL = \mu + 3\frac{\sigma}{\sqrt{n}} = 2000 + 3\frac{4}{\sqrt{5}} = 2000 + 5.367 = 2005.37$$

$$LCL = \mu - 3\frac{\sigma}{\sqrt{n}} = 2000 - 3\frac{4}{\sqrt{5}} = 2000 - 5.367 = 1994.63$$

EXAMPLE 17.1

Bottle Filling

TABLE 17.3   **Twenty-Five Samples of Bottle Fill with $n = 5$**   📷 **BottleFill**

Sample	Bottle 1	Bottle 2	Bottle 3	Bottle 4	Bottle 5	Mean	Range
1	2001	1998	2001	2001	1997	1999.6	4
2	1997	2004	2001	2000	2002	2000.8	7
3	2001	2000	2003	1995	1994	1998.6	9
4	2007	2007	2001	2000	1997	2002.4	10
5	1999	2001	1998	2001	1996	1999.0	5
6	2002	2002	1988	1995	2004	1998.2	16
7	2003	1998	1998	1996	2001	1999.2	7
8	2005	2000	1991	1996	1996	1997.6	14
9	1999	1997	2006	1999	1999	2000.0	9
10	2005	1999	1998	2002	2000	2000.8	7
11	2001	1997	2002	2004	2007	2002.2	10
12	2002	1995	1995	1997	2000	1997.8	7
13	2006	2006	1997	1998	1994	2000.2	12
14	2003	1997	2000	2003	2004	2001.4	7
15	2003	2008	1994	1998	1999	2000.4	14
16	1998	1997	1999	2001	1994	1997.8	7
17	1988	1996	2001	2002	2002	1997.8	14
18	2003	2003	1997	1995	2001	1999.8	8
19	2003	2004	1998	1998	2006	2001.8	8
20	2005	2001	2005	2000	2004	2003.0	5
21	2004	1996	2003	2002	1993	1999.6	11
22	1998	1996	2005	1997	1999	1999.0	9
23	2002	2001	1995	2004	2007	2001.8	12
24	2002	2002	1997	1995	2002	1999.6	7
25	2002	1999	2001	1992	1993	1997.4	10
				Average over 25 samples of 5 bottles:		1999.832	9.160

FIGURE 17.5

MINITAB's $\bar{x}$ Chart with Known Control Limits

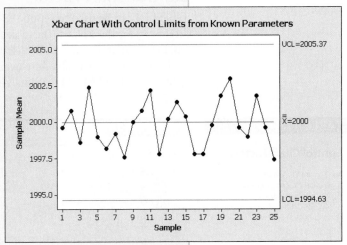

Figure 17.5 shows a MINITAB $\bar{x}$ chart for these 25 samples, with MINITAB's option to specify μ and σ instead of estimating them from the data. Because all the sample means lie within the control limits, this chart shows a process that is *in control*. If a sample mean exceeds UCL or is below LCL, we suspect that the process may be *out of control*. More rules for detecting an out-of-control process will be explained shortly.

Empirical Control Limits

When the process mean μ and standard deviation are unknown (as they often are), we can estimate them from sample data, replacing μ with $\bar{\bar{x}}$ (the average of the means of all samples) and replacing σ with the standard deviation s from a pooled sample of individual X-values. Generally, the centerline and control limits are based on *past* data, but are to be used on *future* data to monitor the process. It is desirable to set the control limits from samples taken independently, rather than using the same data to create the control limits and to plot the control chart. However, this is not always possible.

(17.5) $\quad \text{UCL} = \bar{\bar{x}} + 3\dfrac{s}{\sqrt{n}} \quad$ (upper control limit for $\bar{X}$, unknown μ and σ)

(17.6) $\quad \text{LCL} = \bar{\bar{x}} - 3\dfrac{s}{\sqrt{n}} \quad$ (lower control limit for $\bar{X}$, unknown μ and σ)

There are other ways to estimate the process standard deviation σ. For example, we could use $\bar{s}$, the mean of the standard deviations over many subgroups of size n, with an adjustment for bias. Or we could replace σ with an estimate $\bar{R}/d_2$ where $\bar{R}$ is the average range for many samples and d_2 is a control chart factor that depends on the subgroup size (see Table 17.4). If the number of samples is large enough, any of these methods should give reliable control limits. The $\bar{R}$ method is still common for historical reasons (easier to use prior to the advent of computers). If the $\bar{R}$ method is used, the formulas become:

(17.7) $\quad \text{UCL} = \bar{\bar{x}} + 3\dfrac{\bar{R}}{d_2\sqrt{n}} \quad$ (upper control limit for $\bar{X}$, unknown μ and σ)

(17.8) $\quad \text{LCL} = \bar{\bar{x}} - 3\dfrac{\bar{R}}{d_2\sqrt{n}} \quad$ (lower control limit for $\bar{X}$, unknown μ and σ)

Figure 17.6 shows MINITAB's menu options for estimating control limits from a sample. By default, MINITAB uses the pooled standard deviation, an attractive choice because it directly estimates σ. In Figure 17.6, using the $\bar{R}$ method, the $\bar{x}$ chart is similar to the chart in Figure 17.5, where σ was known, except that the LCL and UCL values are slightly different.

Control Chart Factors

Table 17.4 can be used to set up the control limits from sample data. We only need the first factor (d_2) for the $\bar{x}$ chart (the table also shows D_3 and D_4, which are used to construct control limits for an R chart, to be discussed shortly). The table only goes to $n = 9$ for purposes of illustration (larger tables are available in more specialized textbooks). These factors are built into MINITAB, MegaStat, Visual Statistics, and other computer packages.

TABLE 17.4			

Control Chart Factors

See Laythe C. Alwan, *Statistical Process Analysis* (Irwin/McGraw-Hill, 2000), p. 740, for details of how these factors are derived.

Subgroup Size	d_2	D_3	D_4
2	1.128	0	3.267
3	1.693	0	2.574
4	2.059	0	2.282
5	2.326	0	2.114
6	2.534	0	2.004
7	2.704	0.076	1.924
8	2.847	0.136	1.864
9	2.970	0.184	1.816

FIGURE 17.6

MINITAB's $\bar{x}$ Chart with Estimated Control Limits

To calculate $\bar{\bar{x}}$ and $\bar{R}$, we use averages of 25 sample means and ranges (see Table 17.3):

$$\bar{\bar{x}} = \frac{\bar{x}_1 + \bar{x}_2 + \cdots + \bar{x}_{25}}{25} = \frac{1999.6 + 2000.8 + \cdots + 1997.4}{25} = 1999.832 \quad \textbf{(17.9)}$$

$$\bar{R} = \frac{R_1 + R_2 + \cdots + R_{25}}{25} = \frac{4 + 7 + \cdots + 10}{25} = 9.160 \quad \textbf{(17.10)}$$

Using the sample estimates $\bar{\bar{x}} = 1999.832$ and $\bar{R} = 9.160$, along with $d_2 = 2.326$ for $n = 5$ from Table 17.4, the estimated empirical control limits are

$$\text{UCL} = \bar{\bar{x}} + 3\frac{\bar{R}}{d_2\sqrt{n}} = 1999.832 + 3\frac{9.160}{2.326\sqrt{5}} = 2005.12$$

$$\text{LCL} = \bar{\bar{x}} - 3\frac{\bar{R}}{d_2\sqrt{n}} = 1999.832 - 3\frac{9.160}{2.326\sqrt{5}} = 1994.55$$

Note that these *empirical* control limits (2005.12 and 1994.55) differ somewhat from the *theoretical* control limits (2005.37 and 1994.63) that we obtained using $\mu = 2000$ and $\sigma = 4$, and the *empirical* centerline ($\bar{x} = 1999.83$) differs from $\mu = 2000$. In practice, it would be necessary to take more than 25 samples to ensure a good estimate of the true process mean and standard deviation. Indeed, engineers may run a manufacturing process for days or weeks before its characteristics are well understood. Figure 17.7 shows MegaStat's $\bar{x}$ chart using the sample data to estimate the control limits.

FIGURE 17.7

MegaStat's $\bar{x}$ Chart with Estimated Control Limits

MegaStat *always* uses estimated control limits by the $\bar{R}$ method, and does not permit you to specify known parameters. Also, MegaStat expects the observed data to be arranged as a rectangle, with each subgroup's observations comprising a *row* (like Table 17.3). MegaStat's $\bar{x}$ chart is similar to MINITAB's except for details of scaling.

Detecting Abnormal Patterns

Sample means beyond the control limits are strong indicators of an out-of-control process. However, more subtle patterns can also indicate problems. Experts have developed many "rules of thumb" to check for patterns that might indicate an out-of-control process. Here are four of them (the "sigma" refers to the *standard error of the mean*):

- *Rule 1.* Single point outside 3 sigma.
- *Rule 2.* Two of three successive points outside 2 sigma on same side of centerline.
- *Rule 3.* Four of five successive points outside 1 sigma on same side of centerline.
- *Rule 4.* Nine successive points on same side of centerline.

Violations of Rules 1 and 2 can usually be seen from "eyeball inspection" of control charts. Violations of the other rules are more subtle. A computer may be required to monitor a process to be sure that control chart violations are detected. Figure 17.8 illustrates these four rules, applied to a service organization (an HMO clinic conducting physical exams for babies).

Multiple rule violations are possible. Figure 17.9 shows a MINITAB $\bar{x}$ chart with these four rules applied (note that MINITAB includes many other tests and uses a different

FIGURE 17.8

Red Dots Indicate Rule Violations

FIGURE 17.9

Violations of Rules of Thumb (from MINITAB)

numbering system for its rules). In this illustration, an out-of-control process is shown, with eight rule violations (each violation is numbered and highlighted in red).

Histograms

The normal curve is the reference point for variation inherent in the process or due to random sampling. UCL and LCL are set at ± 3 standard errors from the mean, but we could (and should) also examine ± 2 and ± 1 standard error ranges to see whether the percentage of sample means follows the normal distribution. Recall that the expected percent of samples within various distances from the centerline can be stated as normal areas or percentages:

- Within ± 1 standard deviation or 68.26 percent of the time.
- Within ± 2 standard deviations or 95.44 percent of the time.
- Within ± 3 standard deviations or 99.73 percent of the time.

The distribution of sample means can be scrutinized for symmetry and/or deviations from the expected normal percentages. Figure 17.10 shows an $\bar{x}$ chart and histogram for 100 samples of acidity for a commercial cleaning product. The histogram is roughly symmetric, with 60 sample means between -1 and $+1$ and 97 sample means between -2 and $+2$, while the normal distribution would predict 68 and 95, respectively.

FIGURE 17.10

$\bar{x}$ Chart and Histogram

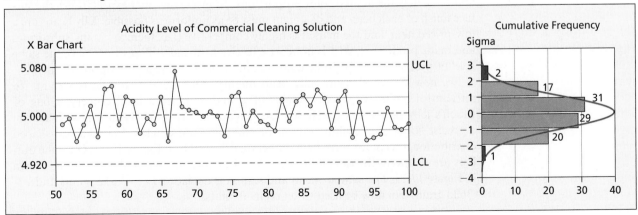

SECTION EXERCISES

17.16 (a) To construct control limits for an $\bar{x}$ chart, name three ways to estimate σ empirically. (b) Why is the $\bar{R}$ method often used? (c) Why is the s method the default in MINITAB?

17.17 For an $\bar{x}$ chart, what percent of sample means should be (a) within 1 sigma of the centerline; (b) within 2 sigmas of the centerline; (c) within 3 sigmas of the centerline; (d) outside 2 sigmas of the centerline; (e) outside 3 sigmas of the centerline? *Note:* "Sigma" denotes the standard error of the mean.

17.18 List four rules for detecting abnormal (special cause) observations in a control chart.

17.19 Set up control limits for an $\bar{x}$ chart, given $\bar{\bar{x}} = 12.50$, $\bar{R} = .42$, and $n = 5$.

17.20 Set up control limits for an $\bar{x}$ chart, given $\mu = 400$, $\sigma = 2$, and $n = 4$.

17.21 Time (in seconds) to serve an early-morning customer at a fast-food restaurant is normally distributed. Set up a control chart for the mean serving time, assuming that serving times were sampled in random subgroups of 4 customers. *Note:* Use this sample of 36 observations to estimate μ and σ. ServeTime

Sample 1	Sample 2	Sample 3	Sample 4	Sample 5	Sample 6	Sample 7	Sample 8	Sample 9
65	56	84	69	75	87	87	99	102
51	87	67	81	80	84	90	61	61
94	84	71	59	76	80	65	84	88
79	70	85	75	88	52	61	79	78

17.22 To print 8.5 × 5.5 note pads, a copy shop uses standard 8.5 × 11 paper, glues the long edge, then cuts the pads in half so that the pad width is 5.5 inches. However, there is variation in the cutting process. Set up a control chart for the mean width of a note pad, assuming that, in the future, pads will be sampled in random subgroups of 5 pads. Use this sample of 40 observations (widths in inches) to estimate μ and σ. NotePads

5.52	5.57	5.44	5.47	5.52	5.46	5.43	5.45
5.49	5.47	5.48	5.51	5.53	5.53	5.48	5.47
5.59	5.51	5.43	5.48	5.53	5.50	5.49	5.52
5.46	5.46	5.56	5.54	5.47	5.44	5.53	5.58
5.55	5.56	5.47	5.44	5.55	5.42	5.45	5.54

Mini Case   17.1

Control Limits for Jelly Beans JellyBeans

The manufacture of jelly beans is a high-volume operation that is tricky to manage, with strict standards for food purity, worker safety, and environmental controls. Each bean's jelly core is soft and sticky, and must be coated with a harder sugar shell of the appropriate color. Hundreds of thousands of beans must be cooled and bagged, with approximately the desired color proportions. To meet consumer expectations, the surface finish of each bean and its weight must be as uniform as possible. Jelly beans are a low-priced item, and the market is highly competitive (i.e., there are many substitutes and many producers), so it is not cost-effective to spend millions to achieve the same level of precision that might be used, say, in manufacturing a prescription drug.

So, how do we measure jelly bean quality? One obvious metric is weight. To set control limits, we need estimates of μ and σ. From a local grocery, a bag of Brach's jelly beans was purchased (see Figure 17.11). Each bean was weighed on a precise scale. The resulting sample of 182 jelly bean weights showed a bell-shaped distribution, except for three high outliers, easily visible in Figure 17.12. Once the outliers are removed, the sample presents a satisfactory normal probability plot, shown in Figure 17.13. The sample mean and standard deviation ($\bar{x} = 3.352$ grams and $s = .3622$ gram) can now be used to set control limits.

Referring to Figure 17.11, some differences in size are visible. Can you spot the three oversized beans? Some consumers may regard "double" beans as a treat, rather than as a product defect. But manufacturers always strive for the most consistent product possible, subject to constraints of time, technology, and budget.

FIGURE 17.11

The Data Set (*n* = 182)

FIGURE 17.12   **Dot Plot for All Data (*n* = 182)**

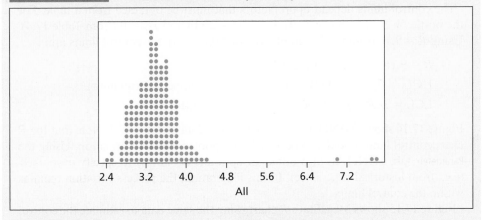

FIGURE 17.13   **Normal Plot for Trimmed Data (*n* = 179)**

17.6 CONTROL CHARTS FOR A RANGE

The $\bar{x}$ chart of sample means by itself is insufficient to tell whether a process is in control because it reveals only *centrality*. We also should examine a chart showing *variation* around the mean. We could track the sample standard deviations (using an *s chart*), but it is more traditional to track the *sample range* (the difference between the largest and smallest items in each sample) using the *R chart*. The sample range is sensitive to extreme values. Nonetheless, its behavior can be predicted statistically, and control limits can be established. The *R* chart has asymmetric control limits because the sample range is not a normally distributed statistic.

Control Limits for the Range

The centerline is obtained by calculating the average range $\bar{R}$ over many samples taken from the process. Estimation of $\bar{R}$ ideally would precede construction of the control chart, using a large number of independent samples, though this is not always possible in practice. Control limits based on samples may not be a good representation of the true process. It depends on the number of samples and the "luck of the draw." The control limits for the *R* chart can be set using either the average sample range $\bar{R}$ or an estimate $\hat{\sigma}$ of the process standard deviation:

(17.11) $\quad \text{UCL} = D_4\bar{R} \quad \text{or} \quad \text{UCL} = D_4 d_2 \hat{\sigma} \quad$ (upper control limit of sample range)

(17.12) $\quad \text{LCL} = D_3\bar{R} \quad \text{or} \quad \text{LCL} = D_3 d_2 \hat{\sigma} \quad$ (lower control limit of sample range)

EXAMPLE 17.2

Bottle Filling: R Chart

The control limits depend upon factors that must be obtained from a table. For the bottle fill data with $n = 5$, we have $D_4 = 2.114$ and $D_3 = 0$ (from Table 17.4). Using $\bar{R} = 9.16$ from the 25 samples (from Table 17.3), the control limits are:

$\bar{R} = 9.16 \qquad$ (centerline for *R* chart)

$\text{UCL} = D_4\bar{R} = (2.114)(9.160) = 19.36 \qquad$ (upper control limit)

$\text{LCL} = D_3\bar{R} = (0)(9.160) = 0 \qquad$ (lower control limit)

Figure 17.14 shows MINITAB's *R* chart for the data in Table 17.3. Note that the *R* chart control limits could also be based on a pooled standard deviation. Using the Parameters tab, MINITAB also offers an option (not shown) to specify σ yourself (e.g., from historical experience). In this illustration, the process variation remains within the control limits.

Figure 17.15 shows MegaStat's *R* chart using the same data to estimate the control limits. The MINITAB and MegaStat charts are similar except for scaling. MegaStat always uses estimated control limits, whereas MINITAB gives you the option.

FIGURE 17.14

MINITAB's *R* Chart with Control Limits from Sample Data

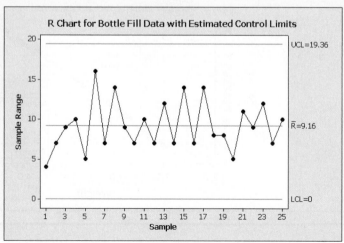

FIGURE 17.15

MegaStat *R* Chart with Estimated Control Limits

17.23 Set up limits for the *R* chart, given $\bar{R} = 0.82$ and $n = 6$.

17.24 Set up limits for the *R* chart, given $\bar{R} = 12$ and $n = 3$.

SECTION EXERCISES

17.7 OTHER CONTROL CHARTS

Attribute Data: *p* Charts

The *p chart* for attribute data plots the *proportion* of nonconforming items using the familiar sample proportion *p*:

$$p = \frac{\text{number of nonconforming items}}{\text{sample size}} = \frac{x}{n} \qquad (17.13)$$

LO 17-6

Make and interpret common control charts ($\bar{x}$, *R*, and *p*).

In manufacturing, *p* used to be referred to as a "defect rate," but the term "nonconforming items" is preferred because it is more neutral and better adapted to applications outside manufacturing, such as service environments. For example, for a retailer, *p* might refer to the proportion of customers who return their purchases for a refund. For a bank, *p* might refer to the proportion of checking account customers who have insufficient funds to cover one or more checks. For Ticketmaster, *p* might refer to the proportion of customers who have to wait "on hold" more than 5 minutes to obtain concert tickets.

The number of nonconforming items in a sample of *n* items is a binomial random variable, so the control limits are constructed as a confidence interval for a population proportion using one of several methods to state the *population* nonconformance rate π:

- Use an assumed value of π (e.g., a target rate of nonconformance).
- Use an empirical estimate of π based on a large number of trials.
- Use an estimate *p* from the samples being tested (if no other choice).

If *n* is large enough to assume normality,* the control limits would be

$$\text{UCL} = \pi + 3\sqrt{\frac{\pi(1 - \pi)}{n}} \qquad (\pi \text{ is the process centerline}) \qquad (17.14)$$

$$\text{LCL} = \pi - 3\sqrt{\frac{\pi(1 - \pi)}{n}} \qquad (\pi \text{ is the process centerline}) \qquad (17.15)$$

The logic is similar to a two-tailed hypothesis test of a proportion. Approximately 99.73 percent of the time, we expect the sample proportion *p* to fall within 3 standard deviations of

---

*To assume normality, we want $n\pi \geqq 10$ and $n(1 - \pi) \geqq 10$. If not, the binomial distribution may be used to set up control limits. MINITAB will handle this, although the resulting control limits may be quite wide.

the assumed centerline (π). If the LCL is negative, it is assumed to be zero (since a proportion cannot be negative). In manufacturing, the rate of nonconformance is likely to be a very small fraction (e.g., .02 or even smaller) so it is quite likely that LCL will be zero.

EXAMPLE 17.3

Cell Phone Manufacture

A manufacturer of cell phones has a .002 historical rate of nonconformance to specifications (i.e., 2 nonconforming phones per 1,000). All phones are tested, and the nonconformance rates are plotted on a p chart, using an assumed value $\pi = .002$. Thus, the control limits are

$$\text{UCL} = .002 + 3\sqrt{\frac{(.002)\,(.998)}{n}} \quad \text{and} \quad \text{LCL} = .002 - 3\sqrt{\frac{(.002)\,(.998)}{n}}$$

Table 17.5 shows inspection data for 100 days of production. Each production run (n) is around 2,000 phones per day, but does vary. Hence, the control limits are not constant, as shown in the p chart in Figure 17.16.

TABLE 17.5 Nonconforming Cell Phones 🖅 CellPhones

Day	Nonconforming (x)	Production (n)	x/n
1	3	2,056	0.00146
2	1	1,939	0.00052
3	4	2,079	0.00192
4	5	2,079	0.00241
5	4	1,955	0.00205
⋮	⋮	⋮	⋮
96	4	1,967	0.00203
97	6	2,077	0.00289
98	3	2,075	0.00145
99	5	1,908	0.00262
100	2	2,045	0.00098

FIGURE 17.16 MINITAB p Chart for Cell Phones

Tests performed with unequal sample sizes

Notice that p stays within the control limits although it touches the LCL twice (not a problem because zero defects is ideal). Although n varies, we can illustrate the control limit calculation by using $\pi = .002$ and $n = 2,000$:

$$\text{UCL} = .002 + 3\sqrt{\frac{(.002)\,(.998)}{2,000}} = .004997$$

$$\text{LCL} = .002 - 3\sqrt{\frac{(.002)\,(.998)}{2,000}} = -.000997$$

Because a negative proportion is impossible, we just set LCL = 0. You will notice that MINITAB's UCL is not quite the same as the calculation above because MINITAB uses a binomial calculation rather than the normal approximation. The difference may be noticeable when $n\pi < 10$ (the criterion for a normal approximation to the binomial). In this example, $n\pi = (.002)(2,000) = 4$, so the binomial method is preferred.

Application: Emergency Patients

Instead of being a rate of *nonconformance* to specifications, *p* could be a rate of *conformance* to specifications. Then

$$p = \frac{\text{number of conforming items}}{\text{sample size}} = \frac{x}{n} \qquad (17.16)$$

Ardmore Hospital's emergency facility advertises that its goal is to ensure that, on average, 90 percent of patients receive treatment within 30 minutes of arrival. Table 17.6 shows data from 100 days of emergency department records.

Day	Seen in 30 Minutes (x)	Patient Volume (n)	x/n
1	87	97	0.900
2	113	122	0.924
3	106	115	0.920
4	84	90	0.928
5	82	92	0.896
⋮	⋮	⋮	⋮
96	128	142	0.900
97	101	112	0.900
98	123	135	0.908
99	128	141	0.908
100	141	149	0.944

TABLE 17.6

Emergency Patients Seen within 30 Minutes
 ERPatients

The average number of patient arrivals per day is around 120, but there is considerable variation. Hence, the control limits are not constant, as shown in the *p* chart in Figure 17.17. Because the sample sizes are smaller than in the cell phone example, the LCL and UCL are more sensitive to the varying sample size, and hence appear more jagged. This process is in control.

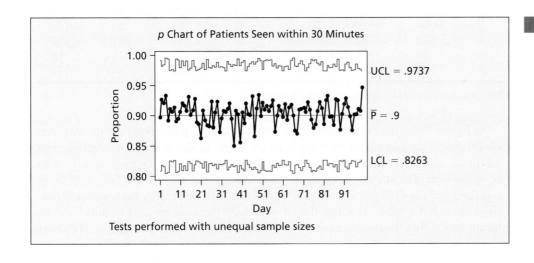

FIGURE 17.17

p Chart for ER Patients

The *p* chart is likely to be used in service operations (e.g., for benchmarking in health care delivery). Rules of thumb for detecting outliers, runs, and patterns apply to the *p* chart, just as for the $\bar{x}$ chart. However, tests for patterns are rarely seen outside manufacturing, except when service sector tasks are ongoing, repeatable, and easily sampled.

Other Control Charts (*s, c, np, I, MR*)

Other common types of control charts include:

- *I* charts (for individual numerical observations).
- *MR* charts (moving range for individual observations).
- *s* charts (for standard deviations).
- *c* charts (for Poisson events).
- *np* charts (for binomial totals).
- zone charts (using six regions based on σ).

The first two are used when *continuous inspection* is possible. When $n = 1$, there is no range, so a *moving range* is used. *I* chart control limits simply are $\mu \pm 3\sigma$ when $n = 1$. Mini Case 17.2 gives an illustration. Interpretation is the same as for any other control chart.

Mini Case   17.2

I-MR Charts for Jelly Beans 📂 JellyBeans2

Table 17.7 shows a sample of weights for 44 Brach's jelly beans (all black) from a randomly chosen bag of jelly beans. Is the weight of the jelly beans in control? To construct the control limits, we use the sample mean and standard deviation from the large trimmed sample in Mini Case 17.1 ($\bar{x} = 3.352$ grams and $s = 0.3622$ gram) with MINITAB's *I-MR* chart option with assumed parameters $\mu = 3.352$ and $\sigma = 0.3622$.

TABLE 17.7	Weights of 44 Black Brach's Jelly Beans						
Obs	Weight	Obs	Weight	Obs	Weight	Obs	Weight
1	3.498	12	3.181	23	3.976	34	3.168
2	3.603	13	3.545	24	3.321	35	2.656
3	4.223	14	3.925	25	3.609	36	2.624
4	7.250	15	3.686	26	3.604	37	3.254
5	3.830	16	3.938	27	3.668	38	3.411
6	3.563	17	3.667	28	3.433	39	2.553
7	2.505	18	3.152	29	3.678	40	4.217
8	3.034	19	3.325	30	3.264	41	3.417
9	3.408	20	3.905	31	3.743	42	3.615
10	3.564	21	3.714	32	3.446	43	1.218
11	3.042	22	3.359	33	3.036	44	3.612

Note: Measurements taken using a Mettler DF360 Delta Range Scale.

In Figure 17.18, the *I* chart (upper one) reveals that two jelly beans (the 4th and 43rd observations) are not within the control limits. There is also evidence of a problem in sample-to-sample variation in the *MR* chart (lower one). The explanation turned out to be rather clear. The 4th jelly bean was a "double-bean" (where two jelly beans got stuck together) and the 43rd jelly bean was a "mini-bean" (where the jelly bean was only partially formed). Figure 17.19 shows that, if we remove these outliers, the trimmed sample means stay within the control limits on the *I* chart (upper one), although the *MR* chart (lower one) still has one odd point. Improved quality control for a high-volume, low-cost item like jelly beans is cost-effective only up to a point. A business case would have to be made before spending money on better technology, taking into account consumer preferences and competitors' quality levels.

FIGURE 17.18 **Before Outliers Removed**

FIGURE 17.19 **After Outliers Removed**

Ad Hoc Charts

We said earlier that any display of a quality metric over time is a kind of control chart. If we set aside the formalities of control chart theory, anyone can create a "control chart" to monitor something of importance. For example, Figure 17.20 is not a "classic" control chart, but it shows a quality metric (patient waiting time in an emergency department) plotted over time. A box plot showing the range and quartiles over time is an *ad hoc* chart, yet it's a useful one. Organizations must develop their own approaches to quality improvement. As long as they begin with measurement, charting, and analysis, they are heading in the right direction.

FIGURE 17.20

Box Plots over Time
AdHoc

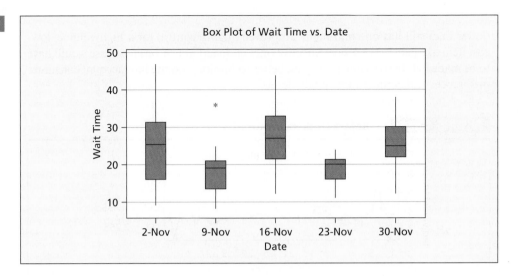

FIGURE 17.20

Box Plots over Time
AdHoc

SECTION EXERCISES

17.25 Why are *p* charts widely used in service applications like health care?

17.26 Create control limits for a *p* chart for a process with $\pi = .02$ and subgroup size $n = 500$. Is it safe to assume normality? Explain.

17.27 Create control limits for a *p* chart for a process with $\pi = .50$ and subgroup size $n = 20$. Is it safe to assume normality? Explain.

17.28 Create control limits for a *p* chart for a process with $\pi = .90$ and subgroup size $n = 40$. Is it safe to assume normality? Explain.

17.8 PATTERNS IN CONTROL CHARTS

The Overadjustment Problem

The $\bar{x}$ chart is a visual hypothesis test for μ, while the *R* chart is a visual hypothesis test for σ. In manufacturing, a control chart is used to guide decisions to continue the process or halt the process to make adjustments. *Overadjustment* or stopping to make unnecessary process corrections (Type I error) can lead to loss of production, downtime, unnecessary expense, forgone profit, delayed deliveries, stockout, or employee frustration. On the other hand, failing to make timely process corrections (Type II Error) can lead to poor quality, excess scrap, rework, customer dissatisfaction, adverse publicity or litigation, and employee cynicism.

Statistics allows managers to balance these Type I and II errors. It has been shown that, in the absence of statistical decision rules, manufacturing process operators tend toward overadjustment, which will actually *increase* variation above the level the process is capable of attaining.

The actions to be taken when a control chart violation is detected will depend on the consequences of Type I and Type II error. For example, if a health insurer notices that processing times for claim payments are out of control (i.e., relative to target benchmarks), the only action may be an investigation into the problem because the immediate consequences are not severe. But in car manufacturing, an out-of-control metal-forming process could require immediate shutdown of the assembly process to prevent costly rework or product liability.

Abnormal Patterns

LO 17-7

Recognize abnormal patterns in control charts and their potential causes.

Quality experts have given names to some of the more common abnormal control chart patterns, that is, patterns that indicate assignable causes:

- **Cycle**   Samples tend to follow a cyclic pattern.
- **Oscillation**   Samples tend to alternate (high-low-high-low) in "sawtooth" fashion.
- **Instability**   Samples vary more than expected.

- **Level shift**   Samples shift abruptly either above or below centerline.
- **Trend**   Samples drift slowly either upward or downward.
- **Mixture**   Samples come from two different populations (increased variation).

These names are intended to help you recognize symptoms that may be associated with known causes. These concepts extend to any time-series pattern (not just control charts).

Symptoms and Assignable Causes

Each $\bar{x}$ chart in Figure 17.21 displays 100 samples, which is a long enough run to show the patterns clearly. However, the $\bar{x}$ charts shown are exaggerated to emphasize the essential features of each pattern. Abnormal patterns like these would generate violations of Rules 1, 2, 3, or 4 (or multiple rule violations) so the process would actually have been

FIGURE 17.21
Common Abnormal Patterns

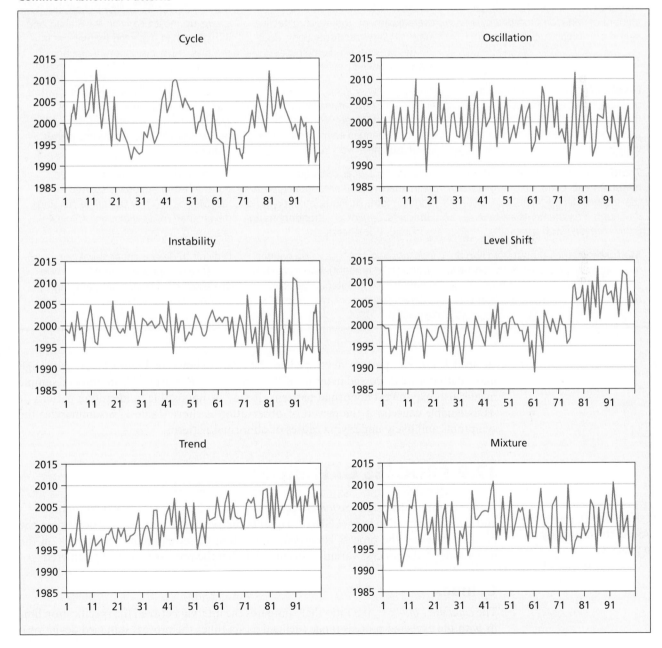

TABLE 17.8	Pattern Descriptions and Assignable Causes	
Pattern Description	*Likely Assignable Causes*	*Detected How?*
Cycle is a repeated series of high measurements followed by a series of low measurements ($+ + + + − − − +$ $+ + − − − − + + + +$, etc.) relative to the centerline. Equivalent to positive autocorrelation in regression residuals.	*Industry:* worn threads or gears, humidity or temperature fluctuations, operator fatigue, voltage changes, overadjustment. *Services:* duty rotations, employee fatigue, poor scheduling, periodic distractions.	May be detected visually (fewer than $m/2$ centerline crossings in m samples) or by a runs test (see Chapter 16) or higher-than-expected tail frequencies in a histogram. Look for violations of Rule 4.
Oscillation is a pattern of alternating high and low measurements ($+ −$ $+ − + − + − +$, etc.) relative to the centerline (a zigzag or sawtooth pattern). Equivalent to negative autocorrelation in regression residuals.	*Industry:* alternating sampling of two machines, two settings, two inspectors, or two gauges. *Services:* attempts to compensate for performance variation on the last task, alternating task between two workers.	May be detected visually (more than $m/2$ centerline crossings in m samples) or by a runs test (see Chapter 16). Process mean stays near the centerline, though process variance may increase. May not violate any rules.
Instability is a larger-than-normal amount of variation preceded by a period of normal, stable variation.	*Industry:* untrained operators, overadjustment, tool wear, defective material. *Services:* distractions, poor job design, untrained employees, flawed sampling process.	May be detectable on the $\bar{x}$ chart, but shows up most clearly on the R chart and in higher-than-expected frequencies in the tails of the histogram. Violations of Rules 1, 2, and 3 are likely.
Level shift is a sudden change in measurements either above or below the centerline. It is a change in the actual process mean. Easily confused with trend.	*Industry:* new workers, change in equipment, new inspector, new machine setting, new lot of material. *Services:* changed environment, new supervisor, new work rules.	Center of the histogram shifts but with no change in variation. Violation of Rule 4 is likely, and perhaps others. May be too few centerline crossings (fewer than $m/2$).
Trend is a slow, continuous drifting of measurements either up or down from the chart centerline. Detectable visually if enough measurements are taken. Easily confused with level shift.	*Industry:* tool wear, inadequate maintenance, worker fatigue, gradual clogging (dirt, shavings, etc.), drying of lubricants. *Services:* inattention, rising workload, bottlenecks.	Process variance may be unchanged, but the histogram grows skewed in one tail. May be too few centerline crossings (fewer than $m/2$). Violation of Rule 4 is likely, and perhaps others.
Mixture is merged output from two or more separate processes. Both may be in control, but with different means, so the overall process variance is increased.	*Industry:* two machines, two gauges, two shifts (day, night), two inspectors, different lots of material. *Services:* different supervisors, two work teams, two shifts.	Difficult to detect, either visually or statistically, especially if more than two processes are mixed. Histogram may be bimodal. Use same tests as for instability.

stopped *before* the pattern developed to the degree shown in Figure 17.21. Although many patterns are discussed in terms of the $\bar{x}$ chart, the R chart and histogram of sample means also may reveal abnormal patterns. It may be impossible to identify a pattern or its assignable cause(s) if the period of observation is short. Table 17.8 summarizes the symptoms and likely underlying causes of abnormal patterns.

17.9 PROCESS CAPABILITY

A business must translate *customer requirements* into an **upper specification limit (USL)** and **lower specification limit (LSL)** of a quality metric. These limits do *not* depend on the process. Whether the process is *capable* of meeting these requirements depends on the magnitude of the process variation (σ) and whether the process is correctly centered (μ).

C_p Index

The *capability index C_p* is a ratio that compares the interval between the specification limits with the expected process range (defined as six times the process standard deviation).

If the process range is small relative to the specification range, the capability index will be high, and conversely. A higher C_p index (a *more capable* process) is always better.

$$C_p = \frac{\text{USL} - \text{LSL}}{6\sigma} \qquad \text{(process capability index } C_p\text{)} \qquad \textbf{(17.17)}$$

A C_p value of 1.00 indicates that the process is barely capable of staying within the specifications *if* precisely centered. Managers typically require $C_p > 1.33$ to allow flexibility in case the process drifts off center. A much higher capability index may be required in some applications.

Example 1: If $\text{USL} - \text{LSL} = 6\sigma$, then $C_p = \dfrac{6\sigma}{6\sigma} = 1.00$

Example 2: If $\text{USL} - \text{LSL} = 8\sigma$, then $C_p = \dfrac{8\sigma}{6\sigma} = 1.33$

Example 3: If $\text{USL} - \text{LSL} = 10\sigma$, then $C_p = \dfrac{10\sigma}{6\sigma} = 1.67$

Figure 17.22 illustrates how a reduction in σ could increase C_p even though the specification limits remain the same. Note that when the distance between the USL and the LSL is 12σ then $C_p = 2.0$.

FIGURE 17.22

Smaller σ Improves Process Capability

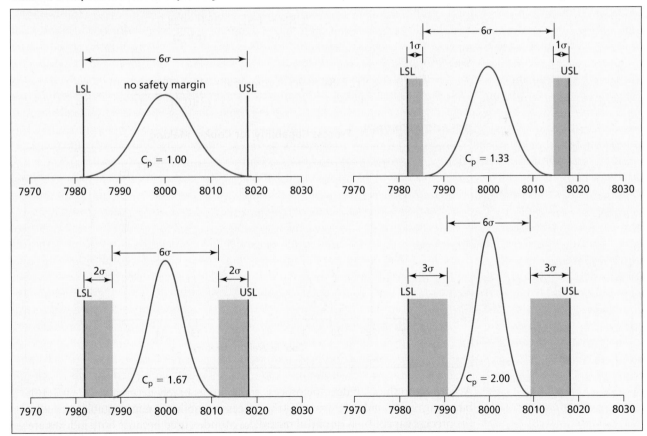

C_{pk} Index

The index C_p is easy to understand but fails to show whether the process is well-centered. A process with acceptable variation could be off-centerline and yet have a high C_p capability index. To remedy this weakness, we define another process capability index called

C_{pk} that looks at each (the distance between each specification limit and the process centerline).

The process capability index C_{pk} simply is the smaller of these two distances (USL $- \mu$ and $\mu -$ LSL) expressed as a fraction of the 3σ distance above or below μ:

(17.18) $$C_{pk} = \frac{\min(\mu - \text{LSL}, \text{USL} - \mu)}{3\sigma}$$ (process capability index C_{pk})

We are assuming that LSL lies below μ (the centerline) and USL lies above μ (the center-line) so that both distances are positive. If both $\mu -$ LSL and USL $- \mu$ are exactly 3σ, then $C_{pk} = 1.00$. A C_{pk} index of 1.00 is the minimum capability, but much higher values are preferred. If $\mu -$ LSL and USL $- \mu$ are the same, then C_{pk} will be identical to C_p. In contrast to the C_p index, the C_{pk} index imposes a penalty when the process is off-center. An animated illustration of both the C_p index and the C_{pk} index can be found at the website http://elsmar.com/Cp_vs_Cpk.html.

EXAMPLE 17.4

Cookie Baking

A bakery is supposed to produce cookies whose average weight, after baking, is 31 grams. To meet quality requirements, it has been decided that USL = 35.0 grams and LSL = 28.0 grams. The process standard deviation is 0.8 gram and the process centerline is set at $\mu = 31$ grams. The company requires a capability index of at least 1.33.

C_p index:

$$C_p = \frac{\text{USL} - \text{LSL}}{6\sigma} = \frac{35.0 - 28.0}{(6)(.8)} = 1.46$$

C_{pk} index:

$$C_{pk} = \frac{\min(\mu - \text{LSL}, \text{USL} - \mu)}{3\sigma} = \frac{\min(31.0 - 28.0, 35.0 - 31.0)}{(3)(0.8)} = \frac{3.0}{2.4} = 1.25$$

FIGURE 17.23   **Process Capability for Cookie Making**

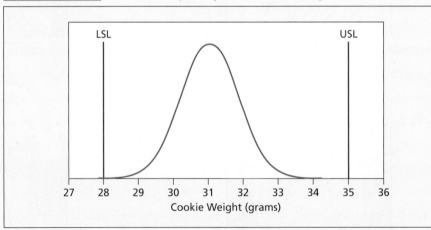

Cookie Weight (grams)

According to the C_p index, the process capability is barely acceptable ($C_p = 1.46$), but using the C_{pk} index ($C_{pk} = 1.25$) the process capability is unacceptable. Actually, the process capability is doubtful regardless of index used because both indexes are uncomfortably close to the company's chosen minimum (1.33). The situation is illustrated in Figure 17.23. In cookie making, management is less concerned about oversized cookies than undersized ones (customers will not complain if a cookie is too big), so the limits are not symmetric, as can be seen in Figure 17.23. Note that their process is correctly centered at $\mu = 31$, even though the specification limits are asymmetric.

Bottle Filling Revisited

Figure 17.24 illustrates several possible situations, using the bottle-filling scenario with symmetric specification limits LSL = 1994 and USL = 2006 and a target μ = 2000. Remember that specification limits are based on customer demands (or engineering requirements) and not on the process itself. *There is no guarantee that the extant process is capable of meeting the requirements.* If it is not, there is no choice but to find ways to improve the process (i.e., by reducing σ) through improved technology, worker training, or capital investment.

FIGURE 17.24

Process Variation versus Specification Limits

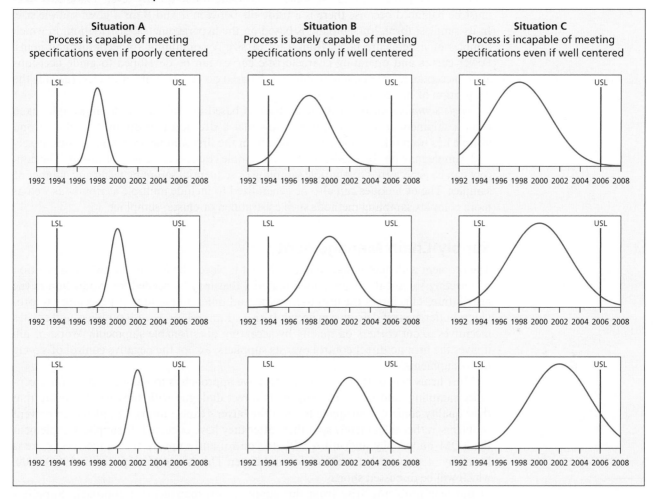

17.29 Find the C_p and C_{pk} indexes for a process with μ = 720, σ = 1.0, LSL = 715, USL = 725. How would you rate the capability of this process? Explain.

17.30 Find the C_p and C_{pk} indexes for a process with μ = 0.426, σ = 0.001, LSL = 0.423, USL = 0.432. How would you rate the capability of this process? Explain.

17.31 Find the C_p and C_{pk} indexes for a process with μ = 55.4, σ = 0.1, LSL = 55.2, USL = 55.9. How would you rate the capability of this process? Explain.

SECTION EXERCISES

17.10 ADDITIONAL QUALITY TOPICS (OPTIONAL)

Acceptance Sampling

The end quality of most manufactured products is strongly affected by the quality of materials purchased from suppliers. Manufacturing firms relied on random sampling inspection of shipments of incoming material until the 1970s. This process is called

acceptance sampling. Although acceptance sampling as a quality control tool is not commonplace today, companies do still use acceptance sampling plans when trying out a new vendor or verifying the capability of a new business process. Elaborate tables and decision rules were created to guide firms in choosing a sampling plan that gave the frequency of sampling, sample size, allowable defect level, and batch size. Different sampling plans were provided based on different combinations of Type I and Type II risks. The best-known are the Dodge-Romig tables, which were originally prepared for Bell Telephone.

In acceptance sampling, *the producer's risk* (α error) is the probability of rejecting material of some stated desirable quality level, while the *consumer's risk* (β error) is the probability of accepting material of some stated undesirable quality level. These two risks must be balanced because there is a trade-off between α and β for a given sample size. In its simplest form, lot sampling is based on the hypergeometric distribution, in which samples of *n* items are taken from a lot of size *N* containing *s* nonconforming items. Power curves and operating characteristic curves can be developed to guide decisions about acceptance or rejection of shipments, based on the attribute of interest (usually the proportion of nonconforming items).

Single sampling means that the decision is based on only one random sample taken from a shipment. *Double sampling* means that a decision is postponed until a second sample has been taken, unless the results from the first sample are unambiguous. A second sample may not be needed if the first sample result is extremely clear-cut. The concept can be generalized to multiple sampling or sequential sampling using any number of samples. The techniques can also be generalized to include multiple attributes as well as more complex sampling methods such as stratified or cluster sampling.

Supply-Chain Management

The problem with acceptance sampling is that it places the firm in the awkward position of rejecting shipments of purchased material that may be needed for production in the near future. This forces the firm to increase lead times and hold larger inventory to provide a buffer against defective material. It also strains relations with suppliers and creates incentives to cut corners on quality by accepting questionable shipments. Worst of all, it gives the firm no direct control over its suppliers, except the negative control of saying no to shipments.

Most firms believe that a more constructive approach is to reduce reliance on acceptance sampling, and instead to engage in direct dialogue with suppliers to ensure that their quality control is adequate to meet the buyer's expectations. The idea is to prevent problems, rather than merely spot them after they have occurred. If suppliers implement the TQM philosophy and utilize SPC to control and improve their processes, there is harmony of purpose between vendor and buyer. This is one principle behind ISO 9000, which will be discussed shortly.

But new problems arise from this supply-chain management approach. Suppliers may be smaller companies that lack the experience and resources needed to invest in training, research, and development, and there may be coordination problems between seller and buyer. Buyers may have to subsidize the process of implementing quality control at the supplier level, for example, by sponsoring training seminars, sharing their managerial experience, and working toward common database and decision support systems. Deming felt that suppliers should not be chosen solely on the basis of lowest cost. Rather, he thought buyers should develop long-term relationships with a small group of suppliers, and then nurture the links with those suppliers. Many firms have done this. But changing the supply-chain relationships can be difficult. Overseas outsourcing makes quality control even more complex. What does a U.S., Canadian, or European original equipment manufacturer do if its low-cost Chinese supplier delivers nonconforming or defective raw materials or parts? How do they work with a Chinese supplier to resolve the problem across thousands of miles and language and cultural barriers?

These nonstatistical problems illustrate why quality management in a global environment requires understanding of international business, as well as behavioral, financial, and supply-chain management. Engineers and technical specialists often find it helpful to study business management (and maybe Chinese). If you require a more detailed understanding of quality management, you will need further training (you can start with the RELATED READING list).

Quality and Design

Quality is closely tied to design. A well-designed process, product, or service is more likely to yield better quality and more customer satisfaction, with less effort and for a longer time. A poorly designed process, product, or service is more likely to yield undesired outcomes, awkward or inconvenient working arrangements, employee frustration in trying to maintain quality, and more frequent problems, breakdowns, and dissatisfied customers.

Firms may know that their products and services could be designed in a better way, but it would take time and cost money. Customer needs must be met today, so they say, "We will nurse along the old design and do the best we can with it." The problem is that, in the longer run, the customers may not be there, as more dynamic competitors capture the market. One lesson of our time is that there is no such thing as a "safe job," even in a large organization. When we can see a better way to do it, change becomes an ally and inertia an enemy. The search for design improvement is an ongoing process, not something done once. If we improve the design tomorrow, even better solutions are likely to be found later on. Successful organizations try to create a climate in which employees are encouraged to suggest new ways of doing things.

Taguchi's Robust Design

The prominence of Japanese quality expert Genichi Taguchi is mainly due to his contributions in the field of *robust design,* which uses statistically planned experiments to identify process control parameter settings that reduce a process's sensitivity to manufacturing variation. In Taguchi's taxonomy, we identify the functional characteristics that measure the final product's performance, the control parameters that can be specified by process engineers, and the sources of noise that are expensive or impossible to control. By varying control parameters in a planned experiment, we can predict control parameter settings that would make the product's performance less sensitive to random variation. Parameter settings are first varied in a few experimental runs. Then, a fractional factorial experimental design is selected (see Chapter 11), using a balancing property to choose pairs of parameter settings. Finally, predictions of improved parameter settings are made and verified in a confirming experiment.

Taguchi's methods are especially useful in manufacturing situations with many process control parameters, which imply complex experimental designs. Once the problem is defined, we rely on well-known experimental design methods. In addition, Taguchi is known for explicitly including in quality measures the total loss incurred from the time the product is shipped, using a quadratic loss penalty based on the squared difference between actual and target quality. His inclusion of customers in the model is considered a major innovation.

Six Sigma and Lean Six Sigma

Six Sigma is a broad philosophy to reduce cost, eliminate variability, and improve customer satisfaction through improved design and better management strategy. *Lean Six Sigma* integrates Six Sigma with supply-chain management to optimize resource flows, while also lowering cost and raising quality. Most of us have heard of the Six Sigma goal of 3.4 defects per million through reduced process variation (i.e., extremely high C_p and C_{pk} indexes), essentially using the tools outlined in this chapter and the DMAIC steps for process improvement. However, there is more to it than statistics, and Six Sigma experts must be certified (Green Belts, Black Belts, Master Black Belts) through advanced training. Six Sigma implementation varies according to the organization, with health care being perhaps the latest major application. Six Sigma knowledge goes beyond the bounds of an introductory statistics class, but if you take a job that requires it, your company will give you advanced training.

ISO 9000

Since 1992, firms wishing to sell their products globally have had to comply with a series of ISO standards, first articulated in 1987 in Europe. These standards have continued to evolve. Now, ISO 9000 and ISO audits (both internal and of suppliers) have become a de facto quality system standard for any company wanting to be a world-class competitor. ISO 9001 includes customer service as well as design of products and services (not just manufacturing). Several other ISO standards have been developed that address environmental management, food safety management, social responsibility, and risk management. The broad scope of the standards requires special training that is not normally part of an introductory statistics class.

Malcolm Baldrige Award

To recognize the importance of achievement in attaining superior quality, in 1988 the United States initiated the *Malcolm Baldrige National Quality Award,* based on seven categories of quality: leadership, information/analysis, strategic planning, human resource development, process management, operational results, and customer satisfaction. The Baldrige Award is given by the president of the United States to firms (large or small, manufacturing or services) that have made notable achievements in design, manufacture, installation, sales, and service.

Advanced MINITAB Features

A glance at MINITAB's extensive menus will tell you that quality tools are one of its strengths. In addition to all types of control charts and cause-and-effect diagrams (fishbone or Ishikawa diagrams), MINITAB offers capability analysis, variable transformations to achieve normality, alternative distributions where the assumption of normality is inappropriate, and gage study for variables and attributes. If you want further study of statistical quality tools, you could do worse than to explore MINITAB's menus, help system, and data sets. Many other general-purpose software packages (e.g., SAS, SPSS) offer similar capabilities.

Future of Statistical Process Control

Automation, numerical control, and continuous process monitoring have changed the meaning of SPC in manufacturing. The integration of manufacturing and factory floor quality monitoring systems in manufacturing planning and control, materials requirements planning (MRP), computer-aided design and manufacturing (CAD/CAM), order entry, and financial, customer service, and support systems have continued to redefine the role of SPC. Automation has made 100 percent testing and inspection attainable in some applications where it was previously thought to be either impossible or uneconomical.

It may be that SPC itself will become part of the background that is built in to every manufacturing organization, allowing managers to focus on higher-level issues. As an analogy, consider that only a few decades ago chart-making required specialists who were skilled in drafting. Now, anyone with access to a computer can make excellent charts. In the service sector of the economy, quality improvement is still at an early level of implementation. In health care, financial services, and retailing, processes are harder to define and tasks are often not as repetitive or as standardized as in manufacturing. Thus, the role of SPC is still unfolding, and every business student needs to know its basic principles.

Mini Case   17.3   **VAIL**RESORTS

ISO 9001/14001 Certification

Since 1992, firms wishing to compete globally have had to comply with a series of standards developed and maintained by the International Organization for Standardization (ISO). ISO 9000 standards address Quality Management Systems (QMS) within an organization. ISO 9001 certification means that an organization has a QMS in place to measure, achieve, and continually improve their customers' quality requirements, whether the organization provides products, services, or a combination of both. The ISO 14000 standards address Environmental Management Systems (EMS). ISO 14001 certification means that an organization is setting environmental objectives, identifying and controlling their environmental impact, and continually improving their environmental performance.

Vail Resorts Hospitality manages contracts within the Grand Teton National Park near Jackson, Wyoming, through the Grand Teton Lodge Company (GTLC). Grand Teton Lodge Company was one of the first Wyoming tourism entities to achieve ISO 14001 certification, a designation that also places them among an elite group of national park concessionaires that have received such certification. GTLC is also ISO 9001 certified, the only hospitality company in the United States to certify their quality management system.

Each year their commitment is verified through independent, third-party audits. Vail Resorts reports that the environmental management system has been successfully recertified each year, including several years with no adverse findings in this process. The GTLC EMS has achieved goals related to the environment such as annually diverting 300 tons of waste from landfills through recycling and reuse and working with their food vendors to develop a line of eco-friendly disposable food containers.

You can read more about the ISO certification process and Vail Resorts' quality and environmental efforts at the following websites: www.iso.org and www.vailresorts.com.

CHAPTER SUMMARY

Quality is measured by a set of attributes that affect **customer satisfaction. Quality improvement** is aimed at **variance reduction. Common cause** variation is normal and expected, while **special cause** variation is abnormal and requires action, such as adjusting the **process** for producing a good or service. Quality is affected by management, resources, technology, and human factors (e.g., training, employee involvement). **Statistical process control** (SPC) involves using **control charts** of key quality metrics to make sure that the processes are **in control.** The **upper control limit** (UCL) and **lower control limit** (LCL) define the range of allowable variation. These limits are usually set **empirically** by observing a process over time. Control charts are used to track the **mean** ($\bar{x}$ chart), **range** (R chart), **proportion** (p chart), and other statistics. Samples may be taken by **subgroups** of n items, or by continuous monitoring with **individual charts** (I charts) and **moving range** (MR) charts. There are **rules of thumb** to identify out-of-control patterns (instability, trend, level shift, cycle, oscillation) and their likely causes. A **capable** process is one whose variability (σ) is small in relation to the **upper and lower specification limits** (USL and LSL) as reflected in the C_p and C_{pk} capability indexes. SPC concepts were first applied to manufacturing but can be adapted to service environments such as finance, health care, and retailing. International **ISO standards** now guide companies selling in world markets, and Six Sigma techniques are widely used to improve quality in service organizations, as well as in manufacturing.

KEY TERMS

acceptance sampling, *750*
Baldrige Award, *752*
business process redesign (BPR), *727*
C_p, *746*
C_{pk}, *748*
common cause variation, *722*
control chart, *729*

continuous quality improvement (CQI), *727*
cycle, *744*
Deming, W. Edwards, *724*
DMAIC, *728*
fishbone chart, *726*
I charts, *742*
instability, *744*

ISO 9000, *752*
level shift, *745*
lower control limit (LCL), *730*
lower specification limit (LSL), *746*
mixture, *745*
MR charts, *742*
oscillation, *744*

Commonly Used Formulas

Control limits for $\bar{x}$ chart (known or historical σ): $\mu \pm 3\dfrac{\sigma}{\sqrt{n}}$

Control limits for $\bar{x}$ chart (sample estimate of σ): $\bar{\bar{x}} \pm 3\dfrac{s}{\sqrt{n}}$

Control limits for $\bar{x}$ chart (using average range): $\bar{\bar{x}} \pm 3\dfrac{\bar{R}}{d_2\sqrt{n}}$

Control limits for R chart (using average range or sample standard deviation with control chart factors from a table):

$$UCL = D_4\bar{R} \quad \text{or} \quad UCL = D_4d_2s$$
$$LCL = D_3\bar{R} \quad \text{or} \quad LCL = D_3d_2s$$

Capability index (ignores centering): $C_p = \dfrac{USL - LSL}{6\sigma}$

Capability index (tests for centering): $C_{pk} = \dfrac{\min(\mu - LSL,\ USL - \mu)}{3\sigma}$

Control limits for p chart: $\pi \pm 3\sqrt{\dfrac{\pi(1 - \pi)}{n}}$

CHAPTER REVIEW

Note: Questions with * are based on optional material.

1. Define (a) quality, (b) process, and (c) productivity. Why are they hard to define?

2. List six general attributes of quality.

3. Distinguish between common cause and special cause variation.

4. In quality improvement, list three roles played by statisticians.

5. Describe the five service quality dimensions.

6. In chronological order, list important phases in the evolution of the quality movement in North America. What is the main change in emphasis over the last 100 years?

7. (a) Who was W. Edwards Deming and why is he remembered? (b) List three of Deming's major ideas and explain them in your own terms.

8. List three influential thinkers other than Deming who made contributions to the quality movement and state their contributions.

9. (a) Briefly explain each acronym: TQM, BPR, SQC, SPC, CQI, DMAIC. (b) List the steps in the continuous quality improvement model.

10. (a) What is shown on the $\bar{x}$ chart? (b) Name three ways to set the control limits on the $\bar{x}$ chart. (c) How can we obtain good empirical control limits for the $\bar{x}$ chart? (d) Why are quality control samples sometimes small?

11. Explain the four rules of thumb for identifying an out-of-control process.

12. (a) What is shown on the R chart? (b) How do we set control limits for the R chart?

13. Name the six abnormal control chart patterns and tell (a) how they may be recognized and (b) what their likely causes might be.

14. (a) State the formulas for the two capability indexes C_p and C_{pk}. (b) Why isn't C_p alone sufficient? (c) What is considered an acceptable value for these indexes? (d) Why is an *in-control* process not necessarily *capable?*

15. (a) What is shown on the p chart? (b) How do we set control limits for the p chart? (c) Why might the p chart control limits vary from sample to sample?

*16. Briefly explain (a) the overadjustment problem, (b) *ad hoc* control charts, (c) acceptance sampling, (d) supply-chain management, (e) Taguchi's robust design, (f) the Six Sigma philosophy, (g) ISO 9000, and (h) the Malcolm Baldrige Award.

Instructions: You may use MINITAB, MegaStat, or similar software to assist you in the control chart questions. Data sets for the exercises are on the CD.

CHAPTER EXERCISES

connect

17.32 Explain each chart's purpose and the parameters that must be known or estimated to establish its control limits.

 a. $\bar{x}$ chart
 b. R chart
 c. p chart
 d. I chart

17.33 Define three possible quality metrics (not necessarily the ones actually used) to describe and monitor: (a) your performance in your college classes; (b) effectiveness of the professors in your college classes; (c) your effectiveness in managing your personal finances; (d) your textbook's effectiveness in helping you learn in a college statistics class.

17.34 Define three quality metrics that might be used to describe quality and performance for the following services: (a) your cellular phone service (e.g., Verizon); (b) your Internet service provider (e.g., AOL); (c) your dry cleaning and laundry service; (d) your physician's office; (e) your hairdresser; (f) your favorite fast-food restaurant.

17.35 Define three quality metrics that might be used to describe quality and performance in the following consumer products: (a) your personal vehicle (e.g., car, SUV, truck, bicycle, motorcycle); (b) the printer on your computer; (c) the toilet in your bathroom; (d) a PDA (e.g., Palm Pilot); (e) an HDTV display screen; (f) a light bulb.

17.36 Based on the cost of sampling and the presumed accuracy required, would sampling or 100 percent inspection be used to collect data on (a) the horsepower of each engine being installed in new cars; (b) the fuel consumption per seat mile of each Northwest Airlines flight; (c) the daily percent of customers who order low-carb menu items for each McDonald's restaurant; (d) the life in hours of each lithium ion battery installed in new laptop computers; (e) the number of medication errors per month in a large hospital?

17.37 Why are the control limits for an R chart asymmetric, while those of an $\bar{x}$ chart are symmetric?

17.38 Bob said, "We use the normal distribution to set the control limits for the $\bar{x}$ chart because samples from processes follow a normal distribution." Is Bob right? Explain.

17.39 Bob said, "They must not be using quality control in automobile manufacturing. Just look at the J.D. Power data showing that new cars all seem to have defects." (a) Discuss Bob's assertion, focusing on the concept of variation. (b) Can you think of processes where zero defects *could* be attained on a regular basis? Explain. (c) Can you think of processes where zero defects *cannot* be attained on a regular basis? *Hint:* Consider activities like pass completion by a football quarterback, 3-point shots by a college basketball player, or multiple-choice exams taken by a college student.

17.40 Use your favorite Internet search engine to look up any four of the following quality experts. Write a one-paragraph biographical sketch *in your own words* that lists his contributions to quality improvement.

 a. Walter A. Shewhart
 b. Harold F. Dodge
 c. Harry G. Romig
 d. Joseph M. Juran
 e. Genichi Taguchi
 f. Kaoru Ishikawa
 g. Armand V. Feigenbaum

17.41 Make a fishbone chart (cause-and-effect diagram) like the following for the reasons you have ever been (or could be) late to class. Use as many branches as necessary. Which factors are most important? Which are most easily controlled?

17.42 Make a fishbone chart (cause-and-effect diagram) for the reasons your end-of-month checkbook balance may not match your bank statement. Use as many branches as necessary. Which factors are most important? Which are most easily controlled?

17.43 Make a fishbone chart (cause-and-effect diagram) for the reasons an airline flight might be late to arrive. Use as many branches as necessary. Which factors are most important? Which are most easily controlled?

CAPABILITY

17.44 A process has specification limits of LSL = 540 and USL = 550. The process standard deviaton is $\sigma = 1.25$. Find the C_p and C_{pk} capability indexes if (a) the process mean is 545; (b) the process mean is 543.

17.45 In painting an automobile, the thickness of the color coat has a lower specification limit of 0.80 mil and an upper specification limit of 1.20 mils. Find the C_p and C_{pk} capability indexes if (a) the process mean is 1.00 mil and the process standard deviation is 0.05 mil; and (b) the process mean is .90 mil and the process standard deviation is 0.05 mil.

17.46 Moisture content per gram of a certain baked product has specification limits of 120 mg and 160 mg. Find the C_p and C_{pk} capability indexes if (a) the process mean is 140 mg and the process standard deviation is 5 mg; and (b) the process mean is 140 mg and the process standard deviation is 3 mg.

$\bar{x}$ CHARTS

17.47 The yield strength of a metal bolt has a mean of 6,050 pounds with a standard deviation of 100 pounds. Twenty samples of three bolts were tested, resulting in the means shown below. (a) Construct upper and lower control limits for the $\bar{x}$ chart, using the given product parameters. (b) Plot the data on the control chart. (c) Is this process in control? Explain your reasoning.
  📁 **Bolts-M**

6,107	6,031	6,075	6,115	6,039	6,079	5,995	6,097	6,114	6,039
6,154	6,054	6,028	6,002	6,062	6,094	6,051	6,031	5,965	6,082

17.48 Refer to the bolt strength problem 17.47. Assume $\mu = 6,050$ and $\sigma = 100$. Use the following 24 *individual* bolt strength observations to answer the questions posed. (a) Prepare a histogram and/or normal probability plot for the sample. (b) Does the sample support the view that yield strength is a normally distributed random variable? (c) Are the sample mean and standard deviation about where they are expected to be?   📁 **Bolts-I**

6,121	6,100	6,007	6,166	6,164	6,032	6,276	6,151
6,054	5,836	6,024	6,105	6,033	6,066	6,079	6,192
6,028	6,087	5,983	6,040	6,062	6,054	6,100	5,983

17.49 In painting an automobile at the factory, the thickness of the color coat has a process mean of 1.00 mil and a process standard deviation of 0.07 mil. Twenty samples of five cars were tested, resulting in the mean paint thicknesses shown below. (a) Construct upper and lower control limits for the $\bar{x}$ chart, using the given process parameters. (b) Plot the data on the control chart. (c) Is this process in control? Explain your reasoning.   📁 **Paint-M**

0.996	0.960	1.016	1.017	1.001	0.988	1.006	1.073	1.032	1.021
0.984	1.019	0.997	1.024	1.033	1.030	0.994	0.980	0.977	1.037

17.50 Refer to the paint thickness problem 17.49. Assume $\mu = 1.00$ and $\sigma = 0.07$. Use the following 35 *individual* observations on paint thickness to answer the questions posed. (a) Prepare a histogram and/or normal probability plot for the sample. (b) Does the sample support the view that paint thickness is a normally distributed random variable? (c) Are the mean and standard deviation about as expected?   📁 **Paint-I**

1.026	0.949	1.069	1.105	0.995	0.955	1.080
0.932	1.014	0.899	1.031	1.042	1.022	1.082
1.111	0.995	1.005	1.004	0.964	1.065	0.909
0.912	0.978	1.037	0.992	1.010	0.974	0.977
0.905	1.008	0.971	0.951	1.200	1.065	0.972

17.51 The temperature control unit on a commercial freezer in a 24-hour grocery store is set to maintain a mean temperature of 23 degrees Fahrenheit. The temperature varies because people are constantly opening the freezer door to remove items, but the thermostat is capable of maintaining temperature with a standard deviation of 2 degrees Fahrenheit. The desired range is 18 to 30 degrees Fahrenheit. (a) Find the C_p and C_{pk} capability indexes. (b) In words, how would you describe the process capability? (c) If improvement is desired, what might be some obstacles to increasing the capability?

17.52 Refer to the freezer problem 17.51 with $\mu = 23$ and $\sigma = 2$. Temperature measurements are recorded four times a day (at midnight, 0600, 1200, and 1800). Twenty samples of four observations are shown below. (a) Construct upper and lower control limits for the $\bar{x}$ chart, using the given process parameters. (b) Plot the data on the control chart. (c) Is this process in control? Explain your reasoning. 📊 **Freezer**

Sample	Midnight	At 0600	At 1200	At 1800	Mean
1	25	26	23	23	24.25
2	22	23	28	22	23.75
3	20	24	25	21	22.50
4	21	25	22	23	22.75
5	21	23	21	23	22.00
6	26	25	27	26	26.00
7	21	23	25	20	22.25
8	25	23	22	25	23.75
9	22	24	24	22	23.00
10	27	23	26	25	25.25
11	24	23	20	21	22.00
12	25	21	23	20	22.25
13	26	21	21	23	22.75
14	26	22	26	22	24.00
15	21	24	20	19	21.00
16	23	26	23	23	23.75
17	23	21	24	21	22.25
18	25	22	22	23	23.00
19	24	20	21	22	21.75
20	24	21	23	21	22.25

17.53 Refer to the freezer data's 80 *individual* temperature observations in problem 17.52. (a) Prepare a histogram and/or normal probability plot for the sample. (b) Does the sample support the view that freezer temperature is a normally distributed random variable? (c) Are the sample mean and standard deviation about where they are expected to be? 📊 **Freezer**

17.54 A Nabisco Fig Newton has a process mean weight of 14.00 g with a standard deviation of 0.10 g. The lower specification limit is 13.40 g and the upper specification limit is 14.60 g. (a) Describe the capability of this process, using the techniques you have learned. (b) Would you think that further variance reduction efforts would be a good idea? Explain the pros and cons of such an effort. *Hint:* Use the economic concept of opportunity cost.

17.55 A new type of smoke detector battery is developed. From laboratory tests under standard conditions, the half-life (defined as less than 50 percent of full charge) of 20 batteries are shown below. (a) Make a histogram of the data and/or a probability plot. Do you think that battery half-life can be assumed normal? (b) The engineers say that the mean battery half-life will be 8,760 hours with a standard deviation of 200 hours. Using these parameters (not the sample), set up the centerline and control limits for the $\bar{x}$ chart for a subgroup size of $n = 5$ batteries to be sampled in future production runs. (c) Repeat the previous exercise, but this time, use the sample mean and standard deviation. (d) Do you think that the control limits from this sample would be reliable? Explain, and suggest alternatives. 📊 **Battery**

8,502	8,660	8,785	8,778	8,804	9,069	8,516	9,048	8,628	9,213
8,511	8,965	8,688	8,892	8,638	8,440	8,900	8,993	8,958	8,707

17.56 A box of Wheat Chex cereal is to be filled to a mean weight of 466 grams. The lower specification limit is 453 grams (the labeled weight is 453 grams) and the upper specification limit is 477 grams (so as not to overfill the box). The process standard deviation is 2 grams. (a) Find the C_p and C_{pk} capability indexes. (b) Assess the process capability. (c) Why might it be difficult to reduce the variance in this process to raise the capability indices? *Hint:* A single Wheat Chex weighs .3 g (30 mg).

17.57 Refer to the Wheat Chex problem 17.56 with $\mu = 465$ and $\sigma = 3$. During production, samples of three boxes are weighed every 5 minutes. (a) Find the upper and lower control limit for the $\bar{x}$ chart. (b) Plot the following 20 sample means on the chart. Is the process in control? 📊 **Chex-M**

465.7	463.7	466.0	466.3	463.0	468.3	465.0	463.3	462.0	463.0
465.7	467.0	463.3	466.0	465.3	465.3	463.0	466.7	466.3	466.3

17.58 Refer to the Wheat Chex box fill problem 17.56 with $\mu = 465$ and $\sigma = 3$. Below are 30 *individual* observations on box fill. (a) Prepare a histogram and/or normal probability plot for the sample. Does the sample support the view that box fill is a normally distributed random variable? Explain. (b) Is the mean of these 20 same means where it should be? 📂 **Chex-I**

461	465	462	469	463	465	462	465	467	467
460	467	466	466	465	465	462	458	470	460
465	466	464	460	465	465	466	464	465	461

17.59 Each gum drop in two bags of Sathers Gum Drops was weighed (to the nearest .001 g) on a sensitive Mettler PE 360 Delta Range scale. After removing one outlier (to improve normality), there were 84 gum drops in the sample, yielding an overall mean $\bar{x} = 11.988$ g and a pooled standard deviation $s = .2208$ g. (a) Use these sample statistics to construct control limits for an $\bar{x}$ chart, using a subgroup size $n = 6$. (b) Plot the means shown below on your control chart. Is the process in control? (c) Prepare a histogram and/or normal probability plot for the pooled sample. Does the sample support the view that gum drop weight is a normally distributed random variable? Explain. 📂 **GumDrops**

Sample	x_1	x_2	x_3	x_4	x_5	x_6	Mean
1	11.741	11.975	11.985	12.163	12.317	12.032	12.036
2	12.206	11.970	12.179	12.182	11.756	11.975	12.045
3	12.041	12.120	11.855	12.036	11.750	11.870	11.945
4	12.002	11.800	12.092	12.017	12.340	12.488	12.123
5	12.305	12.134	11.949	12.050	12.246	11.839	12.087
6	11.862	12.049	12.105	11.894	11.995	11.722	11.938
7	11.979	12.124	12.171	12.093	12.224	11.965	12.093
8	11.941	11.855	11.587	11.574	11.752	12.345	11.842
9	12.297	12.078	12.137	11.869	11.609	11.732	11.954
10	11.677	11.879	11.926	11.852	11.781	11.932	11.841
11	12.113	12.129	12.156	12.284	12.207	12.247	12.189
12	12.510	11.904	11.675	11.880	12.086	12.458	12.086
13	12.193	11.975	12.173	11.635	11.549	11.744	11.878
14	11.880	11.784	11.696	11.804	11.823	11.693	11.780

p CHARTS

17.60 Past experience indicates that the probability of a post-surgical complication in a certain procedure is 6 percent. A hospital typically performs 200 such surgeries per month. (a) Find the control limits for the monthly p chart. (b) Would it be reasonably safe to assume that the sample proportion x/n is normally distributed? Explain.

17.61 A large retail toy store finds that, on average, a certain cheap (under $20) electronic toy has a 5 percent damage rate during shipping. From each incoming shipment, a sample of 100 is inspected. (a) Find the control limits for a p chart. (b) Plot the 10 samples below on the p chart. Is the process in control? (c) Is the sample size large enough to assume normality of the sample proportion? Explain. 📂 **Toys**

Sample	X	n	X/n
1	3	100	0.03
2	5	100	0.05
3	4	100	0.04
4	7	100	0.07
5	2	100	0.02
6	2	100	0.02
7	0	100	0.00
8	2	100	0.02
9	7	100	0.07
10	6	100	0.06

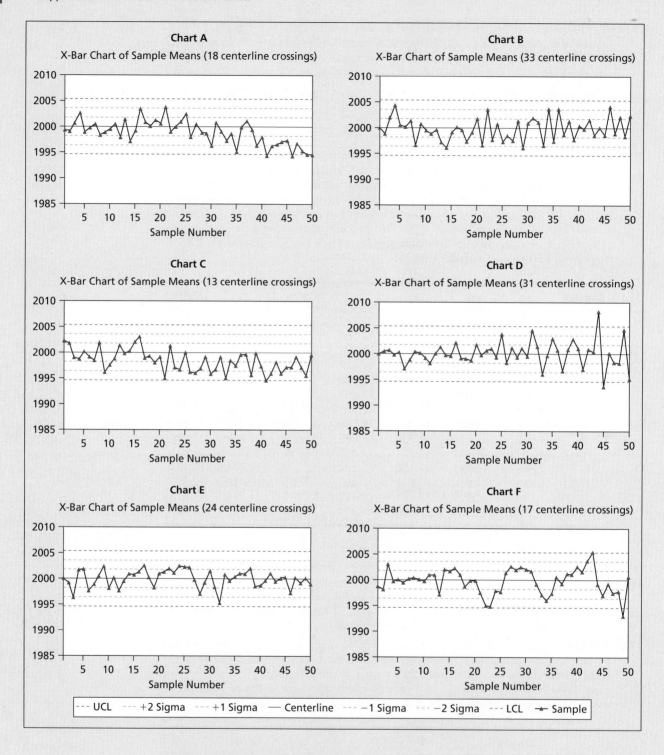

PATTERNS IN CONTROL CHARTS

17.62 Which abnormal pattern (cycle, instability, level shift, oscillation, trend, mixture), if any, exists in each of the $\bar{x}$ charts shown above? If you see none, say so. If you see more than one possibility, say so. Explain your reasoning.

17.63 Referring to Charts A–F, which Rules (1, 2, 3, 4) are violated in each chart? Make a photocopy and circle the points that violate each rule.

17.64 Refer to the bolt strength problem 17.47. Assuming $\mu = 6{,}050$ and $\sigma = 100$ with $n = 3$, then LCL = 5,876.8 and UCL = 6,223.2. Below are five sets of 20 sample means using $n = 3$. Test each set of means for the pattern suggested in the column heading. This is a visual judgment question, though you can apply Rules 1–4 if you wish. ✉ **Bolts-P**

Up Trend?	Down Trend?	Unstable?	Cycle?	Oscillate?
5,907	6,100	6,048	6,079	6,122
6,060	6,009	5,975	6,029	5,983
5,987	6,145	6,092	6,006	6,105
5,919	6,049	5,894	6,012	6,024
6,029	6,039	6,083	6,098	6,123
6,114	5,956	6,069	6,124	6,022
6,063	6,103	6,073	6,092	6,082
6,084	6,140	5,972	6,114	6,018
5,980	6,054	6,112	6,071	6,031
6,056	6,062	5,988	6,097	6,107
6,078	6,042	6,006	6,038	6,031
6,118	6,152	6,226	6,099	6,047
6,051	5,961	5,989	6,000	6,055
6,021	5,926	6,111	6,004	6,041
6,068	6,109	6,026	6,054	5,972
6,157	5,904	6,057	6,083	5,987
6,041	6,049	6,098	6,148	6,043
6,129	6,042	6,082	6,071	6,137
6,026	5,847	6,050	6,095	5,930
6,174	6,033	6,084	6,092	6,057

17.65 Refer to the paint problem 17.49 with $\mu = 1.00$ and $\sigma = .07$. With $n = 5$, LCL = .906 and UCL = 1.094. Below are five sets of 20 sample means using $n = 5$. Test each set of means for the pattern suggested in the column heading. This is a visual judgment question, though you can apply Rules 1–4 if you wish. 📂 **Paint-P**

No Pattern?	Up Trend?	Down Trend?	Unstable?	Cycle?
0.996	0.995	1.007	0.999	0.964
0.960	0.942	1.000	0.986	1.025
1.016	0.947	1.011	0.950	0.988
1.017	1.011	0.989	0.982	1.000
1.001	0.983	0.999	0.967	1.023
0.988	0.989	1.000	0.972	1.019
1.006	0.978	1.025	0.977	1.035
1.073	0.958	0.963	1.015	1.043
1.032	1.034	1.060	0.970	1.044
1.021	1.058	1.020	1.016	0.993
0.984	1.058	0.977	0.979	0.994
1.019	0.958	0.985	0.934	0.988
0.997	1.030	1.033	0.975	0.991
1.024	1.022	0.975	1.100	1.001
1.033	0.976	0.939	0.976	1.011
1.030	1.024	1.007	0.976	1.015
0.994	1.032	0.994	1.029	1.000
0.980	0.994	0.990	0.987	1.010
0.977	1.016	0.925	0.954	1.061
1.037	1.039	0.907	1.011	1.001

DO IT YOURSELF

17.66 Buy a bag of M&Ms. (a) As a measure of quality, take a sample of 100 M&Ms and count the number with incomplete or illegible "M" printed on them. (b) Calculate the sample proportion with defects. (c) What ambiguity (if any) did you encounter in this task? (d) Do you feel that your sample was large enough? Explain.

17.67 Examine a square meter (or another convenient unit) of paint on your car's driver door. Be sure the area is clean. (a) Tally the number of paint defects (scratch, abrasion, embedded dirt, chip, dent, rust, other). You may add your own defect categories. (b) Repeat, using a friend's car that is either older or newer than yours. (c) State your findings succinctly.

17.68 Buy a box of Cheerios (or your favorite breakfast cereal). (a) As a measure of quality, take a sample of 100 Cheerios, and count the number of Cheerios that are broken. (b) Calculate the sample proportion with defects. (c) What ambiguity (if any) did you encounter in this task? (d) Do you feel that your sample was truly random? Explain.

Web Data Sources

Source	Web Site
American Society for Quality (books, training, videos)	www.qualitypress.asq.org
Deming Society (philosophy, references)	www.deming.org
Juran Institute	www.juran.com
Quality Digest Magazine (current issues)	www.qualitydigest.com
Quality University (training videos)	www.qualityuniversity.com

RELATED READING

Besterfield, Dale H. *Quality Control*. 8th ed. Prentice-Hall, 2008.

Bossert, James L. *Supplier Management Handbook*. 6th ed. ASQC, 2004.

Brussee, Warren. *Statistics for Six Sigma Made Easy*. McGraw-Hill, 2004.

Evans, James R., and William M. Lindsay. *Management and the Control of Quality*. 8th ed. South-Western, 2011.

Foster, S. Thomas. *Managing Quality*. 4th ed. Prentice Hall, 2010.

George, Michael L.; David T. Rowlands; and Bill Kastle. *What Is Lean Six Sigma?* McGraw-Hill, 2003.

Jonglekar, Anand M. *Statistical Methods for Six Sigma*. Wiley, 2003.

Kemp, Sid. *Quality Management Demystified*. McGraw-Hill, 2006.

Montgomery, Douglas C. *Introduction to Statistical Quality Control*. 6th ed. Wiley, 2008.

Norton, Mick. *A Quick Course in Statistical Process Control*. Pearson, 2005.

Pyzdek, Thomas. *The Six Sigma Handbook*. 3rd ed. McGraw-Hill, 2009.

CHAPTER 17 Online Learning Resources

The Online Learning Center (OLC) at www.mhhe.com/doane4e has several *LearningStats* demonstrations to help you understand quality management. Your instructor may assign one or more of them, or you may decide to download the ones that sound interesting.

Topic	LearningStats Demonstrations
Quality overview	Quality Overview
	Process Control Overview
Capability	Capability Explained
	Capability Indexes
	Moving Range
Control chart patterns and rules	Control Chart Patterns
Other	What Is Six Sigma?

Key: = PowerPoint   = Excel

APPENDIX A

BINOMIAL PROBABILITIES

Example: $P(X = 3 \mid n = 8, \pi = .50) = .2188$

This table shows $P(X = x)$.

π

n	x	.01	.02	.05	.10	.15	.20	.30	.40	.50	.60	.70	.80	.85	.90	.95	.98	.99
2	0	.9801	.9604	.9025	.8100	.7225	.6400	.4900	.3600	.2500	.1600	.0900	.0400	.0225	.0100	.0025	.0004	.0001
	1	.0198	.0392	.0950	.1800	.2550	.3200	.4200	.4800	.5000	.4800	.4200	.3200	.2550	.1800	.0950	.0392	.0198
	2	.0001	.0004	.0025	.0100	.0225	.0400	.0900	.1600	.2500	.3600	.4900	.6400	.7225	.8100	.9025	.9604	.9801
3	0	.9703	.9412	.8574	.7290	.6141	.5120	.3430	.2160	.1250	.0640	.0270	.0080	.0034	.0010	.0001	—	—
	1	.0294	.0576	.1354	.2430	.3251	.3840	.4410	.4320	.3750	.2880	.1890	.0960	.0574	.0270	.0071	.0012	.0003
	2	.0003	.0012	.0071	.0270	.0574	.0960	.1890	.2880	.3750	.4320	.4410	.3840	.3251	.2430	.1354	.0576	.0294
	3	—	—	.0001	.0010	.0034	.0080	.0270	.0640	.1250	.2160	.3430	.5120	.6141	.7290	.8574	.9412	.9703
4	0	.9606	.9224	.8145	.6561	.5220	.4096	.2401	.1296	.0625	.0256	.0081	.0016	.0005	.0001	—	—	—
	1	.0388	.0753	.1715	.2916	.3685	.4096	.4116	.3456	.2500	.1536	.0756	.0256	.0115	.0036	.0005	—	—
	2	.0006	.0023	.0135	.0486	.0975	.1536	.2646	.3456	.3750	.3456	.2646	.1536	.0975	.0486	.0135	.0023	.0006
	3	—	—	.0005	.0036	.0115	.0256	.0756	.1536	.2500	.3456	.4116	.4096	.3685	.2916	.1715	.0753	.0388
	4	—	—	—	.0001	.0005	.0016	.0081	.0256	.0625	.1296	.2401	.4096	.5220	.6561	.8145	.9224	.9606
5	0	.9510	.9039	.7738	.5905	.4437	.3277	.1681	.0778	.0313	.0102	.0024	.0003	.0001	—	—	—	—
	1	.0480	.0922	.2036	.3281	.3915	.4096	.3602	.2592	.1563	.0768	.0284	.0064	.0022	.0005	—	—	—
	2	.0010	.0038	.0214	.0729	.1382	.2048	.3087	.3456	.3125	.2304	.1323	.0512	.0244	.0081	.0011	.0001	—
	3	—	.0001	.0011	.0081	.0244	.0512	.1323	.2304	.3125	.3456	.3087	.2048	.1382	.0729	.0214	.0038	.0010
	4	—	—	—	.0005	.0022	.0064	.0284	.0768	.1563	.2592	.3602	.4096	.3915	.3281	.2036	.0922	.0480
	5	—	—	—	—	.0001	.0003	.0024	.0102	.0313	.0778	.1681	.3277	.4437	.5905	.7738	.9039	.9510
6	0	.9415	.8858	.7351	.5314	.3771	.2621	.1176	.0467	.0156	.0041	.0007	.0001	—	—	—	—	—
	1	.0571	.1085	.2321	.3543	.3993	.3932	.3025	.1866	.0938	.0369	.0102	.0015	.0004	.0001	—	—	—
	2	.0014	.0055	.0305	.0984	.1762	.2458	.3241	.3110	.2344	.1382	.0595	.0154	.0055	.0012	.0001	—	—
	3	—	.0002	.0021	.0146	.0415	.0819	.1852	.2765	.3125	.2765	.1852	.0819	.0415	.0146	.0021	.0002	—
	4	—	—	.0001	.0012	.0055	.0154	.0595	.1382	.2344	.3110	.3241	.2458	.1762	.0984	.0305	.0055	.0014
	5	—	—	—	.0001	.0004	.0015	.0102	.0369	.0938	.1866	.3025	.3932	.3993	.3543	.2321	.1085	.0571
	6	—	—	—	—	—	.0001	.0007	.0041	.0156	.0467	.1176	.2621	.3771	.5314	.7351	.8858	.9415
7	0	.9321	.8681	.6983	.4783	.3206	.2097	.0824	.0280	.0078	.0016	.0002	—	—	—	—	—	—
	1	.0659	.1240	.2573	.3720	.3960	.3670	.2471	.1306	.0547	.0172	.0036	.0004	.0001	—	—	—	—
	2	.0020	.0076	.0406	.1240	.2097	.2753	.3177	.2613	.1641	.0774	.0250	.0043	.0012	.0002	—	—	—
	3	—	.0003	.0036	.0230	.0617	.1147	.2269	.2903	.2734	.1935	.0972	.0287	.0109	.0026	.0002	—	—
	4	—	—	.0002	.0026	.0109	.0287	.0972	.1935	.2734	.2903	.2269	.1147	.0617	.0230	.0036	.0003	—
	5	—	—	—	.0002	.0012	.0043	.0250	.0774	.1641	.2613	.3177	.2753	.2097	.1240	.0406	.0076	.0020
	6	—	—	—	—	.0001	.0004	.0036	.0172	.0547	.1306	.2471	.3670	.3960	.3720	.2573	.1240	.0659
	7	—	—	—	—	—	—	.0002	.0016	.0078	.0280	.0824	.2097	.3206	.4783	.6983	.8681	.9321
8	0	.9227	.8508	.6634	.4305	.2725	.1678	.0576	.0168	.0039	.0007	.0001	—	—	—	—	—	—
	1	.0746	.1389	.2793	.3826	.3847	.3355	.1977	.0896	.0313	.0079	.0012	.0001	—	—	—	—	—
	2	.0026	.0099	.0515	.1488	.2376	.2936	.2965	.2090	.1094	.0413	.0100	.0011	.0002	—	—	—	—
	3	.0001	.0004	.0054	.0331	.0839	.1468	.2541	.2787	.2188	.1239	.0467	.0092	.0026	.0004	—	—	—
	4	—	—	.0004	.0046	.0185	.0459	.1361	.2322	.2734	.2322	.1361	.0459	.0185	.0046	.0004	—	—
	5	—	—	—	.0004	.0026	.0092	.0467	.1239	.2188	.2787	.2541	.1468	.0839	.0331	.0054	.0004	.0001
	6	—	—	—	—	.0002	.0011	.0100	.0413	.1094	.2090	.2965	.2936	.2376	.1488	.0515	.0099	.0026
	7	—	—	—	—	—	.0001	.0012	.0079	.0313	.0896	.1977	.3355	.3847	.3826	.2793	.1389	.0746
	8	—	—	—	—	—	—	.0001	.0007	.0039	.0168	.0576	.1678	.2725	.4305	.6634	.8508	.9227
9	0	.9135	.8337	.6302	.3874	.2316	.1342	.0404	.0101	.0020	.0003	—	—	—	—	—	—	—
	1	.0830	.1531	.2985	.3874	.3679	.3020	.1556	.0605	.0176	.0035	.0004	—	—	—	—	—	—
	2	.0034	.0125	.0629	.1722	.2597	.3020	.2668	.1612	.0703	.0212	.0039	.0003	—	—	—	—	—
	3	.0001	.0006	.0077	.0446	.1069	.1762	.2668	.2508	.1641	.0743	.0210	.0028	.0006	.0001	—	—	—
	4	—	—	.0006	.0074	.0283	.0661	.1715	.2508	.2461	.1672	.0735	.0165	.0050	.0008	—	—	—
	5	—	—	—	.0008	.0050	.0165	.0735	.1672	.2461	.2508	.1715	.0661	.0283	.0074	.0006	—	—
	6	—	—	—	.0001	.0006	.0028	.0210	.0743	.1641	.2508	.2668	.1762	.1069	.0446	.0077	.0006	.0001
	7	—	—	—	—	—	.0003	.0039	.0212	.0703	.1612	.2668	.3020	.2597	.1722	.0629	.0125	.0034
	8	—	—	—	—	—	—	.0004	.0035	.0176	.0605	.1556	.3020	.3679	.3874	.2985	.1531	.0830
	9	—	—	—	—	—	—	—	.0003	.0020	.0101	.0404	.1342	.2316	.3874	.6302	.8337	.9135

									π									
n	x	.01	.02	.05	.10	.15	.20	.30	.40	.50	.60	.70	.80	.85	.90	.95	.98	.99
10	0	.9044	.8171	.5987	.3487	.1969	.1074	.0282	.0060	.0010	.0001	—	—	—	—	—	—	—
	1	.0914	.1667	.3151	.3874	.3474	.2684	.1211	.0403	.0098	.0016	.0001	—	—	—	—	—	—
	2	.0042	.0153	.0746	.1937	.2759	.3020	.2335	.1209	.0439	.0106	.0014	.0001	—	—	—	—	—
	3	.0001	.0008	.0105	.0574	.1298	.2013	.2668	.2150	.1172	.0425	.0090	.0008	.0001	—	—	—	—
	4	—	—	.0010	.0112	.0401	.0881	.2001	.2508	.2051	.1115	.0368	.0055	.0012	.0001	—	—	—
	5	—	—	.0001	.0015	.0085	.0264	.1029	.2007	.2461	.2007	.1029	.0264	.0085	.0015	.0001	—	—
	6	—	—	—	.0001	.0012	.0055	.0368	.1115	.2051	.2508	.2001	.0881	.0401	.0112	.0010	—	—
	7	—	—	—	—	.0001	.0008	.0090	.0425	.1172	.2150	.2668	.2013	.1298	.0574	.0105	.0008	.0001
	8	—	—	—	—	—	.0001	.0014	.0106	.0439	.1209	.2335	.3020	.2759	.1937	.0746	.0153	.0042
	9	—	—	—	—	—	—	.0001	.0016	.0098	.0403	.1211	.2684	.3474	.3874	.3151	.1667	.0914
	10	—	—	—	—	—	—	—	.0001	.0010	.0060	.0282	.1074	.1969	.3487	.5987	.8171	.9044
12	0	.8864	.7847	.5404	.2824	.1422	.0687	.0138	.0022	.0002	—	—	—	—	—	—	—	—
	1	.1074	.1922	.3413	.3766	.3012	.2062	.0712	.0174	.0029	.0003	—	—	—	—	—	—	—
	2	.0060	.0216	.0988	.2301	.2924	.2835	.1678	.0639	.0161	.0025	.0002	—	—	—	—	—	—
	3	.0002	.0015	.0173	.0852	.1720	.2362	.2397	.1419	.0537	.0125	.0015	.0001	—	—	—	—	—
	4	—	.0001	.0021	.0213	.0683	.1329	.2311	.2128	.1208	.0420	.0078	.0005	.0001	—	—	—	—
	5	—	—	.0002	.0038	.0193	.0532	.1585	.2270	.1934	.1009	.0291	.0033	.0006	—	—	—	—
	6	—	—	—	.0005	.0040	.0155	.0792	.1766	.2256	.1766	.0792	.0155	.0040	.0005	—	—	—
	7	—	—	—	—	.0006	.0033	.0291	.1009	.1934	.2270	.1585	.0532	.0193	.0038	.0002	—	—
	8	—	—	—	—	.0001	.0005	.0078	.0420	.1208	.2128	.2311	.1329	.0683	.0213	.0021	.0001	—
	9	—	—	—	—	—	.0001	.0015	.0125	.0537	.1419	.2397	.2362	.1720	.0852	.0173	.0015	.0002
	10	—	—	—	—	—	—	.0002	.0025	.0161	.0639	.1678	.2835	.2924	.2301	.0988	.0216	.0060
	11	—	—	—	—	—	—	—	.0003	.0029	.0174	.0712	.2062	.3012	.3766	.3413	.1922	.1074
	12	—	—	—	—	—	—	—	.0002	.0022	.0138	.0687	.1422	.2824	.5404	.7847	.8864
14	0	.8687	.7536	.4877	.2288	.1028	.0440	.0068	.0008	.0001	—	—	—	—	—	—	—	—
	1	.1229	.2153	.3593	.3559	.2539	.1539	.0407	.0073	.0009	.0001	—	—	—	—	—	—	—
	2	.0081	.0286	.1229	.2570	.2912	.2501	.1134	.0317	.0056	.0005	—	—	—	—	—	—	—
	3	.0003	.0023	.0259	.1142	.2056	.2501	.1943	.0845	.0222	.0033	.0002	—	—	—	—	—	—
	4	—	.0001	.0037	.0349	.0998	.1720	.2290	.1549	.0611	.0136	.0014	—	—	—	—	—	—
	5	—	—	.0004	.0078	.0352	.0860	.1963	.2066	.1222	.0408	.0066	.0003	—	—	—	—	—
	6	—	—	—	.0013	.0093	.0322	.1262	.2066	.1833	.0918	.0232	.0020	.0003	—	—	—	—
	7	—	—	—	.0002	.0019	.0092	.0618	.1574	.2095	.1574	.0618	.0092	.0019	.0002	—	—	—
	8	—	—	—	—	.0003	.0020	.0232	.0918	.1833	.2066	.1262	.0322	.0093	.0013	—	—	—
	9	—	—	—	—	—	.0003	.0066	.0408	.1222	.2066	.1963	.0860	.0352	.0078	.0004	—	—
	10	—	—	—	—	—	—	.0014	.0136	.0611	.1549	.2290	.1720	.0998	.0349	.0037	.0001	—
	11	—	—	—	—	—	—	.0002	.0033	.0222	.0845	.1943	.2056	.1142	.0259	.0023	.0003
	12	—	—	—	—	—	—	—	.0005	.0056	.0317	.1134	.2501	.2912	.2570	.1229	.0286	.0081
	13	—	—	—	—	—	—	—	.0001	.0009	.0073	.0407	.1539	.2539	.3559	.3593	.2153	.1229
	14	—	—	—	—	—	—	—	—	.0001	.0008	.0068	.0440	.1028	.2288	.4877	.7536	.8687
16	0	.8515	.7238	.4401	.1853	.0743	.0281	.0033	.0003	—	—	—	—	—	—	—	—	—
	1	.1376	.2363	.3706	.3294	.2097	.1126	.0228	.0030	.0002	—	—	—	—	—	—	—	—
	2	.0104	.0362	.1463	.2745	.2775	.2111	.0732	.0150	.0018	.0001	—	—	—	—	—	—	—
	3	.0005	.0034	.0359	.1423	.2285	.2463	.1465	.0468	.0085	.0008	—	—	—	—	—	—	—
	4	—	.0002	.0061	.0514	.1311	.2001	.2040	.1014	.0278	.0040	.0002	—	—	—	—	—	—
	5	—	—	.0008	.0137	.0555	.1201	.2099	.1623	.0667	.0142	.0013	—	—	—	—	—	—
	6	—	—	.0001	.0028	.0180	.0550	.1649	.1983	.1222	.0392	.0056	.0002	—	—	—	—	—
	7	—	—	—	.0004	.0045	.0197	.1010	.1889	.1746	.0840	.0185	.0012	.0001	—	—	—	—
	8	—	—	—	.0001	.0009	.0055	.0487	.1417	.1964	.1417	.0487	.0055	.0009	.0001	—	—	—
	9	—	—	—	—	.0001	.0012	.0185	.0840	.1746	.1889	.1010	.0197	.0045	.0004	—	—	—
	10	—	—	—	—	—	.0002	.0056	.0392	.1222	.1983	.1649	.0550	.0180	.0028	.0001	—	—
	11	—	—	—	—	—	—	.0013	.0142	.0667	.1623	.2099	.1201	.0555	.0137	.0008	—	—
	12	—	—	—	—	—	—	.0002	.0040	.0278	.1014	.2040	.2001	.1311	.0514	.0061	.0002	—
	13	—	—	—	—	—	—	—	.0008	.0085	.0468	.1465	.2463	.2285	.1423	.0359	.0034	.0005
	14	—	—	—	—	—	—	—	.0001	.0018	.0150	.0732	.2111	.2775	.2745	.1463	.0362	.0104
	15	—	—	—	—	—	—	—	—	.0002	.0030	.0228	.1126	.2097	.3294	.3706	.2363	.1376
	16	—	—	—	—	—	—	—	—	.0003	.0033	.0281	.0743	.1853	.4401	.7238	.8515

APPENDIX

POISSON PROBABILITIES

Example: $P(X = 3|\lambda = 2.3) = .2033$

This table shows $P(X = x)$.

	λ														
x	**0.1**	**0.2**	**0.3**	**0.4**	**0.5**	**0.6**	**0.7**	**0.8**	**0.9**	**1.0**	**1.1**	**1.2**	**1.3**	**1.4**	**1.5**
0	.9048	.8187	.7408	.6703	.6065	.5488	.4966	.4493	.4066	.3679	.3329	.3012	.2725	.2466	.2231
1	.0905	.1637	.2222	.2681	.3033	.3293	.3476	.3595	.3659	.3679	.3662	.3614	.3543	.3452	.3347
2	.0045	.0164	.0333	.0536	.0758	.0988	.1217	.1438	.1647	.1839	.2014	.2169	.2303	.2417	.2510
3	.0002	.0011	.0033	.0072	.0126	.0198	.0284	.0383	.0494	.0613	.0738	.0867	.0998	.1128	.1255
4	—	.0001	.0003	.0007	.0016	.0030	.0050	.0077	.0111	.0153	.0203	.0260	.0324	.0395	.0471
5	—	—	—	.0001	.0002	.0004	.0007	.0012	.0020	.0031	.0045	.0062	.0084	.0111	.0141
6	—	—	—	—	—	—	.0001	.0002	.0003	.0005	.0008	.0012	.0018	.0026	.0035
7	—	—	—	—	—	—	—	—	—	.0001	.0001	.0002	.0003	.0005	.0008
8	—	—	—	—	—	—	—	—	—	—	—	—	.0001	.0001	.0001

	λ														
x	**1.6**	**1.7**	**1.8**	**1.9**	**2.0**	**2.1**	**2.2**	**2.3**	**2.4**	**2.5**	**2.6**	**2.7**	**2.8**	**2.9**	**3.0**
0	.2019	.1827	.1653	.1496	.1353	.1225	.1108	.1003	.0907	.0821	.0743	.0672	.0608	.0550	.0498
1	.3230	.3106	.2975	.2842	.2707	.2572	.2438	.2306	.2177	.2052	.1931	.1815	.1703	.1596	.1494
2	.2584	.2640	.2678	.2700	.2707	.2700	.2681	.2652	.2613	.2565	.2510	.2450	.2384	.2314	.2240
3	.1378	.1496	.1607	.1710	.1804	.1890	.1966	.2033	.2090	.2138	.2176	.2205	.2225	.2237	.2240
4	.0551	.0636	.0723	.0812	.0902	.0992	.1082	.1169	.1254	.1336	.1414	.1488	.1557	.1622	.1680
5	.0176	.0216	.0260	.0309	.0361	.0417	.0476	.0538	.0602	.0668	.0735	.0804	.0872	.0940	.1008
6	.0047	.0061	.0078	.0098	.0120	.0146	.0174	.0206	.0241	.0278	.0319	.0362	.0407	.0455	.0504
7	.0011	.0015	.0020	.0027	.0034	.0044	.0055	.0068	.0083	.0099	.0118	.0139	.0163	.0188	.0216
8	.0002	.0003	.0005	.0006	.0009	.0011	.0015	.0019	.0025	.0031	.0038	.0047	.0057	.0068	.0081
9	—	.0001	.0001	.0001	.0002	.0003	.0004	.0005	.0007	.0009	.0011	.0014	.0018	.0022	.0027
10	—	—	—	—	—	.0001	.0001	.0001	.0002	.0002	.0003	.0004	.0005	.0006	.0008
11	—	—	—	—	—	—	—	—	—	—	—	.0001	.0001	.0001	.0002	.0002
12	—	—	—	—	—	—	—	—	—	—	—	—	—	—	.0001

	λ														
x	**3.1**	**3.2**	**3.3**	**3.4**	**3.5**	**3.6**	**3.7**	**3.8**	**3.9**	**4.0**	**4.1**	**4.2**	**4.3**	**4.4**	**4.5**
0	.0450	.0408	.0369	.0334	.0302	.0273	.0247	.0224	.0202	.0183	.0166	.0150	.0136	.0123	.0111
1	.1397	.1304	.1217	.1135	.1057	.0984	.0915	.0850	.0789	.0733	.0679	.0630	.0583	.0540	.0500
2	.2165	.2087	.2008	.1929	.1850	.1771	.1692	.1615	.1539	.1465	.1393	.1323	.1254	.1188	.1125
3	.2237	.2226	.2209	.2186	.2158	.2125	.2087	.2046	.2001	.1954	.1904	.1852	.1798	.1743	.1687
4	.1733	.1781	.1823	.1858	.1888	.1912	.1931	.1944	.1951	.1954	.1951	.1944	.1933	.1917	.1898
5	.1075	.1140	.1203	.1264	.1322	.1377	.1429	.1477	.1522	.1563	.1600	.1633	.1662	.1687	.1708
6	.0555	.0608	.0662	.0716	.0771	.0826	.0881	.0936	.0989	.1042	.1093	.1143	.1191	.1237	.1281
7	.0246	.0278	.0312	.0348	.0385	.0425	.0466	.0508	.0551	.0595	.0640	.0686	.0732	.0778	.0824
8	.0095	.0111	.0129	.0148	.0169	.0191	.0215	.0241	.0269	.0298	.0328	.0360	.0393	.0428	.0463
9	.0033	.0040	.0047	.0056	.0066	.0076	.0089	.0102	.0116	.0132	.0150	.0168	.0188	.0209	.0232
10	.0010	.0013	.0016	.0019	.0023	.0028	.0033	.0039	.0045	.0053	.0061	.0071	.0081	.0092	.0104
11	.0003	.0004	.0005	.0006	.0007	.0009	.0011	.0013	.0016	.0019	.0023	.0027	.0032	.0037	.0043
12	.0001	.0001	.0001	.0002	.0002	.0003	.0003	.0004	.0005	.0006	.0008	.0009	.0011	.0013	.0016
13	—	—	—	—	.0001	.0001	.0001	.0001	.0002	.0002	.0002	.0003	.0004	.0005	.0006
14	—	—	—	—	—	—	—	—	—	.0001	.0001	.0001	.0001	.0001	.0002
15	—	—	—	—	—	—	—	—	—	—	—	—	—	—	.0001

λ

x	4.6	4.7	4.8	4.9	5.0	5.1	5.2	5.3	5.4	5.5	5.6	5.7	5.8	5.9	6.0
0	.0101	.0091	.0082	.0074	.0067	.0061	.0055	.0050	.0045	.0041	.0037	.0033	.0030	.0027	.0025
1	.0462	.0427	.0395	.0365	.0337	.0311	.0287	.0265	.0244	.0225	.0207	.0191	.0176	.0162	.0149
2	.1063	.1005	.0948	.0894	.0842	.0793	.0746	.0701	.0659	.0618	.0580	.0544	.0509	.0477	.0446
3	.1631	.1574	.1517	.1460	.1404	.1348	.1293	.1239	.1185	.1133	.1082	.1033	.0985	.0938	.0892
4	.1875	.1849	.1820	.1789	.1755	.1719	.1681	.1641	.1600	.1558	.1515	.1472	.1428	.1383	.1339
5	.1725	.1738	.1747	.1753	.1755	.1753	.1748	.1740	.1728	.1714	.1697	.1678	.1656	.1632	.1606
6	.1323	.1362	.1398	.1432	.1462	.1490	.1515	.1537	.1555	.1571	.1584	.1594	.1601	.1605	.1606
7	.0869	.0914	.0959	.1002	.1044	.1086	.1125	.1163	.1200	.1234	.1267	.1298	.1326	.1353	.1377
8	.0500	.0537	.0575	.0614	.0653	.0692	.0731	.0771	.0810	.0849	.0887	.0925	.0962	.0998	.1033
9	.0255	.0281	.0307	.0334	.0363	.0392	.0423	.0454	.0486	.0519	.0552	.0586	.0620	.0654	.0688
10	.0118	.0132	.0147	.0164	.0181	.0200	.0220	.0241	.0262	.0285	.0309	.0334	.0359	.0386	.0413
11	.0049	.0056	.0064	.0073	.0082	.0093	.0104	.0116	.0129	.0143	.0157	.0173	.0190	.0207	.0225
12	.0019	.0022	.0026	.0030	.0034	.0039	.0045	.0051	.0058	.0065	.0073	.0082	.0092	.0102	.0113
13	.0007	.0008	.0009	.0011	.0013	.0015	.0018	.0021	.0024	.0028	.0032	.0036	.0041	.0046	.0052
14	.0002	.0003	.0003	.0004	.0005	.0006	.0007	.0008	.0009	.0011	.0013	.0015	.0017	.0019	.0022
15	.0001	.0001	.0001	.0001	.0002	.0002	.0002	.0002	.0003	.0003	.0004	.0005	.0006	.0007	.0008	.0009
16	—	—	—	—	—	.0001	.0001	.0001	.0001	.0001	.0002	.0002	.0002	.0003	.0003
17	—	—	—	—	—						.0001	.0001	.0001	.0001	.0001

λ

x	6.1	6.2	6.3	6.4	6.5	6.6	6.7	6.8	6.9	7.0	7.1	7.2	7.3	7.4	7.5
0	.0022	.0020	.0018	.0017	.0015	.0014	.0012	.0011	.0010	.0009	.0008	.0007	.0007	.0006	.0006
1	.0137	.0126	.0116	.0106	.0098	.0090	.0082	.0076	.0070	.0064	.0059	.0054	.0049	.0045	.0041
2	.0417	.0390	.0364	.0340	.0318	.0296	.0276	.0258	.0240	.0223	.0208	.0194	.0180	.0167	.0156
3	.0848	.0806	.0765	.0726	.0688	.0652	.0617	.0584	.0552	.0521	.0492	.0464	.0438	.0413	.0389
4	.1294	.1249	.1205	.1162	.1118	.1076	.1034	.0992	.0952	.0912	.0874	.0836	.0799	.0764	.0729
5	.1579	.1549	.1519	.1487	.1454	.1420	.1385	.1349	.1314	.1277	.1241	.1204	.1167	.1130	.1094
6	.1605	.1601	.1595	.1586	.1575	.1562	.1546	.1529	.1511	.1490	.1468	.1445	.1420	.1394	.1367
7	.1399	.1418	.1435	.1450	.1462	.1472	.1480	.1486	.1489	.1490	.1489	.1486	.1481	.1474	.1465
8	.1066	.1099	.1130	.1160	.1188	.1215	.1240	.1263	.1284	.1304	.1321	.1337	.1351	.1363	.1373
9	.0723	.0757	.0791	.0825	.0858	.0891	.0923	.0954	.0985	.1014	.1042	.1070	.1096	.1121	.1144
10	.0441	.0469	.0498	.0528	.0558	.0588	.0618	.0649	.0679	.0710	.0740	.0770	.0800	.0829	.0858
11	.0244	.0265	.0285	.0307	.0330	.0353	.0377	.0401	.0426	.0452	.0478	.0504	.0531	.0558	.0585
12	.0124	.0137	.0150	.0164	.0179	.0194	.0210	.0227	.0245	.0263	.0283	.0303	.0323	.0344	.0366
13	.0058	.0065	.0073	.0081	.0089	.0099	.0108	.0119	.0130	.0142	.0154	.0168	.0181	.0196	.0211
14	.0025	.0029	.0033	.0037	.0041	.0046	.0052	.0058	.0064	.0071	.0078	.0086	.0095	.0104	.0113
15	.0010	.0012	.0014	.0016	.0018	.0020	.0023	.0026	.0029	.0033	.0037	.0041	.0046	.0051	.0057
16	.0004	.0005	.0005	.0006	.0007	.0008	.0010	.0011	.0013	.0014	.0016	.0019	.0021	.0024	.0026
17	.0001	.0002	.0002	.0002	.0003	.0003	.0004	.0004	.0005	.0006	.0007	.0008	.0009	.0010	.0012
18	—	.0001	.0001	.0001	.0001	.0001	.0001	.0002	.0002	.0002	.0003	.0003	.0004	.0004	.0005
19	—	—	—	—	—	—	.0001	.0001	.0001	.0001	.0001	.0001	.0001	.0002	.0002
20	—	—	—	—	—	—	—	—	—	—	—	—	.0001	.0001	.0001

(continued)

									λ						
x	8.0	8.5	9.0	9.5	10.0	11.0	12.0	13.0	14.0	15.0	16.0	17.0	18.0	19.0	20.0
0	.0003	.0002	.0001	.0001	—	—	—	—	—	—	—	—	—	—	—
1	.0027	.0017	.0011	.0007	.0005	.0002	.0001	—	—	—	—	—	—	—	—
2	.0107	.0074	.0050	.0034	.0023	.0010	.0004	.0002	.0001	—	—	—	—	—	—
3	.0286	.0208	.0150	.0107	.0076	.0037	.0018	.0008	.0004	.0002	.0001	—	—	—	—
4	.0573	.0443	.0337	.0254	.0189	.0102	.0053	.0027	.0013	.0006	.0003	.0001	.0001	—	—
5	.0916	.0752	.0607	.0483	.0378	.0224	.0127	.0070	.0037	.0019	.0010	.0005	.0002	.0001	.0001
6	.1221	.1066	.0911	.0764	.0631	.0411	.0255	.0152	.0087	.0048	.0026	.0014	.0007	.0004	.0002
7	.1396	.1294	.1171	.1037	.0901	.0646	.0437	.0281	.0174	.0104	.0060	.0034	.0019	.0010	.0005
8	.1396	.1375	.1318	.1232	.1126	.0888	.0655	.0457	.0304	.0194	.0120	.0072	.0042	.0024	.0013
9	.1241	.1299	.1318	.1300	.1251	.1085	.0874	.0661	.0473	.0324	.0213	.0135	.0083	.0050	.0029
10	.0993	.1104	.1186	.1235	.1251	.1194	.1048	.0859	.0663	.0486	.0341	.0230	.0150	.0095	.0058
11	.0722	.0853	.0970	.1067	.1137	.1194	.1144	.1015	.0844	.0663	.0496	.0355	.0245	.0164	.0106
12	.0481	.0604	.0728	.0844	.0948	.1094	.1144	.1099	.0984	.0829	.0661	.0504	.0368	.0259	.0176
13	.0296	.0395	.0504	.0617	.0729	.0926	.1056	.1099	.1060	.0956	.0814	.0658	.0509	.0378	.0271
14	.0169	.0240	.0324	.0419	.0521	.0728	.0905	.1021	.1060	.1024	.0930	.0800	.0655	.0514	.0387
15	.0090	.0136	.0194	.0265	.0347	.0534	.0724	.0885	.0989	.1024	.0992	.0906	.0786	.0650	.0516
16	.0045	.0072	.0109	.0157	.0217	.0367	.0543	.0719	.0866	.0960	.0992	.0963	.0884	.0772	.0646
17	.0021	.0036	.0058	.0088	.0128	.0237	.0383	.0550	.0713	.0847	.0934	.0963	.0936	.0863	.0760
18	.0009	.0017	.0029	.0046	.0071	.0145	.0255	.0397	.0554	.0706	.0830	.0909	.0936	.0911	.0844
19	.0004	.0008	.0014	.0023	.0037	.0084	.0161	.0272	.0409	.0557	.0699	.0814	.0887	.0911	.0888
20	.0002	.0003	.0006	.0011	.0019	.0046	.0097	.0177	.0286	.0418	.0559	.0692	.0798	.0866	.0888
21	.0001	.0001	.0003	.0005	.0009	.0024	.0055	.0109	.0191	.0299	.0426	.0560	.0684	.0783	.0846
22	—	.0001	.0001	.0002	.0004	.0012	.0030	.0065	.0121	.0204	.0310	.0433	.0560	.0676	.0769
23	—	—	—	.0001	.0002	.0006	.0016	.0037	.0074	.0133	.0216	.0320	.0438	.0559	.0669
24	—	—	—	—	.0001	.0003	.0008	.0020	.0043	.0083	.0144	.0226	.0328	.0442	.0557
25	—	—	—	—	—	.0001	.0004	.0010	.0024	.0050	.0092	.0154	.0237	.0336	.0446
26	—	—	—	—	—	—	.0002	.0005	.0013	.0029	.0057	.0101	.0164	.0246	.0343
27	—	—	—	—	—	—	.0001	.0002	.0007	.0016	.0034	.0063	.0109	.0173	.0254
28	—	—	—	—	—	—	—	.0001	.0003	.0009	.0019	.0038	.0070	.0117	.0181
29	—	—	—	—	—	—	—	.0001	.0002	.0004	.0011	.0023	.0044	.0077	.0125
30	—	—	—	—	—	—	—	—	.0001	.0002	.0006	.0013	.0026	.0049	.0083
31	—	—	—	—	—	—	—	—	—	.0001	.0003	.0007	.0015	.0030	.0054
32	—	—	—	—	—	—	—	—	—	.0001	.0001	.0004	.0009	.0018	.0034
33	—	—	—	—	—	—	—	—	—	—	.0001	.0002	.0005	.0010	.0020
34	—	—	—	—	—	—	—	—	—	—	—	.0001	.0002	.0006	.0012
35	—	—	—	—	—	—	—	—	—	—	—	—	.0001	.0003	.0007
36	—	—	—	—	—	—	—	—	—	—	—	—	.0001	.0002	.0004
37	—	—	—	—	—	—	—	—	—	—	—	—	—	.0001	.0002
38	—	—	—	—	—	—	—	—	—	—	—	—	—	—	.0001
39	—	—	—	—	—	—	—	—	—	—	—	—	—	—	.0001

APPENDIX

C-1

STANDARD NORMAL AREAS

Example: $P(0 < z < 1.96) = .4750$

This table shows the normal area between 0 and z.

z	.00	.01	.02	.03	.04	.05	.06	.07	.08	.09
0.0	.0000	.0040	.0080	.0120	.0160	.0199	.0239	.0279	.0319	.0359
0.1	.0398	.0438	.0478	.0517	.0557	.0596	.0636	.0675	.0714	.0753
0.2	.0793	.0832	.0871	.0910	.0948	.0987	.1026	.1064	.1103	.1141
0.3	.1179	.1217	.1255	.1293	.1331	.1368	.1406	.1443	.1480	.1517
0.4	.1554	.1591	.1628	.1664	.1700	.1736	.1772	.1808	.1844	.1879
0.5	.1915	.1950	.1985	.2019	.2054	.2088	.2123	.2157	.2190	.2224
0.6	.2257	.2291	.2324	.2357	.2389	.2422	.2454	.2486	.2517	.2549
0.7	.2580	.2611	.2642	.2673	.2704	.2734	.2764	.2794	.2823	.2852
0.8	.2881	.2910	.2939	.2967	.2995	.3023	.3051	.3078	.3106	.3133
0.9	.3159	.3186	.3212	.3238	.3264	.3289	.3315	.3340	.3365	.3389
1.0	.3413	.3438	.3461	.3485	.3508	.3531	.3554	.3577	.3599	.3621
1.1	.3643	.3665	.3686	.3708	.3729	.3749	.3770	.3790	.3810	.3830
1.2	.3849	.3869	.3888	.3907	.3925	.3944	.3962	.3980	.3997	.4015
1.3	.4032	.4049	.4066	.4082	.4099	.4115	.4131	.4147	.4162	.4177
1.4	.4192	.4207	.4222	.4236	.4251	.4265	.4279	.4292	.4306	.4319
1.5	.4332	.4345	.4357	.4370	.4382	.4394	.4406	.4418	.4429	.4441
1.6	.4452	.4463	.4474	.4484	.4495	.4505	.4515	.4525	.4535	.4545
1.7	.4554	.4564	.4573	.4582	.4591	.4599	.4608	.4616	.4625	.4633
1.8	.4641	.4649	.4656	.4664	.4671	.4678	.4686	.4693	.4699	.4706
1.9	.4713	.4719	.4726	.4732	.4738	.4744	.4750	.4756	.4761	.4767
2.0	.4772	.4778	.4783	.4788	.4793	.4798	.4803	.4808	.4812	.4817
2.1	.4821	.4826	.4830	.4834	.4838	.4842	.4846	.4850	.4854	.4857
2.2	.4861	.4864	.4868	.4871	.4875	.4878	.4881	.4884	.4887	.4890
2.3	.4893	.4896	.4898	.4901	.4904	.4906	.4909	.4911	.4913	.4916
2.4	.4918	.4920	.4922	.4925	.4927	.4929	.4931	.4932	.4934	.4936
2.5	.4938	.4940	.4941	.4943	.4945	.4946	.4948	.4949	.4951	.4952
2.6	.4953	.4955	.4956	.4957	.4959	.4960	.4961	.4962	.4963	.4964
2.7	.4965	.4966	.4967	.4968	.4969	.4970	.4971	.4972	.4973	.4974
2.8	.4974	.4975	.4976	.4977	.4977	.4978	.4979	.4979	.4980	.4981
2.9	.4981	.4982	.4982	.4983	.4984	.4984	.4985	.4985	.4986	.4986
3.0	.49865	.49869	.49874	.49878	.49882	.49886	.49889	.49893	.49896	.49900
3.1	.49903	.49906	.49910	.49913	.49916	.49918	.49921	.49924	.49926	.49929
3.2	.49931	.49934	.49936	.49938	.49940	.49942	.49944	.49946	.49948	.49950
3.3	.49952	.49953	.49955	.49957	.49958	.49960	.49961	.49962	.49964	.49965
3.4	.49966	.49968	.49969	.49970	.49971	.49972	.49973	.49974	.49975	.49976
3.5	.49977	.49978	.49978	.49979	.49980	.49981	.49981	.49982	.49983	.49983
3.6	.49984	.49985	.49985	.49986	.49986	.49987	.49987	.49988	.49988	.49989
3.7	.49989	.49990	.49990	.49990	.49991	.49991	.49992	.49992	.49992	.49992

APPENDIX

CUMULATIVE STANDARD NORMAL DISTRIBUTION

Example: $P(z \leq -1.96) = .0250$

This table shows the normal area less than z.

z	.00	.01	.02	.03	.04	.05	.06	.07	.08	.09
−3.7	.00011	.00010	.00010	.00010	.00009	.00009	.00008	.00008	.00008	.00008
−3.6	.00016	.00015	.00015	.00014	.00014	.00013	.00013	.00012	.00012	.00011
−3.5	.00023	.00022	.00022	.00021	.00020	.00019	.00019	.00018	.00017	.00017
−3.4	.00034	.00032	.00031	.00030	.00029	.00028	.00027	.00026	.00025	.00024
−3.3	.00048	.00047	.00045	.00043	.00042	.00040	.00039	.00038	.00036	.00035
−3.2	.00069	.00066	.00064	.00062	.00060	.00058	.00056	.00054	.00052	.00050
−3.1	.00097	.00094	.00090	.00087	.00084	.00082	.00079	.00076	.00074	.00071
−3.0	.00135	.00131	.00126	.00122	.00118	.00114	.00111	.00107	.00104	.00100
−2.9	.0019	.0018	.0018	.0017	.0016	.0016	.0015	.0015	.0014	.0014
−2.8	.0026	.0025	.0024	.0023	.0023	.0022	.0021	.0021	.0020	.0019
−2.7	.0035	.0034	.0033	.0032	.0031	.0030	.0029	.0028	.0027	.0026
−2.6	.0047	.0045	.0044	.0043	.0041	.0040	.0039	.0038	.0037	.0036
−2.5	.0062	.0060	.0059	.0057	.0055	.0054	.0052	.0051	.0049	.0048
−2.4	.0082	.0080	.0078	.0075	.0073	.0071	.0069	.0068	.0066	.0064
−2.3	.0107	.0104	.0102	.0099	.0096	.0094	.0091	.0089	.0087	.0084
−2.2	.0139	.0136	.0132	.0129	.0125	.0122	.0119	.0116	.0113	.0110
−2.1	.0179	.0174	.0170	.0166	.0162	.0158	.0154	.0150	.0146	.0143
−2.0	.0228	.0222	.0217	.0212	.0207	.0202	.0197	.0192	.0188	.0183
−1.9	.0287	.0281	.0274	.0268	.0262	.0256	.0250	.0244	.0239	.0233
−1.8	.0359	.0351	.0344	.0336	.0329	.0322	.0314	.0307	.0301	.0294
−1.7	.0446	.0436	.0427	.0418	.0409	.0401	.0392	.0384	.0375	.0367
−1.6	.0548	.0537	.0526	.0516	.0505	.0495	.0485	.0475	.0465	.0455
−1.5	.0668	.0655	.0643	.0630	.0618	.0606	.0594	.0582	.0571	.0559
−1.4	.0808	.0793	.0778	.0764	.0749	.0735	.0721	.0708	.0694	.0681
−1.3	.0968	.0951	.0934	.0918	.0901	.0885	.0869	.0853	.0838	.0823
−1.2	.1151	.1131	.1112	.1093	.1075	.1056	.1038	.1020	.1003	.0985
−1.1	.1357	.1335	.1314	.1292	.1271	.1251	.1230	.1210	.1190	.1170
−1.0	.1587	.1562	.1539	.1515	.1492	.1469	.1446	.1423	.1401	.1379
−0.9	.1841	.1814	.1788	.1762	.1736	.1711	.1685	.1660	.1635	.1611
−0.8	.2119	.2090	.2061	.2033	.2005	.1977	.1949	.1922	.1894	.1867
−0.7	.2420	.2389	.2358	.2327	.2296	.2266	.2236	.2206	.2177	.2148
−0.6	.2743	.2709	.2676	.2643	.2611	.2578	.2546	.2514	.2483	.2451
−0.5	.3085	.3050	.3015	.2981	.2946	.2912	.2877	.2843	.2810	.2776
−0.4	.3446	.3409	.3372	.3336	.3300	.3264	.3228	.3192	.3156	.3121
−0.3	.3821	.3783	.3745	.3707	.3669	.3632	.3594	.3557	.3520	.3483
−0.2	.4207	.4168	.4129	.4090	.4052	.4013	.3974	.3936	.3897	.3859
−0.1	.4602	.4562	.4522	.4483	.4443	.4404	.4364	.4325	.4286	.4247
−0.0	.5000	.4960	.4920	.4880	.4841	.4801	.4761	.4721	.4681	.4641

This table shows the normal area less than z.

z	.00	.01	.02	.03	.04	.05	.06	.07	.08	.09
0.0	.5000	.5040	.5080	.5120	.5160	.5199	.5239	.5279	.5319	.5359
0.1	.5398	.5438	.5478	.5517	.5557	.5596	.5636	.5675	.5714	.5753
0.2	.5793	.5832	.5871	.5910	.5948	.5987	.6026	.6064	.6103	.6141
0.3	.6179	.6217	.6255	.6293	.6331	.6368	.6406	.6443	.6480	.6517
0.4	.6554	.6591	.6628	.6664	.6700	.6736	.6772	.6808	.6844	.6879
0.5	.6915	.6950	.6985	.7019	.7054	.7088	.7123	.7157	.7190	.7224
0.6	.7257	.7291	.7324	.7357	.7389	.7422	.7454	.7486	.7517	.7549
0.7	.7580	.7611	.7642	.7673	.7704	.7734	.7764	.7794	.7823	.7852
0.8	.7881	.7910	.7939	.7967	.7995	.8023	.8051	.8078	.8106	.8133
0.9	.8159	.8186	.8212	.8238	.8264	.8289	.8315	.8340	.8365	.8389
1.0	.8413	.8438	.8461	.8485	.8508	.8531	.8554	.8577	.8599	.8621
1.1	.8643	.8665	.8686	.8708	.8729	.8749	.8770	.8790	.8810	.8830
1.2	.8849	.8869	.8888	.8907	.8925	.8944	.8962	.8980	.8997	.9015
1.3	.9032	.9049	.9066	.9082	.9099	.9115	.9131	.9147	.9162	.9177
1.4	.9192	.9207	.9222	.9236	.9251	.9265	.9279	.9292	.9306	.9319
1.5	.9332	.9345	.9357	.9370	.9382	.9394	.9406	.9418	.9429	.9441
1.6	.9452	.9463	.9474	.9484	.9495	.9505	.9515	.9525	.9535	.9545
1.7	.9554	.9564	.9573	.9582	.9591	.9599	.9608	.9616	.9625	.9633
1.8	.9641	.9649	.9656	.9664	.9671	.9678	.9686	.9693	.9699	.9706
1.9	.9713	.9719	.9726	.9732	.9738	.9744	.9750	.9756	.9761	.9767
2.0	.9772	.9778	.9783	.9788	.9793	.9798	.9803	.9808	.9812	.9817
2.1	.9821	.9826	.9830	.9834	.9838	.9842	.9846	.9850	.9854	.9857
2.2	.9861	.9864	.9868	.9871	.9875	.9878	.9881	.9884	.9887	.9890
2.3	.9893	.9896	.9898	.9901	.9904	.9906	.9909	.9911	.9913	.9916
2.4	.9918	.9920	.9922	.9925	.9927	.9929	.9931	.9932	.9934	.9936
2.5	.9938	.9940	.9941	.9943	.9945	.9946	.9948	.9949	.9951	.9952
2.6	.9953	.9955	.9956	.9957	.9959	.9960	.9961	.9962	.9963	.9964
2.7	.9965	.9966	.9967	.9968	.9969	.9970	.9971	.9972	.9973	.9974
2.8	.9974	.9975	.9976	.9977	.9977	.9978	.9979	.9979	.9980	.9981
2.9	.9981	.9982	.9982	.9983	.9984	.9984	.9985	.9985	.9986	.9986
3.0	.99865	.99869	.99874	.99878	.99882	.99886	.99889	.99893	.99896	.99900
3.1	.99903	.99906	.99910	.99913	.99916	.99918	.99921	.99924	.99926	.99929
3.2	.99931	.99934	.99936	.99938	.99940	.99942	.99944	.99946	.99948	.99950
3.3	.99952	.99953	.99955	.99957	.99958	.99960	.99961	.99962	.99964	.99965
3.4	.99966	.99968	.99969	.99970	.99971	.99972	.99973	.99974	.99975	.99976
3.5	.99977	.99978	.99978	.99979	.99980	.99981	.99981	.99982	.99983	.99983
3.6	.99984	.99985	.99985	.99986	.99986	.99987	.99987	.99988	.99988	.99989
3.7	.99989	.99990	.99990	.99990	.99991	.99991	.99992	.99992	.99992	.99992

APPENDIX

STUDENT'S *t* CRITICAL VALUES

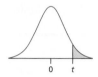

This table shows the *t*-value that defines the area for the stated degrees of freedom (*d.f.*).

	Confidence Level						Confidence Level				
	.80	.90	.95	.98	.99		.80	.90	.95	.98	.99
	Significance Level for Two-Tailed Test						Significance Level for Two-Tailed Test				
	.20	.10	.05	.02	.01		.20	.10	.05	.02	.01
	Significance Level for One-Tailed Test						Significance Level for One-Tailed Test				
d.f.	.10	.05	.025	.01	.005	d.f.	.10	.05	.025	.01	.005
1	3.078	6.314	12.706	31.821	63.657	36	1.306	1.688	2.028	2.434	2.719
2	1.886	2.920	4.303	6.965	9.925	37	1.305	1.687	2.026	2.431	2.715
3	1.638	2.353	3.182	4.541	5.841	38	1.304	1.686	2.024	2.429	2.712
4	1.533	2.132	2.776	3.747	4.604	39	1.304	1.685	2.023	2.426	2.708
5	1.476	2.015	2.571	3.365	4.032	40	1.303	1.684	2.021	2.423	2.704
6	1.440	1.943	2.447	3.143	3.707	41	1.303	1.683	2.020	2.421	2.701
7	1.415	1.895	2.365	2.998	3.499	42	1.302	1.682	2.018	2.418	2.698
8	1.397	1.860	2.306	2.896	3.355	43	1.302	1.681	2.017	2.416	2.695
9	1.383	1.833	2.262	2.821	3.250	44	1.301	1.680	2.015	2.414	2.692
10	1.372	1.812	2.228	2.764	3.169	45	1.301	1.679	2.014	2.412	2.690
11	1.363	1.796	2.201	2.718	3.106	46	1.300	1.679	2.013	2.410	2.687
12	1.356	1.782	2.179	2.681	3.055	47	1.300	1.678	2.012	2.408	2.685
13	1.350	1.771	2.160	2.650	3.012	48	1.299	1.677	2.011	2.407	2.682
14	1.345	1.761	2.145	2.624	2.977	49	1.299	1.677	2.010	2.405	2.680
15	1.341	1.753	2.131	2.602	2.947	50	1.299	1.676	2.009	2.403	2.678
16	1.337	1.746	2.120	2.583	2.921	55	1.297	1.673	2.004	2.396	2.668
17	1.333	1.740	2.110	2.567	2.898	60	1.296	1.671	2.000	2.390	2.660
18	1.330	1.734	2.101	2.552	2.878	65	1.295	1.669	1.997	2.385	2.654
19	1.328	1.729	2.093	2.539	2.861	70	1.294	1.667	1.994	2.381	2.648
20	1.325	1.725	2.086	2.528	2.845	75	1.293	1.665	1.992	2.377	2.643
21	1.323	1.721	2.080	2.518	2.831	80	1.292	1.664	1.990	2.374	2.639
22	1.321	1.717	2.074	2.508	2.819	85	1.292	1.663	1.988	2.371	2.635
23	1.319	1.714	2.069	2.500	2.807	90	1.291	1.662	1.987	2.368	2.632
24	1.318	1.711	2.064	2.492	2.797	95	1.291	1.661	1.985	2.366	2.629
25	1.316	1.708	2.060	2.485	2.787	100	1.290	1.660	1.984	2.364	2.626
26	1.315	1.706	2.056	2.479	2.779	110	1.289	1.659	1.982	2.361	2.621
27	1.314	1.703	2.052	2.473	2.771	120	1.289	1.658	1.980	2.358	2.617
28	1.313	1.701	2.048	2.467	2.763	130	1.288	1.657	1.978	2.355	2.614
29	1.311	1.699	2.045	2.462	2.756	140	1.288	1.656	1.977	2.353	2.611
30	1.310	1.697	2.042	2.457	2.750	150	1.287	1.655	1.976	2.351	2.609
31	1.309	1.696	2.040	2.453	2.744	∞	1.282	1.645	1.960	2.326	2.576
32	1.309	1.694	2.037	2.449	2.738						
33	1.308	1.692	2.035	2.445	2.733						
34	1.307	1.691	2.032	2.441	2.728						
35	1.306	1.690	2.030	2.438	2.724						

Note: As *n* increases, critical values of Student's *t* approach the *z*-values in the last line of this table. A common rule of thumb is to use *z* when *n* > 30, but that is *not* conservative.

APPENDIX

CHI-SQUARE CRITICAL VALUES

This table shows the critical value of chi-square for each desired right-tail area and degrees of freedom (*d.f.*)

Example for *d.f.* = 4

.05

0   9.488

d.f.	.995	.990	.975	.95	.90	.10	.05	.025	.01	.005
1	0.000	0.000	0.001	0.004	0.016	2.706	3.841	5.024	6.635	7.879
2	0.010	0.020	0.051	0.103	0.211	4.605	5.991	7.378	9.210	10.60
3	0.072	0.115	0.216	0.352	0.584	6.251	7.815	9.348	11.34	12.84
4	0.207	0.297	0.484	0.711	1.064	7.779	9.488	11.14	13.28	14.86
5	0.412	0.554	0.831	1.145	1.610	9.236	11.07	12.83	15.09	16.75
6	0.676	0.872	1.237	1.635	2.204	10.64	12.59	14.45	16.81	18.55
7	0.989	1.239	1.690	2.167	2.833	12.02	14.07	16.01	18.48	20.28
8	1.344	1.646	2.180	2.733	3.490	13.36	15.51	17.53	20.09	21.95
9	1.735	2.088	2.700	3.325	4.168	14.68	16.92	19.02	21.67	23.59
10	2.156	2.558	3.247	3.940	4.865	15.99	18.31	20.48	23.21	25.19
11	2.603	3.053	3.816	4.575	5.578	17.28	19.68	21.92	24.72	26.76
12	3.074	3.571	4.404	5.226	6.304	18.55	21.03	23.34	26.22	28.30
13	3.565	4.107	5.009	5.892	7.042	19.81	22.36	24.74	27.69	29.82
14	4.075	4.660	5.629	6.571	7.790	21.06	23.68	26.12	29.14	31.32
15	4.601	5.229	6.262	7.261	8.547	22.31	25.00	27.49	30.58	32.80
16	5.142	5.812	6.908	7.962	9.312	23.54	26.30	28.85	32.00	34.27
17	5.697	6.408	7.564	8.672	10.09	24.77	27.59	30.19	33.41	35.72
18	6.265	7.015	8.231	9.390	10.86	25.99	28.87	31.53	34.81	37.16
19	6.844	7.633	8.907	10.12	11.65	27.20	30.14	32.85	36.19	38.58
20	7.434	8.260	9.591	10.85	12.44	28.41	31.41	34.17	37.57	40.00
21	8.034	8.897	10.28	11.59	13.24	29.62	32.67	35.48	38.93	41.40
22	8.643	9.542	10.98	12.34	14.04	30.81	33.92	36.78	40.29	42.80
23	9.260	10.20	11.69	13.09	14.85	32.01	35.17	38.08	41.64	44.18
24	9.886	10.86	12.40	13.85	15.66	33.20	36.42	39.36	42.98	45.56
25	10.52	11.52	13.12	14.61	16.47	34.38	37.65	40.65	44.31	46.93
26	11.16	12.20	13.84	15.38	17.29	35.56	38.89	41.92	45.64	48.29
27	11.81	12.88	14.57	16.15	18.11	36.74	40.11	43.19	46.96	49.64
28	12.46	13.56	15.31	16.93	18.94	37.92	41.34	44.46	48.28	50.99
29	13.12	14.26	16.05	17.71	19.77	39.09	42.56	45.72	49.59	52.34
30	13.79	14.95	16.79	18.49	20.60	40.26	43.77	46.98	50.89	53.67
31	14.46	15.66	17.54	19.28	21.43	41.42	44.99	48.23	52.19	55.00
32	15.13	16.36	18.29	20.07	22.27	42.58	46.19	49.48	53.49	56.33
33	15.82	17.07	19.05	20.87	23.11	43.75	47.40	50.73	54.78	57.65
34	16.50	17.79	19.81	21.66	23.95	44.90	48.60	51.97	56.06	58.96
35	17.19	18.51	20.57	22.47	24.80	46.06	49.80	53.20	57.34	60.27
36	17.89	19.23	21.34	23.27	25.64	47.21	51.00	54.44	58.62	61.58
37	18.59	19.96	22.11	24.07	26.49	48.36	52.19	55.67	59.89	62.88
38	19.29	20.69	22.88	24.88	27.34	49.51	53.38	56.90	61.16	64.18
39	20.00	21.43	23.65	25.70	28.20	50.66	54.57	58.12	62.43	65.48
40	20.71	22.16	24.43	26.51	29.05	51.81	55.76	59.34	63.69	66.77
50	27.99	29.71	32.36	34.76	37.69	63.17	67.50	71.42	76.15	79.49
60	35.53	37.48	40.48	43.19	46.46	74.40	79.08	83.30	88.38	91.95
70	43.28	45.44	48.76	51.74	55.33	85.53	90.53	95.02	100.4	104.2
80	51.17	53.54	57.15	60.39	64.28	96.58	101.9	106.6	112.3	116.3
90	59.20	61.75	65.65	69.13	73.29	107.6	113.1	118.1	124.1	128.3
100	67.33	70.06	74.22	77.93	82.36	118.5	124.3	129.6	135.8	140.2

Area in Upper Tail

Note: For *d.f.* > 100, use the Excel function =CHISQ.INV.RT(α,degrees of freedom).

APPENDIX F

CRITICAL VALUES OF $F_{.10}$

This table shows the 10 percent right-tail critical values of F for the stated degrees of freedom (d.f.).

Denominator Degrees of Freedom (df_2)	Numerator Degrees of Freedom (df_1)										
	1	2	3	4	5	6	7	8	9	10	12
1	39.86	49.50	53.59	55.83	57.24	58.20	58.91	59.44	59.86	60.19	60.71
2	8.53	9.00	9.16	9.24	9.29	9.33	9.35	9.37	9.38	9.39	9.41
3	5.54	5.46	5.39	5.34	5.31	5.28	5.27	5.25	5.24	5.23	5.22
4	4.54	4.32	4.19	4.11	4.05	4.01	3.98	3.95	3.94	3.92	3.90
5	4.06	3.78	3.62	3.52	3.45	3.40	3.37	3.34	3.32	3.30	3.27
6	3.78	3.46	3.29	3.18	3.11	3.05	3.01	2.98	2.96	2.94	2.90
7	3.59	3.26	3.07	2.96	2.88	2.83	2.78	2.75	2.72	2.70	2.67
8	3.46	3.11	2.92	2.81	2.73	2.67	2.62	2.59	2.56	2.54	2.50
9	3.36	3.01	2.81	2.69	2.61	2.55	2.51	2.47	2.44	2.42	2.38
10	3.29	2.92	2.73	2.61	2.52	2.46	2.41	2.38	2.35	2.32	2.28
11	3.23	2.86	2.66	2.54	2.45	2.39	2.34	2.30	2.27	2.25	2.21
12	3.18	2.81	2.61	2.48	2.39	2.33	2.28	2.24	2.21	2.19	2.15
13	3.14	2.76	2.56	2.43	2.35	2.28	2.23	2.20	2.16	2.14	2.10
14	3.10	2.73	2.52	2.39	2.31	2.24	2.19	2.15	2.12	2.10	2.05
15	3.07	2.70	2.49	2.36	2.27	2.21	2.16	2.12	2.09	2.06	2.02
16	3.05	2.67	2.46	2.33	2.24	2.18	2.13	2.09	2.06	2.03	1.99
17	3.03	2.64	2.44	2.31	2.22	2.15	2.10	2.06	2.03	2.00	1.96
18	3.01	2.62	2.42	2.29	2.20	2.13	2.08	2.04	2.00	1.98	1.93
19	2.99	2.61	2.40	2.27	2.18	2.11	2.06	2.02	1.98	1.96	1.91
20	2.97	2.59	2.38	2.25	2.16	2.09	2.04	2.00	1.96	1.94	1.89
21	2.96	2.57	2.36	2.23	2.14	2.08	2.02	1.98	1.95	1.92	1.87
22	2.95	2.56	2.35	2.22	2.13	2.06	2.01	1.97	1.93	1.90	1.86
23	2.94	2.55	2.34	2.21	2.11	2.05	1.99	1.95	1.92	1.89	1.84
24	2.93	2.54	2.33	2.19	2.10	2.04	1.98	1.94	1.91	1.88	1.83
25	2.92	2.53	2.32	2.18	2.09	2.02	1.97	1.93	1.89	1.87	1.82
26	2.91	2.52	2.31	2.17	2.08	2.01	1.96	1.92	1.88	1.86	1.81
27	2.90	2.51	2.30	2.17	2.07	2.00	1.95	1.91	1.87	1.85	1.80
28	2.89	2.50	2.29	2.16	2.06	2.00	1.94	1.90	1.87	1.84	1.79
29	2.89	2.50	2.28	2.15	2.06	1.99	1.93	1.89	1.86	1.83	1.78
30	2.88	2.49	2.28	2.14	2.05	1.98	1.93	1.88	1.85	1.82	1.77
40	2.84	2.44	2.23	2.09	2.00	1.93	1.87	1.83	1.79	1.76	1.71
50	2.81	2.41	2.20	2.06	1.97	1.90	1.84	1.80	1.76	1.73	1.68
60	2.79	2.39	2.18	2.04	1.95	1.87	1.82	1.77	1.74	1.71	1.66
120	2.75	2.35	2.13	1.99	1.90	1.82	1.77	1.72	1.68	1.65	1.60
200	2.73	2.33	2.11	1.97	1.88	1.80	1.75	1.70	1.66	1.63	1.58
∞	2.71	2.30	2.08	1.94	1.85	1.77	1.72	1.67	1.63	1.60	1.55

Denominator Degrees of Freedom (df_2)	Numerator Degrees of Freedom (df_1)										
	15	20	25	30	35	40	50	60	120	200	∞
1	61.22	61.74	62.05	62.26	62.42	62.53	62.69	62.79	63.06	63.17	63.32
2	9.42	9.44	9.45	9.46	9.46	9.47	9.47	9.47	9.48	9.49	9.49
3	5.20	5.18	5.17	5.17	5.16	5.16	5.15	5.15	5.14	5.14	5.13
4	3.87	3.84	3.83	3.82	3.81	3.80	3.80	3.79	3.78	3.77	3.76
5	3.24	3.21	3.19	3.17	3.16	3.16	3.15	3.14	3.12	3.12	3.11
6	2.87	2.84	2.81	2.80	2.79	2.78	2.77	2.76	2.74	2.73	2.72
7	2.63	2.59	2.57	2.56	2.54	2.54	2.52	2.51	2.49	2.48	2.47
8	2.46	2.42	2.40	2.38	2.37	2.36	2.35	2.34	2.32	2.31	2.29
9	2.34	2.30	2.27	2.25	2.24	2.23	2.22	2.21	2.18	2.17	2.16
10	2.24	2.20	2.17	2.16	2.14	2.13	2.12	2.11	2.08	2.07	2.06
11	2.17	2.12	2.10	2.08	2.06	2.05	2.04	2.03	2.00	1.99	1.97
12	2.10	2.06	2.03	2.01	2.00	1.99	1.97	1.96	1.93	1.92	1.90
13	2.05	2.01	1.98	1.96	1.94	1.93	1.92	1.90	1.88	1.86	1.85
14	2.01	1.96	1.93	1.91	1.90	1.89	1.87	1.86	1.83	1.82	1.80
15	1.97	1.92	1.89	1.87	1.86	1.85	1.83	1.82	1.79	1.77	1.76
16	1.94	1.89	1.86	1.84	1.82	1.81	1.79	1.78	1.75	1.74	1.72
17	1.91	1.86	1.83	1.81	1.79	1.78	1.76	1.75	1.72	1.71	1.69
18	1.89	1.84	1.80	1.78	1.77	1.75	1.74	1.72	1.69	1.68	1.66
19	1.86	1.81	1.78	1.76	1.74	1.73	1.71	1.70	1.67	1.65	1.63
20	1.84	1.79	1.76	1.74	1.72	1.71	1.69	1.68	1.64	1.63	1.61
21	1.83	1.78	1.74	1.72	1.70	1.69	1.67	1.66	1.62	1.61	1.59
22	1.81	1.76	1.73	1.70	1.68	1.67	1.65	1.64	1.60	1.59	1.57
23	1.80	1.74	1.71	1.69	1.67	1.66	1.64	1.62	1.59	1.57	1.55
24	1.78	1.73	1.70	1.67	1.65	1.64	1.62	1.61	1.57	1.56	1.53
25	1.77	1.72	1.68	1.66	1.64	1.63	1.61	1.59	1.56	1.54	1.52
26	1.76	1.71	1.67	1.65	1.63	1.61	1.59	1.58	1.54	1.53	1.50
27	1.75	1.70	1.66	1.64	1.62	1.60	1.58	1.57	1.53	1.52	1.49
28	1.74	1.69	1.65	1.63	1.61	1.59	1.57	1.56	1.52	1.50	1.48
29	1.73	1.68	1.64	1.62	1.60	1.58	1.56	1.55	1.51	1.49	1.47
30	1.72	1.67	1.63	1.61	1.59	1.57	1.55	1.54	1.50	1.48	1.46
40	1.66	1.61	1.57	1.54	1.52	1.51	1.48	1.47	1.42	1.41	1.38
50	1.63	1.57	1.53	1.50	1.48	1.46	1.44	1.42	1.38	1.36	1.33
60	1.60	1.54	1.50	1.48	1.45	1.44	1.41	1.40	1.35	1.33	1.29
120	1.55	1.48	1.44	1.41	1.39	1.37	1.34	1.32	1.26	1.24	1.19
200	1.52	1.46	1.41	1.38	1.36	1.34	1.31	1.29	1.23	1.20	1.15
∞	1.49	1.42	1.38	1.34	1.32	1.30	1.26	1.24	1.17	1.13	1.00

CRITICAL VALUES OF $F_{.05}$

This table shows the 5 percent right-tail critical values of F for the stated degrees of freedom ($d.f.$).

Denominator Degrees of Freedom (df_2)	Numerator Degrees of Freedom (df_1)										
	1	2	3	4	5	6	7	8	9	10	12
1	161.4	199.5	215.7	224.6	230.2	234.0	236.8	238.9	240.5	241.9	243.9
2	18.51	19.00	19.16	19.25	19.30	19.33	19.35	19.37	19.38	19.40	19.41
3	10.13	9.55	9.28	9.12	9.01	8.94	8.89	8.85	8.81	8.79	8.74
4	7.71	6.94	6.59	6.39	6.26	6.16	6.09	6.04	6.00	5.96	5.91
5	6.61	5.79	5.41	5.19	5.05	4.95	4.88	4.82	4.77	4.74	4.68
6	5.99	5.14	4.76	4.53	4.39	4.28	4.21	4.15	4.10	4.06	4.00
7	5.59	4.74	4.35	4.12	3.97	3.87	3.79	3.73	3.68	3.64	3.57
8	5.32	4.46	4.07	3.84	3.69	3.58	3.50	3.44	3.39	3.35	3.28
9	5.12	4.26	3.86	3.63	3.48	3.37	3.29	3.23	3.18	3.14	3.07
10	4.96	4.10	3.71	3.48	3.33	3.22	3.14	3.07	3.02	2.98	2.91
11	4.84	3.98	3.59	3.36	3.20	3.09	3.01	2.95	2.90	2.85	2.79
12	4.75	3.89	3.49	3.26	3.11	3.00	2.91	2.85	2.80	2.75	2.69
13	4.67	3.81	3.41	3.18	3.03	2.92	2.83	2.77	2.71	2.67	2.60
14	4.60	3.74	3.34	3.11	2.96	2.85	2.76	2.70	2.65	2.60	2.53
15	4.54	3.68	3.29	3.06	2.90	2.79	2.71	2.64	2.59	2.54	2.48
16	4.49	3.63	3.24	3.01	2.85	2.74	2.66	2.59	2.54	2.49	2.42
17	4.45	3.59	3.20	2.96	2.81	2.70	2.61	2.55	2.49	2.45	2.38
18	4.41	3.55	3.16	2.93	2.77	2.66	2.58	2.51	2.46	2.41	2.34
19	4.38	3.52	3.13	2.90	2.74	2.63	2.54	2.48	2.42	2.38	2.31
20	4.35	3.49	3.10	2.87	2.71	2.60	2.51	2.45	2.39	2.35	2.28
21	4.32	3.47	3.07	2.84	2.68	2.57	2.49	2.42	2.37	2.32	2.25
22	4.30	3.44	3.05	2.82	2.66	2.55	2.46	2.40	2.34	2.30	2.23
23	4.28	3.42	3.03	2.80	2.64	2.53	2.44	2.37	2.32	2.27	2.20
24	4.26	3.40	3.01	2.78	2.62	2.51	2.42	2.36	2.30	2.25	2.18
25	4.24	3.39	2.99	2.76	2.60	2.49	2.40	2.34	2.28	2.24	2.16
26	4.23	3.37	2.98	2.74	2.59	2.47	2.39	2.32	2.27	2.22	2.15
27	4.21	3.35	2.96	2.73	2.57	2.46	2.37	2.31	2.25	2.20	2.13
28	4.20	3.34	2.95	2.71	2.56	2.45	2.36	2.29	2.24	2.19	2.12
29	4.18	3.33	2.93	2.70	2.55	2.43	2.35	2.28	2.22	2.18	2.10
30	4.17	3.32	2.92	2.69	2.53	2.42	2.33	2.27	2.21	2.16	2.09
40	4.08	3.23	2.84	2.61	2.45	2.34	2.25	2.18	2.12	2.08	2.00
50	4.03	3.18	2.79	2.56	2.40	2.29	2.20	2.13	2.07	2.03	1.95
60	4.00	3.15	2.76	2.53	2.37	2.25	2.17	2.10	2.04	1.99	1.92
120	3.92	3.07	2.68	2.45	2.29	2.18	2.09	2.02	1.96	1.91	1.83
200	3.89	3.04	2.65	2.42	2.26	2.14	2.06	1.98	1.93	1.88	1.80
∞	3.84	3.00	2.60	2.37	2.21	2.10	2.01	1.94	1.88	1.83	1.75

Denominator Degrees of Freedom (df_2)	Numerator Degrees of Freedom (df_1)										
	15	20	25	30	35	40	50	60	120	200	∞
1	245.9	248.0	249.3	250.1	250.7	251.1	251.8	252.2	253.3	253.7	254.3
2	19.43	19.45	19.46	19.46	19.47	19.47	19.48	19.48	19.49	19.49	19.50
3	8.70	8.66	8.63	8.62	8.60	8.59	8.58	8.57	8.55	8.54	8.53
4	5.86	5.80	5.77	5.75	5.73	5.72	5.70	5.69	5.66	5.65	5.63
5	4.62	4.56	4.52	4.50	4.48	4.46	4.44	4.43	4.40	4.39	4.37
6	3.94	3.87	3.83	3.81	3.79	3.77	3.75	3.74	3.70	3.69	3.67
7	3.51	3.44	3.40	3.38	3.36	3.34	3.32	3.30	3.27	3.25	3.23
8	3.22	3.15	3.11	3.08	3.06	3.04	3.02	3.01	2.97	2.95	2.93
9	3.01	2.94	2.89	2.86	2.84	2.83	2.80	2.79	2.75	2.73	2.71
10	2.85	2.77	2.73	2.70	2.68	2.66	2.64	2.62	2.58	2.56	2.54
11	2.72	2.65	2.60	2.57	2.55	2.53	2.51	2.49	2.45	2.43	2.41
12	2.62	2.54	2.50	2.47	2.44	2.43	2.40	2.38	2.34	2.32	2.30
13	2.53	2.46	2.41	2.38	2.36	2.34	2.31	2.30	2.25	2.23	2.21
14	2.46	2.39	2.34	2.31	2.28	2.27	2.24	2.22	2.18	2.16	2.13
15	2.40	2.33	2.28	2.25	2.22	2.20	2.18	2.16	2.11	2.10	2.07
16	2.35	2.28	2.23	2.19	2.17	2.15	2.12	2.11	2.06	2.04	2.01
17	2.31	2.23	2.18	2.15	2.12	2.10	2.08	2.06	2.01	1.99	1.96
18	2.27	2.19	2.14	2.11	2.08	2.06	2.04	2.02	1.97	1.95	1.92
19	2.23	2.16	2.11	2.07	2.05	2.03	2.00	1.98	1.93	1.91	1.88
20	2.20	2.12	2.07	2.04	2.01	1.99	1.97	1.95	1.90	1.88	1.84
21	2.18	2.10	2.05	2.01	1.98	1.96	1.94	1.92	1.87	1.84	1.81
22	2.15	2.07	2.02	1.98	1.96	1.94	1.91	1.89	1.84	1.82	1.78
23	2.13	2.05	2.00	1.96	1.93	1.91	1.88	1.86	1.81	1.79	1.76
24	2.11	2.03	1.97	1.94	1.91	1.89	1.86	1.84	1.79	1.77	1.73
25	2.09	2.01	1.96	1.92	1.89	1.87	1.84	1.82	1.77	1.75	1.71
26	2.07	1.99	1.94	1.90	1.87	1.85	1.82	1.80	1.75	1.73	1.69
27	2.06	1.97	1.92	1.88	1.86	1.84	1.81	1.79	1.73	1.71	1.67
28	2.04	1.96	1.91	1.87	1.84	1.82	1.79	1.77	1.71	1.69	1.66
29	2.03	1.94	1.89	1.85	1.83	1.81	1.77	1.75	1.70	1.67	1.64
30	2.01	1.93	1.88	1.84	1.81	1.79	1.76	1.74	1.68	1.66	1.62
40	1.92	1.84	1.78	1.74	1.72	1.69	1.66	1.64	1.58	1.55	1.51
50	1.87	1.78	1.73	1.69	1.66	1.63	1.60	1.58	1.51	1.48	1.44
60	1.84	1.75	1.69	1.65	1.62	1.59	1.56	1.53	1.47	1.44	1.39
120	1.75	1.66	1.60	1.55	1.52	1.50	1.46	1.43	1.35	1.32	1.26
200	1.72	1.62	1.56	1.52	1.48	1.46	1.41	1.39	1.30	1.26	1.19
∞	1.67	1.57	1.51	1.46	1.42	1.39	1.35	1.32	1.22	1.17	1.00

CRITICAL VALUES OF $F_{.025}$

This table shows the 2.5 percent right-tail critical values of F for the stated degrees of freedom ($d.f.$).

Denominator Degrees of Freedom (df_2)	Numerator Degrees of Freedom (df_1)										
	1	2	3	4	5	6	7	8	9	10	12
1	647.8	799.5	864.2	899.6	921.8	937.1	948.2	956.6	963.3	968.6	976.7
2	38.51	39.00	39.17	39.25	39.30	39.33	39.36	39.37	39.39	39.40	39.41
3	17.44	16.04	15.44	15.10	14.88	14.73	14.62	14.54	14.47	14.42	14.34
4	12.22	10.65	9.98	9.60	9.36	9.20	9.07	8.98	8.90	8.84	8.75
5	10.01	8.43	7.76	7.39	7.15	6.98	6.85	6.76	6.68	6.62	6.52
6	8.81	7.26	6.60	6.23	5.99	5.82	5.70	5.60	5.52	5.46	5.37
7	8.07	6.54	5.89	5.52	5.29	5.12	4.99	4.90	4.82	4.76	4.67
8	7.57	6.06	5.42	5.05	4.82	4.65	4.53	4.43	4.36	4.30	4.20
9	7.21	5.71	5.08	4.72	4.48	4.32	4.20	4.10	4.03	3.96	3.87
10	6.94	5.46	4.83	4.47	4.24	4.07	3.95	3.85	3.78	3.72	3.62
11	6.72	5.26	4.63	4.28	4.04	3.88	3.76	3.66	3.59	3.53	3.43
12	6.55	5.10	4.47	4.12	3.89	3.73	3.61	3.51	3.44	3.37	3.28
13	6.41	4.97	4.35	4.00	3.77	3.60	3.48	3.39	3.31	3.25	3.15
14	6.30	4.86	4.24	3.89	3.66	3.50	3.38	3.29	3.21	3.15	3.05
15	6.20	4.77	4.15	3.80	3.58	3.41	3.29	3.20	3.12	3.06	2.96
16	6.12	4.69	4.08	3.73	3.50	3.34	3.22	3.12	3.05	2.99	2.89
17	6.04	4.62	4.01	3.66	3.44	3.28	3.16	3.06	2.98	2.92	2.82
18	5.98	4.56	3.95	3.61	3.38	3.22	3.10	3.01	2.93	2.87	2.77
19	5.92	4.51	3.90	3.56	3.33	3.17	3.05	2.96	2.88	2.82	2.72
20	5.87	4.46	3.86	3.51	3.29	3.13	3.01	2.91	2.84	2.77	2.68
21	5.83	4.42	3.82	3.48	3.25	3.09	2.97	2.87	2.80	2.73	2.64
22	5.79	4.38	3.78	3.44	3.22	3.05	2.93	2.84	2.76	2.70	2.60
23	5.75	4.35	3.75	3.41	3.18	3.02	2.90	2.81	2.73	2.67	2.57
24	5.72	4.32	3.72	3.38	3.15	2.99	2.87	2.78	2.70	2.64	2.54
25	5.69	4.29	3.69	3.35	3.13	2.97	2.85	2.75	2.68	2.61	2.51
26	5.66	4.27	3.67	3.33	3.10	2.94	2.82	2.73	2.65	2.59	2.49
27	5.63	4.24	3.65	3.31	3.08	2.92	2.80	2.71	2.63	2.57	2.47
28	5.61	4.22	3.63	3.29	3.06	2.90	2.78	2.69	2.61	2.55	2.45
29	5.59	4.20	3.61	3.27	3.04	2.88	2.76	2.67	2.59	2.53	2.43
30	5.57	4.18	3.59	3.25	3.03	2.87	2.75	2.65	2.57	2.51	2.41
40	5.42	4.05	3.46	3.13	2.90	2.74	2.62	2.53	2.45	2.39	2.29
50	5.34	3.97	3.39	3.05	2.83	2.67	2.55	2.46	2.38	2.32	2.22
60	5.29	3.93	3.34	3.01	2.79	2.63	2.51	2.41	2.33	2.27	2.17
120	5.15	3.80	3.23	2.89	2.67	2.52	2.39	2.30	2.22	2.16	2.05
200	5.10	3.76	3.18	2.85	2.63	2.47	2.35	2.26	2.18	2.11	2.01
∞	5.02	3.69	3.12	2.79	2.57	2.41	2.29	2.19	2.11	2.05	1.94

Denominator Degrees of Freedom (df_2)	Numerator Degrees of Freedom (df_1)										
	15	20	25	30	35	40	50	60	120	200	∞
1	984.9	993.1	998.1	1001	1004	1006	1008	1010	1014	1016	1018
2	39.43	39.45	39.46	39.46	39.47	39.47	39.48	39.48	39.49	39.49	39.50
3	14.25	14.17	14.12	14.08	14.06	14.04	14.01	13.99	13.95	13.93	13.90
4	8.66	8.56	8.50	8.46	8.43	8.41	8.38	8.36	8.31	8.29	8.26
5	6.43	6.33	6.27	6.23	6.20	6.18	6.14	6.12	6.07	6.05	6.02
6	5.27	5.17	5.11	5.07	5.04	5.01	4.98	4.96	4.90	4.88	4.85
7	4.57	4.47	4.40	4.36	4.33	4.31	4.28	4.25	4.20	4.18	4.14
8	4.10	4.00	3.94	3.89	3.86	3.84	3.81	3.78	3.73	3.70	3.67
9	3.77	3.67	3.60	3.56	3.53	3.51	3.47	3.45	3.39	3.37	3.33
10	3.52	3.42	3.35	3.31	3.28	3.26	3.22	3.20	3.14	3.12	3.08
11	3.33	3.23	3.16	3.12	3.09	3.06	3.03	3.00	2.94	2.92	2.88
12	3.18	3.07	3.01	2.96	2.93	2.91	2.87	2.85	2.79	2.76	2.73
13	3.05	2.95	2.88	2.84	2.80	2.78	2.74	2.72	2.66	2.63	2.60
14	2.95	2.84	2.78	2.73	2.70	2.67	2.64	2.61	2.55	2.53	2.49
15	2.86	2.76	2.69	2.64	2.61	2.59	2.55	2.52	2.46	2.44	2.40
16	2.79	2.68	2.61	2.57	2.53	2.51	2.47	2.45	2.38	2.36	2.32
17	2.72	2.62	2.55	2.50	2.47	2.44	2.41	2.38	2.32	2.29	2.25
18	2.67	2.56	2.49	2.44	2.41	2.38	2.35	2.32	2.26	2.23	2.19
19	2.62	2.51	2.44	2.39	2.36	2.33	2.30	2.27	2.20	2.18	2.13
20	2.57	2.46	2.40	2.35	2.31	2.29	2.25	2.22	2.16	2.13	2.09
21	2.53	2.42	2.36	2.31	2.27	2.25	2.21	2.18	2.11	2.09	2.04
22	2.50	2.39	2.32	2.27	2.24	2.21	2.17	2.14	2.08	2.05	2.01
23	2.47	2.36	2.29	2.24	2.20	2.18	2.14	2.11	2.04	2.01	1.97
24	2.44	2.33	2.26	2.21	2.17	2.15	2.11	2.08	2.01	1.98	1.94
25	2.41	2.30	2.23	2.18	2.15	2.12	2.08	2.05	1.98	1.95	1.91
26	2.39	2.28	2.21	2.16	2.12	2.09	2.05	2.03	1.95	1.92	1.88
27	2.36	2.25	2.18	2.13	2.10	2.07	2.03	2.00	1.93	1.90	1.85
28	2.34	2.23	2.16	2.11	2.08	2.05	2.01	1.98	1.91	1.88	1.83
29	2.32	2.21	2.14	2.09	2.06	2.03	1.99	1.96	1.89	1.86	1.81
30	2.31	2.20	2.12	2.07	2.04	2.01	1.97	1.94	1.87	1.84	1.79
40	2.18	2.07	1.99	1.94	1.90	1.88	1.83	1.80	1.72	1.69	1.64
50	2.11	1.99	1.92	1.87	1.83	1.80	1.75	1.72	1.64	1.60	1.55
60	2.06	1.94	1.87	1.82	1.78	1.74	1.70	1.67	1.58	1.54	1.48
120	1.94	1.82	1.75	1.69	1.65	1.61	1.56	1.53	1.43	1.39	1.31
200	1.90	1.78	1.70	1.64	1.60	1.56	1.51	1.47	1.37	1.32	1.23
∞	1.83	1.71	1.63	1.57	1.52	1.48	1.43	1.39	1.27	1.21	1.00

CRITICAL VALUES OF $F_{.01}$

This table shows the 1 percent right-tail critical values of F for the stated degrees of freedom (*d.f.*).

Denominator Degrees of Freedom (df_2)	Numerator Degrees of Freedom (df_1)										
	1	2	3	4	5	6	7	8	9	10	12
1	4052	4999	5404	5624	5764	5859	5928	5981	6022	6056	6107
2	98.50	99.00	99.16	99.25	99.30	99.33	99.36	99.38	99.39	99.40	99.42
3	34.12	30.82	29.46	28.71	28.24	27.91	27.67	27.49	27.34	27.23	27.05
4	21.20	18.00	16.69	15.98	15.52	15.21	14.98	14.80	14.66	14.55	14.37
5	16.26	13.27	12.06	11.39	10.97	10.67	10.46	10.29	10.16	10.05	9.89
6	13.75	10.92	9.78	9.15	8.75	8.47	8.26	8.10	7.98	7.87	7.72
7	12.25	9.55	8.45	7.85	7.46	7.19	6.99	6.84	6.72	6.62	6.47
8	11.26	8.65	7.59	7.01	6.63	6.37	6.18	6.03	5.91	5.81	5.67
9	10.56	8.02	6.99	6.42	6.06	5.80	5.61	5.47	5.35	5.26	5.11
10	10.04	7.56	6.55	5.99	5.64	5.39	5.20	5.06	4.94	4.85	4.71
11	9.65	7.21	6.22	5.67	5.32	5.07	4.89	4.74	4.63	4.54	4.40
12	9.33	6.93	5.95	5.41	5.06	4.82	4.64	4.50	4.39	4.30	4.16
13	9.07	6.70	5.74	5.21	4.86	4.62	4.44	4.30	4.19	4.10	3.96
14	8.86	6.51	5.56	5.04	4.69	4.46	4.28	4.14	4.03	3.94	3.80
15	8.68	6.36	5.42	4.89	4.56	4.32	4.14	4.00	3.89	3.80	3.67
16	8.53	6.23	5.29	4.77	4.44	4.20	4.03	3.89	3.78	3.69	3.55
17	8.40	6.11	5.19	4.67	4.34	4.10	3.93	3.79	3.68	3.59	3.46
18	8.29	6.01	5.09	4.58	4.25	4.01	3.84	3.71	3.60	3.51	3.37
19	8.18	5.93	5.01	4.50	4.17	3.94	3.77	3.63	3.52	3.43	3.30
20	8.10	5.85	4.94	4.43	4.10	3.87	3.70	3.56	3.46	3.37	3.23
21	8.02	5.78	4.87	4.37	4.04	3.81	3.64	3.51	3.40	3.31	3.17
22	7.95	5.72	4.82	4.31	3.99	3.76	3.59	3.45	3.35	3.26	3.12
23	7.88	5.66	4.76	4.26	3.94	3.71	3.54	3.41	3.30	3.21	3.07
24	7.82	5.61	4.72	4.22	3.90	3.67	3.50	3.36	3.26	3.17	3.03
25	7.77	5.57	4.68	4.18	3.85	3.63	3.46	3.32	3.22	3.13	2.99
26	7.72	5.53	4.64	4.14	3.82	3.59	3.42	3.29	3.18	3.09	2.96
27	7.68	5.49	4.60	4.11	3.78	3.56	3.39	3.26	3.15	3.06	2.93
28	7.64	5.45	4.57	4.07	3.75	3.53	3.36	3.23	3.12	3.03	2.90
29	7.60	5.42	4.54	4.04	3.73	3.50	3.33	3.20	3.09	3.00	2.87
30	7.56	5.39	4.51	4.02	3.70	3.47	3.30	3.17	3.07	2.98	2.84
40	7.31	5.18	4.31	3.83	3.51	3.29	3.12	2.99	2.89	2.80	2.66
50	7.17	5.06	4.20	3.72	3.41	3.19	3.02	2.89	2.78	2.70	2.56
60	7.08	4.98	4.13	3.65	3.34	3.12	2.95	2.82	2.72	2.63	2.50
120	6.85	4.79	3.95	3.48	3.17	2.96	2.79	2.66	2.56	2.47	2.34
200	6.76	4.71	3.88	3.41	3.11	2.89	2.73	2.60	2.50	2.41	2.27
∞	6.63	4.61	3.78	3.32	3.02	2.80	2.64	2.51	2.41	2.32	2.18

Denominator Degrees of Freedom (df_2)	Numerator Degrees of Freedom (df_1)										
	15	**20**	**25**	**30**	**35**	**40**	**50**	**60**	**120**	**200**	**∞**
1	6157	6209	6240	6260	6275	6286	6302	6313	6340	6350	6366
2	99.43	99.45	99.46	99.47	99.47	99.48	99.48	99.48	99.49	99.49	99.50
3	26.87	26.69	26.58	26.50	26.45	26.41	26.35	26.32	26.22	26.18	26.13
4	14.20	14.02	13.91	13.84	13.79	13.75	13.69	13.65	13.56	13.52	13.47
5	9.72	9.55	9.45	9.38	9.33	9.29	9.24	9.20	9.11	9.08	9.02
6	7.56	7.40	7.30	7.23	7.18	7.14	7.09	7.06	6.97	6.93	6.88
7	6.31	6.16	6.06	5.99	5.94	5.91	5.86	5.82	5.74	5.70	5.65
8	5.52	5.36	5.26	5.20	5.15	5.12	5.07	5.03	4.95	4.91	4.86
9	4.96	4.81	4.71	4.65	4.60	4.57	4.52	4.48	4.40	4.36	4.31
10	4.56	4.41	4.31	4.25	4.20	4.17	4.12	4.08	4.00	3.96	3.91
11	4.25	4.10	4.01	3.94	3.89	3.86	3.81	3.78	3.69	3.66	3.60
12	4.01	3.86	3.76	3.70	3.65	3.62	3.57	3.54	3.45	3.41	3.36
13	3.82	3.66	3.57	3.51	3.46	3.43	3.38	3.34	3.25	3.22	3.17
14	3.66	3.51	3.41	3.35	3.30	3.27	3.22	3.18	3.09	3.06	3.01
15	3.52	3.37	3.28	3.21	3.17	3.13	3.08	3.05	2.96	2.92	2.87
16	3.41	3.26	3.16	3.10	3.05	3.02	2.97	2.93	2.84	2.81	2.76
17	3.31	3.16	3.07	3.00	2.96	2.92	2.87	2.83	2.75	2.71	2.66
18	3.23	3.08	2.98	2.92	2.87	2.84	2.78	2.75	2.66	2.62	2.57
19	3.15	3.00	2.91	2.84	2.80	2.76	2.71	2.67	2.58	2.55	2.49
20	3.09	2.94	2.84	2.78	2.73	2.69	2.64	2.61	2.52	2.48	2.42
21	3.03	2.88	2.79	2.72	2.67	2.64	2.58	2.55	2.46	2.42	2.36
22	2.98	2.83	2.73	2.67	2.62	2.58	2.53	2.50	2.40	2.36	2.31
23	2.93	2.78	2.69	2.62	2.57	2.54	2.48	2.45	2.35	2.32	2.26
24	2.89	2.74	2.64	2.58	2.53	2.49	2.44	2.40	2.31	2.27	2.21
25	2.85	2.70	2.60	2.54	2.49	2.45	2.40	2.36	2.27	2.23	2.17
26	2.81	2.66	2.57	2.50	2.45	2.42	2.36	2.33	2.23	2.19	2.13
27	2.78	2.63	2.54	2.47	2.42	2.38	2.33	2.29	2.20	2.16	2.10
28	2.75	2.60	2.51	2.44	2.39	2.35	2.30	2.26	2.17	2.13	2.07
29	2.73	2.57	2.48	2.41	2.36	2.33	2.27	2.23	2.14	2.10	2.04
30	2.70	2.55	2.45	2.39	2.34	2.30	2.25	2.21	2.11	2.07	2.01
40	2.52	2.37	2.27	2.20	2.15	2.11	2.06	2.02	1.92	1.87	1.81
50	2.42	2.27	2.17	2.10	2.05	2.01	1.95	1.91	1.80	1.76	1.69
60	2.35	2.20	2.10	2.03	1.98	1.94	1.88	1.84	1.73	1.68	1.60
120	2.19	2.03	1.93	1.86	1.81	1.76	1.70	1.66	1.53	1.48	1.38
200	2.13	1.97	1.87	1.79	1.74	1.69	1.63	1.58	1.45	1.39	1.28
∞	2.04	1.88	1.77	1.70	1.64	1.59	1.52	1.47	1.32	1.25	1.00

Solutions to Odd-Numbered Exercises

CHAPTER 1

1.9 No, association does not imply causation. See Pitfall 5.

1.11 a. All combinations have same chance of winning so method did not "work."

b. No, same as any other six numbers.

1.13 A reduction of .2% may not seem important to the individual customer, but from the company's perspective it could be significant depending on how many customers they have.

1.15 Disagree. The difference is practically important. 0.9% of 231,164 is 2,080 patients.

1.19 a. Analyze the 80 responses but make no conclusions about nonrespondents.

b. No, study seems too flawed.

1.21 Agree. Be wary of Pitfall 2.

1.23 Disagree. Tom fell for Pitfall 2.

1.25 a. Attendance, study time, ability level, interest level, instructor's ability, prerequisites.

b. Reverse causation? Good students make better decisions about their health.

c. No, causation is not shown.

1.27 A major problem is that we don't know number of students in each major.

a. Likely fewer philosophy majors to begin with.

b. Likely more engineers want an MBA, so they take it.

c. Causation not shown. Physics may differ from marketing majors (e.g., math skills).

d. The GMAT is just an indicator of academic skills.

1.29 a. Most would prefer the graph, but both are clear.

b. The number of salads sold reached a maximum in May and decreased steadily toward the end of 2005.

CHAPTER 2

2.1 a. categorical   b. categorical   c. discrete numerical

2.3 a. continuous numerical

b. continuous numerical (often reported as an integer)

c. categorical   d. categorical

2.5 a. cross-sectional   b. time series

c. time series   d. cross-sectional

2.7 a. time series   b. cross-sectional

c. time series   d. cross-sectional

2.9 a. ratio   b. ordinal   c. nominal   d. interval

e. ratio   f. ordinal

2.13 a. Interval, assuming intervals are equal.

b. Yes (assuming interval data).

c. 10-point scale might give too many points and make it hard for guests to choose between.

2.15 a. Census   b. Sample or census

c. Sample   d. Census

2.17 a. Parameter   b. Parameter

c. Statistic   d. Statistic

2.19 a. Convenience   b. Systematic

c. Judgment or biased

2.25 a. Telephone or Web.   b. Direct observation.

c. Interview, Web, or mail.   d. Interview or Web.

2.27 Version 1: Most would say yes. Version 2: More varied responses.

2.29 a. Continuous numerical   b. Categorical

c. Discrete numerical

2.31 a. Ordinal   b. Interval   c. Ratio

2.33 Q1 Categorical, nominal   Q2 Continuous, ratio

Q3 Continuous, ratio   Q4 Discrete, ratio

Q5 Categorical, ordinal   Q6 Categorical, ordinal

Q7 Discrete, ratio   Q8 Continuous, ratio

Q9 Discrete, ratio   Q10 Categorical, ordinal

Q11 Continuous, ratio   Q12 Discrete, ratio

Q13 Categorical, ordinal   Q14 Categorical, nominal

Q15 Categorical, ordinal

2.35 a. time series   b. cross-sectional   c. cross-sectional

d. time series

2.37 a. Census   b. Sample

c. Census

2.39 a. Statistic   b. Parameter   c. Parameter

2.41 a. Complaint   b. Patient visits, discrete. Waiting time, continuous.

2.43 a. No, census costly, perhaps impossible.

2.45 a. Cluster sampling

b. No, population effectively infinite.

2.47 a. Census   b. Sample

c. Sample   d. Census

2.49 a. Cluster sample.   b. Cluster sample.

c. Random Sample of tax returns.   d. Statistic based on sales, not a sample.

2.51 a. Cluster sampling, neighborhoods are natural clusters.

b. Picking a day near a holiday with light trash.

2.53 a. Yes, 11,000/18 > 20.   b. 1/39

2.55 Convenience. Cost and Time.

2.57 Education and income could affect who uses the no-call list.

a. They won't reach those who purchase such services. Same response for b and c.

Surveys and Scales

2.59 a. Rate the effectiveness of this professor. 1—Excellent to 5—Poor.

b. Rate your satisfaction with the president's economic policy. 1—Very Satisfied to 5—Very dissatisfied.

c. How long did you wait to see your doctor? Less than 15 minutes, between 15 and 30 minutes, between 30 minutes and 1 hour, more than 1 hour.

2.61 a. Ordinal.   b. Intervals are equal.

CHAPTER 3

3.1 a.

Frequency	Stem	Leaf
1	0	9
5	1	56889
7	2	1145667
10	3	1222334559
1	4	2
24		

b.

c. Skewed left, central tendency approximately 30, range from 9–42.

3.3 Sarah's calls are shorter.

3.5 a.

b. Skewed left, central tendency approximately 80, majority of data from 50 to 100, two outliers at 18 and 27.

3.7 Sturges' Rule suggests about 6 bins. Slight right skew.

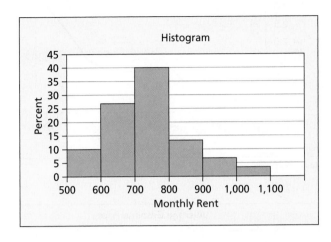

3.9 a. 7 bins, width = 5, Sturges' Rule = 6 bins

b. 8 bins, width = 10, Sturges' Rule = 6 or 7 bins

c. 10 bins, width = 0.15, Sturges' Rule = 9 bins

d. 8 bins, width = 0.01, Sturges' Rule = 8 bins

3.11 a.

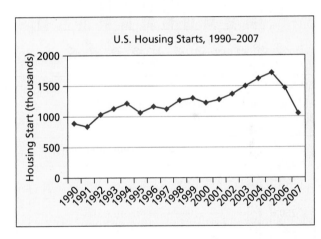

b. Increasing trend until 2005, then sharp decrease.

3.13 Decreasing at a decreasing rate.

3.15 a.

Source: www.fueleconomy.gov.

b.

Source: www.fueleconomy.gov.

c. Line chart is preferred by most analysts.

3.17 a.

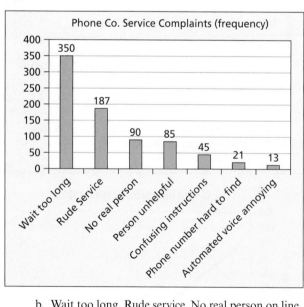

b. Wait too long, Rude service, No real person on line
c. Wait too long

3.19 a. Default pie is clear, but rather small (can be dragged larger).
b. Visually strong, but harder to read due to rotation.
c. Clear, easy to read.

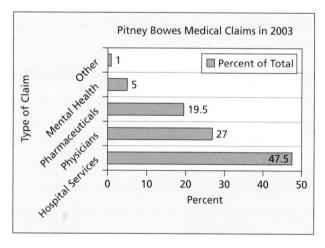

3.21 a. To show more detail, you could start the graph at (.80,100).
b. There is a moderate negative linear relationship.

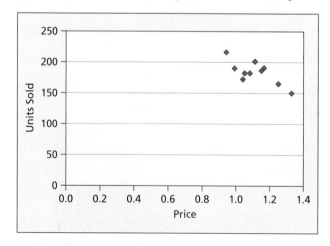

3.23 a. To show more detail, you could start the graph at (20,20).

b. There is a moderate positive linear relationship.

b.

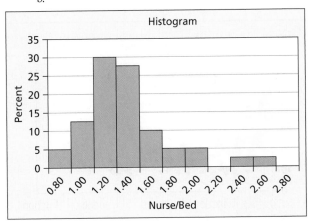

c. Skewed to the right. Half of the data values are between 1.2 and 1.6.

3.25   a.

Frequency	Stem	Leaf
3	0	249
6	1	227778
5	2	14557
4	3	0025
1	4	4
3	5	013
2	6	26
0	7	
1	8	4
1	9	9

3.29   a. MegaStat's dotplot.

b. MegaStat's histogram.

b.

c. Heavily skewed to the right. Central tendency approximately 3 minutes.

c. Skewed right.

3.27   a.

3.31

3.33 a.

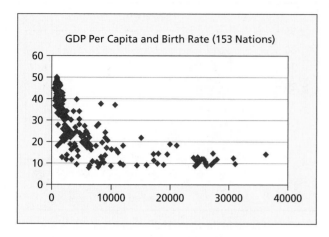

b. Negative, Nonlinear, Moderate relationship.

3.35 a. Horizontal bar chart with 3D visual effect.
b. Strengths: Good proportions and no distracting pictures. Weaknesses: No labels on X and Y axes, title unclear, 3D effect does not add to presentation.
c. Vertical bar chart without visual effect and label on X axis.

3.37 a. Exploded pie chart.
b. Strengths: Information complete, colorful. Weaknesses: Hard to assess differences in size of pie slices.
c. Sorted column chart with OPEC and non-OPEC countries color coded.

3.39 a. Pie chart.
b. Strengths: Source identified, answers the question posed. Weaknesses: "Other" category quite large.
c. Might change title: Distribution of Advertising Dollars in the United States, 2001. Some might prefer a column chart.

3.41 a. Line chart with pictures.
b. Pictures distracting, implies irresponsibility, does show source of data.
c. Take out pictures, show a simple line chart.

3.43 a.

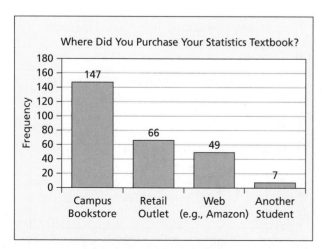

b. Yes, pie chart could be used.

3.45 a.

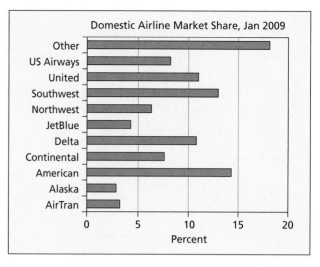

b. Yes, a pie chart could be used.

3.47 a.

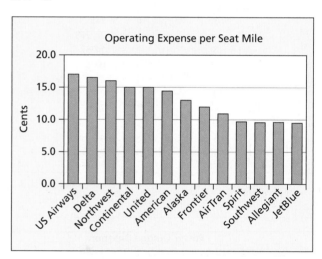

b. Yes, a bar chart could be used. But a table may be clearest, because the large quantity of data tends to clutter the graphs.

3.49 a.

b. Yes, a pie chart would work.

3.51 a.

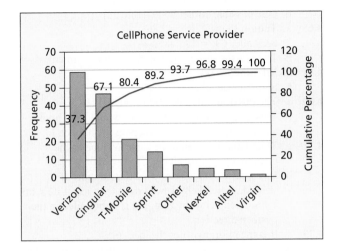

b. Verizon, Cingular, T-Mobile.

CHAPTER 4

4.1 a. mean = 2.83, median = 1.5, mode = 0.
b. mean = 68.33, median = 72, mode = 40.
c. mean = 3.04, median = 3.03, no mode.

4.3 a. Continuous data, skewed right, no mode. Median best choice.
b. Mostly one rider, mode best choice.
c. Symmetric distribution, mean and median the same, and two modes. Mean best choice.

4.5 a. Mean = 75.5, median = 80.5, mode = 93.
b. Skewed left.
c. Mode not a useful measure. The value 93 appears only 3 times out of 24 observations.

4.7 a. $\bar{x}$ = 27.34, median = 26, mode = 26.
b. No, $\bar{x}$ is greater than the median and mode.
d. Slightly skewed right.

4.9 b. $\bar{x}$ = 4.48, median = 2, mode = 1.
c. No, $\bar{x}$ > median > mode.
d. Skewed right.

4.11 a. TRIMMEAN(A1:A50,.2).   b. 5.   c. 10.

4.13 a. Mean = 100, median = 0, mode = 0, midrange = 325. Geometric mean is undefined because there are values equal to 0.
b. Choose the mean. Midrange would overestimate total expected expenses.

4.15 a. $\bar{x}$ = 27.34, midrange = 25.50, geometric mean = 26.08, 10% trimmed mean = 27.46.
b. The measures are all close, especially the mean and trimmed mean.

4.17 a. $\bar{x}$ = 4.48, midrange = 15.0, geometric mean = 2.6, 10% trimmed mean = 3.13.
b. The data are skewed right.

4.19 a. Sample A: $\bar{x}$ = 7, s = 1. Sample B: $\bar{x}$ = 62, s = 1. Sample C: $\bar{x}$ = 1001, s = 1.
b. The standard deviation is not a function of the mean.

4.21 Hybrid: 5.1%. Gas: 7%. The hybrid had more consistent gas mileage relative to the mean than the gasoline vehicle.

4.23 a. Stock A: CV = 21.43%. Stock B: CV = 8.32%. Stock C: CV = 36.17%.
b. Stock C
c. Directly comparing standard deviation would not be helpful in this case because the means have different magnitudes.

4.25 a. $\bar{x}_A$ = 6.857, s_A = 1.497, $\bar{x}_B$ = 7.243, s_B = 1.209.
b. CV_A = 0.218, CV_B = 0.167.
c. Consumers preferred sauce B.

4.27 At least 75% of the data will fall within ±2 standard deviations so: .75 × 400 = 300.

4.29 a. z = 2.4.   b. z = 1.   c. z = 0.6.

4.31 a. Bob's GPA = 3.596.
b. Sarah's weekly work hours = 29.978.
c. Dave's bowling score = 96.

4.33 b. 18 (z = 2.30) and 20 (z = 2.64) are unusual observations. 26 (z = 3.67) and 29 (z = 4.18) are outliers.
c. 87.7% lie within 1 standard deviation and 93.8% lie within 2 standard deviations. 87.7% is much greater than the 68% specified by the empirical rule. The distribution does not appear normal.

4.35 b. Strongly skewed right.

4.37 a. Q_1 ≈ 3300, Q_2 ≈ 3900, and Q_3 ≈ 4300.
b. x_{min} ≈ 2400 and x_{max} ≈ 4800.
c. Left skewed.

4.39 a. Q_1 = 1, Q_3 = 5. The middle 50% of the calls last between 1 and 5 minutes.
b. *Midhinge* = 3. Calls typically last 3 minutes.
c. The data are heavily skewed to the right.

4.41 a.

b. Strong, positive linear association.
c. r = .9620.

4.43

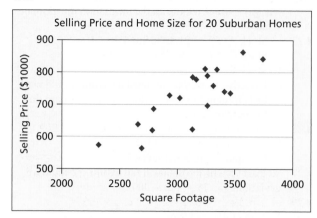

b. $r = .8338$
c. Yes, there is a strong positive linear relationship.

4.45 Using Chebyshev's Theorem, at least 88.9%.

4.47 a. $z = 3.128$.   b. Outlier, $z > 3$.

4.49 a. Allison's final exam = 90.1.
b. Jim's weekly grocery bill = $35.60.
c. Eric's daily video game time = 3.09 hours.

4.51 a. Standard deviation = 2.
b. Assumed a normal distribution.

4.53 a. $\bar{x} = 26.71$, median = 14.5, mode = 11, and midrange = 124.5.   b. $Q_1 = 7.25$, $Q_3 = 20.75$, *Midhinge* = 14.
c. The geometric mean is only valid for data greater than zero.

4.55 a. Mean = 66.85, median = 69.5, and mode = 86.
b. Mean and median fairly close.
c. No, mode not typical; continuous numerical data with few repeats.
d. Difficult to describe shape based only on mean and median. Might conclude somewhat symmetric.

4.57 a. Stock funds: $\bar{x} = 1.329$, median = 1.22. Bond funds: $\bar{x} = 0.875$, median = 0.85.
b. Stock funds: $s = 0.5933$, $CV = 44.65\%$. Bond funds: $s = 0.4489$, $CV = 51.32\%$.
c. The stock funds have less variability relative to the mean.

4.59 a. mean = 6,807, median = 6,646.
b. Slightly skewed right.   c. There is no mode.

4.61 a. $\bar{x} = 3,012.44$, median = 2,550.5.
b. The typical cricket club's income is approximately £2.5 million.

4.63 a.

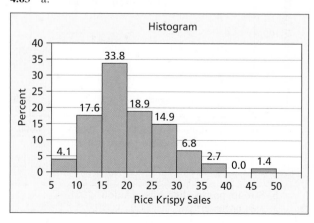

b. Skewed right.
c. Mean = 20.12, standard deviation = 7.64.
d. One possible outlier at 49 (store 22).

4.65 a. Tuition Plans: $CV = 42.86\%$,
S&P 500: $CV = 122.48\%$.
b. The CV shows *relative* risk for each investment.

4.67 a. Midrange = 0.855.
b. Standard deviation = .0217.

4.69 a. The distribution is skewed to the right.
b. This makes sense; most patrons would keep books about 10 days with a few keeping them much longer.

4.71 a. Would expect mean to be close in value to the median, or slightly higher.
b. Life span would have normal distribution. If skewed, more likely skewed right than left. Life span is bounded below by zero, but is unbounded in the positive direction.

4.73 a. It is the midrange, not the median.
b. The midrange is influenced by outliers. Salaries tend to be skewed to the right. Community should use the median.

4.75 a. and c.

	Week 1	Week 2	Week 3	Week 4
Mean	50.00	50.00	50.00	50.00
Sample standard deviation	10.61	10.61	10.61	10.61
Median	50.00	52.00	56.00	47.00

b. Based on the mean and standard deviation, it appears that the distributions are the same.
d.

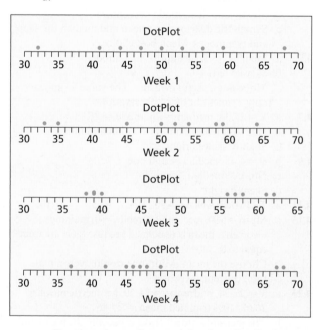

e. Based on the medians and dotplots, distributions are quite different.

4.77 a. $\bar{x} = 9.458$.   b. $s = 10.855$.
c. No, the distribution is skewed right.
d. To prevent bins with zero frequencies.

4.79 a. $\bar{x} = 60.2$, $s = 8.54$, $CV = 14.2\%$.
b. No. The class widths increase as the data values get more spread out.

4.83 a.

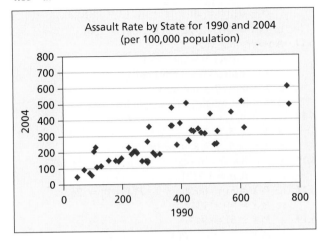

b. $r = .8332$.

c. The rates are positively correlated.

d. 1990: mean = 331.92, median = 3.7, Std Dev = 172.914. 2004: mean = 256.6, median = 232, Std Dev = 131.259.

CHAPTER 5

5.1 a. S = {(V,B), (V,E), (V,O), (M,B), (M,E), (M,O), (A,B), (A,E), (A,O)}

b. Events are not equally likely. Barnes and Noble probably carries more books than other merchandise.

5.3 a. S = {(L,B), (L,B'), (R,B), (R,B')}

b. Events are not equally likely. More right-handed people than left-handed people.

5.5 Empirical.

5.7 Empirical.

5.9 Classical

5.11 Empirical.

5.13 a. Not mutually exclusive.

b. Mutually exclusive.

c. Not mutually exclusive.

5.15 a. $P(A \cup B) = .4 + .5 - .05 = .85$.

b. $P(A \mid B) = .05/.50 = .10$.

c. $P(B \mid A) = .05/.4 = .125$.

5.17 a. $P(S) = .217$.   b. $P(S') = .783$.

c. Odds in favor of S: $.217/.783 = .277$.

d. Odds against S: $.783/.217 = 3.61$

5.19 a. $X = 1$ if the drug is approved, 0 otherwise.

b. $X = 1$ if batter gets a hit, 0 otherwise.

c. $X = 1$ if breast cancer detected, 0 otherwise.

5.21 a. $P(S') = 1 - .246$. There is a 75.4% chance that a female aged 18–24 is a nonsmoker.

b. $P(S \cup C) = .246 + .830 - .232 = .844$. There is an 84.4% chance that a female aged 18–24 is a smoker or is Caucasian.

c. $P(S \mid C) = .232/.830 = .2795$. Given that the female aged 18–24 is a Caucasian, there is a 27.95% chance that she is a smoker.

d. $P(S \cap C') = P(S) - P(S \cap C) = .246 - .232 = .014$. $P(S \mid C') = .014/.17 = .0824$. Given that the female aged 18–24 is *not* Caucasian, there is an 8.24% chance that she smokes.

5.23 a. $P(A \mid B) = P(A \cap B)/P(B) = .05/.50 = .10$.

b. No, A and B are not independent because $P(A \mid B) \neq P(A)$.

5.25 a. $P(V \cup M) = .73 + .18 - .03 = .88$.

b. $P(V \cap M) \neq P(V)P(M)$ therefore V and M are not independent.

5.27 "Five nines" reliability means $P(\text{not failing}) = .99999$. $P(\text{power system failure}) = 1 - (.05)^3 = .999875$. The system does not meet the test.

5.29 Ordering a soft drink is independent of ordering a square pizza. $P(\text{ordering a soft drink}) \times P(\text{ordering a square pizza}) = .5(.8) = .4$. This is equal to $P(\text{ordering both a soft drink and a square pizza})$.

5.31 a. $P(\text{Recycles}) = .34$.

b. $P(\text{Don't Recycle} \mid \text{Lives in Deposit Law State}) = .30$.

c. $P(\text{Recycle and Live in Deposit Law State}) = .154$.

d. $P(\text{Recycle} \mid \text{Lives in Deposit Law State}) = .70$.

5.33 a. $P(D) = .5064$.   b. $P(R) = .1410$.

c. $P(D \cap R) = .0513$.   d. $P(D \cup R) = .5962$.

e. $P(R \mid D) = .1013$.   f. $P(R \mid P) = .1628$.

5.35 *Gender* and *Major* are not independent. For example, $P(A \cap F) = .22$. $P(A)P(F) = .245$. Because the values are not equal, the events are not independent.

5.37

5.39 Let A = using the drug. $P(A) = .04$. $P(A') = .96$. Let T be a positive result. False positive: $P(T \mid A') = .05$. False negative: $P(T' \mid A) = .10$. $P(T \mid A) = 1 - .10 = .90$. $P(T) = (.04)(.90) + (.05)(.96) = .084$. $P(A \mid T) = (.9)(.04)/.084 = .4286$.

5.41 Let W = suitcase contains a weapon. $P(W) = .001$. $P(W') = .999$. Let A be the alarm trigger. False positive: $P(A \mid W') = .02$. False negative: $P(A' \mid W) = .02$. $P(A \mid W) = 1 - .02 = .98$. $P(A) = (.001)(.98) + (.02)(.999) = .02096$. $P(W \mid A) = (.98)(.001)/.02096 = .04676$.

5.43 $_{20}C_5 = 15{,}504$.

5.45 a. $26^6 = 308{,}915{,}776$.

b. $36^6 = 2{,}176{,}782{,}336$.

c. $32^6 = 1{,}073{,}741{,}824$.

5.47 a. $10^6 = 1{,}000{,}000$.

b. $10^5 = 100{,}000$.

c. $10^6 = 1{,}000{,}000$.

5.49 a. $7! = 5{,}040$ ways.   b. No, too many!

5.51 a. $_8C_3 = 56$.   b. $_8C_5 = 56$.

c. $_8C_1 = 8$.   d. $_8C_8 = 1$.

5.57 Empirical.

5.59 a. An empirical probability using response frequencies from the survey.

5.61 a. Empirical or subjective.

5.63 a. Subjective.

5.65 a. Empirical or subjective.

5.69 Odds *against* a 2004 Audi being stolen: 78 to 1.

5.71 P(Butler making it to the NCAA finals) = $1/(200 + 1) = .005$.

5.73 a. $26^3 10^3 = 17,576,000$.
　　　b. $36^6 = 2,176,782,336$.
　　　c. 0 and 1 might be disallowed because they are similar in appearance to letters like O and I.
　　　d. Yes, 2.2 billion unique plates should be enough.
　　　e. $34^6 = 1,544,804,416$.

5.75 Order does not matter. $_7C_3 = 35$.

5.77 a. P(Two aces) = $(4/52)(3/51) = 0.00452$.
　　　b. P(Two red cards) = $(26/52)(25/51) = 0.245098$.
　　　c. P(Two red aces) = $(2/52)(1/51) = 0.000754$.
　　　d. P(Two honor cards) = $(20/52)(19/51) = 0.143288$.

5.79 No, $P(A)P(B) \neq .05$.

5.81 P(at least one gyro will operate) = .99999936. Yes, they've achieved "five-nines" reliability.

5.83 Assuming independence, P(3 cases won out of next 3) = $.7^3 = .343$.

5.85* Assuming independence, P(4 adults say yes) = $.56^4 = 0.0983$.

5.87* See the Excel Spreadsheet in *Learning Stats:* 05-13 Birthday Problem.xls.
　　　For 2 riders: P(no match) = .9973.
　　　For 10 riders: P(no match) = .8831.
　　　For 20 riders: P(no match) = .5886.
　　　For 50 riders: P(no match) = .0296.

5.89* a. i. .4825 ii. .25 iii. .19 iv. .64 v. .09 vi. .015
　　　b. Yes, the vehicle type and mall location are dependent.

5.91 a. i. .5588 ii. .5294 iii. .19 iv. .64 v. .09 vi. .015.
　　　b. No, $P(A-) = .4705$ and $P(A- \mid F-) = .3684$. Interest rates moved down 47% of the time and yet the forecasters' predictions of a decline showed a 37% accuracy rate.

5.93*

	Cancer	No Cancer	Totals
Positive Test	4	500	504
Negative Test	0	9496	9496
Totals	4	9996	10000

P(Cancer | Positive Test) = $4/504 = 0.00794$.

5.95* Let D = applicant uses drugs and T = applicant has positive test result.

$$P(D \mid T) = \frac{P(T \mid D)P(D)}{P(T \mid D)P(D) + P(T \mid D')P(D')}$$
$$= \frac{.036}{.036 + .144} = .20.$$

CHAPTER 6

6.1 Only A is a PDF because $P(x)$ sum to 1.

6.3 $E(X) = 2.25$, $V(X) = 1.6875$, $\sigma = 1.299$, right-skewed.

6.5 $E(X) = 5000(.01) + (0)(.999) = \$50$, add \$25, charges \$75.

6.7 $E(X) = 250(.3) + 950(.3) + 0(.4) = \$360$ million.

6.9 a. $\mu = (20 + 60)/2 = 40$,
　　　$\sigma = \sqrt{[(60 - 20 + 1)^2 - 1]/12} = 11.83$.
　　　b. $P(X \geq 40) = .5122$, $P(X \geq 30) = .7561$.

6.11 Answers may vary.
　　　a. 1 = correct, 0 = incorrect.
　　　b. 1 = insured, 0 = uninsured.
　　　c. 1 = busy, 0 = not busy.
　　　d. 1 = lost weight, 0 no weight loss.

6.13 a. $X = 0$, 1, or 2.
　　　b. $X = 4$, 5, 6, or 7.
　　　c. $X = 4$, 5, 6, 7, 8, 9, or 10.

6.15 a. $\mu = 0.8$, $\sigma = 0.8485$　　b. $\mu = 4$, $\sigma = 1.5492$
　　　c. $\mu = 6$, $\sigma = 1.7321$

6.17 a. $P(X = 5) = .0074$.　　b. $P(X = 0) = .2621$.
　　　c. $P(X = 9) = .1342$.

6.19 a. $P(X \leq 3) = .9437$
　　　b. $P(X > 7) = 1 - P(X \leq 7) = .0547$
　　　c. $P(X < 3) = P(X \leq 2) = .0705$

6.21 a. $P(X > 10) = .9183$.　　b. $P(X \geq 4) = .4059$.
　　　c. $P(X \leq 2) = .9011$.

6.23 a. $P(X = 0) = .10737$
　　　b. $P(X \geq 2) = .62419$
　　　c. $P(X < 3) = .67780$
　　　d. $\mu = n\pi = (10)(.2) = 2$
　　　e. $\sigma = \sqrt{(10)(.2)(1 - .2)} = 1.2649$
　　　g. Skewed right.

6.25 a. $P(X = 0) = .0916$.　　b. $P(X \geq 2) = .6276$.
　　　c. $P(X < 4) = .9274$.　　d. $P(X = 5) = .0079$.

6.27 a. $P(X = 16) = .0033$.
　　　b. $P(X < 10) = .1753$.
　　　c. $P(X \geq 10) = .8247$.

6.29 a. $\lambda = 1$, $\mu = 1.0$, $\sigma = 1$
　　　b. $\lambda = 2$, $\mu = 2.0$, $\sigma = 1.414$
　　　c. $\lambda = 4$, $\mu = 4.0$, $\sigma = 2.0$

6.31 a. $P(X = 6) = .1042$.　　b. $P(X = 10) = .1048$.
　　　c. $P(X = 4) = .0912$.

6.33 a. $\lambda = 4.3$, $P(X \leq 3) = .37715$
　　　b. $\lambda = 5.2$, $P(X > 7) = .15508$
　　　c. $\lambda = 2.7$, $P(X < 3) = .49362$

6.35 a. $P(X > 10) = .1841$.　　b. $P(X \leq 5) = .7851$.
　　　c. $P(X \geq 2) = .9596$.

6.37 a. $P(X \geq 1) = .8173$.　　b. $P(X = 0) = .1827$.
　　　c. $P(X > 3) = .0932$.　　d. Skewed right.

6.39 a. Add-ons are ordered independently.
　　　b. $P(X \geq 2) = .4082$.　　c. $P(X = 0) = .2466$.
　　　d. Skewed right.

6.41* Let $\lambda = n\pi = (500)(.003) = 1.5$
　　　a. $P(X \geq 2) = 1 - .55783 = .44217$
　　　b. $P(X \leq 4) = .93436$　c. Yes, $n \geq 20$ and $\pi \leq .05$

6.43* a. Set $\lambda = \mu = (200)(.03) = 6$
　　　b. $\sigma = \sqrt{(200)(.03)(1 - .03)} = 2.412$
　　　c. $P(X \geq 10) = 1 - .91608 = .08392$
　　　d. $P(X \leq 4) = .28506$
　　　e. Yes, $n \geq 20$ and $\pi \leq .05$.

6.45* a. $E(X) = 2.3$.
　　　b. $P(X = 0) \approx .1003$, $P(X > 2) = .4040$.
　　　c. Yes, $n \geq 20$ and $\pi \leq .05$.

6.47 Distribution is symmetric with small range.

6.49 a. X = number of incorrect vouchers in sample.
　　　b. $P(X = 0) = .06726$　　c. $P(X = 1) = .25869$

d. $P(X \geq 3) = 1 - .69003 = .30997$
e. Fairly symmetric

6.51* a. $3/100 < .05$, OK.   b. $10/200 = .05$, OK.
c. $12/160 > .05$, not OK.   d. $7/500 < .05$, OK.

6.53* a. $P(X = 0) = 0.34868$ (B) or $.34516$ (H).
b. $P(X \geq 2) = .26390$ (B) or $.26350$ (H).
c. $P(X < 4) = .98720$ (B) or $.98814$ (H).
d. $n/N = 10/500 = .02$, so set $\pi = s/N = 50/500 = .1$.

6.55* a. $P(X = 5) = .03125$ when $\pi = .50$
b. $P(X = 3) = .14063$ when $\pi = .25$
c. $P(X = 4) = .03840$ when $\pi = .60$

6.57* a. $\mu = 1/\pi = 1/(.50) = 2$
b. $P(X > 10) = (.50)^{10} = .00098$

6.59* a. $\mu = 9500 + 7400 + 8600 = \$25,500$ (Rule 3), $\sigma^2 = 1250 + 1425 + 1610 = 4285$ (Rule 4), $\sigma = 65.4599$.
b. Rule 4 assumes independent monthly sales (unlikely).

6.61* a. If Y = Bob's point total then $\mu_Y = 400$, $\sigma_Y = 11.18$.
b. No, 450 is more than 3 standard deviations from the mean.

6.63 $E(\text{loss}) = \$0(.98) + \$250(.02)$
$= \$5. E(\text{loss}) > \text{Insurance}$
so purchase insurance.

6.65 a. $\pi = .80$ (answers will vary).
b. $\pi = .300$ (answers will vary).
c. $\pi = .50$ (answers will vary).
d. $\pi = .80$ (answers will vary).
e. One trial may influence the next.

6.67 a. $P(X = 5) = .59049$ b. $P(X = 4) = .32805$
c. Strongly right-skewed

6.69 a. $P(X = 0) = .06250$
b. $P(X \geq 2) = 1 - .31250 = .68750$
c. $P(X \leq 2) = .68750$ d. Symmetric.

6.71 a. =BINOM.DIST(3,20,0.3,0)
b. =BINOM.DIST(7,50,0.1,0)
c. =BINOM.DIST(6,80,0.05,1)
d. =1−BINOM.DIST(29,120,0.2,1)

6.73 a. $P(X = 0) = .48398$
b. $P(X \geq 3) = 1 - P(X \leq 2) = 1 - .97166 = .02834$
c. $\mu = n\pi = (10)(.07) = 0.7$ defaults

6.75 Binomial with $n = 16$, $\pi = .8$:
a. $P(X \geq 10) = 1 - P(X \leq 9) = 1 - .02666 = .97334$.
b. $P(X < 8) = P(X \leq 7) = .00148$.

6.77 Let X = number of no shows. Then:
a. If $n = 10$ and $\pi = .10$, then $P(X = 0) = .34868$.
b. If $n = 11$ and $\pi = .10$, then $P(X \geq 1) = 1 - P(X = 0)$
$= 1 - .31381 = .68619$.
c. If they sell 11 seats, not more than 1 will be bumped.
d. If X = number who show ($\pi = .90$). Using $1 -$
BINOM.DIST(9, n, .9,1) we find that $n = 13$ will
ensure that $P(X \geq 10) \geq .95$.

6.79 a. Because calls to a fire station within a minute are
most likely all about the same fire, the calls are not
independent.
b. Answers will vary.

6.81 a. $P(X = 5) = .0872$.   b. $P(X \leq 5) = .9349$.
c. $\lambda = 14$ arrivals/5 min interval.   d. Independence.

6.83 a. $P(X = 0) = .7408$.   b. $P(X \geq 2) = .0369$.

6.85 a. Assume independent cancellations.
b. $P(X = 0) = .22313$ c. $P(X = 1) = .33470$
d. $P(X > 2) = 1 - .80885 = .19115$
e. $P(X \geq 5) = 1 - .98142 = .01858$

6.87 a. Assume independent defects with $\lambda = 2.4$.
b. $P(X = 0) = .09072$ c. $P(X = 1) = .21772$
d. $P(X \leq 1) = .30844$

6.89* $P(\text{at least one rogue wave in 5 days}) = 1 - P(X = 0) = .9892$.

6.91 a. Assume independent crashes.
b. $P(X \geq 1) = 1 - .13534 = .86466$
c. $P(X < 5) = P(X \leq 4) = .94735$
d. Skewed right.

6.93* a. $E(X) = (200)(.02) = 4$.
b. Poisson approximation: $P(X = 0) = .0183$,
binomial function: $P(X = 0) = .0176$.
c. Poisson approximation: $P(X = 1) = .0733$,
binomial function: $P(X = 1) = .0718$.
d. Yes, $n \geq 20$ and $\pi \leq .05$.

6.95* a. $E(X) = n\pi = (5708)(.00128) = 7.31$.
b. Poisson approximation: $P(X < 10) = .7977$,
$P(X > 5) = .7371$.   c. Yes, $n \geq 20$ and $\pi \leq .05$.

6.97* a. $P(X \geq 4) = 1 - P(X \leq 3) = .5182$.
b. Assume calls are independent.

6.99* a. $\mu = 1/.25 = 4$.   b. $P(X \leq 6) = .8220$.

6.101* a. $\mu = 1/\pi = 1/(.08) = 12.5$ cars
b. $P(X \leq 5) = 1 - (1 - .08)^5 = .3409$

6.103* a. $\mu = 1/\pi = 1/(.05) = 20$
b. $P(X \geq 30) = 1 - P(X \leq 29) = .2259$.

6.105* a. $(233.1)(0.4536) = 105.734$ kg
b. $(34.95)(0.4536) = 15.8533$ kg
c. Rule 1 for the μ, Rule 2 for σ.

6.107 $\mu_{X_1 + X_2} = \mu_1 + \mu_2 = 3420 + 390 = 3810$ ml,
$\sigma_{X_1 + X_2} = \sqrt{\sigma_1^2 + \sigma_2^2} = \sqrt{10^2 + 2^2} = 10.2$ ml.

6.109* Rule 1, $\mu_{vQ+F} = v\mu_Q + F = (2225)(7) + 500 = \$16,075$
Rule 2, $\sigma_{vQ+F} = v\sigma_Q = (2225)(2) = \$4,450$
Rule 1, $E(PQ) = P\mu_Q = (2850)(7) = \$19,950$
$E(TR) - E(TC) = 19,950 - 16,075 = \$3,875$

6.111* a. $\mu_{X+Y} = \$70 + \$200 = \$270$.
b. $\sigma_{X+Y} = \sqrt{10^2 + 30^2 + 2 \times 400} = \$42.43$.
c. The variance of the total is greater than either of
the individual variances.

CHAPTER 7

Note: Using Appendix C or Excel will lead to somewhat
different answers.

7.1 a. D   b. C   c. C

7.3 a. Area $= bh = (1)(.25) = .25$, so not a PDF (area is not 1).
b. Area $= bh = (4)(.25) = 1$, so could be a PDF (area is 1).
c. Area $= \frac{1}{2}bh = \frac{1}{2}(2)(2) = 2$, so not a PDF (area is
not 1).

7.5 a. $\mu = (0 + 10)/2 = 5$, $\sigma = \sqrt{\dfrac{(10 - 0)^2}{12}} = 2.886751$.

b. $\mu = (200 + 100)/2 = 150$, $\sigma = \sqrt{\dfrac{(200 - 100)^2}{12}} = 28.86751$.

c. $\mu = (1 + 99)/2 = 50$, $\sigma = \sqrt{\dfrac{(99 - 1)^2}{12}} = 28.29016$.

7.7 A point has no area in a continuous distribution so $<$
or $\leq$ yields the same result.

7.9 Means and standard deviations differ (X axis scales are
different) and so do $f(x)$ heights.

7.11 For samples from a *normal distribution* we expect about 68.26% within $\mu \pm 1\,\sigma$, about 95.44% within $\mu \pm 2\,\sigma$, and about 99.73% within $\mu \pm 3\,\sigma$.

7.13 Using Appendix C-1:
a. $P(0 < Z < 0.50) = .1915$
b. $P(-0.50 < Z < 0) = P(0 < Z < 0.50) = .1915$.
c. $P(Z > 0) = .5000$.
d. Probability of any point is 0.

7.15 Using Appendix C-2:
a. $P(Z < 2.15) - P(Z < -1.22) = .9842 - .1112 = .8730$
b. $P(Z < 2.00) - P(Z < -3.00) = .9772 - .00135 = .97585$ c. $P(Z < 2.00) = .9772$
d. Probability of any point is 0.

7.17 Using Appendix C-2:
a. $P(Z < -1.28) = .1003$.   b. $P(Z > 1.28) = .1003$.
c. $P(Z < 1.96) - P(Z < -1.96) = .975 - .025 = .95$.
d. $P(Z < 1.65) - P(Z < -1.65) = .9505 - .0485 = .902$.

7.19 $P(Z > 1.75) = .0401$, $.0401 \times 405 = 16.24$. About 16 women ran faster than Joan.

7.21 Using Appendix C-2:
a. $z = -1.555$ (the area .06 is halfway between .0606 and .0594).
b. $z = .25$ (the closest area to .6 is .5987).
c. $z = -1.48$ (closest area is .0694).

7.23 Using Appendix C-2:
a. $-0.84 < Z < 0.84$ (the closest area is .2995).
b. $z = 2.05$ (closest area is .9798).
c. $-1.96 < Z < 1.96$.

7.25 $= \text{NORM.S.INV}(.10) = -1.28$. The runners must finish 1.28 standard deviations below the mean.

7.27 a. $P(X < 300) = P(Z < 0.7143) = .7625$
b. $P(X > 250) = 1 - P(Z < -2.86) = .9979$
c. $P(275 < X < 310) = P(Z < 1.43) - P(Z < -1.07) = .9236 - .1423 = .7813$

7.29 $P(X \ge 24) = P(Z \ge 1.92) = 1 - .9726 = .0274$.

7.31 $P(X > .5) = .0062$ or 6.2%.

7.33 a. $Z = 1.282$, $X = 13.85$.   b. $X_L = 7.98$, $X_U = 12.02$
c. $Z = -0.842$, $X = 7.47$.   d. $Z = -1.282$, $X = 6.15$.

7.35 a. $P(X > x) = .05$, $z = 1.645$, $x = 124.52$ oz.
b. $P(X < x) = .50$, $z = 0$, $x = 114$ oz.
c. $P(x_L < X < x_U) = .95$, $z = \pm 1.96$, $x_L = 100.28$ oz., $x_U = 127.72$ oz.
d. $P(X < x) = .80$, $z = .842$, $x = 119.89$.

7.37 a. $Z = (8.0 - 6.9)/1.2 = 0.92$, so $P(Z < 0.92) = .8212$ (82nd percentile).
b. $Z = 1.282$, $X = 8.44$ lbs
c. $Z = \pm 1.960$, $X = 4.55$ lbs to 9.25 lbs

7.39 $P(X \le X_L) = .25$ and $P(X \ge X_U) = .25$. Solve for X_L and X_U using $z = \pm 0.67$. $X_L = 18$ and $X_U = 21$. The middle 50% of occupied beds falls between 18 and 21.

7.41 Using Appendix C-2: Use $z = 0.52$ (closest area is .6985). Solve the following for σ:
$0.52 = (\$171 - \$157)/\sigma$, $\sigma = \$26.92$.

7.43 a. NORM.DIST(110,100,15,TRUE) − NORM.DIST(80,100,15,TRUE) = .6563
b. NORM.DIST(2,0,1,TRUE) − NORM.DIST(1.5,0,1,TRUE) = .0441
c. NORM.DIST(7000,6000,1000,TRUE) − NORM.DIST(4500,6000,1000,TRUE) = .7745
d. NORM.DIST(450,600,100,TRUE) − NORM.DIST(225,600,100,TRUE) = .0667

7.45 a. $1 - \text{NORM.DIST}(60,40,28,\text{TRUE}) = 0.2375$
b. NORM.DIST(20,40,28,TRUE) = 0.2375
c. $1 - \text{NORM.DIST}(10,40,28,\text{TRUE}) = 0.8580$

7.47 Normality OK because $n\pi = (1000)(.07) = 70 \ge 10$, $n(1 - \pi) = (1000)(.93) = 930 \ge 10$. Set $\mu = n\pi = 70$ and $\sigma = \sqrt{n\pi(1 - \pi)} = 8.0684571$.
a. $P(X < 50) = P(Z < -2.54) = .0055$ (using $X = 49.5$)
b. $P(X > 100) = P(Z > 3.78) = 1 - P(Z \le 3.78) = 1 - .99992 = .00008$ (using $X = 100.5$)

7.49 Normality OK. Set $\mu = 180$, $\sigma = 4.242641$.
a. $P(X \ge 175) = P(Z \ge -1.30) = 1 - P(Z \le 1.30) = 1 - .0968 = .9032$ (using $X = 174.5$)
b. $P(X < 190) = P(Z \le 2.24) = .9875$ (using $X = 189.5$)

7.51 Set $\mu = \lambda = 28$ and $\sigma = \sqrt{28} = 5.2915$.
a. $P(X > 35) = 1 - P(Z \le 1.42) = 1 - .9222 = .0788$ (using $X = 35.5$)
b. $P(X < 25) = P(Z \le -0.66) = .2546$ (using $X = 24.5$)
c. $\lambda = 28 \ge 10$, so OK to use normal.
d. .0823 and .2599. Yes, it is good.

7.53 a. $P(X > 7) = e^{-\lambda x} = e^{-(0.3)(7)} = e^{-2.1} = .1225$
b. $P(X < 2) = 1 - e^{-\lambda x} = 1 - e^{-(0.3)(2)} = 1 - e^{-0.6} = 1 - .5488 = .4512$

7.55 $\lambda = 2.1$ alarms/minute or $\lambda = .035$ alarm/second
a. $P(X < 60$ seconds$) = 1 - e^{-\lambda x} = 1 - e^{(-0.035)(60)} = 1 - .1225 = .8775$
b. $P(X > 30$ seconds$) = e^{-\lambda x} = e^{(-0.035)(30)} = .3499$
c. $P(X > 45$ seconds$) = e^{-\lambda x} = e^{(-0.035)(45)} = .2070$

7.57 a. $P(X > 30$ sec$) = .2466$.   b. $P(X \le 15$ sec$) = .5034$.
c. $P(X > 1$ min$) = .0608$.

7.59 $\lambda = 4.2$ orders/hour or $\lambda = .07$ order/minute.
a. Set $e^{-\lambda x} = .50$, take logs, $x = 0.165035$ hr (9.9 min).
b. Set $e^{-\lambda x} = .25$, take logs, $x = 0.33007$ hr (19.8 min).
c. Set $e^{-\lambda x} = .10$, take logs, $x = 0.548235$ hr (32.89 min).

7.61 MTBE = 20 min/order so $\lambda = 1/\text{MTBE} = 1/20$ order/min.
a. Set $e^{-\lambda x} = .50$, take logs, $x = 13.86$ min.
b. Distribution is very right-skewed.
c. Set $e^{-\lambda x} = .25$, take logs, $x = 27.7$ min.

7.63 a. $\mu = (0 + 25 + 75)/3 = 33.3333$
b.
$$\sigma = \sqrt{\frac{0^2 + 75^2 + 25^2 - (0)(75) - (0)(25) - (75)(25)}{18}}$$
$= 15.5902$
c. $P(X < 25) = (25 - 0)^2/((75 - 0)*(25 - 0)) = .3333$
d. Shaded area represents the probability.

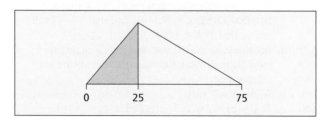

7.65 a. D   b. C   c. C

7.67 a. $\mu = (25 + 65)/2 = 45$ b. $\sigma = 11.54701$
c. $P(X > 45) = (65 - 45)/(65 - 25) = 0.5$
d. $P(X > 55) = (65 - 55)/(65 - 25) = 0.25$
e. $P(30 < X < 60) = (60 - 30)/(65 - 25) = 0.75$

7.69 a. Right-skewed (zero low bound, high outliers likely).
b. Right-skewed (zero low bound, high outliers likely).
c. Normal.   d. Normal.

7.71 a. =NORM.S.DIST(1,1) = .8413, 84th percentile.
b. =NORM.S.DIST(2.571) = .9949, 99th percentile.
c. =NORM.S.DIST(-1.7141) = .0433, 4th percentile.

7.73 a. =NORM.INV(0.5,450,80) = 450
b. =NORM.INV(0.25,450,80) = 396.04
c. =NORM.INV(.1,450,80) = 347.48,
=NORM.INV(.9,450,80) = 552.52
d. =NORM.INV(0.05,450,80) = 318.42

7.75 a. Q_1 = \$6.77   b. Q_2 = \$7.00
c. 90th percentile = \$7.45

7.77 a. =1$-$NORM.DIST(130,115,20,TRUE) = .2266
b. =NORM.DIST(100,115,20,TRUE) = .2266
c. =NORM.DIST(91,115,20,TRUE) = .1151

7.79 a. $P(28 < X < 32) = P(X < 32) - P(X < 28) = .8413 - .1587 = .6826$
b. $P(X < 28) = .1587$
c. 75% of 30 is 22.5, so $P(X < 22.5) = P(Z < -3.75) = .00009$

7.81 $P(1.975 < X < 2.095) = P(-2.00 < Z < +2.00) = .9544$, so 4.56% will not meet specs.

7.83 Using Appendix C-2: $P(X \geq 230) = P(Z \geq 1.64) = .0505$.

7.85 $P(X \leq 90)$ = NORM.DIST(90,84,10,TRUE) = .7257.

7.87 a. $P(X > 5200) = 1 -$ NORM.DIST(5200,4905,355, TRUE) = 0.2030

7.89 a. 5.3% below John.   b. 69.2% below Mary.
c. 96.3% below Zak.   d. 99.3% below Frieda.

7.91* Probability of making it to the airport in 54 minutes or less is .5000 for A and .0228 for B, so use route A. Probability of making it to the airport in 60 minutes or less is .8413 for A and .5000 for B, so use route A. Probability of making it to the airport in 66 minutes or less is the same for routes A and B.
a. $P(X < 54)$ *Route A*: =NORM.DIST(54,54,6,TRUE) = .5000
    Route B: =NORM.DIST(54,60,3,TRUE) = .0228
b. $P(X < 60)$ *Route A*: =NORM.DIST(60,54,6,TRUE) = .8413
    Route B: =NORM.DIST(60,60,3,TRUE) = .5000
c. $P(X < 66)$ *Route A*: =NORM.DIST(66,54,6,TRUE) = .9772
    Route B: =NORM.DIST(66,60,3,TRUE) = .9772

7.93 =NORM.S.INV(.20) = -0.842, so $x = \mu + z\sigma = 12.5 + (-0.842)(1.2) = 11.49$ inches

7.95 For any normal distribution, $P(X > \mu) = .5$ or $P(X < \mu) = .5$. Assuming independent events:
a. Probability that both exceed the mean is $(.5)(.5) = .25$
b. Probability that both are less than the mean is $(.5)(.5) = .25$
c. Probability that one is above and one is less than the mean is $(.5)(.5) = .25$ but there are two combinations that yield this, so the likelihood is: $.25 + .25 = .50$.
d. $P(X = \mu) = 0$ for any continuous random variable.

7.97 Normality OK because $n\pi \geq 10$ and $n(1 - \pi) \geq 10$. Set $\mu = n\pi = (.25)(100) = 25$ and σ = SQRT(.25*100*(1 - .25)) = 4.3301. Then $P(X < 19.5)$ = NORM.DIST(19.5,25,4.3301,1) = .1020.

7.99 Set $\mu = n\pi = (.25)(100) = 25$ and σ = SQRT(.25*100*(1 - .25)) = 4.3301.
a. z = NORM.S.INV(.95) = 1.645 so $x = \mu + z\sigma = 25 + 1.645(4.3301) = 32.12$

b. z = NORM.S.INV(.99) = 2.326 so $x = \mu + z\sigma = 25 + 2.326(4.3301) = 35.07$
c. Q1 = NORM.INV(0.25,25,4.3301) = 22.08
Q2 = NORM.INV(0.5,25,4.3301) = 25.00
Q3 = NORM.INV(0.75,25,4.3301) = 27.92

7.101 Set $\mu = n\pi = (.02)(1500) = 30$ and σ = SQRT(.02* 1500*(1 $-$ .02)) = 5.4222. Then
a. $P(X > 24.5) = 1 - P(X < 24.5) = 1-$NORM.DIST(24.5,30,5.4222,1) = .8448
b. $P(X > 40.5) = 1 - P(X < 40.5) = 1-$NORM.DIST(40.5,30,5.4222,1) = .0264

7.103 a. $P(X > 100,000$ hrs.) = .2397.
b. $P(X \leq 50,000$ hrs.) = .5105.
c. $P(50,000 \leq X \leq 80,000) = .6811 - .5105 = .1706$.

7.105 a. $P(X \leq 3$ min) = .6321.
b. The distribution is skewed right so the mean is greater than the median.

7.107* a. $\mu = (300 + 350 + 490)/3 = 380$
b.
$$\sigma = \sqrt{\frac{300^2 + 350^2 + 490^2 - (300)(350) - (300)(490) - (350)(490)}{18}}$$
$= 40.21$
c. $P(X > 400) = (490 - 400)^2/((490 - 300)(490 - 350)) = .3045$

7.109* a. $\mu = (500 + 700 + 2100)/3 = 1100$
b.
$$\sigma = \sqrt{\frac{500^2 + 700^2 + 2100^2 - (500)(700) - (500)(2100) - (700)(2100)}{18}}$$
$= 355.90$
c. $P(X > 750) = (2100 - 750)^2/((2100 - 500)(2100 - 700)) = .8136$
d. Shaded area represents the probability.

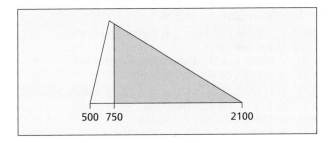

CHAPTER 8

8.1 a. 16   b. 8   c. 4
8.3 a. (96.71, 103.29).
b. (1917.75, 2082.25).
c. (496.71, 503.29).
8.5 a. (4.0252, 4.0448).
b. (4.0330, 4.0370).
c. Both are outside expected range.
8.7 a. $\sigma_{\bar{x}} = \sigma/\sqrt{n} = 0.25/\sqrt{10} = 0.0791$.
b. (3.345, 3.655).
8.9 a. (11.06, 16.94).
b. (33.68, 40.33).
c. (115.12, 126.88).
8.11 a. (2.3177, 2.4823).
b. (2.302, 2.498).
c. (2.2712, 2.5288).

8.13 a. (254.32, 285.68).   b. (258.91, 281.09).
c. (262.16, 277.84).   d. Width decreases as n increases.
8.15 (20.225, 21.775).
8.17 (0.27278, 0.27342).
8.19 a. 2.262, 2.2622.   b. 2.602, 2.6025.
c. 1.678, 1.6779.
8.21 a. $d.f. = 9$, $t = 2.262$, (255.6939, 284.3061).
b. $d.f. = 19$, $t = 2.093$, (260.6398, 279.3602).
c. $d.f. = 39$, $t = 2.023$, (263.6027, 276.3973).
d. Width decreases.
8.23 a. (33.01, 58.31).   b. Increase n or decrease 95%.
8.25 a. (742.20, 882.80).
8.27 a. (81.87, 88.13) for Exam 1, (82.79, 94.41) for Exam 2, (73.34, 78.66) for Exam 3.
b. Exams 1 and 2 overlap.   c. Unknown σ.
8.29 a. Yes   b. Yes   c. No, $.08 \times 100 = 8 < 10$.
8.31 a. .062   b. .0877   c. .1216
8.33 a. (.2556, .4752).   b. Yes, normal.
8.35 a. (.013, .083).   b. Yes, normal.
8.37 a. (.1416, .3290).   b. Yes, normal.
8.39 a. (47.518, 52.482).   b. (47.042, 52.958).
c. (46.113, 53.887).
8.41 (.4575, .5225).
8.43 25
8.45 a. $\sigma = R/6 = 16.67$.   b. 43
8.47 385
8.49 a. $\sigma = R/6 (21 - 16)/6 = 0.833$ b. 31
8.51 a. 1692   b. Stratify (e.g., income)
8.53 a. 2401   b. Stratify (e.g., age)
8.55 a. 125   b. Conduct inspection of a sample of 125. AA fleet size is much larger.
8.57 (1.01338, 1.94627).
8.59 (5.88, 10.91).
8.61 a. Uneven wear.   b. (0.8332, 0.8355).
c. Normality.   d. 95
8.63 a. (29.443, 39.634).   b. Varying methods.
c. Raisin clumps.
8.65 a. FCPF = .9333. b. No, $n^* 20 = 500 > 187$.
8.67 a. (19.245, 20.69).   b. Small n.
8.69 a. (33.013, 58.315). Using the FPCF (34.0690, 57.2590).
b. 119   c.* (21. 26, 40.14).
8.71 a. (29.078, 29.982).   b. 116
8.73 (4.38, 6.80), $\chi_L^2 = 17.71$, $\chi_U^2 = 42.56$
8.75 a. (48.515, 56.965).   b. Outliers   c. 75
8.77 a. (.125, .255).   b. Yes   c. 463
8.79 136
8.81 a. (.258, .322).   b. Yes
8.83 (.595, .733).
8.85 a. Margin of error = .035 for 95% CI.   b. Greater
8.87 a. (.393, .527).   b. Yes
8.89 a. No   b. (.0044, .0405).
8.91 .04 for 95% CI.
8.93 a. 385   b. n would increase to 1537.

CHAPTER 9

9.1 a. 50   b. 10   c. 1
9.3 a. H_0: Employee not using drugs.
H_1: Employee is using drugs.
b. Type I error: Test positive for drugs when not using.
Type II error: Test negative for drugs when using.

c. Employees fear Type I, while employers fear both for legal reasons.
9.5 False negative: Brakes are OK when they are not. Consequences can be dangerous such as a car wreck.
9.7 H_0: $\mu = 2.5$ mg vs. H_1: $\mu \neq 2.5$ mg.
9.9 H_0: $\mu \leq 4$ min vs. H_1: $\mu > 4$ min.
9.11 a. Reject in lower tail.   b. Reject in both tails.
c. Reject in upper tail.
9.13 a. $z_{calc} = 2.98$.   b. $z_{calc} = -1.58$.   c. $z_{calc} = 2.22$.
9.15 a. $z_{.025} = \pm 1.96$.   b. $z_{.10} = 1.2816$.
c. $z_{.01} = -2.3264$.
9.17 a. H_0: $\mu \leq 3.5$ mg vs. H_1: $\mu > 3.5$ mg.
b. $z_{calc} = 2.50$.
c. Yes, $z_{crit} = 2.33$ and $2.50 > 2.33$.
d. p-value = .0062.
9.19 a. $z = 1.50$, p-value = .1336.
b. $z = -2.0$, p-value = .0228.
c. $z = 3.75$, p-value = .0001.
9.21 p-value = .0062. The mean weight is heavier than it should be.
9.23 a. Reject H_0 if $z > 1.96$ or $z < -1.96$.
b. $z = 0.78$. Fail to reject H_0.
9.25 $z = 3.26$, p-value = .0006.
9.27 H_0: $\mu = 1.967$ vs. H_1: $\mu \neq 1.967$, $t_{calc} = -1.80$, p-value = .0719. Fail to reject H_0.
9.29 a. Using $d.f. = 20$, $t_{.05} = \pm 1.725$.
b. Using $d.f. = 8$, $t_{.01} = 2.896$.
c. Using $d.f. = 27$, $t_{.05} = -1.703$.
9.31 a. $t_{calc} = -3.33$.   b. $t_{calc} = -1.67$.
c. $t_{calc} = 2.02$.
9.33 a. p-value = .0836.
b. p-value = .0316.
c. p-value = .0391.
9.35 a. $t = 1.5$, p-value = .1544.
b. $t = -2.0$, p-value = .0285.
c. $t = 3.75$, p-value = .0003.
9.37 a. H_0: $\mu \geq 400$ vs. H_1: $\mu < 400$. Reject H_0 if $t_{calc} < -1.476$. $t_{calc} = -1.977$ therefore reject H_0.
b. Yes decision close at $\alpha = .05$ c. p-value = .0525.
d. Could be important to a contractor.
9.39 a. H_0: $\mu \geq \$216$ vs. H_1: $\mu < \$216$. Reject H_0 if $t_{calc} < -1.729$. $t_{calc} = -2.408$ so reject H_0.
b. p-value = .0132.
9.41 H_0: $\mu \geq 1.6$ vs. H_1: $\mu > 1.6$, $t_{calc} = 1.14$, p-value = .1306. Fail to reject H_0.
9.43 a. p-value = .1079. Fail to reject H_0.
b. (3.226, 3.474) includes 3.25.
9.45 a. $z = 2.0$, p-value = .046.
b. $z = 1.90$, p-value = .029.
c. $z = 1.14$, p-value = .127.
9.47 a. No.   b. No.   c. Yes.
9.49 a. H_0: $\pi \geq .997$ versus H_1: $\pi < .997$. Reject H_0 if the p-value is less than 0.05.
b. Yes.
c. Type I error: Throw away a good syringe.
Type II error: Keep a bad syringe.
d. p-value = .1401 ($z = -1.08$)
9.51 a. H_0: $\pi \geq .50$ versus H_1: $\pi < 0.50$. If the p-value is less than .05, reject H_0.
b. p-value = .0228.
c. Yes, cost could be high if call volume is large.

9.53 p-value ≈ 0. More than half support the ban.
9.55 a. p-value $= .143$. Standard is being met.
　　　b. Less than five defects observed, cannot assume normality.
9.57 a. .4622　b. .7974　c. .9459
9.59 a. .0924　b. .3721　c. .7497
9.61 No, p-value $= .2233$
9.63 p-value $= .0465$. Reject H_0.
9.65 p-value $= .6202$. Fail to reject H_0.
9.67 a. P(Type I error) $= 0$.
　　　b. You increase the P(Type II error).
9.69 a. H_0: User is authorized.
　　　　H_1: User is unauthorized.
　　　b. Type I error: Scanner fails to admit an authorized user. Type II error: Scanner admits an unauthorized user.
　　　c. Type II is feared by the public.
9.71 H_0: $\pi \le .02$ vs. H_1: $\pi > .02$.
9.73 P(Type I error) $= 0$.
9.75 a. Type I: deny access to authorized user, Type II: allow access to an unauthorized user.
　　　b. The consequences of a false rejection are less serious than a false authorization.
9.77 a. H_0: $\mu \le 20$ min vs. H_1: $\mu > 20$ min.
　　　b. $t_{calc} = 2.545$.
　　　c. Yes. Using $d.f. = 14$, $t_{.05} = 1.761$, $2.545 > 1.761$.
　　　d. p-value $= .0117 < .05$. Yes.
9.79 a. A two-tailed test.
　　　b. Overfill is unnecessary while underfill is illegal.
　　　c. Normal (known σ).
　　　d. Reject if $z > 2.576$ or if $z < -2.576$.
9.81 a. H_0: $\mu \ge 90$
　　　　H_1: $\mu < 90$
　　　b. $t_{crit} =$ T.INV(.01,7) $= -2.998$.
　　　c. $t = -0.92$. Fail to reject H_0.
　　　d. At least a symmetric population.
　　　e. p-value $= .1936$.
9.83 a. H_0: $\mu \ge 2.268$
　　　　H_1: $\mu < 2.268$
　　　　If the p-value is less than .05, reject H_0.
　　　　p-value $= .0478$. Reject H_0.
　　　b. Usage wears them down.
9.85 p-value $= .0228$. Reject H_0.
9.87 p-value $= .0258$. Fail to reject (close decision) H_0.
9.89 H_0: $\pi \le .1$ vs. H_1: $\pi > .1$, $z_{calc} = 0.8819$. $0.8819 < 1.645$ (z_{crit}); therefore, fail to reject H_0.
　　　b. p-value $= .1889$.
9.91 p-value $= .0192$. Reject H_0. Important to players and universities.
9.93 p-value $= .0017$. Reject H_0.
9.95 a. Yes, $z = 1.95$, p-value $= .0253$.
　　　b. Yes.
9.99 p-value $= .0794$. Fail to reject H_0.
9.101 H_0: $\pi = .50$ vs. H_1: $\pi > .50$. $P(X \ge 10 \mid n = 16, \pi = .5) = .2272$. Fail to reject H_0.
9.103 a. $(0, .0125)$
　　　b. $np < 10$.
　　　c. Goal is being achieved.
9.105 $\beta = 1 -$ power. The power values are:
　　　$n = 4$: .2085, .5087, .8038, .9543
　　　$n = 16$: .5087, .9543, .9996, 1.0000

9.107 a. H_0: $\mu \le 106$ vs. H_1: $\mu > 106$. $t_{calc} = 130.95$; so reject the null hypothesis.
　　　b. H_0: $\sigma^2 \ge .0025$ vs. H_1: $\sigma^2 < .0025$. $\chi^2 = 12.77$; therefore, we would fail to reject the null hypothesis.

CHAPTER 10

Note: Results from Excel except as noted (may not agree with Appendix C, D, or E due to rounding or use of exact $d.f.$).

10.1 a. H_0: $\mu_1 - \mu_2 \ge 0$ vs. H_1: $\mu_1 - \mu_2 < 0$, $t = -2.148$, $d.f. = 28$, $t_{.025} = -2.048$, p-value $= .0202$, so reject H_0.
　　　b. H_0: $\mu_1 - \mu_2 = 0$ vs. H_1: $\mu_1 - \mu_2 \ne 0$, $t = -1.595$, $d.f. = 39$, $t_{.05} = \pm2.023$, p-value $= .1188$, so can't reject H_0.
　　　c. H_0: $\mu_1 - \mu_2 \le 0$ vs. H_1: $\mu_1 - \mu_2 > 0$, $t = 1.935$, $d.f. = 27$, $t_{.05} = 1.703$, p-value $= .0318$, so reject H_0.
10.3 a. H_0: $\mu_1 - \mu_2 = 0$ vs. H_1: $\mu_1 - \mu_2 \ne 0$. Using $d.f. = 190$, $t_{.005} = 2.602$. $t_{calc} = -6.184 < -2.602$. Reject H_0.
　　　b. Using $d.f. = 190$, p-value $= 3.713$E-09.
10.5 a. H_0: $\mu_1 - \mu_2 \le 0$ vs. H_1: $\mu_1 - \mu_2 > 0$, $t = 1.902$, $d.f. = 29$, $t_{.01} = 2.462$, can't reject H_0.
　　　b. p-value $= .0336$. Would be significant at $\alpha = .05$.
10.7 H_0: $\mu_1 - \mu_2 = 0$ vs. H_1: $\mu_1 - \mu_2 \ne 0$. $t = -3.55$, $d.f. = 11$, p-value $= .0045$. Reject H_0.
10.9 H_0: $\mu_S - \mu_F \ge 0$ vs. H_1: $\mu_S - \mu_F < 0$, $t_{calc} = -1.813$, p-value $= .0424 > .05$. Reject H_0.
10.11 a. $(-1.16302, 0.80302)$.
　　　b. $(-1.15081, 0.79081)$.
　　　c. Assumptions did not change conclusion.
　　　d. μ_1: $(7.95, 9.33)$, μ_2: $(8.10, 9.54)$.
10.13 H_0: $\mu_d \le 0$, H_1: $\mu_d > 0$, $t = 1.93$, $d.f. = 6$, and p-value $= .0509$, so can't quite reject H_0 at $\alpha = .05$.
10.15 H_0: $\mu_d \le 0$, H_1: $\mu_d > 0$, $t = 2.86$, $d.f. = 9$, and p-value $= .0094$, so reject H_0 at $\alpha = .10$.
10.17 H_0: $\mu_d \ge 0.5$ vs. H_1: $\mu_d < 0.5$, $t_{calc} = 1.821$, p-value $= .9597 > .05$. Fail to reject H_0.
10.19 H_0: $\mu_d = 0$, H_1: $\mu_d \ne 0$, $t = -1.71$, $d.f. = 7$, and p-value $= .1307$, so can't reject H_0 at $\alpha = .01$.
10.21 a. $z_{calc} = -1.310$, p-value $= .0951$.
　　　b. $z_{calc} = 1.787$, p-value $= .0370$.
　　　c. $z_{calc} = 1.577$, p-value $= .1149$.
10.23 a. H_0: $\pi_1 - \pi_2 \ge 0$ vs. H_1: $\pi_1 - \pi_2 < 0$, $\bar{p} = .4200$, $z = -2.431$, $z_{.01} = -2.326$, p-value $= .0075$, so reject at $\alpha = .01$.
　　　b. H_0: $\pi_1 - \pi_2 = 0$ vs. H_1: $\pi_1 - \pi_2 \ne 0$, $\bar{p} = .37500$, $z = 2.263$, $z_{.05} = \pm1.645$, p-value $= .0237$, reject at $\alpha = .10$.
　　　c. H_0: $\pi_1 - \pi_2 \ge 0$ vs. H_1: $\pi_1 - \pi_2 < 0$, $\bar{p} = .25806$, $z = -1.706$, $z_{.05} = -1.645$, p-value $= .0440$, reject at $\alpha = .05$.
10.25 a. H_0: $\pi_1 - \pi_2 \ge 0$ vs. H_1: $\pi_1 - \pi_2 < 0$, $\bar{p} = .26000$, $z = -2.280$.
　　　b. $z_{.01} = -2.326$, can't reject at $\alpha = .01$ (close decision).
　　　c. p-value $= .0113$
　　　d. Normality OK because $n_1 p_1 = 42$, $n_2 p_2 = 62$, both exceed 10.
10.27 H_0: $\pi_1 - \pi_2 = 0$ vs. H_1: $\pi_1 - \pi_2 \ne 0$, $\bar{p} = .11$, $z = 2.021$, $z_{.025} = \pm1.960$ ($p = .0432$) so reject at $\alpha = .05$ (close decision).

10.29 a. $H_0: \pi_1 - \pi_2 = 0$ vs. $H_1: \pi_1 - \pi_2 \neq 0$, $p_1 = .07778$, $p_2 = .10448$, $\bar{p} = .08502$, $z = -0.669$, critical value is $z_{.025} = 1.960$, and p-value $= .5036$, so cannot reject at $\alpha = .05$.

b. Normality not OK because $n_1 p_1 = 14$ but $n_2 p_2 = 7$.

10.31 a. $H_0: \pi_1 - \pi_2 \leq .10$, $H_1: \pi_1 - \pi_2 > .10$, $p_1 = .28125$, $p_2 = .14583$, $\bar{p} = .22321$, $z = 0.66$, and critical value is $z_{.05} = 1.645$.

b. p-value $= .2546$, cannot reject at $\alpha = .05$

10.33 $(-.1584, .1184)$.

10.35 $(.0063, .1937)$.

10.37 a. $H_0: \sigma_1^2 = \sigma_2^2$ versus $\sigma_1^2 \neq \sigma_2^2$. Reject H_0 if $F > 4.76$ or $F < .253$. ($df_1 = 10$, $df_2 = 7$.) $F = 2.54$ so we fail to reject the null hypothesis.

b. $H_0: \sigma_1^2 = \sigma_2^2$ versus $\sigma_1^2 < \sigma_2^2$. Reject H_0 if $F < .264$ ($df_1 = 7$, $df_2 = 7$). $F = .247$ so we reject the null hypothesis.

c. $H_0: \sigma_1^2 = \sigma_2^2$ versus $\sigma_1^2 > \sigma_2^2$. Reject H_0 if $F > 2.80$ ($df_1 = 9$, $df_2 = 12$). $F = 19.95$ so we reject the null hypothesis.

10.39 $H_0: \sigma_1^2 = \sigma_2^2$ versus $\sigma_1^2 < \sigma_2^2$. Reject H_0 if $F < .355$ ($df_1 = 11$, $df_2 = 11$). $F = .103$ so we reject the null hypothesis. The new drill has a reduced variance.

10.41 a. $H_0: \pi_M - \pi_W = 0$ vs. $H_1: \pi_M - \pi_W \neq 0$. Reject the null hypothesis if $z < -1.645$ or $z > 1.645$.

b. $p_M = .60$ and $p_W = .6875$.

c. $z = -.69$, p-value $= .492$. The sample does not show a significant difference in proportions.

d. Normality can be assumed because both $n_1 p_1 \geq 10$ and $n_2 p_2 \geq 10$.

10.43 a. $H_0: \pi_1 - \pi_2 \leq 0$ vs. $H_1: \pi_1 - \pi_2 > 0$.

b. Reject if $z > z_{.05} = 1.645$.

c. $p_1 = .98000$, $p_2 = .93514$, $\bar{p} = .95912$, $z = 4.507$.

d. Reject at $\alpha = .05$.   e. p-value $= .0000$.

f. Normality is OK because $n_1(1 - \pi_1) = 17$ and $n_2(1 - \pi_2) = 48$, both > 10.

10.45 a. $H_0: \pi_1 - \pi_2 = 0$ vs. $H_1: \pi_1 - \pi_2 \neq 0$.

b. $p_1 = .17822$, $p_2 = .14300$, $\bar{p} = .14895$, $z = 1.282$, p-value $= .2000$. Because z is within ± 1.960 for a two-tail test at $\alpha = .05$ and p-value exceeds $.05$, we fail to reject H_0.

10.47 a. $H_0: \pi_1 - \pi_2 = 0$ vs. $H_1: \pi_1 - \pi_2 \neq 0$, $p_1 = .38492$, $p_2 = .48830$, $\bar{p} = .44444$, $z = -2.506$. Because z does not exceed ± 2.576, we cannot reject H_0.

b. Two-tailed p-value $= .0122$.

c. Normality OK because $n_1 p_1 = 97$, $n_2 p_2 = 167$ both exceed 10.

d. Gender interests may imply different marketing strategies.

10.49 a. $H_0: \pi_1 - \pi_2 \geq 0$ vs. $H_1: \pi_1 - \pi_2 < 0$, $p_1 = .14914$, $p_2 = .57143$, $\bar{p} = .21086$, $z = -8.003$. Because $z < -2.326$, we conclude that pilots are more likely to approve of night-flying without non-instrument rating.

b. Left-tailed p-value $= .0000$.

c. Normality assumption OK because $n_1 p_1 = 61$, $n_2(1 - p_2) = 30$ both exceed 10.

10.51 $H_0: \mu_B - \mu_A \geq 0$ vs. $H_1: \mu_B - \mu_A < 0$, $t_{calc} = -1.581$, p-value $= .0607 > .05$. Fail to reject H_0.

10.53 a. $H_0: \pi_1 - \pi_2 \geq 0$ vs. $H_1: \pi_1 - \pi_2 < 0$. Reject the null hypothesis if $z < -1.645$ or p-value $< .05$. p-value $= .0914$, fail to reject H_0.

b. Yes, normality is met.

10.55 a. $H_0: \mu_1 - \mu_2 \leq 0$ vs. $H_1: \mu_1 - \mu_2 > 0$. Assuming equal variances, $t = 4.089$ with $d.f. = 84$. Because the p-value is $.0000$, reject H_0 at $\alpha = .01$.

10.57 a. $H_0: \pi_1 - \pi_2 \geq 0$ vs. $H_1: \pi_1 - \pi_2 < 0$, $p_1 = .1402$, $p_2 = .2000$, $\bar{p} = .16396$.

b. $z = -2.777$ and left-tailed p-value $= .0027$. Because $z < -2.326$, reject H_0.

c. Normality OK because $n_1 p_1 = 104$, $n_2 p_2 = 98$ both exceed 10.

d. Many people can't afford them or lack insurance to pay for them.

10.59 a. $H_0: \mu_1 - \mu_2 \leq 0$ vs. $H_1: \mu_1 - \mu_2 > 0$. Assuming unequal variances, $t = 1.718$ with $d.f. = 16$ (using Welch's adjustment). Because the p-value is $.0525$, we fail to reject H_0 at $\alpha = .05$.

b. If we had looked at the same firm in each year, the test would have more power.

10.61 a. Dot plots suggest that the new bumper has less downtime, but variation is similar.

b. $H_0: \mu_1 - \mu_2 \leq 0$ vs. $H_1: \mu_1 - \mu_2 > 0$.

c. Assuming equal variances, reject H_0 if $t < -1.729$ with $d.f. = 19$.

d. $\bar{x}_1 = 5.917$, $s_1 = 3.423$, $\bar{x}_2 = 8.889$, $s_2 = 4.961$, $s_p^2 = 17.148$, $t = -1.63$, p-value $= .0600$, so fail to reject H_0 at $\alpha = .05$.

10.63 a. $H_0: \mu_1 - \mu_2 \leq 0$ vs. $H_1: \mu_1 - \mu_2 > 0$, $t = 7.08$, $d.f. = 28$, p-value ≈ 0. Reject H_0.

b. $H_0: \sigma_1^2 = \sigma_2^2$ versus $\sigma_1^2 \neq \sigma_2^2$. Reject H_0 if $F < .3357$ or $F > 2.9786$ ($df_1 = 14$, $df_2 = 14$). $F = 2.778$ so we fail to reject the null hypothesis.

10.65 a. $H_0: \mu_1 - \mu_2 \leq 0$ vs. $H_1: \mu_1 - \mu_2 > 0$.

b. Reject H_0 if $t > 2.438$ with $d.f. = 35$.

c. $\bar{x}_1 = 117,853$, $s_1 = 10,115$, $\bar{x}_2 = 98,554$, $s_2 = 14,541$, $s_p^2 = 152,192,286$, $t = 4.742$.

d. Reject H_0 at $\alpha = .01$. Men are paid significantly more.

e. p-value $= .0000$. Unlikely result if H_0 is true.

10.67 a. Dot plots show strong skewness, but means could be similar.

b. $H_0: \mu_1 - \mu_2 = 0$ vs. $H_1: \mu_1 - \mu_2 \neq 0$. Assume equal variances.

c. Reject H_0 if $t > 2.663$ or if $t < -2.663$ with $d.f. = 58$.

d. $\bar{x}_1 = 50.333$, $s_1 = 81.684$, $\bar{x}_2 = 50.000$, $s_2 = 71.631$, $s_p^2 = 5{,}901.667$. Because $t = .017$ we cannot reject H_0.

e. p-value $= .9866$. Sample result well within chance range.

10.69 a. $H_0: \mu_1 - \mu_2 = 0$ vs. $H_1: \mu_1 - \mu_2 \neq 0$.

b. For equal variances, $d.f. = 55$, reject H_0 if $t < -2.004$.

c. Because $t = -3.162$ ($p = .0025$) we reject H_0 at $\alpha = .05$. Mean sales are lower on the east side.

10.71 $H_0: \sigma_1^2 = \sigma_2^2$, $H_1: \sigma_1^2 \neq \sigma_2^2$, $df_1 = 30$, $df_2 = 29$. For $\alpha/2 = .025$, $F_R = F_{30,29} = 2.09$, and $F_L = 1/F_{29,30} \cong 1/F_{25,30} = 1/2.12 = .48$. Test statistic is $F = (13.482)^2/(15.427)^2 = 0.76$, so we can't reject H_0.

10.73 $H_0: \mu_d = 0$ vs. $H_1: \mu_d \neq 0$. $t = -0.87$. p-value $= .4154$ (from MegaStat). Fail to reject the null hypothesis.

10.75 a. $H_0: \mu_1 - \mu_2 = 0$ vs. $H_1: \mu_1 - \mu_2 \neq 0$, $t = -1.10$, $d.f. = 22$, p-value $= .2839$. Fail to reject H_0.

b. $H_0: \sigma_1^2 = \sigma_2^2$ versus $\sigma_1^2 \neq \sigma_2^2$. Reject H_0 if $F < 0.188$ or $F > 5.3197$ ($df_1 = 11$, $df_2 = 11$). $F = 2.59$ so we fail to reject the null hypothesis.

10.77 a. $H_0: \sigma_1^2 \leq \sigma_2^2$, $H_1: \sigma_1^2 > \sigma_2^2$, $df_1 = 11$, $df_2 = 11$. For a right-tail test at $\alpha = .025$, Appendix F gives $F_R = F_{11,11} \cong F_{10,11} = 3.53$. The test statistic is $F = (2.9386)^2/(0.9359)^2 = 9.86$, so conclude that Portfolio A has a greater variance than Portfolio B.

b. These are independent samples. $H_0: \mu_1 - \mu_2 = 0$ vs. $H_1: \mu_1 - \mu_2 \neq 0$. $\bar{x}_1 = 8.5358$, $s_1 = 2.9386$, $\bar{x}_2 = 8.1000$, $s_2 = .9359$. Assuming unequal variances with $d.f. = 13$ (with Welch's adjustment) we get $t = 0.49$ with p-value $= .6326$, so we cannot reject H_0 at $\alpha = .025$.

10.79 $(-.0153, .2553)$. Yes, the interval includes zero.

10.81 a. $(-2.51, 0.11)$.   b. No.

10.83 a. $(-.4431, -.0569)$.   b. Normality is not met.

10.85 a. $H_0: \mu_M - \mu_F \leq 0$ vs. $H_1: \mu_M - \mu_F > 0$.

b. $t_{calc} = 2.616$.

c. Reject H_0 if $t_{calc} > 2.896$.

d. p-value $= .0094 < .01$. Reject H_0.

e. $F_{calc} = 7.169$, p-value $= .0047$. Assume unequal variances.

CHAPTER 11

11.1 a. 40.

b. 5.

c. $H_0: \mu_1 = \mu_2 = \mu_3 = \mu_4 = \mu_5$ vs. H_1: At least one mean is different.

d. $F_{crit} = 2.6415$.   e. $F_{calc} = 1.80$.

f. Fail to reject H_0.

11.3 a. $H_0: \mu_1 = \mu_2 = \mu_3 = \mu_4 = \mu_5$ vs. H_1: At least one mean is different.

b. $df_1 = 4$, $df_2 = 25$.

c. $F_{crit} = 2.18$.

d. Reject H_0.

e. p-value $=$ F.DIST.RT(2.447,4,25) $= .0726$

11.5 a. $H_0: \mu_A = \mu_B = \mu_C$, H_1: Not all means are equal.

b. One-factor, $F = 5.31$, p-value $= .0223$.

c. Reject H_0 at $\alpha = .05$.

d. Plant B mean likely higher, Plant C lower.

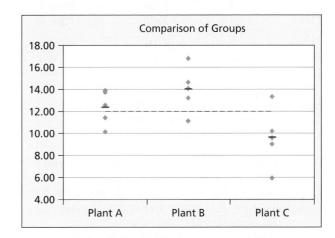

11.7 a. $H_0: \mu_1 = \mu_2 = \mu_3 = \mu_4$, H_1: Not all equal.

b. One-factor $F = 3.52$, p-value $= .0304$.

c. Reject H_0 at $\alpha = .05$. GPAs not the same.

d. Marketing and HR likely higher, accounting and finance lower.

11.9 a. 6.

b. $c = 4$, $n - c = 30$.

c. $T_{4,30} = 2.72$.

11.11 Only Plant B and Plant C differ at $\alpha = .05$ ($t = 3.23$) using MegaStat Tukey test.

11.13 Only marketing and accounting differ at $\alpha = .05$ (Tukey $t = 3.00$).

11.15 a. $H_0: \sigma_1^2 = \sigma_2^2 = \sigma_3^2$ vs. H_1: At least one variance is different.

b. $df_1 = 3$, $df_2 = 4$.

c. $H_{3,4} = 15.5$.

d. $H_{calc} = 7.68$.

e. Fail to reject H_0.

11.17 $H_{calc} = 7.027/2.475 = 2.839$. Critical value from Table 11.5 $= 15.5$ ($df_1 = c = 3$, $df_2 = n/c - 1 = 4$). Fail to reject equal variances.

11.19 $H_{calc} = 8.097$. Critical value from Table 11.5 $= 10.4$ ($df_1 = c = 4$, $df_2 = n/c - 1 = 6$). Fail to reject null.

11.21 a. H_0: Mean absenteeism same in all four plants, H_1: Mean absenteeism not the same in all four plants.

b. ANOVA table: Two factor without replication.

c. Plant means differ, $F = 41.19$ ($p = .0002$). Blocking factor $F = 8.62$ ($p = .0172$) also significant.

d. Plants 1, 2 below overall mean, Plants 3, 4 above.

ANOVA table: Two factor without replication

Source	SS	df	MS	F	p-value
Treatments (plant)	216.25	3	72.083	41.19	.0002
Blocks (date)	30.17	2	15.083	8.62	.0172
Error	10.50	6	1.750		
Total	256.92	11			

Mean	n	Std. Dev	Factor Level
20.333	3	1.528	Plant 1
18.000	3	2.000	Plant 2
29.000	3	2.646	Plant 3
25.000	3	2.646	Plant 4
21.500	4	4.041	04-Mar
25.250	4	5.377	11-Mar
22.50	4	5.508	18-Mar

11.23 a. H_0: Mean scores same for all five professors, H_1: Mean scores are not the same.
c. For "professor effect" ambiguous, $F = 3.26$ ($p = .0500$), blocking factor not significant.
d. Clagmire above overall mean; Ennuyeux slightly below; plots suggest no strong differences.

11.25 a. *Rows:* H_0: Year means the same, H_1: Year means differ. *Columns:* H_0: portfolio type means the same, H_1: portfolio type means differ. *Interaction(Year $\times$ Type):* H_0: no interaction, H_1: There is an interaction effect.
b. ANOVA table: Two factor with replication (5 observations per cell).
c. Year ($F = 66.82$, $p < .0001$) is highly significant. Portfolio ($F = 5.48$, $p = .0026$) differs significantly, and significant interaction ($F = 4.96$, $p = .0005$).
d. p-values are very small, indicating significant effects at $\alpha = .05$. Year is strongest result.
e. Interaction plot lines do cross and support the interaction found and reported above.

ANOVA table: Two factor with replication (5 observations per cell)

Source	SS	df	MS	F	p-value
Factor 1 (portfolio)	1,191.584	2	595.7922	66.82	<.0001
Factor 2 (year)	146.553	3	48.8511	5.48	.0026
Interaction	265.192	6	44.1986	4.96	.0005
Error	427.980	48	8.9162		
Total	2,031.309	59			

11.27 a. *Rows:* H_0: Age group means same, H_1: Age group means differ. *Columns:* H_0: Region means same, H_1: Region means differ. *Interaction (Age $\times$ Region):* H_0: no interaction, H_1: interaction.
b. ANOVA table: Two factor with replication (5 observations per cell).
c. Age group means ($F = 36.96$, $p < .0001$) differ dramatically. Region means ($F = 0.5$, $p = .6493$) don't differ significantly. Significant interaction ($F = 3.66$, $p = .0010$).
d. Age group p-value indicates very strong result, interaction is significant at $\alpha = .05$.
e. Interaction plot lines do cross and support the interaction found and reported above.

11.29 a. H_0: $\mu_1 = \mu_2 = \mu_3 = \mu_4$, H_1: Not all the means are equal.
b. Graph shows mean Freshmen GPA is lower than overall mean.
c. $F = 2.36$ ($p = .1000$), fail to reject H_0 at $\alpha = .05$, no significant difference among GPAs.
d. Reject H_0 if $F > F_{3,21} = 3.07$.
e. Differences in mean grades large enough (.4 to .7) to matter, but not significant, so cannot be considered important.
f. Large variances within groups and small samples rob the test of power, suggests larger sample within each group.
g. Tukey confirms no significant difference in any pairs of means.
h. $H_{calc} = (0.6265)^2/(0.2826)^2 = 4.91$, which is less than Hartley's critical value 13.7 with $df_1 = c = 4$ and $df_2 = n/c - 1 = 5$, so conclude equal variances.

11.31 a. H_0: $\mu_1 = \mu_2 = \mu_3$, H_1: Not all means are equal.
b. Graph suggests Type B a bit lower, C higher than the overall mean.
c. $F = 9.44$ ($p = .0022$) so there is a significant difference in mean cell outputs.
d. Reject H_0 if $F > F_{2,15} = 3.68$.
e. Small differences in means, but could be important in a large solar cell array.
f. Sounds like a controlled experiment and variances are small, so a small sample suffices.
g. Tukey test shows that C differs from B at $\alpha = .01$ and from A at $\alpha = .05$.
h. $H_{calc} = (4.57)/(4.00) = 1.14$, less than Hartley's 10.8 with $df_1 = c = 3$ and $df_2 = n/c - 1 = 5$, conclude equal variances.

11.33 a. H_0: $\mu_1 = \mu_2 = \mu_3 = \mu_4$, H_1: Not all means equal.
b. Graph shows B higher, D lower.
c. $F = 1.79$ ($p = .1857$) so at $\alpha = .05$ no significant difference in mean waiting times.
d. Reject H_0 if $F > F_{3,18} = 3.16$.
e. Differences in means might matter to patient, but not significant so can't be considered important.
f. Variances large, samples small, so test has low power.
g. Tukey test shows no significant differences in pairs of means.
h. $H_{calc} = (11.90)^2/(6.74)^2 = 3.121$, less than the Hartley's 20.6 with $df_1 = c = 4$ and $df_2 = n/c - 1 = 4$ so conclude equal variances.

11.35 a. *Columns:* H_0: Surface has no effect on mean braking distance, H_1: Surface does affect distance. *Rows:* H_0: Pumping method has no effect on mean braking distance, H_1: Pumping method does affect distance.
b. Graph suggests differences (ice is greater than the other two).
c. Surface: $F = 134.39$ ($p = .0002$), reject H_0. Surface has a significant effect on mean stopping distance. Braking method: $F = 0.72$ ($p = .5387$), cannot reject H_0. Braking method has no significant effect on stopping distance.
d. Reject H_0 if $F > F_{2,4} = 6.94$.
e. For surface, differences large enough to be very importance in preventing accidents.
f. Replication would be desirable, if tests are not too costly.
g. Tukey test shows a difference between ice and the other two surfaces.
h. $H_{calc} = 1.37$ (for Method) and $H_{calc} = 14.5$ (for Surface). Cannot reject the hypothesis of equal variances.

11.37 a. $H_0: \mu_1 = \mu_2 = \mu_3 = \mu_4 = \mu_5$; H_1: Not all means equal.

    b. Graph suggests that Chalmers is higher and Ulysses is lower.

    c. $F_{calc} = 6.19$ ($p = .0019$) so reject H_0. There are significant differences in means.

    d. Reject H_0 if $F_{calc} > F_{4,21} = 2.84$ at $\alpha = .05$.

    e. Significant and probably important to clients.

    f. Sample may be limited by number of clinics in each town.

    g. Chalmers differs from all except Villa Nueve, while other means do not differ significantly.

    h. $H_{calc} = (11.171)^2/(6.850)^2 = 2.659$ does not exceed Hartley's $H_{crit} = 25.2$ with $df_1 = c = 5$ and $df_2 = n/c - 1 = 26/5 - 1 = 4$ so conclude equal variances.

11.39 a. $H_0: \mu_1 = \mu_2 = \mu_3 = \mu_4 = \mu_5$, H_1: Not all means equal.

    b. Graph shows no differences in means.

    c. $F = 0.39$ ($p = .8166$), cannot reject H_0. No significant difference in the mean dropout rates.

    d. Reject H_0 if $F > F_{4,45} = 2.61$.

    e. Differences not significant, not important.

    f. Could look at a different year. But sample is already fairly large.

    g. Tukey shows no significant differences in pairs.

    h. $H_{calc} = (10.585)^2/(3.759)^2 = 7.93$, exceeds Hartley's 7.11 with $df_1 = c = 5$ and $df_2 = n/c - 1 = 9$ so conclude unequal variances.

11.41 In this replicated two-factor ANOVA, the response (days until expiration) is significantly related to *Brand* (row factor, $F_{calc} = 3.39$, $p = .0284$) and strongly related to *Store* (column factor, $F_{calc} = 7.36$, $p = .0021$). Freshness is important to customers. Sample sizes could be increased because bag inspection is not difficult.

11.43 In this two-factor ANOVA without replication (randomized block), the response (trucks produced per shift) is weakly related to *Plant* (row factor, $F_{calc} = 2.72$, $p = .0912$) and strongly related to *Day* (column factor, $F_{calc} = 9.18$, $p = .0012$). Productivity is important to car companies. Sample sizes could be increased because daily production is routinely recorded for each shift.

11.45 a. Two Factor ANOVA.

    b. Instructor gender p-value ($p = .43$) exceeds $\alpha = .10$; instructor gender means do not differ. Student gender p-value ($p = .24$) exceeds $\alpha = .10$; student gender means do not differ (p-value $> \alpha = .10$). For interaction, the p-value ($p = .03$) suggests significant interaction effect (at $\alpha = .05$).

    c. Unlikely that a gender effect was overlooked due to sample size; test should have very good power.

11.47 a. $F_{calc} = (1069.17)/(12270.28) = 0.0871$.

    b. p-value $= .9666$.

    c. $F_{3,36} = 2.87$.

    d. No significant difference in means.

11.49 a. Two-factor ANOVA without replication (randomized block).

    b. 4 rows, 4 columns, 1 observation per cell.

    c. At $\alpha = .05$, plant location is not significant ($p = .1200$) while noise level is quite significant ($p = .0093$).

11.51 a. Two factor, either factor could be of research interest.

    b. Pollution affected freeway ($F = 24.90$, $p = .0000$) and by time of day ($F = 21.51$, $p = .0000$).

    c. Variances for freeway 2926.7 to 14333.7, for time of day 872.9 to 14333.6. Ratios are large (4.90 and 16.42), suggesting possibly unequal variances.

    d. For freeway, $df_1 = c = 4$ and $df_2 = n/c - 1 = 20/4 - 1 = 4$, Hartley's critical value 20.6, so conclude equal variances. Time of day, $df_1 = c = 5$ and $df_2 = n/c - 1 = 20/5 - 1 = 3$, Hartley's critical value is 50.7 so conclude equal variances.

11.53 a. One factor.

    b. Between groups $df_1 = 4$ and $df_1 = c - 1$ so $c = 5$ bowlers.

    c. p-value 0.000, reject null, conclude at least two samples are significantly different.

    d. Sample variances 83.66 to 200.797, $F_{max} = 200.797/77.067 = 2.61$. Hartley's test, $df_1 = c = 5$ and $df_2 = n/c - 1 = 67/5 - 1 = 12$, critical value is 5.30. Not enough variation to reject null hypothesis of homogeneity.

CHAPTER 12

12.1 For each sample: $H_0: \rho = 0$ vs. $H_1: \rho \neq 0$

Sample	df	r	t	t_α	Decision
a	18	.45	2.138	2.101	Reject
b	28	−.35	−1.977	1.701	Reject
c	5	.6	1.677	2.015	Fail to reject
d	59	−.3	−2.416	2.39	Reject

12.3 b. −.7328.   c. $t_{.025} = 3.182$.

    d. $t = -1.865$, fail to reject.   e. p-value $= .159$.

12.5 b. .531   c. 2.131   d. 2.429   e. Yes, reject.

12.7 a. Each additional *Sq Ft* increases price $150.

    b. $425,000.   c. No, *SquareFeet* cannot be zero.

12.9 a. For each additional year in median age there is an average of 35.3 fewer cars stolen per 100,000 people.

    b. 255 cars per 100,000 people.

    c. No, median age cannot be zero.

12.11 a. Each one unit increase in *PowerDistanceIndex* means an increase of 1.75 international franchises.

    b. 101.25.

    c. No, cannot have negative number of franchises.

12.13 a. Earning an extra $1,000 raises home price by $2,610.

    b. No.   c. $181,800, $312,300.

12.15 a. Blazer: Each year reduces price by $1,050. Silverado: Each year reduces price by $1,339.

    b. Intercept could indicate price of new car.

    c. $10,939.

    d. $15,896.

12.17 a. $\hat{y} = 14.42$, $e = 3.58$, underestimate.

    b. $\hat{y} = 13.3$, $e = -7.3$, overestimate.

12.19 b. *Wait Time* $= 458 - 18.5$ *Operators*.

    d. $R^2 = .5369$.

12.21 $\hat{y} = 0.458x + 11.155$, $R^2 = .2823$.

12.23 b. $H_0: \beta_1 = 0$ vs. $H_0: \beta_1 \neq 0$.   c. p-value $= .0269$, (1.3192, 10.8522).   d. Slope is significantly different from zero because the p-value is less than .05.

12.25 a. $\hat{y} = 557.45 + 3.00x$.   b. (1.2034, 4.806).

    c. $H_0: \beta_1 \leq 0$ vs. $H_1: \beta_1 > 0$, p-value $= .0009$, reject H_0.

12.27 a. $\hat{y} = 1.8064 + .0039x$.
 b. Intercept: $1.8064/.6116 = 2.954$, slope: $.0039/.0014 = 2.786$ (may be off due to rounding).
 c. $d.f. = 10$, $t_{.025} = \pm 2.228$.
12.29 a. $\hat{y} = 6.9609 - 0.053x$.
 b. $(-0.1946, 0.0886)$. Interval does contain zero, slope is not significantly different from zero.
 c. t test p-value $= .4133$. Conclusion: slope is not significantly different from zero.
 d. F statistic p-value $= .4133$. Conclusion: No significant relationship between variables.
 e. $0.74 = (-0.863)^2$.
12.31 a. $\hat{y} = -31.1895 + 4.9322x$.   b. $(2.502, 7.362)$. Interval does not contain zero, the slope is greater than zero.   c. t test p-value is 0.0011. Conclusion: the slope is positive.   d. F statistic p-value $= .0011$. Conclusion: significant relationship between variables.   e. $(4.523)^2 = 20.46$.
12.33 b. 95% confidence interval: $(0.3671, 1.1477)$, 95% prediction interval: $(-0.4662, 1.9810)$.
 c. 95% confidence interval for μ_Y: $(-0.205, 1.4603)$.
 d. The second interval is much wider.
12.35 Normality assumption is reasonable. Residual plot shows signs of nonconstant variance.
12.37 a. 33.02 mpg.   b. 5.13.   c. 2.527.
 d. This is an unusual observation, not an outlier.
12.39 a. $h = .1850 > .0541$, high leverage.   b. $h = .0304 < .0541$, not high leverage.   c. $h = .0952 > .0541$, high leverage.
12.57 $t_{critical} = 2.3069$ (from Excel). From sample: $t = 2.3256$. Reject H_0.
12.59 a. 1515.2.   b. No.   c. $(1406.03, 1624.37)$.
12.61 a. $y = 1743.57 - 1.2163x$.   b. $d.f. = 13$. $t_{critical} = 2.160$.
 c. Slope is significantly different from zero.
 d. $(-2.1671, -0.2656)$. Interval indicates slope is significantly less than zero.
 e. $7.64 = (-2.764)^2$
12.63 a. $r = -.3871$
 b. From sample: $t = -2.688$. For a two-tailed test, $t_{.005} = 2.7012$. Fail to reject H_0.
12.65 b. $r = .749$.
 c. $d.f. = 13$. For a two-tailed test, $t_{.025} = 2.160$, $t_{calc} = 4.076$. Reject H_0.
12.69 b. $y = -4.2896 + 0.171x$, $R^2 = .2474$. Fit is poor.
12.71 a. No significant relationship between variables. (p-value $= .774$).
 b. No, study time and class level could be predictors. (Answers will vary.)
12.73 a. The negative slope means that as age increases, price decreases.
 b. Intercepts could be asking price of a new car.
 c. The fit is good for the Explorer, Pickup, and Taurus.
 d. Additional predictors: condition of car, mileage.

CHAPTER 13

13.1 a. *Net Revenue* $= 4.31 - 0.082\,ShipCost + 2.265\,PrintAds + 2.498\,WebAds + 16.7\,Rebate\%$
 b. Positive coefficients indicate an increase in net revenue; negative coefficients indicate a decrease in net revenue.

c. The intercept is meaningless.
 d. \$467,111.
13.3 a. *Ovalue* $= 2.8931 + 0.1542\,LiftWait + 0.2495\,AmountGroomed + 0.0539\,SkiPatrolVisibility - 0.1196\,FriendlinessHosts$.
 b. Overall satisfaction increases with an increase in satisfaction for each coefficient except for friendliness of hosts. This counterintuitive result could be due to an interaction effect.
 c. No.
 d. 4.5831.
13.5 a. $df_1 = 4$ (numerator) and $df_2 = 45$ (denominator).
 b. $F_{.05} = 2.61$. Using $df_1 = 4$ and $df_2 = 40$.
 c. $F = 12.997$. Yes, overall regression is significant.
 d. $R^2 = .536$. $R^2_{adj} = .495$.
13.7 a. $df_1 = 4$, $df_2 = 497$.
 b. Using App. F, $df_1 = 4$ and $df_2 = 200$, $F_{.05} = 2.42$.
 c. $F_{calc} = 12.923$. Yes, overall regression is significant.
 d. $R^2 = .0942$, $R^2_{adj} = .0869$.
13.9 a. and c. See Table.

Predictor	Coef	std error coef	t-value	p-value
Intercept	4.31	70.82	0.0608585	0.9517414
ShipCost	−0.082	4.678	−0.0175289	0.9860922
PrintAds	2.265	1.05	2.1571429	0.0363725
WebAds	2.498	0.8457	2.9537661	0.0049772
Rebate%	16.697	3.57	4.6770308	.0003

 b. $t_{critical} = 2.69$. *WebAds* and *Rebate%* differ significantly from zero.
13.11 a. and c.

Predictor	Coef	std error coef	t-value	p-value
Intercept	2.8931	0.3680	7.8617	2.37E-14
LiftWait	0.1542	0.0440	3.5045	.0005
AmountGroomed	0.2495	0.0529	4.7164	3.07E-06
SkiPatrolVisibility	0.0539	0.0443	1.2167	.2245
FriendlinessHosts	−0.1196	0.0623	−1.9197	.0557

 b. $t_{.005} = 2.586$. *LiftWait* and *AmountGroomed* differ significantly from zero.
13.13 $\hat{y}_i \pm 2.032(3620)$: $\hat{y}_i \pm 7355.84$.
 Quick Rule $\hat{y}_i \pm 2s$: $\hat{y}_i \pm 7240$.
13.15 a. Number of nights needed and number of bedrooms.
 b. Two: *SwimPool* $= 1$ if there is a swimming pool and *ParkGarage* $= 1$ if there is a parking garage.
 c. *CondoPrice* $= \beta_0 + \beta_1 NumNights + \beta_2 NumBedrooms + \beta_3 SwimPool + \beta_4 ParkGarage$.
13.17 a. $ln(Price) = 5.4841 - 0.0733\,SalePrice + 1.1196\,Sub\text{-}Zero + 0.0696\,Capacity + 0.04662\,DoorFzBot - 0.34322\,DoorFzTop - 0.70961\,DoorFz - 0.88201\,DoorNoFz$.
 b. *SalePrice*: p-value $= .0019$, *Sub-Zero*: p-value $= 2.24$E-14, *Capacity*: p-value $= 2.71$E-31, *2DoorFzBot*: p-value $= .5650$, *2DoorFzTop*: p-value $= 3.68$E-19, *1DoorFz*: p-value $= 1.19$E-07, *1DoorNoFz*: p-value $= 8.59$E-09.
 c. 0.3432.
 d. Side freezer.
13.19 a. Positive nonlinear relationship. Yes, nonlinear model appropriate.

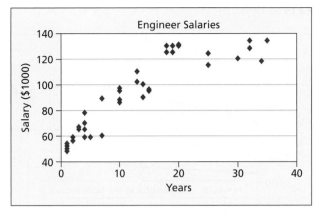

b. $R^2 = .915$, $F_{calc} = 194.99$, p-value $= 4.84 \times 10^{-20}$. Yes, model significant.

c. *Years: p*-value $= 5.5 \times 10^{-14}$, *YearsSq: p*-value $= 6.21 \times 10^{-8}$. Yes, the predictors are both significant.

13.21 a. *LiftOps* and *Scanners* ($r = .635$), *Crowds* and *Lift-Wait* ($r = .577$), *AmountGroomed* and *TrailGr* ($r = .531$), *SkiSafe* and *SkiPatrolVisibility* ($r = .488$).

b. All VIFs are less than 2. No cause for concern.

13.23 a. Not high.   b. High.   c. High.

13.43 There are no quantitative predictor variables and the sample size is too small relative to number of predictors.

13.45 Overall regression not significant (F statistic p-value $= .371$), $R^2 = 0.117$ indicates poor fit. Conclusion: No apparent relationship between cost per load and predictors type of washer and type of detergent used.

13.47 a. Coefficients make sense, except for *TrnOvr*, which would be expected to be negative.   b. No.

c. With 6 predictors, should have minimum of 30 observations. We have only 23 so sample is small.

d. Rebounds and points highly correlated.

13.49 a. Experience lowers the predicted finish time.   b. No.

c. If the relationship is not strictly linear, it can make sense to include a squared predictor, such as seen here.

13.51 The first three predictors (*Income, Unem, Pupil/Tea*) are significant at $\alpha = .05$, but adding the fourth predictor (*Divorce*) yields a weak p-value (.1987) and R^2 and R^2_{adj} barely improve when *Divorce* is added.

CHAPTER 14

14.1 a.

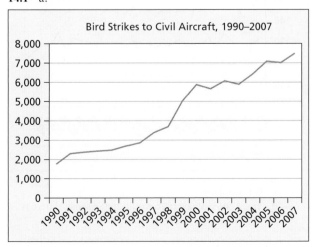

b. More planes in the air.

c. Linear: $y_t = 1008.5 + 361.51t$ ($R^2 = .9503$); quadratic: $y_t = 1277.8 + 280.73t + 4.2515t^2$ ($R^2 = .9531$); exponential: $y_t = 1724.4e^{.0886t}$ ($R^2 = .9489$).

d. Linear is simplest, exponential increases too rapidly.

e. Linear: 7877, 8239, 8600; quadratic: 8146, 8593, 9048; exponential: 9284, 10,144, 11,084.

14.3 a. Decreasing trend.

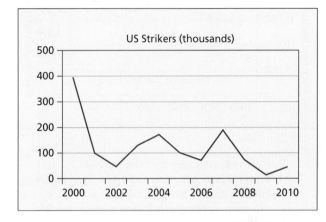

b. Erosion of unskilled jobs, globalization, tougher bargaining.

c. Linear: $y_t = 229.38 - 18.109t$ ($R^2 = .3258$); quadratic: $y_t = 291.87 - 46.948t + 2.2403t^2$ ($R^2 = .3706$); exponential: $y_t = 229.56e^{-0.161t}$ ($R^2 = .3552$).

d. Linear predicts negative strikes (impossible). Quadratic has best fit but predicts a rise that doesn't fit the trend. Exponential seems most plausible for future forecasts.

e. Use exponential trend. 2011: 33,254 strikers; 2012: 28,309 strikers; 2013: 24,099 strikers.

14.5 a. Linear ($R^2 = .8667$).

b. More healthy diet choices.

c. $y_t = 596.79 + 19.95t$.

d. Increased capacity needed for production and distribution.

e. Using $t = 7$, $y_7 = 596.79 + 19.95(7) = 736$.

14.7 Graph shows negative trend and cyclical pattern. Fit improves as α increases (i.e., as we give more weight to recent data). Forecasts are similar for each value of α.

Alpha	.10	.20	.30
Mean Squared Error	0.039	0.028	0.021
Mean Absolute Percent Error	3.8%	3.1%	2.7%
Percent Positive Errors	42.3%	46.2%	51.9%
Forecast for Period 53	4.30	4.37	4.43

14.9 a. Seasonality exists, but not a significant trend.

b. Fit is not very good ($R^2 = .416$, $R^2_{adj} = .216$), and no months show significant seasonality at $\alpha = .05$.

c. Forecasts for 2008:

Period	Forecast	Period	Forecast
January	2,529.75	July	2,618.25
February	2,631.75	August	2,518.50
March	3,249.75	September	2,977.00
April	3,256.75	October	2,692.75
May	3,263.25	November	2,606.50
June	2,936.50	December	3,025.25

14.11 a. Dual-scale graph is needed due to differing magnitudes.

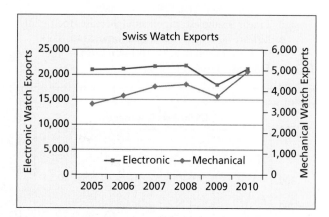

b. Electronic sales are higher than mechanical, had a drop in 2009 but on the rise again. Mechanical sales are smaller, also had a drop in 2009 but on the rise again, appearing to grow at a faster rate than electronic.

c. Electronic sales are falling at 1.3%: $y_t = 21668e^{-0.013t}$ ($R^2 = 0.105$), while sales of mechanical watches are rising at 5.49%: $y_t = 3320.6e^{0.0549t}$ ($R^2 = 0.581$).

d. Fascination with electronic gadgets may be waning and/or competitors may be moving in on the Swiss watch industry. They may have a stronger specialty niche.

e. Linear forecasts for 2011, 2012, and 2013 follow. Electronic: 19,939, 19,697, 19,456; mechanical: 4,844, 5,070, and 5,295. 2009 sales might be off due to the recession.

14.13 a.

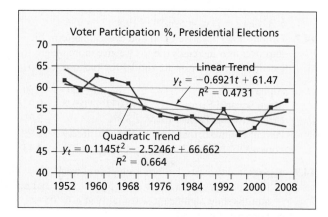

b. The trend was decreasing until 1996 but has been increasing since then.

c. See graph for trend models.

d. Choose the quadratic, which shows an increase after 1996 and has a better fit.

e. Using the quadratic model: 2012 forecast is 55.6%.

14.15 a.

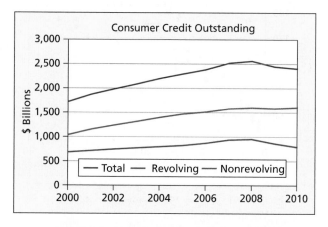

b. Increasing trend with a maximum in 2008 followed by a decrease over the next few years.

c. Total credit linear $y_t = 77.227t + 1762.5$ ($R^2 = 0.8536$), quadratic: $y_t = -10.078t^2 + 198.16t + 1500.4$ ($R^2 = 0.9669$). Revolving linear: $y_t = 57.291t + 1065.8$ ($R^2 = 0.9212$), quadratic: $y_t = -5.8531t^2 + 127.53t + 913.62$ ($R^2 = 0.9962$). Nonrevolving linear: $y_t = 20.036t + 696.15$ ($R^2 = 0.5772$), quadratic: $y_t = -4.2261t^2 + 70.75t + 586.27$ ($R^2 = 0.7774$).

d. Forecasts in table.

	Total	*Revolving*	*Nonrevolving*
2011	2427.09	1601.13	826.71
2012	2373.230	1582.34	791.81
2013	2299.35	1551.83	748.45

14.17 a. Graphs will vary.

b. Whole milk down, low-fat milk up. Fruit juices up slightly, beer and wine level or down slightly. Hard liquor is down sharply.

c–d. Answers will vary, but defend using specific criteria (past fit, recent fit, believability, Occam's Razor).

e. Answers will vary.

14.19 a.

b. It is unlikely.

d. Yes, a moving average would make sense. There is not much of a decreasing trend.

14.21 a.

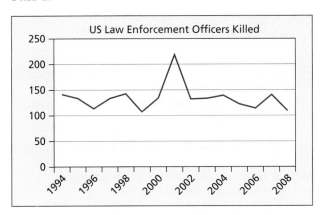

b. No trend. Spike in number killed in 2001. Most likely these numbers include deaths during 9/11.
c. No, a trend would not be helpful.
d. Best forecast is average over all years: 128 without 2001, 134 with 2001.

14.23 a.

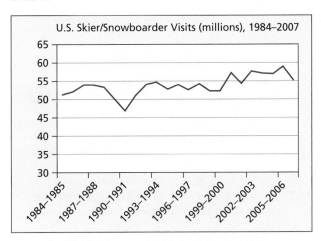

b. Yes, a linear trend would work.
c. Using the linear trend: $y_{07-08} = 56.933$ million.

14.25 a. Steady upward trend.
b. Growing population, bigger cars, rising world demand.
c. Linear: $y_t = 39.667 + 441.59t$ ($R^2 = .9188$); exponential: $y_t = 667.17e^{0.2067t}$ ($R^2 = 0.9108$)
d. Forecast for 2010: Linear: $y_{11} = 4897$, exponential $y_{11} = 6482$. Believable, given continued role of oil in the U.S. economy.
e. Consumers, producers, government, refiners (i.e., all of us).

14.27 a. Rate declines, then increases.
b. The following graph shows $\alpha = .20$. Other graphs similar.
c. For these data $\alpha = .20$ seems to track the recent data well, yet provides enough smoothing to iron out the "blips." It gives enough weight to recent data to bring its forecasts above 1.80 (lagging but reflecting the recent rise in rates). In contrast, $\alpha = .05$ or $\alpha = .10$ provides too much smoothing, so they give a forecast below 1.80. While $\alpha = .50$ gives a good "fit," it does not smooth the data very much.

d. Smoothing methods are useful since there is no single, consistent trend.

14.29 a. Upward trend with seasonal pattern.
b. Yes (make a bar chart to see this clearly).
c. MegaStat's indexes are adjusted so they sum to 12.000. The average monthly index is 1.000.

Month	Index	Month	Index
Jan	0.7976	Jul	1.3630
Feb	0.7943	Aug	1.2422
Mar	0.9843	Sep	0.9347
Apr	0.8057	Oct	0.9246
May	1.0755	Nov	0.9305
Jun	1.2470	Dec	0.9006

d. Highest: summer (June, July, August); Lowest: winter (January, February).
e. MegaStat trend after deseasonalizing: $y_t = 21469 + 382.11t$ ($R^2 = .6200$).

14.31 a.

b. There is a positive trend up until early 2009 and then a decreasing trend. This corresponds to the recession.

Month	Index	Month	Index
Jan	1.014	Jul	0.993
Feb	0.997	Aug	1.001
Mar	0.985	Sep	1.000
Apr	0.986	Oct	1.001
May	0.989	Nov	1.011
Jun	0.991	Dec	1.033

c. Seasonal indexes show higher borrowing in December and January and lower borrowing in March, April, and May. Borrowing during December makes sense because of Christmas.

14.33 a.

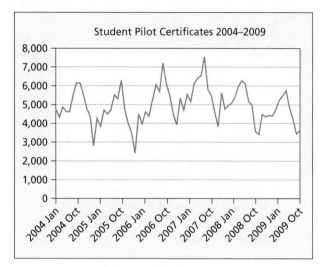

Time trend is not significant; however, there is a seasonal effect. Using December as a base month (omitted), the seasonal binary coefficients show that summer months (Jun, Jul, Aug) are significantly higher and winter months (Oct, Nov, Feb) are significantly lower. The fitted regression (including the insignificant variables) is *Permits* = 3229 + 2.17 *Time* + 1524 *Jan* + 1017 *Feb* + 1537 *Mar* + 1381 *Apr* + 1816 *May* + 2465 *Jun* + 2587 *Jul* + 3195 *Aug* + 2028 *Sep* + 1499 *Oct* + 652 *Nov*.

Variables	Coefficients	Std Error	t (d.f. = 59)	p-value
Intercept	3,229.43	249.273	12.955	6.67E-19
Time	2.17	3.022	0.718	.4759
Jan	1,523.52	305.221	4.992	5.62E-06
Feb	1,016.52	304.907	3.334	.0015
Mar	1,536.68	304.622	5.045	4.63E-06
Apr	1,380.51	304.368	4.536	2.87E-05
May	1,816.18	304.142	5.971	1.44E-07
Jun	2,464.51	303.947	8.108	3.59E-11
Jul	2,587.01	303.782	8.516	7.38E-12
Aug	3,194.67	303.647	10.521	3.71E-15
Sep	2,027.84	303.541	6.681	9.37E-09
Oct	1,498.84	303.466	4.939	6.80E-06
Nov	652.34	303.421	2.150	.0357

b. Forecasts for 2010 are obtained from the fitted regression using *Time* = 73, 74, . . . , 84 and the binary predictors from the spreadsheet. MegaStat gives these predictions:

Month	Forecast	Month	Forecast
Jan	4,911	Jul	5,988
Feb	4,406	Aug	6,598
Mar	4,929	Sep	5,433
Apr	4,775	Oct	4,906
May	5,213	Nov	4,062
Jun	5,863	Dec	3,412

CHAPTER 15

15.1 a. H_0: *Earnings* are independent of *Approach*.
b. Degrees of Freedom = $(r - 1)(c - 1)$ = $(4 - 1)(3 - 1) = 6$.
c. CHISQ.INV(.01,6) = 16.81.
d. Test statistic is 127.57 (*p*-value = .0000) so reject null at α = .01.
e. *No Clear Effect* and *Business Combinations* contribute the most.
f. All expected frequencies exceed 5.
g. *p*-value is near zero (observed difference not due to chance).

15.3 a. H_0: *Verbal* and *Quantitative* are independent.
b. Degrees of Freedom = $(r - 1)(c - 1)$ = $(3 - 1)(3 - 1) = 4$.
c. CHISQ.INV(.005,4) = 14.86.
d. Test statistic is 55.88 (*p*-value = .0000), reject null at α = .005.
e. *Under 25* and *Under 25* contributes the most.
f. Expected frequency is less than 5 in two cells.
g. *p*-value is nearly zero (observed difference not due to chance).

15.5 a. H_0: *Completion Rate* and *Email Notice* are independent.
b. Degrees of Freedom = $(r - 1)(c - 1)$ = $(2 - 1)(2 - 1) = 1$.
c. CHISQ.INV.RT(.025,1) = 5.024.
d. Test statistic is 5.42 (*p*-value = .0199), reject null at α = .025.
e. *Completed* and *No* contribute the most.
f. All expected frequencies exceed 5.
g. *p*-value is less than .025 (observed difference did not arise by chance).
h. z = 2.33 (*p*-value = .0199 for two-tailed test).

15.7 χ^2_{calc} = 5.44, *p*-value = .2447, fail to reject H_0. The sample shows the distribution of visits has stayed the same.

15.9 a. Bars are similar in length. Vanilla and Mocha are the leading flavors.
b. If uniform, e_j = 84/4 = 21 for each flavor.
c. Test statistic is 0.86 with *d.f.* = 4 − 1 = 3 (*p*-value = .8358). Chi-square critical value for α = .05 is 7.815, so sample does not contradict the hypothesis that sales are the same for each beverage.

15.11 Expected frequency is 56/7 = 8 for each age group. Test statistic is 10.000 (*p*-value = .1247). At α = .05, critical value for *d.f.* = 7 − 1 = 6 is 12.59. Cannot reject the hypothesis that moviegoers are from a uniform population.

Age Class	Obs	Exp	O−E	(O−E)²/E
10 < 20	5	8.000	−3.000	1.125
20 < 30	6	8.000	−2.000	0.500
30 < 40	10	8.000	2.000	0.500
40 < 50	3	8.000	−5.000	3.125
50 < 60	14	8.000	6.000	4.500
60 < 70	9	8.000	1.000	0.125
70 < 80	9	8.000	1.000	0.125
Total	56	56.000	0.000	10.000

15.13 Sample mean $\lambda = 4.948717949$, test statistic 3.483 (p-value = .4805) with $d.f. = 6 - 1 - 1 = 4$. The critical value for $\alpha = .05$ is 9.488; cannot reject the hypothesis of a Poisson distribution.

X	P(X)	Obs	Exp	O−E	(O2E)²/E
2 or Less	0.12904	3	5.032	−2.032	0.821
3	0.14326	5	5.587	−0.587	0.062
4	0.17724	9	6.912	2.088	0.631
5	0.17542	10	6.841	3.159	1.458
6	0.14468	5	5.643	−0.643	0.073
7 or More	0.23036	7	8.984	−1.984	0.438
	1.00000	39	39.000	0.000	3.483

15.15 From sample, $\bar{x} = 75.375$, $s = 8.943376$. Set $e_j = 40/8 = 5$. Test statistic is 6.000 (p-value = .306) using $d.f. = 8 - 2 - 1 = 5$. Critical value for $\alpha = .05$ is 11.07; cannot reject the hypothesis of a normal distribution.

Score	Obs	Exp	Obs−Exp	Chi-Square
Under 65.09	5	5.000	0.000	0.000
65.09 < 69.34	3	5.000	−2.000	0.800
69.34 < 72.53	5	5.000	0.000	0.000
72.53 < 75.38	3	5.000	−2.000	0.800
75.38 < 78.22	9	5.000	4.000	3.200
78.22 < 81.41	7	5.000	2.000	0.800
81.41 < 85.66	4	5.000	−1.000	0.200
85.66 or more	4	5.000	−1.000	0.200
Total	40	40.000	0.000	6.000

15.17* The probability plot looks linear, but p-value (.033) for the Anderson-Darling test is less than $\alpha = .05$. This tends to contradict the chi-square test used in Exercise 15.15. However, the Kolmogorov-Smirnov test ($D_{Max} = .158$) does not reject normality (p-value > .20). Data are a borderline case, having some characteristics of a normal distribution. If we have to choose one test, the A-D is the most powerful.

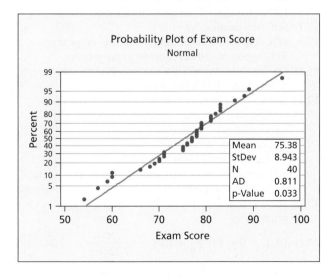

15.19 Is *Satisfaction* independent of *Pay Category?* For $d.f. = (r - 1)(c - 1) = (3 - 1)(2 - 1) = 2$, critical value is CHISQ.INV.RT(.05,2) = 5.991. Test statistic is 4.54 (p-value = .1032); cannot reject the null at $\alpha = .05$. *Salaried* and *Dissatisfied* contribute the most. All expected frequencies exceed 5. The p-value suggests that observed difference would arise by chance 103 times in 1,000 samples if the two variables really were independent, which is not very convincing.

15.21 Is *Grade* independent of *Hand-In Order?* For $d.f. = (r - 1)(c - 1) = (2 - 1)(2 - 1) = 1$, critical value CHISQ.INV.RT(.10,1) = 2.706. Test statistic is 0.23 (p-value = .6284) so cannot reject the null at $\alpha = .10$. *"B" or Better* and *Later Hand-In* contribute the most. All expected frequencies exceed 5. For a two-tailed test of proportions, $p_1 = .4000$, $p_2 = .3333$, $\bar{p} = .3673$, $z = 0.48$ (p-value = .6284), which agrees with the chi-square test.

15.23 a. Is *Reading* independent of *Language?* For $d.f. = (r - 1)(c - 1) = (3 - 1)(4 - 1) = 6$ the critical value is CHISQ.INV.RT(.10,6) = 10.64. Test statistic is 4.14 (p-value = .6577), so we cannot reject the null at $\alpha = .10$. Four cells (each corner) have expected frequencies below 5.

15.25 Is *Smoking* independent of *Race?* For $d.f. = (r - 1)(c - 1) = (2 - 1)(2 - 1) = 1$, critical value is CHISQ.INV.RT(.005,1) = 7.879. For males, test statistic is 5.84 (p-value = .0157); can't reject the null at $\alpha = .005$. For females, test statistic is 14.79 (p-value = .0001) so reject the null at $\alpha = .005$. *Black* and *Smoker* contribute the most in each test. All expected frequencies exceed 5. The two-tailed test of proportions agrees.

15.27 For $d.f. = (r - 1)(c - 1) = (2 - 1)(2 - 1) = 1$, critical value CHIINV(.10,1) = 2.706, test statistic is 1.80 (p-value = .1792) so fail to reject the null at $\alpha = .10$. The lower left cell contributes most. All expected frequencies exceed 5. The two-tailed test of proportions ($z = 1.342$) agrees with the chi-square test. Interestingly, the relationship seems to be inverse (i.e., rates tend to rise when they are predicted to fall).

15.29 For the 2×2 table, $d.f. = 1$, critical value is CHISQ.INV.RT(.05,1) = 3.841, test statistic is 7.15

(p-value = .0075) so reject null at α = .05. For the 3 × 3 table, $d.f.$ = 4, critical value is CHISQ.INV.RT(.05,4) = 9.488, test statistic is 12.30 (p-value = .0153), so reject null at α = .05. All expected frequencies exceed 5.

15.31 With $d.f. = (r - 1)(c - 1) = (3 - 1)(3 - 1) = 4$, the critical value is CHISQ.INV.RT(.01,4) = 13.28. The test statistic is 54.18 (p-value = .0000) so we reject the null at α = .01. All expected frequencies exceed 5.

15.33 χ^2_{calc} = 43.36, p-value = 2.84 × 10^{-7}; therefore, reject H_0. The sample shows the distribution of car colors has changed.

15.35 For $d.f.$ = 4 − 1 = 3, critical value is CHISQ.INV.RT (.05,3) = 7.815, test statistic is 6.045 (p-value = .1095) so we cannot reject hypothesis that Oxnard follows U.S. distribution.

15.37 For $d.f.$ = 6 − 1 = 5, critical value is CHISQ.INV.RT (.10,5) = 9.236, test statistic is 4.40 (p-value = .4934) so we can't reject the hypothesis that the die is fair.

15.39 Estimated mean is λ = 1.06666667. For $d.f.$ = 4 − 1 − 1 = 2, critical value is CHISQ.INV.RT(.025,2) = 7.378, test statistic is 4.947 (p-value = .0843) so can't reject the hypothesis of a Poisson distribution.

X	f_j	$P(X)$	e_j	$f_j - e_j$	$(f_j - e_j)^2/e_j$
0	25	0.344154	20.64923	4.35077	0.917
1	18	0.367097	22.02584	−4.02584	0.736
2	8	0.195785	11.74712	−3.74712	1.195
3 or more	9	0.092964	5.57781	3.42219	2.100
Total	60	1.000000	60.00000	0.00000	4.947

15.41 Mean is λ = 0.702479339 run/inning. For $d.f.$ = 4 − 1 − 1 = 2, critical value is CHISQ.INV.RT(.05,2) = 5.991, test statistic is 64.02 (p-value = .0000) so reject hypothesis that runs per inning are Poisson. In hockey, goals are independent events, while in baseball they are not.

15.43* Answers will vary, but most should confirm the normal distribution and intended μ and σ.

15.45* Answers will vary, but most should confirm the Poisson distribution and intended λ.

CHAPTER 16

16.1 R = 14, z = −0.133 (p-value = .8942). Fail to reject H_0.

16.3 R = 15, z = 0.697 (p-value = .4858). Results are random.

16.5 a. Sample median = 53.75. W = 234.5, z = 0.7174, p-value = .48. Median is not significantly different from 50.

b. Close to a normal distribution. Parametric t test could be justified.

16.7 a. z = 1.319, p-value = .1872. No difference in medians.

b. t = 1.62, p-value = .0606 (assuming equal variances). Same decision but p-value closer to .05.

16.9 a. H = 5.724, p-value = .1258. No difference in medians.

b. Yes, F = 2.71, p-value = .055.

c. Can assume normality for Energy and Retail. Health and Leisure are less obvious.

16.11 χ^2 = 4.950, p-value = .2925. No difference in median ratings.

16.13 a.

2004	2005	2004	2005
6	7	17	20
5	5	16	16
10	10	4	4
13	14	14	19
15	15	11	13
19	18	1	1
3	3	20	17
7	6	2	2
8	8	18	12
12	11	9	9

b. r_s = .9338.   c. Yes, z_{calc} = 4.07, p-value = .0000.

e. Pearson: r = .996.

f. Nonnormal data justify use of Spearman rank correlation.

16.15 R = 28, z = 0.775 (p-value = .4383). Results are random.

16.17 R = 22, z = 1.419 (p-value = .1559). Results are random.

16.19 R = 9, z = −1.647 (p-value = .0996). Results are random.

16.21 z = −1.039, p-value = .2988. No difference in medians.

16.23 From MegaStat Wilcoxon – Signed-Rank Paired Data Test: z = −1.481, p-value = .1386. Medians do not differ.

16.25 z = −3.086, p-value = .0020. The medians differ.

16.27 H = 1.46, p-value = .4819. No difference in medians.

16.29 H = 9.026, p-value = .0110. The medians differ.

16.31 χ^2_{calc} = 2.731, p-value = .6038. No difference in median waiting times by day of week.

16.33 r_s = .67, $r_{.05}$ = .374. Significant rank correlation.

16.35 r_s = .696, $r_{.05}$ = .468. Significant rank correlation.

16.37 r_s = .812, $r_{.05}$ = .444. Significant rank correlation.

CHAPTER 17

17.1 a. *Productivity:* ratio of output to input, measures efficiency.

b. *Quality control:* used to ensure product/service quality.

c. *Process control:* used to ensure process conformance to specifications.

17.3 Common cause comes from within the process. Special cause originates outside the process.

17.5 Define metrics, collect data, track variation.

17.7 See www.deming.org

17.9 SQC applies statistical controls to the end product. SPC applies statistical controls to the process.

17.11 Quality improvement is a continuous cycle that repeats. See Section 17.3 for the steps.

17.13 Service blueprints and service transaction analysis.

17.15 a. Sampling frequency depends on cost and physical possibility of sampling.

b. For normal data, small samples may suffice for a mean (Central Limit Theorem).

c. Large samples may be needed for a proportion to get sufficient precision.

17.17 Expect 68.26 percent, 95.44 percent, 99.73 percent respectively.

17.19 $UCL = \bar{\bar{x}} + 3\dfrac{\bar{R}}{d_2\sqrt{n}} = 12.5 + 3\dfrac{.42}{2.326\sqrt{5}} = 12.742$

$LCL = \bar{\bar{x}} - 3\dfrac{\bar{R}}{d_2\sqrt{n}} = 12.5 - 3\dfrac{.42}{2.326\sqrt{5}} = 12.258$

17.21 Estimated σ is $\bar{R}/d_2 = 30/2.059 = 14.572$, UCL = 98.37,
LCL = 54.63

$$\bar{\bar{x}} = \frac{\bar{x}_1 + \bar{x}_2 + \cdots + \bar{x}_9}{9}$$

$$= \frac{72.25 + 74.25 + \cdots + 82.25}{9} = 76.5$$

$$\bar{R} = \frac{R_1 + R_2 + \cdots + R_9}{9}$$

$$= \frac{43 + 31 + \cdots + 41}{9} = 30$$

17.23 $\bar{R} = .82$ (centerline)
UCL = $D_4\bar{R} = (2.004)(.82) = 1.64328$
LCL = $D_3\bar{R} = (0)(.82) = 0$

17.25 Services are often assessed using percent conforming or acceptable quality, so we use p charts.

17.27 Yes, safe to assume normality. UCL = .8354, LCL = .1646.

17.29 By either criterion, process is within acceptable standard ($C_p = 1.67$, $C_{pk} = 1.67$).

17.31 Fails both criteria, especially C_{pk} due to bad centering ($C_p = 1.17$, $C_{pk} = 0.67$).

17.33 Answers will vary. Examples:
  a. GPA, number of classes retaken, faculty recommendation letters (Likert).
  b. Knowledge of material, enthusiasm, organization, fairness (Likert scales for all).
  c. Number of bounced checks, size of monthly bank balance errors, unpaid Visa balance.
  d. Number of print errors, clarity of graphs, useful case studies (Likert scales for last two).

17.35 Answers will vary. Examples:
  a. MPG, repair cost.
  b. Frequency of jams, ink cost.
  c. Frequency of re-flushes, water consumption.
  d. Battery life, ease of use (Likert scale).
  e. Cost, useful life, image sharpness (Likert scale).
  f. Cost, useful life, watts per lumen.

17.37 $\bar{x}$ is normally distributed from the Central Limit Theorem for sufficiently large values of n (i.e., symmetric distribution) while the range and standard deviation are not.

17.39 a. Variation and chance defects are inevitable in all human endeavors.
  b. Some processes have very *few* defects (maybe zero in short run, but not in long run).
  c. Quarterbacks cannot complete all their passes, etc.

17.41 Answers will vary (e.g., forgot to set clock, clock set incorrectly, couldn't find backpack, stopped to charge cell phone, had to shovel snow, clock didn't go off, traffic, car won't start, can't find parking).

17.43 Answers will vary (e.g., weather, union slowdown, pilot arrived late, crew change required, deicing planes, traffic congestion at takeoff, no arrival gate available).

17.45 a. $C_p = 1.33$, $C_{pk} = 1.33$.
  b. $C_p = 1.33$, $C_{pk} = 0.67$.

17.47 a. UCL = 6223, LCL = 5877.
  b. Chart violates no rules.   c. Process is in control.

17.49 a. UCL = 1.0939, LCL = 0.9061.
  b. Chart violates no rules.   c. Process is in control.

17.51 a. $C_p = 1.00$, $C_{pk} = 0.83$.
  b. Process well below capability standards (both indices less than 1.33).
  c. Technology, cost, door not closed tightly, frequency of door opening.

17.53 Sample mean of 23.025 and standard deviation of 2.006 are very close to the process values ($\mu = 23$, $\sigma = 2$). Histogram is symmetric, but perhaps platykurtic (chi-square or Anderson-Darling test needed).

17.55 a. Histogram is arguably normal, but somewhat bimodal (chi-square or Anderson-Darling test needed).
  b. $\mu = 8760$, $\sigma = 200$, UCL = 9028, LCL = 8492.
  c. $\bar{x} = 8785$, $s = 216.14$, UCL = 9075, LCL = 8495,
  d. Sample is small, may have unreliable estimates of μ and σ.

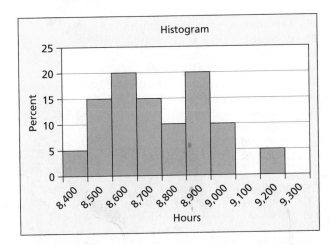

17.57 a. UCL = 470.2, LCL = 459.8.
  b. No rules violated. Process in control.

17.59 a. UCL = 12.22095, LCL = 11.75569, centerline = 11.98832.
  b. Process appears to be in control.
  c. Histogram approximates normal distribution.

17.61 a. UCL = .1154, LCL = 0.
  b. Sample 7 hits the LCL, otherwise in control.
  c. Samples are too small to assume normality ($n\pi = 5$). (Better to use MINITAB's binomial option.)

17.63 Chart A: Rule 4.
Chart B: No rules violated.
Chart C: Rule 4.
Chart D: Rules 1, 4.
Chart E: No rules violated.
Chart F: Rules 1, 2.

17.65 Each pattern is clearly evident, except possibly instability in third series.

Answers to Exam Review Questions

CHAPTERS 1–4

1. a. inferential;   b. descriptive;   c. inferential
2. c. independent judgment is needed
3. b. anecdotal data ($n = 1$)
4. a. numerical;   b. categorical;   c. numerical
5. a. ratio (true zero);   b. ordinal;   c. nominal
6. a. continuous;   b. continuous;   c. discrete
7. a. convenience;   b. simple random;   c. systematic
8. c. Computer software makes it easy, and inexpensive, to generate random numbers.
9. a. Likert only if distances have meaning
10. a. sampling error cannot be eliminated
11. Skewed right, no outliers, Sturges $k \cong 6$
12. c. range is $-1 \le r \le +1$
13. a. small n and sum to 100%
14. $\bar{x} = 12$, $s = 5.701$, CV = 47.5%
15. a. $\bar{x} = 59.3$, median = 58.5, modes 55, 58, 62 (not unique)
    b. mean or median best   c. $Q_1 = 55$, $Q_2 = 62.25$.
16. a. slight positive correlation;
    b. $r = 0.5656$ (not very linear)

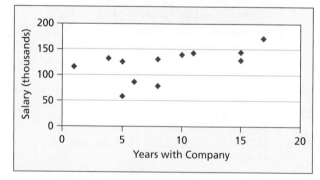

17. b. GEOMEAN(Data) requires all $x_i > 0$
18. a. $z = (x - \mu)/\sigma = (81 - 52)/15 = 1.93$ (not an outlier)
19. b. log scales are less familiar to most

CHAPTERS 5–7

1. a. empirical;   b. subjective;   c. classical
2. a. 40/200 = .20;   b. 50/90 = .5556;
   c. 100/200 = .50
3. no, since $P(A)\,P(B) = (.30)(.70) = .21 \ne P(A \cap B) = .25$
4. b. would be true if $P(A \cap B) = 0$
5. c. $U(a, b)$ has two parameters
6. c. $.60(1000) + .30(2000) + .10(5000) = 1700$

7. a. .2565;   b. .4562;
   c. .7576;   d. Poisson, $\lambda = 2.5$
8. a. .1468;   b. .0563;   c. .7969;
   d. binomial, $n = 8$, $\pi = .20$
9. a. $\mu = n\pi = (50)(.30) = 15$;
   b. $\sigma = \sqrt{n\pi(1 - \pi)} = \sqrt{(50)(.30)(.70)} = 3.24$
10. a. binomial ($n = 8$ trials, π unknown)
    b. Poisson (arrivals, λ unknown);
    c. discrete uniform ($a = 0$, $b = 9$)
11. c. $X =$ trials until first success in geometric
12. a. points have no area, hence no probability
13. a. Normal PDF is always symmetric about the mean
14. Using Appendix C:
    a. $P(Z > 1.14) = .1271$;
    b. $P(-.71 < Z < +0.71) = .5222$;
    c. $P(Z < 0) = .5000$.
    Using Excel:
    a. .1265;   b. .5249;   c. .5000
15. Using Table 7.9:
    a. $\mu + 1.645\sigma = 70 + 1.645(7) = 81.52$;
    b. $\mu - 1.282\sigma = 70 - 1.282(7) = 61.04$;
    c. $\mu + 0.675\sigma = 70 + 0.675(7) = 74.73$
16. a. gives cumulative left tail area
17. Using $\lambda = 1.2$:
    a. $P(X < 1.5) = 1 - e^{-\lambda x} = 1 - e^{(-1.2)(1.5)} = .8347$;
    b. $P(X > 0.5) = e^{-\lambda x} = e^{(-1.2)(0.5)} = .5488$;
    c. $P(X > 1) - P(X > 2) = e^{(-1.2)(1)} - e^{(-1.2)(2)} = .3012 - .0907 = .2105$ (if X is expressed in minutes)
18. Using $\lambda = 1.2$:
    a. Solve $e^{-\lambda x} = .05$ to get $x = 2.496$ min (149.8 sec);
    b. Solve $e^{-\lambda x} = .75$ to get $x = 0.2397$ min (14.38 sec);
    c. MTBE $= 1/\lambda = (1/1.2) = 0.83$ min (50 sec)
19. a. This is a correct rule of thumb (set $\mu = \lambda$ and $\sigma = \sqrt{\lambda}$)
20. c. Triangular is skewed unless b is halfway between a and c.

CHAPTERS 8–10

1. a. CLT applies to $\bar{X}$. Sample *data* may not be normal.
2. a. consistent;   b. efficient;
   c. unbiased
3. b. It is conservative to use t *whenever* σ is unknown, regardless of n.
4. a. $d.f. = n - 1 = 8$, $t_{.025} = 2.306$, so $\bar{x} \pm t\frac{s}{\sqrt{n}}$ gives $13.14 < \mu < 16.36$;
   b. Unknown σ.

5. a. $n = 200$, $z = 1.96$, $p = 28/200 = .14$,
    so $p \pm z\sqrt{\frac{p(1-p)}{n}}$ gives $.092 < \pi < .188$;
    b. $np = 28 > 10$ and $n(1 - p) = 172 > 10$.
    c. Using $z = 1.645$ and $E = \pm .03$ the formula $n = \left(\frac{z}{E}\right)^2$
    $\pi(1 - \pi)$ gives $n = 363$ (using $p = .14$ for π from
    preliminary sample) or $n = 752$ (using $\pi = .50$ if we
    want to be very conservative)
6. c. Normality OK since $np = 17.5 > 10$.
7. b. Type I error is rejecting a true H_0.
8. b. $z_{.025} = \pm 1.960$
9. a. $H_0: \mu \geq 56$, $H_1: \mu < 56$;
    b. Using $\bar{x} = 55.82$, $\sigma = 0.75$ (known), and $n = 49$, we
    get $z_{\text{calc}} = \frac{\bar{x} - \mu_0}{\sigma/\sqrt{n}} = -1.636$;
    c. $z_{.05} = -1.645$;
    d. fail to reject (but a very close decision)
10. a. $H_0: \mu \leq 60$, $H_1: \mu > 60$;
    b. Using $\bar{x} = 67$, $s = 12$, and $n = 16$, we get $t_{\text{calc}} = \frac{\bar{x} - \mu_0}{\sigma/\sqrt{n}}$
    $= 2.333$;
    c. For $d.f. = n - 1 = 15$, $t_{.025} = 2.131$;   d. reject
11. a. $\alpha = P(\text{reject } H_0 \mid H_0 \text{ is true})$
    b. True. As the sample size increases, critical values
    of $t_{.05}$ increase because the $d.f.$ increase, gradually
    approaching $z_{.05}$.
12. a. $H_0: \pi \leq .85$, $H_1: \pi > .85$, $p = 435/500 = .87$,
    $z_{\text{calc}} = \frac{p - \pi_0}{\sqrt{\frac{\pi_0(1 - \pi_0)}{n}}} = 1.252$, $z_{.05} = 1.645$, not a
    significant increase;
    b. $n\pi_0 = (500)(.85) = 425 > 10$ and
    $n(1 - \pi_0) = (500)(.15) = 75 > 10$
13. a. independent samples, unknown variances, $t_{\text{calc}} =$
    -2.034 (regardless whether equal or unequal
    variances assumed);
    b. two-tailed test, $t_{.025} = \pm 2.0739$ (if equal variances
    assumed, $d.f. = 22$) or $t_{.025} = \pm 2.0796$ (if unequal
    variances assumed, $d.f. = 21$);
    c. reject $H_0: \mu_1 = \mu_2$ in favor of $H_1: \mu_1 \neq \mu_2$.

14. a. $H_0: \pi_1 \leq \pi_2$, $H_1: \pi_1 > \pi_2$, $p_1 = 150/200 = .75$,
    $p_2 = 140/200 = .70$, $\bar{p} = .725$, $z_{\text{calc}} = 1.120$, $z_{.025} = 1.96$
    Colorado not significantly greater
15. a. paired t-test;
    b. $d.f. = n - 1 = 5 - 1 = 4$, left-tailed test, $t_{.10} = -1.533$
    c. $t_{\text{calc}} = -1.251$, fail to reject, second exam not signifi-
    cantly greater
16. a. Reject if *small p*-value
17. a. $F_{\text{calc}} = s_1^2/s_2^2 = (14^2)/(7^2) = 4.00$;
    b. $\alpha/2 = .05/2 = .025$, $F_L = 0.2123$ ($d.f. = 7, 11$)
    and $F_R = 3.7586$ ($d.f. = 7, 11$), reject $H_0: \sigma_1^2 = \sigma_2^2$.

CHAPTERS 11–13

1. c. In ANOVA, each population is assumed normal.
2. b. Hartley's F_{max} test compares variances (not means).
3. $F_{\text{calc}} = (744/4)/(751.5/15) = 3.71$, $F_{4,15} = 3.06$
4. a. 3;
    b. 210;
    c. No, *p*-value $= .9055 > .05$;
    d. No, *p*-value $= .3740 > .05$
5. Two-tailed test, $t_{\text{calc}} = 2.127$, $d.f. = 28$, $t_{.005} = 2.763$,
    fail to reject.
6. b. In correlation analysis, neither variable is assumed
    dependent.
7. a. $R^2 = SSR/SST = (158.3268)/(317.4074) = .4988$.
8. b. $d.f. = n - 2 = 25$, $t_{.025} = 2.060$
9. a, c. Both formulas give the same t_{calc}.
10. a. false (residual is within $\pm 1 s_{yx}$);
    b. true;
    c. true
11. a. Evans' Rule suggests $n/k \geq 10$.
12. b. $R_{\text{adj}}^2 \leq R^2$ always; big difference would suggest weak
    predictors
13. a. because their 95% CIs do not include zero
14. c. *p*-value $< .05$ for X_3 (clearly) and X_4 (barely)
15. b. $d.f. = 38$, $t_{.005} = \pm 2.712$, so only X_3 is significant
    ($t_{\text{calc}} = -5.378$)

Writing and Presenting Reports

Business recruiters say that written and oral communication skills are critical for success in business. Susan R. Meisinger, president and CEO of the Society for Human Resource Management, says that "[i]n a knowledge-based economy a talented workforce with communication and critical thinking skills is necessary for organizations and the United States to be successful." Yet a survey of 431 human-resource officials in corporate America found a need for improvement in writing (www.conference-board.org). Table I.1 lists the key business skills needed for *initial* and *long-range* success, as well as some common *weaknesses*.

For Initial Job Success	For Long-Range Job Success	Common Weaknesses
Report writing	Managerial accounting	Communication skills
Accounting principles	Managerial economics	Writing skills
Mathematics	Managerial finance	Immaturity
Statistics	Oral communication	Unrealistic expectations

Mini Case — I.1

Can You Read a Company Annual Report?

Many people say that company annual reports are hard to read. To investigate this claim, Prof. Feng Li of the University of Michigan's Ross School of Business analyzed the readability of more than 50,000 annual reports. One of his readability measures was the Gunning-Fog Index (GFI) which estimates how many years of formal education would be needed in order to read and understand a block of text. For company annual reports, the average GFI was 19.4. Since a college graduate will have 16 years of education, almost a Ph.D. level of education is apparently required to read a typical firm's annual report. Li also found that annual reports of firms with lower earnings were harder to read. (See http://accounting.smartpros.com/x53453.xml; and *Detroit Free Press,* June 7, 2006, p. E1.)

Rules for "Power" Writing

Why is writing so important? Because someone may mention your report on warranty repairs during a meeting of department heads, and your boss may say, "OK, make copies of that report so we can all see it." Next thing you know, the CEO is looking at it! Wish you'd taken more care in writing it? To avoid this awkward situation, set aside 25 percent of your allotted project time to *write* the report. You should always outline the report *before* you begin. Then complete the report in sections. Finally, ask trusted peers to review the report, and make revisions as necessary. Keep in mind that you may need to revise more than once. If you have trouble getting started, consult a good reference on technical report-writing.

While you may have creative latitude in how to organize the flow of ideas in the report, it is essential to answer the assigned question succinctly. Describe what you did and what conclusions you reached, listing the most important results first.

Use section headings to group related material and avoid lengthy paragraphs. Your report is your legacy to others who may rely on it. They will find it instructive to know about difficulties you encountered. Provide clear data so others will not need to waste time checking your data and sources. Consider placing technical details in an appendix to keep the main report simple.

If you are writing the report as part of a team, an "editor-in-chief" must be empowered to edit the material so that it is stylistically consistent, has a common voice, and flows together. Allow enough lead time so that all team members can read the final report and give their comments and corrections to the editor-in-chief.

Avoid Jargon   Experts use jargon to talk to one another, but outsiders may find it obscure or even annoying. Technical concepts must be presented so that others can understand them. If you can't communicate the importance of your work, your potential for advancement will be limited. Even if your ideas are good and hundreds of hours went into your analysis, readers up the food chain will toss your report aside if it contains too many cryptic references like SSE, MAPE, or 3-Sigma Limits.

Make It Attractive   Reports should have a title page, descriptive title, date, and author names. It's a good idea to use footers with page numbers and dates (e.g., Page 7 of 23— Draft of 10/8/12) to distinguish revised drafts.

Use wide margins so readers can take notes or write comments. Select an appropriate typeface and point size. Times Roman, Garamond, and Arial are widely accepted.

Call attention to your main points by using subheadings, bullets, **boldfaced type**, *italics,* large fonts, or color, but use special effects sparingly.

Watch Your Spelling and Grammar   To an educated reader, incorrect grammar or spelling errors are conspicuous signs of sloppy work. You don't recognize your errors— that's why you make them. Get someone you trust to red-pencil your work. Study your errors until you're sure you won't repeat them. Your best bet? Keep a dictionary handy! You can refer to it for both proper spelling and grammatical usage. Remember that Microsoft specializes in software, not English, so don't rely on spelling and grammar checkers. Here are some examples from student papers that passed the spell-checker, but each contains two errors. Can you spot them quickly?

Original	*Correction*
• "It's effects will transcend our nation's boarders."	(its, borders)
• "We cannot except this shipment on principal."	(accept, principle)
• "They seceded despite there faults."	(succeeded, their)
• "This plan won't fair well because it's to rigid."	(fare, too)
• "The amount of unhappy employees is raising."	(number, rising)

Organizing a Technical Report

Report formats vary, but a business report usually begins with an *executive summary* limited to a *single page.* Attach the full report containing discussion, explanations, tables, graphs, interpretations, and (if needed) footnotes and appendices. Use appendices for backup material. Paste your graphs and tables *into the main report* where you refer to them, and format them nicely. Each table or graph needs a title and a number. A common beginner's error is to attach a bunch of Excel printouts and graphs at the end of a technical report; most readers won't take the time to flip pages to look at them. Worse, if you put all your tables and graphs at the end, you may be tempted not to spend time formatting them nicely. There is no single acceptable style for a business report but the following would be typical:

- Executive Summary (1 page maximum)
- Introduction (1 to 3 paragraphs)
  - Statement of the problem
  - Data sources and definitions
  - Methods utilized
- Body of the Report (as long as necessary)
  - Break it into sections
  - Each section has a descriptive heading
  - Use subsection headings as necessary
  - Discuss, explain, interpret everything
  - Tables and graphs, as needed
- Conclusions (1 to 3 paragraphs)
  - Restatement of findings
  - Limitations of your analysis
  - Future research suggestions
- Bibliography and Sources
- Appendices (if needed for lengthy or technical material)

General tips:

- Avoid huge paragraphs (break them up).
- Include page numbers to help the reader take notes.
- Check spelling and grammar. Ask others to proofread the report.

Writing an Executive Summary

The goal of an **executive summary** is to permit a busy decision maker to understand what you did and what you found out *without reading the rest of the report*. In a statistical report, the executive summary *briefly* describes the task and goals, data and data sources, methods that were used, main findings of the analysis, and (if necessary) any limitations of the analysis. The main findings will occupy most of the space in the executive summary. Each other item may only rate a sentence or two. The executive summary is limited to a single page (maybe only two or three paragraphs) and should avoid technical language.

An excellent way to evaluate your executive summary is to hand it to a peer. Ask him/her to read it and then tell you what you did and what you found out. If the peer cannot answer precisely, then your summary is deficient. The executive summary must make it *impossible to miss your main findings*. Your boss may judge you and your team by the executive summary alone. S/he may merely leaf through the report to examine key tables or graphs, or may assign someone to review your full report.

Rules for Presenting Oral Reports

The goals of an oral report are *not the same* as those of a written report. Your oral presentation must only *highlight* the main points. If your presentation does not provide the answer to an audience question, you can say, "Good question. We don't have time to discuss that further here, but it's covered in the full report. I'll be happy to talk to you about it at the end of the presentation." Or give a brief answer so they know you did consider the matter. Keep these tips in mind while preparing your oral presentation:

- Select just a few key points you most want to convey.
- Use simple charts and diagrams to get the point across.
- Use **color** and *fonts* creatively to **emphasize a point.**

- Levity is nice on occasion, but avoid gratuitous jokes.
- Have backup slides or transparencies just in case.
- Rehearse to get the timing right (don't go too long).
- Refer the audience to the written report for details.
- Imagine yourself in the audience. Don't bore yourself!

The Three Ps

Pace   Many presenters speak too rapidly—partly because they are nervous and partly because they think it makes them look smarter.

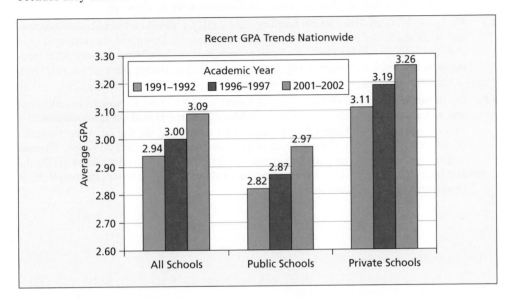

FIGURE I.1

Pictures Help Make the Point

Source: Copyright © 2005 Stuart Rojstaczer. Used with permission.

Slow down! Take a little time to introduce yourself, introduce your data, and explain what you are trying to do. If you skip the basic background and definitions, many members of the audience will not be able to follow the presentation and will have only a vague idea what you are talking about.

Planning   Create an outline to organize the ideas you want to discuss. Remember to keep it simple! You'll also need to prepare a verbal "executive summary" to tell your audience what your talk is about. Before you choose your planned opening words, "*Our team correlated robbery with income,*" you should ask yourself:

- Is the audience familiar with correlation analysis?
- Should I explain that our data came from the FBI and the 2010 U.S. Census?
- Will they know that our observations are averages for the 50 U.S. states?
- Will they know that we are talking about per capita robbery rates (not total robberies)?
- Will they know that we are using per capita personal income (not median family income)?
- Should I show them a few data values to help them visualize the data?

Don't bury them in detail, but make the first minute count. If you ran into problems or made errors in your analysis, it's OK to say so. The audience will sympathize.

Check the raw data carefully—you may be called on to answer questions. It's hard to defend yourself when you failed to catch serious errors or didn't understand a key definition.

Practice   Rehearse the oral presentation to get the timing right. Maybe your employer will send you to training classes to bolster your presentation skills. Otherwise consider videotaping yourself or practicing in front of a few peers for valuable feedback. Technical presentations may demand skills different from the ones you used in English class, so don't panic if you have a few problems.

APPENDIX EXERCISES

I.1   Use your favorite web search engine to search for each key term, and print one or two excerpts from websites that you found particularly interesting or useful. (a) "technical writing"; (b) "scientific reports"; (c) "presentation tips."

I.2   Go to the McGraw-Hill *OnLine Learning Center* (OLC) website www.mhhe.com/doane4e and select the folder called Appendix I—Business Reports. Download the document Executive Summaries.docx that contains actual executive summaries from project reports by 16 student teams. There were three introductory statistics students on each team. Their assignment was to forecast the annual revenue for a company of their choice and to write a report. The project instructions are shown in the document. Choose *three* of their executive summaries and grade them (A, A–, B+, B, B–, C+ and so on). List specific strengths and weaknesses, using the criteria for an effective executive summary in Appendix I. Write the same kinds of comments that you would think an instructor would write.

I.3   Go to the McGraw-Hill *OnLine Learning Center* (OLC) website www.mhhe.com/doane4e and select the folder called Appendix I—Business Reports. Download the document Oral Presentation Tips.pdf. (a) Think of an oral presentation you have heard recently. After reading these tips, write three suggestions that would have helped the speaker improve. (b) Which of these tips seem most relevant for you? Why?

I.4   Go to the McGraw-Hill *OnLine Learning Center* (OLC) website www.mhhe.com/doane4e and select the folder called Appendix I—Business Reports. Download the document Fog Index Project.docx. (a) Follow the instructions for calculating the *Fog Index* from samples of 100 words from each of three types of publications (company annual report, business magazine, scholarly journal). (b) Report your results in the indicated table format. (c) Do the Fog Index results support your prior expectations about the degree of writing complexity in these three types of publications?

Excel Statistical Functions

Descriptive Statistics	2007 Function	2010 Function
Number of data items	COUNT(Data)	COUNT(Data)
Largest data value	MAX(Data)	MAX(Data)
Smallest data value	MIN(Data)	MIN(Data)
Mean	AVERAGE(Data)	AVERAGE(Data)
Median	MEDIAN(Data)	MEDIAN(Data)
Mode (returns first mode only)	MODE(Data)	MODE.SNGL(Data)
Mode (array function for multiple modes; highlight output range and use Ctrl-Shift-Enter)	----------------	{MODE.MULT(Data)}
Geometric mean (positive data values only)	GEOMEAN(Data)	GEOMEAN(Data)
Quartile k (old Excel method),* e.g., $k = 3$ for Q_3	QUARTILE(Data, k)	QUARTILE.INC(Data, k)
Quartile k (mainstream),* e.g., $k = 3$ for Q_3	----------------	QUARTILE.EXC(Data, k)
Percentile p (old Excel method),* e.g., $p = .25$ for Q_1	PERCENTILE(Data, p)	PERCENTILE.INC(Data, p)
Percentile p (mainstream),* e.g., $p = .25$ for Q_1	----------------	PERCENTILE.EXC(Data, p)
Sample standard deviation	STDEV(Data)	STDEV.S(Data)
Sample covariance for (X, Y) data pairs	----------------	COVARIANCE.S(XData, YData)
Population standard deviation	STDEVP(Data)	STDEV.P(Data)
Population variance for (X, Y) data pairs	COVAR(XData, YData)	COVARIANCE.P(XDdata, YData)
Standardize an X value (use sample mean and standard deviation if μ and σ unknown)	STANDARDIZE(Data, μ, σ)	STANDARDIZE(Data, μ, σ)
Correlation coefficient for (X, Y) data pairs	CORREL(XData, YData)	CORREL(XData, YData)
Average deviation around the mean	AVEDEV(Data)	AVEDEV(Data)
Slope of simple X-Y regression	SLOPE(XData, YData)	SLOPE(XData, YData)
Intercept of simple X-Y regression	INTERCEPT(XData, YData)	INTERCEPT(XData, YData)
R-squared for simple X-Y regression	RSQ(XData, YData)	RSQ(XData, YData)

*See Chapter 4, Section 4.5 for explanation of interpolation methods for percentiles and quartiles. Excel's old method was rather unconventional, while its new method agrees with mainstream statistical packages.

Discrete Probability Distributions	2007 Function	2010 Function
Binomial distribution		
PDF: Returns probability $P(X = x)$	BINOMDIST(x, n, π, 0)	BINOM.DIST(x, n, π, 0)
CDF: Returns probability $P(X \leq x)$	BINOMDIST(x, n, π, 1)	BINOM.DIST(x, n, π, 1)
Inverse CDF: Returns x for $P(X \leq x) = \alpha$	CRITBINOM(n, π, α)	BINOM.INV(n, π, α)
Poisson distribution		
PDF: Returns probability $P(X = x)$	POISSON(x, λ, 0)	POISSON.DIST(x, λ, 0)
CDF: Returns probability $P(X \leq x)$	POISSON (x, λ, 1)	POISSON.DIST(x, λ, 1)
Inverse CDF: Returns x for $P(X \leq x) = \alpha$	----------------	----------------
Hypergeometric distribution		
PDF: Returns probability $P(X = x)$	HYPGEOMDIST(x, n, s, N)	HYPGEOM.DIST(x, n, s, N, 0)
CDF: Returns probability $P(X \leq x)$	----------------	HYPGEOM.DIST(x, n, s, N, 1)
Inverse CDF: Returns x for $P(X \leq x) = \alpha$	----------------	----------------

Continuous Probability Distributions	2007 Function	2010 Function
Normal distribution		
PDF: Returns height of $f(x)$	NORMDIST($x, \mu, \sigma, 0$)	NORM.DIST($x, \mu, \sigma, 0$)
CDF: Returns probability $P(X \leq x)$	NORMDIST($x, \mu, \sigma, 1$)	NORM.DIST($x, \mu, \sigma, 1$)
Inverse CDF: Returns x for $P(X \leq x) = \alpha$	NORMINV(α, μ, σ)	NORM.INV(α, μ, σ)
Standard normal distribution		
PDF: Returns height of $f(z)$	----------------	NORM.S.DIST($z, 0$)
CDF: Returns probability $P(Z \leq z)$	NORMSDIST(z)	NORM.S.DIST($z, 1$)
Inverse CDF: Returns z for $P(Z \leq z) = \alpha$	NORMSINV(α)	NORM.S.INV(α)
Exponential distribution		
PDF: Returns height of $f(x)$	EXPONDIST($x, \lambda, 0$)	EXPON.DIST($x, \lambda, 0$)
CDF: Returns probability $P(X \leq x)$	EXPONDIST($x, \lambda, 1$)	EXPON.DIST($x, \lambda, 1$)
Inverse CDF: Returns x for $P(X \leq x) = \alpha$	----------------	----------------
Student's t distribution		
PDF: Returns height of $f(t)$	----------------	T.DIST($t, df, 0$)
CDF: Returns probability $P(t \leq t_0)$	1-TDIST($t_0, df, 1$) only if $t_0 > 0$	T.DIST($t_0, df, 1$)
Inverse CDF: Returns t_0 for $P(t \leq t_0) = \alpha$	----------------	T.INV(α, df)
F distribution		
PDF: Returns height of $f(x)$	----------------	F.DIST($x, df_1, df_2, 0$)
CDF: Returns probability $P(X \leq x)$	1-FDIST(x, df_1, df_2)	F.DIST($x, df_1, df_2, 1$)
Inverse CDF: Returns F_0 for $P(F \leq F_0) = \alpha$	FINV($1 - \alpha, df_1, df_2$)	F.INV(α, df_1, df_2)

Common Hypothesis Tests	2007 Function	2010 Function
Normal distribution*		
Left-tailed p-value for test statistic z_{calc}	NORMSDIST(z_{calc})	NORM.S.DIST($z_{calc}, 1$)
Right-tailed p-value for test statistic z_{calc}	1-NORMSDIST(z_{calc})	1-NORM.S.DIST($z_{calc}, 1$)
Two-tailed p-value for test statistic z_{calc}	2*(1-NORMSDIST($|z_{calc}|$))	2*(1-NORM.S.DIST($|z_{calc}|, 1$))
Critical z value for left-tailed test at α	NORMSINV(α)	NORM.S.INV(α)
Critical z value for right-tailed test at α	NORMSINV($1 - \alpha$)	NORM.S.INV($1 - \alpha$)
Critical z values for two-tailed test at α	$\pm$NORMSINV($\alpha/2$)	$\pm$NORM.S.INV($\alpha/2$)
Student's t distribution*		
Left-tailed p-value for test statistic t_{calc}	TDIST($|t_{calc}|, df, 1$)	T.DIST($t_{calc}, df, 1$)
Right-tailed p-value for test statistic t_{calc}	TDIST($|t_{calc}|, df, 1$)	T.DIST.RT(t_{calc}, df)
Two-tailed p-value for test statistic t_{calc}	TDIST($|t_{calc}|, df, 2$)	T.DIST.2T($|t_{calc}|, df$)
Critical value of t_α for left-tailed test at α	$-$TINV($2\alpha, df$)	T.INV(α, df)
Critical value of t_α for right-tailed test at α	TINV($2\alpha, df$)	T.INV($1 - \alpha, df$)
Critical values of $t_{\alpha/2}$ for two-tailed test at α	$\pm$TINV(α, df)	$\pm$T.INV.2T(α, df)
F distribution		
Left-tailed p-value for test statistic $F_{calc} < 1$	1-FDIST(F_{calc}, df_1, df_2)	F.DIST($F_{calc}, df_1, df_2, 1$)
Right-tailed p-value for test statistic $F_{calc} > 1$	FDIST(F_{calc}, df_1, df_2)	F.DIST.RT(F_{calc}, df_1, df_2)
Two-tailed p-value for folded F_{calc} test	2*FDIST(F_{calc}, df_1, df_2)	2*F.DIST.RT(F_{calc}, df_1, df_2)
Critical value for left-tailed test at α	1/FINV(α, df_2, df_1)	F.INV(α, df_1, df_2)
Critical value for right-tailed test at α	FINV(α, df_1, df_2)	F.INV($1 - \alpha, df_1, df_2$)
Critical value for folded F test at α	FINV($\alpha/2, df_1, df_2$)	F.INV.RT($\alpha/2, df_1, df_2$)
Chi-square distribution		
Left-tailed p-value for test statistic χ^2_{calc}	1-CHIDIST(χ^2_{calc}, df)	CHISQ.DIST($\chi^2_{calc}, df, 1$)
Right-tailed p-value for test statistic χ^2_{calc}	CHIDIST(χ^2_{calc}, df)	CHISQ.DIST.RT(χ^2_{calc}, df)
Two-tailed p-value for test statistic χ^2_{calc}	2*CHIDIST(χ^2_{calc}, df)	2*CHISQ.DIST.RT(χ^2_{calc}, df)
Critical value for left-tailed test at α	CHIINV($1 - \alpha, df$)	CHISQ.INV(α, df)
Critical value for right-tailed test at α	CHIINV(α, df)	CHISQ.INV.RT(α, df)
Critical value for two-tailed test at α	CHIINV($\alpha/2, df$)	CHISQ.INV($1 - \alpha/2, df$)

*For the normal and Student's t distributions, the symbols $|z_{calc}|$ and $|t_{calc}|$ are used to denote absolute values for functions that require a positive argument. The $\pm$ symbol is used in two-tailed z and t tests to indicate that left- and right-tail critical values are the same except for sign.

Hypothesis Test Calculations	2007 Function	2010 Function
t-test for two means: returns a two-tailed p-value for a test of zero difference in two data arrays	TTEST(Data1, Data2, Tails, Type) where Tails = 1 or 2 and Type 1 = paired (must have $n_1 = n_2$) 2 = equal variances assumed 3 = unequal variances assumed	T.TEST(Data1, Data2, Tails, Type) where Tails = 1 or 2 and Type 1 = paired (must have $n_1 = n_2$) 2 = equal variances assumed 3 = unequal variances assumed
F-test of two variances: returns a 2-tailed p-value for equality of variances in two arrays	FTEST(Data1, Data2)	F.TEST(Data1, Data2)
χ^2 goodness-of-fit test of k frequencies: returns a 2-tailed p-value assuming $k - 1$ degrees of freedom (assumes no parameters estimated). No warning if array frequencies do not have the same sum (as they should).	CHITEST(Data1, Data2) where Data1 is an array of k observed frequencies and Data2 is an array of k expected frequencies	CHISQ.TEST(Data1, Data2) where Data1 is an array of k observed frequencies and Data2 is an array of k expected frequencies

Other Useful Stats Functions	2007 Function	2010 Function
Rank (average for ties)	----------------	RANK.AVG(x, Data, k) where x is a cell reference in array Data, $k = 0$ (descending), $k = 1$ (ascending)
Rank (no correction for ties)	RANK(x, Data, k) where x is a cell reference in array Data, $k = 0$ (descending), $k = 1$ (ascending)	RANK(x, Data, k) where x is a cell reference in array Data, $k = 0$ (descending), $k = 1$ (ascending)
Random uniform ($0 \le x < 1$)	RAND()	RAND()
Random integers ($a \le x \le b$)	RANDBETWEEN(a, b)	RANDBETWEEN(a, b)
Confidence interval half-width $\pm z\, \sigma/\sqrt{(n)}$ (margin of error) using normal distribution with known standard deviation σ and confidence $1 - \alpha$	CONFIDENCE(α, σ, n)	CONFIDENCE.NORM(α, σ, n)
Confidence interval half-width $\pm t\, s/\sqrt{n}$ (margin of error) using Student's t distribution with unknown standard deviation s and confidence $1 - \alpha$	----------------	CONFIDENCE.T(α, s, n)
Sum of squares of an array of data values around their mean	DEVSQ(Data)	DEVSQ(Data)
Frequency of items in a data array using bin upper limits in bin array (highlight output range and use Ctrl-Shift-Enter)	{FREQUENCY(Data, Bins)}	{FREQUENCY(Data, Bins)}

For more information about the Excel 2010 statistical functions, see Function Improvements in Microsoft Office Excel 2010 (http://go.microsoft.com/fwlink/?LinkId=186148).

PHOTO CREDITS

INDEX